Visual Basic.NET Programming

Business Applications with a Design Perspective

Visual Basic.NET Programming

Business Applications with a Design Perspective

Jeffrey J. Tsay

Prentice Hall
Upper Saddle River, New Jersey 07458

Library of Congress Cataloging-in-Publication Data
Tsay, Jeffrey J.
    Visual Basic.NET programming / Jeffrey Tsay.— 2nd ed.
        p. cm.
    ISBN 0-13-009421-8
    1. Microsoft Visual BASIC.   2. BASIC (Computer program language)   3. Microsoft .NET.
I. Title.
    QA76.76.B3 T753 2003
    005.2'768—dc21

                                                                    2002151817

Publisher and Vice President:: Natalie E. Anderson
Executive Editor: Jodi McPherson
Senior Project Managers, Editorial: Eileen Clark and Thomas Park
Editorial Assistant: Jodi Bolognese
Marketing Manager: Sharon Turkovich
Manager, Production: Gail Steier de Acevedo
Project Manager, Production: Audri Anna Bazlen
Associate Director, Manufacturing: Vincent Scelta
Manufacturing Buyer: Natacha St. Hill Moore
Design Manager: Maria Lange
Art Director: Pat Smythe
Book Designer: Graphic World Inc.
Cover Design: John Romer
Line Art Studio: Matrix Publishing Services
Full-Service Composition: Impressions Book and Journal Services, Inc.
LCover Printer: Phoenix
Printer/Binder: Von Hoffman - Owensville

10 9 8 7 6 5 4 3 2 1
ISBN 0-13-0094218

Brief Contents

Preface XIX

1 Introduction 1

2 Introduction to Visual Basic Programming 17

3 User Interface Design: Visual Basic Controls and Events 59

4 Data, Operations, and Built-In Functions 113

5 Decision 165

6 Input, Output, and Procedures 205

7 Repetition 251

8 Arrays and Their Uses 295

9 Database and ADO.NET 355

10 Special Topics in Data Entry 413

11 Menus and Multiple-Form Applications 459

12 Object-Based Programming .513

13 Object-Oriented Programming 557

14 Beyond the Core 591

Appendix A Data Management Using Files 639

Appendix B Graphics, Animation, Drag and Drop 667

Appendix C Number Systems and Bit-Wise Operations 695

Index 709

Contents

Preface XIX

1 Introduction 1

1.1 What Is Visual Basic?. 2
Evolution of Visual Basic 2
Characteristics of Visual Basic. 3
Visual Basic as a Language and as a Processor 4
Editions of Visual Basic.NET 5
1.2 Overview of Visual Basic Program Development. 5
Criteria for a Sound Application Program 6
Steps in Program Development 8
1.3 How to Use This Book 10
Learning the Language: An Analogy 10
Conventions for Syntax Specification. 11
The Case for Hands-On 11
Beyond the Content Coverage 13
Summary 13
Review Questions. 14

2 Introduction to Visual Basic Programming 17

2.1 Navigating the Integrated Development Environment 18
Starting the IDE. 18
Customizing the VS.NET IDE 18
Starting a New Project 19
The Menu Bar and the Toolbar 20
The Toolbox 21
The Form and the Code Window 22
The Solution Explorer 22
The Properties Window 23
Exiting the VB IDE 24
2.2 Your First Visual Basic Program. 24
A Simple Program Walkthrough 24
Handling VB Program Files. 28
2.3 Some Basic Concepts. 30
Understanding the Integrated Development Environment. 30
Coding Mechanics 31
Interfaces of VB Objects 32
Defaults 35
2.4 Exploring More Properties. 35
Common Properties 35
Changing the Font for the Label: An Exercise 37
The AutoSize Property. 37

2.5   Getting Help from the Help Menu 37
       The Index Tab 37
       Help Text and Hyperlinks 38
       Alternative Ways to Explore 38

2.6   Naming Objects 39
       Object Naming Convention 39
       Changing the Object Names in the Project 39

2.7   Overview of the Code Structure 42
       Statements That Bring Results and Execute Sequentially 42
       Statements That Direct Flow of Execution Control. 42

2.8   Revising the First Program 44
       Organizing Project and Solution Folder 44
       The Visual Interface. 45
       Coding the Revised Project 47
       Completing the Development Cycle. 50

       Summary 51

       Explore and Discover 52

       Exercises 53

       Projects 56

3   User Interface Design: Visual Basic Controls and Events   59

3.1   Obtaining Open-Ended Input from the User: Text Box and Masked
       Edit Control 60
       Text Property of the Text Box 60
       The Masked Edit Box Control 62
       Comparing the Text Properties of the Two Controls. 65
       Clearing the Text Property 65
       Selecting (Highlighting) a Portion of the Text 66
       The ClipText Property 67

3.2   Arranging Many VB Controls on a Form: Group Box and Tab Controls. . . 68
       The Group Box 69
       The Tab Control. 71

3.3   Data with Limited Number of Choices: Radio Buttons and Check Boxes. . 74
       The Radio Button. 74
       Check Boxes for Independent Choices 76

3.4   Longer List of Known Items: List Boxes and Combo Boxes 78
       The List Box Control 78
       The Need for the Combo Box 83

3.5   Graphics in the Visual Interface 86
       The Picture Box. 86

3.6   VB Controls in the Design of a Data-Entry Interface: Recapitulation 87

3.7   Naming the Controls and Setting the Tab Order 88
       Naming Convention: Suggested Name Prefixes 88
       Setting the Tab Order. 89

3.8   Some Commonly Used Events 89
       Setting the Initial State at Runtime: The Form Load Event. 90
       Various Uses of the Click Event. 90
       SelectedIndexChanged and DoubleClick Events. 91
       Viewing the Key Entered: The KeyPress Event 93
       Before the User Does Anything in a Control: The Enter Event. 93
       As the User Leaves the Field: The Leave Event. 94

3.9   **An Application Example** **95**
The Environ-Pure Project 95
The Visual Interface 96
Setting the Tab Order 98
Coding the Event Procedures 99
Testing the Project 102

Summary **102**

Explore and Discover **103**

Exercises **105**

Projects **110**

4   Data, Operations, and Built-In Functions   113

4.1   **Classification and Declaration of Data** **114**
Declaring Constants 114
Declaring Variables 115
Checking for Variable Declarations 116
Rules for Variable Declaration 117

4.2   **Scope and Lifetime of Variables** **118**
Form (Class)-Level Declaration 118
Procedure-Level Declaration 118
Static Declaration 119
Scope and Lifetime: A Recap 121
Scope and Program Modularity 122
Constant and Variable Naming Convention 123

4.3   **Numeric Data and Types** **123**
Byte and Char Types 124
Boolean Type 124
Short, Integer, and Long Types 124
Single and Double Types 125
Other Numeric Data Types 126
Declaring Numeric Data Types 126
The Object Data Type 126
Strict Implicit Type Conversion 127
The Assignment Statement 128
Numeric Operations 130
Data Type Conversions 131
Computing Net Sale: An Application Example 132
The Format Function 136

4.4   **Built-In Numeric Functions** **137**
Mathematical Functions 137
Conversion Functions 139
Date/Time Functions 140
Using Functions 142

4.5   **String Data** **142**
Declaring String Variables 143
String Operations and Built-In Functions 143
The Calculating Vending Machine: An Example 149

Summary **154**

Explore and Discover **155**

Exercises **160**

Projects **163**

5   Decision   165

5.1   Logical Expressions 166
Relational Operators. 166
Assignment Statements 168
Logical Operators. 168
Operational Precedence 170

5.2   The If Block. 171
Simple If Block 172
The If. . . Then. . . Else. . . End If Block. 172
The If. . . Then. . . ElseIf. . . Then. . . Else. . . End If Block 174
Nesting If Blocks 176
Additional Notes on Coding the If Block 179

5.3   The Select Case Block 183
Syntax Structure. 183
Nesting Select Case Blocks 187
A Note on Block Level Declaration. 193

Summary 193

Explore and Discover 195

Exercises 199

Projects 202

6   Input, Output, and Procedures   205

6.1   Introduction to Input and Output. 206
The MsgBox Function 206
Files. 209
File Dialog Boxes 214

6.2   Procedures: Subs and Functions. 216
Writing a Sub Procedure 217
Calling a Sub Procedure. 218
Passing Data to Sub Procedures 220
Terminating a Procedure Before Reaching the End: Exit Sub or Return 222
Event Procedures and General Sub Procedures. 223
Function Procedures. 223
Using the Function Procedure 225
Additional Notes on General Procedures 225
Uses of General Procedures 230

6.3   An Application Example. 230
The Contacts Project 230
The User Interface 231
Designing the Code Structure. 232
Coding the Project 233
Coding the Event Procedures 234
Additional Remarks 237

Summary 237

Explore and Discover 239

Exercises 244

Projects 247

7   Repetition   251

7.1   The Do...Loop Structure 252
Example 1. Showing a Sequence of Numbers. 252

Example 2. Reading a Name List and Populating a List Box 253
The Endless Loop 255
Do Loop Without a Condition on Either Statement. 255
Example 3. Computing the Value of an Infinite Series 255
Example 4. Finding the Solution to an Equation Numerically. 258

7.2   The For...Next Structure **261**
Example 5. Listing a Sequence of Numbers 262
Example 6. Listing Who's Invited (the Invitation Project) 263
Example 7. Every Other Day 264
Example 8. Displaying a String on Two Lines (the ShowTwoLines Project) 264
Nesting the Loops 266
Example 9. Matching Up Teams in a League 267
Example 10. What Is Your Chance to Win? 268
The For Each...Next Structure 270
Referencing Objects in a Collection by Index 272

7.3   Additional Notes on Coding Repetition **272**
Do Versus For 272
For Versus For Each 273
Tips for Efficiency 273

7.4   An Application Example **275**
The W-4 Form Project 275
Design Considerations 275
The Visual Interface. 275
Coding the Project 276

Summary **282**

Explore and Discover **283**

Exercises **287**

Projects **292**

8   Arrays and Their Uses   295

8.1   One-Dimensional Arrays **296**
Creating One-Dimensional Arrays 296
Dynamic Arrays. 297
Passing Arrays to Procedures and Returning an Array from a Function. 299
Determining the Boundary of an Array. 299

8.2   Sample Uses of Arrays **300**
Simplified Selection. 300
Table Look Up. 302
Tracking Random Occurrences. 303
Simulation 305
Random Sampling Without Replacement 307

8.3   Sorting and Searching **310**
Selected Algorithms for Sorting 311
Bubble Sort 311
Straight Insertion Sort 315
Shell Sort. 317
Quick Sort 319
Comparison of Performance. 324
Sequential Search and Binary Search 324

8.4   The Collection Object **326**
Using the Collection Object 326

8.5   Two-Dimensional Arrays **330**
Tables 331

Matrices 334
Game Boards 334

8.6   **Additional Notes on Arrays** **335**
Preserving Data in ReDim 335
Displaying Array Contents in the List Box or Combo Box 335
Releasing an Array: The Erase Statement 335
Array Properties and Methods 335
Appropriate Use of Arrays 337

8.7   **An Application Example** **337**
The "Sales by Product" Project 337
Algorithm 338
Coding the Project 338

Summary **341**

Explore and Discover **342**

Exercises **346**

Projects **352**

9   Database and ADO.NET   355

9.1   **Introduction to Database** **356**
Table Definitions 356
Indexes, the Primary Key, and the Foreign Key 356
Introduction to the SQL 357

9.2   **Using ADO.NET** **361**
Brief Introduction to ADO.NET Terminology and Concept 362
Working with the Data Adapter 362
Using Parameters for Query 370
Viewing Data Record by Record 372
Updating the Database 374
The Case of Immediate Updating 379

9.3   **Working with ADO.NET by Code** **382**
Coding the Products Search Project 382
Maintaining the Phonebook Database by Code 385
Using Data Commands 389
Saving Data "Locally" 390
Browsing Database Table Definitions (Schema) 390
The Data Reader 395

9.4   **Multiple Data Tables in a Dataset and the Data Relation** . . . **397**
Browsing the Database Schema with the Use of Data Relation 398
A Concluding Comment 400

Summary **400**

Explore and Discover **402**

Exercises **404**

Projects **409**

10   Special Topics in Data Entry   413

10.1   **Principles of GUI Design** **414**
Simplicity and Clarity 414
Flexibility 414
Consistency 415

Immediate Feedback 415
Forgiveness 415
Pleasant Appearance 416

10.2   Designing a User-Friendly Keyboard **417**
Handling the Enter Key 417
Auto Tabbing 419
Arrow Keys Up and Down 420
Providing Access Keys 420
Using the Tab Control 422

10.3   Additional Considerations on Friendly GUI Design **423**
Detecting Unsaved Data 423
Handling Unsaved Data When the Program Is Quitting 424

10.4   Checking for Data-Entry Errors **425**
When the User Presses a Key 426
When the User Is Done with the Field 431
When the User Is Ready to Proceed 435

10.5   Handling Errors **438**
A User's Nightmare in Previous Versions 438
The Try. . . Catch. . . Finally. . . End Try Structure 440

10.6   Providing Visual Clues **442**
Listing Prime Numbers: An Illustrative Example 443
The Prime Number Computing Algorithm 444
The Cursor 444
Messages for Progress Status 445
The Progress Bar 446

Summary **448**

Explore and Discover **449**

Exercises **453**

Projects **457**

11 Menus and Multiple-Form Applications   459

11.1   The Main Menu **460**
Creating a Menu 460
Context (Pop-Up) Menus 463
Assigning Access and Shortcut Keys 463
Invoking an Action 463
Levels of Menus 464

11.2   The Tree View **464**
Setting Up Nodes in the Tree View 464
Coding with the Tree View 466

11.3   Multiple-Form Applications **468**
Adding a Form to a Project 468
Starting Up and Calling a Form 469
Modal and Modeless Forms 470
Closing and Hiding Forms 471
Sharing Data Between Forms 472
The Standard Module 474
A Multiple-Form Example 478

11.4   MDI Applications **484**
Differences Between MDI and SDI in Behavior 485
Creating an MDI Application 485

11.5 **Coding an MDI Project: An Example** **485**
Features of the Project 486
Creating the Interface 486
Coding the Project 488
Code in the Standard Module 488
Handling Events in the Child Form 489
Handling Events in the MDI Form 489
Building the Find Dialog Box 493
Creating MDI Applications: A Recap 497
Additional Remarks 498

11.6 **Designing a Large Project** **498**
Modular Design 499
Factoring to Minimize Code 500
Layered Standard Modules 500
Object-Oriented Programming 500

Summary **500**

Explore and Discover **502**

Exercises **508**

Projects **510**

12 Object-Based Programming   513

12.1 **Classes and Objects: Basic Concepts** **514**
Object and Class Defined 514
Instance and Static Members 514
Advantages of Object-Oriented Programming 514

12.2 **Building and Using a Class** **515**
Differences Between the Class Module and the Standard Module 515
Adding a Class Module to a Project 517
Creating the Fixed Asset Class 517
Creating a Property 518
Creating a Method 520
Using the FixedAsset Class 523
Default Property Setting and the Constructor 523
Building and Using a Class: A Recapitulation 524

12.3 **Adding Features to the Class** **525**
Enumerated Constants 525
Throwing Exceptions 527
Implementing Events in a Class 529
A Class with an Event: An Example 529
Hooking Event Handlers 534

12.4 **Nested Classes** **535**
Developing the Depositor Class 536
Using the Depositor Class 538
Additional Remarks 539

12.5 **The Visual Element in an Object** **539**
Treating the Form as an Object 539
A Count Down Clock 540
Using the Count Down Clock 541

Summary **542**

Explore and Discover **543**

Exercises 548

Projects 554

13 Object-Oriented Programming   557

13.1   Inheritance 558
Inheritance Hierarchy 558
Why Inheritance? 558
An Inheritance Example 558
Inheriting from VS.NET Classes 561
Creating Event Arguments 563
Hiding Members from Classes Outside the Class Hierarchy 565
The MustInherit and NotInheritable Classes 567

13.2   Inheriting a Form at Design Time 567
A Data Entry Form Example 568

13.3   Polymorphism 570
Inheritance-Based Polymorphism 571
Using Polymorphism 573
Interface-Based Polymorphism 576
Multiple Inheritances 580

13.4   Additional Topics 580
Garbage Collection and the Finalizer 580
Creating User Defined Exceptions 580

Summary 581

Explore and Discover 582

Exercises 587

Projects 589

14 Beyond the Core   591

14.1   Using the Windows Registry 592
A Simple Text Browser Project 592
Remembering the Default Font 594
Additional Remarks 596

14.2   Creating Components 597
Creating a Component with No Visual Element 597
Testing the DBSchemaBrowser Component 602
Using the Component in Any Project 604
Creating a Component with Visual Elements 605
Testing and Using the New Control 606
The User Control 608

14.3   Developing Web Forms Applications 608
Basic Concepts 608
ASP.NET 609
Requirements for ASP.NET Development 610
Creating a Simple Web Forms Application 610
Data Access with Web Forms 615
Data Validation 618
A Course Login Form 619

14.4   Creating and Using Web Services 621
Creating A Web Service 622
Accessing a Web Service 626
Additional Remarks 630

Summary 631

Explore And Discover 632

Exercises 636

Projects 638

Appendix A Data Management Using Files   639

A.1   Working with Sequential Files 640
    Opening a File 640
    Reading Data from a File 641
    Output with Sequential Files 646

A.2   The Structure 648
    Defining the Structure 648
    Declaring and Using a Structure Variable 648

A.3   Working with Binary Files 649
    Differences between the Binary File and the Sequential File 649
    Opening a File with the Binary Mode 650
    Output and Input with a Binary File 650
    Saving and Retrieving an Array 651

A.4   Working with Random Files 652
    An Example 653
    Opening a File for Random Mode 654
    Performing Input and Output with a Random File 655
    Completing the Example 656
    Additional Remarks 658
    A Technical Note 659

A.5   Design Considerations 659
    File Characteristics and Suitable Applications 659

Summary 660

Explore and Discover 661

Exercises 664

Appendix B Graphics, Animation,
Drag and Drop   667

B.1   Drawing Graphs 668
    Basic Concepts 668
    The Graphic Object 669
    The DrawRectangle and DrawEllipse Methods 671
    The Fill Methods and the Brushes 672
    An Example: Christmas Lights 674
    The DrawString Method and Fonts 677

B.2   Animation 679
    The Flying Butterfly 680
    Rotating Light Colors 682
    The Rolling Wheel 684

B.3   Drag and Drop 688
    Keeping a Disk in the Holder: An Example 689
    Dragging Texts Among Controls 690

Summary 691

Explore and Discover 692

Exercises 693

Appendix C Number Systems and Bit-Wise Operations   695

C.1   Number Systems 696

Converting Between the Two Systems 696

From Binary to Decimal. 696

From Decimal to Binary. 696

The Hex Decimal Representation 697

Converting Between Hex and Decimal Numbers 697

Representing Hex Numbers in VB 698

Why Discuss Number Systems? 698

C.2   Bit-Wise Operation of Logical Operators 698

The Not, And, Or, Xor Operators 699

Various Uses of the Logical Operators 699

Summary 703

Explore and Discover 704

Exercises 707

Index   709

Preface

Dedication

To My Parents

Introduction

I have been looking for a visual basic textbook that:

- **Helps students clearly see the practical applications of visual basic (VB) features.** Due to the voluminous number of features available, students new to VB programming tend to get lost as to how to best utilize a particular VB feature. A textbook that clearly illustrates the application contexts of these features can help the student understand and appreciate these features easily and promptly.

- **Provides proper coverage in both programming topics and design issues.** As a programming textbook, it should not only introduce VB language elements but also properly discuss programming logic and algorithms. In addition, a proper attempt to teach programming applications will inevitably involve a discussion of design choices; thus, design issues must also be properly considered in the discussion.

- **Enables the instructor to focus on important topics.** The textbook should provide sufficient technical information to which students can refer. This allows the instructor to emphasize key points without spending a tremendous amount of class time explaining details.

- **Reinforces important topics effectively.** The textbook should provide plenty of examples to illustrate how important VB features can be applied, and how programming logic and algorithms can be implemented. In addition, it should provide a sufficient number of exercises for the student to practice to hone their programming skills.

- **Provides a guide for the student to use the VB integrated development environment (IDE) not only as a programming tool, but also as a learning device and as a source of technical information.** Many of the VB features can be learned by simply "playing" with the VB IDE. In addition, the Help file contains a wealth of technical information and is available at the student's fingertips. The textbook should provide pedagogical devices that guide the student towards using these resources. A student equipped with this learning skill will be able to continue to develop on their own after completing the course.

While existing textbooks satisfy some of these needs, none appear to meet all the criteria. As an attempt to satisfy the needs of my class, I wrote some handouts, which were met with enthusiastic responses from my students. My efforts evolved into a complete textbook.

Features

This book has been written with the previously stated goals in mind. It contains the following features:

Application Context

While retaining the typical organizational structure of presenting VB topics, the book provides clear application contexts. For example, Chapter 3, "User Interface Design: Visual Basic Controls and Events," introduces many VB controls. Instead of beginning with introducing the features of each control one by one, the chapter first discusses an application scenario and then presents the control that is most suitable given the application requirement(s). All chapters are written with a similar flavor. Chapter 8, "Arrays and Their Uses," includes a discussion of practical array uses that call for different programming logic and techniques. Most chapters include application examples that help the student see how the materials learned in the particular chapter can be put together in an application. Most chapters also involve discussions of programming logic and/or algorithms.

Design Orientation

Chapter 3 also serves as an example of the design orientation that this textbook emphasizes. In the process of introducing each VB control for the application context, the chapter provides a guide to design choices for the visual interface. Of course, design issues are not limited to the visual interface. Given a set of application requirements, many different code elements and code structures can be assembled to obtain the same result. Wherever more than a single plausible alternative can accomplish the same goal, this textbook points out the difference and suggests a choice, if applicable. For example, as early as Chapter 2, "Introduction to Visual Basic Programming," the text suggests that the form Close method is preferred to the End statement to terminate a program.

While most textbooks appear to shy away from discussing design issues probably as an attempt for simplicity, proper discussion of the issues helps the student gain a clearer understanding and prepares the student to be a better software developer.

Code Examples

This textbook provides many code examples. Good code examples help students learn more effectively for several reasons. They show the programming context for the code, illustrate good programming practice, and also serve as an "analogy" by which the student can extend the code to other applications.

Most of the code examples are not just code fragments but complete procedures. A beginner can be faced with countless uncertainties as to how to use a code fragment properly. For example, a beginner can be uncertain as to whether a method of a control can only be used in an event of the same control. A code example with a control's event procedure that includes the use of yet another control's method can easily clarify the doubt in the beginner's mind without any additional words.

Although it is desirable to give code examples in complete procedures, it is also important that the key point is not buried in tedious details and countless lines of code. The code examples have been carefully structured to illustrate the point without being unnecessarily complex.

Attention to Interactions among Control Interfaces

VB is an event-driven language. Event procedures are executed when events occur. While most events are triggered by user actions, the same events can also be triggered by code; therefore, some event procedures can be executed for no "obvious" reasons, causing unexpected results. To the beginner, these unexpected results are mysterious and can be frustrating in an attempt to trace the source of error. This textbook calls particular attention to and suggests ways to avoid these potential problems. The instructor should benefit from not having to help the student hunt for the mysterious bug.

Special Boxes

Three types of special boxes are used throughout the textbook: *Tip*, *Try This*, and *Look It Up*. Tip boxes alert the student to special coding tips and/or potential programming pitfalls. They draw the student's attention to some particular programming techniques. Try This boxes encourage the student to experiment with code and observe the outcomes. These hands-on experiments help the student retain knowledge. Look It Up boxes guide the student to additional technical information in the MSDN help file on a particular VB feature. Students who follow the instruction will gradually develop the habit and capability of searching for answers from this valuable resource.

End of Chapter Assignments

Starting from Chapter 2, each chapter contains three types of assignments: Explore and Discover Exercises, Exercises, and Projects. Explore and Discover Exercises include hands-on exercises that allow the student to explore, experiment, and inspect results. They are designed to be a "learn-by-doing" tool. Students who perform these exercises will learn more than what the chapter covers and retain the knowledge more easily. Innovative students should also be able to follow the pattern and devise their own "tools" to make their own discoveries when no answer is readily available.

The Exercises are designed for the student to apply what they learn in the chapter. Each chapter contains many exercises with a wide range of varieties. Instructors should have no difficulty with finding those exercises they deem most suitable for the course objectives. The student is encouraged to work on as many as time allows to become truly proficient.

The Projects require the assembly of concepts and techniques from the current chapter as well as previous chapters. These projects will require major efforts by the student, and can be considered as devices for integration of the learned programming knowledge.

About This Edition

This edition retains all significant features in the previous edition. Its contents, however, have been completely updated to reflect the sweeping changes that come with VB.NET. Similar to previous versions, VB.NET is available as a part of the complete package of Microsoft Visual Studio. NET (VS.NET). Different from the previous versions, however, all the languages in VS.NET are supported by the same "common language runtime" (recognized as the .NET framework), allowing VB.NET to tab into other languages' powerful features not previous available. In many ways, this new VB version is different from its previous versions. Changes in the language include those in language elements, control names, control interfaces, and inclusion of true object-oriented features, just to list a few. As a result of these changes, the language is not only productive (for rapid application development), but also powerful as a software development tool. This edition of the textbook incorporates all these significant changes in the language. In addition, several changes are made in the organization and topics. These changes include:

- Chapter 13, "Selected Topics in Input and Output" is replaced with "Object-Oriented Programming" (OOP), which discusses inheritance and polymorphism. Along with this change, Chapter 12 is renamed "Object-Based Programming," which discusses topics in basic OOP concepts and encapsulation.
- Topics in API, automation, and creating ActiveX DLL are dropped from Chapter 14, "Beyond the Core." In their places are "Creating Components," "Developing Web Forms Applications," and "Creating and Using Web Services." These changes reflect

the new features of the language. "Creating Components" illustrates how a component can be easily created and used in various applications. "Web Forms" and "Web Services" reflect the current trend toward sharing computing resources through the network (intranet and internet).

- Chapters 9 and 8 of previous edition are now Chapters 8 and 9. This sequence is more consistent with the traditional arrangement of presenting arrays before topics in database; however, teachers who prefer to teach topics in database first should encounter no problem.

Background of Students

The contents of this book have been successfully field-tested with two groups of students: business graduate students without programming background and undergraduate students who have taken one or more programming courses. Both groups of students should have some exposure to the Windows operating system as a user. They should have a good understanding of the Windows' basic terms and concepts. For example, they should know how to start a program, how to use the mouse to navigate around, and how to create a file or folder.

Regardless of the background, if you are a student inspired to be a proficient software developer, you should find this book worth studying and keeping as a reference. It discusses many intriguing programming problems and design issues not found in a typical textbook.

Organization

There is a consensus among VB instructors that students have a harder time understanding and developing programming logic than designing the user interface. The proposed treatment, however, varies. Two alternatives have emerged: introducing programming elements (such as flow of execution control) first and introducing almost all essential VB controls at the beginning. The latter approach appears to produce better results.

While students may have difficulty developing programming logic, their hardest challenge is the clear understanding of the context of their code in the VB environment. VB is an event-driven language. Its code behaves in quite a different manner from that in the procedure-oriented language. Students can see the effect of their code only after they clearly understand the relationship between the actions of the user/system and the code they place in the event procedure; that is, they can see the complete picture only after they have a good understanding of events and event procedures.

Introducing more controls at the beginning does not hinder students' progress in developing the ability to handle programming logic. On the contrary, with the broad exposure to VB controls, they become acquainted with events more readily. In addition, they are better able to design a user interface that is more efficient for data entry and for code.

Because of this consideration, Chapter 3 introduces many controls in the context of data entry. It emphasizes the design choices for different controls. Other controls are introduced in the chapters where the controls are needed. Students' responses to this approach have been very positive.

Chapter 1, "Introduction," provides an overview of the book. Topics in Chapters 2 through 7 are considered essential and should be studied in sequence. Chapters 8 through 13 (Chapters 12, "Object-Based Programming," and 13, "Object Oriented Programming," as a unit), however, are fairly "modular". Any chapter can be studied without the background of the other, although some assignments at the end of the chapter do assume the knowledge of previous chapters.

Instructors who want to teach files can use Appendix A, "Data Management Using Files," at any point after Chapter 7, "Repetition." The appendix contains summary tables that compare different file structures. The student should find them helpful in understanding different VB file modes. Instructors who want to teach graphics should be able to use Appendix B, "Graphics,

Animation and Drag and Drop," after Chapter 7. Appendix C, "Number Systems and Bit-wise Operations," can be taught in conjunction with Chapter 5, "Decision."

As a special note, topics covered in Chapter 10 "Special Topics in Data Entry," are seldom found in a typical textbook; however, many instructors consider these topics important. The chapter can be deemed as an application of VB programming techniques. The student may be intrigued by the "tricks" employed to minimize code and to generalize its applicability in performing data validation. Hopefully, the student will be inspired to develop code in a similar fashion.

A Note on Printing Style

As you read this text, please note the following print style:

- New terms and technical concepts are italicized.

- Each code indent level is represented by four spaces. Some code lines are too long to be printed physically in one line. The code continuation is printed on the next line with a two-space indent. These lines should be treated as single lines in the code window, instead of as multiple lines as seen in the printed text.

- Text in bold font represents an item or concept and should be read as a single unit in the context. For example, in the sentence, "The computer displays **Male button is on,**" the boldfaced text is a message displayed by the computer.

For the Instructor

Instructor Resources

Resources available to instructors include the Instructor's CD and additional support by a companion website as highlighted below:

Instructor's Resource CD-ROM. The Instructor's Resource CD-ROM that is available with *Visual Basic .NET Programming* contains:

- Instructor's Manual in Word and PDF

- Solutions to all questions and exercises from the book and website

- PowerPoint lectures with PresMan software

- A Windows-based test manager and the associated test bank in Word format with over 1,500 new questions

Tools for Online Learning. This text is accompanied by a companion website at **www.prenhall.Com/tsay** This website is designed to bring you and your students a richer, more interactive web experience. Features of this new site include the ability for you to customize your home page with real-time news headlines, current events, exercises, an interactive study guide, and downloadable supplements.

For the Student

Welcome to *Visual Basic.NET Programming*!

After the publication of the first edition, I received feedback from many readers stating that this book is easier to understand than other books they have used before. I believe this is attributable to the textbook's features, especially the application context and step-by-step explanation of programming logic. To help you learn more effectively, Chapter 1 offers suggestions on how to use the book. The companion website, **http://www.prenhall.com/tsay**, also provides code examples selected from the text and solutions to all odd-numbered exercises and projects.

It is worth noting that when you work on a programming problem, you will learn much more effectively by attempting it on your own without referring to the solution first. The provided solutions should be reviewed only after you complete your own work. If you are able to solve a substantial number of the odd-numbered problems in a chapter, you probably have a good understanding of the topics in that chapter.

The development of this book has benefited from the comments of my previous students. No doubt, your comments will be valuable as well, and are not only welcome but also much appreciated. Please send your feedback to jefftsay@uta.edu

Acknowledgement

This book would not have been possible without the enthusiasm and support of Alex Von Rosenburg, executive editor of Prentice Hall. Thanks should also be extended to many people at Prentice Hall for their diligent involvement with the book in various aspects: Susan Rifkin, Melissa Whitaker, Jodi McPherson, Thomas Park and the production team Audri Anna Bazlen, Gail Steier, Pat Smythe.

I want to thank Ampapat Suchiva for her tireless efforts in proofreading several versions of the original manuscript and for her suggestions for improvement of the contents. A special thanks goes to a generous friend, whom I got to know via the Internet, Ben Wu. He reviewed the draft of the entire original manuscript plus a substantial portion of the second edition and provided many constructive comments and suggestions.

I am grateful to the following reviewers whose constructive suggestions help shape the contents and writing style of this textbook:

Larry Andrew	Western Illinois University
Kelly J. Black	California State University
David Cooper	New River Community College
Marvin Harris	Lansing Community College
Paul C. Jorgensen	Grand Valley State University
Susan K. Lippert	George Washington University
Pati Milligan	Baylor University
Paula Velluto	Bunker Hill Community College
John F. Walker	Dona Ana Branch Community College - New Mexico State University
John Russo	Wentworth Institute of Technology
Eugene Thomas	Indiana University/Kelley School of Business
Doug Waterman	Fox Valley Technical College
Becca Wemhoff	Iowa State University
Shelly Hawkins	Western Washington University
Jim Forkner	Pennsylvania State University

Susan Pazourek and Chris Panell's technical editing helps to refine and strengthen many topics and to eliminate quite a few errors in the manuscripts for the revised edition. Of course, I retain the responsibility for all the remaining errors.

I am also indebted to the following students and friends for their contributions in various ways to this book:

Dan Burns, Mark Eakin, Doug Allison, Bruce Campbell, Phawinee Chaiwattana, Li-Ju Christine Chen, Meei-Ling Chen, Iris Shihyin Chien, James Garth Dimock, Christine Ding-tsyr Gau, Yi-Hsien Huang, Aygun Sarioglu, Jeffrey Nevin Scroggins, Nora Shen, and Ada Yu Yin.

I have been on a VB Internet discussion group since the date when it was sited in Texas A&M University. The group moved to a server hosted by L-Soft, International and has since become two separate groups. The addresses are:

VISBAS-L@PEACH.EASE.LSOFT.COM and
VISBAS-BEGINNERS@PEACH.EASE.LSOFT.COM.

I have benefited much more from the discussions than I have contributed. To those active participants, I sincerely express my thanks.

Dr. David Leuthold, professor emeritus of political science of the University of Missouri-Columbia has been my inspiration, mentor and role model. His advice and encouragement are deeply appreciated. My good friend and an experienced book author, Professor Lanny Solomon also provided advice in the development and writing process.

To say that writing this book is a family endeavor is not an exaggeration. My daughters, Carolyn and Angela, helped with editing the prospectus and the first few chapters of the original manuscripts. My son, Jonathan, helped with capturing the screens for production. My wife, Nora, read and tested the hands-on instructions of the first few chapters. During the intensive book-writing periods, she single-handedly shouldered various responsibilities and obligations so that I could remain focused on the book. Without you, Nora, I know I would have not progressed this far. Writing this book reminds me of the good old days when I was writing my dissertation. Nora, thank you!

Jeff Tsay

1 Introduction

This book introduces you to Visual Basic (VB) programming. It is oriented toward business applications, with a design perspective. Many business applications involve data-entry operations. On appearance, data entry appears to be a fairly simple programming problem; however, once you start to develop this type of application program, you will encounter many intriguing issues. For example, as soon as you start to design the data-entry screen, you will wonder how to best design the visual interface—thus, you will be faced with interface design issues. In addition, you will have to develop code to validate the data entered by the user because data accuracy is of the utmost importance to any business. Here, you may encounter a lot of duplicate code—thus, you will need to design the code structure to minimize duplication. Business applications also involve data storage and processing; therefore, you will need to deal with data management issues and develop algorithms to process data efficiently. This book is oriented toward handling these issues.

This chapter gives an overview of VB programming. Naturally, when you are learning VB programming, your first question is, "What is Visual Basic?" Section 1.1 provides some explanations. Section 1.2 examines what constitutes a sound application program. This section also discusses the steps involved in developing a program. Section 1.3 provides some suggestions on how to use this book.

After completing this chapter, you should be able to:

- Explain what Visual Basic is.
- Contrast the operating environment of Visual Basic with that of programs developed using procedure-oriented languages.
- Set forth the criteria for a sound application program.
- Enumerate the steps to develop a program.
- Understand the importance of hands-on experience in learning a programming language.

1.1 What Is Visual Basic?

Evolution of Visual Basic

Visual Basic evolves from *BASIC*, an acronym for *Beginner's All-Purpose Symbolic Instruction Code*, which was created in the 1960s. Its syntax is similar to *FORTRAN,* another programming language that was developed to handle *For*mula *Tran*slation. However, BASIC was used primarily for interactive computing, while FORTRAN was used in the batch-processing environment where each program was run as a job without human interaction or intervention. When microcomputers were introduced, BASIC was the language available in nearly all makes, such as Tandy, Apple, and so on. Its power was fairly limited because of hardware limitations. When the personal computer (PC) became available, Microsoft introduced GW-BASIC with its disk operating system (DOS).

As you may be aware, programs written in BASIC (any version) need to be processed by a *language processor* (a *program* that processes the BASIC program) before their instructions can be understood and executed by the computer. The BASIC language processors up to that point were *interpreters* that read one line of BASIC code at a time, interpreted the code, and carried out the activities called for by the instructions. Because of the overhead associated with interpreting the code, the execution was very slow.

To improve execution speed, BASIC *compilers* were introduced. A version of the BASIC compilers by Microsoft is *Quick Basic*. A compiler is another kind of language processor that translates a *source program,* such as a program written in Quick Basic, into the machine language or some pseudo-code that is fairly close to the machine language. The resulting program is recognized as the *object program,* or *executable,* in modern terminology. Because of the elimination of the overhead of interpretation, the object program runs much faster than a source program under an interpreter.

As you can see from the diagram in Figure 1.1, the key difference between an interpreter and a compiler is the output. The interpreter takes the source program along with the data as input and produces the results that the source program calls for. Under this arrangement, each time you need to run the source program, you will need to invoke the interpreter. In contrast, the compiler takes only the source program as input and produces an object program in a lower-level language. The object program must be run along with required data to produce the results. Note that the object program can be run many times with different input, and without being compiled again as long as the source program is not changed.

Despite its speed, Quick Basic has its drawbacks, especially by today's standards:

- It is a procedure-oriented language. When it runs, the program, instead of the user, dictates the sequence of activities to be carried out. The user is not allowed any flexibility.

- Its interface is text based instead of graphics based. The appearance is not attractive. The keyboard is used nearly exclusively to obtain user input or commands. In many cases, text-based input is more susceptible to errors, and may not be as efficient as other gadgets that are available in the graphics-based environment, such as check boxes, radio buttons, and combo boxes.

- Programs take a long time to develop and are difficult to change, especially when the change involves the visual interface. The programmer needs to track all the details relating to the location, size, and color of all boxes and texts drawn onscreen. A minor change can call for painstaking efforts by the programmer to ensure that everything is done correctly.

After the graphic user interface (*GUI*)-based Windows operating system was introduced for PCs, *Visual Basic* arrived in 1991. The first version of VB had two editions: one for DOS, and another for the Windows system. As the Windows system gained in popularity, the later versions of VB were designed only for the Windows operating systems. Earlier versions of VB were written for 16-bit operating systems because 32-bit operating systems were not yet available. There were two editions of VB in version 4: one for 16-bit operating systems, such as Windows 3.0, and another for 32-bit operating systems, such as Windows NT and Windows 95. Since version

Figure 1.1

Difference between
Interpreter and Compiler

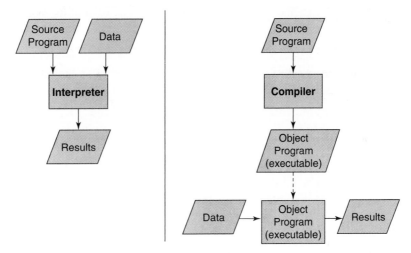

Difference between interpreter and compiler: the former produces
results of computations; the latter produces an object program, which
needs to be loaded into the memory to run in order to obtain the results.

5, all editions have been made exclusively for 32-bit operating systems. Version 6 expanded several language features, and supported ActiveX Data Objects (ADO) for data access. The current version, VB.NET, is a result of a sweeping overhaul to the language, and offers the object-oriented features of modern programming languages. The following table briefly highlights the *milestones* of the evolution of VB.

Year	Milestone	Remark
1964	BASIC	For interactive computing in *mainframe* computers
1970's	BASIC	In various microcomputers/PC (BASIC and GW-Basic)
1985	BASIC and Quick Basic	Processed by compilers
1991	Visual Basic	For Windows or for DOS
1992	Visual Basic 2	For Windows only
1993	Visual Basic 3	For Windows only; enhanced with data access capability
1996	Visual Basic 4	For 16 bit or 32 bit Windows systems
1997	Visual Basic 5	For 32 bit Windows systems only
1998	Visual Basic 6	For 32 bit Windows systems only
2001	Visual Basic.NET	Object oriented; sweeping overhaul

Characteristics of Visual Basic

The vocabulary and syntax of VB are derived from BASIC; however, VB differs significantly from BASIC in several respects:

- VB provides a set of visual objects (recognized as controls) that can be drawn easily onto a window (called a form). These controls eliminate the need to develop the code to construct the visual interface. The layout of the windows that contain the controls can be changed easily by dragging and dropping the controls to a new location, without necessitating a change in the code. The process for program development and revision becomes much easier and requires much less time and effort.

- The code structure of VB is *object-oriented*, whereas that of BASIC is *procedure-oriented*. In BASIC, there is no object. Its code usually follows the following syntax:

  Verb Operand List

For example, to display a line of text in BASIC, such as "Display this line", the code will look like the following:

```
Print "Display this line."
```

Although some VB code still retains this form, most of its code is structured around objects. The syntax appears as follows:

```
Object.Method (parameter list)
```

where the so-called method is the action or activity to be carried out.

To display the same line using VB, you would code the following:

```
Console.WriteLine("Display this line.")
```

As you can see, Console is recognized as an object. Its WriteLine method will write the line on the object, which is the console.

Object-oriented coding is easier because the object and the action are identified separately, resulting in a more concise set of vocabulary. In BASIC, you must remember to use Lprint to print on the printer and Print to print onscreen. In VB, you use the same WriteLine method to display (print) on different objects. It is also more consistent with the user's activity in the GUI environment. For example, when you are editing a document with a word processor, you highlight a block of text (identify the object) and then instruct the computer what to do with it (indicate an action such as cut or paste).

Note that an object-oriented language offers many more advantages than merely simplified syntax. One significant advantage is code reusability through *inheritance*, a feature that allows the programmer to extend the functionality from existing code without having to directly modify the original source code. This feature was not available in the previous versions of VB. VB.NET is a full-fledged object-oriented language that offers many exciting features of modern computer languages.

VB is an *event-driven* rather than procedure-oriented language. As discussed earlier in this chapter, when a procedure-oriented program runs, it dictates the sequence of operations. This means the programmer must predefine the sequence when developing the program. In addition, changing the sequence of operations requires revising the program. On the other hand, an event-driven program does not dictate the sequence of operations. The user can instruct the computer to perform whatever operations the program is capable of, in any sequence he or she desires. This offers the user flexibility. Any changes in the sequence of operations will not call for revising the program. In this sense, an event-driven program is easier to develop, and requires fewer revisions.

Event-driven programs, however, present the programmer with a different kind of challenge. In many instances, an activity can be carried out only after some prerequisite actions have been taken or data are ready. For example, when the user clicks the Send button in an email application, the target email address, the subject line, and the body of message must all be filled in first. When the user initiates the action, there is no guarantee that the prerequisites have been met. As a programmer, you must find ways to ensure that the prerequisites are there.

Visual Basic as a Language and as a Processor

From the preceding discussion, you understand that VB is a programming language used to write programs to make the computer perform desired tasks. It has its own vocabulary and grammatical rules (syntax). These elements can be combined to form a program, which is the complete set of instructions designed to perform the defined tasks.

You have also learned that the program you write in the VB language will need to be processed by a VB language processor, which is also a computer program. In most instances, the VB language processor is also referred to as Visual Basic. When we say that you can write a program in VB.NET, we mean that you can write a VB.NET program that VB.NET (the processor) can understand and process. As such, the term Visual Basic can actually mean two different things—the language and the processor—in different contexts, or the language and the processor at the same time.

When you are developing a VB program, you will work with a software program that does more than just process your program. It provides an environment in which you can draw the visual interface, write the code, compile and test the program, and make additional changes. For VB.NET, this processor is recognized as the Visual Studio Integrated Development Environment (IDE), which is actually capable of handling not just VB but also several other languages. You will explore the IDE further in Chapter 2, "Introduction to Visual Basic Programming."

Statement and Code. A VB program can consist of many instructions. An instruction that is complete in meaning and can stand alone like a sentence is recognized as a *statement*. Usually, you will use a line to write a statement. Some statements are very long. In such cases, the statement can be spanned over several lines. The mechanic of spanning a statement over multiple lines is explained in Chapter 2. Statements in a program are collectively recognized as *code*. The following sample code fragment comes from Chapter 7, "Repetition:"

```
For I = 0 To lstNames.SelectedItems.Count - 1
    'Show names selected
    Console.WriteLine(lstNames.SelectedItems(I))
Next I
```

Each line in this code is complete in meaning and, therefore, is a statement.

Editions of Visual Basic.NET

In this book, you will learn the VB language pertaining to the features available in the VB.NET language processor. VB.NET is available as a part of the complete package of the Visual Studio .NET (VS.NET). There are actually four different editions of VS.NET:

- Visual Studio .NET Professional Edition: This edition includes features for building .NET-based applications, such as Web services, Web forms, Windows forms, .NET framework, and common language runtime. It also includes languages such as VB.NET, Visual C++ .NET, and Visual C# .NET, as well as the unified integrated development environment.

- Visual Studio .NET Academic Edition: This edition has all the features of the Professional Edition plus tools and code samples specifically designed for faculty and students.

- Visual Studio .NET Enterprise Developer Edition: This edition includes all available features in the .NET Professional Edition and tools to develop database applications such as MS SQL server 2000, and some of the Enterprise life-cycle tools such as Microsoft Visual SourceSafe® 6.0c and enterprise template project type.

- Visual Studio .NET Enterprise Architect Edition: This edition includes all the features available in the preceding edition with the complete package for the enterprise life-cycle tools and the full versions of the service technologies such as MS Windows 2000 Advanced Server, MS Exchange Server, and MS BizTalk Server.

In addition, there is a VB.NET Standard Edition that has the core VB language features that were stripped off some features in the Professional Edition. This book focuses on the features available in the Professional Edition.

1.2 Overview of Visual Basic Program Development

Before you get involved in the details of actually developing a VB program, it is important that you become aware of the criteria for a sound program. These criteria provide benchmarks against which the quality of your programs can be compared, and thus serve as the guide for your application development. In addition, you should also be acquainted with the program development cycle. A good understanding of the cycle will equip you with a step-by-step roadmap to developing your program so that you can be more efficient and effective in carrying out your programming endeavor. This section discusses these two aspects.

Criteria for a Sound Application Program

How do you judge the soundness of an application program? As a programmer, you examine the program in two completely different perspectives: *external* and *internal*. You first inspect the program from an external perspective, and judge it in terms of the application requirements. The criteria include the following:

- *Functionality.* The program must meet the requirements of the application; that is, it must deliver the functionality called for by the application. For example, if an order-processing application needs to update both the customer records and the on-hand quantities of all products ordered, the program cannot be considered complete until it can perform both functions. In short, can the program do what it is expected to do?

- *Efficiency.* The program should also perform the required functions efficiently. The program should minimize the consumption of computer resources, including computer time and storage space. I have seen a general ledger package that takes several minutes of computer time to post 10 transactions from a general journal to a general ledger, almost as fast (slow) as a person can handle the task manually. Such a program obviously fails the efficiency test.

- *User-Friendliness.* The concept of user-friendliness is not new. The ancient concept stipulated that the message to the user be clear, meaningful, and in a friendly tone; however, with the GUI environment, this concept encompasses a much wider variety of user expectations. Briefly, a user-friendly program should do the following:
  - Provide the user with maximum mobility around the user interface.
  - Be consistent in appearance and behavior among different windows.
  - Provide the user with supports in using the program to perform the task. Examples of support include providing dialog boxes for lookup and online help.
  - Be flexible in accommodating user's tastes and preferences.
  - Guard the user against errors and mistakes. If not handled carefully in the program, some errors caused by the user can crash the application, resulting in loss of data. The program should properly handle all errors and mistakes by the user to prevent accidental loss of data or causing any inconvenience to the user.

From the perspective of the programmer, the program not only should satisfy the external requirements as outlined above, but also should be developed with a set of *internal standards*. The code developed for a program should have the following characteristics:

- *Consistency in Coding Style.* There is a set of coding conventions that the programmer should follow when developing code. These conventions include coding mechanics such as properly indenting blocks of code for visual clues to the code structure and naming objects with predefined prefixes for easy identification of the types of objects involved. Code developed with a consistent style is much easier to read and understand. As an illustration, look again at the code fragment on page 5. It is indented properly, providing a clue that it is a code block. The name *lstNames* also follows the naming convention; it contains a three-letter prefix, lst, indicating the type of object it represents.

- *Code Clarity and Readability.* In addition to the consistent coding style, other factors can also make code clearer and easier to understand. For example, if the names used to represent data in your program are meaningful, your program will become much easier to read and follow. The person who reviews the code can easily associate the names with the data they represent, making the tracing of programming logic much easier. As an example, you also might have inferred that lstNames in the preceding code sample contains names. In many cases, the purpose or meaning of some code may not be clear. Adding comments can make the program easier to understand. In the preceding code example, the lines that start with a single quote (also known as the apostrophe ') are comment lines.

- *Modularity in Code Design. Modularity* refers to the design of code structure so that each block of code is isolated from the rest of the program; that is, each block can perform its designated task without depending on the state of other blocks and without being interfered with by the actions of other parts. In this way, each block of code is independent of the others. Program logic and flow of execution are localized, and much easier to trace. Such a code structure is easier to debug, review, and revise.

- *Elegant Algorithms.* An algorithm is a systematic approach to solving a programming problem. It usually involves the iterative application of a group of defined steps to arrive at the solution. An algorithm is said to be elegant when its logic is easy to trace and implement, and is efficient in terms of its speed and storage requirements. Given a fairly complex problem, an infinite number of algorithms can be constructed to solve it. Some are efficient; some are not. For example, the sorting problem (arranging data elements in order) has a simple goal, yet literally hundreds of algorithms exist for sorting. For a fairly large volume of data, the difference in speed between the best and the worst algorithm is a factor of several hundred times. Careful identification and selection of algorithms for your program can make it perform much more efficiently.

- *Code Maintainability.* Often, the requirements of a program change over time. A change in the requirements necessitates revision of the program; thus, efforts are involved in maintaining the program. All the internal factors just mentioned have an impact on code maintainability; however, code maintainability is not limited to the aforementioned factors. This is particularly true in VB. Some code by nature is more generally applicable than other code. *General applicability* refers to the attribute of certain code blocks that will not necessitate any revision even when the program requirements are changed. For example, in many cases, you may need to clear the content of the controls (visual objects) in the visual interface. One way to perform this is to refer to the controls by name and assign a certain value to these controls. In VB, you can assign the same value to these controls without referring to their specific names. The latter approach is more generally applicable because no matter how the names of the controls are changed, you can still use the same code to perform the task. The use of the more generally applicable code will undoubtedly result in a program that is much more maintainable. An example is provided in Chapter 7.

The diagram in Figure 1.2 summarizes this discussion.

How are these criteria for sound programs treated in this book? The functionality issue depends on the programmer's understanding of the application requirements. All the other issues are considered throughout the book where applicable. In most cases, your attention is called to why a certain problem is solved with a particular block of code instead of other alternatives. The performance implications of different code structures and algorithms are considered where applicable. In addition, a significant portion of Chapter 8, "Arrays and Their Uses," is also used to present different sorting algorithms. This will stimulate your mind, and you will become more critical in selecting and devising a suitable algorithm to solve the problem at hand. The user-friendliness criterion is very important, especially in the context of data-entry screens and user interfaces. Chapter 10, "Special Topics in Data Entry," is devoted in particular to treating this topic thoroughly.

Figure 1.2

External and internal
criteria for sound
programs

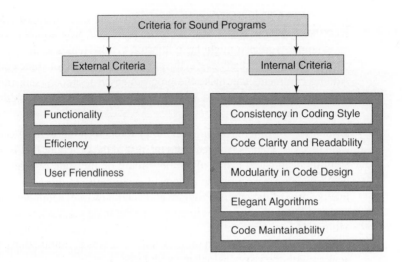

Steps in Program Development

When you are ready to develop an application program, there is a fairly standard set of steps you should follow. Your progress will be much smoother when you observe these steps, which can be outlined as follows:

1. *Analyze and Define the Problem.* As discussed previously in this chapter, the first requirement of a sound program is that it must meet the needs of the application. A clear understanding of the problem and goals is the first step in developing the program. Only when the needs and requirements of the program are clearly understood can you determine how the program is to look and act.

TIP

When developing a program, you can save a lot of time, headaches, and effort in revision and rework if you know its exact requirements/specifications at the very beginning. Analyze the problem carefully and define the requirements clearly before proceeding.

2. *Design the Visual Interface.* Based on your analysis and understanding of the problem, you will be able to design the visual interface for the program. You will start to work with the IDE. You will need to decide what data fields should appear on a form. This process can become quite involved. VB provides various visual objects (controls) that you can use to represent these data fields. It takes a careful analysis to determine which VB control will be the best given the nature of a data field. Chapter 3, "User Interface Design: Visual Basic Controls and Events," provides an analytical framework for this purpose.

3. *Define User-Program Interaction.* The user interface consists of the *visual aspect* as described earlier in this chapter, and the *behavior* in which your program responds to the user's actions and to what happens in the computer internally. You will need to determine what your program should do in detail. The user's actions and system activities are recognized as *events*. User actions that can trigger events include pressing a key, clicking a control, or making a selection from a menu. System activities can also trigger events. Examples of these activities include loading and closing a form. You must first be aware what events will be triggered when each of these actions occurs. Based on how you decide your program should react, you will place the code in the pertinent event to respond accordingly. Some of those commonly seen events are discussed in Chapter 3. Additional events are discussed in other chapters, where the events need to be handled.

4. *Design the Code Structure.* On appearance, the code you will develop to respond to an action should be placed in the event that the action triggers. Your code structure will simply be dictated by the responses you want your program to carry out. In reality, however, it can be much more complex. You will be introduced to various complex situations. Suffice it to say, it pays to analyze the complex situation thoroughly before writing any code. As your program grows into multiple modules (a module is a code window that contains your code), you will also discover that many code blocks can be shared so the appropriate module(s) in which to place these blocks can become an issue. Your design of the code structure can have far-reaching implications on the maintainability of your code. The importance of this design phase cannot be overemphasized. Some authors maintain that most (more than 60%) of your time and effort should be expended on this endeavor to produce a sound program. Some of these design issues are discussed in Chapter 10, "Special Topic in Data Entry," Chapter 11, "Menus and Multiple Form Applications," and Chapter 13, "Object-Oriented Programming." The context of the discussions in these chapters pertains to minimizing code duplication and dealing with the issues associated with large projects.

5. *Write Code.* Based on your design, you will then develop the code to perform the activities that your program requires. In addition to ensuring that the code performs what is called for, you should pay particular attention to your coding style. As mentioned, this includes the mechanical aspects of indenting and following the naming conventions. You will start to learn about this aspect beginning in Chapter 2.

6. *Test and Edit the Program.* Unless a program is very short, it is rare that the program anybody develops will run correctly the first time. The program can have various kinds of errors:

   - *Syntax errors* result from the failure to follow the rules to put various code elements together.

   - *Semantic errors* result from the difference between what the programmer codes and what the programmer actually means. For example, the programmer may code the statement, A = B = C thinking that the three variables will have the same value after its execution; however, the statement actually has quite a different meaning in VB.

   - *Logic errors* result from the differences between what the programmer believes a block of code will do and what the program actually does. This type of error is the trickiest and can take days or even weeks to resolve in some complex situations. In most cases, you will test run your program and discover some unexpected problems or results. You will then modify your code to solve the problems you have identified and test it again. You will repeat the process until no problem or unexpected result is encountered.

   Testing and editing code constitute most of your effort in the coding activity. To minimize the possibility of encountering mysterious logic errors, it is advisable to break the code into small blocks and test it often. This makes it easier to identify the range of code that causes the error. A smaller number of statements make the error source easier to track down and correct.

7. *Place the Program into Production.* After a program is thoroughly tested, it is ready to be placed in actual use. A program that works with live data and produces real results is called a *production program*. When you are developing and testing the program, you work in the IDE. A program to be placed in production should be compiled to produce a separate object program. This object program (an executable file) can then run without the IDE. Additional explanations of the IDE and the compiled executable file are discussed in Chapter 2.

Figure 1.3 summarizes the steps of program development.

Figure 1.3

Steps of program
development

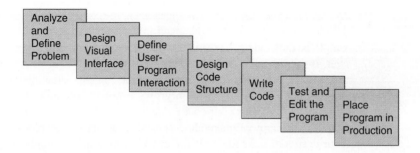

When a beginner is working on a programming exercise, some of these steps may be combined, or may not be applicable. For example, the exercise may be so simple that it requires little analysis of the problem or design of code structure. Once you understand the goal, you can start to work on designing the visual interface, writing the code, and testing the program. As you proceed and the problems become more complex, however, it pays to revisit this complete roadmap. You will appreciate the importance of those steps that you initially could do without.

1.3 How to Use This Book

This section offers a few suggestions on how to use this book. It should be stressed that hands-on practice is the key to successfully learning a programming language. You learn to program by programming, just like you learn to swim by swimming, not by observing. Perhaps, another analogy can help illustrate the point.

Learning the Language: An Analogy

In many ways, learning a computer language is no different from learning a human language to convey ideas. Before you can speak a language fluently, you must build a wide vocabulary. You will also need to know the rules to put the vocabulary together to convey an idea. The sentences must be structured correctly. Without the correct structure, these sentences will be hard to understand. In the case of computer languages, the computer will simply refuse to understand.

It is also important to note that a grammatically correct sentence may not necessarily convey exactly the idea that you have in mind. For example, the two sentences, "You like a dog" and "You are like a dog" are both grammatically correct. But you know how different the reactions can be from your listener. In VB, the statement A = B = C may have quite a different meaning from what you may think. (Wait until Chapter 5, "Decision," for the explanation.) You must also choose the right vocabulary to express the right ideas. Furthermore, even if the sentences convey the correct meaning, you may find that there are better ways to convey the same thing; that is, different sentences may have different effectiveness in conveying the same idea.

The previous discussion suggests that there are four aspects of speaking a language (writing a VB program):

1. Vocabulary

2. Grammar (syntax rules)

3. Semantics (meaning)

4. Effectiveness

To express yourself well in a language as a speaker or writer, not just as a listener or reader, you need to build a large vocabulary, follow the syntax rules, clearly understand the meanings of the vocabulary, and find the proper expression to convey the ideas effectively. It takes a lot of practice to learn to speak a new language fluently and convey ideas effectively. At the beginning, even a very simple sentence bears repetition to gain the desired level of familiarity.

Conventions for Syntax Specification

Syntax rules were mentioned in the previous subsection. In this textbook, when introducing new VB features, the syntax rules for code are often explained. The following table lists the conventions used in this text.

Syntax Rule	Example	Remark
Regular typed words represent exact words to be used in code.	`Option Strict On`	Every word should be typed as it appears
Italicized letters represent a concept, a placeholder to be replaced with a specific item.	`Dim VariableName As Integer`	*VariableName* should be replaced with a variable name in actual coding.
Mutually exclusive alternatives are separated by vertical bars ("|").	`ByRef¦ByVal`	Either ByRef or ByVal can be specified.
Items specified in brackets are optional.	`[ParameterList]`	A parameter list can be present or omitted.
Brackets with items separated by vertical bars indicate one item or none can be specified.	`[ByRef¦ByVal]`	Either ByRef or ByVal can be specified or omitted.
Braces with items separated by vertical bars indicate one item must be specified.	`{On¦Off}`	Either On or Off must be specified.
The plus (+) sign indicates that two keys should be pressed at the same time.	`Ctrl+R`	The Ctrl key and the R key must be pressed simultaneously.
Ellipsis (…) indicates the omission of some parts.	`Dim Variable1 [As data type] [, Variable2 [As data type]]...`	More can be specified.

The Case for Hands-On

When you are developing a VB program, you will be the speaker or writer of the language, not just a listener or reader. To be good at VB programming, you will do exactly as you would to learn a new human language. You will learn the vocabulary of VB. You will also learn the rules to combine the elements to form expressions and statements that express what you want the computer to perform. As you progress, you will also discover different ways of getting the same result. In many instances, the different ways may have different performance implications. You will be faced with design choices, and will select the more effective and efficient approach.

From learning the vocabulary to making an intelligent design choice, the development of your proficiency takes a lot of hands-on practice, which enables you to do the following:

- Gain familiarity not only with the IDE, but also with the vocabulary and syntax rules of VB without exerting stress on your memory. Many details are involved in each code line. They do not stand out in your memory until you actually write the code. Familiarity will make you much more efficient in handling the same or a similar problem. You will find your second attempt takes much less time than the first one. Familiarity improves your efficiency and enhances your confidence.

- Gain a more in depth understanding of the interrelationship between different parts of the code. You will be able to see the effect of the code you place in different events more readily. This level of understanding allows you to develop and trace programming logic more easily.

- Identify opportunities for code improvement. Some programming problems can appear different in their context but call for the same or similar solution. The first time you encounter the problem, you might just be glad that you have a solution. The second time, you may see some faults of your original solution and attempt to improve on it. In the process, you will explore, experiment, and discover new solutions. As a result, you will gain even more knowledge. You will be able to write programs that perform effectively, much like a speaker delivering an effective speech.

You have seen how to code to display a line of text on the Console object. Write a line of code in VB to display the following text:

```
Practice makes perfect.
```

How do you feel about your experience with this experiment? As easy as the code may be, you should find that there are details to pay attention to. Only hands-on can provide this additional insight. The solution is given immediately before the summary section.

To repeat, merely reading the text is not enough. You may gain some knowledge of VB by reading, but you still need the hands-on practice to obtain the familiarity, the deep understanding, and the skills for effective delivery. This book provides many devices that facilitate your hands-on practice with VB. To gain that hand-on knowledge, do the following:

- Try the examples in each chapter, and ensure that all the results are as expected. In most cases, you can try the examples as you read. As you work with the examples, you become familiar with the code structure and its use.

- Test the code in the "Try This" boxes. These boxes allow you to see the effect of the code and provide you with a deeper understanding. The benefit of these exercises can be immense.

- Complete the "Explore and Discover" exercises. These exercises deal with topics that are not discussed in detail in the text, and broaden your working knowledge of VB. They are designed so that you find answers to VB questions in a fun way. They serve to illustrate how you can explore VB on your own. Hopefully, by working with this group of exercises, you will become more adventuresome and daring, willing to try anything without being afraid of encountering an error. After you develop this mental capacity toward VB and the computer, whenever you have an intriguing question, you will be able to devise your own code strategy to test your question, discover the answer, and figure out how and why your code works out the way it does. You will be able to learn a lot on your own.

- Work on the exercises and projects suggested by your instructor—and even more, if you can find time. These assignments give you an opportunity to put together what you learn from the text in a meaningful way. The acid test of your VB programming skill rests in whether you can successfully develop the code to perform the requirements of these assignments. These assignments vary in difficulty and fields of applications. They challenge you in different ways and can be very interesting and intriguing. The ample exercises offer plenty of choices in taking on the challenge.

- Have a thorough understanding of a chapter before proceeding to the next. This is particularly important for the first seven chapters. Each chapter is built on the preceding ones. Together, the first seven chapters form the foundation for the remainder of the book. This also means that *the first few chapters deserve a lot of your study time*. I have had some students who thought that the first few chapters were fairly easy, and thus devoted relatively little time to studying this material. These students had to work twice as hard later just to catch up, while those who worked hard initially had a much easier time and more fun with the later chapters.

Keep this in mind: Programming is more of an art than a science. The more you do, the better and the faster you can program. Hands on. Hands on. And more hands on.

Beyond the Content Coverage

There is so much to learn about VB. It includes many controls and objects that can be used in a wide range of applications. These controls and objects have many features. It takes several books just to document all these features. As a result, it is impossible for a textbook to cover all aspects of this language.

This book, however, provides a special feature that can help equip you to explore, learn, and expand your knowledge in VB on your own. Starting from Chapter 3, each chapter contains several special boxes titled "Look It Up." These boxes show you what types of information on VB you can obtain from the online help file. These boxes also serve as a reminder that a lot of valuable information is available at your fingertips and are intended to help you build a habit of looking up your questions in the online help file. Follow the instructions and perform all the suggested lookups. You will learn a lot more by just doing this. Better yet, getting familiarized with the help file can be the best resource in your study of VB.

After you become acquainted with the help file, you will be able to appreciate the wealth of information that is readily available. While you are writing your program, the help file is there for your use. It provides many details that textbooks may not have. Above all, it covers *all* the features of VB. If you decide to pursue a topic not covered in this book, you will be able to proceed comfortably by browsing the file for the needed information. Chapter 2 has a section that shows you how to browse the online help file.

TIP

The solution to the "Try This" box in the preceding section is as follows:

```
Console.WriteLine("Practice makes perfect.")
```

Common mistakes include (1) failing to include a dot (.) between Console and WriteLine, (2) failing to enclose the text in a pair of double quotes (not single quotes), and (3) failing to enclose the quoted text in a pair of parentheses.

Summary

- Visual Basic evolves from BASIC, which by the modern standard, has several drawbacks, including inflexibility in accommodating user needs, unattractive user interface, and low maintainability.
- Visual Basic has several advantages:
  - Its visual elements allow easy changes in user interface design.
  - The object-oriented syntax is easier for the programmer to develop the vocabulary and remember the syntax. More importantly, the object-oriented language enhances code reusability.
  - It is event-driven. This allows the user the flexibility to decide the sequence of activities to carry out in performing a task.
- The term, Visual Basic can refer to the language, the software processing a program written in that language, or even both.
- A sound program should possess the quality that meets both the external and internal criteria. The external criteria include functionality, efficiency, and user-friendliness. The internal criteria include consistency in coding style, code clarity and readability, modularity in code design, elegant algorithms, and code maintainability.
- You should follow the standard set of steps in developing application programs. These steps are: (1) analyze and define the problem; (2) design the visual interface; (3) define the user-program interaction; (4) design the code structure; (5) write code; (6) test and edit the program; and (7) place the program into production.

- Learning a programming language is like learning a human language. You learn to build a large vocabulary, follow the syntax rules, understand clearly the meanings of the vocabulary, and find the proper expression to convey the ideas effectively.

- It takes a lot of practice to become a proficient programmer. Hands-on is the only way to develop the necessary skills.

- It is strongly recommended that you do the following in using this book:

  - Try the examples in each chapter.

  - Test the code in the "Try This" boxes.

  - Complete the "Explore and Discover" exercises at the end of each chapter.

  - Work on all assignments suggested by your instructor.

  - Understand each chapter thoroughly before proceeding to the next. This is particularly important for the first seven chapters.

  - Perform all the lookups as suggested in the "Look It Up" boxes.

Review Questions

1-1.   What is Visual Basic? Is it a language, or is it a program?

1-2.   What is an interpreter? A compiler? Based on the discussion in the text, if both are available (separately) to process a source program, which one will you use? (*Hint:* Your choice should depend on the stage of your program development because one is more convenient but the other is more efficient in execution. Note also that fortunately, you do not have to make such a choice for VB. Chapter 2 explains why.)

1-3.   How is Visual Basic different from its predecessor, BASIC?

1-4.   What is *inheritance*? How does inheritance enhance code reusability?

1-5.   What is an event? How is programming in an event-driven language such as Visual Basic different from that in a procedure-oriented language?

1-6.   Explain the following terms:

Program

Statement

Code

1-7.   Computers are becoming faster in speed and larger in memory and storage size. Why should the programmer still be concerned about program efficiency in speed and in storage usage? (*Hint:* Your computer may be performing more than one task at a time.)

1-8.   What does *user-friendliness* mean? What constitutes a user-friendly program?

1-9.   Why is it important to observe consistency in coding style?

1-10.   What factors can enhance code clarity and readability?

1-11.   What does *modularity* mean? Why is it an important consideration in code design?

1-12.   How do you judge whether an algorithm is elegant?

1-13.   What factors affect the maintainability of a program?

1-14.   Enumerate the steps that a programmer should follow in developing a program. What can happen if these steps are not followed?

1-15.   Why is hands-on practice important to learning Visual Basic? What benefits can you gain by doing a lot of hands-on practice?

1-16.   What benefits can you gain by developing a habit of browsing the online help file?

2. Introduction to Visual Basic Programming

This chapter provides a hands-on overview of the Visual Basic (VB) program development cycle. Chapter 1, "Introduction," enumerated the steps involved in the cycle. Chapter 1 also explained that in developing a simple VB program, several of those steps could be combined. After you understand the programming goal, you can design the user interface, develop the necessary code, and then run and test your code. You will revise the code and repeat the run-test process until the program works exactly as wanted. All these activities are carried out in the Integrated Development Environment (IDE). A thoroughly tested program to be used in production (to perform the real work) should be compiled into an executable. You subsequently can use that program without the IDE. This chapter will begin by introducing the IDE, and conclude by showing the steps to run an executable.

After completing this chapter, you should be able to:

- Navigate the IDE.
- Appreciate the use of a form.
- Create controls on a form and adjust their sizes.
- Understand the events, properties, and methods of controls.
- Understand how the code and events work in a VB program.
- Open and save a VB project.
- Understand the coding mechanics and the naming convention.
- Get help from the MSDN help system.
- Enumerate the types of statements in a program.
- Run an executable without the IDE.

2.1 Navigating the Integrated Development Environment

This section introduces the IDE. You will learn how to start the IDE and will have a brief visit of the important parts in it, such as the menu bar, the toolbar, and the toolbox.

Starting the IDE

VB.NET is one of the languages provided in the Microsoft Visual Studio.NET (VS.NET). To program in VB, you begin with starting the VS.NET IDE. To start the IDE, do the following steps:

1. Click the Start icon at the lower left corner of the desktop to open the Start menu (Figure 2.1).
2. Highlight the Programs option by resting the mouse pointer on the item. A submenu should appear, as shown in Figure 2.1.
3. Highlight the Microsoft Visual Studio.NET (folder) option. Another submenu should appear. Again, see Figure 2.1.
4. Click the Microsoft Visual Studio.NET (program) option to open the VS.NET IDE.

Customizing the VS.NET IDE

The IDE is capable of handling several programming languages. When it starts, its appearance may differ, depending on its previous setting. You can customize the IDE to suit your needs and preference by performing the following steps:

Figure 2.1

Sequence of menus to invoke VS.NET IDE

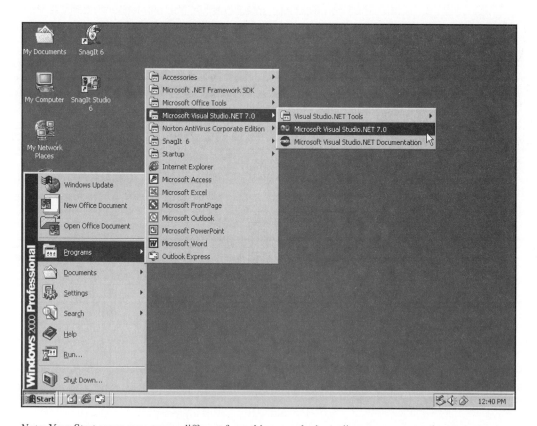

Note: Your Start menu may appear different from this example depending on your operating system.

1. Clicking the My Profile option in the IDE Start Page.
2. Choose the proper selections from the combo boxes or radio buttons. The following table shows a list of recommended choices. Figure 2.2 shows the Start Page after all these choices are made.

Box	Setting
Immediately below "Profile:"	(Custom)
Keyboard Scheme	Visual Basic 6
Window Layout	Visual Basic 6
Help Filter	Visual Basic and Related
Show Help	External Help
At Startup	Show Start Page

You can always come back to this page to reset or change your choices when you start the IDE. The Help Filter should be set to Visual Basic and Related so that when you search the help file, you will not accidentally get into a totally unfamiliar area and become lost. Also, having the Show Help set to External Help should allow you more mobility in going back and forth between the help text and the code you are currently working on. Note that when you change to this option, you will get a message, "Changes will not take effect until Visual Studio is restarted." Click the OK button in the message box to proceed.

Starting a New Project

After you have made the customizations in the Start Page, click the Get Started option. The Start Page will show a list of previous projects. Below the list, you should see the Open Project and New Project buttons (see Figure 2.3).

Figure 2.2

Customizing the IDE

Regardless of where you were in the Start page, click My Profile to customize your IDE.

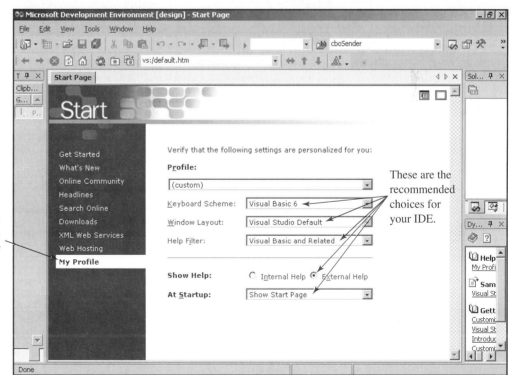

Figure 2.3
The Get Started page

This box gives a list of projects that you recently worked on.

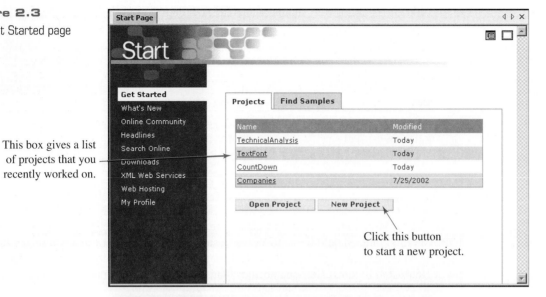

Figure 2.4
The New Project dialog box

Then click this OK button.

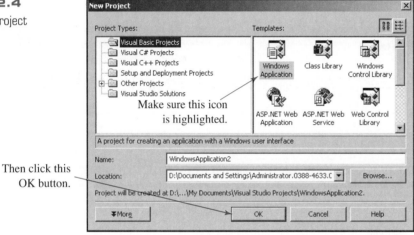

To start a new project, follow these steps:

1. Click the New Project button. The New Project dialog box should appear (see Figure 2.4).

2. If necessary, highlight the Windows Application icon in the Templates pane.

3. Type the proper name and location (file path) in their respective text boxes. Because you just are exploring, use the same name and location as supplied by the IDE; that is, take the default and do nothing.

4. Click the OK button.

The IDE will appear with a blank form in the center as well as several other elements (see Figure 2.5). The following subsections introduce these elements.

The Menu Bar and the Toolbar

The menu bar and toolbar are found under the title bar of the IDE, as shown in Figure 2.5. The *menu bar* provides many menu items. These items are similar to most of the Windows applications. For example, the Edit menu contains options such as the familiar Cut, Copy, Paste, and Select All options found in the word processing application. Click on some of these menu items and explore the available options. These menu items will be discussed when they are needed.

The *toolbar* appears below the menu bar. It provides shortcuts to the menu bar. All the options available here are also available in the menus; however, the items on the toolbar allow you to gain quick access to the options. If you need to know what option an icon on the toolbar repre-

Figure 2.5

The IDE for Visual Basic

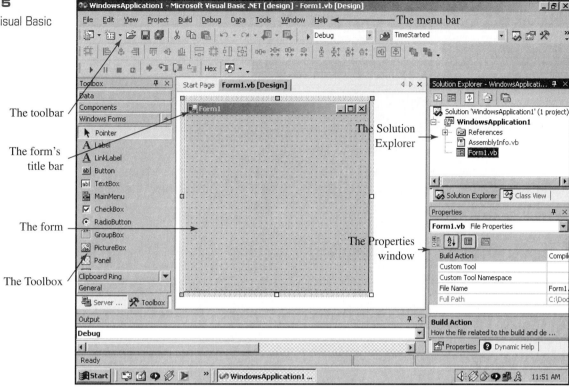

Figure 2.6

TheToolTip

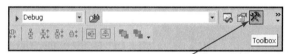

Rest the mouse pointer on one of these icons and
a ToolTip text will appear to show what the icon is for.

sents, simply rest the mouse pointer on the icon. A ToolTip will appear to indicate what the icon is for (see Figure 2.6).

The ToolTip feature is available for all the icons in the IDE. Get acquainted with these icons by resting the mouse pointer on each of them.

The Toolbox

On the left side of the IDE is the *Toolbox*, which contains various icons along with text (see Figure 2.5). These icons represent various VB controls, which are visible objects that can be drawn on the form. You will see some of these controls in action in the next section. (*Note:* If you do not see the Toolbox, click the View menu and select the Toolbox option. Alternatively, click the Toolbox icon on the toolbar.)

Notice that there are three tabs immediately below the Toolbox title bar. (They actually look like buttons.) Clicking one of these tabs will make the box show different items. For example, if you click the Data tab, a fairly small list of items will appear. Notice also that the other two tabs now appear at the bottom of the box (see Figure 2.7). Click the Windows Forms tab to restore its original appearance. As you can see, the list of items is longer than the box can show. To find the items in the bottom part of this tab, press (point and hold down the mouse) the down arrow button by the Clipboard Ring tab. To go back to the top of the list, press the up arrow button by the Windows Forms tab.

Notice also that there are two small buttons on the right end of the Toolbox title bar. If you click the *Close (X) button*, the Toolbox will disappear. (To make it reappear, click the Toolbox

Figure 2.7

Contents of different tabs in the Toolbox

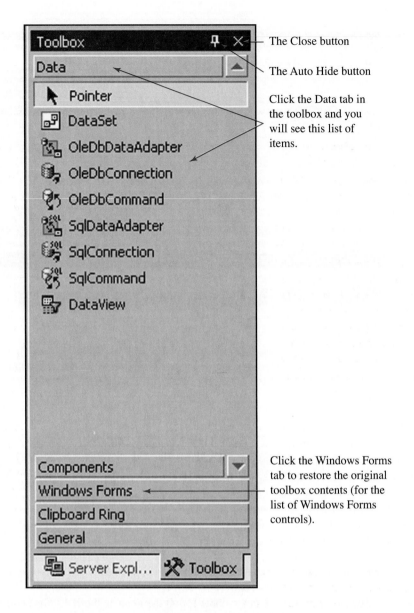

The Close button

The Auto Hide button

Click the Data tab in the toolbox and you will see this list of items.

Click the Windows Forms tab to restore the original toolbox contents (for the list of Windows Forms controls).

icon in the toolbar.) If you click the *Auto Hide button*, the Toolbox will show only a small vertical bar on the side. Rest the mouse pointer on this vertical bar to make the box appear. As soon as you move the mouse pointer away from the Toolbox, it hides again. To suppress the Auto Hide feature, make the Toolbox appear and then click the Auto Hide button. The Auto Hide button toggles between on and off.

The Form and the Code Window

In the center of the IDE, you should see a form with a title bar, Form1, as shown in Figure 2.5. The form is what you use to design the visual interface in VB. Behind the form is the code window in which you write your code. If you double-click the form, the code window will appear. If you click the X (Close) button on the upper right corner of this window, it will disappear and the form will reappear on top. Another way to toggle the appearance/disappearance of the form and the code window is to use the *Solution Explorer*.

The Solution Explorer

The Solution Explorer is located on the upper right corner of the IDE. This window shows all the forms, references, classes, and modules that your current VB project(s) contain(s), as seen in

Figure 2.5. (*Note:* If you do not see this window, click the View menu and select the Solution Explorer option. Alternatively, press Ctrl+R.)

There are five icons immediately below the Solution Explorer title bar: the *View Code, View Designer, Refresh, Show All Files,* and *Properties* icons (see Figure 2.5). If you do not see all these icons, click the form. To identify a particular icon, rest the mouse pointer on the item until its ToolTip appears. Click the View Code icon, and the code window will appear in the middle of the IDE screen in place of the form. Click the View Designer icon, and the form will appear over the code window. When developing a project, you will use these two icons often because you will need to toggle between the Code and Form views. If you have more than one form in your project, the form displayed is the one that is highlighted and the code is the one associated with this form. The Refresh icon refreshes the display of those items in this Solution Explorer window. The Properties icon shows the Properties window (or Properties page) of the item you highlight in the Solution Explorer. For example, if you click AssemblyInfo.vb in the Solution Explorer window and then click the Properties icon, you will see this file's properties displayed in the Properties window, located at the lower right corner of the screen. The Show All Files icon toggles the display of all files under each category, such as References, within the solution and can be useful when you have many forms and modules in a solution.

Solutions and Projects. As a side note, you may wonder what a *solution* is. A solution is a container in which items are developed and put together for an application. Physically, it is a file folder. A solution can consist of one or more *projects*. A project can consist of forms, classes, and modules, all of which work together as a logical unit. When you have the project compiled, it typically produces an executable program (.exe file) or dynamic link library (.DLL file). A typical simple solution can consist of one project in which there is one form.

Look at the Solution Explorer again. Below the icons, you should see the Solution icon with the solution title—'WindowsSolution1', in your case. It also indicates that it contains one project. Below the solution title is the Project icon with project title—WindowsApplication1, which is the same as the solution title. Be aware of the existence of these icons and titles. You will need to deal with them from time to time.

The Properties Window

The *Properties window* (Figure 2.8) lies below the Solution Explorer window on the right side of the screen. Immediately below the title of the Properties window is an Object box that shows the object being displayed. (Forms and VB controls are collectively referred to as objects.) If you click the drop-down button on its right side, a drop-down list will display all objects on the form. You can select an object from the list by clicking the item of interest. *(Note:* If you do not see this

Figure 2.8

The Properties window

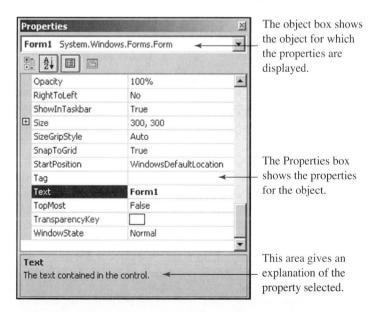

The object box shows the object for which the properties are displayed.

The Properties box shows the properties for the object.

This area gives an explanation of the property selected.

window, click the View menu and select the Properties Window option. Alternatively, press F4 or click the Properties Window icon in the toolbar.)

In the middle of this window is the *Properties box* that displays the properties of the selected object. You can use this window to set the value for various properties of the object. A *property* is a special type of data associated with the object. The object acts, behaves, and/or appears differently, depending on the values of its various properties. There is a vertical scrollbar on the right side of the Properties window that you can use to scroll up and down in the window to view the property settings. Below the list of properties is a small window that explains the property selected in the window. If you click a different property, different explanatory text will appear in this area. Note that different types of objects have different properties. You can explore and learn about the properties of an object by clicking different properties in this window, and viewing the text in this area.

Between the Object box and the Properties box, there are four icons: *Categorized, Alphabetic, Properties,* and *Property Pages.* The Categorized and Alphabetic icons determine the order in which the properties are displayed in the Properties window. When the Alphabetic icon is selected, properties are displayed in alphabetic order. If you would rather that they be displayed by categories, you can select the Categorized icon. In this case, properties will be displayed in groups by their effect on appearance, behavior, and so on of the object. The Properties and Property Pages icons determine whether the Properties window or Property pages will be displayed for the object shown in the Object box. For example, if you click the WindowsApplication1 project icon in the Solution Explorer window, the Object box will show this project. If you then click the Property Pages icon, the WindowsApplication1's Property pages will appear. Not all objects have the Property pages. In those cases, the Property Pages icon will be disabled. Clicking on it will have no effect.

Exiting the VB IDE

You have completed a brief tour of the VS.NET IDE. To exit the software, click the Close (X) button on the upper right corner of the IDE window, or click the File menu and then click the Exit option. A message box will appear with the message, "Save changes to the following items?". Click the No button to end.

2.2 Your First Visual Basic Program

You have just completed a brief tour of the IDE. As explained at the beginning of this chapter, the VS.NET IDE is where you work to develop a VB program (project). You are probably eager now to learn to write your first VB program. You will first walk through a program development cycle so that you can get a hands-on feel. The concepts behind all the work will then be explained.

A Simple Program Walkthrough

This program displays "Welcome To Visual Basic.NET!!!" in a label on a form when you click a button with the text "Say Welcome." The first step is to start the IDE, and create a solution folder. To do so, follow these steps:

1. Click the Start button on the lower left corner of the desktop. Highlight Programs in the Start menu. Highlight Microsoft Visual Stuio.NET (folder) in the Programs menu; then click the Microsoft Visual Studio.NET icon (program) in the submenu. (*Note:* The appearance and wording may differ depending on your operating system.) The Start Page should appear similar to Figure 2.3, if you have customized your profile as suggested in the preceding section. If you have not yet customized the IDE, do so before proceeding.

2. Click the New Project button in the center of the screen to start a new project.

3. Make sure the Windows Application icon in the Templates pane is highlighted when the New Project dialog box appears (see Figure 2.4).

4. Assign a proper name for the solution. Enter **Welcome** as the name in place of the name that automatically appears in the Name text box.

5. Click the OK button. (For simplicity, do not change the folder location. This aspect will be discussed later.) The IDE should show a form in the center and all the other elements discussed in the preceding section.

You are now ready to work on the program. This project involves three VB objects: a form, a label, and a button. As you can see, the form is readily available in the IDE at this point. You will, however, need to bring the label and the button from the Toolbox that is located on the left side in the IDE. To develop the Welcome project, follow these steps:

1. Resize the form so that its width is about one-quarter of the screen width, and its height is also about one-quarter of the screen height. You can resize the form by dragging one of the sizing handles on the sides and corners of the form. You drag by holding down the mouse button and moving away from the original point. Figure 2.9 shows the sizing handles of the form.

2. Draw a label on the form. Double-click the Label icon in the Toolbox, shown in Figure 2.9. You should see the label with the text Label1 at the upper left corner of the form. Drag the label to the center of the form; then, drag a sizing handle on the right so the label is wide enough to hold about 30 characters.

3. Draw a button on the form.

    3.1. Click the Button icon on the Toolbox.

    3.2. Point the mouse on the form below the label control; then drag down and to the right corner for about 1/3" × 1".

    3.3 Release the mouse. You will see the new shape and size of the button (Figure 2.10).

Figure 2.9

Sizing handles

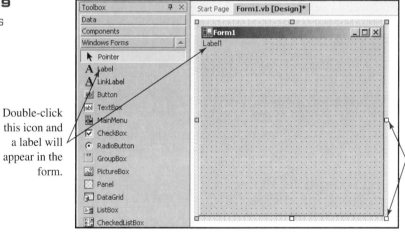

Double-click this icon and a label will appear in the form.

Sizing handles that you can drag to change the size of an object (form).

Figure 2.10

Drawing a control on the form

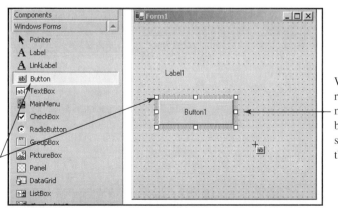

First, click the Button icon in the Toolbox. Then place the mouse pointer here, and drag down and to the right.

When you release the mouse button, you should see this button.

You can resize the button by dragging one of the its sizing handles, the same way you resized the form and the label.

4. Change the button's Text property to "**Say Welcome**." You change the property setting through the Properties window. If you do not see the window onscreen, click the Properties Window option in the VB View menu, or press F4.

   4.1. Click the button on the form so that the Properties window shows the properties of this button.

   4.2. Use the scrollbar of the window to find the Text property. Type **"Say Welcome"** to replace Button1 in the text box (Figure 2.11).

5. Add code to the code window.

   5.1. Double-click the button on the form (not the icon in the Toolbox, nor the form itself). The code window will appear in place of the form. You should see some code lines in the code window, as shown in Figure 2.12.

   5.2. Add two lines of code to the code template as shown on page 27.

Figure 2.11

Setting the Text property for Button1

Make sure that the object box displays Button1 by clicking Button1 in the form.

Click the Text property and then enter "Say Welcome" in the box.

Figure 2.12

The code window

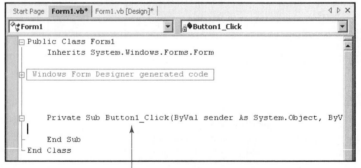

You should see the code window with these code lines after you double-click Button1 in the form.

```
Private Sub Button1_Click(ByVal Sender As System.Object, ByVal
    e As System.EventArgs) Handles Button1.Click
    ' Make the label display the Welcome message
    Label1.Text = "Welcome to Visual Basic.NET!!!"
End Sub
```

Notice that a small window showing various choices will appear immediately after you type "**Label1.**" including the dot (see Figure 2.13). This small window is recognized as the *IntelliSense* and provides all the legitimate choices for Label1. As you enter additional letters in the code, you will see different items in the IntelliSense highlighted. When you see Text highlighted, you can continue to type the remaining letters, enter the equal sign (=), or press the spacebar to complete that portion of the code line.

6. Run the program. Click the Start button in the toolbar, click the Start option in the Debug menu, or press F5.

7. Click the Say Welcome button in the running form. You should see the label now displays, "Welcome to Visual Basic.NET!!!" instead of its original Label1 (Figure 2.14).

Congratulations! You have successfully completed a VB project. Click the Close (X) button on the form's title bar to end the project. To exit the IDE, click File in the menu bar and then click Exit. Alternatively, click the Close button of the IDE. When asked whether to save changes, click the Yes button.

Figure 2.13
The IntelliSense

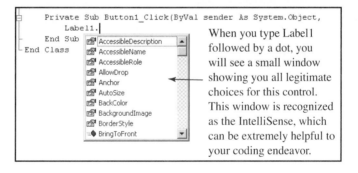

Figure 2.14
The Welcome project
in action

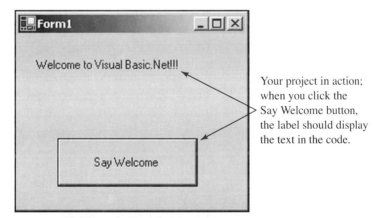

TIP

When entering code, beware of the difference between the lowercase L and the number 1. To the human eyes, l (lowercase L) and 1 (numeral 1) look similar. To the computer, however, they are completely different. Some beginners tend to be careless in distinguishing the two. The consequence can range from an obvious syntax error with an immediate fix, to days of searching for a mysterious bug in the program. A similar situation exists between the letter O (or its lowercase o) and the number 0.

Handling VB Program Files

When you make changes in your project if your IDE options have not been changed since its installation, these changes will automatically be saved in the folder name that you gave. The folder should have the same name as the solution.

Reopening a Project. When you start the IDE, you can reopen the project by clicking the Open Project button in the Start page. An Open Project dialog box will appear. You can then browse to find the project you want to open (see Figure 2.15). Alternatively, if it is a recent project, you may see it in the list of recent projects at the center of the IDE. You can click on the name to open the project.

If you are already working on a project and would like to switch to another one, you can do the following:

1. Click the File menu in the menu bar.
2. Select the Open option.
3. Click Project in the submenu (see Figure 2.16).
4. The Open Project dialog box will appear. You can then browse to find the project.

Figure 2.15

The Open Project dialog box

Figure 2.16

Opening an existing project from the File menu

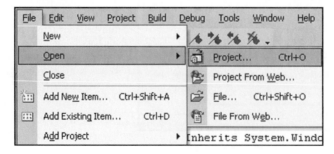

If the project is one that you worked recently, you may switch to it with this shortcut:

1. Click the File menu in the menu bar.
2. Select the Recent Projects option.
3. Find and click the project in the list of recent projects.

Saving Changes Automatically? As stated previously in this chapter, the IDE will automatically save all changes you make in the project by installation default. If you would rather have a chance to decide whether you want to save or not, you can change the option. To effect this option, follow these steps:

1. Click the Tools menu in the menu bar.
2. Click Options. An Options Dialog box will appear.
3. Expand the Environment folder on the left pane, if it is closed.
4. Click the Projects and Solutions node under the Environment folder on the left pane.
5. Select Prompt to save changes to open documents (Figure 2.17).
6. Click the OK button.

Each time you run your project after making changes, the IDE will prompt you to save the changes. You can make your choice at that time.

Starting a New Project While In Another Project. Suppose you have finished a project, and decide to create a new project. You can remain in the IDE and start a new project by following these steps:

1. Click the File menu in the menu bar.
2. Select the New option.
3. Click Project.
4. The New Project dialog will appear (See Figure 2.4). You can then start a new project.

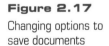

Changing options to save documents

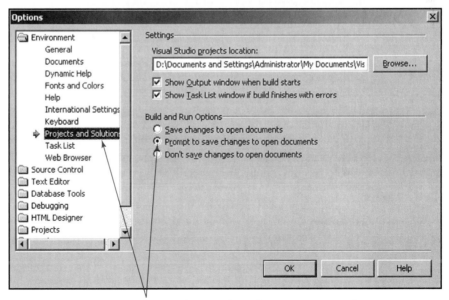

Click Projects and Solutions on the left pane. Then select Prompt to save changes to open documents. If you do so, the IDE will prompt you whether to save the documents each time you run your project after making changes.

Organizing Your Projects and Solutions. If you do not choose a location when you create a new project, the IDE creates the new folder within the folder under which the previous project was saved. If this is the first project it creates, it will save it under the Visual Studio Projects folder, located under the My Documents folder. The Welcome project that you created in the previous example should be there if the setting has not been changed since the IDE's installation. As you proceed, you will eventually create many projects and solutions. For better organization, you probably will not want to have all these folders created directly under the Visual Studio Projects folder. You will need to consider how these solutions should be organized on your disk. This aspect will be discussed later in this chapter.

2.3 Some Basic Concepts

This section introduces you to a few basic concepts that you need to know before you can feel at ease writing a simple program. They include the programming environment, the coding mechanics, and other basic programming concepts.

Understanding the Integrated Development Environment

Take another look at the steps you just took to develop the Welcome project. When you were resizing the form, and bringing both the label and the button to the form, you were in the *design phase* of your project. This phase is called *design time*. At design time, you work with the visual aspect of your project. The elements that you bring from the Toolbox onto the form are called *controls*. When you run the project by clicking the Start button on the toolbar, your project enters *runtime*. In this phase, the code in your project comes to life, responding to events triggered by either the user's or the system's actions. When you clicked the Say Welcome button, the button's Click event occurred. The code you wrote in Sub Button1_Click was then triggered in response. The line

```
Label1.Text = "Welcome to Visual Basic.NET!!!"
```

tells the computer to move the "Welcome to Visual Basic.NET!!!" text string to the Text property of Label1. The *Text property* of Label1 is then changed and displayed on the label. When your program quits, you still remain in the development environment, ready for another round of modification to the project.

Program Development in the Good Old Days. In the old DOS environment, when programs were developed in procedure-oriented languages such as COBOL, all the visual aspect of a program was written in code. Additional code was—as is now—also needed to handle computations. The code was written with a text editor and saved as a file. The file was then input into a language processor and recognized as a compiler that translated the source program into machine executable code (in machine language), which was saved as a separate file. This executable file was run to produce the results that the developer desired. (*Note:* Quick Basic worked a bit differently.) In effect, a programmer had to work with three different programs at different phases of the program development activities to obtain results: an editor at design time, a compiler at compile time, and the compiled program at run time (see Figure 2.18). You can imagine how long it could take (and how tedious it was) to develop a bug-free program that could be used formally for business data processing.

Program Development in the VS IDE. In contrast, when you are developing a program in VB.NET, all the activities in visual design, code editing, and testing can be carried out in a single environment. While you are entering code, the IDE checks for apparent syntax errors and also compiles your code. When you run your program, the IDE makes your program execute without having to leave the development environment and is thus recognized as the Integrated Development Environment.

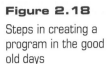

Figure 2.18

Steps in creating a program in the good old days

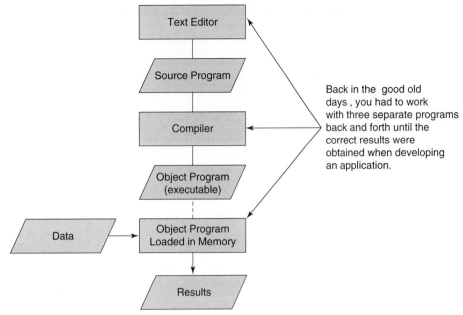

Back in the good old days , you had to work with three separate programs back and forth until the correct results were obtained when developing an application.

Coding Mechanics

You may have noticed that there are two lines of code inside the preceding Button1_Click event procedure:

```
' Make the label display the Welcome message
Label1.Text = "Welcome to Visual Basic.NET!!!"
```

Only the second line causes an action, however. The first line is a comment statement.

Comments on Code. A comment statement starts with a tick (') mark or a Rem (for Remark) keyword. When VB sees a line beginning with a tick mark (apostrophe) or Rem, it ignores the line. The following line will have the same effect as the line with a tick mark in the preceding code:

```
Rem Make the label display the Welcome message
```

You can also write comments at the end of a code line, as follows:

```
Label1.Text = "Welcome to Visual Basic.NET!!!" 'Show Welcome
```

or

```
Label1.Text = "Welcome to Visual Basic.NET!!!" Rem Show Welcome
```

The programmer usually uses comments to provide clues to the purposes of the code. Comments enhance the readability and understandability of the program and are an indispensable part of the program documentation. A well-documented program is much easier to maintain. You should use comments for your program whenever applicable. When you come back to your programs at a later date, you will appreciate your own thoughtfulness if your code is accompanied by plenty of comments.

Furthermore, if you write a program for a company, another programmer may have to update your code in the future. If it is properly commented, the programmer will have a much easier time figuring out what your program does and how it should be changed.

Showing Blocks of Code Lines. The text editor in the IDE that you use to write code will automatically indent the code lines for you, making the program you develop highly readable. You can also insert blank lines between any code lines. If your procedure consists of several blocks of code, each dealing with a specific task, inserting blank lines between these blocks can make each block stand out and provide a visual clue to the logical structure of your procedure.

Line Continuation. There may be times when you will have to code a long, complex statement. You may find it desirable to break such a statement into several lines. You can do this by using a space followed by an underscore (_) at end of the line and then continue the remainder of the code in the next line, as shown in the following code.

```
Label1.Text = _
"Welcome to Visual Basic.NET"
```

Do not break a string constant into multiple lines, such as:

```
Label1.Caption = "Welcome _
To Visual Basic" X
```

In the first line, the compiler considers the space and the underscore as a part of the string literal; the compiler thus fails to recognize these characters as symbols for line continuation. The *correct code* should be as follows:

```
Label1.Caption = "Welcome" _
& " To Visual Basic"
```

where the & character is the concatenation operator that joins two strings. String operations are discussed in Chapter 4, "Data, Operations, and Built-in Functions."

Multiple Statements on a Line. You can have more than one statement on a line by inserting a colon between statements. For example, you can code the following:

$$HourlyPay = 10 : Area = Height * Width$$

Although there is nothing wrong with the syntax, you may not want to code your program this way because the statements are harder to read, and you can miss the flow of your program logic when reviewing the code.

Interfaces of VB Objects

You have worked with a form and two controls. Forms and controls are collectively recognized as objects. Each type of object provides different functionality. For example, forms serve as containers for other objects and as windows for the visual interface. Labels are used to display text, which is usually simple messages or instructions for the user. Buttons are used to initiate specific actions when the user clicks them. All objects provide interfaces for your code. These interfaces include properties, events, and methods (Figure 2.19). The following sections take a closer look at each.

Properties. Objects have *properties*—special types of data associated with the objects. Most properties relate to the appearance of the objects. Other properties determine how an object behaves. Many properties can be set at either design time or runtime, while other properties can be set only at design time. Still others can be set or available only at runtime. In code, you refer to a property of an object by the following syntax:

Figure 2.19

The three interfaces of an object

Objects have three types of interfaces: properties, events, and methods.

```
Object.Property
```

The object name and the property name are separated by a dot (.). There should be no spaces in between. For example, you can refer to the background color property of the label named Label1 by coding:

```
Label1.BackColor
```

To set its background color to red, you will code:

```
Label1.BackColor = Color.Red
```

where Color.Red is a constant name recognized in VB and represents the red color. Many controls have common properties which will be explored in the next section.

Events. In addition to properties, objects also have *events* that are user or system actions recognized by the object. As you can see from the Welcome project, the button has a Click event. When the user clicks the button, the *Click event* is raised (triggered). Different objects recognize different events. As discussed in Chapter 1, "Introduction," VB is an event-driven language. When a VB project starts to run, it waits for events to occur and then responds by executing the code written to handle these events accordingly. You write code for each of the events that you want the program to handle. The procedure written to handle an event is called an *event procedure* or *event handler*. Event procedures have the following syntax structure:

```
Private Sub ObjectName_Event(parameter list) Handles Object.Event
        <Code to handle the event>
End Sub
```

The first line of the procedure starts with Private Sub, which is used to indicate the beginning of a Sub procedure. The object name identifies the object of interest, and the object and event are separated by an underscore. The event name is followed by a pair of parentheses that enclose a list of parameters. Typically, the parameter list looks similar to the following:

```
ByVal Sender As System.Object, ByVal e As System.EventArgs
```

As you can see, the list has two parameters. The first parameter identifies the message sender, or the object that makes the call. The second parameter gives the event arguments. Its contents will vary depending on the event. These parameters will be explored further in other chapters where applicable.

The End Sub line physically defines the end of the procedure; that is, any lines beyond this point have nothing to do with this procedure. When execution control drops down to this line, it will return to the point where this procedure was triggered;— that is, it will return to the message sender. In most cases, this means the computer will be waiting for another event to invoke another event procedure.

TIP

You might have discovered some confusing terminology in the previous discussion. The term, *control* has been used in two different contexts. Initially, those objects dragged into the form from the Toolbox were introduced as *controls*. The flow of execution in a program, however, is also referred to as *control* in the previous paragraph. For clear differentiation, this book uses *execution control* to refer to execution flow. Unless the context is clear, the term *VB control* will be used to refer to VB objects.

Exploring Available Events of an Object. You can find what events an object can recognize and what parameters each event procedure has by exploring the code window (see Figure 2.20).

The *Object box* at the upper left corner has a list of all the objects on the form. You can see the names of these objects by clicking the drop-down button. The *Procedure box* on the right shows

Figure 2.20

The Object box and the Procedure box

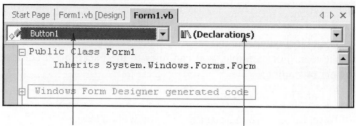

The Object box contains all the objects used in the current form.

The Procedure box lists all the events recognized by the object selected in the object box. Always use these two boxes to obtain the event procedure code template.

the list of events the object on the left recognizes. If you click an event in this list, an event procedure template will appear in the code window. This is the standard way to start writing code to handle a particular event.

TIP Always use the procedure template provided by VB to code an event procedure. When in the code window, first select the object name from the object box; then select the event from the procedure box. The event procedure template will appear in the code window.

A project can have many event procedures. The relative position of these procedures is not important. Procedures get invoked by the events, and are not executed in the order they are placed in the code window. In contrast, the order of the code lines within the procedure is very important. In general, these lines are executed top down, line by line—or more accurately, statement by statement. The result of executing a line may depend on the results from the previous lines. Any lines that are placed out of order can cause an erroneous result.

TRY THIS In the code window of your current project, select (Base Class Events) from the Object box on the left; then select KeyPress from the Procedure box on the right. You should see the following event procedure template in the code window:

```
Private Sub Form1_KeyPress(ByVal sender As System.Object,
    ByVal e As System.Windows.Forms.KeyPressEventArgs) Handles
    MyBase.KeyPress

End Sub
```

You may want to try a few more, just for fun and familiarity.

Methods. Finally, objects have *methods*—actions that objects are capable of performing. For example, SetBounds is a method that many objects have. The following code will set bounds for (move) the label you have created to a random location on the form. For the time being, however, do not worry about how the code works.

```
Label1.SetBounds(Rnd() * Width, Rnd() * Height, Label1.Width,
    Label1.Height)
```

The syntax to use a method is as follows:

Object.Method (Parameter List)

Notice that there is a dot between the object and the method, as is the case in the code for the property. Some methods have required parameters; some have optional parameters; other methods require no parameters. Notice also that there is a pair of parentheses enclosing the parameter list. This pair is required, even when the method requires no parameter.

These parameters provide information for the method to perform proper actions. For example, the SetBounds method just shown requires four parameters. Its syntax appears as follows:

Object.SetBounds (*x, y, Width, Height*)

where Object = a control or form.

x, y = a pair of numbers indicating the coordinate at which the left side and top edge of the object should be aligned.

Width, Height = a pair of numbers giving the width and height of the object.

The preceding statement tells the label to set its boundary at (move to) a position in which its upper left corner is at the point as defined by the first two parameters, keeping its width and height the same as its previous size.

Insert the Label1.SetBounds code line to the Button1_Click event procedure you created in the previous section. Run the project and then click the Say Welcome button as many times as you want. You should see the Welcome label move all over the form. Remove this line of code to continue this chapter.

Defaults

In earlier versions of VB, you might encounter code that was not explicit in its expression; however, it could still be acceptable to VB. This occurred because when VB encountered missing or unspecified elements in an expression, it filled in the blank by assuming a certain default element.

In the current version, VB allows defaults only under very strict conditions. After all, code with defaults is not very clear. The programmer might assume something while VB actually does something else; therefore, using defaults in code can cause errors that may be hard to uncover. Avoid using defaults in your code by all means.

Default Property Setting. Most objects have many properties. When an object is initiated, each of these properties is assigned with an assumed setting (value). This setting is referred to as the default setting of the property. For example, you may have already discovered that the default settings (values) of the Text property for the first label, button, and form are Label1, Button1, and Form1, respectively. In most cases, default property settings are the proper settings for your project. In addition, not all the properties of an object have significant bearings on the performance of the project. These default property settings are usually left untouched.

2.4 Exploring More Properties

In this section, you will explore some more properties of the three objects—form, label, and button. It has been mentioned that all three objects have the Text property. Recall that you changed the Text property of the button from "Button1" to "Say Welcome" at design time by using the Properties window. You also have used code to change the Text property of the label from "Label1" to "Welcome to Visual Basic.NET!!!" Why not try to change the form's Text property to "My First VB Project"? You can do this either at design time using the Properties window (follow the same steps for the button), or by code (double-click the form to obtain the form load code template and place the code in that event). In general, if you do not anticipate the property setting to change when your program runs, it is easier and more efficient to set it at design time.

Common Properties

Forms and labels have many common properties. If you carefully examine the Properties window of each object, you should be able to identify quite a few. The following is a short sample list of these common properties and their uses:

Property	Uses	Default Setting
BackColor	Background color.	Gray; standard color for buttons
Enabled	When set to True, it is accessible by the user; when set to False, it is not accessible to the user.	True
Font	Font for text displayed in the object.	MS Sans Serif 8.25
ForeColor	Foreground (text) color.	Black; standard text color
Location	A pair of numbers representing a coordinate at which the object's left upper corner is to be aligned.	
Size	A pair of numbers giving the width and height of the object.	

Of course, any of these property settings can be changed. You may have noticed that as you move the objects around, the values in their Location property change. Furthermore, as you resize the objects, the values in their Size property also change.

Note also that at runtime, you can also set the Left and Top properties (in addition to the Location property) to change the location of an object. For example, the following code will place the left margin of Label1 100 pixels from the left margin of the form (without changing the label's vertical position or size).

```
Label1.Left = 100
```

Figure 2.21

The Font property box and the Font dialog box

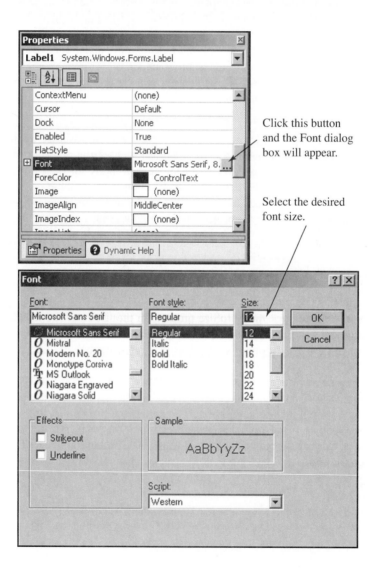

Changing the Font for the Label: An Exercise

As an exercise, change the font size of the label in your project to 12. Follow these steps:

1. Click the label's Font property in the Properties window. An ellipsis button should appear in the property box.
2. Click the ellipsis button. A Font dialog box will appear (Figure 2.21).
3. Click 12 in the Size box.
4. Click the OK button.

The AutoSize Property

You might discover that the size of the label you previously drew is not large enough to hold the text. Of course, you can resize the label by using its sizing handle, as you did with the form before; however, there is another way that is much more convenient. You can set the label's *AutoSize property* to True. The label automatically adjusts its size based on its text content.

2.5 Getting Help from the Help Menu

At this moment, you might find the large number of properties of these objects overwhelming; however, understand that they are made available to make your job as a programmer easier. After you become familiar with these properties, you might want to actively look for their help to make your job easier. Most of the time, you may wonder what features a newly encountered property provides. The answer is most likely at your fingertips. VS.NET comes with a comprehensive online help system. For example, to find out more about the AutoSize property of the label control, you can do the following:

1. Click the Help menu on the menu bar. You will see a drop-down list with many options such as Contents, Index, and Search.
2. Click the Index option. The Visual Studio.NET Combined Collection dialog box should appear.

The Index Tab

You can explore the Index tab in various ways. For now, focus on how you can use the Index tab to find the answer to the question, "What is the AutoSize property of the label control?" To search for an answer, do the following:

1. Enter AutoSize in the Look For box on the left pane. The list box will display many topics.
2. Double-click the AutoSize property in the list box. You will see an Index Results list box in the lower center pane displaying several items.
3. Double-click Label.AutoSize Property. The upper center pane displays the results (see Figure 2.22).

The Remarks section of the screen gives additional information on how its different settings (True and False) affect the behavior of the object.

TIP

You can get many of your VB questions answered by browsing the Help file. Get acquainted with the online Help feature as soon as you can. Whenever you have a question about a control, property, event, or method, simply look it up from the online Help feature.

Figure 2.22

The Index tab of the VS.NET help screen

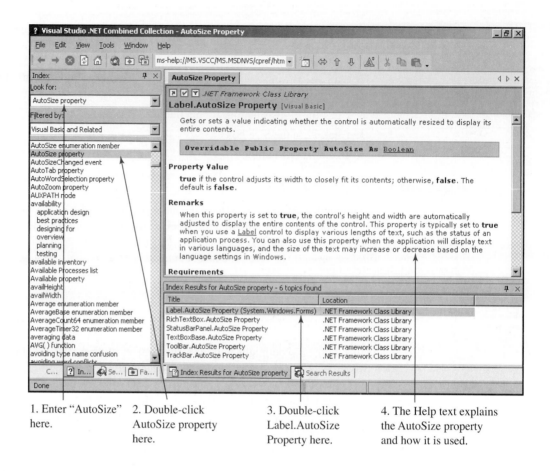

1. Enter "AutoSize" here. 2. Double-click AutoSize property here. 3. Double-click Label.AutoSize Property here. 4. The Help text explains the AutoSize property and how it is used.

Help Text and Hyperlinks

In the upper-right pane, you can see several terms underlined and in light blue color. These terms are hyperlinks to additional information, much like the hypertext you see when browsing Internet web pages.

Click the word Label, and the pane will display the text that explains the Label control. You can discover additional information related to your original search, and continue to explore using these links.

TIP

A quick way to find an explanation for the AutoSize property of the Label control is to highlight the AutoSize property in the Properties window and then press F1. The context sensitive Help screen will display the help page for the property.

Alternative Ways to Explore

There are other ways to explore the Help file. For example, if you click the Contents tab, you will see a book icon labeled Visual Studio.NET. Click the book icon, and an array of book icons with various topics will appear. One of these is Visual Basic and Visual C#. Click the Expand (+) button on the left side of the book icon (or double-click the book icon itself. You should now be able to explore various VB topics. This is a convenient way to get general information about a specific VB topic; however, if you have a specific question such as a method, a property, or an event, using the Index tab can make your search easier. Alternatively, you can also use the Search option in the Help menu. When you look for help this way, the search results show not only the titles found but also the location and the rank of each title. You can also specify how the search should be done and presented—whether it should be limited to titles, match related words, or highlight search hits.

In this book, you will be reminded of the Help file by a special Look It Up box. You can learn more on your own by reading the help text. You will also know what specific type of knowledge you can gain by following the pointer in the box. Because these pointers are related to specific topics, this textbook will often refer to the Index tab just presented.

Be aware that the help file is not prepared exclusively for VB, as the file name implies. Therefore, you may run into topics of which you are totally unaware. This is the reason why you should limit your search to topics related only to VB by selecting Visual Basic and Related in the Filtered By box at the top of the left pane. The box should display this if you have customized your IDE as suggested in Section 2.1, "Navigating the Integrated Development Environment."

2.6 Naming Objects

The three objects used in the Welcome example have another common property—Name. Unlike the Text property, the Name property can be set only at design time. When naming an object, be as descriptive as possible. A descriptive name provides clues to what the object is used for in a project. This can be particularly helpful when you need to review or modify the code in the future. In other words, descriptive names enhance code clarity and maintainability.

Object Naming Convention

Companies adopt naming standards for their projects. These standards typically include rules on how objects should be named. A commonly used standard is to use the first three letters in lowercase to indicate the type of object, followed by a descriptive name. For example, the three objects used in this chapter—form, label, and button—have the following name prefixes:

Object Type	Prefix	Example
Form	frm	frmWelcome
Label	lbl	lblWelcome
Button	btn	btnQuit

A more complete list of these prefixes is given in the next chapter, and these prefixes will be referred to and used whenever a new object is encountered. In this book, this standard will be followed to help you develop a sound naming habit.

TIP

When naming objects, make them as descriptive as you can. Include the standard three-letter prefix as a part of their names. Code clarity and maintainability are greatly enhanced with this practice.

Changing the Object Names in the Project

You can implement the aforementioned naming standard in your example project by following these steps:

1. Change the label name to lblWelcome. You can do this by using the Properties window. The steps are as follows:

   1.1. Click the label in the form.

   1.2. Select the Name property in the Properties window. The Name property appears near the top of the Properties list in both Categorized and Alphabetic views.

   1.3. Type `lblWelcome` in the box.

It is a good habit to test the program whenever a change is made. After you have changed the label name, start the project by clicking the Start button. An error message will appear, indicating errors in build and asking whether to continue (see Figure 2.23).

Click the No button. The Debug window immediately below the form should display the following message:

The name 'Label1' is not declared (see Figure 2.24).

Click the View Code icon in the Solution Explorer window to inspect the code in the code window. You should see Label1 in the following line underlined:

```
Label1.Text = "Welcome to Visual Basic.NET!!!"
```

This occurs because after you change the label's name, there is no control on the form with the name Label1. To correct this error, change the line as follows:

```
lblWelcome.Text = "Welcome to Visual Basic.NET!!!"
```

Now run the project again. This time the project should run without any problems.

2. Change the name of the button to `btnWelcome`; then start the project, and click the button. This time, the program runs without any problem. If you inspect the code, you will notice that a part of the Button1_Click line has been changed. Previously, at the end of the line, it had "Handles Button1.Click." Now, however, it shows "Handles btnWelcome.Click."

The IDE is smart in updating your changes; however, the code is not clear. For clarity and ease of review in the future, you should replace "Button1" in the procedure header to "btnWelcome." The corrected event procedure should appear as follows:

```
Private Sub btnWelcome_Click(ByVal Sender As System.Object, ByVal
     e As System.EventArgs) Handles btnWelcome.Click

        'Make the label display thee Welcome message

        lblWelcome.Text = "Welcome to Visual Basic.NET!!!"

End Sub
```

3. Change the name of the form to `frmWelcome` and then run the program again. This time, an error message appears, indicating errors in build and asking whether to continue. Click the No button. You should see the following message displayed in the Debug window.

Figure 2.23

An error message

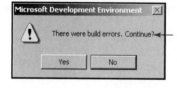

When you change the label name to lblWelcome and then try to run the project, an error message will display.

Figure 2.24

Diagnostics in the Debug window

The Debug window immediately below the form (or code window) tells you what went wrong in your program.

```
Startup code 'Sub Main' was specified in 'Welcome.Form1', but
'Welcome.Form1' was not found.
```

Basically, the system is still looking for a form named Form1, but you have changed it to frmWelcome. To fix this problem, right-click the Welcome project in the Solution Explorer window. A context menu will appear. Click Properties at the bottom of the menu (see Figure 2.25). The Property Pages dialog box will appear.

Select frmWelcome in the Startup Object box (Figure 2.26) and then click the OK button. Run the program again. The program should run without any problem.

Note that any time you change the name of the first form in your project, you will most likely encounter this same problem. In most cases, you use this form as the startup object for your project. It is important to remember how you can fix this problem.

Figure 2.25

Context menu for project

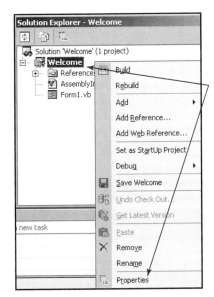

Right-click the Welcome project to display the context menu; then click Properties to invoke the Property Pages dialog box.

Figure 2.26

The Property Pages dialog box

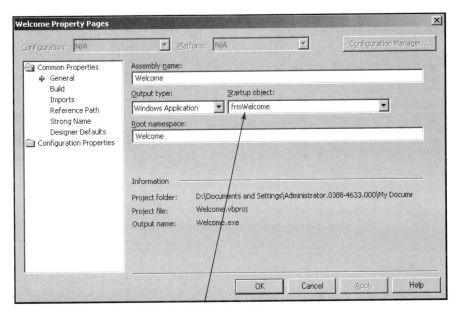

Select frmWelcome from this box to fix the problem after you change the form name.

From this exercise, you have learned:

- To become aware of observing sound naming standards
- To test the code as often as possible
- To name all the objects before placing any code in the code window
- How to change the startup object for a project

TIP

When developing a project, always make sure that all objects have been named properly before starting to place any code in the code window. This helps to eliminate the possibility of encountering mysterious errors in code associated with the names.

2.7 Overview of the Code Structure

You have learned that the code in event procedures handles the events and that when developing code for them, you should use the event procedure templates provided by the IDE. You have also learned that the order of the procedures in the code window is not important because they are invoked by the event, not by the order in which they appear. Also, in general, code in a procedure is executed top down. But is there some kind of code in a procedure that will not get executed in sequence?

In terms of the order in which statements are executed, there are basically two types of statements: statements that bring results and execute sequentially, and statements that direct flow of execution control. You will study each of these types in detail in later chapters, but take a brief look at each type here.

Statements That Bring Results and Execute Sequentially

Most statements bring results such as relocating an object onscreen or moving data from one location to another in the memory. For example, you have seen the following statement that moves the label to a random location in the form:

```
Label1.SetBounds(Rnd() * Width, Rnd() * Height, Label1.Width,
    Label1.Height)
```

You have also seen the statement:

```
lblWelcome.Text = "Welcome to Visual Basic.NET!!!"
```

This statement moves the text string "Welcome to Visual Basic.NET!!!" to the Text property of the label named lblWelcome. Statements of this type are recognized as *assignment statements*, and are the most commonly seen statements in VB programs.

These types of statements are executed sequentially in the order they appear in a procedure. There are many more of these types of statements. You will encounter many of them throughout the remainder of this book.

Statements That Direct Flow of Execution Control

From time to time, you will encounter situations in which you need to change the sequence of execution in your code. For example, you may need to execute a block of code only if a certain condition is true; you may need to repeat the execution of a block of code for a certain number of times; or you may want to leave (jump away from) a block of code when your program reaches a certain point of execution.

Conditional Execution. If you need to execute a block of code that depends on a certain condition, you may need to use the If block. Its syntax appears as follows:

```
If Condition Then
    Statements to be executed when Condition is True
Else
    Statements to be executed when Condition is False
End If
```

where *Condition* is an expression that can be evaluated to either True or False.

For example, suppose you want to set the BackColor property of the label lblWelcome to either blue or green, depending on the value of the random number given by the Rnd function. You can code the following:

```
If Rnd() <.5 Then
    lblWelcome.BackColor = Color.Blue
Else
    lblWelcome.BackColor = Color.Green
End If
```

Rnd is a random number generator that returns a fractional number in the range of 0 and 1. Color.Blue and Color.Green are named constants that VB recognizes to be values for the blue and green colors. The preceding code block will set the background color of the label to blue if the random number has a value less than .5; otherwise, it will set it to green. There are other code structures used to handle execution of different statements based on certain conditions. Chapter 5, "Decision," discusses these in more detail.

Repetition. In many other situations, you may need to execute a block of code repetitively. One way to handle this is to use the *For . . . Next loop*. The code syntax for this structure is as follows:

```
For Counter = Starting Value To Ending Value
    Statements to be repeated
Next Counter
```

Suppose you need to write 10 numbers, 1 through 10, in the immediate window. You can use this structure in the following manner:

```
For Counter = 1 To 10
    Console.WriteLine(Counter)
Next Counter
```

When this block of code is executed, Counter will start with a value of 1. The statement inside the For block (that is; Console.WriteLine(Counter)), is then executed, resulting in the number 1 being displayed in the immediate window. The next statement, Next Counter, will send the execution control back to the For statement. Counter is then increased by 1 to 2, which is in turn displayed when the WriteLine statement is executed. The loop will continue until Counter is greater than 10. The execution control is then transferred to the statement immediately below the block. Other variations and ways of coding repetitions are discussed in detail in Chapter 7, "Repetition."

Code That Jumps. There are statements that can jump (skip) the remainder of code in a block or a procedure. These statements include GoTo (which results in execution flow that is hard to trace and *should be avoided by all means*), Exit Do, Exit For, Exit Sub, and Exit Function. When there is a need to use each of these statements, their uses will be explained.

An event procedure that contains various code structures discussed previously is given in Figure 2.27.

Figure 2.27

A sample procedure with various code structure

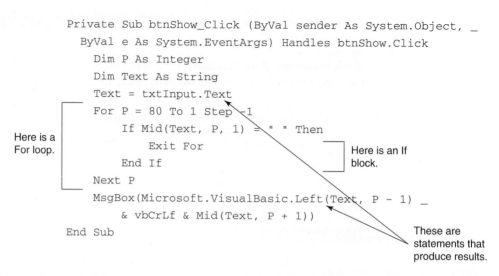

```
Private Sub btnShow_Click (ByVal sender As System.Object, _
    ByVal e As System.EventArgs) Handles btnShow.Click
    Dim P As Integer
    Dim Text As String
    Text = txtInput.Text
    For P = 80 To 1 Step -1
        If Mid(Text, P, 1) = " " Then
            Exit For
        End If
    Next P
    MsgBox(Microsoft.VisualBasic.Left(Text, P - 1) _
        & vbCrLf & Mid(Text, P + 1))
End Sub
```

Here is a For loop.

Here is an If block.

These are statements that produce results.

2.8 Revising the First Program

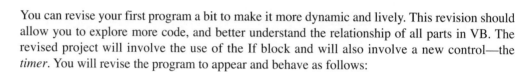

You can revise your first program a bit to make it more dynamic and lively. This revision should allow you to explore more code, and better understand the relationship of all parts in VB. The revised project will involve the use of the If block and will also involve a new control—the *timer*. You will revise the program to appear and behave as follows:

1. The Welcome to Visual Basic.NET!!! sign will automatically appear when the program starts, and will have a larger font and more lively colors: blue foreground and red background.

2. When the program starts, the Welcome sign (the label) will appear from the right margin of the form and move smoothly across the form. After it completely disappears from the form, it will reappear from the right margin again. This will continue on and on.

3. The program will end when you click a button with the text Quit.

Organizing Project and Solution Folders

Rather than modifying the project from the previous one, you will start with a new project. This will allow you to consider the folder organization for your solutions. Follow these steps:

1. Start the IDE using the procedure outlined in Section 2.1 until you see the New Project dialog box as shown in Figure 2.4.

2. Enter **Welcome02** in the Name box.

3. Click the Browse button on the Location box. The Project Location dialog box will appear. Verify that the current folder is Visual Studio Projects (Figure 2.28).

4. Create a new folder under Visual Studio Projects, and name it **Examples**. To do so,

   4.1. Click the Create New Folder icon in the dialog box.

   4.2. Enter **Examples** in the Name box (see Figure 2.29).

   4.3. Click the OK button in the New Folder dialog box.

5. Create a new folder under Examples and name it **Chapter02**. Verify that the current folder is Examples; then:

   5.1. Click the Create New Folder icon.

   5.2. Enter **Chapter02** in the Name box.

   5.3. Click OK.

6. Click Open in the Project Location dialog box.

Figure 2.28

The Project Location
dialog box

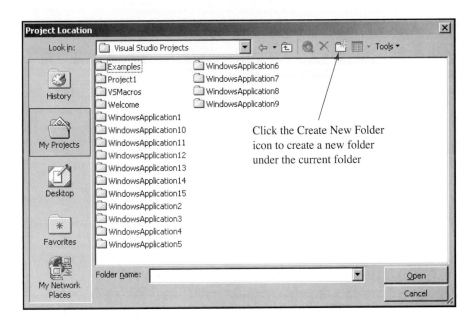

Click the Create New Folder
icon to create a new folder
under the current folder

Figure 2.29

The New Folder dialog
box

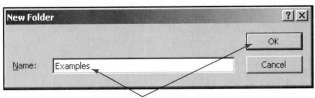

Enter the new folder name
and then click OK.

7. Click the OK button in the New Project dialog box (see Figure 2.30).

The previous steps create the new project with the following folder path:

```
\…\My Documents\Visual Studio
   Projects\Examples\Chapter02\Welcome02
```

This structure allows you to locate a project fairly easily. Subsequent examples will follow this convention; that is, all examples will be created under the Examples folder with a proper chapter subfolder and an appropriate name to identify the project.

The Visual Interface

You can now set up the visual interface as shown in Figure 2.31. Follow these steps:

1. Draw a label and button on the form, taking care of their locations and sizes by following the steps outlined for the previous Welcome example.

2. Set several properties for the label.

2.1. Set its name property to lblWelcome. Use the Properties window to achieve the desired setting. Refer to Section 2.6, "Naming Objects," for specific steps to change the name property for an object.

2.2. Set its Text property to "Welcome to Visual Basic.NET!!!" by using the Properties window. The steps involved should be similar to those used to change the Text property of the button to Say Welcome in the Welcome example.

2.3. Set its AutoSize property to True.

2.4. Set its Font property to Monotype Corsiva, 24, Bold, and Italic. If your computer does not have this font, set it to your favorite font. The steps to set the font were presented in Section 2.4, "Exploring More Properties."

Figure 2.30

Creating a new project under a folder organization

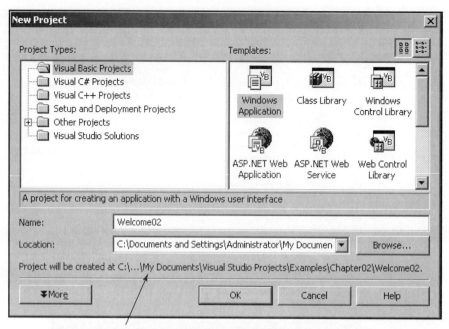

The steps as described will create the new project under this folder organization.

Figure 2.31

The Visual Interface of the revised Welcome project

2.5. Set its BackColor property to red by using the Properties window. Click this property in the Properties window, click the drop-down button in the Property box, click the Custom tab, and select the red color from the color pane.

2.6. Set its ForeColor to blue in the same manner as in step 2.5.

2.7. Make sure the label is placed vertically in the middle of the form.

3. Set the form name to **frmWelcome** and its Text property to **Welcome**.

4. Set the project's Startup object to frmWelcome. Refer to Section 2.6 for the necessary steps.

5. Move the button to the lower right corner of the form. Set its Name property to **btnQuit** and its Text property to **Quit**.

6. Add a timer to the form by pressing the down arrow button by the Clipboard Ring to find this control. Notice that this control will appear in the area below the form, but not on the form. It will not appear when your program runs. Change its name to **tmrWelcome**. (Note that the name prefix for the timer is *tmr*.) Set its Enabled property to True, and its interval to 250. You will learn what this number means later in this section. The form should appear similar to the one shown in Figure 2.31.

Coding the Revised Project

Now turn your attention to what code you need for this revised project. Because all the required properties of all controls have been set, your main focus is to make the label move across the form. Here is the list of questions you need to answer:

1. How do you place the label on the right margin of the form?
2. How do you move the label smoothly across the form?
3. How do you know the label has disappeared from the form?

Placing the Label on the Right Margin of the Form. The label has a Left property, which locates the label's left side on the form. The right margin of the form should have the value of the entire width of the form (see Figure 2.32). If you set the Left property of the label to the form's width, the label will be placed on the right margin of the form. The code should be as follows:

```
lblWelcome.Left = Me.Width
```

In which event procedure should you place the preceding statement? You want this line to be executed as soon as the project starts. The event that is raised when the project starts is the *Form Load event* that occurs when the form is being loaded into memory. This event is where you can place code that sets initial values for various properties and data before the occurrence of any other events; therefore, you will place the previous statement in this event. To get the event code template from the code window, do the following:

1. Select Base Class Events from the Object box.
2. Select the Load event from the procedure box. The procedure template should appear in the code window. Alternatively, double-click the form. The code will appear with the form load event procedure template.

The code should appear as follows:

```
Private Sub frmWelcome_Load(ByVal sender As System.Object, ByVal e
    As System.EventArgs) Handles MyBase.Load
        'Place the label on the right margin of the form.
        lblWelcome.Left = Me.Width
End Sub
```

Moving the Label Across the Form. To move the label across the form, you can use the SetBounds method discussed previously in this chapter; however, you will need to provide (code) the four required parameters. Alternatively, you can set the label's Left property.

Figure 2.32

Aligning the label on the right margin of the form

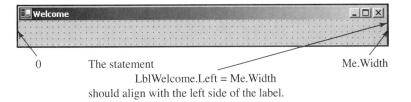

0   The statement   Me.Width
        LblWelcome.Left = Me.Width
    should align with the left side of the label.

Each time this property changes, the label repositions itself horizontally. For example, you can code:

```
lblWelcome.Left = lblWelcome.Left - lblWelcome.Width / 10
```

This statement will subtract one-tenth of the label's width from its current Left property value and assign the result to that property, causing the label to move to the left by one-tenth of the label's width. Notice that the equal sign in the statement does not mean equal, but rather to move data from the right side to the left side of the equal sign.

Now, imagine that you have a button, and you place this statement in its Click event. Each time you click the button, the label will move to the new position. If you can click the button at an even tempo, the label will move smoothly across the form. It is, of course, hard for anybody to click the button evenly. And even if you can, you will get tired quickly! That's why you use the timer.

The *timer* keeps track of time. At design time, you can see its appearance below the form and set its properties. At run time, it disappears completely. When enabled, all it does is keep track of time. The timer has one event—the Tick event—that is similar to a Click event; when the Tick event is raised (triggered), the code in the event procedure is executed. The Tick event, however, is not raised by a click, but rather by the time interval you set for its Interval property. An interval value of 1 is equivalent to one one-thousandth of a second. If you set its interval property to 250, the Tick event will be triggered every quarter of a second. You can think that the timer ticks every quarter of a second; if you place the preceding statement to set the label's Left property in this Tick event, the label will move left every quarter of a second by one-tenth of the label's width. The code should appear as follows:

```
Private Sub tmrWelcome_Tick(ByVal sender As System.Object, ByVal e
    As System.EventArgs)   Handles tmrWelcome.Tick
        lblWelcome.Left = lblWelcome.Left - lblWelcome.Width / 10
End Sub
```

To enter the code shown, do the following:

1. Make sure that the timer's name has been set to **tmrWelcome**. Click the timer below the form, and check its name in the Properties window. Verify that the Enabled property is set to True, and the Interval property is set to 250.

2. Double-click the timer. The timer's Tick event procedure should appear in the code window.

3. Type in the preceding code line.

Determining Whether the Label Has Completely Disappeared. If you test the program now, the label will appear from the right margin of the form and then gradually move to the left until it disappears; however, it will not reappear. So how can you tell if the label has completely disappeared from the form? The Left and Top properties of all the controls on the form are set relative to the upper left corner of the form, which has a coordinate value (0,0). When the label's Left property has a value zero, the label's left margin is aligned with the left margin of the form (see Figure 2.33). At that time, the entire width of the label still appears on the form. This means when the label's Left property plus its width is less than 0, the entire label has moved out of or disappeared from the form. At this point, it will be time to move the label to the right margin of the form again; an If block can be coded as follows:

```
If lblWelcome.Left + lblWelcome.Width <= 0 Then
    lblWelcome.Left = Me.Width 'place the label on the right
        margin of the form
Else
End If
```

The If statement tests whether the Left property plus the Width property is less than 0. If so, the line below it (the assignment statement) will be executed. The assignment statement moves the label to the right margin of the form, as explained previously in this chapter.

Figure 2.33

Welcome banner on the left margin of the form

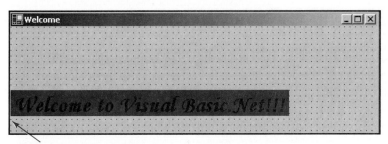

When the label reaches this point, its Left property has a value, 0.
When it moves further left, its Left property will be negative.
When it moves further left for its entire length, its Left property
plus its width will be 0.

You now need to determine what code you should place between Else and End If. This will be the situation that the label can still be seen on the form. That's when the label should move in the normal way. The complete Timer Tick event procedure should appear as follows:

```
Private Sub tmrWelcome_Tick(ByVal sender As System.Object, ByVal e
    As System.EventArgs) Handles tmrWelcome.Tick
    If lblWelcome.Left + lblWelcome.Width <= 0 Then
    ' Label has disappeared from the form. Place it on the right
      margin.
    lblWelcome.Left = Me.Width 'Place the label on the right
      margin of the form
    Else
    ' Label can be seen. Keep moving to the left.
    lblWelcome.Left = lblWelcome.Left - lblWelcome.Width / 10
    End If
End Sub
```

Modify your timer procedure to match the preceding code.

Ending the Program. All the questions raised at the beginning of coding this revised project have been answered. All that is left now is to consider how the program should end. Like all Windows-based programs, your project unloads when the user clicks the Close button in its control box. Although many users will click the Close button to quit, it is a good practice to provide the user with a more formal way to exit. The Quit button is used for this purpose. You can use the form's Close method to terminate the program. The code should appears as follows:

```
Private Sub btnQuit_Click(ByVal Sender As System.Object, ByVal e
    As System.EventArgs) Handles btnQuit.Click
    Me.Close()
End Sub
```

In the code Me is a special name for the current form. The Close method will close the form, ending the project in effect. Notice that all methods require a pair of parentheses even if no parameters are required.

TIP

Another way to quit a program is to use the End statement:

```
Private Sub btnQuit_Click(ByVal Sender As System.Object, ByVal
    e As System.EventArgs) Handles btnQuit.Click
    End
End Sub
```

There are some differences in the effects of the Close method and the End statements. This aspect is discussed in more detail in Chapter 11, "Menus and Multiple-Form Applications," when you work with multiple forms. Suffice it to say that the Close method is considered less abrupt and a better way to exit.

Revised Project in Summary. The complete code should include three event procedures, as follows:

1. The Form (frmWelcome) Load procedure to place the banner (label) on the right margin of the form
2. The tmrWelcome Tick procedure to move the banner across the form and replace the banner on the right margin again
3. The btnQuit Click procedure to terminate the program

Test your project. You can also try to click the form's Maximize button so that the form will cover the entire screen. Enjoy the Welcome banner as it moves across the form to say Welcome!!!

Completing the Development Cycle

All the aforementioned steps in revising the example program enable you to develop a working program. After a program is thoroughly tested and runs without any problem, it can be placed into production. As you may recall from Chapter 1, this should be the last step of the application (program) development cycle. In this step, the program is compiled into an executable file. From then on, you use the compiled version (the executable) to process live data. You will no longer need to use the IDE to run that program. Actually, when you test run your program, the IDE compiles and saves the executable file at the same time. You can use the Windows Explorer to browse down the path and find your Welcome02 folder. Below the folder, there is a Bin folder that should contain the Welcome02.exe file.

So, how do you run the compiled program? The executable file will run in exactly the same way as all other executables. When you find it in the folder, double-click the icon to run. Alternatively, you can use the Run option of the Start menu to start the program. This will be similar to the way you run many of the setup programs when you install some software. If you would rather have the program appear in the Program submenu of the Start menu so that it can be run like some of your major applications such as Word, Excel, or VS.NET, you will need to create a shortcut in your system. The steps for both alternatives are described briefly next.

To run the Welcome executable using the Run option of the Start menu, follow these steps:

1. Click the Start button on the desktop.
2. Click the Run option to open the Run dialog box.
3. Type the path of your Welcome02 executable into the Open combo box, or use the Browse button to find the Welcome02 executable.
4. Click the OK button to run.

To add the Welcome02 executable to the Programs submenu, follow these steps:

1. Click the Start button on the desktop.
2. Highlight the Settings option. A submenu will appear.
3. Click the Taskbar & Start Menu option. A Taskbar Properties dialog box will appear.
4. Click the Advanced tab.
5. Click the Add button to open the Create Shortcut dialog box.
6. Enter the path for your Welcome02 executable in the Command Line text box—(C:\. . .\Examples\Chapter02\Welcome02\bin\Welcome02.exe). Alternatively, use the Browse button to locate your Welcome02 executable and then click the OK button.
7. Click the Next button. The Select Program Folder dialog box will appear.
8. Select a folder in which you would like the Welcome02 executable to be included, such as Programs or Accessories, and click the Next button. (You can also create a new folder for your executable by clicking the New Folder button.) The Select a Title for the Program dialog box will appear.

9.   Enter a title for the executable in the text box, such as **Say Welcome**.

10.   Click the Finish button; then click the OK button in the Taskbar Properties dialog box.

Note that these steps assume the operating system is Windows 2000; other operating systems will require different steps. The Windows Help file contains detailed information and step-by-step instructions.

Summary

- Starting the VS.NET IDE is similar to starting any Windows program. You begin with clicking the Start button. Highlight the Programs menu and the Microsoft Visual Studio.NET folder; then click Microsoft Soft Visual Studio.NET.

- At the Start page of the IDE, be sure to make the proper choices to customize your environment.

- The IDE's menu bar provides you with all action choices. The toolbar offers many shortcuts to the IDE menus.

- The Toolbox contains many controls and components that you can use to design and develop your program.

- The form allows you to design all the visual elements of the user interfaces of your program. The code window behind the form serves as the container in which you write your code.

- The Solution Explorer window shows the files that are contained in your solution, which contains your project(s) among other elements.

- The Properties window shows the properties of a selected object. You can use this window to set and view the settings of the properties for the object.

- To develop a simple program, you:

  - Draw the needed controls on the form

  - Adjust the sizes and locations of the form and controls

  - Set other properties of the objects

  - Place code in the proper events

  - Test and revise the code until it runs as expected

- The IDE enables you to write code, compile the program, and test run without having to leave the environment.

- It is a good practice to insert comment lines in your code to provide additional information on the code, including the purpose of certain code statements.

- If a code line becomes too lengthy, you can break it by typing a space and an underscore (_) and then continue the remaining code on the next line.

- Objects have three types of interfaces: properties, methods, and events. Properties are special types of data that can affect the objects' appearance or behavior. Methods are procedures that can be called to perform some specific actions. Events are triggered by the user or system actions. The event procedures are where you write the code that runs in response to these events.

- The VS.NET help file provides a wealth of information on VB among other languages. Develop a habit of browsing the file for additional information. The habit can pay a huge dividend in your career development.

- Follow the object naming conventions. They add clarity and readability to your code. Before writing any code, make sure that the objects to be used in code are properly named.

- Programming statements can be classified into two types based on flow of logic: those that produce results, and those that direct flow of execution.

- Four objects are introduced in this chapter: the form, label, button, and timer. The form serves as a visual container in which you can draw controls and is the window for the user visual interface. The label is used to display text that gives the user clues or instructions. The button is used for the user to trigger actions, usually by clicking on it. The timer is used to keep track of time. Its Tick event allows code to be executed at a regular time interval.

- The revised program assembles several programming elements. It utilizes the four objects introduced, and also shows how the If structure can be used to execute different code blocks under different conditions.

- The IDE automatically produces the executable file while you develop your program. You can run the executable just like all other Windows programs.

Explore and Discover

2-1. **Border Property of the Label.** Draw a label onto a new standard form. Look for the BorderStyle property in its Properties window. (If you do not see this window, press F4.) What is the current setting? Change this setting to Fixed3D. How does the label appear now? It should look like a three-dimensional box.

2-2. **BackColor Property of the Label.** Use the label created in exercise 2-1. Click the BackColor property in the Properties window. You should see a down-arrow button. Click that button. You should see a window with three tabs: Custom, Web, and System. Click one tab; then click another. What do you see under each tab? Select white from an item of any tab. The label should now look like a text box in a typical window.

2-3. **TextAlign Property of the Label.** Use the same label in exercise 2-2. Make sure the AutoSize property is set to False. Widen the label so that there is extra space beyond the text Label1, and set the TextAlign property to MiddleCenter. Check the position of Label1 in the label. Where does it appear? Change the property to TopRight. Check the position of the text again. Where does it appear?

2-4. **Font Property of the Button.** Draw a button on a new form. Can you change the font to Courier 12? (Yes, the button has the Font property. Follow the steps discussed earlier in this chapter.)

2-5. **BackColor Property of the Button.** Use the button in exercise 2-4. Change its BackColor property to red. (Refer to exercise 2-2 for additional clues. Look for the color in the Custom tab.) Do you see any change in color in the button?

2-6. **Anchor Property.** Use the same button in exercise 2-5. Run the project, and maximize the form by clicking the Maximize button. Where does the button appear in the form? End the project. Change its Anchor property to Bottom, Right. (Click off the two bars that are currently on and click on the other two that are current off.) Run the project and then maximize the form again. What do you see this time? Most controls have this property. You can use it to set the control's position relative to the form.

2-7. **Icon Properties of the Form.** Click the form's Icon property in the Properties window. You should see an ellipsis button indicating choices. Click that button. You should see an Open (icon file) dialog box. Find and select an icon in your system. Try one from the following folder.

C:\Program files\Microsoft Visual Studio.NET\Common7\Graphics\Icons\Computer
Check the upper left corner of the form. What do you see?

2-8. **WindowState Property of the Form.** The form's WindowState property can be set to one of the three values: Normal, Minimized, and Maximized. Run the project each time after you change the setting to one of these values.

Run the project with its WindowState property set to Normal. You should see the Minimize, Maximize, and Close buttons on the right side of the form's title bar. Click each of these buttons. What happens?

The form also has the MaximizeBox and MinimizeBox properties. Set one of these properties to False. Run the project. Inspect the right side of the form's title bar. Do you see any change?

2-9. **ControlBox Property of the Form.** Set the form's ControlBox property to False and then inspect its title bar. Run the project. You can no longer end the project by clicking the Close button on the title bar—it is no longer there. Terminate the project by clicking the Stop Debugging button on the toolbar, or click the Stop Debugging option in the Run menu.

2-10. **AcceptButton and CancelButton Properties of the Form.** Start a new project. Draw a label and two buttons on the form. Set the Name property of the label to **lblShow**. Set the Text property of one button to **Default** and its Name property to **btnDefault**. Set the Text property of the other button to Cancel and its Name property to **btnCancel**. Enter the following code in the btnDefault click event:

```
lblShow.Text = "Default button has been clicked."
```

Enter the following code in the btnCancel click event:

```
lblShow.Text = "Cancel button has been clicked."
```

(*Hint:* Obtain the event procedure templates by the steps discussed earlier in this chapter.)

Run the program and then press the Return key followed by the Esc key. Do you see any text change in the label?

Now set the form's AcceptButton property to **btnDefault** and the CancelButton property to **btnCancel**. Run the program again. Press the Enter key. Look at the label. "Default Button has been Clicked" should appear. Press the Esc key. What do you see now? What can you conclude about the AcceptButton and CancelButton properties of the form?

2-11. **The Dock property.** Continue from exercise 2-10, set the label's Dock property to Top, and check where it appears in the form. Change that property to different settings and inspect the label's location on the form. Most controls have this property, which can be handy in the design of user interface. You will use it in chapter 11, "Menus and Multiple Form Applications."

2-12. **Various IDE Windows below the Code Window.** Run the project you created for exercise 2-10. Take a look at the window below the code window. What do you see? Notice the two rows of tabs and buttons below this window. (Your system may show only one row.) Click each of these and observe what you see. Click the Output tab. Select Debug from the box immediately below the Output title bar. This window gives status or actions at various stages of execution. It is also the area for output from the Console object that was mentioned in Chapter 1.

Exercises

In the following exercises, make sure that all objects in your projects are named properly before you start your coding.

2-13. **Beeper.** Set a new form's Text Property to **Beeper** and name the form **frmBeeper**. Give the code such that the computer will make a sound when the user clicks on your form. (*Hint:* The event is Form Click. The command to make a sound is Beep.)

2-14.   Say Yes, Say No. Use a label control and two buttons. One button has the text, "Say yes;" the other, "Say no."

Provide the code so that when your program runs, the label will display "Yes!" when the Say yes button is clicked, and "No!" when the Say no button is clicked. (*Hint:* Name the buttons btnYes and btnNo and the label lblYesNo. Set the Text property of the label in the Click event of each button.)

2-15.   Move Left, Move Right. Use one label and two buttons. Set the label's Text property to **I can move!**, Font property to MonoType Corsiva 24, BorderStyle property to Fixed3D, and background color to Blue. (*Note:* If your computer does not have MonoType Corsiva, use your favorite font as a substitute.) Set one button's Text property to **Move Left** and name to **btnMoveLeft**. Set the other button's Text property to **Move Right** and name to **btnMoveRight**.

Provide the code so that as the program runs, the label will move to the left by one-half of the label's width if the Move Left button is clicked, and will move to the right by the same distance if the Move Right button is clicked. (*Hint:* The line given below will move the label named lblMover to the right by one-half of its width.)

```
lblMover.Left = lblMover.Left + lblMover.Width / 2
```

2-16.   Showing Intention of Move. Modify exercise 2-15 to handle the keyboard. At run time, when the user uses the Tab key to move the focus to the Move Left (Right) button, the label (lblMover) will display "I will move left (right)". When the user presses the Return key, the label will move as promised. (*Hint:* When the user tabs to a control, the control's Enter event is raised. When the user presses the Return key on a button, the Click event is raised.)

2-17.   Move Up, Move Down. Use one label and two buttons. Set the label's Font property to Bookman Old Style Bold Italic 20, BorderStyle property to Fixed3D, Backcolor to Green, and Text property to **I can move!**. (*Note:* If your computer does not have Bookman Old Style, use your favorite font as a substitute.) Set one button's text to **Move Up** and name to **btnMoveUp**. Set the other button's text to **Move Down** and name to **btnMoveDown**. Provide the code so that as the program runs, the label will move up by twice the height of the label when the Move Up button is clicked, and will move down by the same distance when the Move Down button is clicked. (*Hint:* The property to set an object's vertical position is Top. You can get more hints from exercise 2-15.)

2-18.   Random Movement. Use one label and one button. Set the label's Text property to **I don't necessarily move**. Set its color, font, and border style to make it look attractive. Set the button's text to **Move**. Provide the code so that as the project runs, the label will move to a random location only about half of the time when you click the Move button. (*Hint:* Use an If statement:

```
If Rnd() >= .5 Then
     'the statement to move the label
End If
```

An example to move a label to a random location is given in the text.)

2-19.   Make It Red, Make It Blue. Use one label control and two buttons. Set the form's text to **Color Exercise**. Set the label's text to **Show My Color**, border style to Fixed3D, and font to Times New Roman 20. Set one button's Text Property to **Make it Red**; set the other to **Make it Blue**. When the program runs, the label will change its background color to red and foreground color to green, or background color to blue and foreground color to white, depending on which button is clicked. (*Hint:* The names for colors red, blue, green, and white are Color.Red, Color.Blue, Color.Green, and Color.White, respectively.)

2-20.   Change Color or Not. When the user clicks on the form, its background will be red if the random number (VB's Rnd function) is less than .5; otherwise, it will be blue. (*Hint:* Use an If statement with the following structure:

```
If Rnd() < .5 Then
    ' set the form's background color to Red
Else
    ' set the form's background color to Blue
End If
```

The event is Form Click.)

2-21.   Floating Banner. Modify the revised Welcome project in the text so that the Welcome sign (label) will appear from the bottom center of the form and then move up every half of a second by one-quarter of the label's height until it disappears from the form; then make it reappear from the bottom center again, and repeat the movement. The program should quit when the user clicks a button with the text **Quit**.

2-22.   Controlling the Action. Modify exercise 2-21 by adding one more button to the form. Name this button **btnControl**. When the program starts, the button has the text **Go** and the banner is hidden. When the user clicks the **Go** button, the button's text is changed to **Halt** and the banner starts to float as described in exercise 2-21. The banner's movement will continue until the user click this Halt button. In such case, the banner stops floating, and the button's text is changed to **Go** again. Clicking this button will toggle the banner's action. When the user clicks the Quit button, the program ends. (Hint: Use the If structure in the btnControl Click event to handle the Halt and Go. Set the timer's Enabled property to True to trigger the Tick event, and to False to halt the action. Also, assign **Halt** or **Go** to the button's Text property depending on the conditions.)

2-23.   Coding a Long Statement. Draw a label and a button on a new form. Name the label **lblLongStatement**. Make sure that its size is large enough to hold a long text. Name the button **btnSetStatement**. Provide the code so that when the user clicks the button, the following text will appear in the label:

"This is an example of a statement which, if one absolutely had to be thoroughly descriptive, could be described as rambling. If one wanted to be even more excruciatingly accurate, however, they could state that this statement consists of not only one but two long-winded sentences that could have easily been rewritten to be more concise had the purpose of this exercise been anything other than to create a long chain of words that created a need to be broken up into several lines."

Note: Break the statement into several lines.

2-24.   Changing Mood. Draw two picture boxes as well as a timer on a new form. Name them **picHappy**, **picSad**, and **tmrMood**, respectively. Place picHappy in the center of the form. Set the Visible property of picSad to False; then set the Image property of picHappy to a happy face image that you find in your computer; set picSad to a sad face image.

Provide code so that at run time, the picture at the center of the form will show the happy face for one second and then change to sad face for another second, alternately. (*Hint:* In the Form Load event, assign the Left and Top properties of picSad with those of picHappy. Set the timer interval to 1000. In its Tick event, reverse the Visible property of each picture box— from True to False and vice versa. If you enjoy this exercise, modify the problem to animate traffic lights, which you should be able to find in your computer.)

Projects

2-25. **The Rotating Banner.** Modify the Welcome project in this chapter so that as soon as the left margin of the banner disappears from the form's left side, it reappears from the right as shown in Figure 2.34. (*Hint:* This involves a trick. You need to set up two identical labels. Call them **lblWelcome1** and **lblWelcome2**. Start the first label the same way as the example project in the text; then, in the Timer Tick event, allow it to move in the same manner without the If block. Make the second label follow the first label with the distance between the left margins of the two labels equal to the form's width. When the second label starts to disappear from the form, assign its Left property to the first label's [use an If block to handle this].)

2-26. **Random Position, Random Size, Random Color.** Use one label and one button. Set the form's Text property to Randomizer. Set the label's border style to Fixed3D and text to **I change as I wish**. Change its font and font size to your liking. Place the button at the upper left corner of the form and then name it **btnMove**.

Provide the code so that when the program runs and the user clicks on the button, the form will move to a random location and its size will change simultaneously. Its background color will be red or blue, depending on whether the value of the random number (VB's Rnd function) is greater than .5. The label will move to a random location within the form. Its background color will be white if the form's background is blue; otherwise, it will be green. (*Hint:* The following statements will move the form to a random location in the screen, and will have the form's size changed as well.

```
Dim W, X, Y, H
X = Rnd * Screen.PrimaryScreen.Bounds.Width
Y = Rnd * Screen.PrimaryScreen.Bounds.Height
W = Rnd * Screen.PrimaryScreen.Bounds.Width
H = Rnd * Screen.PrimaryScreen.Bounds.Height
Me.SetBounds(X, Y, W, H)
```

Beware that W must be wide enough to accommodate the widths of the label and the button. H must be high enough to accommodate the height of the label and the button. For the form and the controls to stay visible, X must be less than Screen.PrimaryScreen.Bounds.Width – W, and Y must be less than Screen.PrimaryScreen.Bounds.Height – H. Use the If statement to adjust these values. Use the following code to ensure that the label does not go out of the form's boundary.

Figure 2.34

The rotating banner

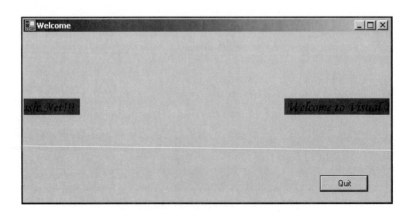

```
'Set label's position based on form width and height
Dim LX, LY
LX = W * Rnd()
If LX > Me.Width - lblMover.Width Then
    LX = Me.Width - lblMover.Width
End If
LY = H * Rnd()
If LY > Me.ClientSize.Height - lblMover.Height Then
    LY = Me.ClientSize.Height - lblMover.Height
End If
lblMover.Left = LX
lblMover.Top = LY
```

Use the If block to set the color for the form and the label.)

2-27.   **Random Changes at Regular Time Intervals.** Modify the project in exercise 2-26 so that the form will change its position, size, and color every half of a second. When the user clicks the button with the text **Quit**, the program quits.

3. User Interface Design: Visual Basic Controls and Events

I n Chapter 2, "Introduction to Visual Basic Programming,", you explored four Visual Basic (VB) objects—the form and three controls—and some of their capabilities. There are, of course, more VB objects and controls. Many of the controls have features that can make your design of a data-entry screen more powerful and user-friendly. This chapter presents various data-entry/user-interface situations. For each situation, you will learn the appropriate VB control(s) to use. In addition, when you place many VB controls on a form, you may discover that the sequence in which the user tabs through these controls is not exactly what you had in mind. This chapter shows how this sequence can be modified.

As explained in Chapter 2, each VB control has its own events. These events are raised or triggered when some situation occurs in the system or when the user takes an action. You can place code in the procedures that are associated with these events so that the computer behaves exactly as you would like; therefore, these events are where you give your program life and personality. You will explore a few of the events most commonly used in data-entry operations. All the code you place in your project will directly or indirectly relate to one or more of these events, so it is important that you have a thorough understanding of them.

fter completing this chapter, you should be able to:

- Have a clear understanding of the important features and the role each of the following VB controls plays in the user interface for data-entry operations:
  - Text box
  - Group box
  - Radio button
  - List box
  - Masked edit box
  - Tab
  - Check box
  - Combo box
- Set the tab order for the controls placed on the form.
- Understand the nature and uses of the following events:
  - Form Load
  - KeyPress
  - Click, DoubleClick, and SelectedIndexChanged
  - Enter and Leave

3.1 Obtaining Open-Ended Input from the User: Text Box and Masked Edit Control

As an example, imagine that you would like to develop a VB program to keep track of your friends' names and phone numbers. Your first step, as explained in Chapter 2, is to design the visual interface. In this process, you will need to place VB controls onto the form for the user to enter the name and phone number. The VB control that enables you to enter any type of data is the text box. As its name suggests, the text box specializes in handling text data.

Text Property of the Text Box

Similar to the label and the button, the text box has a property called *Text*. At design time, you can set this property to any text, which will then be displayed at runtime, much like the label you saw in Chapter 2. Unlike the label, however, the text box also allows the user to enter and edit its content at runtime. The text can then be further processed, or simply saved for future use.

As an exercise, place a text box in a new form by double-clicking the TextBox icon in the Toolbox. You will see TextBox1 displayed in the box (Figure 3.1). Adjust its size by dragging one of its sizing handles, and change its location by dragging the control from inside the boundary as you see fit. Because you are interested in using the text box for inputting your friend's name, you should name the control **txtName** and clear the text to make it a blank. You can change the control's name by typing **txtName** in the Name property in the Properties window. To clear the text box, delete **TextBox1** from the control's Text property.

Make sure that there is no remaining blank space when clearing the text box's Text property. An invisible extra space can create problems for beginners when they try to compare the property with a pre-determined text in code.

Look at the form again and you will realize that a blank box in a form means little to the user because it provides no clue as to what the user is supposed to do with it. You can place a label with proper text such as **Name (Last, First Init.)** by the text box. Such a clue is indispensable. Text boxes are almost always accompanied with labels when used for input purposes. Your result should look similar to that shown in Figure 3.2.

After you have the label and the text box in the form, you can run the program and enter your name into the text box. To see what the computer can do with what you have entered, you will write code to make the computer display the content of the text box when you click on the form.

Figure 3.1

Bringing a text box to a form

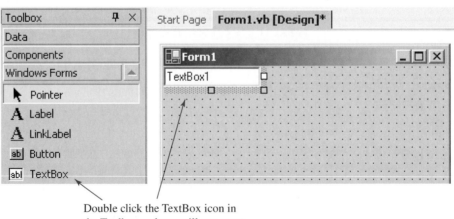

Double click the TextBox icon in the Toolbox and you will see a text box appear in the form.

Figure 3.2

Making the label and text box work together

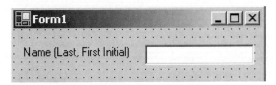

A text box should always be accompanied by a label to provide clues as to what is to be entered.

The form has a Click event. Place the code in this event to display the message. Enter the following code:

```
Private Sub Form1_Click(ByVal sender As System.Object, ByVal e As
    System.EventArgs) Handles MyBase.Click
        MsgBox("Your name is " & txtName.Text)
End Sub
```

Recall that to create a code template for an event procedure, you need to use the object box and procedure box in the code window. Refer to Figure 2.20 for specifics.

Both the label and text box controls can be used to display text. So, how do you decide which one to use? If you don't want the user to change its content, use the label. If you need the user's input or if you want to allow the user to copy and paste from the box, use the text box. You can make a label look similar to a text box by setting its BackColor property to ActiveCaptionText (White) and BorderStyle property to Fixed3D.

Run the program again. Enter your name and then click the form. You should see a message box displaying the message, "Your name is " along with your name. End the program before proceeding.

In the preceding code, the & operator concatenates the text string "Your name is " with the content of the text box named txtName. If you enter "Smith, John" as your name in the text box, the resulting text string will be "Your name is Smith, John." Figure 3.3 shows the result. String operations are discussed in more detail in Chapter 4, "Data, Operations, and Built-In Functions." The MsgBox displays the text in a dialog box, and waits until the user acknowledges the message by clicking the OK button. The MsgBox is discussed further in Chapter 6, "Input, Output, and Procedures."

Figure 3.3

Showing what's entered in the text box

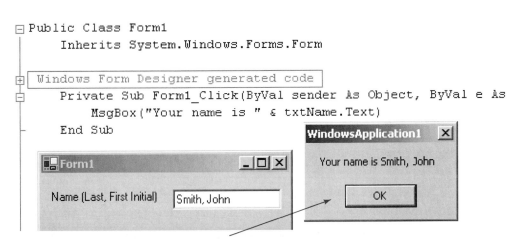

With the code, MsgBox will display this message when you click the form. Click the OK button to make the message box disappear.

You can create the phone number field on the form in the same manner:

1. Add a label and then change its text to **Phone Number**.
2. Add another text box. Change its Name property to **txtPhone** and clear its box by clearing its Text property.

The user interface is now ready for another test. Start the program, and try to enter a friend's name and phone number. A sample result is shown in Figure 3.4.

Understanding the Focus. Because you have more than one control to accept input, you can enter data into a control only when it has the focus. A user can set the focus of a control by clicking on it, or by pressing the Tab key repetitively until the focus reaches that control. When the text box gets the focus, a blinking cursor will appear in its box.

You can also use the Focus method to set focus on a particular text box control. For example, the following statement will set the focus on txtName.

```
txtName.Focus
```

This method can be useful when you find a need to set the focus on some control after certain operations. For example, assume you have added a button named btnSave to the form and imagine the user has just clicked the Save button, triggering the Click event procedure to save data onscreen. After the data are saved, however, the focus remains on the button. By including the statement, you can make it convenient for your user to continue the data-entry operation. The code structure should appear as follows:

```
Private Sub btnSave_Click(ByVal Sender As System.Object, ByVal e As
    System.EventArgs) Handles btnSave.Click
    ' Statements to save data
    MsgBox("Data saved") 'Tell the user data have been saved
    ' Reset focus on the first control
    txtName.Focus()
End Sub
```

The Masked Edit Box Control

Back to the phone number example, keying in the name should be a simple and smooth process; however, the phone number field has a defined pattern. The area code, which is enclosed in a pair of parentheses, is followed by a hyphen, a three-digit prefix, another hyphen, and the four-digit number. The parentheses and hyphens are in fixed positions. If you have a control that can show these fixed characters automatically, you will not only force the user to follow the pattern, but also save the user four keystrokes, a nearly 30% improvement in keying efficiency. The *masked edit control* is a VB control that can handle this defined pattern. This control has a *Mask property,* which, when left blank, will cause the control to act like a standard text box, but the property can be set to expect and conveniently enforce a desired input pattern.

Figure 3.4

Text boxes in action

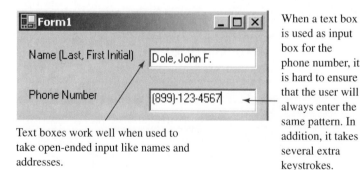

Text boxes work well when used to take open-ended input like names and addresses.

When a text box is used as input box for the phone number, it is hard to ensure that the user will always enter the same pattern. In addition, it takes several extra keystrokes.

Adding the Masked Edit Box Control. This control is not a standard (intrinsic) VB control, but can be added to the project. To add the masked edit box control, follow these steps:

1. Click the Tools menu and then click the Customize Toolbox option (Figure 3.5). The Customize Toolbox dialog box will appear.
2. Click the COM Components tab in the dialog box if it is not selected.
3. Click the Microsoft Masked Edit Control version 6.0 check box (Figure 3.6), and click the OK button.

Figure 3.5

Tools menu and the Customize Toolbox option

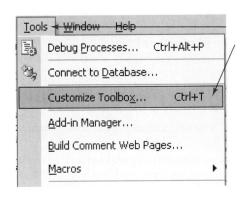

Click the Tools menu then select the Customize Toolbox option to invoke the Customize Toolbox dialog box. Note that you can press Crtl+T to accomplish the same.

Figure 3.6

The Customize Toolbox dialog box

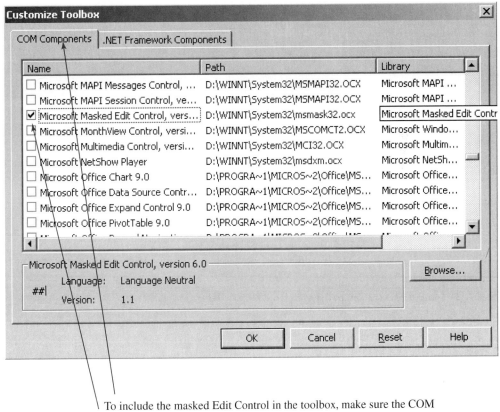

To include the masked Edit Control in the toolbox, make sure the COM Components tab is selected. Then locate and check Microsoft Masked Edit Control, version 6.

The masked edit control icon ##| will appear in VB's Toolbox. To include this control in your project, follow these steps:

1. Delete the text box for phone number. Click on the text box on the form and then press the Delete key.

2. Place a masked edit in place of the text box. The masked edit control should appear at the end of the Toolbox. Press the down arrow button at the bottom of the Toolbox to scroll through the list of controls.

   2.1. Click the masked edit icon in the Toolbox.

   2.2. Draw this control in the same place where the text box was. Adjust its size and position properly.

   2.3. Change its Name property to **mskPhone**.

The Mask Property. As mentioned, the masked edit box has a Mask property. Set this property to **(###)-###-####**; you should see the mask appear in the control's box in the form (Figure 3.7).

Start the program and try it. A sample is shown in Figure 3.8.

The # symbol in the mask is a placeholder for a required digit, and the parentheses and hyphens are literals. At runtime, the literals present themselves in their respective positions, but the # signs disappear. Many more mask characters are available for different uses. For example, an A mask character is a placeholder for a required alphanumeric character. Explore the Help file for many additional mask features of this control, as suggested in the Look It Up box that follows.

Figure 3.7

Masked edit and its Mask property

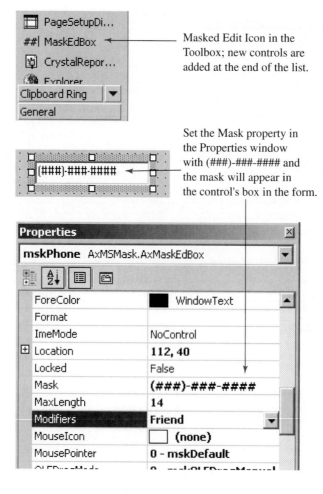

Masked Edit Icon in the Toolbox; new controls are added at the end of the list.

Set the Mask property in the Properties window with (###)-###-#### and the mask will appear in the control's box in the form.

Figure 3.8

Masked edit box in action

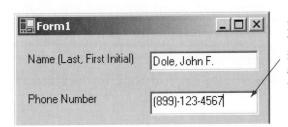

Here's a masked edit box in action. With its Mask property set as shown in the text, the parentheses and dashes are automatically displayed. The box will not accept any nonnumeric keys.

Search the online help screen using **mask property** as the keyword in the Index tab. The page for MaskedEdit ActiveX Control provides a complete list of mask characters used in the mask property of the masked edit box. You will most likely need to visit this page from time to time when you have a special requirement for the masked edit box.

Comparing the Text Properties of the Two Controls

Both the text box and masked edit box have the Text property that holds the exact content of the box. There are some differences in the property between the two controls, however. The Text property of the text box is available at both design time and runtime; that is, you can set this property at both design time and runtime by code. In addition, the user can key anything into the text box at runtime.

In contrast, the Text property of the masked edit box is not available at design time. You can set its value only by code or by the user's key input at runtime. If you assign its value by code, the value must conform to the pattern dictated by the box's mask. For example, if you have set the Mask property for a masked edit box named mskPhone as (###)-###-####, your code to assign a phone number to this control must be in the same pattern as shown in the following assignment statement. Otherwise, a runtime error will result.

```
mskPhone.Text = "(123)-456-7890"
```

When the user enters a key that does not conform to the expected pattern by its mask, the masked edit box will not accept the key, and the cursor stays at the same position as if nothing had happened (it might make a beeping sound). For example, if you try to enter a letter into mskPhone, it will ignore your attempt because its mask expects only numbers. In real applications, the user introduces most of the data errors. The Mask property ensures that only the proper type of key is entered, thus the masked edit box can help enhance data accuracy. The following table summarizes the differences in the Text property behavior between the text box and the masked edit box.

Difference in	Text Box	Masked Edit Box
Availability	Design time and runtime	Only in runtime
Keyboard entry	Any key	Based on the mask
Data assignment by code	Any text	Must be in accordance with the mask

Clearing the Text Property

You may find it desirable to clear the text box or the masked edit box. You can clear the text box easily by assigning a zero-length string (a string that contains nothing) to the Text property as follows:

```
txtName.Text = ""
```

You cannot do exactly the same for the masked edit box because this control expects an exact match of the pattern as specified in the mask; however, you can clear the mask first. Without the mask, the masked edit behaves exactly like a text box. It will allow you to assign a zero-length string to its Text property. After this is done, you should restore the mask so that the user can enter data only with the expected pattern. The following code shows how this is done:

```
mskPhone.Mask = ""                      'To clear the mask
mskPhone.Text = ""                      'To clear the edit box
mskPhone.Mask = "(###)-###-####"        'To restore the mask
```

TIP

At print time, the Text property of the masked edit does not appear to be accessible (either read or write) as documented in the MSDN. Use the control's SelText property as a workaround. Assuming the Mask property is set properly, the following code will provide the equivalence of the Text property:

```
mskPhone.SelStart = 0
mskPhone.SelLength = Len(mskPhone.Mask)
' Print the content
Console.WriteLine(mskPhone.SelText)
```

To clear the text box before the bug is fixed, use the following code:

```
mskPhone.SelStart = 0
mskPhone.SelLength = Len(mskPhone.Mask)
mskPhone.SelText = "(   )-  -    "
```

Selecting (Highlighting) a Portion of the Text

Imagine that you are working with a word processor such as Word. At times, you might find a need to highlight a portion of the text so that you can perform operations such as delete, cut, and paste. Both the text box and the masked edit box support these operations. Suppose in your code you need to know what text is highlighted. You can use the *SelectedText* (*SelText*) *property* of the text box (masked edit) to show the text that is highlighted, and the *SelectionStart* (*SelStart*) and *SelectionLength* (*SelLength*) *properties* of the text box (masked edit) to show the position at which the highlight starts and the length of the selection. Note that the first position has a value of 0 for the SelectionStart property.

TRY THIS

Draw a text box and a button on a new form. Name the text box **txtName,** and clear its text. Name the button **btnShow** and then set its text to Show. Enter the following code:

```
Private Sub btnShow_Click(ByVal Sender As System.Object, ByVal
    e As System.EventArgs) Handles btnShow.Click
    MsgBox("SelectedText=" & txtName.SelectedText & _
    ". SelectionStart=" & txtName.SelectionStart & "."
        SelectionLength=" & txtName.SelectionLength)
End Sub
```

Run the project. Enter some text in the text box, and highlight a portion of the text; then click the Show button. What do you see?

You can also use the SelectionStart and SelectionLength properties in code to select (highlight) a portion of the text. For example, the following code will highlight the content of a text box named txtName when the user tabs into the control (Figure 3-9).

```
Private Sub txtName_Enter(ByVal sender As System.Object, ByVal e
    As System.EventArgs) Handles txtName.Enter
    txtName.SelectionStart = 0 'Set the cursor at the beginning
    'Highlight the text from the beginning
    txtName.SelectionLength = Len(txtName.Text)
End Sub
```

Figure 3.9

Highlighted text box

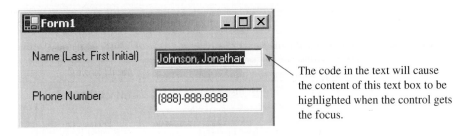

The code in the text will cause the content of this text box to be highlighted when the control gets the focus.

The code is placed in the txtName's *Enter event* procedure, which is triggered when the user presses the Tab key to move the focus to txtName. Its SelectionStart property is set to 0 to place the cursor at the beginning of the text. The following expression:

```
Len(txtName.Text)
```

involves the use of the *Len function*, which returns the length of the parameter enclosed in the pair of parentheses (txtName.Text). The SelectionLength property of txtName is then set to this returned value. Because the SelectionLength property highlights the text starting from the current cursor position (which is set at the beginning by the SelectionStart property), the entire text in txtName will be highlighted. Functions are discussed further in Chapter 4.

In general, the key you enter into a text box is inserted to the existing text. This is recognized as the Insert mode. Another mode of typing is recognized as the type over mode, in which whatever you type replaces the existing text. You can make a text box perform the type over mode with a simple block of code. Recall that the key you enter replaces the highlighted text; therefore, all you have to do is highlight the next position in the text box as soon as the user enters a key. The text box has a *TextChanged* event, which occurs when its text changes (when your key is entered). You can use this event to do the trick:

```
Private Sub txtName_TextChanged(ByVal sender As System.Object,
    ByVal e As System.EventArgs) Handles txtName.TextChanged
        'Ensure the cursor is placed in a proper position
        If txtName.SelectionStart < 0 Then
            txtName.SelectionStart = 0
        End If
        'highlight the character where the cursor is</P>
    txtName.SelectionLength = 1
End Sub
```

The ClipText Property

In addition to the Text property, the masked edit box also has the *ClipText property*. The difference between the two properties is that the Text property has the exact content in the box, including the literal characters in the mask; but the ClipText property has only the text without the literal. Usually, this is what the user actually enters. In the preceding code example, which assigned (123)-456-7890 to mskPhone.Text, the control's ClipText property will be 1234567890 and its Text property will be (123)-456-7890.

Draw one text box, one masked edit box, and a button on a new form. Name them **txtName**, **mskBirthDate**, and **btnShow**, respectively. Set the mask property of mskBirthDate to ##-##-####. Set the Text property of btnShow to Show and then double-click the button in the form to show the code window. Enter the following lines of code:

```
Private Sub btnShow_Click(ByVal Sender As System.Object, ByVal
  e As System.EventArgs) Handles btnShow.Click
    MsgBox("Name is " & txtName.Text)
    MsgBox("Birthdate text is " & mskBirthDate.Text)
    MsgBox("Birthdate clip text is " & mskBirthDate.ClipText)
End Sub
```

Run the program. Key in some data, click the Show button, and see how these Text and ClipText properties work. This exercise should also allow you to gain some experience and proficiency of working with the IDE. *Note:* If the Text property of the masked edit does not work properly, use the following code as a workaround:

```
mskBirthDate.SelStart = 0
mskBirthDate.SelLength = Len(mskBirthDate.Mask)
MsgBox("Birthdate text is " & mskBirthDate.SelText)
```

The following table provides a summary of the new properties discussed in this section.

Property	Applicable Object	Use/Remark
Text	Text box	For the user to enter data; value can be set at design time or assigned by code at runtime; for example, txtName.Text = "John Smith".
	Masked edit box	For the user to enter data; not available at design time; entered data or value assigned must be in accordance with the mask pattern.
Mask	Masked edit box	To define the pattern for the expected data type; for example, a # will expect a number for the corresponding position in the Text property.
SelectionStart*	Text box	To set the cursor position in the field (control); for example, the code txtName.SelectionStart = 1 will place the cursor at the second position of the field.
SelectionLength*	Text box	To select a portion of the text; for example, the statement txtName.SelLength = 3 will select (highlight) three characters in the field beginning at the current cursor position.
SelectedText*	Text box	Returns the text string that is currently highlighted.
ClipText	Masked edit box	Returns the string that is not a literal part of the mask; for example, a masked edit box with the mask ##-##-#### and containing a text string of "12-31-1999" will return a value 12311999.

* The counterpart properties for the masked edit are SelStart, SelLength, and SelText.

3.2 Arranging Many VB Controls on a Form: Group Box and Tab Controls

Suppose you are designing an entry screen for an account file used by a hospital. The screen will be used to collect not only personal data about the account holder and their employer, but also information on the holder's health insurance. One obvious difference from the previous situation is the number of data fields on the form. How does this affect your design? As the number of fields increases, you need to ensure that the form layout looks neat, logical, and uncluttered. That is, VB controls placed on the form should be aligned neatly with each other and be grouped properly. Furthermore, the grouping of these fields should appear to be logical and intuitive to the user.

Figure 3.10

The group box

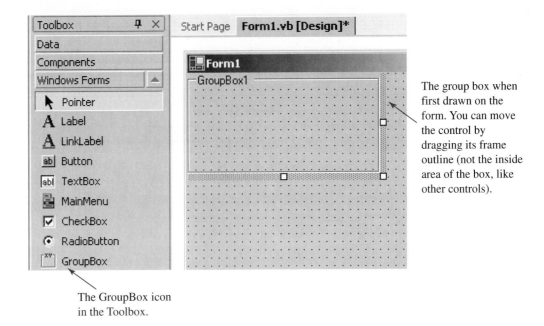

The group box when first drawn on the form. You can move the control by dragging its frame outline (not the inside area of the box, like other controls).

The GroupBox icon in the Toolbox.

The Group Box

A VB control often used to help group related data fields is the *group box.* As its name suggests, the group box provides a box within which a group of controls can be placed (Figure 3.10). It has a Text property that can be used to indicate its content. When used properly, the group box not only provides a means of grouping controls logically, but also facilitates an organized arrangement of the form layout.

Design Time Behavior. Controls within the group box are treated as one logical unit. When the box is moved, all controls inside the box move with it. If you delete the group box, all controls within it are also deleted. Because the group box has the capability to hold other controls, it is recognized as a type of *container*.

Placing Controls in a Group Box. At design time, to place a control in the group box, draw the control in the group box. You can also first draw a control onto the form and then drag it into the group box. In either case, the control becomes a logical part of the group box and will be handled accordingly. When you move the group box, the control will move with the group box.

Place a group box in the left upper corner of a new form and then double-click the TextBox icon in the Toolbox. The text box should appear in the group box. Move the group box. Notice that the text box moves with the group box, showing that the text box is a logical part of the group box.

A simplified form layout with two group boxes is presented in Figure 3.11 as an illustration. The steps to draw a control onto a form were discussed in Chapter 2. The added layer of the group box makes drawing the controls in the group boxes a bit more complex. To create the interface in Figure 3.11, follow these steps:

1. Draw two group boxes on a new form. Adjust the size and position of the group boxes so that they look similar to those in the figure.

2. Draw five labels inside the left group box. After a label is drawn into the group box, you can adjust its position so that it will be located properly.

Figure 3.11
Group boxes

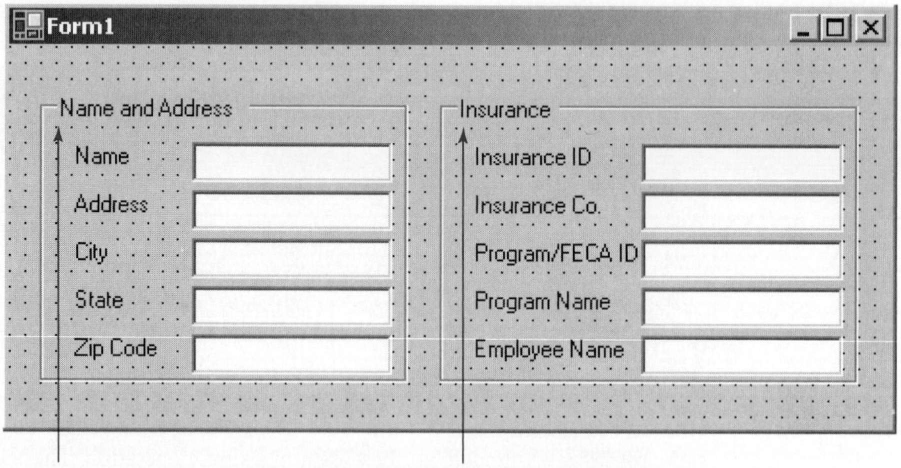

Here are two group boxes usd in the user visual interface. Other
controls that are drawn inside these containers are treated as a logical
unit. You can set the Text property of the group box to show the content.

3. Draw five text boxes onto the left group box using the same steps as for the labels. Adjust their sizes and positions so that they look similar to the five text boxes in the figure.

4. Set the Text property for the left group box to **Name** and **Address**.

5. Set the Text properties for the labels in the left group box so that they appear as **Name**, **Address**, **City**, **State**, and **Zip Code**, respectively. You may want to set the AutoSize properties to True for all labels before setting their Text properties.

6. Clear the text in the text boxes.

7. Repeat steps 2 through 6 to draw controls inside the right group box.

TIP

When setting various properties of several controls of the same type, work with one property at a time instead of one control at a time. As you switch from one control to another, the same property you have just worked on will be highlighted in the Properties window, making it easy to locate the property and change its setting.

As a reminder, before you start to write any code for the project, set the Name properties of all the controls to be referenced in the code.

Runtime Behavior, Visible Property, and Enabled Property. At runtime, all controls contained in the group box control are treated as a single unit. For example, assuming the left group box control in Figure 3.11 is named grbAcctHolderAddr, executing the following code will make the entire group box invisible. None of the controls in the group box can be seen.

```
grbAcctHolderAddr.Visible = False
```

Similarly, the following code will disable all controls in that group box; that is, none of the text boxes in the group box can receive focus or accept any input from the user.

```
grbAcctHolderAddr.Enabled = False
```

Most of the VB controls have the *Visible and Enabled properties*. The default values of these properties are True. They can be set at design time or by code. At runtime, a control with its *Visible property* set to False will be invisible as if it did not exist. After the property is changed to True, the control will appear again. You can manipulate this property with your code to hide the control when it is not needed in your program context, and to show it only when it is needed.

When a VB control, such as a text box, has the focus, the user can key in data. A control can receive focus only when it is enabled. A disabled control with its Enabled property set to False cannot receive focus or input. Its appearance will also change to light gray to indicate its disabled status. Figure 3.12 shows this contrast.

The Tab Control

Now consider the hospital account screen further. The data to be collected are far more detailed than what have been just presented. For example, concerning personal data, the hospital needs not only the account holder's name and address but also additional identification (such as gender and date of birth), phone numbers, spouse, and so on, not to mention additional information on the holder's insurance. It is impractical, if not impossible, to include all these data elements in one screen, yet it is highly desirable to treat all these data as one single logical unit. You want to save, retrieve, and update all these data in a single operation. The VB control that can help handle this situation is the tab control, which you have already seen in action in the IDE. Recall the Customize Toolbox dialog box that you worked with to bring the masked edit box into the Toolbox. The dialog box consists of two tabs, each containing logically related data elements. The VB control that presents tabs and allows the user to view among these tabs is called the *tab control.* Figure 3.13 shows the TabControl icon and its initial appearance on a form.

You can set the number of tabs, each tab's individual Text property as well as other properties in the TabPage Collection Editor dialog box. To access this dialog box, click the TabPages property in the control's Properties window; then click the button on the right of the box. With this dialog box, you can add a tab by clicking the Add button. You can set each individual tab's properties, such as name, back color, text, and so on, by highlighting the tab name in the upper left

Figure 3.12
Enabled and disabled labels

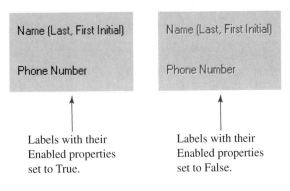

Labels with their
Enabled properties
set to True.

Labels with their
Enabled properties
set to False.

Figure 3.13
The TabControl icon and appearance

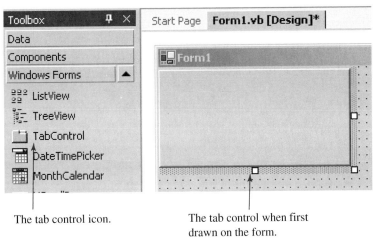

The tab control icon.

The tab control when first
drawn on the form.

box and then setting the properties in the Properties window on the right (Figure 3.14). To remove a tab, highlight the tab name and click the Remove button.

Similar to the group box control, each of these tabs serves as a container. Various VB controls, including the group box, can be drawn in it. At runtime, the user can move between these tabs by clicking the tab captions. The control's *SelectedIndex property* value tells you which tab your user is working on. (The first tab has a SelectedIndex value of 0.) You can also use code to change the tab by assigning a value to the control's SelectedIndex property. For example, the following statement will make a tab control named tabAcctInfo show its third tab. (Note again the SelectedIndex property for the first tab is 0.)

```
tabAcctInfo.SelectedIndex = 2
```

Figure 3.15 shows the redesigned—but still simplified—hospital account holder entry form, using the tab control as the main grouping device.

To create the interface on a new form, follow these steps:

1. Draw a tab control onto the form and then adjust the size of the control.

2. Customize the tab using its TabPage Collection Editor dialog box, as illustrated in Figure 3.14. Do the following:

    2.1. In the dialog box, change the number of tabs to five by clicking the Add button five times.

    2.2. Set the individual tab's Text properties. Do the following:

        2.2.1. Click TabPage1 in the left box.

        2.2.2. Set the Text property in the Properties window on the right of the dialog box. Make it show Account.

        2.2.3. Set the Text properties for all other tabs in the same manner.

3. Draw controls into the first tab. Notice that there is a group box used to group the radio buttons for gender. You may want to draw the group box first. (The radio button is discussed in the next section, but drawing the control on the form is the same as drawing other controls.)

4. Draw controls onto the other tabs. The details, including fields to include, are left up to you.

5. Draw the buttons onto the form. Notice that they are not drawn inside the tab control. Change the Text properties of these buttons as well as the form.

More discussion on the tab control is presented in Chapter 10, "Special Topics in Data Entry." The following table lists the new properties discussed in this section.

Property	Applicable Object	Use/Remark
Visible	The form and all controls that can appear during runtime	The object will be visible if this property is set to True; invisible, if False. For example, the code lblAddress.Visible = False will make the label lblAddress disappear.
Enabled	The form and all controls	To enable or disable a control; a disabled control cannot receive focus and thus cannot accept any user input; an object is enabled if this property is set to True; disabled, if False. The code grbID.Enabled = False will disable all controls in the group box named grbID.
SelectedIndex	Tab	To set or return the tab's index position; for example, the code tabAccount.SelectedIndex = 1 will show the second tab of the tab control named tabAccount.

Figure 3.14

The TabPages Properties window and TabPage Collection Editor dialog box

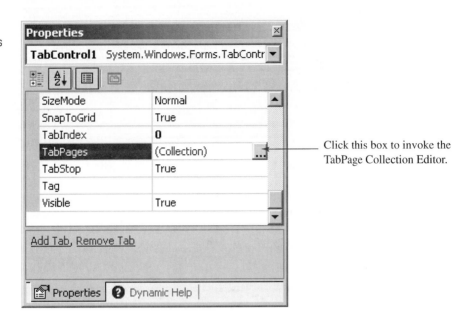

Click this box to invoke the TabPage Collection Editor.

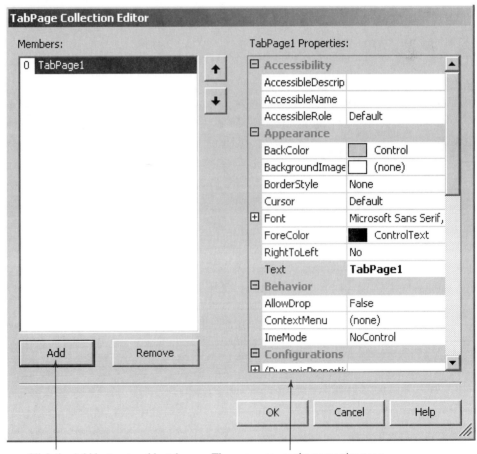

Click the Add button to add a tab page. Then you can use the properties page on the right to set various properties.

Figure 3.15

Sample use of tab control for visual interface

The tab control consists of a number of tab pages, each of which is added when you click the Add button in the TabPage Collection Editor. The properties of each page are set in the tab page's properties window (Figure 3.14). To allow tab text (titles) to appear in multiple rows, set the control's MultiLine property to True. Note that the control's Properties window is available in the IDE like all other controls, while each page's properties are set in the TabPage Collection Editor dialog box.

3.3 Data with Limited Number of Choices: Radio Buttons and Check Boxes

Again, consider the hospital account holder information screen. One blank to be filled in for identification purpose must be gender. You can add another text box and ask the user to fill in either M (for male) or F (for female); however, this choice is not really optimal. A careless user might enter O (for other). An interface designed this way will require additional code to ensure the validity of entered data.

The Radio Button

One VB control that can be conveniently used for this purpose is the *radio button* (Figure 3.16). This control has Text and Checked properties. The text in the Text property is displayed next to the button, and is typically used to show the choice. Its Checked property is set to either True or False to indicate whether this option is chosen. A radio button with its Checked property set to True will show a dot bullet in its button; otherwise, the button will be empty.

How Radio Buttons Work in Groups. When the Checked property of one radio button is set to True, the same properties of all other radio buttons in the same group will

Figure 3.16

The radio button

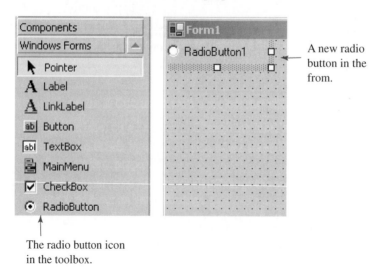

A new radio button in the from.

The radio button icon in the toolbox.

automatically be set to False. If one button is clicked on, all others in the group will be turned off. For the gender question, two radio buttons can be brought into the group box. One can have the Text property set to Male, and the other to Female. At design time, you can also set a default choice by setting the Checked property of either button to True. Figure 3.17 shows the gender radio buttons within a group box as a part of the account tab.

Notice that *all* radio buttons on a form constitute a single group. Only one radio button can be selected from a group. To have more than one group of radio buttons in a form, you must place each group in a different container, such as a group box or a tab page.

At runtime, when an off button is clicked, it will be turned on and its Checked property will be set to True. *Clicking an on button will not result in any change.* You can presume the on status in the Click event. As an illustration, assume that the two buttons used for gender are named rbtFemale and rbtMale. The following code will cause a message box to display **Female button is clicked** or **Male button is clicked** when you click the button.

```
Private Sub rbtMale_Click(ByVal sender As System.Object, ByVal e
    As System.EventArgs) Handles rbtMale.Click
      MsgBox("Male button is clicked")
End Sub

Private Sub rbtFemale_Click(ByVal sender As System.Object, ByVal e
    As System.EventArgs) Handles rbtFemale.Click
      MsgBox("Female button is clicked")
End Sub
```

Notice again that clicking a radio button that is already on will not turn it off; therefore, there is no need to check the Checked property of the button in the Click event.

In data-entry operations, usually no immediate response by the computer is needed when the user makes a choice among the radio buttons. So, when the user is ready to save the result, say by clicking a Save button, how does the computer know which button is on? Your code must test the Checked property of the radio button. For example, the following code shows which button is on at the time the button named btnSave is clicked (Figure 3.18).

```
Private Sub btnSave_Click(ByVal Sender As System.Object, ByVal e
    As System.EventArgs) Handles btnSave.Click
      If rbtMale.Checked Then
          MsgBox("Male button is on.")
      Else
          MsgBox("Female button is on.")
      End If
          ' Place the code to save data here
End Sub
```

Figure 3.17

Radio button in a group box

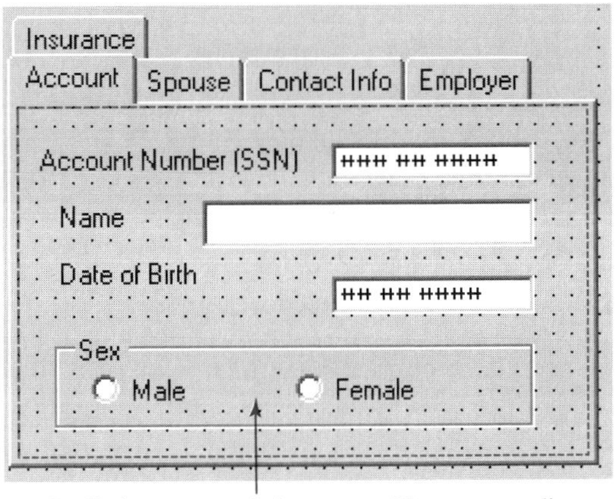

Radio buttons work in groups. These two radio buttons for choice of gender are placed in a group box, independent of the other groups in this form.

Figure 3.18

Radio button in action

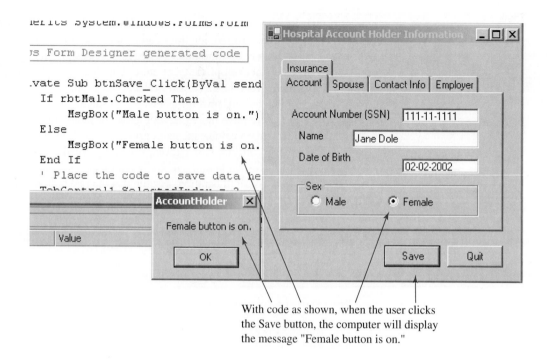

With code as shown, when the user clicks
the Save button, the computer will display
the message "Female button is on."

As explained in Chapter 2, the If statement can have the following structure:

```
If condition Then
    Statements to execute if the condition is true
Else
    Statements to execute if the condition is false
End If
```

Recall that the Checked property of a radio button is either True or False. The If statement
will test to see whether this value is True for rbtMale. If it is, the computer displays **Male button
is on**. If not, it will display **Female button is on**. An If block structured this way must be closed
with the End If statement. Chapter 5, "Decision," discusses the If statement in more detail. (Note
that the code presumes that one of the radio buttons is checked. To ensure the code works properly, set the Checked property of either radio button to True at design time.)

Check Boxes for Independent Choices

For data with a limited number of items that are mutually exclusive, radio buttons are ideal; however, what if these choices are not mutually exclusive, but rather are independent? For example,
a health survey questionnaire may ask the respondent whether he or she regularly has breakfast,
lunch, and dinner. The respondent may regularly have all, or skip any of the three meals. In such
situation, the check box control will be suitable.

The check box appears similar to the radio button (Figure 3.19). It also has the Text property
and the Checked property. The Text property can display text in a manner similar to the radio
button. The Checked property has a value of True if the check box is clicked on; and False, otherwise. As noted, however, the check boxes work independently of each other. Any number of
them can be set on at the same time, regardless of the status of the other check boxes. When
clicked on (checked), its squared box shows a check mark (✓). If clicked again, the check mark
disappears, suggesting it is turned off. This behavior differs from that of the radio button, which
once clicked on will stay on until another button in the same group gets clicked on. Therefore, in
the check box's Click event, you cannot assume that the box is on. Your code must test its
Checked property. The following code tests if a check box named chkBreakfast is on.

Figure 3.19

Check boxes: icon, appearance, and in action

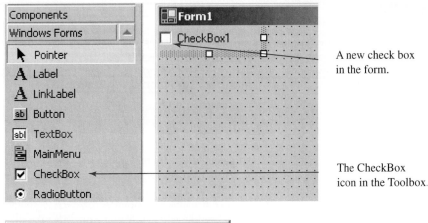

A new check box in the form.

The CheckBox icon in the Toolbox.

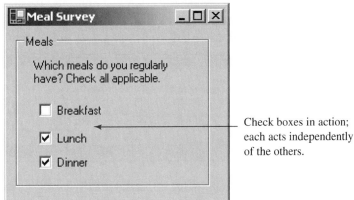

Check boxes in action; each acts independently of the others.

```
Private Sub chkBreakFast_Click(ByVal sender As System.Object,
    ByVal e As System.EventArgs) Handles chkBreakFast.Click
    If chkBreakFast.Checked Then
        MsgBox("The respondent regularly has breakfast!")
    Else
        MsgBox("The respondent does not eat breakfast regularly.")
        End If
End Sub
```

The If statement checks the value of the Checked property. If it is True, the message immediately below the If statement is displayed; otherwise, the message in the Else block is displayed.

Theoretically, a check box with a text **Male?** or **Female?**will suffice to ascertain a person's gender. But such a design choice will not be politically correct albeit efficient. As a software developer or systems designer, you should not only be concerned about efficiency but also other factors such as users' needs, corporate policy, various systems environmental considerations, and so on.

Difference in the Click Event Between the Check Box and the Radio Button. When you click a check box that is off, it will be turned on and vice versa. In either case, the Click event is raised; therefore, you need to test the Checked property of the check box in the Click event. This differs from the way the radio button responds.

The following code is *not useful*:

```
Private Sub rbtMale_Click(ByVal sender As System.Object, ByVal
    e As System.EventArgs) Handles rbtMale.Click
    If rbtMale.Checked Then
        MsgBox("Male button is clicked.")
    Else
        MsgBox("Female button is clicked.")
    End If
End Sub   X
```

This code is not useful because a radio button can only be turned on when it is clicked; thus, the Else portion of the code will never be executed. Refer to the subsection dealing with the radio button for the correct code.

You should use the CheckedChanged event instead, which is triggered when the control's Checked property changes. The following code will work (note the difference in event names):

```
Private Sub rbtMale_CheckedChanged(ByVal Sender As
    System.Object, ByVal e As System.EventArgs) Handles
    rbtMale.CheckedChanged
    If rbtMale.Checked Then
        MsgBox("Male button is clicked.")
    Else
        MsgBox("Female button is clicked.")
    End If
End Sub
```

The CheckState Property. The check box has a CheckState property that the radio button does not. This property interacts with the Checked property. Usually, the CheckState property is not used. Inquisitive readers can gain additional insight by working on 3.9 of the Explore and Discover exercises at the end of this chapter.

3.4 Longer List of Known Items: List Boxes and Combo Boxes

A principle that was implicitly stated in the preceding section is that whenever the expected data are known with a limited number of items, your program should provide these items for the user to select, rather than prompting the user to enter (into a text box, for example). Such design reduces the number of keystrokes, thus enhancing the data-entry accuracy and efficiency. In addition, there won't be a need to check for entry errors, thus making the program simpler and faster.

What if the number of known items is not just a few, but quite a few? For example, a college can have a large number of departments, but the departments are known and seldom change. Using radio buttons to identify a department may not sound practicable, but you should still resist the use of text boxes for this purpose. The data that the user enters can contain errors. Furthermore, it can take the user many keystrokes to complete the entry. One possible solution is to use data codes—call it department ID—in place of the complete department names. Your program will still need to verify the accuracy of entered data, however, even though such a design should reduce the number of keystrokes. A good solution is to use the list box or combo box.

The List Box Control

The list box is as it sounds—a box that contains a list, such as department names in the college of business, names of students in a VB class, or fixed assets a company owns. When the list of elements in the box is longer than the physical height of the list box control, the list box shows a

Figure 3.20

List box: icon and appearance

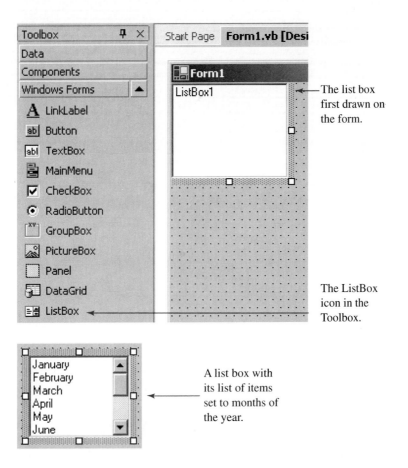

The list box first drawn on the form.

The ListBox icon in the Toolbox.

A list box with its list of items set to months of the year.

vertical scrollbar that the user can use to scroll up and down to browse its content. The item that the user clicks is identified as the list's *SelectedItem property*. The list box's *SelectedIndex property*, also set in the Click event, indicates the position of the item clicked. For example, suppose the list box in Figure 3.20 is named lstMonths. If the user clicks March in the list, lstMonths.SelectedItem will show March, and lstMonths.SelectedIndex will give a value of 2. Note that the first position in the list has a SelectedIndex value of 0, not 1. You can also use code to select an item. For example, the following code will select the first item in the list and thus set the SelectedItem property to January.

```
LstMonths.SelectedIndex = 0
```

Populating the List Box. How do you build a list for the list box? If you have a short list with known data that will not change, you can create the list at design time. To do so, follow these steps:

1. Click the list box in the form.
2. Click the Items property in the Properties window.
3. Click the ellipsis (…) button in the property box. The String Collection Editor will appear (Figure 3.21).
4. Key your list into the box. At the end of each list item, press Enter to enter the next item.
5. Click the OK button when the list is complete.

If you have a fairly long list or the data items are not known at design time, you will need to build the list by code using the *Items.Add method*. This method has the following syntax:

```
Listboxname.Items.Add(ItemToAdd)
```

Figure 3.21

The Items property and the String Collection Editor

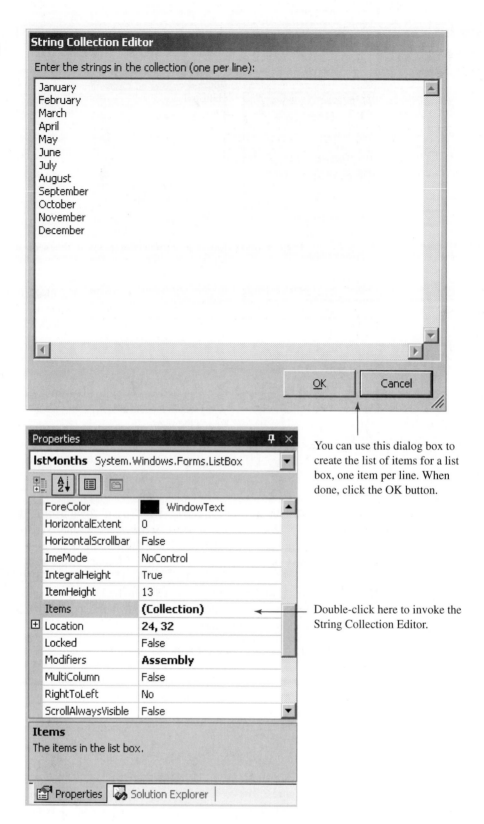

You can use this dialog box to create the list of items for a list box, one item per line. When done, click the OK button.

Double-click here to invoke the String Collection Editor.

For example, the following code will add John Wayne to the list box named lstMyFriends.

```
lstMyFriends.Items.Add("John Wayne")
```

The Items.RemoveAt Method. You can also use the code to remove any item from the list box using the *Items.RemoveAt method.* For example, the following code will remove the third item from the list.

```
lstMyFriends.Items.RemoveAt(2)
```

Note that when you remove an item from the list, all subsequent indices are automatically adjusted. In this example, the previous fourth item will now have an index value of 2 because it is now the third item.

The Items.Count Property. The list box has an *Items.Count property* that gives the number of items in the list box. At any time, its value represents the actual count. Because the list's SelectedIndex starts at 0, the highest SelectedIndex value is Items.Count − 1. The Items.Count property of lstMonths as shown previously in this section will give a value 12, and its highest SelectedIndex value should be 11.

The SelectionMode Property. The list box has an interesting property, the *SelectionMode property.* It can have four alternative settings: None, One, MultiSimple, or MultiExtended. The default setting is One, meaning only one item can be selected from the list box. If the setting is None, nothing can be selected from the list. The user cannot click and select any item at runtime. If the property is set to MultiSimple or MutiExtended, the list box will allow multiple selections from its content (Figure 3.22). The difference between these two settings lies in the way the list box responds to the mouse click and combinations of keys.

Use the keywords SelectionMode enumeration to search the Index tab for explanation of how the list box behaves under different SelectionMode settings.

The Sorted Property. At design time, the Sorted property of the list box can be set to False (default) or True. When the property is set to False, items in the box will appear in the order as originally set. If the property is set to True, items will appear in ascending order regardless of when the item is added to the list. This can be convenient for the user when searching for an item.

The Checked List Box, a Variant. VB.NET also has a control recognized as *the checked list box.* This control has the same properties as the list box except for its appearance. While the standard list box displays each item as plain text, the checked list box displays a check box in front of each item, making it look like a check box (Figure 3.23). This control, however, appears to be of limited use because it allows for only one selection even when multiple items are checked. (It does not support either of the multi-selection settings of the SelectionMode property.)

Figure 3.22

List box with different settings of SelectionMode property

When the SelectionMode property is set to One, you can select only one item.

When the SelectionMode property is set to either MultiSimple or MultiExtended, you can select more than one item.

Figure 3.23

The checked list box

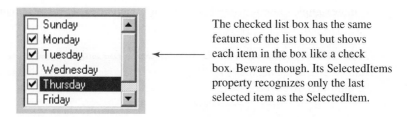

The checked list box has the same features of the list box but shows each item in the box like a check box. Beware though. Its SelectedItems property recognizes only the last selected item as the SelectedItem.

Versatility of the List Box. The versatility of the list box is impressive, but how does this relate to data entry? The list box was introduced as an alternative to radio buttons and check boxes when there are too many known items to show onscreen. The list box has the capability to hold many items, and it requires only limited space because its vertical scrollbar can be used to browse various parts of its content. When its SelectionMode property is set to One, it is a good alternative to radio buttons. When its SelectionMode property is set to MultiSimple or MultiExtended, it becomes a good alternative to check boxes. In addition, the list box has the flexibility to add items to the list either at design time or at runtime without the need to adjust its visual appearance.

The SelectedItem and SelectedIndex Properties. How does your program know which item in the list box is selected? As explained previously in this section, when the user clicks an item, the list box sets its Text and SelectedIndex properties. When the SelectionMode property is set to One, the item clicked is the item selected and highlighted. Your program can then use either the SelectedItem property or the SelectedIndex property to identify what is selected.

Identifying the Selected Items. When the list box is set to accept multiple selections; that is, when the SelectionMode property is set to either MultiSimple or MultiExtended, the list box behaves similar to the check box; that is, the user can select or deselect an item by clicking it. The SelectedItem and the SelectionIndex properties give the first item selected and nothing more. You need different ways to identify whether an item is selected, and what the selected items are.

To determine whether an item is selected, you can use the *GetSelected method.* This method has the following syntax:

```
Listbox.GetSelected(Index)
```

This method checks if the item in the index is selected. If so, it returns a value of True; otherwise, False. For example, the following code shows how you can decide whether the first item of a list box named lstMajors is selected.

```
If lstMajors.GetSelected(0) Then
    MsgBox("The first item is selected.")
Else
    MsgBox("The first item is not selected.")
End If
```

Notice that the index begins with 0, thus GetSelected(0) refers to the first element in the list. Note also that the parameter (the value in the pair of parentheses) does not have to be a constant. It can also be a variable—a name that represents some value. Recall Chapter 2 examined a code structure for the For loop:

```
For Counter = 1 to 10
    Statements to be executed
Next Counter
```

Statements inside the structure will be executed 10 times. The first time, Counter will have a value 1; second time, 2; and so on until Counter is greater than 10. Also, as mentioned previously in this section, the first item in the list box has an index of 0 and the last item will have an index of Items.Count – 1. If you are interested in inspecting whether each item in the list is selected, you can code the following:

```
For I = 0 to lstMajors.Items.Count - 1
    If lstMajors.GetSelected(I) Then
        MsgBox("Item no. " & I & " is selected.")
    Else
        MsgBox("Item no. " & I & " is not selected.")
    End If
Next I
```

Again, as mentioned in Chapter 2, the & operator concatenates two strings into one. If the first item is selected, the message box will display the following:

```
Item no. 0 is selected.
```

Chapter 7, "Repetition," discusses loops in more detail.

The Items Property. Take a look at the Items property. This property sets or returns the items in the list box. The first item has the index value of 0. In the preceding example, if the first item in the majors list is accounting and if it is checked, you can make the computer display **accounting is selected** by coding the following:

```
If lstMajors.Selected(0) Then
    MsgBox(lstMajors.Items(0) & " is selected.")
End If
```

To display all selected items, you can code the following:

```
For I = 0 to lstMajors.Items.Count - 1
    If lstMajors.GetSelected(I) Then
        MsgBox(lstMajors.Items(I) & " is selected.")
    End If
Next I
```

The GetSelected method allows you to inspect all items in the list box, but what if you are interested in only those items that are actually selected? In this situation, you can rely on the *SelectedItems property*. This property gives the list of items that are selected. The SelectedItems.Count property gives the number of items selected. The following code will more efficiently accomplish exactly the same as the preceding code:

```
For I = 0 to lstMajors.SelectedItems.Count - 1
    MsgBox(lstMajors.SelectedItems(I) & " is selected."
Next I
```

TIP

Use the SelectedIndices property to identify the positions of those items corresponding to the SelectedItems property.

The Need for the Combo Box

Similar to the radio button and the check box, the list box provides a fixed set of choices for the user, and does not allow the user to add additional items directly into the box. There are cases in which it is necessary for the user to add more items at runtime. For example, you may provide a list of Zip codes in a list box for your user to choose from, but a new customer may have a Zip code different from any existing ones. This is a case in which the combo box comes in handy. The *combo box*, as the name suggests, provides a combination of a text box and a list box (Figure 3.24). Its Text property represents the content of the text box area. Under certain *DropDownStyle property* settings (discussed later in this subsection), its text box area can be used to enter data, similar to a typical text box; and its list box can be used to select an item like a list box.

Figure 3.24

Combo box: icon and appearance

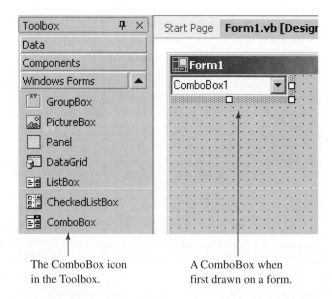

The ComboBox icon in the Toolbox.

A ComboBox when first drawn on a form.

Similar Properties. The combo box has many properties that behave exactly the same as those of the list box:

- The combo box has the SelectedItem and SelectedIndex properties that identify the item that the user selects. When the SelectedIndex property is set by code, the SelectedItem property is automatically set to the associated item.

- The combo box has the Sorted property and behaves the same as the list box.

- The combo box has the Items property, whose items are indexed in exactly the same manner as the list box.

- The combo box has the Items.Count property that gives the number of items in its list, just like the list box.

Similar Methods. The combo box also has the Items.Add and Items.RemoveAt methods to add and remove items from its list. Note that an item entered into its text box area will not be automatically added to its list; that is, when another item appears in the text box, whatever was previously entered will be lost. If you need to keep the entered text in its list box, you will need to write code to handle it. Suppose you have a combo box named cboZipCode in your form. To add (to its list) the item that has just been entered into its text box area, you can code the following:

```
cboZipCode.Items.Add(cboZipCode.Text)
```

As you can see in the code, the text area is recognized as its Text property. The code will add whatever appears in the combo box's text box into its list.

The DropDownStyle Property. The combo box has the DropDownStyle property, which the list box does not have. The available settings include the following:

- DropDown (default): Under this setting, the combo box will show a fixed-height text box with a drop-down button which, when clicked, will drop down to display the list. The user can either make a selection from the list provided or type in the data.

- Simple: Under this setting, you can adjust its height like the list box. Both the text box and the list will appear. The user can either make a selection from the list or enter the data in the text box.

- DropDownList: Under this setting, the combo box looks exactly the same as the DropDown setting; however, the user can only make a selection from the list, and is not allowed to enter any data.

Figure 3.25

Combo boxes with
different settings of
DropDownStyle property

When the DropDownStyle
property is set to DropDown,
you can either enter the text
or select an item from the
drop-down list.

When the DropDownStyle
property is set to Simple,
the control shows both the
box and the list. You can
either enter the text or
select an item from the list.

When the DropDownStyle
property is set to DropDownList,
you can only select an item from
the drop-down list. Notice the
difference in the highlighted box
between this setting and the
DropDown setting.

Figure 3.25 shows combo boxes with different DropDownStyle settings.

Notice that when its DropDownStyle is set to DropDown or DropDownList, it requires only as much space as a single-line text box. Its text box clearly shows what has been selected or entered. In contrast, the list box requires more space to meaningfully display the list, and has no capability to accept items the user may desire to key in.

On the other hand, the list box also has some properties that are not available in the combo box. For example, the combo box does not have the SelectionMode property, which allows multiple selections. Only one item can be selected from its list, therefore the combo box can be used as an alternative only to radio buttons and not to check boxes.

Between the List Box and Combo Box. Because there are many similarities and some differences between the list box and the combo box, how do you decide which control to use given a certain circumstance? Here is a list of decision rules you can consider:

1. Does the situation involve multiple selections? If so, the list box is the clear choice; otherwise, consider factors listed next.

2. Is the available space in the form an important issue? If so, the combo box is the clear choice.

3. Is the list complete? If the user has to be given an opportunity to enter an item not already in the list, the combo box is the clear choice.

4. How important is it to show the result (choice) clearly and explicitly? If it is important, the combo box is the best choice.

If you cannot decide from these guidelines, consider how each control will affect the layout of your form. The control that will give a more pleasing look in your form layout should be your choice.

The following table summarizes the properties pertaining to the list box and combo box.

Property	Applicable Object	Use/Remark
Items.Count	List box, combo box	Returns the number of items in the list.
SelectedIndex	List box, combo box	Returns or sets a number pointing to the position of the item clicked or selected by code; for example, the code: cboWeekDays.SelectedIndex = 3 will select the fourth item in the combo box named cboWeekDays. The item (Wednesday) will appear in the box. (Recall that the index for items begins with zero.)

continues

Property	Applicable Object	Use/Remark
SelectionMode	List box	When set to None, no item can be selected from the list box; to One, only one item can be selected; otherwise, multiple items can be selected (MultiSimple or MultiExtended).
Sorted	List box, combo box	When set to True, items in the list will appear in ascending order.
Items	List box, combo box	Gives the items in the list, indexed with a value starting at 0; for example, lstMonths.Items(3) will give the fourth item (April) in the list.
GetSelected (method)	List box	Returns a True or False value that indicates whether a particular item in the list box is selected; for example, lstMonths.GetSelected (0) will give a value True if the first item (January) is selected.
DropDownStyle	Combo box	Can be DropDown, Simple, or DropDownList. Refer to the text in this section for details of behavior under each setting.
SelectedItem	List box, combo box	Gives the item selected (clicked) from the list.
Text	Combo box	Gives or sets the content of the text box area of the combo box.

3.5 Graphics in the Visual Interface

In many applications, you may find it desirable to add graphics such as pictures and icons in the visual interface to make it lively. In such cases, you can use the picture box.

The Picture Box

The picture box has an image property that you can use to load pictures at either design time or runtime. Its icon and appearance are shown in Figure 3.26.

Figure 3.26

The picture box: icon and appearance

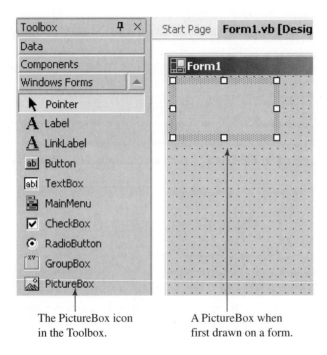

The PictureBox icon in the Toolbox.

A PictureBox when first drawn on a form.

Setting the Picture Property. How do you bring a picture into the picture box? At design time, you can set its *Image property*. Click that property in the control's Properties window and then click the button in the property box. An Open (file) dialog box appears for you to specify a file containing a picture. This control supports files with various formats such as bitmap (bmp), icon (ico), metafile (wmf), JPEG (jpg), and GIF (gif). If you decide to remove the picture, you can right-click the Image property box and then select the Reset option. At runtime, you can use the *Image.FromFile method* to load a picture. For example, you can code the following:

```
picFamily.Imgage = Image.FromFile _
    ("C:\Program Files\Microsoft Visual " & _
    " Studio.NET\Common7\Graphics\icons\Elements\CLOUD.ico")
```

You can remove the picture by assigning Nothing to the control's Image property:

```
picFamily.Image = Nothing
```

Depending on the setting of the *SizeMode property* of the control, the picture image and the picture box can behave differently. When the property is set to Normal (default), the size of the picture box drawn into the form sets the boundary for the picture brought into the picture box. If the picture is smaller than the box, it shows in the upper left corner of the box. On the other hand, if the picture is larger than the picture box, only its upper left portion will be shown in the box. When the property is set to StretchImage, the size of the image is adjusted to fit in the picture box. When the property is set to AutoSize, the picture box's size is adjusted to the size of the image. Finally, when the property is set to Center Image, the image will appear in the center of the picture box. The size of neither the picture box nor the image is adjusted.

Images for Actions. The picture box has a Click event, too, so you can use a picture box in place of a button for the user to click and initiate actions. Note, however, that the button also has an Image property, which you can use to set images. Both the image and the text can appear. You can properly align both by setting the *ImageAlign* and *TextAlign* properties. One of the Explore and Discover exercises in this chapter gives you hands-on practice.

3.6 VB Controls in the Design of a Data-Entry Interface: Recapitulation

You have been introduced to many VB controls in this chapter. These controls have been considered in the context of data-entry interface design. In the process, a few design principles have been presented, including the following:

1. Minimize the number of user keystrokes to improve data-entry efficiency as well as to minimize potential errors.
2. Present the layout of the form neatly (uncluttered).
3. Group logically related data fields together.

The text box is considered the most versatile control in accepting any kind of text or numeric data from the user; however, the user must key in every character the data field is expected to contain. The longer the data field, the higher the possibility that the user will enter a wrong key, in addition to the lengthier time for the entry. Whenever the text box is used as a field for data input, you should be prepared to write code to check for data validity. Alternatives to the text box should be considered when applicable. One such situation is when the input fits a specific pattern, such as dates and Social Security numbers. In such cases, masked edit boxes should be used to help reduce the number of keystrokes and filter out keys that do not fit the expected pattern.

Another situation in which alternatives to the text boxes can be considered is when the data elements are known before the program starts. In this case, if the number of available choices is small, such as gender or names of meals, radio buttons and check boxes should be used. The key criterion in choosing between these two types of controls is whether the known choices are mutually exclusive or independent of each other. If the choices are mutually exclusive, you should use radio buttons. If the choices are independent of each other, you should use check boxes.

As the number of known items grows, or if the items can change, the list box or combo box should be considered. The choice between the two depends on several factors, such as the nature of the choice (mutual exclusiveness), space availability in the form, possibility that data have to be added by the user, and their visual effect on the form layout. If the available known choices are not mutually exclusive, you can use only the list box, which has the SelectionMode property whose setting determines whether multiple selections are allowed. Otherwise, you can decide between the two VB controls based on additional characteristics of the data. If at runtime the list of known data is not exhaustive, and thus the user may still have to enter data not already included in the list, you should use the combo box. In addition, if space on the form is limited, the combo box will be preferred; otherwise, whichever gives a better fit for the layout should be chosen.

Containers such as group boxes are presented as a necessity to group logically related radio buttons in order for the latter to function properly. Containers are also desirable and needed to group logically related data fields together. They not only make the layout of the form neater, but also make it easier for the user to anticipate the type of data fields in the group. This can enhance data-entry efficiency. As the number of data fields for a data entry screen becomes too big, the tab control can be used. In such case, each tab should contain data of the first level major grouping. Other containers can then be used for the subgroupings.

The picture box can be used to enhance the appearance and attractiveness of visual interfaces. The picture box can also be used for the user to initiate actions because it also has a Click event. Note, however, that the button can also display images. The choice between the two is a matter of style. In general, the button uses less system resources, and should be the preferred alternative in this context.

3.7 Naming the Controls and Setting the Tab Order

This section discusses the naming convention for VB controls and setting the tab order for the controls on a form. A consistent naming convention for controls makes your code easier to read and understand because the name provides a clue to the control used. The order in which the VB controls in a form receive their focuses when the user presses the Tab key is recognized as the tab order. This order is an important part of the user interface design and must be set properly. An order that appears random to the user can cause frustration and decrease the effectiveness of your program.

Naming Convention: Suggested Name Prefixes

Many VB controls have been introduced in this chapter. In Chapter 2, it was strongly recommended that all VB controls be named with three letter prefixes to enhance code clarity. This standard was observed wherever VB control was used, and is important in developing a good coding habit. To refresh your memory and for your convenience, the following table shows the controls you have seen so far with the suggested prefixes.

VB Object	Prefix
Check box	chk
Combo box	cbo
Button	btn
Form	frm
Group box	grb
Label	lbl
List box	lst

VB Object	Prefix
Masked edit	msk
Radio button	rbt
Picture box	pic
Tab control	tab
Text box	txt
Timer	tmr

Setting the Tab Order

As stated at the beginning of this section, the tab order is the order in which the VB controls in a form receive their focuses when the user presses the Tab key. This order is determined by the control's *TabIndex property*, which is set in the order the control is brought into the form. The first control brought to the form will have its TabIndex value set to 0. When you test your program, you may find the tab order not in accordance with your original design. In addition, when you are designing an interface with many data elements, you may have to insert controls into or delete controls from the form, making it necessary to adjust the tab order again.

You can set the TabIndex properties of these controls to the desired values. To set them to the desired order, follow these steps:

1. Make sure the form appears in the IDE. Click the form so that it has the focus.
2. Click the View menu in the menu bar.
3. Select the Tab Order option. The form will display the current tab index for each control at the control's upper left corner.
4. Click each control in the order that you want it to receive focus, first one first. The new tab index value for each control will appear as you click. Figure 3.27 shows a form with the tab orders of the controls being reset.
5. To restore the form's original appearance without the tab indices shown, click the View menu and then click the Tab Order option.

3.8 Some Commonly Used Events

The preceding discussion focused on which VB controls to use and how to arrange them on a form. You will still need to place the code in the project before it will work the way you want. You have had a general idea that the code should be placed in certain events. The next question, naturally, is in which event to place specific code. This, of course, depends on what you want to accomplish. The following discussion considers various programming requirements and the proper events in which to place code.

Figure 3.27

Setting tab orders

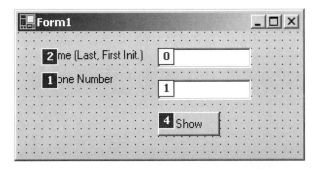

After the Tab Order option in the View menu is selected, all controls in the form will show their current tab order settings with the blue background color. Click the controls in the order you want to set their tab indices. In this figure, the name box has been clicked first; and the phone number, second.

Setting the Initial State at Runtime: The Form Load Event

In many cases, when your program starts and before the computer shows your form, you want certain controls and variables to be in a specific state. For example, you may want to populate a list box with data that are not available until runtime. Or, you may want a combo box to show an initial choice. In what event should you place the code for this purpose? It is the Form Load event.

The *Form Load event* occurs when the form is loaded into the memory and before the form is displayed. At this stage, all the controls' properties are set to their initial states; that is, their default settings or the settings that you made for them during design time. You may want to change some of these settings so that the controls will appear the way you want when the form first appears.

Imagine that your form has a combo box named cboWeekdays with its list set at design time to Sunday, Monday, and so on. You would like for this box to show Sunday (the first element in its list) as soon as the program starts. How can you do this?

First, recall that one way to set a desired selection for the list box is to assign a proper value to its SelectedIndex. You can do the same for the combo box. Because Sunday is the first position in the list, you can assign 0 to that property. (Again, recall that the first item has an index value of 0.) The code should appear as:

```
cboWeekDays.SelectedIndex = 0
```

So where should this line go? Because you want to show the setting as soon as the program starts, the code should be placed in the Form Load event. Assuming the form name has not been changed, the complete code should appear as:

```
Private Sub Form1_Load(ByVal Sender As System.Object, ByVal e As
    System.EventArgs) Handles MyBase.Load
        cboWeekDays.SelectedIndex = 0
End Sub
```

TIP

You might be tempted to code the described requirement as follows:

```
cboWeekDays.Text = "Sunday"
```

This line of code may not always work, however. When the DropDownStyle is set to DropDownList, the Text property will be read-only and cannot be set by direct assignment. In this case, you can make the combo box display the desired text only by setting the SelectedIndex property.

Various Uses of the Click Event

In many instances, you can place the code in a Click event to perform some specified task when the user clicks on an object. The event is most often used in conjunction with the button, radio button, and check box.

Buttons. The Click event procedures most often seen are related to the button, whose text typically indicates to the user what to expect. For example, you may have a program for the user to enter certain data required to perform certain computation. When the user is ready for your program to compute, he or she will click a button with a text **Compute**. In this case, it is certainly clear to you that you will place your code to perform the computation in the button's Click event. As another example, in most forms, a button is used for the user to end the program. Typically, the button is named btnQuit and its Text property is set to Quit. Remember how the code was presented previously? Here it is again:

```
Private Sub btnQuit_Click(ByVal Sender As System.Object, ByVal e
    As System.EventArgs) Handles btnQuit.Click
        Me.Close()
    End Sub
```

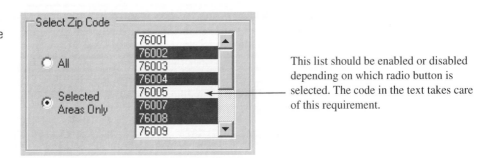

Figure 3.28

Conditionally enabling the list box by selection of radio buttons

This list should be enabled or disabled depending on which radio button is selected. The code in the text takes care of this requirement.

Radio Buttons and Check Boxes. When the user clicks a radio button or a check box, the Click event is triggered. You can place code in the control's Click event if a certain response is expected. For example, in a mailing label printing application, the user has a choice of printing all members or only those in the Zip code areas selected from a list box named lstZipCode. The user indicates the choice by clicking one of the two radio buttons—rbtAll or rbtSelected. It is obvious that when the user chooses to print all members, any selections made from the list box will be meaningless; thus, the list box should be disabled. On the other hand, when the user chooses to select Zip codes from the list box, the latter should be enabled. In short, depending on which radio button is clicked, the list box is enabled or disabled. Figure 3.28 shows a sample visual interface with such a design. The code should be placed in the Click event of each radio button and should appear as follows:

```
Private Sub rbtAll_Click(ByVal sender As System.Object, ByVal e As
    System.EventArgs) Handles rbtAll.Click
      ' All members should be printed; disable the list box
      lstZipCode.Enabled = False
End Sub
Private Sub rbtSelected_Click(ByVal sender As System.Object, ByVal
    e As System.EventArgs)   Handles rbtSelected.Click
      ' Only members in selected zip code areas should be printed.
      ' Enable the list box
      lstZipCode.Enabled = True
End Sub
```

SelectedIndexChanged and DoubleClick Events

The list box and combo box have the *SelectedIndexChanged event*, which behaves very much like the Click event. The SelectedIndexChanged event is triggered when the user clicks an item, causing a change in the selected item.

List Boxes. The use of the SelectedIndexChanged event in conjunction with these two controls varies. As you have already seen, when the user selects an item in these two controls, their SelectedIndex and SelectedItem properties are set to the item. You can use this event to retrieve the selection made by the user. For example, you may want to show the current choice in the text box txtName as soon as the user clicks an item in the list box lstName. The event to place the code will be lstName_SelectedIndexChanged, and you will assign the list's text property to that of the text box. The code will appear as follows:

```
Private Sub lstName_SelectedIndexChanged(ByVal sender As
    System.Object, ByVal e As System.EventArgs) Handles
    lstName.SelectedIndexChanged
      'Show the item selected in the textbox
      txtName.Text = lstName.SelectedItem
End Sub
```

Sometimes, you may want to be sure that when the user initiates an action, he means what he is doing; for example, to delete an item when he clicks on it. In such cases, the DoubleClick event would be better than the SelectedIndexChanged event because there is less chance for the user to accidentally double-click on an item. As an illustration, if you want the user to indicate which item to delete from a list box, named lstCandidate, you may instruct the user to double-click the item to remove. In this case, the event in which to place the code will be lstCandidate_DoubleClick. The item to be removed from the box is indicated by the SelectedIndex property. Remember that when the user clicks an item, the SelectedIndex and SelectedItem properties are set to this item, provided that the SelectionMode is set to One. Note also the SelectedIndexChanged event is always triggered before the DoubleClick event. The code will appear as follows:

```
Private Sub lstCandidate_DoubleClick(ByVal sender As
   System.Object, ByVal e As System.EventArgs) Handles
   lstCandidate.DoubleClick
      lstCandidate.Items.RemoveAt(lstCandidate.SelectedIndex)
End Sub
```

Combo Box Events. Notice that the combo box does have a Click event in addition to the SelectedIndexChanged event; however, the Click event may not behave in a manner as one might expect. If the control's DropDownStyle property is set to either DropDown or DropDownList, the Click event occurs when the user presses the drop-down button to cause the list to drop down, not when he or she makes the selection from the list. The Click event may work as you expected only when its DropDownStyle property is set to Simple. In this case, however, the Click event occurs not only when you click on an item in its list box, but also when you click on its text box. In short, the combo box's Click event has too many ramifications and usually is not a good choice to handle the user's click on the control.

The *SelectedIndexChanged event* is still the event to use in response to the user's selection of an item in the combo box. Regardless of the DropDownStyle property setting, this event is triggered literally when the SelectedIndex changes. This is what happens when the user makes a selection in the combo box's list box.

Notice, however, the SelectedIndexChanged event occurs not just when the user makes a selection, but also whenever there is a change in the SelectedIndex property. The event can be triggered when your code assigns a value to the SelectedIndex property. In short, the SelectedIndexChanged event for the list box and combo box should work almost like the Click event for the button and radio button, but be aware that that event can be triggered by code. The following Try This box shows you how this possibility can cause some potential problems.

Bring a combo box into a new form. Name the combo box **cboWeekDays**. At design time, set its Items property to contain Sunday, Monday all the way through Saturday. Place the following in the code window:

```
Private Sub Form1_Load(ByVal Sender As System.Object, ByVal e
   As System.EventArgs) Handles MyBase.Load
      'Show the first item when the program starts
      cboWeekDays.SelectedIndex = 0
End Sub
Private Sub cboWeekDays_SelectedIndexChanged(ByVal Sender As
   System.Object, ByVal e As System.EventArgs) Handles
   cboWeekDays.SelectedIndexChanged
      'Remove the item selected by the user
      cboWeekDays.Items.RemoveAt(cboWeekDays.SelectedIndex)
End Sub
```

Run the program, and check the list in the combo box. Do you see Sunday in it? No. It has been removed because when your program starts, the Form Load event sets the SelectedIndex of the combo box, which triggers the SelectedIndexChanged event. In that event procedure, the item pointed to by the current SelectedIndex is removed. All these happen without any selection made by the user. Beware!

Viewing the Key Entered: The KeyPress Event

In many cases, you may want to inspect the key that the user enters into a control for various purposes. For example, you may want your program to perform a series of actions when the user presses the Enter key. Or, you may want to ensure that only certain types of keys, such as numeric keys, are entered into a text box. When the user presses a key, the control's *KeyPress event* is triggered. This event occurs after a key is pressed, but before the key is shown in the control. When the event is triggered, the system also passes a structure—the event argument object—that contains the *KeyChar* and *Handled properties*. The KeyChar property gives the key pressed by the user and the Handled property allows you to indicate whether you have handled the key in the event procedure. You can inspect the KeyChar and perform properly actions. For example, suppose you want to ensure that the user does not enter a question mark in a text box named txtAddress. Your code will most likely appear as follows:

```
Private Sub txtAddress_KeyPress(ByVal sender As System.Object,
   ByVal e As System.Windows.Forms.KeyPressEventArgs) Handles
   txtAddress.KeyPress
      If e.KeyChar = "?" Then
         ' This is a question mark
         MsgBox("No question mark, please.") 'Display a message
         e.Handled = True 'Tell the system you have handled the key
            and to suppress the key
      End If
End Sub
```

In this event procedure, the key that the user presses (KeyChar) is passed to the procedure as a part of the event argument object, e (thus you code e.KeyChar to refer to the key pressed) and is compared with the question mark ("?"). If they are equal, the message **No question mark, please**. is displayed. In addition, the Handled property is set to True to tell the system that the event has been handled properly. There is no need for the system to process the key further. This, in effect, suppresses the key pressed because the key has not been, and will not be, displayed in the text box.

The KeyPress event procedure includes a KeyPressEventArgs parameter (named e). This parameter is different from that in a Click event. It is worth repeating that when you code an event procedure, you should always use the procedure template provided by VB rather than create your own event procedure header. All the parameters in an event procedure are predefined and are automatically provided in the procedure template. (You should never change any part of the parameter list.) This way, you will never have to figure out what parameters the event header should have. The steps to obtain a procedure template were explained in Chapter 2.

When you double-click a control on a form, a default procedure template for the control is automatically shown in the code window. This provides a convenient shortcut to the code window and the event procedure. Be very careful when doing this. The event procedure template that is given to you this way may not be exactly the one you want. For example, when you double-click a text box, its TextChanged event procedure template will appear, but you may actually want to use the KeyPress event. Placing the correct code in a wrong event procedure unintentionally is a frequent error for beginners. Pay extra attention to avoid this type of mistake.

Before the User Does Anything in a Control: The Enter Event

Sometimes when the user tabs into a field or clicks the field to set the focus, you want your program to perform some preparatory activities, such as keeping the current content of the control in a variable (as a backup) or highlighting the content to facilitate editing. When the user tabs into a control, the control's Enter event is triggered. The code placed in this event will be executed as soon as the control gets the focus. For example, you want to keep the current content of a text box named txtName before the user starts doing anything on the field, so that when the user presses the Esc key, you can restore the content. You can code the following:

```
Private Sub txtName_Enter(ByVal sender As System.Object, ByVal e
   As System.EventArgs) Handles txtName.Enter
     PreviousName = txtName.Text
End Sub
```

Note that the preceding code only keeps the content of the text box in a variable named PreviousName. To restore the content when the user presses the Esc key, more code will be needed. You should be able to complete this exercise by the time you finish Chapter 4.

As the User Leaves the Field: The Leave Event

When the user finishes working with a field (VB control), he or she leaves that field. Usually, this is the moment you want to perform additional operations on a field, such as converting all letters in the field to uppercase letters. When the user leaves a field, the Leave event is triggered. As with all previous events, you can place code in this event to perform any operations you deem desirable. For example, if you want all characters entered into a field named txtUser to be converted to the uppercase, you can place the code in the control's Leave event as follows:

```
Private Sub txtUser_Leave(ByVal sender As System.Object, ByVal e
   As System.EventArgs) Handles txtUser.Leave
     txtUser.Text = UCase(txtUser.Text)
End Sub
```

In the preceding code, UCase is a built-in function that converts a text string to uppercase letters. The statement instructs the computer to convert the content of txtUser to the uppercase and then assign the result to the text property of txtUser.

Prior to VB6, *LostFocus* was the event in which the field level data validation code was placed. (The LostFocus event is still available in VB.NET. Stay away from it if you can.) There are, however, potential problems with placing the data validation code in this event. For the convenience of data validation, VB.NET introduces two new events—*Validating* and *Validated*—that occur after the Leave event but before the LostFocus event. Data validation is discussed in Chapter 10.

The following table summarizes the events discussed in this section:

Event	Applicable Controls	Trigger	Uses
Form Load	Form	When the form is loaded into memory	To initialize values of variables and properties
Click	Form, button, radio button, check box	When the user clicks the control	To carry out some activities initiated by the user
Double-Click	List box, combo box	When the user double-clicks the control (the SelectedIndexChanged event is also triggered with this event)	To carry out the activities initiated by the user
SelectedIndexChanged	List box, combo box	When the value of the SelectedIndex property is changed either by user action (click) or by code	To carry out the activities initiated by the user
KeyPress	Text box, mask edit box, form	When the user presses a key	To carry out certain activities or verify the validity of the key

Event	Applicable Controls	Trigger	Uses
Enter	Text box, masked edit box	When the control receives focus as a result of tabbing to the control	To perform some preparatory activities such as highlighting the text
Leave	Text box, masked edit box	When the focus is leaving the control as a result of tabbing from the control or clicking another control	To perform finishing touch activities such as converting to uppercase letters or checking field level validity

Notice that the Applicable Controls column lists the controls that are most commonly seen with the event, rather than all the controls that recognize the event. Some events, such as Enter and Leave, are recognized by almost all controls; however, these events are usually used in conjunction with only a few controls.

3.9 An Application Example

You have been introduced to many VB controls and several of their related events. You may be wondering how all these pieces of puzzles can be put together to perform a task. Here, you consider an example for this purpose. The example pertains to an order-entry screen for a manufacturer of water filters. Before you proceed further into any details, please note that the main purpose of the example is to show which controls should be used in a given situation, and where (in which event) a particular segment of code should be placed. So that your attention can be focused on the key interest, it is necessary to simplify the problem. Please ignore some potential ramifications as you proceed. In addition, please work along as you read. You will have a much better understanding of the subject if you actually work on the problem while reading.

The Environ-Pure Project

The Environ-Pure Company manufactures two models of water filters—Puri-Clear and Environ-Safe. Models are added and deleted as new technology evolves, as well as when the company's market strategy shifts. The products are sold through three distributors who redistribute the products to the retailers. The company is negotiating with several potential distributors as additional channels of distribution. Typically, the distributors place a purchase order for one model at a time, with a quantity ranging from 500 to 2,500 units. Regular orders are delivered by the company's own trucks. Occasionally, some orders need to be rushed. In such cases, the company ships them either through U.P.S. or through a special carrier arranged by the distributor.

You are assigned to design a user interface to take orders from the distributors. The screen should capture the following data elements:

1. Date of the order
2. Distributor number
3. Model number
4. Quantity ordered
5. Whether this is a rush order
6. If so, how the order should be delivered (U.P.S. or a special carrier)

You should also provide code that makes the program behave properly.

The Visual Interface

As has been repeated several times, the first step in developing a VB project is to design the visual interface. In this step, you consider what VB control should be used for each of the required data elements.

> After you understand the requirements for your project, carefully analyze the nature of the data field so that you can use the best control for its purpose. The most suitable control for the data field can make both the data entry operation, and your code efficient and effective.

Date of Order. A date field has a specific format. The masked edit box appears to be the best choice. Name this control **mskDate**. In addition, set its Mask property to "##-##-####" at design time.

Distributor Number. As the project description states, there are only two distributors. The data field under consideration has a limited number of choices. Controls that may be appropriate would seem to be either the check box or radio button. Notice that only one distributor can place an order; therefore, the control that comes to mind immediately is the radio button. However, in this case, the radio button is probably not the best choice because the number of distributors can change over time, as the project description implies. If you use the radio buttons, each time the company adds or deletes a distributor, the visual interface will need to be revised. Obviously, this is not an ideal solution.

As discussed previously in this chapter, the other possible VB controls for known choices are the list box or combo box. In the real-world application, the names of the distributors can be added to these controls from a file or database maintained by the user. The use of either the list box or combo box can eliminate the need to revise the program as a result of any change in distributors.

Should you use the list box or the combo box? If you go through the list of criteria for determining the appropriate control between the two, you should find the two controls tie almost all the way. This suggests that the appearance of the control is the determining factor. You would like for the control to appear as a box for a single line input, so your best choice for this purpose would be the combo box. Name it **cboDistributor**.

Model Number. The factors to consider for the control for the model number are similar to those for the distributor number. The dynamic nature of known items (adding and dropping models) and the appearance consideration suggest that you should also use the combo box. Name this control **cboModel**.

Note that the model number should be selected from the list of existing models, not keyed in by the user. This means that the DropDownStyle property of cboModel should be set to DropDownList, not the default setting, DropDown. The model numbers should be added to the combo box using the Items.Add method when the program starts, and not set at design time by editing the List property. In real applications, these models should be read from a file or database maintained by the user. Databases and files are discussed in later chapters.

All these same considerations also apply to the distributor number; therefore, the DropDownStyle property of cboDistributor should also be set to DropDownList.

Quantity Ordered. The main consideration here is that keys entered into this data field should be numeric. There is a range of values (500 to 2,500) that is considered typical. It appears that the number entered should not exceed four digits. Either a text box or a masked edit box should be suitable. You will use the text box for this purpose and name it **txtQuantity**. In addition, you should also set the *MaxLength property* of this control to 4. This property gives the maximum number of characters the user can enter in the box. Setting the maximum length will ensure that the user cannot accidentally enter a number that exceeds the reality.

Use the MaxLength property to limit the number of characters the user can enter into a text box when the number can be determined at design time. This can help eliminate unexpected extra keys into the box, which can cause problems for your program.

Special Instructions. Finally, you need to determine whether the order is a rush order. Because this is a yes-or-no question, it appears that the check box will serve as a good visual interface. Name it **chkRush**. In addition, when it is a rush order, you should also record the type of delivery: U.P.S. or special carrier. Because the user will be choosing between the two types of carriers (mutually exclusive choices), radio buttons appear to be the most appropriate. Name them **rbtUPS** and **rbtSpecialCarrier**.

As a side note, you may argue that the combo box can be a better choice than the radio buttons in this case, based on the same considerations given to distributor numbers and model numbers. Yes, you are right. Your choice here is based more on the interest to demonstrate how radio buttons can be used.

Buttons and the Form. In addition to the data fields already considered, you should also provide a means for the user to save data and end the program. You can do this by adding two buttons to the form. One will be named **btnSave** with the text **Save**; another, named **btnQuit** with the text **Quit**.

You should also set the proper Text and Name properties for the form. You will name the form **frmSalesOrder** and set its text to **Environ-Pure Sales Order Entry Form**.

Grouping and Layout. After you have decided what VB controls to use for all required data fields, you can consider how these controls should be arranged. The VB controls for special delivery instructions are logically related; therefore, they should be grouped together, perhaps within a group box. The other fields all pertain to the order itself; thus they can be grouped in another group box. All these fields should have proper labels to indicate the nature of the field. The buttons are usually placed at the bottom or the right side of the form. In this form, the layout should look neat when the two buttons are placed at the bottom.

When you have to place several controls on a form, be sure to take advantage of the group box. Group boxes can help your form layout appear neat and logical.

With all these considerations, you can now draw two group boxes and all labels onto a form. You will also set the Text properties for all controls properly as shown in Figure 3.29.

You will then add the other controls you considered. Notice that you may need to add the masked edit control to the Toolbox if the control is not added yet. (Refer to the discussion of the masked edit box at the beginning of this chapter for specifics.) Here you need to set several properties of each control properly. These properties have already been discussed and are summarized in the following table:

Field/Button	Type of Control	Property	Setting
Date of Order	Masked edit box	Name	mskDate
		Mask	##-##-####
Distributor No.	Combo box	Name	cboDistributor
		DropDownStyle	DropDownList
Model No.	Combo box	Name	cboModel
		DropDownStyle	DropDownList

continues

Figure 3.29

Initial visual layout for the project

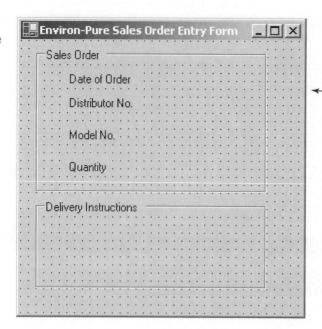

The initial layout for the project should have (1) the form's Text property set, (2) two group boxes with text set to "Sales Order" and "Delivery Instructions," and (3) four labels with their Text properties properly set.

Field/Button	Type of Control	Property	Setting
Quantity Ordered	Text box	Name	txtQuantity
		Text	(blank)
		MaxLength	4
Rush Order?	Check box	Name	chkRushOrder
		Text	Rush Order?
U.P.S.	Radio button	Name	rbtUPS
		Text	U.P.S.
Special Carrier	Radio button	Name	rbtSpecialCarrier
		Text	Special Carrier
Save button	Button	Name	btnSave
		Text	Save
Quit button	Button	Name	btnQuit
		Text	Quit
Form	Form	Name	frmSalesOrder
		Text	Environ-Pure Sales Order Entry form

The resulting form layout appears as Figure 3.30.

Pay particular attention to the appearance of the masked edit box and the two combo boxes. The string ##-##-#### should appear in the date field if the Mask property of the masked edit box is set properly. Also, the combo boxes should be blank if their DropDownStyle properties are set to DropDownList.

Setting the Tab Order

After all controls are placed in proper position, you should test their tab order. You can do so by running the program. Before you can run the program, however, you need to do one more thing. Recall that whenever you change the name of the startup form, you will need to change the Startup object in the project's Property Pages dialog box. Right-click the project icon in the Solution Explorer window and then click the Properties option at the bottom of the pop-up context menu. Select frmSalesOrder as the Startup object. (Refer to Section 2.6 in Chapter 2 for further details.)

After you have the project's Startup object changed, you can run the program by clicking the Start button. To test the controls' tab order, verify that the focus is on the masked edit (date of order) when the program starts; then press the Tab key repetitively to see if the focus is set on the

Figure 3.30

The visual interface for Environ-Pure

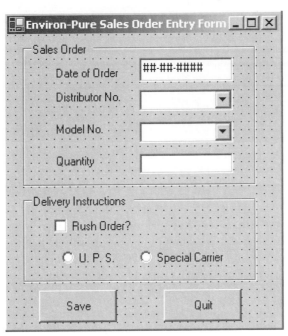

The completed visual interface should contain one masked edit box, two combo boxes, one textbox, one check box, two radio buttons, and two buttons. Make sure these controls are properly named. Also notice that the mask for the masked edit box should appear. In addition, the two combo boxes should display blanks if their DropDownStyle properties have been set to DropDownList.

controls in the order you want. That is, the focus should go in the order of Date, Distributor Number, Model Number, Quantity, Rush Order, U.P.S. (or Special Carrier), Save, and, finally, Quit. Note that at runtime, you can tab to only one of the radio buttons; therefore, you should also test their tab order at design time.

If the tab order is not exactly the way you desire, you can use the Tab Order option in the View menu to set the TabIndex property of all controls properly as discussed in Section 3.7.

Coding the Event Procedures

With the visual interface in place, you can now focus on the action aspect of the project. You need to consider in which events to place what code. This, of course, depends on what you would like the program to do. Consider one VB control (data field) at a time.

Date of Order. Your main concern here is the accuracy of the date entered by the user. One possibility is for the computer to fill the date into the control automatically. For simplicity, you will not do it this way now. Notice that the masked edit box with the proper mask in place will automatically check to ensure that all keys are numeric. Numeric data, however, do not guarantee that the entire field is a valid date. At some point, you will need to check that the masked edit box has a valid date.

Which event should you use? You can decide whether the masked edit box has a valid date only when the field is complete, that is, when the user leaves the field. As explained previously, VB.NET provides an event purely for the field level data validation, the Validating event. You will place the code in this event. How do you check for a valid date? There is a built-in function, *IsDate*, that checks exactly whether a string is a valid date. If the string is a valid date, the function returns a True value; otherwise, False. (Built-in functions are discussed in more detail in Chapter 4.) You can use this function to perform the test. The code appears as follows:

```
Private Sub mskDate_Validating(ByVal sender As System.Object,
    ByVal e As System.ComponentModel.CancelEventArgs) Handles
    mskDate.Validating
    If IsDate(mskDate.Text) Then
        ' the control has a valid date; do nothing
    Else
        ' the control has an invalid date; display a message
        MsgBox("Please enter a valid date.")
        ' Reset the focus to this control
        e.Cancel = True
    End If
End Sub
```

In the code, when an invalid date is found in the masked edit box, a message is displayed. The event also includes a parameter, Cancel. When this parameter is set to True, the focus will be reset to the current control; otherwise, the focus will move to the next control. Additional issues concerning data validation are discussed in Chapter 10.

If the Text property of the masked edit fails to perform as documented in the MSDN, use the following code in place of the If statement in the preceding validating event procedure:

```
mskDate.SelStart = 0
mskDate.SelLength = Len(mskDate.Mask)
If IsDate(mskDate.SelText) Then
```

Distributor Number. As explained previously, you need to add the list of distributors to the combo box by code. For simplicity, you will assume that these distributor numbers are 100 and 101. You also know that the Items.Add method can be used. The question is where the code should be placed. Recall that these numbers should already be in the combo box as soon as the program starts, suggesting that form load is the event to place the code. The code should appear as follows:

```
Private Sub frmSalesOrder_Load(ByVal sender As System.Object,
    ByVal e As System.EventArgs) Handles MyBase.Load
    ' Add distributor numbers to cboDistributor
    ' In real applications, numbers are read from a file or database
    cboDistributor.Items.Add(100)
    cboDistributor.Items.Add(101)
End Sub
```

Model Number. Similar to the distributor numbers, model numbers should be added to the combo box as soon as the program starts. The Form Load procedure presented previously should be modified as follows:

```
Private Sub frmSalesOrder_Load(ByVal sender As System.Object,
    ByVal e As System.EventArgs) Handles MyBase.Load
    ' Add distributor numbers to cboDistributor
    ' In real applications, numbers are read from a file or database
    cboDistributor.Items.Add(100)
    cboDistributor.Items.Add(101)
    ' Add model numbers to cboModel
    ' In real applications, models are read from a file or database
    cboModel.Items.Add("Puri-Clear")
    cboModel.Items.Add("Environ-Safe")
End Sub
```

In addition to getting model numbers into the combo box ready for selection, assume also that the Puri-Clear model is the most commonly ordered model. To save the user from having to make the selection, you would like to set the model as the user's default choice whenever the user moves to this field. Note that this model is the first item in the list; therefore, you can set the combo box's SelectedIndex to 0 to effect the choice. But where should you place the code? Again, recall that you would like for this to happen as soon as the user moves to this field; that is, when the control gets the focus. The event to use is this control's Enter event. The code appears as follows:

```
Private Sub cboModel_Enter(ByVal sender As System.Object, ByVal e
    As System.EventArgs) Handles cboModel.Enter
    ' set the first item as the choice
    cboModel.SelectedIndex = 0
End Sub
```

Quantity Ordered. This is a text box. You would like to ensure that the user enters only numeric keys. In what event should the code be placed? As explained, as soon as the user presses a key, the KeyPress event is triggered. The proper event to place the code is the KeyPress event of this control, txtQuantity. For simplicity, the code to check for errors is left out and only a comment indicating where the code should be placed is given. You will learn more about error checking in Chapter 10.

```
Private Sub txtQuantity_KeyPress(ByVal sender As System.Object,
   ByVal e As System.Windows.Forms.KeyPressEventArgs) Handles
   txtQuantity.KeyPress
      ' Place key error checking routine here
End Sub
```

Special Delivery Instructions. When the user clicks the check box for **Rush Order?**, the check box is checked or unchecked. The ensuing selection of types of delivery (U.P.S. or special carrier) makes sense only when the check box is checked. You should not allow the user to make any selection between the two radio buttons when the check box is unchecked; that is, you should enable or disable the two radio buttons when the check box is checked or unchecked. As implied in the opening statement, the code should be placed in the check box's Click event:

```
Private Sub chkRushOrder_Click(ByVal sender As System.Object,
   ByVal e As System.EventArgs) Handles chkRushOrder.Click
      If chkRushOrder.Checked Then
          ' the check box is checked, enable both Radio buttons
          rbtUPS.Enabled = True
          rbtSpecialCarrier.Enabled = True
      Else
          ' the check box is unchecked, disable both Radio buttons
          rbtUPS.Enabled = False
          rbtSpecialCarrier.Enabled = False
      End If
End Sub
```

If you test the program at this point, you should notice that when the program starts, the check box is unchecked (a good thing because most orders are not rush orders). The two radio buttons, however, are also enabled. This is not a good state because you want to disable them when the rush order check box is unchecked. Go back and set (at design time) the Enabled properties of both radio buttons to False. Note that if you can't get the program to start, you will know how to correct the problem when you reach the next subsection, "Testing the Project."

TIP

Always disable the controls for input purposes that do not expect any user input or action in the context. This saves the user's time and eliminates the confusion by the user. Be sure to enable these controls again when the context requires the user input.

Buttons. As you recall, it is customary to place code in the Click event to handle all expected activities when the user clicks a button. Although you show the Save button, for simplicity, you will note that code to save the screen should be placed in the button's Click event without providing the actual code. You would, however, place a line of code to display the message, "Data saved."

```
Private Sub btnSave_Click(ByVal Sender As System.Object, ByVal e
   As System.EventArgs) Handles btnSave.Click
      ' Place the routine to save data here
      ' then display the following message
      MsgBox("Data saved.")
End Sub
```

The code to terminate the program has been presented in this chapter as well as the preceding chapter. It is left for you to complete as an exercise.

Testing the Project

You have now completed the project. It's time to test it to see whether it works as expected. Click the Start button. If you encounter a Build error pertaining to the Startup object, refer to the subsection on setting the tab order to set the Startup object for the project properly.

If everything goes correctly, you should be able to see that the visual layout looks like Figure 3.30. In addition, when you run the program, you should be able to verify the following:

- The date of order field does not accept any nonnumeric keys, although no message is displayed. Furthermore, it will display an error message when you leave the field with an invalid date.

- When you click the distributor number field and the model number field, you should be able to see their proper contents.

- When you tab to the model number field, it should automatically display the Puri-Clear model.

- The quantity field will not allow you to go over four digits. Make sure its MaxLength property is set to 4 if it lets you enter more than that.

- When the Rush Order check box is unchecked, the two radio buttons are disabled; but when the former is checked, the two are enabled.

- When you click the Save button, the computer displays the Data saved message.

- When you click the Quit button, the program ends. (You are to provide the code to handle this.)

In the process of testing the program, you may find some typing errors. You may even find that you have placed code in a wrong event. If you believe that you have done everything correctly but the program still does not work properly, you may want to check the names of the controls you use in the code against those in the form. Unmatched names for presumably the same control can give you a source for unsolved mysteries.

Summary

- When deciding on what VB control to use for a data field to take input from the user, observe the following general guidelines:
  - Use text boxes for open-ended data.
  - Use masked edit boxes for data items with a defined pattern, such as date and social security number.
  - Use radio buttons for data of limited number of known, constant (such as sex, names of meals, and so on), and mutually exclusive choices.
  - Use check boxes for data of limited number of known, constant, and independent choices.
  - Use list boxes for data of a varying number of known items or a relatively large number of known items that require independent choices.
  - Use list boxes or combo boxes for data of a varying number of known items or a relatively large number of known items that require mutually exclusive choices.
  - Use group boxes to group related data fields on a form to make the user interface appear organized and logical.
  - Use the tab control to group a large number of data fields that must be presented at the same time. When both the group boxes and tab controls are used, use the tab control for the first (higher) level grouping.
  - Use picture boxes to spice up the appearance of the form if you find it desirable.

- You can change the tab order of controls on the form by using the Tab Order option of the View menu. The option is available only when the form has the focus.
- Use (place code in) the Form Load event to initialize values of variables or set initial states of control properties.
- Use the Click event to respond to the user's click on buttons, radio buttons, and check boxes. Use the list box's DoubleClick event for actions that may have severe consequence, such as removing items.
- Use the SelectedIndexChanged event to respond to the user's click on (selection of) items in list boxes and combo boxes. Be aware that the event can also be triggered by code that assigns a value to the SelectedIndex property.
- Use the KeyPress event to preview the user's key in the text box or masked edit box.
- Use the Enter event to perform preparatory tasks when the user reaches this data field (control); for example, highlight the text or present a default choice.
- Use the Validating, Validated, or Leave event to perform finishing touch activities, such as change all letters to the uppercase.
- The Environ-Pure project serves as an example to illustrate how to decide what controls to use and what events to place proper code.

Explore and Discover

3-1.   How Does the Text Box Handle It? Draw a text box on your form. Try to draw it taller than its initial height. Can you? (See exercise 3-3 for the answer.) Run your project. Type a paragraph from this textbook into the text box. What happens to the extra characters that you cannot see in the box? Press the Home key. What do you see? Press the End key. What do you see? Press each of the arrow keys until it reaches the beginning or end of the text. You should have a good idea of how each key works with the text box. Notice that the left-arrow key and up-arrow key behave the same way. So do the right-arrow and down-arrow keys.

3-2.   The PasswordChar Property of the Text Box. Set the PasswordChar property of the text box to "*" (You can try to enter "**" and see what happens.) Observe what is displayed in the text box afterwards. Run the project. Enter some words in the text box. What is displayed?

3-3.   The MultiLine Property of the Text Box. Continued from exercise 3-1. Set the Multiline property of the text box to True. Now try to draw it tall. You should be able to. Run the project again. Type the same paragraph into the text box. How many lines of the text do you see? What happens to the extra characters that you could not see in the box? Press the Home key. What do you see? Press the End key. What do you see? Now try pressing the Ctrl+Home and Ctrl+End keys. How do they work? Press each of the arrow keys until it reaches the beginning or end of the text. You should have a good idea how each key works with the text box. Do the left-arrow and up-arrow keys behave the same way now? How about the right-arrow and down-arrow keys?

3-4.   The ScrollBars Property of the Text Box. Continued from exercise 3-3.

A. Set the Multiline property to False. Observe what happens to the text box's height. Set the ScrollBars property to each of the Horizontal, Vertical, and Both settings. For each setting of the ScrollBars property, run the program and then enter the same paragraph. What do you observe? There should be no difference between any settings.

B. Set the Multiline property to True. Draw the text box taller and then set the ScrollBars property to each of the Horizontal, Vertical, and Both settings. For each setting of the ScrollBars property, run the program and then enter the same paragraph. What do you observe? How many lines of text do you see in each case? In addition to arrow keys, you should also be able to navigate the text box with the scrollbar. Do you notice any difference between the Vertical and Both settings? There should be none. (Continue to C to see why.)

C. Set the Multiline property to True and ScrollBars to Both. Also set the Wordwrap property to False. Run the program again, and enter a long paragraph. What do you notice? You must press the Enter key to move to the next line and the horizontal scrollbar is now working because the Wordwrap property is turned off.

3-5.   The Anchor Property of the Label. Bring a label to the form. Run the project. Observe its position relative to the upper left corner and the lower right corner. Maximize the form. Observe its relative position again. To which corner does it appear to anchor its position? End the project. The Anchor property in the Property window of the Label should have the (Top, Left) setting. Click the down arrow icon and then click each of the Anchor indicators once so that they show the Anchor setting to be (Bottom, Right). Run the project again. Maximize the form. Where is the label now? Is its position anchored with the upper left corner or lower right corner? Inspect the Property Window of other controls. Most of them should also have this property.

3-6.   The TextAlign Property of the Button. In exercise 2-3, you explored how the label's TextAlign property works. The button also has the TextAlign property; however, it works a bit differently from the label. Bring a button to the form. Leave **Button1** as its default Text property. Draw the button at least twice as tall and as wide as the text, **Button1**. Try each of the nine different settings for the button's TextAlign property and then inspect the position the text appears in the button.

3-7.   The PromptChar Property of the Masked Edit Box. Bring a masked edit box into a new form. (*Note:* you may need to bring this VB control into the Toolbox as explained earlier in this chapter.) Set its Mask property to ##-##-#### and then start the program. When the control gets the focus, what is displayed in the box? (You should be able to see underscores and dashes ["-"].) Change the PromptChar property to a space. Run the project again. You can see only the dashes. This fine point can be important when you need to check the number of characters the user has entered.

3-8.   Clicking the Radio Button and the Check Box. Draw a check box and a radio button on a new form. Run the project. Click the check box repetitively; then click the radio button repetitively. Do you observe any difference in response?

3-9.   The Checked and CheckState Properties of the Check Box. Draw a check box on a new form. Do the following in sequence (don't reset) to inspect how the Checked and CheckState properties interact with each other.

A. Set the Checked property to True, and inspect the setting of the CheckState property. Also observe what happens to the check box in the form.

B. Set the CheckState property to UnChecked, and inspect the setting of the Checked property. Also observe what happens to the check box in the form.

C. Set the CheckState property to Checked, and inspect the setting of the Checked property. Also observe what happens to the check box in the form.

D. Set the CheckState property to Indeterminate, and inspect the setting of the Checked property. Also observe what happens to the check box in the form.

E. Set the Checked property to False, and inspect the setting of the CheckState property. Also observe what happens to the check box in the form.

Have you got a good feel about how the two properties interact?

3-10.   **The Dock Property of the Picture Box.** Bring a picture box into a form. Set its Dock property to one of the six possible settings. Observe how it appears on the form after each change of settings. Do you see how the Dock property works? Inspect the property window of other controls. Most controls have this property, too.

3-11.   **Checking the Check Boxes in a Checked List Box.** Use a button and a checked list box. Name the button **btnCheck** and set its Text property to **Check**. Name the checked list box **lstWeekDays**. Set its Items property to **Sunday, Monday, through Saturday**. Give the following code in the btnCheck Click event procedure. Run the project. Click the button. What do you see in the checked list box? Which days are checked? Can you still check and uncheck every item? You should be able to.

```
Private Sub btnCheck_Click(ByVal Sender As System.Object, ByVal e
    As System.EventArgs) Handles btnCheck.Click
        lstWeekDays.SetItemChecked(0, True)
        lstWeekDays.SetItemChecked(2, True)
        lstWeekDays.SetItemChecked(4, True)

End Sub
```

3-12.   **Use of Image with the Button.** Draw button on a form. Set its Text property to Call. Set its Image property to a Phone picture. (Your computer most likely has one.) How does the button appear? The text and the image probably overlap each other. Look for the control's TextAlign property in the Properties window and then set it to MiddleRight. Now look for the ImageAlign property and then set it to MiddleLeft. How do the image and text appear now? Of course, you can set these properties with other settings that make the button look nice, given a specific situation.

Exercises

3-13.   **Most Suitable Control for Each Data Element.** For each of the following data elements, determine what is the most suitable VB control to use for input. If more than one control can be suitable, state the conditions under which each will be better.

 A. Address

 B. Description of a product

 C. Inventory ID (No.)

 D. Eye color of a person

 E. Hair color

 F. Nationality

 G. Division of a company

 H. Student classification:

 - Undergraduate student

 - Graduate student pursuing a master degree

 - Graduate student pursuing a Ph. D. degree

 I. Features of a website such as:

 - Does it have a site map?

 - Does it have an "about company" link?

 - Does it have an investor relation link?

 - Does it have a financial reporting link?

 - Does it show a current stock quote?

 J. State code such as AZ, TX, and so on

K. A convention survey asking the participant whether they would be interested in serving in one of the following capacities (only one can be selected):

- Session chairperson
- Paper presenter
- Paper critic

L. Course and section number

M. Student ID number

N. Driver's License number

O. A series of questions in a hospital admission questionnaire such as:

- Have you been hospitalized before?
- Have you had any major surgery before?
- Are you allergic to any medicine?
- Has anybody in your family had a heart condition?

3-14.   Which Event to Use? For each of the following situations, determine in which event procedure you should place your code:

A. When the user clicks a button with the text **Save**, your program needs to save the data onscreen.

B. As soon as the user makes a selection among four radio buttons, your program needs to display an appropriate message.

C. As soon as the user checks on or off a check box, your program needs to make another VB control visible or invisible.

D. As soon as the user enters a key into a masked edit box, your program needs to check to see whether it is a Return key.

E. As soon as the user enters a key into a text box, your program needs to determine whether it is an Esc key.

F. As soon as the user enters a key into a combo box, your program needs to determine whether it is an uppercase letter.

G. When the user tabs into or clicks a combo box, your program needs to highlight the content of the entire box.

H. Your program needs to determine whether the Social Security number in a masked edit box represents a valid employee when the user leaves the box.

I. As soon as the user makes a selection in a list box, your program needs to know if it is the fifth item in the list.

J. As soon as the user clicks on an item in a combo box, your program needs to move that item to a text box.

3-15.   Make It Double. Here's a project that will double a number entered by the user.

1. Draw a label on a new form. Change the label's Text property to Enter a number.

2. Draw a text box by the right side of the label. Change its Name property to txtNumber. Clear its Text property.

3. Add another label below Label1. Change the second label's Name property to lblResult and then clear its Text property.

4. Add a button below the text box. Change its Text property to Double, and Name property to btnDouble.

5. Add the following code to the code window. (*Hint:* Use the event procedure template provided by VB before adding the statement inside the procedure.)

```
Private Sub btnDouble_Click(ByVal Sender As System.Object, ByVal e
    As System.EventArgs) Handles btnDouble.Click
        lblResult.Text = "Twice of " & txtNumber.Text & _" is " &
        Val(txtNumber.Text) + Val(txtNumber.Text)
End Sub
```

Run the program and make sure the results are as expected.

3-16.   Make It Do More. Modify the preceding project as follows:

1. Add two more buttons. Change the first button's Text property to **Half**, and the Name property to **btnHalf**. Change the second button's Text property to **Square** and the Name property to **btnSquare**.

2. Add code so that:
   - When the user clicks the Half button, your program will display in lblResult the following message (assuming the user enter a number 10):

   ```
   Half of 10 is 5
   ```

   - When the user clicks the Square button, your program will display in lblResult the following message (assuming the user enter a number 10):

   ```
   Square of 10 is 100
   ```

   (*Hint:* To obtain one half of a number, code:

   ```
     Val(txtNumber.Text) / 2
   To obtain the square of a number, code:
   Val(txtNumber.Text) * Val(txtNumber.Text)
   ```

3-17.   Hello! Text Box for Input. Use a label, a text box, and two buttons. Set their properties as follows:

Control	Property	Setting
Label	Text	Enter a Name
Text box	Text	(cleared)
	Name	txtName
Button	Text	Hello
	Name	btnHello
Button	Text	Quit
	Name	btnQuit

Provide the code to perform the following:

When your project runs, you will enter a name into the text box. When you click the Hello button, the computer will display a message showing Hello! followed by the name you've just entered in the text box. After you click the OK button in the message box, the computer clears the text box and waits for further actions. When you click the Quit button, your program quits.

3-18.   Checking for Date Validity, Use of Masked Edit Box. Use a label, a masked edit box, and two buttons. Set their properties as follows:

Control	Property	Setting
Label	Text	Enter a Date
Masked edit box	Mask	##-##-####
	Name	mskDate
Button	Text	Check
	Name	btnCheck
Button	Text	Quit
	Name	btnQuit

When your project runs, the user will enter a date into the masked edit box. When you click the Check button, the computer will check to see whether the date entered is valid. If it is a valid date, the computer displays a message, **It's a valid date**. Otherwise, the computer displays a message, **Please enter a valid date**. After you click the OK button in the message box, the computer clears the masked edit box and waits for further actions. When you click the Quit button, your program quits. (*Hint:* Refer to the application example for code to check date validity. The way to clear a masked edit box is also presented in the text.)

3-19.   **Events and Messages.** Use a label, a text box, and a masked edit box. Align them vertically down. Set the label's AutoSize property to True and clear its Text property. Set the Mask property of the masked edit box to ##-##-####. At runtime, when the user tabs to (or clicks) the text box, the label will display **Enter your name**. When the user tabs to the masked edit box, the label will display **Enter your birth date**. (*Hint:* Place code in the Enter event procedure of each of the two controls.)

3-20.   **Activity Monitor.** Imagine you have a data-entry screen. For security reasons, you don't want it to stay inactive for a long period. (Your user is probably away from the desk. Somebody else can peek or even poke at the data.) You decide that if the computer is inactive for five minutes, the program should automatically quit. Write the code to handle this requirement. (*Hint:* Use a timer and set its Enabled property to True and its Interval property to 5 minutes, although while testing, you might want to set it to a shorter time period. When some user activity occurs, either the mouse will move or the keyboard will be pressed. You can use the form's KeyDown and MouseMove events to disable and enable the timer again. Also, set the form's KeyPreview property to True.)

3-21.   **Practicing Form Layout and Use of Container.** Draw your favorite credit card on a new form. (*Hint:* Use a group box to draw the outline. Also, use the label to draw horizontal or vertical lines.)

3-22.   **Practicing Form Layout and Use of Container.** Draw your driver's license on a form. (*Hint:* Use a picture box to hold your own picture.)

3-23.   **Practicing Form Layout and Use of Container.** Create a student entry form that contains a tab control with three tabs. The first tab contains identification data with **ID** as its tab text. It has controls to ascertain the following data: name, student number, sex, and date of birth. The second tab contains contact information with **Contact Info** as its tab text. It has controls to ascertain the following data: current address and phone number, permanent address, and email address. The third tab contains academic information with **Academic Info** as its tab text. It has controls to ascertain the following data: whether the student has a high school diploma and if so, the school name; whether the student has an undergraduate degree and if so, the name of the degree and the awarding institution; whether the student has any advanced degrees and if so, the name(s) of the degree(s) and the awarding institution(s) (allow three different degrees);

and the degree the student is currently pursuing. Because all degrees offered by the university are known, a combo box with all known degrees (enter a few degrees available at your college) should be used for this field. Outside the tab control, there should be two buttons: one for Save, and the other for Quit.

Be sure to use the most appropriate control for each field. Also add group boxes where appropriate.

3-24.   Setting Colors in Different Events. Use two text boxes and one button. Name the text boxes **txtName** and **txtAddress**. Set the button's Name property to **btnQuit** and the BackColor property to red. At runtime, when each of the text boxes receives focus, the text color is black. When it loses focus, its text color turns to blue. (*Hint:* The relevant events for the text boxes are Enter and Leave. The names of the colors are Color.Blue and Color.Black.)

3-25.   Adding Items to Combo Box. Use a combo box and a button. Set the button's Text property to **Add**. Provide the code so that when you click the Add button, whatever you have typed in the combo box is added to the combo list. Give proper names to these controls.

3-26.   I Give You. You Give Me. List Boxes. Use two list boxes. Call them **lstEast** and **lstWest**. Use the Items property to add the following 12 oriental zodiac symbols to lstEast. Provide the code so that whichever symbol you click in one list box moves to the other list box. (*Hint:* Code in each list box's SelectedIndexChanged event, and use its Items' Add and RemoveAt methods.)

Rat	Rabbit	Horse	Rooster
Bull	Dragon	Sheep	Dog
Tiger	Snake	Monkey	Boar

3-27.   Invitation to the Party. Use a list box and a button. Use the list box's Items collection to add five of your friends' names. Set the button's Text property to **Invite**; then provide the code to do the following:

At runtime, click the names of your friends who you plan to invite to your birthday party. When you click the Invite button, the program will display a message box for each friend who will be invited; for example, **Jerry will be invited to my birthday party**. (*Hint:* You need to use the For loop.)

3-28.   Passing Data Between Controls. Use a combo box, a list box, and a button. Set the button's Text property to **Add**. At runtime, when you click the button, whatever you have typed in the combo box is added to the list box (not the combo box); however, when you double-click the list box, the item appears in the list of the combo box and disappears from the list box. Give each control a proper name. (The event name for double-click is DoubleClick.)

3-29.   Enabling and Disabling Controls Depending on the Check Box. Draw a group box in a new form; then draw inside the group box a check box, a label, and a text box. Name the check box **chkFreqFlier**. Set its Text property to **Are you a frequent flier of our company?** Name the label **lblFreqFlier**. Set its Text property to **Frequent Flier Number**. Place the text box on its right side. Clear its Text property. Name it **txtFlierNumber**. Set the Enabled property of both the label and the text box to False. When your project runs, if the check box is checked on, both the label and the text box will be enabled. If the check box is clicked off, both the label and the text box will be disabled. (*Hint:* The event to code is chkFreqFlier_Click.) (*Note:* To spice up the appearance, draw a picture box inside the group box. Set its Picture property to an airplane image. You can find an icon file for the airplane in your system.)

3-30.   **Enabling and Disabling Controls Depending on Radio Buttons.** Draw a group box on a new form. Set its Text property to **Payment Method**. Next, draw three radio buttons in the group box. Name them **rbtCash**, **rbtCheck**, and **rbtCreditCard**. Set their Text properties to **Cash, Check, and Credit Card**, respectively. Place a label and a combo box below the three radio buttons but still within the group box. Name the label **lblCreditCard**. Set the label's Text property to **Credit Card Type**. Name the combo box **cboCreditCard**. Set its Items property to hold **Visa, Master Card, American Express, Diner's Club, and Discover**. Set the rbtCash's Checked property to True. Set the Enabled properties of lblCreditCard and cboCreditCard to False; then provide code to perform the following:

When your project runs, if the credit card radio button is clicked, your program will enable both the label and the combo box. In addition, the combo box's SelectedIndex property is set to zero (0)l; otherwise, both the label and the combo box are disabled. (*Hint:* Beware. If you use the Click event, you'll have more than one event to take care of the requirement. That is, the event[s] that the credit card radio button is turned off is not this radio button's Click event. You can use the CheckedChanged event to take care of both.)

Projects

3-31.   **The Jury Selection Questionnaire.** A jury selection system has the following questionnaire.

Have you had any major injury?

Are you a citizen of the United States?

Your place of birth _____

Date of birth _____

How many years have you lived in this county?

Driver license number_____

List counties and states you have lived since 1985

Are you or your relatives in law enforcement?

   If so, who?

Your occupation _____

Work phone _____

Employer_____

   How long_____ years

Spouse's name_____

Spouse's employer_____

Spouse's occupation_____

   How long_____ years

Number of children _____

Home phone_____

Required: Design a form for this questionnaire, using the most suitable VB control for each question. (*Hint:* Add containers wherever appropriate. Give each control for input purposes a meaningful name.)

3-32.   **The Alumni Association Database.** Your school would like to maintain a database for its alumni association. The database will include information on the alumnus' personal identification such as name, gender, date of birth; academic records such as major, highest degree, and year and term of last degree; contact information such as address, home phone, and email address; spouse's name and work phone; work-related data such as position, company name, address, and work phone number; and association history such as the year the alumnus joining the association, date, and amount of the last association dues paid.

Required: Design a form for such purpose. Add additional data elements wherever you see fit. Use the most suitable VB control for each data element. (*Hint:* Add containers wherever appropriate. Give each control for input purposes a meaningful name.)

3-33.   The Account Holder File. A clinic needs a data-entry screen to enter account holder data. The following data elements must be entered.

    Insured's (account holder's) name

    Insured's address (number, street)

    City, state, and Zip code

    Insured's telephone number

    Insured's policy group or Feca Number

    Insured's date of birth

    Sex

    Employer's name

    Insurance plan name or program name

    Type of insurance

        Medicare, Medicaid, Champus, Champva, Group health plan, Feca, or Others

    Is there another health benefit plan?

        If so, give the following:

            Other insured's name

            Other insured's policy or group number

            Other insured's date of birth

            Sex

            Employer's name

            Insurance plan name or program name

Required: Design an interface for such purpose. When the question, **Is there another health benefit plan?** is answered affirmatively, all controls used to take input for the other insured should be all enabled; otherwise, they should be disabled. (*Hint:* Use the Tab control. Separate data between the primary insured and the other insured. Also, use group boxes wherever applicable.)

4. Data, Operations, and Built-In Functions

So far, you have learned more than a dozen Visual Basic (VB) controls, and have explored their important features. These controls present themselves as great tools for building an elegant graphic user interface. Data obtained from the interface, however, usually need to be further handled before they become truly useful. In many cases, complex computations must also be performed; the results are then displayed. In this chapter, you will study various aspects of data and the operations/computations that the computer can perform on them.

After you complete this chapter, you should be able to:

- Differentiate among different types of data.
- Declare data types properly for constants and variables.
- Appreciate the importance of having the IDE check variables for their declaration.
- Differentiate and appreciate the implications of the scope and lifetime of variables under different declarations.
- Understand the nature of the assignment statement.
- Recognize and use various arithmetic expressions and functions.
- Understand the usefulness of strict type checking.
- Recognize and use various string functions.
- Understand better how data and VB controls are used together in a project.

4.1 Classification and Declaration of Data

Consider the following code:

```
MsgBox("Your age is " & 24)
```

As simple as this statement is, two different types of data are involved. The text enclosed in a pair of quotation marks is a *string*, whereas the number, 24, is *numeric* data. A string consists of zero or more characters; numeric data are numbers that can be used for various computations, and can be further classified into many different types. The first level of data classification by type can be depicted as in Figure 4.1.

All data must be stored somewhere in the computer memory before they can be retrieved for additional manipulation or display. If a memory location with some data is expected to change as a result of operations, it is recognized as a *variable*. A variable must be given a name so that you can refer to it. Data that present themselves "as is" and are never expected to change are recognized as *constants*. A constant can go without a name but can also be given a name. A constant without a name has to be presented and used as literal. A constant that is given a name and is referenced accordingly is recognized as a *named constant*. This classification can be depicted as in Figure 4.2.

To summarize, data can be classified by type into numeric and string, and by variability into constant and variable. The following table shows the classifications:

	Numeric	String	Name Required?
Constant	Numeric constant	String constant	No
Variable	Numeric variable	String variable	Yes

Declaring Constants

Before a named constant can be used in your program, you must make sure that VB can recognize it. Some named constants are predefined and automatically recognized. These are called *system constants*. You have seen some of these constants in the preceding chapters. For example, you have seen named constants for colors such as Color.Green, Color.Blue, and Color.Red. You have also seen true or false named constants—True and False. Other named constants must be declared before VB can recognize them. These are called *symbolic constants*. You use the *Const statement* to declare a symbolic constant. The syntax is as follows:

```
Const name [As data type] = literal
```

For example, the following statement declares the named constant Zero to have a constant value of 0. As the syntax in the preceding example suggests, you can also omit As Integer from the declaration without affecting the result.

Figure 4.1

Classification of data by type

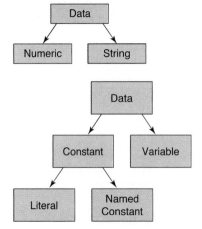

Figure 4.2

Classification of data by variability

```
Const Zero As Integer = 0
```

Why Name Constants? Properly named constants can enhance the understandability of the code. When reviewing code, you may not recognize the specific meaning of a particular value, such as 0 or -1. This is particularly true when the constants are used as the property setting of a VB control. Instead, if you code these constants as False (for 0) and True (for -1) in setting the Checked property of a check box, anyone, including yourself, should be able to follow the code much more easily. In addition, in some cases, you may find it necessary to later change the value of a constant. Using a named constant, you need to make the correction in only one place—where the constant is declared. In contrast, you will have to search the entire program for the constant to change if the constant literal was used.

Declaring Variables

Under certain option settings in your project, variables can be used without being declared. It is a good habit, however, to declare all variables used. The reasons for this are given later in the section, "Why Force Yourself into Declaring All Variables?" To declare a variable, you can use the *Dim statement*. The syntax is as follows:

```
Dim Variable1 [As data type][, Variable2 [As data type]]...
```

For example, you can code the following:

```
Dim TheName as String, SSN as Integer
Dim Rate, PresentValue As Double
```

The first statement declares a variable, TheName, as the String type variable, and another variable named SSN as an Integer type. The second statement declares both the variables, Rate and PresentValue, as the Double type. (Numeric data types are explained in Section 4.3, "Numeric Data and Types," and the String type is discussed in Section 4.5, "String Data.")

Note that for code clarity, it is advisable to declare only one variable per line. (Many companies have adopted this coding standard.) Thus, a better way to code the preceding first line is as follows:

```
Dim TheName As String
Dim SSN As Long
```

Initializing Value with Declaration. When you declare only a variable per line, you can also assign an initial value to the variable as shown in the following example:

```
Dim TheName As String = "John Doe"
```

In this line, the variable TheName is declared as a String type, and is given "John Doe" as its initial value. A string variable without an initial value is initialized as a zero length string.

Using Type Suffixes. A variable or symbolic constant can also be declared with a trailing special character that signifies a data type. These special characters, such as $, %, and &, are called *type-declaration characters* or *type suffixes*, and are listed in Section 4.3. The following statement with type-declaration characters will have the same effect as the previous example.

```
Dim TheName$
Dim SSN&
```

Recall in Chapter 2, "Introduction to Visual Basic Programming," the importance of using meaningful names for VB objects was emphasized. This observation can certainly be extended and applied to all types of names, including constants and variables. As you can see, declarations using type suffixes are not as easy to understand as those using data type names. For code clarity, always use data type names instead of type suffixes.

For program readability, always give your variables and constants meaningful names. Use the data type names instead of type suffixes to declare the data types for the variables and constants.

Checking for Variable Declarations

You have control over having VB check if the variables used in your program have been declared properly by the use of the Option Explicit statement, which has the following syntax:

```
Option Explicit {On¦Off}
```

The statement must be placed before any other statement in the code window, except for other Option statements to be discussed later in this chapter. If you code,

```
Option Explicit Off
```

VB will not check whether any variable you use has been declared. The default—is Option Explicit On. It is strongly recommended that you use the default. With the default, the compiler immediately underlines any variable that is not declared.

Create a new project. Place the following code in the form Load event.

```
A = B
```

You will immediately see that both A and B are underlined. Rest the mouse pointer on the underline to see the IntelliSense, indicating that the name is not declared.

Why Force Yourself into Declaring All Variables? The advantages of declaring all variables include the following.

- A variable not declared may give you unexpected results. This kind of error is hard to uncover.
- This practice helps identify misspelled variables that can cause unexpected results.
- Declaring all variables can help you catch syntax errors that you unexpectedly make. For example, suppose you mean to assign a string "Ben" to the variable TheName, but fail to enclose Ben in a pair of double quotes. Your statement will look like:

```
TheName = Ben
```

With Option Explicit On, the editor will tell you the variable Ben has not been declared. With the option off, both variables will have a zero length string.

- If you declare a variable with proper capitalization, the same capitalization will be maintained automatically by VB throughout the program. For example, if you declare a variable as HourPay, VB will change it in your program to HourPay regardless of how you type the variable, such as hourpay or HOURPAY. This enables you to immediately check if you have typed in a name properly. Proper capitalization also enhances the readability of your program.

Ensuring Automatic "Option Explicit On" in Your Project. What if the compiler does not enforce variable declaration in your project? As stated previously, you can code the Option Explicit On statement in the code window, which is recognized as a module. The statement will be in effect for that particular module. If your project has more than one module, you will need to code the statement in each module. You can actually verify and opt to have the compiler enforce variable declaration for the entire project without any code. The settings for several Options are accessible in the project's Property Pages dialog box. To access the Option's setting, follow these steps:

1. Right-click the project in the Solution Explorer window.
2. Click the Properties option (the last option in the pop-up menu). The project's Property Pages dialog box appears.
3. Click the Build option under the Common Properties folder.
4. Select On in the combo box for Option Explicit, as shown in Figure 4.3.

TIP

Experienced programmers know the importance of having all the variable names spelled correctly. A minor error in spelling a variable name can result in mysterious errors in the program, and cause numerous hours of hunting for the bug. Always ensure that Option Explicit On is the setting for your project.

Rules for Variable Declaration

When you are declaring variables or named constants, some rules must be observed. Any violation of the rules will result in a syntax error. These rules include:

- A variable or constant name can contain any combination of letters and numbers, must begin with a letter or underscore, and must have at least one letter or digit if it begins with an underscore.
- If the variable is a reserved keyword, it must be enclosed with a pair of brackets, such as [Case]. (Case is a reserved keyword. You will learn about it in Chapter 5, "Decision.")
- A variable must not contain any embedded period, such as Your.Name, or embedded special characters used for data type declaration, such as The%Completed.

Figure 4.3

Setting Option Explicit On

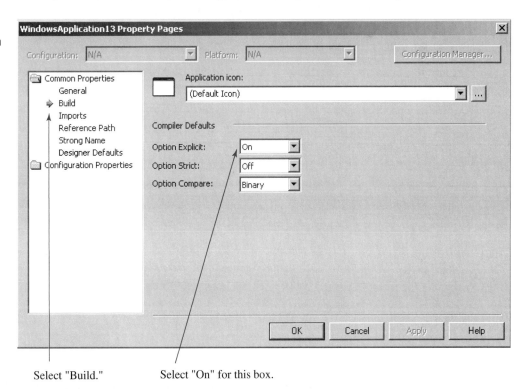

Select "Build."   Select "On" for this box.

4.2 Scope and Lifetime of Variables

The code window associated with the form is recognized as the *class module*. Before discussing the placement of variable declaration statements, take a look at this module first. When you first create a new project, the module (code window) appears as in Figure 4.4.

Notice the following two statements:

```
Public Class Form1
End Class
```

These two statements define a class, which is the template for an object. All statements pertaining to the class must be placed between these two statements. Classes will be discussed in detail in Chapter 12, "Object Based Programming," and Chapter 13, "Object Oriented Programming." Also, notice the line **Windows Form Designer Generated Code** as shown in Figure 4.4. If you click the Expand (+) button on the left, you should see many lines of code that are generated by the Form Designer. Click the Compress (-) button if you have expanded the code. In general, these lines should be left alone. Most of the code that you place in the module should be placed between this line and the End Class statement. (Option statements such as Option Explicit should be placed at the beginning before the Class statement.) All the event procedures that you have coded have been placed in this area. If you have any variable declaration statements to be placed outside of any procedure, you should place them in this area first, before any code for any procedure. This area will be called the *general declaration area*.

Variables and constants have their scope and lifetime (duration). *Scope* refers to how widely a variable is recognized (accessible); *lifetime* refers to how long a variable remains in computer memory. The placement of a variable declaration can affect both the scope and the duration of that variable.

Form (Class)-Level Declaration

Variables and constants declared with a Dim statement in the general declaration area are the *class level* variables and constants. They are recognized by and accessible to all procedures in the class. In addition, they exist as long as the class does; that is, their values are preserved until the form is destroyed. In a single form application, the form is destroyed when the project ends. The life of a form is discussed in more detail in Chapter 11, "Menus and Multiple-Form Applications."

Procedure-Level Declaration

Variables and constants declared in a procedure (within the Sub … End Sub structure) are recognizable only in that procedure. They are said to be the *procedure level* or *local* variables and constants. The same names used in other procedures refer to different memory locations, and have nothing to do with those in the current procedure. Because these variables are independent of

Figure 4.4

The Initial Code window

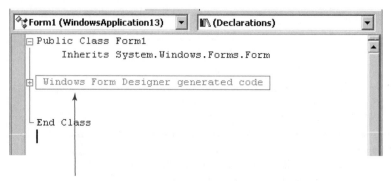

Use this area for class level declaration of variables. Place all event procedures below this "general declaration area."

each other, you can declare different data types in different procedures using the same name. For example, it is legitimate to have the following declarations for I:

```
Private Sub btnTest1_Click(ByVal Sender As System.Object, ByVal e
    As System.EventArgs) Handles btnTest1.Click
    Dim I as Integer
    ' additional code lines
End Sub
Private Sub btnTest2_Click(ByVal Sender As System.Object, ByVal e
    As System.EventArgs) Handles btnTest2.Click
    Dim I as Long
    ' additional code lines
End Sub
```

Such a practice, however, creates confusion even for yourself when you review the code later. Avoid this practice by all means.

Lifetime of Variables Declared in a Procedure with Dim. Variables declared with a Dim statement in a procedure exist as long as the procedure is in action. When the procedure ends, these variables are said to be out of scope and disappear. When the procedure is called again, these variables are reinitialized. They no longer have their previous values. They will be reset to zero if they are numeric variables, or to a zero-length string if they are string variables.

Static Declaration

If you want a local variable to preserve its value for the duration of the form, not just of the procedure, you can use the Static statement for the declaration. When you declare a variable with the *Static statement,* the value of that variable will be preserved and will not be reinitialized between each call of the procedure. The following example illustrates the difference between a variable declared with a Dim statement and one with a Static statement:

```
Private Sub Form1_Click(ByVal sender As System.Object, ByVal e As
    System.EventArgs) Handles MyBase.Click
    Dim I as Integer
    Static J as Integer
    I = I + 1
    J = J + 1
    MsgBox( "I = " & I & ". J = " & J)
End Sub
```

When you run this program and then click on the form repetitively, you will notice that the message box continues to display 1 for I, but increases the value for J each time (see Figure 4.5).

Scope of Static Variables. If a static variable lives as long as the form, how then is it different from a class level variable? They differ in scope. A static variable, which can be declared only inside a procedure, is a local variable, recognized only in the procedure. On the other hand, a class level variable is recognized by all procedures in the same form. For example, suppose you have a form with a button named btnTest. Consider the following code:

```
Dim K as Integer 'Place this line right after the Inherits
    statement
Private Sub Form1_Click(ByVal sender As System.Object, ByVal e As
    System.EventArgs) Handles MyBase.Click
    Static J as Integer
    K = K + 1
    J = J + 1
    MsgBox( "K = " & K & ". J = " & J)
End Sub
```

You should be able to enter and run the routine without any problem. If you then enter the following code, however, you will notice that although you can enter the first MsgBox statement without any problem, the second MsgBox will have its variable J underlined. The compiler will

Figure 4.5

Effect of static
declaration

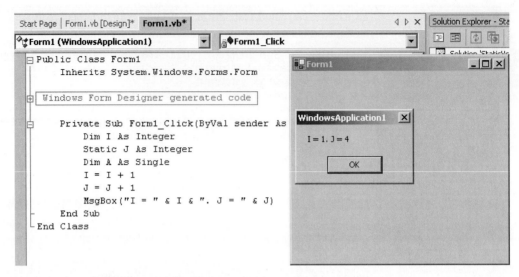

With the given code, each time you click
the form, J is *increased* by 1, while I
remains as 1.

tell you that J is not declared because a Static variable in another procedure is local to that procedure, and is not recognized in any other procedure.

```
Private Sub btnTest_Click(ByVal Sender As System.Object, ByVal e
    As System.EventArgs) Handles btnTest.Click
    MsgBox("K = " & K)
    MsgBox ("J = " & J)
End Sub    X
```

Block Level Declaration. Procedure level declarations can be placed anywhere in
the procedure before the variables in question are used. If you declare a variable within an If
block, however, the variable will be recognized only within the block. After the execution leaves
the block, the variable is out of scope. If you subsequently attempt to use it, the compiler will tell
you that it is not declared.

Overlapping Declarations in Form and Procedure. What happens
when a class level variable is also declared in a procedure? The one declared in the procedure is
a different variable, a local variable with the same name. VB recognizes the variable of the narrowest scope. This procedure recognizes only the local variable, not the class level variable;
other procedures where no variable of the same name is declared recognize the class level variable. To see the effect, draw a button in a new form. Name it **btnTest,** and set its Text property to
Test; then enter the following code:

```
Dim K as Integer 'Place this line in the general declaration area
Private Sub Form1_Click(ByVal sender As System.Object, ByVal e As
    System.EventArgs) Handles MyBase.Click
    K = K + 1
    MsgBox("K = " & K)        'You will see a different K each time
        you click the form.
End Sub
Private Sub btnTest_Click(ByVal Sender As System.Object, ByVal e
    As System.EventArgs) Handles btnTest.Click
    Dim K as Integer
    K = K + 1
    MsgBox("K = " & K)        'You will always see 1 when you click
        the button.
End Sub
```

Run the project. You should see that each time you click the form, K is increased by 1. The class level variable K is recognized; however, when you click the button repetitively, you will continue to see K equal to 1. In this procedure, the local procedure level variable is used. To refer to the class level variable K in the second procedure, qualify it with Me. While K references the procedure level variable, Me.K references the class level variable.

Note, however, that you cannot have overlapping declarations in procedures and blocks; if you declare a variable in a procedure, you cannot declare another variable with the same name inside a block, such as an If block, in that procedure.

Scope and Lifetime: A Recap

To recapitulate, variables have different scopes and lifetimes, depending on where and how they are declared. A variable declared at the form (class) level is recognized by all procedures; a variable declared in a procedure is recognized only in that procedure. If the same variable name is declared in different contexts (in the form and/or in different procedures), the variable declared in the procedure is the one recognized inside the procedure.

Besides its scope, a variable also has its lifetime. A form level variable has its value preserved until the form is destroyed. The value of a procedure level variable is reinitialized each time the procedure is called if the variable is declared with a Dim statement. If it is declared with a Static statement, however, the procedure level variable's value is preserved until the form is destroyed.

The following table provides a summary of the scope and duration of variables.

Declaration	Scope	Duration
Dim A As Integer (in the general declaration area)	Form (class) level variable recognized by all procedures	The value is preserved for as long as the form exists.
Dim B As Integer (inside a procedure)	Procedure level (local) variable recognized only in that procedure	As soon as the procedure ends, the value is gone.
Dim C As Integer (inside a block)	Block level variable recognized only in that block	As soon as the execution control leaves the block, the name is not recognized.
Static D As Integer (allowed only inside a procedure)	Procedure level (local) variable recognized only in that procedure	The value is preserved for as long as the form exists.

Declaring Constants. The value of named constants cannot be changed. Although they have similar scope and lifetime as variables, it would seem more appropriate to use the same names for the same types and values throughout the project. One potential problem is that broad scope constants declared at different places in a project may result in name collision; same names have different values and types. To guard against such a problem, declare all constants in one place in your program. This practice enhances the consistency and maintainability for the project.

Additional Note on Declaration. The preceding discussion on declaring variables and constants dealt with projects with only one form. Will there be any difference in declaration when a project has more than one form? Yes. In this case, you may need to consider whether a variable declared in one module *at the class level* (local variables are local, anyway) should be available (accessible) to the other modules. Two commonly used access modifiers (modifiers that define the scope) are *Public* and *Private*. You can declare variables as follows:

```
Public Dim YourVariable As Double
Private Dim MyVariable As Single
```

When a variable is declared with an access modifier, you can omit the keyword Dim. Typically, the declarations appear as follows:

```
Public YourVariable As Double
Private MyVariable As Single
```

A variable declared as Public is accessible to all other modules in the project; a variable declared as Private is recognized only in that class, and so is a variable declared with a Dim statement at the class level. The following two declarations have the same effect:

```
Dim MyVariable As Integer
Private MyVariable As Integer
```

Variable accessibility will be discussed in more detail in Chapter 11, "Menus and Multiple-Form Applications," which discusses multiple form projects.

The discussion of declaration of variables so far has focused on their use for elementary data types. Variables can be (and are) also used to reference other types such as structures (combinations of elementary data types, discussed in Appendix A, "Data Management Using Files"), enumerations (groupings of constant names, discussed in Chapter 12, "Object Based Programming"), and objects such as controls. In the case of elementary data types, structures, and enumerations, variables are ready to be used after they are declared. In the case of objects, however, it usually takes two steps: one step to declare the variable as the type, and another step to create (instantiate) and associate the object with the variable. As an example, consider the case of the Random object (an object that you can use in place of the Rnd function). To use it, you will first declare a variable of the Random type as follows:

```
Dim R As Random
```

In the second step, you will create the Random object with the New keyword, and assign it to the variable R as shown below:

```
R = New Random()
```

From that point on, you will be able to use the variable R to generate random numbers that suit your need. (Note that Random is followed by a pair of parentheses.)

Understanding Objects. Technically, Random as a type is similar to an icon in the Toolbox, such as the Text Box icon. The icon in the Toolbox is not yet an object. It is simply a template from which you can create instances of objects. For examples, you can draw many text boxes onto a form, creating many instances of text boxes from the template. The formal term for the template is *class*; for the instance(s), *object*. The action of creating an object (instance) from the class is termed *instantiation*. Use these terminologies to restate the two preceding steps: You first declared the variable R as the Random class; you then created an instance of the Random class and associated it with R.

In many cases, the two steps are combined into one—that is, the object is created and associated with the variable at the same time when the variable is declared. Again, the New keyword is used to create the object. The following statement accomplishes both steps:

```
Dim R As New Random()
```

The use of the Random object will be discussed later in this chapter. This discussion of declaration of variables (and the terms, object and class) may not appear very clear to you. This is natural because of the huge body of knowledge in VB that you need to absorb in a short period. You may want to come back and revisit this section a few more times to gain additional familiarity and understanding.

Scope and Program Modularity

As you can see from the previous discussion, a variable declared in the general declaration area is recognized by all procedures in the class. This also means that only one memory location is used to handle the variable. You may be tempted to declare all variables at the class level for convenience and to conserve memory; however, you should avoid this programming practice.

When a variable is recognized by all procedures, it is shared by all procedures. When the value of this variable is changed in one procedure, the result affects *all* procedures. In some cases (and too often), such a change may not be expected when you write your code. This coding practice makes the resulting program difficult to maintain. In addition, because of the duration of the class level variables, the memory use is not necessarily minimized; therefore, the general rule is to declare each variable with a scope as narrow as possible—that is, to the extent possible, declare the variables you need to use in the procedures where you need them and declare variables at the class level only if they absolutely have to be shared by more than one procedure. By declaring variables with the narrowest scope possible, you keep procedures independent of each other, which is the basic foundation of modular design.

When you absolutely need for the procedures to share certain variables, try to design your code such that each of these variables is assigned/changed in as few procedures as possible. This makes it easier to trace the source of the change when there is a problem. If the value of a variable needs to be changed to perform some operations within a procedure, and such a change is not intended for all other procedures, you should take care to restore the original value of the variable. This can be done by the use of a temporary variable, for example, a properly declared variable named TempVar, as shown in the following code fragment:

```
TempVar = YourVariable 'Save the original value
YourVariable = New Value 'Change the variable to a new value
' Your code that uses the New value
YourVariable = TempVar 'Restore the value at the end
```

Constant and Variable Naming Convention

Some companies also adopt naming conventions for constants and variables in addition to those that they use for controls. The rules for variables typically stipulate that there should be a one-character prefix for the scope, followed by another three-character prefix for the data type. For example, a module level integer variable can have a prefix mint, where m indicates the scope (module level) and int represents its data type. This naming notation is recognized as the Hungarian notation. The purpose of such rules is to enhance the readability of the code.

Some well-known authors, however, maintain that such a practice appears to be overkill, and can make the code extra long by adding an overhead to the coding effort. This textbook will not follow this convention in using variables and constants; however, you should be aware that such a convention does exist.

4.3 Numeric Data and Types

Now turn your attention to numeric data types. VB has different ways of storing and handling numbers, depending on the *types* you declare for them. Some data types can handle only numbers without decimal points; others can handle a wide *range* of numeric values, from a very small fraction to a huge value. In addition, some data types have a low *precision*. They can be accurate for only a few significant digits. Others have a high precision, capable of holding many significant digits. Some selected numeric data types used in VB are given in the following table.

Data Type	Size in Bytes	Value Range	Type Suffix for Variable	Type Suffix for Literal Constant
Byte	1	0 to 255	(None)	(None)
Char	2	0 to 65535	(None)	C
Boolean	2	True or False	(None)	(None)
Short	2	-32,768 to 32,767	(None)	S
Integer	4	-2,147,483,648 to 2,147,483,647	%	I
Long	8	-9,223,372,036,854,775,808 to 9,223,372,036,854,775,807	&	L

continues

Data Type	Size in Bytes	Value Range	Type Suffix for Variable	Type Suffix for Literal Constant
Single	4	1.401298E-45 to 3.402823E+38 (in magnitude)	!	F
Double	8	4.94065645841247E-324 to 1.79769313486231E+308 (in magnitude)	#	R
Date	8	0:00:00 on January 1, 0001 through 11:59:59 PM on December 31, 9999		# (Enclose)
Decimal	16	79,228,162,514,264,337,593,543,950,335 (in magnitude; with 28 places to the right or left of the decimal)	@	D

Notice the last two columns in the table. The Type Suffix for Variable column shows the character to append to a variable to indicate the data type in declaration. As noted previously, declaring data with type suffixes makes the code less readable. Do not use them in your own code. They are listed here for your reference in case you encounter them when reviewing someone else's code. The Type Suffix for Literal Constant column shows the character to append to a literal to force or make explicit its data type. For example, to indicate that the number 12345 is of the Decimal type, you code:

    12345D

Also note that to show a date literal, you must enclose the constant with a pair of pound (#) signs, such as #12/31/2002#.

Byte and Char Types

As you can see from the preceding table, *Byte* type data can handle only a small range of values with a very narrow range and low precision (fewer than three complete digits); it cannot handle negative values. Its use is rather limited for computational purposes. The Char type has a wider range and higher precision; however, it usually is not used for computational purposes, either. Both the Byte and Char types are typically used to handle string data.

Character strings are coded either in ASCII code or Unicode. The ASCII code uses one byte of data storage to represent a character, while the Unicode uses two bytes. The ASCII code has a limited capability in representing characters only up to 256 different symbols. This range is sufficient to handle languages such as English, but insufficient for many other languages. As a result, the Unicode is used more universally because of its capability of representing up to 65,535 different symbols. As you may have already guessed, the Byte type is suitable for handling the ASCII code data, while the Char type is suitable for the Unicode data.

Boolean Type

Boolean type data are used to store the logical state—True (-1) or False (0). In contrast to Byte data, Boolean data are often used, although there are only two values. Many properties of VB controls can accept only Boolean data. These properties, such as Visible or Enabled, must be set to the desired state for the VB controls to work properly. Also, the If statement always involves the use of Boolean data.

Short, Integer, and Long Types

The *Short type* uses two bytes to store data. This data type is often used for counters, which seldom exceed several thousands. The *Integer* type uses four bytes to store data and is commonly used for computations dealing with integer numbers. It is also used as the index for elements in a list. The *Long* type uses eight bytes to store data. The Short, Integer, and Long types use exactly the same internal coding scheme to represent numbers, but have different ranges and precisions as the table shows.

When the result of a numeric operation exceeds the capacity that a data type can handle, an *overflow error* will occur at runtime. In those cases in which you are not sure how big an integer number may be, you should use the Long type to be on the safe side.

Single and Double Types

In contrast to the Short, Integer, and Long types, the *Single* and *Double* types can handle data with fractional numbers and decimal points. These two data types use the *floating point* coding scheme to store data. This coding scheme breaks the stored data into two portions: One portion is used to keep track of the exponent, while the other portion stores the base value (mantissa) of the data. As an illustration, the number 123.45 can be expressed as 1.2345×10^2. The mantissa value, 1.2345, is stored in one part of the storage area while the exponent, 2, is stored in another part. This form of representation can also be used in code, where the mantissa is presented first followed by a symbol E (for exponent) and the exponent value. Here are some examples:

Actual Value	Floating Point Representation
34500	3.45E4
-34500	-3.45E4
.0002345	2.345E-4
-.0002345	-2.345E-4

Both the Single and Double data types can handle a wide range of values, as shown in the previous table; however, the Single type has a precision of approximately seven significant digits. This means if you have an amount like 1234567.89 that must be stored accurately, you *should not* use the Single type because the last few digits of the amount will be lost. If you need to use a floating point type to handle your data, you should keep this in mind. Note that you can append a suffix (F for single and R for Double) to the literal to explicitly show its type (force the compiler to handle it as such). For example, if you want 3.45 to be handled as Double, you can code:

```
3.45R
```

TRY THIS

Type the following code in the code window of a new project without any VB control. Run the project and then click the form. What does the message box display? Change Single to Double in the Dim statement. Run the program again. What do you see this time?

```
Private Sub Form1_Click(ByVal sender As System.Object, ByVal e
    As System.EventArgs) Handles MyBase.Click
    Dim Amount As Single
    Amount = 1234567.89
    MsgBox("The amount is " & Amount)
End Sub
```

The characteristics of the eight numeric data types discussed in this subsection can be summarized as follows:

Data Type	Value Range	Precision	Speed*	Remark
Byte	Small	Low	NA	Seldom used for computation purposes but for handling character strings in ASCII code
Char	Medium	High	NA	Seldom used for computation purposes but for handling character strings in Unicode
Boolean	Small	Low	NA	Often used to represent state, such as True or False, On or Off
Short	Small	Low	2	Often used as counters
Integer	Medium	High	1	Used for integer computations; cannot handle decimal point
Long	Medium large	High	3	Used for computations with large integer values; cannot handle decimal point
Single	Large	Medium	4	Can be accurate for about seven significant digits
Double	Very large	Very high	5	Requires twice the storage of the Integer or Single type

* 1= fastest; 5= slowest

TIP

When you are uncertain as to how many significant digits the actual data may be, use the data type with higher precision for the variable. Your program may become slower, and will consume more storage space. (Between Short and Integer, the latter is faster.) Nevertheless, you are assured that your program will not encounter a serious unexpected problem. Story has it that the stock market crashed once because a computer program used by a large bank in New York City failed to process all transactions when the assumed maximum number of transactions was exceeded on that day. *Program robustness should outweigh the efficiency consideration.*

Other Numeric Data Types

In addition to the numeric data types described previously, there are also data types of Decimal and Date. They use 16 and 8 bytes of storage, respectively. The Decimal type can handle 29 significant digits, and you can put the decimal point up to 28 places to the right or left of the number. The Date type is used to handle date/time data, as the name implies. Basically, it uses the double floating point representation to handle the data. Its fractional part is used to keep track of time; the integer part is for the date value.

Declaring Numeric Data Types

As explained in Section 4.1, "Classification and Declaration of Data," you can declare a numeric variable using the following syntax:

```
Dim name As data type
```

or

```
Dim name+type suffix
```

You probably have noticed in the first table that not all data types can be declared with a type suffix. Again, for code clarity, avoid declaring variables with type suffixes.

Here are some examples of variable declarations:

```
Dim NewRec As Boolean    'Declare NewRec as Boolean type
Dim NumberOfEmployees As Integer    'Declare # of employees as
    integer
Dim RecordCount As Long    'Declare RecordCount as long
Dim HourPay As Single    'Declare hour pay as single
Dim BillsIncome As Double    'Declare Bill's income as double
Dim Amount As Decimal    'Declare Amount as Decimal
```

The Object Data Type

What if you declare a variable without explicitly giving its type? The variable is then given the Object data type. This is also the data type that VB assumes for you if you use a variable without declaration and you have an Option Explicit Off statement. The Object data type can take on any type of data, numeric or string. In a way, it is a versatile type with a lot of flexibility and capability; however, this versatility can also cause unexpected results and a lot of confusion. Consider the following code:

```
Dim V As Object
V = "1.23"
V = V + "45"
```

What result do you expect? V will contain a string "1.2345" because both V and "45" are strings, and the + symbol is considered a string concatenation operator (see the string section that follows for more explanation). But what do you expect from the following?

```
V = "1.23"
V = V + 45
```

The answer is 46.23. Because 45 is a number, VB considers + as an addition operator. It thus converts the string "1.23" to the number 1.23 and then performs the addition. After the last statement, V is no longer a string but rather a floating point Double type! See the confusion that the Object type can cause?

In addition to the potentially unexpected result and confusion, the Object type also uses more computer memory to store, and is slower because of the additional complexity involved in handling this data type. *Stay away from this data type as much as possible.*

Strict Implicit Type Conversion

The confusing results from using the Object type is partially caused by VB's permissive data type conversion rules. By default, VB allows the programmer to write code without much concern about how data should be converted from one type to another. This convention appears to be convenient for the beginner to learn the language; however, it also can result in mysterious bugs in the program. The programmer might believe that the compiler does one thing, while it actually does another. The best way to avoid this kind of problem is to explicitly perform data conversion by code. For example, in the preceding example, if you mean for the expression to perform a string operation, you should code:

```
V = CStr(V) + CStr(45)
```

In the code, CStr is a function that converts the argument, V (and 45) into a string. In section 4.4, "Built-in Numeric Functions," a group of data conversion functions are presented. Note that although at this point in the code V has functioned as a string, the CStr function is still needed under the strict conversion rule because V (being of the Object type) can be any data type at execution time.

You can have the complier force you to observe strict data conversion rules by adding a line of code at the beginning of the module:

```
Option Strict On
```

When the strict data conversion rule is on, you can implicitly convert data from a type of narrower range to that of a wider range, such as from Single to Double, but not the other way. In this case, if you really mean to do it, you will need to use one of the conversion functions explicitly. As you can infer, when your program does not have this line of code, you are in effect coding with Option Strict Off by default. It is recommended that you have this option on. Programs coded with explicit data type conversion code are easier to understand because the code explicitly shows the intended data type of each element, and is less error prone. You can have the compiler enforce strict data type conversion rules for the project without any code by setting Option Strict On in the project's Property Pages. The steps are exactly the same as turning on Option Explicit, as shown in Figure 4.3. This textbook will follow strict data conversion rules as soon as you learn those data conversion functions in Section 4.4.

Place the following code in a button click event.

```
Dim V As System.Object
V = "1.23"
V = V + 45
MsgBox("v=" & V)
MsgBox(V.GetType().ToString)
```

In the code, the GetType method returns the data type of the object. When you run the program and click the button, you should see in the message box that V = 46.23 and the data type is System.Double. Add the following line at the beginning of your code window (before any statement).

```
Option Strict On
```

Check the code in your Click procedure again. You should see V underlined. Change the code as follows and test the program again. What do you see this time?

```
Dim V As Object
V = "1.23"
V = CStr(V) + CStr(45)
MsgBox("v=" & CStr(V))
MsgBox(V.GetType().ToString)
```

Comment out the Option Strict On statement before proceeding further.

The Assignment Statement

You are now ready to learn about numeric operations. Before doing so, however, take another look at the assignment statement. Consider the following statement:

```
HourPay = 12.50
```

The equal sign (=) in the statement instructs the computer to move data resulting from the operation(s) on the right side to the variable on its left side. Statements with this structure are recognized as assignment statements, and are the most common statements in nearly all programs. In addition, to assigning a constant to a variable, you can also assign the value of a variable to another variable:

```
HourPay = StandardHourPay
```

It is important to note that because the result on the right side will be moved to the left, *any variables appearing on the right side must have been assigned with proper values* before execution reaches the statement. In the previous statement, you assume StandardHourPay is another variable and has been declared and assigned some value before execution reaches this line.

You can also assign data entered in the VB control to a variable. For example, the following code will assign to the variable HourPay whatever number the user enters into the text box named txtHourPay (see Figure 4.6).

```
HourPay = txtHourPay.Text
```

Figure 4.6

Moving data between text box and variable

```
Private Sub btnShow_Click(ByVal sender As System.Object, ByV
    Dim HourPay As Single
    HourPay = txtHourPay.Text
    lblResult.Text = "Entered hour pay is " & HourPay
End Sub
End Class
```

This illustration shows that you can assign data entered into the text box to a variable, whose content can then be displayed.

TIP

Keep in mind that the language has strict syntax rules that govern how each type of statements should be constructed. In the case of the assignment statement, there can be only one variable on the left side. The following statements will result in *compile errors*:

```
I, J = 1
I and J = 1   X
```

Also, the result of the following statement may not be what you expected:

```
I = J = 1   ?
```

In some languages, this may mean I and J both are assigned a value 1. But in VB, this line means to compare whether J is equal to 1. If so, assign a value True to I; otherwise, assign False.

Notice that the left side of an assignment statement must be a variable or a control property whose value can be set at runtime. Notice also that the equal sign in the statement does not mean *equal*, but represents an instruction to move the result on the right side to the variable on the left. You can write a statement such as the following:

```
I = I + 1
```

This statement says to add 1 to the value of I and then move the result to I. The effect is that I is increased by 1. Note that VB.NET has special syntax for operations that can produce the same effect. The syntax appears as follows:

```
Variable Operation = Operand
```

where *Variable* = the variable to appear on the left side of the assignment statement (the first operand)

> *Operation* = the mathematical operation such as + (addition), - (subtraction), * (multiplication), or / (division)
>
> *Operand* = the other (second) operand in the operation.

For example, the same effect of the preceding statement can be obtained with the following line:

```
I + = 1
```

The following table shows the effects of a few examples using this special syntax:

Example	Equivalent Statement	Effect
I += 2	I = I + 2	Increase the value of I by 2
I += I	I = I + I	Double the value of I
I -= 3	I = I - 3	Decrease the value of I by 3
I *= 3	I = I * 3	Triple the value of I
I /= 2	I = I / 2	Halve the value of I

Swapping Two Values. After assigned a new value, the variable loses its previous content. It is important to remember that if you still need the original value of the variable, you will have to keep it in another variable before assigning a new value to it. For example, suppose you need to swap the values for two variables, named AdamsPay and JonesPay. The following code will *not* get the desired results:

```
AdamsPay = JonesPay
JonesPay = AdamsPay   X
```

This code fails because the first line assigns JonesPay (for example, 5,000) to AdamsPay. AdamsPay now has the value of 5,000, no matter what it had previously. This in effect results in both variables containing the same value, JonesPay. The second line assigns 5,000 to JonesPay, which was the original value of JonesPay anyway.

How do you solve this problem? As suggested, because you will need the original value of AdamsPay, you should find a way to keep its value before the variable is assigned with another value. You can do this by introducing a temporary variable to hold the original value of AdamsPay. After this is done, JonesPay can be assigned to AdamsPay, and the value in the temporary variable (Adams' original value) can then be assigned to JonesPay. The diagram in Figure 4.7 shows how this algorithm works.

The following code accomplishes swapping the values of the two variables:

```
TempVar = AdamsPay
AdamsPay = JonesPay
JonesPay = TempVar
```

In the future, you may see many situations where, at the first glance, the problem appears pretty difficult to tackle. In such cases, your solution may lie in an introduction of an additional variable. It is important to remember this point.

Draw a button onto a new form. Set its Name property to **btnSwap** and its Text property to **Swap**. Enter the following code. Run the program, click the button, and observe the result. You should be able to verify the swap.

```
Private Sub btnSwap_Click(ByVal Sender As System.Object, ByVal
    e As System.EventArgs) Handles btnSwap.Click
    Dim TempVar As Single
    Dim AdamsPay As Single
    Dim JonesPay As Single
    AdamsPay = 5000
    JonesPay = 7500
    TempVar = AdamsPay
    AdamsPay = JonesPay
    JonesPay = TempVar
    MsgBox("After the swap, AdamsPay is " & AdamsPay & _
        " JonesPay is " & JonesPay)
End Sub
```

Numeric Operations

Refer back to the discussion of the assignment statement, the code that appears on the right side of the equal sign is recognized as *expression*, which can be a constant, a variable, or any operations on any combinations of constants and variables that result in a value. The symbols used to express *arithmetic operations* in VB are similar to the daily arithmetic symbols and are listed in the following table.

Figure 4.7

Swapping data between two variables

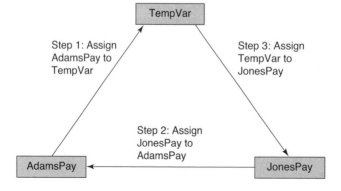

Symbol	Arithmetic Operations	Example	Meaning
-	Negation (unary)	-A	Negative value of A
+	Addition	A + B	A plus B
-	Subtraction	A - B	A minus B
*	Multiplication	A * B	A times B
/	Division	A / B	A divided by B
\	Integer division	A \ B	A divided by B
^	Power	A ^ B	A^B
Mod	Modulus	A Mod B	Remainder of A divided by B

The following are examples of valid expressions:

```
Salary + Commission
Mph * Hours
(Fahrenheit - 32) * 5 / 9
3.1416 * R ^ 2
20 Mod 3
```

The Mod operation divides the first operand by the second operand, and returns the remainder. The last expression, 20 Mod 3, will give 2 as a result because the remainder of 20/3 is 2.

Operational Precedence. When you combine several arithmetic operations in one expression, the order of execution resembles the ordinary arithmetic rules of precedence as follows (from highest to lowest):

Power (^)

Unary negation (-)

Multiplication and division (*, /)

Integer division (\)

Mod (Mod)

Addition and subtraction (+, -)

When the expression involves two or more operations of the same level of precedence, the execution goes from left to right.

Use of Parentheses. In many cases, you may find this order not exactly what you want. You can use parentheses to change the order of execution. An operation enclosed in a pair of parentheses will always be performed first. You can place as many pairs of parentheses as you want in an expression. You can also nest the parentheses. In this case, operations in the innermost pair will be performed first. Here are some examples of expressions using parentheses:

```
(7 + 8) * 3
(1 + Rate) ^ N ' compound interest for n periods
H * (A * X ^ (1 + B)) 'total costs for the learning curve effect
```

Data Type Conversions

If an arithmetic operation in an expression has two operands that are of different data types, VB will have to perform conversion to make them the same type before it can proceed with the computation. In addition, if the result of the expression has a different data type from that of the variable on the left side of the assignment statement, VB will also make a conversion before moving the result to the variable. For example, consider the following code:

```
Dim I As Integer
    I = .5 * 20
```

There will be two conversion operations in executing the preceding code. In the code, .5 is a floating point constant; 20 is an integer constant. To make the two operands compatible, the number with smaller range or precision will be converted to the one with higher range and precision. Before the multiplication operation, 20 is converted to a Double floating point number. The multiplication is then carried out in a Double floating point operation. The result is a Double floating point value (10), which is then converted back to an integer number before it can be stored in an Integer variable.

As pointed out previously in this chapter, while VB will carry out these conversions automatically by default, it is advisable that you write your code explicitly to take care of the data conversions for semantic clarity and error minimization.

Computing Net Sale: An Application Example

You have learned a lot about numeric data in this chapter. These are in addition to those VB controls you learned in Chapter 3, "User Interface Design: Visual Basic Controls and Events." Have you been wondering how all these can be put together into an application? The purpose of this example is to show you how VB controls and numeric data can be used together for a simple but practical application. Please work along as you read.

The Net Sale Project. A retailer's gross receipts consist of cash and credit cards. Both cash and credit card receipts are deposited daily in the bank. Before making the deposit, the owner needs to figure out her net receipts (which will be her actual amount of deposit). Cash is deposited on a one-for-one basis, meaning there is no discount or fee; however, she has to pay the bank a processing fee of 2.5% for all credit card receipts. You are to develop a project to compute the net receipts that she can use to prepare her deposit slips.

Input, Process, and Output. One way to analyze the project is to examine the input, process, and output of the project. It is usually easier to consider the output first. What the retailer needs to know is the net receipts that include both cash and net credit card receipts. It would also be nice to show the amount of credit card processing fees. The input should include the amount of cash and gross credit card receipts.

The process (computation) should be fairly simple. There will be no change in cash receipts between the gross and net amount. The credit card processing fee can be computed from the gross credit card receipts. The formula should be as follows:

```
ProcessingFees = GrossCreditCardReceipts x .025
```

This analysis can be shown as in the following table.

Input	Processing	Output
Cash receipts	None	Cash receipts
Gross credit card receipts (GCCR)	GCCR × .025	Credit card processing fees (CCPF)
	GCCR – CCPF	Net credit card receipts

In addition, it would be nice to show total gross and net receipts. The retailer can use the total gross amount to verify the entered data. The total net receipt amount can be used for the preparation of deposit slips.

The Visual Interface. What VB controls should you use to obtain input from the user? Both cash receipts and credit card receipts are numeric. The exact amounts vary from day to day. It would appear that text boxes are the most suitable VB controls to use. Output can also be displayed in text boxes; however, you do not want the user to accidentally change the results, so labels would be a better choice. You can make the labels look similar to text boxes by properly setting their BackColor and BorderStyle properties. You can also set both text boxes and all labels to display amounts right-justified so that they will feel and appear right. For code clarity, you can use a named constant for the processing fee rate. You will also use variables to store computational data before the values are displayed in the output labels.

When should the computation be carried out and displayed? For simplicity, the computation will be done when the user clicks on a button with a text Compute. It would also be nice to provide the user a button to quit. A sketch of the interface design is presented in Figure 4.8.

As you may recall, you learned in Chapter 3 that text boxes by themselves give no clues to the user about what they are or what the user should do. When you translate this sketch into a VB form layout, you must also add proper labels. The resulting visual interface appears as seen in Figure 4.9.

The settings of selected properties of the VB objects used are summarized in the following table.

Named Object	Description	Property	Setting
txtCash	For cash input	TextAlign	Right
txtCreditCards	For credit card input	TextAlign	Right
lblGrossReceipts	To display gross receipts	BackColor	White
		BorderStyle	Fixed3D
		TextAlign	MiddleRight
lblProcessingFees	To display processing fees	BackColor	White
		BorderStyle	Fixed3D
		TextAlign	MiddleRight

continues

Figure 4.8

A sketch of input, process, and output of the receipts project

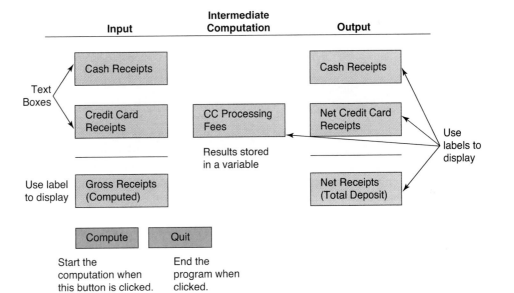

Figure 4.9

Visual interface for the net sale project

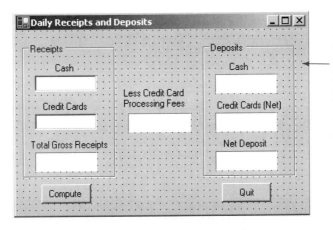

In this application, the user will enter Cash and credit card receipts on the left column. When he or she clicks the Compute button, all other amounts will be computed and displayed. The "boxes" for all the computed amounts are labels to prevent accidental changes by the user.

Named Object	Description	Property	Setting
lblNetCash	To display cash receipts	BackColor	White
		BorderStyle	Fixed3D
		TextAlign	MiddleRight
lblNetCreditCards	To display net credit cards	BackColor	White
		BorderStyle	Fixed3D
		TextAlign	MiddleRight
lblNetReceipts	To display net receipts	BackColor	White
		BorderStyle	Fixed3D
		TextAlign	MiddleRight
btnCompute	To perform computations	Text	Compute
btnQuit	To end the program	Text	Quit

Declaring the Variables and Constant. Before writing any code, try to identify the variables to use and their data types. In addition, you should also consider whether to name any constant to be used in the project. From the analysis, you know that:

- Cash and credit cards entered will be used in computations. You can use variables to hold the data entered into the text boxes. For computations, variables are faster and easier to reference than the properties of controls.

- You need variables to hold credit card processing fees and the net credit card receipts.

TIP

If you need to refer to a property several times in a procedure, assign it to a variable first; then use the variable from then on. The code executes faster with a variable than with a property of an object. Of course, if the property setting changes, the variable will need to be reassigned with the new setting.

The next question is: What data type should each variable be? In the previous discussion, it was suggested that the same data type be used for all the variables in a statement to avoid the problem with conversion. Because all these variables will be used to handle amounts, they will involve decimal points. This excludes the Integer and Long types from consideration. The floating point (Single and Double) and Decimal types are the potential candidates. You may recall that the Single type can handle only about six or seven significant digits. If the retailer has a gross sale in excess of $100,000.00, the Single type will not have enough precision (field width) to handle the amount. The choice should be between Double and Decimal. The Decimal type has the advantage of being accurate, but is slower in speed than the Double type. Assume that the processing speed is the most important criterion for this project. Your choice will then be the Double type for all variables. With all these considerations, you will now place the following code in the *btnCompute Click event* procedure:

```
Dim Cash As Double
Dim CreditCards As Double
Dim ProcessingFees As Double
Dim NetCreditCards As Double
```

Because a variable should be declared before it is used, it makes sense to place all the preceding lines at the beginning of the procedure. Doing so also has another advantage. When you need to check the declaration for a particular variable, it is much easier to locate at the predetermined location.

How do you handle the credit card processing rate? Using a named constant for the rate appears to have some advantages. The name itself can give a clear purpose for the computation. More important, if the rate literal is used in several places in the project, when there is a change in the rate, you may have to search over the entire project to make the corrections. On the other hand, if you use a named constant, you define it at only one place and, therefore, revise the rate only once at the same place. With this consideration, you will place the following line in the general declaration area in the code window:

```
Const CreditCardRate As Double = 0.025
```

Again, the constant is declared as the Double type to be consistent with all the variables used to avoid data type conversion. Placing the declaration in the general declaration area will make the constant recognizable in all procedures.

Computations. Before considering any code, please note that you will not deal with strict type conversion at this point. After you have the variables declared, you can assign the content of the text boxes to them:

```
'Store user entered data in variables
Cash = txtCash.Text
CreditCards = txtCreditCards.Text
```

These variables can then be used in the computations. The credit card processing fees are computed by multiplying the (gross) credit card receipts by the processing fee rate:

```
' Perform fees computations
ProcessingFees = CreditCards * CreditCardRate
```

The net credit card receipts is the difference between the gross credit card receipts and the processing fees.

```
' Find net credit card deposit
NetCreditCards = CreditCards - ProcessingFees
```

Displaying the Results. You are now ready to display the results. Net cash will be the same as its original amount. Both the computational results will be displayed in their corresponding labels.

```
' Display results
lblNetCash.Text = Cash
lblProcessingFees.Text = ProcessingFees
lblNetCreditCards.Text = NetCreditCards
```

The totals can be displayed by adding cash and gross/net credit card receipts.

```
' Display totals
lblNetReceipts.Text = Cash + NetCreditCards
lblGrossReceipts.Text = Cash + CreditCards
```

You also need to provide code to end the program execution. This is done in the btnQuit Click event procedure. As explained in Chapter 2, a good way to handle this is to close the form:

```
Me.Close
```

The Complete Code. Putting everything together, the complete code appears as follows:

```
'Place the following constant declaration in the general
  declaration area
Const CreditCardRate As Double = 0.025
Private Sub btnCompute_Click(ByVal Sender As System.Object, ByVal
  e As System.EventArgs) Handles btnCompute.Click
    Dim Cash As Double
    Dim CreditCards As Double
    Dim ProcessingFees As Double
    Dim NetCreditCards As Double
    'Store user entered data in variables
    Cash = txtCash.Text
    CreditCards = txtCreditCards.Text
    ' Perform fees computations
    ProcessingFees = CreditCards * CreditCardRate
```

```
          ' Find net credit card deposit
          NetCreditCards = CreditCards - ProcessingFees
          ' Display results
          lblNetCash.Text = Cash
          lblProcessingFees.Text = ProcessingFees
          lblNetCreditCards.Text = NetCreditCards
          'Display totals
          lblNetReceipts.Text = Cash + NetCreditCards
          lblGrossReceipts.Text = Cash + CreditCards
      End Sub
      Private Sub btnQuit_Click(ByVal Sender As System.Object, ByVal e
         As System.EventArgs) Handles btnQuit.Click
          Me.Close()
      End Sub
```

An Issue of Presentation. Have you been working on our example? If you have (and you should), it is time to test run the program to see if it gives the correct and desired results. The program should work. You might, however, discover one minor problem. When the credit card receipts have a fractional number, the resulting amounts on the form do not appear to be neatly presented; some may have no decimal points, and others may have a decimal point with several digits to the right. Is there a way to force the computer to display two decimal places for all amounts so that they appear neatly aligned by the decimal point? The answer lies in the Format function.

The Format Function

The Format function provides a wide variety of formatting capabilities. The syntax is as follows:

```
Format(Expression, Formatting String)
```

where Expression represents any valid expression that evaluates to either a string or a number to be formatted, and Formatting string represents a string that specifies the format.

The formatting string can be a user-defined string or a name recognized by VB. For example, VB recognizes the name Standard, which will show the number with commas (as thousand separators) and a period with two decimal places; for example, Format(3000, "Standard") will give the result: 3,000.00. The following table lists selected named numeric formats.

FormatName	Meaning	Example Code	Result
Currency, C, or c	Display the dollar sign before the number with thousand separator and two digits to the right of the decimal point.	Format(3000, "Currency")	$3,000.00
Fixed, F, or f	Display at least one digit to the left and two digits to the right of the decimal point.	Format(3000.1, "Fixed")	3000.10
General Number, G or g	Display number without thousand separator	Format(3000, "G")	3000
Percent	Display number multiplied by 100 with a percentage sign (%) appended to the right with two digits to the right of the decimal point.	Format(0.25, "Percent")	25.00%
Scientific E, or e	Use standard scientific notation.	Format(1234, "Scientific")	1.234E+03
Standard, N, or n	Display numbers with thousand separator and two digits to the right of the decimal point.	Format(3000,"Standard")	3,000.00

You can also provide your own user-defined formatting string. The following table gives a selected list of characters that you can use to form the formatting string.

Character	Explanation	Code Example	Result
#	Place holder; either the number or nothing	Format(5, "###")	5
0	Place holder; either the number or 0	Format(5, "000")	005
.	Decimal place holder	Format(5, "###.00")	5.00
,	Thousand separator	Format(5000, "#,###.00")	5,000.00
+, -, $, (,)	Literal	Format(5000, "$#,###.00")	$5,000.00
%	Percent (multiplied by 100)	Format(5, "###.00%")	500.00%

Back to the example, you can use the Format function with the Standard format to display all the amounts in the form. To do so, the statement to display (net) cash should be changed to the following:

```
lblNetCash.Text = Format(Cash, "Standard")
```

All other statements to display the amounts should be changed similarly. You will notice that "Standard" appears in several lines of code. You can, instead, use a symbolic constant, such as FmtStandard, in place of the literal "Standard." You can declare the constant next to the declaration of credit card processing rate:

```
Const FmtStandard As String = "Standard"
```

The statement to display (net) cash can then be changed to the following:

```
lblNetCash.Text = Format(Cash, FmtStandard)
```

All other amounts, including the two text boxes, can be formatted in a similar fashion. In case you decide to change the format later, such as to Currency, all you will have to do is to change the constant value. Notice that because FmtStandard is a constant name, it should not be enclosed in a pair of double quotes when placed in the Format function as the second parameter.

You can also use the FormatNumber function to format a number. Use the keyword FormatNumber in the Index tab of the help file for details on how to use the function.

For a complete list of the characters used for the user defined format string for numbers, use the keyword Format function to search the Index tab; then select user-defined numbers to view the table.

A Side Note on Design. In the previous example, the credit card rate was treated as a constant. In a real application, this may not be a good design because the rate can change. Each time the change occurs, you will need to change and recompile the program. A well thought out design should call for the rate to be saved in some file/database and read in when your program starts. I have seen a commercial program with the social security tax rate hard-coded in the program. When the client company called for an update, the software company charged the client service fees. Don't you think this practice is taking advantage of their own poor design?

4.4 Built-In Numeric Functions

VB.NET also provides many functions and objects that can be used to handle conversion, mathematical, and financial operations. This section discusses selected conversion and mathematical functions that are commonly used.

Mathematical Functions

The following table lists three mathematical functions.

138 CHAPTER 4 DATA, OPERATIONS, AND BUILT-IN FUNCTIONS

Function	Use	Code Example	Result
Fix(x)	Returns the integer portion of x by truncation	Fix(3.6)	3
Int(x)	Returns the integer portion of x by truncation	Int(3.6)	3
Rnd(x)	Returns a random number in the range of 0 to 1 (but less than 1) (See the following for additional explanation.)	Rnd()	Fractional random number

Fix and *Int* differ in their way of handling negative values. Fix truncates the fraction; Int gives the next negative integer smaller than the parameter. For example, Fix(-3.3) will return -3, whereas Int(-3.3) will return –4 *Rnd* is a random number generator that returns a fractional number of the Single type between 0 and 1 each time it is called. Depending on the value of the parameter given, it returns different results. If the parameter is a negative value, that value is used as the seed and results in the same random number if the same parameter is used. If the parameter is equal to zero, it returns the most recently generated random number. If no parameter is given, or if the parameter is greater than zero, it returns a random number in the sequence.

Rnd uses a seed to start the random number sequence. To avoid repeating the same sequence each time you run a program, you can use the *Randomize statement* to set a different seed as follows:

```
Randomize
```

The Randomize statement uses the system timer as the seed for the random number sequence. Because it is virtually impossible to have the same timer value repeated, there is no chance that the same sequence of random numbers will be generated.

The Random Object. In the preceding section, you saw the Random object used as an example to illustrate how a variable should be declared and associated with an object. The use of this object, which provides two methods of random number generation, is now explored. The *NextDouble method* takes no parameter, and returns a random number (of the Double type) that is greater than or equal to 0.0 and less than 1.0, providing the same functionality of the Rnd function. The *Next method* takes up to two integer parameters. When no argument is specified, the method returns an integer random number. When one argument is specified, the method returns a random number less than the argument. When two arguments are specified, the method returns a random number that is greater than or equal to the first argument, but less than the second argument. The second argument must be at least equal to the first argument; otherwise, you will encounter an argument out of range exception. The following statements will generate a random number between 1 and 100, inclusive:

```
Dim Rand As New Random()
Dim R As Integer
R = Rand.Next(1, 101)
```

As you can see, when you need to generate a series of integer random numbers within a range, this method is more convenient to use than the Rnd function. Note that the Random object randomizes its seed when it is instantiated. There is no need to use the Randomize statement.

Methods in the Math Object. VB.NET also provides a Math object that contains many methods for mathematical computations. The following table gives a selected list of these methods:

Function	Use	Code Example	Result
Abs(x)	Returns the absolute value of x	Abs(-3.2)	3.2
Ceiling(x)	Returns the smallest whole number Larger than or equal to x	Ceiling(2.3)	3
Cos(x)	Returns the cosine value of x, where x is an angle in radians	Cos(3.14159265359)	-1
Exp(x)	Returns the value of e^x	Exp(1)	2.71828182845905
Floor(x)	Returns the largest whole number smaller than or equal to x	Floor(2.3)	2
Log(x)	Returns the natural logarithm of x	Log(2.71828182845905)	1
Log10(x)	Returns the common logarithm of x	Log10(100)	2
Max(a, b)	Returns the larger of the two numbers	Max(10, 100)	100
Min(a, b)	Returns the smaller of the two numbers	Min(10, 100)	10
Round(x)	Returns a whole number nearest to x	Round(5.6)	6
Sign(x)	Returns the sign (1, 0, or –1) of x	Sign(-9)	-1
Sin(x)	Returns the sine value of x, where x is an angle in radians	Sin(0)	0
Sqrt(x)	Returns the square root of x	Sqrt(100)	10

To use these methods, precede the method name with Math and a dot, similar to any typical method in an object. For example, to obtain the square root of 100, you code:

```
Math.Sqrt(100)
```

TIP

The Math object also provides two commonly used constants in math: E and PI. You can conveniently use PI to perform trig computations. For example, you can code the following to obtain the cosine value at 180 degrees:

```
Math.Cos(Math.PI)
```

Use the keyword Math to search the Index tab of the help file for all members in the Math objects.

A Side Note on Referencing Object Methods. Are you wondering about the difference in the treatment of objects between Random and Math? To use the Random object, you have to create (instantiate) and associate it with a variable. But to use the Math object, you have not done so. What causes the inconsistency—or more appropriately, difference—in treatment? The difference has to do with the types of methods in these objects. Technically, Math is a class. Methods provided in the Math class are static. These methods exist without having to be instantiated. You can directly reference *static methods* and properties by using the class name, instead of the name of the instance (object) instantiated from the class.

On the other hand, the methods in the Random class are instance methods. You must have an instance of the class before you can reference these methods. And you must qualify the method name with the instance (object) name, not the class name.

Conversion Functions

The following table lists selected data conversion functions.

Function	Use	Code Example	Result
CBool(x)	Returns a Boolean type value; all nonzero values converted to True	CBool(1)	True
CByte(x)	Returns a Byte type value	CByte("12")	12
CDate(x)	Returns a Date/Time type value	CDate("31-Dec-98")	12/31/1998 12:00:00 AM
CDbl(x)	Returns a Double type value	CDbl("12.34")	12.34
CDec(x)	Returns a Decimal type value	CDec("12.34")	12.34
CInt(x)	Returns an Integer type value	CInt("12.34")	12
CLng(x)	Returns a Long type value	CLng("12.34")	12
CShort(x)	Returns a Short type value	CShort("12.34")	12
CSng(x)	Returns a Single type value	CSng("12.6")	12.6

In all the conversion functions listed in the table, x is an expression that can be evaluated to a numeric value. These functions typically are used to convert from one numeric data type to another; however, they can also be used to convert strings that appear to human beings as numbers. For example, the expressions CLng("3,456") and CLng("$3,456") will both yield a result of 3456. The expression CLng(" ") will cause an error because a blank space is not considered a number.

You may have noticed that the preceding example program to compute net receipts behaves exactly as described here, although the content of the text box is assigned to the numeric variable directly without calling any conversion function. The Text property of the text box is of the String type; however, those variables are declared to be the Double type. As noted previously in this chapter, in the absence of Option Strict specification, when the data type of the expression (source) is different from the variable on the left side (target) of an assignment statement, a data conversion will occur. One of these conversion functions is automatically called.

Note also, the Int and Fix functions differ from CInt and CLng in that the former pair truncate the fractional portion from the result, and the latter round the number. Using the number 5.5 in Int or Fix will have a result of 5, but will have a result of 6 with CInt or CLng.

Date/Time Functions

Date/Time functions are listed in the following table.

Function	Use	Code Example	Result
Today *	Returns current date as set in the computer	Today	Today
Now*	Returns current date and time as set in the computer	Now	Current date and time
TimeOfDay*	Returns current time as set in the computer	TimeofDay	Current time
Day(Date)	Returns the day of the Specified date	Day(#12/31/2001#)	31
Month(Date)	Returns the month of the specified date	Month(#12/31/2001#)	12
Year(Date)	Returns the year of the Specified date	Year(#12/31/2001#)	2001
DateSerial(year, month, day)	Returns a date given the year, month, and day in the parameter	DateSerial(2002, 5, 31)	5/31/2002
DateValue(Date)	Returns a date given a string such as "02-28-1998" as the parameter	DateValue("May-31-2002")	05/31/2002
DateAdd(interval, number, date)	Returns a Date/Time value after adding the specified date by the specified number of intervals	DateAdd(DateInterval.Month, 2 ,#03-31-2002#)	05/31/2002

* Technically, these three are properties of the System.DateTime object rather than functions. You can use them not only to return values, but also to set the date/time for your system.

Note that the Day function must be qualified by Microsoft.VisualBasic in order for the IDE to accept your code.

The DateAdd function is a versatile function in handling Date/Time data. You specify the interval parameter by using the DateInterval enumeration. For example, to indicate an interval in year, you code DateInterval.Year. The number parameter requires an integer, while date can be any Date/Time value (Note that a date literal must be enclosed by a pair of the # sign). For example, the following expression:

```
DateAdd(DateInterval.Second, 5, Now)
```

will return a Date/Time value that represents 5 seconds from now.

If you need to perform Date/Time calculations, use the keywords "DateAdd function" and "DateDiff function" to search the index tab of the help file. These two topics give you specific details and fine points for various computations.

Formatting Date Data. Recall that you can use the Format function to format numeric data. You can also use the same function to format date/time. The following table shows a list of selected predefined date/time formats.

Format Name	Meaning	Code Example	Result
General Date, or G	Display a date and/or time	Format(#12/31/2002#, "General Date")	12/31/2002 12:00 AM
Long Date, or D	Display a date in the computer's long date format	Format(#12/31/2002#, "Long Date")	Tuesday, December 31, 2002
Medium Date	Display a date in the medium date format	Format(#12/31/2002#, "Medium Date")	Tuesday, December 31, 2002
Short Date or d	Display a date in the computer's short date format	Format(#12/31/2002#, "Short Date")	12/31/2002
Long Time or T	Display a time using the computer's long time format, including hours, minutes, and seconds	Format(#3:23:25 PM#, "Long time")	3:23:25 PM
Medium Time	Display a time using the computer's medium time format	Format(#3:23:25 PM#, "Medium time")	3:23:25 PM
Short Time or t	Display a time using the computer's short time format	Format(#3:23:25 PM#, "Short time")	3:23 PM

You can also use the FormatDateTime function to format date/time data. Use the keyword FormatDateTime to search in the Index tab of the help file for information on how it can be used.

Of course, you can also create your own user-defined formatting string to format date/time. The following table gives a selected list of examples.

Code Example	Result	Comment
Format(#2/23/2002#, "MM/dd/yyyy")	02/23/2002	M for month, d for day, y for year; number of characters defines maximum number of output digits
Format(#2/23/2002#, "M/d/yy")	2/23/02	
Format(#2/23/2002#, "d-MMM")	23-Feb	MMM specifies 3 characters for month
Format(#2/23/2002#, "MMMM yy")	February 02	MMMM specifies full month name
Format(#2:35:6 pm#, "HH:mm:ss")	14:35:06	H for hour (24 hour clock), m for minute, s for seconds; number of characters defines maximum number of digits displayed
Format(#2:35:06 PM#, "h:m:s tt")	2:35:6 PM	h for hour (12 hour clock); tt shows AM or PM

Use the keyword Format function to search the Index tab of the help file; then double-click user-defined dates/times under the format function heading for a complete list of characters for date/time formatting.

VB also provides financial functions that can be used to compute annuity, mortgage payments, and depreciation amounts. You can find these functions by searching the online Help file with the keyword Financial functions.

Using Functions

You can use functions in any expressions in the same way you use a constant or variable. Here are some examples, assuming all variables involved have been properly declared and assigned with proper values:

```
TheWidth = Math.Abs (X1 - X2) 'width of a rectangle
GrossPay = CDbl (HourRate) * CDbl(HoursWorked) 'compute gross pay
' Compute total time under the learning curve model
TotalTime = InitTime * Units ^ _
    (1R + Math.Log(LearningRate) / Math.Log (2R))
Sample = Sqr(100 * Rnd()) 'square root of 100 times a random
    number
MsgBox("Today is " & Today) ' Display today
```

4.5 String Data

As explained previously, a string consists of zero or more characters. The String data type is usually used to handle text such as names and addresses. It is also used for data code. For example, the characters M and F can be used to represent male and female. A string literal must be enclosed in a pair of quotes. String variables are used to store string data as shown in the following:

```
LastName = "Smith"
```

The code moves the string literal "Smith" to the variable named LastName. You can also assign data in a control or a variable to another variable. For example, the following code will assign to the variable LastName the text that the user has entered in the text box named txtLastName.

```
LastName = txtLastName.Text
```

Declaring String Variables

You can declare a string variable with the following syntax:

```
Dim Name As String
```

For example, you can code:

```
Dim Address As String
```

All strings in VB.NET are *variable-length strings*. A variable-length string variable can contain any number of characters. Its length depends on what is assigned to it.

String Operations and Built-In Functions

You cannot perform computations on string data; however, you can perform concatenation on strings. The concatenation operation joins two separate strings. You can use either + or & as the symbol for the concatenation operation. Here are two examples of concatenations:

```
EmployeeName = "John " + "Smith"
EmployeeName = txtFirstName.Text & " " &  txtLastName.Text
```

The first line will result in the string "John Smith" being assigned to the variable EmployeeName. In the second line, the content of the text box named txtFirstName is first concatenated with a blank space. The result is then concatenated with the content of the text box named txtLastName. Finally, this result is assigned to the variable EmployeeName. If txtFirstName contains the string "John" and txtLastName contains the string "Smith," EmployeeName will have the string "John Smith" as the result.

The Ambiguous + Operator. Both + and & symbols can be used for the concatenation operation; however, the + operator can be ambiguous. This is particularly true when one of the operands involved is a string, and the other is a number. Consider these lines:

```
Dim Text As String
Text = "123" + "123"
Text = "123" + 123
Text = "ABC" + 123
```

The first line will result in Text containing the string "123123" as expected. The second line, however, will result in text containing a string value of "246." Because 123 is a number, VB considers + an addition operation, instead of concatenation; therefore, "123" is first converted to a number 123. The two numbers are then added together. The resulting value is converted to a string before it is assigned to the variable Text.

The third line will cause a runtime Invalid cast exception. Again, VB treats the expression as a numeric addition first. When it is unable to successfully convert the string "ABC" to a number, it issues an error message. As you can see, using the + operator for string concatenation can cause confusing results. Avoid using it by all means.

If you mean to have string concatenations for the previous examples, the following lines will produce the correct results:

```
Dim Text as String
Text = "123" & "123"
Text = "123" & 123
Text = "ABC" & 123
```

Because VB knows the & operator is only used for string concatenation, it will first convert 123 into a string "123" in the last two lines. The first two lines will result in a string of "123123," and the third line results in "ABC123."

On Strict Conversion Again. If you observe strict data type conversion, you would not have coded some of the above lines as they were. In each of those lines that involved mixed types of data, you would convert one of the operands into the type of the other operand to ensure that the meaning is clear. For example, line 2 in the above two cases can be coded as follows (imagine the value 123 is actually represented by a numeric variable):

```
Text = "123" + CStr(123)
Text = "123" & CStr(123)
```

No ambiguity will result as to what kind of operation you expect to perform. From this point on, this textbook will observe strict data conversion throughout the remainder of this book; this is a good practice to follow. Set Option Strict On in your project to make the compiler force you to observe strict conversion rules.

Type the following code in the code window of a new project with Option Strict Off. Run the project, click the form, and observe the results; then replace the + symbol with the & symbol. Repeat the test, and you should be able to get a good feel about how VB treats the two symbols.

```
Private Sub Form1_Click(ByVal sender As System.Object, ByVal e
    As System.EventArgs) Handles MyBase.Click
    Dim Text123 As String
    Dim TextABC As String
    Text123 = "123" + 123
    MsgBox("Text123 is " & Text123)
    TextABC = "ABC" & 123
    MsgBox("TextABC is " & TextABC)
End Sub
```

Because the & symbol is also used as a type suffix, you must be sure that there is a space between this symbol and the variable before it to avoid a syntax error. For example, the expression:

```
FirstName& " " & LastName   X
```

will cause an error. But the following expression (notice the space before &):

```
FirstName & " " & LastName
```

will produce no error.

Built-In String Functions. In addition to the concatenation operation, many built-in string functions can be used to manipulate string data. The following table lists selected functions.

Function Name	Syntax	Use
Asc	Asc(*char*)	Returns the ASCII key code value of a character (one byte); for example, Asc("A") returns 65.
AscW	AscW(*char*)	Returns the key code value of a character (two bytes); for example, AscW("A"C) returns 65.
Chr	Chr(*n*)	Returns a character with an ASCII value n; for example, Chr(65) returns "A".
ChrW	ChrW(*n*)	Returns a character in Unicode with a value n; for example, ChrW(65) returns "A"C.
Val	Val(*S*)	Converts the string S to a numeric value; for example, Val("-23.5") returns –23.5.

Function Name	Syntax	Use
Str	Str(*n*)	Converts a number n into a string; for example, Str(-23.5) returns "–23.5".
StrReverse	StrReverse(*S*)	Returns a string of the mirror image of the string S; for example, StrReverse("AB") returns "BA".
Lcase	LCase(*S*)	Returns the lowercase of the string S; for example, LCase("AbC") returns "abc".
Ucase	UCase(*S*)	Returns the uppercase of the string S; for example, UCase("AbC") returns "ABC".
Space	Space(*n*)	Generates a string with n blank spaces; for example, Space(1) returns " ".
Left	Left(*S*, *n*)	Returns a string with the first n characters of the string S; for example, Left("My Name", 2) returns "My".
Right	Right(*S*, *n*)	Returns a string with the last n characters of the string S; for example, Right("My Name", 4) returns "Name".
Mid	Mid(*S*, *b*, [*n*])	Returns a string of n characters that starts at the bth position in S; for example, Mid("My Name", 2, 3) returns "y N".
InStr	InStr([*p*], *S*, *c*)	Returns the position in S at which the content matches the string c. The comparison will start at position p. If p is omitted, it will start at position 1; for example, InStr("My Name", "y") returns 2.
InStrRev	InStrRev(*S*, *c*, [*p*])	Returns the position in S at which the content matches the string c. The comparison goes backward from position p. If p is omitted, it will start from the end; for example, InStrRev("02-02-43", "-") returns 6.
Len	Len(*S*)	Returns the length of the string; for example, Len("My Name") returns a value 7.
Ltrim	LTrim(*S*)	Returns a string with all leading blank spaces trimmed off; for example, LTrim(" My ") returns "My ".
Rtrim	RTrim(*S*)	Returns a string with all trailing blank spaces trimmed off; for example, RTrim(" My ") returns " My".
Trim	Trim(*S*)	Returns a string with all the leading and trailing spaces trimmed off; for example, Trim(" My ") returns "My".
Replace	Replace(*S*, *a*, *b*)	Replaces all a's in S with b; for example, Replace("Jeff", "f", "s") returns "Jess".

Note that both the Left and Right functions must be qualified by Microsoft.VisualBasic; the actual code to reference to the Left function should be as follows:

```
Microsoft.VisualBasic.Left(MyString, Number)
```

If you encounter a design time error when coding a built-in function and you are sure the function name is correct, try to qualify the name with Microsoft.VisualBasic. The error may be caused by name conflicts. Examples of built-in functions requiring the qualifier include Left, Right, Timer, and Day.

Asc and Chr Functions. The Asc function returns the ASCII key code value of a character. For example, the ASCII key code value for A is 65; therefore, Asc("A") will return a value of 65. The Chr function converts a key code value to a character and can be considered the complement of the Asc function. Chr(65) returns a character A.

What do you need this pair of functions for? These functions provide a convenient way to perform computation on characters, which can become pretty tedious otherwise. For example, suppose you are developing a Scrabble game. You probably would need to provide a capability to generate a string of random letters. The Chr function makes this fairly easy.

You know there are 26 letters in the English alphabet; therefore, you need to generate a random number within the range of 26 so that each number will correspond to a letter. The following code should accomplish this:

```
Dim Rand As New Random()
Rand.Next(0, 26)
```

Recall that the Next method of the Random object returns an Integer number greater than or equal to the first argument but less than the second argument. The second statement should return an integer in the range of 0 and 25. Because A has an ASCII value of 65, adding 65 to the result of the Next method should produce the ACSII value of the random letter. You can then use the Chr function to convert this ASCII value to display the letter.

```
MsgBox("The next random letter is " & Chr(Rand.Next(0, 26) + 65))
```

As another illustration, suppose you want to display the next letter following the one that the user has entered in a text box named txtLetter when the user clicks a button named btnNext. What code will you provide in the button's Click event procedure? You will first obtain the key-code value of the current letter (using the ASC function). Add 1 to that value to get the keycode value of the next letter and then convert the result to the letter (using the Chr function). The code can appear as follows:

```
Private btnNext_Click(ByVal Sender As System.Object, ByVal e As
   System.EventArgs) Handles btnNext.Click
      Dim KeyAscii As Integer
      'Get the ASCII value of the letter
      KeyAscii = Asc(txtLetter.Text)
      MsgBox("The next letter is " & Chr(KeyAscii + 1))
End Sub
```

In this illustration, you assume the user will not enter the letter Z or more than one letter in the text box.

The preceding discussion deals with the ASCII code. If you are dealing with characters in Unicode code, the proper functions to use are the AscW and CharW functions. The only difference between these two functions and the two just discussed is that the AscW and ChrW pair deals with the Unicode (two bytes), while the Asc and Chr pair deals with the ASCII code (one byte).

Val and Str Functions. The Val function converts a string into a numeric value. For example, Val("123") will return a value 123. The Str function does the opposite. It converts a number into a string. For example, Str(123) will return a string " 123". Note that there is a leading blank space before the string "123". This can be important if you intend to check the length of the resulting string. If you do not want the leading blank space for any reason, you should use the Format function instead. For example, Format(123,"General Number") will return a string "123".

Note that the Val function ends its attempt to convert a string as soon as it encounters a nonnumeric character, thus Val("1B2") will return 1 with no error. In addition, Val("3,456") will return a value 3; however, CLng("1B2") will result in an error, whereas CLng("$3,456") will return a value of 3456. In a text box, such as, txtUnitsSold, you may expect that the user will enter numbers with commas; therefore, one of the conversion functions should be used. You may also anticipate that the user will leave the box blank or enter an invalid string. In such a case, the Val function will be safer. Thus, you are faced with a dilemma of choosing the appropriate function to use. One possible solution is to use yet another function to decide which function to use. The function *IsNumeric(S)* can be used to test whether the string parameter S is a valid numeric string. If it is, the function returns a value True; otherwise, False. Your solution can look like the following:

```
If IsNumeric(txtUnitsSold.Text) Then
    UnitsSold = CLng(txtUnitsSold.Text)
Else
    UnitsSold = CLng(Val(txtUnitsSold.Text))
End If
```

You can even insist that the user enter a valid number before accepting the data. In this case, your code in the Else block will be a message requesting the user to enter a valid number.

LCase and UCase Functions. The LCase function returns a lowercase string. For example, LCase("ABC") will return a string "abc." The UCase function returns the uppercase string, so UCase("abc") will give "ABC".

Space Function. The function Space(n) will generate a string with n blank spaces.

Left, Right, and Mid Functions. The Left, Right, and Mid functions deal with the substring of a string. Left(S, n) returns the first n characters of the string S; therefore, Left("Upper",2) returns "Up". Note that this function has a name conflict with the Left property of the form. To differentiate properly between this function and the Left property, this function must be coded as:

```
Microsoft.VisualBasic.Left(S, n)
```

Right(S, n) returns the last n characters in string S; therefore, Right("Upper",3) will return "per". Note that this function also has a name conflict, and must be qualified with Microsoft.VisualBasic. The Mid(S, b, n) returns a string of n characters in S beginning from the bth position. Mid("Upper", 2, 3) will return "ppe". If the third parameter is omitted, all the remaining string starting from the Bth position will be returned. For example, Mid("Upper", 2) will return "pper".

Mid can also be used as the target of a string assignment. For example, assume the string variable MyStr contains a string "Uppercase". The following code will change the string to "Upperhand":

```
Mid(MyStr, 6, 4) = "hand"
```

In this statement, the four characters in MyStr starting from the sixth position are replaced with a string "hand". The last argument in Mid is an optional argument. If it is omitted, either the remaining length of MyStr or the length of the expression on the right side of the assignment (whichever is shorter) is used. The following table summarizes the examples discussed concerning these functions.

Code	Result (Value of A)
A = Microsoft.VisualBasic.Left("Upper", 2)	"Up"
A = Microsoft.VisualBasic.Right("Upper", 3)	"per"
A = Mid("Upper", 2, 3)	"ppe"
A = Mid("Upper", 2)	"pper"
A = "Uppercase"	
Mid(A, 6, 4) = "Hand"	"UpperHand"

The InStr and InStrRev Function. The InStr(S, ss) function returns the position in S where its substring matches the string ss. For example, InStr("ABCDE", "CD") will return a value 3. Actually, the complete syntax for the function is as follows:

```
InStr([p], S, ss, [Compare])
```

where *p* = the position in S at which to begin the search

   S = the string to be searched on

   Ss = the substring to search for

   Compare = a value to specify the type of comparison and should be either CompareMethod.Text or CompareMethod.Binary. If CompareMethod.Text is specified, the search is not case sensitive; that is, "abc" and "ABC" are treated as equal.

Using this syntax, the expression InStr("12-31-1999", "-") will return a value 3 and the expression InStr(4, "12-31-1999","-") will return a value 6. The InStrRev function has the following syntax:

```
InStrRev(S, ss, [p], [Compare])
```

where all the parameters have exactly the same meaning as those parameters in the InStr function. The positions in which the parameters are placed in the two functions are different, however. Also note that to specify the fourth parameter for the InStr function, you must also provide the value for the first parameter, as shown in the second through fifth code examples in the following table.

Code	Result (Value of Pos)
Pos = InStr("Containing", "in")	6
Pos = InStr(1, "Containing", "in")	6
Pos = InStr(7, "Containing", "in")	8
Pos = InStr(7, "Containing", "In")	0
Pos = InStr(7, "Containing", "In", CompareMethod.Text)	8
Pos = InStrRev("Containing", "in")	8
Pos = InStrRev("Containing", "In", CompareMethod.Text)	8

These functions and the substring functions (Left, Right, Mid) together form a very useful group of functions in parsing strings. An illustration is provided in the next subsection.

The Len Function. The Len function returns the length of the string, including blank spaces. The string "" containing nothing between the quotes has a length zero; therefore, Len("") will return a value of 0.

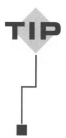

If you need to check whether a string (say, MyStr) is of zero length, your code is more efficient with:

```
If Len(MyStr) = 0 Then
```

than with:

```
If MyStr = "" Then
```

Trim, Ltrim, and Rtrim Functions. If you are interested only in the length of the visible characters in a string, you can use the Trim function to trim off the spaces and obtain the length accordingly. Len(Trim(MyString)) gives the length of the string with no leading or trailing spaces. If you are interested in trimming off only the leading spaces of any string, you can use the LTrim function to do the job. Furthermore, if you are interested in trimming off only the trailing spaces, you should use the RTrim function.

Search the Contents tab of the help file. Expand the following items (book icons) in sequence: Visual Studio .NET -> Visual Basic and Visual C # -> Reference -> Visual Basic Language -> Visual Basic Language and Run-Time Reference -> Keywords and Members by Task; then locate and click String manipulation keywords summary. You will find a list of functions organized by purpose and use. These functions can make your job of manipulating strings much easier. You should find Replace, Split, as well as those format functions useful.

Figure 4.10

The vending machine in action

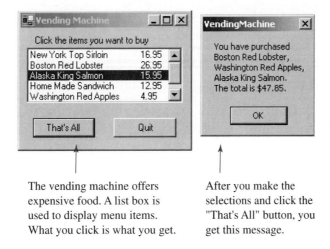

The vending machine offers expensive food. A list box is used to display menu items. What you click is what you get.

After you make the selections and click the "That's All" button, you get this message.

The Calculating Vending Machine: An Example

To illustrate how some of the previously mentioned string handling functions can be used to solve a programming problem, consider an example. In this project, a list box is used as the display of a vending machine. The customer buys an item by clicking on it. The visual interface of the project in action is given in Figure 4.10. At runtime, this program behaves in the following manner:

- When the user clicks an item in the list box (named lstVending), he or she buys it. Clicking on the same item multiple times means buying the same item multiple times. (No confirmation. No refund. It's a vending machine, after all.) The price is added to the total. (*Note:* Make sure that the SelectionMode property is set to One.)

- When the user finishes the purchase, he or she clicks a button (named btnShow) with the text **That's all**. The computer will then display all the items purchased as well as the total, as shown in Figure 4.10.

- When the user clicks another button (named btnQuit) with the text Quit, the program ends.

Setting Up the Vending Machine. The list box will display the items available as the program starts. So, how do you add the items to the vending machine? You can use the list box's Items.Add method to add the food items along with their prices. (In a real application, food items and their prices can be read from a file or database.) You would also like to align the prices in a column. This can be accomplished by inserting a *tab character* between the food item and its price. The key code constant for the tab character (Chr(9)) is defined in VB as vbTab. You will have six items in the vending machine. The code should be placed in the Form Load event procedure:

```
Private Sub frmVendingMachine_Load(ByVal sender As System.Object,
    ByVal e As System.EventArgs) Handles MyBase.Load
    lstVending.Items.Add("New York Top Sirloin" & vbTab & "16.95")
    lstVending.Items.Add("Boston Red Lobster" & vbTab & "26.95")
    lstVending.Items.Add("Alaska King Salmon" & vbTab & "15.95")
    lstVending.Items.Add("Home Made Sandwich" & vbTab & "12.95")
    lstVending.Items.Add("Washington Red Apples" & vbTab & "4.95")
    lstVending.Items.Add("Florida Orange Juice" & vbTab & "5.95")
End Sub
```

Notice that the length of each item varies slightly. The price of each item has a slightly different length, too, however the use of the tab character (vbTab) helps align the prices fairly evenly.

Use the keyword **constants** to search the Index tab of the help file. You will find all kinds of predefined constants that you can use in your program. The subtopic, miscellaneous, gives constants that are used in printing and display, such as tab, linefeed, and so on.

A Side Note on Coding Mechanics. Notice the repetitive references to lstVending.Items in the previous procedure. A coding structure exists that allows you to use a shorthand reference to the same object or collection. This involves the use of the With…End With structure, which has the following syntax:

```
With Object
      Statements
End With
```

Inside the With block, any statement that begins with a dot will be automatically qualified with the object. For example, the preceding Form Load event procedure can be rewritten as follows:

```
Private Sub frmVendingMachine_Load(ByVal sender As System.Object,
   ByVal e As System.EventArgs) Handles MyBase.Load
      With lstVending.Items
         .Add("New York Top Sirloin" & vbTab & "16.95")
         .Add("Boston Red Lobster" & vbTab & "26.95")
         .Add("Alaska King Salmon" & vbTab & "15.95")
         .Add("Home Made Sandwich" & vbTab & "12.95")
         .Add("Washington Red Apples" & vbTab & "4.95")
         .Add("Florida orange Juice" & vbTab & "5.95")
      End With
End Sub
```

All the .Add statements will be interpreted as lstVending.Items.Add because the With statement refers to lstVending.Items. This structure is not only convenient for coding, but also efficient for execution. The reference to the object is set for all statements in the block, thus avoiding the need to locate the object for each statement individually.

When you have a block of code that refers to an object several times, use the **With…End With** structure to reference the object. Your coding will be more efficient. The code executes faster, and the code is easier to read.

Determining the Item the Customer Has Chosen. When the user makes a selection by clicking an item in the vending machine, what does the computer know? You may recall that the item is identified by the list box's SelectedItem property, as well as the SelectedIndex property. This item will be referenced several times in the program. You will assign the text to a variable, which is named TheItem. You can code the following:

```
TheItem = lstVending.SelectedItem 'store the clicked item in a
      variable
```

Obtaining the Item Name. How do you get the food item name from this string? Recall that the string has both the name and the price. You know that the tab character separates the item and its price. If you know the position of the tab character, you should be one step closer to solving your problem. You can use the InStr function to find this position. If you use the variable TabPos to keep track of the position, you can code the following:

```
' Find the position of vbTab in the selected item
TabPos = InStr(TheItem, vbTab)
```

The item name starts at the beginning of the string, and ends one position before the tab character position. It can be computed as follows:

```
Microsoft.VisualBasic.Left(TheItem, TabPos - 1)
```

Putting Items Bought Together. The question then is what should you do with this result? Consider this list:

One, two, three, …

When you have only one item such as **One**, you will show only the item One. If you have more than one item, you want to insert a comma between the two items; that is, in addition to adding the item, you also add a comma and a space. If you use a variable named ItemsBot to track the items purchased, you will assign the item name to ItemsBot when this item is the first one; that is:

```
ItemsBot = Microsoft.VisualBasic.Left(TheItem, TabPos - 1) 'For
    the first item
```

If the item is not the first one, you will add a comma (with a space) as well as the item name to the existing string. The code should be as follows:

```
ItemsBot = ItemsBot & ", " & Microsoft.VisualBasic.Left(TheItem,
    TabPos - 1)
```

Showing Items on Separate Lines. Here is an additional thought. What if you want to show each item on a separate line? This ensures that the text to be displayed is wrapped properly. The character combination Chr(13) & Chr(10)—recognized as carriage return and line feed—will make the computer display what follows it in the next line. This constant has a predefined name vbCrLf. To make each item appear on a separate line, you can insert this named constant to the preceding code:

```
ItemsBot = ItemsBot & ", " & vbCrLf & _
    Microsoft.VisualBasic.Left(TheItem, TabPos - 1)
```

Telling the First Item from Others. Finally, you can tell whether the current item is the first item purchased by checking the length of ItemsBot. If the current item is the first one, nothing has been bought before. The length of ItemsBot will be zero. The code to add the item name to the list ItemsBot should be as follows:

```
If Len(ItemsBot) = 0 Then
    'First item, just keep the item name
    ItemsBot = Microsoft.VisualBasic.Left(TheItem, TabPos - 1)
Else
    'Not the first item; add a comma, and concatenate the new item
    ItemsBot = ItemsBot & ", " & _
        vbCrLf & Microsoft.VisualBasic.Left(TheItem, TabPos - 1)
End If
```

Obtaining the Price. So far, you have taken care of the list of items bought. How do you get the price from TheItem? Recall that the price starts from one position beyond the tab character, and extends to the end of TheItem. The Mid function can be used neatly to find the price string:

```
Mid(TheItem, TabPos + 1)
```

Recall that the Mid function takes three parameters. When the last parameter is omitted, it returns the remainder of the string beginning with the position specified in the second parameter.

Accumulating the Total. You will use the variable Total to keep track of the total purchases by the customer. The price string obtained previously should be converted to numeric data before it is added to Total. You can use the Val function to convert the price string, such as:

```
' Add the purchase price to total
Total = Total + CSng(Val(Mid(TheItem, TabPos + 1)))
```

The Complete Code for a Selected Item. As described in the project requirements, the customer buys an item when he or she clicks on it; therefore, all the preceding code should be placed in the lstVending SelectedIndexChanged event procedure. The complete event procedure appears as follows:

```
Private Sub lstVending_SelectedIndexChanged(ByVal sender As
   System.Object, ByVal e As System.EventArgs) Handles
   lstVending.SelectedIndexChanged
     Dim TabPos As Integer
     Dim TheItem As String
     TheItem = lstVending.Text 'store selected item in a variable
     ' Find the position of vbTab in the clicked item
     TabPos = InStr(TheItem, vbTab)
     If Len(ItemsBot) = 0 Then
         ' first item, just keep the item name
         ItemsBot = Microsoft.VisualBasic.Left(TheItem, TabPos
         - 1)
     Else
         'Not the first item; add a comma, a CrLf
         'and concatenate the new item
         ItemsBot = ItemsBot & ", " & vbCrLf & _
         Microsoft.VisualBasic.Left(TheItem, TabPos - 1)
     End If
     ' add the purchase price to total
     Total = Total + CSng(Val(Mid(TheItem, TabPos + 1)))
End Sub
```

Declaring the Variables Used. Notice that four variables have been used: ItemsBot, Total, TheItem, and TabPos. You need to consider their data types and scope. In terms of their data types:

- Both ItemsBot and TheItem are used to handle string data. They should be declared as the String type.

- Total is used to accumulate the purchase amount. Because the total does not require a number of many digits but can be a fractional number, it can be declared as a Single floating point variable.

- TabPos is used to keep the position of vbTab in the string TheItem, which does not have many characters; therefore, TabPos can be declared as an Integer variable. (A Short variable is also appropriate, but the Integer type computes faster.)

In terms of their scope:

- Both TheItem and TabPos are used only in the lstVending Click event procedure. You should declare (and have declared) them in that procedure.

- Both ItemsBot and Total, however, are used in both lstVending Click procedure and btnShow Click procedure (discussed next). They should be placed in the general declaration area:

```
Dim ItemsBot As String
Dim Total As Single
```

TIP Beware that you are not allowed to break a string constant into multiple lines as shown below:

```
lblDemo.Text = "This is a demonstration of _
   an extremely long string message" X
```

In the first line, the compiler considers the space and the underscore as a part of the string literal; it fails to recognize it as an underscore for line continuation. The correct code should be:

```
lblDemo.Text = "This is a demonstration of  " _
   & "an extremely long string message"
```

Handling "That's All". Finally, consider handling the event when the user clicks the button with the text "That's All". This is the event where your program should tell the user what he or she purchased as well as the total amount. The list of purchased items has been collected in the lstVending Click procedure. You would like for the computer to show a message such as the following:

```
You have purchased
Boston Red Lobster,
Florida Orange Juice.
The total is $32.90.
```

More Text on Separate Lines. If you examine the tentative output carefully, you should notice that both the first line and the last line of output are on separate lines from the purchase list. In addition, there is a period at the end of the purchase list as well as the end of the total. This means vbCrLf and the period should be added at the proper places. Notice also the amount displayed has a $ sign, and there should be two decimal places, suggesting that the total should be formatted with the Currency format. The code should appear as follows:

```
MsgBox("You have purchased" & vbCrLf & ItemsBot & "." & _
   vbCrLf & "The total is " & Format(Total, "Currency") & ".")
```

Um, Not Yet: A Finishing Touch. There is another fine point you should consider. What if the user clicks the "That's All" button before clicking any item? Using the previous line will result in the following message:

```
You have purchased
   .
The total is $0.00.
```

Although that's not too bad, it does not appear very neat. You would rather inform the user that he or she has not yet selected any item. Recall that you can test whether any item has been purchased by checking the length of ItemsBot; therefore, the more complete code is as follows:

```
If Len(ItemsBot) = 0 Then
    MsgBox("You have not selected any item yet.")
Else
    MsgBox("You have purchased" & vbCrLf & ItemsBot & "." & _
    vbCrLf & "The total is " & Format(Total, "Currency") & ".")
End If
```

Reinitializing Data for the Next Customer. After the message is displayed, you should also clear ItemsBot and Total so that the vending machine will be ready for another customer. To do this, you can assign a zero-length string to ItemsBot and a value 0 to Total:

```
ItemsBot =""
Total = 0
```

Complete Code, "That's All". Recall that the name of the button is btnShow. The complete procedure to handle the event when the customer clicks the That's All button should appear as follows:

```
Private Sub btnShow_Click(ByVal Sender As System.Object, ByVal e
    As System.EventArgs) Handles btnShow.Click
    If Len(ItemsBot) = 0 Then
        MsgBox("You have not selected any item yet.")
    Else
        MsgBox("You have purchased" & vbCrLf & ItemsBot & "."
          & _
          vbCrLf & "The total is " & Format(Total, "Currency")
            & ".")
        ItemsBot = ""
        Total = 0
    End If
End Sub
```

Finally, you should also take care of the event when the user clicks the Quit button:

```
Private Sub btnQuit_Click(ByVal Sender As System.Object, ByVal e
    As System.EventArgs) Handles btnQuit.Click
    Me.Close()
End Sub
```

Additional Remarks. The vending machine example involved four event procedures:

1. The Form Load event procedure to prepare the list box to show food items
2. The lstVending Click procedure to accumulate the customer's purchases
3. The btnShow Click procedure to display the result
4. The simple btnQuit Click procedure to close the form

Run and test the program. If everything works correctly, you should be able to verify that the computer:

- Displays in the list box all the items with their prices as soon as the program starts
- Displays a reminder message if you click the That's All button before making any selection
- Accumulates and displays correctly the items and the total prices you have purchased when you click the That's All button after you have made selections
- Ends the project when you click the Quit button

Summary

- Data can be classified by use in computation into two broad categories: numeric and string.
- Data can also be classified by variability into variables and constants. Each variable must have a name, while a constant may or may not have a name—although in general, it is advisable to give a name to a constant.
- Constants are declared with the keyword Const. Variables are declared with the keyword Dim (or Static for local static variable).
- Variables and constants declared at the class level are recognized by all procedures in the class and are of the class level scope. If they are declared with the modifier Public, they are also accessible to other modules and, therefore, can be of the global scope.
- Variables and constants declared inside a procedure (but outside of all code blocks) are recognizable only in that procedure and have the local scope. Variables and constants declared within a block, such as an If block, are recognizable only inside the block and have the block scope.

- Variables and constants of the class scope exist in the program for as long as the class exists.

- Procedure level variables declared with Dim exist for as long as the procedure comes into action. Each time the procedure is called, the variables get reinitialized. To preserve the values of previous calls, declare the variables with Static.

- Block level variables are out of scope, and no longer exist outside of the block.

- Variables should be declared with a scope as narrow as possible. Constants should be declared with a broad scope. All constants used in a project should be declared in the same area for ease of code management.

- Numeric data can be further classified by internal code scheme into Byte, Char, Boolean, Short, Integer, Long, Date, Single, Double, and Decimal. These data types have different ranges and precisions, and each is suitable for different type of computational need. Of these types, Asc and Chr are typically used in handling string data, and are seldom used for computation. In terms of speed, the Integer type is the fastest.

- The Object data type is capable of handling any type of data and, therefore, is very flexible; however, it is slow and can produce results that may be unexpected. Beginners are advised to stay away from this data type.

- You can use the Next method of the Random object to generate integer random numbers conveniently. To use the object, declare a variable of the Random type (class) and then associate it with an instance (object) of the Random class created (instantiated) by the use of the New keyword.

- VB is capable of performing various kinds of computations. The symbols for operations used in code are similar to those used in math. The operational precedence in VB is the same as in math.

- The Net Sale Computation example is used to illustrate how data are moved and used from the user interface into the memory storage (variables) for computation and how results are displayed back.

- The Format function can be used to format numeric data as well as date and time.

- VB provides many functions and methods to handle mathematical computations as well as conversion of data from one type to another.

- To minimize unexpected results caused by automatic data conversion provided by VB, always explicitly use data conversion functions to convert data so that operands in an expression are compatible. It is strongly recommended that Option Strict On is set for the project.

- VB also provides many functions for string manipulation.

- The vending machine example serves to show how various string handling functions can be used in an application.

Explore and Discover

4-1.   Declaring Static Variables in the General Declaration Area. Place the following line in the form's general declaration area. What do you see? Static declarations at the class level are not allowed.

```
Static A As Integer
```

4-2.   Declaring with Public or Private modifier. Place the following code in the general declaration area. Do you see any problem?

```
Public Salary As Decimal
Private Wage As Decimal
```

Now cut and paste the code into an event procedure—say, form click. What do you see? You can't declare variables with these modifiers inside a procedure. They are for module/class level declarations only.

4-3.   Implicit Type Declaration. Turn Option Strict off. Place the following code in the form click event:

```
Dim A
A = "a"
MsgBox(A.GetType().ToString)
```

Run the program and then click the form. What do you see? (The GetType method gets the data type of the object and ToString gives the string of the data type.) A variable declared with no explicit type is given the Object type whose specific type depends on the type of data actually assigned to the variable.

Now set Option Strict On. Check the code the again. An implicit type declaration is not allowed. If you really mean for the variable to be of the Object type, you must code:

```
Dim A As Object
```

4-4.   Data Type: Comparing Single, Double, and Long Types. Enter the following code in a new form. Run the project and then click any part of the form. Examine the results in the immediate window.

```
Private Sub Form1_Click(ByVal sender As System.Object, ByVal e As
    System.EventArgs) Handles MyBase.Click
    Dim D As Double
    Dim C As Long
    Dim S As Single
    D = 123456789
    S = CSng(D)
    C = CLng(D)
    Console.WriteLine("D = " & D)
    Console.WriteLine("S = " & S)
    Console.WriteLine("C = " & C)
End Sub
```

What results do you see? Especially, what value does S have?

Now change the line for D to:

```
D = 0.0000123456789
```

Repeat the testing process. What results do you see? Particularly, what value does C have?

4-5.   The Rnd Function. Draw three buttons on a new form and name them btnForward, btnRecent, and btnSeed. Set their Text properties to Forward, Recent, and Seed, respectively; then type in the following code:

```
Private Sub btnRecent_Click(ByVal Sender As System.Object, ByVal e
    As System.EventArgs) Handles btnRecent.Click
    Console.WriteLine(Rnd(0))
End Sub
Private Sub btnForward_Click(ByVal Sender As System.Object, ByVal
    e As System.EventArgs) Handles btnForward.Click
    Console.WriteLine(Rnd(1))
End Sub
Private Sub btnSeed_Click(ByVal Sender As System.Object, ByVal e
    As System.EventArgs) Handles btnSeed.Click
    Console.WriteLine(Rnd(-1.23))
End Sub
```

Run the program. Click each button repetitively a few times and then click each button once. Have you got a good feel about the effect of each of the parameter values for Rnd? If not, look up in the Index tab of the online Help file using Rnd as the keyword.

4-6.   Some Date/Time Functions. Draw a button on a new form. Name it btnToday, and set its Text property to **Today**. Type in the following code:

```
Private Sub btnToday_Click(ByVal sender As System.Object, ByVal e
   As System.EventArgs) Handles btnToday.Click
     Dim D As Date
     D = Now
     Console.Write("Year = " & Year(D))
     Console.Write("Month = " & Month(D))
     Console.Write("Day =" & Microsoft.VisualBasic.Day(D))
End Sub
```

Run the project and then click the button. What do you think the following functions do? Now, Year, Month, and Day.

4-7.   The DateAdd Function. Draw a button on a new form, name it btnNextMonth, and set its Text property to Next Month. Type in the following code.

```
Dim D As Date = #07/01/2002#
Private Sub btnNextMonth_Click(ByVal sender As System.Object,
   ByVal e As System.EventArgs)  Handles.btnNextMonth.Click
     D = DateAdd(DateInterval.Month, 1, D)
     Console.WriteLine(D)
End Sub
```

Run the project. Click the Next Month button repetitively. What results do you see? Isn't this a convenient way to find the same day of the next month, such as, 07/01/2002, 08/01/2002, 09/01/2002, and so on?

But beware. Change the date in the Dim statement to:

```
#01-31-2002#
```

Repeat the experiment. What results do you get? Does everything turn out to be what you expected? Were you expecting to see month end dates?

There are many other uses of the DateAdd function, depending on the first parameter you specify. Check out the online Help file, using the keyword DateAdd function.

4-8.   Problem with Broad Scope Variables. Create a new project. Draw a list box on the form and then name it **lstWeekDays**. Set its Items property (collection) to **Sunday**, **Monday**, **Tuesday**, through **Saturday**. Set its SelectionMode property to MultiSimple. Draw two buttons on the form. Name them **btnChangeColor** and **btnShowSelected** and then set their Text properties to **Change Color** and **Show What's Selected**, respectively. Declare I in the general declaration area as follows:

```
Dim I As Integer
```

In the btnChangeColor click event, enter the following code:

```
I + = 1
If I > 1 Then I = 0
If I = 0 Then
  LstWeekDays.BackColor = Color.Red
Else
  lstWeekDays.BackColor = Color.Blue
End If
```

In the btnShowSelected click event, enter the following code:

```
For I = 0 To lstWeekDays.SelectedItems.Count - 1
    Console.WriteLine(lstWeekDays.SelectedItems(I))
Next
```

Run the project, and click the Change Color button. What do you see? Each time you click, the list box's color changes from blue to red and from red to blue. Keep it red. Select one or two items in the list box and then click the Show What's Selected button. After all selected items are displayed, click the Change Color button again. Does it change the color? Click the button one more time. Does it change this time? What happened?

When you have items selected in the list box and clicked the Show what's Selected button, I is left with a value of 1 or greater after the click event is executed. Because it is a class level variable, the value is preserved. When you click the Change Color button, that value of I is increased by 1, resulting in a value greater than 1. The If statement changes it to 0; therefore, the list box's BackColor is set to Red, the same as what is already there (showing no change). Do you see how a broad scope variable can cause problems or confusion?

4-9. **The SelectedText Property of the Text Box.** Draw a text box and a button on a new form. Name the text box **txtTest,** and set its HideSelection property to False. Name the button **btnHighLight**, and set its Text property to **Highlight**. Enter the following code:

```
Private Sub Form1_Click(ByVal sender As System.Object,  ByVal e As
    System.EventArgs) Handles MyBase.Click
        Console.WriteLine(txtTest.SelectedText)
End Sub
Private Sub btnHighLight_Click(ByVal sender As System.Object,
    ByVal e As System.EventArgs) Handles btnHighLight.Click
        txtTest.SelectionStart = 2
        txtTest.SelectionLength = 3
    End Sub
```

Run the project. Enter some long text in the text box. and then do the following:

A. Click the form. Do you see anything?

B. Highlight a portion of the text box. Click the form. What do you see? Whatever you highlight should appear in the immediate window. Highlight a few different portions, and click the form to get a good feel.

C. Click the Highlight button. What do you see in the text box? The setting of the HideSelection property makes the highlight show.

D. Click the form. What do you see?

You should have a good feel about the read capability of the SelectedText property.

4-10. **The SelectedText Property of the Text Box (continued).** Add a button to the preceding project. Name it **btnInsert**, and set its Text property to Insert. Enter the following code:

```
Private Sub btnInsert_Click(ByVal sender As System.Object, ByVal e
    As System.EventArgs) Handles btnInsert.Click
        txtTest.SelectedText = "***Inserted***"
End Sub
```

Run the program. Enter some text into the text box, and do the following:

A. Place the cursor anywhere in the text box and then click the Insert button. What do you see?

B. Highlight a portion of the text and then click the Insert button. What do you see this time? Is the highlighted text still in the text box?

C. Click the Highlight button and then click the Insert button. What do you see?

The write capability of the SelectedText property can be conveniently used to replace or insert text into a text box.

4-11. **Scope of Variables.** Type in the following code:

```
Dim A As Integer = 1
Dim B As Integer = 2
Private Sub Form1_Click(ByVal sender As System.Object, ByVal e As
   System.EventArgs) Handles MyBase.Click
    Dim B As Integer
    Console.WriteLine("A =" & A)
    Console.WriteLine("B =" & B)
End Sub
```

Run the project and then click the form. Why is A equal to 1, but B equal to 0?

4-12. **Scope and Lifetime of Variables.** Enter the following code, and run the program. Click the form a few times. What do you observe? Why is B always 1, while A and C have different values after each form click?

```
Dim A As Integer
Private Sub Form1_Click(ByVal sender As System.Object, ByVal e As
   System.EventArgs) Handles MyBase.Click
    Dim B As Integer
    Static C As Integer
    A = A + 1
    B = B + 1
    C = C + 1
    Console.WriteLine("A =" & A)
    Console.WriteLine("B =" & B)
    Console.WriteLine("C =" & C)
End Sub
```

4-13. **Lengths of Different Types of Variables.** Do you want to know the length (number of bytes) a type of variable uses? Insert this code in the form click event. Run the program and then click the form. What do you see?

```
Dim A As Date
Console.WriteLine("Length of A is " & Len(A))
```

Change the type in the Dim statement to another to find the length of the type of interest.

4-14. **Which way is Faster?** Insert the following code in a button click event. Run the program and then click the button. How much time does it take?

```
Dim I As Integer
Dim S As String
Dim T As Double
T = Microsoft.VisualBasic.Timer()
S = Space(32000)
For I = 1 To 32000
    Mid(S, I, 1) = "a"
Next I
MsgBox("Time used " & Microsoft.VisualBasic.Timer() - T)
```

Now try the following code:

```
Dim I As Integer
Dim S As String
Dim T As Double
T = Microsoft.VisualBasic.Timer()
   For I = 1 To 32000
         S = S &  "a"
   Next I
MsgBox("Time used " & Microsoft.VisualBasic.Timer() - T)
```

How much time does it take this time? (Note: In VB6, the first method is much faster, but in VB.NET the reverse is true. There are many changes between the two versions. You just can't assume that what works better in one version will work equally well in the other.)

Exercises

4-15. **Converting Temperature.** The relationship between the two measurement systems of temperature can be expressed as follows: Fahrenheit = 32 + Celsius * (9/5). Design a project with two text boxes (with proper labels) and two buttons. When the user clicks the Convert to Fahrenheit button, your program will convert the number in the text box containing the Celsius data into Fahrenheit degrees and show the result in the text box for the Fahrenheit data. When the user clicks the Convert to Celsius button, the opposite conversion takes place.

4-16. **Converting Measurements.** A mile is equal to 1.60935 kilometers. One kilogram is equal to 2.20462 pounds. One acre is equal to 4046.85 square meters. On a new form, draw six text boxes with proper labels such as Miles, Kilometers, and so on, and two buttons. Set one button's Text property to **Convert to Metric**. Set the other button's Text property to **Convert to British**.

Provide the code so that when the user clicks the Convert to British button, your program will convert the data in the text boxes containing the metric data into British/American measurements and show the results in the proper text boxes. When the user clicks the other button, the opposite conversion occurs.

4-17. **The Area and the Length of the Hypotenuse of a Right Triangle.** The area of a right triangle is computed by multiplying the two sides of the right angle, divided by 2. The length of the hypotenuse is equal to the square root of the total of the sides squared. Design a project to compute the area and the hypotenuse. The user is expected to click a Compute button after entering the values of the sides. There should also be a Quit button.

4-18. **Testing Divisibility.** Develop code to test whether a number, N, can be evenly divided by another number, D. Use two text boxes for the user to enter N and D, respectively, with a proper label for each. After the user has entered the numbers, he or she clicks a button with the text Test. Your program will display a message indicating whether N can be evenly divided by D. (*Hint:* Use the Mod operator.)

4-19. **Applying Strict Type Conversion.** The net receipts example in the text (p. 132) assumes Option Strict Off. Modify the project by setting Option Strict On; then revise the code so that there is no syntax error.

4-20. **Next Letter.** The Next Letter example in this chapter (p. 146) assumes that the user does not enter a letter Z. Modify the program so that if the user enters Z, your program will show A as the next letter.

4-21.   **Last Day of the Previous Month.** Write an expression that will give the last day of the previous month. Show the result in a text box. (*Hint:* The last day of the previous month is one day before the first day of the current month. You will need to use the following date/time functions: DateSerial, Day, Month, and Year.)

4-22.   **Automatically Filling the Date.** Write a statement that will fill a masked edit control named mskDateofOrder with today's date with a mask "##-##-####." Suppose you want this effect each time the control has focus. In which event should the statement be placed?

4-23.   **Julian Date.** The Julian date represents a date by a five-digit number. The first two digits represent the year, and the last three digits represent the date sequence number in that year. For example, 99001 represents January 1, 1999. Write two short routines—one to convert a Julian date to a regular (Gregorian) date/time value and another to convert a date/time value to a Julian date. (*Hint:* You should find DateAdd and DatePart useful.)

To test your routines, draw two text boxes and two buttons on a new form. Set the Text property of one button to **Julian** and another to **Gregorian**. Use one text box (with a Julian Date label) to enter a Julian date; the other (with a Gregorian Date label) to enter the date in the mm/dd/yyyy format. When the user clicks the Gregorian button, your program will convert the Julian date in the Julian Date text box and display in the Gregorian Date text box a date in the mm/dd/yyyy format. Conversely, when the user clicks the Julian button, the regular (Gregorian) date is converted to a Julian date.

4-24.   **Rotation Encryption.** A plain text string can be encrypted by rotating each letter in the text by 13 positions in the alphabet. For example, A (first position in the alphabet) will be rotated into N (fourteenth position in the alphabet); and N to A (13 + 14 = 27, which goes back to 1).

An interesting feature of this encryption algorithm is that you can use it to both encrypt and decrypt. For example, the string POKE will be encrypted into CBXR, but applying the same algorithm on CBXR will result in POKE.

Draw a text box and a button onto a new form. Provide the code so that when the user enters a text string in the text box and clicks the button, the text will be encrypted by the rotation algorithm just described. The result should be displayed in the same text box. The text should be restored when the user clicks the button again (if your routine works properly). Assume the user is allowed to enter only uppercase letters. (*Hint:* Use a For loop. You should find the functions Mid, Asc, Chr, and the Mod operator useful.)

4-25.   **Elapse Time.** Draw two buttons on a new form. Name them **btnStart** and **btnStop,** and set their texts to **Start** and **Stop,** respective. Provide the code so that when you click the Start button, your program starts to measure the elapse time; when you click the Stop button, your program will tell you how long it has been since you clicked the Start button. Note that when your program starts, you should disable the Stop button. When you click the Start button, the Stop button should be enabled and the Start button disabled.

4-26.   **The Name Enforcer.** Nearly all words in a name, such as personal name, street name, and so on, start with an uppercase letter. Assume that you will not accept any uppercase letter after the first in a word. Provide the code to enforce this rule while the user is entering the name for a text box named txtName; that is, perform the uppercase to lowercase conversion automatically no matter what case—upper or lower—the user enters the letter. Note that there can be more than one word in the text box. (*Hint:* Place the code in the KeyPress event. The first letter of a word is either the first character in the text box, or one whose left side is a space. You need to use the built-in functions Asc, Chr, Ucase, and Lcase.)

Note: The built-in function, StrConv can perform this process on an entire string; but here, the problem requires the immediate conversion as each character is being entered.

4-27. **Computing the Economic Order Quantity.** The economic order quantity can be computed by the following formula:

```
Q* = Square Root of (2*P*D/S)
```

Where   P = cost to place an order

   D = annual demand

   S = annual cost to carry an item

Design a project that will take P, D, and S as input (use text boxes), compute the EOQ, and display the result in a label because you do not want the user to enter any number here. (*Note:* Include two buttons: one to handle computation and another to quit.)

4-28. **Future Value of a Deposit.** The future value of a deposit (loan) compounded annually can be computed as follows:

$$F = D (1 + Rate)^n$$

Where D = amount of deposit (loan)

   Rate = annual percentage rate

   N = number of years

Design a project to compute the future value of a deposit.

Question: Can the user use your program to determine how long it will take to double his or her money? How?

4-29. **Finding Last Name and First Name.** A label has a Text **Name (Last, First)**. A text box is on its right for the user to enter the name. When the user clicks the Show button, your program will compute the last name and first name, and display the results using the MsgBox statement for example **Your name is John Smith**. (Note that the user is expected to enter a name in the format like, "Smith, John.") When the user clicks the Quit button, your program unloads.

4-30. **Handling the Esc Key.** Suppose in exercise 4.29, you want the text box to restore its previous content when the user presses the Esc key while entering a new name. Provide the code to implement this requirement. (*Hint:* You need to place the code in the Enter event and the KeyPress event. The keycode value for the Esc key is Keys.Escape. Use the AscW function to find the keycode value for the key pressed [KeyChar].)

4-31. **Replacing characters.** Write a program that will display the date for today in short time format, such as 12/31/2002; however, you want the separators between month, day, and year to be dashes (-) instead of slashes (/).

4-32. **Searching and Highlighting.** Set up a form with two text boxes with proper labels. The first one will be used to enter the search word, and the second one will contain a long string of text to be searched on (name it txtLongText). This text box has several lines. (Set its

MultiLine property to True.) When your program starts, the user enters a long text into the second box; then each time the user enters a search word and clicks on the Find Next button, your program will look for that word in the second text box. If the search word is found, it is highlighted in the second text box; otherwise, the message **Word Not Found** will be displayed (use the MsgBox statement). (*Hint:* Set the HideSelection property of the second text box to False. Use CompareMethod.Text as the fourth parameter for the InStr function to make the search not case sensitive.)

4-33. **Repetitive Searching and Highlighting.** Continuing from exercise 4-32, you would like to allow the user to click the Find Next button repetitively. Each time the user clicks the Search button, your program will find and highlight the next matching word in the second text box. When there are no more matches, the message Word Not Found will be displayed. (*Hint:* Use the first optional parameter of the InStr function to specify the position to start searching. If the current search is a new search, it should start from position 1; otherwise, it should start from the previous position plus the length of the word being searched. You will need static variables to keep track of the previous position and word being searched.)

4-34. **Repetitive Search and Replace.** Modify the project in exercise 4-33. Add a text box, with proper label, and a button. Set the button's Text property to **Replace**. Provide the code so that when this button is clicked, the text found in txtLongText will be replaced with the text in the new text box. Make sure that when no matching text is found, or when the new text box contains no replacement text, a proper error message is displayed. (*Hint:* See exercise 4-10 for string replacement.)

Projects

4-35. **Computing Daily Receipts.** At the end of each day, a restaurant owner needs to determine the amount of sales, credit card processing fees, sales taxes, and net receipts. The cash register gives a tally of the amounts received by category. A sample of the tally appears as follows:

Cash	$1,569.82
American Express	4,031.99
Other Credit Cards	5,903.22
Total	11,505.03
Food	$8,135.03
Liquor	2,320.00
Beer	1,050.00
Total	11,505.03

American Express (AE) credit card receipts are mailed to AE, which will deduct a 4.25% processing fee and make a direct deposit in the restaurant's bank account in two weeks. Statements are mailed to the restaurant. Cash and other credit card receipts are deposited in the bank the same night. These credit cards are subject to a 2.45% processing fee, which will be subtracted from the restaurant's account balance and shown in the monthly bank statement.

The food sales include a 7.25% sales tax. The liquor sales are subject to 10% liquor tax, and beer sales are subject to a 7% beer tax. Both liquor and beer taxes are expenses of the restaurant, whereas sales taxes are withholdings; therefore, the amount of food sales to be reported for this sample should be $8,135.03/(1 + .0725). The restaurant owner will report and remit all these withholdings and taxes to the state tax authorities every month.

Required: Design a project to compute the net receipts (monetary), bank deposit, credit card processing fees, net sales, net revenues (net of fees and taxes), and taxes (withholdings and expenses) owed to the state tax authorities. Your visual interface should be neat, clear, and uncluttered.

4-36. **The Virtual Vending Machine.** Imagine that on the third floor of the Business School building there is this Do-It-Yourself Vending Machine. On the top row of its display (screen), it clearly identifies itself as the Almighty Virtual Vending Machine. This sign is shown as a blinking light. (Make it look like a neon sign.) On the left side of this sign, there's a picture (image of your choice). On the right side of the sign, there's a clock that shows the current date and time, and ticks every second. (*Hint:* Use one timer for the blinking light, and another timer for the date/time clock. Set the fonts of the labels to make them look neat.)

In the middle of the screen is a list of the menu choices. It shows six of your favorite dishes with prices; however, this list box is tall enough to show only four items. From this list, a customer can select any number of items to purchase. (*Note:* Use the list box. Set its foreground and background colors such that it will look like a vending machine. Use the Items.Add method to create the menu list. Concatenate a tab character between each item and its price.)

On the left side of this list box, there's a check box for the customer to indicate whether the customer is a student at your college. If so, the box (with proper label) below the check box is enabled so that the customer can enter the student ID; otherwise, this box and its related label are disabled. (*Hint:* Use a group box to contain the check box and the ID field, which should be the user's Social Security number.)

On the right side of the list box, two radio buttons allow the customer to identify the payment method: cash or credit card. If the choice is credit card, the combo box below it (with proper label) is enabled to allow the customer to indicate the type of the credit card: Visa, Diners Club, Master Card, Discover, or American Express; otherwise, the combo box and its label are disabled. (*Hint:* Use another group box to contain the radio buttons and the combo box. Set the default credit card to Visa. The combo box should not accept any other kind of credit cards.)

At the bottom of the screen, there are two buttons. The left one has a text **Buy**; the right one, **Bye**. When the Buy button is clicked, the computer should display the items the customer has chosen, total purchase, and indicate the payment method. If the customer is a student at your college, the customer is entitled to a 20% discount. The following is a sample display (use the message box for this purpose):

```
You have purchased chicken noodle soup, cheesecake, and beer.
The total purchase is $12 with a 20% discount. Net amount is
   $9.60.
You paid with a Visa credit card.
```

If the customer is not a student of your college, the middle line will read as follows:

```
The total purchase is $12 with no discount.
```

The machine will reset to its original state after the message is displayed. When the Bye button is clicked, the program ends. (*Note:* This project is different from the example in the chapter. You can no longer use the list box's SelectedIndexChanged event to keep track of what the customer has bought. Instead, you should figure out what has been selected in the Buy button's Click event. You will need to use a For loop to test what has been selected in the list box.)

5. Decision

Beginning with Chapter 2, "Introduction to Visual Basic Programming," you have seen the need for an If statement (or block) to make a program work properly. It is not an exaggeration to claim that you just cannot write a program without the use of the If block. This is true because however simple a programming problem may be, it is bound to involve some decisions; that is, depending on the condition of one thing, something else will have to be handled differently. For example, suppose your program has a check box, which is used to ascertain whether a patient of a clinic is insured. If so, you want to enable a group box for the user to enter insurance information; otherwise, the group box will be disabled. You will need to use the If block to determine whether the check box is checked or unchecked, and to execute the proper code accordingly.

When you used the If block previously, you basically looked at the syntax. It is now time to take a closer look at its structure and additional details. Sometimes, various alternative actions need to be taken depending on the result obtained from a single expression, a situation commonly referred to as branching. In such a case, coding with the If block structure can become cumbersome. VB provides an alternative structure, the Select Case block, to handle this situation more concisely. This structure is examined in this chapter.

Both the If block and the Select Case block structures involve the use of logical expressions, which are expressions that can be evaluated to a Boolean value, True or False. For you to thoroughly understand both structures, it is best to have a basic understanding of logical expressions first.

After you finish this chapter, you should be able to:

- Understand relational and logical operators and use them in logical expressions.
- Code the If block structure to solve various programming problems that involve decisions.
- Appreciate and design various alternatives to the If block.
- Understand and use the Select Case block structure.

5.1 Logical Expressions

As you may recall, a simple If statement has the following syntax:

```
If Condition Then Statement
```

Where *Condition* represents an expression that can be evaluated to True or False, and *Statement* represents a VB statement such as the assignment statement explained in previous chapters.

The conditional expression is recognized as the logical expression. Two types of operators are used to construct a logical expression: relational operators and logical operators. Take a look at relational operators first.

Relational Operators

Relational operators are used to compare the operands, and decide whether the relation is true. For example, you can use the equal operator to test whether two variables, A and B, are equal by coding:

```
If A = B Then MsgBox("A and B are equal")
```

When A is actually equal to B, the expression is True and the message, **A and B are equal** will be displayed; otherwise, the expression will be False, and the message will not be displayed. The following table provides a list of the relational operators.

Relational Operator	Example	Remark/Explanation
=	A = B	The result is True when A is actually *equal* to B; otherwise, False.
<>	A <> B	The result is True when A is *not equal* to B; otherwise, False.
>	A > B	The result is True when A is *greater than* B; otherwise, False.
>=	A >= B	The result is True when A is *greater than or equal to* B; otherwise, False.
<	A < B	The result is True when A is *less than* B; otherwise, False.
<=	A <= B	The result is True when A is *less than or equal to* B; otherwise, False.

Numeric Comparisons. Typically, relational operators are used to compare numeric data. For example, the following code checks whether the hours worked in a week entered by the user is greater than or equal to 168. If so, a message box is displayed.

```
If Val(txtHoursWorked.Text) >= 168 Then
    MsgBox("Have you ever slept?", MsgBoxStyle.Question)
    txtHoursWorked.Focus
End If
```

In the code, if the number of hours worked is found to be greater than or equal to 168, the message box displays a question mark with a message teasing the user. (Additional details concerning the use of the MsgBox statement are presented in Chapter 6, "Input, Output, and Procedures.") The text box's Focus method is then used to reset the focus on the text box so that the user can correct the number.

Recall that the minimum requirement for a user-friendly program is that the message should provide concise information in a friendly tone. The message displayed in the above code is not really a good example. A better message would be:

```
MsgBox( "The maximum number of hours allowed per week is 60.",
    MsgBoxStyle.Information)
```

Additionally, if the upper limit is 60, the hours worked should be compared with 60, not 168.

Potential Problem with Conversion. When the operands involved are of different data types, a conversion will have to take place before the comparison is done. Occasionally, a conversion can bring about some unexpected result. Consider this example:

```
Const RateS As Single = 0.095
Const RateD As Double = 0.095
Private Sub btnCompare_Click(ByVal Sender As System.Object, ByVal
    e As System.EventArgs) Handles btnCompare.Click
    Dim A As Single, D As Double
    A = RateS * 99895
    D = RateD * 99895
    If A = D Then
        MsgBox("A and D are equal.")
    Else
        MsgBox("A and D are not equal.")
    End If
End Sub
```

You can test the code by placing a button in a new form, naming it **btnCompare**, and setting its Text property to **Compare**; then, type in the preceding code and click the button after you start the project. The message A and D are not equal is displayed when you click the Compare button. Why? If you inspect the computational results, D has a value of 9490.025, but A has 9490.024. A is less accurate because its data type is Single, and is unable to represent the data with the exact precision.

Although the advice is to always use the same data type to avoid data conversion in any operations, including comparisons, you occasionally may be faced with a situation when it is necessary to perform mixed-data type comparisons. In such a case, instead of comparing for equality, you can avoid the problem by allowing a very small difference between the two values. For example, you can work around the problem with the previous example by modifying the code for the comparison as follows:

```
If Math.Abs((A - D) / D) < 0.000001 Then
```

In this statement, you assume that you are willing to accept a relative difference of 10^{-6} as virtually equal; however, this approach will do well only if D is not close to zero. If D is anywhere near zero, you should check the absolute difference, that is, Math.Abs(A – D), instead of the relative difference.

String Comparisons. The familiar relational operators can also be used to compare string data. For example, you can compare to see whether a name entered in a text box such as txtName is the same as the variable CustName by coding the following:

```
If txtName.Text = CustName Then . . .
```

Notice that all the six relational operators can be used in string expressions. The question is how are the string data compared? For example, is **A** greater than **a**? No. The comparison is based on the keycode value of the characters. Because **A** has a keycode value of 65, and **a** has a value of 97, **a** is greater than **A**.

Note that this result is obtained based on VB's default setting for comparison, *Option Compare Binary*. You can change the setting to *Option Compare Text*, under which the comparison is not case sensitive; that is, a and A are considered equal. Similar to other option settings, such as Option Explicit and Option Strict, you can place Option Compare Text at the beginning of a module (code window) to effect text comparison; or, you can set the option in the project's Property Pages. The steps are exactly the same as setting Option Explicit, which is described in Chapter 4, "Data, Operations, and Built-in Functions."

LOOK IT UP

Search the Index tab of the help file for the keyword KeyCode enumeration member. It shows the predefined keycode names of most keys.

Comparing Strings with Unequal Lengths. What happens when two strings are not of the same length? Basically, the comparison is carried out from left to right in pairs, one character after another until an inequality is found or one of the strings runs out of characters; therefore, the string "b" is greater than "abcd" because the first character in the first string, "b" is greater than the first character in the second string. Also, the string "ab" is greater than "a". The latter string runs out of characters before an inequality can be determined.

TIP

When you set Option Compare Text, all string comparisons will no longer be case sensitive. In some cases, you may want to preserve the case sensitive comparison; that is, set Option Compare Binary, but occasionally need to perform character comparison that is not case sensitive. In such cases, you can use the UCase or LCase functions before the comparison is performed. For example, the code:

```
If UCase(txtName.Text) = UCase(CustName)  Then ...
```

will result in True for a name McCord and MCCORD, or any variations of upper- or lowercase spellings on either side of the equality comparison.

Assignment Statements

Notice that in addition to being used in If statements, the logical expression can also be a part of an assignment statement. That is, you can assign the result of a comparison (or logical operation, explained in the following section) to a numeric variable as follows:

```
D = A = B
```

In this statement, the first = represents the assignment operation (move the result of the operation on the right side to the variable on the left), and the second = is the equality comparison operator that compares whether A and B are equal. In this example, assuming D is a Boolean variable, it will have a value True if A is indeed equal to B; otherwise, it will have a value False. If D is of any kind of numeric data type other than Boolean, an implicit data type conversion will be required. The result will be –1 if A is equal to B; otherwise, it will be 0.

Of course, similar to any typical assignment statement, the result of a comparison can also be assigned to a property setting of any VB control that expects True or False. For example, suppose you would like to enable or disable a check box named chkDorm, depending on whether the variable, Score, is greater than or equal to 80. You can code the following:

```
chkDorm.Enabled = Score >= 80
```

This statement will enable the chkDorm check box when Score is greater than or equal to 80; otherwise, the check box will be disabled.

Logical Operators

Logical operators are primarily used in logical expressions to perform operations on Boolean data. For example, the following code tests whether the conditions that the purchase amount (named Purchase) is greater than $10,000, and that the account has no previous balance (named Balance) are both true:

```
Status = Purchase > 10000 And Balance = 0
```

Notice that there is the And logical operator between the two comparisons. The And operator requires both of the comparisons to be True to produce a result of True; that is, the variable, Status, will have a value True if the purchase amount is greater than $10,000 and the previous balance is equal to zero.

The following table provides a list of the logical operators often used in programs.

Logical Operator	Example	Remark/Explanation
Not	Not (A = B)	The Not operator negates the operand on its right; therefore, in the example if A is equal to B, the entire expression will be False.
And	Purchase > 10000 And Balance = 0	When the expressions on both sides of the And operator are True, the result is True; otherwise, False.
AndAlso	Purchase > 10000 AndAlso Balance = 0	The result is the same as the And operator, but the operator works differently. When the first expression is false (Purchase is not greater than 10000), the entire expression is false. The second portion is not evaluated.
Or	Purchase > 10000 Or Balance = 0	When either expression on both sides of the Or operator is True, the result is True; otherwise, False.
OrElse	Purchase > 10000 OrElse Balance = 0	The result is the same as the Or operator, but the operator works differently. When the first expression is True (Purchase is greater than 10000), the entire expression is true. The second portion is not evaluated.
Xor	Purchase >10000 Xor Balance = 0	When exactly one of the two expressions on both sides of the Xor (exclusive Or) operator is True, the result is True; otherwise False. That is, when both sides are True or when both are False, the result is False.

Notice the difference between And and AndAlso and that between Or and OrElse. In general, And and AndAlso should produce the same result; so do Or and OrElse. The differences lie in their ways of obtaining the results and the implication thereof. Both the AndAlso and OrElse operators employ a quick out algorithm. In the case of AndAlso, the result is true only if both operands (expressions) are true, similar to the And operator; however, in the process of evaluation, when the first expression is false, it knows the result must be false and therefore will not evaluate the second expression. By the same token, in the case of OrElse, the result is true if the first expression is true. The operator will not evaluate the second expression. On the other hand, both the And and Or operators evaluate both of their operands regardless of the outcome of the first expression; therefore, AndAlso and OrElse are more efficient. This point is discussed further in Section 5 of this chapter. You may then wonder why there is a need for the And and Or operators. The answer is given at the end of this sub-section.

Uses of Logical Operators. Here are two examples of using the logical operators:

Example 1. A clinic patient who is insured and assigns the right to claim the insurance will be charged a co-payment, while his insurance company will pay for the remaining charges. Assume that the variables, Insured and Assigned, have a value "Y" if the patient is insured and has assigned the insurance claim to the clinic. To compute the charge to each party, you can code the following:

```
If Insured = "Y" AndAlso Assigned = "Y" Then
    ChargeToPatient = CoPay
    ChargeToInsurance = TotalCharge ' ChargeToPatient
End If
```

Example 2. A store will give a 20% discount to a customer who is either a student or has purchased at least $1,000 worth of goods. Assume that the chkStudent check box is used to identify whether a customer is a student, and the Purchase variable represents the amount of purchase. The computation of discount can be coded as follows:

```
If chkStudent.Checked OrElse Purchase >= 1000 Then
    Discount = Purchase * .2
End If
```

The Xor Operator. Although the first five logical operators correspond well to the daily life connotation, the Xor operator may call for some additional explanation. As explained in the table, this operator sets the result to True only if exactly one of its two operands is True. An easy way to understand how it works is to think of it as an inequality operator; that is, when its two Boolean operands are not equal, the result is true. As its name implies, this operator is most useful in handling a situation where the conditions are mutually exclusive. For example, when making a journal entry in accounting records, the user can enter only a debit or credit amount for an account involved in that transaction. Assume the two text boxes, txtDebit and txtCredit, are used for the user to enter the amount, and only positive amounts can be entered. The following code can be used to check that one and only one amount is entered:

```
If Val(txtDebit.Text) > 0 Xor Val(txtCredit.Text) > 0 Then
    ' Only one amount has been entered; OK
Else
    'Either both are zero or both amounts are entered.
    'Display a message
    MsgBox "Please enter exactly one amount for the account."
End If
```

Bit-Wise Operations. The logical operators, except for AndAlso and OrElse, actually operate on a bit-wise basis. When the operands are numeric data of Short, Integer, or Long type rather than the Boolean type, the results can be different from what are expected. Appendix C, "Number Systems and Bit-wise Operations," discusses the additional fine points and some of the uses of these operators in this aspect.

Operational Precedence

Chapter 4 listed the operational precedence of various numeric operators used in an expression. All these rules still hold for all conditional expressions used in an If statement, but now there are two more types of operators: relational and logical operators. How are these new operators ranked? These new operators rank lower in their operational precedence than any of the numeric operators. In addition, the relational operators have precedence over the logical operators, among which Not has the highest precedence followed by And. The following is the list of operators again, ranking from the highest to the lowest in operational precedence:

1. Power (^)
2. Unary negation (-)
3. Multiplication and division (*, /)
4. Integer division (\)
5. Remainder (Mod)
6. Addition and subtraction (+, -)
7. Equal (=)
8. Not equal (<>)
9. Less than, Greater than (<, >)
10. Greater than or equal to (>=)
11. Less than or equal to (<=)
12. Not
13. And, AndAlso
14. Or, OrElse and Xor

Too many rules to remember? If you think so, use parentheses to explicitly express the order of operations. Parentheses help add clarity to what needs to be done first.

Want to verify that the And operator actually takes precedence over the Or operator? Consider the following code:

```
MsgBox(True Or True And False)
```

If Or and And rank equal in precedence, the result should be False; however, if And has the precedence, the result should be True.

Enter the code in the form's click event, run the program, and click the form. What do you see?

Now you have seen how relational and logical operators work. These operators are used to construct logical expressions, which most likely are used in If statements. It is time to take a closer look at the If statement (block).

5.2 The If Block

Recall that a simple If statement has the following syntax:

```
If Condition Then Statement
```

When the expression in the condition portion is True, the statement portion is executed; otherwise, it is ignored. For example, you can code the following:

```
If Score > = 90 Then Grade = "A"
```

This statement says if Score is greater than or equal to 90, an "A" is assigned to Grade. If Score is less than 90, nothing is assigned to Grade because the statement portion is ignored.

Note that the condition can be any logical expression. In addition, recall that an expression can be as simple as a variable, control property, or constant, as explained in Chapter 4; therefore, it is correct to code the following:

```
If rbtMale.Checked Then Sex = "M"
```

This statement says if rbtMale.Checked is True, assign "M" to the variable, Sex. Because the Checked property of the radio button rbtMale is either True or False (which is what the computer is checking for), there is no need to code:

```
If rbtMale.Checked = True Then Sex = "M"
```

Any expression that can be evaluated to a Boolean value (either True or False) can be placed in the condition portion:

```
If CBool(A) Then cboZipCode.SelectedIndex = 0
```

Note that A is assumed to be a numeric variable in this line. The SelectedIndex property of the combo box, cboZipCode, will be set to 0 when A is any value but zero. Recall again that a numeric expression is converted to True when it is nonzero and False when zero.

In practice, you will find that the simple If statement is seldom used because in most cases either more than one statement will have to be executed or a more complex If structure is called for. Actually, this simple If statement can become a point of confusion. Use the simple If block discussed immediately below even if only one statement is to be executed. It offers the flexibility of adding more statements to execute. It is also easier to trace the logic of your program.

Simple If Block

When a condition is true, you may need to execute more than one statement. In such cases, the previous simple structure would be deficient. The following simple If block will serve the purpose better:

```
If Condition Then
    Statements to be executed
End If
```

Notice that the first line of the block starts with an If, and ends with the keyword Then. There should be no other expression or statement (except for comments) after Then; otherwise, the line will be interpreted as a simple If statement explained previously. Also notice that the block ends with an "End If" statement. All statements within these two lines will be executed when the condition in the If line is True. Consider the following code in an event procedure:

```
Private Sub chkSort_Click(ByVal Sender As System.Object, ByVal e
    As System.EventArgs) Handles chkSort.Click
    If chkSort.Checked Then
        cboSortField1.Enabled = True
        cboSortField2.Enabled = True
    End If
End Sub
```

The If statement checks to see whether the chkSort check box is checked. If so, both the combo boxes containing sort field 1 and sort field 2 are enabled. (*Note:* To test the preceding code, set the Enabled property of the two combo boxes to False at design time.)

What happens to the two combo boxes in the previous example if the check box is clicked off? Nothing inside the If block will be executed. Both can be either enabled or disabled before the event procedure is triggered; however, once enabled, no code inside the procedure will disable the two combo boxes.

What if you really mean to disable the two combo boxes when the check box is clicked off? Given what you have learned in this chapter so far, one way to solve this is to code the procedure as follows:

```
Private Sub chkSort_Click(ByVal Sender As System.Object, ByVal e
    As System.EventArgs) Handles chkSort.Click
    cboSortField1.Enabled = False
    cboSortField2.Enabled = False
    If chkSort.Checked Then
        cboSortField1.Enabled = True
        cboSortField2.Enabled = True
    End If
End Sub
```

In the code, the two combo boxes will always be disabled first (regardless of the check state of the check box) and then enabled if the check box is found checked.

The If. . . Then. . . Else. . . End If Block

Although the previous code gives the correct result, you probably feel weird about it. Apparently, it is not completely efficient because it always disables the combo boxes even when they will be enabled immediately inside the If block. Is there an If block structure that allows the execution of a group of statements when a condition is True, and another group when the condition is False? Yes, there is—it was covered in Chapter 2. The syntax structure appears as follows:

```
If Condition Then
    Statements to be executed when condition is True
Else
    Statements to be executed when condition is False
End If
```

With this structure, we can code the preceding example as follows:

```
Private Sub chkSort_Click(ByVal Sender As System.Object, ByVal e
    As System.EventArgs) Handles chkSort.Click
    If chkSort.Checked =vbChecked Then
        cboSortField1.Enabled = True
        cboSortField2.Enabled = True
    Else
        cboSortField1.Enabled = False
        cboSortField2.Enabled = False
    End If
End Sub
```

This code will not only produce correct results but literally do what you expect it to, which is enable the combo boxes only when the check box is clicked on and disable them only when the check box is clicked off.

Beware of the code structure. Some VB beginner may fail to see the *syntax error* in the following structure:

```
If A > B Then Console.WriteLine(A)
Else Console.WriteLine(B)    X
End If
```

When an If statement ends with an executable statement (as in the first line), VB considers the If block complete; therefore, the Else and End If statements below will have no context. *The correct structure* should be:

```
If A > B Then
    Console.WriteLine(A)
Else
    Console.WriteLine(B)
End If
```

Leaving One Side Out. Note that with this syntax structure, it is okay to omit statements from either the True or False side of the block. For example, the following code should cause no syntax problem:

```
Private Sub chkCitizen_Click(ByVal Sender As System.Object, ByVal
    e As System.EventArgs) Handles chkCitizen.Click
    If chkCitizen.Checked Then
        'Respondent is a citizen. No problem.
    Else
        'Respondent is not a citizen. Reject the service.
        MsgBox("You are not qualified to serve as a Juror.")
    End If
End Sub
```

This event procedure is triggered when the user clicks the check box that asks whether the respondent is a citizen. As you can imagine, the check box is used in a data entry screen for the jury selection questionnaire. If the box is checked off, the qualification message is displayed. In this example, a statement is provided only on the False side of the block. You may wonder why not directly test whether the check box is unchecked as follows:

```
If chkCitizen.Checked = False Then
    'Respondent is not a citizen. Reject the service.
    MsgBox("You are not qualified to serve as a Juror.")
End If
```

Both blocks of preceding code should work properly. The second block appears to be more concise; however, some companies have coding standards that require all conditions in the If statement be expressed in affirmation. They maintain that such a coding standard makes the code easier to review because of code logic uniformity.

It is also perfectly acceptable to provide code for only the True side of the If block as illustrated in the following code:

```
Private Sub txtName_Validating(ByVal sender As System.Object, _
    ByVal e As System.ComponentModel.CancelEventArgs) Handles
    txtName.Validating
      If Len(Trim(txtName.Text)) = 0 Then
          MsgBox("Please enter name before proceeding further.")
          e.Cancel = True 'Reset focus on txtName
      Else
      End If
End Sub
```

This event procedure is invoked when the user moves away from a text box named txtName. The If statement checks whether the VB control is blank. If so, an error message is displayed. In addition, the Cancel property of the event argument object e is set to True, which in effect resets the focus back on txtName. As mentioned in Chapter 3, "User Interface Design: Visual Basic Controls and Events," the Validating event is triggered when the user leaves the control and before the focus is set on the next control. The event is used to perform field-level data validation, which is discussed more thoroughly in Chapter 10, "Special Topics in Data Entry."

Note that the previous If block can actually do without the Else line. You can think of the Else statement as being there as a reminder that no statement has been coded on the False side.

The If...Then...ElseIf...Then...Else...End If Block

Many times, a decision can be much more complicated than that in the previous example; that is, several conditions, rather than just the either or situation, will determine the conclusion. For example, a teacher may assign an A to any score greater than or equal to 90, a B if the score is greater than or equal to 80, and a C to all other scores. Is there an If block that can handle this situation conveniently? Yes! The syntax appears as follows:

```
If Condition1 Then
    Statements to be executed when condition1 is True
ElseIf Condition2 Then
    Statements to be executed when condition2 is True
ElseIf Condition3 Then
    Statements to be executed when condition3 is True
Else
    Statements to be executed when none of the above
        conditions are True
End If
```

In this structure, you can have as many ElseIf statements as desired following the If statement. You can then code a catch all Else statement after all of the ElseIf statements. It is an error to place an ElseIf after an Else statement. Again, the entire block is closed with an End If statement.

When the block is executed, the conditions in the If block are tested one after another top down (condition1, condition2, and so on) until one condition is true. At that point, those statements under that condition are executed, and the remainder of the If block is skipped. If none of the conditions are true, the statements in the Else portion (if any) are executed.

Using this structure, the teacher's grade assignment problem can be coded as follows:

```
If Score >= 90 Then
    Grade = "A"
ElseIf Score >= 80 Then
    Grade = "B"
Else
    Grade = "C"
End If
```

The code will first check whether Score is greater than or equal to 90. If so, A is assigned to Grade and the remainder of the If block is ignored. If the first condition is not true, the ElseIf statement checks to see whether Score is greater than or equal to 80. If so, B is assigned to Grade and the remaining part of the If block is ignored. On the other hand, if the condition in the ElseIf statement is not true, the statement in the Else block will be executed; that is, C is assigned to Grade.

Beware! The following code will not obtain the desired results:

```
If Score < 80 Then
    Grade = "C"
ElseIf Score >= 80 Then   X
    Grade = "B"
ElseIf Score >= 90 Then
    Grade = "A"
    End If
```

Why? If the score is less than 80, a C is assigned; otherwise, the ElseIf Score >= 80 will be always true, resulting in a B being assigned. There will be no A even if the score is 100. When you are coding this If structure, always test the most restrictive condition first.

Varying the Criteria. Of course, this structure can be used to handle more complex situations. Consider this investment decision example. An independent oil exploration company will invest in an oil exploration project if a pretest indicates that the probability of finding oil is at least 50%; otherwise, the net present value of the project will have to be greater than $1 million. If not, the company will invest only if the project will cost less than $100,000. The decision rule can be depicted as in Figure 5.1.

Note that unlike the previous example, at each stage of the decision, a different factor is involved in this problem. This, however, poses no problem to this If structure. Assume Invest is a Boolean variable indicating whether to invest. Also, the variables, Probability, NPV, and Cost, have been assigned proper values. One way to solve the problem is to code the following:

```
If Probability >= .5 Then
    Invest = True 'Invest when the probability of success is high
ElseIf NPV >= 1000000 Then
    Invest = True 'Invest when the expected return is high
ElseIf Cost <= 100000 Then
    Invest = True 'Invest when the cost is low
Else
    Invest = False ' don't invest if none of the above is true
End If
```

A Key Validation Procedure: Another Example. Similar to the previous "If Then Else" block, any part of the "If Then ElseIf Then" structure may leave out statements without causing a syntax problem. To illustrate, consider a data-entry key validation routine. You would like to be sure that keys entered into a text box named txtNumber are numbers. If not, you want to display an error message and suppress the key. How do you code this?

As you may recall, when the user presses a key, the KeyPress event is triggered and the KeyChar of the key is also passed as one of the event arguments to this event procedure. In coding this event, you should inspect the key to see if it is numeric.

Be aware that not all the keys that are nonnumeric are bad keys for this data validation purpose. The control keys, such as the Enter key and the Backspace key, are also captured in the

Figure 5.1

Decision rules for the investment decision

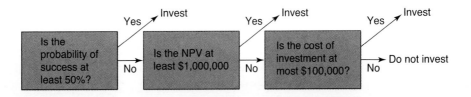

KeyPress event. All these control keys have a keycode value lower than 32 (the keycode value of the spacebar, a constant named Keys.Space).

You should also display an error message, and suppress the key if it does not belong to either of the previous two groups of keys.

How do you check for a numeric key? The Keys enumeration provides constant names for all keys. The keycode values of the keys 0 and 9 are Keys.D0 (48) and Keys.D9 (57), respectively. You can compare the keycode value of the key pressed to see if it is in this range. One way to implement the key validation procedure is as follows:

```
Private Sub txtNumber_KeyPress(ByVal sender As System.Object,
   ByVal e As System.Windows.Forms.KeyPressEventArgs) Handles
   txtNumber.KeyPress
     Dim KeyAscii As Integer
     KeyAscii = AscW(e.KeyChar) 'Convert the character to a numeric
       keycode
     If KeyAscii < Keys.Space Then
        ' These are control keys, ignore.
     ElseIf KeyAscii >= Keys.D0 AndAlso KeyAscii <= Keys.D9 Then
        ' These are numeric keys, ignore.
     Else
        ' These are neither control keys nor numeric keys.
        ' Display an error message
        MsgBox("Please enter numeric keys only.")
        e.Handled = True ' Suppress the key
     End If
End Sub
```

In this code example, no statement appears in either the If or the ElseIf portion of the If block; however, the code works exactly the way you want it to. The key pressed by the user (KeyChar) is first converted to an integer variable (KeyAscii) using the AscW function, which gives the numeric value of a key in unicode. The KeyAscii value is first compared with Keys.Space (32). If the value is less than 32, the key is a control key; otherwise (the ElseIf block), the value is checked to see whether it is within the range of numeric keys. If not (the Else block), an error message is displayed. In addition, the event's Handled argument is assigned a value of True. Assigning True to this argument tells the system that the key has been handled properly and not to process it further. This, in effect, suppresses the key, and no key will appear in the text box.

TIP

Do you want to know the keycode values of the numeric keys? Try the following code in the form click event:

```
Dim I As Integer
For I = Asc("0") To Asc("9")
    MsgBox(Chr(I) & " " & I)
Next I
```

You can also find the keycode value of a key name in your code by resting the mouse pointer on the key name. For example, if you have Keys.D0 in your code, just rest the mouse pointer on D0. You should see the IntelliSense shows a declared constant value of 48.

Nesting If Blocks

Any of the If blocks can be further nested to handle complex conditions. As an illustration, assume a teacher's grading system requires that a student must have not only a score of 90 or better, but also a perfect attendance to earn an A; otherwise, a B is given. A student with a score in the range of 80 to 89 must have at least a 90% attendance record to earn a B. All other students will get a C. These decision rules are depicted in the flowchart in Figure 5.2.

Figure 5.2

Flowchart of grade assignment

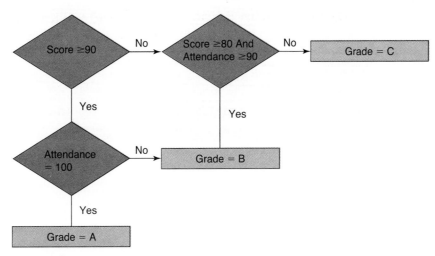

Figure 5.3

Grade assignment

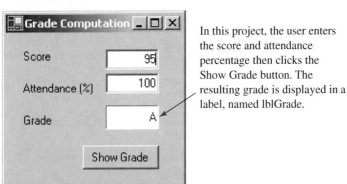

In this project, the user enters the score and attendance percentage then clicks the Show Grade button. The resulting grade is displayed in a label, named lblGrade.

The two text boxes in the user interface shown in Figure 5.3 are used to enter both the score (txtScore) and the attendance percentage (txtAttendance). When the user clicks on the Show Grade button (btnGrade), the grade is displayed in the label named lblGrade. The following code provides a solution:

```
Private Sub btnGrade_Click(ByVal Sender As System.Object, ByVal e
    As System.EventArgs) Handles btnGrade.Click
    Dim Score As Integer
    Dim Attendance As Integer
    Dim Grade As String
    Score = Val(txtScore.Text)
    Attendance = Val(txtAttendance.Text)
    If Score >= 90 Then
        If Attendance = 100 Then
            Grade = "A"
        Else
            Grade = "B"
        End If
    ElseIf Score >= 80 AndAlso Attendance >= 90 Then
        Grade = "B"
    Else
        Grade = "C"
    End If
    lblGrade.Text = Grade
End Sub
```

In the preceding code, the score and attendance percentage are obtained from the two text boxes, txtScore and txtAttendance, respectively. The score is first compared with 90. If it is greater or equal to 90, the second-level If statement checks whether the attendance percentage is equal to 100. If so, an A grade is assigned; otherwise, a B grade is assigned. The ElseIf statement checks whether the score is greater than or equal to 80 and the attendance is at least 90. If so, a B grade is assigned; otherwise, a C grade is assigned. The resulting grade is displayed in a label, named lblGrade.

Will This Work? You may wonder why not just code as follows to solve the previous problem:

```
If Score>=90 AndAlso Attendance = 100 Then
    Grade = "A"
ElseIf Score >= 80 AndAlso Attendance >= 90 Then        ?
    Grade = "B"
Else
    Grade = "C"
End If
lblGrade.Text = Grade
```

This would appear much simpler. But *the modified code would not work correctly.* The initial problem states that if a student has a score of at least 90 as well as perfect attendance, they will earn an A. Without perfect attendance, they will earn a B. The original solution produces the correct result. The modified code will assign a C to a student who has a score of 100 but with an 80% attendance! The 80% attendance will fail not only the If test, but also the ElseIf test, thus falling into the catch all Else block for an assignment of a grade C.

Rule for Nesting. When If blocks are nested, one rule to keep in mind is that one block should enclose the other, constituting a relationship of the inner and outer blocks. It is not logical (and, therefore, not allowed) to intertwine any If blocks. Figure 5.4 shows both the acceptable and unacceptable nesting blocks.

If Blocks: A Summary of Syntax. In terms of syntax, the If block can be structured several ways. The following table provides a summary.

Figure 5.4

Legitimate and illegitimate nesting of If blocks

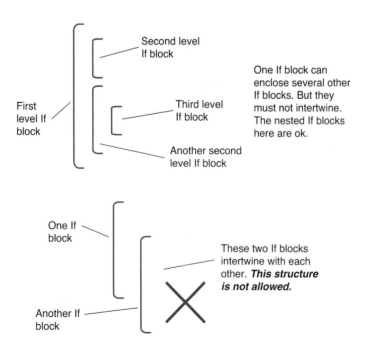

Syntax Structure	Example	Remark
If *condition* Then *statement*	If rbtMale.Checked Then Sex = "M"	This is not a preferred coding structure.

If *Condition* Then
    Statement(s)
End If
	If Len(txtName.Text) = 0 Then
	    MsgBox("Must have a name")
	    e.Cancel = True
	End If
		Use this structure to handle situations in which one or more statements must be executed when a certain condition is True, but no action is required when the condition is False.

If *Condition* Then
    Statements
Else
    Statements
End If
	If chkPrintAll.Checked Then
	    lstZipCode.Enabled = False
	Else
	    lstZipCode.Enabled = True
	End If
		Use this structure to handle situations in which a group of statements need to be executed when the condition is True; otherwise, another group of statements are to be executed.

If *Condition1* Then
    Statement group 1
ElseIf *Condition2* Then
    Statement group 2
ElseIf *Condition3* Then
    Statement group 3
Else
    Statement group 4
End If
	If rbtBreakfast.Checked Then
	    Charge = 4.50
	ElseIf rbtLunch.Checked Then
	    Charge = 7.50
	ElseIf rbtDinner.Checked Then
	    Charge = 10. 50
	Else
	    Charge = 0
	End If
		Use this structure when a series of mutually exclusive conditions will require different actions, or cause different results.

Additional Notes on Coding the If Block

Because most programming problems involve many decisions, If blocks are used extensively in programs. It is desirable to consider several issues before leaving this topic.

Indenting. When If blocks are used, the programming logic becomes less than straightforward because some statements may or may not be executed based on the result of the If expression. Keeping track of all possible results can become challenging. Therefore, it is important to provide as much visual aid as possible in the code to facilitate future review and current logic development/tracing.

One important aspect of this is to indent the code properly. Fortunately, the IDE editor indents your code automatically. Basically, all statements in each portion of the If block are indented. In a nested block, the inside If block skeleton (If, ElseIf, Else, and End If) is indented just like the inside statements. In addition, the statements inside the inner If block are further indented. Such a layout clearly indicates the level of logical nesting. (Note that the compiler will even catch your failure to include a matching End If statement.) After completing the coding of a complex structure of nested If block, take advantage of this extra help by the editor and exam the structure carefully for hints about proper placement of your code block.

Use of Comments. The importance of using comments (remarks) in programs cannot be overemphasized. Comments can be especially helpful to people who review code that contains many If statements. In many cases, the meaning of the expressions (conditions) in the If statement is not self-explanatory. Comments help you and the reviewer follow the logic of the code much more easily. Consider the following statement:

```
If KeyAscii < Keys.Space Then
```

Without any comments with it, it may take a while for a beginner to figure out what the If statement is attempting to accomplish. Adding a remark similar to the following line can make it much easier for anybody who reads the code:

```
' These are control keys and can be ignored
```

Syntax and Semantic. Beware that you can be syntactically correct, but end up with a wrong result. Consider the following code:

```
If 21 <= Age <= 35 Then
    MsgBox("You are a young adult")
End If
```

?

The code is meant to test whether the variable, Age is in the range of 21 to 35; however, if you test the code, you will find that the message box always displays "You are a young adult" even when Age is 100! Why? In the execution, 21 is first compared with Age to see whether the relation <= is True, yielding an implicit numeric value of either –1 (for True) or zero (for False). When this result is compared with 35, it is always less than 35, so the result is always True.

Note that you can obtain the above result only if you turn off Option Strict (the default). If you set Option Strict On, the compiler will tell you that the implicit conversion from Boolean (result of 21 <= Age) to the data type of 35 (say, Integer) is not allowed. Another good reason to set Option Strict On, isn't it?

TIP

The correct code to check the age range of 21 and 35 is:

```
If  21 <= Age AndAlso Age <= 35 Then
```

Efficiency. Another issue concerning the use of the If block relates to the efficiency (speed of execution) versus the clarity of code. Consider this line of code (used in some countries to determine whether a person is a candidate for military draft):

```
If Sex = "M" And Age >= 16 Then
```

Although the line of code is clear, it is not as efficient as the following code:

```
If Sex = "M" AndAlso Age >= 16 Then
```

In the first code sample, three operations are always involved in the expression: Sex is compared with "M," Age is compared with 16, and an And operation is performed on the results from the two comparisons. On the other hand, in the second code sample, when the first expression is false (Sex is not equal to "M"), the AndAlso operator will not evaluate the second expression but conclude that the result is false; therefore, this operator is more efficient than the And operator. Note that the use of the AndAlso operator has the same effect as the following code structure:

```
If Sex = "M" Then
    If Age >= 16 Then
```

As you can see, the code line using the AndAlso operator appears to be simpler and should be the preferred way of coding.

Note also the order of the expressions in the If condition can affect the efficiency. The probability of a person being a male is approximately 50%, but the probability of a person being 16 or older is much higher. With the current code, the chance that the second expression is tested is only one half. If the order of the expressions is reversed, however, the chance that Age >= 16 is true is much higher, resulting in more need to evaluate the second expression (Sex = "M") before a conclusion can be reached. The current code is more efficient than if you reverse the order of the two expressions.

Similarly, the OrElse operator is more efficient than the Or operator in evaluating the condition in the If statement. Because the OrElse operator stops evaluating the second expression as soon as it finds first expression in the condition is true, you should place those expressions with higher probability of being true first. For example, suppose you are writing a program to diagnose a disease that always causes abnormal body temperature, mostly fever but occasionally below normal temperature. Your code will be more efficient if you write:

```
If Temperature > 100 OrElse Temperature < 97
```

Code Clarity and Alternatives. As already mentioned, when the code involves too many If blocks (especially nested ones), it can become challenging to trace the logic. The effects of the code can become much harder to figure out. Are there any alternatives? Yes, the possibilities include the following:

- *Use of the IIf (immediate If) function*—The IIf function has the syntax:

```
IIf(Condition, expression 1, expression 2)
```

This function returns the value of expression 1 when the condition is evaluated to be True; otherwise, it returns the value of expression 2. For example, in the following statement:

```
A = IIf(X > 0, Y, Z)
```

A will have a value Y when X > 0; otherwise, it will have a value of Z.

The IIf function is known to be slow. All three arguments passed to the functions are evaluated before a value is returned, so, it may not truly be a good alternative to the If block.

- *Computations*—With careful analysis, many of the apparent needs for the If block can be converted into computational formulas. Consider the following code that you used in one of the previous illustrations.

```
Private Sub chkSort_Click(ByVal Sender As System.Object,
    ByVal e As System.EventArgs) Handles chkSort.Click
    If chkSort.Checked Then
        cboSortField1.Enabled = True
        cboSortField2.Enabled = True
    Else
        cboSortField1.Enabled = False
        cboSortField2.Enabled = False
    End If
End Sub
```

The procedure enables or disables the cboSortField1 and cboSortField2 combo boxes, depending on whether the chkSort check box is checked. An alternative way to code the procedure is given as follows:

```
Private Sub chkSort_Click(ByVal Sender As System.Object,
    ByVal e As System.EventArgs) Handles chkSort.Click
    cboSortField1.Enabled = chkSort.Checked
    cboSortField2.Enabled = chkSort.Checked
End Sub
```

In the code, both combo boxes' Enabled properties are assigned the value of chkSort's Checked property. Recall that the value of this property is True when the check box is checked on; and False when the check box is checked off. When the check box is checked (unchecked), both combo boxes' Enabled properties will be set to True (false), causing the two combo boxes to be enabled (disabled). (Again, to test the code, set the Enabled property of the two combo boxes to False at design time.)

As another example, assume that a bookstore sells only three book titles. A customer can buy only one copy of each book, but can buy any combination of the three books. The chkBook1, chkBook2, and chkBook3 check boxes are used to represent whether the customer wants each of the books. Their prices are represented by the variables Price1, Price2, and Price3, respectively. When the customer is ready to check out, the cashier clicks on the check boxes and the button btnCompute to compute the total pur-

Figure 5.5

Visual interface for the
Only-Three bookstore

This bookstore sells only three books. After the customer makes
selections, the cashier clicks the Compute button to get the total
purchase. The "text box" is actually a label, named lblTotal. You
can make it appear this way by setting its BackColor to white and
BorderStyle to Fixed3D.

chase. The result is displayed in the label lblTotal. The visual interface appears as in
Figure 5.5.

One possible solution to this problem is as follows:

```
Private Sub btnCompute_click(ByVal Sender As System.Object,
  ByVal e As System.EventArgs) Handles btnCompute.Click
    Dim Total as Single
    Total = 0
    If chkBook1.Checked Then
        Total = Price1
    End If
    If chkBook2.Checked Then
        Total = Total + Price2
    End If
    If chkBook3.Checked Then
        Total = Total + Price3
    End If
    lblTotal.Text = Format(Total, "Standard")
End Sub
```

Because the Checked property is True when it is checked and False when it is
unchecked, the preceding code can be converted into a computational formula. The
modified code appears as follows:

```
Private Sub btnCompute_Click(ByVal Sender As System.Object,
  ByVal e As System.EventArgs) Handles btnCompute.Click
    Dim Total As Single
    Total = Math.Abs(CSng(chkBook1.Checked)) * Price1 + _
    Math.Abs(CSng(chkBook2.Checked)) * Price2 + _
    Math.Abs(CSng(chkBook3.Checked)) * Price3
    lblTotal.Text = Format(Total, "Standard")
End Sub
```

How does the code work? Consider the first book. If it's check box is checked,
chkBook1.Checked will be True, which when converted to Single is –1. The Math.Abs
method will give 1 as a result. The following expression

```
Math.Abs(CSng(chkBook1.Checked)) * Price1
```

will result in a value of Price1. On the other hand, if the check box is off, the result will
be zero. The same is true for the expressions for the other two books. Adding the results
of the three expressions should yield the correct total. The next line of code uses the
Format function to format the value into a string, which is then displayed in (assigned to)
the lblTotal label . As in the enabling/disabling combo boxes example, the computational
alternative has much shorter code, and the If condition is embedded in the formula.

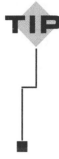

The following code will also produce the correct result for this example, and is more efficient because the Math.Abs method is called only once.

```
Dim Total As Single
Total = CSng(chkBook1.Checked) * Price1 +
  CSng(chkBook2.Checked) * Price2 _
+ CSng(chkBook3.Checked) * Price3 _
Total = Math.Abs(Total)
lblTotal.Text = Format(Total, "Standard")
```

In the previous code, focus was placed on computing the total and no attention was paid to how Price1, Price2, and Price3 obtained their values. They should be declared as class level variables, and can be initialized in the Form Load event. So that you can focus on the current discussion, a simple solution is given here. A better solution is given in exercise 5-29.

```
Dim Price1 As Single
Dim Price2 As Single
Dim Price3 As Single
Private Sub Form1_Load(ByVal sender As System.Object, ByVal
  e As System.EventArgs) Handles MyBase.Load
    Price1 = 35
    Price2 = 45
    Price3 = 60
End Sub
```

Return to the discussion of computing the total. Although the alternative appears to be more concise, you must not get carried away with this approach. The meaning of the code may not be as apparent or intuitive as the If block. Sometimes, this alternative approach may not produce the correct result or execute efficiently. When you decide to code a problem using computational formulas in place of the If block, be sure that you test the code thoroughly. In addition, provide comments in the code to explain how the formula works so that the formula will not become a mystery when you review it in the future.

- *Use of the Select Case Block*—If the conditions in the "If. . . ElseIf" block depend on the different results of the same expression, one good alternative to the If block is the Select Case Block. This is explained in the next section.

5.3 The Select Case Block

As explained in Section 5.2, an alternative to the If block is the Select Case block, which is particularly useful when the decision depends on the result of one single expression. Consider the previous example of assigning a grade based strictly on the student's score. The grade will be A, B, or C if the score is at least 90, 80, or below 80, respectively. This problem can be conveniently solved by the use of the Select Case block.

Syntax Structure

The Select Case block has the following syntax structure:

```
Select Case Expression
  Case Criterion 1

      Statements (group1) to be executed when criterion 1 matches the result of expression
```

```
Case Criterion 2
```

Statements (group 2) to be executed when criterion 2 matches the result of expression

.
.

```
Case Criterion n
```

Statements (group n) to be executed when criterion n matches the result of expression

```
Case Else
```

Statements (group n+1) to be executed when none of the above criteria match the result of expression

```
End Select
```

Where the expression can be any kind, such as numeric, string, or logical, and the criteria should have the same type as the expression. Each criterion can consist of a list of single values and ranges.

As an illustration, using the Select Case block, the grading problem discussed in the preceding section can be coded as follows:

```
Select Case Score
    Case Is >= 90
        Grade = "A"
    Case 80 To 90
        Grade = "B"
    Case Else
        Grade = "C"
End Select
```

As you can see from the illustration, Score is the expression whose value will be evaluated against the criteria stated in the Cases. The first Case (Is >= 90) has an open range; that is, any Score value greater or equal to 90 will belong to this Case, and will result in the statement Grade = "A" being executed. The second Case has a closed range (where both ends are specified), and is expressed with the keyword To. A score in the range of 80 to 90 will result in the statement Grade = "B" being executed. Finally, if none of the cases are true, the statement(s) in the catch all Case Else will be executed.

TIP

When specifying the range in the Case statement, always specify the lower value first; otherwise, the criterion will never be True. In checking the range, the computer assumes the first number is the lower end of the range, and the second value is the higher end. That is, the following Case will never be True:

```
Case 90 To 80   X
```

Mutual Exclusiveness of Cases. Notice that the cases are mutually exclusive; that is, only one of the case blocks will be executed. The testing of cases starts from the top and proceeds down. As soon as a criterion (Case) is found true, no more comparisons will be performed. In the previous example, when a score is 90, "A" will be assigned to Grade. The second case will never be tested (even though 90 is also a value in the second case), resulting in a correct assignment decision.

Why not just code the second case "Case 80 to 89"? This will work correctly as long as Score is an integer (Long, Integer or Short) variable; however, if Score is a variable that can take on a fractional value, a score of 89.99 will not belong to this case and will become a "Case Else".

Draw a text box on a new form. Enter the following code in the form's click event:

```
Select Case Val(TextBox1.Text)
    Case 0 To 60 'First message
        MsgBox("The number is in the range of 0 and 60.")
    Case 50 To 100 'Second message
        MsgBox("The number is in the range of 50 and 100.")
End Select
```

Run the program; then enter a number in the range of 50 and 60. You will always see the first message displayed. The second message is displayed only when you enter a value greater than 60. Do you see how the block works when the criteria in the Case statements are not mutually exclusive?

Beware of the logic error like the following:

```
Select Case Age
    Case Is >= 5
        Admission = Half
    Case Is>= 12
        Admission = One                X
    Case Else
        Admission = 0
End Select
```

You will see that all admissions will be either zero or half priced when the routine runs. Why? Consider the age of 20. It is greater than 5, so the statement Admission = Half will be executed even though the age is greater than 12. To correct the error, place Case Age Is >= 12 as the first criterion. Always place the most restrictive criterion as the first case when coding this structure.

Detailed Syntax Rules. When coding the criteria, observe the following syntax rules:

- To specify a value to test for equality, give the value. For example, "Case 80" would mean to compare whether the expression in the Select Case statement (the expression, such as Score) is equal to 80.

- To specify several values to test for equality, separate the values in the list with commas. For example, "Case 80, 81, 85" would mean to compare whether the expression is equal to 80, 81, or 85.

- To specify a closed range, insert the keyword To between the lower- and upper-end values. For example, "Case 80 To 90" would mean to test whether the expression is within the range of 80 to 90 (inclusive). Note that the first value must be less than or equal to the second value.

- To specify an open range, use the keyword Is. For example, "Case Is < 0" would mean to test whether the expression is negative.

You can combine all these situations in one Case statement by separating the criteria with commas. For example, you can code the following:

```
Case 50, 80 To 90, Is < 0
```

Can you see what's wrong with the following code?

```
Select Case Age
Case Age >= 12
    'Statements            X
Case Age >= 5
    'Statements
Case Else
    'Statements
End Select
```

The variable Age should be removed from each Case statement. As coded, the first case statement will compare Age with 12 first, resulting in a value of either True or False before this value is compared with Age (the expression specified in the Select Case statement). You will see that the statements in the Case Else block always get executed. If you have set Option Strict On, you will be informed of the conversion restriction that should alert you to the problem. Always set Option Strict On to avoid unexpected problems.

Variations in the Case Structure. Similar to the If block, you can omit statements from any of the cases. For example, in the preceding section, you used the If block to check for numeric keys for a txtNumber text box. That routine can be replaced by the use of the Select Case block as follows:

```
Private Sub txtNumber_KeyPress(ByVal sender As System.Object,
   ByVal e As System.Windows.Forms.KeyPressEventArgs) Handles
   txtNumber.KeyPress
   Dim KeyAscii As Integer
   KeyAscii = AscW(e.KeyChar)
   Select Case KeyAscii
      Case Is < Keys.Space
         ' These are control keys; ignore
      Case Keys.D0 To Keys.D9
         'These are numeric keys; ignore
      Case Else
         ' These are neither control keys nor numeric keys;
         ' display an error message
         MsgBox("Numeric key only, please.")
         e.Handled = True 'Suppress the key
   End Select
End Sub
```

This code allows only numeric keys. What if you also expect a decimal point to be entered? The keycode value for period (decimal point) is 46. (There is no predefined name for this key.) To accommodate this, you can insert the following line:

```
Case 46
```

Without any statement following this Case, no message will be displayed, similar to the previous two Cases.

Because all three cases are handled in the same way (do nothing), you could combine the three cases together:

```
Select Case KeyAscii
Case Is < Keys.Space, Keys.D0 To Keys.D9, 46
' Legitimate keys; do nothing
Case Else
' Unexpected keys; display a message
   MsgBox("Numeric key only, please.")
   e.Handled = True 'suppress the key
End Select
```

Note that in the first Case statement, commas are used to separate the three criteria. It is interesting to point out that this Case provides a good example of a list of all types of criteria allowed by the syntax: open-ended range, closed range, and single value. Of course, you can add more to the list. For example, if you also expect negative numbers, you can also include 45 (key code for -) in the Case line:

```
Case Is < Keys.Space, Keys.D0 ToKeys.D9, 45, 46
```

Note that when coding individual values in the list, their order does not really matter; however, for convenience and clarity, you should list them in the order that gives you the clearest meaning.

Dealing with Constants. The use of the numeric values 45 and 46 in the previous code should cause you to be concerned about code clarity. When you come back to review the code after a while, you may not know what these two values represent. One possible solution is to use the Asc function. Recall that this function gives the ASCII value of a key. In place of 45 and 46, you can code the following:

```
Case Is < Keys.Space, Keys.D0 To Keys.D9, Asc("-"), Asc(".")
```

The code is clearer; however, it will execute a bit slower because the Asc function will need to be called to give the ASCII values of the two keys. Another alternative is to declare two constants for the two keys and then use them wherever they are needed. For example, you can declare the following:

```
Const KeyMinus As Integer = 45
Const KeyPeriod As Integer = 46
```

Then code the Case statement as follows:

```
Case Is < Keys.Space, Keys.D0 To Keys.D9, KeyMinus, KeyPeriod
```

This approach takes a bit more code, but the code is both efficient and clear.

Enter "Case < Keys.Space" in the code window for the previous example; then move the cursor to another line. You will see the line you have just entered is changed to "Case Is < Keys.Space". The IDE does more than you expect. This also indicates that the IDE checks the syntax of each line you enter as soon as you move away from it.

Nesting Select Case Blocks

You can nest Select Case blocks in the same way as the If blocks are nested. That is, within each Case of a Select Case block, you can code another Select Case block. The nesting can practically go as deep as you would like. Beware of the problem with clarity, though. As in the case of the If blocks, you should never intertwine a Select Case block with another.

An Example. As an illustration of nesting the Select Case blocks, assume that a university charges tuition based on the student's residence status and the number of hours taken, as shown in the following table.

Hours Taken	In State	Out of State	International
1–5	850	1,250	1,700
6–8	1,000	1,500	2,000
9–11	1,300	2,000	2,700
12–over	1,500	2,300	3,200

You are to design a project to determine the student's tuition when the student enrolls. How should you proceed?

Figure 5.6

Visual Interface for
Tuition Calculation

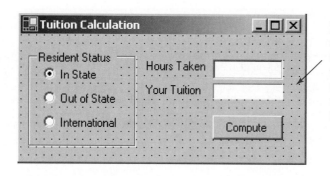

In this application, the user
selects the residence status,
enters the number of hours
taken, and then clicks the
Compute button. The
tuition is displayed in the
label named lblTuition.

As usual, you will need to design the visual interface first. The student must declare a residence status among the three categories. These categories represent mutually exclusive alternatives that will most likely remain unchanged for a long while, so radio buttons will be a good
choice. The number of hours taken can be entered into a text box. The visual design can appear
as in Figure 5.6.

A list of the properties of the VB controls used in code is given in the following table.

Control	Property	Setting	Remark
Radio button	Text	In State	
	Name	rbtInState	
	Checked	True	As the default option
Radio button	Text	Out Of State	
	Name	rbtOutOfState	
Radio button	Text	International	
	Name	rbtInternational	
Text box	Name	txtHoursTaken	To enter hours taken
Label	Name	lblTuition	To display tuition
	BackColor	White	Used so the label will look like a text box
	BorderStyle	Fixed3D	
Button	Text	Compute	To initiate tuition computation
	Name	btnCompute	

Notice that the Checked property of the rbtInState radio button is set to True so that it can be
used as the default status. When the user clicks the Compute button, your program will show the
result in the lblTuition label.

How can your program determine a student's tuition? There are several different ways to handle this. One possibility is to use the nested Select Case blocks. As you can see from the previous
table, two factors jointly determine the amount of tuition: residence status and hours taken.
Either of these factors can be considered the first level of branching. Suppose you use the hours
taken as the first level. You can then use the following skeleton to code the problem:

```
Private Sub btnCompute_Click(ByVal Sender As System.Object, ByVal
  e As System.EventArgs) Handles btnCompute.Click
    Dim Tuition As Decimal
    Select Case Val(txtHoursTaken.Text)
    Case 1 to 5
        'For the first bracket
    Case 6 To 8
        'For the second bracket
    Case 9 to 11
        'For the third bracket
    Case Else
        '12 or more hours
    End Select
    lblTuition.Text = Format(Tuition, "Standard") 'Display the
      tuition
End Sub
```

Within each Case, you can code the tuition based on the residence status. Should you also use the Select Case structure? You can, but it takes a bit more analysis. Instead, begin with the more straightforward If block first. Inspect the table again; under the 1-5 hours bracket, you see that a student with an in state, out of state, and international status will pay 850, 1250, 1700, respectively. The first bracket can be coded as follows:

```
Select Case Val(txtHoursTaken.Text)
    Case 1 to 5 'For the first bracket
        If rbtInState.Checked Then
            Tuition = 850
        ElseIf rbtOutOfState.Checked Then
            Tuition = 1250
        Else
            Tuition = 1700
        End If
    Case 6 To 8 'For the second bracket
    Case 9 to 11 'For the third bracket
    Case Is >= 12   '12 or more hours
End Select
```

The rest of the brackets can be coded in a similar fashion, and is left to you as an exercise (5-30). For simplicity, the case where the user enters a zero or nothing was also left out. The additional code to take care of this is also left to you as an exercise.

Note that the If block can be conveniently used here to handle the radio buttons because the state (Checked property) of each button is a different expression. Using the Select Case structure to handle multiple expressions like this can be a challenge. By syntax, the Select Case structure is more natural to branch based on one single expression.

Identifying the Radio Button Selected. To force the use of Select Case structure to handle radio buttons, a commonly used approach is to introduce a class level variable, whose value can then be set in the Click event of each radio button. For example, when rbtInState, rbtOutOfState, or rbtInternational is clicked, the variable ResidenceStatus can be set to 0, 1, or 2. ResidenceStatus can then be used as an expression in the Select Case statement. The following code should set the value of ResidenceStatus properly.

```
Dim ResidenceStatus As Integer
Private Sub rbtInState_Click(ByVal Sender As System.Object, ByVal
  e As System.EventArgs) Handles rbtInState.Click
    ResidenceStatus = 0
End Sub
Private Sub rbtOutOfState_Click(ByVal Sender As System.Object,
  ByVal e As System.EventArgs) Handles rbtOutOfState.Click
    ResidenceStatus = 1
End Sub
Private Sub rbtInternational_Click(ByVal Sender As System.Object,
  ByVal e As System.EventArgs) Handles rbtInternational.Click
    ResidenceStatus = 2
End Sub
```

After the residence status is determined, you can add the following Select Case block to determine the tuition of the first bracket of hours taken.

```
Select Case ResidenceStatus
    Case 0 'In State
        Tuition = 850
    Case 1 'Out of State
        Tuition = 1250
    Case 2 'International
        Tuition = 1700
End Select
```

The complete code for the button Click event procedure using the nested Select Case blocks can then appear as follows:

```
Private Sub btnCompute_Click(ByVal Sender As System.Object, ByVal
    e As System.EventArgs) Handles btnCompute.Click
    Dim Tuition As Decimal
    Select Case Val(txtHoursTaken.Text)
        Case 1 To 5 'First bracket
            Select Case ResidenceStatus
                Case 0 'In State
                    Tuition = 850
                Case 1 'Out of State
                    Tuition = 1250
                Case 2 'International
                    Tuition = 1700
            End Select
        Case 6 To 8 'Second bracket
            Select Case ResidenceStatus
                Case 0 'In State
                    Tuition = 1000
                Case 1 'Out of State
                    Tuition = 1500
                Case 2 'International
                    Tuition = 2000
            End Select
        Case 9 To 11 'Third bracket
            Select Case ResidenceStatus
                Case 0 'In State
                    Tuition = 1300
                Case 1 'Out of State
                    Tuition = 2000
                Case 2 'International
                    Tuition = 2700
            End Select
        Case Is >= 12 '12 hours or more
            Select Case ResidenceStatus
                Case 0 'In State
                    Tuition = 1500
                Case 1 'Out of State
                    Tuition = 2300
                Case 2 'International
                    Tuition = 3200
            End Select
    End Select
    lblTuition.Text = Format(Tuition, "Standard") 'Display tuition
End Sub
```

The logic in this procedure appears fairly straightforward. Identifying the radio button selected, however, takes some analysis. Incidentally, there is a trick that you can use with the Select Case structure to identify fairly easily the radio button selected, but it takes some inverted thinking. Rather than explaining its logic here, the trick is presented in the Explore and Discover exercise (5-11) for you to examine.

More on the Syntax of Select Case. Because the tuition is jointly determined by the student's residence status and hours taken, can you code the cases as shown here?

```
Select Case ResidenceStatus And HoursTaken
    Case 0 And 1 To 5      ?
    .
    .
End Select
```

No. Although "ResidenceStatus And HoursTaken" can be considered as an expression, it means something different to the computer than what a beginner may have in mind. Recall that the expression in the Select Case statement is first evaluated to arrive at a value that will be used to match against the criteria in the Cases. In an attempt to evaluate the expression, the computer will first perform a logical And operation on the variables ResidenceStatus and HoursTaken.

Suppose that ResidenceStatus has a value zero (0). No matter what value HoursTaken may be, the result of the And operation will be a zero. (Recall that zero is equal to False and the And logical operator requires that both of its operands be True for the result to be True; otherwise, the result will be False, which is a zero.) The first Case statement that has a zero will be considered the match. Assuming there are no other problems, the result will be both unexpected and unpredictable.

Now, consider this statement:

```
Case 0 And 1 To 5
```

1 To 5 is a range expression; however, an And operator is on its left, which is not expected; therefore, the statement has a syntax error.

Mixing the Select Case Structure with the If Block. As you may have already noticed in the preceding example, a Select Case structure can have If blocks within its structure. Conversely, an If block can also contain Select Case structures. There is no restriction to which structure can enclose the other as long as the nesting constitutes a relationship of the inner and outer blocks, as discussed in the preceding section.

An Alternative Design. The tuition example can be designed somewhat differently. For example, instead of using the text box to enter hours taken and radio buttons for residence status, you can use two combo boxes for both. The first combo box can be used to display the residence status; and the second one, for the brackets of hours taken. The visual interface can then appear as in Figure 5.7.

A list of the properties of the controls used in code is given in the following table.

Control	Property	Setting	Remark
Combo box	Name	cboResidenceStatus	
	DropDownStyle	DropDownList	To disallow user entry
Combo box	Name	cboHoursTaken	
	DropDownStyle	DropDownList	To disallow user entry
Label	Name	lblTuition	To display tuition
	BackColor	White	So that the label will look like a text box
	BorderStyle	Fixed 3D	
Button	Text	Compute	To initiate tuition computation
	Name	btnCompute	

Figure 5.7

Alternative user interface design for tuition calculation

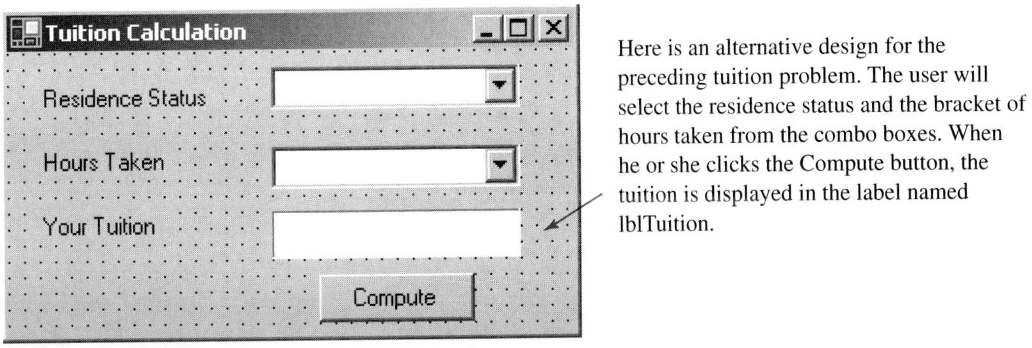

Here is an alternative design for the preceding tuition problem. The user will select the residence status and the bracket of hours taken from the combo boxes. When he or she clicks the Compute button, the tuition is displayed in the label named lblTuition.

In the Form Load event, the two combo boxes can be populated using the Items.Add method as follows:

```
Private Sub frmTuitionCalculation_Load(ByVal sender As
   System.Object, ByVal e As System.EventArgs) Handles MyBase.Load
      With cboResidenceStatus.Items
          'Populate combo box with residence status
          .Add("In State")
          .Add("Out Of State")
          .Add("International")
      End With
      cboResidenceStatus.SelectedIndex = 0 'Set default status (In
        state)
      With cboHoursTaken.Items
          'Populate combo box with brackets of hours taken
          .Add("1 to 5")
          .Add("6 to 8")
          .Add("9 to 11")
          .Add("12 or More")
      End With
      cboHoursTaken.SelectedIndex = 3
End Sub
```

Notice that the code has also included statements to set the SelectedIndex properties of both combo boxes. This will make the items corresponding to the SelectedIndex values appear in the controls' text boxes as the default selections when the program starts.

The Click event procedure for the button can then be modified with the following code skeleton:

```
Private Sub btnCompute_Click(ByVal Sender As System.Object, ByVal
   e As System.EventArgs) Handles btnCompute.Click
      Dim Tuition As Decimal
      Select Case cboResidenceStatus.SelectedIndex
          Case 0 'In state
              Select Case cboHoursTaken.SelectedIndex
                  Case 0 ' 1 to 5 hours
                  Case 1 ' 6 to 8 hours
                  Case 2 ' 9 to 11 hours
                  Case 3 ' 12 or more hours
              End Select
          Case 1 'Out Of state
              'Similar to the Case for In state
          Case 2 'International
              'Similar to the Case for In state
      End Select
      lblTuition.Text = Format(Tuition, "Standard")
End Sub
```

With the comments in the structure, you should be able to complete the remaining code, which is left to you to complete.

Notice that in the procedure, the residence status is used as the first-level Select Case structure. This is done to show that either of the two factors can be the first level without affecting the result. This structure should appear to you logically more natural because you typically would check the residence status before asking about the number of hours taken.

Notice also that the Select Case statements now use the combo boxes' SelectedIndex properties as the expressions. Because the DropDownStyle properties of both controls are set to DropDownList, the user cannot enter any data into the text portion of the combo box. Instead, the user can select an item from the list. Such an action will set the controls' SelectedIndex properties.

Which Design Do You Prefer? The original design has the advantage of code clarity. When you review the code, you should be able to have a good feel about what the code is supposed to do; however, it is not flexible. For example, if the hours taken for each bracket change, and the number of brackets remain the same, you will need to change the program to handle the new situation. The second design has the advantage of code brevity. It is also more flexible in handling the changes in data. Although you use the Items.Add method to populate the combo boxes, in a real application, the items should be read from a file or database. A change in the hours taken for each bracket will not necessitate a revision in the program as long as the number of brackets remains the same. The code, however, is not as clear because the SelectedIndex itself says very little about the underlying data. In such a case, it is important that you include comments to provide the additional details.

There are actually other alternatives to handle this problem. Another alternative that is even more flexible is considered in an exercise in Chapter 8. These alternatives are presented here to illustrate the use of the Select Case structure and the If block to solve a problem. Hopefully, each alternative will stimulate your mind and make you more resourceful in identifying solutions to your next problem.

A Note on Block Level Declaration

Declaration of variables at the block level was discussed in Chapter 4, "Data, Operations, and Built-In Functions." It was mentioned that variables declared at this level have a block scope. But what constitutes a block in this context? In the case of the If structure, each of the If, ElseIf, and Else blocks is independent of each other, so the following declarations pose no problem.

```
If A = B Then
    Dim I As Integer
ElseIf A > B Then
    Dim I As Integer
Else
    Dim I As Integer
End If
```

Each of the variables named I is separate and distinct from the other variables of the same name; when the execution leaves the block where I is declared, it will no longer be recognized. Note, however, you cannot declare I in these blocks if you have declared a procedure level variable with the same name. By the same token, if you have inner blocks in one of these blocks, you will not be able to (and should not) declare another I.

These same rules apply to the Select Case structure. You can declare the same variable in each of the mutually exclusive Case blocks, but you cannot make any of these declarations if you have already declared a variable of the same name at the procedure level, nor can you declare the same variable in an inner block (either Case or If block).

Summary

- This chapter introduces two structures commonly used to handle decisions: the If structure and the Select Case structure.
- The If structure involves testing whether the expression following the If keyword is True or False. In most cases, this expression contains the relational operators and/or logical operators.
- The relational operators include =, <>, >, <, >=, and <=. Each compares its two operands to determine whether the stated relation, such as equal, is True.
- Commonly used logical operators include Not, And, Or, Xor, AndAlso, and OrElse. The first four operators perform operations on their operands on a bit-wise basis. (Additional details are discussed in Appendix C, "Number Systems and Bit-wise Operations.") The last two operators strictly operate on Boolean data, and employ the quick out algorithm—that is, as soon as the operators are able to draw conclusion on the result, they stop evaluating any expressions thereafter.
- String comparisons can be either Binary (in which the uppercase of any letters is not considered equal to the lowercase of the same letters) or Text (in which the uppercase of any letters is considered equal to the lowercase of the same letters). You make your

choice by either coding Option Compare Text (or Binary) in the module or setting Option Compare in the project's Property Pages dialog box.

- If you consider the operational precedence confusing or hard to memorize, use pairs of parentheses to enclose the expression(s) that you want performed first.

- You can construct the If structure in four different ways:

  - Simple If statement:

    ```
    If condition Then Statement
    ```

  - Simple If block:

    ```
    If condition Then
        Statements
    End If
    ```

  - If...Else block:

    ```
    If condition Then
        Statements
    Else
        Statements
    End If
    ```

  - If...ElseIf...Else block

    ```
    If condition1 Then
        Statements
    ElseIf condition2 Then
        Statements
    ElseIf condition3 Then
            . . .
    Else
        Statements
    End If
    ```

- If blocks can be nested.

- The practical meaning of the condition (expression) in the If structure may not be very clear. It is advisable to include comments to explain the purpose.

- The computer evaluates logical or relational expressions in a mechanical way, which can be quite different from the way you interpret them; for example, 20 <= Age <= 35. Be aware of the difference. Also, set Option Strict On. It can help identify some of the potential problems.

- For logical expressions, the AndAlso and OrElse operators are more efficient than the And and Or operators.

- In some cases, computations can replace the use of If blocks. The code is typically shorter and can be more efficient, but the resulting code may not be as clear. Weigh the alternatives carefully when you have a choice.

- The Select Case structure can be used to replace the If...ElseIf...Else...End If structure when the branching depends on the result of one single expression.

- The Select Case structure can be nested and can also be nested with the If structure. There is no restriction as to which structure must contain the other structure.

- The tuition calculation example was used to illustrate how the Select Case structure can be nested. Two alternative interface designs were presented. They yielded different solutions with interesting trade-offs between program flexibility and code clarity.

- You can declare block level variables in both the If blocks and the Case blocks, but you cannot declare the same variable in an inner block as the one in the outer block.

Explore and Discover

5-1. Use of Logical Operators. Relational operators work on both numeric and string data. Can logical operators do the same? Try the following statements. (*Note:* Set Option Strict Off. To test these statements, place them in the Form Click event procedure with a Dim A as Integer statement at the beginning; then insert a line of code to display the result between the lines below.)

```
A = "34" And "32"
A = "34" Or 32
A = "XY" Or "AB"
```

Why do the first two run, but not the last? (*Answer:* Logical operators work on numeric data only. Data type conversions are performed automatically by VB in the first two cases, making the code executable. It is impossible to convert the strings to numbers in the last case. So, the operation fails.)

5-2. Comparing the And and the AndAlso operators. Enter the following code in the form click event.

```
Dim A As Integer = 64000
Dim B As Integer = 64000
If A > 64000 And (A * B) < 192000 Then
    MsgBox("B is less than 3")
Else
    MsgBox("B is a least 3")
End If
```

Run the program and then click the form. What do you find? Because the And operator evaluates both expressions, you have an overflow error when the computer is evaluating A * B. Now replace the And operator in the If statement with the AndAlso operator. Run the program, and click the form again. Do you still have the same problem? You should not, because when the expression A > 64000 is not true, the AndAlso operator will not evaluate the second expression.

5-3. Comparing the Or and the OrElse operators. Enter the following code in the form click event. Run the program and then click the form. What do you see?

```
Dim A As Integer = 64000
Dim B As Integer = 64000
If A + B > 64000 Or (A * B) > 64000 Then
    MsgBox("Either the sum or the prodcut will be greater than
        64000.")
Else
    MsgBox("Neither the sum or the product will be greater than
        64000.")
End If
```

Now change the Or operator to OrElse, and test the program again. Do you still run into the same problem?

5-4. What is passed to an event procedure? Create a new project. Draw a text box on the form as well as in the code window; then create a KeyPress event for the text box. (Select TextBox1 from the object box on the upper left corner of the code window; then select the KeyPress procedure from the procedure box on the upper right corner.) Inside the event procedure, type "**e.**" (without quotes but with the period). The IntelliSense should display a list of choices. You should see KeyChar and Handled among the list.

Create a MouseDown event procedure. Inside the procedure type "**e.**" again. What do you see this time?

You know that e is a structure that contains the event arguments passed to your event procedure. Not all events have the same arguments. To find more explanation for the arguments in the key-press event, search the Index tab of the Help file using KeyPressEventArgs as the keyword.

5-5. **What is Its Numeric Value?** Set Option Strict Off in your new project. Draw a check box on the form, name it **chkTest,** and set its Text property to **Test**; then enter the following code:

```
Private Sub chkTest_Click(ByVal sender As System.Object, ByVal e
    As System.EventArgs) Handles chkTest.Click
    Dim I As Integer
    I = chkTest.Checked
    MsgBox("Checked = " & chkTest.Checked)
    MsgBox("I = " & I)
End Sub
```

Run the project and then click the check box a few times. What do you see in the intermediate window? True gives a numeric value of –1, and False gives 0.

5-6. **Handling Data Type Conversion.** Refer to Exercise 5-5. Set Option Strict On. What do you see in the code window? The following statement is underlined because option strict does not allow a Boolean value to be converted to an integer implicitly:

```
I = chkTest.Checked
```

Change the statement to the following, and test the program again. It should work properly.

```
I = CInt(chkTest.Checked)
```

5-7. **Assigning a Value to the Boolean Variable.** Set Option Strict Off in your new project. Place a text box and a button on the form; then name the text box **txtNumber** and the button **btnCheck**. Set the button's Text property to **Check**. Enter the following code:

```
Private Sub btnCheck_Click(ByVal Sender As System.Object, ByVal e
    As System.EventArgs) Handles btnCheck.Click
    Dim BoolTest As Boolean
    Dim TheNumber As Single
    TheNumber = Val(txtNumber.Text)
    BoolTest = TheNumber
    MsgBox("The resulting Boolean value is " & BoolTest)
    If BoolTest = TheNumber Then
        MsgBox("BoolTest and TheNumber are equal.")
    Else
        MsgBox("BoolTest and TheNumber are Not equal.")
    End If
End Sub
```

Run the program, enter any number (try at least these numbers: -1, 0, 1000, -30, and 0.005), and click the button. What does the computer display? What conclusion can you draw from this experiment? What do you also learn? (*Answer:* Any nonzero value will be converted to True for a Boolean variable. Only a value of 0 is interpreted as False. Beware of the potential problem with comparing a Boolean variable with another variable of another data type after assigning the same value to both.)

5-8. **Handling Data Conversions.** Refer to Exercise 5-7, and set Option Strict On. What do you see in the code window? You should see many underlines because the compiler no long permits implicit conversions. You need to convert data explicitly. Revise the code as follows:

```
Private Sub btnCheck_Click(ByVal sender As System.Object, ByVal e
    As System.EventArgs) Handles btnCheck.Click
    Dim BoolTest As Boolean
    Dim TheNumber As Single
    TheNumber = CSng(Val(txtNumber.Text))
    BoolTest = CBool(TheNumber)
    MsgBox("The resulting Boolean value is " & BoolTest)
    If CSng(BoolTest) = TheNumber Then
        MsgBox("BoolTest and TheNumber are equal.")
    Else
        MsgBox("BoolTest and TheNumber are Not equal.")
    End If
End Sub
```

Test the program again. Does it work the same way as the preceding exercise? Is there any advantage of coding the program with setting Option Strict On? It forces you to state explicitly what you mean to do. When errors are caused by implicit conversions, it is harder to identify their sources because what we assume and what the computer actually does may not be the same.

5-9. **Playing with the Truth.** Set Option Strict Off. Place the following code in the form click event:

```
Dim B As Boolean
Dim L As Long
Dim S As String
B = 3 = 3
L = 3 = 3
S = 3 = 3
MsgBox("B = " & B & ", L = " & L & ", S = " & S)
MsgBox("Len(B) = " & Len(B) & ",Len(L) = " & Len(L) _
    & ", Len(S) = " & Len(S))
S = L
MsgBox("S = " & S & ", Len(S) = " & Len(S))
```

Run the project and then click on the form. Does everything turn out to be as expected?

Set Option Strict On. Do you see many underlines indicating syntax problems with the code? Again, setting Option Strict On is one way to detect potential problems with the code.

5-10. **Inverting the Range of the Case Criterion.** Draw a button and a text box on a form; name the button **btnCheck**, and set its Text property to **Check**. Name the text box **txtNumber** and then clear its text. Enter the following code:

```
Private Sub btnCheck_Click(ByVal sender As System.Object, ByVal e
    As System.EventArgs) Handles btnCheck.Click
    Select Case Val(txtNumber.Text)
        Case 90 To 10 'Note that these two values are inverted
            MsgBox("The value is in the range")
        Case Else
            MsgBox("The value is out of the range")
    End Select
End Sub
```

Run the program, and enter any number between 10 and 90. Which message does the computer display? When the range of the criterion is inverted, the criterion will never be tested to be true.

5-11. **Inverting the Criterion for the Select Case Block.** Typically, the Select Case statement involves a certain expression whose value will vary depending on one or more of the variables or control properties used in the expression. Seldom will you see a single constant used as the expression; however, consider the following code used in the event procedure btnTest click.

```
Private Sub BtnTest_Click(ByVal Sender As System.Object, ByVal e
    As System.EventArgs) Handles btnTest.Click
    Select Case True
        Case rbtOne.Checked
            MsgBox("Radio button1 is selected.")
        Case rbtTwo.Checked
            MsgBox("Radio button2 is selected.")
        Case rbtThree.Checked
            MsgBox("Radio button3 is selected.")
        Case Else
            MsgBox("No radio button is selected.")
    End Select
End Sub
```

Does it mean anything to you? Here, the constant True is used as the expression, whereas the Checked property of each radio button is used as the criterion. The comparison is inverted.

Draw on a new form a button, a group box, and three radio buttons inside the group box. Name the button btnTest. Name the three radio buttons rbtOne, rbtTwo, and rbtThree. Enter the preceding code. Start the program. Click one (or none) of the radio buttons. Then click the button. What do you find? It's a tricky way to test which radio button in a group is selected, isn't it?

5-12. **Block Level Declaration.** In an event procedure, declare three variables I, J, and K as Integer; then insert the following code:

```
If J > K Then
    Dim I As Integer
Else
    Dim I As Integer
End If
```

Do you see Dim I underlined in each case? Remove the procedure level declaration for I from the event procedure. Do you still see the underlines? You are allowed to declare the same variable in mutually exclusive blocks.

Now try to enter the following code; that is, insert another If bock with the same declaration:

```
If J > K Then
    Dim I As Integer
    If J > K Then
        Dim I As Integer
    End If
Else
    Dim I As Integer
End If
```

Do you see any code underlined? Multiple declarations of the same variable are not allowed in a block where the variable is still in scope. Try to declare any variables, such as K, L, and M, and observe the results. Is any part of the code underlined?

5-13. **Block Level Declaration.** Replicate the block declarations in the preceding exercise with the Select Case structure. You should be able to conclude that the compiler treats the If block and the Select Case block in the same manner for variable declarations.

Exercises

5-14. **Sorting Two Random Numbers.** Draw a button on a new form. Name it **btnShow** and then set its Text property to **Show**.

Provide the code so that when the user clicks the button, your program will display two random numbers in the range of 0 to 1, smaller one first. (*Hint:* Swap the values if the random numbers are out of order.)

5-15. **Sorting Two Random Numbers in a Lottery.** Modify the preceding project so that the random numbers are in the range of 1 to 50, representing the first two numbers drawn from a lottery. Again, the smaller number should be shown first. In addition, the two numbers should not be the same.

5-16. **Sorting Three Random Numbers in a Lottery.** Modify the preceding project so that the program will display three numbers instead of two. (*Hint:* As each number is drawn, make sure it is not the same as the previous one[s]. Sort the first two numbers in order.; then compare the third number with the smaller one. If the third one is smaller, you have found the order; otherwise, compare the third one with the larger number.)

5-17. **Ordering Names.** Write a routine so that it will display two names in alphabetic order regardless the order the names are given. Note that the comparison should not be case sensitive.

Test your routine by drawing two text boxes and a button on a new form. When your program runs, it will display the names entered in the text boxes in alphabetic order when the user clicks the button.

5-18. **Toggling a Button.** Create a new project, and draw a button on the form. Name the button **btnTraffic**. Provide the code so that when the program starts, the button's text will display **Go**. When the user clicks the button, it will display **Stop**. When the user clicks the button again, it displays **Go** again. Each subsequent click will cause the button to alternate its text between **Go** and **Stop**.

5-19. **I Know What's on Your Mind.** Design a game that will guess the letter that is on the player's mind. The player is to pick one of the first four letters in the alphabet (a, b, c, or d) without revealing it. Your program is allowed to ask the player two questions. In each question, it presents two letters and asks whether the player's letter is on the list. Your program should be able to tell the player the letter the user has picked after the two questions. (*Hint:* Suppose the lists your program presents are: a, d [first list] and a, c [second list]. The following table shows the letter the player picked.)

First Answer	Second Answer	Letter Picked
Yes	Yes	A
Yes	No	D
No	Yes	C
No	No	B

5-20. **Make the Game More Interesting.** Refer to Exercise 5-19, and revise the game to make it more interesting. Instead of limiting on the first four letters of the alphabet, modify your code so that it will show four consecutive letters, such as m, n, o, p, beginning with a letter randomly generated by your program. Your program will then instruct the player to pick any letter from the four and proceed to ask two questions in the same manner as described in Exercise

5-19. (*Hint:* Use the Next method of the Random object to generate a random number in the range of 0 and 22. Use this random number—say, R—to produce the four consecutive letters [the second letter should be Chr(65 + R)]. Assign these four letters to four variables.)

5-21. **Rotating Background Colors.** Write a procedure that rotates the background color of a label, lblSign, in blue, red, green, yellow, and back to blue each time the user clicks a button named btnChange with a text, "Change." (*Hint:* In the event procedure, type the keyword, Color. Then type a dot [period]. The IntelliSense should display the list of color names you need in your code. Use a Static long integer variable to keep track of the count. Use the Mod operator to generate the number sequence 0, 1, 2, 3, 0, 1 . . . and so on, which can then be used in a Select Case block.)

5-22. **Rotating Background Colors Automatically.** Modify the preceding project so that the colors are rotated automatically every half of a second after your program starts. (*Hint:* You may need to also modify the code so that the count will be limited to 0, 1, 2, and 3; that is, not to allow the number to grow any larger. If you allow the number to keep increasing and let the program run for a long while, the number may exceed the variable's upper limit causing an overflow error.)

5-23. **Alternative Solution to the Exploration Problem.** The oil exploration investment decision problem presented in this chapter has an alternative solution. Write a line of code using relational and logical operators to come up with a correct value for the variable Invest. (*Question:* Which coding alternative executes more efficiently?)

5-24. **Random Judgment.** When your program starts, it automatically displays one of the three questions on a label named lblQuestion. (Provide three favorite questions of your own. Use the Rnd function to decide which question to display.) Below the displayed question is a text box named txtAnswer for the user to type in the answer. When the user presses the Enter key, your program will display (using MsgBox) either "Yeah! You are right!" or "Nah! You are wrong!," depending on the number given by the Rnd function; that is, when the random value is less than 0.5, your program will display the "Yeah!" message; otherwise, it will display the "Nah!" message. (*Hint:* Place your code in the text box's KeyPress event and then check for the Keys.Return. On the form, use a label to instruct the user to press the Enter key when they complete the answer.)

5-25. **What Number Is on My Mind?** When the user clicks on the button named btnPlay with the text **Play** your program generates a number in the range of 1 to 1,000. The user will guess the number by typing a number in a text box named txtNumber, and clicking the Check button named btnCheck. If the guess is too low, your program will display a message, "Nope. Higher." If it is too high, it will display, "Nah! Lower." When the answer is correct, your program says, "Yes, you've got it. But it takes *n* seconds for you to find out." where *n* is computed from the time the Play button is clicked until the time a correct answer is obtained. (*Hint:* Use the Microsoft.VisualBasic.Timer function to keep track of time.)

5-26. **Port of Entry.** When you come back at the port of entry from a trip to a foreign country, the officer from the Immigration and Naturalization Service (a computer guarding the entrance) displays a check box with a question, "Are you a U.S. citizen?" If you check the box, the computer displays a text box with the label "Enter U.S. Passport Number." If you uncheck the box, the computer displays three text boxes with proper labels, "Nationality," "Passport Number," and "Visa Number," respectively. Design the proper visual interface and then provide the necessary code. (*Question:* Can you do this one without using the If block?)

5-27. **Long-Term Assets.** A part of a long-term asset entry screen has a check box with the text "Depreciable Asset?" When the box is checked, a text box with the label "Estimated Life" and a combo box with the label "Depreciation method" are enabled; otherwise, they are disabled. The allowable depreciation methods are straight-line, sum-of-years' digit, ACRE, modified ACRE, and double-declining balance methods. The most often used method is the straight-line method. (Populate the combo box with the Items.Add method in the form load procedure.) (*Question:* Can you do this without using the If block? The routine will be shorter if you do it this way.)

5-28. **Broker's Commission.** A broker charges her commission based on the amount of trading involved. If the amount is less than $1,000, the commission rate is 2%. *Additional* commission on the amount between $1,000 and $5,000 is 1%; between $5,000 and $20,000 is 0.5%; and above $20,000 is 0.025%. There is a minimum charge of $15.

The user interface to compute the commission should allow the user to enter the Date, Ticker Symbol, Price, and Number of Units (shares). When the program starts, the date field should be automatically filled with the current date. When the user clicks the Compute button, the computer should display the amount of trade as well as the commission in two labels with text box appearance, separately.

5-29. **Revisiting the Only-Three Bookstore Problem.** In the Only-Three Bookstore example in the text, the prices (Price1, Price2, and Price3) are assigned in the form load procedure. Actually, the prices are also shown on the texts of the check boxes. A good design should obtain the same data from only one source so that the results are always consistent. Assume that the check boxes' Text properties should be the sole source of data. Modify the project so that the form load procedure will assign the prices as given in the check boxes' Text properties. (*Hint:* Use the InStr function to obtain the position of the "$" in the text; then use the CSng function to convert the string to the Single type.)

5-30. **The Tuition Problem.** In Section 5.3 of this chapter, after the tuition problem is introduced, a partial solution was given using an If block as the second-level nesting. Complete the remaining code. For consistency, all the remaining second-level nesting should use the If block.

5-31. **Year-End Bonus.** A company determines the year-end bonuses for its employees based on rank and performance. The bonus is computed as a percentage of the employee's annual salary as given in the following table.

Rank	Excellent	Good	Mediocre
High	100%	75%	50%
Middle	80%	50%	30%
Low	60%	25%	15%

Your form should provide an interface for the user to specify the employee's rank, performance level, and the employee's annual salary. When the user clicks the Compute button, your program will show the amount of bonus for the employee in a label, which should have the appearance of a text box.

Projects

5-32. **Computing the FICA Withholding.** The FICA tax is computed based on a person's annual income. The formula consists of two parts: the Social Security tax and Medicare tax. A few years ago, the Social Security tax rate was 6.2%, and had an upper limit of an annual income of $45,000; that is, there was no Social Security tax on any income above $45,000. The Medicare tax rate was 1.45% with an upper limit on an annual income of $120,000; that is, there was no Medicare tax on any income above $120,000.

For the purpose of your programming practice, assume the same tax rate and bracket. Each time an employee is paid, your company has to withhold Social Security taxes based on the employee's current and previous income and withholding. In a real-world situation, the employee's previous income and withholding would have been kept in a file (database), and read in after an employee number was entered. In this project, your program will make the user enter the employee's previous income as well as the current income. Your program will then proceed to compute the previous and current FICA withholding when the user clicks the Compute button. Your program should display the previous and current withholding as well as the total income and withholding including the current amounts. (*Hint:* To compute the current withholding, compute the total withholding based on total income and then subtract the previous withholding based on previous income from it. This is much easier than if you try to compute the current withholding directly.)

Design a user interface for this purpose. Use three group boxes—one for previous data, another for current data, and the other for total amounts. Use text boxes for fields that require user input, but use labels for fields that will be computed by your program. Change the BackColor and BorderStyle settings for these labels so that they look like text boxes. You should add two buttons: one for computation and the other for quitting.

Provide code for the computation and display of results as specified.

The following table can be used to verify the accuracy of your program:

Previous Income (Entered)	Previous Withholding (Computed)	Current Income (Entered)	Current Withholding (Computed)
0	0	10,000	765
40,000	3,060	5,000	382.50
40,000	3,060	10,000	455
40,000	3,060	80,000	1,470
40,000	3,060	100,000	1,470
80,000	3,950	40,000	580
80,000	3,950	80,000	580

5-33. **Computing Total for Guest Check.** A restaurant offers two kinds of drinks: St. Helen Volcano ($15) and Bloody Mary ($12). They are so strong that diners are allowed to order only one drink per day. Appetizers include shrimp cocktail ($5.95), seasoned mushrooms ($6.45), and hibachi-style crab rangoon ($6.75). Diners can order any combinations, but are restricted to only one drink and one appetizer. Entrees include Maine lobster ($24.95), New York strip steak ($21.95), and oriental vegetables ($28.95). The portions are so large that no diner should order more than one. Finally, desserts include spice cake ($8.75) and Ginseng ice cream ($8.75). Diners can order either, both, or none.

Design a user interface that servers of the restaurant can use to enter the order for each diner. Restrict your choice of VB controls to only radio buttons and check boxes. Use as many group boxes as you deem desirable to group items on the form.

Provide necessary code so that when the server clicks the Compute button, the computer will display in the lblTotal label the total charges for a diner. (*Hint:* You may find the code much shorter using formulas as an alternative to If blocks.)

5-34. **Computing the Total for a Guest Check: A Variation.** Modify the code in the previous exercise (5-33) to satisfy the requirement that the restaurant would rather not have the Compute button, but for the computer to display the total as soon as the server clicks on any of the available choices on the restaurant menu. Be aware that when a check box is clicked, it can be checked or unchecked.

Input, Output, and Procedures

This chapter introduces two topics. Section 6.1 provides introductory topics to input and output features available in VB, which are essential to your understanding of input and output concepts. In addition, some of these features provide a convenient means for you to design sound interactions between your program and the user. Section 6.2 discusses the uses of general procedures in structuring VB code. The advantages of using general procedures are too significant to overemphasize, and are outlined at the end of that section after you gain a good working knowledge of general procedures. This chapter concludes with an example that represents an attempt to show how all the pieces you learn from this chapter can be put together.

After completing this chapter, you should be able to:

- Use the MsgBox function to ascertain the user's response when your program needs a decision/direction from the user.
- Develop code to handle text files for input and output.
- Use file dialog boxes to prompt for file paths.
- Appreciate the need to create and use general procedures.
- Write and use general procedures.
- Differentiate between the situations in which a sub and a function should be written.
- Determine when a parameter is needed for a general procedure.

6.1 Introduction to Input and Output

When your program starts, the variables in the program must be initialized first either with constants or with values provided from external sources, such as users' actions (keystrokes or mouse clicks) or an existing file. The process of obtaining data from a source external to the CPU (central processing unit) is referred to as *input*.

The data that the variables in your program contain are stored in memory. As soon as your program terminates, all these data will not longer exist in the CPU. Some of the data are temporary in nature, and can be discarded without any problem. Others, however, need to be displayed (for the user to view their values), printed on a hard copy, or saved in some intermediate storage device such as hard disks for future uses. The process of sending the data in the CPU to an external device is referred to as output. This section introduces a few possible means that you can use in VB for input and output.

VB provides various ways that your program can obtain input or produce output. Recall in Chapter 3, "Some Visual Basic Controls and Events," you learned that at least six VB controls could be used to obtain input from the user. A text box, for example, can be used for the user to enter data. Indeed, some of those controls can also be used to display output. For example, you can display any data in the same text box. This section explores three additional ways for input and output:

- The MsgBox function
- Files
- File dialog boxes

The MsgBox Function

You have seen MsgBox used to display a pop-up message. When used to display a message (as output), the MsgBox function has the following syntax:

```
MsgBox(Prompt[, Buttons] [, Title])
```

where Prompt = a text string that is displayed on the message box.

Buttons = a message box style enumeration value specifying the button(s) and icon the pop-up message box is to display; when omitted, an OK button is displayed. To specify the enumeration, code MsgBoxStyle followed by a dot and the enumeration name, such as MsgBoxStyle.OkOnly.

Title = an optional text string to be displayed as the title of the pop-up message box; when omitted, the project name is displayed.

The buttons parameter specifies what button(s) and icon the message box is to display. Some of the sample values are listed in the following table:

MsgBoxStyle Constant	Display	Type
OKOnly	OK button only	Button(s)
YesNoCancel	Yes, No, and Cancel buttons	
YesNo	Yes and No buttons	
RetryCancel	Retry and Cancel buttons	
Critical	Critical Message icon	Icon
Question	Warning Query icon	
Information	Information Message icon	

You can specify one group of buttons and one icon to display at the same time. To display a group of buttons and an icon together, insert an "Or" logical operator between the two values as the second parameter. If nothing is specified, the OK default button will be displayed. Two examples of the uses of MsgBox follow.

Simple Message. Suppose you want to display a message in your payroll program informing the user that the maximum allowable number of hours worked per week is 60; you can code the following:

```
MsgBox("Maximum allowable hours worked per week is 60.", _
    MsgBoxStyle.Information, "Payroll Entry")
```

The code will display in the message box not only the message, but also an Information icon. It will also show "Payroll Entry" as its title. Because nothing is said about the buttons to display, the default OK button will be displayed (see Figure 6.1).

Notice again that you can specify an icon along with a group of buttons to display in the message box by performing the Or logical operation on the icon and buttons values for the second parameter. For example, you can make it display Yes and No buttons instead of the default OK button as well as the Information icon by coding the following:

```
MsgBox("Maximum allowed hours worked per week is 60.", _
    MsgBoxStyle.Information Or MsgBoxStyle.YesNo, "Payroll Entry")
```

The Yes and No buttons, however, do not seem to make any sense in this message. They are usually used when the message box is used to prompt for the user response rather than to display a straight message.

TIP

If you set Option Strict Off, you can code the following

```
MsgBoxStyle.Information + MsgBoxStyle.YesNo
```

in place of MsgBoxStyle.Information Or MsgBoxStyle.YesNo in the preceding code; however, technically, the Or operator is the correct operator to use. The values in the MsgBoxStyle enumeration are actually flags that represent the on and off states of different bits. Refer to Appendix C, "Number Systems and Bit-wise Operations," for flags and bit-wise operations.

Using MsgBox to Obtain the User Response. The MsgBox function can be used to obtain the response from the user. When used for this purpose, its has the following syntax:

```
Response = MsgBox(prompt[, buttons] [, title])
```

Depending on the button the user clicks on the message box, the MsgBox returns a different value. The possible returned values are enumerated as MsgBoxResult-type values with the same names as the buttons. The following table is a sample of the possible responses:

Figure 6.1

A sample message box

The third parameter is displayed here.

MsgBoxStyle. Information in the second parameters will make the message box display this icon.

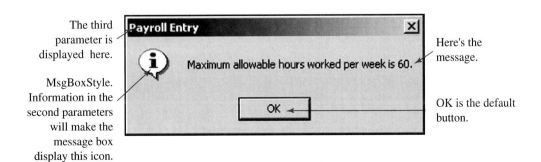

Here's the message.

OK is the default button.

Button Clicked	MsgBoxResult Constant
Cancel	Cancel
Abort	Abort
Yes	Yes
No	No

Suppose your form has a text box named txtName, which is cleared when data on the form are saved. When the user clicks the Close (X) button on the title bar, if the control contains data, it would mean that data have not yet been saved. You would like to warn and then ask the user if it is OK to quit. One solution is to place the code in the form's Closing event to handle this situation. The *Form Closing event* occurs immediately before the form is being closed. It occurs when the user clicks the form's Close button, or when the form's Close method is being executed. The event has a Cancel argument—e.Cancel—that when set to True will cancel the Close operation.

Using this event procedure, the code can appear as follows:

```
Private Sub Form1_Closing(ByVal sender As System.Object, ByVal e
    As System.ComponentModel.CancelEventArgs) Handles MyBase.Closing
    Dim Response As Integer
    If Len(Trim(txtName.Text)) > 0 Then
        'The text box contains data.
        'Ask the user whether he or she really means to quit.
        Response = MsgBox("Data not yet saved. Ok to quit?", _
        MsgBoxStyle.Question Or MsgBoxStyle.YesNo, "Testing")
            'Display the "?" icon as well as yes and no buttons
        If Response = MsgBoxResult.Yes Then
            ' User clicks the Yes button;
            ' Do nothing (allow program to proceed to close)
        Else
            ' User clicks the No button, cancel the close operation
            e.Cancel = True
        End If
    End If
End Sub
```

In this procedure, the first If statement checks if the txtName text box contains any nonblank text. If so, the message box displays the warning message with the question mark icon and the Yes and No buttons (see Figure 6.2). Note that the buttons parameter specifies to display the question icon as well as the Yes and No buttons. If the user clicks the Yes button, a value MsgBoxResult.Yes will be returned. (Notice that this enumeration is different from MsgBoxStyle, which is used for displaying message and not for comparing results.) The program will proceed normally (close); otherwise, True is assigned to the Cancel parameter and the closing process will be canceled.

The MsgBox function provides a facility for simple dialogs between your program and the user. It is most appropriate in the following situations:

Figure 6.2

Message with a question icon and two buttons

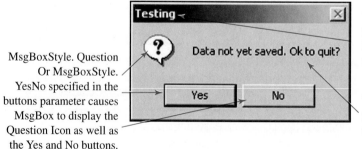

MsgBoxStyle. Question Or MsgBoxStyle. YesNo specified in the buttons parameter causes MsgBox to display the Question Icon as well as the Yes and No buttons.

When the title parameter is omitted, the message box displays the name of the project.

The string specified as the prompt parameter is displayed here.

- When your program needs to convey a simple message to the user. Examples include messages that do the following:
  - Indicate that a file has been saved
  - Inform the user that an entry is not acceptable
  - Instruct the user to take a certain action, such as inserting a disk in a drive

- When your program needs a direction (among a few available choices) from the user. Examples include the following:
  - Informing the user of the failure of an operation, such as unable to read a specified file, and prompting whether to try again, skip the operation, or quit
  - Warning the user of the possibility of losing data, such as when instructed to delete a file, and prompting whether to proceed the operation

Search the keyword MsgBox Function (Visual Basic language reference) in the Index tab of the Help file. It explains in more details of all the parameters. It also provides a complete list of button values you can specify for the box to display as well as the values indicating the button clicked.

Files

VB provides different ways to handle files. In this section, you will explore the use of two objects that can be used to read and write text files. These two objects are available under the System.IO namespace, which is explained later in this chapter. Traditionally, files are handled by various commands. This traditional approach of file accesses is presented in Appendix A, "Data Management Using Files."

When you work with files using objects in System.IO, several key steps are involved:

1. Declare an object variable to indicate the object type by which your code is to perform input or output. The two objects that can be used to read or write text files are StreamReader and StreamWriter.

2. Create the object. In this step, your program associates the object in your program with the physical file residing in the intermediate storage device, such as the hard drive or floppy disk. Traditionally, this step is recognized as Open the File. A file that is associated with the StreamReader is said to be opened for input, while a file that is associated with the StreamWriter is said to be opened for output.

3. Use the object's proper method to perform file operations, such as reading/writing data from/onto the file. Most of the file activities of your program relate to this aspect.

4. Close the object. This process dissociates your program from the physical file, and ensures that all I/O operations are completed by the system.

Declaring the Object Variable. If you want to read data from an existing file, you will use the StreamReader. If you want to write data onto a file, you use the StreamWriter. The syntax appears as follows:

```
Dim InputFileName As System.IO.StreamReader
Dim OutputFileName as System.IO.StreamWriter
```

where InputFileName and OutputFileName can be any legitimate names.

The declaration indicates that the variable is of the object type, System.IO.StreamReader (System.IO.StreamWriter). Assuming that you want to read a file containing names and phone numbers, you can declare a phone file as follows:

```
Dim PhoneFileI As System.IO.StreamReader
```

As discussed in Chapter 4, "Data, Operations, and Built-in Functions," be aware that this declaration simply indicates that the variable, PhoneFileI is of the StreamReader type but a StreamReader object has not yet been created.

Creating the Object. In this step, you create the object and associate it with a physical file in your computer systems. For example, assume the phone file is located at C:\Temp\PhoneFile.txt. You can use the following code to create the object (open the file).

```
PhoneFileI = New
    System.IO.StreamReader("C:\Temp\PhoneFile.txt")
```

The New keyword creates a new StreamReader object and associates the object with the physical file specified in the string (opens the file). The resulting object is assigned to PhoneFileI. From this point on, when you make any reference to PhoneFileI, you are actually referring to the object that deals with the file. Notice that the physical file, such as C:\Temp\PhoneFile.txt, must exist before you can associate it with the StreamReader. If the file does not exist, execution of the preceding statement will result in a runtime error.

Combining Declaration and Creation of An Object. In the preceding discussion, you are shown two steps to associate an object variable with an object. As explained in Chapter 4, you can actually combine the two steps in some cases. For example, the following statement will declare the variable PhoneFileI and associate it with the physical file at the same time:

```
Dim PhoneFileI As New
    System.IO.StreamReader("C:\Temp\PhoneFile.txt")
```

Notice the New keyword in the statement. This keyword works exactly the same way as in the previous assignment statement. Which way is preferable? It depends on how the variable is going to be used. The one-step approach appears to be convenient; however, if the variable is declared in a procedure, the object will not be accessible to another procedure, and will be out of scope as soon as the procedure ends. If it is declared at the class level, the filename must be known at design time. Apparently, its applicability is limited. The two-step approach is more flexible if the object needs to be accessible to more than one procedure.

Reading Data from a File. The StreamReader provides several methods that you can use to read data from the file. The following table shows methods that are of particular interest:

Method	Explanation
Peek	Returns the next character in the stream but does not advance the current position; returns −1 if there is no more data (end of file is reached)
Read	Reads one character or a number of specified characters starting from current position
ReadLine	Reads one line of data starting from current position
ReadToEnd	Reads the remainder of the entire file starting from current position
Close	Dissociates the object from the physical file

Depending on the organization of the existing file and the application, you will find each of these methods useful. The ReadLine method will be most useful when you organize your data on a line by line basis. For example, suppose that you have created the Append I PhoneFileI object shown in the preceding code example. The file contains your friends' names and phone numbers and appears as follows:

```
8172223838, John Dole
2145559999, Jane Smith
```

To read your friends' data one person at a time, the ReadLine method should be most appropriate. As an example, assume your form has a button named btnRead. When you click the button, you want to read one line of data into the variable PhoneAndName and then display the result. Your code can appear as follows:

```
Dim PhoneFileI As System.IO.StreamReader
Private Sub Form1_Load(ByVal sender As System.Object, ByVal e As
   System.EventArgs) Handles MyBase.Load
    PhoneFileI = New
      System.IO.StreamReader("C:\Temp\PhoneFile.txt")
End Sub
Private Sub btnRead_Click(ByVal Sender As System.Object, ByVal e
   As System.EventArgs) Handles btnRead.Click
    Dim PhoneAndName As String
    PhoneAndName = PhoneFileI.ReadLine()
    MsgBox(PhoneAndName) 'Show the line
End Sub
```

The first time the procedure is executed, the PhoneFileI object will read the first line of data into the variable PhoneAndName, so the variable will hold the value "8172223838, John Dole". The second time the procedure is executed, the variable will have the data on the second line.

Of course, if you want to separate the phone from the name, you will need to parse the string. A possible solution is to add the following code:

```
Dim TheName As String
Dim ThePhone as String
Dim P As Integer
P = Instr(PhoneAndName, ",") 'find position of comma
ThePhone = Microsoft.VisualBasic.Left(PhoneAndName, P - 1)
TheName = Mid(PhoneAndName, P + 2) 'There's a space after comma
```

As a technical side note, at the end of each line in a text file, there is an end of line marker that the computer uses to separate one line from the other. The marker consists of two character codes: Return (13, that is Keys.Return) and Line Feed (10). VB provides the named constant vbCrLf for this marker. Recall that you used this constant in Chapter 3, "User Interface Design: Visual Basic Controls and Events," to display texts on different lines. Although the marker is not visible to you, it is important to be aware of its existence. The awareness helps you understand how the text file is handled internally.

Testing for the End of File Condition. In the preceding example, if you continue to click the Read button and execute the ReadLine method, the file will eventually run out of data. Further attempt to read the file will result in a runtime error. Your code should check for the end of file condition before executing the ReadLine method. One way to perform this test is to use the Peek method. As indicated in the preceding table, the Peek method previews the next character in the input stream without advancing the current position. When the end of file is reached, this method returns a value –1. The complete code to test the end of file condition, read and parse the data, and display the result is given as follows:

```
Private Sub btnRead_Click(ByVal Sender As System.Object, ByVal e
   As System.EventArgs) Handles btnRead.Click
    Dim PhoneAndName As String
    Dim TheName As String
    Dim ThePhone As String
    Dim P As Integer
    If PhoneFileI.Peek() = -1 Then
        'end of file has been reached
        MsgBox("No more data") 'display the eof message
        Exit Sub 'leave the procedure
    End If
    PhoneAndName = PhoneFileI.ReadLine()
    P = InStr(PhoneAndName, ",") 'find position of comma
    ThePhone = Microsoft.VisualBasic.Left(PhoneAndName, P - 1)
    TheName = Mid(PhoneAndName, P + 2) 'There's a space after comma
    MsgBox("The phone is " & ThePhone & ". The name is " & TheName
      & ".")
End Sub
```

Pay particular attention to the If block in the code. The If statement uses the Peek method to test against –1. If it is true, a message indicating no more data is displayed. The next statement, *Exit Sub*, will leave the procedure without executing any of the remaining code in the event procedure. Additional explanation of this statement is given in the next section of this chapter.

To test the above procedure, be sure to include the code to declare the PhoneFileI variable and the form Load procedure to create the object to associate with the physical file, as given on page 211.

Reading an Entire File. The ReadToEnd method reads from the current position to the end of the file. This method is handy when you need to read the entire file in one operation. All you have to do is to create a StreamReader object and then use this method to read the file. For example, suppose you would like to read the entire file into a text box named txtDoc from "C:\Temp\PhoneFile.txt." You can code the following:

```
Dim TheInputFile As System.IO.StreamReader
TheInputFile = New
  System.IO.StreamReader("C:\Temp\PhoneFile.txt")
txtDoc.Text = TheInputFile.ReadToEnd()
```

This should be a handy way to display the file content in a text box. You can even allow the user to edit the text as in the word processing operations. Of course, to display the text properly, you should set the text box's MultiLine property to True and its Scrollbars property to Vertical.

Note that as previously discussed, you can declare and create an object at the same time. The preceding code can be modified as follows:

```
Dim TheInputFile As New
  System.IO.StreamReader("C:\Temp\PhoneFile.txt")
txtDoc.Text = TheInputFile.ReadToEnd()
```

The Close Method. When you are done with a file, you should dissociate it from the StreamReader object for several reasons. You may need to use the same file with different mode, such as from output to input mode. The dissociation eliminates the possibility that your program will accidentally perform unexpected operations on the file. It releases the computer resources associated with that file and ensures that all file operations you have performed are actually carried out by the computer. The StreamReader's *Close method* dissociates the file from the object. To close TheInputFile in the preceding example, you will code:

```
TheInputFile.Close()
```

Output with Files. To output data onto a text file, you can create a StreamWriter object and then use its Write or WriteLine method to write the text. The syntax to create the StreamWriter appears as follows:

```
StreamWriterObject = New System.IO.StreamWriter(FileName,
  AppendMode)
```

where StreamWriterObject = a variable that is declared to be of the StreamWriter Type.
FileName = a string giving the file path
AppendMode = a Boolean value. Regardless of this value, if the physical file does not exist, a new file is created. On the other hand, if the file already exists and if the Boolean value is True, new data will be written at the end of the existing contents (old data preserved); otherwise, the existing contents will be erased.

The following statements will associate the StreamWriter, PhoneFileO, with the Phone file discussed in the previous example. Note that its related StreamReader, PhoneFileI, must be closed if you have previously created the association for other purposes.

```
Dim PhoneFileO As System.IO.StreamWriter 'Place this line in
  the general declaration area
'Place the following line in an event procedure to create a
  StreamWriter with the append mode
PhoneFileO = New
  System.IO.StreamWriter("C:\Temp\PhoneFile.txt", True)
```

You can then use the WriteLine method to add more phone numbers and names.

The WriteLine Method. The *WriteLine* method will write the text data on the file, and add an "end of line" maker; that is, vbCrLf. The next output operation will start from the next line. This method has the following syntax:

```
StreamWriterObject.WriteLine(StringToOutput)
```

where StreamWriterObject = the object created to write the stream.
StringToOutput = a string expression to be written to the file.

For example, you have a masked edit box named mskPhone, and a text box named txtFriend in a form. You would like to save the data entered by the user onto the file associated with PhoneFileO. You can use the following statement:

```
PhoneFileO.WriteLine(mskPhone.ClipText & ", " &
    txtFriend.Text)
```

The line of output data in the file will appear as follows:

```
2146668392, Allen Jones
```

Recall that the ReadLine method of the StreamReader explained previously in this subsection reads one line of data at a time. You can think of the ReadLine and WriteLine methods as complementary I/O methods.

Notice a difference between the Write and the WriteLine method. As discussed, the WriteLine method always adds an end of line marker, but the Write method does not; therefore, if you use the Write method to output to a file, the next output operation (either using the Write or WriteLine method) will start at where the previous output ends, not at the beginning of a new line—even if the file is closed and opened again for output operations.

Close the StreamWriter. After you use the StreamWriter to write data to the file, and before your program ends, *be sure you have code to close the StreamWriter*. This is imperative. Without closing the StreamWriter, the output operations may not be complete, and your data may be lost in the process. In the Explore and Discover exercises at the end of this chapter, you explore the consequence of not closing the StreamWriter and learn alternatives to ensure that the data are written to the file. Still, closing the StreamWriter is the most direct and efficient way to achieve this purpose. To close the StreamWriter in the preceding example, you code:

```
PhoneFileO.Close()
```

In what event should the statement be placed? This depends on the application at hand. Assume in the preceding example, a phone number and a name are written on the file each time a button is clicked. This would suggest that the StreamWriter should be active as long as the program is in action. The most appropriate time to close the StreamWriter will probably be just before the form is closed. In such a case, the code to close the StreamWriter should be placed in the form closing event.

Always make sure that you have code to close a StreamWriter before the program ends to ensure all data are written to the file. This is the most direct and efficient way to ensure that all necessary output operations are complete.

About System.IO. You have seen that some objects and functions in your code are qualified with other names. For example, the StreamReader and StreamWriter are qualified with System.IO. This pertains to the way VS.NET is organized. The huge software contains many class libraries (libraries that provide classes [templates for objects]), commands, and so forth that are developed by different groups. Because of the huge vocabulary of the software, it is unavoidable that some identifiers in one part conflict with those in another part. To resolve this issue, the software is organized into *namespaces*. Within each namespace, identifier names must be unique, but the same identifier names can be used in another namespace. To differentiate an identifier (of the same name) in one namespace from the one in another namespace, you qualify the name with the name space. Recall that the Left function discussed in Chapter 4 must be qualified with Microsoft.VisualBasic because Left is also a property of the form.

All namespaces coming with VS.NET begin with System or Microsoft. When VS.NET starts, it automatically includes some of these namespaces for references based on the profile setting for your project. Among these are Microsoft.VisualBasic, which provides most of the VB functionality, and System.Windows.Forms, which provides functionality for forms and controls. As you may guess by now, the StreamReader and StreamWriter are in the System.IO namespace, which is not automatically included (imported) in the project. That is why your code needs to qualify them with the namespace System.IO.

You can leave out the namespace qualification for the two objects if you *import* the namespace into your project. To import System.IO, place the following code as the first line in the module (before the Class statement):

```
Imports System.IO
```

After you have this line in place, you will no longer need to qualify the StreamReader or StreamWriter. For example, you can code the following line without encountering any error:

```
Dim MyFileReader As StreamReader
```

File Dialog Boxes

The files created using the StreamWriter can be viewed and edited by the use of the Microsoft Notepad program. Files created by Notepad can also be input to your program using the StreamReader with the ReadLine and ReadToEnd methods.

Talking about Notepad, you probably notice that each time you use it to open or save a file, it displays a dialog box for you to specify the file in your computer system. Wouldn't it be nice if you can have the same facilities in VB to specify the file? VB.NET provides the open file dialog and save file dialog controls to do these.

The open file dialog is used when you want to open a file; therefore, its default title is Open. The save file dialog is used when you want to save a file, so its default title is Save As. Similar to the timer control, these two controls are visible at design time, allowing the programmer to set their properties. At runtime, however, they do not appear until invoked by code. Figure 6.3 shows their appearance at design time.

These two controls have a few different properties; however, they also have several common properties that you can set at design time or by code to perform the services you need. The following table lists some of these properties:

Figure 6.3

File dialogs: icons and appearances at design time

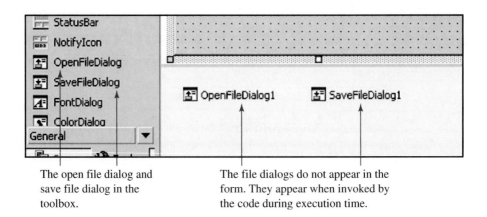

The open file dialog and save file dialog in the toolbox.

The file dialogs do not appear in the form. They appear when invoked by the code during execution time.

Property	Explanation	Example	Effect
Filter	Show only the types of file extension as specified.	.Filter ="Text File (*.*) I*.txt"	Only file with the txt extension will be shown in the dialog box
Title	A string to be displayed on the title bar of the dialog box in place of the default Open or Save As	.Title ="Where is the File?"	The dialog box title bar will display **Where is the File?**
FileName	Sets or returns the filename specified by the user	MyFileName = .FileName	MyFileName will hold the current FileName property
AddExtension	If set to True, file extension will be added in the file specification	.AddExtension = True	

The Filter Property. The Filter property allows you to specify what types of files you would like the file dialog to display. For each type of file you want to specify, you must give the description and the filter, separated by a I (pipe) symbol. For example, assume that you have an OpenFileDialog named cdlOpenFile, and you want it to show only files with the txt extension. (The cdl name prefix is the acronym for common dialog boxes, which include the file, font, color, and print dialog boxes.) You can specify the following:

```
cdlOpenFile.Filter = "Text Files (*.txt)¦*.txt"
```

In the preceding code, the string "Text Files (*.txt)" gives the description of the type of file your user will be looking for. The filter "*.txt" (following the I) specifies that the system will display all files with the txt file extension. The * is a wildcard specification that indicates to ignore the matching (all names are considered a match).

You can also separate additional filters by additional I symbols. The following line will allow either text files or all files to be possible filters, depending on which filter the user chooses.

```
cdlOpenFile.Filter = "Text File (*.txt)¦*.txt¦All Files
    (*.*)¦*.*"
```

To illustrate how one of these dialog boxes can be used for file specifications, suppose in the previous phone file example (for input) that all you know is that there is such a file. The file can be located at any folder with any name, so you want your user to specify the location for input using the OpenFileDialog. Again, assume the control has been named cdlOpenFile. Your code to open the file (associate the file with a StreamReader) can appear as follows:

```
'Title on the dialog box
cdlOpenFile.Title = "Where is the phone file?"
'Display only txt files
cdlOpenFile.Filter = "Text Files (*.txt)¦*.txt"
cdlOpenFile.ShowDialog()   ' Display the open dialog box
' cdlFile.FileName below is obtained from the ShowDialog
   method
PhoneFileI = New System.IO.StreamReader(cdlOpenFile.FileName)
```

When the ShowDialog method is executed, the dialog box will appear as in Figure 6.4.

After the user browses through the computer and selects the proper file, the filename is stored in the control's FileName property, which can then be used as the string for the file specification in the StreamReader creation statement.

Additional Notes. Both the OpenFileDialog and SaveFileDialog have *CheckFileExists* and *CheckPathExists* properties. When these Boolean properties are Set to True, the controls will check whether the file (folder) entered by the user in the dialog box exists. If not, the dialog box displays a message box to inform the user that the file (folder) must exist before it will accept the entry. Of course, setting the CheckFileExists property to True is more meaningful for the OpenFileDialog than for the SaveFileDialog. Set this property to True for the OpenFileDialog. It can save your program from failure when the user fails to provide a filename for an existing file.

Figure 6.4

An open file dialog in action

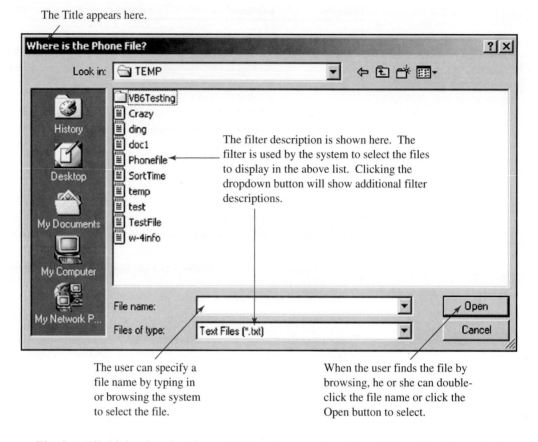

The Title appears here.

The filter description is shown here. The filter is used by the system to select the files to display in the above list. Clicking the dropdown button will show additional filter descriptions.

The user can specify a file name by typing in or browsing the system to select the file.

When the user finds the file by browsing, he or she can double-click the file name or click the Open button to select.

The SaveFileDialog has the *OverwritePrompt property*, which when set to True will also check whether the specified file already exists. If it does, the dialog box warns the user that the file already exists and then asks the user whether the file should be overwritten. Setting the property to True can protect the user against accidental loss of valuable data.

The preceding code example assumes that the user will always choose or enter a valid file-name when the OpenFileDialog displays the dialog box. What if the user simply clicks the Cancel button? The FileName property will contain a zero length string. The creation of the StreamReader will fail, resulting in an execution time error. To guard against this potential problem, you can test the length of the filename before attempting to create the StreamReader object. The code can appear as follows:

```
If Len(cdlOpenFile.FileName) > 0 Then
    PhoneFileI = New
       System.IO.StreamReader(cdlOpenFile.FileName)
    'Other statements
End If
```

6.2 Procedures: Subs and Functions

Consider the student registration application. The user first enters the student's ID number as well as all the courses and section numbers that the student intends to enroll. When the user clicks the Process button, the program will proceed to process the request by going through the following steps:

1. Verifying that the student number is valid and the student is allowed to enroll

2. Looking for all previous unpaid invoices, campus police tickets, and library fines owed by the student

3. Verifying for each course the student requests to enroll:

    3.1. that the course and the section number are valid

    3.2. that the class is not yet full

    3.3. that the student has the prerequisites to take the course

4. Computing the total tuition and previous balance

5. Issuing the invoice

6. Updating the student's record

7. Updating all the class records

The list can go even longer, but the point is simple: In this situation, if you place all the code in the button's Click event procedure, it will be hard to follow the program flow of logic. The program will be too long and difficult to read, understand, debug, change, or maintain. The solution to this problem is to divide the program into several subprograms, each handling a predefined special task, such as one of the major steps outlined. The button's Click event procedure will then provide just an outline of the steps by calling these subprograms. This arrangement will dramatically reduce the number of lines in the event procedure. Because each subprogram handles a smaller task, it is easier to develop code and to understand.

A partial, conceptual solution to the previous problem would probably be similar to the following:

```
Private Sub btnProcess_Click(ByVal Sender As System.Object, ByVal
    e As System.EventArgs) Handles btnProcess.Click
    If BadStudentID(IDNumber) Then
        MsgBox("Needs a valid student ID number to proceed.")
        Exit Sub
    End If
    FindUnPaidRecords(IDNumber)
        .
        .
        .
End Sub
```

Each procedure referenced inside the event procedure can be written separately as a *Sub* or as a *Function* procedure and can be placed anywhere in the class in the same area as the event procedures. Both types of procedures are different from the event procedure in that the event procedure is typically invoked by the occurrence of an event, whereas the former are invoked by a reference of their names in the code. These procedures are recognized as general (or separate) procedures, as a distinction from the event procedure. The key difference between Sub and Function procedures is that the latter returns a value, whereas the former does not. Additional distinctions are explained in the subsection "Additional Notes on General Procedures," later in this chapter. For now, the classification of procedures can be summarized as follows.

Procedure Type	How Invoked	Returns a Value?	Remark
Event	Triggered by event	No	
Sub	Referenced by name	No	Collectively recognized as general or separate
Function	Referenced by name	Yes	procedures

Writing a Sub Procedure

So, how do you create a Sub procedure? A Sub procedure is declared with a *Sub* keyword with the following syntax structure:

```
[Private¦Public] Sub SubProgramName(Parameter List)
    Statements for the sub program
```

```
     End Sub
```

where SubProgramName can be any valid name for an identifier, and ParameterList represents a list of parameters.

Note that the parameter list can range from none to many and has the following syntax:

```
[ByVal¦ByRef] Param1 As DataType1, [ByVal¦ByRef]  Param2 As
    DataType2,. . . .
```

The *ByVal* and *ByRef* keywords indicate whether the parameter will be passed by value or by reference (address). When ByVal is specified, a copy of the value of the parameter is passed to the procedure. On the other hand, if ByRef is specified, the address of the parameter is passed. The default is ByVal.

The following examples are valid subprogram headers.

```
Private Sub BringData()
Private Sub SearchPreviousInvoice(ByVal IDNumber as Long)
Public Sub Enroll(ByRef ID As Long, ByVal CourseSection As String)
```

The *Private* or *Public Modifier* declares the scope of the procedure. A private procedure is recognized only in the current form or class. A public (default) procedure is accessible to all modules in the project; that is, it can be called from another form or module.

Although the number of parameters for a procedure is determined by the task requirement, it is always difficult to use a procedure with too many parameters. Limiting the number to 5 or fewer appears to be a good rule of thumb; otherwise, try your best to order the list in a logical way so that you can easily remember the parameters needed one after another. Alternatively, try to redesign the code structure to see if it is possible to reduce the number of parameters needed.

The statements that are inside the procedure will be executed line by line in sequence when the procedure is invoked. The following Sub procedure computes and displays the area for a circle given its radius.

```
Private Sub ComputeArea(ByVal Radius As Double)
    ' This Sub computes and displays the area of a circle
    'given a radius, which is expected to be of the Double type
    Dim Area As Double
    Area = Math.Pi * Radius * Radius
    MsgBox( "The area of a circle with a radius of " _
        & Radius & " is " & Area)
End Sub
```

In this example, you declare the procedure to be Private; that is, the procedure will be recognizable and accessible only in this form. The procedure is named ComputeArea. It expects a parameter of the Double type and the parameter will be recognized in this procedure as Radius. Inside the procedure, this parameter is used to compute the area of a circle, and the resulting area is displayed by the MsgBox statement.

Calling a Sub Procedure

You can call (invoke) a Sub procedure by using the following syntax:

```
[Call] SubName(argument list)
```

To call the Sub just written, you can code the following:

```
Call ComputeArea(10)
```

or

```
ComputeArea(10)
```

Notice that you must enclose the argument(s) with a pair of parentheses in either case. Notice also that you pass an argument with a value 10 to the Sub, ComputeArea, but the argument is recognized in ComputeArea as the parameter, Radius. That is, Radius is a symbolic name for any value that the calling procedure passes to the Sub. If you change the value to 8, 8 will still be recognized by the Sub as Radius. The relationship between an argument and a parameter in this context can be depicted as the following diagram:

```
ComputeArea(10)
Private Sub ComputeArea(ByVal Radius As Double)
```

In addition, you can also use different variables as arguments to call the Sub. For example, assume that you have declared both A and B as Double and assigned proper values to both variables. You can obtain the proper results by using the following statements:

```
ComputeArea(A)
ComputeArea(B)
```

To test how it works, enter the Sub procedure in the module in the same area as you would for event procedures; then draw a new button on the form. Name it **btnCompute,** set its Text property to **Compute**, and enter the following code:

```
Private Sub btnCompute_Click(ByVal Sender As System.Object, ByVal
    e As System.EventArgs) Handles btnCompute.Click
    Dim A As Double
    Dim B As Double
    A = 10
    B = 8
    ComputeArea(A)
    ComputeArea(B)
End Sub
```

Run the project and then click the button. The message box should first display the area of the circle for a radius 10; then, for 8.

Code Reusability with the General Procedure. This simple illustration has also demonstrated a powerful use of general procedures. Much like the use of variables to handle different data values, you can use a procedure to even handle different variables that require the same computational formulas or processing steps. You can use the same Sub repetitively anytime you need to handle a similar situation, even when the variables involved are not the same; therefore, general procedures enhance the reusability of your code.

To further illustrate this point, suppose you have a program that allows the user to set the Text, ForeColor, and BackColor properties of certain controls. Rather than writing the code for each specific control, you can write a generic Sub for this purpose, and call it wherever you need to perform the task. The Sub can appear as follows:

```
Private Sub SetControlProperties(ByRef TheControl As Control,
    ByVal TheText As String, ByVal TheForeColor As Color, ByVal
    TheBackColor As Color)
    With TheControl
        .Text = TheText
        .ForeColor = TheForeColor
        .BackColor = TheBackColor
    End With
End Sub
```

This Sub takes four parameters. The first parameter is a control, the second is the text, and third and the fourth are the colors, as indicated in the header. Inside the procedure, the specified control's Text, ForeColor, and BackColor properties are assigned the values given by the parameters.

If you want to set the properties for the control named txtName, you can call the Sub using the following code:

```
SetControlProperties(CType(txtName, Control), "Jeff Tsay",
    Color.Blue, Color.Aqua)
```

If you want to set the properties for a button named btnSave, you can use this same Sub:

```
SetControlProperties(CType(btnSave, Control), "Save",
    Color.Blue, Color.Red)
```

Notice how the first argument in each statement is specified. With Option Strict On, the specific type of control, such as textbox, cannot be passed as a generic control. The CType function is used to explicitly convert each specific type to the generic control.

Position and Type of Argument. An important point you must remember in calling a Sub is that the data or objects you pass as arguments are recognized by their positions, not by their names. With SetControlProperties's header as defined previously, if you try to call it with a statement such as the following:

```
SetControlProperties("Jeff Tsay", Color.Blue, Color.Aqua,
    txtName)  X
```

you will get three parameters underlined by the compiler. The Sub expects the first parameter to be a control, but "Jeff Tsay" is a string, not a control. The same reason goes for the second and fourth parameters.

You may be wondering why then the statement:

```
ComputeArea(10)
```

did not result in the same error. (Recall that ComputeArea expects a Double type parameter, but the number 10 is an integer.) The explanation is that even under Option Strict On, the compiler allows implicit data conversion from a narrower range (Integer) to a wider range (Double).

Passing Data to Sub Procedures

This subsection takes a closer look at how data can be passed to sub procedures. In the preceding discussion, all data are passed by position. However, they can be passed either by position or by name. The following discussion provides additional details.

Passing Data By Position. The preceding subsection stresses that data passed to the Sub procedure are recognized by position, not by name. This is true even when the data types of the arguments match those parameters expected by the Sub. For example, consider the following Sub:

```
Private Sub MakeTwice(ByRef Two As Double, ByVal One As Double)
    Two = One + One
End Sub
```

This procedure doubles the value of the second parameter, and assigns the result to the first one. If in another procedure you have two variables, such as X and Y (both declared to be the Double data type and assigned with proper values), and you use the following statements:

```
MakeTwice(Y, X)
MsgBox(X & Y)
```

you should see that Y has a value twice of X. In addition, if you use the statements:

```
MakeTwice(X, Y)
MsgBox(X & Y)
```

you should see that X has a value twice of Y.

This holds even if you use the variables Two and One in the calling procedure. To test, try the following code, and be sure to include the MakeTwice Sub.

```
Private Sub Form1_Click(ByVal sender As System.Object, ByVal e As
   System.EventArgs) Handles MyBase.Click
      Dim One as Double, Two As Double
      One = 1
      Two = 2
      MakeTwice(Two, One)
      MsgBox("One = " & One & " Two " & Two)
      MakeTwice(One, Two)
      MsgBox("One = " & One & " Two = " & Two)
   End Sub
```

Run the project. When you click the form, you should see the first message box display two numbers: 1 and 2 the first time for the variables One and Two. The results are obtained as expected when the arguments are passed to the Sub as shown next.

```
      MakeTwice(Two, One)
      Private Sub MakeTwice(ByRef Two As Double, ByVal One As Double)
```

The second message box, however, will display the numbers 4 and 2 for the variables One and Two. Again, the results are obtained (perhaps not as expected for some beginners) when the arguments are passed as shown next:

```
      MakeTwice(One, Two)
      Private Sub MakeTwice(ByRef Two As Double, ByVal One As Double)
```

The variable Two in the calling procedure is passed to MakeTwice as One, which is then doubled inside the procedure and assigned to the parameter named Two; however, the corresponding variable in the calling procedure to this parameter is the variable One. The result in the calling procedure is that One has twice the value of Two.

Passing Data by Name. There is actually a way to pass data by the parameter name. Using this approach, the position of the parameter will no longer be important. The syntax to pass data by name is as follows:

SubName(Parameter1 := Argument1[, Parameter2 := Argument2] . . .)

The := symbol is used to indicate that the left side is the parameter name, whereas the right side is the argument. Parameter1 can be a parameter in any position. It does not have to be the first parameter in the parameter list in the Sub procedure's header.

Consider the following statement in previous example again.

```
      MakeTwice(X, Y)
```

Using the named parameter syntax, you can have the same result by coding:

```
      MakeTwice(Two := X, One := Y)
```

or

```
      MakeTwice(One := Y, Two := X)
```

Of course, you can also code the following for the first statement in the above Form Click event procedure:

```
      MakeTwice(Two := Two, One := One)
```

or

```
      MakeTwice(One := One, Two := Two)
```

Again, keep in mind that the name on the left of the := symbol is the parameter name, and the name on the right is the argument to be passed.

ByVal and ByRef Again. A derived question in the previous discussion is, "Why can a procedure change the value of a variable in *another* procedure?" This is because in your code, you specified ByRef for the parameter, Two. The argument's address, rather than its value, was passed. Whatever operations are performed on the parameter are actually performed on the argument. Any change made on the parameter is actually made on the argument.

If you do not want a procedure to accidentally change the value of any variables passed to it, use the *ByVal* keyword (default) in its header. For example, the header:

```
Private Sub MakeTwice(ByVal Two As Double, ByVal One As Double)
```

will cause only the values of the arguments to be passed to this procedure, not their addresses. That is, a copy of the argument, not the argument itself, is passed to the procedure. The effect is this: Whatever changes made to the parameters inside the Sub procedure will not cause any change in the variables used as arguments in the calling procedure.

In the previous example, the use of *ByVal* will make no sense because there will be no way to obtain the intended result because ByVal nullifies all desired effect of doubling the value of one of the variables; however, not all the Subs are written for the purpose of changing the values of some parameters.

ByVal is compatible with other languages. It is also true that in general, passing data ByVal executes faster than ByRef.

There is another way to have the effect of ByVal if you do not want the variable passed to a procedure gets its value changed. Enclose the variable with a pair of parentheses. For example, you can code:

```
MakeTwice ((Y), (X))
```

The arguments then will be taken as expressions, forcing the compiler to create two dummy variables to pass the data to the called procedure. Whatever changes made to the dummy variables are discarded as soon as the called procedure ends.

Terminating a Procedure Before Reaching the End: Exit Sub or Return

In some cases, your program logic in a procedure may be such that when certain conditions arise, there is no need to proceed further to execute the remainder of the code in the Sub. In such cases, you can use the Exit Sub or the Return statement to terminate the Sub procedure. The effect will be the same as if the Sub has reached the End Sub statement. For example, assume you have a Sub to save an inventory part in a file. The part number must be greater than 100; otherwise, it is considered invalid. Your Sub may appear as follows:

```
Private Sub SavePart(ByVal ID As Integer, ByVal PartName As
   String)
      If ID <= 100 Then
         MsgBox("The ID number is not valid. Part not saved.")
         Exit Sub 'You can substitute Return for Exit Sub here
      End If
      ' The routine to save the part will continue from here
End Sub
```

Exit Sub Versus End Sub. If both End Sub and Exit Sub (and Return) statements terminate a procedure, what is the difference between the two? The End Sub statement actually serves two purposes. It not only terminates a Sub procedure when the execution control reaches that point, but also physically defines the boundary of a Sub procedure. It tells the compiler that the procedure ends here. No other statements beyond this point should be considered a part of this procedure. On the other hand, the Exit Sub (Return) statement terminates the Sub at that point and returns execution control to the calling procedure. Because no other statements inside the procedure will be executed after the control reaches this statement, the Exit Sub (Return) statement is usually included in an If block; that is, you would want to terminate a Sub only when certain conditions occur.

Event Procedures and General Sub Procedures

At this point, you may wonder about the differences between the event procedures and the general Sub procedures. After all, both have the keyword Sub. The two differ in several aspects:

- Event procedures are triggered by events. As you recall, these events are results of something occurring in the systems or the results of the user's actions. There is no explicit call in the code to invoke an event procedure. In contrast, the general Sub procedures must be triggered (invoked) by code. That is, somewhere in the code, the name of the general Sub procedure must be referenced, and only when this line of code is executed will the general Sub be invoked. Note, however, an event procedure can also be invoked by an explicit call like the way a general Sub is called.

- A corollary of the preceding difference is that in general, you will find general Subs are called from an event procedure or another general Sub procedure; however, it is rare that a general Sub calls an event procedure even though it is permissible to do so.

- By convention, the name of an event procedure follows a specific syntax structure. The first part of it is the name of the object with which the event is associated, and the second part is the name of the event. These two parts are connected with an underscore. For example, the name for the Form1's Load event procedure is Form1_Load. Form1 is the name of the object and Load is the event. Between Form1 and Load, there is the underscore ("_"). More important, at the end of the name header, there is a Handles clause that begins with the keyword Handles followed by the name of the object, a dot (.), and the name of the event. In this clause, the name must be the object name and the event must be one recognized by the object. (Additional variations in naming event handlers are discussed in Chapter 12, "Object Based Programming.") In contrast, you can create any name for a general Sub procedure as long as the name can be considered a legitimate identifier name.

- The number, order, and data type of parameters for event procedures are predefined by the system. You cannot change these elements in any event procedure. In contrast, you have complete freedom in deciding these elements in the general procedures that you create.

- In terms of scope, the event procedure must be Private, whereas the Sub procedure can either be Private or Public.

These differences are summarized in the following table.

Difference in	Event Procedure	General Sub Procedure
Trigger	Event (triggered by the occurrence of the event)	Referenced by code (called by another procedure)
Caller	Seldom called from another procedure	Must be called by another procedure, which can be an event or general procedure
Name syntax	Should observe the following structure: ObjectName_EventName (variations discussed in Chapter 12)	Can use any legitimate identifier name as the name of a Sub
Parameter list	Predefined by VB	Designed by the programmer
Scope	Private	Public (default) or Private

Function Procedures

Consider the previous MakeTwice Sub procedure example again. The example is used to illustrate how arguments passed to a Sub are handled. If you carefully reexamine the design, you should realize that there is a better way to structure the code. Recall that in the Sub, one parameter (One) was used to compute the value of the other (Two), which could then be used by the calling procedure. That is, the Sub procedure was used to generate one result based on the value of another parameter. In such a case, a Function (instead of a Sub) procedure is a better choice. The key difference between a Sub and a Function procedure is that the latter returns a value, whereas the former does not.

The Function Procedure Header. So, how do you create a Function procedure? The Function procedure is declared with the Function keyword with the following syntax:

```
[Public¦Private] Function Name(parameter list) [As Type]
    'Statements (including Exit Function or Return)
    Name = Expression
End Function
```

As you can see in the syntax, the Function procedure header has the scope descriptor (Public or Private) and the parameter list (similar to the Sub procedure); however, the function header accepts a Type declaration, whereas the Sub does not. The Type declaration at the end of the function header specifies the type of data that the function will return. Inside the Function procedure, the function name should appear at least once on the left side of an assignment statement. The value so assigned is the value returned to the caller. Alternatively, you can use the Return statement to return a value. The syntax appears as follows:

```
Return(Expression)
```

The Differences Between Subs and Functions. There are several differences between Sub and Function procedures.

- Because the Function procedure is expected to return a value to the calling procedure, you should provide a Type declaration at the end of the header. (With Option Strict On, you must specify the type.) The type declared here is the data type of the value to be returned by the function. The Sub procedure is not expected to return a value. A Type declaration in its header is not allowed.

- Both types of procedures will contain statements that carry out computations. In a Function procedure, however, at least one statement should have the effect of returning a value. This can be either an assignment statement that has the function name on the left side or a Return statement with an expression as its parameter. The execution of this statement will cause the value of the expression to be returned to the calling procedure. On the other hand, the name of the Sub procedure must not appear in any assignment statement.

- Because the Function procedure returns a value, its name is typically used as a part of an expression, whereas the Sub procedure is used as a statement (when referenced without the keyword "Call") or a part of a statement (when referenced with the keyword "Call").

Writing a Function Procedure. To illustrate the structure of a function, you can rewrite the MakeTwice Sub into a Function procedure called Twice as follows:

```
Private Function Twice(ByVal One As Double) as Double
    Twice = One + One
End Function
```

or

```
Private Function Twice(ByVal One As Double) as Double
    Return(One + One)
End Function
```

The function is named Twice, and is declared to be a Double type because it is expected to return a value of this type. Inside the first example procedure, the parameter One is doubled, and the result is assigned to Twice—the name of the Function procedure. This statement enables the function to return the value computed. In the second example procedure, the Return statement first doubles the parameter value of One and then returns the result to the caller. If none of the statements inside a Function procedure either assigns a value to the function name (in this case, Twice) or has a Return statement with an expression, the function will return a value of zero (or a zero-length string if the function is expected to return a string).

The preceding function can then be used by other procedures as follows:

```
Two = Twice(10)
```

or, assuming a proper declaration and assignment of value have been made for A,

```
MsgBox("Twice of " & A & " is " & Twice(A))
```

Note that similar to the Sub procedure, the argument passed to the function does not have to be named One (the name used for the parameter) but can be any constant, variables, or expressions of the same type.

As another example, the previous Sub to compute the area of a circle can be rewritten as a function as follows:

```
Private Function AreaOfCircle(ByVal Radius As Double) As Double
    ' This function computes and returns the area of a circle
    'given a radius, which is expected to be of the Double type
    AreaOfCircle = Math.Pi * Radius * Radius
End Function
```

In this function, you make the function only compute and return the area, but have omitted the code to display the result. This choice is by design, not by the restriction on a function.

Using the Function Procedure

From the preceding examples, you must have noticed that the way to use/invoke a function is by the reference of the Function procedure's name. Arguments passed to a function must be enclosed in a pair of parentheses. Because the function is expected to return a value, the name of the function typically appears in an expression. That is, a function can be used exactly like a constant or a variable, in exactly the same way as built-in functions. But a Sub cannot be used in the same manner. The only difference between a built-in function and a general function procedure is that the former is predefined (built-in) in the system, whereas you are the one to define the latter whenever you choose to use one.

Additional Notes on General Procedures

You have been introduced to the basic syntax and concepts on general procedures. This subsection considers additional important issues and features regarding these kinds of procedures.

Function Versus Sub. Those examples in the discussion of Function procedures may make you wonder when you should create a Sub and when you should create a Function procedure. The key distinction between the two types of general procedures is that one returns a value, and the other does not. In general, when there is a need for the procedure to return a value, the procedure should be written as a function. This includes the following situations:

- When the value returned from a function will be used like a variable in an expression; therefore, all computational problems that obtain a result based on a list of parameters naturally fall in this category.

- When there is a need to determine whether the computations/actions performed by the procedure are successful. For example, the execution of the procedure may fail because of some external conditions; for example, required files are missing or not available, or an operation is canceled by the user. In such cases, the procedure can be written as a function and then returns an execution code to indicate whether the execution was successful, which can be used by the calling procedure to determine the proper courses of actions.

If the procedure is not required to return any value but just to carry out some activities, it will be more appropriate to create this procedure as a Sub.

Naming the General Procedure. All identifier names should be descriptive. Names for procedures are no exception. Because the Sub procedures will be more related to actions, it is advisable to use names that begin with a verb; for example, SaveCustomerRecord, DisplayAssetItem, and ClearScreen. The names for Function procedures are a bit trickier. Those functions for computational results are usually given the nomenclature of the values they return; for example, AreaOfCircle, CubeRoot, and GrossPay. Those functions used to carry out actions but expected to provide a return code are usually given names that begin with a verb, too. They can be easily confused with Subs. Fortunately, the confusion does not cause coding problems. When you do not need a return value from a function of this kind, you can use it as if it were a Sub by referencing the name without assigning the result to another variable. For example, suppose you have a function CheckDate that returns a value True and displays an error message when a String parameter passed to it is not a valid date. The function appears as follows:

```
Function CheckDate(TheDate As String) As Boolean
    'This function checks if a string contains a valid date
    'in the mm/dd/yyyy format and
    'returns a value True when the date is invalid
    If IsDate(TheDate) AndAlso
      Val(Microsoft.VisualBasic.Left(TheDate, 2)) <= 12 Then
        'This appears to be a valid date. Do nothing
        Return(False) 'Return False to caller
    End If
    'Execution will reach here only if it fails the above test.
    'Display an error message and set the return code to True
    MsgBox("Must have a valid date to proceed.")
    Return(True)
End Function
```

But suppose in your code, all you need is to display an error message if the string variable BirthDate is invalid. Its return code will not be used. You can still use the function just like a Sub as follows:

```
CheckDate(BirthDate)
```

You can even invoke it by using the Call statement syntax as follows:

```
Call CheckDate(BirthDate)
```

The CheckDate Function. Perhaps some explanation of the code in the CheckDate function is in order. The function takes a string, TheDate, as its only parameter. It assumes that the date is in the mm/dd/yyyy format. In the procedure, it first uses the IsDate function to check whether the string appears to be a valid date. If so, it further checks to see whether the first two digits in the string are not greater than 12. This is necessary because IsDate accepts strings in several different date formats, including the dd/mm/yyyy format. The string "31/12/2002" will be considered valid, although it should be considered invalid in the CheckDate function. The second expression in the If statement ensures that the month portion of the string is not greater than 12.

If a string passes both tests, it should be a valid date. The Return statement will return a value False. If the string fails either test of the IsDate or the second expression, it is considered invalid. The MsgBox function is used to display an error message. In addition, the Return statement will return a value True, indicating the string is not a valid date.

Documenting General Procedures. A procedure typically is written to perform a much more complex task than the examples illustrated previously; therefore, it is important to document the procedure properly with remarks (comments) when it is being developed. These comments should include at least the following:

- The purposes of the procedure
- What is returned if the procedure is a function
- A description of the required parameters
- Assumptions made
- The algorithm used if the problem is fairly complex

All the examples given previously are coded with this in mind. If you did not notice the comments given at the beginning of each procedure, you may want to take another look now. Of course, additional comments pertinent to any code in the procedure should be added, just as you would typically do for an event procedure.

Recursion. All the VB procedures are recursive; that it, each procedure can call itself. This feature can be a powerful programming tool. A complex programming problem can be solved with an algorithm that recursively (repetitively) divides the problem into a smaller problem of the same nature until the latter is simple enough to solve.

A classical example of the use of recursion is the computation of n factorial (n!). When n is large enough, the problem calls for a fairly long series of computations; however, the problem can be subdivided into a problem of n (n - 1)! That is, if you are able to obtain the result of (n - 1)!, all you have to do to obtain the result is to multiply n by the factorial of one less. You can now solve the problem of (n - 1)! in the same manner; that is, if you think of (n - 1) as n', n'! can be solved with the same algorithm. This divide and conquer method can be continued until the n at hand is a value one (1); then, there is no need to divide the problem any further. The result is 1. This value can be returned to the previous level, which can then multiply, obtain the result, and return to yet another previous level. The process repeats until it reaches the original problem level. There the problem is solved.

The following table shows the process of arriving at the solution for 4! based on the description in the preceding paragraph.

Problem-Solving Description	Example	Solution Return Process	Solution
1. Original problem	4!	10. Obtain result and return	24
2. Divide the problem	4 x 3!	9. Obtain result and return	4 x 6
3. Divide the next problem 3!	3 x 2!	8. Obtain result and return	3 x 2
4. Divide the next problem 2!	2 x 1!	7. Obtain result and return	2 x 1
5. Solve the problem 1!	1	6. Return result to preceding level	1

Column 1 shows the solution process, and column 2 shows the numeric example based on the process. Column 3 shows how the result is obtained at each subsequent step, and should be read from bottom to the top with its corresponding numeric results in column 4.

How can this process be implemented in VB? The following code provides the solution:

```
Private Function Factorial(N As Integer) As Long
    ' This function computes the value of N!
    ' where N is an integer
    ' Assumption: N is a number not to exceed 20
    ' Otherwise, overflow will result
    If N > 1 Then
        Factorial = N * Factorial (N - 1)
    Else
        Factorial = 1
    End If
End Function
```

This function literally implements the algorithm just described. When n is greater than 1, the function calls itself to find the result of the factorial of 1 less than the current n. The result returned from this call is then multiplied and returned to the caller, which can be itself. Only when n reaches a value not greater than 1 does the function consider the problem simple enough to find the solution (1), and return to the previous level.

The following table shows the execution process for an initial parameter value 4.

N	Function Call	Call Return (from Bottom to Top)
Initial call	Factorial (4)	24
4	4 * Factorial(3)	4 * 6
3	3 * Factorial(2)	3 * 2
2	2 * Factorial(1)	2 * 1
1	Return 1	1

To use a recursive procedure is no different from any other typical procedure. For example, after entering the code for the previous Factorial function, if you place the following statement in a button Click event, you should see a message box displaying, "Factorial(4) = 24".

```
MsgBox("Factorial(4) = " & Factorial(4))
```

Cascading an Event Procedure. Even the event procedure is recursive; that is, an event procedure can trigger the same event and invoke itself within itself. In general, recursion for event procedures occurs by accident, not by design. They are written to handle events. Triggering an event to handle the event itself just does not make much sense. You should take care not to code an event procedure that causes recursion of itself. As an illustration of event cascading, consider the following code:

```
Private Sub txtNumber_TextChanged(ByVal Sender As System.Object,
    ByVal e As System.EventArgs) Handles txtNumber.TextChanged
    txtNumber.Text = CStr(1 + Val(txtNumber.Text))
End Sub
```

The code is placed in the text box's *TextChanged* event that occurs when the value of the text box changes. The programmer may think the code will increase the number entered by the user by 1; however, when you run the project and press a numeric key into the text box, you will encounter an unhandled error. Why? Initially, the number entered by the user is increased by 1 and then assigned to the Text property of the text box. This action causes a change in the text box and thus triggers another TextChanged event, invoking the event procedure itself before the current event procedure ends. This process continues until the computer runs out of stack memory.

Actually, the code was placed in that event procedure because of the misunderstanding of the TextChanged event, which occurs after *each* key is entered or after an assignment of data to the text box. If the intent was to increase the value in the text box by 1 after the field has been properly entered, the code should be placed in either the text box's Validating or Leave event when the user leaves the field.

If you encounter an unhandled error in your program, consider recursion as a possible source of error. If you use a recursive procedure, make sure it can exit without calling itself. If the error occurs in an event procedure, examine the code carefully. Look at the left side of the assignment statements for the control name associated with the event. When you find one, check to ensure that the statement does not trigger the same event.

Optional Parameters. The general procedure can have optional parameters that can be omitted when the procedure is called. An optional parameter is specified with the keyword Optional, and must be provided with a default value. All parameters following an optional parameter must be optional; the syntax to specify the header for a general procedure is as follows:

```
[Public¦Private] {Sub¦Function}([required parameter
    list][,optional parameter list])
```

where the optional parameter list can be specified as:

```
Optional {ByVal¦ByRef} Name1 As Type1[, Optional {ByVal¦ByRef}
    Name2 As Type2]. . . .
```

The following are valid examples of specifying optional parameters:

```
Sub AnyGeneralProc(ByVal A As Integer, Optional ByVal B As single
    = -9999, Optional ByVal C as Double = -9999)
Private Function QuickCount(Optional ByVal FirstCount As _
    Integer = 0, Optional ByVal SecondCount As Integer = 0 ) _
    As Integer
```

Because both of the QuickCount parameters are optional, when you invoke the function, you can provide both parameters or omit either or both of the parameters as follows:

```
QuickCount(X, Y)
QuickCount(X)
QuickCount(, Y)
QuickCount()
```

The omitted parameter will have a value zero as specified in the header.

You have seen built-in functions that allow optional parameters. For example, the Rnd function allows omission of its only parameter, and the Mid function allows the omission of its last parameter. Typically, for the convenience of coding the calling procedure, a procedure can be written to allow optional parameters if their values can be assumed or derived. Consider a function that computes the net pay for employees. The net pay depends on the total earnings that include gross pay, commissions, and tips. But not all employees have all three elements. In this case, you can make the commissions and tips optional and code the header as follows:

```
Function NetPay(ByVal GrossPay As Double, _
    Optional ByVal Commission As Double = 0, _
    Optional ByVal Tip As Double = 0) As Double
      'Statements to compute net pay
End Function
```

To compute the net pay for an employee who has gross pay and tips but no commission, you can then code:

```
Amount = NetPay(GrossPay,, Tip)
```

Overloading Procedures. You can write two or more different procedures (Sub or Function) with the same name as long as they have different parameter lists in number, type, or both. For example, suppose you want to write a generalized function that gives you the smaller of two values that can be either of Long type of String type. You can code the function as follows:

```
Function Smaller(ByVal A As Long, ByVal B As Long) As Long
    If A <= B Then
        Return (A)
    Else
        Return (B)
    End If
End Function
Function Smaller(ByVal A As String, ByVal B As String) As String
    If A <= B Then
        Return (A)
    Else
        Return (B)
    End If
End Function
```

You can then use the function to obtain the smaller of two values as long as the two parameters are both either of the Long type or the String type similar to the following:

```
MsgBox("The smaller of 23 and -10 is " & Smaller(23, -10))
MsgBox("The smaller of X and b is " & Smaller("X", "b"))
```

Of course, you can add additional functions to handle other data types. This feature, recognized as overloading, makes it convenient to call procedures of similar functionality without having to differentiate between data types or the number of parameters. (Note that the Math.Min function does exactly what our example here attempts to do. Smaller is used as an example because of its simplicity.)

To explicitly indicate that a procedure overloads another, precede the Function or Sub keyword with the Overloads keyword. A more explicit header for the Smaller function should be:

```
Public Overloads Function Smaller(ByVal A As Long, _
    ByVal B As Long) As Long
```

Note that if you precede one of the overloading procedures with the Overloads keyword, you must do the same for all procedures with the same name.

Uses of General Procedures

You may wonder why go through all the trouble of creating general procedures. After all, you may end up with more lines of code. In addition, the calls and returns between procedures impose overhead in handling all the housekeeping tasks inside the computer, which can slow down the program. These drawbacks, however, must be weighed against the advantages of creating and using these procedures. Here are some of their important advantages:

- General procedures facilitate top-down and modular design. A huge, complex task can be broken down into smaller, manageable tasks, each written as a procedure. When designed this way, the main program is much easier to read, and its logic is much easier to trace. The programmer can focus on requirements of the main task at the beginning, and then take care of the details of smaller tasks later. Several programmers can even work together on the same project, each taking care of some of the lower-level procedures. This is the advantage cited at the beginning of this section.

- Problems can be isolated, making the program easier to understand, debug, and revise.

- Procedures can be made reusable. Carefully designed general (public) procedures can be called from any part of the project, eliminating the need to repeat similar code in different parts of the project. This not only reduces the size of the program, but also simplifies the coding. Later, if the procedure needs to be revised or corrected, the programmer needs to focus on only one place (the procedure). Any change made to the procedure applies to all parts of the project that call the procedure, making it much easier (and more efficient and effective) to maintain the code.

- Function procedures can make code easier to understand. A function procedure returns a value that can be used just like a constant or variable in a formula. The meaning of the formula can be clear to the developer and the reader/reviewer. The complexity of the computations is isolated from the main focus of the problem. This structure of code will be much easier to review and understand than one that includes complex code to carry out the computations of the formula.

- Recursion simplifies problem solving. Wherever a complex problem can be subdivided into simpler problems using the same algorithm, a recursive procedure can be developed. This makes the program much shorter and easier to code.

6.3 An Application Example

This section presents a project that will use some of the features you have learned in this chapter. This project involves uses of file dialog boxes, file input and output, and general procedures. It also considers a few code design issues.

The Contacts Project

This program (Contacts) will be used to maintain a file that contains your friends' phone numbers and names. This file has been created as a text file, so it will be easy to handle the file with the StreamReader and StreamWriter. Note that a file can only be opened either for input or for output (or append) mode; that is, it cannot be associated with the StreamReader and the StreamWriter at the same time. When a file needs to be updated (edit, add, or delete records), you will need to handle it as follows:

1. Open (create) a new output file.
2. Read the original file, and let the user inspect the records one at a time.
   - If a record needs no correction, it can be saved in the new file as is; otherwise, the user can make the change and then save the record.
   - If a record needs to be deleted, the user will choose not to save it in the new file.
   - To add a new record, the user enters the new data and then saves it.

The User Interface

The form should contain data fields for the user to enter the phone number and name. These two fields can also be used to display the record read from the existing phone file.

- The field for the phone number is a masked edit box.
- The field for the name is a text box.

The form should also contain four buttons for the user to initiate actions to do the following:

- Read a record from the existing file.
- Save the record displayed on the fields. These can be either from the file or entered by the user.
- Clear the fields so that the user can enter new data.
- Quit.

The form should also include an open file dialog named cdlOpenFile to prompt for file path to open for input, as well as a save file dialog named cdlSaveFile to prompt for file path to save (for output). Finally, this form should include a group box to hold the data fields (with their proper labels). The resulting visual interface appears as Figure 6.5.

The following table provides a list of controls along with selected properties referenced in the code.

Control	Property	Setting	Remark
Open file dialog	Name	cdlOpenFile	To prompt for input file path
	CheckFileExists	True	To make sure the file exists
Save file dialog	Name	cdlSaveFile	To prompt for output file path
	OverwritePrompt	True	To ensure an existing file not accidentally erased
Masked edit Box	Name	mskPhone	Phone field
	Mask	(###)-###-####	
Text box	Name	TxtName	Name field
Button	Name	btnRead	To read a record
	Text	Read	
Button	Name	btnSave	To save a record
	Text	Save	
Button	Name	btnClearScreen	To clear the screen
	Text	Erase	
Button	Name	btnQuit	To close file and quit
	Text	Quit	

Figure 6.5

Visual interface for the Contacts project

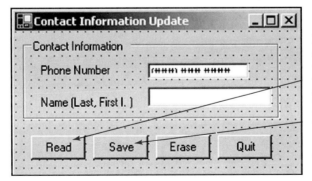

In this application, existing contact data are read from an existing file when the Read button is clicked. Whatever appears on the "Contact Information" group box will be saved onto another file when the Save button is clicked. An open file dialog and a save file dialog are used to prompt for the file paths.

The program should behave in the following manner:

- As soon as the program starts, it should display an open file dialog box to prompt the user for the phone file and then a save file dialog box to prompt for the name to save as the new file.
- When the user clicks the Read button, it reads a record from the existing file and then places the record in the masked edit box and the text box. When the file runs out of records, the program displays a message to such an effect.
- When the user clicks the Save button, the data is saved on the new file; then, the data fields onscreen are cleared.
- When the user clicks the Erase button, the data fields onscreen are cleared.

Designing the Code Structure

If you inspect the program's requirements closely, several points should draw your attention:

- The open and save file dialog boxes will be used to prompt for file paths: the open file dialog for the input file, and the save file dialog for the output file. Recall that it takes several lines of code before the dialog box's ShowDialog method is used to prompt for a file; however, most of the statements will be the same for both situations. This condition presents itself as a possibility to create a general procedure that can be called to handle both prompts. Should this procedure be a Sub or a function? Recall that the key difference between the two is in whether the procedure returns a value. It seems that requiring the procedure to return the filename will make the procedure more convenient to use. The programmer will not need to look for or remember the name of the file dialog box to obtain the result; therefore, the procedure should and will be coded as a function, and will be called GetTheFileName.
- There are two situations in which clear screen is called for—when the data is saved and when the Erase button is clicked. Again, creating a general procedure to handle the clearing will shorten the code. There is no need for the procedure to return a value. This procedure will be coded as a Sub, and will be named ClearScreen.
- All other requirements can be implemented in the event procedures directly.

Given these considerations, you will create two general procedures, and handle all other requirements in the event procedures.

Determining the Parameters for the General Procedures. The preceding discussion suggests that two general procedures should be created: ClearScreen and GetTheFileName. What parameters, if any, should each procedure have?

Obviously, the action to clear the screen will be the same regardless of the situation that triggers the call; there will be no need for ClearScreen to require any parameters. In determining the parameters for the GetTheFileName function, several factors should be considered:

- There are two file dialogs in the program. The function needs to know which one to use. One easy way to handle this is to pass the specified dialog as a parameter.
- The program will prompt for two different files. The user should be properly informed of which file the program is looking for. Recall that both file dialog boxes have the Title property that can be used to specify the title. The title can be used to display the prompt. The calling procedure can specify the title. This procedure can then display the proper one, so the title should be one of the parameters required by the procedure.
- What types of files should appear in the dialog box? Recall that the file dialog boxes have a Filter property by which you can specify the type of files to display in the dialog box. For this project, you could allow only the text file and hard-code the file filter in the procedure; however, if you would like the procedure to be more general, you should

also allow different file filters to be specified. This means another required parameter should be the file filter.

- You should also consider the file's existence status. When the function is prompting for the existing phone file for input, it should expect that the file has already existed. Because the open file dialog will be used in this case, its CheckFileExists property should be set to True at design time as shown in the preceding table. On the other hand, when it prompts for the output file, if the file already exists, it should caution the user that the file will be written over. Because the save file dialog will be used in this case, its WriteOverPrompt property should be set to True, again as shown in the preceding table. These two situations can be handled at design time. No code or parameter for the function is called for.

Coding the Project

Based on the preceding discussion, you are now ready to write the code for the project. Consider the two general procedures first.

The GetTheFileName Function. This procedure should be a function instead of a Sub. It should also take three parameters—one for the file dialog, another for the title, and the other for the file filter. The header of the procedure should appear as follows:

```
Private Function GetTheFileName(ByVal TheDialog As FileDialog, _
    ByVal TheTitle As String, ByVal TheFilter As String) As String
```

Notice that the type of the function is declared to be As String because you expect the function to return a filename of the String type. The function is declared as a Private procedure because you do not expect it to be called by other forms or modules.

The calling procedure will then supply as its arguments: the file dialog (TheDialog), the dialog title (TheTitle) and the file filter (TheFilter) when calling this function. Inside this function, the TheTitle parameter can then be assigned to the dialog box's Title property, and the TheFilter parameter, the Filter property. The complete procedure should appear as follows:

```
Private Function GetTheFileName(ByVal TheDialog As FileDialog, _
    ByVal TheTitle As String, ByVal TheFilter As String) As String
    With TheDialog
        .Title = TheTitle
        .Filter = TheFilter
        .ShowDialog()
        Return (.FileName) 'Return the filename to caller
    End With
End Function
```

The detail working of most statements in this procedure has been explained in the first section of this chapter. The way to use this procedure is further discussed in the next subsection, "Coding the Event Procedures."

Notice the following statement:

```
Return(.FileName)
```

This statement returns the filename obtained by the dialog box from the ShowDialog method (the line above this statement) to the calling procedure (caller).

The ClearScreen Procedure. The ClearScreen procedure clears the masked edit box and the text box. The code should be fairly straightforward, and should appear as follows:

```
Sub ClearScreen()
Dim Temp As String
    'See chapter 3 for an explanation of the following code
    'Clear the masked edit box
    Temp = mskPhone.Mask 'Save the mask
    mskPhone.Mask = "" 'Clear the mask
```

```
                         mskPhone.Text = "" ' Clear the text
                         mskPhone.Mask = Temp ' Restore the mask
                         ' Clear the text box
                         txtName.Text = ""
                     End Sub
```

> **TIP**
>
> If the Text property of the masked edit does not work properly, use the following routine as a
> workaround to clear the box.
>
> ```
> mskPhone.SelStart = 0
> mskPhone.SelLength = Len(mskPhone.Mask)
> mskPhone.SelText = Space(Len(mskPhone.Mask))
> ```

Coding the Event Procedures

Recall that as soon as the project starts, the program will prompt the user for the path of the input file and then for the output file. In addition, there are four buttons to allow the user to initiate various activities.

Prompting for the File Paths. Because the program will prompt for the file paths as soon as the project starts, the code should be placed in the Form Load event. The prompt will involve calls to the GetTheFileName function, which requires three parameters, one of which is the file filter. As discussed previously, the expected file type should be the text file; the file extension should be txt. Just in case the user might use a different file extension, you will also allow all other file extensions. The filter string should be just a constant for the purpose of this example. It is suggested that constants be declared at a broader scope so that other procedures can use the same. You will place the declaration of the filter string in the general declaration area.

```
Const FileFilter As String =  "Text Files (*.txt)¦*.txt¦All Files
   (*.*)¦*.*"
```

After the file paths are obtained, the input file should be associated with a StreamReader; the output file should be associated with a StreamWriter. These files should remain open throughout the life of the project because the program will continue to read and write while the project is running. This consideration should also hint that the StreamReader and StreamWriter associated with the files should be recognized by all the event procedures dealing with the files; therefore, the two object variables should be declared as the class-level variables. On the other hand, filenames are needed only at the time they are to be opened. Recall that in general, all variables should be declared with a scope as narrow as possible, so you will declare the filenames in the Form Load procedure while declaring the StreamReader and StreamWriter in the general declaration area.

In summary, the general declaration area should contain the declaration of two object variables and a constant as follows:

```
Const FileFilter As String = "Text Files (*.txt)¦*txt¦All Files
   (*.*)¦*.*"
Dim ContactReader As System.IO.StreamReader
Dim ContactWriter As System.IO.StreamWriter
```

The Form Load procedure will declare the variables, prompt for the file paths, and open the files (associate files with the StreamReader and StreamWriter). It should appear as follows:

```
Private Sub frmContacts_Load(ByVal sender As System.Object, ByVal
   e As System.EventArgs) Handles MyBase.Load
     Dim InFileName As String
     Dim OutFileName As String
     'Prompt for the existing input file path
```

```
      InFileName = GetTheFileName(cdlOpenFile, "Where is the Phone
        File?", FileFilter)
      'Prompt for the output file path
      OutFileName = GetTheFileName(cdlSaveFile, "Specify Filename to
        Save", FileFilter)
      'Open phone file to read
      ContactReader = New System.IO.StreamReader(InFileName)
      ' Open output file to write
      ContactWriter = New System.IO.StreamWriter(OutFileName)
  End Sub
```

Using the GetTheFileName Function. Notice how the GetTheFileName function is invoked. In the first case, to prompt for the existing input file, the open file dialog (cdlOpenFile) is passed as the file dialog, and the constant literal **Where is the Phone File?** is passed as the TheTitle parameter. This should make the open file dialog display a title to prompt for the phone file. For simplicity, the program assumes the phone file has already existed and takes no steps in creating a new one. Before testing this project, create a text file with one phone number and name using Notepad.

In the second case, to prompt for the output file path, the save file dialog (cdlSaveFile) is passed as the file dialog, and the constant literal **Specify Filename to Save** is passed as the TheTitle parameter so that the dialog box can display it to prompt for the output file.

The two files are then opened as (associated with) ContactReader and ContactWriter, which are declared as class-level object variables to be recognizable by other event procedures. Note that in this event procedure, there is no testing for file validity. Several things can go wrong in this procedure. For example, the user may click the Cancel button in response to the prompt for the file path. This will result in a zero-length string being returned as the filename, causing an invalid filename error when the procedure attempts to open the file. Also, the user may specify the same filename for both input and output by mistake. This will cause a conflict in an attempt to open the file both for input and output. Adding additional If blocks to guard against these potential errors is left to you as an exercise.

Reading the Phone File. When the user clicks the Read button, your program should read a record such as the phone number and name, and display the data on the masked edit and text box controls. The code to read and write the file depends on how the data appear in the data file. You expect the file to have one record per line. Each record has a phone number and name that are separated with a comma followed by a blank space. A sample file appears as follows:

```
8172726009, Tsay, Jeffrey J.
3333838, Handler, Henry H.
4809359999, Tuff, Tiffany T.
.
.
```

If the file runs out of records, a message should be displayed and the execution for the procedure should be terminated with the Exit Sub or Return statement. The code for the event procedure should appear as follows:

```
Private Sub btnRead_Click(ByVal Sender As System.Object, ByVal e
    As System.EventArgs) Handles btnRead.Click
    Dim PhoneName As String
    Dim PhoneNo As String
    Dim Name As String
    Dim P As Integer
    If ContactReader.Peek() = -1 Then
        MsgBox("No more phone records.")
        Exit Sub
    End If
    PhoneName = ContactReader.ReadLine()
    P = InStr(PhoneName, ",")
    PhoneNo = Microsoft.VisualBasic.Left(PhoneName, P - 1)
```

```
        Name = Mid(PhoneName, P + 2) 'skip the space after comma to
          get the name
        mskPhone.Text = Format(Val(PhoneNo), "(000)-000-0000")
        txtName.Text = Name
    End Sub
```

On the Format String. Notice how the phone number is formatted. The masked edit box has the mask "(###)-###-####," as shown in the visual interface. You can actually use the Mask property as the format string for the phone number; however, if the phone number has fewer digits than the specified format, the resulting string will not fit the mask, producing an error. For example, if the actual number is 3333838, the resulting string will be "()-333-3838." On the other hand, the format string "(000)-000-0000" will force zeros to fill in the leading missing digits, resulting in a string "(000)-333-3838," which will be acceptable to the masked edit box given the mask.

Saving the Data Fields. When the user clicks the Save button, the program is expected to save the data onscreen onto the output file. The data can come from the Read operation either with or without the user's correction and from the user's direct entry into the data fields. A simple WriteLine statement should take care of creating a record. To be sure that there are data to be saved, the program should also check whether the name field is blank. In addition, after the record is saved, the data fields should be cleared by calling the ClearScreen procedure. The complete code for the event procedure appears as follows:

```
    Private Sub btnSave_Click(ByVal Sender As System.Object, ByVal e
      As System.EventArgs) Handles btnSave.Click
        If Len(Trim(txtName.Text)) = 0 Then
            MsgBox("Please enter a valid name.")
            Exit Sub
        End If
        ContactWriter.WriteLine(mskPhone.ClipText & ", " & _
          txtName.Text) 'Write the phone number and name
        ClearScreen()
    End Sub
```

Notice that the masked edit box's ClipText property (not the Text property) is saved. This property strips the mask's literal (parentheses and dashes) from the text string so that only the digits entered by the user are saved.

Erasing the Data Fields. The user can choose to erase the data fields when he or she sees no need to preserve the record. The user can then proceed to read another record, or enter his or her own data. The event procedure can be easily taken care of by a call to the ClearScreen Sub as shown next:

```
    Private Sub btnClearScreen_Click(ByVal Sender As System.Object,
      ByVal e As System.EventArgs) Handles btnClearScreen.Click
        ClearScreen()
    End Sub
```

Terminating the Program. Finally, terminating the program is a simple procedure that should close the form.

```
    Private Sub btnQuit_Click(ByVal Sender As System.Object, ByVal e
      As System.EventArgs) Handles btnSave.Click
        Me.Close
    End Sub
```

Also, as noted previously, the ContactReader and ContactWriter objects associated with the files should be closed, too. Should the code also be placed in the Quit button's click event? You should be aware that the form can also be closed if the user click the Close button in the form's title bar. In this case, the Quit button's click event will not be triggered. Placing the code there will not close the objects.

The form closing event will always be triggered regardless how the form is closed,—by code or by the user's click on the Close button. Those objects should be closed in this event. The code appears as follows:

```
Private Sub frmContacts_Closing(ByVal sender As System.Object,
   ByVal e As System.ComponentModel.CancelEventArgs) Handles
   MyBase.Closing
      ContactReader.Close()
      ContactWriter.Close()
End Sub
```

Additional Remarks

The preceding procedures should complete the requirements for the project. Before leaving this example, keep in mind that it is presented only for the purpose of illustrating how the various parts you have learned in this chapter can be pieced together. Please note the following points in particular:

- This program assumes that the phone file has already existed. To test the code for this example, you should create a text file first, perhaps with Notepad. The phone number should be the first field, and the name should be the second field of each record (line). Be sure to separate the phone and the name with a comma followed by a space.

- When you work with the program as the user, you should feel very nervous about the accuracy of the results. For example, if you repetitively click the Read button, the program will continue to read the records from the existing file. There is no warning that the previous record has not yet been saved. Also, the records in the old file that have not been read before the program quits will not be saved. All these situations can certainly cause the new file to miss records that should have been kept. The needed refinements to guard against potential losses of data are left to you as an exercise.

- In general, you would rather have a way to update/edit a record randomly; that is, you would rather have the ability to recall a record for edit at random choice instead of having the program dictate the sequence in which records are retrieved. The approach used in the example will take too long and cost unnecessary effort and attention (plus potential errors) of the user. A better approach would be to structure the file so that it is capable of being randomly accessed, or to save the records in a database table. In either case, a record can be retrieved and updated directly. New records can also be added to the file (database table) without any need to deal with the existing records. Databases are discussed in Chapter 9, "Database and ADO.NET." The use of random files is discussed in Appendix A, "Data Management Using Files."

- Despite the shortcomings of the example project just noted, you should be able to appreciate the reasons for creating those general (separate) procedures and the design for the parameter(s) called for by each procedure. In addition, you should also notice the contexts in which various statements such as Exit Sub can be used.

Summary

- MsgBox can be used not only to display messages, but also prompt the user for direction to guide the flow of control in your program.
- The StreamReader can be used to associate with (to open) a file for input purposes. It provides various input capabilities:
  - The ReadLine method can read one line at a time.
  - The ReadToEnd method can read the entire file in one operation.
  - The Peek method offers a way to test whether the end of file has been reached.

- The StreamWriter can be used to associate with (to open) a file for output purposes. Its WriteLine method will add an end of line marker, ensuring the next output operation begins with a new line. Its Write method will write the text without adding the end of line mark, so the next output operation will start from where the previous output ends (will continue on the same line).

- When no additional input (output) operation is needed, the StreamReader (StreamWriter) should be closed to release the resources associated with the object. In the case of StreamWriter, closing the object ensures that all data are properly written to the file.

- VS.NET is organized into various namespaces. Object names that are in a namespace not imported into the project must be qualified by the namespace; for example, StreamReader must be qualified by System.IO.

- You can import a namespace by placing an Imports statement at the beginning of the module.

- File dialogs (open file dialog and save file dialog) can be used to prompt the user to specify the filename. Always set the Filter property so that only pertinent files are displayed in the dialog box.

- General procedures (also recognized as separate procedures) provide many advantages. Before writing large block of code in an event procedure, analyze the problem and then determine whether the code can be simplified by creating separate Subs and Functions. These separate procedures can be invoked anywhere in the event procedure.

- General procedures differ from event procedures in that the former must be invoked by a reference of the procedure name; the latter are triggered by events.

- Subs differ from functions in that the former do not return any value; the latter do.

- General procedures enhance code reusability because they can accept different variables as parameters as long as the data types match or conversions are allowed.

- In general, parameters are passed by position. With proper syntax, parameters can be passed by name.

- Parameters can be passed by value (ByVal) or by reference (ByRef). By value is the default.

- Sub procedures can be terminated before the flow of control reaches the procedure end (End Sub) by the use of Exit Sub or Return statement.

- Function procedures can be terminated before the flow of control reaches the procedure end (End Function) by the use of Exit Function or Return statement. The former does not return a value. The latter can be coded with an expression, such as Return(X), to return a value.

- A function can be used in an expression like a constant, a variable, or a built-in function. The only difference between a general function and a built-in function is that the former is defined by the programmer and the latter is predefined and provided by the system.

- As in all cases, the names of general procedures (Subs and functions) should be meaningful. Inside each procedure, proper comments should be inserted to enhance it understandability.

- All procedures (including event procedures) in VB are recursive. Recursion can be powerful in solving complex programming problems when these problems can be divided into smaller problems of the same nature; but invoking an event procedure recursively seldom has practical meaning.

- A procedure can have optional parameters. All parameters following the first optional parameter must also be optional.

- More than one procedure can have the same procedure name. Procedures coded this way are said to be overloaded. The parameters of these procedures must be different in *number*, in *type*, or in both.

- The application example (Contacts) shows how general procedures can be useful and how they can be designed to accept meaningful parameters.

Explore and Discover

6-1.   Default Button for the MsgBox Function. Enter the following code in the form click event of a new project. Note the different way of specifying the buttons and icon.

```
Dim Answer As Integer
Answer = MsgBox("Cannot find the file. Proceed?", _
  vbYesNoCancel Or vbQuestion)
MsgBox(Answer)
```

Run the project and then click the form. What do you see the message box display as the default button? Press the spacebar. What value do you see in the second message box?

Revise the first MsgBox statement as follows:

```
Answer = MsgBox("Cannot find the file. Proceed?", _
  vbYesNoCancel Or vbQuestion Or vbDefaultButton2)
```

Run the project again and then click the form. What do you see the message box display as the default button? Press the spacebar. What value do you see in the second message box this time?

6-2.   Closing a Program without Closing a StreamWriter. Place the following code in the form click event. Note that to test this project, you need to have a Temp folder in Drive C. Change the path to some other folder if you do not want to create a Temp folder. Run the project, click the form, and end the program. Use Notepad to view the file. Do you see any text in the file?

```
Dim MyFileWriter As New
  System.IO.StreamWriter("c:\temp\test.txt")
MyFileWriter.WriteLine("This is a test line")
```

The line written by the object MyFileWriter was not actually written on the file when your program ends. Now, add the following line to the code.

```
MyFileWriter.Close()
```

Again, run the program and then click the form. Use Notepad to view the file. What do you see this time? It is important to close the StreamWriter to ensure that data are actually written onto the file.

6-3.   The AutoFlush Property of the StreamWriter. Modify the code in exercise 6-2 as follows:

```
Dim MyFileWriter As New
  System.IO.StreamWriter("c:\temp\test.txt", True)
MyFileWriter.AutoFlush = True
MyFileWriter.WriteLine("This is a test line")
```

Run the program and then click the form. Use Notepad to view the file. What do you see this time? When the StreamWriter's AutoFlush property is set to True, the StreamWriter automatically flushes its buffer (forces the operating system to write on the file and clear the data in the file buffer). The data are actually written onto the file even when you do not close the

StreamWriter; however, in this manner, the file buffer is not efficiently used. Setting the property to True slows down your computer, especially when your program has large amount of data to output.

6-4. **The Flush Method of the StreamWriter.** Modify the code in exercise 6-3 as follows:

```
Dim MyFileWriter As New
   System.IO.StreamWriter("c:\temp\test.txt", True)
MyFileWriter.WriteLine("This is a test line")
MyFileWriter.Flush()
```

Run the program and then click the form. Use Notepad to view the file. What do you see this time? The StreamWriter's flush method flushes the file buffer and causes the data to be actually written onto the file; however, its effect is still not the same as closing the object. The resources associated with the file are not released. The file is not actually closed; if you click the form again, your program will encounter an error for attempting to open a file already in use. This same problem holds with setting the AutoFlush property to True. What lesson have you learned from this exercise? Always close the StreamWriter and StreamReader when it is no longer needed.

6-5. **Append Versus Output Mode.** Draw two buttons on a new form. Name the first one **btnAppend**, and set its Text property to **Append**. Name the second one **btnOutput** and set its Text property to **Output**. Enter the following code:

```
Private Sub btnOutput_Click(ByVal Sender As System.Object, ByVal e
   As System.EventArgs) Handles btnOutput.Click
   Dim MyFileWriter As New
   System.IO.StreamWriter("C:\Temp\TestFile.txt", False)
   MyFileWriter.WriteLine("ABCD")
   MyFileWriter.Close()
End Sub

Private Sub btnAppend_Click(ByVal Sender As System.Object, ByVal e
   As System.EventArgs) Handles btnAppend.Click
   Dim MyFileWriter As New
   System.IO.StreamWriter("C:\Temp\TestFile.txt", True)
   MyFileWriter.WriteLine("ABCD")
   MyFileWriter.Close()
End Sub
```

Note that the only difference between the two procedures is in the second parameter in creating the object—in the Dim statement where the object is created, one specifies False; the other, True.

Run the project. Click the Append button and then use Notepad to inspect the file. Each time you click the Append button, you should see one more line of ABCD when you view the file with Notepad.

Click the Output button and then inspect the file again. What do you see? Click as many times as you want. You should always see only one line of ABCD in the file. The Output mode (the second parameter set to False) erases the previous content of the file; the Append mode (the second parameter set to True) appends data at the end of the existing file.

6-6. **Creating the StreamWriter at the Class Level?** Can you create the StreamReader or StreamWriter at the class level? Place the following code in the general declaration area to find out.

```
Dim MyFileWriter As New
   System.IO.StreamWriter("C:\Temp\TestFile.txt", True)
```

6-7.   **Using The Color Dialog.** Draw a color dialog and a button on a new form. Name the button **btnSetColor** and set its Text property to **Set Color**. Type in the following code:

```
Private Sub btnSetColor_Click(ByVal sender As System.Object, ByVal
    e As System.EventArgs) Handles btnSetColor.Click
      ColorDialog1.ShowDialog()
      Me.BackColor = ColorDialog1.Color
End Sub
```

Run the project, click the Set Color button, and select a color. What do you see? The color dialog obtains the setting for its Color property from the user by its ShowDialog method. Its Color property setting can then be used in the program.

6-8.   **The InputBox Function.** Draw a text box onto a new form. Enter the following code in the form click event.

```
TextBox1.Text = InputBox("What is your name?",  "Name Prompt",
    "Debbra Solomon")
```

Run the project, click the form, and carefully inspect the dialog box. Can you associate the code with the text in the dialog box? After you click the form, do the following (one each time) and inspect the result in the text box:

  A.   Click the OK button.
  B.   Press the Enter key.
  C.   Click the Cancel button.
  D.   Enter your name in the box and then click the OK button.
  E.   Enter your name in the box and then click the Cancel button.

Have you got a good feel about how the InputBox function behaves? This function allows the program to obtain data from the user on the fly, and can be used conveniently to test your program logic under certain circumstances. It cannot, however, be used in a serious data-entry application because it pops up only when called, and input from the function can be verified only afterward (not while the data is being typed in); therefore, it is not further discussed in the text.

6-9.   **Relationship of Argument and Parameter.** Use two buttons. Name one **btnTestA,** and the other **btnTestB**. Set their Text properties to "Test A" and "Test B," respectively. Enter the following code.

```
Sub Messenger(ByVal C As Integer)
    MsgBox("I get a value " & C)
End Sub
Private Sub btnTestA_Click(ByVal sender As System.Object, ByVal e
    As System.EventArgs) Handles btnTestA.Click
    Dim A As Integer
    A = 100
    Call Messenger(A)
End Sub
Private Sub btnTestB_Click(ByVal sender As System.Object, ByVal e
    As System.EventArgs) Handles btnTestB.Click
    Dim B As Integer
    B = 120
    Messenger(B)
End Sub
```

Run the project and then click each button. What message do you see? Notice that you can use two different syntactical expressions to call a Sub procedure. Also, how are A and B related to C in this illustration?

6-10. **Positions of Arguments and Parameters.** Use a button, and name it **btnTest**. Set its Text property to **Test**. In its Click event procedure and a separate Sub procedure named Divider, give the code as follows:

```
Private Sub btnTest_Click(ByVal sender As System.Object, ByVal e
    As System.EventArgs) Handles btnTest.Click
    Dim A As Single
    Dim B As Single
    A = 4
    B = 2
    Divider(B, A)
End Sub

Sub Divider(ByVal A As Single, ByVal B As Single)
    MsgBox("The quotient is " & A / B)
End Sub
```

Click the button. Is there anything puzzling to you? Recall that arguments passed to a Sub procedure are recognized by their positions, not by their names. What is recognized in the event procedure as A is recognized as B in Divider. It's the position, not the name, of the variable in the argument list that matters.

6-11. **Passing by Name.** (continued from exercise 6-10). If you pass the arguments without referencing the names of the parameters, they are recognized by position, as shown in the preceding exercise. As explained in the text, however, there is a way in which you can pass the arguments by the parameter names. For example, without any change to the Divider Sub in the preceding exercise, you can rewrite the Test Click event procedure as follows:

```
Private Sub btnTest_Click(ByVal sender As System.Object, ByVal e
    As System.EventArgs) Handles btnTest.Click
    Dim A As Single
    Dim B As Single
    A = 4
    B = 2
    Divider (B := B, A := A)
End Sub
```

Run the program and then click the button. Do you see the correct result? Inspect the syntax carefully. The := symbol is used to indicate the parameter assignment. The name on the left side of the := symbol is the parameter name. The name on its right is the argument.

Replace the line in the event procedure to call Divider as follows:

```
Divider(B := 2, A := 4)
```

Run the project again. Do you still obtain the correct result?

When you use this syntax, the positions of the parameters no long matter. They are recognized by name. Can you think of situations in which the use of named parameters is more convenient?

6-12. **Optional Parameters.** VB provides a way to write procedures that require optional parameters. For example, suppose you are interested in a function that will return the largest value from a list of two or three arguments. You can code the function as follows:

```
Function Biggest(ByVal X1 As Long, ByVal X2 As Long, _
    Optional ByVal X3 As Long = -9999999999) As Long
    Dim X As Long
    If X1 >= X2 Then
        X = X1
```

```
        Else
            X = X2
        End If
        If X3 = -9999999999 Then
        ElseIf X3 > X Then
            X = X3
        End If
        Biggest = X
    End Function
```

Note that the third parameter starts with the keyword Optional, which denotes that the parameter can be omitted. A default value must be specified as shown. To check whether it is present (passed from the calling procedure), your code checks against the default value.

Try the preceding code with the following code placed in the form click event:

```
        MsgBox(Biggest(12, 34, 53))
```

Are there other situations in which optional parameters can be useful?

6-13.   Overloading a Procedure. Add the following code to the project in exercise 6-12.

```
    Function Biggest(ByVal X1 As String, ByVal X2 As String, _
        Optional ByVal X3 As String = "") As String
        Dim X As String
        If X1 >= X2 Then
            X = X1
        Else
            X = X2
        End If
        If X3 = "" Then
        ElseIf X3 > X Then
            X = X3
        End If
        Biggest = X
    End Function
    Place the following code in the form click event:
        MsgBox(Biggest(12, 34, 53))
        MsgBox(Biggest("d","V"))
```

Run the program and then click the form. What do you see? Although you have two functions of the same name in the class, the compiler knows which one to use because the two functions have different number or types of parameters. Notice also that you are not required to specify the third parameter because it is optional.

6-14.   Effect of ByVal and ByRef. Draw a button on a new form, name it **btnTest,** and set its Text property to **Test.** In its Click event procedure and a separate Sub procedure named Setter, give the following code:

```
    Sub Setter(ByVal C As Integer, ByRef D As Integer)
        C = 10
        D = 10
    End Sub

    Private Sub btnTest_Click(ByVal sender As System.Object, ByVal e _
        As System.EventArgs) Handles btnTest.Click
        Dim A As Integer
        Dim B As Integer
        Setter A, B
        MsgBox("After setting the values, A = " & A & " and B = " & B))
    End Sub
```

Click the button. Why don't you get the same result for A and B? Recall that a ByVal parameter uses a copy of the value of the argument. Any change to that parameter will not cause a corresponding change to the argument passed to the Sub procedure.

6-15. **Expressions as Arguments.** (Continued from exercise 6-14). Suppose the previous Setter procedure is revised as follows:

```
Sub Setter(ByRef C As Integer, ByRef D As Integer)
    C = 10
    D = 10
End Sub
```

The parameters will be passed by reference; however, you code the calling event procedure as follows:

```
Private Sub btnTest_Click(ByVal Sender As System.Object, ByVal e
    As System.EventArgs) Handles btnTest.Click
    Dim A As Integer
    Dim B As Integer
    Setter((A), (B))
    MsgBox("After setting the values, A = " & A & " and B = " & B)
End Sub
```

What results do you obtain when you test the program? Why are A and B's values not set to 10? The pairs of parentheses enclosing the variables make each argument an expression, not the original variable. Expressions are passed to procedures by value, not by reference, no matter how the parameters are declared in the header of the procedure.

Exercises

6-16. **Using the MsgBox Function.** Add the masked edit box control to your project. Draw a masked edit box and a button on the form. Name the masked edit box **mskPhone**, and set its Mask property to "(###)-###-####." Set its Prompt Character property to a blank space, set the button's Text property to **Save**, and name it **btnSave**.

Provide code so that when the button is clicked, your program will check whether the user has entered a 10-digit number. If not, your program should display a message (use the MsgBox function) indicating that the phone number field is incomplete and then ask the user whether it is okay to save. If the user clicks the No button, the focus is set on the masked edit box and the Save procedure is exited. When the masked edit box has a legitimate number or when the user indicates that it is okay to save, the program displays a message stating that the record has been saved. (Do not provide code to actually save the record.)

6-17. **Ensuring Data Are Saved.** Add code to the Contacts example in Section 6.3 so that when the Read button is clicked, your program will check whether the name field has any data. If so, your program will display a message box asking the user whether to save the data before reading another record. The message box should display three buttons: Yes, No, and Cancel. If the user clicks the Yes button, your program should save the data fields before reading in another record. If the user clicks the No button, your program should proceed to read another record. If the Cancel button is clicked, your program should neither save the record nor read another record.

6-18. **Ensuring Data Are Saved** (continued from exercise 6-17). Refer to the Contacts example in Section 6.3 again. Add code to the project so that the remaining records in the original file can be saved when the user wants to quit. The additional code should work as follows:

1. When the user clicks the Quit or Close button, the program checks to see whether the original file contains any unread data. If not, the program quits; otherwise, the program proceeds to step 2.
2. Displays a message (use the MsgBox function) warning the user of the unread/unsaved data and asks the user whether the data should be copied into the new file. The MsgBox function should display a Question icon with three buttons: Yes, No, and Cancel.
3. If the Yes button is clicked, your code will copy the remaining records in the old file to the new one and then quit. If the No button is clicked, your program quits. If the Cancel button is clicked, your program does not quit. (*Hint:* Place your code in the Form Closing event.)

6-19.   The WhatFollows Function. Write a function that will take either the Integer type or String type as its parameter. If the parameter is of the Integer type, the function increases the magnitude of the value by 1, and returns the result (that is, if the value is 3, the function returns 4; if the value is –3, the function returns –4). If the parameter is a letter, the function returns the next letter; for example if the parameter value is "c", the function returns "d". If the parameter is not a letter, it returns the same value as the original parameter. (*Hint:* Use the overloading feature. Write two functions with the same name.)

6-20.   A Personal Memo Project. Design and write code for a project that will open your personal memo (a file with the path "C:\My Documents\MyMemo.txt"), and display the content in a text box. Set its MultiLine property to True. You can then edit the content, and save the updated version with the same filename.

6-21.   Save a Record (Data Entry Screen). Suppose that a form has a masked edit box and two text boxes. They are named mskSSN, txtLastName, and txtFirstName, respectively. You would like for the data entered to be saved as a record in fixed-length format (one record per line); that is, data in each field are to have the same length (pad with blank spaces, if necessary). The lengths for the fields should be 9, 12, and 12, respectively. Write a Sub to save data entered.

From what event procedure should the Save Record procedure be called? Is there a reason why the Save routine should be written as a separate procedure?

6-22.   Read and Display a Record. Write a general Sub procedure to read the data saved in the preceding exercise and then display the results in the three VB controls.

From what event procedure should the Read Record procedure be called? Is there a reason why the Read routine should be written as a separate procedure?

6-23.   The Missing Data Function. Write a function to return a Boolean value True if the text string passed to this function contains only blank spaces or zero length; otherwise, the function returns False. Name the function **Missing**. Its header should appear as follows:

```
Function Missing(TheText As String) As Boolean
```

6-24.   Random Uppercase Letters. Write a function that will return a random uppercase letter. Test the function as follows:

1. Draw a text box, with proper label, and a button on a new form.
2. Name the button **btnGenerate**.
3. Provide the code so that when the user clicks the button, the function is called and the letter it generates is displayed in the text box.

6-25. **The Month-End Function.** Write a function that will take the month and year as its parameter, and return a string that represents the last day of that month; for example, MonthEnd(2, 2004) will return the string "02/29/2004." (*Hint:* Use the DateSerial function. The last day of a month is one day before the first day of the next month.)

6-26. **The Julian Date Function.** Write a function that will return a Julian date given a valid date string such as "01/01/1999." A Julian date is a date represented by a five-digit number whose first two digits represent the year, and the last three digits give the sequence number of the day in the year. For example, the Julian date for 01/01/1999 is 99001.

6-27. **The GetTheFileName Function.** Use an OpenFileDialog and a SaveFileDialog in a form. Write a function that will prompt the user for a filename, and return it as a string. The function should have the following header:

```
Function GetTheFileName(ForWhat As String, Filter As String) _
    As String
```

The parameter ForWhat expects an "O" (for "Open") or "S" (for "Save"). The parameter Filter expects a string specifying the file filter, as explained in the chapter. Make sure that when "O" is specified, the dialog box will insist that the file must exist; and when "S" is specified, the user will be warned if the file already exists.

The function will return the filename (a string) specified by the user in the dialog box. If the user clicks the Cancel button in the dialog box, the function should return a zero-length string.

6-28. **The Grade Function.** Write a function that will return a letter grade. The function expects an integer parameter that represents the score. The grading system is based on the typical 90, 80, 70, and so on, cut-off criteria.

6-29. **String of Specified Length.** Write a function that will take a string and an integer parameter and return a string of the length as specified in the second parameter. If the string parameter is longer than the specified length (L), the function will return the first L characters of the string. If the string is shorter than the specified length, the function will return the string with additional spaces padded at the end.

6-30. **Numeric String of Specified Length.** Write a function that will take two integers as its parameters. The first parameter represents the number to be converted to a string and returned. The second parameter specifies the length of the returned string. If the string to be returned is longer than the specified length, its extra characters on the left are truncated. If the string is shorter than the specified length, it should be padded with spaces on its left.

6-31. **The Present Value of an Annuity Function.** The present value of the annuity of one dollar ($1), P, can be computed by the following formula:

```
P = (1 - (1 + R) -n) / R
```

where R is the rate of interest per period, and N is the number of periods.

Write a function with the following header to perform the computation

```
Function PresentValue(R As Double, N As Integer) As Double
```

Compare the results obtained from this function with the results from using the built-in PV function. Use the keyword PV function to search the Index tab of the online Help file for additional information on how to use the function.

6-32.   **Recursive Function.** Write a recursive function to compute the following series.

```
S = 1 + 2 + 3 + . . . + N
```

The function should have the following header.

```
Function Series(N As Integer) As Long
```

(*Hint:* Rewrite the formula as follows:

```
S = N + (N - 1) + (N - 2) + . . . + 2 + 1)
```

6-33.   **Recursive Function.** Write a recursive function to approximate the following infinite series.

$$S = B + B / D + B / D^2 + B / D^3 + . . .$$

Where D is greater than 1.

The function should have the following header.

```
Function Series(B As Double, D As Double) As Double
```

(*Hint:* Rewrite the formula as follows:

$$S = B + (B + (B / D + (B / D^2 + . . .))) / D$$

The series can be evaluated by the beginning value (B) plus the series that begins with the current beginning value divided by D. Terminate the function when B/D is very small—say, .1E-10.

Projects

6-34.   **Revisiting the FICA Computation Project.** Refer to exercise 5-32 in the previous chapter. Modify the FICA withholding computation project so that the previous data come from an existing file, and the resulting year-to-date (y-t-d) data are saved onto a new file.

The existing file contains the y-t-d data on all employees who have been paid previously. Each record consists of employee Social Security number (SSN), employee name, y-t-d pay, and FICA withholding. A sample record from the data file appears as follows:

```
"111-11-1111", "John Smith", 10000, 465
```

Your program should have buttons to Read, Compute, Save, and Quit. These buttons should align across the top of the form. You should add controls to display the employee SSN and name in the form, while all other data fields in your visual interface remain the same.

Your project should behave in the following manner.

- When the project starts, it should prompt for the existing (y-t-d) file and the file to which updated data will be saved. To simplify your code, create an empty y-t-d file using Notepad for the first round before testing your program.

- When the user clicks the Read button, your program will read a record from the existing file. If the file runs out of records, your program should display a message to that effect. The pay data will be displayed in the group box for the previous period, and the employee SSN and name should be displayed in the proper controls. Before your program proceeds to read, it should check to see whether the data in the current screen have been saved. If not, it should prompt the user whether to save and should save the data if so instructed. (See requirement 4 for instructions on what to save.)
- The user should enter current pay in the group box for current data and then click the Compute button. Your program will then display the results in the proper fields as described in exercise 5-32.
- When the user clicks the Save button, the data in the group box for cumulative total should be saved in the same format as the previous sample record. All fields on the form should then be cleared.
- Data on new employees can be entered when all the fields are cleared. The user should enter the employee SSN, name, and current pay. Click the Compute button and then click the Save button. (This is what you should do to create a y-t-d file for the first round.)
- When the user clicks the Quit or Close button on the title bar, your program should check whether the existing file has any unread data. If so, it should copy all these records to the new file, and display a message informing the user of this action.

(*Note:* This project emulates a sequential file processing system although it is much simplified.)

6-35.   **A Mini Word Processor.** Develop a project that will provide the following word processing capabilities: opening a file; allowing the user to edit, search, and replace text; and saving text onto a file. The user interface should have buttons for Open, Search, Save, and Quit across the top of the form; a text box for text editing and processing at the center of the form; and a group box for search and replace. The group box should be placed below the text box, and should contain a text box for search text, another text box for replace text, a button with a Find Next text, another with a Replace text, and the other with an OK text. The text boxes in the search group box should be accompanied with proper labels.

The application should behave as follows:

- When the project starts, all the buttons across the top of the form and the text box (txtDoc) for word processing should appear. The form should have space enough to show all these controls. (The aforementioned group box is not visible. In addition, there is no space in the form to hint its existence.) The user can start entering and editing text or click the Open button to bring text from an existing file. (*Hint:* Set the group box's Visible property to False. Compute the form's Height property using the Top and Height properties of txtDoc.)
- When the user clicks the Open button, a dialog box should appear to prompt for an existing file; then the data should be retrieved and displayed in the text box. Note that before your program retrieves data from an existing file, if the text box contains text and has been changed, your program should prompt the user whether to save the change. (*Hint*: Use a class-level variable to keep track of the change. Set it to False when the file is first open, or when the text is saved; then set it to True when the text changes.)
- When the user clicks the Save button, or when the user indicates to save in requirement 2, your program should prompt for an output file path. The text will then be saved in the specified file path.

- When the user clicks the Search button, the group box for Search and Replace will appear below txtDoc. (*Hint*: Compute the form's Height property using the group box's Top and Height property.) After the group box appears:

   A. When the user clicks the Find Next button, your program will search the text in txtDoc for the text specified in the Search text box. If a match is found, it will be highlighted; otherwise, the program displays a Not Found message.
   B. When the user clicks the Replace button, whatever appears in the Replace text box will replace the highlighted text in txtDoc. (*Hint*: See exercise 4-10 in Chapter 4 for hints for replacing text.)
   C. When the user clicks the OK button, the group box disappears, and the form goes back to its previous size.
   D. When the user clicks the Quit button, the program should check to ensure that the changes in the text have been saved. If not, it should prompt the user whether to save. If so, handle the saving operation as specified in requirement 3.

7. Repetition

One of the most powerful features of the computer is its capability to execute a group of instructions repetitively while the data handled by these instructions change. With this capability, many tasks that are repetitive in nature can be handled with much shorter code and greater flexibility. Imagine a payroll routine that computes for each employee the gross pay, various deductions, and the net pay. The steps to handle each employee's pay are basically the same. Only the data—the employee and the pay—in question change. Without the capability to execute the group of instructions repetitively, the same code will have to be repeated for each employee. The length of code will be sizable, to say the least. Worse yet, the number of repetitions in code, which vary with the number of employees to be paid, will have to be known beforehand. Each time the number of employees changes, the program will have to be modified—an extremely tedious task.

Many of the problems (much more than can be imagined) handled by the computer are repetitive in nature. To list a few, populating a list box or combo box, reversing a string, computing the square root of a number (searching for the root of any function in general), and listing the content of a file all require repeating a selected group of instructions.

In VB, there are several structures by which you can construct code for repetition. In each of these structures, the repetition starts with a keyword, such as Do or For, in an opening statement and ends with another keyword, such as Loop or Next, in the closing statement. Statements enclosed physically inside the two statements are repeated until a certain condition is satisfied. Because the execution of the group of statements starts from the opening statement top down, ends at the closing statement, and starts over again from the opening statement, the repetition looks like a loop and is commonly so referenced. This chapter provides detailed discussions of these structures.

After completing this chapter, you should be able to:

- Understand all variations of the Do...Loop structure.
- Develop code that calls for the use of the Do...Loop structure with all variations.
- Understand the For...Next structure with different values and signs of the increment parameter.
- Develop code that requires the use of the For...Next structure.
- Understand and develop code that calls for the use of nested loop structures.

7.1 The Do...Loop Structure

One of the structures for repetition is the *Do...Loop structure*. You can construct the Do...Loop structure with either of the following syntaxes:

```
Do [{While¦Until} Condition]
        Statements to be repeated
Loop
```

or

```
Do
        Statements to be repeated
Loop [While¦Until} Condition]
```

where *condition* = any expression that can be evaluated to True or False; any expression that can be used in an If statement can be used here.

While = the keyword that will make the loop continue as long as the condition is true, and
Until = the keyword that will make the loop continue as long as the condition is false.

When the loop ends, the execution continues to the line below the Loop statement. The following examples illustrate how the various variations of the Do...Loop structure work.

Example 1. Showing a Sequence of Numbers

Suppose you would like to know the sequence of numbers in the range of 1 and 1,000, which are successively doubled beginning with 1. To solve the problem, you can do the following:

1. Create a variable such as N, and assign it a value 1.

2. Show N in a list box.

3. Double N.

4. Compare N with 1,000. If N is less then 1,000, repeat steps 2 and 3; otherwise, end the process.

A flowchart that depicts the process is presented in Figure 7.1.

The flowchart gives a visual hint that the connector (A) and the decision (N <1,000) form a loop. The routine can look similar to the following:

Figure 7.1

A flowchart to display a
sequence of numbers

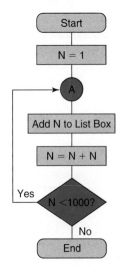

```
Private Sub Form1_Click(ByVal sender As System.Object, ByVal e As
    System.EventArgs) Handles MyBase.Click
    Dim N As Integer
    N = 1
    Do
        lstNumbers.Items.Add(N)
        N = N + N
    Loop While N < 1000
End Sub
```

Before the loop is executed, N is set to 1. Within the loop, the value N is added to the lstNumbers list box, using the control's Items.Add method. N is then added to itself, doubling its value in effect. When the loop reaches the end (the Loop statement), N is compared with 1,000. The While condition states that if N is less than 1,000, the repetition continues. The execution transfers back to the beginning of the loop (the Do statement). The two statements inside the loop will be executed again. This cycle continues until N is greater than or equal to 1,000; then the While condition is no longer true. The execution control goes to the statement immediately below the Loop statement. In this case, the End Sub statement is reached, and the Form Click event procedure ends.

The process can be depicted with the following execution table.

Iteration No.	N (in lstNumbers)	N (After doubling)
1	1	2
2	2	4
3	4	8
4	8	16
.	.	.
10	512	1024

Notice that the Loop While statement can be rewritten with the Until keyword as follows:

```
Loop Until N >= 1000
```

Replacing this statement for the preceding Loop While line will have exactly the same result as the original routine. Try both ways. The last number you should see in the list box is 512.

Example 2. Reading a Name List and Populating a List Box

Suppose you have created a list of names with one name per line, and kept it in a file located at c:\friends\namelist.txt. The content of the file appears as follows:

```
Andrea Aaron
Ben Bennett
.
.
Zeff Zenor
```

You would like to populate the lstNames list box with these names as soon as your program starts. To do this, you must first open the file (associate the file with a StreamReader); then your program should do the following:

1. Read a name from the file.
2. Add the name to the list box using the Items.Add method.
3. Repeat steps 1 and 2 until the file runs out of names.

Assume the StreamReader associated with the file is NameFileReader, and the list box name is lstNames. The first approximation of the repetition should appear as follows:

```
Do
    ' Read a name from NameFile
    TheName = NameFileReader.ReadLine()
    ' Add the name to the list box
    lstNames.Items.Add(TheName)
Loop Until NameFileReader.Peek() = -1 'Check for EOF
```

In this structure, when the loop is executed, the computer will read the name from the file and then add it to the list box before the execution reaches the Loop statement, where the EOF condition is tested. Recall that the StreamReader's Peek method returns the next character in the file without moving the current position, and it returns a value –1 when the EOF is reached. Because the Loop statement uses the keyword Until, the loop will continue when the Peek method does not return –1; that is, EOF is not reached.

Dealing with an Empty File. As long as there is at least one name in the file, the preceding code structure will perform properly without any error; however, if the file happens to be empty, this structure will have a problem. When it attempts to read the name the first time, the EOF is reached and an error occurs. The program will fail.

To guard against this possibility, the EOF condition should be tested at the beginning of the loop; that is, the condition should be placed in the Do statement. If the file is empty, no statements inside of the loop will be executed. The loop should appear as follows:

```
Do Until NameFileReader.Peek() = -1 'Check for EOF
    ' Read a name from NameFile
    TheName = NameFileReader.ReadLine()
    ' Add the name to the list box
    lstNames.Items.Add(TheName)
Loop
```

The Complete Procedure. Because you want to populate the list box as soon as the program starts, you should place the code in the Form Load event procedure as shown here:

```
Private Sub Form1_Load(ByVal sender As System.Object, ByVal e As
    System.EventArgs) Handles MyBase.Load
    Dim TheName As String
    Dim NameFileReader As New
      System.IO.StreamReader("C:\Friends\NameList.txt")
    Do Until NameFileReader.Peek() = -1 'Check for EOF
        ' Read a name from NameFile
        TheName = NameFileReader.ReadLine()
        ' Add the name to the list box
        lstNames.Items.Add(TheName)
    Loop
    NameFileReader.Close()
End Sub
```

In the procedure, the Dim statement declares the variable NameFileReader as a StreamReader. The New keyword creates a StreamReader object that is associated with the NameList.txt file. After the file is associated with the StreamReader, the Do...Loop structure will perform the required repetition until it exhausts the records in the file.

Difference in Effect Between the Two Structures. The preceding discussion suggests that whether the statements inside the loop will be executed at least once depends on the placement of the condition in the Do or Loop statement. Placing the condition with the Do statement can prevent those statements from being executed; placing the condition with the Loop statement ensures that those statements will be executed at least once.

If the execution of those statements strictly depends on the condition, you should place the condition in the Do statement; however, if those statements must be executed at least once or if it is inconsequential whether the condition is checked before entering the loop, you may place the condition in the Loop statement. For example, the code given in Example 1 can be changed to the following without affecting the result or exposing any potential possibility for errors:

```
Private Sub Form1_Click(ByVal sender As System.Object, ByVal e As
    System.EventArgs) Handles MyBase.Click
    Dim N As Integer
    N = 1
    Do While N < 1000
```

```
        lstNumbers.Items.Add(N)
            N = N + N
      Loop
   End Sub
```

Why? You know for certain that the first time the loop is executed the value of N will be 1 and thus is less than 1,000. When the loop is executed enough times that N is at least 1,000, the loop will end regardless of whether the checking is performed with Do or with Loop.

The While...End While Loop. As a side note, the Do While...Loop structure has a cousin in syntax: *While...End While*. With this syntax structure, you can code the loop as follows:

```
   While N < 1000
       lstNumbers.Items.Add(N)
           N = N + N
   End While
```

This code will produce exactly the same result. (Note that there is no Until... End Until Structure.)

The Endless Loop

Notice that in the previous structures, some of the statements inside the loop must produce some result that causes the condition to be False in conjunction with the keyword While, or True in conjunction with the keyword Until; otherwise, the loop will execute endlessly, resulting in an undesirable trap. Thoroughly test your program to prevent this situation from happening.

Do Loop Without a Condition on Either Statement

If you inspect the syntax of the Do...Loop structure again, you may discover that the While/Until condition is optional; that is, the entire structure can do without any While/Until condition. For example, it is perfectly legitimate to have a Do...Loop structure as follows:

```
   Do
         'Statements to be executed
   Loop
```

Similar to the preceding structures, there must be some condition(s)—plus some statements—inside the loop that can terminate the loop; otherwise, the loop will repeat endlessly. Typically, this structure is used when the condition to be checked is neither at the beginning nor at the end of the group of statements to be executed. The following example illustrates this situation.

Example 3. Computing the Value of an Infinite Series

Consider the following series:

$$S = 1/2 + (1/2)^2 + (1/2)^3 + \dots$$

Is there a way to approximate the value of the series numerically? The series starts with a value of 1/2. Each subsequent value to be added is half of the previous value. Although the addition is supposed to be carried out infinitely, your intuition is that at a certain point, the number in the series will be so small that any further addition will not alter the tangible value of the result. You can certainly stop the addition, or get out of the loop, at that time. For practical purposes, you can consider 0.1E-07 (10^{-8}) very small.

Let *S* be the variable to accumulate the value for the series, and *V* be the variable to represent the value at each point of the series.

The algorithm to compute the series can be described as follows:

1. Set V to 1, and S to 0.

2. Divide V by 2; that is, V = V/2.

3. Compare V with the very small number. If V is less than that number, terminate the computation; otherwise, proceed to step 4.

4. Add V to S; that is, S = S + V.

5. Go to step 2 and repeat the process.

With this algorithm, the following code can be written to approximate the result:

```
Dim S As Single
Dim V As Single
V = 1
S = 0
Do
    V = V / 2
    If V < .1E-07 Then Exit Do
    S = S + V
Loop
MsgBox("The value of the series is " & S)
```

The following execution table shows the value of S and V at various stages.

Iteration No.	Value of V	Value of S
0	1	0
1	1/2	1/2
2	$(1/2)^2$	$(1/2) + (1/2)^2$
3	$(1/2)^3$	$(1/2) + (1/2)^2 + (1/2)^3$
.	.	.
.	.	.
.	.	.
N	$(1/2)^n$	$(1/2) + (1/2)^2 + \ldots + (1/2)^n$

The Exit Do Statement. Notice how the loop is ended in the previous routine. You place an If statement among the group of statements inside the loop. Each time the statement is reached (after V has been divided by 2), it checks whether V is very small (when V < 0.1E-07). If the value is not very small, execution will drop down to the next statement, and V will be added to S. When V is very small, the *Exit Do statement* will be executed, terminating the loop. When this statement is executed, the execution control is transferred to the statement immediately following the Loop statement; that is, the MsgBox statement, exactly like the situation in which the condition with the Until/While keyword is True.

Place the preceding code in an event procedure and then test the result. (*Note:* VB will automatically convert the number 0.1E-07 to 0.00000001.) It should print 1 as the result.

Are you wondering whether the computation of series has any practical application in business? Yes, there are problems of this nature in business. Exercise 7-28 provides an example.

TIP

The statement to terminate the While...End While loop from inside is the *Exit While* statement.

Viewing Data in the Loop. In many cases in the process of testing your program, you need to inspect the values of the variables in the loop. Their values at different stages can provide clues as to how the program executes as well as to why a program fails to produces the expected results. In the preceding example, you may wonder how the values of V and S change at different stages of execution. One straightforward way is, of course, just to insert statements that display the values. This approach, however, has some drawbacks. You have to not only take time to insert these statements initially, but also take care to remove them afterwards.

A more convenient alternative is to set the *breakpoint* using the IDE's debugging facility. At design time, while in the code window, locate the statement of interest and then click on the left margin of the code window. You will see the statement highlighted in brown color as shown in

Figure 7.2

Setting the breakpoint

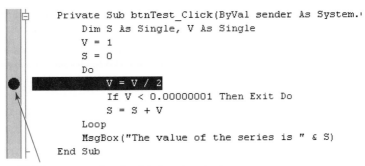

```
Private Sub btnTest_Click(ByVal sender As System.'
    Dim S As Single, V As Single
    V = 1
    S = 0
    Do
        V = V / 2
        If V < 0.00000001 Then Exit Do
        S = S + V
    Loop
    MsgBox("The value of the series is " & S)
End Sub
```

Click here to set a breakpoint. A statment set
as the breakpoint will be higlighted with brown
color. To clear the breakpoint, click the circle.

Figure 7.2. At runtime, the execution breaks at this statement, waiting for your action. You can then rest the mouse pointer on any variable of interest. The value of the variable will be displayed. To have the execution move forward step-by-step, press the F8 key. Each time you press F8, the execution moves forward by one step. (Again, you can inspect the value of any variable at any time.) You can cancel the break point by clicking the circle of the highlighted line to clear the breakpoint. To resume normal execution, click the Start button in the toolbar again.

You can customize the behavior of the debugger by the various settings it allows. To view and set these settings, click the Tools menu and then select the Options option. In the Options dialog box, open the Debugging folder on the left pane. You can then select one of the four items under the folder to specify the settings, as shown in Figure 7.3. To learn about the specific effect of a particular setting, press F1 to view the related help page.

Figure 7.3

Configuring the debugger

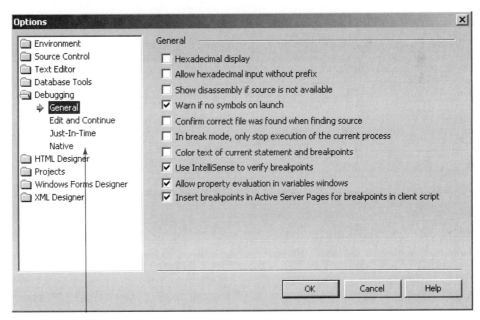

When you select the Options option in the Tools menu, this Options dialog appears. You can use it to configure the debugger. Open (by clicking) the Debugging folder. Click an item under the folder and all available settings under the item will appear. To learn about the specific effect of a setting, press the F1 key to view the related help page.

You can actually set as many breakpoints as you want. Whenever the execution hits a breakpoint, it breaks. If you have set many breakpoints, you can use the Clear All Breakpoints option in the Debug menu to clear all breakpoints at one time. Of course, the use of breakpoints is not limited to checking values in loops. You can use it in any part of your program where you have a need to examine the variables.

TIP

Set the breakpoint on the statement from which you want to start inspecting the values of variables. Clear it after it is no longer needed. This approach is much simpler than inserting statements to display the values of the variables.

Example 4. Finding the Solution to an Equation Numerically

You have learned how to perform computations repetitively using the Do...Loop structure. Repetition is a powerful feature that you can use to solve various mathematical problems. To illustrate, consider the following equation:

```
a xᶜ = 4,000
where a = 100
    c = 1 + log(.8)/log(2)
```

You are to write a VB program to find the solution (the value of x that makes the equation true). One possible way, of course, is to perform some analysis or algebraic manipulation so that you can express x in terms of all the other values. You can then just code the formula into your program. In this case, it should work.

Sometimes the equation is so complex, however, that it defies any analysis. It will then be impossible to solve the problem *analytically*. In such a case, you may still be able to use the computer to find the solution *numerically*. Pretend that this problem is complex enough that you would rather solve it numerically.

Where do you start? First, examine the left side and let y be the function; that is, let $y = a\ x^c$.

You can then plot the function as shown in Figure 7.4.

Notice that the x value at which the y value is equal to 4,000 is the solution. As you can see, the function increases monotonically with respect to x. In such a case, there is a fairly simple but efficient way to find the solution.

An Algorithm for the Numerical Solution. Inspect the chart again. Notice that for any x value beyond the solution, y is greater than 4,000, and below the solution y is less than 4,000. Now, suppose you know that x must fall in a certain range; you can do the following:

1. Compute the midpoint of the range of x.

2. Find the new y for the midpoint of x.

Figure 7.4

The function

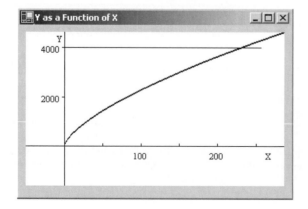

3. Compare the resulting y with 4,000.

   3.1. If y is less than 4,000, this x value is too small. You can then change the lower bound of the range to this midpoint.

   3.2. If y is greater than 4,000, this x value is too large. You can change the upper bound of the range to this midpoint.

In either case, you have narrowed the possible range of the solution by half of the current range. The revised range can again be used to compute a new midpoint, which will give a clue to revising the range of the solution.

When this trial-and-error method is repeated a sufficient number of times, you will find the range is so small that any value within it can be considered a good approximation to the solution. This method of finding a solution of an equation numerically is recognized as the *half interval method*. Figure 7.5 illustrates graphically how this trial-and-error method is carried out.

Searching for the Initial Range. How do you set the initial range to search for the solution? In this example case, it is obvious that the lower bound cannot be anything less than 0. The upper bound can be identified by a reverse half interval method. Suppose you try a value for x at 1. You should find the function gives a y value that is smaller than 4,000. So, you can double this value of x and try again. If it is still smaller than 4,000, you can double x again. You can repeat this process until you obtain an x value that results in a y value greater than 4,000. This x value can then be used as the upper bound.

In sum, the procedure to find the numerical solution can be stated by the pseudo-code as follows:

1. Find an appropriate upper bound:

   1.1. Let x = 1.

   1.2. Double x.

   1.3. Compute y for the given x.

   1.4. If y is less than 4,000, repeat 1.2 through 1.3; otherwise, proceed to step 2.

2. Find the numerical approximation (solution) using the half interval method:

   2.1. Let Low = 0, and High = x, which is obtained in step 1. (Low and High represent the lower and upper bounds of the range to search for the solution.)

   2.2. Compute x = (Low + High)/2.

Figure 7.5

The half interval method at work

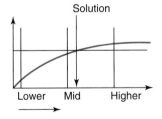

If the midpoint of the range is lower than the solution, then replace the lower point with the midpoint to narrow the range for the next iteration.

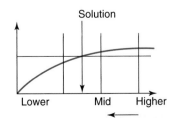

If the midpoint of the range is higher than the solution, then replace the higher point with the midpoint to narrow the range for the next iteration.

2.3. Compute y for the given x.

2.4. If y is less than 4,000, let Low = x (that is, adjust the lower bound); otherwise, let High = x (that is, adjust the upper bound).

2.5. If (High − Low) is still not small enough, repeat steps 2.2 through 2.4; otherwise, terminate the search. x is a good approximation to the solution.

Suppose the user will click a button named btnSolve to initiate the computation. The complete procedure using this algorithm can be coded in VB as follows:

```
Private Sub btnSolve_Click(ByVal sender As System.Object, ByVal e
    As System.EventArgs) Handles btnSolve.Click
    Dim R As Double
    Dim C As Double
    Dim A As Double
    Dim Y As Double
    Dim T As Double
    Dim Low As Double
    Dim High As Double
    Dim X As Double
    R = 0.8
    A = 100
    T = 4000
    C = 1 + Math.Log(R) / Math.Log(2)
    ' Search for a point that Y(X) > T
    X = 1
    Do
        X = X + X
        Y = A * X ^ C
    Loop Until Y >= T
    ' Search for X using the half interval method
    Low = 0
    High = X
    Do
        X = (High + Low) / 2
        Y = A * X ^ C
        If Y < T Then
            ' Too low; adjust lower bound
            Low = X
        Else
            ' Too high; adjust upper bound
            High = X
        End If
    Loop Until (High - Low) / X < 0.000001
    MsgBox("X = " & X)
End Sub
```

Notice that you have assigned 0.8 to a variable R, 100 to A, and 4,000 to T. You can redesign the project so that the values of these variables can be obtained from data entered through text boxes. The modification is left to you as an exercise.

The Termination Criterion. Notice that you used the formula (High − Low)/X to determine whether the range of the true solution is small enough. The criterion is based on a precision *relative* to the value of the solution. In contrast, you can also use *absolute* precision as the criterion by comparing the difference between High and Low with a very small value without dividing by X. In general, the relative precision is better, especially when X is relatively large. When X is near zero, however, you may encounter an overflow problem with the computation of the relative precision.

The Real-World Meaning of the Example. Is there a real-world meaning of the preceding example? Yes. You have just solved a learning curve problem, which asks, "If the first product unit takes 100 hours (A) to complete, how many units can we produce if we have 4,000 hours (T), assuming our factory has a 0.8 learning rate (R)?" Often used in the aircraft manufacturing industry, the learning curve model asserts that because of the task complexity, the initial time (A) to complete a unit of product takes longer. As the experience (production) doubles, the average time required to perform the same task decreases by a constant percentage, R. The formula you see at the beginning of this example is the one to compute the total hours required to produce X units. The solution to the problem is approximately 230.5 units. This is intriguing because if every unit takes 100 hours to produce (the initial time), you can produce only 40 units with 4,000 hours available!

As a side note, perhaps you have also learned a moral. When you first attempted to solve this problem, you were unaware of the problem's practical meaning. As long as you know how the function behaves, your knowledge (or the lack) of the practical meaning of the problem should not affect your ability to solve the programming problem.

You may encounter a situation in which the code contains a loop that will continue until the user clicks a button (say, btnStop). Apparently, the loop cannot include the click event procedure that is triggered when the button is clicked. How can you then terminate the loop when the event is fired? Here is the solution. Declare a class level Boolean variable (say, GoodBye). Set the variable to True in the button's click event procedure; that is, to code:

```
Dim GoodBye As Boolean
Private Sub btnStop_Click(ByVal sender As System.Object, ByVal
    e As System.EventArgs) Handles btnStop.Click
    GoodBye = True
End Sub
```

Assume the Do…Loop has no other termination conditions in the opening or closing statement. The loop can be structured as follows:

```
Do Until GoodBye
    ' Place all other statements for the loop here.
    Application.DoEvents() 'Release execution control to
        the system
Loop
```

Notice that there is an Application.DoEvents statement inside the loop. The statement releases execution control to the system for it to perform system level activities, including checking for the Button Click event so that the Boolean variable GoodBye can be set properly. Without the DoEvents statement, the loop will never terminate.

7.2 The For…Next Structure

The preceding section focused on the Do…Loop structure, and briefly mentioned the While…End While structure. Both of these structures perform the repetition based on the value of a condition (True or False). This section discusses the For…Next structure that performs repetition based on a counter. The For…Next structure has the following syntax:

```
For Counter = Starting Value To Ending Value [Step Increment]
    Statements to be executed
Next [Counter]
```

where *Counter* = a variable to serve as the counter in the repetition; it starts with the *starting value* and is added by the *increment* in each iteration.

Starting Value = an expression that can be evaluated to a numeric value, which will be assigned to *Counter* when the loop starts.

Ending Value = an expression that can be evaluated to a numeric value, which will be compared with *Counter*.

Increment = an optional parameter that will be added to *Counter* for each iteration. *Increment* can be either a positive or a negative value; if this parameter is omitted, 1 is the default value.

As the syntax shows, the For...Next structure starts a loop with the For statement and ends with the Next statement. The counter in the Next statement is optional; however, you are strongly urged to include the counter name in the statement for code clarity.

When the loop starts, the counter is set to the starting value for the first iteration. The increment is then added to the counter for each of the subsequent iterations. At the beginning of each iteration, the counter value for the upcoming iteration is first compared with the ending value. Either the statements inside the loop will be executed, or the loop will terminate, depending on the sign of the increment and the result of comparison.

A Closer Look at the Increment. Notice that the increment can be either positive or negative. If the increment is positive, the loop will end as soon as the counter is greater than the ending value. If the starting value is greater than the ending value, the loop will terminate immediately and the statements inside the loop will never be executed.

On the other hand, if the increment is negative, the loop will end as soon as the counter is less than the ending value. In this case, if the starting value is less than the ending value, statements inside the loop will never be executed. The two flowchart fragments in Figure 7.6 show how the For...Next loop works with positive and negative increment.

Notice that when the increment is negative, adding it to the counter will decrease the value of the counter. The following examples illustrate how the For...Next loop can be used.

Example 5. Listing a Sequence of Numbers

Suppose you would like to show by code the numbers 1 through 10 in the list box. What would be the easiest to do? You can use the For...Next loop, setting the starting value to one (1) and ending value to 10 with an increment of 1. You can then use the Items.Add method to add the value of the counter inside the loop. The code should appear as follows:

```
Dim Counter As Integer
'Clear the current content to prevent multiple lists
lstNumbers.Items.Clear
For Counter = 1 To 10
    lstNumbers.Items.Add(Counter)
Next Counter
' execution will continue here after the above loop is done
```

Recall that in the For statement, if the Step optional parameter is omitted, the increment defaults to 1. In the preceding code, when the loop starts, the starting value 1 is assigned to the

Figure 7.6

For loops with positive and negative increment

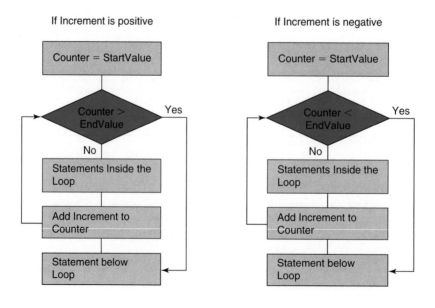

variable Counter. The list box's Items.Add method inside the loop is then executed, adding the current value of Counter into the list box.

In the next iteration, the default increment 1 is added to Counter, resulting in 2, which is compared with the ending value 10. Because 2 is not greater than 10, the statement inside the loop is executed. The iteration continues until Counter has a value of 11, which is greater than the ending value 10. The loop is then terminated. The execution control is transferred to the statement immediately below the Next statement. (Try the routine in a form Click event. Click the form a few times, and inspect the results.)

Example 6. Listing Who's Invited (the Invitation Project)

In Example 2, you saw how the lstNames list box was populated with the list of your friends' names in a file. Suppose the list box's SelectionMode property has been set to MultiSimple. You can select as many names as you want. When you click the btnInvite button with a text Invite, you would like the computer to display in a message box the list of friends whom you plan to invite to your birthday party (see Figure 7.7 for a sample result). How can you do that? (Eventually, you want to modify the program so that the computer will print a personal invitation to each of the friends invited.)

Recall that the list box has a SelectedItems property, and the property is indexed. SelectedItems(0) gives the first selected item, and SelectedItems(1) gives the second. Notice that the index of the property in the pair of parentheses does not have to be a constant. It can be a variable. If you use a variable for the index and have a way to change this variable such that it will go 0, 1, 2, and so on until the end of the list, you would be able to list all the items in the SelectedItems property.

If you set up a For loop with a beginning number 0 and an increment 1, the loop's counter will go 0, 1, 2 and so on, exactly the same values you would like for the index of the SelectedItems property to be. The Counter of the loop can then be used as the index. What is the value of the index for the last item in the list box? Recall that the SelectedItems.Count property gives the number of items selected. Because the index of SelectedItems starts with 0, the last item should have an index of SelectedItems.Count −1; for example, if three items are selected, giving a Count of 3, they will be indexed 0, 1, and 2. The code to show the list of friends to be invited should appear as follows:

```
Private Sub btnInvite_Click(ByVal sender As System.Object, ByVal e
    As System.EventArgs) Handles btnInvite.Click
    Dim MyMsg As String
    Dim I As Integer
    MyMsg = "I'll invite the following friends to my birthday
      party:"
    For I = 0 To lstNames.SelectedItems.Count - 1
        MyMsg = MyMsg & vbCrLf & CStr(lstNames.SelectedItems(I))
    Next I
    MsgBox(MyMsg)
End Sub
```

In the procedure, the string "I'll invite...party:" is placed before the loop starts because you want the line to appear in the message only once, and before any of your friends' names. The For statement sets the starting value for the counter, I to 0, and the ending value to the number of

Figure 7.7

Displaying names selected from a list box

selected items (SelectedItems.Count) minus 1. Inside the loop, the existing value of MyMsg is concatenated with the carriage return—vbCrLf, the end of line marker—and with the name corresponding to the index that has the value of the current Counter. The carriage return makes the subsequent string containing the name appear on the next line. Figure 7.7 shows the results of a sample run. The following execution table depicts the process of executing the For loop.

Iteration	I	SelectedItem(I)	Resulting MyMsg
Before loop			I'll invite the following friends to my birthday party:
1	0	Andrea Aaron	I'll invite the following friends to my birthday party: Andrea Aaron
2	1	George Gunther	I'll invite the following friends to my birthday party: Andrea Aaron George Gunther
3	2	Lisa Latimer	I'll invite the following friends to my birthday party: Andrea Aaron George Gunther Lisa Latimer

Example 7. Every Other Day

You have made a decision to run every other day in the month of October beginning on October 1. You would like to show in a list box all the days you should run as a reminder. How can you do this? You can still use the counter in a loop to represent the days that you are supposed to run. The only difference in this problem from Example 5 is that the increment is no longer 1 but 2; therefore, the routine can appear as follows:

```
Dim Counter As Integer
lstNumbers.Items.Clear
lstNumbers.Items.Add("I am determined to run on the following
  days of October:")
For Counter = 1 to 31 Step 2
    lstNumbers.Items.Add(Counter)
Next Counter
```

In this example, the Step parameter is specified explicitly as 2; therefore, Counter will begin with the starting value of 1. After the first iteration, it is increased by 2, resulting in 3 being added to the list box. The following numbers should appear in the list box below the text string:

1 3 5 7 9 11 13 15 17 19 21 23 25 27 29 31

TIP

In some languages, there is a restriction that the counter as well as the increment for the For loop must be Integer (or Long) variables. There is no such restriction in VB; however, it is always advisable that both the counter and the increment are of the same data type. This will eliminate the need for data conversion and avoid unexpected problems, some of which are illustrated in the Explore and Discover exercises at the end of this chapter.

Example 8. Displaying a String on Two Lines (the ShowTwoLines Project)

Suppose you have a text string that is longer than 80 characters, but shorter than 140. You would like to display it in a message box in two lines, and you don't want the first line to be longer than 80 characters. How can this be done?

Assume your text string has embedded spaces between positions 1 and 80. One way to handle this is to search the string backward for a blank space starting from the 80th position. This space position can then be used as the split point; everything on the left can be printed on the first line, and the remainder on the second.

To search for the space backward, you can compare each character in the string with the space character beginning with the 80th position, and go backward until the comparison is true. Recall that you can use the Mid function to extract a character from a string. The code to search for a blank space for this purpose should appear as follows:

```
Dim P As Integer
For P = 80 to 1 Step -1
    If Mid(Text, P, 1) = " " Then
        Exit For
    End If
Next P
```

In the preceding code, P is used as the counter with a starting value of 80. Inside the loop, the Mid function extracts a character at position P. This character is then compared with the space character. If the comparison is not True, nothing is done within the If block. The Next P statement transfers execution control to the For statement. In the next iteration, a value -1 is added to P. As long as P is greater than or equal to 1, the loop will continue. When the text string's position P is a space, the comparison will be True. The statement inside the If block will then be executed. The *Exit For statement* will immediately terminate the loop, and transfer the execution control to the statement immediately following the Next P statement, much like the Exit Do statement for the Do...Loop structure.

For example, assume the two words near position 80 are "getting excited" and are positioned as follows:

Position	69	70	71	72	73	74	75	76	77	78	79	80	81	82	83
Character	g	e	t	t	i	n	g		e	x	c	i	t	e	d

The following execution table depicts how the For loop is executed.

Iteration	P	Mid(Text, P, 1)	= " "	Action
1	80	i	False	(Next P)
2	79	c	False	(Next P)
3	78	x	False	(Next P)
4	77	e	False	(Next P)
5	76	(space)	True	Exit For

When the loop terminates, P should have a value of 76. After the position is found for the space, you can display the string in two separate lines as follows:

```
MsgBox(Microsoft.VisualBasic.Left(Text, P - 1) & vbCrLf & _
    Mid(Text, P + 1))
```

Recall that vbCrLf is the end of line marker, and will force the ensuing string to be displayed in the next line. The result will be similar to the following:

```
. . . getting
excited . . .
```

To test the preceding code, convert the problem into a project called **ShowTwoLines**. Here are the steps to create the visual interface:

1. Draw a text box on a new form, and name it **txtInput**. This text box will be used to input the text string, which will be approximately 140 characters long.

2. Draw a label above the text box. Use **Enter the text here:** as its text.

3. Add a button to the form, and name it **btnShow**. The resulting visual interface should be similar to that shown in Figure 7.8.

After the user enters the text string in txtInput, the user will click the button to initiate printing the text string in two lines.

Figure 7.8

Showing a long string in two lines

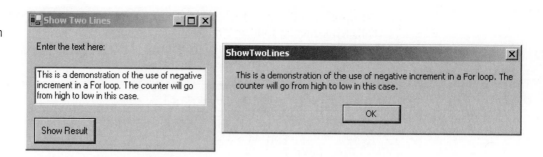

With this modification, your code should be placed in the btnShow Click event. The complete code for the procedure should appear as follows:

```
Private Sub btnShow_Click(ByVal sender As System.Object, ByVal e
    As System.EventArgs) Handles btnShow.Click
    Dim P As Integer
    Dim Text As String
    Text = txtInput.Text
    For P = 80 To 1 Step -1
        If Mid(Text, P, 1) = " " Then
            Exit For
        End If
    Next P
    MsgBox(Microsoft.VisualBasic.Left(Text, P - 1) & vbCrLf & _
        Mid(Text, P + 1))
End Sub
```

Notice that you have added the declaration for the variable Text. Because the source of the text string is the text box txtInput, Text is assigned with the Text property of that control. If everything goes well, the program should display in the message box the text you have entered in the text box in two lines when you click the button. A sample output from the project is shown in Figure 7.8.

The code does not test whether the string is actually longer than 80 characters. If the string is not, the code will fail because the Mid function begins with testing the character at the 80th position. The additional code to safeguard against this error is left to you as an exercise.

Note that the preceding For loop was one way to find the position of a character in a string backward before VB6 was available. As you may recall, the InStrRev string function, discussed in Chapter 4, "Data, Operations, and Built-In Functions," can perform the same computation much more effectively. A statement such as the following:

```
P = InStrRev(Text, " ", 80)
```

will give the same result as the For loop. Practically, you should use the For loop for this purpose only if you are using an older version of VB. Even so, this example should give you a fairly good idea about how a For loop works with a negative increment.

Nesting the Loops

Similar to the If blocks, the loop structures—the Do, While, and For structures—can be nested; that is, a Do…Loop structure can contain several Do…Loop structures inside itself. Similarly, a For…Next structure can contain several For…Next structures inside itself. In addition, a Do…Loop structure can also contain For…Next structures, and vice versa. The nesting can go practically any levels deep. The nested structure can appear as follows:

```
            For I = 1 To 20
                Statements to be executed (Level 1)
                For J= I to 40
                    Statements to be executed (Level 2)
                    For K = J to 1 Step - 1
                        Statements to be executed (Level 3)
                    Next K
                    Statements to be executed (Level 2)
                Next J
                Statements to be executed (Level 1)
            Next I
```

Notice that the loops cannot be interposed; that is, one loop can contain another, and the inner loop must be complete before the end of the outer loop. In addition, you should not use the same counter variable for any inner one loop. Example 9 illustrates the use of a nested loop structure.

TIP

When you are coding nested loops, you may want to have all the loop structures in place before starting to write the detailed code. After you start to focus on the detailed logic of your program, it is easy to become lost as to which part of the program you are in.

In some other cases, it may be easier to start with the innermost loop first and work outward one step at a time. After you finish the inner loop, you can treat it like a procedure that solves a problem. You can then use it to solve a bigger problem that is being handled in the outer loop.

Example 9. Matching Up Teams in a League

Suppose there are eight teams in a sport league. In a season, each team is to play with all other teams exactly once. You would like to list all the possible games showing which team is to play against the other team. How can this be done?

Consider the situation for Team 1. The team will play all the other teams, that is, Teams 2 through 8. You can list all these other teams the team will play against. How about Team 2? It will also play against all seven other teams. You should notice that the game Team 2 against Team 1 is the same game as Team 1 against Team 2. This game has already been listed for Team 1. There is no need to list this one again. So, for Team 2, you only need to list Teams 3 through 8. To avoid listing the same games, the general rule is to list as the opponents only those teams whose numbers are higher than the current team you are considering. This analysis yields the following table.

Pivotal Team	Opponents to List
1	2, 3, . . . 7, and 8
2	3, 4, . . . 7, and 8
3	4, 5, . . . 7, and 8
.	
.	
6	7 and 8
7	8

Notice that Team 8 is not listed as a pivotal team because it has been listed as the opponent to *all* other teams already.

Let *Team* be the focal team and *Other* be the other team that Team will play against; then the following code should display in a list box all the games for the league during a season.

```
For Team = 1 To 7
    For Other = Team + 1 to 8
        lstGames.Items.Add("Team " & Team & _
            " against Team " & Other)
    Next Other
Next Team
```

The inner For loop actually displays the other teams that Team will be playing against. The counter Other starts with a value Team + 1. As explained, all games against any teams with a team number smaller than this team have already been listed. The following table shows the results at different states of the two loops.

Team	Other	Game
1		
	2	Team 1 against Team 2
	3	Team 1 against Team 3
	.	
	.	
	7	Team 1 against Team 7
	8	Team 1 against Team 8
2		
	3	Team 2 against Team 3
	4	Team 2 against Team 4
	.	
	8	Team 2 against Team 8
.	.	
	.	
7		
	8	Team 7 against Team 8

Note that the inner loop with the counter Other repeats seven times. Each time, Other starts with a different value. When Team is 1, Other starts with 2; when Team is 2, Other starts with 3. The inner loop always ends after Other reaches 8. A total of 28 games should be displayed when the routine ends.

Example 10. What Is Your Chance to Win?

Nested loops are often used to solve complex computational problems. It is therefore important for you to become familiar and comfortable with their working. Here is another illustrative problem that calls for the use of nested loops: The probability for a gambler to win a hand of blackjack against the house is 49%. What is the chance to win at least 60 hands out of 100?

To solve this problem *analytically*, you will need to find the formulas to compute the probability to win 60 through 100 out of 100 hands and then sum the results. You can imagine how long the formula may look.

An alternative is to solve the problem *numerically by simulation*. You can use the random numbers generated by the computer to simulate the event and outcome. The resulting experience can then be used as an approximation to the probability of interest.

For example, the probability to win a hand is 49%, so you can draw a random number and then examine its value. If it is less than or equal to 0.49, you can consider that you have won a hand; otherwise, you have lost. Given sufficient repetition, the probability of winning will be approximately 49%, using this simulation scheme. To simulate playing a hand, you will draw a random number, and examine whether it is less than or equal to 0.49.

In the original problem, the question is the chance of winning 60 hands out of 100. You can simulate playing 100 hands. As each hand is played, you can determine whether you win or lose, and accumulate the number of hands won. At the end of this experiment, you can check to see how many hands you have won. If you have won at least 60 hands, you can claim it a success by the definition of the problem.

Let R be the random number, and *Wins* be the number of hands won; then the previous discussion can be translated into the following pseudo-code:

1. Let Wins = 0.

2. Repeat steps 2.1 and 2.2 100 times.

    2.1. Draw a random number, R.

    2.2. If R is less than or equal to 0.49, add 1 to Wins.

3. If Wins is greater than or equal to 60, you have succeeded in winning 60 hands out of 100.

The code to implement the algorithm can appear as follows:

```
Wins = 0
For I = 1 To 100
    R = Rnd()
    If R <= 0.49 Then
        Wins = Wins + 1
    End If
Next I
If Wins >= 60 Then
    ' Claim that you have succeeded
End If
```

Notice that a For...Next loop has been used to play 100 hands. Inside the loop, a hand is played by drawing a random number, and the outcome (win or loss) is determined by comparing the random number with 0.49.

The preceding code gives the result of one experiment; that is, you experiment by playing 100 hands and see whether you succeed. To approximate the probability of success, you will need to experiment many times, some successful, others unsuccessful. The probability of success can then be approximated by the relative frequency by dividing the number of successes by the total number of experiments. Assume you experiment 1,000 times. The algorithm can be described as follows:

1. Repeat steps 1.1 and 1.2 1,000 times.

    1.1. Experiment with 100 hands, and count the number of wins (W).

    1.2. If Wins is greater than or equal to 60, add 1 to Successes.

2. The probability of success equals Successes/1,000.

The code to implement the algorithm should appear as follows:

```
For J = 1 To 1000
    ' Include the experiment to play 100 hands here
    If Wins >= 60 Then
    ' Claim that you have succeeded
        Successes = Successes + 1
    End If
Next J
ProbOfSuccess = Successes / 1000
```

The Complete Simulation Procedure. Assuming the computation will be initiated by a click on a button named btnSimulate, the complete procedure can appear as follows:

```
Private Sub btnSimulate_Click(ByVal sender As System.Object, ByVal
    e As System.EventArgs) Handles btnSimulate.Click
    Dim R As Single
    Dim Wins As Single
    Dim Successes As Single
    Dim I As Integer
    Dim J As Integer
    Dim ProbOfSuccess As Single
    Randomize() 'Randomize the random number sequence
    For J = 1 To 1000
        Wins = 0
        For I = 1 To 100
            R = Rnd()
            If R <= 0.49 Then
                Wins = Wins + 1
            End If
        Next I
        If Wins >= 60 Then
            ' Claim that you have succeeded
            Successes = Successes + 1
        End If
    Next J
```

```
        ProbOfSuccess = Successes / 1000
        MsgBox("Probability of winning 60 hands out of 100 is " &
          ProbOfSuccess)
    End Sub
```

Notice that the Randomize statement has been inserted at the beginning of the program so that a different series of random numbers will be generated each time the simulation is performed. Test the program. You will see that the result oscillates around 2%. Does it surprise you?

Additional Remarks. The accuracy of the program depends primarily on the quality of the random number generator. If the random numbers are truly random, the results can be very accurate when the number of experiments is large.

Of course, you can modify the program so that it can be used to simulate a broad number of intriguing probability problems. For instance, in the previous example, the probability of winning a hand, the number of hands played, and the number of experiments are fixed at 0.49, 100, and 1,000, respectively. You can replace these simulation parameters with variables, and allow the user to specify their values. The program can then be used to answer a question such as "If the probability for a particular baseball player (say, Barry Bonds) to hit a home run each time he is at bat is 10%, what is the probability that he hits two or more home runs in a game when he is at bat five times?" The desired revision is left to you as an exercise.

The For Each...Next Structure

A variation of the For... Next structure is the For Each...Next structure, which has the following syntax:

```
For Each Object In Collection
    Statements to be Executed
Next [Object]
```

where *Object* = an object variable that represents an object such as a text box.

Collection represents a variable or predefined term that represents a set of object items; for example, the term Controls represents all the VB controls in a container. The expression Me.Controls represents the controls in the form.

It is probably easier to show you how the For Each structure works by example than by explanation of concept. The following code will count the number of text boxes in a form:

```
Dim Ctrl As Control
Dim Count As Integer
For Each Ctrl In Me.Controls
    If TypeName(Ctrl) = "TextBox" Then
        Count += 1
    End If
Next Ctrl
```

As you can see in the code, the variable Ctrl is declared to be of a Control type, and Count is declared to be an Integer. Count is used to count the number of text boxes. In the For Each statement, the variable Ctrl is set to a control in the form. Inside the loop, the *TypeName function* returns a string representing the type name of the control. For example, if the control is a TextBox, the function returns a string "TextBox." The string is compared with "TextBox," and if the two are equal, Count is increased by 1. In the next iteration, Ctrl is set to the next control in the Controls collection. The loop continues until the Controls collection runs out of the control object; that is, until all controls in the form have been enumerated.

Note that in the code, Me qualifies Controls. In VB.NET, each control container has its own Controls collection. All controls in the form but not within a container control, such as group box, are included in the form's Controls collection. Those controls within a container control are included in the container's Controls collection, but not in the form's Controls collection. To enumerate those controls within a container control, qualify Controls with the container name. For example, to refer to those controls in a group box named GroupBox1, you should code:

```
GroupBox1.Controls
```

Another way to identify the type of a control/object is to use the TypeOf keyword; however, it can be used only in the If statement as follows:

```
If TypeOf(Ctrl) Is TextBox Then
     'Other statements
End If
```

Notice that the Is operator must be used to test the type.

Clearing Text Boxes and Masked Edit Boxes in a Form. With this understanding, you should be able to explain why the following code clears all the text boxes and masked edit boxes in the form:

```
Dim Ctrl As Control
Dim Temp As String
Dim TheMaskedEdit As AxMSMask.AxMaskEdBox
For Each Ctrl In Me.Controls 'Enumerate controls in the form
    Select Case TypeName(Ctrl)
        Case "TextBox"
            ' If the control is a text box
            Ctrl.Text = "" 'Clear the text box
        Case "AxMaskEdBox"
            ' If the control is a Masked Edit box
            TheMaskedEdit = CType(Ctrl, AxMSMask.AxMaskEdBox)
            Temp = TheMaskedEdit.Mask 'Save the mask
            TheMaskedEdit.Mask = "" 'Clear the mask
            TheMaskedEdit.Text = "" 'Clear the text box
            TheMaskedEdit.Mask = Temp 'Restore the mask
    End Select
Next Ctrl
```

The routine uses the For Each…Next loop to enumerate through all the controls in the form. If a control is a text box, a zero-length string is assigned to its Text property to clear the text box. If a control is a masked edit box, a few more steps are needed. The generic object variable, Ctrl, is converted to the masked edit type (axMSMask.AxMaskEdBox) using the *CType function*. The function converts the object in its first parameter to the type specified in the second parameter. The result is then assigned to an object of the masked edit type as declared in one of the Dim statements. This conversion step is necessary because the generic object does not recognize the Mask property. The masked edit's Mask property is saved before the Mask is cleared. Its text box is then cleared, and the Mask property is restored. This method to clear the text box of the masked edit box was explained in Chapter 3, "User Interface Design: Visual Basic Controls and Events."

If the Text property of the masked edit box does not behave as documented, use the following code as a workaround to clear its text box:

```
' If the control is a Masked Edit box
TheMaskedEdit = CType(Ctrl, AxMSMask.AxMaskEdBox)
Temp = TheMaskedEdit.Mask 'Save the mask
If Len(Temp) = 0 Then
    ' There no mask; use the length of the control's
      ClipText property
    Temp = Space(Len(TheMaskedEdit.ClipText))
End If
TheMaskedEdit.SelStart = 0
TheMaskedEdit.SelLength = Len(Temp)
TheMaskedEdit.SelText = Space(Len(Temp)) 'Clear the text
  box
```

The Advantages of Generality. You may be wondering whether you would need a routine like this one at all. After all, when you develop a project and design the visual interface, you certainly know all the text boxes and the mask edit boxes in the form. Will it not be equally convenient to just code like the following?

```
txtName.Text = ""
```

The answer is that the loop approach is better in most cases, especially for an application with many controls on a form. You do not need to know the names of the controls to make the code work properly. In addition, one statement, or a group of statements such as:

```
Ctrl.Text = ""
```

will take care of clearing all controls of the same type.

Furthermore, when the visual interface is changed, such as addition or deletion of some controls, you do not have to worry about revising the code. It is generalized and will work properly for all text boxes and masked edit boxes. This generalized nature of the code enhances code maintainability.

TIP

So, how do you find out the type name of different controls? Use the TypeName function. The following routine will show the names and type names of all the controls in the form.

```
Dim Ctrl As Control
For Each Ctrl In Me.Controls
    MsgBox(Ctrl.Name & " " & TypeName(Ctrl))
Next
```

Referencing Objects in a Collection by Index

Notice that you can also reference objects in a collection by index. Objects in the Controls collection, for example, can be referenced in a manner similar to the Items collection in the list box. The first object in the Controls has an index of zero. The Controls collection also has a Count property that gives the number objects in the collection; therefore, the following code fragment can also count the number of text boxes on a form:

```
Dim I As Integer
Dim Count As Integer
For I = 0 To Me.Controls.Count - 1
    If TypeName(Me.Controls(I)) = "TextBox" Then
        Count += 1
    End If
Next I
```

7.3 Additional Notes on Coding Repetition

You have seen all the structures to construct code for repetition. Have you wondered under what situations you should use which structure (a question of *suitability*)? In addition, recall that statements within the loop will be repeated many times. Any performance efficiency/inefficiency associated with these statements can be magnified dramatically (a question of *speed* or efficiency). Are there tips that can enhance the efficiency of code for loops? Here are some notes in these regards.

Do Versus For

The key difference between the Do structure and the For structure is the absence or presence of the counter. This difference makes one structure more suitable than the other for certain situations. The following discussion provides additional details.

Suitability. The Do…Loop structure (and its variant, While…End While structure) has no counter; the For…Next structure does. In nearly all cases, one structure can be used in place of the other; however, one structure will appear to be more suitable than the other for a given situation. Basically, the For…Next structure is clearly intended for a situation in which the lower and the upper limit as well as the increment are known; the Do…Loop structure is designed for the situation in which such parameters are undeterminable.

For example, when reading an entire text file record by record, it will be difficult for the program to determine ahead of time how many records, or lines, there are in the file. In such a situation, it will be more appropriate to use the Do…Loop structure and check for the EOF condition to terminate the loop. Even if there is a need to use a counter while the input process is in progress, such as displaying the record number being read, a variable can be used to perform the count in the Do loop. You will be still better off not to use the For…Next structure by assuming an arbitrary upper limit and then checking for the EOF condition inside the loop. Such an approach leaves open the possibility that in the future the arbitrary upper limit might be unexpectedly exceeded when the file grows too large.

On the other hand, the For…Next structure will be more suitable when its parameter values are known. Take the computation of the series of 1, 2, 3, to n, for example. At the time of computation, the value of n is certainly known, as are the starting value and the increment; therefore, it is natural that the For…Next structure is used. Although you can still accomplish the requirement by using the Do…Loop structure, you will find that more lines of code are needed. The code will not be as concise and easy to understand.

Speed. How does the For…Next structure compare with the Do…Loop structure in terms of speed? In general, the difference is negligible. In fact, the performance difference of the two structures depends more on the way the condition in the Do loop is coded and on the data types of the parameters in the For loop than on the structures themselves.

For example, similar to the condition in the If statement, a complex logical expression such as A >= B And C = D Or Not (X = Y And W < V) in the Do or Loop statement will be much slower than a simple expression such as A <> B. In the case of For loops, using variables of Decimal or Double type to serve as counter will certainly take more time to execute than using variables of the Short, Integer or Long type. Because loops are to be executed many times, their performance difference will be magnified and more noticeable. One of the Explore and Discover exercises at the end of this chapter illustrates the difference in speed between the Integer counter and the Decimal counter for the For…Next loop.

For Versus For Each

The For Each…Next structure is a convenient way to enumerate objects—especially of different types—in a collection, as you have seen in the example of enumerating all controls in a form. When you learn more about multiple form applications and databases in later chapters, you will find more opportunities to use this structure.

Note, however, that in many cases, the objects in a collection are of the same type. Usually, in such cases, the For…Next with a counter instead of with the keyword Each can also be used. When this is the case, the For…Next structure is usually more efficient than the For Each…Next structure.

Tips for Efficiency

To repeat the point, because loops are to be executed many times, the efficiency or inefficiency of the group of statements in the loops is magnified. It is far more important to examine the code in the loops—especially the innermost loops—very closely. Here are a few tips to improve the efficiency in coding the loops:

- Move all constant assignments/operations out of the loop. For example, consider the following loop:

```
For I = 1 To 20000
    A = 10 + B
    ' Other statements
Next I
```

where none of the other statements inside the loop change the value of A or B. The code will be more efficient if it is rearranged as follows:

```
A = 10 + B
For I = 1 To 20000
    ' Other statements
Next I
```

- *Replace complex mathematical operations with simpler ones.* For example, the present value of an ordinary annuity of $1 for n years can be computed by the following formula:

$$P = (1 + r)^{-1} + (1 + r)^{-2} + \ldots + (1 + r)^{-n}$$

Assuming the proper values for R and N have been obtained, a straightforward way to code the formula will be as follows:

```
Dim PresentValue As Double
Dim I As Integer
PresentValue = 0
For I = 1 To N
    PresentValue = PresentValue + (1 + R) ^ (-I)
Next I
```

The preceding code, however, is not efficient for two reasons. The value of $(1 + R)$ will never change inside the loop. It will be more efficient to perform the computation before the loop. Also, the ^ operator takes much more time than a simple multiplication. The following code can accomplish the same and would be much more efficient:

```
Dim PresentValue As Double
Dim Factor1 As Double
Dim FactorN As Double
Dim I As Integer
PresentValue = 0
FactorN = 1        ' The present value of a dollar for n
  years
Factor1 = 1 / (1 + R) 'The inverse factor, i.e., (1 +
  r) ^ (-1)
For I = 1 To N
    FactorN *=  Factor1 'Compute V = V ^ I
    PresentValue += FactorN
Next I
```

The following execution table shows the state of each iteration.

I	FactorN	PresentValue
1	$(1 + r)^{-1}$	$(1 + r)^{-1}$
2	$(1 + r)^{-2}$	$(1 + r)^{-1} + (1 + r)^{-2}$
.		
N	$(1 + r)^{-n}$	$(1 + r)^{-1} + (1 + r)^{-2} + \ldots + (1 + r)^{-n}$

- *Avoid data type conversions inside the loop.* In the previous example, some might not see a need for the variable Factor1 or FactorN to be of the Double type; however, as long as PresentValue is of the Double type, making either Factor1 or FactorN (or both) as a Single type variable will force data type conversion inside the loop, creating additional work for the computer.

- *Replace reference to a control's property by a variable.* It takes longer to refer to a control's property than to a variable. For repetitive references in a loop, a variable should be used. For example, consider the following code:

```
For I = 1 To Len(txtName.Text)
    Ch = Mid(txtName.Text, I , 1)
    ' Other statements
Next I
```

The code will be more efficient if it is rearranged as follows, assuming TheText has been declared as a String variable:

```
TheText = txtName.Text
For I = 1 To Len(TheText)
    Ch = Mid(TheText, I, 1)
    ' Other statements
Next I
```

7.4 An Application Example

Loops are used extensively in programs but can be difficult for the beginner to understand. To illustrate how they can be used in a practical problem, consider a simplified aspect of a payroll system. When a new employee is hired, the payroll department needs to establish an employee record for the employee so that proper payroll withholdings can be handled. An aspect of this involves the completion of a W-4 form that requires the employee to enter information concerning employee's tax status, such as the marital status and number of dependents. This simplified W-4 form example focuses on the programming steps, rather than the information required.

The W-4 Form Project

The project involves the entry of the employee W-4 form. Assume one or more new employees will be entered into the W-4 file each time the program runs and that the company has fewer than 100 employees. The program will require the entry of the following data:

- Employee Social Security number
- Name (last, first)
- Sex
- Number of dependents

The data will be saved in a file called W-4Info.txt as a fixed-length file (the length of each field remains constant), one line per record. The following lists additional specifications.

Design Considerations

One important consideration of the project is that there should be no duplicate employee records. To handle this, you will populate the existing employee records in a list box. As each new employee is to be saved, the list box will be searched for the new Social Security number (SSN). If the SSN is found, an error message will be displayed and the record will not be saved; otherwise, the record will be saved. In addition, it will be added to the list box so that any future duplicate entry can be identified.

The Visual Interface

You will use the following controls to handle the data fields:

Data Field	Control
Employee Social Security number	Masked edit box
Name (last, first)	Text box
Sex	Radio buttons
Number of dependents	Text box

To make the form appear uncluttered, you will use a group box to group all these fields. In addition to the VB controls for these data fields, you will add a list box to list the existing employees, as mentioned previously. Furthermore, you should also have two buttons: one to save the data, and another to end the program.

The properties for these controls should be set to proper values. Some selected ones are as listed in the following table.

Control (Field)	Property	Setting
Group box	Name	grbW4Info
	Text	W-4 Information
Masked edit box (S-S-N)	Name	mskSSN
	Mask	###-##-####
Text box (Employee Name)	Name	txtName
	MaxLength	24
Radio button (for male)	Name	rbtMale
	Text	Male
	Checked	True
Radio button (for female)	Name	rbtFemale
	Text	Female
Text box (No. of dependents)	Name	txtNoOfDependents
	MaxLength	3
List box (to list employees)	Name	lstEmployees
Button	Name	btnSave
	Text	Save
Button	Name	btnQuit
	Text	Quit

The visual interface appears as in Figure 7.9.

Coding the Project

The code needs to handle the following situations:

- As soon as the program starts, the list box should be populated with employee records in the W-4 info file. This will involve associating the file with a StreamReader object, having the StreamReader read the records one at a time in a loop, and adding each record to the list box as it is read. The file needs to be closed by closing the StreamReader and then reopened with a StreamWriter object so that data for additional employees can be saved during the remaining duration of the program.

- When the user clicks the Save button, several major steps should be carried out:

  There should be an input validation routine to ensure that data entered are legitimate. For simplicity, you will check only the employee's Social Security number to ensure that duplicate records for the same employee will not be allowed.

  The data should be saved in the W-4 Info file. In addition, the same record should appear in the list box.

  The screen should be cleared to facilitate the entry of the next record.

- When the user clicks the Quit button, the program should end.

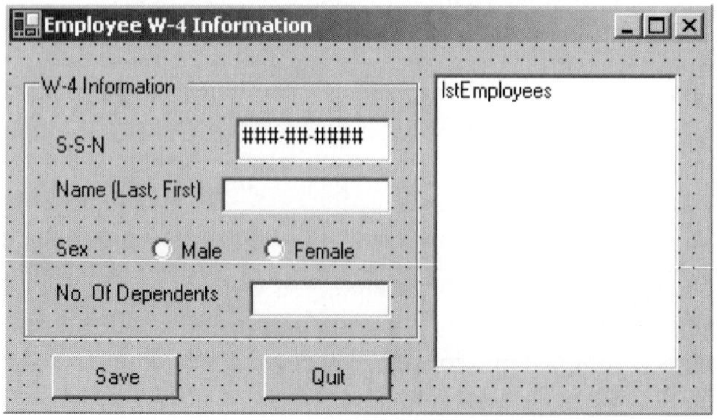

Figure 7.9

The visual interface for W-4 form entry

Populating the List Box. The list box will be populated with all existing employee records. Assuming the file has been associated with a StreamReader W4FileReader, how can this be accomplished? For simplicity, you will assume all fields in the record will be kept in the list box. You can set up a loop, and read the file one record (line) at a time (in each iteration). As the record (named EmpRec) is read, it is added to the list box. The code in Example 2 can be easily modified to handle this:

```
Do Until W4FileReader.Peek() = -1
    EmpRec = W4FileReader.ReadLine()
    lstEmployees.Items.Add(EmpRec)
Loop
```

As already stated, this should be done as soon as the program starts, and it should be placed in the Form Load event. This event procedure should also do the following:

1. Open the file for input (associate the file with the StreamReader, W4FileReader).

2. Close the StreamReader (W4FileReader) after all records have been read.

3. Associate the file with a StreamWriter; for example, W4FileWriter, with the Append specification because you will be adding new records for the remaining duration of the program.

The complete code for the Form Load event procedure appears as follows:

```
Dim W4FileWriter As System.IO.StreamWriter
Private Sub Form1_Load(ByVal sender As System.Object, ByVal e As
   System.EventArgs) Handles MyBase.Load
    Dim EmpRec As String
    Dim W4FileReader As New System.IO.StreamReader("C:\Temp
      \w-4info.txt") 'Open the file to read
    ' Read employee w-4 info file and populate the list box
    Do Until W4FileReader.Peek() = -1
        EmpRec = W4FileReader.ReadLine()
        lstEmployees.Items.add(EmpRec)
    Loop
    ' Input complete; close the file
    W4FileReader.Close()
    ' Reopen the file for Append
    W4filewriter = New System.IO.StreamWriter("C:\temp
      \w-4info.txt", True)
End Sub
```

Note that the variable W4FileWriter is declared in the general declaration area at the class level. This is necessary because the variable will also be used in another event procedure in which the employee W-4 records are saved; however, the variable W4FileReader is declared inside the form load procedure because no other event procedure will need to use it to read the file. Note also that this routine will not run when it attempts to open the W-4 Info file for Input if the file does not exist. You should create an empty file with Notepad before testing this program.

Handling the Save Button. As indicated previously, when the user clicks the Save button, the program should do the following:

1. Ensure that the current entry is not a duplicate of an existing record.

2. Save the record, if it is a new one.

3. Clear the screen.

These steps can be coded in the btnSave click event procedure as follows:

```
Private Sub btnSave_Click(ByVal sender As System.Object, ByVal e
    As System.EventArgs) Handles btnSave.Click
        ' Make sure s-s-n does not already exist
        ' Don't save the record if it does exist
        If SSNExists() Then Exit Sub
        ' Save the employee record
```

```
' Also add the record to the list box
SaveRec()
' Clear screen and reset the default radio button
ClearScreen()
' Set focus on the first control for the convenience of the
  user
mskSSN.Focus()
End Sub
```

This coding design takes advantage of using general procedures for the top-down design. Each major step is coded either as a function or as a Sub and is invoked from this procedure. The code should be self-explanatory.

The first step is to make sure the Social Security number entered does not already exist in the file. To do this, the event procedure calls a function, SSNExists, which returns a value of True or False, depending on whether the Social Security number actually exists. How does the function carry out the checking? To understand how it is done, you need to understand the format of the records saved first.

Saving a W-4 Record. As mentioned, the file is created as a fixed-length file; that is, each field in the file remains constant. Assume the lengths for SSN, name, sex, and number of dependents are 9, 24, 1, and 3, respectively. The lengths for SSN and sex should pose no problem because their field lengths appear fixed. For ease of browsing the file, you will also pad a blank space between each field.

How do you handle the length for name? Note that the actual length of names can vary. You can solve this problem by creating a function (SetLength) that will take a string, and set its length according to the specified length. The function appears as follows:

```
Function SetLength(ByVal Text As String, ByVal L As Integer) _
  As String
'This function returns a string of the specified length L,
'given Text as the first parameter
    If Len(Text) >= L Then
        Return (Microsoft.VisualBasic.Left(Text, L))
    Else
        Return (Text & Space(L - Len(Text)))
    End If
End Function
```

As you can see from the function's header, the function takes two parameters. The first parameter is the string itself, and the second parameter is used to specify the desired length. Inside the procedure, the length of the string (Text) is compared with the desired length. If the former is greater or equal to the latter, the first L (desired length) characters of the string are returned. On the other hand, if the string is shorter than the desired length, it is padded with additional spaces to make it of the exact desired length.

How do you ensure that the number of dependents will be always three characters long? You can handle this in several different ways. This is a numeric field, but you are not sure whether the user will always enter a number, or enter additional spaces after the number; therefore, the first step is to convert the content of the text to a number using the Val function, and convert it back to string using the CStr function. You can then pad on its left side with spaces. One way to do it without involving an explicit use of the If block is to always pad the result with three spaces and then take only the three characters on the right. The code will appear as follows:

```
'Generate a string (from a number) of length 3 with spaces
'padded on the left
Microsoft.VisualBasic.Right(Space(3) & _
  Cstr(Val(txtNoOfDependents.Text)) , 3)
```

The following code for Sub SaveRec should save the employee record in the format you want.

```
Sub SaveRec()
    ' This Sub saves an employee w-4 record
    ' It also adds the same to the list box
```

```
        Dim TheName As String
        Dim Sex As String
        Dim EmpRec As String
        TheName = SetLength(txtName.Text, 24)
        If rbtMale.Checked Then
            Sex = "M"
        Else
            Sex = "F"
        End If
        EmpRec = mskSSN.ClipText & " " & TheName & " " & Sex & " " _
          & Microsoft.VisualBasic.Right(Space(3) & _
          CStr(Val(txtNoOfDependents.Text)), 3)
        W4FileWriter.WriteLine(EmpRec)
        ' Also add to the list box
        lstEmployees.Items.Add(EmpRec)
        ' Tell the user what has been done
        MsgBox("Employee data for " & Trim$(TheName) & " Saved")
    End Sub
```

Notice that in the code, you also convert what the user specifies as the employee's sex by the radio buttons—rbtMale and rbtFemale—to a string variable, Sex, which is assigned a value "M" or "F", depending on which radio button is clicked. Notice also that the variable EmpRec is used to prepare the employee W-4 record to be saved. In addition, the ClipText property, not the Text property of the masked edit box for S-S-N is used, so there will be no embedded dash (-) in the saved SSN. After the W-4 Info record is assembled, it is saved to the file. The same record is also added to the list box for content consistency and to facilitate the prevention of duplicate employee records.

Checking for Existence of an S-S-N. Now you know the Social Security number is the first field in the file and the list box. Searching for the SSN involves the comparison of the data entered in the masked edit box with the first field of each item in the list box until a match is found or the list box runs out of items. To speed up the operation, a string variable SSN can be used to store the data extracted from the masked edit box. (Recall that data stored in variables can be accessed much faster than those properties in controls.) The pseudo-code to search for the SSN can appear as follows:

1. Let SSN = the number extracted from the masked edit box.
2. For each I = 0, 1, 2… item count in the list box minus 1, perform the following:
   2.1. Compare SSN with the SSN in the Ith item in the list box. If the two are equal, conclude that SSN exists and exit the function; otherwise, proceed to next I.
3. When all items are compared, exit the function.

How do you extract data in the first field (SSN) of a list item? Each item (record) in the list box can be accessed by the list box's Items(I) property. To extract the first sub-string from a string, you can use the Left function. Because the SSN field has a length of 9, the expression Left(CStr(lstEmployees.Items(I)), 9) should return the SSN of the Ith (0th being the first) employee. (Notice that the CStr function is used to convert lstEmployees.Items(I) to the String type because Items(I) is of the Object type.) How do you set the value for I? The value can vary in the range of 0 through Items.Count -1. This range can be used to set up the counter of a For loop. The following code tests the existence for a given S-S-N and returns a value True when the SSN is found:

```
    Function SSNExists() As Boolean
        ' This function checks if the SSN in the masked edit box
        ' already exists; if so, it displays an error message
        ' Returns True; otherwise, it returns False
        Dim SSN As String
        Dim I As Integer
        SSN = mskSSN.ClipText
        For I = 0 To lstEmployees.Items.Count - 1
```

```
                         If SSN =
                           Microsoft.VisualBasic.Left(CStr(lstEmployees.Items(I)),
                           9) Then MsgBox("S-S-N already in file", vbInformation)
                             Return (True)
                         End If
                     Next I
                     Return (False)
                 End Function
```

In the loop, when SSN (the entered SSN) is found to be equal to one of the SSNs in the list box, a message is displayed. The function then terminates with a return value True; otherwise, the search continues until the end of the loop. The function returns a value of False.

The FindString Method. As a side note, the list box and the combo box of VB.NET have the *FindString method* that returns the position of the string in the box that starts with the specified string. If the string is not found, the method returns a value –1. The method has the following syntax:

```
    Object.FindString(StringToSearch, [BeginningPosition])
```

If the second parameter is specified, the search will start at this specified position. The preceding SSNExists function can be rewritten as follows:

```
    Function SSNExists() As Boolean
        ' This function checks if the SSN in the masked edit box
        ' already exists; if so, it displays an error message
        ' Returns True; otherwise, it returns False
        Dim SSN As String
        SSN = mskSSN.ClipText
        If lstEmployees.FindString(SSN) >= 0 Then
            MsgBox("S-S-N already in file", vbInformation)
            Return (True)
        End If
    End Function
```

The code here is definitely much simpler. The previous code is used to illustrate how the For loop can be used. (And was also the typical way to find the matching string in the previous versions.) Also note that the list box and the combo box also have the FindStringExact method that returns the position of the string in the box that exactly matches the specified string. This method has exactly the same syntax as the FindString method.

TIP

Use the FindString and FindStringExact methods of the list box and combo box to search for a match in the box. They make your code much simpler.

Clearing the Screen. The third major step in the Save event procedure is to clear to screen. The previous code example to clear the text boxes and masked edit boxes on the screen (form) can be copied and used here. Notice, however, that you have qualified Controls with grbW4Info (name for the group box which contains all data entry boxes) so that the routine will clear all text boxes and masked edit boxes in that container. Can you write a routine that can clear the screen, regardless of whether the text boxes and masked edit boxes are in any container control? Yes. This challenge is left to you as an exercise at the end of this chapter.

This W-4 info screen also has radio buttons. What you would like to accomplish is to reset the default button, such as set rbtMale on. To do this in the For Each loop appears to be a bit trickier. You will take the direct approach of setting the Checked property of rbtMale to True. The complete code for this Sub appears as follows:

```
    Sub ClearScreen()
        Dim Ctrl As Control
        Dim Temp As String
```

```
     Dim TheMaskedEdit As AxMSMask.AxMaskEdBox
     'Enumerate controls in the group box
     For Each Ctrl In grbW4Info.Controls
         Select Case TypeName(Ctrl)
             Case "TextBox"
                 ' If the control is a text box
                 Ctrl.Text = "" 'Clear the text box
             Case "AxMaskEdBox"
                 ' If the control is a Masked Edit box
                 TheMaskedEdit = CType(Ctrl, AxMSMask.AxMaskEdBox)
                 Temp = TheMaskedEdit.Mask 'Save the mask
                 TheMaskedEdit.Mask = "" 'Clear the mask
                 TheMaskedEdit.Text = "" 'Clear the text box
                 TheMaskedEdit.Mask = Temp 'Restore the mask
         End Select
         rbtMale.Checked = True
     Next Ctrl
End Sub
```

As a technical side note, if the Text property of the masked edit fails to clear, refer to the tip in the "For Each…Next Structure" subsection of Section 7.2 for a workaround.

Don't forget to Close the StreamWriter. As pointed out in Chapter 6, "Input, Output, and Procedures," it is extremely important that the StreamWriter be closed before the program ends; otherwise, the data may not be written to the file. The output will be incomplete. As noted in Chapter 6, the most appropriate event to close the object is the form's closing event. The code appears as follows:

```
Private Sub Form1_Closing(ByVal sender As System.Object, ByVal e
   As System.ComponentModel.CancelEventArgs) Handles MyBase.Closing
      W4FileWriter.Close()
End Sub
```

Finally, when the user clicks the Quit button, the program should end. This is left to you as an exercise. This completes the code for the application example. The following table lists all the procedures developed for this application:

Procedure name	Procedure type	Page	Remark
Form1_Load	Event	277	Open the W4 file for input
			Populate the list box with records read from the W4 file
			Close the W4 file
			Reopen the W4 file for append
btnSave_Click	Event	277–278	Call four other procedures related to the "save record" operations
SetLength	General function	278	Returns a string with the specified length
SaveRec	General sub	278–279	Saves the record (as entered on the screen) to the W4 file
			Add the new record to the list box
			Displays a "record saved" message
SSNExists	General function	279–280	Returns a Boolean value indicating whether the specified SSN already exists. (Note that there are two versions. Include only one to test.)
ClearScreen	General sub	280–281	Clears the text boxes and masked edit box and also resets rbtMale as the default selection
Form1_Closing	Event	281	Closes the W4 file
btnQuit	Event		To terminate the program (you code)

Testing the Program. Run the program. You should be able to observe the following:

- As soon as the program starts, you should be able to see the existing employees in the list box. If you do not see all fields for the employee in the list box, stop the program and then set the list box's *HorizontalScrollBar property* to True, or make the list box wider.

- After you have entered data for an employee and clicked the Save button:

  If the SSN already exists, the program should display a message box and wait for your additional action.

  If the SSN is new, the data will be saved and the screen will be cleared. In addition, the computer will display a message indicating that the data have been saved. Also, the new record is added to the list box.

- When you click the Quit button, the program terminates, assuming you have entered the proper code.

- When you run the program again, all data that you previously entered should appear in the list box. If not, check to see if you have the code to close the StreamWriter, W4FileWriter.

Additional Remarks. This application example was made as simple as possible. As simple as it is, however, it illustrates how useful and widely used loops are. You have seen that all the following activities involve the use of loops:

- Populating the list box
- Reading records from a file
- Looking for certain data in a list (list box is just an example)
- Clearing edit boxes in a container

You may have also noticed that each situation calls for a different loop structure. The implication is that you should not rely exclusively on only one structure. Become well acquainted with all of them, and you will become more proficient in programming in VB.

If you compare this example with the one at the end of the preceding chapter for the phone file update, you may find some differences in design. For instance, the current example involves only one file. Recall that a case was made in Chapter 6 that updating a text file sequentially calls for the use of two files (one for input and one for output). The current example imposes additional restrictions. Records can only be added to the file. No record can be recalled for editing, nor can a record be deleted from the file. In addition, the entire file is read into a list box. This is feasible only when the file is fairly small.

Summary

- There are basically two types of structures for repetition: one based on condition, and the other based on counter. The Do...Loop structure is based on condition; the For...Next structure is based on counter.

- In the Do...Loop structure, a condition expression can be placed either with Do or with Loop. The condition can be any expression that evaluates to a Boolean value (either True or False). The condition must start with a keyword either While or Until. If the keyword is While, the repetition continues as long as the condition expression is True. If the keyword is Until, the repetition continues as long as the condition expression is False.

- In the Do...Loop structure, if neither the Do statement nor the Loop statement has a condition, the loop can only be terminated with an Exit Do statement (or other statements that terminate the procedure) inside the loop.

- The Do While...Loop structure is equivalent to the structure of While...End While. To exit the latter structure, use the Exit While statement.

- The For…Next structure has the following syntax:

```
For Counter = Starting Value To Ending Value [Step
    Increment]
        Statements to be executed
Next [Counter]
```

When the loop starts, the counter is set to the starting value and compared with the ending value. If it passes the ending value, the loop is terminated. In each of the subsequent iterations, the current value of the counter is added by the increment and compared with the ending value. Again, if it passes the ending value, the loop is terminated. The comparison to determine whether the counter's value passes the ending value depends on the sign of the increment. If the increment is positive, the counter is considered to have passed the ending value when the counter is greater. If the increment is negative, the counter is considered to have passed the ending value when the counter is less.

- The default increment in the For…Next structure is 1.

- The For Each…Next structure relies on the enumerator to enumerate all the objects in a collection. The loop ends when all objects in the collection have been enumerated.

- The Do…Loop structure (and its variant, the While…While End structure) is most proper when the repetition depends on certain known conditions; for example, reaching the end of the file. The For…Next structure is most suitable when the beginning and ending value of the counter are known before the execution of the loop. The For Each…Next can be very useful in enumerating objects in a collection.

- Many mathematical problems whose complexity in the equation defies analysis can be solved numerically by approximating the solution iteratively. These numerical methods can also be applied in many business problems. (For a sample, see exercise 7-33 and project 7-38 at the end of this chapter.)

- Loops execute statements within their structures many times; therefore, they magnify the efficiency of the code noticeably. Always analyze code within the repetition structure (especially the innermost loop) very carefully to ensure code efficiency. Tips to enhance code speed include:

    Move the constant assignment statement out of the loop.

    Replace a complex computation inside the loop with a simpler one.

    Assign object properties to variables outside of the loop, and use the variables inside the loop.

- The application example shows how different repetition structures can be put together to solve a practical problem.

Explore and Discover

7-1. **Conditions with Both the Do and Loop Statements.** Enter the following code in the form click event:

```
Dim I As Integer
Dim C As Integer
I = -10
Do Until I > 0
    I = I + 1
    C = I - 1
Loop While C < 0
```

You should notice that the keyword While is underlined. Place the mouse cursor on the word. What does the IDE say?

7-2. Changing the Parameters of a For Block. Enter the following code:

```
Private Sub Form1_Click(ByVal sender As System.Object, ByVal e As
    System.EventArgs) Handles MyBase.Click
    Dim I As Integer
    Dim K As Integer
    Dim Z As Integer
    Dim Total As Integer
    K = 1
    Z = 10
    For I = K To Z
        Total = Total + I
        K = 10
    Next I
    MsgBox(Total)
End Sub
```

Run the project and then click the form. What is the value of Total? Does the change in value for K inside the loop affect the loop?

7-3. **Changing the Parameters of a For Block.** (continued from exercise 7-2) Test the following code:

```
Private Sub Form1_Click(ByVal sender As System.Object,  ByVal e As
    System.EventArgs) Handles MyBase.Click
    Dim I As Integer
    Dim K As Integer
    Dim Z As Integer
    Dim Total As Integer
    K = 1
    Z = 10
    For I = K To Z
        Total = Total + I
        Z = 1
    Next I
    MsgBox(Total)
End Sub
```

What is the value of Total? Does the change in value for Z inside the loop affect the loop?

7-4. **Changing the Parameters of a For Block.** (continued from exercise 7-3) Test the following code:

```
Private Sub Form1_Click(ByVal sender As System.Object, ByVal e As
    System.EventArgs) Handles MyBase.Click
    Dim I As Integer
    Dim K As Integer
    Dim Z As Integer
    Dim Total As Integer
    Dim S as Integer
    K = 1
    Z = 10
    S = 1
    For I = K To Z Step S
        Total = Total + I
        S = 2
    Next I
    MsgBox(Total)
End Sub
```

What is the value of Total? Does the change in the value of S inside the loop affect the loop? What is your conclusion concerning the effect of changing the parameter values of the For loop?

7-5. **Changing the Counter of a For Block.** Test the following code:

```
Private Sub Form1_Click(ByVal sender As System.Object, ByVal e As
    System.EventArgs) Handles MyBase.Click
    Dim I As Integer
    Dim K As Integer
    Dim Z As Integer
    Dim Total As Integer
    Dim S as Integer
    K = 1
    Z = 10
    S = 1
    For I = K To Z Step S
        Total = Total + I
        I = 10
    Next I
    MsgBox(Total)
End Sub
```

What is the value of Total? Why is the result different from that of previous exercises? The parameters for the loop are set the first time the loop is executed and remain the same. The counter value (which is allowed to be changed inside the loop) is always compared with the ending value each time the For statement is executed. (*Note:* Changing the counter value inside the loop can make it difficult to trace the code logic. Avoid such a coding practice.)

7-6. **Fractional Progression.** Type the following code in the form click event procedure. Run the project, and observe the result:

```
Dim I As Single
Dim C As Integer
For I = 1 To 100 Step 0.1
    C = C + 1
Next I
MsgBox("C = " & C)
```

Is the result what you expected? How do you explain it?

7-7. **Fractional Progression.** (continued from exercise 7-6) Make sure you have set Option Strict On. Change the declaration for I in the preceding problem to the following:

```
Dim I As Integer
```

Do you see a portion of the following line highlighted?

```
For I = 1 To 100 Step 0.1
```

Place the mouse point on the highlighted line to find out why.

7-8. **Fractional Progression.** (continued from exercise 7-7) Place the following code as the first line in the code window of the preceding project.

```
Option Strict Off
```

Now run the project. What result do you obtain? Why does the code result in an error? Click the Break button on the error message box. Place the mouse pointer on the variable C in the For loop. What value do you see? That value basically indicates that C has an overflow condition. Why does the program result in an overflow for C? The loop turns out to be an endless one. I is an integer. After I is added by 0.1, it is truncated to be 1; therefore, the counter never increases, regardless of how many iterations the loop executes. You can see this effect by setting the breakpoint on the For statement, pressing F8, and examining the value of I for a few iterations.

7-9.   **Counter Value After Exit For.** Consider the following code:

```
Dim I as Integer
For I = 1 To 10
    If I = 5 Then Exit For
Next I
MsgBox (I)
For I = 1 To 10
Next I
MsgBox (I)
```

Place the code in an event procedure, such as a button Click or Form Click event, and test it. What results do you obtain? When the loop is terminated by Exit For, the value of the counter is exactly what it is within the loop. When the loop is terminated from the For statement by comparing the counter value with the ending value, the counter value should be one increment value as specified in the Step parameter away from the ending value.

7-10.   **The Puzzling Fractional Increment.** Test the following code in the form click event:

```
Dim S As Single
For S = 0 To 2 Step 0.2
Next S
MsgBox(S)
```

What is the last number in the message box? Is it 2, which is what you should expect? As explained in Chapter 4, Single type variables have a precision of approximately seven significant digits. Some numbers are hard for this type of variables to represent exactly. Repetitively adding 0.2 to S causes the variable to be minutely off its true value. Do you see the potential problem with using the Single type variable, especially as a counter? (Contributed by Wen-Hao Chuang via Ben Wu, both of Indiana University.)

7-11.   **Use of the For Each…Next Structure.** Draw a few different types of controls on a form. Give each a name of your favorite; then test the following code in the form click event:

```
Dim V As Object
For Each V In Me.Controls
    MsgBox(V.Name)
Next V
```

Does it work properly? Set Option Strict Off if you see V.Name underlined. Do you see the flexibility of the For Each…Next? Notice also that V is declared as Object, which can also be any type of data. When you set Option Strict Off, you have much more flexibility in your code. But when your code does not produce the expected results, you may not know the exact statement that causes the problem.

7-12.   **Does It Really Matter What Data Type the Counter Is?** Draw two buttons on a new form. Name one **btnInteger** and set its Text property to **Integer**. Name the other **btnDecimal** and set its Text property to **Decimal**. Enter the following code:

```
Private Sub btnInteger_Click(ByVal sender As System.Object, ByVal
    e As System.EventArgs) Handles btnInteger.Click
    Dim I As Integer
    Dim J As Integer
    Dim T As Double
    T = Microsoft.VisualBasic.Timer
```

```
        For I = 1 To 10000
            For J = 1 To 10000
            Next J
        Next I
        MsgBox(Microsoft.VisualBasic.Timer - T)
    End Sub
    Private Sub btnDecimal_Click(ByVal sender As System.Object, ByVal
      e As System.EventArgs) Handles btnDecimal.Click
        Dim I As Decimal
        Dim J As Decimal
        Dim T As Double
        T = Microsoft.VisualBasic.Timer
        For I = 1 To 10000
            For J = 1 To 10000
            Next J
        Next I
        MsgBox(Microsoft.VisualBasic.Timer - T)
    End Sub
```

Notice that the only difference between the two procedures is the type of data declared for the counters. Click the Integer button. Observe the time displayed in the message box. Do the same with the Decimal button. Do you see a difference in the time it takes to execute each procedure? Decimal counters use much more time than Integer counters in getting an empty loop executed.

Exercises

7-13. Series. Write a routine to compute the total of $1+ 2 + 3 +. . . + n$, where n is taken from a text box. The result is displayed in the Text property of the lblSeries label when the user clicks the btnCompute button.

7-14. Factorial. Write a routine to compute the product of $1 \times 2 \times 3 \times . . . \times n$, where n is taken from a text box. The result is displayed in the text of a label called lblFactorial when the user clicks a button named btnCompute. Use the Double data type for the result. (*Remarks:* Recall that this problem was solved by the use of recursive procedures. Most problems that can be solved by recursion can also be solved by iteration. Iteration can be easier for the computer, but recursion is typically easier for human beings to solve a complex problem.)

7-15. Setting the SelectedIndex Property of Combo Boxes in a Form. Write a Sub procedure and name it **ComboSetter**; set the SelectedIndex property of all combo boxes in your form to zero when the user clicks the button with a text **Set Default**. Your procedure should not explicitly refer to the names of the combo boxes. Test the program using a form that contains combo boxes mixed with other controls. Make sure each combo box contains at least one item. The Sub should be invoked by a call from a button's Click event procedure. (*Hint:* Use the For Each loop to enumerate all controls and the TypeName function to identify the combo boxes in the form.)

7-16. Are All Text Boxes Blank? Write a routine to check whether all text boxes in a form are blank. When the user clicks the button with the text **All Blank?**, your program will display either the message **Yes. All text boxes are blank**, or the message **No. Some text boxes contain data**, depending on the state of the text boxes. (*Hint:* Use the For Each loop to enumerate all controls and the TypeName to identify the text boxes in the form. *Note:* Write the routine as a function that returns a Boolean value; then use this function from the Click event procedure.)

7-17. Reversing a String. Develop the code to reverse a string; that is, given a string "abcde," your code will produce "edcba" as a result. Test your code by taking the string from a text box named **txtOriginal** into which the user enters the data and displaying the result in the Text property of a label named **lblReversed**. (*Note:* VB.NET has a reverse string function—

StrReverse—to handle this; however, the purpose of this exercise is for you to practice using the loop—don't allow yourself to use that built-in function.)

7-18. **Encrypting a String.** Write code to encrypt a string in a text box named **txtUserName** using the 13 rotation algorithm. This rotation algorithm replaces each letter in the string with a letter in the alphabet 13 positions from it. For example, the letter a (first position) will be replaced by n (14th position), b will be replaced by o, and so on. n is then replaced by a, o is replaced b, and so on. The result should be displayed in the same txtUserName text box when the user clicks the button named **btnEncrypt** with the text **Encrypt/Decrypt**. (*Hint:* Use a For loop to work on each character in the string at a time. Use the Mid function to extract a character from the string. Examine whether it is a letter. If it is, find its keycode value, and use it to find its position in the alphabet. Add 13 to the position, and obtain its remainder against 26. The remainder gives the encrypted position. Convert that position to the corresponding letter. You will need to use the ASC and Char functions.)

7-19. **Counting the Number of Periods in a Paragraph.** Write a function to count the number of periods in a text string (paragraph), which is passed to the function as a parameter. Test the function by calling it from an event procedure. (*Hint:* Use the InStr function in a Do loop. Take advantage of its first [optional] parameter.)

7-20. **Counting the Number of Words in a Paragraph.** Write a function that will return the number of words in a text string passed to the function as a parameter. (*Hint:* Trim off the leading and trailing spaces of the text. The number of words should be equal to the number of groups of spaces; that is, a group of consecutive spaces should be counted as one.)

7-21. **Counting the Number of Radio Buttons in a Form.** Write a routine to count the number of radio buttons in a form by using the For Each...Next structure. Test your code by drawing five radio buttons on a form in addition to one text box, one picture box, one list box, and one button. The button should have a name **btnCount** with the text **Count**. After you click the Count button, your routine should display the message **There are 5 radio buttons on the form**.

7-22. **Listing All Controls in a Form.** Recall that if the form has a container control such as group box, Me.Controls will not enumerate any of the controls contained in the container control in the For Each...Next enumeration. Write a Sub procedure that will display the names of all controls in the form, regardless of whether the controls are in a container or in the form itself. (*Hint*: Each control has a Controls collection that has the Count property. This property indicates whether this control contains any other controls. Your Sub should recursively go deeper into each layer of the container.)

7-23. **Clearing the Contents of All Text Boxes and Masked Edit Boxes in the Form.** Modify exercise 7-22 so that it will clear all the text boxes and masked edit boxes in the form.

7-24. **Adding an Item to the Combo Box.** Set up a new form such that it will contain the following fields for data entry:

Field	Control	Control Name
Name	Text box	txtName
Address	Text box	txtAddress
Zip code	Combo box	cboZipCode

There should be two buttons: one with the text **Save**, and the other with the text **Quit**.

When the user clicks the Save button, your program checks whether the Zip code entered in the combo box (cboZipCode.Text) already exists in its list. If not, this new Zip code is added to the list.

7-25.   Populating and Saving the Content of a Combo Box. Modify exercise 7-24 in the following manner:

- When the program starts, the combo box will be populated with a list of Zip codes in a file called ZipCodeList.txt.
- When the user clicks the Save button, if the Zip code is new, it is added to the combo box's list and saved in the file. (*Hint:* In the Form Load event, after the combo box is populated, close the file; then reopen it for Append. Close this file in the form's Closing event.)

7-26.   Generalized Routine for Series Computation. Write a function to compute the value of an infinite series of the form:

$$S = a + a\,(1/d) + a\,(1/d)^2 + a\,(1/d)^3 + \ldots + a\,(1/d)^n$$
$$\text{where } d > 1$$

The function should have the following header:

```
Function Series(A As Double, D as Double) As Double
```

Test your routine by calling it from a button Click event. The values of a and d should be taken from two text boxes whose values are entered by the user.

7-27.   Computing the Present Value of an Annuity. The present value of an annuity can be computed with the following formula:

$$P = a\,(1 + r)^{-1} + a\,(1 + r)^{-2} + a\,(1 + r)^{-3} + \ldots + a\,(1 + r)^{-n}$$

where *a* = the amount of payment per period

r = the interest rate per period

n = the number of periods

p = the present value of the annuity

Write a routine to compute p and then display the result when the user clicks the button with the text Compute. The values of a, r, and n are to be taken from the text boxes named **txtAmount**, **txtRate**, and **txtPeriod**. (*Note:* Do not use the PV built-in function for this purpose; instead, set up a For loop to perform the computation.)

7-28.   Computing the Present Value of a Perpetual Annuity. Consider the problem in exercise 7-27 again. Suppose n (the number of periods) is infinite; such an annuity is recognized as perpetual annuity. Modify your routine to compute the result.

7-29.   The Present Value of a Bond. A coupon bond pays an interest semiannually at the stated rate of its coupon, such as 6%. On the date of maturity, it pays its face value of $1,000 per unit, in addition to its interest coupon. Because the coupon rate can seldom be the same as the market rate that fluctuates daily, the price or present value of the bond is seldom the same as its face value. The formula to compute the present value (price) of a coupon bond is as follows:

$$P = c\ (1 + r)^{-1} + c\ (1 + r)^{-2} + c\ (1 + r)^{-3} + \ldots + c\ (1 + r)^{-2n} + f\ (1 + r)^{-2n}$$

where P = the present value (price) of the bond

c = coupon rate x Face value / 2

r = market rate / 2

n = number of years to maturity

f = face value (usually $1,000)

Write a function to compute the price of a bond given the coupon rate, market rate, years to maturity, and face value. Set all of these as the function's parameters.

Your visual interface should include three text boxes for the user to enter the coupon rate, the market rate, and years to maturity. You can assume that the face value is $1,000. You should also have a box (a label with an appearance similar to a text box) to display the result of computation (price). There should also be two buttons: one to initiate the computation, and the other to end the program. Invoke the function from the Click event of the button to initiate computation and display the result.

7-30. **Computing the Square Root of a Number.** The square root of a number can be computed by a set of iterative formulas:

$$D = (X_n^2 - A)\ /\ (2\ X_n)$$
$$X_{n+1} = X_n - D$$

where A = the number for which to compute the square root

X = the square root of A

n = the subscript of X, denoting the number of iterations

The formulas state that you can start with any positive number for X as an approximation for the square root of A. (You can start with A, except when it is zero. In the case of zero, there no need to compute. The root is zero.) A better approximation can then be computed by subtracting from the current approximation (X_n) a value D, which is computed by the formula just given.

Each approximation will move closer to the true square root of A. When D (the amount of adjustment/correction) is sufficiently small, the new X can be considered a good approximation to the root. You can then stop the iteration (repetition). You can consider D sufficiently small when $Abs(D\ /\ X) < 0.0000001$.

Write a function (call it SquareRoot) to compute the square root of any positive number using this method. Test your program by taking a number from a text box entered by the user and displaying the result in the text of a label. Compare your result with the result given by the Math object's Sqrt method.

7-31. **Computing the Cube Root of a Number.** Refer to exercise 7-30. In a similar fashion, the cube root of a number can be computed by a set of iterative formulas:

$$D = (X_n - A\ /\ X_n^2)\ /\ 3$$
$$X_{n+1} = X_n - D$$

Write a function to compute the cube root of any positive number using the same iterative method. Test your results with the following numbers: 1, 8, 27, 64, and 125. The solution should be 1, 2, 3, 4, and 5.

7-32. Computing the Economic Order Quantity (EOQ): The Sequential Method. The relevant cost of an inventory replenishment policy has an optimum point with respect to the quantity reordered each time. The total inventory cost for such a purpose is given as follows:

```
TCC = CC x (Q / 2)
TOC = PC x (D / Q)
TIC = TCC + TOC
```

where Q = the quantity to order each time

CC = the cost to carry an item per period

PC = the cost to place an order

D = the total demand (units) per period for the product

TCC = total carrying costs

TOC = total ordering costs

TIC = total relevant inventory cost

You can compute the total relevant inventory cost beginning with Q = 1; then perform the cost computation when Q is increased by 1 each time. Initially, you will find the cost decreases as Q increases. Eventually, you will find the total cost increases as Q increases. The EOQ is the quantity at which the total cost is the lowest—before it starts to increase as Q increases.

Write a routine to compute the Q at which the total inventory cost is the lowest, using this method. Your visual interface should include three text boxes for the user to enter the total demand per period, the carrying cost per unit per period, and the cost to place an order. You should also have a box (a label with an appearance like a text box) to display the result (EOQ). In addition, you should have two buttons: one to initiate the computation, and one to end the program.

7-33. Computing the EOQ with the Half Interval Method. The preceding problem can be solved using another, more efficient algorithm. If you draw a graph depicting the cost behavior of the total carrying costs and the total order costs, you will notice that a Q below the optimum EOQ, the total ordering costs, is higher than the total carrying costs. A Q above the EOQ, however, has higher total carrying costs than the total ordering costs. You can start by setting a very low quantity, such as 1, and call it Low, and a very high quantity, such as 10 times the demand, and call it High, so that you are ensured that the EOQ is in between the two quantities.

You can approximate the EOQ by finding the half point of the Low and High; that is, Q = (High + Low) / 2); then compute the total carrying costs and the total ordering costs. If the total carrying costs are higher than the total ordering costs, Q is too high (higher than the EOQ according to the previous explanation). You should then adjust the high bound by setting High = Q; otherwise, you should adjust the low bound. You can then repeat this computational process until High and Low are very close to each other;, for example, a difference less than 0.1. There you have the solution. (This method of arriving at a numerical solution is recognized as the half interval method as explained in this chapter.)

Write a routine to compute the EOQ using this method. The visual interface should be the same as in the preceding exercise.

7-34.   Listing All Available Lottery Numbers. Assume that a lottery involves the random selection (without replacement) of three balls from a box. The box contains 25 numbers labeled from 1 to 25. Write a routine that will list all possible combinations of numbers for the lottery. Place the results in a list box.

7-35.   Clearing Selections of a List Box. Write a Sub procedure that will take a list box as its parameter and clear all selections in the list box. (*Note:* Just deselect; do not remove the item[s].) Note that if the SelectionMode is set to one, all you have to do is is to set the SelectedIndex to -1; otherwise, you will also need to deselect all selected items.

7-36.   Clearing All Controls. Write a Sub procedure that will clear all controls in a form that are used to accept the user input. These controls should include text boxes, masked edit boxes, radio buttons, check boxes, combo boxes, and list boxes. Deselect items selected in combo boxes and list boxes, but do not clear the items from these controls. Refer to exercise 7-35 for the fine points concerning deselecting items in the list box.

7-37.   Generalizing the Simulation Example. Modify the blackjack simulation program in example 10 so that it can be used for a general class of problems. Your project should allow the user to specify the following:

1. The probability of success per trial (winning a hand)
2. The minimum desired number of successes per 100 trials, such as winning at least 60 out of 100 hands
3. The number of experiments—this was assumed to be 1,000 in the example

Test your project by answering the following question: "Assume the probability that Mark McGwire hits a home run each time that he is at bat is 10%. He is at bat five times per game. What is the probability that he hits 70 home runs in a season of 162 games?"

Without revising the program, can you use it to answer the question, "For Mark McGwire to have a 50% probability to hit 70 home runs in a season, at what rate (probability) must he be able to hit a home run each time he is at bat?" (*Hint:* Try different values of the probability to win per trial until the probability of success is around 50%. You can minimize your trials by mimicking the half interval method.)

Projects

7-38.   Finding the Effective Rate of a Bond. Refer to exercise 7-29 for the computation of the bond price (present value). In the financial market, the bond price is found through the bid and ask process (quote). When you are buying or selling a bond, you know the price first. As an investor, you, of course, would want to know the effective (market) interest rate of the bond given the price. You are to develop a project for such a purpose.

Input: The user will enter the coupon rate, the years to maturity, and the price of the bond. The price is quoted as if the face value were 100, so a quote of 101 actually means 101% of the face value.

Output: The computed market rate should be displayed in a label's text, which should look like a text box and be accompanied by another label with a proper text.

Computation: The bond price changes inversely with the market rate of interest. The higher the market rate, the lower the bond price. You should first write a function to compute the bond price (present value) given the market rate, coupon rate, and years to maturity as the parameters (call this function BondPrice) (refer to the formula in exercise 7-29). The rate that makes the present value of the bond equal to the current bond price is the market (effective) rate on the bond. You can approximate the market rate by using the half interval method. For any practical problem, you can assume the market rate will be between 0% and 100%. Your algorithm to find the market rate will be as follows:

1. Set the lower rate to 0, and the higher rate to 1.
2. Compute the midpoint of the lower rate and higher rate.
3. Use the midpoint rate to compute the bond price using the BondPrice function.
4. Compare the computed bond price with the bond price given by the user.
   A. If the computed price is higher than the one given, the current midpoint rate is lower than the true market rate. Adjust the lower rate by setting the lower rate to the current midpoint rate.
   B. Otherwise, adjust the higher rate by setting the higher rate to the current midpoint rate.
5. Repeat steps 2 through 4 until the lower rate and the higher rate are very close to each other. Consider the two rates very close when their difference is less than 0.1E-06.

7-39.   **Updating the Accounts Receivable File: Sequential File Processing.** Develop a project that will update customer balances in an accounts receivable master file using a customer transaction file. Each record in the accounts receivable master file consists of two data fields and is structured as follows:

Field	Length	Description
Account number	5 digits	xxxxx
Account balance	10 digits	xxxxxx.xx; begins at position 7

Sample records of the file appear as follows:

```
10001 8000.00
10002 10000.00
   .
   .
```

Each record in the transaction file consists of four data fields and is structured as follows:

Field	Length	Description
Date	10 characters	mm/dd/yyyy
Account number	five digits xxxxx;	begins at position 12
Charge or credit	one character	C or D; in position 18; C = Credit; D = Charge
Amount	nine digits	xxxxxx.xx; begins at position 20

Sample records of the file appear as follows:

```
01/10/1999 10002 D 7000.00
01/05/1999 10002 C 5000.00
   .
   .
```

Both files are text files created with the StreamWriter.WriteLine method (one record per line), and have been sorted in ascending order by the account number.

To update the account balances, your program needs to read both files and use the data to create a new account receivable (customer balance) file. Note that the customer master file contains all valid accounts. An account number in the transaction file that fails to match one in the master file represents an invalid number. The transaction record should be logged in an error log file and discarded.

Hints:

1. You need to use four files for the duration of your program. These are the existing account receivable master file (for Input), the transaction file (for Input), the updated account receivable file (for Output), and the error log file. Note that the new master file should have the same format as the existing one.

2. Use a button's Click event to initiate the update process.

3. The major steps involved in the update are as follows:

   3.1. Read transaction records for an account (TFAcctNo) until a different account or end of file (EOF) is encountered. For each record for the same account, accumulate the transaction amount. Note that you have an unprocessed transaction record here.

   3.2. Read a customer master record. If the account number (MFAcctNo) is smaller than the one from the transaction file (TFAcctNo), this master record has no current transactions. Simply output the record onto the new account receivable master file and repeat step 3.2. If MFAcctNo equals TFAcctNo, update the balance with the amount accumulated from step 3.1 and output the result onto the new master file. If MFAcctNo is greater than TFAcctNo, TFAcctNo is invalid; print an error log (message) in the error log file.

   3.3. If it is not the EOF of the transaction file, set the TFAcctNo and the accumulated transaction amount to the last record read in step 3.1, and repeat steps 3.1 and 3.2; otherwise, copy all the remaining records in the old master file to the new master file and then quit.

8. Arrays and Their Uses

So far, most of the variables you have used have been scalar variables. That is, each of these variables holds one value, a number or a string. There may be times when you will encounter a situation in which your program needs to handle a large group of homogeneous data, and it needs to access these data back and forth. In this case, using array variables will be more elegant and/or efficient. An array is a collection of more than one element of data, and is collectively recognized by the same variable name. Each element in the array is indexed with the variable's subscript(s). You can refer to these elements by their indexes.

Although the concept of arrays appears simple, their applications can be fascinating. Their uses can make many complex problems much easier to solve. One interesting problem is sorting, which involves arranging data in order. The goal is simple and well defined, but the algorithms to solving the problem are diverse and intriguing.

An array can have one or more subscripts. The number of subscripts of an array is also referred to as the rank or the number of dimensions; therefore, an array with two subscripts is recognized as a two-dimensional array. Although most of this chapter is devoted to discussing uses of one-dimensional arrays, the last section deals with two-dimensional arrays.

After completing this chapter, you should be able to:

- Create and use one-dimensional arrays.
- Understand some practical applications of one-dimensional arrays.
- Appreciate and implement several sorting algorithms.
- Use the Collection object as a means of handling a list of controls.
- Create and use two-dimensional arrays.

8.1 One-Dimensional Arrays

This introductory section deals with the technical aspects of handling one-dimensional arrays. Topics include creating one-dimensional arrays, dynamic arrays, arrays as parameters between procedures, and determining array boundaries. This discussion provides the background information required for the remainder of this chapter.

Creating One-Dimensional Arrays

To declare a one-dimensional array, use the Dim statement with the following syntax:

```
Dim Name([upper bound]) As Type
```

where *Name* = any unique name that is legitimate as a variable name

Upper bound = an integer representing the upper value of the subscript

Type = any data type, such as Integer, Long, and so on

Scope of Array Variables. Similar to the declaration of scalar variables, the declaration of array variables can be placed in the general declaration area or in a procedure. Array variables declared in the general declaration area are class-level variables, and are recognized by all procedures in the form. Array variables declared in a procedure are local (procedure-level) variables.

Declaration Examples. Here are some examples of valid array declarations:

```
Dim A(5) As Double
Dim Student(50) As String
Dim Balance() As Decimal
```

The first Dim statement declares A to be a variable containing six elements of the Double type with a subscript range of 0 to 5, as shown here:

```
A(0)  A(1)  A(2)  A(3)  A(4)  A(5)
```

The second Dim statement declares the Student string variable to contain 51 elements with a subscript range of 0 to 50, as shown next:

```
Student(0)  Student(2)  ...  Student(49)  Student(50)
```

The third statement declares a Decimal variable, Balance, to contain unknown number of elements. Usually, a variable declared this way is used to receive results from a function that generates varying number of elements. In other cases, the number of elements is not known until runtime. The array is then resized when it is needed. Examples will be provided in the next subsection.

Referencing Elements in an Array. After the array is declared, you can refer to individual elements in the array by the use of an index (subscript). For example, Student(0) refers to the first element in the Student array; therefore, you can code the following:

```
Student(0) = "Angela Allen"
```

This statement will assign the text string (name) "Angela Allen" to the first element of the Student array. You can then use the element just as you would any scalar variable. For example, to display the name, you can code the following:

```
MsgBox("The first student in the array is " & Student(0))
```

Similarly, A(5) refers to the sixth element in A. Notice that A's smallest subscript value is 0.

Using Variables as the Index. The index in the pair of parentheses does not have to be a constant. It can also be a variable or any expression that results in a numeric value. If you have declared an Amount array variable (say, with an upper bound of 9999), you can code the following:

```
Amount(N) = 100
```

Depending on the value of N, 100 will be assigned to the corresponding element. That is, if N is 2,000, Amount(2000) will be assigned with a value 100. (Note that N should be an Integer variable.) The ability to handle an expression as the index greatly enhances the flexibility and power of arrays, as you will see in the examples in the next section. Here are some simple uses of this capability:

Example 1. The following code lists all the names of students (assuming that the array has been properly populated with the names):

```
' List Student(0) Through Student(50)
For I = 0 to 50
    Console.WriteLine(Student(I))
Next I
```

Recall that in the For loop, the counter I will vary from the starting value (0) to the ending value (50) with the specified increment. Because the increment is not specified, its default is 1; therefore, the loop will execute 51 times, with I taking on 0, 1, 2, 3, . . . 49, 50. The following execution table shows the process:

Iteration	I	Element of Student(I) Referenced	Example Result
1	0	Student(0)	Angela Allen
2	1	Student(1)	Bob Bunker
.	.	.	.
.	.	.	.
51	50	Student(50)	Zeff Ziegler

Example 2. The following code increases each element in Scores() (again, assuming that the array has been properly declared and populated with values) by 5.

```
' Add 5 points to Scores(0) through Scores(50)
For I = 0 To 50
    Scores (I) += 5
Next I
```

Dynamic Arrays

When the size of an array cannot be determined until runtime, you can use the ReDim statement to resize the array when the information on its size is available. But you must have the variable declared as an array first. The syntax for the ***ReDim statement*** is as follows:

```
ReDim Name1(UpperBoundExpression1)
[,Name2(UpperBoundExpression2)] . . .
```

The ReDim statement can be placed only within procedures; that is, you are not allowed to use the ReDim statement in the general declaration section. The following are examples of valid uses of the ReDim statement.

```
ReDim A(10)
ReDim Employees(EmployeeCount)
ReDim Holder(3 * N)
ReDim Balance(2000), Amount(CustomerCount - 1)
```

If you use a variable as a part of an expression to compute the subscript of an array, the variable must have its proper value before the ReDim statement is executed. In the preceding examples, you assumed proper values have been assigned to the variables EmployeeCount, N, and CustomerCount in lines 2, 3, and 4.

Note again that in the preceding ReDim statements, you assumed that the variables, A, Employees, and Holder have been declared as one-dimensional array variables. The ReDim statement cannot change the data type or rank (number of dimensions) of the variable.

Scope of ReDimed Variables. If the ReDim statement can be used only within procedures, does it mean that all variables sized with the ReDim statement are procedure-level (local) variables? Not necessarily. It depends on where the variable is actually declared (by the Dim statement). If the variable is declared in a procedure, it is a local variable and can be ReDimed only in that procedure; however, if you declare the variable in the general declaration area, it is a class level variable as shown here:

```
Dim Employees() As String 'Note I don't have to declare the size
    here although I may.
```

In a procedure, you can declare its actual size:

```
Private Sub Form1_Load(ByVal sender As System.Object, ByVal e As
    System.EventArgs) Handles MyBase.Load
    Dim N As Integer
    ' various statements, including one that sets the value of N
    ReDim Employees(N)
    ' other statements
End Sub
```

Declaring Dynamic Arrays with Initial Values. You can declare initial values for a dynamic array by enclosing the constants in a pair of braces. For example, the following code should cause A to contain three elements with the values 12, 24, and 36.

```
Dim A() As Integer = {12, 24, 36}
```

Assigning Array Values. You can also assign a list of values to an array, using the braces to form the list. Assume you have declared B as an Integer array. You can then use a statement similar to the following to assign values to it:

```
B = New Integer() {3, N, 5}
```

Notice how the expression on the right is constructed. The New keyword must be used. In addition, the keyword for the data type, such as Integer, must be followed by a pair of parentheses to indicate an array. The data elements in the pair of braces can be either constant or scalar variables of the same type.

Enter the following code in the form click event.

```
Dim I As Integer
Dim N As Integer
Dim B() As Integer
N = 5
B = New Integer() {3, N, 5}
For I = 0 To 2
    Console.WriteLine(B(I))
Next I
```

Run the project, click the form, and examine the results. You now know how to construct a list values for an array. You also know that variables can be included in the list, just like constants.

Passing Arrays to Procedures and Returning an Array from a Function

Sometimes, an entire array needs to be passed to another procedure for computation or data manipulation. To pass an array to a procedure, the called procedure must be written to expect an array as its parameter. The parameter in the header should be followed by a pair of parentheses. The following example illustrates the syntax:

```
Function Sum(A() As Double) As Double
    '  statements
End Function
```

To pass an array, such as Salary, in another procedure to the Sum function, you can code the following:

```
Total = Sum(Salary)
```

Here you assume that the variable Salary has been properly declared as an array of the Double type. Note that Salary as an argument should not be followed by a pair of parentheses.

Can a function be made to return an array? Yes. In the header, add a pair of parentheses after the type specification. For example, the following header indicates that the Sequence function returns an integer array:

```
Function Sequence(N As Integer) As Integer()
```

Again, notice the pair of parentheses following "As Integer." Without the pair, the function is expected to return a scalar value. With the pair, the function is expected to return an array. The code to actually generate the results is left to you as exercise 8-37.

Determining the Boundary of an Array

If you inspect the Sum function in the preceding example again, you may notice that any Double array can be passed to it. The array parameter passed each time may not have the same size. How does the function know the ending subscript value to perform the summation? The *UBound function* gives the upper boundary of an array. For example, UBound(A) will return the largest subscript of A; therefore, the preceding Sum function can be written as follows:

```
Function Sum(A() As Double) As Double
    ' This function returns the total of a Double type array, A()
    Dim Total As Double
    Dim I as Integer
    For I = 0 To UBound(A)
        Total = Total + A(I)
    Next I
    Return(Total) 'Return total to the caller
End Function
```

Suppose in the Form Click event procedure, you code the following:

```
Private Sub Form1_Click(ByVal sender As System.Object, ByVal e As
    System.EventArgs) Handles MyBase.Click
    Dim Salary(2) as Double
    Dim CashNeeded As Double
    ' Populate the Salary array with pay data
    ' In real operations, data will be read from a file
    Salary(0)=40000
    Salary(1)=80000
    Salary(2)=55000
    ' Compute total salary to arrive at cash needed for payroll
    CashNeeded = Sum(Salary)
    MsgBox("We need " & CashNeeded & " dollars.")
    ' additional statements follow
End Sub
```

When the Sum function is invoked, the upper bound of the array parameter A will be exactly 2 because Salary's subscript has 2 as its upper bounds. The For loop in the Sum function will be set up equivalently to the following:

```
For I = 0 To 2
```

All elements in Salary will be involved in the computation. Test the preceding procedures. You should see the total cash needed is 175,000.

TIP

The function to find the lower boundary of an array is LBound. In VB.NET, all arrays have a lower boundary of 0, so the LBound function is not as indispensable in VB.NET as in the previous versions of VB.

8.2 Sample Uses of Arrays

In addition to their uses in simplifying repetitive operations (as illustrated in the preceding examples), arrays can be used to solve various programming problems. It is difficult to exhaust the list of their uses. The following examples represent a small sample.

Simplified Selection

What is considered your normal weight? This depends on your sex, height, and frame size. For simplicity, consider only the case of males with a medium frame. The following table gives an abbreviated list.

Height (In Shoes)	Normal Weight
5'2"	118–129
5'3"	121–133
5'4"	124–136
.	
.	
.	
6'3"	167–185
6'4"	172–190

Suppose your program is expected to give an answer when the user enters the height and clicks the Show button. How can this be handled in code? (Assume the height is given in two text boxes: txtFeet and txtInches.)

When the program starts, you can populate the normal weight in an array, with each element holding the weight value for each different height. There should be 15 different heights (from 62 inches to 76 inches); therefore, the array should have 15 elements. In response to repetitive queries, the height entered in the text boxes can be converted to inches, which can then be used to compute the index to obtain the weight stored in the Weight array. The Form Load event procedure may appear as follows:

```
' Declare an array to hold weights for heights from 5'2" to 6'4"
Dim Weights(14) As String
Private Sub Form1_Load(ByVal sender As System.Object, ByVal e As
    System.EventArgs) Handles MyBase.Load
    ' populate the weight array with data
    ' In real application, data will be read from a file
    Weights(0) = "118-129" 'For 5'2"
    Weights(1) = "121-133" 'For 5'3"
    .
```

```
      .
      Weights(14) = "172-190" 'For 6'4"
   End Sub
```

The preceding code appears tedious. In a real application, the data should be stored in a file. The data will be read and assigned to each element one at a time with a loop. (See the following example for an illustration.)

How can the stored data be used when the user enters the height and clicks the Show button? As explained, the entered height will first be converted to inches. This value can then be used to compute the index to obtain the weight data. The computation should be fairly straightforward. Consider the weight for the height of 62 inches (5'2"). It is stored in the first element (with a 0 index). The weight for 63 inches is stored in the second element. To compute the index, all you have to do is subtract 62 from the height. This relationship is shown in the following table:

Height in inches	Subtract 62 to obtain the index	Look in Weight(Index)	The value is
62	0	Weight(0)	"118–129"
63	1	Weight(1)	"121–133"
.	.		
76	14	Weight(14)	"172–190"

The following code should solve the problem:

```
Private Sub btnShow_Click(ByVal Sender As System.Object, ByVal e
   As System.EventArgs) Handles btnShow.Click
   Dim Inches As Integer
   ' Convert height to inches
   Inches = CInt(Val(txtFeet.Text) * 12 + Val(txtInches.Text))
   ' Display the weight
   MsgBox("Your normal weight should be " & Weights(Inches - 62) _
      & " lbs.")
End Sub
```

Suppose a person's height is 5'3". This height measurement will be converted to 63 inches by executing the line to convert the height, so Weights(Inches - 62) refers to Weights(1), which contains the string "121-133." The message box will display the following:

Your normal weight should be 121-133 lbs.

In Contrast to the Code Using Select Case. Note that the last line of code can also be done by the use of the Select Case structure as follows, assuming a variable, named Weight, has been declared as String:

```
Select Case Inches
Case 62
    Weight  = "118-129"
Case 63
    Weight = "121-133"
Case 64
    .

    .
Case 76
    Weight = "172-190"
End Select
MsgBox("Your normal weight should be " & Weight & " lbs.")
```

The code using this structure not only is much longer but also will have to be revised when the data change—over the years, the normal height and weight relationship may change. When you use the array and the data are stored in the file, however, the data can be updated without the need to revise the program.

Table Look Up

Imagine the information service desk of a midsize company. When a customer calls in to ask for the phone number of a particular employee, the clerk will use your program to find the needed information in response. How should you code this program?

Looking Up the Array. There are, of course, several ways to accomplish this. One possibility is to keep all the employees' names and phone numbers in two separate arrays; for example, Employees() and Phones(). These arrays can be populated as soon as the program starts. When the clerk enters a name in a text box such as txtName, and clicks a button such as Search, your program can search through the Employees array, find the match, and give the corresponding phone number. If the arrays have been populated properly, the following code should accomplish the search:

```
Private Sub btnSearch_Click(ByVal sender As System.Object, ByVal e
    As System.EventArgs) Handles btnSearch.Click
    Dim TheName As String, I As Integer
    TheName = txtName.Text 'Get the name entered by the user
    For I = 0 To EmployeeCount -1
        If TheName = Employees(I) then
            ' The ith employee has the name searched for.
            ' Give the ith phone number along with the name.
            MsgBox("The phone number for " & TheName _
                & " is " & Format(Phones(I), "(000)-000-0000"))
            Exit Sub
        End If
    Next I
    MsgBox("Employee name " & TheName & " not found.")
End Sub
```

In this procedure, the name of the employee to look up from the Employees array is taken from the text box txtName. A For loop is then used to compare TheName with each element (name) in the Employees array. The I loop counter will vary from 0 to EmployeeCount − 1 (where EmployeeCount is a class-level variable used to represent the number of employees). When I is 0, TheName will be compared with Employees(0), the first employee name in the list. When I is 1, TheName will be compared with Employees(1), and so on. If a match is found, a message box will display the employee's name and phone number (Phones(I)), which is presented with the proper format. The procedure is then terminated with the Exit Sub statement. If no match is found, the loop will continue until all employees in the list are compared. When the loop ends, the list of employees has been exhausted without a match. A message indicating the employee name is not found is thus displayed.

Populating the Array. In the previous procedure, you assumed that the value of the variable EmployeeCount has been set properly. How is the value of this variable set, and how are the two arrays populated? Assume that the employee phone file has been properly created, and the phone number and the employee name are separated with a tab character (vbTab) in each record. The following code should accomplish populating the arrays and setting the value for EmployeeCount:

```
Dim Phones(500) As Long
Dim Employees(500) As String
Dim EmployeeCount As Integer
Private Sub Form1_Load(ByVal sender As System.Object, ByVal e As
    System.EventArgs) Handles MyBase.Load
    ' When the project starts, this routine populates the Phones()
    ' and Employees() arrays
    Dim TheRecord As String
    Dim PhoneNumber As Long
    Dim TheName As String
    Dim P As Integer
    Dim PhoneFile As IO.StreamReader
```

```
            First, Open the file
            PhoneFile = New IO.StreamReader("C:\Employees\Phones.txt")
            ' Populate the arrays
            Do Until PhoneFile.Peek = -1
                TheRecord = PhoneFile.ReadLine()
                P = InStr(TheRecord, vbTab)
                PhoneNumber = CLng(Microsoft.VisualBasic.Left(TheRecord, P
                    - 1))
                TheName = Mid(TheRecord, P + 1)
                Phones(EmployeeCount) = PhoneNumber
                Employees(EmployeeCount) = TheName
                EmployeeCount += 1
            Loop
            ' Close the file
            PhoneFile.Close()
        End Sub
```

You may have noticed that populating an array from a file is basically the same as populating a list box or combo box. You are exactly right. The steps are identical. Only the "objects" that you are populating are different. Also, you use the Items.Add method to add items (elements) to the controls, but you use the assignment statement to add elements to arrays.

Tracking Random Occurrences

Arrays can conveniently be used to keep track of the occurrence of random events; for example, the number of times each customer called during a period, the number of purchase orders issued for each parts inventory, and the number of times each depositor made deposits in a month. All of these involve frequency counting.

Frequency Count. As an illustration of how arrays can simplify frequency count, consider this simple problem. You would like to know that given 1,000 random numbers in the range of 0 to 9, how many times each number appears. The first reaction is probably to code the count routine as follows (assume all variables except Rand have been properly declared):

```
Dim Rand As New Random()
For I = 1 to 1000
    Number = Rand.Next(10) 'Generate a random # in range 0 - 9
    If Number = 0 Then Freq0 += 1
    If Number = 1 Then Freq1 += 1
        .
        .
    If Number = 9 Then Freq9 += 1
Next I
```

Notice the variables Freq0 through Freq9. Each is serving a similar purpose. Why not use an array, such as Freq() instead? If you declare the variable Freq() as follows:

```
Dim Freq(9) As Integer
```

you can use it in the following manner:

```
If Number = 0 Then Freq(0) += 1
If Number = 1 Then Freq(1) += 1
    .
    .
```

Now, inspect this line carefully:

```
If Number = 0 Then Freq(0) += 1
```

The If condition tests whether Number is equal to zero. If so, Freq(0) is increased by 1. Note that if Number is zero, Freq(Number) and Freq(0) both refer to the same element. When Number is zero, you can code the following:

```
Freq(Number) += 1
```

That is, you do not need the If condition to accumulate total count for zero. It turns out that all the lines below this one are the same way. There is no need to test the value of Number! All you have to code to count the frequency is the following:

```
Freq(Number) += 1
```

This statement has the effect that when Number is zero, Freq(0) is increased by 1, and when Number is 1, Freq(1) is increased by 1, and so on as shown in the following table.

When Number Is	Freq(Number) Refers to	Effect of Freq(Number) += 1
0	Freq(0)	Freq(0) is increased by 1.
1	Freq(1)	Freq(1) is increased by 1.
.		
.		
9	Freq(9)	Freq(9) is increased by 1.

The statement can be used to replace *all* the 10 statements in the previous loop! The previous routine can now be rewritten as follows:

```
Dim I As Integer
Dim Rand As New Random()
Dim Number As Integer
Dim Freq(9) As Integer
For I = 1 To 1000
    Number = Rand.Next(10)
    Freq(Number) += 1
Next I
```

To see the results after the count, you can code the following:

```
For I = 0 To 9
    Console.WriteLine(I & " " & Freq(I))
Next I
```

You can test the program by placing the preceding two loops in the Form Click event. Inspect the results. The total of frequency counts for all numbers should be 1,000. Notice that the use of the array simplifies the code not only for counting but also for output.

TIP

Beginners tend to associate the range of the loop counter with the size of the array involved in the loop. Beware of this general tendency (and misconception). The two are not necessarily related. If you inspect the second loop in the previous example, the counter and the size of the Freq variable do correspond to each other because the counter is used to retrieve the content of each element in the array. In the first loop, however, the counter goes from 1 to 1000, not 0 to 9 (lower and upper bounds of the array). They are completely independent of each other.

Counting Letters. Would you like to know how often each letter of the alphabet is used in daily life? Assume you have a text box named txtText for the user to enter a long text string. When the user is ready, they click the Count button.

How should your program proceed to count? Recall that the key code value for A and Z are 65 (Keys.A) and 90 (Keys.Z), respectively. Before any letter is counted, it can be converted to uppercase. Its key code value will then have to fall in the range of Keys.A (65) through Keys.Z (90); therefore, if you declare an array variable LetterCount as follows:

```
Dim LetterCount(25)
```

you will be able to use it to count the frequency of each letter in a fashion similar to the previous example. The following code represents a sample solution:

```
Dim LetterCount(25) As Integer
Dim I As Integer
Dim Text As String
Dim Ascii As Integer
Text = Ucase(txtText.Text) 'Get upper case of the entered text
For I = 1 To Len(Text)
    ' Obtain the ASCII value of the character being inspected
    Ascii = Asc(Mid(Text, I, 1))
    Select Case Ascii
        Case Keys.A To Keys.Z
            ' alphabet, count its frequency
            LetterCount(Ascii - Keys.A) += 1
        Case Else
            ' non-alphabetic characters, ignore
    End Select
Next I
```

The For. . . Next loop is used to inspect each character in the text string (from the first through the last character) one at a time using the Mid function. The key code value of each character is then obtained using the Asc function. If it falls within the range of alphabet values, the key code value is subtracted by the key code value of A and the result is then used in the frequency count, in a similar fashion to the frequency count for random numbers. (Note that if the letter is A, subtracting its key code value, Ascii by Keys.A result in a zero; therefore, its count is tracked by LetterCount(0). By the same token, B's count is tracked by LetterCount(1) and so forth.) If the ASCII value falls out of the range of the alphabet, it is ignored.

Do you want to inspect the results? The following code will display the results in a list box named lstResults:

```
' Output the results into a list box
lstResults.Items.Clear()
For I = 0 To 25
    lstResults.Items.Add(Chr(I + Keys.A) & _
        vbTab & LetterCount(I))
Next I
```

You can test the preceding code by placing both routines in the btnCount Click event (assuming the Count button mentioned previously is named btnCount).

The two frequency counting examples can easily be modified to count the frequency of scores and letter grades for a class when data are available in a file or database table. They can be generalized to handle all the problems mentioned at the beginning of this subsection. Exercises 8-25 and 8-26 provide additional problems of this nature for you to practice.

Simulation

Because of their capability to accumulate frequency count easily, arrays can also be used conveniently to simulate/approximate probabilities in conjunction with the use of random numbers. As an illustration, consider the case of obtaining the number of good output units under uncertainty. Assume the product spoilage rate in a production process is 2%; that is, 98% of the product going through the process will turn out to be good. What is the probability that you will obtain 100, 101, . . . or more good units, when you put 105 raw units in a batch through the process? You can, of course, solve this problem analytically; however, it will take a long time to get the formula right, assuming you have average math skills, and obtain the correct computation thereof.

With the computer, you can use an alternative approach, which involves using random numbers to simulate the event and accumulate the experiences. (This kind of simulation is recognized as Monte Carlo simulation.) You can simulate whether a unit from the process is good or bad by drawing a random number. Because the probability of getting a spoiled unit is 2%, if the random number is higher than .02, you can claim that it is a good unit; otherwise, it is spoiled. If you simulate this inspection of good/bad output units 105 times, you should be able to find how many units turn out to be good. This experiment is equivalent to running 105 raw units through the process, and counting the number of good units. If you run the experiment 1,000 (or even 10,000) times, you should be able to count the number of times good output units equal 100, 101, . . . or more units.

The following discussion shows how to code this simulation process step by step. Assume that the variable GoodUnits is used to accumulate the number of good units in each experiment. When you inspect a unit of output and find it to be good, you add 1 to GoodUnits. (A random number greater than or equal to .02 represents the event of obtaining a good unit.) The code appears as follows:

```
If Rnd() >=.02 Then
    GoodUnits += 1
End If
```

Each batch consists of 105 units, so you need to inspect 105 times:

```
GoodUnits = 0 'Before the process, there is no good unit.
For I = 1 to 105
    If Rnd() >=.02 Then
        GoodUnits += 1
    End If
Next I
```

After the inspection, the value of GoodUnits represents the number of good units produced from this batch. This experience can be accumulated by a frequency count. Assume that the array variable GoodUnitCount is declared with a proper range of its subscript. You can place the following line immediately below the loop:

```
GoodUnitCount(GoodUnits) += 1
```

You have just finished simulating one batch of production. To arrive at a probability distribution, you need to repeat the experiment many times. For the interest of fairly accurate approximation, repeat the experiment 1,000 times. In addition, to make the code complete, you also show the proper declaration for all the variables used:

```
Dim I As Integer
Dim J as Integer
Dim GoodUnits As Integer
Dim GoodUnitCount(105) As Integer
' Randomize to get a different sequence of random numbers
Randomize()
For J = 1 to 1000
    ' Set good units to 0 at start of each production run
    GoodUnits = 0
    'Inspect a batch and count the number of good units
    For I = 1 to 105
        If Rnd() >=.02 Then
            GoodUnits += 1
            End If
    Next I
    ' Accumulate the frequency for good units
    GoodUnitCount(GoodUnits) += 1
Next J
```

Notice that GoodUnitCount is declared with an upper bound of the subscript of 105. This allows the possibilities that, in a production run, the entire batch can be either all bad or all good. Notice also that before the inspection of a batch, the variable GoodUnits is assigned a value of 0. This must be done; otherwise, the count from the previous batch will be carried over, resulting in an extremely unreasonable large number (much greater than 105 units). Note also that you place the Randomize statement before the simulation starts so that the random number sequence will be different each time the program is run.

Are you interested in the results of the simulation? You can place the results in a list box named lstResults:

```
For I = 0 To 105
    lstResults.Items.Add(I & vbTab & GoodUnitCount(I))
Next I
```

You can place these statements along with the preceding code in a button Click event. Alternatively, you can place them in a Sub procedure and then call the procedure from a button Click event. The following table is a sample result from one simulation.

Number of Good Units	Frequency
98	3
99	14
100	33
101	97
102	194
103	278
104	262
105	119

Because the random number sequences will differ in each simulation, the results will vary slightly; however, the results should give a pretty good approximation of the probability of obtaining a specified number of good units. (The preceding results show that there is approximately a 98.3% probability that you will get 100 or more good units if you place a batch of 105 raw units into production, given a spoilage rate of 2%.) If you are interested in more stable or accurate results, you can increase the number of experiments. Of course, it will then take longer to compute the results.

Random Sampling Without Replacement

Consider the drawing of a lottery. There are 50 balls, numbered from 1 to 50. Six balls will be drawn. None of the drawn balls will be placed back in the bin; therefore, none of the six numbers will be repeated. (This type of problem is recognized as random sampling without replacement.) You want your program to emulate the drawing; that is, your program will display six random numbers in the range of 1 to 50, without repetition when the user clicks the Draw button. How do you proceed?

Drawing a Ball. Drawing a random number in the range of 1 to 50 can be done with the following statements:

```
Dim Rand As New Random()
BallNumber = Rand.Next(1, 51)
```

The first statement declares and associates the Rand variable with a random object. Recall that the Next method of the Random object generates a random number in the range of the two specified integers (at least equal to the lower specified number but less than the higher specified number). Rand.Next should generate a random integer in the range of 1 and 50.

Avoiding Repetition. The preceding statement does not guarantee that some of the six numbers drawn will not be the same. You need to find a way to verify that a new number has not already been drawn.

There are two possible ways to accomplish this. Consider an *intuitive approach* first. As soon as you draw a number, you can compare it with all those numbers previously drawn. If a match is found, you should draw another number (discard the current number) and compare again until the new number has no match with the previously drawn numbers. This number is then included in the numbers already drawn. When the total number of numbers drawn is equal to six, your program has done the job, can display the results, and quit.

You can use a variable, for example, NumbersDrawn, to count the number of numbers drawn. To keep track of the numbers drawn, you can set up an array—for example, Ball(5). Each time a number is drawn, you can use a For loop, varying the counter from 0 to NumbersDrawn - 1 to compare this new number with the ones drawn to determine whether the number is already drawn. So that you can easily determine whether a match is found at the end of the loop, you can use another variable such as NotFound. Before the loop, you can assume the new number has no match; therefore, set NotFound to True. If a match is found within the loop, the variable is set to False and the loop is terminated.

The description can be translated into the following code:

```
Dim Rand As New Random()
Dim BallNumber As Integer
Dim NumbersDrawn As Integer
Dim NotFound As Boolean

BallNumber = Rand.Next(1, 51) 'Draw a random number
NotFound = True 'Assume this number is not already drawn
For I = 0 To NumbersDrawn - 1
    If BallNumber = Balls(I) Then
        'A match is found; so NotFound is false
        NotFound = False
        Exit For 'and terminate the search
    End If
Next I
If NotFound Then
    ' The current ball number is indeed new
    Balls(NumbersDrawn) = BallNumber 'Keep the ball number
    NumbersDrawn += 1 'Increase the number count
End If
```

Notice how a new number is added to the "already drawn" list. The current value of NumbersDrawn is used as the subscript to identify the position in the array Balls where the ball number is stored because the index starts with a lower bound of 0. That variable is then increased by 1.

The routine should be repeated as long as NumbersDrawn is less than six. You should enclose the preceding code within a Do loop as follows:

```
Do
    ' Place all the above statement here
Loop While NumbersDrawn < 6
```

Complete Code for the Intuitive Approach. Assume the routine will be triggered by the user's click on a button named btnDraw. The complete procedure can appear as follows:

```
Private Sub btnDraw_Click(ByVal sender As System.Object, ByVal e
    As System.EventArgs) Handles btnDraw.Click
    Dim I As Integer
    Dim NumbersDrawn As Integer
    Dim BallNumber As Integer
    Dim Balls(5) As Integer
    Dim NotFound As Boolean
    Dim Rand As New Random()
    Do
        BallNumber = Rand.Next(1, 51)
        NotFound = True
        For I = 1 To NumbersDrawn
            If BallNumber = Balls(I) Then
                NotFound = False
                Exit For
            End If
        Next I
        If NotFound Then
            Balls(NumbersDrawn) = BallNumber
            NumbersDrawn += 1
        End If
    Loop While NumbersDrawn < 6
    lstNumbers.Items.Clear() 'Clear the list box
    ' Show results
```

```
        For I = 0 To 5
            lstNumbers.Items.Add(Balls(I))
        Next I
    End Sub
```

Notice that in this code, you have included proper declarations for all variables used in the procedure. A For. . . Next loop is also used at the end to display the results by adding the drawn numbers to a list box named lstNumbers.

Another Approach. The preceding routine keeps track of the numbers that have been drawn. Alternatively, you can focus on each number in the entire range. That is, when a number is drawn, you can ask whether the ball has been drawn, not by comparing the numbers that have been drawn but by checking a "marker" for the particular number. If the marker is not turned on, the ball has not yet been drawn, and you can display the number and turn its marker on; otherwise, it has been drawn, and the number should be discarded.

If you want to set up a marker for each ball, you will need 50 markers because there are 50 balls. The marker should be an array with 50 elements. Let the array name be AlreadyPicked. You can then declare it as follows:

```
        Dim AlreadyPicked(49) As Boolean
```

Now imagine you have drawn the number 3. You can test the value of AlreadyPicked(2) (the third element) to determine whether it has already been drawn. If AlreadyPicked(2) is False, you can set it to True and display 3; otherwise, you can ignore the number and repeat the drawing. Notice that 3 is just a particular number. Any number you draw (BallNumber) should work the same way. The routine to obtain a legitimate (non-repeated) ball number can be coded as follows:

```
        Do
            BallNumber = Rand.Next(1, 51) 'Draw a number
            ' If the number has been drawn, repeat the drawing.
        Loop While AlreadyPicked(BallNumber - 1)
        AlreadyPicked(BallNumber - 1) = True
        lstNumbers.Items.Add(BallNumber) 'display the number
```

You need six numbers, so the routine should be repeated six times. You can accomplish this by enclosing the preceding routine in a For. . . Next loop as follows:

```
        For I = 1 to 6
            ' Place the above drawing routine here
        Next I
```

Complete Code for the Second Approach. To test this approach, you can draw another button on the same form. Name it **btnDrawAlt** and set its Text property to **Draw, Alternative Way**. The complete code should appear as follows:

```
    Private Sub btnDrawAlt_Click(ByVal sender As System.Object, ByVal
        e As System.EventArgs) Handles btnDrawAlt.Click
        Dim AlreadyPicked(49) As Boolean
        Dim BallNumber As Integer
        Dim I As Integer
        Dim Rand As New Random()
        lstNumbers.Items.Clear() 'Erase previous output
        For I = 1 To 6
            Do
                BallNumber = Rand.Next(1, 51) 'Draw a ball
                ' If it is already picked, then repeat the drawing
            Loop While AlreadyPicked(BallNumber - 1)
            AlreadyPicked(BallNumber - 1) = True 'Mark the ball drawn
            lstNumbers.Items.Add(BallNumber)  'Display the number
        Next I
    End Sub
```

When you run the project, you should be able to verify that each time you click the button, six unique numbers in the range of 1 to 50 are displayed in the list box. These numbers should vary randomly from one round to the next.

Notice that with this approach, there is no need to have another array, Balls(), which keeps track of all the ball numbers drawn. Each number is added to the list box when it is determined to be legitimate. These numbers are also implicitly kept in the AlreadyPicked array. The position of the element that has been set to True represents the ball number that has been drawn; for example, if AlreadyPicked(4) is True, 5 is a number that has been drawn. The following loop should also give the numbers that have been drawn:

```
      For I = 0 To 49
          If AlreadyPicked(I) Then
              ' I+1 has been picked
              Console.WriteLine(I + 1) 'Print the ball number
          End If
  Next I
```

Comparing the Two Approaches. When you inspect the two procedures, you should notice that the first approach requires longer code but takes a smaller array, whereas the second approach requires shorter code but takes a longer array. The second approach should be faster because the loop to determine whether a ball (number) has been drawn requires a test on one element of the array; that is, AlreadyPicked(BallNumber – 1). In contrast, the first approach requires the execution of a loop. Only after the loop is completely executed can the routine conclude that the number has not been drawn. Thus, there is a trade-off between speed and space (storage) used.

You will encounter many problems of similar nature and, therefore, be faced with the same design issue as to which approach to use given a situation. If speed of execution is the most important consideration, you should use the second approach. You should use the first approach only when the number of elements to keep track of (balls to draw) is relatively small. When this number approaches the total potential number (50 in this example), you will always be better off using the second approach.

8.3 Sorting and Searching

The main purpose of this section is to acquaint you with various sorting and searching algorithms, which should enable you to become more capable of dealing with new programming problems. The algorithms can provide you with new insight as to how a programming problem is solved. VB.NET has built-in methods for sorting and searching, so the reason for discussing this topic is not its direct application but rather to help you build a foundation for programming skills.

The main advantage of keeping data in an array is that the array allows you to conveniently handle the data in it randomly without any restriction. One of the uses of arrays is sorting: Data in the array can be arranged in either ascending or descending order. The sorted data can then be output or further processed.

Human beings prefer sorted data. Sorted data are easier to browse, and they facilitate lookup. Even computers have a better time with sorted data. More efficient search/processing algorithms can be used with sorted data. Thus, if an array is to be searched repetitively for different search values, it pays to sort the array first. In batch processing (where transactions are collected into a batch and then all are processed at one time), transactions sorted in the same order as their master records (such as customer accounts) eliminate the need to search the master file back and forth to update the affected master records. In this case, sorting is a necessity for efficient processing.

Selected Algorithms for Sorting

You may be amazed that as simple as the goal of sorting is, virtually countless algorithms to sort data exist. This section discusses the following algorithms:

- Bubble sort
- Insertion sort
- Shell sort
- Quick sort

A careful study of the sorting algorithms allows you to appreciate the performance differences as well as helps you develop the capability to design elegant solutions to new programming problems.

A study of sorting algorithms is both important and interesting. Nearly 30 years ago, Donald E. Knuth, a well-known computer scientist, asserted that nearly 20% of the computer resources at that time were used to perform sorting, according to a survey. This would suggest several alternative explanations: Sorting is important and indispensable in computer applications; sorting is not conducted efficiently; or, sorting has been used unnecessarily. A careful study of sorting algorithms could help improve at least the first two situations.

Bubble Sort

In the bubble sort, each element in the array is compared with the next element. If these elements are out of order, they are swapped. When one round of comparisons (and the resulting swaps) is done, the largest value in the array will be placed at the right-most position as a result. In the next round, one fewer element needs to be compared. This process continues until the last round in which only two elements need to be compared.

The process is illustrated in the following example.

Position	1	2	3	4	5
Value	38	51	23	56	34

The comparisons start from left to right, element by element. The first element, 38, is compared with the second element, 51. Because they are in order, nothing is performed. The second element, 51, is then compared with the third element, 23. Because they are out of order, the two elements are swapped. The result appears as follows:

Position	1	2	3	4	5
Value	38	**23**	**51**	56	34

The third element, now 51, is compared with the fourth element, 56; then 56 is compared with 34, resulting in another swap. After the first round of comparison, the array will appear as follows:

Position	1	2	3	4	5
Value	38	23	51	**34**	**56**

Notice that the largest element in the array is now at the right-most position.

The same process of comparisons for the second round will start from position 1 again, but will stop at position 4, resulting in the second largest element being moved into this position. This process is repeated until all elements are placed in their proper position.

Comparing and Swapping.   How do you implement such an algorithm? Assume X() is the array to be sorted, and the Ith element is to be compared with the next element. The following statements should accomplish the comparison and swap:

```
If X(I) > X(I+1) Then
    ' out of order; swap
    Temp = X(I)
    X(I) = X(I+1)
    X(I+1) = Temp
End If
```

The Number of Elements to Compare. What range of I should the preceding code execute? I should always start with the lower bound of the array. In the first round, it should go until I + 1 is the last element of the array; that is, I should be one less than the upper bound of the array. In the second round, this number should be one less than the preceding round; the next round, one further less, and so on. Before you have a formula to compute this value, you can name a variable, H, to represent the value. The loop to complete a round of comparisons can then appear as follows:

```
For I = 0 To H
    If X(I) > X(I+1) Then
        ' out of order; swap
        Temp = X(I)
        X(I) = X(I+1)
        X(I+1) = Temp
    End If
Next I
```

The Number of Rounds of Comparisons. One round of comparisons will move only one element, the largest in the range considered, to its proper position. If the array X has n elements, it will take n – 1 rounds of comparisons to complete the sort. The sort will take n – 1, not n rounds because the smallest will automatically be placed in its position when the second smallest element is moved to its proper position. This means the preceding For loop should be executed n – 1 times. In other words, the loop should be enclosed by another loop that will execute n – 1 times.

```
For J = 0  To UBound(X) - 1
    ' place the above For I loop here
Next J
```

Computing the Number of Comparisons for Each Round. You still need to compute H before the For I loop is reached. As stated previously, the first time H should have a value of one less than the upper bound of the array, and should decrease by 1 in each subsequent round. This can be done by setting its initial value before the For J loop and then decreasing it by 1 inside the J loop.

```
H = UBound(X)
For J = 0 To UBound(X) -1
    H -= 1
    ' place the above For I loop here
Next J
```

The Bubble Sort Sub Procedure. A sort routine is best written as a separate Sub procedure, which can then be called by any other procedure that needs a sort operation. Following this consideration, the complete Bubble Sort routine can be presented as follows:

```
Sub BubbleSort(ByVal X() As Integer)
    Dim I As Integer
    Dim J As Integer
    Dim H As Integer
    Dim Temp As Integer
    H = UBound(X)
    For J = 0 To UBound(X) - 1
        H -= 1
        For I = 0 To H
            If X(I) > X(I + 1) Then
                ' out of order; swap
                Temp = X(I)
                X(I) = X(I + 1)
                X(I + 1) = Temp
            End If
        Next I
    Next J
End Sub
```

Figure 8.1

Visual interface for sorting

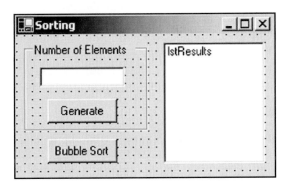

Testing the Procedure. To test the procedure, you can design a visual interface similar to the one shown in Figure 8.1. As you may surmise, the visual interface includes the following:

- A group box that contains a text box and a button. The text box is named txtNumber, and will be used to specify the number of elements for the array to be sorted. The button is named btnGenerate, and has the text "Generate". This button will be used to generate the random numbers specified in the txtNumber text box.
- Another button with the text "Bubble Sort". This button is named btnBubble, and will be used to initiate the sorting.
- A list box named lstResults. This will be used to show the sorting results.

Expected Behavior of the Testing Project. When the program starts, the user is expected to enter a number in the text box. When the user clicks the Generate button, your program will set the upper bound of the array X() to the number in the text box minus 1 and then generate random numbers to populate the entire array. The values of the random numbers will be in the range of 0 to this number. When the user clicks the Bubble Sort button, your program will call the Bubble Sort Sub procedure, and populate the list box with the sorting results.

Declaring the Array. Because the array X() to hold the random numbers will be used in several procedures, it should be declared at the class level. In addition, its upper bound will change, depending on the number the user enters in the text box; therefore, it should be declared as a dynamic array. Its declaration in the form class should appear as follows:

```
Dim X() As Integer
```

Generating the Random Numbers. The random numbers will be generated when the user clicks the Generate button. The button's Click event procedure can appear as follows:

```
Private Sub btnGenerate_Click(ByVal sender As System.Object, ByVal
    e As System.EventArgs) Handles btnGenerate.Click
    Dim Number As Integer
    Dim I As Integer
    Dim Rand As New Random()
    Number = CInt(txtNumber.Text)  'Take the number from the user
    ReDim X(Number - 1) 'Set X()'s upper bound to Number
    For I = 0 To Number - 1
        X(I) = Rand.Next(Number) 'Populate X() with random numbers
    Next I
End Sub
```

In this procedure, the number entered in the text box is assigned to the variable Number; then, X() is dynamically dimensioned with its upper bound set to Number – 1. In the For loop, each element of X() is assigned a random number, in the range of 0 to Number – 1 (inclusive).

Calling the Sorting Sub and Displaying the Results. When the user clicks the Bubble Sort button, your program should call the Bubble Sort Sub procedure and then display the results. This event procedure appears as follows:

```
Private Sub btnBubble_Click(ByVal sender As System.Object, ByVal e
    As System.EventArgs) Handles btnBubble.Click
    Dim I As Integer
    Dim TheTime As Double
    TheTime = Microsoft.VisualBasic.Timer()
    BubbleSort(X) 'Call BubbleSort to sort the array
    Console.WriteLine(Microsoft.VisualBasic.Timer() - TheTime)
    lstResults.Items.Clear() 'Clear all previous data
    For I = 0 To UBound(X)
        'Populate the list box with sorted data
        lstResults.Items.Add(X(I))
    Next I
End Sub
```

You can test your Bubble Sort procedure with the visual interface in Figure 8.1 and the preceding event procedures. Run the project. Enter a number in the text box. Click the Generate button and then the Bubble Sort button. You can then inspect the numbers in the list box to ensure that they are in order. (*Note:* Be sure that the list box's Sorted property is set to False, the default.)

Computing Time Used. Notice that to see how much time the sort routine takes, two additional statements have been added. Before calling the Bubble Sort procedure, TheTime (declared as Double) is assigned a value returned by the *Timer function*, which returns a value (of the Double type) in seconds that represents the current time. (Note that the Timer function must be qualified by Microsoft.VisualBasic because of name conflict with the Timer control.) After the Sub is called, TheTime is subtracted from Timer to obtain the time it takes to perform the sorting. The result is displayed in the immediate window. Although this way of determining the time consumed is not very precise, it should give you a good idea about sorting efficiency of a particular algorithm.

Notice also that the list box is first cleared with its Items.Clear method before it is populated with the sorted data. This is necessary because the user may click the Bubble Sort button several times in the duration of the program. Without that statement, the newly sorted results will be mixed with the previous ones, making it difficult to examine the results.

A Remark on Sorting Efficiency. The speed of a sorting algorithm depends mainly on two factors: the number of comparisons and the amount of data movements.

Recall that the number of comparisons involved in bubble sort varies from round to round, ranging from n – 1 in the first round to 1 in the last round, so the total is $1 + 2 + \ldots + (n - 1) = n(n - 1)/2$. This number is in the order of n^2 and can become huge when n is large. In addition, the number of data movements can be equally huge. If you inspect the process closely, you should find that a big element located on the left side will take many swaps before reaching its final position on the right side of the array. Bubble sort is considered the least efficient sorting algorithm.

Simple Selection Sort. One way to alleviate the data movement problem in the bubble sort algorithm described is to select the proper element for one position at a time; that is, instead of comparing neighboring elements in each round, the program can compare one fixed element with other elements. For example, you can start with finding the largest element in the array by comparing the last element with all other elements. If the other element is greater than this last element, the two elements are swapped. The new element in the last position is then considered the new champion until another element in the array is found to be greater. At that time, another swap will take place. This modification should reduce the number of swaps and is left to you as an exercise at the end of this chapter.

Straight Insertion Sort

Imagine that in the sorting process, an additional array is used for output purposes. Each element from the original (input) array is placed into the output array in sorted order. When all elements from the original array are moved to the output area, the sorting is complete. To ensure that a new element from the input array is placed in the output array in sorted order, it is compared with the elements already in the output array to determine its proper position. After this position is identified, this new element is inserted in that position. This algorithm can be illustrated as follows.

The first element is moved into the output area.

Position	1	2	3	4	5
Input (Original)	38	51	23	56	34
Output	**38**				

The second element, 51, will then be moved to the output area. It is first compared with the existing element in output, 38. Because 51 is greater, it is placed at the end of the output area, resulting in the following:

Position	1	2	3	4	5
Input (Original)	38	51	23	56	34
Output	38	**51**			

The third element will now be moved. When it is compared with the elements in the output area, you find that it should be inserted at position 1. The result will appear as follows:

Position	1	2	3	4	5
Input (Original)	38	51	23	56	34
Output	**23**	38	51		

where 23 is inserted at position 1.

This process continues until all elements in the original array are moved into the output area.

In actual implementation, there is no need to set aside another array for output purposes. Recall that the number of output elements is equal to the number of elements already moved from the input array. Because all the elements in the output area are also the same as those already moved from the input array, the area in the input array can be used to hold the output.

The algorithm involves two major activities when an element is moved from the input area to output: determining the proper position of the new element and inserting the new element in its proper position.

You can write a function (for example, FindPos) to find the proper position for the new element and a Sub procedure to perform the insertion.

The *FindPos function* will search the output area sequentially until the new element is less than the element in the output or the output area is exhausted. Either of these conditions identifies the new element's proper position. For example, if the output area has 38 and 51, and the new element is 23, the function should return the first position, as shown next:

Position	1	2	3
Output	**38**	51	

23 should be inserted here; 0 (the index for the first position) should be returned.

```
Function FindPos(ByVal X() As Integer, ByVal V As Integer, ByVal L
    As Integer) As Integer
    ' This function searches and returns the proper position
    ' for a value V in an array whose elements in the range of its
    ' lower bound and (L - 1)th position are sorted (L is imagined
    ' to be the extra position to accommodate an additional
      element to be inserted)
```

```
            Dim I As Integer
            For I = 0 To L - 1
                If V < X(I) Then
                        Return (I)
                End If
            Next I
            Return (L)
        End Function
```

The Insert Sub Procedure. Assume P is the position in the array X() at which to insert the Lth element. In this case, all elements starting at P through L – 1 will need to be shifted to the right by one position first. The Lth element can be placed at the Pth position to complete the insertion. The steps can be depicted as follows:

Step 1: Move elements to the right.

Position	1	2	3
Output	38	51	

Step 2: Insert the new element.

Position	1	2	3
Output	23	38	51

```
    Sub Insert(ByVal X() As Integer, ByVal P As Integer, _
      ByVal L As Integer)
        ' This procedure performs an insertion of X(L) at position P of
        ' Array X(); L is also the upper boundary of the sorted area
        Dim I As Integer
        Dim Temp As Integer
        Temp = X(L)  ' keep the element to be inserted
        ' Move every element in the range of p to L - 1
        ' by one position to the right
        For I = L - 1 to P Step -1
            X(I + 1) = X(I)
        Next I
        ' Insert the new element at position P
        X(P) = Temp
    End Sub
```

Note that in this routine, L serves two purposes. The element in this position is the one to be inserted. In addition, L identifies the upper boundary of the area where an insertion is to take place. Notice also that the elements are moved to the right, last elements first to avoid overwriting existing data.

The Insertion Sort Procedure. The Insertion Sort Sub procedure can be implemented by calling these two procedures iteratively:

```
    Sub InsertionSort(ByVal X() As Integer)
        Dim I As Integer
        Dim P As Integer
        For I = 1 To UBound(X)
            P = FindPos(X, X(I), I)  'Find position for X(I)
            ' Insert X(I) to position P of the sorted area
            Insert(X, P, I)
        Next I
    End Sub
```

Notice that the For loop starts with 1, the second position of the array. The first element does not need to be sorted. Within the loop, the FindPos function is used to identify the proper position of X(I). The area to search for this position is between 0 and I. (The area between the lower bound and I – 1 contains the sorted elements. X(I) should be placed at position I if it is greater than all elements in this area.) After this proper position—P—is identified, the Insert Sub procedure inserts X(I) into the output area with an upper boundary set at I.

Insertion Sort Versus Bubble Sort. When data in the array are placed randomly, this algorithm requires fewer comparisons than a bubble sort. As a new element is compared with the elements in the sorted output area, the expected number of comparisons is half of the elements in the sorted area, whereas the previous two algorithms require comparisons of all possible pairs of elements. Because data movements in insertion sort involves shifting positions (to the right) rather than swapping, fewer data movements are needed than in the preceding algorithm; therefore, straight insertion sort is faster than bubble sort.

Testing Insertion Sort. The simplest way to test this algorithm is to use the same interface and event procedures as for the bubble sort, as shown in the following steps:

1. Add the three procedures presented in this subsection (the FindPos function, the Insert sub, and the InsertionSort sub) to the same module (code window).

2. Add another button to the form. Name it **btnInsertion** and then set its Text property to **Insertion Sort**.

3. Add the following event procedure:

```
Private Sub btnInsertion_Click(ByVal sender As System.Object,
   ByVal e As System.EventArgs) Handles btnInsertion.Click
      Dim I As Integer
      Dim TheTime As Double
      TheTime = Microsoft.VisualBasic.Timer()
      InsertionSort(X) 'Call InsertionSort to sort the array
      Console.WriteLine(Microsoft.VisualBasic.Timer() - TheTime)
      lstResults.Items.Clear() 'Clear all previous data
      For I = 0 To UBound(X)
          lstResults.Items.Add(X(I)) 'Add sorted element to the
             list box
      Next I
   End Sub
```

Notice that the only difference between this procedure and the btnBubble Click procedure is the statement that calls the sort routine. Here, the Sub procedure, InsertionSort (instead of BubbleSort), is called.

To test the InsertionSort Sub, you can do the following:

1. Enter a number in the text box.
2. Click the Generate button.
3. Click the Insertion Sort button. (Be sure to skip the Bubble Sort button to obtain fair results.)

To obtain a truly fair comparison between the two sorting algorithms, you should populate the same random numbers in two different arrays. Each array can then be sorted by each sorting routine to obtain the sorting time. Such a modification is left to you.

Binary Insertion Sort. The number of comparisons in the preceding algorithm can be further reduced if the binary search algorithm is used to search for the position for a new element. The binary search algorithm is explained in the subsection "Sequential Search and Binary Search" later in this section. Implementing this sorting algorithm is left to you as an exercise at the end of this chapter.

Shell Sort

You may have noticed that in the bubble sort, each element is moved toward its proper position one swap at a time. Many swaps are usually involved before each element reaches its final position. One approach to improve this slow movement is to initially perform the comparisons of an element with another approximately half the array away. A swap of these two elements will thus accomplish a big move. The comparisons continue until no further swap is called for. This interval of comparisons can then be cut in half. The same process is repeated. Eventually, the interval will be equal to one. When it finally finishes the comparisons with this interval, you can be sure that all elements are sorted in order. (At this stage, the sort is similar to the bubble sort, but requires much fewer swaps and rounds of comparison.)

The following example illustrates how Shell sort is performed:

Position	1	2	3	4	5
Value	38	51	23	56	34

The initial interval is computed to be slightly smaller than half of the array; that is, 2 in this case. The first element, 38, is then compared with the third element, 23. Because the two elements are out of order, they are swapped:

Position	1	2	3	4	5
Value	**23**	51	**38**	56	34

The second element, 51, is then compared with the fourth element, 56, and 38 with 34, resulting in another swap:

Position	1	2	3	4	5
Value	23	51	**34**	56	**38**

The comparisons have reached the end. Because the current round resulted in swaps, another round of comparisons with the same interval should be performed; that is, 23 with 34, 51 with 56, and 34 with 38. No swap occurs. So, the interval is reduced by half to 1, and another round of comparisons is performed until no swap occurs.

Assume X() is the array to be sorted. You can first compute the interval as follows:

```
Interval = CInt(Math.Ceiling(UBound(X) / 2))
```

Does the formula appear more complex than necessary? Actually, it is written this way to take care of a fine point. The reason will be explained shortly.

A For loop as shown here should complete a round of comparisons:

```
For I = 0 UBound(X) - Interval
    If X(I) > X(I + Interval) Then
        ' Out of order, swap
        Temp = X(I)
        X(I) = X(I + Interval)
        X(I + Interval) = Temp
    End If
Next I
```

The For statement sets the position of the element on the left to be compared and starts at the lower bound of the array. It should end when I + Interval is greater than the upper bound of X; that is, I should go as high as I + Interval = UBound(X). Thus, the ending value for I is Ubound(X) – Interval.

This loop is to be repeated until no swap occurs. To keep track of swaps, you can use a Boolean variable, Swapped. The variable can be set to False before executing the For loop. If a swap occurs, it is set to True. Before the outer loop is repeated, this variable can be tested, and another round of comparisons is performed only if Swapped is True.

```
Do
    Swapped = False
    For I = 0 to UBound(X) - Interval
        If X(I) > X(I + Interval) Then
            ' Out of order, swap
            Temp = X(I)
            X(I) = X(I + Interval)
            X(I + Interval) = Temp
            Swapped = True
        End If
    Next I
Loop While Swapped
```

When the outer loop is finished, it is time to reduce the interval size by half and then repeat another round of comparisons until the interval size is zero. The entire sort procedure using the Shell sort algorithm should appear as follows:

```
Sub ShellSort(ByVal X() As Integer)
    Dim Interval As Integer
    Dim I As Integer
    Dim Swapped As Boolean
    Dim Temp As Integer
    Interval = CInt(Math.Ceiling(UBound(X) / 2))
    Do Until Interval = 0
        Do
            Swapped = False  ' assume no swap
            For I = 0 To UBound(X) - Interval
                If X(I) > X(I + Interval) Then
                    ' Out of order, swap
                    Temp = X(I)
                    X(I) = X(I + Interval)
                    X(I + Interval) = Temp
                    ' Swap occurs, so set swapped to true
                    Swapped = True
                End If
            Next I
        Loop While Swapped
        ' Reduce the interval by half
        Interval = CInt(Interval / 2)
    Loop
End Sub
```

Notice that two different formulas are used to compute Interval. The second formula computes Interval by converting into the integer value the quotient of the previous Interval divided by 2. CInt rounds its parameter; however, when the fractional portion is exactly .5, it rounds the parameter to the nearest even number. That is, if the parameter is 1.5, it will be rounded to 2; but if the parameter is .5, it will be rounded to 0. This is exactly what you want for it to do in the second formula. But consider the formula at the beginning. If X has two elements (thus its UBound is 1), Interval will be 0 if you use the same formula as the second one. This will mean that when X has two elements, the array will never be sorted. To ensure that Interval will be at least one, the Ceiling function, which gives the smallest integer greater than or equal to the parameter, is first used to round the number up before the result is converted to an integer by the CInt function.

You can implement a test procedure by following the same steps as outlined in the preceding subsection. Test the program, and you should find that this algorithm is much faster than those previously discussed.

Quick Sort

You may recall that in the bubble sort, in each round of comparisons, the algorithm attempts to identify which element in the array should be moved to a destination position. In other words, a destination is waiting for an element that qualifies. In the quick sort, the goal is inverted. The algorithm looks for the proper position for the given data element at hand. Specifically, when the sorting operation starts, the first element in the array is considered the pivotal element. The algorithm looks for the proper final position in the array to place this pivotal element. This is done by first comparing the pivotal element with the array elements backward (right to left) until the pivotal element is greater than the element in the array. The pivotal element is swapped with this element; then the pivotal element (in its new position) is compared with elements in the array forward (left to right) until it is found to be smaller than another element in the array. A swap takes place, and the comparisons go backward again.

The backward-forward sequence of comparisons/swaps continues until all elements in the array have been compared with the pivotal element. At this point, no element on the left side of the pivotal element is greater than and no element on its right is less than the pivotal element. The pivotal element has found its proper position. This process also ensures that all elements on the left side are smaller than all elements on the right side of the pivotal element; no further sorting between the two sides is necessary. The elements on each side can then be sorted separately using the same algorithm.

The following example illustrates how the pivotal element is placed in its proper position.

Position	1	2	3	4	5
Value	**38**	51	23	56	34

The first element, 38, is the pivotal element. At first, the comparisons start from right to left until the pivotal element is greater than the element in the array. This occurs immediately when 38 is compared with the fifth element, 34. A swap takes place:

Position	1	2	3	4	5
Value	**34**	51	23	56	**38**

Comparisons now turn forward. (Notice that 38 is the pivotal element.) The second element, 51, is compared with 38. They are out of order. Another swap takes place:

Position	1	2	3	4	5
Value	34	**38**	23	56	**51**

Comparisons then go backward again. 38 is compared with 56 and then with 23, where another swap takes place:

Position	1	2	3	4	5
Value	34	**23**	**38**	56	51

At this point, all elements have been compared with 38. The pivotal element has found its proper position. Note that all elements on its left side are smaller than 38, and all elements on its right side are greater. The sub-arrays on both sides (as depicted in the following illustration) can be sorted by the same algorithm:

Position	1	2	3	4	5
Value	34	23	38	56	51

Header for Quick Sort. Before you start coding for this algorithm, you should note that you will use the same procedure to sort sub-arrays. This means that this sort Sub procedure will have to call itself; that is, it will be used as a recursive procedure. Each sub-array has a different range of elements to sort. The range can be defined by the beginning and ending positions of the sub-array; therefore, the header of this Sub procedure should look a bit different from the previous sort procedures:

```
Sub QuickSort(ByVal X() as Integer, ByVal BegPos as Integer, ByVal
    EndPos as Integer)
```

where *X()* is the array to be sorted, and *BegPos* and *EndPos* define the range of the sub-array to sort. Of course, when the routine is initially called, these variables will cover the entire range—0 and UBound(X)—of the array.

You will use two variables—I and J—to keep track of the positions for forward and backward comparisons, respectively. Initially, I starts at the beginning of the range, and J starts at the end:

```
I = BegPos
J = EndPos
```

The first element is the pivotal element:

```
Pivot = X(I)
```

Comparing Backward. The comparisons will first go backward. For any element J in the array, if it is found to be greater than or equal to Pivot, you will go one position to the left; otherwise, a swap takes place, and the backward comparison ends:

```
If Pivot =< X(J) Then
    ' In order, go one position left
    J = J - 1
Else
    ' out of order; swap and terminate the loop
    X(I) = X (J)
    X(J) = Pivot
    Exit Do
End If
```

Note that before the swap, X(I) and Pivot are the same. There is no need to assign X(I) to Pivot in the swap process. This comparison routine should be enclosed in a Do loop. If the comparisons exhaust all the items; that is, I = J, the loop should also end. The complete code for backward comparisons should appear as follows:

```
Do Until I >= J
    If Pivot <= X(J) Then
        ' In order, go one position to the left
        J = J - 1
    Else
        ' out of order; swap and terminate the loop
        X(I)  = X (J)
        X(J) = Pivot
        Exit Do
    End If
Loop
```

Comparing Forward. After this loop ends, the process should proceed to the next phase to compare forward. The code can be written in a similar fashion as follows:

```
Do Until I >= J
    If Pivot >= X(I) Then
        ' In order, go one position to the right
        I = I + 1
    Else
        ' out of order; swap and terminate the loop
        X(J) = X (I)
        X(I) = Pivot
        Exit Do
    End If
Loop
```

Again, notice that at this point before the swap, Pivot and X(J) are the same (see the swap in the preceding loop). There is no need to assign X(J) to Pivot at the beginning of the swap.

The Outer Loop. The preceding two loops should be repeated as long as some elements still have not been compared with Pivot; that is, another (outer) loop as shown below should enclose the two preceding loops:

```
Do Until I >= J
    ' Place both of the above loops here
Loop
```

Sorting the Sub-arrays. The preceding code completes the process of placing the pivotal element in its proper position. As stated at the beginning of this subsection, after this is done, the sub-arrays on both sides of the pivotal element can be sorted using the same algorithm. The following two lines of code should be placed immediately after the preceding loops:

```
QuickSort (X, BegPos, J - 1)  'Sort the subarray on left side
QuickSort (X, J + 1, EndPos) ' sort the subarray on right side
```

Terminating the Procedure. The procedure so written will continue to call itself unless you provide additional code to end the recursive process. The procedure should discontinue further sorting under the following circumstances:

- There is only one element in a sub-array; therefore, there will be no need to sort.
- There are only two elements in a sub-array, so you can perform a simple comparison to see whether they are out of order. If so, a swap can be performed; otherwise, nothing further needs to be done. In either case, there is no need to perform additional sorting.

This analysis suggests the following code:

```
'One or fewer elements, no need to sort
If EndPos - BegPos < = 0 Then Exit Sub
If EndPos - BegPos = 1 Then
    ' This subarray has two elements, check to see if they are
    ' out of order
    If X(BegPos) > X(EndPos) Then
        ' Out of order, swap
        Temp = X(BegPos)
        X(BegPos) = X(EndPos)
        X(EndPos) = Temp
    End If
    Exit Sub
End If
```

These lines should be placed at the very beginning of the procedure.

The Better, the Worse. The code previously presented basically completes the quick sort algorithm in its original form. When used to sort an array with random elements, it is fast because this method preserves the results of comparisons and involves few unnecessary data movements. Recall that all elements found to be smaller than the pivotal element are placed on its left, and all elements greater are on its right. Therefore, none of the elements on the left need to be compared with those on the right, eliminating many unnecessary comparisons that occur in the bubble sort. The process of searching for the proper position of the pivotal element also moves each element near its proper position. When used to sort an array that is already in order, however, the number of comparisons degenerates to the bubble sort because at the end of each round, the pivotal element is placed at the beginning of the array, resulting in only one side being sorted. The next pivotal element will again be compared with the remainder of the entire array.

Solving the Paradox. One proposal to alleviate this problem is to select a random element (instead of the first element) as the pivotal element. Another proposal is to use the midpoint of the array as the pivotal element. If you use the midpoint approach, you will first swap the midpoint element with the first element and then proceed with the sorting as previously presented. That is, you will add the following statements:

```
M = CInt((BegPos + EndPos) / 2 ) 'Find mid point
' Use mid point element as the pivotal element
' Also swap the mid point element with the first element
Pivot = X(M)
X(M) = X(BegPos)
X(BegPos) = Pivot
```

These statements will replace the line Pivot = X(I) presented previously.

The Stack Space Issue. Another issue concerning quick sort is the amount of stack space needed. The Sub procedure calls itself when sorting the sub-arrays on both sides of the pivotal element. The parameters passed to the procedure itself are kept in the memory stack. If not carefully managed, the routine can run out of stack space before the sort routine is complete. The solution is to ensure that the shorter sub-array is sorted first. To implement this solution, the calls to sort the subarrays can be rewritten as follows:

```
      If J - BegPos <= EndPos - J Then
          ' Left side is shorter, sort it first
          QuickSort(X, BegPos, J - 1) 'Sort the left subarray
          QuickSort(X, J + 1, EndPos) ' sort the right subarray
      Else
          ' Right side is shorter, sort it first
          QuickSort(X, J + 1, EndPos) ' sort the right subarray
          QuickSort(X, BegPos, J - 1) 'Sort the left subarray
      End If
```

The complete Quick Sort routine as modified appears as follows:

```
Sub QuickSort(ByVal X() As Integer, ByVal BegPos As Integer, ByVal
   EndPos As Integer)
   Dim Temp As Integer
   Dim Pivot As Integer
   Dim M As Integer
   Dim I As Integer
   Dim J As Integer
   If EndPos - BegPos <= 0 Then Exit Sub 'One or fewer elements,
       ' no need to sort
       If EndPos - BegPos = 1 Then
           ' This subarray has two elements.
           ' Check whether they are out of order
           If X(BegPos) > X(EndPos) Then
               ' Out of order, swap
               Temp = X(BegPos)
               X(BegPos) = X(EndPos)
               X(EndPos) = Temp
           End If
           Exit Sub 'No need to do anything more
       End If
       ' Here is the typical quick sort
       I = BegPos    'initial left position for forward comparisons
       J = EndPos    'initial right position for backward comparisons
       M = CInt((BegPos + EndPos) / 2)  'Midpoint of array
       Pivot = X(M) ' Use midpoint of array as pivotal element
       X(M) = X(BegPos) ' Swap midpoint with first element
       X(BegPos) = Pivot
       ' Find the proper position for Pivot
       Do Until I >= J
           ' Check backward
           Do Until I >= J
               If Pivot <= X(J) Then
                   ' In order, go one position to the left
                   J = J - 1
               Else
                   ' out of order; swap and terminate the loop
                   X(I) = X(J)
                   X(J) = Pivot
                   Exit Do
               End If
           Loop
           ' Check forward
           Do Until I >= J
               If Pivot >= X(I) Then
                   ' In order, go one position to the right
                   I = I + 1
               Else
                   ' out of order; swap and terminate the loop
                   X(J) = X(I)
                   X(I) = Pivot
                   Exit Do
               End If
           Loop
       Loop
```

```
                    ' Sort subarrays
                    If J - BegPos <= EndPos - J Then
                        ' Left side is shorter, sort it first
                        QuickSort(X, BegPos, J - 1)    'Sort the left subarray
                        QuickSort(X, J + 1, EndPos) ' sort the right subarray
                    Else
                        ' Right side is shorter, sort it first
                        QuickSort(X, J + 1, EndPos) ' sort the right subarray
                        QuickSort(X, BegPos, J - 1)    'Sort the left subarray
                    End If
                End Sub
```

This completes the discussion of the quick sort algorithm. As a reminder, the code to call this sort routine is a bit different, and should appear as follows:

```
QuickSort(X, 0, UBound(X))
```

The next subsection presents sample empirical performance results of various sorting algorithms. You should find the quick sort algorithm gets its name for a good reason.

Comparison of Performance

As you can see, some of the algorithms are pretty simple; but others are more involved. In general, if two algorithms give the same performance, you would rather use the simpler one. The additional complexity can be justified only with better performance. So, how do they compare in terms of speed? The following table shows the time used to sort varying numbers of elements by these algorithms using a Pentium IV 1.4 GHz machine.

Number of Elements	Bubble Sort	Insertion Sort	Shell Sort	Quick Sort
4000	0.12017	0.05007	0	0
8000	0.48069	0.17024	0.01001	0
16000	1.92276	0.67096	0.03004	0
32000	7.68104	2.61376	0.07010	0.01001
64000	30.87440	10.63529	0.18026	0.02003

The leftmost column shows the number of integer numbers (generated by the formula given in bubble sort) being sorted. The numbers in the table are time in seconds. Because the numbers are randomly generated, the results can be different if you attempt to replicate the experiments; however, you should be able to make several general observations:

- Quick sort and Shell sort far outperform the other algorithms.
- As the number of elements to sort doubles, the first two algorithms approximately quadruple the time used; the latter two algorithms slightly more than double.

The nearly linear relationship between the number of elements to sort and time required suggests that the last two algorithms are not only more efficient, but also steadier performers.

Sequential Search and Binary Search

After data in an array are sorted in order, they can be searched with more efficient algorithms. Data stored randomly can be searched only sequentially. The table lookup example given previously, such as looking for the phone number given an employee's name, shows how a sequential search can be coded. The average number of comparisons required to find an item will be half of the number of elements in the array.

Improved Sequential Search with Sorted Data. The number of comparisons can be reduced if the data are arranged in order, even with the same sequential search method. How? Because the data are in order, if the data in the array is found to be greater than the search key, there is no need to search further. All data beyond this point will be greater than the search key. The search can therefore be terminated with the conclusion **Data Not Found**. This idea can be implemented with the following code for the same lookup problem, assuming employee names are sorted in ascending order.

```
Private Sub btnSearch_Click(ByVal sender As System.Object, ByVal e
    As System.EventArgs) Handles btnSearch.Click
    Dim Name As String
    Dim I As Integer
    Name = txtName.Text
    For I = 0 To EmployeeCount -1
        If Name = Employees(I) then
            MsgBox("The phone number for " & Name _
                & " is " & Format(Phones(I), "(000)-000-0000"))
            Exit Sub
        ElseIf Name < Employees(I) Then
            ' The name in array is greater than the search key;
            ' There's no such an employee
            Exit For
        End If
    Next I
    MsgBox("Employee name " & Name & " not found.")
End Sub
```

The Binary Search. The preceding search can be even more efficient if the binary search algorithm is used. This algorithm begins by setting the lower and upper boundary of the search to the entire range of the array. It then starts the search at the midpoint of the array. If the search key is greater than the data at the midpoint, the item being searched (if it exists) must be in the upper half of the array; the lower boundary can be adjusted to this midpoint. On the other hand, if the search key is less than the element in the array, the item being search must be in the lower half; therefore, the upper bound is adjusted. The midpoint of this new search boundary is then computed. The search continues, each time narrowing the search boundary by half until the item is found or there is only one item in the range (lower and upper bounds are the same; this means data for the search key does not exist). This algorithm is similar to the half interval method introduced in Chapter 7, "Repetition," to find a numerical solution for a mathematical function. (See Figure 7.4 for a sketch of the algorithm.) Using this algorithm, the preceding lookup problem can be coded as follows:

```
Private Sub btnSearch_Click(ByVal sender As System.Object, ByVal e
    As System.EventArgs) Handles btnSearch.Click
    Dim Name As String
    Dim I As Integer
    Dim Lower As Integer
    Dim Upper As Integer
    Name = txtName.Text
    Lower = 0
    Upper = EmployeeCount -1
    Do
        I = (Lower + Upper) \ 2 'Compute the mid point
        If Name = Employees(I) Then
            MsgBox("The phone number for " & Name _
                & " is " & Format(Phones(I), "(000)-000-0000"))
            Exit Sub
        ElseIf Name > Employees(I) Then
            ' the name in array is less than the search key;
            ' Adjust the lower bound
            Lower = I + 1
        Else
            ' The name in array is greater than the search key;
            ' Adjust the upper bound
            Upper = I - 1
```

```
            End If
        Loop Until Lower = Upper
        If Name = Employees(Upper) Then
        Msg Box("The phone number for " & Name _
            & " is " & Format(Phones(I), "(000)-000-0000"))
        Else
            MsgBox("Employee name " & Name & " not found.")
        End If
    End Sub
```

Notice that after the Do loop, Name is compared with Employees(Upper) to determine for the last time that the name is actually not in the array. This is necessary because when Lower and Upper reach the same value, a new I value has not been computed.

Before leaving this example, note that the binary search method is commonly used. VB.NET provides a BinarySearch method that is explained at the end of this chapter. The purpose here is to show you the algorithm itself, and hope you will be able use it to solve other similar problems.

8.4 The Collection Object

The collection object collects items in a list. The items in its list can be of different types, including objects. This flexibility makes it convenient in handling diverse programming situations. To create a collection object, you can make the following declaration:

```
Dim Name As New Microsoft.VisualBasic.Collection()
```

You can add items to the collection with its Add method, which has the following syntax:

```
CollectionName.Add(Item[, Key])
```

As stated, Item can be any type, such as an integer number, a text box, and so on. Key must be a string that uniquely identifies the item. (Attempting to add a duplicate key will result in an error.) Items in the collection are indexed from 1 to the number of items, unlike many other objects you have met, which are typically indexed with 0 as the first element. If keys are also added to the collection, you can either use the key or the numeric index to retrieve an item, using the Item property with the following syntax:

```
CollectionName.Item(Index¦ key)
```

The collection allows you to remove items from the list, using its Remove method with syntax similar to the Item property:

```
CollectionName.Remove(Index¦key)
```

Finally, the collection has the Count property that gives the number of items in the list.

Using the Collection Object

In this section, your interest in the collection object stems from the need to handle controls as an array. VB.NET does not support control arrays; however, you may encounter situations in which the visual interface design of your application requires the flexibility of control arrays. For example, consider the data entry screen for a program that evaluates the merits of an investment project. The user will enter the project life in years and then enter the cash flow for each year. The cash flows should be entered in text boxes, the number of which should vary based on the project life. A sample visual interface is shown in Figure 8.2. As you can see, the number of text boxes for the cash flows and their related labels should depend on the number of years specified in the text box for the project life. The text boxes for cash flows should appear when the user clicks the Ready button or presses the Enter key in the text box for the project life ("how many years"). There are at least two challenges:

Figure 8.2

Visual interface for the
Cashflow Entry Form

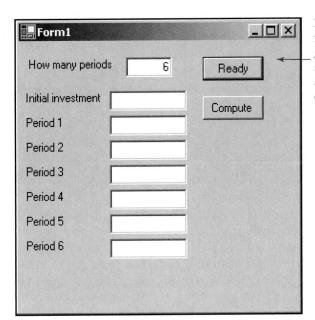

In this project, the text boxes
for cash flow amounts should be
generated only after the user
specifies the number of periods
and either clicks the Ready button
or presses the Enter key.

- The controls (labels and text boxes) should be added to the form during runtime, and should depend on the number specified by the user.
- To handle the user input flexibly, the text boxes must be handled in a way similar to an array.

Before considering these challenges, take a look at the controls drawn to the form at design time in the following table first:

Control	Name	Remark
Label	Label1	To display the text "How many periods"
Text box	txtPeriods	To enter number of periods (project life in years)
Button	btnReady	To invoke the procedure to add labels and text boxes
Button	btnCompute	To invoke the computation routine

Adding Controls to the Form by Code. VB controls are objects. They can be added to the form similar to other objects such as the stream reader. The main difference is that controls should be visible in the form; therefore, in the code, you must specify those properties that pertain to the visual elements—for example, size, location, and text properties. Also, the form has a Controls collection, as explained in Chapter 7. A newly added control must also be added to that collection, using the *Add method*. The following code should add a label to a form.

```
Dim lblSample As Label

LblSample = New Label()
With lblSample
    .Text = "This is a sample"
    .Location = New Point(5, 20) 'Set Left at 5 and Top at 20
    .AutoSize = True 'So that I don't have to specify its size
End With
Me.Controls.Add(lblSample)
```

The Dim statement declares that lblSample is of the Label type. The next statement creates a new label. The statements within the With . . . End With block set up the visual properties for the label. Its Location property is assigned a Point object at (5, 20), which is five pixels from the left margin, and 20 pixels from the top margin of its container (the form). This statement is equivalent to assigning 5 to the label's Left property, and 20 to its Top property. The last statement adds lblSample to the form's Controls collection.

TIP

> If you have more than one control to add to the form, you can use the AddRange method that expects a collection of controls as its parameter. A collection of controls can be created with the following syntax:
>
> ```
> New Control(){Control1, Control2, ...}
> ```
>
> The following statement will add Label1 and Label2 to the form.
>
> ```
> Me.Controls.AddRange(New Control() {Label1, Label2})
> ```

You may wonder why you use a separate statement to create a new label, instead of using the New keyword in the Dim statement. In this case, either way will produce the same result; however, keep in mind that there is some difference between the two approaches. When a new label is created using an assignment statement with the New keyword, as in the code, each time this statement is executed, a new label is created. If it is placed in a loop, many labels can be created. If you use the New keyword in the Dim statement, you create the label at that time. Only when that statement is invoked again will another label be created.

Creating a Specified Number of Text Boxes. Back to the cash flow project, assume that the number of periods specified is N. You will then need to generate N + 1 text boxes (period 0 for initial investment). You can use a For loop in which a text box is created. The code can appear as follows:

```
Dim txtCashflow As TextBox
Dim I as Integer
Dim N as Integer
N = CInt(Val(txtPeriods.Text))
For I = 0 To N
    txtCashflow = New TextBox() 'Create a new text box
    With txtCashflow
        .Size = New Size(80, 20) 'Width=80; Height=20
        .Location = New Point(95, 50 + I * 25)
        .TabIndex = 1 + I 'Set the tabindex
        'Align the text on the right
        .TextAlign = HorizontalAlignment.Right
    End With
    Me.Controls.Add(txtCashflow)
Next I
```

With this code, you are able to generate the desired number of text boxes. Note again that each time the first statement within the For loop is executed, a new text box is created, although all of these text boxes are initially given the same name, txtCashflow. After you leave the loop, however, you will have difficulty referring to each individual text box. You can still refer to the text box most recently created using the variable name, txtCashflow. With the current code, however, you no longer have a way to make a reference to those previously created text boxes. Trick? Add each text box to a collection object while you can still reference it. Later, you can refer to each text box by the collection's Item property.

Assuming you have declared a collection named cllCashflow, you can add a statement like the following to keep the reference for the text boxes:

```
cllCashflow.Add(txtCashflow)
```

Complete Code to Create the Project Interface. You are now ready to develop the code to create the visual interface for your cash flow project. You will place the code in a sub procedure for the reason to be explained later. The procedure appears as follows:

```
Dim txtCashflow As TextBox
Dim lblCashflow As Label
Dim cllCashflow As New Microsoft.VisualBasic.Collection()
Private Sub ShowBoxes()
    Dim I As Integer
    Dim N As Integer
    N = CInt(Val(txtPeriods.Text))
    If N = 0 Then Exit Sub 'Do nothing if N is zero
    For I = 0 To N
        lblCashflow = New Label()
        With lblCashflow
            If I = 0 Then
                .Text = "Initial investment"
            Else
                .Text = "Period " & I
            End If
            .AutoSize = True
            .Location = New Point(5, 50 + I * 25)
        End With
        txtCashflow = New TextBox() 'Create a new textbox
        With txtCashflow
            .Size = New Size(80, 20) 'Width=80; Height=20
            .Location = New Point(95, 50 + I * 25)
            .TabIndex = 1 + I 'Set the tabindex
            'Align the text on the right
            .TextAlign = HorizontalAlignment.Right
        End With
        cllCashflow.Add(txtCashflow)
        Me.Controls.AddRange(New Control() {lblCashflow,
          txtCashflow})
    Next I
    btnReady.TabIndex = N + 2
    btnCompute.TabIndex = N + 3
End Sub
```

Notice the last two statements within the loop. The newly created txtCashflow text box is added to the collection as explained previously. The two newly created controls (the label and text box) are now added to the form's Controls collection, using the *AddRange method* instead of the Add method. The AddRange method expects a control array as its parameter. The control array is created with exactly the same syntax as creating any data array as explained in Section 8.1. Notice also the two statements below the loop. They set the TabIndex properties for the two buttons that were drawn on the form at design time so that the user can tab through the text boxes before running into the buttons.

Invoking the ShowBoxes Sub. The ShowBoxes sub can be invoked in two different events: when the user clicks on the Ready button, or when the user presses the Enter key in the text box named txtPeriods. These two event procedures can be coded as follows:

```
Private Sub btnReady_Click(ByVal sender As System.Object, ByVal e
  As System.EventArgs) Handles btnReady.Click
    ShowBoxes()
End Sub
Private Sub txtPeriods_KeyPress(ByVal sender As System.Object,
  ByVal e As System.Windows.Forms.KeyPressEventArgs) Handles
  txtPeriods.KeyPress
    If e.KeyChar = ControlChars.Cr Then
        ShowBoxes()
        e.Handled = True 'No further process needed
    End If
End Sub
```

Referencing the Text Boxes in the Collection. As mentioned previously in this chapter, you use the collection object because you want to have a way to reference to the text boxes created at runtime. Suppose the user clicks the Compute button after entering relevant data in the cash flow boxes. How can you obtain the values entered in the text boxes and then assign them to an array? The following code should do the trick:

```
Private Sub btnCompute_Click(ByVal sender As System.Object, ByVal
    e As System.EventArgs) Handles btnCompute.Click
    Dim I As Integer
    Dim CashFlow() As Double
    Dim N As Integer
    N = cllCashflow.Count - 1
    ReDim CashFlow(N)
    For I = 0 To N
        'Convert the collection item to text box
        txtCashflow = CType(cllCashflow.Item(I + 1), TextBox)
        CashFlow(I) = Val(txtCashflow.Text)
    Next I
    'Other statements
End Sub
```

Notice that each item in the collection is a generic object, which does not have the Text property. To retrieve this property, you must first assign the item in the collection to a variable of the text box type; however, under strict implicit conversion rule (Option Strict On), the compiler requires an explicit conversion from a generic object to a control like the text box. The CType function is therefore used to explicitly convert Item I + 1 to the TextBox type, and the result is assigned to txtCashflow, which has been declared in the general declaration area.

Additional Note. The labels and text boxes that you created in the preceding examples are not capable of handling events. This capability can be important. For example, you may want to use the KeyPress event to ensure that keys entered in the text boxes are numeric only. With minor modifications, you can add this capability. This topic is discussed in Chapter 12, "Object-Based Programming."

8.5 Two-Dimensional Arrays

As stated at the beginning of this chapter, array variables can have more than one dimension. Consider the case of two-dimensional variables. The syntax to declare a two-dimensional variable is as follows:

$$\text{Dim Name}(UB_1, UB_2) \text{ As } Type$$

where *Name* = any legitimate variable name

UB_n = an integer representing the upper bound for the nth subscript

Type = any valid data type

As you can see, the only difference between a two-dimensional array and one-dimensional array is the number of subscript(s). When a variable has more than one subscript, use commas to separate the subscripts. The following are examples of valid declarations of two-dimensional arrays:

```
Dim A(9, 9) As Integer
Dim Weights(Row, Col) As String
```

The first line declares a 10 × 10 Integer array, A, depicted as follows:

```
A(0, 0)  A(0, 1)  A(0, 2)     . . .    A(0, 9)
A(1, 0)  .           .             .    A(1, 9)
.            .           .             .    .
A(9, 0)                                A(9, 9)
```

The second line declares a Weights String table whose size depends on the values of the variables, Row and Col. These two variables should exist, and have been assigned proper values before the Dim statement is executed.

Two-dimensional arrays can be used to handle various kinds of two-dimensional data. The following discussion explains how they can be used to represent tables, matrices, and even game boards.

Tables

Revisit the weight lookup example from the first section. The weight table shown there was only for males with a medium frame. What happens to the small- and large-frame males? Actually, the complete weight table appears as follows:

Height (in Shoes)	Small Frame	Medium Frame	Large Frame
5'2"	112–120	118–129	126–141
5'3"	115–123	121–133	129–144
5'4"	118–126	124–136	132–148
5'5"	121–129	127–139	135–152
5'6"	124–133	130–143	138–156
5'7"	128–137	134–147	138–156
5'8"	132–141	138–152	147–166
5'9"	136–145	142–156	151–170
5'10"	140–150	146–160	155–174
5'11"	144–154	150–165	159–179
6'	148–158	154–170	164–184
6'1"	152–162	158–175	168–189
6'2"	156–167	162–180	173–194
6'3"	160–171	167–185	178–199
6'4"	164–175	172–190	182–204

Refining the Weight Lookup Project. You can design a project similar to the previous one with this more complete set of data to respond to any normal-weight queries. The weights shown in the preceding table can be read into a two-dimensional array. The user can specify the height and the frame size and then click a Show Normal Weight button. The program can then retrieve a cell (an element) from the table, and display it in a label. The visual interface appears as in Figure 8.3.

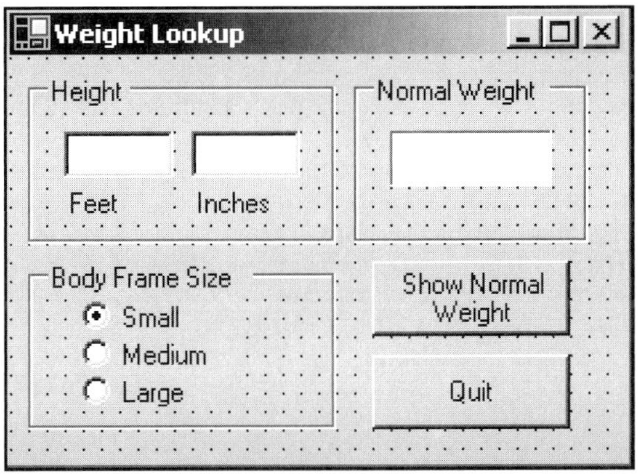

Figure 8.3

Visual interface for the Weight Lookup project

The following table lists the controls and properties used in the code.

Control	Property	Setting	Remarks
Text box	Name	txtFeet	To specify height
Text box	Name	txtInches	
Label	Name	lblNormalWeight	To display normal weight for the given height
Radio button	Name	rbtBodyFrameS	To specify body frame
	Text	Small	
Radio button	Name	rbtBodyFrameM	
	Text	Medium	
Radio button	Name	rbtBodyFrameL	
	Text	Large	
Button	Name	btnShow	To initiate the computation and display of normal weight
	Text	Show normal weight	
Button	Name	btnQuit	To terminate the program
	Text	Quit	

Code Requirements. The program should satisfy the following requirements:

- As soon as the program starts, the weight table needs to be populated with data read in from a file.
- When the user clicks the Show Normal Weight button, the program needs to convert the height into inches and identify the radio button clicked for the frame size.
- Use the numbers obtained in the preceding bullet point to retrieve and display the weight data in the label.

Coding the Project. Now consider the code for the project. The first step is to populate the Weights() table as the project starts. Assume the data file appears as follows:

```
62, 112-120, 118-129, 126-141
63 . . .
  .
  .
  .
76 . . .                          182-204
```

The table can then be populated as follows:

```
Dim Weights(14, 2) As String
Private Sub Form1_Load(ByVal sender As System.Object, ByVal e As
  System.EventArgs) Handles MyBase.Load
    Dim Col As Integer
    Dim Row As Integer
    Dim Height As Integer
    Dim TheRecord As String
    Dim HeightNWeight() As String
    Dim WeightFile As IO.StreamReader
    ' Open weight file located in the same Bin folder as this
      program
    WeightFile = New IO.StreamReader("MaleWeights.txt")
    ' Populate the weight table
    Do Until WeightFile.Peek() = -1
        TheRecord = WeightFile.ReadLine()
        HeightNWeight = Split(TheRecord, ",")
        Row = CInt(HeightNWeight(0)) - 62
        For Col = 0 To 2
            Weights(Row, Col) = HeightNWeight(Col + 1)
        Next Col
    Loop
End Sub
```

The array variable, Weights is declared as a 15 × 3 table. The 15 rows will accommodate the heights from 5'2" to 6'4" and the three columns will accommodate the three body frame sizes. The StreamReader, WeightFile reads in the data one record (line) at a time. The record is assigned to the TheRecord variable, which is parsed into a string array using the *Split function*. The Split function has the following syntax:

```
Split(StringToParse, Delimiter)
```

It breaks the string into sub-strings based on the specified delimiter, and returns the sub-strings as a one-dimensional array. For example, the expression Split("AB,C,DEF", ",") will return a string array with "AB," "C," and "DEF." The expression Split(TheRecord, ",") should return an array with the height as the first element followed by three weight ranges for different frame sizes. The result is assigned to the HeightNWeight variable. The row position to store the weight data is computed by subtracting 62 from the height (in inches). In the For loop, the weights (from the record) are then assigned to the Weights table in the calculated row position. Notice that the first element in HeightNWeight is the height, and its second element holds the normal weight range for the small body frame. Thus, its position Col + 1 holds the data that should be assigned to the Col of Weights.

When the Show button is clicked, the program needs to convert the height to inches and identify which of the frame radio buttons is clicked. Converting the height is easy, as shown in the previous example:

```
Inches = CInt(txtFeet.Text) * 12 + CInt(txtInches.Text)
```

To compute the row position in the Weights table, you can subtract 62 from Inches; that is,

```
Row = Inches - 62
```

But how do you identify which radio button was clicked last, and therefore the column position? You will use the approach explained in the Explore and Discover exercise 5-11. After you identify the row and column, the element (cell), Weights(Row, Col) should give the weight that corresponds to the height and body frame computed previously. The code to handle the event when the user clicks the Show button should appear as follows:

```
Private Sub btnShow_Click(ByVal sender As System.Object, ByVal e
    As System.EventArgs) Handles btnShow.Click
    Dim Inches As Integer
    Dim Row As Integer
    Dim Col As Integer
    Inches = CInt(txtFeet.Text) * 12 + CInt(txtInches.Text)
    Row = Inches - 62
    'The following Select Case structure identifies the column
    'position
    Select Case True
        Case rbtBodyFrameS.Checked
            Col = 0 'Column for small frame
        Case rbtBodyFrameM.Checked
            Col = 1 'Column for medium frame
        Case rbtBodyFrameL.Checked
            Col = 2 'Column for large frame
    End Select
    lblNormalWeight.Text = Weights(Row, Col) 'Show normal weight
        range
End Sub
```

Can you see the benefits of using a table (array) for selection? Without the Weights table as an array, the alternative will be to code the project using the Select Case structure. Compare this solution with the solution to the tuition problem illustrated in Chapter 5, "Decision." Using that approach, you will also need to nest the Select Case structure because the selection involves two factors, the height and the body frame size. The code will be much longer and not as neat, elegant, or flexible.

Matrices

A matrix consists of a rectangular array of numeric elements in rows and columns. It is mainly used in matrix algebra to handle various linear algebraic problems. The two-dimensional array fits exactly the definition of a matrix, and can be used to perform any matrix operations. For example, by definition, adding two matrices calls for the addition of the corresponding elements in the two matrix operands. Suppose the two matrices as represented by two two-dimensional arrays are A and B. The matrix operation A + B will mean performing A(I, J) + B(I, J) for the entire range of both subscripts. A and B must have the same dimensions. The following function procedure adds the two matrices and returns the results to the caller.

```
Function MatrixAdd(ByVal A(,) As Double, ByVal B(,) As Double) _
   As Double(,)
      Dim I As Integer
      Dim J As Integer
      Dim C(,) As Double
      ReDim C(UBound(A, 1), UBound(A, 2))
      For I = 0 To UBound(A, 1)
          For J = 0 To UBound(A, 2)
              C(I, J) = A(I, J) + B(I, J)
          Next J
      Next I
      Return (C)
End Function
```

In this procedure, the loop counters I and J are set to start from 0 to the upper bound of their respective subscripts.

Notice how the header is specified. The two parameters (A and B) and As Double are each followed by a pair of parentheses. A comma is placed in each pair to indicate the *rank* (number of dimensions) of the array. Without the comma, each is presumed to be a one-dimensional array; therefore, As Double(,) in the header indicates that the function will return a two-dimensional array. Notice also the arguments used in the UBound functions. When the array has more than one subscript, you can specify the subscript number for which you want the boundary. UBound(A, 1) tells the function to return the upper bound of the first subscript; and UBound(A, 2) tells the function to return the upper bound of the second subscript. When the optional second parameter (the subscript number) is omitted, the first subscript is the default.

Game Boards

Two-dimensional arrays can also be used to represent boards used in games that call for the placement of different markers or stones on the board. For example, in a tic-tac-toe game, two players will mark alternately on a 3 × 3 board with X's and O's. The first player who can place three of the same marks in a straight line (vertically, horizontally, or diagonally) wins the game. You can use a two-dimensional variable such as Status to keep track of the marks that the players place on the board while your program draws the marks on the screen. For example, when the first player places an X mark on position (1,1), you can code the following:

```
Status(1, 1) = 1
```

You can use any nonzero value to represent one side and another value—for example, -1—to represent the other side. A zero value in a position will indicate that the position is not yet marked (occupied) and is available; otherwise, an attempt to mark the position will be considered illegitimate. Each time a player marks a position, your program will need to determine whether your program can declare the winner.

In addition to keeping track of the status internally, you will also need to consider how the game should be represented externally; that is, what will be used to represent the board and the marks onscreen. One way is to actually draw the X and O marks on a picture box, which can be used to represent the board. You should be able to do this after you study Appendix B, "Graphics,

Animation, Drag and Drop." Another way, which uses more computer resources, is to use nine labels to represent the nine positions on the board. As illustrated previously, you can create labels and any controls at runtime; however, in such a case, you will need the capability to handle events for these labels; for example, when the user clicks on a label that is not yet marked, the program needs to draw a mark. You will revisit this programming challenge in Projects 12–25 in Chapter 12. Suffice it to say that the two-dimensional array can be handily used to represent the state of the board.

8.6 Additional Notes on Arrays

The preceding discussion focuses on the practical uses of arrays. This section presents several additional aspects and issues concerning arrays that deserve your attention.

Preserving Data in ReDim

Each time you use the ReDim statement to change the size of an array, the previous content of all elements will be reinitialized (to 0 for numeric variables and to zero-length string for string variables). You can preserve their previous contents, however, by using the keyword Preserve in the ReDim statement. For example, assume a class-level array variable Students() has been previously populated with text strings, and you would like to expand its size by doubling its upper bound without losing its previous contents. You should be able to accomplish this by the following statement:

```
ReDim Preserve Students(2 * UBound(Students))
```

Displaying Array Contents in the List Box or Combo Box

It is easy to display the content of a one-dimensional array in a list box or combo box. All you have to do is to set the control's *DataSource property* to the array. For example, assume you have a list box named lstX on your form, and a one-dimensional array named X. To display the content of X in lstX, you can code:

```
lstX.DataSource = X
```

Note that when the content of X changes, you will need to execute the same statement to update the list box. Assigning a control's DataSource property with an object is referred to as to bind the data to the control. More about data binding will be discussed in Chapter 9, "Database and ADO.NET."

Releasing an Array: The Erase Statement

You can release the resources used by an array by using the Erase statement. For example, suppose the array variable Employees has been populated with a department's employee names, and you no longer need it. You can use the following statement to release the memory used by the variable.

```
Erase Employees
```

The array will then have nothing. All its previous contents are gone, and it has zero elements.

Array Properties and Methods

NET treats all arrays as objects. As such, they are given built-in properties and methods. For example, each array has the *Length property* that gives the length of the array, and the *Rank property* that gives the number of dimensions of the array. To illustrate, assume X is an array. The following expression will return the number of elements in X:

```
X.Length
```

The CopyTo Method. The CopyTo method allows a convenient way to copy data from an entire array into another. For example, assume X and Y have the same length, and you want to copy the contents of X to Y. You can code the following:

```
X.CopyTo(Y, 0)
```

The second parameter specifies the index of the target array (Y) into which to start copying data. If you specify 1 instead of 0, the copy operation begins with the second element in Y; that is, the first element of X will go into the second element of Y, and the second element of X will go into the third element of Y, and so forth. In such a case, Y will have to have at least one more element than X; otherwise, an error will result.

TIP

Beware of the following statement when both are declared as array variables:

```
Y = X
```

It does not produce any syntax error, but it may not give what you want. The statement copies the pointer of X to Y. After the statement, both X and Y refer to the same array. Whatever changes you make to one of the two variables will be reflected in the other variable. Tricky, huh?

Generic Array Methods. The preceding discussion pertains to properties and method for specific arrays. In addition to these interfaces, the *Array object* also has many generic methods that can operate on any arrays. The following lists a few selected methods of particular interest.

The Clear Method. The Clear method allows you to reinitialize a portion of an array, and has the following syntax:

```
Array.Clear(Name, BeginningIndex, Length)
```

The following statement will reinitialize 10 elements in the array named A beginning from the second element:

```
Array.Clear(A, 1, 10)
```

Notice that in the statement the object is Array and not A, the array variable. Although the statement A.Clear(A, 1, 10) will still work correctly, the code can appear confusing.

The Sort Method. The Sort method sorts an array in order. For example, assume that you have an array, X. You can sort it by the following statement:

```
Array.Sort(X)
```

You can even specify the range to sort. For example, the following statement will sort five elements in X starting from the second position.

```
Array.Sort(X, 1, 5)
```

The Reverse Method. The Reverse method will reverse the order of the elements in an array. For example, assume X has {1, 2, 3} as its contents. The following statement will result in X containing {3, 2, 1}

```
Array.Reverse(X)
```

The Binary Search Method. If you have a sorted array, the Binary Search method can be used to search the array more efficiently as explained previously. Assume X is an Integer array. The following expression will return the position in which 5 is found. If the search value is not found, the method returns a negative value.

```
P = Array.BinarySearch(X, 5)
```

Use the "array class" keyword to search the Index tab of the Help file; then click All Members under the found list to browse for all available array properties and methods for their uses. In most cases, each method can perform different tasks depending on the parameters specified.

Appropriate Use of Arrays

As you can see from the preceding examples, arrays can be useful and powerful. They are often used in conjunction with loops. For this reason, arrays tend to be overused by the beginner when the program calls for the use of loops. As an illustration, suppose you would like to read a file and list its content. Simple? Assume the StreamReader named DataFile has been associated with the physical file. After learning about arrays, a beginner would tend to code as follows:

```
Dim DataRec(5000) As String
Dim Counter As Integer
Dim I as Integer
Do Until DataFile.Peek() = -1
    DataRec(Counter) = DataFile.ReadLIne()
    Counter = Counter + 1
Loop
For I = 1 To Counter
    1stRecords.Items.Add(DataRec(I))
Next I
```

?

That is, the entire file is read in and kept in the memory before each record is added to the list box 1stRecords for display. If the data in a file can be handled in one single pass (reading from the beginning through the end), there is actually no need to use an array.

The same goal can indeed be accomplished with the following code:

```
Dim DataRec As string
Do Until DataFile.Peek() = -1
    DataRec = DataFile.ReadLine
    1stRecords.Items.Add(DataRec)
Loop
```

Arrays use much more memory than scalar variables. When there is no need to use arrays, they should be avoided. In general, you will need an array if the group of data will need to be worked on back and forth (usually more than one time) or randomly such that the order cannot be predicted. Hopefully, the examples in this chapter have shown you the proper context where arrays are called for.

8.7 An Application Example

This chapter concludes with an application example that requires the accumulation of total sales by product. The project shows how arrays can be used to solve a practical business problem.

The "Sales by Product" Project

Your company sells 25 different products. The sales transactions are kept in a text file. Each record contains a field representing the product (product code) and another field for the sales amount. These records are kept in ascending order by the transaction date, not by the product code. You are interested in obtaining the total sales by product. The results should be displayed in a list box.

Algorithm

How can the sales be accumulated by product when the file is not sorted in the order of product code? There are several ways, each with variations in details. This example will follow an approach that uses two arrays: one to keep track of the product codes already encountered, and the other to accumulate total sales for the corresponding products. This can be depicted as follows:

Product Codes	D	A	C	. . .	K
Sales by Product	Sales for D	Sales for A	Sales for C	. . .	Sales for K

How do you keep track of product codes? As each record is read, its product code is compared with the ones already in the product code array. The number of codes already in the array can be tracked by a counter variable; for example, ProductCount. If the current product code is not found, the current (new) product code should be placed in the position pointed by ProductCount and ProductCount should then be increased by 1. (Recall that the first element of the array is indexed as zero.) This approach is similar to the first method of generating a random lottery number discussed previously in this chapter.

How do you accumulate the sales for the corresponding product? The preceding search for the product code should give the position of the product code in the array. Call the position ProductPos. This value can then be used as the subscript for the array SalesByProduct to add the current sales; that is, the total sales by product can be accumulated with the following statement:

```
'Increase the array element by Sales Amount
SalesByProduct(ProductPos) += Sales
```

Coding the Project

Suppose the routine to perform the computation is invoked when the user clicks the btnCompute button. This routine should do the following:

1. Read the sales records.
2. Build the product code array, and accumulate the total sales by product.
3. Display the results in a list box.

Because the accumulation of sales hinges on the successful creation of the product code array, consider this aspect in more detail. To show how this array can be built, assume the first few records in the file are those shown in the following table. For simplicity, pay attention only to product code.

Record No.	Product Code	Sales Amount (Not Shown)
1	D	
2	A	
3	D	
4	C	

When the first record is read, the product code array is empty and the product count is zero. The current product code in record one (that is, D) will be compared with all elements in the product code array, which is still empty; therefore, D is not found. You will place D in the product code array at the position pointed by the product count and then increase the product count by 1. The state in the memory can be represented as in the following table.

Record No.	Product Code	Content of Product Codes (Array)	Product Count
1 (before processing)	D	(Empty)	0
1 (after processing)	D	D	1

After the second record is read and before it is processed, the memory state will be the same as after processing the first record, except for the current product code from the record, which is now A. The same steps just outlined will be repeated. Again, A is not found in the array, so the product code A is added to the array, and the product count is increased by 1. The states of memory should be as shown in the following table.

Record No.	Product Code	Content of Product Codes (Array)	Product Count
1 (before processing)	D	(Empty)	0
1 (after processing)	D	D	1
2 (after processing)	A	D, A	2

When the third record is read, the current product code will be D, which is already in the array. There will be no change to the product codes array. The product code position will be identified and used to accumulate the sales amount.

Because the product codes can appear in any order, they will be searched sequentially. The search routine appears as follows:

```
For I = 0 To ProductCount - 1
    If ProductCode = ProductCodes(I) Then
        ' A match is found, set the product position and
        ' terminate the loop
        ProductPos = I
        Exit For
    End If
Next I
```

If the product code is not found, you will need to add it to the array. As shown in the lottery number example in Section 8.2, you will need an indicator to determine whether the product code is in the array. Here, you will use the value of ProductPos for this purpose.

How? As shown in the preceding code, if the product code is found, ProductPos will be set to its position in the array. The position has to be in the range of 0 to ProductCount - 1. If you set ProductPos to ProductCount before the loop, you can check whether this value has changed. If it has not changed, the product code is not found and you can add the current product code to the array. The code can appear as follows:

```
ProductPos = ProductCount
For I = 0 To ProductCount - 1
    If ProductCode = ProductCodes(I) Then
        ' Product code is found, get this position and
        ' exit the loop
        ProductPos = I
        Exit For
    End If
Next I
If ProductPos = ProductCount Then
    ' No change in product pos as initially set.
    ' This means the product code is not found
    ' Update count and add the code to array
    ProductCount += 1 'Increase count by 1
    ' and keep the current code in the array
    ProductCodes(ProductPos) = ProductCode
End If
```

The preceding code deals with a product code read from a record. Of course, you will need to open and read the file. Reading records from the file will take another loop, which should be the outer loop of the preceding routine. For simplicity, assume that each transaction in the file has only two fields: product code and sales. Further assume that the two fields in each record are separated by a Tab character (vbTab). The following code should satisfy the project's requirements:

```
Private Sub btnCompute_Click(ByVal sender As System.Object, ByVal
    e As System.EventArgs) Handles btnCompute.Click
    Dim I As Integer
    Dim SalesFile As IO.StreamReader
    Dim ProductPos As Integer
```

```
            Dim ProductCount As Integer
            Dim CodeNSales As String
            Dim CNS() As String
            Dim ProductCode As String
            Dim Sales As Double
            Dim ProductCodes(24) As String
            Dim SalesByProduct(24) As Double
            ' Step 1: Find the file in the same (BIN) folder
            ' as this program
            SalesFile = New IO.StreamReader("Sales.txt")
            ' Step 2: read and accumulate sales by product
            Do Until SalesFile.Peek() = -1
                CodeNSales = SalesFile.ReadLine()
                'Parse the record into two fields
                CNS = Split(CodeNSales, vbTab)
                ProductCode = CNS(0) 'The first field is product code
                Sales = CDbl(CNS(1)) 'The second field is sales
                ' Search for the product code in Product codes array
                ' Assume this product code is not in array;
                ' in that case the product position will be the same
                ' as the current count
                ProductPos = ProductCount
                For I = 0 To ProductCount - 1
                    If ProductCode = ProductCodes(I) Then
                        ' Product code is found, get this position
                        ' and exit the loop
                        ProductPos = I
                        Exit For
                    End If
                Next I
                If ProductPos = ProductCount Then
                    ' No change in product pos as initially set;
                    ' this means the product code is not found
                    ' Update count and add the code to array
                    ProductCount += 1 'Increase count by 1
                    ' and keep the current code in the array
                    ProductCodes(ProductPos) = ProductCode
                End If
                ' Add current sales to corresponding total
                SalesByProduct(ProductPos) += Sales
            Loop
            ' Step 3: Show results in the list box
            For I = 0 To ProductCount - 1
                lstSales.Items.Add(ProductCodes(I) & vbTab & _
                    SalesByProduct(I))
            Next I
        End Sub
```

The procedure begins with associating the sales file with the StreamReader, SalesFile; then, in the outer loop, the StreamReader reads a line into the variable, CodeNSales, which is parsed into an array CNS with the delimiter, vbTab. The first element is assigned to ProductCode; the second element is converted to Sales. (Of course, you can use the old trick of using the InStr function to find the position for vbTab in CodeNSales and then obtain the product code and sales. Here you use a different approach with an interest to show the use of the Split function.) Next comes the routine to search for the product code and set the value for the product position, including handling the addition of a new product code; then the statement:

```
            SalesByProduct(ProductPos) += Sales
```

adds the current sales to the total sales at the position ProductPos. If the current product code is D (refer to the illustration at the beginning of this example), ProductPos should have a value of 0. Thus, the statement will in effect appear as follows:

```
            SalesByProduct(0) + = Sales
```

Consequently, the current sales will be added to the first element, which corresponds to the position of Product D, of the array SalesByProduct. In sum, this statement tells the computer to add current sales to the total sales of the current product code.

Finally, step 3 in the code uses a For loop to populate the list box with the accumulated sales by product using the Items.Add method. If the Sorted property of the list box is set to True, the list box will show the sales in ascending order by the product code.

As stated at the beginning of this example, other algorithms can be used to solve the same problem. For example, you can sort the file by product code first; then, the accumulation of sales by product basically involves going through the sorted data arrays in sequential order, and adding the sales with the same product code together. The implementation of this algorithm is left to you.

Summary

- You can declare a one-dimensional array variable with a Dim statement. The variable should be followed by a pair of parentheses. If an expression is placed inside the pair of parentheses, it must be evaluated to an integer. The value inside the parentheses gives the upper bound of the array.

- All array indices begin with zero.

- An element of an array can be referenced by an integer expression in the pair of parentheses following the variable.

- The scope of an array is determined by exactly the same rules as the scalar variable.

- The lifetime of an array is determined by exactly the same rules as the scalar variable.

- An array's length can be changed by the use of the ReDim statement.

- An array of values can be constructed by enclosing the elements with a pair of braces. Commas must be inserted between elements.

- When a procedure expects an array parameter, the parameter name must be followed by a pair of parentheses. If the parameter is expected to be two dimensional, the pair of parentheses should also enclose a comma.

- The UBound function gives the upper bound of the array specified in the parameter.

- Arrays have many uses. This chapter gives examples that show the following:
  - Simplified selection
  - Table lookup
  - Tracking random occurrence
  - Simulation
  - Random sampling without replacement

- Several selected sorting algorithms were discussed to acquaint you with some sample methods to solve programming problems.

- The sequential search and binary search methods were also discussed. The binary search method is an efficient algorithm to search a long list of ordered items.

- The collection object can be used to collect a list of related items. It can be used to handle a group of controls (or other objects). The text shows how it can be used to handle a group of text boxes more conveniently and flexibly.

- Two-dimensional arrays can be used to handle tables, matrices, and game boards.

- To preserve the contents of an array while it is being re-dimensioned (with the ReDim statement), use the Preserve keyword. To release the content of an array so that it contains nothing, use the Erase statement.

- Arrays are treated as objects. As such, they have inherent properties and methods. The Rank and Length properties as well as the CopyTo, Clear, Sort, Reverse, and BinarySearch methods were discussed.

- Although arrays have many uses, beginners should be aware that not all problems call for the use of arrays. Arrays use more memory than scalar variables. Be sure that you use an array only when its use is called for.

Explore and Discover

8-1. Relative Position of a Named Constant for Use. Try each of the following pairs of statements separately in the general declaration section in a new form; then run the project:

```
1.    Const HUNDRED As Integer = 100
      Dim A(HUNDRED) As Integer
2.    Dim A(HUNDRED) As Integer
      Const HUNDRED As Integer = 100
```

Does the computer accept both? (Yes. Also, use the UBound function to check the upper bound of A for both.) What do you infer as the rule concerning the use of a named constant in the declaration of an array?

8-2. Use of a Variable for Array Declaration. Place the following code in the Form Click event:

```
Dim N as Integer
N = 10
Dim A(N) As Integer
Console.WriteLine(LBound(A) & " " & UBound(A))
```

Run the project and then click the form. What result do you see? As long as the value of a variable to define the size of an array is known before the Dim statement, the statement is executed properly.

8-3. Static Arrays. Can you declare a static array in a procedure? If so, how is it different? You can try the following code to find out.

```
Private Sub btnTest_Click(ByVal sender As System.Object, ByVal e
   As System.EventArgs) Handles btnTest.Click
   Dim I As Integer
   Dim A(5) As Integer
   Static B(5) As Integer
   For I = 0 To 5
       A(I) += + 1
       B(I) +=  + 1
   Next I
   Console.Write("A: ")
   For I = 0 To 5
       Console.Write(A(I))
   Next I
   Console.WriteLine()
   Console.Write("B: ")
   For I = 0 To 5
       Console.Write(B(I))
   Next I
   Console.WriteLine()
End Sub
```

Run the project, and click the btnTest button several times. Do you see any differences between the values of elements in arrays A and in B?

8-4.   **Use of ReDim.** Create a new project. Type the following code in the Form Click event procedure:

```
Dim N As Integer
Dim A() As Integer
N = 10
ReDim A(N) As Integer
Console.writeline(LBound(A) & " " & UBound(A))
```

Is any line highlighted for syntax error? The ReDim statement does not allow any redefinition of data type, even if there is no change. Remove As Integer from the ReDim statement. Run the project and then click the form. Is it working properly now?

8-5.   **Use of ReDim.** (continued from exercise 8-4). Comment out the Dim A statement from the event procedure in exercise 8-4. Is any line highlighted for syntax error? The variable in a ReDim statement must be declared in a Dim statement first.

8-6.   **Using Functions to Declare Subscript Range.** Place the following code in the Form Click event.

```
Dim A(100) As Integer
Dim B() As Long
ReDim B(UBound(A))
sole.WriteLine(UBound(B))
```

Run the project and then click the form. What do you see in the immediate window? What do you learn from this exercise? The range of an array subscript in a ReDim statement can be any expression as long as it can be resolved to an integer.

8-7.   **Content of an Array After ReDim.** Draw a button on a new form. Name it **btnReDim** and set its Text property to **Re Dim**; then enter the following code:

```
Dim A() As Integer
Private Sub Form1_Click(ByVal sender As System.Object, ByVal e As
  System.EventArgs) Handles MyBase.Click
    Dim I As Integer
    ReDim A(10)
    For I = 0 To 10
        A(I) = CInt(Rnd * 100)
    Next I
    ShowMe(A)
End Sub
Private Sub btnReDim_Click(ByVal sender As System.Object, ByVal e
  As System.EventArgs) Handles btnReDim.Click
    ReDim A(12)
    ShowMe(A)
End Sub
Sub ShowMe(X() As Integer)
    Dim I As Integer
    For I = 0 To UBound(X)
        Console.Write(X(I) & " ")
    Next I
    Console.WriteLine()
End Sub
```

Run the project, and click the form. What numbers do you see in the immediate window? Now click the ReDim button. What numbers do you see in the immediate window?

8-8. **Preserving Content of an Array After ReDim.** Change the btnReDim Click event procedure in exercise 8-7 as shown in the following code. Add the Preserve key word to the ReDim statement, and run the project again. Click the form. What numbers do you see? Click the Re Dim button. What numbers do you see? What difference does the keyword Preserve make?

```
Private Sub btnReDim_Click(ByVal sender As System.Object, ByVal e
    As System.EventArgs) Handles btnReDim.Click
    ReDim Preserve A(12)
    ShowMe(A)
End Sub
```

8-9. **Changing the Number of Subscripts and the Preserve Keyword.** Change the event procedure in exercise 8-8 to the following:

```
Private Sub btnReDim_Click(ByVal sender As System.Object, ByVal e
    As System.EventArgs) Handles btnReDim.Click
    ReDim Preserve A(4, 4)
End Sub
```

What do you see? The variable A as initially declared is expected to be a one-dimensional array, but the ReDim statement now is trying to change its rank, which is not allowed. To make this statement work, you need to change the declaration for A to:

```
Dim A(,) As Integer
```

(Notice the comma inside the pair of parentheses.) This will cause errors in all other procedures in which A was coded as a one-dimensional array. The following exercise explores the use of two-dimensional arrays.

8-10. **ReDim and Preserve with a Multidimensional Array.** Draw a button on a new form. Name it **btnReDim** and then set its Text property to **Re Dim**. Enter the following code:

```
Dim A(,) As Integer 'Note the presence of a  comma
Private Sub Form1_Click(ByVal sender As System.Object,  ByVal e As
    System.EventArgs) Handles MyBase.Click
    ReDim A(10, 10)
End Sub
Private Sub btnReDim_Click(ByVal sender As System.Object, ByVal e
    As System.EventArgs) Handles btnReDim.Click
    ReDim A( 4, 10)
End Sub
```

Run the project. Click the form and then click the Re Dim button. Did you get an error message? Now change the ReDim statement in the btnReDim Click event procedure to the following:

```
ReDim Preserve A(4, 10)
```

Run the project. Click the form and then click the Re Dim button. Again, did you get an error message? Now change this ReDim statement to:

```
ReDim Preserve A(10, 4)
```

Repeat the experiment: Run the project, click the form, and click the Re Dim button. Did you experience any problems this time? You can change the second (last) subscript, but not the first (others) in a ReDim statement with the Preserve keyword.

8-11.   **Returning an Array from a Function.** Can a function return an array? Yes. The following function will return a sequence of 1, 2, 3, . . . N in an array.

```
Function Sequence(ByVal N As Integer) As Integer()
    Dim A() As Integer
    Dim I As Integer
    ReDim A(N)
    For I = 0 To UBound(A)
        A(I) = I
    Next I
    Return(A)
End Function
```

Note how the function is declared. Note also the last line within the procedure. The entire array A is returned with the Return statement.

To test the function, enter the preceding code in the code window. Also enter the following in Form Click event procedure.

```
Dim B() As Integer
Dim I As Integer
B = Sequence(5) 'Generate a sequence of 1, 2, ...5
For I = 0 To UBound(B)
    Console.WriteLine(B(I))
Next I
```

Note how B is declared and assigned. Run the project, and click the form. What do you see?

8-12.   **What Do You Really Get?** Place the following code in the Form click procedure. Run the project, click the form, and examine the results. Do you see anything puzzling? When one array is assigned another array, its pointer is replaced by that of the other array. The two arrays in effect are pointing to the same area and thus are the same.

```
Dim X() As Integer
Dim Y() As Integer
Dim I As Integer
Y = New Integer() {1, 2, 3, 4, 5}
X = Y
X(2) = 1000
For I = 0 To 4
    Console.Write(X(I) & " ")
Next I
Console.WriteLine()
For I = 0 To 4
    Console.Write(Y(I) & " ")
Next I
Console.WriteLine()
```

8-13.   **Another Way to Copy.** In the text, elements in one array can be copied to another, using the CopyTo method. You can also use the Copy method. Change the assignment statement in exercise 8-12 as follows. Run the program, click the form, and examine the results. Are they different from those in exercise 8-12?

```
'X = Y 'Comment out  this statement
Dim X(UBound(Y))
Array.Copy(Y, X, 5) 'This is the way to copy
```

8-14.   Why Add? Enter the following code in the Form Click event:

```
Dim MyLabel As New Label()
With MyLabel
    .Location = New Point(10, 20)
    .Size = New Size(90, 25)
    .Text = "This is my label"
End With
```

Run the project and then click the form. Do you see the label? Now add the following statement at the end:

```
Me.Controls.Add(MyLabel)
```

Run the project, and click the form again. This time, do you see the label? A control must be added to the form's Controls collection before it can appear in the form.

8-15.   Rank of an Array. Enter the following code:

```
Dim A() As Integer ={1,3,5,7}
```

Do you see any hint of error by the compiler? Everything should be fine. Now, change A() to A(,). What do you see? The compiler is expecting a two-dimensional array, but the pair of braces initializes a one-dimensional array.

8-16.   Rank of an Array. (continued from exercise 8-15) Enter the following code:

```
Dim A(,) As Integer ={{1,3},{5,7}}
```

Do you see any hint of error? To construct a higher rank array, use inner braces. The innermost pair of braces contains the values for the rightmost dimension. Verify the assertion with the following routine:

```
Dim I, J As Integer
For I = 0 To 1
    For J = 0 To 1
        Console.Write(A(I, J))
    Next J
    Console.WriteLine()
Next I
```

Exercises

8-17.   Random Roll Calls with Repetition. Create a text file with a class roll of 15 names, one line each. Use Notepad, and save the result. Draw a button on a new form. Name the button **btnCall** and set its Text property to **Call**. Develop the code to perform the following:

1.   As soon as the program starts, populate an array named Students with the names in the file.
2.   When the user clicks the Call button, a student's name drawn randomly from the array will be displayed with the MsgBox. The name of each student can be repeated.

8-18.   Random Roll Calls Without Repetition. Modify the program in exercise 8-17 so that the following can be handled properly:

1.   The number of students in the file may change, and the array Students will accommodate a huge class of 400 students.

2. When the user clicks the Call button, a student's name drawn randomly from the array will be displayed with the MsgBox. The name of each student cannot be repeated.

(*Hint:* This is a sampling-without-replacement problem.)

8-19.   Computing the Value of a Polynomial Function. Write a function to compute the value of a polynomial function of any degree. The header should appear as follows:

```
Function Polynomial(A() As Double, X As Double) as Double
```

where A() is an array containing the coefficients of the polynomial function and X is the value of the variable in the polynomial function.

For example, given the following function:
$$f(x) = 3 x^4 + 10 x^3 - 12 x^2 + 5 x - 20$$

the array parameter A should contain 3, 10, -12, 5, and -20.

The function should return the value of the formula given any value of x. Test the result using 1 and 2 individually as the value of x.

8-20.   Computing Average, Max, and Min. Draw two buttons on a new form. Name them **btnPopulate** and **btnCompute**. Give each its proper text. Provide the code to ensure that the following occurs:

1. When the Populate button is clicked, the array Scores is populated with random integers ranging from 65 to 100. The array should have 60 elements.
2. When the Compute button is clicked, the average, high, and low scores are computed and displayed in a message box.

8-21.   Finding the Two Largest Numbers. Modify exercise 8-20 so that when the Compute button is clicked, the two highest scores are displayed in a message box.

8-22.   Finding the n (n <= 5) Largest Numbers. Modify the program in exercise 8-21 so that when the Compute button is clicked, the n highest scores are displayed in a message box. The number n is specified by the user in a text box named txtNumber; add this control to the form. (*Hint:* Use another array and—call it Highest—to keep track of the n highest scores. Refer to the insertion sort algorithm for hints to populate this array, treating this array as the sorted output. Note, however, that the highest value should be placed at the first position.)

8-23.   Which Checks Are Still Outstanding? Suppose you have written 100 checks, numbered 1001 through 1100, in a month. When you receive the monthly statement from the bank, you keep the check numbers that have been returned to a file. Design a project that will show you the checks that are still outstanding after your program reads through the checks returned file.

8-24.   Who Has Not Yet Checked In? In an exclusive club meeting, all 200 members are all expected to attend. As each member checks in, the member reports their membership number (501 to 700). Assume the check-in procedure is computerized. The user is to enter a membership number and then click the Check In button. At any time, you can request the list of members (membership numbers) who are still outstanding. The outstanding list should be populated in a list box. Note that a member is not allowed to check in twice. (Your program should detect this error.)

8-25.   **Counting Frequency of Random Numbers Ranging from 0 to 99.** Modify the frequency-counting example in the subsection "Tracking Random Occurrences" of section 8.2 so that the random numbers involved are 0 through 99, instead of 0 through 9. Display the results in a list box.

8-26.   **How Many Times Did Each Patient Visit the Clinic Last Year?** A clinic maintains a file recording all patient visits. The file is arranged in ascending order by date (first field of each record). Other fields in each record include the patient number (second field) and the diagnosis code. The physician would like to know how many times each patient visited the clinic last year. The patient number ranges from 20,001 to 25,000.

Develop a project that can provide this information. Display the results in a list box. Each line in the list box will give the patient number and the number of times the patient visited the clinic. (*Note:* For simplicity, instead of reading data from a file, use random numbers in the range of 20,001 and 25,000 to represent the patient numbers. Assume the file contains 40,000 patient visit records.)

8-27.   **Searching for a Number in an Array and Returning the Position.** Draw a text box and a button on a new form. Name the text box **txtNumber** and the button **btnSearch**. Clear the Text property of the text box. Set the button's Text property to **Search**; then provide the code to accomplish the following:

1. When the project starts, populate an array (named EmployeeNos) of 10,000 elements with random numbers ranging from 10,000 to 50,000. Each number in the array should be unique.
2. Write a function to search for a number in an array. It should return the position of the array in which the number is found; otherwise, it should return a value of –1. The header of the function should appear as follows:

```
Function FindPos(Numbers() As Integer, SearchKey As Integer)
    As Integer
```

3. When the user clicks the button, the computer searches for the number entered in the text box in the array by using the function developed in number 2, and displays a message similar to the following if the number is found:

```
Employee no. 10538 is found in position 92 of the array.
```

If the number is not found, the message should appear as follows:

```
Employee no. 30348 is not found in the array.
```

8-28.   **Lookup: Your Grade Given a Score.** Suppose a teacher has the following grading system:

Score Range	Grade
88 and over	A
75–87	B
60–74	C
Below 60	D

Instead of using the Select Case structure, you would rather use two arrays to handle this problem. Develop a project that will display the grade in a message box when the user enters a score in a text box named **txtScore** and clicks a button named **btnGrade**. (*Hint:* You need to keep only the lower score of each grade to decide the grade.)

8-29. **Probability of at Least Two Persons with the Same Birthday in a Gathering with 34 People.** What is the probability that in a group of 34 people, at least two people will have the same birthday? Develop a project to simulate (approximate) this probability. You can set up an array with 365 elements, each representing a day in the year. Generate 34 random days in the year (with a value range from 1 to 365) and then use the array to keep track of how many birthdays fall in each day. If any day (element in the array) has more than 1 count, you have found at least one incident of the same birthday in this experiment.

If you do this experiment 1,000 times, and count the number of times you find the occurrence of the same birthday, you can approximate the probability by dividing the count by 1,000.

8-30. **Probability of at Least n Persons with the Same Birthday in a Gathering of p People.** Modify the program in exercise 8-29 so that the number of people having the same birthday and the number of people in a party can be any number specified by the user.

8-31. **Probability of Exactly n (n = 2 to p) Persons with the Same Birthday in a Gathering of p People.** Consider the experiment in exercise 8-30. How many times do 2, 3, 4, . . . p people have the same birthdays? (*Hint:* Use another array to count the frequency of the counts that are greater than 1.)

8-32. **Chances of Winning.** Assuming that as a blackjack player, you have 49% probability of winning a hand. Develop a project to allow yourself to approximate the probability of winning exactly 30, 31, 32, . . . or more hands out of 50. Use the Monte Carlo simulation method illustrated in the "Simulation" subsection of 8.2. (The results should be returned as an array.)

8-33. **Good Product Units from a Sequential Process.** Suppose a product takes two processes to complete. A batch of raw materials is placed at the beginning of the first process. At the end, units are inspected for quality. Good units are then placed into the second process. At the end, another inspection is performed. Assuming the probabilities of obtaining good units are 97% and 98% for processes 1 and 2, respectively, develop a project to compute the probability of obtaining at least g (such as 1,000) good units when r (such as 1,100) units of raw materials are placed in production at the beginning of process 1. (Show separate probability for each good unit count; such as 1000, 1001, . . . and so on.)

8-34. **Parse a Text String into Words.** Assume that a text string contains many words, all separated by blank spaces. There can be one or more spaces between two words. Write a Function procedure that will parse the string and extract all words in the string and then return them in an array. The text string will be passed to this function as a parameter. See exercise 8-11 for a function returning an array. (*Note:* There is a function, Split, that can perform this requirement. Do not use that function. Create one from scratch for yourself.)

8-35. **List All Prime Numbers up to 60,000.** Write a Sub procedure that will list all the prime numbers from 1 to 60,000. A prime number is one that can be evenly divided only by 1 or itself. The first smallest prime numbers are 1, 2, 3, 5, and 7. (*Hint:* Identify these numbers from the smallest. Use an array to store all the identified prime numbers. Test whether a number is a prime number by checking the remainder of this number divided by all the identified prime numbers. If a number cannot be evenly divided by any prime numbers that are less than the square root of this number, this number is a prime number.)

Test your program as follows:

1. Draw a button and a list box on a new form.
2. When the user clicks the button, the event procedure should call your prime number procedure to obtain the results. Populate the results in the list box mentioned in step 1.

8-36. **The Sequence Function.** Write a function that will return an integer array representing the specified sequence of numbers. The function should allow the following different kinds of specifications (all parameters are of the integer type):

Specification	Returns
Sequence(n)	{1, 2, 3, . . . N}
Sequence(3, 2, 4)	{3, 5, 7, 9}

(Hint: Modify exercise 8-11. Use optional parameters or overload the function.)

8-37. **Load Text Boxes, Obtain Cash Flow, and Compute the Net Present Value of an Investment Project.** Develop a project to calculate the net present value of an investment project. When your program starts, the form has two text boxes with proper labels and one button. The text boxes expect the user to enter the required rate of return for the project and the expected life of the project. As soon as the user finishes entering the expected life by pressing the Enter key, your program should show additional text boxes with proper labels for the user to enter the cash inflow for each period of the expected life. Note the total number of text boxes should be one more than the number of periods so that the user can also enter the amount of initial investment. When the user clicks the Compute button, your program computes and displays the net present value in a label, which should appear like a text box.

8-38. **Computing the Internal Rate of Return for a Project.** For a typical simple project that has a negative initial cash flow (investment) followed by a series of positive cash flows, there is a rate that makes the net present value of the project equal to zero. This rate is referred to as the internal rate of return. You are to design a project that will compute the internal rate of return for a project based on the same setting as given in exercise 8-37. (Change the label "Required rate of return" to "Initial guess"; or delete this label and the related text box.)

8-39. **Revisiting the Tuition Computation Problem.** Consider the tuition computation problem presented in Chapter 5 again. Design a project to carry out the "computation" using an array to hold the tuition data. The interface should appear the same as in the second approach.

8-40. **Weight Lookup Program Continued.** The following table shows the normal weight for women. Modify the weight lookup program presented in Section 8.2 so that you can also inquire about women's normal weight, given the height. You will need to add two radio buttons for the user to indicate the gender of the person of interest. (*Hint:* This can be handled several ways. One way is to use two tables to store the weights: one for men and another for women. The table to look up the weight will then depend on which of the radio buttons for gender is clicked.)

Height	Small Frame	Medium Frame	Large Frame
4'10"	92–98	96–101	104–119
4'11"	94–101	98–110	106–122
5'	96–104	101–113	109–125

Height	Small Frame	Medium Frame	Large Frame
5'1"	99–107	104–116	112–128
5'2"	102–110	107–119	115–131
5'3"	105–113	110–122	118–134
5'4"	108–116	113–126	121–138
5'5"	111–119	116–130	125–142
5'6"	114–123	120–135	129–146
5'7"	118–127	124–139	133–150
5'8"	122–131	128–143	137–154
5'9"	126–135	132–147	141–158
5'10"	130–140	136–151	145–163
5'11"	134–144	140–155	149–168
6'	138–148	144–159	153–173

8-41.   **Binary Search for a Match.** It is well known that when searching a sorted array, the binary search algorithm is much more efficient than the sequential search. Write a binary search function with the following header:

```
Function BinarySearch(X() As Long, SK As Long) as Integer
```

where X() is a sorted array and SK is the value (search key) to search for.

The function will return the position of the array at which SK is found. If SK is not found in the array, the function will return a value of –1. Compare your results with the BinarySearch method of the Array object.

8-42.   **A Possible Improvement on the Bubble Sort.** A suggested method to improve the performance of the bubble sort is to add a counter in the inner loop. The counter will count the number of swaps. If there is no swap after the loop is complete, the counter will be zero. This will be an indication that all the elements in the array are already in order; therefore, the process can be terminated immediately. The counter adds overhead to the sorting process, but allows the algorithm to perform faster when the array to be sorted is already pretty much in order. Modify the code in the text to implement this improvement.

8-43.   **Simple Selection Sort.** Write a Sub procedure to perform the simple selection sort as described in Section 8.3.

8-44.   **Reverse Simple Selection Sort.** The simple selection sort as described in exercise 8-43 has an alternative. Instead of selecting the largest element first, you can start with selecting the smallest element first and placing it in the first position of the array. You can then proceed to find the second, third, ... and nth smallest elements in the same manner. Modify the program presented in exercise 8-43 to implement this alternative sorting algorithm for simple selection.

8-45.   **Binary Insertion Sort.** Write a Sub procedure to perform the binary insertion sort as described in Section 8.3.

8-46.   **Improved Shell Sort.** Empirical studies have found that Shell sort is most efficient when the intervals of sort are computed as follows:

```
Interval 1 = 1
Interval k + 1 = 3 x Interval k + 1
And stops when Interval k + 2 > Number of elements to be sorted
```

That is, the intervals can be computed as follows:

K Value	Interval
1	1
2	3 x 1 + 1 = 4
3	3 x 4 + 1 =13
4	3 x 13 + 1 = 40
5	3 x 40 + 1 =121
6	3 x 121 + 1 = 364

An array with 300 elements should be sorted with the sort intervals set to 40, 13, 4, and 1 according to this table because two steps below it, the interval 364 is greater than the number of elements 300. Modify the Shell sort routine as presented in Section 8.3 to implement this improvement.

8-47. Reverse Quick Sort. You may have noticed that in the quick sort algorithm, if you use the last element in the array instead of the first element as the pivotal element, the comparisons should start forward first until a swap is called for; then followed by backward comparisons. The backward/forward comparison sequence in search for the proper position for the pivotal element as presented in Section 8.3 is changed to a forward/backward sequence. Just for the fun of it, revise the quick sort procedure to implement this modification.

Projects

8-48. Demand During Lead Time with Random Lead Time Days and Random Daily Demand. The demand for a product during a lead time period (between the day you place a purchase order and the day you actually receive the goods) is determined by two factors: the lead time in days, and the demand in each of these days. The lead time period (in days) is subject to a random distribution, as is the demand each day during this period. Suppose the lead time period has a probability distribution as follows:

Lead Time (No. of Days)	Probability	Cumulative Probability
13	.3	.3
14	.5	.8
15	.2	1.0

Also assume the daily demand for the product is subject to the following probability distribution:

Daily Demand in Units	Probability	Cumulative Probability
30	.2	.2
31	.6	.8
32	.2	1.0

If you inspect the two tables, you should see that the total demand during each lead time period can vary from 390 (13 x 30) to 480 (15 x 32), subject to a joint probability distribution. Develop a project to simulate (approximate) the probability of demand during lead time for this company. Your output should appear as follows:

Demand During a Lead Time Period	Probability
390	0
391	.01
392	.
.	.
.	.
480	0

(*Hint:* Consider the simulation for the actual demand for a day. If you draw a random number, and it turns out to be .5, you can assert that the demand for that day is 31. You draw this conclusion because the number falls in the cumulative probability that includes 31. Similarly, if the random number is .9, you can claim the demand for that day is 32. To simulate daily demand, you can use two arrays: one holding the cumulative probability, and another holding the daily demand. After you obtain a random number, you can search the cumulative probability array and then identify the position, which is used to obtain the actual daily demand from the daily demand array. If you repeat this simulation for a lead time period and add all the daily demand, you will come up with the demand for a lead time period. But how do you know the days of a lead time period? You use the same simulation method, but a different pair of arrays. Refer to the first table for needed data. If you repeat the simulation for 1,000 lead time periods, you will be able to count the number of times each demand quantity occurs.)

8-49. Finding Connected Groups in a Go Game Board. A Go game board has a dimension of 19 × 19 lines. Two players take turns in placing their stones (black versus white) on the intersections. The objective is to occupy as big a territory as possible. A group of isolated stones of one player is captured if it is completely surrounded by the opponent's stones without empty intersections inside the group.

One aspect of programming the game is to identify the groups of stones that are connected. Two stones of the same side (color) are connected if both are on the same line (vertical or horizontal; that is, on the row or column) and next to each other on the other dimension. For example, the two stones at 9,10 and 9,11 are connected because they are on the same row and are next to each other by column. Many stones placed on the board can be connected to one another vertically and horizontally to form a group.

The Challenge: When your program starts, the user will enter the number of stones to be placed on the board. Use a text box for this purpose. Your program will proceed to simulate where these stones are placed on the board. The next step is the key challenge: to identify the number of connected groups (as described in the preceding paragraph) and the stones belonging to each group. To simplify the problem, assume all stones on the board are of the same color and played by the same player.

Internal Representation: Various schemes can be used to represent the status of the game board internally. For example, an intersection, Board(Row, Col) has a value zero if it is not occupied by either side and has a value of –1 if occupied by the Black side and a value of 1 if occupied by the White side. Because you are assuming only one side is playing, you can use either –1 or 1 to indicate that a stone has been placed at the intersection.

Simulating the Intersection Points Occupied (Played): You can use a pair of random numbers to simulate the intersection point at which the player places the stones. More specifically, if you declared the Board as Board(18, 18), you will need to generate a pair of random number Row and Col, each within the range of 0 to 18. Notice that an intersection may have been occupied already. In that case, another pair of Row and Col must be generated until an empty intersection is found. Refer to the "Sampling Without Replacement" subsection in Section 8.2 for hints to identify whether a number has already been selected.

(*Hint:* Note that a stone may be connected to as many as four other stones, which can in turn be connected to other stones. It would be much easier to use a recursive procedure to identify the group; however, you will need to avoid double counting, which involves including an intersection that has already been included/connected. This will result in an endless connection loop. Use another array with the same dimension as the board to identify the group to which a particular intersection belongs.)

Displaying Results: Use a list box to show the result. One way to show the results is as follows:

Group 1:

1, 1
1, 2
1, 3
2, 1
3, 1

Group 2:

10, 12
11, 12
12, 12

where each pair of numbers represents the coordinate of the intersection. Enjoy your challenge!

9 Database and ADO.NET

All organizations must keep records of their activities, both financial and nonfinancial, to satisfy their own information needs and meet legal requirements. The activities required to create, store, and retrieve these data are recognized as *data management*. There are two general approaches to data management: the file-oriented approach and the database approach. The file-oriented approach focuses on individual application systems' needs. Each application system develops and handles its own files. On the other hand, the database approach takes an enterprise view on the data. When more than one application system uses the same set of data, the set of data will be shared by these applications. The management of data under shared ownership can become very complex and therefore calls for specialized software, which is recognized as the database management system (DBMS).

This chapter presents topics related to using ADO.NET (ActiveX Data Objects) to work with the database.

After completing this chapter, you should be able to:

- Understand the concept of relational database.
- Know how to construct SQL statements.
- Understand the concepts of dataset, data table, and data row.
- Configure the data adapter to work with the database.
- Generate the dataset using the Data menu.
- Use the data adapter in conjunction with the dataset, data table, and data row to maintain the database strictly by code.
- Use the data command without involving the data adapter to perform various database operations.
- Use the connection object to obtain database schema information.
- Create and use the data relation to handle parent-child data tables in a dataset.

9.1 Introduction to Database

A *database* is defined as a collection of stored data that are managed by the database management system (DBMS). There are several conceptual models for the database. One of these models is the relational database model. Under this model, a database is a collection of tables, each consisting of rows and columns. Each row represents a record, and a column represents a *field*, which is the smallest data element that has practical meaning. Examples of fields include the transaction date, Social Security number, and employee name. This model is popular because it's easy to understand. Almost all the current commercial database software packages for personal computers are built under this model. Microsoft Access, SQL Server, FoxPro, Dbase, Btrieve, and Oracle9*i* are all examples of relational database software.

Table Definitions

Two distinct types of activities are required to create a database. Before a database comes into existence, you will need to define tables and fields for the database. For example, if you are designing a payroll database, you will include at least an Employees table to keep data pertaining to all employees, and a Paychecks table to record all paychecks paid to employees. For each table in the database, you will further specify the fields and their respective data types. For example, the Employees table will probably have at least the following fields:

Field Name	Data Type	Length
Employee Number	Long Integer	
Last Name	String	15 characters
First Name	String	15 characters
Middle Initial	String	1 character
Sex	String (M or F)	1 character

After the tables and fields in a database are defined in the table definition phase, the user will be able to store and retrieve data from the tables. In many applications, the VB program is used to serve as the front-end interface, while the database engine is used as the backbone to handle the actual storage and retrieval of the data.

DDL and DML. Perhaps a few technical terms should be defined here. In the preceding discussion, the language that is used to define tables is referred to as the *data definition language (DDL)*. The result of using the language that defines an overall view of the structure of the database is referred to as the *schema* of the database. Some software enables the user to further define the user's own partial views of the database. These definitions are recognized as *subschemata*.

The language that allows the user to manipulate the data is recognized as the *data manipulation language (DML)*. Examples of the types of data manipulation that can be performed include updating, editing, adding, and deleting records.

Indexes, the Primary Key, and the Foreign Key

In many applications, you will need to search the table for needed data. To facilitate the search, you can create indexes to the table. An index allows the computer to find the location of a record given a field value. For example, assume the employee whose employee number is 1001 is the 50th record in the table. If the table has the employee number as one of its indexes, when you specify the employee number 1001 using the index, the computer will be able to identify that the record is located at the 50th position, and retrieve it quickly. An index can be built on one or several fields. For example, an index can be built on the Employee Number field; another index can be built on the combination of the Last Name, First Name, and Middle Initial fields.

Index Uniqueness. When you create an index, you need to indicate whether it should be unique. A *unique index* will not allow a new record with the same index value as an existing one to be added. Some indexes by nature should be unique. For example, in the Employees table, the

Employee Number index should be unique; otherwise, you will encounter difficulty in identifying an employee given an employee number. In the Paychecks table, the Check Number index should be unique, as well. (You won't write two checks with the same check number, will you?) On the other hand, some indexes by nature will never be unique. For example, in the Employees table, if you decide to build an index on Sex, the index will have approximately half of the records with the same field value!

A *primary key* is an index of which each value is *uniquely identified* with a record. By definition, a primary key *must* be a unique index, although not all unique indexes are primary keys. In a way, this distinction is more conceptual than technical. There can be only one primary key in a table. In addition, the primary key of each record must not be missing (recognized as the *entity integrity rule*). You can call a unique index the primary key of a table only if it is identified with the record. Without a value for the primary key, there will be no way to identify the record. The employee number should be the primary key of the Employee table, whereas the check number should be the primary key of the Paychecks table.

The primary key of a table is often also used in another table to establish a relation/reference to the record in that table. For example, there should be an Employee Number field in the Paychecks table to indicate to whom the check is paid. The Employee Number in the Paychecks table can be considered the *foreign key* to the Employees table.

Introduction to the SQL

The SQL (Structured Query Language) is a standard database query language supported by all relational database software. VB provides ways to interact with the database software that will interpret and act on the SQL. A good understanding of the SQL will enable you to code VB programs that can interact with the database software smoothly. The following discussion covers some basics of the SQL that pertain to the MS Jet data engine (for MS Access). Different software can have its own "dialect." If you use different software (server) for your database, you should consult the particular software manual for the specific vocabulary, which can be slightly different from what's presented here.

The Basic Syntax for the Select Statement. The Select statement of the SQL is used to construct a data table (collection of rows) from the database and has the following basic syntax:

```
Select Field1[, field2][, . . .] From Table [Where Criteria]
       [Order by fields to sort];
```

where *field1, field2,. . .* = the list of fields in the table to be included in the results

Table = the name of the table to be queried

Criteria = the criteria to include records; only records satisfying the criteria will be returned

Fields to sort = records included will be sorted by the fields specified here

The statement should conclude with a semicolon (;) although in most cases, its absence will not cause any problem.

Notice that the selection and sort criteria are optional. A very simple SQL statement can appear as follows:

```
Select EmployeeNumber From Employees;
```

The preceding statement will result in a datatable that contains a column of all the employee numbers from the Employees table. Note that the EmployeeNumber field name is one word. MS Access allows a field name to be created with embedded spaces. In such a case, you will need to enclose the name in a pair of brackets to avoid confusing the database engine (server) in interpreting the code. If the field name in the database table is "Employee Number," the preceding SQL code will have to be changed to the following:

```
Select [Employee Number] From Employees;
```

Note, however, that you should avoid creating table or field names with embedded spaces. Most DBMS do not allow names of this structure. The following discussion assumes that field and table names are not created with embedded spaces.

Selecting More Than One Field. To select more than one field, you will list the fields, separated by commas. To select both the Employee Number and Name, you will code the following:

```
Select EmployeeNumber, LastName, FirstName From Employees;
```

Note that commas are used to separate the field names.

Sorting the Returned Table. You may want the previous results sorted by last name and then by first name. You can use the "*Order By*" clause to handle this:

```
Select EmployeeNumber, LastName, FirstName From
    Employees Order by LastName, FirstName;
```

Notice that SQL and VB do not have the same syntax rules. For example, in SQL, if you need to continue to the next line, you do not code any line continuation marker.

You can also specify whether the sort is in ascending or descending order by adding the *Asc* or *Desc* keyword after the sort field in the Order clause. For example, the following code will sort the last name in descending order and first name in ascending order:

```
Select EmployeeNumber, LastName, FirstName From
    Employees Order by LastName Desc, FirstName Asc;
```

Specifying All Fields in the Record. Rather than selecting only a few specific fields, what if you would like to select all fields in the Employees table while sorting the same way as done previously? You can use the wildcard "*" character to indicate all fields in the table:

```
Select * From Employees
    Order by LastName, FirstName;
```

Selecting a Specific Record. What if you want only the record for employee number 1001? You can specify this criterion by using the "Where" clause with the "=" operator:

```
Select * From Employees
    Where EmployeeNumber = 1001;
```

Specifying a Range. Note that the comparison criterion described can also be other "relational" operators, which were presented in Chapter 5, "Decision." For example, if you want all the records for employee numbers in the range of 1,000 and 2,000, you can code the following:

```
Select * From Employees
    Where (EmployeeNumber >= 1000) And (EmployeeNumber <= 2000);
```

Notice the use of the logical operator And. Specifying the criteria for the SQL is similar to specifying the conditions for an If statement in VB. Or and Not are also recognized logical operators in the SQL. Also, the two pairs of parentheses are used to enhance code clarity; they are not required.

Matching a Name. When the query involves a text string, the string should be enclosed in a pair of either single or double quotes. Because it is easier to handle the single quotes than double quotes in VB code, you should use the single quotes. For example, suppose you would like the record for the employee named Charles Smith. The SQL statement should appear as follows:

```
Select * From Employees
    Where (LastName = 'Smith') And (FirstName = 'Charles');
```

Note that the MS Access string comparisons are not case sensitive; that is, the preceding query will produce all records that contain the name "Charles Smith," whether they are uppercased, lowercased, or any combination thereof.

Matching a Partial Text. If your search requires a partial match of a text string such as all last names that begin with "Sm," you should use the Like operator instead of the relational (comparison) operator(s). For example, the following SQL will select all employees with a last name that begins with "Sm," such as Smart, Smiley, and Smith:

```
Select * From Employees
    Where LastName Like 'Sm%';
```

What if you want to limit the records to those last names with only five characters (excluding Smiley in the previous example)? You will still use the Like operator. Instead of using the "%" wildcard specification, however, you can use the "?" character, which represents a positional parameter that does not require a match. You can code the following:

```
Select * From Employees
    Where LastName Like 'Sm???';
```

The three "?"s ensure that only those last names with five characters are selected for comparison; then as long as the first two characters are "Sm," the record is considered to have satisfied the search criterion. (Note again that MS Access string comparisons are not case sensitive.)

The Inner Join and Outer Join. Suppose that in the previous payroll application you would like to retrieve all fields of all checks. In addition, you would like to include the names of employees to whom each check is paid. The Paychecks table should have an Employee Number field to identify the employee being paid; however, it should not have the Employee Name fields because they are already available in the Employees table. The query involves fields that are in two tables: all fields in the Paychecks table, and the Employee Name fields in the Employees table. These records should be matched by the Employee Number in the two tables.

Inner Join. You can use the Inner Join clause to join the two tables, and obtain the desired results:

```
Select Employees.LastName, Employees.FirstName, Paychecks.*
    From Paychecks Inner Join Employees
    On Paychecks.EmployeeNumber = Employees.EmployeeNumber;
```

Notice how the fields are listed. Because the selection involves two tables, the field names should be qualified with the table names. Because the Last Name and First Name fields are in the Employees table, they are coded as follows:

```
Employees.LastName, Employees.FirstName
```

In addition, to indicate all fields in the Paychecks table, you code the following:

```
Paychecks.*
```

If a field name exists in only one table, you can omit the table name. Because LastName and FirstName appear only in the Employees table, you can also code the SQL as follows:

```
Select LastName, FirstName, Paychecks.*
    From Paychecks Inner Join Employees
    On Paychecks.EmployeeNumber = Employees.EmployeeNumber;
```

For code clarity, it is preferable to qualify the field name with the table name.

The Inner Join operation will return only those records that have the matching fields specified by the "On" criterion. In this example, only those checks with matching employee numbers in the Employees table will be returned. Neither employees who have no paychecks nor paychecks without matching employee numbers in the Employees table will be included. If you want either of these types of records, you should use the Left or Right (outer) Join clause.

Outer Join. There are two types of outer join clauses: the Right Join and the Left Join. The Right Join clause will include all records in the second table regardless of whether or not they have a match on the first table. The Left Join clause will include all records in the first table regardless of whether or not they have a match on the second table. For example, if you are interested in *all* checks paid, regardless of whether they have matching employee numbers in the Employees table, you can code the following:

```
Select Employees.LastName, Employees.FirstName, Paychecks.*
   From Paychecks Left Join Employees
   On Paychecks.EmployeeNumber = Employees.EmployeeNumber;
```

This statement will return all checks paid. (Paychecks is the first [left] table used in the SQL.) If the check has a matching employee number, the name will be included; otherwise, there will be no name.

Hopefully, your company will never have this type of paycheck. In a well-designed database, there should be a primary key–foreign key relation for the employee number between the two tables. You can then impose the *referential integrity* rule, which stipulates that a foreign key cannot be entered without the existence of a corresponding primary key. That is, in this case, the employee number in a paycheck must have a corresponding employee number in the Employees table; otherwise, the paycheck cannot be saved into the Paychecks table.

The previous SQL will not list employees who are not paid. If you are interested in retrieving *all* employees, whether they are paid or not, you will use the Right Join clause; that is, you will code the following:

```
Select Employees.LastName, Employees.FirstName, Paychecks.*
   From Paychecks Right Join Employees
   On Paychecks.EmployeeNumber = Employees.EmployeeNumber;
```

If you need to include the Where or Order clause while using the Inner/Outer Join clause, you will place it after the preceding lines. For example, if you are interested in only those checks with an amount greater than $10 and would like to sort the result by name, you can code the following:

```
Select Employees.LastName, Employees.FirstName, Paychecks.*
   From Paychecks Inner Join Employees
   On Paychecks.EmployeeNumber = Employees.EmployeeNumber
   Where (Paychecks.Amount > 10)
   Order By Employees.LastName, Employees.FirstName;
```

Adding, Updating, and Deleting Records. The Select statement selects records from tables and returns the results. The SQL also provides statements that allow you to add, update, or delete records from a table. To add a record to a table, you use the *Insert statement*, which has the following syntax:

```
Insert Into TableName(Field1, Field2,...) Values(Value1, Value2,
   ...);
```

For example, you can use the following statement to add a new employee record to the Employees table:

```
Insert Into Employees(EmployeeNumber, LastName, FirstName)
   Values(123456789, "Doe", "John");
```

To change the contents of a record, use the *Update statement*, which has the following syntax:

```
Update TableName Set Field1=Value1, Field2=Value2 Where Condition
```

For example, you can use the following statement to change the first name of employee number 123456789:

```
Update Employees Set FirstName = 'Jonathan' Where  EmployeeNumber
   = 123456789
```

To delete a record from a table, use the *Delete statement*, which has the following syntax:

```
Delete From TableName Where Condition
```

To delete employee number 123456789 from the Employees table, you will code:

```
Delete From Employees Where EmployeeNumber = 123456789
```

The Create Table Statement. The SOL statements introduced so far provide you with the capability to manipulate data in the database. The SQL can also be used to define tables (schema) in a database; that is, the SQL also has the DDL capability. For example, you can use the *Create Table statement* to create a new table. The syntax appears as follows:

```
Create Table TableName (Field1 Type[(Length)]
   [, Field2 Type[(Length)]. . .);
```

where *TableName* = name of the new table to be created

Field1, Field2 . . . = name of the nth field in the new table

Type = data type (as recognized in the database, not necessarily the same as in VB); for example, Text (for String in VB) and Integer (for Integer in VB)

Length = length of the (Text) field

The following code will create a new table for a phone directory that contains two fields, Phone and Name:

```
Create Table PhoneDirectory (Phone Text(10), Name Text(50));
```

This discussion provides the necessary background to explore ADO.NET. A thorough discussion of the SQL requires an entire book, and is beyond the scope of this chapter. Consult a book on database programming for a complete treatment of the subject.

9.2 Using ADO.NET

Prior to VS.NET, the *ActiveX data objects* (*ADO*) was the main technology used to handle not only the database (whether local or remote) but also various data "stores" (data that are stored in any form, not just the database format). These objects provide a standard programming interface for you to use in developing the code to handle data. Theoretically, after you learn the ADO, you should have no need to learn other technology to access any kind of data from your VB program, such as Excel files and email messages.

As you can imagine, different kinds of databases require different database servers to manage them. For example, the MS Access database is driven by the *MS Data Jet Database Engine*; however, Oracle has its own database server for the Oracle database. Many of these servers are *ODBC* (open database connectivity) *compliant*, meaning they provide a cross-platform database-independent interface to access the database.

Built upon the same vision, VS.NET introduces a new technology, ADO.NET. It is interesting to note that there are more differences than similarities between ADO and ADO.NET in concept and in code. ADO.NET envisions an operating environment where data are maintained across the network. As such, it is keen on issues concerning network traffic and load (burden) on database server resources; therefore, it provides features that facilitate data creation and maintenance performed locally in memory. Connections to the data source (database) are expected to be minimum. Some of these aspects will be discussed later in this chapter.

From your point of view, you learn to work with ADO.NET so that you can get access to the underlying data that your program needs to handle. ADO.NET provides a uniform set of objects that you can use to handle all kinds of data, alleviating the need to learn different interfaces/code for different kinds of data. This chapter focuses only on the use of ADO.NET to handle the MS Access database as an introduction to database and to ADO.NET technology.

Brief Introduction to ADO.NET Terminology and Concept

This subsection introduces a few new terms and concepts essential to your understanding of ADO.NET.

Dataset, Data Table, Data Row, and Data Column. *ADO.NET* builds data in memory. Data are kept in the *dataset*. A dataset is a memory resident collection of data tables. Similar to a database table, a data table has rows and columns. Rows are indexed by numbers. The first row has an index value of zero (0); columns are also accessible by index; and the first column has an index of zero (0), too. Columns, however, can also be referenced with a string that represents the column name. For example, if a column has a name "Name," you can reference that column as Columns("Name").

Technically, the rows (columns) are called *data rows* (*data columns*). All datasets, data tables, data rows, and data columns are objects. Each type has its own properties and methods. Although a dataset contains data tables, and data tables are organized by data rows and data columns (therefore appear to have a structural hierarchy), you can create independent data tables and data columns. The following code shows how these objects can be declared:

```
Dim MyDataset As New Dataset()
Dim MyDataTable As New DataTable()
Dim MyDataColumn As New DataColumn()
```

As discussed in Chapter 4, "Data, Operations and Built-in Functions," the New keyword in the declaration creates a new object of the object type for the variable declared. Without the New keyword, the variable is not associated with any object, and is recognized only as of the type declared. Before the variable can be referenced, it must be assigned with an (existing) object of the declared type. Because you declare a variable so that you can reference and use it, it is usually more convenient to declare it with the New keyword. Note that the DataRow object cannot be created with the New keyword. Typically, it is created with the NewRow method, as illustrated later in this chapter.

The Data Adapter. The *data adapter* is an object that serves as an interface between the dataset (or data table) and the data source (database). You use the data adapter to bring data from the data source to the dataset (or data table). You will then perform various operations on the data in the dataset, such as add or modify records. When you are ready to update the data source, based on the changes you have made on the dataset, you call the data adapter to perform the task. You can think of the data adapter as the *actor* on data, while the dataset (and those objects of lower hierarchy) is the *holder* of data.

ADO.NET provides two types of data adapters: the SQL data adapter, and the OleDB data adapter. The former specializes in working with the SQL server, and the latter works with any generic database server. Because you will work with MS Access, you will use only the OleDb data adapter. For brevity, the OleDb data adapter will be referred to simply as the data adapter.

The data adapter is available at design time and can also be used exclusively by code. Its use at design time will be discussed first.

Working with the Data Adapter

To illustrate how to work with the data adapter at design time, consider a simple project that involves the grocertogo database, which comes with VS.NET. (If you follow the standard installation procedure, the database should be located under the C:\Program Files\Microsoft Visual Studio .NET\FrameworkSDK\Samples\QuickStart\aspplus\samples\grocertogo\data folder.) The database contains several tables, one of which is the Products table. The following discussion shows the steps to access this table and display its contents in a data grid as shown in Figure 9.1. The major steps include:

Figure 9.1

Sample result: data grid bound to a dataset filled with data by data adapter

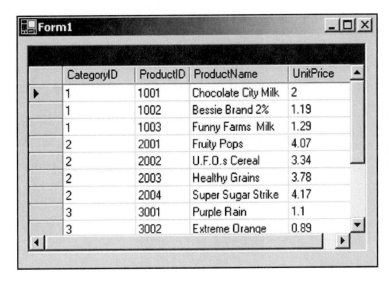

This project will cause all products in the Products table to be displayed in the data grid.

1. Add the data adapter to the project and then configure the data adapter.
2. Generate the dataset.
3. Bind the data grid to the dataset by setting the control's DataSource Property.
4. Fill the dataset with data from the data source (database).

Adding and Configuring the Data Adapter. ADO.NET controls are located in the Data tab of the toolbox. To add and configure the data adapter, do the following:

1. Click the Data tab of the Toolbox, as shown in Figure 9.2. Its contents will appear.
2. Double-click the OleDbDataAdapter icon. The Data Adapter Configuration Wizard will appear, as shown in Figure 9.3.
3. Click the Next button to proceed. You will be prompted to choose your data connection.
4. Set up the connection using the Data Link Properties dialog box:
   4.1. Click the New Connection button in the dialog box, shown in Figure 9.4. The Data Link Properties dialog box will appear.
   4.2. Click the Provider Tab and then select Microsoft Jet 4.0 OLE DB Provider (Figure 9.5).
   4.3. Click the Next button on the Provider tab. The Connection tab will appear.
   4.4. Click the . . . (dialog) button by the entry box (Figure 9.6). The Select Access Database dialog box (open file dialog) will appear. Browse your system to find the grocertogo.mdb database.

Figure 9.2

The Data Tab on the Toolbox

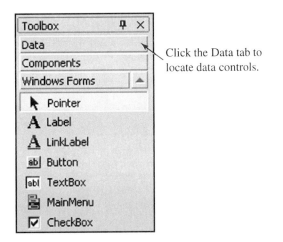

Click the Data tab to locate data controls.

Figure 9.3

Invoking the Data
Adapter Configuration
Wizard

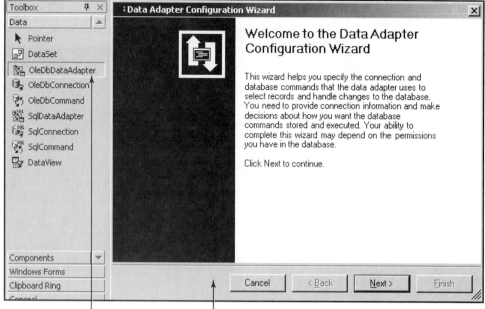

Double click the oleDbDataAdapter icon
and the Data Adapter Configuration
Wizard will appear.

Figure 9.4

Choosing the data
connection

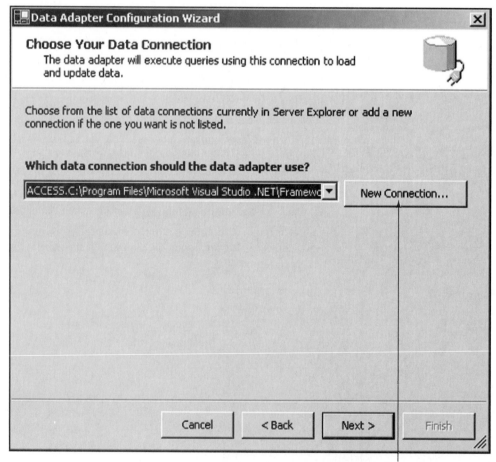

Click the New Connection
button to select a database
file to connect.

Figure 9.5

The Data Link Properties dialog box

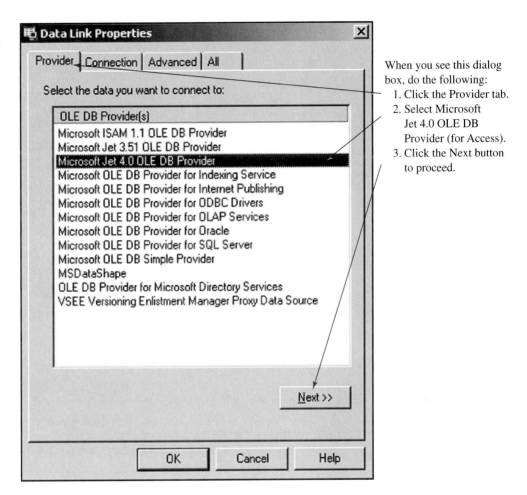

When you see this dialog box, do the following:
1. Click the Provider tab.
2. Select Microsoft Jet 4.0 OLE DB Provider (for Access).
3. Click the Next button to proceed.

4.5. Verify that the database name has been specified correctly, and click the Test Connection button to make sure that the connection is correct. Click the OK button in the Data Link Properties dialog box (see Figure 9.6).

4.6. Click the Next button in the Data Adapter Configuration Wizard as shown in Figure 9.7.

5. Select the radio button for the Use SQL Statements option when prompted to choose the query type (Figure 9.7); then click the Next button.

6. Enter the following SQL in the box (see Figure 9.8):

```
SELECT CategoryID, ProductID, ProductName, UnitPrice FROM
Products
```

7. Click the Next button. You should see that the Data Adapter Configuration Wizard indicates that it is unable to generate the Update and Delete commands (see Figure 9.9). This problem occurs because the Products table has no primary key; however, this does not affect the task here.

8. Click the Finish button. You should see OleDbDataAdapter1 and OleDbConnection1 appear below the form (just like the file dialogs would appear).

9. Change the name of OleDbDataAdapter1 to odaProducts by clicking the control and then changing its name in the Properties window.

These steps add the data adapter and its associated connection to the form. The Connection object associates with a database similar to the way the StreamReader (Writer) associates with a file; however, in most cases, the data adapter automatically manages the connection to the database.

Figure 9.6

Specifying a database name

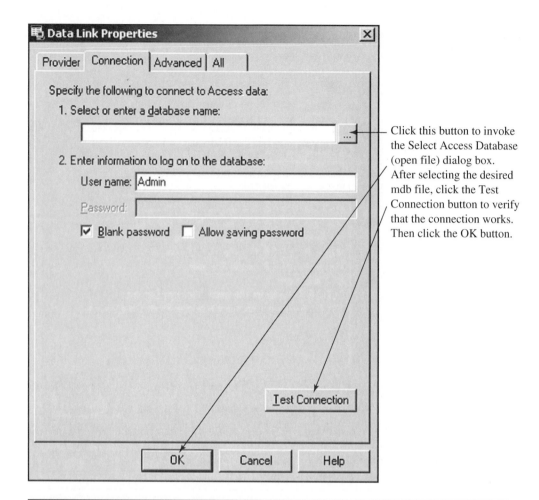

Click this button to invoke the Select Access Database (open file) dialog box. After selecting the desired mdb file, click the Test Connection button to verify that the connection works. Then click the OK button.

Figure 9.7

Choosing the query type

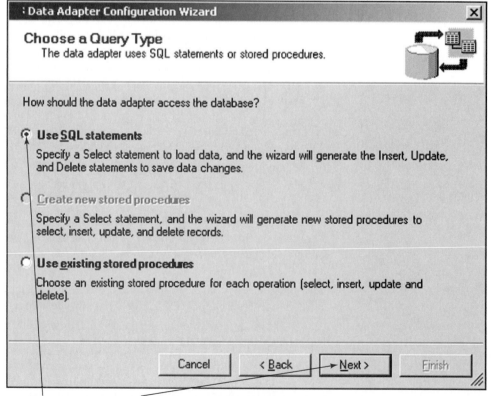

Select "Use SQL statement" then click the Next button.

Figure 9.8

Specifying the Select SQL statement

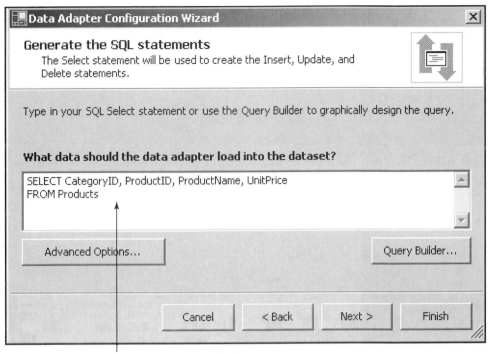

Enter this SQL statement here. You can use the Query Builder to create the same statement if you are familiar with the Query by Example feature of the MS Access.

Figure 9.9

Configuration message from the Data Adapter Configuration Wizard

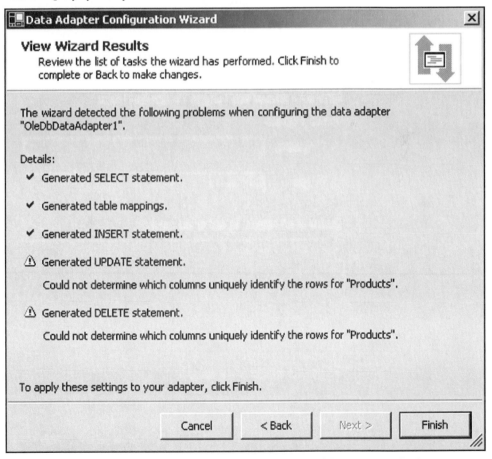

After configuring the data adapter with the Products table of the grocertogo database, you will see this message indicating problems with generating UPDATE and DELETE statements. The problems arise because the Products table has no primary key. But the problems will not affect our current task.

Generating the Dataset. The next major step is to generate the dataset. Based on the information obtained from the preceding step (the connection and the Select SQL), ADO.NET can generate a dataset with its schema coded in XML. To create the dataset, follow these steps:

1. Click the form so that it will have the focus.
2. Click the Data menu in the menu bar; then select the Generate Dataset option as shown in Figure 9.10. The Generate Dataset dialog box will appear.
3. Change the dataset name in the New text box to DsProducts, and make sure that the check box for Add this Dataset to the Designer is checked (see Figure 9.11).
4. Click the OK button.

After these steps, the dataset is added to the project and its schema name (DsProducts.xsd) should appear under the project in the Solution Explorer, as shown in Figure 9.12.

Figure 9.10

The Data menu

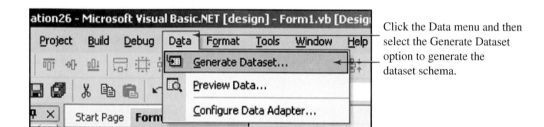

Click the Data menu and then select the Generate Dataset option to generate the dataset schema.

Figure 9.11

The Generate Dataset dialog box

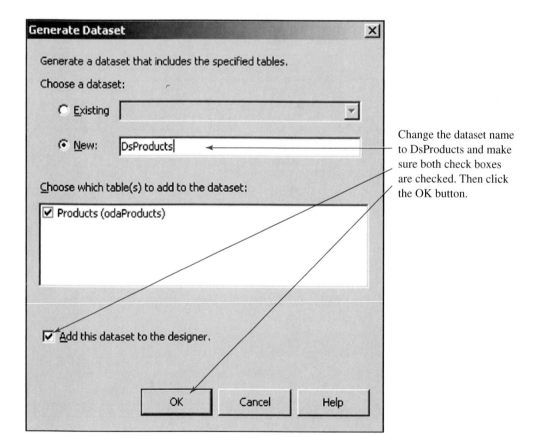

Change the dataset name to DsProducts and make sure both check boxes are checked. Then click the OK button.

Figure 9.12

Result of generating a
dataset

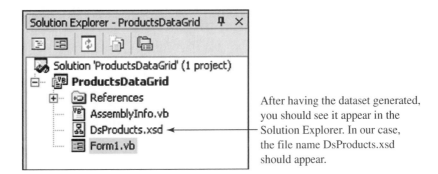

After having the dataset generated,
you should see it appear in the
Solution Explorer. In our case,
the file name DsProducts.xsd
should appear.

Binding the Data Grid. After the dataset exists, you can bind controls to the dataset to display its content. One of the controls that is convenient for this purpose is the data grid. The steps to bind the data grid to the dataset are as follows:

1. Draw a data grid on the form. (If your Toolbox is still displaying the Data tab, click the Windows Forms tab at the bottom of the Toolbox and then locate the DataGrid icon.) Double-click the DataGrid icon; then adjust the size of the grid in the form (see Figure 9.13).

2. Change the data grid's name to dtgProducts using its Properties window.

3. Set the data grid's *DataSource property* to DsProducts1.Products, as shown in Figure 9.14.

Filling the Dataset. You will not see of the any result if you run the program now. The dataset is still empty, so you need to provide the code to fill the dataset with data. The data adapter's Fill method should be used to perform this task. Suppose you want the dataset to be filled with data as soon as the program starts. The code should appear as follows:

```
Private Sub Form1_Load(ByVal sender As System.Object, ByVal e As
    System.EventArgs) Handles MyBase.Load
    'Fill the datatable with data from source
    odaProducts.Fill(DsProducts1.Products)
End Sub
```

Figure 9.13

The Data Grid

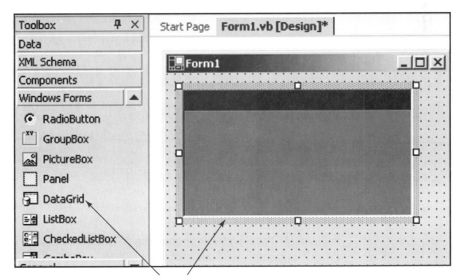

Double click the DataGrid icon
in the toolbox. When the grid
appears in the form, adjust
its position and size.

Figure 9.14

Setting the DataSource property of the data grid

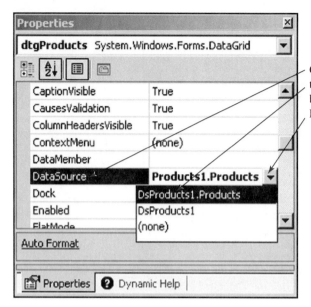

Click the DataSource property then click the down arrow button and select DsProducts1. Products as the setting.

Another way to code the Fill method for the same results is:

```
odaProducts.Fill(DsProducts1, "Products")
```

The way as shown in the text can be used only when the dataset is generated during design time. The syntax shown in this box can be used for the dataset that is generated either at design time or runtime.

The procedure has only one statement, which uses the data adapter's Fill method to fill the Products data table in the dataset. Because the data grid is bound to the data table, you should also see that the result is displayed in the data grid (refer back to Figure 9.1).

Note that the dataset resides in memory. It remains independent of its data source. You can do whatever you want with the dataset; however, until you use the data adapter's Update method to update the data source, the latter remains unchanged.

Using Parameters for Query

The preceding illustration fills the dataset with the data from the entire Products table. In many cases, you are interested only in a subset of an entire table. For example, you may be interested in retrieving products only in a certain category ID, such as 1. In such a case, you should set up the SQL query with a parameter, and provide the value during runtime.

Suppose you want to create a project that will display in a data grid all the Products whose category ID matches the value specified by the user in a text box. You can set up the project as follows:

1. Draw a text box, a label, a button, and a data grid on the form. Name the text box **txtSearch**, the data grid **dtgProducts**, and the button **btnSearch**. Clear the text for the text box and then set the proper texts for the label and the button.

2. Add an OleDb data adapter to the form by performing basically the same steps as the preceding example with the exception that the SQL should be specified as follows:
```
SELECT CategoryID, ProductID, ProductName, UnitPrice FROM Products
    WHERE (CategoryID = ?)
```

3. Name the data adapter **odaProducts**.

4. Generate the dataset, and name it **DsProducts** in the process, again following the same steps as shown in the preceding subsection.

5. Bind the data grid to the datatable, DsProducts1.Products. The steps are exactly the same as the preceding example.

6. Add the code to fill the datatable:

```
Private Sub btnSearch_Click(ByVal sender As System.Object, ByVal e
  As System.EventArgs) Handles btnSearch.Click
    odaProducts.SelectCommand.Parameters("CategoryID").Value =
      txtSearch.Text
    DsProducts1.Clear() 'Clear the dataset before filling data
    'Fill the Products datatable
    odaProducts.Fill(DsProducts1.Products)
End Sub
```

A sample run is shown in Figure 9.15.

Notice that the code is placed in the search button's click event because you want the program to fill the dataset after the user enters the category ID and clicks the button. In the code, the first statement assigns the content of the text box to the CategoryID parameter of the data adapter's SelectCommand. The data adapter has four command properties: *SelectCommand, InsertComand, UpdateCommand*, and *DeleteCommand*. These properties are automatically set when you specify the SQL statement in the process of adding and configuring the data adapter to the form. Recall when you were configuring the data adapter, before you clicked the Finish button, the Data Adapter Configuration Wizard showed you the statements it generated (refer back to Figure 9.9). Note also the data adapter was unable to generate proper Update and Delete statements because the database table (Products) had no primary key. The adapter automatically selects the appropriate command property to use when instructed to interact with the data source. The Fill method uses the SelectCommand. In the preceding SQL statement, the Where clause was specified as:

```
WHERE (CategoryID = ?)
```

The question mark (?) in the clause indicates that the value is to be supplied, and is recognized as a *parameter*, which is given the parameter name CategoryID (same as the specified column name). At runtime, when the user enters a 2 in the text box and then clicks the button, the first statement in the event procedure equivalently sets up the SQL statement as follows:

```
SELECT CategoryID, ProductID, ProductName, UnitPrice FROM Products
  WHERE (CategoryID = 2)
```

The Fill method in the third statement will use the specification to fill the dataset.

Note that the second statement that uses the dataset's *Clear method* has been included to clear the dataset so that it will be empty before being filled with the new data. Without the use of this statement, the data table will retain the old data, and the new data will be added.

Figure 9.15

Sample run with a specified parameter

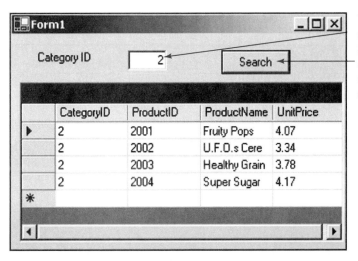

When the user enter a category ID and clicks the Search button, the data grid displays all products whose category ID matches the specified value.

Viewing Data Record by Record

The preceding examples use the data grid to show all rows (records) in a data table. What if you want to display the result one record at a time? For example, you may want to show the result as shown in Figure 9.16.

You can develop the project with the following steps:

1. Set up the user interface. The form has two group boxes: one for search specification, another to display the result. The second group box also contains two buttons for the user to browse the next or previous record. The following table shows the names of the controls involved.

Control	Name	Comment
Text box	txtSearch	For user to enter search text
Text box	txtCategoryID	To display the CategoryID field
Text box	txtProductID	To display the ProductID field
Text box	txtProductName	To display the ProductName field
Text box	txtUnitPrice	To display the UnitPrice field
Button	btnSearch	To select records from source
Button	btnNext	To move to the next record
Button	btnPrevious	To move to the previous record

2. Add a data adapter to the form. The steps are exactly the same as the preceding example. Make sure that the SQL statement is as follows:

   ```
   SELECT CategoryID, ProductID, ProductName, UnitPrice FROM Products
      WHERE (CategoryID = ?)
   ```

   If you need to go back to the Data Adapter Configuration Wizard after you finish working with it, right-click the data adapter below the form and then select the Configure Data Adapter option from the pop-up context menu.

3. Name the data adapter **odaProducts**.

4. Generate the dataset using the Generate Dataset option in the Data menu. (Click the form before clicking the Data menu.) Be sure to name the dataset **DsProducts** in the process.

Figure 9.16

Display data record by record

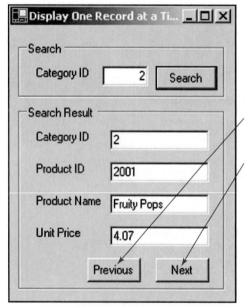

This project provides the visual interface that displays the selected data in the data table one row (record) at a time. When the user clicks the Next button, the next record (row) is displayed. When the user clicks the Previous button, the previous record is displayed.

5. Bind txtCategoryID to the CategoryID field of the Products table in the dataset using the text box's Properties window.

    5.1. Expand the DataBindings property. (Click the + button on its left.)

    5.2. Click the Text property in the Data Binding box; then click the down arrow button.

    5.3. Expand DsProducts1.

    5.4. Expand Products.

    5.5. Select CategoryID in the list, as seen in Figure 9.17.

6. Bind txtProductID, txtProductName, and txtUnitPrice respectively to the ProductID, ProductName, and UnitPrice fields of the Products table, following the same procedure outlined in step 5.

7. Write code to fill the dataset. The code is the same as the preceding example:

```
Private Sub btnSearch_Click(ByVal sender As System.Object, ByVal e
    As System.EventArgs) Handles btnSearch.Click
    odaProducts.SelectCommand.Parameters("CategoryID").Value =
    txtSearch.Text
    DsProducts1.Clear() 'Clear the dataset before filling data
    'Fill the Products datatable
    odaProducts.Fill(DsProducts1.Products)
End Sub
```

8. Provide the code to display the next (previous) record. When controls are bound to fields in a datatable, there is a BindingContext object in the form that keeps track of the position of the data (through yet another object, called CurrencyManager, which is invisible in the coding context anyway). Initially, the binding is set to the first position (0). When this position is changed, the controls will display different data. If you want to display the next record, increase the position by 1. The following code should accomplish your goal:

```
Private Sub btnNext_Click(ByVal sender As System.Object, ByVal e
    As System.EventArgs) Handles btnNext.Click
    Me.BindingContext(DsProducts1, "Products").Position += 1
End Sub
```

Similarly, the following code will make the text boxes display the previous record when the user clicks the Previous button.

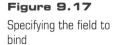

Figure 9.17

Specifying the field to bind

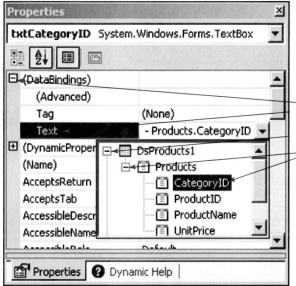

To bind a control to a field in a data table, (1) expand the data bindings property (click + on its left; it shows the list and the + button turns into -) (2) make the Text's dropdown box display the contents (click Text then click the drop down arrow) (3) Expand the dataset (DsProducts1) (4) Expand the datatable (Products), and (5) select the field (CategoryID).

```
Private Sub btnPrevious_Click(ByVal sender As System.Object, ByVal
    e As System.EventArgs) Handles btnPrevious.Click
    Me.BindingContext(DsProducts1, "Products").Position -= 1
End Sub
```

Notice that in the code the binding context object is qualified with Me. The code will actually work fine without the qualification; however, the binding context can exist in container controls, such as group boxes, too. You can create different binding contexts when you have container controls in the form to display data of different contexts. In such a case, you will need to qualify the binding context with the proper container name.

The dataset can contain more than one data table. You can also create relationships among these data tables, much like the way you work with database table. Some of these capabilities are explored in the Explore and Discover exercises at the end of this chapter. In the next subsection, you turn your attention to updating the data source (database) through the dataset.

Updating the Database

The preceding examples showed how to retrieve data from the database into the dataset and how to display the data on the form. After data are brought into the dataset, you can make any changes in it. For example, you can add new rows (records) to the data table. You can update any data in any rows. You can also delete any unwanted rows. Keep in mind, however, that any changes you make to the dataset have no effect on the database (source) until you call the data adapter's Update method to effect the changes. The typical sequence of steps required to maintain a database using ADO.NET is as follows:

1. Retrieve relevant data from the database into the dataset (as shown in the preceding examples).
2. Make desired changes, including Add, Update, or Delete operations in the dataset.
3. Call the data adapter's Update method to update the database.

The following example illustrates how to perform each of these steps.

The Phonebook Example. Consider a simple example. Suppose you have a phonebook database that contains a table with your friends' names and phone numbers. The phone number is the primary key. Use the user interface as shown in Figure 9.18 to handle the database maintenance. You will *not* bind any VB control to the dataset, so you have sole control over the exact actions to take. (Before proceeding further, use MS Access to create the Phonebook database as described. Name the database **Phonebook**. Create a table and then name it **tblPhonebook**. In the table, create two fields: Phone and Name. Select Text as the data type for

Figure 9.18

Visual interface for
Phonebook Maintenance

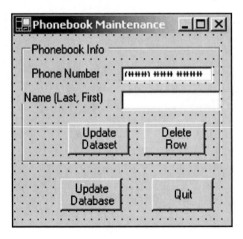

both fields, and make Phone the primary key. Close the database before beginning to work on this Visual Basic project.)

The program will work in the following manner:

- The user will enter a name and a phone number into the proper controls and then click the Update Dataset button. This will cause the program to either add a new row or change an existing row in the dataset, depending on whether the phone number already existed in the data table.
- The user can also click the Delete button to delete a record.
- The user can make as many changes (add, update, or delete) as they desire.
- When the user clicks the Update Database button, the database will be updated.
- When the user clicks the Quit button, the program quits.

The following table shows the settings for the properties of the controls in the form:

Control	Property	Setting	Remark
Group box	Text	Phonebook Info	
Label	Text	Name (Last, First)	
Label	Text	Phone Number	
Text box	Name	txtName	For the user to enter the name
	Text	(cleared)	
Masked edit box	Name	mskPhone	For the user to enter phone number
	Mask	(###)-###-####	
Button	Name	btnUpdateDataset	To initiate changes to the dataset
	Text	Update Dataset	
Button	Name	btnDeleteRow	To delete record (row) from data table
	Text	Delete Row	
Button	Name	btnUpdateDatabase	To update the database
	Text	Update Database	
Button	Name	btnQuit	To end the project
	Text	Quit	

Setting Up the Data Adapter and Creating the Dataset. After the user interface is created, you will bring an OLE DB data adapter onto the form and configure the data adapter in the process. You will then generate the dataset, using the Data menu's Generate Dataset option. The steps involved here are the same as the preceding examples and can be briefly described as follows:

1. Double-click the OleDbDataAdapter icon in the Toolbox.
2. Configure the connection and the SQL Select statement using the Data Adapter Configuration Wizard. In this step, you specify the Phonebook database that you created earlier for the connection. Also, have the SQL Select statement specified as follows:

```
SELECT Name, Phone FROM tblPhonebook
```

3. Change the OleDbDataAdapter name to **odaPhonebook**.
4. Generate the dataset by clicking the Data menu (make sure the form has the focus before clicking) and then selecting the Generate Dataset option. Name the dataset to be generated **DsPhonebook**.

Again, you are *not* binding the dataset to any control; however, you still need to fill the dataset with the data from the database. This should be done as soon as the program starts, so you will place the following statement in the *form load* event:

```
odaPhonebook.Fill(DsPhonebook1.tblPhonebook)
```

The OleDbDataAdapter's Fill method accepts several different parameters. The preceding statement can also be coded as:

```
odaPhonebook.Fill(DsPhonebook1, "tblPhonebook")
```

Adding New Rows to a Data Table. After the user enters the data in the form, the user will click the Update Dataset button to add or update the content of the dataset. For the time being, assume the data pertains to a new record and, therefore, will be added to the dataset as a new row. The following code should accomplish this requirement:

```
Private Sub btnUpdateDataset_Click(ByVal sender As System.Object,
   ByVal e As System.EventArgs) Handles btnUpdateDataset.Click
      Dim TheRecord As DataRow 'Declare a datarow
      'Create a new row of the same structure as that
      'in the datatable
      TheRecord = DsPhonebook1.Tables("tblPhonebook").NewRow
      TheRecord("Phone") = mskPhone.ClipText
      TheRecord("Name") = txtName.Text
      'Add the new row to the datatable
      DsPhonebook1.Tables("tblPhonebook").Rows.Add(TheRecord)
End Sub
```

In the code, the variable, TheRecord is declared to be a DataRow, which is assigned as a *NewRow* of the data table, tblPhonebook. (Note that this name corresponds to the table in the database.) This step is necessary for the data row to have the same data columns as the data table. The next two statements assign data in the controls on the form to the corresponding columns in the data row, TheRecord. Finally, TheRecord is added to the tblPhonebook data table using the *Rows.Add method* of the data table.

Notice how each column in the data row is referenced. The columns for Phone and Name are referenced as TheRecord("Phone") and TheRecord("Name"). You can also code them as TheRecord(0) and TheRecord(1); however, the latter code is less clear. You will need to put extra effort in deciding which column has the index value 0 (or 1).

Determining Whether Data Entered Belong to an Existing Record. The preceding code assumes that the data entered are new, and therefore need to be added. You need a way to determine whether the data are actually new. There are several possible ways. Perhaps, the easiest is to use the *Select method* of the data table. The method takes as its first parameter a filter string that has the syntax similar to the SQL Select statement. For example, the following expression will return all rows that contain the name, "Doe, John:"

```
DsPhonebook1.Tables("tblPhonebook").Select("Name = 'Doe,
   John'")
```

As a side note, "Doe, John" in the statement is enclosed in a pair of inner single quotes because it is a string (which is recognized as text in MS Access). The Select method takes a string parameter, so "Name =... " is enclosed in a pair of double quotes. In addition, "Doe, John" itself is a string in the SQL context, and therefore must also be enclosed. The parameter inside the pair of parentheses following Select (without the enclosing double quotes) should appear as Name = 'Doe, John'. In SQL syntax, you can also enclose the string with a pair of double quotes; however, if you use double quotes, you will need to use two double quotes in place of each one inside when they are enclosed in another pair of double quotes. This makes it both hard to code and read, so it is always simpler to enclose SQL string parameters in single quotes.

Notice that the Select method can return multiple rows; therefore, the target of the assignment statement must be a variable that represents multiple rows. Let FoundRows be the variable to take multiple rows; then you will declare the variable as follows:

```
Dim FoundRows() As DataRow
```

Notice the pair of parentheses immediately following the variable, FoundRows. It indicates that the number of rows is not yet determinable. A variable declared to contain multiple elements is recognized as an array. Arrays were discussed in detail in Chapter 8, "Arrays and Their Uses."

In the example project, the primary key is the phone number, so you should search for the phone number in the data table. The code to look for the phone number given in the masked edit box should appear as follows:

```
FoundRows = _
  DsPhonebook1.Tables("tblPhonebook").Select("Phone='" & _
  mskPhone.ClipText & "'")
```

Notice the single quotes immediately after "Phone=" and within the double quotes at the end of statement. They are needed because the Phone field is specified as a Text field in the database table. If the Clip Property of mskPhone is 1234567890, the value inside the pair of parentheses of the Select method should appear as: Phone='1234567890'. Because the phone number is the primary key, you expect the Select method to return either zero or one row. The array has a Length property, which gives the number of elements in it. You can compare this property with 0 to determine whether the phone number represents a new record. The code structure should be like the following:

```
If FoundRows.Length = 0 Then
    ' This is a new record
Else
    'This is an existing record
End If
```

Modifying Existing Rows. How do you modify the existing row? The variable, FoundRows in the preceding code actually corresponds to exactly the same row(s) in the data table; that is, the variable holds no new (separate) rows, but simply points to the same row(s) in the data table. Any modifications made to the variable will be reflected in the data table. In your project, you need to modify only the name because the phone number is the same as found. The code appears as follows:

```
FoundRows(0) ("Name") = txtName.Text
```

Notice the 0 enclosed in the pair of parentheses. As explained previously, when the phone number exists, the Select method should return one row. Like items in a list box, arrays are indexed with 0 being the first element. Also ("Name") indicates the Name column in the row.

The complete code to handle the Update Dataset button click event appears as follows:

```
Private Sub btnUpdateDataset_Click(ByVal sender As System.Object, _
  ByVal e As System.EventArgs) Handles btnUpdateDataset.Click
    Dim TheRecord As DataRow 'Declare a datarow
    Dim FoundRows() As DataRow
    FoundRows = _
      DsPhonebook1.Tables("tblPhonebook").Select("Phone='" & _
      mskPhone.ClipText & "'")
    If FoundRows.Length = 0 Then
        'This is a new record; add
        'Create a new row of the same structure as that
        'in the datatable
        TheRecord = DsPhonebook1.Tables("tblPhonebook").NewRow
        TheRecord("Phone") = mskPhone.ClipText
        TheRecord("Name") = txtName.Text
        'Add the new row to the datatable
        DsPhonebook1.Tables("tblPhonebook").Rows.Add(TheRecord)
    Else
        'The phone number already exists; update the name
        FoundRows(0)("Name") = txtName.Text
    End If
End Sub
```

Deleting a Row. When the user clicks the Delete button, the row with the same phone number as entered should be deleted from the data table. The record must exist prior to the deletion; otherwise, a runtime error will occur. To guard against this error, the code should determine whether the record actually exists; therefore, the program should first search for the record in the data table. This can be done using the data table's Select method, as shown previously. If the record exists, it can be deleted using the data table's *Delete method*. The code appears as follows:

```
Private Sub btnDeleteRow_Click(ByVal sender As System.Object,
    ByVal e As System.EventArgs) Handles btnDeleteRow.Click
    Dim FoundRows() As DataRow
    FoundRows = _
      DsPhonebook1.Tables("tblPhonebook").Select("Phone='" & _
      mskPhone.ClipText & "'")
    If FoundRows.Length = 0 Then
        'No such record; display a message
        MsgBox("Record not found")
    Else
        'Record exists; delete it
        FoundRows(0).Delete()
    End If
End Sub
```

The code structure is similar to that for updating the dataset. Notice the statement to delete the row. As explained previously, FoundRows(0) represents the row found in the data table. Its Delete method will delete this row from the datatable.

Updating the Database. The preceding event procedures allow the user to either enter a new record or update existing records in the dataset as well as to delete existing rows. When the user completes the task, the user most likely would like for the database to reflect all changes made in the dataset. The Update Database button in the user interface is used for this purpose. When the user clicks this button, the event procedure should call the data adapter's *Update method* to perform the update. The code appears as follows:

```
Private Sub btnUpdateDatabase_Click(ByVal sender As System.Object,
    ByVal e As System.EventArgs) Handles btnUpdateDatabase.Click
    odaPhonebook.Update(DsPhonebook1)
    DsPhonebook1.AcceptChanges()
End Sub
```

Notice the parameter specified in the Update method is the dataset. If the dataset contains more than one data table, this call will cause all related tables in the database to be updated. If you want only one table to be updated, you can specify the data table instead of the dataset in the parameter. For example, the following statement should accomplish the same thing in our example project:

```
odaPhonebook.Update(DsPhonebook1, "tblPhonebook")
```

Notice also the dataset's *AcceptChanges method* is called *after* the database update. When you make changes to the dataset, it keeps track of all changes by maintaining different versions of each row. These versions can be current, original, modified, and deleted. When you call the data adapter, it knows what command to call to update the database by examining these changes. After the update is performed, the dataset itself should retain only the current version of each row. The AcceptChange method updates the dataset itself. The code to quit is left to you to complete.

After you create the Phonebook database as suggested at the beginning of this example and then proceed through this example, you are ready to test this project. Enter a phone number and name, and click the Update Dataset button. Repeat this process a few times with different phone numbers and names. In the process, you can also delete a few records and then click the Update Database button. After you quit, verify the results using MS Access to browse your Phonebook database to see if all the records you have entered, but not deleted appear in the tblPhonebook table.

TIP

Do not call the dataset's AcceptChanges method before the database is updated. If you do, the data adapter will not be able to identify what changes have been made, and will not make proper calls for various update commands. As a result, the database will not be updated (reflect any change in the dataset).

Additional Notes on the Phonebook Project. The example project can be enhanced in several ways. For example, after the data onscreen are used to update the dataset, the screen should be cleared so that the user can conveniently enter another record. Also, you can bind a data grid to the dataset. This would allow the user to view the current states of all changes made to the dataset.

Perhaps you are wondering why in the example all the database maintenance activities are done on the dataset before a call to update the database is made. In other words, why don't you just take a record from the user, find the record in the database, and perform the required "update" operation (add, update, or delete) immediately? The answer lies in the fact that ADO.NET envisions an operating environment that database applications operate over the network. In such a case, the scalability (capability of the server to handle the varying number of connections) of the system is always a concern. ADO.NET is introduced to support disconnected datasets; that is, the dataset can and should reside in the client computer memory without maintaining a connection to the data source (database), which typically locates in another server computer. Each call to update the database requires opening a connection when the Update command is being carried out and then closing the connection immediately afterwards. The data adapter automatically opens and closes the connection during the update (or fill) operation. Under such circumstances, frequent trips to the database will tie up a lot of resources of the system; therefore, it is not efficient to update the data source (database) each time a single change is made.

On the other hand, be aware that transporting many records across the network can slow down the network. It is therefore important to construct the Select SQL so that only the pertinent records are selected for maintenance. For example, if a user is responsible for maintaining employee records for a particular department, only those records pertaining to the department—and not all records in the related table—should be retrieved.

The Case of Immediate Updating

There may be cases where it is more efficient to update the database immediately after each single change. For example, in some applications, the user may have only one or two updates to make each time. It will then not be efficient to marshal many records across the network between the data source and the dataset. Only the few relevant records should be handled. You can modify the phonebook example to illustrate how immediate updating can be accomplished. Figure 9.19 shows the revised visual interface.

This program will work in the following manner:

- When the user clicks the Update button, the record entered in the control will either be added to or updated immediately in the database, depending on whether it already exists.
- When the user clicks the Delete button, the record will be deleted immediately from the database if the record exists; otherwise, an error message is displayed.
- When the user clicks the Quit button, the program quits.

Because an immediate update of the database will involve the dataset in the same step, there is no need for a button for dataset updating. But the interface does include a Delete button to illustrate the use of the data table's Delete method. The following table shows the property settings for the controls on the form.

Figure 9.19

Microsoft procedural syntax

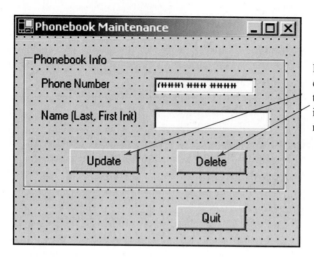

In this illustration, when the user clicks the update or delete button, the change intended for the database is immediately made. Thus, there is no button pertaining to the dataset.

Control	Property	Setting	Remark
Group box	Text	Phonebook Info	
Label	Text	Name (Last, First Init)	
Label	Text	Phone Number	
Text box	Name	txtName	To enter name
	Text	(Cleared)	
Masked edit box	Name	mskPhone	To enter phone number
	Mask	(###)-###-####	
Button	Name	btnDelete	To delete record
	Text	Delete	
Button	Name	btnUpdate	To update database
	Text	Update	
Button	Name	btnQuit	To quit

Setting Up the Data Adapter. If the database is to be updated immediately, the data adapter should fetch only the relevant record from the database and nothing more; therefore, the SQL Select statement should be as follows:

```
Select Name, Phone From tblPhonebook Where Phone = ?
```

This statement is similar to the previous example that uses a parameter to retrieve data.

Filling the Dataset. The dataset cannot be filled when the program starts because the data adapter's Select command requires the Phone parameter, which is not set yet. Instead, it should be filled when the user clicks the Update button. At that time, the program should fetch the pertinent record from the database using the phone number because it is the primary key. Subsequent action will depend on whether the record exists. The following code will fetch the pertinent record:

```
odaPhonebook.SelectCommand.Parameters("Phone").Value =
    mskPhone.ClipText
DsPhonebook1.Clear()
odaPhonebook.Fill(DsPhonebook1)
```

Notice that the dataset is cleared before it is filled. This is necessary in this example because the dataset may contain records from previous operations, and you are interested only in the record to be fetched.

Updating the Database. If the record exists, it should be modified; otherwise, the record entered in the form should be added to the database. After an attempt to fetch the record, if the record does not exist, the data table should have zero rows; therefore, the following code should accomplish the update:

```
Private Sub btnUpdate_Click(ByVal sender As System.Object, ByVal e
    As System.EventArgs) Handles btnUpdate.Click
    Dim TheRecord As DataRow
    odaPhonebook.SelectCommand.Parameters("Phone").Value =
      mskPhone.ClipText
    DsPhonebook1.Clear()
    odaPhonebook.Fill(DsPhonebook1)
    If DsPhonebook1.Tables("tblPhonebook").Rows.Count = 0 Then
        'New record. Add.
        TheRecord = DsPhonebook1.Tables("tblPhonebook").NewRow
        TheRecord("Phone") = mskPhone.ClipText
        TheRecord("Name") = txtName.Text
        DsPhonebook1.Tables("tblPhonebook").Rows.Add(TheRecord)
    Else
        'Existing record. Modify.
        DsPhonebook1.Tables("tblPhonebook").Rows(0)("Name") =
          txtName.Text
    End If
        odaPhonebook.Update(DsPhonebook1)
End Sub
```

In the code, after attempting to fetch the record with the entered phone number, the program checks the data table's *Rows.Count property* to see if it is 0. If it is, the record is added to the dataset in exactly the same manner as the preceding example; otherwise, the name column in the first row of the retrieved record is assigned with the text entered in the name text box (txtName). Note that in this example, there is no need to select the record from the dataset because you know the record filled in this row has the same phone number as entered—which was used to fetch the record to begin with. In either case, the data adapter's Update method is called to update the database. The adapter's AcceptChanges method is not called because the dataset will not be used (will be cleared) in any subsequent operation.

Deleting the Record. If the user clicks the Delete button, the program should first attempt to fetch the record with the same phone number as specified. If the record exists, it will be deleted; otherwise, a message is displayed. The code appears as follows:

```
Private Sub btnDelete_Click(ByVal sender As System.Object, ByVal e
    As System.EventArgs) Handles btnDelete.Click
    odaPhonebook.SelectCommand.Parameters("Phone").Value =
      mskPhone.ClipText
    DsPhonebook1.Clear()
    odaPhonebook.Fill(DsPhonebook1)
    If DsPhonebook1.Tables("tblPhonebook").Rows.Count = 0 Then
        'Record does not exist; display error message
        MsgBox("Record not found")
    Else
        'Record exists; delete
        DsPhonebook1.Tables("tblPhonebook").Rows(0).Delete()
        odaPhonebook.Update(DsPhonebook1)
    End If
End Sub
```

The code to delete the record is similar to the previous example. The Delete method is called. It indicates to delete the first row (.Rows(0)) in the data table, which represents the record retrieved. The next statement calls the data adapter's Update method to update the dataset. As explained previously, the Update method will use the relevant command to update the database based on the row states in the dataset. In this case, it will use the Delete command to instruct the database to delete the record.

The code for the Quit button is left for you to complete.

Additional Note on Immediate Updating. If your MS Access table uses an autonumber field as the primary key, it will be tricky to maintain the table using the approach that makes all changes in the dataset before the database is updated. Your immediate updating approach is a workaround.

You have seen two update approaches representing two extremes in terms of timing of updating. Is there a middle way? And what are the advantages and disadvantages? An attempt to answer these questions is presented in exercise 9-30 at the end of this chapter.

9.3 Working with ADO.NET by Code

In the preceding section, the uses of the data adapter and the dataset for data retrieval and maintenance were discussed. The data adapter was drawn onto the form at design time. Many of the activities were carried out automatically. While performing these activities at design time is convenient, you might find it to be more flexible to work with ADO.NET by code. For example, at design time, you may not know the name of the database because your program may eventually be installed in another computer and be used by someone else. In this case, configuring the data adapter at design time will appear to be impractical. This section discusses working with ADO.NET by code.

When you work with ADO.NET by code, you will not draw any data adapter on the form. Instead, you will use code to create the data adapter and configure it properly. Some of the key steps include:

- Declare a variable and then associate it with the data adapter so that you can refer to it in the program.

- Declare a variable and then associate it with the connection object and set up the connection string so that the data adapter can use it to interact with the database.

- Set up the various command objects in the data adapter so that the data adapter can call the proper ones while interacting with the database. These commands include Select, Insert, Update, and Delete. As you may recall, the Select command is used when the data adapter performs the Fill method; the Update command is called to modify existing records; the Insert command is called to add new records; and the Delete command is called to delete records from the database.

- Set up the parameters for the command objects. In most cases, the commands are set up with parameters whose values are obtained at the time the commands are called. This step provides each command with proper information on how/where to obtain the data.

After you properly configure the data adapter, the next step is to generate the dataset. The data adapter provides the *FillSchema method* that can be used to create the dataset (table) schema from the database. You can also bind the dataset to a control such as the data grid for the user to view the data.

The steps outlined above represent the main differences when you use the data adapter by code. The remaining steps to work with the dataset and the database are exactly the same as discussed previously in this chapter. For example, you will use the data adapter's Fill method to populate the dataset with the pertinent data, or its Update method to update the database. You will use the same dataset or data table methods to perform the desired operations.

Coding the Products Search Project

To illustrate, consider the user interface shown in Figure 9.15 again. The project allows the user to enter a search string to retrieve Products from the grocertogo database. Suppose you want to create the same project, but without drawing the data adapter on the form. How do you proceed? As explained previously, declare one variable and then associate it with the data adapter; then declare another variable with the connection. You also need a variable to hold the dataset. These variables can be declared in the general declaration area as follows:

```
Dim odaProducts As New OleDb.OleDbDataAdapter()
Dim cnnGrocertogo As New OleDb.OleDbConnection()
Dim dsGrocertogo As New DataSet()
```

Setting Up the Connection String. The connection object is used by the data adapter to connect to the database. As discussed earlier in this chapter, the data adapter opens and closes the connection automatically. All you need to do is to set up the connection properly, and include it in the code where a connection object is needed. The connection object requires a connection string, which provides information on the provider and the data source. You may recall that in previous examples, the provider for MS Access is Microsoft.Jet.OLEDB.4.0. The data source specifies the location of the database (grocertogo.mdb). These are the exact parameters that should be specified in the connection object's connection string. The code appears as follows:

```
cnnGrocertogo.ConnectionString = _
   "Provider=Microsoft.Jet.OLEDB.4.0;Data Source=" & _
   "C:\Program Files\. . .\grocertogo.mdb"
```

Note that the path for the file grocertogo.mdb is incomplete. You should provide the correct path for that file in your system. Alternatively, you can add a routine to prompt the user for the file path, using the open file dialog.

Notice that "data source" in the connection string specification consists of two separate words. If you combine the two words in the string, the attempt to open the database will fail with an unhandled exception.

Setting Up Command Objects for the Data Adapter. Each of the data adapter's commands (Select, Insert, Update, and Delete) is an OleDbCommand object, which requires two parameters: the command text, and the connection. You have seen the command text before; it is the SQL statement required to execute the command. For example, the command text for the Select command for your example project (as shown before) is:

```
Select CategoryID, ProductID, ProductName, UnitPrice FROM Products
   Where (CategoryID = ?)
```

You can use a variable to refer to this string. To do so, you can declare a variable as follows:

```
Dim SelectSQL As String = "Select CategoryID, & _
   " ProductID, ProductName, UnitPrice FROM Products " & _
   " Where (CategoryID = ?)"
```

You can then set up the Select command as follows:

```
odaProducts.SelectCommand = OleDb.OleDbCommand(SelectSQL,
   cnnGrocertogo)
```

For your example project, you do not need the other commands, and therefore do not have to set them up because all you are doing is retrieving data from the grocertogo database. If you need the other commands, the code will be similar.

Setting Up the Parameters for Commands. As you can see, the command text in the Select command requires a parameter as represented by the question mark (?). You need to inform the command how this parameter will provide the value. Basically, you specify the name of the parameter; you add to the parameter list using the Parameters' *Add method*, which takes up to four parameters as follows:

```
.Add(Name, Type, Length, SourceColumn)
```

- Name = a string that represents the parameter name; for convenience, the name is typically specified as the same as the source column.

- Data Type = the data type that corresponds to that in the database; note that text data should be specified as BSTR.
- Length = length of the data field.
- Source Column = name of the column in the database table.

The following code accomplishes this step:

```
odaProducts.SelectCommand.Parameters.Add("CategoryID",
    Data.OleDb.OleDbType.BSTR,  50, "CategoryID")
```

Generating the Dataset Schema. After the data adapter is properly configured, the next step is to generate the dataset schema. At this point, the dsProducts dataset variable is empty. The first step is to add a table with the name "Products," using the *Tables.Add method*. The code appears as follows:

```
dsProducts.Tables.Add("Products")
```

You can then call the data adapter's FillSchema method to fill the dataset schema. The *FillSchema method* has the following syntax:

```
FillSchema(Dataset, SchemaType, Table)
```

where schema type can be either source or mapped.

The following code will generate the schema for the Grocertogo dataset:

```
odaProducts.FillSchema(dsGrocertogo, SchemaType.Mapped,
    "Products")
```

How does the data adapter know from where to obtain the schema information? Recall that when you set up the Select command, you specified the connection, which has its connection string pointing to the grocertogo.mdb file path. The data adapter uses this information to connect to the database, and obtain the schema information (such as columns in the table and the corresponding data types) thereof.

Binding the Dataset to a Control. In the previous Products search project, the dataset was bound to a data grid called dtgProducts. Binding the dataset to the control by code is straightforward. Simply assign the dataset with its table name to the DataSource property of the control. The code appears as follows:

```
dtgProducts.DataSource = dsGrocertogo.Tables("Products")
```

Handling the Products Search Project by Code: The Complete Code. All the preceding code should be placed in the form load event so that as soon as the project starts the data adapter and the dataset are ready to act. The code should appear as follows:

```
Dim cnnGrocertogo As New OleDb.OleDbConnection()
Dim odaProducts As New OleDb.OleDbDataAdapter()
Dim dsGrocertogo As New DataSet()
Private Sub Form1_Load(ByVal sender As System.Object, ByVal e As
    System.EventArgs) Handles MyBase.Load
    Dim TheDatabase As String
    Dim SelectSQL As String = "Select CategoryID, " _
      "ProductID, ProductName, UnitPrice From Products " & _
      "Where (CategoryID Like ?)"
    'Set up the connection string
    cnnGrocertogo.ConnectionString =
      "Provider=Microsoft.Jet.OLEDB.4.0;Data Source=" & _
 "c:\....\Grocertogo.mdb" 'Be sure to change this line to the
    correct file path in your computer
    'set up the Select command
    odaProducts.SelectCommand = New OleDb.OleDbCommand(SelectSQL,
      cnnGrocertogo)
```

```
'set up the parameter for the Select command
odaProducts.SelectCommand.Parameters.Add("CategoryID",
  Data.OleDb.OleDbType.BSTR, 50, "CategoryID")
'Specify the table name as "Products"
dsGrocertogo.Tables.Add("Products")
'Fill the dataset schema for "Products"
odaProducts.FillSchema(dsGrocertogo, SchemaType.Mapped,
  "Products")
'Bind the dataset to the data grid to display results
dtgProducts.DataSource = dsGrocertogo.Tables("Products")
End Sub
```

When the user clicks the Search button, your program will search the database and fill the dataset with the results. The code is the same as previously shown and should appear as follows:

```
Private Sub btnSearch_Click(ByVal sender As System.Object, ByVal e
    As System.EventArgs) Handles btnSearch.Click
    odaProducts.SelectCommand.Parameters("CategoryID").Value =
      txtSearch.Text
    dsGrocertogo.Clear()
    odaProducts.Fill(dsGrocertogo, "Products")
End Sub
```

There are different ways of setting up the command text and connection for the SelectCommand. For example, you can create the SelectCommand first and then assign the CommandText and Connection properties as shown below:

```
odaProducts.SelectCommand = New OleDb.OleDbCommand()
With odaProducts.SelectCommand
    .CommandText = SelectSQL
    .Connection = cnnGrocertogo
End With
```

Maintaining the Phonebook Database by Code

The preceding example showed how to code the data adapter and dataset in a data search project. You will now work with a project that maintains the database. Consider the phonebook project again. This time, you will maintain the database by code. In addition, you will revise the project requirements as follows:

- As soon as the project starts, the computer will prompt the user for the file path of the phonebook database.
- As soon as the user selects/enters the file path, the program will display the database contents in a data grid.
- When the user clicks the Update Dataset or the Delete button (after entering proper data), the result is reflected in the data grid.
- When the user clicks on a record on the data grid, the record is displayed on the controls in the form. The user can then perform desired changes and then click either the Update Dataset or Delete button.
- When the user clicks the Update Database button, all the changes to the dataset (including deletion) will be reflected in the phonebook database.
- When the user clicks the Quit button, the program quits.

A sample result is shown in Figure 9.20.

The following table shows the name of the controls used in the code:

Figure 9.20

Visual interface for revised Phonebook project

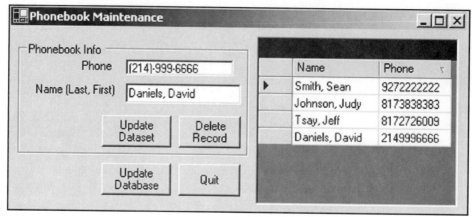

In this project, the data adapter and the dataset are created and handled by code. In addition, a data grid is bound to the dataset (by code) to display its current contents.

Control	Name	Comment
Masked edit box	mskPhone	For phone number entry
Text box	txtName	For name entry
Button	btnUpdateDataset	To update dataset
Button	btnDeleteRow	To delete record
Button	btnUpdateDatabase	To update database
Button	btnQuit	To quit
Data grid	dtgPhonebook	To display contents of the dataset
Open file dialog	cdlOpenFile	To prompt the user for the phonebook file path

The major steps involved in this project are the same as the preceding one; however, in each step, more code is required because of the additional requirements.

Declaring Variables for Connection, Data Adapter, and Dataset. The connection, data adapter, and dataset will be referenced in various procedures in the project, so they are declared in the general declaration area. The declarations appear as follows:

```
Dim cnnPhonebook As New OleDb.OleDbConnection()
Dim odaPhonebook As New OleDb.OleDbDataAdapter()
Dim dsPhonebook As New DataSet()
```

Setting Up the Commands for the Data Adapter. Because the project involves all aspects of maintaining the database, all four commands of the data adapter must be set up. The command text for the Select command can be created as follows:

```
Dim SelectSQL As String = "Select Name, Phone From
    tblPhonebook"
```

The Select SQL statement implies that all rows in the table will be retrieved; therefore, there is no need to create any parameter for this command. The Select command can then be set up in the same manner as shown in the preceding example:

```
odaPhonebook.SelectCommand = New OleDb.OleDbCommand(SelectSQL,
    cnnPhonebook)
```

The Insert command text should appear as follows:

```
Dim InsertSQL As String = "Insert Into tblPhonebook(Name,
    Phone) Values(?, ?)"
```

This Insert SQL statement indicates that the Name and Phone fields will be added, and their values should be supplied from the two corresponding parameters. In addition to setting up the command, two parameters should also be added. The way to code these requirements is the same as explained in the preceding example and should appear as follows:

```
odaPhonebook.InsertCommand = New OleDb.OleDbCommand(InsertSQL,
  cnnPhonebook) 'Set up Insert command
'set up parameters for insert command
odaPhonebook.InsertCommand.Parameters.Add("Name",
  Data.OleDb.OleDbType.BSTR, 50, "Name")
odaPhonebook.InsertCommand.Parameters.Add("Phone",
  Data.OleDb.OleDbType.BSTR, 50, "Phone")
```

The code to set up the Update and Delete commands is similar. In addition, the code to generate the dataset schema, fill the dataset, and bind the data grid to the dataset is the same as the preceding example. All these activities should be performed as soon as the program starts; the code for the complete form load procedure is as follows:

```
Private Sub Form1_Load(ByVal sender As System.Object, ByVal e As
    System.EventArgs) Handles MyBase.Load
    Dim TheDatabase As String
    Dim SelectSQL As String = "Select Name, Phone From
      tblPhonebook"
    Dim InsertSQL As String = "Insert Into tblPhonebook(Name,
      Phone) Values(?, ?)"
    Dim UpdateSQL As String = "Update tblPhonebook Set Name=?
      Where (Phone=?)"
    Dim DeleteSQL As String = "Delete From tblPhonebook Where
      (Phone=?)"
    TheDatabase = GetTheFileName()
    cnnPhonebook.ConnectionString =
      "Provider=Microsoft.Jet.OLEDB.4.0;Data source=" &
      TheDatabase
    With odaPhonebook
        'set up commands
        .SelectCommand = New OleDb.OleDbCommand(SelectSQL,
          cnnPhonebook)
        .InsertCommand = New OleDb.OleDbCommand(InsertSQL,
          cnnPhonebook)
        .UpdateCommand = New OleDb.OleDbCommand(UpdateSQL,
          cnnPhonebook)
        .DeleteCommand = New OleDb.OleDbCommand(DeleteSQL,
          cnnPhonebook)
        'set up parameters for insert command
        .InsertCommand.Parameters.Add("Name",
          Data.OleDb.OleDbType.BSTR, 50, "Name")
        .InsertCommand.Parameters.Add("Phone",
          Data.OleDb.OleDbType.BSTR, 50, "Phone")
        'set up parameters for update command
        .UpdateCommand.Parameters.Add("Name",
          Data.OleDb.OleDbType.BSTR, 50, "Name")
        .UpdateCommand.Parameters.Add("Phone",
          Data.OleDb.OleDbType.BSTR, 50, "Phone")
        'set up parameters for delete command
        .DeleteCommand.Parameters.Add("Phone",
          Data.OleDb.OleDbType.BSTR, 50, "Phone")
    End With
    dsPhonebook.Tables.Add("tblPhonebook") 'Specify table name
    'Fill the schema
    odaPhonebook.FillSchema(dsPhonebook, SchemaType.Mapped,
      "tblPhonebook")
    'Fill the dataset
    odaPhonebook.Fill(dsPhonebook, "tblPhonebook")
    'Bind the data grid to the dataset
    dtgPhonebook.DataSource = dsPhonebook.Tables("tblPhonebook")
End Sub
```

At the beginning of the procedure, the GetTheFileName function is used to prompt the user for the database path, and the result is assigned to a variable named TheDatabase, which is used to construct the connection string for the connection. In this manner, the user is able to specify the database location.

The GetTheFileName function uses the open file dialog to prompt the user for the file location. The code is similar to the example given in Chapter 6, "Input, Output, and Procedures," and appears as follows:

```
Private Function GetTheFileName() As String
    With cdlOpenFile
        .Filter = "MS Access file (*.mdb)¦*.mdb"
        .Title = "Where is the phonebook?"
        .ShowDialog()
        Return (.FileName)
    End With
End Function
```

Coding the Data Grid. After the dataset is filled, its contents are displayed in the data grid because of the data binding. This project will allow the user to select a record from the grid into the controls (the masked edit box and the text box) in the form for editing. When the user makes a selection from the data grid by clicking on a cell, the *CurrentCellChanged event* is triggered. The *CurrentCell property* gives the RowNumber and ColumnNumber of the selected cell. The grid also has the *Item property*, which is indexed by the row and column number (coded as Item(Row, Col)); the first being 0; therefore, Item(0, 0) will represent the content of the first cell. The code to move data from a row in the data grid to the controls appears as follows:

```
Private Sub dtgPhonebook_CurrentCellChanged(ByVal sender As
    System.Object, ByVal e As System.EventArgs) Handles
    dtgPhonebook.CurrentCellChanged
    Dim Row As Integer
    Row = dtgPhonebook.CurrentCell.RowNumber 'Get the current row
    txtName.Text = CStr(dtgPhonebook.Item(Row, 0))
    mskPhone.Text = Format(Val(dtgPhonebook.Item(Row, 1)), "(000)-
        000-0000")
End Sub
```

When the data grid is filled, the first column has the name, and the second column has the phone number because the Select SQL statement specifies name as the first field to retrieve. In the code, column 0 gives the name and column 1 gives the phone number.

If the Text property of the masked edit does not work properly, use the following code as a workaround:

```
mskPhone.SelStart = 0
mskPhone.SelLength = Len(mskPhone.Mask)
mskPhone.SelText = Format(Val(dtgPhonebook.Item(Row, 1)),
    "(000)-000-0000")
```

Maintaining Data in the Dataset. The approach to add, change, and delete records in the dataset is exactly the same as shown in the first phonebook maintenance example in this chapter. The code should appear as follows:

```
Private Sub btnUpdateDataset_Click(ByVal sender As System.Object,
    ByVal e As System.EventArgs) Handles btnUpdateDataset.Click
    Dim TheRecord As DataRow
    Dim FoundRows() As DataRow
    FoundRows =
      dsPhonebook.Tables("tblPhonebook").Select("Phone='" &
      mskPhone.ClipText & "'")
    If FoundRows.Length = 0 Then
        'New record; add row
        TheRecord = dsPhonebook.Tables("tblPhonebook").NewRow()
        TheRecord("Name") = txtName.Text
        TheRecord("Phone") = mskPhone.ClipText
```

```
                    dsPhonebook.Tables("tblPhonebook").Rows.Add(TheRecord)
              Else
                    FoundRows(0)("Name") = txtName.Text
              End If
        End Sub
        Private Sub btnDeleteRow_Click(ByVal sender As System.Object,
           ByVal e As System.EventArgs) Handles btnDeleteRow.Click
              Dim FoundRows() As DataRow
              FoundRows =
                dsPhonebook.Tables("tblPhonebook").Select("Phone='" &
                mskPhone.ClipText & "'")
              If FoundRows.Length = 0 Then
                    'Record not existing; display message
                    MsgBox("Record does not exist")
              Else
                    'Existing; delete
                    FoundRows(0).Delete()
              End If
        End Sub
```

Updating the Database. Again, the approach to update the database is the same as the first phonebook maintenance project. The code should appear as follows:

```
        Private Sub btnUpdateDatabase_Click(ByVal sender As System.Object,
           ByVal e As System.EventArgs) Handles btnUpdateDatabase.Click
              odaPhonebook.Update(dsPhonebook, "tblPhonebook")
              dsPhonebook.AcceptChanges()
        End Sub
```

Recall that you set up the four commands of the data adapter in the form load event; however, they do not appear to be used explicitly anywhere in the project. Rest assured that they are actually used by the data adapter. If you remove them from the code, you will encounter a runtime exception when the data adapter's Update method is called in this btnUpdateDatabase click event procedure.

To complete the project, you should also provide the code to handle the event when the user clicks the Quit button. It is left to you to complete.

Using Data Commands

The preceding example shows how the data adapter uses the commands to interact with the database (select records and maintain the database). When executing a command does not return any record, such as Insert, Update, or Delete, you can actually call the command directly without going through the data adapter. In this case, you can call the command's ExecuteNonQuery method to perform the task. This capability makes it flexible and convenient, not only to maintain the database but also to manipulate the database schema with the DDL.

For example, suppose you would like to add a table called Log to the phonebook database. This table will allow you to keep track of your calls to friends. The Log table will consist of two fields: a phone field, and a date field. You can create a command and then use its ExecuteNonQuery method to accomplish the task. The following code shows how this can be done:

```
              Dim cnnPhonebook As New OleDb.OleDbConnection
              Dim cmdAddLog As New OleDb.OleDbCommand()
              Dim TheDatabase As String
              Dim CreatetableSQL As String = "Create Table Log (Phone
                Text(20), [Date] Time)"
              TheDatabase = GetTheFileName()
              cnnPhonebook.ConnectionString =
                "Provider=Microsoft.Jet.OLEDB.4.0;Data Source=" &
                TheDatabase
              cmdAddLog = New OleDb.OleDbCommand(CreatetableSQL,
                cnnPhonebook)
              cnnPhonebook.Open()
              cmdAddLog.ExecuteNonQuery()
              cnnPhonebook.Close()
```

The code assumes that your project has the GetTheFileName function as shown in the preceding example to prompt the user for the database location. Creating this command takes exactly the same steps and same types of parameters that you used in the preceding example. The CreateTableSQL text string specifies that Phone is a Text (String) field of 20 characters long, and Date is a date/time field. Note that "Date" is a reserve word in MS Access and must be enclosed in a pair of brackets.

Notice that the connection must be opened (using its *Open method*) before the command can be called. The connection should be closed (using its *Close method*) as soon as the database operation is complete.

Saving Data "Locally"

In some cases, you may find it desirable to save the data in the dataset "locally." Recall that the dataset is a memory resident collection of data tables. These tables may not correspond exactly to their data sources. Keeping the current states of the dataset in the client computer (the one where the dataset resides) may enhance systems efficiency because the user can then proceed without having to reconstruct the dataset back to where it was. The dataset can simply be reloaded. In addition, the persisted (saved) dataset can also be used by other applications that understand the structure of the saved data.

The dataset reads and writes data (and schemas) as XML documents. (But you do not really have to know the XML to work with the dataset.) Suppose in the previous phonebook example, you want to save the data in the dataset locally. You can use its *WriteXML method* as follows:

```
dsPhonebook.WriteXML("C:\Temp\Phonebook.XML")
```

Later, you can ready it back using its *ReadXML method* as follows:

```
dsPhonebook.ReadXML("C:\Temp\Phonebook.XML")
```

You can also save the dataset schema information using the *WriteXMLSchema method* as follows:

```
dsPhonebook.WriteXMLSchema("C:\Temp\Phonebook.xsd")
```

To read the same schema, you can use the *ReadXMLSchema method* as follows:

```
dsPhoneBook.ReadXMLSchema("C:\Temp\Phonebook.xsd")
```

Notice the extension for the XMLSchema file is "xsd." Recall that this is exactly the same as the schema created when you used the data adapter to create the dataset at design time. After you have this schema file, you can use it to create a *typed dataset*, which is a derived dataset that incorporates the xsd information on the dataset structure. The datasets that you created using the data adapter at design time are all typed. In contrast, those datasets you created by code are *untyped datasets*. In general, typed datasets are more efficient because you can reference to a particular element in the dataset directly by name, while you must reference the same element as in a collection when the dataset is untyped. For example, in the phonebook example, the tblPhonebook table can be referenced as dsPhonebook1.tblPhonebook when you create the dataset using the data adapter. In contrast, when you create the dataset by code, you reference the same table as dsPhonebook.Tables("tblPhonebook").

Although the typed dataset is more efficient and provides more supports, the untyped dataset has the advantage of flexibility. When the structure of the dataset is not known at design time, your only choice is to use the untyped dataset.

Browsing Database Table Definitions (Schema)

From time to time, you may need to browse through the database to verify the existence of certain tables or columns. ADO.NET connection object provides such a capability with the *GetOleDbSchemaTable method.*

To illustrate the use of this method, consider a project. Suppose you would like to show in a list box named lstSchemaTables all the tables of a database specified by the user. When the user clicks a particular table name in this list box, the field (column) names of this table will show in yet another list box, named lstSchemaColumns. In addition, you will also have the program display the contents of the returned data table. The program begins with the user specifying the database by entering the filename in a text box, or by clicking a Browse button that will invoke an Open File dialog to prompt for the filename.

Figure 9.21 shows the visual interface at runtime. The following table lists the names of the controls used in the code.

Control	Name	Comment
Text box	txtFileName	To enter or display the specified database
Button	btnBrowse	To prompt for the filename using the open file dialog
Data grid	dtgSchema	To display the contents of returned schema
List box	lstSchemaTables	To display the names of the tables in the database
List box	lstSchemaColumns	To display the names of the columns of the selected table
Open file dialog	cdlOpenFile	For the user to select a file

Now consider the code.

Querying the Database Schema. The GetOleDbSchemaTable method returns a data table with the specified schema information. It has the following syntax:

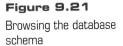

Figure 9.21

Browsing the database schema

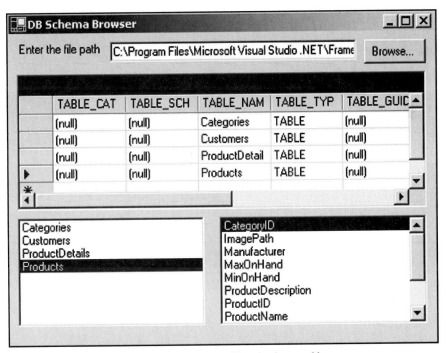

This project allows the user to specify a database and browse its schema. The data grid shows the contents of the returned table from the GetOleDbSchemaTable method when "Tables" is specified as the schema query. The table names in the database are displayed in the list box on the left. The field (column) names of the selected table are displayed in the list box on the right.

```
Connection.GetOleDbSchemaTable(Guid, Criteria)
```

where *Connection* = the connection object to perform the schema query

Guide = "globally unique identifier" specifies the type of schema query; e.g., Tables (for information pertaining to tables in the database) or Columns

Criteria = an Object type array specifying the criteria for the query; different query type will require different array parameters. The following table shows the criteria list for the Tables and Columns queries:

Query Type (Guid)	Criteria	Criteria
Tables	TABLE_CATALOG, TABLE_SCHEMA, TABLE_NAME, TABLE_TYPE	To query for the table names in the database, specify "Table" as the TABLE_TYPE. The criteria array will appear as {Nothing, Nothing, Nothing, "Table"}.
Columns	TABLE_CATALOG, TABLE_SCHEMA, TABLE_NAME, COLUMN_NAME	To query for the column names of a particular table, give the name of the table as the TABLE_NAME. Assume the table name is tblPhonebook. The criteria array will appear as {Nothing, Nothing, "tblPhonebook", Nothing}.

LOOK IT UP

If you are interested in the complete list of the query types and the criteria corresponding to each type, use the keyword "OpenSchema method" (not "GetOleDbSchemaTable method") in the Index tab to search the help file. Be sure that the **Filter by** box in the tab specifies no filter. Double-click the first found topic (at the Host Integration Server: Platform SDK) listed in the Index Results for. . . area. The page provides a list of queries and the corresponding criteria supported for different systems.

To use the method, you need to open the connection and provide the proper parameter values. Because it will return results in data table type, you will begin by declaring two DataTable variables and a connection variable. They should be declared in the general declaration area because they must persist for the entire duration of the project and are declared as follows:

```
Dim cnnDatabase As New OleDb.OleDbConnection()
Dim tblSchemaTables As DataTable 'To hold data related to tables
Dim tblSchemaColumns As DataTable 'To hold data related to columns
```

Before opening the connection, you must first set up its connection string. The code is similar to the preceding example and should appear as:

```
cnnDatabase.ConnectionString =
  "Provider=Microsoft.Jet.OLEDB.4.0;Data Source=" &
  txtFileName.Text
```

As shown above, the GetOleDbSchemaTable method also requires a parameter that specifies the query criteria, which should be an array of the Object type. The criteria vary depending on the schema query type. For example, if the query is for "Tables," this criteria (second) parameter expects an array that specifies four criteria as given in the preceding table. To specify these criteria, you can declare an array variable of the Object type as follows:

```
Dim Criteria(3) As Object
```

The variable Criteria will be indexed from 0 to 3, and will contain four elements. If you are interested in every kind of "tables" in the schema, you will not need to specify any criteria but just pass the variable as the second parameter. Because you are interested in only the "table" type of the TABLE_TYPE (the fourth criterion), you should specify the criteria as follows:

```
Criteria(3) = "Table"
```

The code to query for the tables in the database will then appear as follows:

```
cnnDatabase.Open()
tblSchemaTables =
  cnnDatabase.GetOleDbSchemaTable(Data.OleDb.OleDbSchemaGuid.
  Tables, Criteria)
cnnDatabase.Close()
```

As shown in the preceding table, the object array can be specified as {Nothing, Nothing, Nothing, "Table"}; therefore, an alternative way to code the statement to query for the database schema table without using the "Criteria" variable is:

```
tblSchemaTables =
  cnnDatabase.GetOleDbSchemaTable(Data.OleDb.
  OleDbSchemaGuid.Tables, _
  New Object() {Nothing, Nothing, Nothing, "Table"})
```

The returned result is assigned to the tblSchemaTables data table variable. Notice that the connection must be open before the method can be called. Notice also that you close the connection immediately after the method is executed. This is consistent with the spirit of ADO.NET: Disconnect the connection immediately after its use to release the resource used in the server computer (although in this case, the server computer is the same computer you are actually using to run this program).

After you have the result, you can bind the data table to the data grid and the list box on the left named lstSchemaTables. You have seen how a data grid can be bound to the data table, but how do you bind the list box? This control has the *DataSource property*, and can be coded the same way as the data grid; however, the list box can display only one column in the data table (as opposed to the entire table with the data grid). The column name should be specified in the *DisplayMember property*. The code to bind the list box to show the table name appears as follows:

```
lstSchemaTables.DataSource = tblSchemaTables
lstSchemaTables.DisplayMember =
  tblSchemaTables.Columns("Table_Name").ToString()
```

Take a look at the data grid in the same output. The grid displays the entire content of the returned data table. One of the column headings is TABLE_NAME, which is the column that contains the table names of interest. The second statement in the code specifies this column as the "display member." The column gives an array of the Object type, while the DisplayMember property expects string data; therefore, you must use the column's ToString method to convert to the String type from the Object type as shown in the code.

Now put the code together in a sub procedure to show the table names in a database. The code should appear as follows:

```
Dim cnnDatabase As New OleDb.OleDbConnection()
Dim tblSchemaTables As DataTable 'To hold data related tables
Dim tblSchemaColumns As DataTable 'To hold data related to columns

Private Sub ShowDBSchema()
    Dim Criteria(3) As Object
    Criteria(3) = "Table"
    cnnDatabase.ConnectionString =
      "Provider=Microsoft.Jet.OLEDB.4.0;Data Source=" &
      txtFileName.Text
    cnnDatabase.Open()
    tblSchemaTables =
      cnnDatabase.GetOleDbSchemaTable(OleDb.OleDbSchemaGuid.Tables,
      Criteria)
    cnnDatabase.Close()
    dtgSchema.DataSource = tblSchemaTables
    lstSchemaTables.DataSource = tblSchemaTables
    lstSchemaTables.DisplayMember =
      tblSchemaTables.Columns("Table_Name").ToString()
End Sub
```

Notice how the Guid for the query type is specified. "Tables" is enumerated in the OleDb name space under the OleDbSchemaGuid enumeration. (Enumeration will be discussed in Chapter 12, "Object-Based Programming." For the time being, just think of it as means of listing items under a group name.) It is coded as:

```
OleDb.OleDbSchemaGuid.Tables
```

Recall that when the user clicks the Browse button, or when the user enters the database name in the text box named txtFileName (and presses the Enter key), the table names in the database should be displayed. Each of these two events should call the ShowDBSchema procedure. The two event procedures should appear as follows:

```
Private Sub btnBrowse_Click(ByVal sender As System.Object, ByVal e
    As System.EventArgs) Handles btnBrowse.Click
      txtFileName.Text = GetTheFileName() 'Use the same function as
         shown in the preceding example
      ShowDBSchema()
End Sub

Private Sub txtFileName_KeyPress(ByVal sender As System.Object,
    ByVal e As System.Windows.Forms.KeyPressEventArgs) Handles
    txtFileName.KeyPress
      If AscW(e.KeyChar) = Keys.Return Then
          'enter key; call ShowDBSchema
          ShowDBSchema()
      End If
End Sub
```

Enter the above code and then run the project. (Make sure that the GetTheFileName function is copied from the preceding example.) After the program is working properly, comment out the statement Criteria(3) = "Table" and then run the program again. Examine the contents of the data grid carefully. You should notice that without the Criteria statement, the data grid contains many "tables" that are not user created. They are created by the system, and are usually of no interest to the user.

Querying for the Column Names of a Table. When an item (a table name in the database) in the list box lstSchemaTables is clicked, the field (column) names in that table should appear in another list box, lstSchemaColumns. Again, the GetOleDbSchemaTable method can be used to obtain the column (field) names. Because this method returns a data table, you have declared a DataTable variable to hold the results. The statement to obtain the result appears as follows:

```
tblSchemaColumns =
   cnnDatabase.GetOleDbSchemaTable(OleDb.OleDbSchemaGuid.Columns,
   Criteria)
```

The first parameter (OleDb.OleDbSchemaQuid.Columns) specifies the query type to be "columns" (data fields). As mentioned previously in this chapter, the second parameter varies with the first. As shown in the preceding table, under the "Columns" specification, the second parameter specifies four criteria: TABLE_CATALOG, TABLE_SCHEMA, TABLE_NAME, and COLUMN_NAME. Notice that the third criterion relates to the table name. Because you are interested in only those columns of a particular table, the table name should be specified as the third element of the Criteria parameter. The variable, Criteria, should be set up as follows:

```
Dim Criteria(3) As Object
Criteria(2) = lstSchemaTables.Text
```

The code to populate the list box with the field names of the table selected by the user (by clicking the item) is given as follows:

```
Private Sub lstSchemaTables_SelectedIndexChanged(ByVal sender As
  System.Object, ByVal e As System.EventArgs) Handles
  lstSchemaTables.SelectedIndexChanged
    Dim Criteria(3) As Object
    Criteria(2) = lstSchemaTables.Text
    cnnDatabase.Open()
    tblSchemaColumns =
      cnnDatabase.GetOleDbSchemaTable(OleDb.OleDbSchemaGuid.Columns,
      Criteria)
    cnnDatabase.Close()
    lstSchemaColumns.DataSource = tblSchemaColumns
    lstSchemaColumns.DisplayMember =
      tblSchemaColumns.Columns("Column_Name").ToString()
End Sub
```

The returned data table has a column containing the field names. The column name for this column is Column_Name; therefore, the expression Columns("Column_Name") should give the column names in the database table. For the same reason explained previously, the ToString method must be used to bind the column to the list box. Notice that the code is placed in the list box's SelectedIndexChanged event, which is raised when the user clicks the list box, or when the control's SelectedIndex is assigned a value.

The Data Reader

You may encounter a situation where the data need to be read only once, and either the dataset is huge making it impractical to cache the data in memory or some data fields need to be processed further before they are presented. In such cases, you should find the DataReader object handy. *The DataReader* retrieves a read-only, forward-only stream of data from a database. It reads one row of data at a time, and therefore uses limited system resources.

You create a DataReader object with the data command's *ExecuteReader method*, which can be called after the command is ready to perform a query in the database—that is, its command text must be in place and the connection must be open. The DataReader's *Read method* can then be used to read the data. Each time the Read method is called, it advances to the next record (row) of the returned set. The method also returns a value of True if the record exists, and False if no more data is available. If the record exists, you can obtain the field values in the record in several different ways:

- Use a numeric index. For example, Assume the DataReader object is named MyReader. MyReader(0) (or MyReader.GetValue(0)) will then return the value of the first field.

- Use the field name. For example, MyReader("Name") (or MyReader.Item("Name")) will return the value of the field named Name.

- Use one of the DataReader's data typed accessor methods. Each method allows you to obtain the value in the field's native data type. For example, the GetInt32 method will allow you to obtain a field of the Integer type. The advantage of using this approach is its speed. Data can be obtained without involving data type conversion; however, you must know the field's data type before calling the method. The following table shows a selected list of these methods:

Method	To access VB Data Type
GetDateTime	Date/Time
GetDouble	Double
GetFloat	Single
GetInt16	Short
GetInt32	Integer
GetInt64	Long
GetString	String

All these methods require an index as the parameter that indicates the ordinal position of the data field to access. For example, if you want to retrieve the second field that is an Integer, you will code *TheDataReaderName*.GetInt32(1).

While the data reader is still open, you can use its *GetSchemaTable method* to obtain the schema information about the result set. The method returns a data table with each row containing information pertaining to a data field of the result set and the columns giving the properties of the data fields. The connection is used exclusively by the data reader as long as the data reader is open. As soon as the data reader finishes its job, it should be closed immediately.

To illustrate how the DataReader object can be used, suppose you want to display in a list box all records in the tblPhonebook table that you created and maintained in the previous Phonebook example. Recall that the phone numbers were saved as strings without any extra characters such as dash or parenthesis, but now you want the numbers properly formatted. For example, a phone number 9991234567 will be shown as (999)-123-4567. Also, you would like to show schema information of the result set in a data grid. A sample result is shown in Figure 9.22.

The following table shows the controls used in code:

Control	Name	Remark
Data grid	dtgPhoneBookSchema	To display the schema information on the returned set
List box	lstPhoneBook	To display the contents of tblPhonebook
button	btnReadData	To invoke the procedure to read data from the database

The following event procedure will set up the connection and command, create the DataReader object (named PhonebookReader), and use the object to obtain the schema information of the returned set as well as read the data:

```
Private Sub btnReadData_Click(ByVal sender As System.Object, ByVal
    e As System.EventArgs) Handles btnReadData.Click
    'Declare and create a connection and data command objects
    Dim cnnPhonebook As New OleDb.OleDbConnection()
    Dim cmdPhonebook As New OleDb.OleDbCommand()
    'Declare a data reader and a datatable
    Dim PhonebookReader As OleDb.OleDbDataReader
    Dim PhonebookDataTable As DataTable
    Dim TheName As String
    Dim ThePhone As String
    'Set up connection string
    cnnPhonebook.ConnectionString =
        "Provider=Microsoft.Jet.OleDB.4.0;" & _
        "Data Source=Phonebook.mdb"
```

Figure 9.22

Sample results from the DataReader project

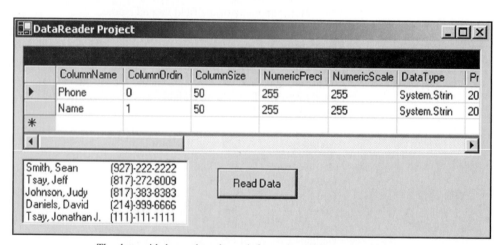

The data grid shows the schema information of the returned set.
The list box shows the contents of the returned set. Because the code uses the DataReader to access the returned set, it is also able to format the phone number for a nicer presentation in the process.

```
'Specify command text and connection for the command
cmdPhonebook.CommandText = "Select Phone, Name From
  tblPhonebook"
cmdPhonebook.Connection = cnnPhonebook
cnnPhonebook.Open()
lstPhonebook.Items.Clear()
'Create the data reader
PhonebookReader = cmdPhonebook.ExecuteReader
'Get the Schema info
PhonebookDataTable = PhonebookReader.GetSchemaTable
'Bind the datatable to the datagrid
dtgPhonebookSchema.DataSource = PhonebookDataTable
'Point to next record if it's available
Do While PhonebookReader.Read()
    'Obtain the first field (Phone); and format it
    ThePhone = Format(Val(PhonebookReader.GetString(0)),
      "(000)-000-0000")
    'Obtain the second field (name) and assign it to the name
    TheName = PhonebookReader.GetString(1)
    lstPhonebook.Items.Add(TheName & vbTab & ThePhone)
Loop
'Close the data reader to release the connection for other uses
PhonebookReader.Close()
'Close the connection to release the resources tied up with it
cnnPhonebook.Close()
End Sub
```

Notice that the DataReader is not created until after the connection is open. If you try to create the DataReader before opening the connection, you will encounter a runtime error. Notice also the DataTable obtained from the GetSchemaTable method is exactly like all other DataTables. It is bound to the data grid to display the schema information of the result set. The data grid shows two rows: one for Phone, and the other for Name because the Select statement in the command text specifies the two data fields.

In the code, the PhonebookReader object's Read method is called in the While statement. This statement serves two purposes. It makes the DataReader point to the next record. Also, the Read method's returned value is tested to determine whether the loop should continue. Recall that the Read method returns a value of True if the next record that it attempts to move exists, and False if the next record does not exist; therefore, the loop will continue only if the next record exists. Each data field in the returned record is accessed with the DataReader's GetString method because both are Text fields in the database table (tblPhonebook). Recall that you can use one of the several approaches to access the data fields, but the use of the data typed accessor methods is the most efficient because they involve no data conversion.

Finally, notice that the DataReader should be closed immediately after it completes its job. This is important because the DataReader uses the connection exclusively. Without closing the DataReader, the connection cannot be used for other purposes.

The code assumes that you place the Phonebook database in the Bin subfolder of the project (solution). You can modify the code so that the user can specify any location for the database. This modification is left to you.

9.4 Multiple Data Tables in a Dataset and the Data Relation

All previous examples involved a dataset that contains one data table. As mentioned in Section 9.2, "Using ADO.NET," a dataset can actually contain many data tables, just like a database. In addition, you can also set up relations between tables. These *data relations* enable you to specify the parent-child relationship, again just like the database. (Note, however, that the relations in a database are not automatically copied onto the dataset.) Most databases contain many tables that have a one-to-many (parent-child) relationship. For example, each customer can have many sales orders, so the Customer table and the Order table have a one-to-many (parent-child) relationship. Conventionally, to retrieve the related child records given a parent record, the Join (inner join or outer join) operation is performed. The resulting table tends to contain many repeated data elements from the parent record. With the data relation, the *GetChildRows method* makes it convenient to retrieve related child rows given a parent row without involving the join operations.

Browsing the Database Schema with the Use of Data Relation

The same schema browser project presented in the preceding section can be used as an example to illustrate the use of multiple data tables and the data relation. Recall in the preceding example the column names are retrieved when a table name is selected. If you do not set the criteria for retrieving the column names, the GetOleDbSchemaTable method will return a data table with all columns for all tables in the schema. This table should be the child table containing details for column names, while the data table for the schema tables is the parent table with its TABLE_NAME column pointing to the TABLE_NAME column of the child table. You can create a relation between these two columns.

You can use the same user interface, but what changes do you need to make in the code to handle the parent-child relationship? The data relation can only be created in a dataset, not in a data table, so you need to declare a data relation in addition to a dataset. Both of these variables should exist throughout the entire life of the project. Of course, you still need the connection and the two data tables to store the database tables and columns. The class level declarations should appear as follows:

```
Dim relTable2Col As DataRelation
Dim dsSchema As New DataSet()
Dim cnnDatabase As New OleDb.OleDbConnection()
Dim tblSchemaTables As New DataTable()
Dim tblSchemaColumns As New DataTable()
```

Retrieving Table and Column Information Without Restriction.
Information on both the schema tables and the schema columns can be retrieved when the connection is open. The code appears as follows:

```
Dim RestrictTable(3) As Object
Dim RestrictColumn(3) As Object
cnnDatabase.ConnectionString =
  "Provider=Microsoft.Jet.OLEDB.4.0;Data Source=" &
  txtFileName.Text
cnnDatabase.Open()
tblSchemaTables =
  cnnDatabase.GetOleDbSchemaTable(OleDb.OleDbSchemaGuid.Tables,
  RestrictTable)
tblSchemaColumns =
  cnnDatabase.GetOleDbSchemaTable(OleDb.OleDbSchemaGuid.Columns,
  RestrictColumn)
cnnDatabase.Close()
```

Notice that you did not set any criteria in the two Object variables used for the criteria parameters. They are still required by the method; however, without any criteria or restriction, all data pertaining to the schema query will be returned. Again, the connection is open for only as long as it takes to retrieved the desired information from the database.

Adding Data Tables to Dataset and Setting Up Relation. Both data
tables can be added to the data set using the dataset *Add method* as shown in the following code:

```
'Add the datatables to the dataset
dsSchema.Tables.Add(tblSchemaTables)
dsSchema.Tables.Add(tblSchemaColumns)
```

The relation between the two tables can then be set up using the dataset's *Relations.Add method* as shown below:

```
'Create the data relation
relTable2Col = dsSchema.Relations.Add("TableColumn",
  tblSchemaTables.Columns("Table_Name"), _
  tblSchemaColumns.Columns("Table_Name"))
```

The Complete ShowSchema Procedure. The complete code for the ShowSchema procedure revised from the preceding example based on the modified requirements appears as follows:

```
Dim relTable2Col As DataRelation
Dim dsSchema As New DataSet()
Dim cnnDatabase As New OleDb.OleDbConnection()
Dim tblSchemaTables As New DataTable()
Dim tblSchemaColumns As New DataTable()
Private Sub ShowSchema()
    Dim RestrictTable(3) As Object
    Dim RestrictColumn(3) As Object
    cnnDatabase.ConnectionString =
      "Provider=Microsoft.Jet.OLEDB.4.0;Data Source=" &
      txtFileName.Text
    cnnDatabase.Open()
    tblSchemaTables =
      cnnDatabase.GetOleDbSchemaTable(OleDb.OleDbSchemaGuid.Tables,
      RestrictTable)
    tblSchemaColumns =
      cnnDatabase.GetOleDbSchemaTable(OleDb.OleDbSchemaGuid.Columns,
      RestrictColumn)
    cnnDatabase.Close()
    'Recreate the dataset
    dsSchema = Nothing 'Make the dataset nothing
    dsSchema = New DataSet() 'Create a new dataset object
    'Add the datatables to the dataset
    dsSchema.Tables.Add(tblSchemaTables)
    dsSchema.Tables.Add(tblSchemaColumns)
    'Create the data relation
    relTable2Col = dsSchema.Relations.Add("TableColumn",
      tblSchemaTables.Columns("Table_Name"), _
    tblSchemaColumns.Columns("Table_Name"))
    'Bind the data grid to the data table for columns
    '(just to see what's in it)
    dtgSchema.DataSource = tblSchemaColumns
    'Bind the list box (for table names) to the data table
    lstSchemaTables.DataSource = tblSchemaTables
    lstSchemaTables.DisplayMember =
      tblSchemaTables.Columns("Table_Name").ToString()
End Sub
```

Notice in the code that two statements to recreate the dataset are also inserted before the data tables are added. The statements are necessary because each time the user specifies another database, the dataset must start from scratch with no previous data or schema. Also, the dataset is now bound to the data table containing schema columns instead of schema tables so you can browse and gain additional insight.

Obtaining and Displaying Child Rows. As in the preceding example, when the user clicks on a table name in the list box on the left (lstSchemaTables), the columns in that table should be displayed in the list box on the right (lstSchemaColumns). The rows (in the data table tblSchemaColumns) containing these columns can be obtained using the GetChildRows method. The syntax appears as follows:

```
ChildRows = ParentTable.Rows(Index).GetChildRows(Relation)
```

The returned child rows should be a data row array. The index gives the position of the particular row, and the relation is the data relation that defines the linkage of the two tables. The code for this example appears as follows:

```
Dim TheChildRows() As DataRow
TheChildRows =
  tblSchemaTables.Rows(lstSchemaTables.SelectedIndex).
  GetChildRows(relTable2Col)
```

When the user selects an item in the list box, the SelectedIndex property is set to point to that item; therefore, this property is the index specified for the row (Rows(lstSchemaTables.SelectedIndex)). There is no easy way to bind a column in a data row array to the list box, so you will need to loop through the array to obtain the elements in the Column_Name column. The code for the event procedure appears as follows:

```
Private Sub lstSchemaTables_SelectedIndexChanged(ByVal sender As
    System.Object, ByVal e As System.EventArgs) Handles
    lstSchemaTables.SelectedIndexChanged
  Dim TheChildRows() As DataRow
  Dim I As Integer
  TheChildRows =
    tblSchemaTables.Rows(lstSchemaTables.SelectedIndex).
    GetChildRows(relTable2Col)
  lstSchemaColumns.Items.Clear()
  For I = 0 To TheChildRows.Length - 1
      lstSchemaColumns.Items.Add(TheChildRows(I)("Column_Name"))
  Next I
End Sub
```

Additional Notes. This project includes the two event procedures as listed. You should also add the GetTheFileName function that prompts the user for the database location. For this application, this approach should be more efficient than the approach followed in the preceding code example. Using this approach, the connection is opened only once. For each database, all schema data are retrieved from the database into the two data tables in memory. All subsequent browsing for the columns in a database table is performed through the data relation. In contrast, in the preceding example, each time a database table is specified, a trip to the database server is required. This also requires establishing the connection. If the database is located in a different computer, the activity will increase the network traffic. In addition, each connection demands additional computing resources from the server computer.

A Concluding Comment

This chapter covered many important concepts and topics in data access and ADO.NET; however, these concepts barely scratch the surface in these areas. It is hoped that the chapter provided you with sufficient background for you to continue to explore and enhance your knowledge in these areas.

Summary

- Two distinct activities are required to create a database. The structure (schema) of the database must be defined first. Data can then be collected, stored, and maintained in the database. The data definition language (DDL) is used to define the database schema, while the data manipulation language (DML) is used to operate and maintain the database.

- A relational database consists of a collection of tables, in which each row represents a record and each column represents an attribute.

- An attribute in a table that uniquely identifies each record in a table is recognized as the primary key. The value of the primary key field of each record must not be missing (the entity integrity rule). A column that contains the primary key of another table is recognized as the foreign key. The foreign key must be either null or a value that exists as the primary key in another table. This rule is recognized as the referential integrity rule.

- The SQL Select statement is used to construct a virtual table from the database; its basic syntax is as follows:

- Select *Field1, Field2, . . .* From *Table1[, Table2,. . .]*

- [Where *(condition1)*[{And | Or}*(Condition2)*] [{And | Or} *(Condition3)*)][. . .]]

- [Order By *Sortfield1* [, *Sortfield2*, [*Sortfield3*. . . .] [Asc|Desc]]

The From portion can also contain Inner Join, Left Join, or Right Join specification.

- The SQL Insert, Delete, and Update statements are used to add, delete, or update records in database tables.

- The SQL Create Table statement is used to create new tables in a database.

- ADO.NET consists of a set of objects, such as the data adapter and the dataset, to handle data. The dataset is a memory resident collection of data tables and is independent of the data source, such as database, while the data adapter serves as an interface between the data sources and the dataset.

- The data adapter provides methods that can be used to extract data from the data source and fill the dataset. The data adapter's Update method can be used to add, delete, and update records in the data source, based on the status of the data rows in the dataset. In performing the operations, the method uses the proper commands (Select, Insert, Delete, and Update) that are either automatically generated during design time when the data adapter is being configured, or created by code if the adapter object is created by code.

- The dataset and the data table each provide a set of methods that can be used to create and modify the contents of the dataset. The dataset's Tables.Add method can be used to add data tables to the dataset. The data table's Rows.Add (Rows.Delete) can be used to add (delete) rows to (from) a data table.

- Changes made to the dataset, such as add and delete, cause certain rows to have several versions, such as current or previously modified. The dataset's AcceptChanges method commits these changes, and makes all data rows current. If you mean to have the data source (database) to reflect all changes made in the dataset, you should call the data adapter's Update method to update the data source before calling the dataset's AcceptChanges method.

- Various controls can be bound to the dataset to display its contents. The data grid can be used for such a purpose to display an entire data table.

- Under typical conditions, the dataset serves as a cache for all changes to be made to the data source. The data adapter's Update method is called only after all changes are complete for a session; however, in some special cases, it may be more efficient to update the data source immediately after a change (add or edit) is made. This chapter gave examples for each approach.

- The dataset that is created by configuring the data adapter and using the Generate Dataset option in the Data menu is a typed dataset, while the dataset created during runtime is an untyped dataset. The typed dataset enjoys more MS support, and can be coded to perform more efficiently by directly referencing the elements of the dataset by code, such as DsPhonebook1.tblPhonebook vs. dsPhonebook.Tables("tblPhoneBook"). The untyped dataset, however, has the flexibility of handling data whose structure (schema) is unknown until runtime.

- You can save the dataset in XML using the dataset's WriteXML method. The saved dataset can be reloaded into a dataset using the ReadXML method. The dataset's schema can be saved with the dataset's WriteXMLSchema method and then reloaded with the ReadXMLSchema method.

- If you do not expect a returned value from an SQL statement, you can use the oleDbCommand's ExecuteNonQuery directly to execute the SQL statement—without the data adapter.

- The connection object provides the GetOleDbSchemaTable method that can be used to retrieve schema information on the database.

- When a dataset consists of more than one table, you can use the dataset's Relations.Add method to set up relations between the data tables. The GetChildRows method returns the rows pertaining to a parent row. The GetParentRow method returns the parent row for a given child row.

Explore and Discover

9-1. **What Are the Contents of the Data Adapter Commands?** Bring an OLE DB data adapter to a new form. In the process, set its connection to the Phonebook database you created for the phonebook examples in the chapter and set the SQL statement to the following:

```
Select Name, Phone From tblPhonebook Where Phone = ?
```

After configuring the data adapter, rename it as **odaPhonebook**. In the form click event, enter the following code:

```
Console.WriteLine(odaPhonebook.SelectCommand.CommandText)
Console.WriteLine(odaPhonebook.InsertCommand.CommandText)
Console.WriteLine(odaPhonebook.DeleteCommand.CommandText)
Console.WriteLine(odaPhonebook.UpdateCommand.CommandText)
```

Run the project and then click the form. What do you see? When you use the data adapter to create a data set, it automatically creates the necessary commands that can be used to update the data source (database) when called for.

9-2. **What Is in the xsd File?** (continued from exercise 9-1) Create the Phonebook dataset in the preceding exercise, naming it **DsPhonebook** in the process. Double-click DsPhonebook.xsd in the Solution Explorer. What do you see? At the bottom of the code window, you should see two icons: DataSet and XML. Click each icon, and examine the code window area closely. The XML code gives the schema of the dataset.

9-3. **What Does the Connection String Specify?** (continued from exercise 9-2) Rename the connection object in the preceding exercise to cnnPhonebook; then add the following code in the form click event:

```
Console.WriteLine(cnnPhonebook.ConnectionString)
```

Run the project, and inspect the immediate window. You should be able to see how connection string is specified.

9-4. **What Is the Parameter Name?** (continued from exercise 9-3) Add the following statement in the form click event:

```
Console.WriteLine(odaPhonebook.SelectCommand.Parameters(0).
  ParameterName)
```

Run the project and then click the form. You should see Phone as the parameter name. The data adapter automatically sets up the parameter name to the same as the field name when you specify a parameter (?) in the SQL select statement.

9-5. **Creating More Than One Data Table in a Dataset at Design Time.** (*Note:* Before working on this exercise, use MS Access to set the CategoryID field in the Categories table of the grocertogo.mdb database as the primary key.) You can create a dataset that contains more than one data table at design time. Create a new project; then try the following steps to create a dataset from the grocertogo database:

1. Add a data adapter to a new project. Configure it so that the grocertogo database is the data source (connection), and the SQL statement is as follows:

   ```
   Select CategoryID, CategoryName From Categories
   ```

   Name the data adapter **odaCategories**.

2. Add another data adapter. Configure it to have the same database as the data source; the SQL statement is as follows:

   ```
   Select CategoryID, ProductID, ProductName From Products
   ```

   Name the data adapter **odaProducts**. (*Note*: Recall that because the Products table has no primary key, not all commands can be successfully generated. This should not affect what you want to accomplish.)

3. Select the Generate Dataset option from the Data menu. Make sure both Categories and Products in the Table(s) box of the Generate Dataset dialog box are checked. Name the dataset **DsCategoryProduct** and then click the OK button in the dialog box.

You should be able to find dsCategoryProduct.xsd in the Solution Explorer. Double-click the file name. If you see some XML text in the area the code window typically occupies, click the Dataset button below the text. You should see two tables. This means you have successfully created a dataset with two tables. (Double-click the form icon in the Solution Explorer to go back to the form.)

9-6. **Creating a Relation at Design Time.** (continued from exercise 9-5) You can create a relation between the two tables in the dataset you created in the preceding exercise. Follow these steps:

1. Double-click dsCategoryProduct.xsd in the Solution Explorer so that the two tables will appear. If the XML text appears, instead of the tables, click the Dataset button below the text.

2. Drag a Relation from the Toolbox into the CategoryID cell of the Products table. When the Edit Relation dialog box appears, verify that Categories is the Parent element and Products is the Child element. Also, both Key Fields and Foreign Key Fields show CategoryID as the key. Click the OK button in the dialog box.

3. Click the File menu and then select the Save DsCategoryProduct.xsd option.

You have now created and saved the Relation in the dataset. The Categories table is the parent table, and the Products table is the child table.

9-7. **Displaying Contents of Related Tables with Bound Controls.** (continued from 9-6) The relation created in the preceding exercise can be used to conveniently display all products in a selected category. Follow these steps to obtain the results:

1. Draw a list box and data grid on the form.

2. Set the DataSource property of the list box to **DsCategoryProduct1**, and the Display Member property to **Categories.CategoryName**.

3. Set the DataSource property of the data grid to **DsCategoryProduct1**, and the DataMember property to **Categories.CategoriesProducts** (name of the relation). Enter the following code in the form load event:

```
odaCategories.Fill(dsCategoryProduct1)
odaProducts.Fill(dsCategoryProduct1)
```

Run the project. Click an item in the list box, and observe the results in the data grid. (Note that you do not need to specify the data table for the Fill method because each data adapter is associated with a particular table.)

Exercises

Note: The grocertogo database referenced in many of the following exercises comes with VB.NET (VS.NET). If you are not familiar with the SQL but are familiar with MS Access, there is a way for you to learn the SQL. Make your query with MS Access first; then, while in query design, you can view the SQL constructed by Access by clicking the SQL View option in the View drop-down menu.

9-8.   Browsing a Database Table with the DataGrid Control. Draw a data grid on a new form. Make the data grid cover the entire available space of the form. (*Hint*: Use the data grid's Dock property.) Name the data grid **dtgProductDetails**.

Bring a data adapter to the form. Configure the data adapter so that the provider is Microsoft Jet OLEDB 4.0, and the data source is the grocertogo database. Set the SQL Select statement as follows:

```
Select * From ProductDetails
```

Create a dataset, and name it **dsGrocerToGo**. Also, set the DataSource property of the data grid to **DsGrocerToGo.ProductDetails**. Provide the code in the form load event to fill the dataset.

Run the project. Browse the table by clicking on the scrollbars (vertical and horizontal) on the data grid.

9-9.   Browsing a Database Table with Bound Text Boxes. Create a new project, and add a data adapter to your project. Draw four labels, four text boxes, and two buttons on a form. Align the labels vertically. Place the text boxes on the right side of the labels, and align them vertically, too. Set the Text properties of the two buttons to Next and Previous.

Name the data adapter **odaProductDetails**. Set its Connection String property so that Microsoft Jet OLEDB 4.0 is the provider, and the grocertogo database mentioned previously is the data source. Set the SQL statement as follows.

```
Select * From ProductDetails
```

Set the pertinent properties of the text boxes so that the following fields in the ProductDetails table may appear in these text boxes:

```
ProductID, Name, Grams, and Percent.
```

Set the Text property of each label to reflect the field name displayed in the corresponding text box.

Provide the proper code so that when the program starts, the first product detail record is shown. When the Next button is clicked, the next record is displayed; when the Previous button is clicked, the previous product detail record is shown.

9-10. **Browsing a Database Table with Bound Label Controls.** Replicate what you did in the preceding exercise on a new form with the following two changes:

1. Use any table in any database available in your computer (other than grocertogo.mdb).
2. Replace the text boxes with the label controls. Make these labels look similar to text boxes by setting their properties properly.

Observe good naming practice; that is, give these labels the field names to which they are bound, but begin with the "lbl" prefix.

9-11. **Browsing a Database Table with the Data Grid Control (One Parameter).** Use the grocertogo database. Set up a project such that only the records (in the ProductDetails table) for a ProductID (specified by the user in a text box) are displayed in a data grid.

9-12. **Browsing a Database Table with the Data Grid (Two Parameters).** The "Using Parameters for Query" example in this chapter allows the user to specify one specific CategoryID. Modify the project to display the same data fields in the data grid within the range of CategoryIDs specified by the user in two text boxes. (*Hint*: Both of the two parameters are related to the same field name. In such a case, the first parameter carries the same name as the field name, while the second one has the same name with a 1 as the suffix, such as CategoryID1.)

9-13. **Browsing Database Tables with the Data Grid Control (SQL).** Set up a project that will display the following data in a data grid for the pertinent records from the grocertogo database when the user clicks a button.

```
CategoryID
CategoryName
ProductName
Name (in ProductDetails table)
Grams
```

Note that the SQL should involve three tables: Categories, Products, and ProductDetails.

9-14. **Populating a Combo Box with Data.** Develop a project that will perform the following, using the grocertogo database:

When the user clicks the Search button after the user enters a portion of the product name in a text box, your program will show all the product names matching the search string in a combo box, sorted by ProductName. (Perform the sorting in the SQL statement.)

9-15. **Populating an Unbound List Box with Data from Database Tables (SQL).** Using the grocertogo database, develop a project that will perform the following:

1. The user interface will let the user specify in two text boxes the range of ProductIDs.
2. When the user clicks the Search button, your code will set up the parameters for the Select command of the data adapter to retrieve all products whose ID falls within this range. The fields to retrieve include ProductID, ProductName, ProductDescription and ServingSize, sorted by ProductName. (*Hint*: Refer to exercise 9-12 for a hint to handle multiple parameters related to the same field name.)
3. The search results should be populated by code in a list box showing all four fields selected. Use vbTab to separate the fields.

9-16.   **Retrieving Data with Items Selected from a List Box.** Use MS Access to create a database called Friends with a table named Directory that has the following fields:

Field Name	Name	Description
Name	Name (Last, First Init)	Text field; make this an index field allowing duplicates
Phone	Phone Number	Text field (no embedded special characters such as parentheses or -); make this the primary key
Address	Street Address	Text field
City	City	Text field
State	State Code	Text field
ZipCode	Zip Code	Text field

You can use this exercise and those following to create your personal directory. So, feel free to add more fields in this table.

Enter five records in the table directly with Access; then develop a project that satisfies the following requirements:

1.   Design a user interface that has all the fields listed in the table. In addition, there should be a list box on the right side of the form to show the names and phone numbers in the table. None of these VB controls should be bound to the dataset.
2.   As soon as your project runs, the list box will be populated with the names along with their phone numbers in the table.
3.   When the user double-clicks a name in the list box, your code will retrieve the record from the table, and show the content in the user interface.

9-17.   **Saving Data Entered in Unbound VB Controls to a Database Table.** (continued from exercise 9-16) Add a Save in Dataset button as well as an Update Database button to the interface you created for exercise 9-16. Provide code to save a new record in the dataset when the user clicks the Save in Dataset button. You may also want to provide code for data validation. The minimum should include ensuring that the name and the phone number have been entered properly. After the record is saved, the screen should be cleared and the list box updated. Your code should display a "Record saved in dataset" message. When the user clicks the Update Database button, the database is updated.

Note that the user can double-click the list box any time to retrieve an existing record; therefore, you should provide code to prevent an accidental loss of entered data. That is, if the user has already entered something in the form, your code should confirm with the user that it is okay to replace the data on the screen.

9-18.   **Adding and Updating Data Entered in Unbound VB Controls to a Database Table.** (continued from exercise 9-17) Modify the code in the preceding exercise such that at the time of saving the record in the dataset, if the phone number is found to be already in the table, your code will verify with the user that this is an update of an existing record. If the user affirms, your program proceeds to update the record; otherwise, your program will inform the user that no two records should have the same phone number (primary key).

Of course, if the phone number is not found in the table, your program should proceed to save the screen as a new record.

9-19. **Replicating Exercises 9-16 Through 9-18 with Different Application Context (Inventory).** Replicate what you did in exercises 9-16 through 9-18 with the Products table of an Inventory database. Make the following modifications:

Field Name	Description	Remarks
ProductID	Product ID	Has a pattern aaa-nn where a = letter; n = number. Make this field the primary key
Name	Product Name	Text string; make this field an index with no duplicate
Description	Description	Text string
Quantity	Quantity on hand	Maximum is 50,000; no fractional unit
Price	Unit cost	Ranges between 20 and 100 with decimal point

9-20. **Logging Phone Calls to Your Friends (Expanding on the Friends Directory Exercises).** By working on exercises 9-16 through 9-18, you have created a database table to keep track of the directory of your friends. Now, you would like to log all the phone calls you make to your friends. To do this, you will create another table called **PhoneLog** in your Friends database. The table has the following fields:

Field Name	Description
RecordID	An auto number field for record identification; make this field the primary key
Date	Date phone call is made; date/time
Phone	The phone number you call (this enables you to identify whom you call)
Duration	Time length of the call
Description	A description of the content of the conversation

Develop a project that will satisfy the following requirements:

1. Design a user interface for the user to enter the logs. Note that RecordID need not be entered (or even shown). You may want to use a list box, similar to the one in exercise 9-15, to show the names and phone numbers.
2. Provide the code to save the logs. Note that a future date would suggest a user error. Also, remember to check the existence of the phone number in the directory.

9-21. **Viewing Phone Logs by Friend.** Using the database you have developed in the exercise 9-21, develop a project that will allow you to review phone calls by friend. The form should have a list box that lists all your friends in the database. There should also be a data grid. When you select a friend in the list, all calls (pertinent rows in the log table) you have made to this friend should appear in the data grid. The dataset should have two data tables that correspond to the database. You should then set up the relation between the two tables and use it to handle the requirement.

9-22. **Purchase Orders.** (continued from exercise 9-19) (*Note:* This project involves multiple forms, and may be more suitable after you have learned to work with multiple forms.) After completing the requirements for 9-19, you would like to create an additional database table to keep track of the purchase orders for the same company. This table should have the following fields:

Field Name	Description
OrderNumber	Purchase order number; a seven-digit numeric field; primary key of the table
Date	Date of purchase order
VendorID	A six-digit numeric field
ProductID	The product ordered
Quantity	Quantity ordered
UnitPrice	Negotiated purchase price

Develop a project that will satisfy the following requirements:

1. Design a user interface for the purpose of performing the purchase order entry. Next to the ProductID field, there should be a button that allows the user to invoke a dialog box to search for the product ID. (We assume that there are many products; therefore, it is not practical to use a list box in the same form for the purpose of search.)

2. Design a dialog box (another form) that will allow the user to search for the product ID. The user will enter a portion of the product name into a text box and then click a Search button. There should be another button for the user to signal that the search is complete. Use a data grid to display the search results.

3. Provide the code to save the data entered in the purchase order entry screen to the database. The code should include data validation routines. Note that the product ID must exist in the Products table. Also, the new purchase price will be considered "unusual" if it is 10% higher or lower than that in the Products table.

4. Provide the code to invoke the product search dialog box. Note that the procedure to invoke the search dialog box should wait until the search is complete before it proceeds to execute the remainder of the code in the procedure. The code should place the search result in the VB control for the product ID field. (*Hint*: To invoke the dialog box, use the following syntax:

   FormObjectName.ShowDialog

   where *Form Name* is the name of the dialog box (form object).

5. Provide the code in the search dialog box to perform the search for the product. When the user clicks the Search button (after entering the search string), your code will display the search results in the data grid. When the user double-clicks an item in the data grid the item is selected. The dialog box will disappear. The selected item is picked up by the code in the purchase order entry form as described in step 4.

9-23. What Tables Are in a Database? Draw a button and a list box on a new form. Name the button **btnBrowse,** and set its Text property to **Browse**. Name the list box **lstTables**. Using the connection object, provide the code to obtain all the user-defined table names from the Phonebook database that you created for exercises 9-16 through 9-18 and 9-21, and to place these names in the list box when the user clicks the Browse button.

9-24. What Fields Are in a Database Table? (continued from exercise 9-23) Add one more list box to the form designed in exercise 9-23. Name this control **lstFields**. Now, add this additional feature to your project: When the user double-clicks on a table name in the lstTables list box, your code will show all the fields of this table in the list box lstFields.

9-25. Using the DataReader. Modify the code in the DataReader example in the text so that the user can specify the location of the Phonebook database.

9-26. Using the DataReader. Using the ProductDetails table in the grocertogo database, develop a project that will display in a list box the three fields (Name, Grams, Percent) for a specified ProductID. The ProductID is taken from a text box. Use a DataReader object to read the data. Also, for efficiency, use data typed accessor methods to access the data fields. (Name and Grams are Text fields. Percent is an Integer field.) The Percent field should be displayed with a % symbol. Insert a tab character between the data fields displayed in the list box.

9-27. Creating DB Tables by Code. Using the connection object (by code only), provide code to create the following two tables for a clinic:

Accounts table

Field Name	Description
Account Number	Numeric; Long integer
Name	Account holder name (Last, First, Init); text
Insurance ID	Text

Patients table

Field Name	Description
Account Number	Numeric; Long integer
Patient Sequence Number	Numeric; integer 0 for the account holder
Name	Patient name
Sex	M or F

(*Note:* Use MS Access to create a blank DB before attempting to add tables to it.)

9-28. **Creating a Dataset with Parent-Child Data Tables.** (refer to exercise 9-22) The database that you created has the Inventory table and the Purchase Orders table. Construct a dataset that contains two data tables corresponding to the database tables. The parent data table should contain ProductID, Name, and Description fields. The child data table should contain ProductID, Date, and Quantity (Ordered) fields. The two data tables are related by ProductID. Display the results in two data grids. When the user clicks a record (row) in the parent data grid, all rows (records) pertinent to that record should appear in the child data grid.

9-29. **Adding and Updating Records with ADO.NET by Code.** Replicate exercises 9-16 through 9-18 using ADO.NET by code only.

9-30. **Adding and Updating Records with ADO.NET.** Replicate exercise 9-19 using the ADO.NET by code only.

9-31. **Building the Dataset "Progressively."** In the text, two extreme approaches to updating the database were presented. The first approach brings all pertinent records from the database table into the dataset, and performs all updates before submitting these changes to the database. The second approach brings only one (or no) record from the database to the dataset, and submits the update immediately. A possible compromise is to start with an empty dataset similar to the second approach. When the user enters any data, the dataset is searched first for the pertinent record. If nothing is found, the database is then searched. If nothing is found in the database, the data is then added as a new record to the dataset; otherwise, the record is brought into and changed in the dataset. The database is updated only at the end of the session or when the user clicks an Update button.

Implement this approach with the phonebook database you created for exercise 9-16. (Ignore the requirements in that exercise.)

Projects

Note: Many of the exercises that are related to each other in this chapter, such as 9-16 through 9-18 plus 9-20 and 9-21, are of the magnitude of a project.

9-32. **Generating an Outstanding Student List.** A professor has maintained a database of outstanding students from his classes since the spring semester of 1995. He wants to generate an HTML file that he can post on his website. The tblOutstandingStudent database table has the following fields:

Field Name	Data Type	Remark
RecordNo	Auto number	Primary key
YearSemester	Long Integer (Integer in VB.NET)	First four digits for year; last two digits for semester; (01=Spring; 02=Summer; 03=Fall); for example, 200201 means spring of 2002
CourseSection	Text	A string representing the course and section number; such as ACCT3303-001
Name	Text	Name of the outstanding student
Rank	Long Integer	1 = highest in the class

The professor teaches up to three classes each semester. Each class can have one to four outstanding students. A sample output from the web page appears as follows:

Spring, 2002

Acct 3301-001	Roth, Michelle Catherine	Scott, Andrea Frances	Powell, Lacey Suzanne	
Acct 3303-501	Thompson, Judith Kay	Ochoa, Reynalda		
Acct 5335-501	Prajuabpansri, Boonsit	Treesupapchaikul, Nitchaporn	Lodal, Brian William	Li, Xiaowei

Fall, 2001

Acct 3303-001	Shackelford, Monica Torres	Atwood, Anna Nikolayevna	
Acct 3303-002	Wang, Dan	Tsai, Hui	
Acct 5315-501	Viwatkunupragan, Pornphan	Liu, Fang-Ting	Blackwood, Joanna Lynn

As you can see, the semester label precedes the list, and the most recent semester is presented first. In each class, the highest ranked student is listed first. Also, the list for each semester is presented in a tabular form. Your challenge is to generate an HTML file from the database table. For simplicity, focus only on generating the tables along with the semester label, and ignore other HTML elements. (*Note*: An HTML file is simply a text file containing additional HTML tags as explained below. Use the StreamWriter to write the output and name it **Outstanding.htm**. Also, use the DataReader to read data from the database. To ensure that data are read in the proper order, use the "Order By" clause in the Select command text.)

As a hint, the following sample HTML code will show the table as given below:

<H3>Fall, 2001</H3>

<TABLE>

<TR>

<TD>A

</TD>

<TD>B

</TD>

</TR>

<TR>

<TD>C

</TD>

<TD>

</TD>

</TR>

</TABLE>

Fall, 2001

A   B
C

HTML Basics:

- Tags are used to specify how texts should be displayed.
- A tag is enclosed in a pair of angled brackets, <>; such as <TABLE>.
- An open tag is usually matched with a closing tag. A closing tag begins with a "/" within the angled brackets, as </TABLE>. When you define a table, you begin with the <TABLE> tag and close the definition with the </TABLE> tag.
- The <TR></TR> pair defines a row.
- The <TD></TD> pair defines a cell. The text enclosed in the pair is displayed in that cell.
- The <H3></H3> pair defines a header of the third level.
- The <BR> tag represents break or absence of an element. The tag does not have a matching closing tag.

10. Special Topics in Data Entry

This chapter considers various issues related to the user interface/data-entry screens. It focuses on designing data-entry screens that can facilitate user efficiency and satisfaction with data entry/interaction. As pointed out in Chapter 1, "Introduction," VB programs operate in the graphical user interface (GUI) environment. Design under this environment is different from the traditional DOS character/keyboard based environment. This chapter first presents important principles that guide the design of the GUI. Several of these principles have been presented and observed in programming practices in previous chapters. This chapter further illustrates how some of these principles can be implemented in your programs.

After completing this chapter, you should be able to:

- Enumerate important principles of a sound GUI design.
- Provide code to enable the user to use the navigation keys, such as the Enter, Up arrow, and Down arrow keys, in a more traditional way by using the SendKeys object.
- Set up access keys for various VB controls to enable the user to move around the data-entry screen more freely and efficiently.
- Implement data entry error-checking routines at three different levels: individual key, field, and screen (form) levels.
- Implement error trapping and handling for your program to be more robust and user-friendly.
- Design and implement visual feedback in a program that involves lengthy processes.

10.1   Principles of GUI Design

Designing a GUI is more an art than a science. There are, however, principles that can be used to guide a sound design. An interface design that strictly follows these principles will result in a much more efficient, effective, and accurate data-entry screen. These principles include simplicity and clarity, flexibility, consistency, immediate feedback, forgiveness, and pleasant appearance. The following discussion considers each of these principles in more detail.

Simplicity and Clarity

All user interfaces (data-entry screens) should have *a simple and clear layout*. For example, each data field should be accompanied by a label that clearly indicates what is to be entered. To enhance neatness of the layout, logically related data should be grouped together within a container such as the group box. When many data fields are required, further grouping can be accomplished by using the Tab control.

Minimal Keystrokes. From the user's viewpoint, simplicity implies that the screen is easy to use. One aspect of this is to require the minimal number of keystrokes by the user to complete the task. You should consider alternatives to text boxes to obtain data from the user. For example, check boxes instead of text boxes can be used where the user is expected to answer Yes or No. Radio buttons or combo boxes can be used for mutually exclusive choices in place of text boxes for the user response. In any case, default values or settings can also be provided.

Recognition Versus Recall. In addition, you should bear in mind that it is much easier for the user to recognize than to recall an item. When the user is expected to enter an item that is already available to your program, such as an item that already exists in a database, it will be helpful if a list box or combo box is used to present data items for the user to choose from. If the list of existing items is too long; for example, customer numbers of an accounts receivable file with thousands of records, a custom dialog box can be provided to facilitate the search for the correct item.

Clear Labeling and Messages. Clarity also means various buttons for important actions should be captioned explicitly. For example, a button to save data should be labeled Save, not OK. The latter should be used only when the user is requested to acknowledge a message.

These points are considered throughout the book, and their uses were emphasized in Chapter 3, "Some Visual Basic Controls and Events," when introducing various VB controls for user interface design. In addition, this book has attempted to observe this principle in all examples. The previous discussion serves as a reminder of this principle.

Flexibility

Your program should provide the user with flexibility in *mobility* and in *customizing* the screen. The user should be given the freedom to move around the screen without undue restrictions. When the user uses the mouse, the user can click on any object onscreen, so the mobility is not an issue. What if the user prefers to use the keyboard? You should still provide a means for the user to move around easily. This can be accomplished by setting up access keys. The implementation of access keys is presented later in this chapter.

Providing flexibility should be balanced against data accuracy and safety. For example, as soon as the user enters a wrong type of key, such as a letter in a numeric field, a message should be clearly displayed. You should regard helping the user catch an entry error at the earliest possible point as a user-friendly design. This will guide the user to enter correct data, and avoid unnecessary keying attempts. Section 10.4 presents error-checking techniques.

Customization and Safety. Under certain circumstances, it is also desirable to provide the user with the ability to customize. For example, the size of a column in an onscreen report can be made adjustable. The tone and loudness of audio feedback (some users may even prefer none) can also be made adjustable. For safety reasons, allowing the user to customize screen or VB control colors may not be desirable. You should at least provide code to guard against choosing the same color for both foreground and background, which renders all entered data invisible.

Consistency

All data-entry screens should have *consistent appearance*. This includes the location of menus, buttons, and icons. Consistent screens make it much easier for the user to anticipate, identify, locate, and respond to relevant items. Wording and terminology displayed in labels and messages should also be consistent. Questions and prompts should be consistent in soliciting responses from users. For example, if a question is worded such that a No answer from the user means that the program should not quit, all questions in a similar context should be worded in the same manner.

Consistent Behavior. Consistency also means that all function and navigation keys should behave the same way throughout all screens. For example, if the Up and Down arrow keys are programmed to move up and down the data fields in one screen, they should behave the same way in all other screens. This eliminates the uncertainty in the user's mind when anticipating the responses from the computer.

Immediate Feedback

By nature, human beings need feedback. Imagine that you are talking on the phone for several minutes without hearing any voice from the other end. Won't you pause and ask, "Hello! Are you still there?" Similarly, the user may start to click various buttons or press different keys when the user sees no response from the computer after clicking a button. Many unexpected consequences might ensue if your program has already started the action after the first click. The importance of immediate proper feedback cannot be overemphasized.

Visual Feedback for Long Processes. When the user clicks a button to initiate a process that may take 1 or 2 seconds to complete, the program should change the mouse pointer to hourglass to indicate that an activity is being carried out. A slightly longer process should display a status message, such as "computing desired prime numbers". A process requiring more than just a few seconds to complete should display a progress bar to show the progress. All these provide a visual feedback to the user, and create a perception of faster process/response by the computer. Section 10.6 demonstrates how these can be implemented in VB.

Immediate Message for Entry Errors. When entering data, if the user presses a key not expected by the program (such as wrong data type), a message should be displayed so that the user is informed and can avoid attempting the same thing unsuccessfully. Any type of data-entry errors should be identified as soon as practicable.

Minimizing Unnecessary Effort. If the user is not expected to enter any data on a particular screen, either the screen should not be made available, or it should be shown on a read-only basis. In no case should the user be allowed to enter the data—only to be informed of the user's ineligibility when the user is ready to save.

Forgiveness

Human beings are prone to making unintentional mistakes. It is unavoidable that the user will press the wrong key or click the wrong button. When a serious consequence can ensue, your program should protect the user from these types of mistakes.

Protecting Against Potential Loss of Data. When the user takes an action that can mean loss of data, a warning message with a request to confirm the action should be displayed. If the user clicks a button to delete a file, a message should appear to confirm the action before the file is actually deleted. Also, when a large quantity of data onscreen is deleted, a way to undo the deletion should also be provided. In addition, if the user decides to leave a screen with unsaved data, a message should be displayed to warn the user of the potential loss of data, and an option should be provided for the user to go back to the screen.

Guard Against Abrupt Program Termination. Sometimes, a wrong answer from the user can cause operational problems to the computer, such as division by zero. Your program can be terminated abruptly. A program that behaves this way cannot be considered user-friendly. You should provide code to take care of potential problems of this nature. This chapter explains how to handle user errors that can cause your program to end abruptly.

Pleasant Appearance

The screen should appear harmonious in color and use of space, drawing the user's attention to the most important element of data on the screen. Colors and graphics that distract attention should be avoided. Although this principle appears to be easy to appreciate, people do vary in their taste. I have seen many "interesting" designs meant to be an enhancement for the presentation. It would seem advisable to seek opinions from experienced graphic designers when one has some unconventional design in color and graphics.

The following table summarizes this discussion, and indicates how each principle is treated in this chapter.

Principle	Applicable Objectives and Suggestions	Remark/Disposition
Simplicity and clarity	Has simple design and clear screen layout	Chapter 3, "Visual Basic Controls and Events," provides general guidelines.
		This principle is observed throughout the text.
	Requires minimal keystrokes for data-entry screens	
	Provides clues for easy recognition of required items	
	Provides clear labeling and instruction	
Flexibility	Allows users maximal latitude in moving around the screen	Section 10.2 discusses design of a user-friendly keyboard.
	Provides ways to customize	A few examples in the text touch the surface of customization.
Consistency	Has consistent appearance	The principle is considered only in general. No technical issue is explicitly treated in this text.
	Implements consistent behavior	
Immediate feedback	Provides visual cues and messages in long processes	Section 10.6 discusses different means of visual feedback.
	Provides immediate messages for errors in data entry	Section 10.4 discusses handling three levels of data validation.
Forgiveness	Warns users of potential loss of data	Section 10.3 illustrates the detection and caution of potential loss of data.
	Guards against potential computer problems and loss of data	Section 10.5 illustrates handling user errors that can cause problems for the program.
Pleasant appearance	Has harmonious screen layout and color.	Not treated in this text

As shown in the table summary, most of these principles are generally observed wherever they are applicable throughout this book. The following sections consider the implementation of some of these principles.

10.2 Designing a User-Friendly Keyboard

One principle stated in the preceding section is that the user should be provided with maximal allowable freedom in mobility around the screen. In data-entry applications, the user usually relies on the keyboard rather than the mouse to perform various activities. One important consideration of this aspect is that the user may expect a particular key to behave in a certain way, which may not be considered standard in the Windows environment. For example, the user may expect the focus to move to the next data field (control) when the user presses the Enter key, a habit that the user might have had since the DOS era. Under the Windows environment, the Tab key is used for the same purpose, whereas the Enter key is usually associated with a button such as Save. Should you then tell the user to change the habit and consider the matter closed? This will appear to ignore the user's need and should not be considered as a user-friendly attitude. This section considers a few of these issues with code solutions.

Handling the Enter Key

This subsection considers the issue cited in the preceding paragraph of this section. How do you make the Enter key move the focus to the next control?

There are ways to change the behavior of the Enter key. For example, for each control, you can test whether the key pressed is the Enter key. If so, you can use the Focus method to set the focus to the next control; however, such an approach is tedious to implement. To set the focus, you will need to identify the control involved. In addition, a group of similar code will need to be repeated for each of the controls involved.

The SendKeys Object. There is a simpler way to handle the Enter key. It involves the use of the SendKeys object, whose Send method allows the program to emulate sending keystrokes to the active window (control) as if the user pressed the keys. The method has the following syntax:

```
SendKeys.Send(Keys)
```

The following statement will send the text string "abcd" to txtName when the user tabs into the control:

```
Private Sub txtName_Enter(ByVal sender As System.Object, ByVal e
    As System.EventArgs) Handles txtName.Enter
      SendKeys.Send("abcd")
End Sub
```

Keys that are not displayed such as Tab, Home, and Delete should be coded with a special code enclosed in a pair of braces. For example, the following code will send a Tab key to the active window (control):

```
SendKeys.Send("{tab}")
```

Windows will then process the key accordingly. Because a normal Tab key moves the focus to the next control, that statement will bring the same effect. Recall that the named system constant vbTab represents the Tab key, Chr$(9). The following statement will accomplish the same:

```
SendKeys.Send(vbTab)
```

Converting the Enter Key. The Enter key can be trapped in the KeyPress event. If you use the Send method to send a Tab key in its place, you in effect convert the Enter key to the Tab key. This will move the focus to the next control. For example, if a form has a text box named txtID, you can code the procedure as follows:

```
Private Sub txtID_KeyPress(ByVal sender As System.Object, ByVal e
    As System.Windows.Forms.KeyPressEventArgs) Handles
    txtID.KeyPress
    If e.KeyChar = vbCr Then
        'The key pressed is the Enter key
        SendKeys.Send(vbTab) 'Send a tab key
        e.Handled = True 'Suppress further processing
    End If
End Sub
```

In the procedure, if the pressed key (e.KeyChar) is equal to vbCr (the Enter key), a Tab key is sent from the program to emulate the pressing of that key by the user. This should cause the Windows operating system to process the key and tab to the next control. The Handled parameter is assigned a value of True, which informs the system that the key has been properly handled. This suppresses the key actually pressed by the user. There will be no further processing of the Enter key. Without such a statement, the system will continue to process the key, and the user will hear a beep (or ding).

Although the preceding code will work, you will soon find a lot of repetitive code to handle the key if the form contains many controls. One elegant way to avoid such a situation is to place the same code in the *Form_KeyPress event* procedure. A form cannot receive focus when there are controls on it; however, it can intercept the keys from most controls, and handle these keys before passing them to the controls when its *KeyPreview property* is set to True. You can create a generic Enter key handler by setting the form's KeyPreview property to True and then entering the following code:

```
Private Sub Form1_KeyPress(ByVal sender As System.Object, ByVal e
    As System.Windows.Forms.KeyPressEventArgs) Handles
    MyBase.KeyPress
    If e.KeyChar = vbCr Then
        'The key pressed is the Enter key
        SendKeys.Send(vbTab) 'Send a tab key
        e.Handled = True 'Suppress further processing
    End If
End Sub
```

A few selected control characters are also enumerated as ControlChars. For example, ControlChars.Tab gives the Tab key, and ControlChar.Cr gives the Enter key.

Auto Tabbing

Many programs move focus to the next field when the current field is filled. This saves the user from having to press the Enter key. The masked edit box will behave this way when its *AutoTab property* is set to True.

The text box can be programmed to work the same way if its *Max Length property* is set to its proper value. Because the focus is expected to move to the next control after the last character is entered, you can consider placing the code in the *TextChanged event*. For example, using the same SendKeys trick, you can implement auto tabbing for the text box named txtID as follows:

```
Private Sub txtID_TextChanged(ByVal sender As System.Object, ByVal
   e As System.EventArgs) Handles txtID.TextChanged
    If txtID.SelectionStart >= txtID.MaxLength Then
        SendKeys.Send(vbTab)  'Tab to the next control
    End If
End Sub
```

The SelectionStart property gives the cursor position of the control. The If statement checks if this position is equal to or greater than the text's MaxLength. If so, a Tab key is sent, resulting in a move of the cursor to the next control.

> To make a masked edit box automatically tab to next control after it is filled with data, set its AutoTab property to True.

Although this code should work, you need to consider two issues. Experienced programmers are reluctant to suggest placing code in the TextChanged event because of the potential of encountering unexpected results. This is because when there is a change in txtID.Text—such as, some value is assigned to it, not necessarily by a key pressed by the user—this event is triggered; therefore, there is always that potential that a Tab key is sent unexpectedly by this procedure.

Also, if a form has many text boxes, there will be a lot of repetitive code. You could minimize the code repetition if there were a way to handle the TextChanged event for all controls at the form level. There's no TextChanged event for all controls at the form level, however.

You could indeed move the code to the form's *KeyUp event* to handle this, with an understanding that it will take some modification and look a bit unnatural.

```
Private Sub Form1_KeyUp(ByVal sender As System.Object, ByVal e As
   System.Windows.Forms.KeyEventArgs) Handles MyBase.KeyUp
    Dim TheBox As TextBox
    If TypeOf (ActiveControl) Is TextBox Then
        TheBox = CType(ActiveControl, TextBox)
        If TheBox.SelectionStart >= TheBox.MaxLength Then
            SendKeys.Send(vbTab)
        End If
    End If
End Sub
```

The KeyUp event occurs when the user releases the key pressed. It occurs after the TextChanged event. When the user presses a key, the events that occur in sequence include KeyDown, KeyPress, TextChanged, and KeyUp.

The event procedure first declares a text box variable, TheBox. It then tests whether the *ActiveControl* is a text box, using the TypeOf function. The ActiveControl represents the control that is active when the key is being pressed and released. The TypeOf function returns the type of an object parameter. This test for the text box is necessary because many controls are capable of accepting a key, but only the text box has both the SelectionStart and MaxLength properties. If the active control is indeed a text box, it is explicitly converted to TheBox, a variable of the TextBox type. You can then reference the SelectionStart and MaxLength properties with this variable, and send the Tab key as shown in the preceding example. When the form's KeyPreview property is set to True, this code should work for all text boxes in the form.

TIP

Wherever the Form's key event procedures (KeyPress, KeyDown, and KeyUp) are used, make sure the form's KeyPreview property is set to True. Many VB projects with key validation procedures fail to work properly just because the programmer forgets to set the form's KeyPreview property to True.

Arrow Keys Up and Down

In a similar fashion, in a form that has controls vertically aligned, the user may expect to use the Up and Down arrow keys to navigate up and down among the fields. The SendKeys object discussed can again be used to do the trick; however, the arrow keys are not trappable in the KeyPress event. Instead, they can be trapped in the *KeyDown event*, which occurs before the KeyPress event. Again, a form-level KeyDown event is available, and can be used to intercept all keys meant for the various controls for input purposes, such as text boxes, masked edit boxes, and so on. The KeyDown event provides the KeyEventArgs as its second argument, e. One of the elements in the argument list is the KeyCode of the key pressed.

The Left, Up, Right, and Down arrow keys have the key code values 37, 38, 39, and 40, respectively. Their corresponding named constants are Keys.Left, Keys.Up, Keys.Right, and Keys.Down. You can check for the Up and Down arrow keys, and handle them with the SendKeys object in a manner similar to the way you handle the Enter key:

```
Private Sub Form1_KeyDown(ByVal sender As System.Object, ByVal e
   As System.Windows.Forms.KeyEventArgs) Handles MyBase.KeyDown
      Select Case e.KeyCode
         Case Keys.Up
            ' Arrow key up; replace it with the Shift+Tab key
            SendKeys.Send("+{tab}")  'Send Shift+Tab key
            e.Handled = True 'Suppress the up-arrow key
         Case Keys.Down
            ' Arrow key down; replace it with the tab key
            SendKeys.Send(vbTab)  'Send tab key
            e.Handled = True 'Suppress the down-arrow key
      End Select
End Sub
```

Notice that the Down arrow key is handled in exactly the same way as the Enter key. Note also that some of the keys used in the Send method have special meanings. For example, the + sign represents the Shift key, and the % symbol represents the Alt key. As explained previously in a Look It Up sidebar in this chapter, if you mean to send a + as a + sign instead of the Shift key, you need to enclose the key in a pair of braces, as {+}. The Up arrow key has a named constant Keys.Up. When this key is pressed, the code will send Shift+Tab to inform the system to move the cursor up to the preceding control.

In this and the preceding subsection, the possibility that the Shift key is pressed is ignored. In some cases, when that key is pressed, some unexpected result can occur. A better alternative involves the use of the application program interface (API), but API is beyond the scope of this textbook.

Providing Access Keys

As discussed at the beginning of this chapter, providing the user with maximal mobility should mean that the user can move from one data-entry box to another wherever it may be in the form with the keyboard, not just with the mouse. You can accomplish this by providing the user with the access keys. This implementation does not even require any code. It involves creating the access keys and then setting up the proper tab orders for the controls.

Accessing a Control with the Text Property by Key. Some controls have the Text properties that are not meant to be changed during runtime; for example, the Text properties of buttons, check boxes, and radio buttons are not expected to change based on user input. You can set up access keys for these controls with their Text properties. Just place an & before the letter in the text that you want to be the access key. For example, suppose you have three controls on the forms: chkStudent (a check box), rbtMale (a radio button), and rbtFemale (another radio button) with the following texts: Student, Male, and Female, respectively. If you set these three texts to &Student, &Male, and &Female, respectively, you should see that S, M, and F in each respective control are underlined as shown in Figure 10.1. When you run the project, pressing Alt+S, Alt+M, Alt+F (in any order) will allow the focus to move to chkStudent, optMale, and optFemale, similar to the way you use the mouse to click on it. (*Note:* if you don't see these letters underlined, press the Alt key.)

> To show an & symbol in the text property for the label, button, check box, and radio button, enter && (two for one) in the desired position.

Accessing a Control Without the Text Property by Key. What if the control such as the combo box or list box that you want to move to does not have a Text property, or the property is to be used for data entry such as the text box and the masked edit box? In general, each of these controls is accompanied by a label control that indicates its content or purpose. For example, a text box named txtName will most likely be accompanied by a label with the text Name. To provide the access key functionality for the text box, you can do the following:

1. Set the access key to the label; for example, set the label's Text property to &Name. Also, make sure that the label's UseMnemonic property is set to True (default).

2. Set the TabIndex for the label and the text box in sequence; for example, set the TabIndex properties for the label and the text box to 0.0 and 0.1, respectively.

At runtime, the label does not receive focus. Any focus set to it will be given to the next control that can receive focus. Therefore, setting the TabIndex property for the label and the text box next to each other will allow the text box to receive the focus when the user presses the access key in the label.

Figure 10.1 shows a simplified data-entry form with access keys properly set up. Draw the same as a practice and notice the following points in particular:

- Place the & before the letter that is underlined in the caption of each control.

- Ensure that the label with the text Name has its TabIndex property set to 0, and that the Name text box has its TabIndex property set to 1. The TabIndex sequence is very important for a control that relies on another control with the Text property to receive the focus.

- Run the project after completing the visual interface. Test to ensure that the access keys work properly.

Figure 10.1

A visual interface with access keys

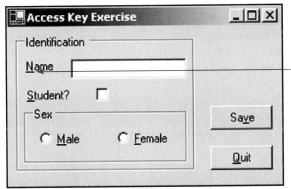

Here is a form with proper access keys. Notice the letter in each caption is underlined. Pressing Alt+<underlined letter> will move focus to that control. To underline the letter, place the & sign before the letter when you set the Text property. The tab indexes for lblName and txtName are set to 0 and 1 respectively. (They must be consecutive to work properly.)

Note also that the Student check box has its text placed before the check box. Set its Check Align property to middle right to show this effect. (There is no need to add a label.)

Using the Tab Control

Chapter 3 presented the Tab control as a container that can be used for a data-entry screen that has to handle a large number of data-entry fields. The following list provides additional points regarding use of the Tab control:

- If you set the multiline property to True (False is the default), when you have the tab captions exceeding the width of the control, the tabs will appear in multiple rows; otherwise, two arrow buttons will appear to allow the user to browse for the tabs. It is usually easier for the user to see all captions when navigating around the tabs, so it is advisable to set the Multiline property to True.

- The control has the Appearance property with different settings: Normal, Buttons, and FlatButtons. With the Normal setting, the Tab control shows its normal appearance at runtime with its clear boundary. With the Buttons setting, each of the tab page's captions is shown as a button, but the user may not be able to tell which controls are within the boundary of the tab page and which are not. With the FlatButton setting, the tab pages appear similar to the Buttons setting, except that the button captions appear flat like labels. You may be able to take advantage of this property to make its appearance fit your requirement.

- The control is actually a collection of tab pages, each as an individual object. Many properties can be set for each tab page individually. For example, you can set the BackColor, ForeColor, BorderStyle, and Font properties for each tab page differently. To set these properties, click the control's TabPages property in the Properties window to invoke the TabPage Collection Editor dialog box.

- At runtime, when you use the Tab key to tab through the controls inside a Tab control, the current tab (text/caption) will receive the focus after the last control on the tab is tabbed—not the next tab of the control. Using the keyboard, you can press Ctrl+Tab to move to the next tab, but only while the tab has the focus. This can prove to be inconvenient.

In general, the user is not really interested in the tab caption when engaging in data-entry operations. The user would rather get to the first control in each tab immediately after accessing (clicking) the tab of interest. One way to do this is to use *Focus method* to set the focus on the first control in each tab. The code can be placed in the Tab control's *SelectedIndexChanged event*.

To illustrate, assume a Tab control named tabAccount has three tabs. The first control in each tab respectively is txtAccountNo, txtInsuranceID, and txtEmployerID. The code will appear as follows:

```
Private Sub tabAccount_SelectedIndexChanged(ByVal sender As
   System.Object, ByVal e As System.EventArgs) Handles
   tabAccount.SelectedIndexChanged
   Select Case tabAccount.SelectedIndex
       Case 0
           ' Set focus on the first control in the first tab
           txtAccountNo.Focus()
       Case 1
           ' Set focus on the first control in the second tab
           txtInsuranceID.Focus()
       Case 2
           ' Set focus on the first control in the third tab
           txtEmployerID.Focus()
   End Select
End Sub
```

Notice that when the SelectedIndexChanged event is triggered, the control's SelectedIndex property is set to the tab selected, and the tab count starts with zero.

10.3   Additional Considerations on Friendly GUI Design

This section considers the potential loss of data onscreen when the program quits. The user may have clicked a wrong (Quit) button unintentionally after an entire screen of data has been entered but not yet saved. To guard against such a possibility, you should detect and warn the user of unsaved data, and allow the user to back out of the Quit button.

Detecting Unsaved Data

When the user clicks the Quit button, a user-friendly program should warn the user of the possibility of losing data if such a situation exists. Your code should first check to see whether the current screen contains any entered data. If you are sure that the user will rely on the keyboard exclusively to enter data, one possible approach to detect unsaved data is to set up a Boolean variable at the class level and then use it to keep track of whether any key has been pressed. The following code fragments illustrate this approach.

In the general declaration section:

```
Dim KeyPressed as Boolean 'Declare a module level variable
```

In the routine that saves the data:

```
KeyPressed = False 'data have been saved; all keys are
    "cleared"
```

In the Form_KeyPress event procedure (*Note:* Remember to set the form's KeyPreview property to True):

```
KeyPressed = True
```

This approach should detect all data entered through the keyboard; however, it will not detect data obtained by copy (or cut) and paste. Because all changes to text boxes and masked edit boxes will trigger the TextChanged event, an alternative is to place the preceding statement in the TextChanged event of each control. This approach should work elegantly if the number of text boxes and masked edit boxes on the form is fairly small.

If the form contains many text boxes and masked edit boxes, and if they are cleared when saved, an alternative is to check whether any control contains any data. The following function (named NotYetSaved) returns a value of True if any nonblank edit box is found.

```
Private Function NotYetSaved(ByVal TheObject As Control) As
    Boolean
    Dim Ctrl As Control
    Dim TheMaskedBox As AxMSMask.AxMaskEdBox
    For Each Ctrl In TheObject.Controls
        Select Case TypeName(Ctrl)
            Case "TextBox"
                If Len(Trim(Ctrl.Text)) > 0 Then
                    Return (True)
                End If
            Case "AxMaskEdBox"
                TheMaskedBox = CType(Ctrl, AxMSMask.AxMaskEdBox)
                If Len(Trim(TheMaskedBox.ClipText)) > 0 Then
                    Return (True)
                End If
            Case Else
                If Ctrl.Controls.Count > 0 Then
                    If NotYetSaved(Ctrl) Then
                        Return (True)
                    End If
                End If
        End Select
    Next Ctrl
End Function
```

This routine uses the For Each loop to enumerate through all controls in the form (or a control) and test whether each text box or masked edit box contains any nonblank data. If one is found, the function returns a value of True and the loop is terminated. You can use this function in the form Closing event to detect unsaved data as illustrated in the following code fragment:

```
If NotYetSaved(Me) Then
    ' Code to handle the case when data are not yet saved
End If
```

Notice how the Case Else portion in the function is coded. When a control is neither the text box nor the masked edit box, the routine checks to see if the control itself contains other controls by checking the Count property of its Controls collection. If the control does, the same NotYetSaved function is called to check for unsaved data in the controls contained in that control. (Recall that Me.Controls enumerates only those controls at the form level. Controls contained in a container such as the group box or the Tab control are not enumerated at the form level.) The recursive capability of VB procedures makes testing for unsaved data at different levels of containers much easier. Also, notice that the function uses a quick out approach. As soon as a control is found to contain data, the function returns True and then exits immediately.

Handling Unsaved Data When the Program Is Quitting

When the user clicks the Close (X) button on the form's control box, or when your code executes the Me.Close statement, two events will be triggered: the form's Closing and the *Closed event*. (It should be easy to infer that the Closing event occurs before the Closed event.) The Closing event provides a Cancel parameter that can be used to cancel the closing operation.

When you want your code to detect whether there are unsaved data on the form, you can place the code in the Closing event. Assume you use the first approach (detecting a key press) in the preceding section. You can code the following:

```
Private Sub Form1_Closing(ByVal sender As System.Object, ByVal e
    As System.ComponentModel.CancelEventArgs) Handles MyBase.Closing
    Dim Ans As Integer
    If KeyPressed Then
        Ans = MsgBox("Data not yet saved.  Ok to quit?",
          MsgBoxStyle.Question Or MsgBoxStyle.YesNo)
        If Ans = vbYes Then
        Else
            e.Cancel = True 'Cancel unload
        End If
    End If
End Sub
```

The statement in the form's KeyPress event procedure in the preceding section will ensure that the Boolean variable KeyPressed will reflect keys entered after data are saved. In the Closing event procedure, this variable is tested. If it is True, there are unsaved data. The MsgBox function is then used to warn the user and obtain the user's direction. If the user decides it is okay to quit, Ans will have a value vbYes (6). If not, the Cancel parameter is assigned a value of True so that the closing operation will be canceled.

If you use the last approach presented in the preceding section, you should include the NotYetSaved function in the class. In addition, the variable KeyPressed in the event procedure should be replaced with the function call NotYetSaved(Me).

LOOK IT UP

The form's Closing event has some additional interesting aspects. Use the keyword "Closing event" to search in the index tab of the help menu for additional discussion.

10.4   Checking for Data-Entry Errors

From the user's viewpoint, the user wants to be informed of an error at the point of its occurrence. This enables the user to make the correction immediately without having to look back for the source data, so the timing in checking for the error is exactly at the point of the error. An error can occur at one of the following three points:

- When the user presses a key
- When the user leaves a data field
- When the user signals that the screen entry is complete, which usually occurs when the user clicks a button such as Save or OK

This section considers checking for errors at each of these three points.

TIP

> The concepts and techniques involved in this section can be fairly complicated. The most effective way to learn the materials is to work along as you read.

To illustrate how error checking can be implemented at each of the three levels, a simplified W-4 data-entry form will be used as an example. Its visual interface appears in Figure 10.2.

The following table gives the controls used for the data fields and the settings of certain selected properties.

Field	Control	Property	Setting	Remark
Employee Number	Text box	Name	txtEmpNo	4 digits, numeric
Employee Name	Text box	Name	txtEmpName	Last, First Initial
Date of Employment	Masked edit box	Name	mskDateOfEmp	To illustrate mask
		Mask	##-???-####	checking
Zip Code	Combo box	Name	cboZipCode	User can select or enter a new Zip code
Number of Dependents	Text box	Name	txtDependents	three digits, numeric

The TabIndex properties of these controls are properly set by row and top-down; that is, the label with the text Employee Number has a TabIndex of zero; txtEmpNo, 1; and so forth.

Notice in particular that the masked edit box mskDateOfEmp has a mask "##-???-####" that expects two digits for the day of the month, three characters for the month, and four digits for the year. Some programmers maintain that such a field design ensures no confusion between month and day; however, it can also cause inconvenience to the user. It requires the user's familiarity. In addition, correcting an entry error can take additional effort. The design is used here simply for the purpose of illustrating how to handle a mask with mixed key types.

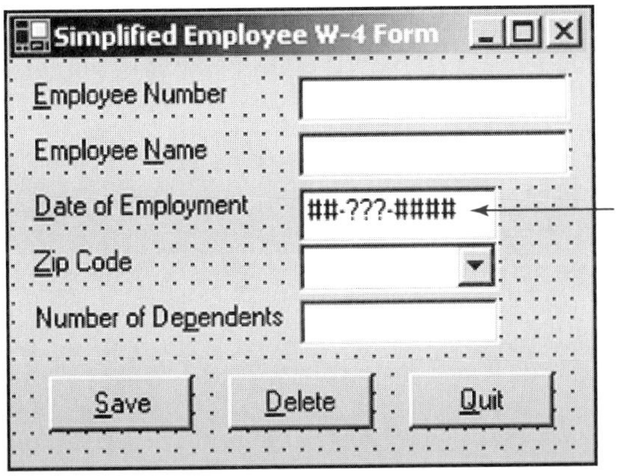

Figure 10.2

Simplified W-4 data-entry form

Simplified Employee W-4 Form

Employee Number

Employee Name

Date of Employment   ##-???-####

The mask is set to expect the Month being entered as a three-letter string, just to illustrate a generalized error checking for the masked edit box.

Zip Code

Number of Dependents

Save   Delete   Quit

Notice also that it is assumed when the program starts, the combo box cboZipcode will be populated with Zip codes stored in the employee database; however, the user can either select a Zip code from its list box, or enter one directly.

When the User Presses a Key

What kind of data-entry errors can your program detect at this level? Because all your program knows is the key the user presses, your program will not be able to tell whether the entire data field is valid. Your program, however, should be able to identify whether the key is numeric or alphabetic. Thus, when the user presses an alphabetic key and the data field is numeric, your program should be able to identify this type of error and inform the user accordingly.

Several types of VB controls accept key input: text boxes, mask edit boxes, and combo boxes. Checking for errors for each of these controls involves slightly different considerations. Consider the text box first.

Working with Text Boxes. Not all the keys pressed by the user are data input. For example, the user may press a control key, a navigation key, or a function key. Only the alphanumeric keys are meant for input. These keys can be checked for validity in the familiar KeyPress event. Recall that the key pressed is passed to the event as KeyChar. You can write code to check for specific types of key errors. For example, if a text box is intended for numeric data only, but the user presses an alphabetic key, the program should catch the error and display a message. The code to check for numeric keys has been illustrated in Chapter 5, "Decision." The code to check for the text box txtNumber is reproduced from that chapter as follows:

```
Private Sub txtNumber_KeyPress(ByVal sender As System.Object,
  ByVal e As System.Windows.Forms.KeyPressEventArgs) Handles
  txtNumber.KeyPress
    Dim KeyAscii As Integer
    KeyAscii = AscW(e.KeyChar)
    Select Case KeyAscii
        Case Is < Keys.Space
            ' These are control keys; ignore
        Case Keys.D0 To Keys.D9
            'These are numeric keys; ignore
        Case Else
            ' These are neither control keys nor numeric keys;
            ' display an error message
            MsgBox("Numeric key only, please.")
            e.Handled = True 'Suppress the key
    End Select
End Sub
```

For this example, the preceding routine can easily be modified to suit your needs. For example, you can place the same code in the KeyPress events for txtEmpNo and txtDependents, respectively to check for numeric keys.

In a similar fashion, you can write an event procedure to check for alphabetic keys for the text box named txtEmpName. The code appears as follows:

```
Private Sub txtEmpName_KeyPress(ByVal sender As System.Object,
  ByVal e As System.Windows.Forms.KeyPressEventArgs)  Handles
  txtEmpName.KeyPress
    Dim KeyAscii As Integer
    KeyAscii = AscW(UCase(e.KeyChar))
    Select Case KeyAscii
        Case Is < Keys.Space
            ' Control key.  Ignore it.
        Case Keys.A To Keys.Z
            ' Letters; do nothing
        Case Else
            ' Not an alphabetic key. Display an error message
            ' and nullify it.
            MsgBox("Alphabet keys only, please.")
```

```
            e.Handled = True
      End Select
   End Sub
```

The key pressed is first converted to uppercase using the UCase function. The key code of the result is then obtained using the AscW function, and assigned to a variable named KeyAscii. If the value is either in the range of control keys or alphabet keys, there will be no need for action; otherwise, a message is displayed and the key is suppressed by setting the Handled parameter to True.

Handling Special Characters. Note also that the code allows for alphabets only; however, the text box for employee names should also allow spaces, commas, and periods. You can add the following Case statement:

```
      Case Keys.Space, 44, 46 ' Space, comma, and period. Ignore.
```

You may have noticed that you use the literal constants for comma and period. There are no predefined constant names for comma or period, although space is defined as Keys.Space. An alternative is to use code Asc(",") and Asc(".") in place of the literal constants. This in effect uses the Asc function to generate the Ascii values. The code appears clear; however, it will execute a bit slower because function calls are involved. Another alternative is to declare the key codes for the two characters in the program with names such as keyComma and keyPeriod. They can then be used along with Keys.Space in the preceding line. For simplicity and clarity, the following code will be used for all later discussion:

```
      Case vbKeySpace, Asc(","), Asc(".")
         ' Space, comma, and period. Ignore.
```

> **TIP**
>
> If you type "Keys." (without quotes but with the period) in a procedure, you should be able to see a complete list of named key code constants.

The Ever-Present Repetitive Code. The preceding coding strategy, which includes error-checking code in each control's KeyPress event procedure, will work fine as long as the number of text boxes on a form is limited. When the number grows large, however, you will soon find the code for the project becomes fat. There will be a lot of duplicate code because each text box checking for the same type of errors will have to repeat exactly the same code in its own KeyPress event procedure. You may have already noticed this problem for txtEmpNo and txtDependents.

Minimizing Code for Key Verification. Two strategies can be used to minimize the code. One approach is to move the preceding code into independent Sub procedures (call them CheckNumeric and CheckAlphabet) and then replace the code in the event procedure with a Sub call. The code structure under this strategy will appear as follows:

```
'(In the General Section:)
Private Sub CheckNumeric(ByVal e As
   System.Windows.Forms.KeyPressEventArgs)
   Dim KeyAscii As Integer
   ' move the code under txtNumeric here
   KeyAscii = AscW(e.KeyChar)
   Select Case KeyAscii
      Case Is < Keys.Space
         ' This is a control key.  Ignore it.
      Case Keys.D0 To Keys.D9
         ' The key is between "0" and "9".
         ' No need to do anything.
      Case Else
         ' This key is not numeric, display an error message
         MsgBox("Numeric data only, please.")
```

```
                              e.Handled = True
                   End Select
         End Sub

         Private Sub CheckAlphabet(ByVal e As
            System.Windows.Forms.KeyPressEventArgs)
               Dim KeyAscii As Integer
               KeyAscii = AscW(UCase(e.KeyChar))
               ' move the code under txtEmpName_KeyPress here
               Select Case KeyAscii
                   Case Is < Keys.Space
                       ' Control key.  Ignore it.
                   Case Keys.A To Keys.Z
                       ' Uppercase and lowercase alphabets.
                       ' Need to do nothing
                   Case Keys.Space, Asc(","), Asc(".")
                       ' Space, comma, and period. Ignore.
                   Case Else
                       ' Not alphabetic key. Display an error message.
                       MsgBox("Alphabet only, please.")
                       'Nullify the key pressed.
                       e.Handled = True
               End Select
         End Sub

         '(The event procedures:)

         Private Sub txtEmpNo_KeyPress(ByVal sender As System.Object, ByVal
            e As System.Windows.Forms.KeyPressEventArgs) Handles
            txtEmpNo.KeyPress
               CheckNumeric(e)
         End Sub

         Private Sub txtEmpName_KeyPress(ByVal sender As System.Object,
            ByVal e As System.Windows.Forms.KeyPressEventArgs) Handles
            txtEmpName.KeyPress
               CheckAlphabet(e)
         End Sub
         Private Sub txtDependents_KeyPress(ByVal sender As System.Object,
            ByVal e As System.Windows.Forms.KeyPressEventArgs) Handles
            txtDependents.KeyPress
               CheckNumeric(e)
         End Sub
```

This strategy works well when the number of text boxes is moderate. The code already looks neat, although you will have to insert the code to call the proper error-checking routines in each KeyPress event procedure. Try the preceding code before continuing.

Key Verification with Form KeyPreview. The other strategy for code minimization with key verification requires no code in the event procedures but the setting of the Tag property of each control. This strategy takes advantage of the form's KeyPreview capability.

As explained in Section 10.2, when the form's KeyPreview property is set to True, all keys that are meant for the text boxes are first previewed by the form in the Form KeyPress event. If you can identify what type of data the current control (text box) expects, you can call the proper error-checking routine (as written previously) accordingly.

The code will be too cumbersome if the name of each control has to be identified individually in this event procedure. Fortunately, all you need to know is the data type (numeric or alphabet) the data field (control) allows. This can be accomplished by setting the control's Tag property to a predetermined value that identifies the particular type. For example, you can use N tag for numeric data and A tag for alphabetic data. The *Tag property* is an extra property provided for the programmer's use and is not used by the control itself; that is, setting the property to any value does not in any way affect the control's behavior or appearance. You can use it for any purpose you see fit.

To illustrate how to implement this strategy, at design time, you can first set the Tag property of txtEmpNo and txtDependents to N and that of txtEmpName to A. Instead of inserting any code in each control's KeyPress event procedure, use the following code:

```
Private Sub Form1_KeyPress(ByVal sender As System.Object, ByVal e
    As System.Windows.Forms.KeyPressEventArgs) Handles
    MyBase.KeyPress
      Select Case ActiveControl.Tag
          Case "A"
              CheckAlphabet(e)
          Case "N"
              CheckNumeric(e)
      End Select
End Sub
```

In the event procedure, ActiveControl in the Select statement refers to the VB control that is currently active when the key is pressed. VB's capability to recognize *ActiveControl* makes the code much more concise. ActiveControl.Tag refers to the Tag property of the active control. This property should be set at design time as explained previously.

TIP

Always make sure that the form's KeyPreview property is set to True when you have code in the form's KeyPress event procedure. Many times the code in the form KeyPress fails to execute, not because of any error in the code but because the developer's neglect to set this property to True. Also, if you mean to have a text box checked for data type error when you use the KeyPress event procedure, be sure to have its Tag property set properly.

Providing Additional Type Checking. The code for CheckAlphabet and CheckNumeric Subs should remain the same. All additional text boxes that require data type checking will only need to have their Tag properties set to either N or A, according to their expected data type. When more data types are used, additional tag values and error-checking Subs can be added under this strategy. For example, the preceding CheckNumeric Sub allows only integers. If another text box allows the decimal point, it will be proper to add another Sub, such as CheckDecimal; then another Tag value such as D can be used for this purpose. The implementation of this additional capability is left to you as an exercise at the end of this chapter.

Note that if you use this last strategy but set no Tag value for a control, no error checking will be performed on the key pressed in this control.

In summary, if a data-entry form has only a few text boxes, error checking can be coded in the control's KeyPress event procedure. If the form contains many text boxes, however, a strategy that works well is to set each control's Tag property to a predetermined value and then invoke the key validation routine in the Form KeyPress event procedure by matching the Tag value. In this case, the form's KeyPreview property must be set to True.

Working with Masked Edit Boxes. As you already know, masked edit boxes are useful in filtering out data-entry errors when a data field has a specific pattern such as dates or Social Security numbers. At design time, you can set the Mask property to the desired pattern, such as ###-##-#### for Social Security numbers. This masked edit box will deny the entry of any nonnumeric key. To keep the user informed, you should display a message when a wrong key is pressed.

If you use the key validation strategy that utilizes the form level KeyPress event, informing the user of a wrong key should involve only setting the proper character in the Tag property. For example, for a mask that expects all numeric characters, such as ##-##-#### or (###)-###-###, you can set the masked edit box's Tag property to N. No additional coding is required.

A Mask with Mixed Keys. A different coding scheme will be needed when a mask requires more than one type of data. In the example, mskDateOfEmp has a mask ##-???-####, suggesting that the first two positions and the eighth through the eleventh positions require numeric keys, whereas the fourth through the sixth positions call for alphabetic keys.

In this case, to be able to inform the user of the type of the expected key, the mask character must be identified. The error message will depend on the mask character. The code in the form's KeyPress event procedure should be modified to expect this variation and can appear as follows:

```
Private Sub Form1_KeyPress(ByVal sender As System.Object, ByVal e
    As System.Windows.Forms.KeyPressEventArgs) Handles
    MyBase.KeyPress
    Select Case ActiveControl.Tag
        Case "A"
            'Expecting alphabetic key
            CheckAlphabet(e)
        Case "N"
            'Expecting numeric key
            CheckNumeric(e)
        Case "M"
            ' Key type depends on the mask of the masked edit box
            CheckMask(e, CType(ActiveControl,
                AxMSMask.AxMaskEdBox))
    End Select
End Sub
```

The last case expects mixed keys based on the mask of a masked edit box. In this case, not only the event argument (e) but also the control itself is passed to a sub procedure named CheckMask. This procedure can be coded as follows:

```
Sub CheckMask(ByVal e As System.Windows.Forms.KeyPressEventArgs,
    ByVal mskControl As AxMSMask.AxMaskEdBox)
    Dim KeyPos As Integer
    Dim MaskChar As String
    KeyPos = mskControl.SelStart + 1
    MaskChar = Mid$(mskControl.Mask, KeyPos, 1)
    Select Case MaskChar
        Case "#"
            CheckNumeric(e)
        Case "?"
            CheckAlphabet(e)
    End Select
End Sub
```

This procedure expects the event argument (e) as its first parameter, and the masked edit box as its second parameter—and therefore the reason why in the preceding event procedure ActiveControl was converted to the masked edit type. It begins with obtaining the position in which the current key is being entered. Recall that the SelStart property gives the cursor position; however, SelStart starts with a value of 0 for the first position. To extract the corresponding mask character, you will need to use the Mid function, which considers the first position of a string position 1 rather than 0; therefore, 1 should be added. The Select Case block uses the extracted MaskChar to determine which Sub procedure to call. It will call CheckNumeric if the mask character is #, and call CheckAlphabet if the mask character is ?.

Checking for Errors at the KeyPress Level: A Recapitulation. If a form has only a few controls, you can use the strategy of checking for valid keys for each control individually. When the form has many controls, however, one strategy that minimizes the code is to take advantage of the form's KeyPreview feature. To perform the key validation at the form's KeyPress level, you should do the following:

- Set the form's KeyPreview property to True.
- Provide the error-checking procedures, each accepting only specific groups of keys. For the example, you should have three Sub procedures: CheckNumeric, CheckAlphabet, and CheckMask.

- Set the Tag property of each control according to the type of keys allowed. For the example, the Tag property should be set as follows:

Control	Tag Property Setting
txtEmpNo	N
txtEmpName	A
mskDateOfEmp	M
cboZipCode	N
txtDependents	N

- In the form's KeyPress event procedure, call the key validation procedures according to the Tag property of the active control to be checked.

This strategy requires a minimal amount of code and maintenance. When you add more VB controls to the form, chances are you need to do nothing about the code but just set their Tag properties. Remember to set the form's KeyPreview property to True to ensure that the form's KeyPress event procedure is activated properly.

When the User Is Done with the Field

Even if each individual key entered has been checked as illustrated, the resulting data field may not necessarily be valid. The user can leave the data field prematurely, resulting in incomplete data, or the entered field may correspond to no reality; for example, 02-DDD-1982 might have been entered as a date, so checking errors at the KeyPress level does not eliminate the need to check for errors at the field level.

The Validating Event and the CausesValidation Property.
When the user finishes entering the data in a field, the user will proceed to the next task by leaving the VB control (that field). A *Leave event* for that control is then raised. You can actually place the field level data validation code in this event; however, VB.NET includes a pair of features that make field level data validation really neat—the *Validating event* and the *CausesValidation property*. The Validating event occurs after the Leave event, but before another (the target) control receives the focus. The CausesValidation property of the target control, when set to True, will cause the original control's Validating event to be raised. The following paragraphs explain how this pair of features can be used to perform field-level data validation.

Checking for Missing Data.
Occasionally, the user may leave a field without keying anything, even though data is required for the field. To check for this error, an independent function can be written. The function can then be called from the Validating event of any control whose data entry is required, not optional. In the example, txtEmpNo should not be allowed to be blank. The code to check for missing data can appear as follows:

```
Private Sub txtEmpNo_Validating(ByVal sender As System.Object,
   ByVal e As System.ComponentModel.CancelEventArgs) Handles
   txtEmpNo.Validating
     If Missing(txtEmpNo.Text) Then
         MsgBox("Must have an employee number to proceed")
         e.Cancel = True
     End If
End Sub
Private Function Missing(Text as String) as Boolean
     Missing = Len(Trim(Text)) = 0
End function
```

In the text box's Validating procedure, the Missing function is called to check for missing data. If the function returns a value of True, an error message is displayed. In addition, the event's Cancel parameter is set to True. When this Boolean parameter is set to True, the control will retain the focus.

Will this Validating event be fired all the time when the user attempts to leave the text box? It depends on the setting of the CausesValidation property of the target control that the user is attempting to move to. For example, if the user is moving the focus to the text box named txtEmpName, which has its CausesValidation property set to True (default), the preceding Validating event will be fired. On the other hand, if the user clicks on the button named btnDelete, whose CausesValidation Property is set to False, the preceding Validate event procedure will not be triggered.

Setting for the CausesValidation Property. For each control that requires checking errors at the field level, you can place the error-checking code in its Validating event procedure; however, should you set the CausesValidation property of all controls in a form to True? In general, before the user moves the focus from one data-entry box to another, you want to be sure that the current control has valid data. You can set this property to True for all VB controls used for data input. This is not the case for some buttons. For example, consider the case of a Quit button. If its CausesValidation property is set to True, when the user decides to quit in the middle of a data field, this field's validation procedure will be triggered, insisting that the user enters valid data before being allowed to quit. Annoying, isn't it? In general, this property of the buttons should be set to False, except for the Save button. All data to be saved should be validated. Setting the button's CausesValidation property to True ensures that the current data field's Validating event will be triggered. As a side note, this is the key difference between using the Leave event and the Validating event. The Leave event will fire regardless of the target control, while the Validating event will fire only if the target control's CausesValidation property is set to True.

TIP

Set the CausesValidation property of all controls to True (default) except for those buttons for delete, quit, or browse operations.

The Missing function compares the length of the trimmed text with 0 and returns a True or False value depending on whether the comparison result is true or false. Note that the first = sign in the formula denotes assignment, whereas the second = sign calls for the comparison of the length with 0. The Trim function will return a zero-length string when the argument text is a string containing only spaces. The Len function will then return a zero. The comparison will result in a value True, which is then assigned to Missing, which is in turn returned to the calling procedure.

Because it is easy to check for missing data directly in a Validating event procedure, one might want to place the code directly in the event procedure instead of using the Missing function. The programmer might question the desirability of a coding structure as shown previously. One reason for showing such a code structure is to illustrate how error conditions common to many controls can be put together. In addition, the previous approach has an advantage of code consistency; all error conditions common to several controls can be coded in a similar manner. Only errors unique to a particular control will be written as additional error-checking code in the Validating event procedure.

For this example, all data-entry boxes should require data. You should therefore provide code in the Validating event of each control. The code for mskDateOfEmp should appear as follows:

```
Private Sub mskDateOfEmp_Validating(ByVal sender As System.Object,
    ByVal e As System.ComponentModel.CancelEventArgs) Handles
    mskDateOfEmp.Validating
    If Missing(mskDateOfEmp.ClipText) Then
        MsgBox("Please enter date of employment.",
          MsgBoxStyle.Information)
        e.Cancel = True
        Exit Sub
    End If
End Sub
```

Notice the ClipText property, not the Text property, is used to check for missing data. As you may recall, the ClipText property gives only the data (keys) that the user has entered and excludes the literal constants that the mask automatically provides, whereas the Text property includes all these characters.

All other controls can be checked for missing data in the same manner as the Validating event procedure for txtEmpNo. The code is left to you to complete.

Other Types of Errors. In general, each data field has its unique requirement in addition to some common error conditions such as missing data. At the field level, there is no elegant way similar to using the Form KeyPress event procedure illustrated previously to factor out the code for even the common error conditions. The following is all you can do to minimize code:

1. Write independent function procedures to return a value signaling an error condition.
2. Call the pertinent functions from the Validating event procedures. These event procedures can test the returned values and perform proper actions accordingly.

Two built-in functions that can be potentially useful to checking data field errors are *IsDate* and *IsNumeric*. The former can be used to test whether a data field, especially a masked edit control, is a valid date. For example, the following code can be placed in the Validating event procedure for a masked edit box named mskDate. It will display an error message when the control contains an invalid date.

```
If IsDate(mskDate.Text) Then
    ' The field appears acceptable, check the month.
    If Val(Microsoft.VisualBasic.Left(mskDate.Text, 2)) <= 12
      Then
        ' This is a valid date.  Do nothing.
    Else
        ' The date is not really valid.
        ' Display an error message.
        MsgBox("Please enter a valid date.")
        e.Cancel = True
    End If
Else
    MsgBox("Please enter a valid date.")
    e.Cancel = True
End If
```

In the preceding code, assume that the masked edit box expects a date in the format mm/dd/yyyy. The IsDate function accepts a date in either the mm/dd/yyyy format or the dd/mm/yyyy format, so both 02/28/1998 and 28/02/1998 will be considered valid. To be sure that the entered date conforms to the first format, the code checks the first two digits (for month) in the field to ensure that it is not greater than 12. Note that the code will not be suitable for the W-4 form example because of the different mask setting.

The IsNumeric function checks whether a data field is a valid numeric field. For example, IsNumeric("1X3") will return a value False, whereas IsNumeric("23.5") will return a value True. This function can be used in a manner similar to the code for IsDate.

You may wonder how a field can still go wrong if each key has been checked for numeric data type. It probably won't if it allows only numeric keys. If the field allows a decimal point, however, the code to check for numeric keys will need to be modified to accept the decimal point. If no additional care is taken to check for more than one decimal point in the field, the user might just happen to leave two or more decimal points. In this case, the IsNumeric function will come in handy as a final check for the field.

TIP

If the Text property of the masked edit box does work properly, you can use the following function as a workaround:

```
Private Function GetMaskedEditText(ByVal TheBox As
   AxMSMask.AxMaskEdBox) As String
      Dim MaskLen As Integer
      MaskLen = Len(TheBox.Mask)
      If MaskLen = 0 Then
          Return (TheBox.ClipText)
      Else
          TheBox.SelStart = 0
          TheBox.SelLength = MaskLen
          Return (TheBox.SelText)
      End If
End Function
```

To reference mskDate.Text, you can code GetMaskedEditText(mskDate) in its place.

Verifying Input with the User. Sometimes, as the user leaves a control, you may find it desirable to warn the user about certain conditions but not necessarily insist that the user enter a correct value. For example, the user may enter 12 in the text box for the number of dependents, named txtDependents. You cannot be sure that the user means 12. Perhaps the user meant to enter either 1 or 2 and, by mistake, left both in. Or, perhaps, the user does have 12 dependents. In such situations, rather than assuming the user is in error or accepting the data outright, you can call it to the attention of the user and then ask if the data should be accepted. Using the MsgBox function can conveniently implement this design concept. The code can appear as follows:

```
Private Sub txtDependents_Validating(ByVal sender As
   System.Object, ByVal e As System.ComponentModel.CancelEventArgs)
   Handles txtDependents.Validating
      Dim N As Integer
      Dim Ans As Integer
      'Use Val to take care of empty box
      N = CInt(Val(txtDependents.Text))
      If N > 5 Then
          Ans = MsgBox("Number of dependents = " & N & _
            ".  Ok to accept?", MsgBoxStyle.YesNo Or
            MsgBoxStyle.Question)
          If Ans = vbYes Then
             ' Ok. Do nothing.
          Else
             ' Not Ok to accept the number
             e.Cancel = True 'Retain focus
          End If
      End If
End Sub
```

The first argument of the MsgBox function displays the number of dependents and then asks whether it is OK to accept this value. The next argument makes MsgBox display both the Yes and No button as well as the ? icon in the message box. If the user clicks the Yes button, the MsgBox returns the value vbYes (6); otherwise, it returns the value vbNo (7). The returned answer value is assigned to the variable Ans. The computer then checks whether the Ans is vbYes. If not, suggesting not to accept the entry, it resets the focus to this control; otherwise, nothing is done, suggesting that the user's action is accepted. Figure 10.3 shows how the program reacts to a sample entry with a questionable value entered for the number of dependents field.

When to Check the Field. The previous sub-section presented the technique to check the field when the user is leaving the field. It should be noted that not all situations call for this design. Consider the case when you are placing a purchase order on a website. You might

Figure 10.3

Confirming a value in
data entry field

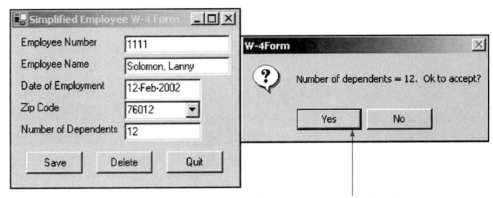

When you are uncertain about the accuracy
of the data entered, ask your user.

feel quite annoyed if the computer insists that you fill in valid data in each field before allowing you to move to the next. After all, you may be just feeling around, and are not even sure if you would complete the form and actually place the order. In such a case, your program will be considered friendlier if it checks all fields only when the user clicks the Submit button. On the other hand, if your program is designed for a high-volume head-down data entry operation in which the user transcribes the data in source documents onto the form (on the computer screen) one document after another, the user will certainly appreciate the program's immediate feedback. It is much easier for the user to correct the error right at the spot than to wait and look for the source of errors at a later point in time.

As a technical note, a test of the initial release of VB.NET indicates that the CauseValidation property and the Validating event do not work as expected; for example, if you have a button click event in which there is a Me.Close statement, the Validating event of the control that you are leaving will fire regardless of the setting of the CauseValidation property of the button. If you encounter a similar problem, check the Microsoft website for service packs that may fix this problem.

When the User Is Ready to Proceed

It would seem that if all data fields have routines to check for keys pressed and Validating event procedures to check for field-level errors, the resulting data screen should be valid when the user is ready to proceed (save, for instance). Not so! For example, the user may complete the first data field correctly and proceed to save the screen, leaving all other fields in the form blank. None of the KeyPress and Validating event procedures written for all subsequent controls would have been triggered.

One possible strategy to ensure that all data fields are entered is to allow the user to proceed only to the next control in the form. Although it is not hard to implement such a strategy, it is too restrictive and is not considered user friendly. This is particularly true when the user is updating a record with only a minor correction. Imagine the trouble of tabbing through a score of data fields to correct an error and then having to tab through another bundle of fields before you reach the Save button!

Calling the Validating Event Procedures from the Save Click Event. Another strategy is to call all the Validating procedures one by one in the Save button Click event procedure. This would appear to work; however, if you simply list all the Validating event procedures in the Save button Click event procedure, you may soon find the project behaves strangely.

To illustrate, assume you have had all the Validating event procedures written for the controls in our example (txtEmpNo, txtEmpName, mskDateOfEmp, cboZipCode, and txtDependents). You can gain this experience by adding the following code, which calls the Validating event procedure of all controls:

```
Private Sub btnSave_Click(ByVal sender As System.Object, ByVal e
    As System.EventArgs) Handles btnSave.Click
    Dim ce As New System.ComponentModel.CancelEventArgs()
    txtEmpNo_Validating(btnSave, ce)
    txtEmpName_Validating(btnSave, ce)
    mskDateOfEmp_Validating(btnSave, ce)                 ?
    cboZipCode_Validating(btnSave, ce)
    txtDependents_Validating(btnSave, ce)
End Sub
```

Run the project, and enter a number in the Employee Number field; then click the Save button. You should see a sequence of error messages followed by the text "Data saved." before you are given a chance to enter any data.

Recall that before this experiment, everything appears to work fine; that is, when a text box was blank, an error message was displayed and the focus was reset if you tried to proceed to the next data field. Why, then, does calling each Validating event procedure in sequence not seem to work properly? The mystery lies in the fact that these Validating procedures are now called and executed one right after another, whereas in the previous case, each of them is triggered by the control's Validating event itself. Previously, as soon as the Validating event procedure finishes, execution control is returned to the system, which waits for another event to be raised. Calling these Validating procedures one after another does not allow execution control to return to the system even when some error is detected.

In addition, there is another problem. Because these procedures are called from the button's Click event and not by the system when the events are fired, the Cancel parameter passed to the procedures are not used by the system to reset the focus but simply returned to the Save button's Click event procedure.

Tricking the System to Trigger the Validating Event. The only way to ensure that Validating event procedures behave properly is for the system to trigger the events. Is there a way to trick the system to do so by code? Recall that to trigger these procedures manually (initiated by the user), the focus should first be set on the first entry box (in this case, txtEmpNo). The user will then press the Tab key repetitively until the Save button is reached. Using code, you can set the focus on the first entry box by the Focus method. To tab through the controls, you can use the SendKeys object to send the Tab key as you did in previous sections. To repeat tabbing, you can use a loop. Your first approximation using this approach should appear as follows:

```
Private Sub btnSave_Click(ByVal sender As System.Object, ByVal e
    As System.EventArgs) Handles btnSave.Click
    txtEmpNo.Focus() 'Set focus on the first control
    Do Until ActiveControl.TabIndex >= btnSave.TabIndex
        SendKeys.Send(vbTab)  'Send the tab key to move focus
    Loop
    MsgBox("Data saved.") ' Pretending                ?
End Sub
```

In the procedure, you first set the focus on the first text box, txtEmpNo, which then becomes the active control. Inside the loop, the SendKeys statement sends a Tab key. If everything works as anticipated, the focus will move to the next control. As the focus moves, ActiveControl will refer to the control currently receiving focus. The Until clause in the Do statement tests to ensure that all controls (for input) have been tabbed through by comparing the TabIndex of the active control with that of the button (btnSave). If it is greater or equal, all the controls for input must have been tabbed through. The focus is back on the Save button. (*Note:* Before testing the procedure, make sure that the TabIndex properties of all the controls are set properly.)

If you run the program and then click the Save button, it will first ask you to enter the employee number. After you enter the number and click the button again, however, you will notice that the computer locks up. Press Ctrl+Enter+Delete to activate the Windows task manager to end this task. (If you feel certain that the program will lock up and do not really want the experience, you can skip this test.)

What happened? Why doesn't the SendKeys object work? Recall that its Send method emulates keys being sent to the Windows operating system. As your program is busily executing the loop, the operating system is not given the time to process the Tab key(s) sent by your program. To ensure that the operating system is given time to handle the environment, such as processing keys entered and mouse clicks by the user or updating the screen appearance, you need to release the execution control to the operating system.

The Application DoEvents Method. The statement to fulfill this is the *DoEvents method of the Application object*. This object provides the methods and properties to manage your application. The DoEvents method is one of the methods that the object provides. The method releases the execution control to the operating system. As soon as the system finishes its work, execution control will return to the statement immediately following the DoEvents statement. The preceding loop should be modified as follows:

```
Do Until ActiveControl.TabIndex >= btnSave.TabIndex
SendKeys.Send(vbTab)  'Send the tab key to move focus
'Release control to the Windows operating system
Application.DoEvents()
Loop              ?
```

If you test run the program again and then click the Save button without entering any data, it still does not work properly. This time, after you enter the employee number and then click the Save button again, it continues to display the message, "Must have a name to proceed." In addition, the focus remains on the text box for employee name. (Click the End button twice to end the program.)

What went wrong this time? Examine the loop again. The Send method sends the Tab key. With the DoEvents method, the operating system is able to attempt to move the focus to the second control; however, an error (missing data) is then detected in the txtName's Validating event, causing the error message to be displayed and the control to retain the focus. The loop is then executed another time with the same sequence of events, and so goes the endless loop. What you need now is to exit the loop (the procedure) when an error is detected.

"Signaling" Error from the Validating Procedures. You need to find a way for the Validating procedures to inform the loop when an error is detected. This can be done by setting up a class-level Boolean variable, such as BadField. When each of the Validating procedures is triggered, if an error is found, the procedure can set the variable to True. The variable can be set to False at the beginning of the loop. Inside the loop, an If statement can be used to test whether the variable is True. If so, the execution control should be returned to the system level (Exit Sub) so that the user can correct the error. The button's Click event procedure should appear as follows:

```
Private Sub btnSave_Click(ByVal sender As System.Object, ByVal e
   As System.EventArgs) Handles btnSave.Click
    BadField = False
    txtEmpNo.Focus() 'Set focus on the first control
    Do Until ActiveControl.TabIndex >= btnSave.TabIndex
        SendKeys.Send(vbTab)  'Send the tab key to move focus
        Application.DoEvents()
        If BadField Then Exit Sub 'Bad field encountered; get out
    Loop
    MsgBox("Data saved.") ' Pretending
End Sub
```

The txtEmpNo Validating procedure should look like the following:

```
Private Sub txtEmpNo_Validating(ByVal sender As System.Object,
   ByVal e As System.ComponentModel.CancelEventArgs) Handles
   txtEmpNo.Validating
     If Missing(txtEmpNo.Text) Then
         MsgBox("Must have an employee number to proceed")
         e.Cancel = True
         BadField = True 'Signal bad field encountered
     End If
End Sub
```

Of course, all other Validating procedures should include the statement to assign True to
BadField where an error is detected. (Place the statement immediately below e.Cancel = True.) In
addition, in the general declaration section, the variable BadField should be declared as follows:

```
Dim BadField as Boolean
```

This statement makes the variable BadField a class-level variable recognizable by all procedures in the form. After you complete this revision, test your program again. It should work
properly.

To summarize, at the screen level, there is an elegant way to trigger all the Validating event
procedures to ensure that all data-entry boxes contain valid data. This is accomplished by doing
the following:

- Setting the focus on the first data-entry box using the Focus method

- Assigning False to a class-level error flag (called it BadField in this example) before
  the loop

- Repetitively sending the Tab key followed by a statement that calls the application
  object's DoEvents method to tab through all data-entry boxes so that the Validating procedures are triggered

- Testing in the loop whether the error flag (BadField) is True; and if so, exiting the procedure (note that these four steps should be coded in the btnSave procedure)

- Setting the error flag (BadField) to True in the Validating procedures where errors are
  found

10.5 Handling Errors

Consider the following program:

```
Private Sub btnSave_Click(ByVal sender As System.Object, ByVal e
   As System.EventArgs) Handles btnSave.Click
     Dim TextFile As IO.StreamWriter
     MsgBox("Please insert a blank diskette in drive A. " _
       & "Click the OK button when ready.")
     TextFile = New IO.StreamWriter("a:\TextFile.txt")
     TextFile.Write(txtContent.Text)
     TextFile.Close()
End Sub
```

As you can see, this program saves whatever the user types in a text box named txtContent to
a file named TextFile.txt in Drive A. Before the Save operation starts, you are careful enough to
remind the user to insert a blank disk in Drive A and then click the OK button when everything
is set. The program has no syntax error or logic error, so it appears to be bug free. Does this mean
that it will work without any problem? The following discussion provides an answer.

A User's Nightmare in Previous Versions

Suppose the preceding program is written with a previous version of VB (using syntax compatible for that version). The answer is yes it will work fine, until an absent-minded user forgets to

Figure 10.4

Possible outcome when saving a file in a previous version

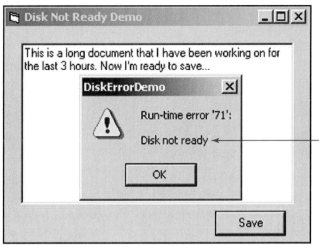

Under a previous version of VB, a user can run into the "Disk not ready" error and lose all his (her) work if the error is not handled properly in the program.

insert a disk before the user clicks the OK button in the message box; then, the system displays a message showing "Run-time Error '71': Disk not ready." If the program has been compiled and is being run from Windows, the only option is to click the OK button. (See Figure 10.4.) The program is then terminated and disappears from the screen, giving the user no recourse.

Slightly Better with the Current Version. Under VB.NET within the IDE, when the user encounters the same problem, the user is given a choice between Continue and Break. (The non-action choice Help as shown in the top of Figure 10.5 explains how Continue and Break are handled.) In either case, the user ends up losing the data. Running the compiled

Figure 10.5

Error messages under VB.NET

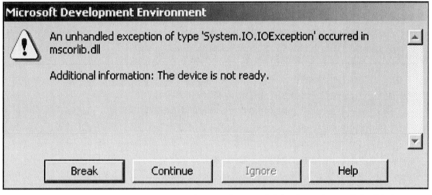

When the user attempts to save a file in drive A without inserting a disk, this is the message he (she) will see if the program runs in the IDE. The program is then terminated regardless of the option he (she) chooses.

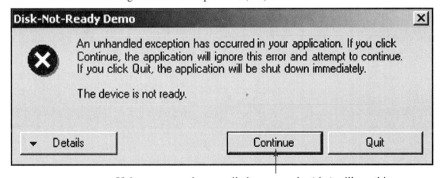

If the user runs the compiled program, he (she) will see this message box, instead. The user will have a chance to go back and try to save the data again if he (she) chooses the Continue option.

version, the user is given the option to Continue or Quit. (The non-action option, Details, gives technical details tracing errors through various routines.) The bottom of Figure 10.5 shows the message box. The user is now given a chance to go back if the user chooses the Continue option; however, the error message can be made clearer to help the user perform their job more easily.

Safeguarding the User. Although it is not the program's (or programmer's) fault that the disk drive is not ready, a program that displays an unclear message or can easily cause the user to lose data is not considered user friendly. As explained in Section 10.1, a sound GUI program should be forgiving; that is, it should not punish the user for making a mistake. Imagine that the user has spent three hours working on the text that represents an important document. Clicking the Save button was the last step to complete the job!

The Try. . . Catch. . . Finally. . . End Try Structure

So, what code can you provide to protect the user from losing data? A structured way to handle runtime errors of this nature is to use the Try. . . End Try structure, which appears as follows:

```
Try
    'Statements that may encounter exceptions
Catch ex1 As TypeOfException1
    'Statements to execute to handle exception of type 1
Catch ex2 As TypeOfException2
    'Statements to execute to handle exception of type 2
    .
.
.
Finally
    'Statements to execute regardless of
    'whether an exception occurs or not
End Try
```

When a statement following the *Try* keyword encounters a runtime error (recognized as an *exception*), execution control is transferred to the *Catch* block. A Catch statement specifies the type of exception to catch, similar to a Case in the Select Case structure. When a match of exception is found, the statements in that Catch block are executed. You can place as many Catch statements as you need to handle different types of exceptions; however, when an exception occurs, only one of these blocks will be executed.

The statements in the *Finally* block will be executed regardless of whether an exception occurs or not. If you have no code to execute following an exception or the Try block, you can omit this block.

In summary, under this structure:

- When there is no runtime error, the code in the Try and the Finally block (if coded) will execute.

- When there is an exception, statements in the Try block will execute up to the statement that encounters the exception. The statements in the Catch block that first matches the exception will then be executed followed by any code in the Finally block. If no match is found, the program will terminate with an unhandled error.

For this example, you can rewrite the code as follows:

```
Private Sub btnSave_Click(ByVal sender As System.Object, ByVal e
    As System.EventArgs) Handles btnSave.Click
    Dim TextFile As IO.StreamWriter
    Dim TheMsg As String
    MsgBox("Please insert a blank diskette in drive A. " _
      & "Click the OK button when ready.")
    Try
        'Possible exception can come from the following statements
        TextFile = New IO.StreamWriter("a:\TextFile.txt")
        TextFile.Write(txtContent.Text)
        TextFile.Close()
```

```
        Catch ex As IO.IOException
            'If it is an IO error, try to find the cause
            "and display an error message
            TheMsg = ex.Message
            If InStr(1, TheMsg, "not ready", CompareMethod.Text) > 0
              Then
                TheMsg = TheMsg & " Please insert a blank disk in
                   drive A."
            ElseIf InStr(TheMsg, "write protected",
              CompareMethod.Text) > 0 Then
                TheMsg = TheMsg & " Please try another disk."
            End If
            MsgBox(TheMsg)
        Finally
            'I can omit this block because
            'there's no additional code to execute
        End Try
    End Sub
```

In the code, only one Catch block is written because you expect only the *IOException* to occur. Take a look at that Catch statement again. An object variable, ex is "declared" as an exception of the IO.IOException type. This statement serves two purposes. The exception specified here can be matched against the exception that actually occurs. In addition, the object variable specified here can be used in the block to perform the desired handling.

In this case, the object's *Message property* is assigned to a variable, TheMsg, which is then parsed for a more specific type of error: device not ready or write-protection error. As you can see from the code, a helpful message is also appended to assist the user in resolving the exception. If the IOException pertains to neither of the two possible causes, no additional message is appended. The resulting message is then displayed so that the user will have a chance to correct and try again—or at least know what went wrong.

Specifying Exceptions. Perhaps, you are wondering what exception you should specify in a Catch statement. Exceptions exist in hierarchies. The System.Exception object (you can code this object as Exception without qualifying it with System because the System namespace is automatically imported into every project) is the base of all exceptions. If you do not know what exception to expect and will handle all exceptions the same way, you can just specify Exception in the Catch statement. It will catch all the possible exceptions thrown in the application.

Many exceptions are derived from this base. For example, ApplicationException, SystemException, and IOException are all derived from it. And DirectoryNotFoundException, EndOfStreamException, FileLoadException, and FileNotFoundException are derived from IOException. You can find a discussion of base exception hierarchy by specifying the keyword "base exceptions" in the Index tab of the Help file. (*Note:* Be sure that the Filter By box specifies Visual Basic and Related, not just Visual Basic. These exceptions pertain to the Common Language Runtime.) You can also find a long list of exceptions in the Exceptions option of the Debug menu. Chances are one of these exceptions meets your error specification requirements.

Note that when you are specifying more than one Catch block, you should specify the most specific exception first. After a Catch statement catches an exception, no other Catch statement will be tested. This is similar to the Select Case situation in which once a Case is found to be True, no other Case criteria will be compared (as noted in Chapter 5). For example, suppose you have a routine to open and read a file. Then, the code may encounter DirectoryNotFoundException and FileNotFoundException when it attempts to open the file. In addition, it may encounter EndOfStreamException when it is reading the file. You should then structure your code in a manner similar to the following, assuming the event handler is named btnRead_Click:

```
    Private Sub btnRead_Click(ByVal sender As System.Object, ByVal e
        As System.EventArgs) Handles btnRead.Click
        Dim TheReader As IO.StreamReader
```

```
                 Dim TheLine As String
                 Try
                     TheReader = New IO.StreamReader("A:\TextFile.txt")
                     Do
                         TheLine = TheReader.ReadLine
                         'other statement to process the line
                     Loop
                 Catch ex As IO.DirectoryNotFoundException
                     'Provide code here to handle this type of error.
                 Catch ex As IO.FileNotFoundException
                     'Provide code here to handle this type of error.
                 Catch ex As IO.EndOfStreamException
                     'Provide code here to handle this type of error.
                 Catch ex As IO.IOException
                     'Note that this exception must be placed after
                     'the preceding three because they are
                     'more specific (derived from this exception).
                     'Provide code here to handle this type of error.
                 Finally
                 End Try
             End Sub
```

In the preceding code, the first three types of exceptions are placed before IOException because they are derived from IOException, and are more specific. Placing IOException before them will cause IOException to catch the error before any of them has a chance, completely defeating the purpose of the code.

In general, you should use the Try structure to handle only the kind of errors caused by the user and not preventable by code. For example, as you have seen previously, there are ways to catch the user's data entry errors, so your program should not wait until your code encounters an error in data conversion and then handle it as an exception. If you heed this suggestion, you should not include the code to catch the EndOfStreamException in the preceding code. Instead, you should check for the end of file condition using the StreamReader's Peek method, as illustrated in Chapter 6, "Input, Output, and Procedures." Also note that when you know the type of exception to expect, you should anticipate and handle this specific exception by providing the proper code. It is not advisable to catch an exception without properly handling it. Doing so can cause even more severe problems for the application and the end user.

TIP

VB.NET also supports the error-handling feature of the previous versions, using the On Error construct; however, the Try. . . End Try structure is considered more structured and robust, and is the preferred approach to error handling.

10.6   Providing Visual Clues

Imagine that you are using a program written by someone else. The program will process a large database in a complex manner, and will take a few hours. When you click the Start Process button, you see nothing taking place. What would be your reaction? You might tend to think that maybe you did not click the button properly or, for whatever reason, that the computer did not register the click, so you would most likely click the button one more time. If nothing happens again, you might click it again and again. What if it turns out that the program actually has started the process on the first and all subsequent clicks? It may take several days before all the repeated processes are completed. For fear that the program may have been so (carelessly) designed that it can ruin your database if you attempt to stop the process, you may have no choice but wait.

As a user, you'd wish that this program had provided immediate visual feedback! When the user clicked the button, if it had somehow acknowledged the click by, say, disabling that button, the user would not have clicked the button another time. (Furthermore, the program should not start the process the second time.) Because it is a long process, the user would rather the computer indicate where the process is as it progresses. Finally, in each processing step, the computer should inform the user of the percentage of completion. All of these steps assure the user that everything is progressing without any problems, alleviating the user's anxiety in deciding what to do next (if anything).

TIP

When a process should be carried out only once in the duration of the project, be sure to disable the button that initiates the process once it is started. For example, assume that the button to initiate a process is named btnProcess. You should then insert a statement to disable the button in its click event as follows:

```
Private Sub btnProcess_Click(ByVal sender As System.Object,
   ByVal e As System.EventArgs) Handle btnProcess.Click
      btnProcess.Enabled = False
      'Other statements to start to process
End Sub
```

A long process should be handled similarly, even if it can be initiated more than once. In the latter case, insert a statement to enable the button at the end of the click event procedure.

Listing Prime Numbers: An Illustrative Example

Now, put yourself in the position of the programmer. How would you implement the preceding list of feedback for the user? To answer this, consider a simpler example. You have a program to compute, and list all the prime numbers up to the number specified by the user in a text box named txtUpperLimit. The results will be displayed in a list box named lstPrimes. The program will start the computation/listing process when the user clicks the Compute button (named btnCompute). The original program appears as follows:

```
Dim Primes() As Integer
Private Sub btnCompute_Click(ByVal sender As System.Object, ByVal
   e As System.EventArgs) Handles btnCompute.Click
      ComputePrimes(CInt(Val(txtUpperLimit.Text)))
End Sub
Sub ComputePrimes(ByVal N As Integer)
   Dim I As Integer
   Dim J As Integer
   Dim Ib As Integer
   Dim SquareRoot As Integer
   Dim PrimeCount As Integer
   Dim IsPrime As Boolean
   ' Step 1: Compute prime numbers up to upper limit
   ReDim Primes(N \ 2)
   Primes(0) = 1 'We know 1 and 2 are prime numbers.
   Primes(1) = 2
   PrimeCount = 2
   For I = 3 To N Step 2
       SquareRoot = CInt(Math.Sqrt(I))
       ' The following loop test if I is a prime number
       IsPrime = True 'Assume I is a prime.
       For J = 2 To PrimeCount - 1
           If (I Mod Primes(J)) = 0 Then
               ' I can be evenly divided by a prime.
               ' It's not a prime
               IsPrime = False
               Exit For
```

```
                            ElseIf SquareRoot < Primes(J) Then
                                ' I cannot be evenly divided beyond this number
                                ' I is a prime number
                                Exit For
                            End If
                        Next J
                        If IsPrime Then
                            ' I is a prime number; add to the list
                            Primes(PrimeCount) = I
                            PrimeCount = PrimeCount + 1
                        End If
                    Next I
                    ' Step 2: Show results in the list box
                    lstPrimes.Items.Clear() 'start the list box afresh
                    lstPrimes.Visible = False 'To speed up the operation
                    ' The next 3 lines ensure that only the largest 64000 primes
                    ' are displayed in the list box
                    Ib = PrimeCount - 64000
                    If Ib < 1 Then Ib = 0
                    For I = Ib To PrimeCount - 1
                        lstPrimes.Items.Add(Primes(I))
                    Next I
                    lstPrimes.Visible = True 'Show the list box
                End Sub
```

The event procedure is triggered when the user clicks the Compute button. The procedure simply calls the ComputePrimes procedure to perform the computation using the number in the text box (txtUpperLimit) as the argument. This Sub procedure also populates the list box with the prime numbers found in the procedure. Additional details are discussed in the following subsection.

As a technical side note, notice the routine to populate the list box. Each time an item is added to the list box, the control updates its appearance. This can take up a lot of time. You can speed up the process by setting the control's Visible property to False before the loop and then setting the same property back to True after everything is populated. The control will not attempt to update its appearance when it is not visible.

The Prime Number Computing Algorithm

The prime number computation Sub consists of two major steps: computing the primes, and showing the primes in the list box. As you know, a prime number is one that can be evenly divided only by the number 1 and itself. The first two prime numbers are 1 and 2. A loop (For I = 3 to N) is set up to examine every odd number starting from 3 through the specified upper limit. Inside the loop, the number is examined by testing whether it can be evenly divided by any previously found prime numbers, using yet another loop (For J = 2 To PrimeCount – 1). As soon as the number is found to be evenly divisible by a prime number, the IsPrime flag is set to False and the inner loop is terminated (Exit For). If the number cannot be evenly divided by any prime number up to the number's square root, it must be a prime number. As each prime number is found, it is added to the prime number list.

In the step to show the list of the prime numbers, the program shows only the last 64,000 prime numbers found in the computation. Also, to simplify the program focus, the code assumes that the user always enters a valid upper limit before clicking the button.

This program can take a long time if the user enters a large number as the upper limit. The following discussion considers how the visual feedback can be implemented.

The Cursor

When you test the program, if you enter a number that exceeds 1,000,000 in the text box, you will start to sense that it takes a while for the computer to complete the task. Depending on the speed of your computer, the specific threshold value may vary. To provide some visual clue to the user that the process has started, the *cursor's* (mouse pointer's) appearance can be changed. Typically, when the computer is waiting for the user to take actions, the mouse pointer is the default (normal) one. After a process has started, you would signal to the user to wait. The cursor typically used for this purpose is the hourglass, recognized as WaitCursor. Most controls (including the form) have the Cursor property (object), which in turn has the Current property that can be referenced with the following syntax:

```
Object.Cursor.Current
```

where *Object* can be the Form, or any control. If omitted, the form (Me) is the default. The cursor shows different shapes based on the setting of the Current property. These shapes are enumerated in Cursors. For example, Cursors.Default refers to the default cursor and Cursors.WaitCursor refers to the hourglass that signals a wait state (the computer is busy doing something).

To signal to the user to wait, when the computation for the prime numbers starts, you can modify the button's Click event procedure as follows:

```
Private Sub btnCompute_Click(ByVal sender As System.Object, ByVal
    e As System.EventArgs) Handles btnCompute.Click
    Dim OldCursor As Cursor
    OldCursor = Me.Cursor.Current 'Keep the current cursor
    Me.Cursor.Current = Cursors.WaitCursor 'Change to WaitCursor
    'Compute prime numbers
    ComputePrimes(CInt(Val(txtUpperLimit.Text)))
    Me.Cursor.Current = OldCursor 'Restore the cursor
End Sub
```

In this modified procedure, the current cursor is preserved with a variable named OldCursor. The Current property is then assigned the value WaitCursor. At this point, the cursor is turned into the hourglass shape. The prime number computation/listing procedure is then called. After the process is complete, the current cursor is restored to its original setting. You should restore the cursor to its original shape, instead of assigning the default setting (Default), to preserve the user's preference. Some users may have assigned a different cursor to the computer as a matter of personal taste.

TIP

Type "**Cursors.**"(without the quotes but with the period) in a procedure, and you should see a list of predefined cursors. Use the following syntax to view the cursor shape:

```
Me.Cursor.Current = Cursors.YourSelection
```

Messages for Progress Status

It is also a good practice to display a message indicating the status (what is taking place) before a long process is undertaken. If a process involves multiple steps, displaying a message at the beginning of each step will make the user feel that the process is going even faster. This can be implemented easily. For example, in the preceding example, you can draw a label on the form. Assume you have named it lblStatus. Before calling the Sub function, you can add a line to the code as follows:

```
lblStatus.Text = "Computing prime numbers.  Please wait."
```

It goes without saying that if the event procedure involves more than just calling the prime number computation routine, you should add a line to change the labels' texts before calling each of these additional procedures. In the prime computation function, there are two major steps: performing the computation, and listing the results. You can add the following statements at the beginning of these steps and at the end of the program:

```
(At the start of prime computations:)
lblStatus.Text = "Computing prime numbers."

(At the start of adding prime numbers to the list box:)
lblStatus.Text = "Populating the list box with prime numbers."

(At the end of the program)
lblStatus.Text = "All done."
```

The Progress Bar

If a process takes a long time to complete, simply displaying the steps being performed is not enough. The user may still be uncertain as to how far the process has progressed. Even a two-second wait may seem to be a long time to the user. To assure the user that the process has been going fine, you can add a *progress bar* to your project, and use it to display the percentage of completion. The progress bar has a rectangular shape, and is used to display the progress in a lengthy process. You can make the progress bar gradually fill its rectangle with the system highlight color by changing its Value property as the process progresses. Figure 10.6 shows the progress bar icon and the control in action when used in the prime number computation project.

The control has *Minimum* and *Maximum properties* with default values of 0 and 100, respectively. Because these can conveniently be used to represent percentages, they can be left unchanged. It has a Value property that can be set either at design time or runtime; however, it should really be set at runtime if it is used to show *progress of a process*. As mentioned, setting this property will make the progress bar fill its rectangle with the system highlight color. To show the progress, you can compute the percentage of the progress and then set the Value property of the progress bar accordingly.

Using the Progress Bar. Because the actual computations are carried out in the sub procedure, you should modify the code in the ComputePrimes sub to use the progress bar. In addition to filling the progress bar, the code should also display the percentage value, using a label named lblPercent. To compute the percentage, you will need to declare a variable, Percent. Also, recall that operations involving control properties take up much more time than involving variables, so you should not continuously assign a value to a control property when the value has not changed. In other words, you should assign Percent to the Label's Text property and the progress bar's Value property only when the value of Percent has changed. To handle this, you will use another variable, PrevPercent, to test for the change. What percentage do you compute? You will take a crude approach by using the number of numbers examined (N); that is:

```
Percent = CInt( (I / N) * 100)
```

This value will not be assigned to the progress bar or the label until it changes by a percentile. You can determine whether it has changed by comparing its value with PrevPercent, so you can code the following:

```
If Percent > PrevPercent Then
    'Percentage has changed.
    'Fill progress bar with new value
    prgPrimeNumbers.Value = Percent
```

Figure 10.6

Progress bar: icon, appearance, and in action

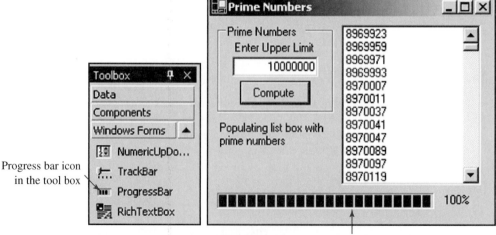

When increasing values are assigned to the progress bar's Value property, the progress bar's rectangle is filled with the system highlight color to show the progress.

```
            lblPercent.Text = Percent & "%" 'Show the value in label
            PrevPercent = Percent   'Update the value of PrevPercent
            Application.DoEvents 'Allow the OS time to update screen
        End If
```

Inside the If block, the computed value of Percent is assigned to the progress bar's Value property as well the label's Text property. Also, it is assigned to PrevPercent so that PrevPercent can be used again to detect changes in the value of Percent. Notice that you also include a statement to call the DoEvents method in the If block. This is to ensure that the Windows operating system is given time to update the screen, such as label texts, while the program is looping through the computations. The percentage computation along with the If block can be placed immediately below the "For I" statement (inside the outer loop).

In a similar fashion, the progress in populating the list box with the prime numbers can be coded. The revised Sub procedure is as follows:

```
Sub ComputePrimes(ByVal N As Integer)
    Dim I As Integer
    Dim J As Integer
    Dim Ib As Integer
    Dim SquareRoot As Integer
    Dim PrimeCount As Integer
    Dim IsPrime As Boolean
    Dim Percent As Integer
    Dim PrevPercent As Integer
    Dim NumbersToDisplay As Integer
    Dim NumberCount As Integer
    ' Step 1: Compute prime numbers up to upper limit
    ReDim Primes(N \ 2)
    lblStatus.Text = "Computing prime numbers."
    'To allow time for Windows to display status
    Application.DoEvents()
    Primes(0) = 1 'We know 1 and 2 are prime numbers.
    Primes(1) = 2
    PrimeCount = 2
    For I = 3 To N Step 2
        SquareRoot = CInt(Math.Sqrt(I))
        Percent = CInt((I / N) * 100)
        If Percent > PrevPercent Then
            'Percentage has changed
            prgPrimeNumbers.Value = Percent 'Fill progress bar
            'Show percentage in label
            lblPercent.Text = Percent & "%"
            'Allow time for Windows to update screen
            Application.DoEvents()
            PrevPercent = Percent 'Update the percentage
        End If
        ' The following loop test if I is a prime number
        IsPrime = True 'Assume I is a prime.
        For J = 2 To PrimeCount - 1
            If (I Mod Primes(J)) = 0 Then
                ' I can be evenly divided by a prime.
                ' It's not a prime
                IsPrime = False
                Exit For
            ElseIf SquareRoot < Primes(J) Then
                ' I cannot be evenly divided beyond this number
                ' I is a prime number
                Exit For
            End If
        Next J
        If IsPrime Then
            ' I is a prime number; add to the list
            Primes(PrimeCount) = I
            PrimeCount = PrimeCount + 1
```

```
                End If
        Next I
        ' Step 2: Show results in the list box
        lblStatus.Text = "Populating list box with prime numbers."
        Application.DoEvents()
        lstPrimes.Items.Clear() 'start the list box afresh
        lstPrimes.Visible = False 'To speed up the operation
        ' The next 3 lines ensure that only the largest 64000 primes
        ' are displayed in the list box
        Ib = PrimeCount - 64000
        If Ib < 1 Then Ib = 0
        NumbersToDisplay = PrimeCount - Ib
        PrevPercent = 0 'Reset value of PrevPercent
        For I = Ib To PrimeCount - 1
            NumberCount += 1
            Percent = CInt(NumberCount / NumbersToDisplay * 100)
            If Percent > PrevPercent Then
                'Percentage has changed
                prgPrimeNumbers.Value = Percent 'Fill progress bar
                'Show percentage in label
                lblPercent.Text = Percent & "%"
                'Allow time for Windows to update screen
                Application.DoEvents()
                PrevPercent = Percent 'Update the percentage
            End If
            lstPrimes.Items.Add(Primes(I))
        Next I
        lstPrimes.Visible = True 'Show the list box
        lblStatus.Text = "All done."
End Sub
```

Summary

- Principles of GUI design include simplicity and clarity, flexibility, consistency, immediate feedback, forgiveness, and pleasant appearance.

- The Enter key can be converted to the Tab key by the use of the SendKeys object, which has a Send method to send keys from a program to the Windows operating system as if the user pressed the keys on the keyboard. This conversion allows the user to press the Enter key to move to the next control (emulate the Tab key). The Up and Down arrow keys can also be programmed in a similar fashion.

- Using the SendKeys object's Send method, you can also make the focus move to the next control when the current control is filled with expected number of characters—a feature called auto-tabbing.

- Access keys allow the user to press Alt+<letter> to move the focus to a particular control. You can set up access keys for controls whose Text properties are not accessible to the user, such as button, radio button, and check boxes, by placing the & symbol before the letter to be used as the access key. For controls whose Text properties change dynamically at runtime, such as the text box, list box, and combo box, set the access key on the labels that are associated with these controls. Be sure that the label's and the related control's TabIndexes are consecutive.

- Before the program quits, it should warn the user when there exists unsaved data to allow the user to decide whether to save. There are different ways to detect unsaved data. For data entry screens that are cleared when data are saved, a generalized program can be written to check through all text boxes and masked edit boxes to see if all are empty.

- Data validation can be performed at three different levels. At the key level, each key entered can be tested to see if it is of the type expected; for example, a numeric field should not allow a non-numeric key. An elegant way to implement key validation is to set the form's KeyPreview property to True, and provide generalized code for its KeyPress event. Each control's Tag property should be set to a letter that represents the type of data expected. At the field level, the field validation routine should be coded in the control's Validating event. (Of course, any routine of generic use should be coded as a separate sub or function procedure, which can then be called by different event procedures.) At the form level, such as at time to save the data, all fields requiring field validation should be checked again to ensure accuracy and completeness. You can trick the system into performing all controls' Validating event procedures by the use of a loop with the SendKeys' Send method and the proper setting of a class-level Boolean variable.

- When you anticipate that the user's mistake can cause a crash of your program, such as failure to place a disk in Drive A when instructed, use the Try. . . End Try error-handling structure to catch and handle the exception. This structured error-handling feature can be useful to handle errors caused by situations outside of your program; however, if the errors are caused by your own code in the program, in most cases, the best way is to add additional code that tests for the conditions to take care of the problems rather than handle them as exceptions.

- If your program will execute a long process, be sure to provide proper visual clues. Depending on the length of the process, one or a combination of the following can be implemented:

  - Change the cursor shape to signal to the user to wait.

  - At the beginning of each major step, display the status (what is being done at the current stage).

  - Use a progress bar to display the percentage of progress.

Explore and Discover

10-1.   Ampersand in the Text Property of the Label. Draw a label on a form. Set its Text property to **John & Jane's Income**. What do you see? Why is there an underline in the label? Because & is used to set the access key for the label. Now try the following:

Set the control's UseMnemonic property to False. What do you see? When you set this property to False, the & in the label will be shown as is. The label cannot be used to set up an access key.

Set the UseMnemonic property to True again; then change the Text property to **John && Jane's Income** (double the & symbol). What do you see this time?

10-2.   Ampersand in the Text Property of the Button. Draw a button on a form, and set its Text property to **Pick & Save**. What do you see? You should see an underline just as in the case of the label. So, how do you get the & symbol to show on a text? Look to the preceding exercise for the answer. Most controls' Text properties (if they exist) behave the same way in this respect. Try the check box and the radio button to prove or disprove this assertion. The exceptions include the text box and rich text box whose Text properties can accept keystrokes from the user at runtime.

10-3.   Access Key of the Button. How does the access key of the button work? When the user presses its access key, is its Click event fired or does it just get focus (its Enter event is triggered)? To answer, draw a text box and a button on a form. Name the button **btnSave** and set its Text property to **&Save**. Enter the following code:

```
Private Sub btnSave_Click(ByVal sender As System.Object, ByVal e
    As System.EventArgs) Handles btnSave.Click
        Console.WriteLine("Click")
End Sub

Private Sub btnSave_Enter(ByVal sender As System.Object, ByVal e
    As System.EventArgs) Handles btnSave.Enter
        Console.WriteLine("Got focus")
End Sub
```

Run the project. Make sure the focus is set on the text box and then press Alt+S. Check the immediate window. Which event is fired? It triggers the Click event, but not the Enter event. There's no visual clue to whether the control has been accessed. Your user may wonder whether your code in the Click event is executed because of the lack of visual clues. Be sure to provide feedback to your user, such as display a "Data saved" message.

10-4. **Key Code Values of Various Keys.** Do you want to know the key code values of various keys? Draw a text box on a form. Name it **txtTest**, and enter the following code:

```
Private Sub txtTest_KeyDown(ByVal sender As System.Object, ByVal e
    As System.Windows.Forms.KeyEventArgs) Handles txtTest.KeyDown
    Console.Write(e.KeyCode)
    Console.Write(" Alt=" & e.Alt)
    Console.Write(" Shift=" & e.Shift)
    Console.WriteLine(" Ctrl=" & e.Control)
End Sub
```

Run the project and then try the following keys:

Arrow keys (of all directions) with and without the Shift key
1 (one) on the regular keypad with and without the Shift key
1 (one) on the numeric keypad with and without the Shift key
Esc
F3 and F4 (be aware that some function keys can get activated in the IDE)
Page Up and Page Down
A with and without the Shift key
Enter on both the keyboard and the numeric keypad

Which key code values surprise you? How about the 1's on different keypads and A with and without the Shift key?

10-5. **Sequence of Keyboard Events.** When a key is pressed on a text box, what keyboard events are fired and in what sequence? To obtain the answer, draw a text box on a form, name it **txtTest**, and clear its Text property. Enter the following code; the count is added to give you clearer messages:

```
Dim Count As Integer
Private Sub txtTest_TextChanged(ByVal sender As System.Object,
    ByVal e As System.EventArgs) Handles txtTest.TextChanged
    Count += 1
    Console.WriteLine("Text changed " & Count)
End Sub

Private Sub txtTest_KeyDown(ByVal sender As System.Object, ByVal e
    As System.Windows.Forms.KeyEventArgs)  Handles txtTest.KeyDown
    Count += 1
    Console.WriteLine("Key Down " & Count)
End Sub

Private Sub txtTest_KeyPress(ByVal sender As System.Object, ByVal
    e As System.Windows.Forms.KeyPressEventArgs) Handles
    txtTest.KeyPress
    Count += 1
    Console.WriteLine("Key Press " & Count)
End Sub

Private Sub txtTest_KeyUp(ByVal sender As System.Object, ByVal e
    As System.Windows.Forms.KeyEventArgs)  Handles txtTest.KeyUp
    Count += 1
    Console.WriteLine("Key Up " & Count)
End Sub
```

Run the project and then set the focus on this text box. Try each of the following and observe the events triggered and their sequence:

> Alphabetic keys
> Numeric keys (on the keyboard and then on the numeric keypad)
> Arrow keys
> Esc, Backspace, and Enter keys
> Delete and Insert keys
> Page up, Page down, Home, and End keys
> Shift, Alt, and Ctrl keys
> Tab key
> Function keys (F1, F2, and so on)

Do these groups give different events? (Some groups should trigger all events, while the others trigger fewer.) A good understanding of these events allows you to select the proper event to place code to suit your requirements.

10-6. **Keyboard Events for the Button.** Modify exercise 10-5 to test on a button. Replace the TextChanged event with the Click event. After experimenting on all nine groups of keys, press the Spacebar. What events does it trigger?

10-7. **Access Key and Keyboard Events.** Modify the Text property of the button in exercise 10-6 to **&Test**. Test the project again. Do you observe any differences between the results you obtain here and previously? (Not really.) This time, also try to press Alt+T while the button has the focus. Try another time while the button does not have the focus. Compare the results between with focus and without focus. (Is there a Click event? a KeyPress event?)

10-8. **Keyboard Events and Key Preview.** Modify the preceding project in the following manner:

1. Set the form's KeyPreview property to True.
2. Add the Keyboard event procedures for the form, each paraphrasing the counterpart of the button as follows:

```
Private Sub Form1_Click(ByVal sender As System.Object,
  ByVal e As System.EventArgs) Handles MyBase.Click
    Count += 1
    Console.WriteLine("Form click " & Count)
End Sub

Private Sub Form1_KeyDown(ByVal sender As System.Object,
  ByVal e As System.Windows.Forms.KeyEventArgs) Handles
  MyBase.KeyDown
    Count += 1
    Console.WriteLine("Form Key Down " & Count)
End Sub

Private Sub Form1_KeyPress(ByVal sender As System.Object,
  ByVal e As System.Windows.Forms.KeyPressEventArgs) Handles
  MyBase.KeyPress
    Count += 1
    Console.WriteLine("Form Key Press " & Count)
End Sub

Private Sub Form1_KeyUp(ByVal sender As System.Object, ByVal
  e As System.Windows.Forms.KeyEventArgs) Handles
  MyBase.KeyUp
    Count += 1
    Console.WriteLine("Form Key Up " & Count)
End Sub
```

Run the project and then press an alphabetic key. What events are triggered? In what order? Each button event is preceded by a form event of the same kind; for example, the button's KeyDown event is preceded by the form's KeyDown event. Were you expecting that all form Keyboard events would precede all the button Keyboard events? Note, however, is the form click event triggered by any key, such as the Spacebar?

Turn off the form's KeyPreview property, and try the same steps again. Do you see any form Keyboard events? (You should not.)

10-9.   **Which Statement Can Have a Runtime Error?** Enter the following code in a new project:

```
Private Sub Form1_Click(ByVal sender As System.Object, ByVal e As
   System.EventArgs) Handles MyBase.Click
      Dim A As Integer
      Dim B As Integer
      Dim C As Double
      A = 50000
      C = A / 0
      B = A * A
End Sub
```

Guess which statement will encounter a runtime error (exception); then run the program, and click the form. What message does the computer display? (The computer should display a message box showing an overflow exception.) Click the Break button in the message box. The exception occurs in the A * A statement, not the A / 0 statement. Rest the cursor at the variable, C. What value do you see? A floating point variable can handle an infinity (thus dividing a value by zero is treated as infinity). But an integer variable cannot handle any value beyond its range, so $50{,}000 \times 50{,}000$ results in an error because the product exceeds the upper limit of the integer variable, $2^{31} - 1$.

Insert the Try. . . Catch. . . Finally. . . End Try error handling structure in the above event so that it will display a "Computations resulted in an overflow" message when an overflow occurs (use System.OverflowException to catch the exception). In addition, it will always display "Execution reaches the end" regardless of whether an overflow error occurs. Test it with different values of A, such as 1, 16,000, 32,000 and 64,000.

10-10.   **Where Is the Error?** Draw a button on a new form. Name the button **btnCompute**. Set its Text property to **Compute** and then enter the following code:

```
Private Sub btnCompute_Click(ByVal sender As System.Object, ByVal
   e As System.EventArgs) Handles btnCompute.Click
      Dim Area As Integer
      Dim Width, Height As Integer
      Try
          Area = 10
          Height = ComputeHeight(Area, Width)
      Catch ex As Exception
          MsgBox(ex.ToString, MsgBoxStyle.Information)
      Finally
          MsgBox("The height is " & Height)
      End Try
End Sub
Function ComputeHeight(ByVal Area As Integer, ByVal Width As
   Integer) As Integer
      ComputeHeight = Area \ Width
End Function
```

Run the project. What messages do you see? Why is the Height zero (according to the message)? Comment out the error handling statements (Try, Catch [and the MsgBox statement immediately following Catch], Finally, and End Try) in the Click event procedure. Run it again. Where do you see the problem (error message)? The ComputeHeight function has a division by zero error because the parameter Width has a zero, which is passed by the Click event procedure.

In the original code, the error handler in the Click event procedure is enabled before the ComputeHeight function is called. The error occurs in the function; however, there is no error handler in that procedure. The error is returned to the caller (Click event), which then handles the error in the Catch block. The Finally block contains the MsgBox statement, which displays the value of Height. Height has not yet been assigned any value because of the error in the function, so the message displays a zero for Height.

Exercises

10-11. **A Visual Interface with Access Keys.** Your company's fixed asset application program requires the following data fields:

Field Name	Description	Control
Asset ID	Has a mask: AAA9999 Where *A* = Any letter *9* = Any digit	Masked edit box
Description	Alphanumeric field for asset description (maximum 32 characters)	Text box
Location	City name such as New York, Dallas, and Los Angeles (maximum 16 characters)	Combo box
Depreciable?	Yes/No to indicate whether asset is depreciable	Check box
Depreciation Method	0-No depreciation 1-Straight-line depreciation 2-ACRS depreciation	Radio buttons
Cost	Numeric field (allow up to 99,999,999.99)	Text box
Life	Economic useful life in years (four digits maximum)	Text box

Design a data-entry screen for this application. The form should also include two buttons: one to save data, and another to Quit. All controls must be assigned a proper access key for the user to access the field using the keyboard. Provide code to handle only the Quit button.

10-12. **A User Interface That Moves Focus with the Up-Arrow, Down-Arrow, and Enter Keys.** (continued from exercise 10-11) Add code to the preceding project so that when the user presses the Enter key or Down arrow key, the focus will move to the next field, and when the user presses the Up arrow key, the focus will move to the preceding field. Also, when the field is filled (reaches maximum length), the focus should automatically move to the next field (control).

10-13. **Programming a User Interface Involving the Tab Control.** (modified from exercises 10-11 and 10-12) Redesign the visual interface for exercise 10-10. Use the Tab control as the container for the data fields. Make the Tab control show two tabs: one with the text **Asset ID**, and the other with the text **Depreciation**. The first tab will contain the first three fields, and the second will contain the last four fields. The buttons should be placed on the form, not on either tab.

Again, all controls should have access keys. In addition, the Tab control should behave as follows:

When the user clicks a tab, the focus should be set on the first control on that tab.

When the user completes the last fields on the tab (by pressing the Enter or Down arrow key), the focus should move to the next logical VB control. That is, the focus should move to the Depreciable field when the user presses the Enter key in the location field and to the Save button when in the Cost field.

The Asset ID field must contain something before the user is allowed to move to the next tab.

10-14. **Allowing the Message Box to Show for Only A Specified Time Period.** Draw a button on a new form. Develop the code so that when the user clicks the button, the message box (MsgBox) will display "Data saved." Your challenge is that if the user does not click the OK button in the message box within 15 seconds, your program will make the message box disappear (as if the user did). (*Hint:* Add a timer, and set its Interval property. In its Tick event, send a key [for you to figure out] using the SendKeys object. In the button's Click event, start the timer before displaying the message box and stop the timer afterwards.)

10-15. **Check for Numeric Keys.** Develop a Sub procedure that will ensure that the key entered is a numeric key. A nonnumeric key will trigger the MsgBox to display an error message. The bad key should be suppressed. Test this Sub by a call from the form's KeyPress event. Set the Tag property to N (numeric) of the VB control to be used to test for this purpose.

10-16. **Check for Numeric Keys with Decimal Point.** Add another Sub to exercise 10-15. This Sub should accept the numeric keys and one (and only one) decimal point in a VB control. An unacceptable key should trigger the MsgBox to display an error message. The bad key should be suppressed. Test this Sub by a call from the form's KeyPress event. Set the Tag property to D (decimal) of the VB control to be used to test for this purpose.

10-17. **Check for Currency Data.** Add another Sub to exercise 10-16. This Sub should accept the numeric keys, dollar sign ($) if it is the first character in the field, commas, and one decimal point. An unacceptable key should trigger the MsgBox to display an error message. The bad key should be suppressed. Test this Sub by a call from the form's KeyPress event. Set the Tag property to C (currency) of the VB control to be used to test for this purpose.

10-18. **Check for Alphabetic Keys.** Add another Sub to the project in exercise 10-17. This Sub should accept only space and alphabetic keys. An unacceptable key should trigger the MsgBox to display an error message. The bad key should be suppressed. Test this Sub by a call from the form's KeyPress event. Set the Tag property to L (letter) of the VB control to be used to test for this purpose.

10-19. **Enforcing Uppercase Alphabetic Keys.** Add another Sub to exercise 10-18. This Sub should accept only space and alphabetic keys. All lowercase letters will automatically be converted to uppercase letters. An unacceptable key should trigger the MsgBox to display an error message. The bad key should be suppressed. Test this Sub by a call from the form's KeyPress event. Set the Tag property to U (uppercase) of the VB control to be used to test for this purpose.

10-20. **Alphabetic and Numeric Keys Only.** Add another Sub to exercise 10-19. This Sub should accept space, alphabetic, and numeric keys, but not any special characters. All lowercase letters will automatically be converted to uppercase letters. An unacceptable key should trigger the MsgBox to display an error message. The bad key should be suppressed. Test this Sub by a call from the form's KeyPress event. Set the Tag property to X (cross) of the VB control to be used to test for this purpose.

10-21.   The Name Enforcer, Again. Add another Sub to exercise 10-20. This Sub should act as the name enforcer. That is, it will accept spaces, letters, a comma, a period, and hyphens, and will automatically convert the first letter of each word to the uppercase letter. An unacceptable key should trigger the MsgBox to display an error message. The bad key should be suppressed. Test this Sub by a call from the form's KeyPress event. Set the Tag property to E (enforcer) of the VB control to be used to test for this purpose.

10-22.   The Mask Handler. Add another Sub to Exercise 10-21. This Sub handles keys based on the Mask property of the masked edit box. An unacceptable key should trigger the MsgBox to display an error message. The bad key should be suppressed. Test this Sub by a call from the form's KeyPress event. Set the Tag property to M (masked) of the VB control to be used to test for this purpose.

10-23.   The Check Date Function. Write a function that will ensure that a text string parameter is a valid date field. (Only a string with the mm-dd-yyyy format should be considered valid.) If so, the function returns a value of False; otherwise, an error message is displayed and the function returns a value of True. Name the function **CheckDate**. Test this function by creating a masked edit box for date entry. When the user leaves the control, your code should check if the date entered is valid. If not, the focus should be reset to this control.

10-24.   The Check Numeric Function. Write a function that will ensure that a text string parameter is a valid numeric field. If so, the function returns a value of False; otherwise, an error message is displayed and the function returns a value of True. Name the function **CheckNumeric**. Test this function by creating a text box for data entry. When the user leaves the control, your code should check whether the text box contains a valid number. If not, the focus should be reset to this control.

10-25.   The Range Checker. Write a function that will ensure that a number is within a specified range. Name this function **CheckRange**. The function takes three parameters (all of the Double type): the number, the lower bound, and the upper bound of the number. If the number is within the range of lower and upper bound, the function returns a value of False; otherwise, it returns a value of True. Test this function with a text box. Assume the valid range of this number is 20,000 to 30,000, inclusive. When the user leaves this control, your code should check to ensure the value is within the range. If it is not, your routine will display an error message and then reset the focus to this control. Note that the keys entered in this text box should be checked for valid numeric keys first.

10-26.   Check Digit. Many programs use the check digit to check the validity of an ID number, such as the bank account number or credit card number. The check digit is usually generated by multiplying each individual digit in the ID number by a sequence of multipliers, which are prime numbers 1, 3, 5, and so on, starting with 1 at the lowest digit. The products (multiplication results) are then summed. The total is divided by yet another (higher) prime number. The resulting remainder (or its complement) is used as the check digit. This method of computing the check digit can be shown as follows:

Account number

7	5	3	6	9	8

Multiplier

11	7	5	3	2	1

Results

77	35	15	18	18	8

Total of results = 77 + 35 + 15 + 18 +18 + 8 = 171
Remainder of 171 / 13 = 2

This digit is then attached as a part of the account number, and given to the account holder, so the preceding account number will be 7536982.

When entering a transaction for this account, this number is entered. The same check digit computation routine is used to ensure that the account number is entered correctly.

Write a function to generate the check digit using the method described. Call the function **GenerateDigit**; then write another function to verify the accuracy of an ID number. Call it **CheckDigit**. It should return a value of True when the check digit is invalid.

To test the functions, draw two buttons and a text box on a form. Name the buttons **btnGenerate** and **btnCheck,** and set their texts to **Generate** and **Check**, respectively. Name the text box **txtIDNumber** and then provide the code to perform the following:

When the user clicks the Generate button, your code will generate the check digit for the ID number entered in the text box. (Note that the ID number must be six digits long.) If the resulting check digit is a two-digit number, your program should advise the user that the ID number should not be used; otherwise, the check digit should be displayed.

When the user clicks the Check button, your code should use the CheckDigit function to verify the number given in the text box. (The user is expected to include the check digit as the last digit of the ID number.) If the check digit is correct, your program will display the message "Accept the ID number."; otherwise, it should display the message "The ID number is not valid."

10-27. **Consistency Test and More.** In the W-4 form of a payroll system, the screen has the following fields:

Field Name	Control	Control Name
S-S-N	Masked edit	mskSSN
Employee Name	Text box	txtName (Last, First Init.)
Date of Birth	Masked edit	mskDOB (mm-dd-yyyy)
Date of Employment	Masked edit	mskDOE (mm-dd-yyyy)
No. of Dependents	Text box	txtNoOfDependents

Design a project for this data-entry screen, and provide code to ensure that all data entered are valid before the record is saved. The error-checking routine should include at least the following:

All keys entered should be checked immediately to ensure they are of the proper type. For the employee name, the first letter of each word should be uppercased. Invoke all key error-checking routines from the form's KeyPress event.

When the user leaves a field, your code should ensure that the data in the field is properly entered. This means:

None of the fields should be left blank.

S-S-N should have nine digits entered by the user.

Employee name should have a comma separating the last name and first name.

Dates entered must be valid.

If the number of dependents is excessive, your code should verify with the user before accepting the number.

The company has a policy not to hire anybody younger than 18 years old. The dates entered should be cross-checked to enforce this policy.

When the user finishes the screen by clicking the Save button, all fields should be checked for validity again. If everything is verified to be valid, your program should display "Data Saved" without actually saving the data. The screen should then be cleared.

10-28. **Protecting Against Disk-Handling Errors.** Modify the error-handling routine in Section 10.5 so that all potential disk errors are properly handled. For example, disk full or bad sectors should be detected. Your program should not only inform the user of the problem and suggest remedial action(s), such as inform the user to insert another diskette, but also provide a choice to quit when the user opts to do so.

10-29. **Visual Feedback.** (refer to exercise 8-33) The project computes the probability of good output units in a two-process production setting, using the Monte Carlo simulation technique. Set the number of experiments to 100,000. This will take a long time to complete the simulation. Implement the following visual feedback for the project:

1. Change the mouse pointer's appearance at the beginning of the simulation.
2. Use a label to indicate that the simulation is in progress.
3. Use a progress bar and label to indicate the percentage of computations completed as the simulation progresses.

Projects

10-30. Refer to Project 3-31 in Chapter 3, "Visual Basic Controls and Events." Complete the following additional requirements for the project:

1. Allow the user to use the Enter key to move to the next control.
2. Allow the user to use the Up and Down arrow keys to move up and down through the controls on the form.
3. Allow the masked edit boxes and text boxes to autotab to the next control when all required keys in the field have been entered. Note that masked edit boxes have the AutoTab property. Setting this property to True will enable the autotabbing without any code.
4. Set up the access keys so that the user can jump among different controls in the form using the keyboard.
5. Provide code to check for all controls in the form such that when a wrong key is pressed in a control, a message is displayed and the key is suppressed.
6. Provide code to perform the field level checks for the following fields:

Field	Type of Errors to Check
Place of Birth	Blank field not allowed
Date of Birth	Valid date; respondent at least 18 years old
Number of Children	Valid range is between 0 and 9; prompt for confirmation if greater than 9

7. When the user clicks the Save button, all three fields presented in requirement 6 should be checked to ensure validity. (*Hint:* This is the screen-level data validation.)

10-31. Refer to Project 3-32 in Chapter 3, and complete the following additional requirements for the project:

1-5. Replicate requirements 1 through 5 as listed in exercise 10-30.
6.   Provide code to perform the field level checks for the following fields:

Field	Type of Errors to Check
Name	Blank field not allowed
Date of Birth	If entered, valid date and older than 18
Address	No blank space
Date Dues Paid	Valid date; no older than 5 years; not a future date

7.   When the user clicks the Save button, all four fields presented in requirement 6 should be checked to ensure validity.

10-32. Refer to Project 3-33 in Chapter 3, and complete the following additional requirements for the project:

1-5. Replicate requirements 1 through 5 as listed in exercise 10-30.
6.   Provide code to handle the tab control so that when a tab is clicked, the first control in the tab receives the focus.
7.   Provide code to perform the field level checks for the following fields:

Field	Type of Errors to Check
Name	Blank field not allowed
Insured's Address	Blank field not allowed
City	Blank field not allowed
State	Blank field not allowed
Zip Code	Blank field not allowed
Date of Birth	Valid date and older than 18
Sex	Must select one

8.   When the user clicks the Save button, all the fields in requirement 7 should be checked to ensure validity.

Menus and Multiple-Form Applications

The previous chapters focused on projects involving only one form. This chapter deals with topics related to large projects. A typical large project involves many forms. Many similar activities and functions will be called for in different forms, so there are plenty of opportunities to reduce redundant code. This requires careful analysis and design of the project. In addition, because many program functions (capabilities) must be provided, menus are used in place of buttons. The purpose of this chapter is to present techniques to handle all these aspects.

fter completing this chapter, you should be able to:

- Create menus.
- Follow proper guidelines in creating menus.
- Use the tree view control.
- Add forms to a project.
- Designate a startup object for the project.
- Properly terminate a project.
- Design and implement ways to share data among forms.
- Create and code MDI applications.
- Appreciate and observe design principles for large projects.

11.1   The Main Menu

When your application needs to provide many functions from which the user can choose, it might not be practical to use buttons to trigger these functions. A large number of buttons can clutter the form, making it look messy as well as making it difficult for the user to locate the needed function or button. In such cases, a menu will be a good alternative.

Creating a Menu

You have seen menus in action in various Windows applications. The VS IDE with which you have been working has a menu bar on which many menus are presented. You can create a similar menu bar and menus in your applications by using the Main Menu control.

Menu Design Considerations.   Before you start to create menus for your application, you should carefully analyze your application to identify all capabilities it needs to provide. Each capability and function that the user can choose to perform will typically become an option in one of the menus. You will then decide how these capabilities should be grouped. There can be various ways to group them, but the most important consideration should be how *logical* and intuitive the menus appear to the user. Another consideration is *consistency* with all other Windows applications.

To illustrate, consider an accounts receivable application system for a family medical clinic. The application is used to keep track of patients' visits and the resulting fees. In most cases, the patients are insured. An insurance company pays the major portion of the fees, and the patient is responsible for a fixed co-pay amount. To obtain payments from the insurance company, the clinic needs to file an insurance claim form for each patient visit, which requires various types of information concerning the patient, the insured, the diagnosis, and the treatment. In many cases, the person responsible for payment on the account is not the patient, but rather somebody else such as the patient's parent who may be insured. The application system must maintain records concerning not only the visits, but also all data pertinent to the patients, accounts, insurance companies, as well as the relationships among these entities. In addition, to support the recording of patient visits, the application system needs to maintain code tables for diagnoses as well as treatments (services provided).

The maintenance of records for all the aforementioned activities and entities requires the following:

- Screens (forms) for data-entry operations
- Reports of various activities (patient visits and payments as well as insurance remittance) for review and verification
- Screens to view activities and entities on files
- Claim forms for fee reimbursement
- Other utility functions for file maintenance operations and system customizations

How should all these functions be grouped for menus? Programmers tend to group functions by their program types; for example, report-generating procedures are grouped together under the menu Reports; however, this approach of grouping may not be most intuitive to the user, who tends to think along the line of business activities. For example, the user most likely would rather see all the software capabilities related to insurance grouped under the menu Insurance. This menu can include procedures and forms that perform maintenance of insurance company information, list insurance companies, print claim forms, as well as generate reports for all outstanding claims.

When designing menus for an application, keep in mind that you develop the application for the user to use. Only those applications that fit the user's needs and meet their application requirements are used and considered successful.

Along the line of designing a menu system that appears intuitive to the user, you should also consider its consistency with other applications. For example, most users are likely to be well acquainted with the word processing software as well as other Windows applications. These applications have the familiar File, Edit, and Help menus; therefore, as long as your application needs to provide similar functions, they should be incorporated in a similar manner. This will alleviate the user's needs to learn to navigate around your software system.

Using the Main Menu Control. After you have designed the menus for your application, you can use the VB.NET's *Main Menu control* to create the menus. To use the Main Menu control, either double-click the MainMenu icon in Toolbox, or click the control and draw it on the form. Either way, the main menu named MainMenu1 will appear in the area below the form, and a rectangle with the text "Type Here" will appear on the upper left corner of the form (Figure 11.1). Whatever you type in the rectangle will become the text for the first menu item. Additional rectangles will appear for you to add items in the menu.

Creating a File Menu Step by Step. To illustrate the steps to create a menu, suppose you need to create a File menu that consists of four options: New, Open, Close, and Exit. You will do the following:

1. Double-click the MainMenu icon in the Toolbox.
2. Enter &File in the rectangle, and press the Enter key when complete. You should see the letter F in File is underlined. You should see two additional rectangles showing Type Here, as shown in Figure 11.2. The rectangle on the right of File allows you to create another item on the menu bar, and the rectangle below File allows you to create a submenu.
3. Enter &New in the rectangle below File. Again, you should see two additional rectangles. The rectangle on the right allows you to create additional submenus, while

Figure 11.1

MainMenu icon and appearance

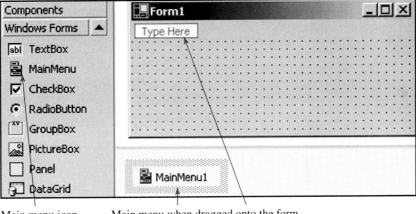

Main menu icon
in the toolbox

Main menu when dragged onto the form
will appear in the area below the form and
show a rectangle in the form.

Figure 11.2

Editing the menu

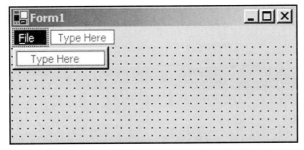

After you enter &File, you should
see File (with F underlined) and two
additional rectangles. The one on the
right allows you to create another menu
on the menu bar and the one below
allows you to create submenu items
(menu options).

the rectangle below allows you to create additional submenu items. Press the Enter key when complete.

4. Do the same to add Open, Close and Exit as the additional submenu items. (Note that x, not E is underlined in Exit. The & symbol should be placed before x.)

Adding a Separator Line. When you click the form, you should be able to see <u>F</u>ile appear in the menu bar of your form. If you click the menu, you should be able to see all the menu options (<u>N</u>ew, <u>O</u>pen, and so on) in the drop-down menu list. Examine the menu list carefully. You may want to add a line (separator) between Exit and all other items above it because this item and others appear to logically belong to different categories. Right-click on Exit and then select the Insert Separator option to add a separator line between Exit and Close. Figure 11.3 shows the resulting file menu with the separator line inserted.

Naming Menu Items. The menu items you have created so far are automatically given the names MenuItem1, MenuItem2, and so on. They should be given appropriate names. To change these names, click on each item and then change the name in the Properties window.

A shortcut to change all menu names is to right-click File on the form (your own menu item, not the File menu for the IDE) to open a context pop-up menu. Select the Edit Names option. The menu names along with their texts will appear as seen in Figure 11.4. You can then proceed to change names by typing the desired names over the existing ones. Be sure to press the Enter key after you complete the editing for each item. When complete, right-click a menu item to invoke the context pop-up menu; then click the EditName option to uncheck and terminate name editing.

In accordance with the naming conventions, menu items are given the prefix mnu; therefore, the menu for File should be given the name mnuFile. The submenu name should include the name of its upper level menu. The name for the menu item New should be mnuFileNew; for Open, mnuFileOpen; for Close, mnuFileClose; and for Exit, mnuFileExit.

Adding New Menu Items in the Menu Bar. When you are ready to add another menu to the menu bar, such as create another top-level menu, click the File menu on the form—the one you have just created, not the File menu in the IDE. You will see two Type

Figure 11.3
A Sample File Menu

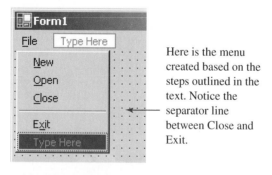

Here is the menu created based on the steps outlined in the text. Notice the separator line between Close and Exit.

Figure 11.4
Editing menu names

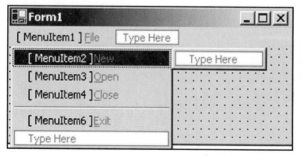

Right-click File (the menu item) and select Edit Names from the context menu. Menu names will appear. You can then edit change these names.

Here rectangles. Enter the menu text (say, Edit) in the rectangle on the right of File to create a new menu.

To add new menu items at the end of a menu, enter the item in the rectangle below a particular menu item. You can also perform Insert New, Delete, Cut, and Paste by right-clicking on the menu list and then selecting the proper option.

Context (Pop-Up) Menus

In some cases, you may find that certain menus do not belong to the menu bar but should be available only in specific situations. Because these menus appear only under certain contexts, they are recognized as *context menus*. Context menus appear only when the user clicks the right mouse button on a particular control. To create a context menu, draw a *Context Menu control* on the form, or simply double-click the context menu icon in the Toolbox. Editing items in the context menu is similar to that for editing a main menu. Here are a few additional points:

- There is no top level menu bar for the context menu.
- You can edit the menu names and items by right-clicking a menu item and then selecting the desired option in the same manner as the main menu.
- You can create as many context menus as you need. For each additional context menu, add a Context Menu control to the form. To edit a particular context menu, click the Context Menu control to make its menu items appear on the form.
- The name of the Context Menu control (the one that appears in the area below the form) should be meaningful. You can change the name using the control's Properties window.
- As mentioned previously, a context menu is triggered when the user right-clicks a control, which must be associated with this context menu. To associate a control with a context menu, set the *Context Menu property* of the control to the context menu. For example, suppose you have created a context menu with the name cmnEdit (which has Copy, Cut, and Paste options) and you want to trigger this menu when the user right-clicks on a text box named txtDocument. You should set the Context Menu property of txtDocument to cmnEdit. A context menu can be associated with many controls, but a control can have only one context menu.

Assigning Access and Shortcut Keys

As you probably have guessed, when you enter an & symbol before a letter in a menu text, the letter becomes the access key for the menu item. For example, &File, which appears in the form as File, has an access key F. The user can press Alt+F to access the File menu. (*Note:* when the program is running, the user may need to press the Alt key for the F letter to show the underline.) In addition to the access key, you can also assign a shortcut key to a menu item by selecting the (shortcut) key in the menu item's Shortcut property in the menu item's Properties window. For example, if you select CtrlC as the shortcut for the Close option, the user will be able to activate the Close option by pressing Ctrl+C. Note that access keys behave differently from short keys in several respects. A menu item is accessible through its access key only when the menu item is visible; the user presses the Alt key plus the underlined letter to activate the menu item. In contrast, a menu item is accessible through the shortcut key anytime the designated shortcut key is pressed regardless of whether the menu item is visible. Also, the shortcut key can be a single key or a key combination. In addition, allowable shortcut keys are predefined. The programmer can designate but not create a shortcut key for a menu item.

Invoking an Action

The menu control has a Click event that occurs when one of the following three situations occurs:

- The menu item is clicked.
- The menu's access key (Alt+<the underlined letter in the Text>) is pressed.
- The menu's shortcut key is pressed.

Coding the event is the same as coding for the Click event procedure of a button. For example, the code for the menu mnuFileExit with the text Exit will be as follows:

```
Private Sub mnuFileExit_Click(ByVal sender As System.Object, ByVal
    e As System.EventArgs) Handles mnuFileExit.Click
    Me.Close()
End Sub
```

Levels of Menus

You can create as many levels of menus as you practically want or need; however, keep in mind that as the levels of menu increase, they could become confusing to the user. When you are designing the menu structure, avoid a design that goes beyond three levels.

Occasionally, a submenu is used for the choice of settings of the operating environment such as the background color or font for an object. In such cases, a custom dialog box (a form created to ascertain specifications/instructions/information from the user) with radio buttons and check boxes can be used as a substitute, and is usually a better alternative.

If you have a complex application that requires multiple levels of menus, a good alternative is to use the tree view. The next section discusses this control.

11.2   The Tree View

When the structure of your application system is complex, an alternative to the main menu is the *tree view*. This control displays a hierarchy of nodes similar to the way the folders and files are displayed in the left pane of the Windows explorer. To use the control, draw it on the form. You can then set up the nodes using the Nodes property in a manner fairly similar to setting up the list for a list box. To illustrate, suppose you need to set up a menu structure (simplified) for a clinic's accounts receivable system as shown in the following table:

Top Level Nodes	Second Level Nodes	Third Level Nodes
File	New Database	
	Open Database. . .	
	Close	
	Exit	
Daily Activities	Appointments	
	Visit and Service Records	
	Reports	Daily Service Summary
		Receipt by Service
		Daily Receipt Summary
Patients and Accounts	Account Information	
	Patients	
Insurance	Print Insurance Claim Forms	
	Aged Receivables Report	
Utilities	Perform Yearend Closing	
	Settings	

Setting Up Nodes in the Tree View

The TreeView icon and a sample of the setup based on the preceding table are shown in Figure 11.5.

Follow these steps to create the tree view nodes:

1. Draw a tree view on the form. Click the TreeView icon in the Toolbox and then draw the control on the form (or simply double-click the icon).

2. Name the control **trvMenu**. Use the control's Properties window to perform this task.

Figure 11.5

The TreeView icon and in action

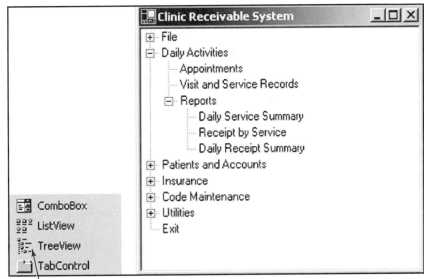

The tree view icon in the toolbox

The tree view displays nodes in a hierarchy and can be used as an alternative to menus of complex structure.

Figure 11.6

Setting the Dock property

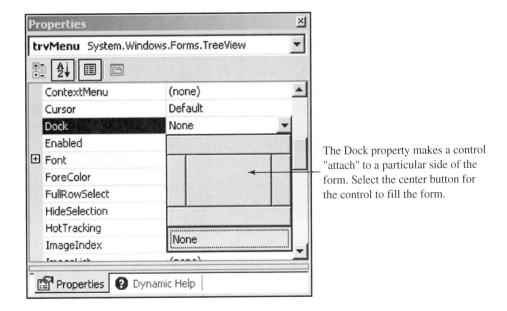

The Dock property makes a control "attach" to a particular side of the form. Select the center button for the control to fill the form.

3. Dock the control on the entire form. Set the control's Dock property with the Fill setting by selecting the center button as shown in Figure 11.6.

4. Set up the nodes:

a. Click the Nodes property in the Properties window; then click the ellipsis (. . .) button on the right. The TreeNode Editor dialog box will appear.

b. Click the Add Root button. You should see Node0 appear in the Label box (see Figure 11.7).

c. Change Node0 in the Label box to **File**.

d. Click the Add Child button. You will see Node1 appear in the Label box. Also observe that this node is added below the File node.

e. Change Node1 to **New database.**

Figure 11.7

The TreeNode editor

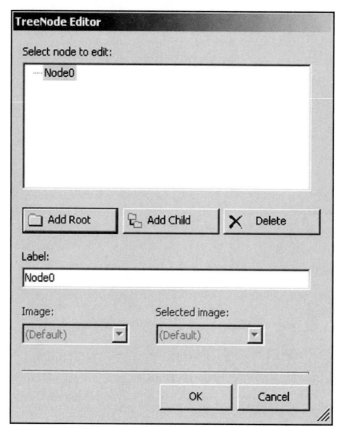

Use this editor to construct the nodes in a tree view. The Add Root, Add Child, and Delete buttons allow you to add root nodes, child nodes, or delete nodes. Change the text for the node in the Label box. You can also add or delete nodes at runtime using the Nodes. Add and Nodes.RemoveAt methods.

f.   Add all other child nodes under the File node. For each additional node, click File in the Select Node to Edit box and then click the Add Child button. Change the text in the Label box to the text specified in the preceding table.

g.   Add the additional nodes indicated in the table. To add an additional top node, click the Add Root button. Repeat steps a through f in step 4 to add additional child nodes.

h.   Click the OK button or press the Enter key when you complete the setup.

The following table gives a summary of what to do to accomplish a specific task when working with the TreeNode Editor:

To	Do This
Add a root note	Click the Add Root button.
Add a child note (to a node at any level)	Click the node and then click the Add Child button.
Change the text for any node	Click the node and then change the text in the Label box.
Delete a node	Click the node and then click the Delete button.

Coding with the Tree View

After you have set up the nodes for a TreeView control, you can write routines to interact with these nodes. The following discussion presents a few pertinent TreeView properties and methods.

Properties and Methods of the TreeView. The tree view has several properties of interest. Its *SelectedNode property* gives the node that the user selects. The *Nodes property* is a collection object for all nodes under a node or the tree view itself. The first line in the following code refers to all root nodes in the tree view; the second line refers to all nodes under the first root node; the third line refers to all nodes under the node that the user currently selects.

```
trvMenu.Nodes
trvMenu.Nodes(0).Nodes
txtMenu.SelectedNode.Nodes
```

The Nodes object also has many properties, one of which is *Count*, which gives the number of nodes under the referenced node. Each node has a *Parent property* that refers to the node's parent. In our example structure, if the SelectedNode is the node for Exit, SelectedNode.Parent refers to the File node.

The tree view also has many methods. The *Nodes.Add method* adds a node. For example, the first statement in the following code will add a root node with the text Others, and the second statement will add a node under the selected node:

```
trvMenu.Nodes.Add("Others")
trvMenu.SelectedNode.Nodes.Add("Others")
```

A node can be removed at runtime using the *RemoveAt method*. For example, the following code will remove the first node under the currently selected node:

```
trvMenu.SelectedNode.Nodes.RemoveAt(0)
```

Triggering Actions. Unlike menus in which each menu item has its own Click event, all nodes in the tree view share the same events. The tree view has the *AfterSelect event* that occurs when the user makes a node selection in the tree view. You can place code in this event to handle different selections. In general, the "actionable" nodes are the end nodes of the tree; that is, nodes that do not have any child node. You can test the Nodes.Count property to decide whether an action is called for. The following code structure provides a template:

```
Private Sub trvMenu_AfterSelect(ByVal sender As System.Object,
    ByVal e As System.Windows.Forms.TreeViewEventArgs) Handles
    trvMenu.AfterSelect
    If trvMenu.SelectedNode.Nodes.Count = 0 Then
        Select Case trvMenu.SelectedNode.Text
            Case "New Database"
                'Statements to handle new database
            Case "Exit"
                Me.Close
            Case . . .
                  .
                  .
        End Select
    End If
End Sub
```

The If statement in the event procedure ensures that the selected node is an end node. The Select Case structure branches to different cases based on the node's Text property. Under each Case block, proper code can be written to handle the required actions. In most cases, this would mean invoking a form for the desired action. Note that it is assumed the texts for all the end nodes are unique. If not, you will also need to test the node's Parent property up to a level that you can uniquely identify the selected node. Also note that if you are sure the Text property for each node (whether actionable or not) is unique, you will not need to test the Nodes.Count property; therefore, the If statement and its associated End If statement can be removed from the sample code.

TIP   In IDE you may encounter a System.ObjectDisposedException error with executing Me.Close in the TreeView's AfterSelect event procedure when you run the project with the Debug button. You should have no problem if you start the project by pressing Ctrl+F5. Also, the compiled executable should run without any problem.

11.3   Multiple-Form Applications

In most practical applications a project can involve many forms, each of which performs a special task such as displaying a report or working as a data-entry screen. This section considers issues related to multiple-form applications.

Adding a Form to a Project

When you start a new VB project, a new form is automatically provided. To add an additional new form to the project:

1. Click the Project menu.
2. Select the Add Windows Form option. The Add New Item dialog box will appear.
3. Select the Windows Form in the Templates pane.
4. Enter the name for the new form at the bottom of the dialog box.
5. Click the Open button.

TIP   Another way to invoke the Add New Item dialog box is to click the project name in the Solution Explorer, select the Add option in the context menu, and click the Add Windows Form option in the submenu.

Switching Among Forms and Code Windows. The form that you add to the project most recently is the one that will appear on top in the center of the IDE. The code window (module) will also be associated with this form.

To switch to another form, double-click the form name in the Solution Explorer window or click the form name and then click the Form icon. To switch to another code window directly, click its form name and then click the View Code icon in the Solution Explorer window. You can also use the Window menu to select the desired form. The list of forms in the project is shown at the bottom of the Window menu.

TIP   The list of forms and their associated code windows that appears in the Window menu is also shown across the top of the Designer's design area where the code appears. The quickest and simplest way to switch among these forms and code windows is to click the desired object on this list.

Figure 11.8

Changing startup object

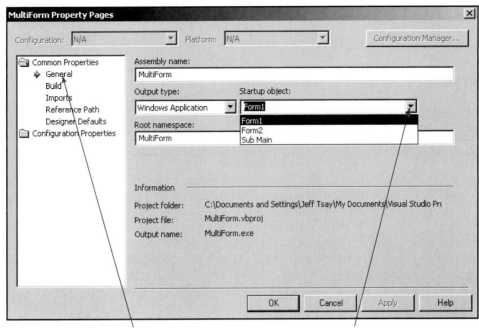

In this dialog box, make sure "General" is selected. Then click the down
arrow button of the startup object box to make your selection.

Starting Up and Calling a Form

When your project starts, only one form will automatically open. The default startup form is the
first form that you create in the project. To start up with another form in the project, you will
need to specify it in the Property Pages dialog box for the project. Recall in Chapter 2,
"Introduction to Visual Basic Programming," how you fixed the problem after you changed the
name for the form? It takes exactly the same steps to change the startup object. Again, to start the
Property Pages dialog box, right-click the Project icon in the Solution Explorer window and then
select the Properties option in the context menu. The dialog box appears as shown in Figure 11.8.

Select General under the common properties folder. You can then click the drop-down arrow
on the Startup object box, and select the desired form. Notice that in the drop-down list, in addition to all the forms you have created, there is also an item called Sub Main. The use of this procedure is discussed in the subsection "The Standard Module" later in this chapter.

Displaying Another Form. At runtime, only the startup form will initially appear.
You will need to provide the code to make the other forms appear. The typical steps are:

1. Declare a variable that can be associated with the form. For example, suppose you add
   a new form to your project, and name it **frmAccountTemplate**. You can declare it with
   the following statement:

   ```
   Dim frmAccount As frmAccountTemplate
   ```

2. In a procedure, create the form and then make it show with its Show method as given
   below:

   ```
   frmAccount = New frmAccountTemplate()
   frmAccount.Show
   ```

Basically, the way to handle a new form—one that is not the startup form—is similar to
creating a new control by code. Recall that the New keyword creates a new object, so
the preceding code will display a new copy of the form each time it is executed. If your
program needs only one copy of the form, you can declare the form in the general dec-

laration area with a New keyword and then use the form's Show method to display the form when called for as follows:

```
'In the general declaration area
Dim frmAccount  As New frmAccountTemplate()
'In a procedure where this form needs to be displayed
frmAccount.Show
```

Understanding the Form. The preceding discussion actually involves three items: the form variable, the form template, and the form created at runtime. The form variable is declared and needed so that you have a way to associate and refer to the form object. The form that you add to the project and design during the design time is actually a form template, similar to any control icon in the Toolbox. Unlike the control that you can draw onto a form at design time to create instances of the control, you can create an instance of the form object only during runtime (except for the startup form, which the system automatically creates for your project). The New keyword in the preceding code is used to create the form object. After created, the *form object* is on its own and behaves much like the startup form in executing code in its code module.

The form variable can have a different life from the form object, depending on how it is declared. If the variable is declared in a procedure, it will be out of scope and cease to exist after the procedure ends. If it is declared in the general declaration area of the startup form, it is similar to other class level variables: It exists for as long as the startup form exists and is recognizable by all procedures. If multiple form objects are created with the same form variable from the same form template, the form variable will be associated with only the object last created. The best way to understand all these variations is to test each possibility. Two Explore and Discover exercises (11-8 and 11-9) at the end of this chapter provide this insight.

Notice that the form variable name has been purposively differentiated from the form template name, such as frmAccount vs. frmAccountTemplate; however, it is acceptable to have the same variable name as the template name. For example, if you have designed a form and named it frmAccount instead of frmAccountTemplate, you can still declare a form variable as follows:

```
Dim frmAccount As frmAccount
```

As you have learned, the first frmAccount refers to the form variable, while the second one refers to the form template. Although the code will still work, you or other people reviewing your code might find it confusing with such coding practice. When you encounter the name in another part of the code, you may not be able to tell whether you meant the form variable or the form template.

Modal and Modeless Forms

The preceding code will show the form in *modeless style*, the default. A form can be displayed in either *modal* or *modeless style*. When displayed as a modeless form, it acts independently of the form that invokes it. All remaining code in the procedure that invokes the form will continue to execute. In addition, the user can change focus among all forms that appear by clicking on the form of interest.

Modal Form and Custom Dialog Box. A modal form will stay on top of the current application. No other forms in the same project can get focus and obtain input until this form is either closed or hidden. In addition, the remaining code in the procedure that invokes the modal form will not be executed until the modal form is either unloaded or hidden.

Modal forms are usually used as custom dialog boxes. A *custom dialog box* is a form designed to solicit special input from the user. For example, in an account data-entry form, the user may have difficulty recalling the account number of an account although the account name is known. In such a case, you may provide a special lookup button that the user can click to look for the account number given an account name. When the button is clicked, another form is displayed to help the user search for the account number. The form designed for such purposes is recognized as a custom dialog box, as opposed to the common dialog box provided by VB.NET to help your code obtain certain information commonly required for input/output operations.

To display a form as modal, use the form's *ShowDialog method* instead of the Show method. The modal form will be discussed later in this chapter.

Closing and Hiding Forms

Recall that the form can be closed with its Close method. When you are closing the form from another form, use the syntax:

```
FormName.Close
```

To close the form in the same module as the form, use the statement:

```
Me.Close
```

A form can be closed not only by code as just shown, but also by the user's clicking the Close button on the form's title bar.

Hiding a Form. To hide a form, use the *Hide method*, which has the following syntax:

```
Object.Hide
```

where Object represents the form to hide. Again, if the code is in the code module of the same form, to hide the form, you will code the following:

```
Me.Hide
```

Hiding a form is equivalent to setting its Visible property to False. Although not visible, the form continues to exist and function. It can be made to reappear with its Show method.

Differences Between Closing and Hiding a Form. Both closing and hiding a form will make the form disappear; however, there are several differences between the two actions:

- The control property settings of a closed form are lost immediately. The form is destroyed as soon as the form object name goes out of scope.
- The control properties of a hidden form continue to be accessible. (Its Visible property is changed to False.) The form may remain in memory even after the form object name goes out of scope. It will be destroyed at time of *garbage collection*, which is discussed in Chapter 12, "Object-Based Programming."
- A hidden form can be made to reappear by using its Show method.
- A closed form cannot be made to reappear by simply using its Show method. It must first be created with the New keyword; therefore, it takes longer to display a closed form than a hidden form.

The Form Activated Event. Because it takes time to reload a form, you may find it desirable to hide (instead of closing) a form to improve performance. You can then use the form's Show method to display the form when it is called again. Often, you will find it desirable to reset the state of the form. For example, you may want to set the focus on the first control in the form. Such a state is automatic when the form is first loaded; however, when the form is hidden, all the states of the form are kept as is. When it is shown again, the focus may not necessarily be on the first control. To ensure this state, you may want to place code in the *Form Activated event*. For example, if the form's first control is mskDate, you will code the following:

```
Private Sub Form1_Activated(ByVal sender As System.Object, ByVal e
    As System.EventArgs) Handles MyBase.Activated
    mskDate.Focus()
End Sub
```

The Form Activated event occurs when the form becomes the active window; when you use the Show method to display the form, the Form Activated event will ensue. Each time the form is activated, however, this event occurs; that is, it can occur many times in the duration of the form's life. In contrast, the Form Load event occurs only once when the form is being loaded.

Be aware that the Activated event can also occur in various contexts. For example, closing or hiding another form currently on top of it or user actions such as clicking on it will activate the form, causing the event to be triggered. An Explore and Discover exercise (11-10) at the end of this chapter is designed to illustrate this situation.

Avoiding Unexpected Execution of the Activated Event. If you have to use the Form Activated event to handle specific situations, you may need to design code to avoid the consequence caused by unexpected trigger of the event. One way is to use a class-level variable to indicate the state of the form, and to allow the code in the Form Activated event to execute only when the state is as expected. For example, suppose you want the Activated event procedure in Form1 to execute only when the form gets reactivated from the hidden state, not when the user closes another form. Assume the code to hide the form is placed in the Quit button (btnQuit). Your code scheme in the form to avoid the unexpected result can be as follows:

```
Dim Hiding As Boolean
Private Sub btnQuit_Click(ByVal sender As System.Object, ByVal e
    As System.EventArgs) Handles btnQuit.Click
    Hiding = True ' I'm hiding now
    Me.Hide()
End Sub

Private Sub Form1_Activated(ByVal sender As System.Object, ByVal e
    As System.EventArgs) Handles MyBase.Activated
    If Hiding Then
        ' I'm getting activated from a hiding state
        mskDate.Focus() 'Set focus to the first control
        Hiding = False 'Now I'm activated.
        'Turn the indicator off.
    End If
End Sub
```

Ending a Project. Chapter 2, "Introduction to Visual Basic Programming," briefly discussed how to end a project. It was suggested that the form's Close method be used instead of using the End statement. The End statement ends the project immediately. No events such as Closing or Closed will be raised when the End statement is executed. This can cause problems. For example, the form may still have unsaved data. Because the Closing event will not be raised, there will be no way to warn the user or to save the data. On the other hand, the Close method will not cause this problem.

Note, however, although closing the startup form will trigger the form's own Closing event, all other forms will terminate without triggering their respective Closing events. When you do use the Closing events in other forms, this can be a serious problem. For example, you may have written code to close a StreamWriter in the form Closing event; but if the event is not triggered when the project ends, the data written by the StreamWrite will be lost. A solution will be presented later in this section.

Sharing Data Between Forms

In multiple-form applications, you may have a need to refer to a property of a control in another form. A control property in one form can be referenced in another form by the syntax:

```
FormName.ControlName.Property
```

To display the Text property of the text box txtName on the form referenced by the variable, frmAccount, you can code in another form (for example, a form to prepare a report) as follows:

```
MsgBox("The account name is " & frmAccount.txtName.Text)
```

Note that the form name here is the form variable name you declare in the code module, not the name of the form template that you create at design time. Note also that because the startup form object—(not the form template)—is not declared as a variable in other forms, it is not possible to refer to any control (and thus its property) in that form. There is, of course, a workaround, which will be discussed in the next subsection.

Declaring Variables for Broader Access. Variables in a form declared with a Dim statement cannot be accessed by another form. To make a variable accessible by other forms, you need to declare it with either the *Public* or *Friend modifier,* instead of Dim or Private. A variable of Public access is accessible to any entity without any restriction. A variable with Friend access is accessible to all modules in the current project. To make the variable AccountName available to other forms, you can code either of the following statements in the general declaration section as follows:

```
Public AccountName As String, or
Friend AccountName As String
```

In other forms, you can refer to this variable by the following syntax:

```
FormName.VariableName
```

To display the AccountName in frmAccount (form variable name, not the form template) in another form, you will code the following:

```
MsgBox("The account name in form account is " &
    frmAccount.AccountName)
```

Recall that you showed a way to display (and therefore to use) multiple copies of the same form. Each copy of the form will have its own copy of variables declared with Public, Friend, Private, Dim, or Static. If the multiple copies of the same form need to share a variable; that is, one copy only, not multiple copies, then the variable should be declared with the *Shared* access. There will be only one copy of the variable for all copies of the forms displayed. A typical use of such a variable is to count the number of copies of forms loaded. For example, you can declare FormCount in the general declaration area as follows:

```
Shared FormCount As Integer
```

In the form's Load event, you can code:

```
FormCount += 1
```

In the form's Closing event, you can code:

```
FormCount -= 1
```

You can then use the variable in the form to find out how many copies of the same are being displayed. A shared variable is said to be static because its value is preserved for the entire duration of the project. Note that a shared variable can be declared with Public, Friend, or Private modifier. (The default is Private; in the preceding example, FormCount is accessible only to the copies of the form and not to any other form). You can also declare the variable as follows:

```
Public Shared FormCount As Integer, or
Friend Shared FormCount As Integer
```

If declared this way, FormCount will have the same Public or Friend access as described previously; that is, it will be accessible to all other modules in the project.

Potential Problems with Accessing Data in a Form Directly. When you refer to data in another form directly as previously shown, you can encounter unexpected problems. Why? You can never be sure that your code is referencing to a form that the user has closed. As mentioned previously, if a form is opened with the ShowDialog method (therefore is used as a dialog box), it is safe to reference the dialog box's contents even if is closed; however, if a form is opened with the Show method, its contents will be lost after it is closed. Whatever your code retrieves can be invalid.

Keeping a Form from Unloading. Ensuring that a form remains in memory can become fairly complicated. For example, although you may use the form's Hide method in code to ensure that the form you will make reference to later remains in memory, this may not be enough. The user may use the Close (x) button to close the form. You can solve this problem by one of the following approaches:

- Set the form's *FormBorderStyle property* to None. In this case, the form will show no title bar (therefore, no control box). The form's appearance may not be exactly what you want.

- Set the form's *ControlBox property* to False to minimize the user's flexibility to maximize or minimize the form.

- Place the code in the Closing event to hide the form and cancel the closing operation as shown next; however, it takes extra code and effort.

```
Me.Hide() 'Hide the form
e.Cancel = True 'Do not close
```

As you can see, the code is fairly simple, but you will need to take care of this for every form whose control properties will be accessed by other forms. You also need to find a way to truly close the form at the end of the project.

A more secure (and easier) way to share data among forms is to use a standard module, discussed in the next section.

The Standard Module

The code you place in a form's code window is kept in a *code module*, which will be called the form module. Other kinds of code modules also exist. The *class module* is used to store code for classes, which are the template of objects. The use of the class module is discussed in Chapter 12, "Object-Based Programming." Finally, the *standard module* is used to contain code and data common to other code modules.

The standard module contains only code and variables. It has no form or any container in which you may place any control or visible object; however, you can use it to keep procedures and data that are global (to the project) in nature. These elements can then be accessible to all modules (form, standard, and class modules) in the project.

Adding Standard Modules to a Project. To add a new standard module to a project, follow these steps:

1. Click the Project menu. Select the Add Module option to open the Add New Item dialog box.

2. Enter the proper name for the module in the name box (begin the name with the mod prefix); then click the Open button.

A project can have as many standard modules as you need. In a large project, you may find it desirable to include more than one module, each specialized in a particular aspect. Procedures that are useful to all projects should be placed in a module (or modules) separated from procedures that are to be used only by forms in a particular project. Modules arranged in this manner can enhance their reusability.

Declaring Variables and Procedures in a Standard Module. You can declare variables and procedures in a standard module in the same way as in a form module. Similar rules for scope and duration apply:

- Variables declared within a procedure are recognized only within the procedure. Variables declared with a Dim statement in the procedure are reinitialized each time the procedure is called. Variables declared with a Static statement retain their values until the project ends.

- Variables declared at the module level with a Dim or Private statement are recognized by all procedures in the module, but are not accessible to other forms or modules. These variables retain their values until the project ends.

- Variables declared with a Public modifier are recognized globally. Variables declared with a Friend modifier are accessible to all procedures in the current project. Both Public and Friend variables retain their values until the project ends.
- Public, Friend, and Private variables can be declared only in the general declaration area. Static variables can be declared only inside a procedure.
- You cannot declare a variable with the Shared access in a standard module because you cannot create multiple copies of the same standard module in a project.

Most of these rules are similar to those explained in Chapter 4, "Data, Operations, and Built-In Functions."

Duration of the Standard Module and Form Module. One difference between the standard module and the form is their time duration. The standard module exists throughout the entire life of the project, whereas the form can be closed and destroyed before the project ends (or loaded after the project starts). Global and module-level variables in the standard module exist for the entire life of the project; in the form, they exist for the entire life of the form, which can be shorter than the life of the project.

Public, Friend, and Private Procedures. The modifiers Public, Friend, and Private are also used to define the scope of Sub and Function procedures and will have exactly the same scope as the variables declared with the same modifiers. For example, consider the following two procedures:

```
Public Sub FirstProc()
    'Statements
End Sub
Private Sub SecondProc()
    'Statements
End Sub
```

FirstProc can be called from any other modules, but SecondProc can be used only within the module.

Also, a procedure that is not preceded by the Public, Friend, or Private keyword is a Public procedure by default. These rules of declaration for procedures apply to procedures in forms as well.

Calling Procedures in Another Module. To call a Public procedure in a standard module, the syntax is exactly the same as if the procedure were in the same form (or standard module); therefore, to call FirstProc from a form, you will code the following:

```
FirstProc()
```

To call a Public procedure in a form, you must qualify the procedure with the form name. For example, assume in a form named frmAccount that there is a public function ComputeBalance, which requires an account number as its parameter and returns a value as the account balance. To use the function from another module (form or standard module), you can code the following:

```
AccountBalance = frmAccount.ComputeBalance(AccountNumber)
```

Of course, here you assume that AccountBalance and AccountNumber have been properly declared, and that AccountNumber has been assigned a proper value.

Another Way to Share Variables Among Modules. Potential problems with accessing data in a form directly have been mentioned because of the possibility that the form is destroyed or closed prematurely. One possible solution is to use a standard module in which you can place all variables to be shared by various forms. The form that provides the value can then assign it to the variable in the standard module. After this is done, whether this form is closed is no longer a concern. All other forms or modules can access the value simply by referencing the variable in the standard module.

In the previous example, suppose various forms need to access the Text property of txtName in the form frmAccount. To use the standard module as the bridge to keep the data, you can first add a declaration in the module as follows:

```
Public AccountName As String
```

In frmAccount, you can then assign the value as follows:

```
AccountName = txtName.Text
```

From then on, in all other forms or modules, you can use the value regardless of the state of frmAccount. Your code in these modules can appear as follows:

```
MsgBox("Account name is " & AccountName)
```

Notice that the (standard) module name does not need to be referenced. The variable name alone is sufficient in most cases.

Variables and Procedures in Multiple Modules. As noted, you can have more than one standard module in a project. Can you then declare the same Public or Friend variable (and procedure) names in these modules? Yes. If you declare the same Public or Friend variable (procedure) name in two standard modules, this name actually represents two different variables (or procedures) in the two modules. To refer to each variable or procedure, you will need to qualify the variable name with the module name. For example, suppose the variable name AccountName is declared as Public in two modules: modAccounts and modInsurance. To refer to that variable in modAccounts from another module, you will need to code the following:

```
modAccounts.AccountName
```

The syntax in referring to these variables/procedures is the same as that for those Public or Friend variable/procedure names declared in a form. If you fail to qualify the variable name with the module name when the former appears in more than one module, you will be informed that "The name <name> is ambiguous between declarations. . . "

Using Sub Main as the Startup Object. The standard module can also contain a special *Sub Main* procedure. This procedure can then be designated as the startup object in place of a form in the project's Property Pages dialog box as discussed previously. The use of Sub Main helps resolve the issues that were mentioned previously, such as:

* The controls and Public (Friend) variables in the startup form object are not accessible by other forms. Controls, module/class level variables, and procedures in a code module are collectively recognized as *members of the module/class*.

* When the startup form closes, all other forms are terminated without triggering their respective Closing events.

Making Contents of the Startup Form Available. The first issue can be resolved by declaring a Public (or Friend) variable for the startup form and start the form in the Sub Main procedure as follows:

```
'Place this code in the standard module
Public frmPayroll As New frmPayrollTemplate()
Public Sub Main()
    Application.Run(frmPayroll) 'Run frmPayroll as the startup form
End Sub
```

It is assumed that the startup form is named frmPayrollTemplate at design time. It is declared as a Public form with the name frmPayroll. Suppose this form has a text box named txtEmployee. You should be able to refer to this control in another module as follows:

```
frmPayroll.txtEmployee
```

Notice the code in Sub Main. Instead of using the form's Show method to display the form, the Application object's *Run method* is used to start the form. Is there a difference? Yes. If you use the form's show method, the form will be displayed but the project will immediately terminate and close the form. For the startup form to continue to appear and accept events, it must be started with the Application's Run method. An application can be terminated with its *Exit method.* When this method is executed, however, the application immediately terminates. No events will be triggered.

Allowing the Closing Event in Each Form to Execute. To allow the Closing event to execute properly when the project terminates involves placing code in several modules. Basically, a Public collection object should be created to keep track of the (non-startup) forms that are loaded and/or removed. When the "startup" form is being closed, the non-startup forms can then be closed first in the startup form's Closing event. The relevant code appears as follows:

```
'In the standard module
'Declare a Public collection object
Public OtherForms As New Collection()

'In the Load event of the non-startup form
'that requires execution of the Closing event
'Include myself in the collection object, using my text as the key
OtherForms.Add(Me, Me.Text)
'In the Closing event of the same form
OtherForms.Remove(Me.Text) 'Remove myself
'Place other pertinent code to execute for form Closing here

'In the Closing event of the "startup" form
Dim I As Integer
Dim Frm as Form
For I = OtherForms.Count To 1 Step - 1
    Frm = CType(OtherForms(I), Form)
    'Close the form in the Collection to trigger its Closing event
    Frm.Close
Next I
' Place other pertinent code for the Closing event here
```

Note that the loop counter—and therefore the collection's index in the loop—starts with the collection Count property and goes down to 1. (Recall that the Collection's index is 1 based, not 0 based.) When an item with a lower index is removed from the collection, the higher indices are adjusted down; therefore, if the item with an index value of 1 is removed first, the highest index will no longer be the collection's Count property, causing an error when the counter reaches that value. Removing the item with the highest index first (as the way your loop does) will not cause this problem.

Notice also that you use the form's Text property as the key for the form to add to and remove from the collection object. This will work only if the Text property of each form is unique; otherwise, a different scheme must be used. This issue is addressed in exercise 11-22 at the end of this chapter.

As an alternative to the "count down" loop, you can remove the first item in the loop instead of an index of varying value as shown next. It will work because, as explained in the text, the collection's indices are adjusted as soon as an item is removed from its list.

```
Dim I As Integer
Dim Frm as Form
For I = 1 To OtherForms.Count
    Frm = CType(OtherForms(1), Form)
    Frm.Close
Next I
```

In addition to resolving the two preceding issues, when the main form takes a long time to load, you can use the Sub Main procedure to alleviate the user's anxiety with waiting for the program to start. How? You can use this procedure to display another form (recognized as the splash form) while loading the main form. The splash form usually displays a logo of the software product for a few seconds and then disappears. By this time, the main form is loaded into memory and is then shown. To make the splash form disappear, you can use a Timer control to close it when the predefined time interval is reach, and thus the timer's Tick event is triggered. You have seen such an arrangement in action: when you load VS.NET, it displays a logo first before the IDE appears.

Assume the main form template is named frmMainTemplate, and the splash form template is named frmSplashTemplate. The code in Sub Main can appear as follows:

```
Dim WithEvents TheTimer As New Timer()
Dim frmSplash As New frmSplashTemplate()
Public frmMain As New frmMainTemplate()
Public Sub main()
    TheTimer.Start() 'Start the timer
    TheTimer.Interval = 4000 'Set the timer interval to 4 seconds
    frmSplash.Show()
    Application.Run(frmMain) 'start the main form
End Sub

Private Sub TheTimer_Tick(ByVal sender As System.Object, ByVal e
    As EventArgs) Handles TheTimer.Tick
    frmSplash.Close()
    TheTimer.Stop() 'Stop the timer
End Sub
```

Use the timer's *Start method* to start the time count. This method turns on the timer by setting its Enabled property to True. Notice TheTimer is declared with the *WithEvents* keyword. When a control's events are to be used in a code module (form or standard module), it must be declared with the WithEvents keyword. In addition, it must be declared at the module level, not in a procedure. The timer's Tick event is used to close the splash form. The Tick event should be triggered in four seconds because the timer's Interval property is set to 4000 in Sub Main. Note that if the main form is loaded within four seconds, it will appear on top of the splash form. Typically, this is what you want because you use the splash form mainly to alleviate the user's anxiety of waiting. But if you mean for the splash form to stay on top until it disappears, you can set the form's TopMost property to True (False is the default).

A Multiple-Form Example

To illustrate how to code an application with multiple forms, consider an example that involves a number guessing game. When the project starts, the program displays an instruction explaining how to play the game, and instructs the game player (user) to enter the player's name and click the Ready button to proceed—to go on to the next form.

The second form has two buttons: Click here to play a game, and Bye. When the first button is clicked, a label and a text box are enabled. In addition, a number in the range of 1 to 1,000 is selected at random, which will be the number for the player to guess. The label instructs the player to enter a number in the text box and then press the Enter key when complete. The program then checks whether the entered number is equal to the selected random number. If so, it displays the message "That's right!" with the player's name, and informs the player of the number of times the player tried and for how long before the correct number was obtained. If the guessed number is not equal to the random number selected, a label below the text box gives a hint indicating whether the actual number is higher or lower.

In addition to showing how each form is started and the variables that can be shared in a multiple form project, this project also touches upon a few technical aspects discussed in the preceding subsections. These aspects are considered later when you code each module.

Setting Up the Guessing Game Project. This project will involve one standard module and two forms. To provide you with a different experience with the IDE, you need to set up the project with a set of different steps. To do so, follow these steps:

1. In the IDE, click the File menu, select the New option, and select Project. The New project dialog box will appear.

2. Select **Empty project** in the Template (right) pane. Enter **GuessingGame** for the project name (in place of Project1); then click the OK button. You will see the IDE without a form or module.

3. Add a module to your project.

   a.   Click the Project menu and then select the Add Module option. The Add New Item dialog box will appear.

   b.   Enter modGuessingGame in the Name box and then click the Open button.

4. Add two forms to your project.

   a.   Click the Project menu and then select the Add Windows Form option. The Add New Item dialog box will appear.

   b.   Enter frmGreetTemplate in the Name box and then click the Open button.

   c.   Repeat steps a and b to add another form named frmGameTemplate.

5. Import proper namespaces. A project created from scratch ("empty") as you have done does not have all the needed namespaces included in it. Follow these steps to import needed namespaces:

   a.   Right-click the Project icon in the Solution Explorer, and select the Properties option. The Property Pages dialog box will appear, as shown in Figure 11.8.

   b.   Click Imports in the left pane. Make sure the following namespaces are in the Project Imports box in the lower right quadrant. If not, enter each of the missing ones (one at a time) in the namespace box (upper right), and click the Add Import button. Here is the list of namespaces to import:

   Microsoft.VisualBasic

   System

   System.Data

   System.Drawing

   System.Windows.Forms

   c.   Click the OK button in the Property Pages dialog box when done.

When you set up the project this way, the IDE automatically sets Sub Main as the startup object for the project. With the module and forms ready, you can proceed to design the visual interface.

Designing the Visual Interface.   The two forms of this project appear as in Figure 11.9. The following table explains the names and purposes of the forms and controls.

Control	Name	Purpose
In frmGreetTemplate		
Text box	txtPlayerName	To obtain player's name
Button	btnReady	To invoke the game form frmGame
Button	btnQuit	To end the program
In frmGameTemplate		
Button	btnStart	To start a game
Text box	txtNumber	For the user to enter the guessed number (*Note:* Also set its Enabled property to False)
Label	lblGuess	The label for txtNumber (*Note:* Also set its Enabled property to False)
Label	lblHint	To display hint telling the player whether the actual number is higher or lower
Button	btnBye	To make the game form disappear

Figure 11.9

Visual interface of the number guessing game

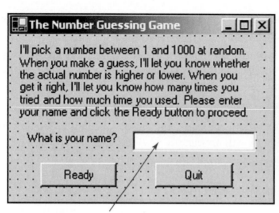

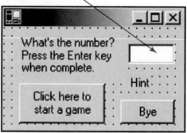

The player will play the number guessing game with this form.

This startup form contains instructions to play the game and prompts for the player's name.

The label, named lblHint, tells the player whether the actual number is higher or lower.

Coding the Project. The project involves one standard module and two forms. Consider the code in each module in the following order:

1. The standard module
2. The startup form (frmGreetTemplate)
3. The game form (frmGameTemplate)

Code in the Standard Module. The standard module provides a code container for the variables to be shared by all forms. It should also have Sub Main to start the project. You may also want to test how the two multiple-form issues previously mentioned (access to objects in the startup form and executing the Closing event in the non-startup form) are actually handled; therefore, you will declare the startup form as a Public variable, and create a collection object to keep track of other forms. The code in this module appears as follows:

```
Module modGuessingGame
    'Create the startup form from the template
    Public frmGreet As New frmGreetTemplate()
    'To be used to keep track of "other forms"
    although there is only one
    Public OtherForms As New Collection()
    Public PlayerName As String 'For all forms to share
    Sub Main()
        Application.Run(frmGreet) 'Run frmGreet as the startup form
    End Sub
End Module
```

Notice that you have declared a collection variable, OtherForms. You will use it to keep track of the other forms to handle proper closing of the non-startup form. Although you know in this project you have only one form other than the startup form and can actually use a simpler approach to keep track of it, pretend that there are many other forms to show the practical use of the collection object in this context.

Code in the Startup Form. Now look at what *should* happen in the startup form (named frmGreetTemplate at design time). As you would expect, when the project starts, this form should appear and wait for the player to enter their name and click the Ready button. The Click event procedure should do the following:

1. Check to ensure the player's name is entered.

2. If the player's name is present, it should proceed to:

    a.   Display the second form (named frmGameTemplate at design time).

    b.   Move the player's name to the Public variable in the standard module for the other
         form to access.

The procedure should appear as follows:

```
'Declare this in the general declaration area
Dim frmGame As frmGameTemplate
Private Sub btnReady_Click(ByVal sender As System.Object, ByVal e
   As System.EventArgs) Handles btnReady.Click
   If Len(Trim(txtPlayerName.Text)) = 0 Then
       'Name has not been entered. Display a message
       MsgBox("Please enter your name to proceed.")
       txtPlayerName.Focus() 'set the focus on the name box
       Exit Sub
   End If
   'Display the game form
   If OtherForms.Count = 0 Then
       frmGame = New frmGameTemplate()
       frmGame.Show()
   End If
   'Keep name in standard module for all forms to share
   PlayerName = txtPlayerName.Text
End Sub
```

The first If block tests whether the player's name is present. If not, a message is displayed and
the focus is set on the text box for the user to enter the name.

The second If block tests whether the OtherForms collection has any item. If it does not, the
code creates the second form (with the New keyword) and displays it. If the collection has any
item, it means the second form (the game form) already exists and nothing is done about the
form. (How OtherForms is used to keep track of the second form will be explained later in this
section.) The last statement in the procedure moves the entered player's name to the PlayerName
variable, which is declared in the standard module as a Public string variable.

When the user clicks the Quit button in the main form at the end of the game, the program
should close. The following familiar code should appear:

```
Private Sub btnQuit_Click(ByVal sender As System.Object, ByVal e
   As System.EventArgs) Handles btnQuit.Click
   Me.Close()
End Sub
```

Ensuring All Forms Are Closed Properly.   As explained previously, if you do
not do anything about the other forms when the startup form is closing, none of the other forms'
Closing events will be triggered. This may cause problems if your code in the Closing events is to
perform important activities at closing; therefore, the following code should also appear:

```
Private Sub frmGreetTemplate_Closing(ByVal sender As
   System.Object, ByVal e As System.ComponentModel.CancelEventArgs)
   Handles MyBase.Closing
   Dim I As Integer
   Dim Frm As Form
   'Make sure other forms are "properly" closed
   For I = OtherForms.Count To 1 Step -1
       Frm = CType(OtherForms(I), Form)
       Frm.Close()
   Next I
End Sub
```

Notice that the routine to close other forms is placed in the form's Closing event, not in the
Quit button's Click event. The code in the Closing event is executed either when the code initi-

ates the closing (as in the Quit button's Click event) or when the user clicks the Close button in the control box. In contrast, the code in the Quit button's Click event is executed only when the user clicks that button.

Because there is only one other form in the project, why use a loop? Can't you just close the other (game) form? Yes, of course; however, when you decide to have more forms in the project in the future, you will need to revise the code, requiring additional maintenance care and effort. In addition, your code will need to test whether the other form still exists before closing it. On the other hand, the code using the loop is general enough so that there will be no maintenance problem in the future.

Code in the Game Form. Now look at the procedures in the second form, frmGameTemplate. Consider the issue of keeping track of the form status with the OtherForms collection variable first. The collection should add the form to its list when this form is loaded, and remove the form from its list when the form is being closed. Clearly, the events to handle these cases should be the form's Load and Closing events. The code to add the form to the collection should appear as follows:

```
Private Sub frmGameTemplate_Load(ByVal sender As System.Object,
    ByVal e As System.EventArgs) Handles MyBase.Load
        'Add the form to the collection, using its text as the key
        OtherForms.Add(Me, Me.Text)
End Sub
```

The Closing Event. When the form is being closed, in addition to removing the form from the collection, you would also like to display a message showing the number of games that the player has played. To accumulate the number of games played, the first thought is to declare a class level variable for such a purpose; however, the result may not be exactly correct. Why? The player can play a few games, and click the Bye button to close the form; then the player can click the Ready button in the first form, and come back to play several games. The player can go back and forth several times before eventually quitting. The number of games should include all. A variable declared with Dim will lose its content when the form is closed. Solution? The variable should be declared with the Shared modifier so that its value is preserved even when the form is closed and reloaded. The code to handle the Closing event appears as follows:

```
'Declare in the general declaration area
Shared GameCount As Integer
Private Sub frmGameTemplate_Closing(ByVal sender As System.Object,
    ByVal e As System.ComponentModel.CancelEventArgs) Handles
    MyBase.Closing
        'Display game statistics
        MsgBox("You played " & GameCount & " games. Bye now.")
        'Remove the form from the collection
        OtherForms.Remove(Me.Text)
End Sub
```

The value of GameCount should be updated when the player guesses the right number for a game. The guessed number is checked when the player enters a number and then presses the Enter key, which triggers the text box's KeyPress event and is discussed later in this section.

Starting the Game. The text box (txtNumber) to enter the guessed number, and its label (lblGuess) should be disabled at design time. This way, the player cannot enter the number before the program is ready for a game—the number to be guessed needs to be set first. When the Click here to start a game button is clicked, the preceding two controls are enabled with the following statements:

```
txtNumber.Enabled = True
lblGuess.Enabled = True
```

A random number in the range of 1 to 1,000 (inclusive) should be picked and kept in the variable TheNumber. Suppose the variable for the Random object is declared to be RandomEngine. The statement should appear as follows:

```
' Pick a random number between 1 and 1000
TheNumber = RandomEngine.Next(1, 1001)
```

In addition, the text box is cleared, and the focus is set on it, ready for the user to guess the number:

```
txtNumber.Text = ""
txtNumber.Focus
```

Finally, the start time should be recorded using the timer function (note that the function must be qualified with Microsoft.VisualBasic because of name conflict with the Timer control) for later computation of time used:

```
'Start counting elapse time
StartTime = Microsoft.VisualBasic.Timer()
```

Because both the start time and the random number are to be shared by other procedures, they should be declared at the module level. The complete procedure appears as follows:

```
Dim TheNumber As Integer
Dim StartTime As Double
Private Sub btnStart_Click(ByVal sender As System.Object, ByVal e
    As System.EventArgs) Handles btnStart.Click
    Dim RandomEngine As New Random()
    'Enabled the number box for guessing
    txtNumber.Enabled = True
    lblGuess.Enabled = True
    'Pick a random number
    TheNumber = RandomEngine.Next(1, 1001)
    txtNumber.Text = ""
    txtNumber.Focus()
    StartTime = Microsoft.VisualBasic.Timer() 'Start counting time
End Sub
```

Responding to an Entered Number. The player is instructed to press the Enter key after entering a number in the text box (see the interface design); therefore, the code to check whether the number entered is correct is placed in the text box's KeyPress event. The procedure will be executed only when the Enter key is pressed.

The entered number should be compared with the number to be guessed (TheNumber). If the two match, a "That's right!" message along with the player's name is displayed. The count for the number of trials is reset, and another game can be played; otherwise, the program shows a hint, either "Higher" or "Lower" depending on the comparison. The code appears as follows:

```
Private Sub txtNumber_KeyPress(ByVal sender As System.Object,
    ByVal e As System.Windows.Forms.KeyPressEventArgs) Handles
    txtNumber.KeyPress
    Static GuessCount As Integer
    Dim TheAnswer As Integer
    If e.KeyChar <> vbCr Then Exit Sub 'Not the Enter key, return
    'No number to test, return
    If Len(Trim(txtNumber.Text)) = 0 Then Exit Sub
    e.Handled = True 'Suppress the Return key
    GuessCount += 1
    TheAnswer = CInt(txtNumber.Text)
    If TheNumber = TheAnswer Then
        'Right answer, give number of attempts and time
        lblHint.Text = ""
        MsgBox("That's right! " & PlayerName & "." & vbCrLf & _
            "It takes you " & GuessCount & " trials " & vbCrLf & _
            "for " & Microsoft.VisualBasic.Timer() _
            - StartTime & " seconds " & vbCrLf & _
            "to get the correct number.")
        GuessCount = 0 'Clear the counter
        txtNumber.Text = "" 'Clear the text box
        'Force the user to click the Start a Game button again
```

```
            lblGuess.Enabled = False
            txtNumber.Enabled = False
            GameCount += 1 'One additional completed game
        ElseIf TheNumber < TheAnswer Then
            lblHint.Text = "Lower"
        Else
            lblHint.Text = "Higher"
        End If
        'Highlight the previous number
        txtNumber.Select(0, Len(txtNumber.Text))
    End Sub
```

The meaning of the code should be apparent. Pay particular attention to the way the player's name is referenced in the first line of the MsgBox statement. The PlayerName variable is used because before this form starts, that variable (declared as Public in the standard module) has already been assigned the Text property of the text box that accepts the player's name in the first (startup) form. Because you have also declared the startup form name as Public in the standard module, you can also reference the text box directly. The control's name should be qualified by the form name (with a dot). The text property of that text box can be coded as follows:

```
        frmGreet.txtPlayerName.Text
```

Notice also that GameCount is increased by 1 each time the player guesses the right number. As explained previously, this variable is declared as Shared, so the value is preserved for the duration of the project even when the game form is closed more than one time.

Quitting the frmGame Form. When the player clicks the Bye button, the form should unload. The familiar code appears again:

```
    Private Sub btnBye_Click(ByVal sender As System.Object, ByVal e As
        System.EventArgs) Handles btnBye.Click
        Me.Close()
    End Sub
```

The need for the Closing Event Procedure in the Startup Form. Recall that in the first (startup) form, there is code in the Closing event that ensures that all forms in the project are closed properly. If this second form is closed by code already, and the player's clicking the Close button in the control box will also close it, why is there a need for the code in that Closing event?

Recall that forms that are not invoked as modal work independently of each other. The user can switch between the two forms at will by clicking on the desired form. The player can set focus on the startup form and then click the Quit or Close button. In this case, the second form will be closed without triggering its Closing event. This is the exact situation of which the code in the Closing event procedure of the startup form was designed to take care.

11.4 MDI Applications

In the preceding section, the forms used in a project have no parent-child relationship with each other. Each form presents itself as a single document; that is, only one document of a similar nature appears in the project at one time. Applications involving forms of this kind are referred to as *single document interface (SDI) applications*. Most real-world applications are of this type. Some applications involve forms of *multiple document interface (MDI)*. Several documents of similar nature are loaded in different windows of the same project at the same time. The familiar applications of this kind are word processing and spreadsheet applications. Additional examples of this style of application include the following:

- Real estate property listing in which several real properties can be shown for review and comparison
- Graphic design in which multiple pictures can be shown for cropping, cutting, pasting, and other drawing/painting operations
- Music composition in which multiple pieces of music can be displayed for the composer to analyze or to cut and paste like in word processing operations

In these applications, multiple documents can be loaded. Each document appears on a window (form) and handles different data (document), but behaves in the same manner and shares the same menu bar. All these documents are child forms of the MDI (parent) form. There is a parent-child relationship between these documents and the MDI form.

Differences Between MDI and SDI in Behavior

You can tell whether an application is SDI or MDI by the manner in which the forms (documents) interact with each other. Here is a selected list of the differences in their behavior and restrictions:

- MDI child forms stay within the boundary of their parent form; SDI forms can appear on any part of the screen, independent of each other's location.
- When the MDI parent form is minimized, all child forms are also minimized; minimizing an SDI form does not affect any other forms.
- When an MDI child form is minimized, its icon stays within the boundary of the MDI (parent) form. When an SDI form is minimized, its icon appears on the taskbar of the Windows system.

Creating an MDI Application

To create an MDI application, you will need at least two forms in your project: one serving as the MDI (parent) container, and the other working as the MDI child form. After you have the forms you need, do the following:

1. Set the MDI form's IsMdiContainer property to True.
2. Indicate the MDI parent-child relationship by code. The syntax appears as follows:

```
MdiChildForm.MdiParent = MdiParentForm
```

In VB.NET, you can have as many MDI (parent) forms as you need in a project, unlike the previous versions of VB which allow only one MDI form. Creating an MDI application involves several issues that are not encountered in an SDI application. The following section discusses these issues by a hands-on example.

11.5   Coding an MDI Project: An Example

To illustrate the special issues involved in an MDI project and how it is put together, consider a simplified example. You will create a program that behaves similar to the Notepad except that the program will be able to handle multiple documents; therefore, you are creating an MDI project. This will involve the following the major steps:

1. Designing the features of the program
2. Creating the MDI interface
3. Implementing the features

Features of the Project

Here are the list of features/capabilities the project is expected to provide:

- As a Notepad application, the program will work mainly with a text file with a .txt extension. It will also allow the user to use other file extensions as long as the file itself contains only text.

- When the project starts, no document will be displayed until the user chooses either to create a new document (New) or open an existing document (Open) from a File menu. There will be only one menu (the File menu) on the menu bar when the program starts, or when there is no open document.

- When there is (are) open document(s), two additional menus, Find and Window, will appear. The Find menu enables the user to search for a text string with a custom Search dialog box. The Window menu provides options to arrange the documents, such as cascade or tile. In addition, it also provides a list of open documents from which the user can select one to work on. In addition, the File menu will be expanded to include the Save and Close options.

- When a document is being closed (child form being unloaded), the program will prompt the user whether to save the document. When the application (project) is being closed, all open documents will be handled similarly.

Creating the Interface

This project requires several forms and a menu bar that changes depending on whether there is a document open. The following discussion considers these details.

Forms and Modules. As explained previously, an MDI application needs at least two forms. In addition, this project needs a form to serve as the Find dialog box. Also, as in most multiple form applications, a standard module can be used to hold various procedures (Subs and Functions) and variables to be shared by the forms in the project; therefore, you will include the following forms and module in this project:

Form or module name	Comments
mdiNotepadTemplate	To serve as the MDI container (parent)
FrmChildTemplate	MDI child form
FrmFindTemplate	To serve as the dialog box to search for text in a document window
ModNotepad	To provide the Sub Main procedure to start the project

Designing the Menu Bar(s). There are several ways to handle the menu bar as described previously. Perhaps the most straightforward way is to use two main menus in the MDI (parent) form. One can be set up to contain only the File menu with the New, Open and Exit options. The other can be set up to have all the menu items for the case when the MDI contains one or more child forms. At runtime, menus can be switched by the following statement:

```
FormName.Menu = MainMenuName
```

You will use this approach. Figure 11.10 shows the MDI form with the two different menus.

Creating and Setting Up the Menus. To create two main menus, draw two main menus on the form, or double-click the MainMenu icon in the Toolbox twice. To name the main menus, click the main menu below the form and then enter the name in the Name property in the Properties window. Name the two main menus **mnuMainNoWin** and **mnuMainWithWin**. To set up the menu items for mnuMainNoWin, click this control (below the form) first; then proceed to enter the text for each menu item, and set its name as described in Section 11.1. Do the same for mnuMainWithWin. Be sure that you click the control below the form before doing anything for this main menu.

Figure 11.10

Two menus in the MDI form

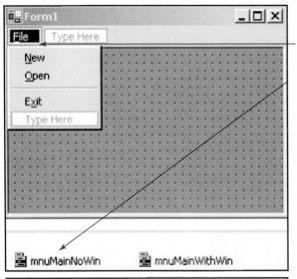

You can have as many main menus as you need in a form. This Mdi form uses two menus. This menu bar (with only one item on the menu bar) is associated with mnuMainNoWin.

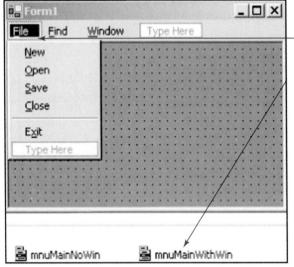

This menu is associated with mnuMainWithWin. At design time, when you click the main menu named mnuMainWithWin, this menu is displayed. If you click mnuMainNoWin on the form, the menu on the top is displayed.

The following table shows the structure of each main menu.

In mnuMainNoWin

First level menu Item: Name	First level menu Item: Text	Second level menu Item: Name	Second level menu Item: Text
MnuFile	&File	mnuFileNew	&New
		mnuFileOpen	&Open
		mnuFileExit	E&xit

In mnuMainWithWin

First level menu Item: Name	First level menu Item: Text	Second level menu Item: Name	Second level menu Item: Text
MnuFile1	&File	mnuFile1New	&New
		mnuFile1Open	&Open
		mnuFile1Save	&Save
		mnuFile1Close	&Close
		mnuFile1Exit	E&xit
MnuFind	Fin&d		
MnuWin	&Window	mnuWinCascade	&Cascade
		mnuWinHorizontal	Tile &Horizontal
		mnuWinVertical	Tile &Vertical

You would like for the Window menu to display the list of windows (open child forms). To enable this capability, click the menu item, &Window (named mnuWin); then set its *MdiList property* (in the Properties window) to True. At runtime, when there are open child forms, you can verify that the Window menu of your MDI form shows a list of child forms' title texts.

The Document on the Child Form. Because the child form will be used to handle the text document, the control to display the document should be placed in this form. The controls that are suitable for this purpose include the text box and the *rich text box control*. For this purpose, the familiar text box will be used to display the document.

Add a text box on the child form, and name it **txtDocument**. Set its MultiLine property to True, Dock property to Fill, and the ScrollBars property to Vertical. This will enable the text box to display and handle the document properly. The child form should appear as in Figure 11.11.

The Custom Search Dialog Box. Details of this form are covered in the subsection "Building the Find Dialog Box" later in this chapter.

Coding the Project

You now have three forms and a standard module to write code. By the sheer number, the project appears pretty complex already. As the code you need to write is discussed, be aware of the specific module in which the code is to be placed.

Code in the Standard Module

This module is used mainly to activate the main (MDI parent) form. When the startup form name is declared as Public in this module, other modules can conveniently reference this form's controls. The code in this module appears as follows:

```
Module modNotepad
    Public mdiNotepad As New mdiNotepadTemplate()
    Sub Main()
        Application.Run(mdiNotepad)
    End Sub
End Module
```

Figure 11.11

Visual interface for the child form

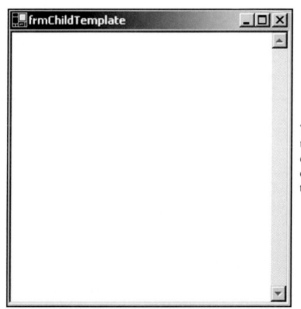

The child form contains only one text box, which is used to edit the document. At runtime, multiple copies of this form can exist in the MDI container (parent) form.

Handling Events in the Child Form

Recall that there is no button or menu in the child form. This form contains only a multi-line text box for text editing. The menus are set up in the MDI (parent) form, and therefore the events associated with the menus should be handled in the parent form; however, recall that different menus will be displayed depending on the number of the child forms. If there is no child form the first simple menu, (mnuMainNoWin) will be used; otherwise, the more complex menu (mnuMainWithWin) will be used. One easy way to keep track of the number of child forms is to use the child form's Load and Closing events. The form count can be increased by 1 when the form is being loaded, and decrease by 1 when being closed. The parent form's menu can then be handled accordingly. The child form's Load event can appear as follows:

```
Public Shared ChildFormCount As Integer
Private Sub frmChildTemplate_Load(ByVal sender As System.Object,
   ByVal e As System.EventArgs) Handles MyBase.Load
     ChildFormCount += 1
     If ChildFormCount = 1 Then
        mdiNotepad.Menu = mdiNotepad.mnuMainWithWin
     End If
End Sub
```

In the procedure, the ChildFormCount variable is increased by 1. Its value is then compared with 1. If it is equal, the parent form's menu is switched to mnu.MainWithWin, the menu bar with more options. Notice that the variable is declared to be Public Shared. It is declared as Shared because it is used to count the number of child forms and should have only one copy for all child forms. It is also declared as Public because its value will also be used in the parent form as you will see later.

Code with similar logic can be placed in the form's Closing event to switch back to the first menu (mnuMainNoWin). In addition, recall that according to the project description, the procedure should also prompt the user whether to save the text (document). If so, it should call a sub to save the content of the text box (txtDocument). Assume that the Sub is available in the parent form because the menu item to save a document is in that form. The code for the child form's event procedure should appear as follows:

```
Private Sub frmChildTemplate_Closing(ByVal sender As
   System.Object, ByVal e As System.ComponentModel.CancelEventArgs)
   Handles MyBase.Closing
     Dim Ans As Integer
     'changes in the textbox has not been saved, ask
     Ans = MsgBox("Save the current document?",
       MsgBoxStyle.Question Or MsgBoxStyle.YesNoCancel)
     If Ans = vbYes Then
        mdiNotepad.SaveDoc() 'Save the current document
     End If
     ChildFormCount -= 1
     If ChildFormCount = 0 Then
        'No more child form, switch to the simple menu
        mdiNotepad.Menu = mdiNotepad.mnuMainNoWin
     End If
End Sub
```

Note that the code assumes that the MDI (parent) form has a public procedure to save the document (SaveDoc()). When the user responds affirmatively to save the document, the procedure is called. The remaining code is fairly straightforward and requires no additional explanation. Admittedly, the code can be refined to test whether there was any change in the text box before prompting the user. In addition, the user can be given a choice to cancel the closing operation when there is unsaved change. These refinements are left to you as an exercise (exercise 11-23).

Handling Events in the MDI Form

Now consider the code in the MDI (parent) form. This form has two main menus. The first main menu has three options in the File menu (named mnuFile): New, Open, and Exit. The second main menu has File, Find, and Window menus. The File menu (named mnuFile1) has New, Open, Save, Close, and Exit options. The Window menu (named mnuWin) has Cascade, Tile Horizontal, and Tile Vertical options. (Refer to the table on p. 487)

It is fairly straightforward to code the event procedure for Exit. Like the SDI application, the Close method should be used. When the MDI (parent) form closes, all its child forms will also close. However, unlike the SDI application, the Closing event in each child form will be raised. Thus, there is no need to close each existing child form explicitly (with code) in order to trigger the Closing event in the child form. The mnuFileExit and mnuFile1Exit Click event procedures should contain the familiar statement to close the form as follows:

```
Private Sub mnuFileExit_Click(ByVal sender As System.Object, ByVal
    e As System.EventArgs) Handles mnuFileExit.Click
    Me.Close()
End Sub
Private Sub mnuFile1Exit_Click(ByVal sender As System.Object,
    ByVal e As System.EventArgs) Handles mnuFile1Exit.Click
    Me.Close()
End Sub
```

The New and Open Menu Options. Both the New and Open menu options appear in both main menus—mnuMainNoWin and mnuMainwithWin. The code for each respective menu option will be the same; therefore, rather than providing the specific code in each event procedure, you should write separate procedures and call them from the events. The code for the events appears as follows:

```
Private Sub mnuFileNew_Click(ByVal sender As System.Object, ByVal
    e As System.EventArgs) Handles mnuFileNew.Click
    OpenNewDoc()
End Sub
Private Sub mnuFile1New_Click(ByVal sender As System.Object, ByVal
    e As System.EventArgs) Handles mnuFile1New.Click
    OpenNewDoc()
End Sub
Private Sub mnuFileOpen_Click(ByVal sender As System.Object, ByVal
    e As System.EventArgs) Handles mnuFileOpen.Click
    OpenExistingDoc()
End Sub
Private Sub mnuFile1Open_Click(ByVal sender As System.Object,
    ByVal e As System.EventArgs) Handles mnuFile1Open.Click
    OpenExistingDoc()
End Sub
```

Now consider the two separate procedures called in these events. The OpenNewDoc Sub should do the following:

- Create a new child form, and display it as a new window in the MDI form.
- Make the child form's title bar display Untitled1, Untitled2, and so on.

Loading a New Child Form. To create and display a new form, follow these steps:

1. Declare a variable of the child form template type with the New keyword. This will create a new child form and associate it with the variable.
2. Use this variable to reference the new form to perform required actions. You would like to show "Untitled" plus the child form count in the form's title bar.

To declare a variable of the form type and create the form at the same time, code the following:

```
Dim frmChild as New Form()
```

The variable frmChild is declared to be of the (generic) form type. A variable so declared can be associated with any types of forms. This form variable will be associated with the form template frmChildTemplate (the name for the child form) that you have created at design time. Therefore, you can also code the following:

```
Dim frmChild as New frmChildTemplate()
```

Is there any difference between the two ways of declarations? Yes. In general, your code is more efficient when the variable type is specific. In addition, your code is not allowed to reference the controls and Public variables in the particular form template under generic form declaration (the first way). With these considerations, you will use the second way of declaration.

To set the form's title bar (Text), code the following:

```
frmChild.Text = "Untitled" & frmChild.ChildFormCount
```

Recall that the variable, ChildFormCount in the child form template was declared as Public Shared. The Public modifier allows another form to reference this static variable with the syntax:

```
FormName.VariableName, or
FormTemplateName.VariableName
```

The complete code to show a new form (document window) appears as follows:

```
Sub OpenNewDoc()
    Dim frmChild As New frmChildTemplate()
    With frmChild
        'Make this MDI form the parent of this child
        .MdiParent = Me
        .WindowState = FormWindowState.Maximized
        .Show()
        .Text = "Untitled" & frmChild.ChildFormCount
    End With
End Sub
```

Notice the line that makes the currently created form the child form of the MDI (parent) form. As mentioned earlier in this section, the form's MdiParent property should be set to the MDI container, which is the form in which the code is written (Me).

Referencing the Active Form. Each time this procedure is executed, a new form is created. Note that the variable frmChild is declared within a procedure, and thus is recognized only in this procedure. So, how do you refer to the form in other procedures or code modules? Recall that there can be several copies of the same form. The child form that is on top is the active form of the MDI (parent) form, so in the standard module, this child form can be referred to as follows:

```
mdiNotepad.ActiveMdiChild
```

In the MDI (parent) form, you can simply refer to it as follows:

```
ActiveMdiChild
```

Loading an Existing Document. Now consider the OpenExistingDoc procedure. This procedure is expected to open an existing document. The specific steps should include the following:

1. Create a new child form.
2. Prompt for the filename, and open the file for input.
3. Read the entire file into the text box in the child form.
4. Assign the child form's Text property with the filename.
5. Make the MDI form the parent of the child form.
6. Maximize and display the form.
7. Close the file.

The first three steps actually open and display the existing document. The fourth step displays the document name (filename) in the child form's title bar. The fifth step assigns the MDI form

(Me) to the child form's MdiParent property, making this form the MDI parent of the newly created (child) form. Steps 6 and 7 take care of additional program details.

To open a file, your program must know the filename, which should be provided by the user. This is commonly done using the common dialog box. Assume a function, GetOpenFileName, for such a purpose is available; then, the OpenExistingDoc procedure can appear as follows:

```
Sub OpenExistingDoc()
    Dim TheTextFile As IO.StreamReader
    Dim frmChild As New frmChildTemplate()
    Dim ThefileName As String
    ThefileName = GetOpenFileName()
    If Len(ThefileName) > 0 Then
        TheTextFile = New IO.StreamReader(ThefileName)
        'Create a new window if everything goes right
        With frmChild
            'Read the entire file
            .txtDocument.Text = TheTextFile.ReadToEnd()
            .Text = ThefileName 'Show the filename in the title bar
            .MdiParent = Me 'Set this window as a child form
            .WindowState = FormWindowState.Maximized
            .Show()
        End With
        TheTextFile.Close()
    End If
End Sub
```

This procedure calls the function GetOpenFileName to obtain an existing file. The function will return the filename if the user selects one; otherwise, a zero-length string is returned. In the OpenExistingDoc Sub, the code checks to ensure that a valid filename is returned. If so, it proceeds to perform the remaining tasks as outlined previously.

Obtaining the Filename. Coding for the function GetOpenFileName should be similar to the code example in Chapter 6, "Input, Output, and Procedures" (using the file dialog box), and appears as follows:

```
Function GetOpenFileName() As String
    Dim cdlFileOpen As New OpenFileDialog()
    With cdlFileOpen
        'Prompt for the file to open
        .Filter = "Text File(*.txt)¦*.txt¦Other Files (*.*)¦*.*"
        .ShowDialog()
        Return (.FileName)
    End With
End Function
```

Note the open dialog box is created in this procedure; therefore, you do not need to draw one on the form to use this procedure. This way of creating a control at runtime was explained in Chapter 8, "Arrays and Their Uses." The code dealing with the use of the Open File dialog was explained in section 6.1 of Chapter 6.

Closing the Window and Saving the Document. The File menu in second main menu (mnuMainWithWin) also contains an option to save the document and another option to close the window. The window is actually the current active MDI child, so the following statement should close the window:

```
Private Sub mnuFile1Close_Click(ByVal sender As System.Object,
    ByVal e As System.EventArgs) Handles mnuFile1Close.Click
        Me.ActiveMdiChild.Close() 'Close the active child window
    End Sub
```

The code to save a file involves the use of the stream writer, which was explained in Chapter 6. The code is left to you as an exercise at the end of this chapter.

Handling the Window Menu Events. The Window menu has three options: Cascade, Tile Horizontal, and Tile Vertical, which refer to how the child forms should be arranged in the MDI workspace. Recall that the code in the OpenNewDoc and OpenExistingDoc Subs to create a new child form each includes a statement to maximize the child form. This, in effect, makes the newly created child form occupy the entire workspace of the MDI form. When several documents are open, this Window menu allows the user to choose a different layout of the documents: cascade, tile horizontal or tile vertical. The MDI form has the *LayoutMdi method*, which can be used to display child forms in several different ways. The LayoutMdi method has the following syntax:

```
MdiForm.LayoutMdi(layout)
```

The named constants for the cascade, tile horizontal, and tile vertical arrangements are MdiLayout.Cascade, MdiLayout.TileHorizontal, and MdiLayout.TileVertical, respectively. The code to handle the Window Click events will appear as follows:

```
Private Sub mnuWinCascade_Click(ByVal sender As System.Object,
    ByVal e As System.EventArgs)  Handles mnuWinCascade.Click
        Me.LayoutMdi(MdiLayout.Cascade)
End Sub

Private Sub mnuWinHorizontal_Click(ByVal sender As System.Object,
    ByVal e As System.EventArgs) Handles mnuWinHorizontal.Click
        Me.LayoutMdi(MdiLayout.TileHorizontal)
End Sub

Private Sub mnuWinVertical_Click(ByVal sender As System.Object,
    ByVal e As System.EventArgs) Handles mnuWinVertical.Click
        Me.LayoutMdi(MdiLayout.TileVertical)
End Sub
```

Invoking the Find Dialog Box. The Find menu's Click event should bring up the Find dialog box (form) for the search of a specified text. The form is named frmFindTemplate. Recall that forms used as dialog boxes should be displayed with the ShowDialog method. The form displayed with this method remains on top until it disappears (is closed or hidden). The code to handle the Click event for the Find menu appears as follows:

```
Private Sub mnuFind_Click(ByVal sender As System.Object, ByVal e
    As System.EventArgs) Handles mnuFind.Click
        Dim frmFind As New frmFindTemplate()
        frmFind.ShowDialog()
End Sub
```

This discussion completes all required code for the MDI parent form.

Building the Find Dialog Box

Now turn your attention to the form to be used to find the specified text in the document (frmFindTemplate). Figure 11.12 shows the visual interface of this custom dialog box, which should behave in the following manner:

- When the user enters the search text in the text box and clicks the Find Next button, the custom dialog box should find and highlight the text in the document that matches the search text.

Figure 11.12

The Find custom dialog box

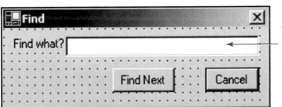

The user will enter the search text in the "Find What?" text box and click the Find Next button to initiate the search.

- When the user clicks the Find Next button another time, the custom dialog box should highlight the next match. When there is no (or no more) text in the document that matches the search text, a message "Text not found" is displayed.
- When the user clicks the Cancel button or the Close button on the title bar, the form should disappear.
- When the user clicks the Find menu in the MDI form again, this dialog box (form) will show the previous search text in the text box. This form should also "remember" the position of the text in the document that was previously highlighted so that any repeated search will start from there.

This form should have the following controls:

- A text box accompanied by a label with proper text, which will be used by the user to enter the text to find. Name it **txtSearch**.
- A button with the text, "Find Next". The user will click this button when they finish entering the search text and are ready to search. Name this button **btnFindNext**.
- Another button with the text, "Cancel". The user will click this button when the user is done with the search. Name this button **btnCancel**.

Setting Up the Visual Interface. Take a look at Figure 11.12 again. Notice that the form does not have either the Maximize or Minimize box. This is the typical appearance of a dialog box as there is no need to maximize or minimize the dialog box. You can get this effect by setting the form's *MaximizeBox* and *MinimizeBox properties* to False. In addition, a dialog box usually also accepts the results, disappears when the user presses the Enter key and cancels the results and disappears when the user presses the Esc key. You can obtain these effects by setting the form's *AcceptButton* and *CancelButton* properties to the respective buttons. In this case, when the user is done with the text search, the user can press either the Enter key or the Esc key to close the dialog box. The Cancel button will close the form, so you can set both the AcceptButton and the CancelButton properties to **btnCancel**.

Close or Hide. This form is fairly light, having few controls and little code. There will be no noticeable performance difference between closing and hiding the form. Hiding the form produces no noticeable advantage; therefore, you will close the form when the user clicks the Cancel buttons:

```
Private Sub btnCancel_Click(ByVal sender As System.Object, ByVal e
    As System.EventArgs) Handles btnCancel.Click
      Me.Close()
End Sub
```

Referencing the Text Box in the Child Form. This dialog box is to be used to search text in the child form's txtDocument text box. While the child form on top can be referenced as ActiveMdiChild, there is no way to directly reference the text box with ActiveMdiChild. The only way to refer to the text box is through a variable of the frmChildTemplate type, so the active child form must be converted to the frmChildTemplate type first. For convenience, the reference to the text box should be saved in the code module for the dialog box. This can be done by assigning the reference to a variable of the text box type declared in the dialog box (refer to the following code). The reference should be available as soon as the dialog box is loaded. therefore, you should place the code to keep the reference in the Form Load event. The code should appear as follows:

```
Dim WorkTextBox As TextBox
Private Sub frmFindTemplate_Load(ByVal sender As System.Object,
  ByVal e As System.EventArgs) Handles MyBase.Load
    Dim frmChild As frmChildTemplate
    frmChild = CType(mdiNotepad.ActiveMdiChild, frmChildTemplate)
    'Keep a reference to Child form's text box
    WorkTextBox = frmChild.txtDocument
    WorkTextBox.HideSelection = False
End Sub
```

As you can see from the code, a class level variable, WorkTextBox, is declared to be of the TextBox type. Inside the Form Load event procedure, a variable named frmChild is declared to be of the frmChildTemplate type, which is then assigned the active MDI child form that is converted to the same type. This conversion allows the reference to the child form's text box by qualifying the control's name with the form variable (frmChild.txtDocument). This reference is then assigned to the WorkTextBox variable. Notice that the assignment of one control and form to another does not create a new identical control or form. Instead, only the pointer to the control (form) is copied. As a result, WorkTextBox actually refers to the text box in the active MDI child form. Note also that the active child form is qualified with the variable mdiNotepad. Recall that this variable is declared as Public and used as the startup (MDI parent) form in the standard module.

Highlighting Text in a Text Box Without Focus. The last statement in the procedure sets the text box's HideSelection property to False. When this property is set to True (default), any selection in the text box will be hidden (not highlighted) if the focus is not on the text box. Setting the property to False allows the selection to be highlighted regardless of the focus. When the dialog box is invoked, it stays on top of the child form and has the focus. It is necessary to set that property to False to highlight the selection for the text found.

Coding for the Find Next Operation. The Find Next event procedure should take care of the following steps/situations:

- It should check to ensure that there is search text in the text box. If there is no search text, the procedure should display the message "Please enter search text" and then exit.

- It should also check to see whether the current search is a continuation of a previous search. This can be determined by comparing the current search text with the previous one. If they are the same, it is a continuation and the search should start from the previously highlighted position plus the length of the search text; otherwise, it is a new search and should start from position one.

- The actual search should use the start position just determined. If no text in the document is found to match the search text, the message "Text not found" should be displayed; otherwise, the text found in the document should be highlighted. As explained in Chapter 3, "Visual Basic Controls and Events," highlighting can be accomplished by the Select method.

- The preceding search text and the highlighted position should be preserved for the next round. These values can be preserved by the use of Shared variables.

The code to handle the FindNext Button Click event appears as follows:

```
Shared PreviousSearchWord As String
Shared Pos As Integer
Private Sub btnFindNext_Click(ByVal sender As System.Object, ByVal
    e As System.EventArgs) Handles btnFindNext.Click
    Dim SearchWord As String
    SearchWord = txtSearch.Text
    If Len(Trim(SearchWord)) = 0 Then
        MsgBox("Please enter search text.",
          MsgBoxStyle.Information)
        Exit Sub
    End If
    If SearchWord = PreviousSearchWord Then
        'Same searchword, continue from previous position
    Else
        'New search word, reset starting position
        Pos = 0
    End If
    Pos = InStr(Pos + 1, WorkTextBox.Text, SearchWord,
      CompareMethod.Text)
    If Pos > 0 Then
```

```
                    'Searchword found, highlight
                    WorkTextBox.Select(Pos - 1, Len(SearchWord))
            Else
                    'Searchword not found, display a message
                    MsgBox("Text not found.")
            End If
            'Keep this for future comparison
            PreviousSearchWord = SearchWord
    End Sub
```

Pay particular attention to the reference to the text box in the child form. It is referenced in this procedure as WorkTextBox, which was declared in the general declaration area and assigned properly in the Form Load event presented previously.

Displaying Previous Search Text. When the search form is closed and invoked later, the controls in the form lose their previous contents. The search text box will no longer have the text previously entered by the user. The two Shared variables, PreviousSearchWord and Pos, help preserve the values. As soon as the form reloads, the previous search text can be assigned back to the search text box. In the Form Load event procedure, you should insert the following statement:

```
        txtSearch.Text = PreviousSearchWord
```

A Few Design Notes. Usually, a dialog box is used to provide a service/data, as is the case here. As such, it should stop at the point where the data is generated, and leave the remaining task of using the data to the calling procedure/form to handle. Such a design will make the code much neater and reusable by other procedures, forms, or even projects; however, for the dialog box to highlight the text found in the calling form while continuing to stay on top (invoked as a modal form), makes such a design tricky. The code (based on the current design) is also used to illustrate how the child form is referenced in other modules. As such, the code in the dialog box loses its general applicability. It should be considered as a specialized dialog box, providing a specific service only to the current project. A possible solution to make this a general dialog box is given as exercise 11-27 at the end of this chapter.

Summary of Procedures. This example includes three forms and one standard module. The code involves many procedures and a lot of details. The following table provides a summary of the procedures in different modules.

Form/Module	Procedure	Procedure Type	Remark
Standard Module	Sub Main	General Sub	Starts the MDI parent form
Child form	frmChildTemplate_Load	Event	Increases child form count, switches (frmChild) main menu when count is 1
	frmChildTemplate_Closing	Event	Prompts whether to save the document; Decreases child form count, switches main menu when count is 0
MDI parent	mnuFileNew_Click	Event	Calls OpenNewDoc in the same form
	mnuFile1New_Click	Event	
	mnuFileOpen_Click	Event	Calls OpenExistingDoc in the same form
	mnuFile1Open_Click	Event	
	mnuFile1Close_Click	Event	Closes the child form
	mnuFile1Save_Click	Event	Calls SaveDoc in the same form (you do it)
	mnuFileExit_Click	Event	Quits

Form/Module	Procedure	Procedure Type	Remark
	mnuFile1Exit_Click	Event	Quits
	OpenNewDoc	General Sub	Creates a new document window (child form)
	OpenExistingDoc	General Sub	Reads an existing document into a document window (child form)
	SaveDoc	General Sub	Save current window (txtDocument) in active child form (left to you to complete)
	mnuFind_Click	Event	Calls frmSearch
	mnuWinCascade_Click	Event	Cascades child forms
	mnuWinTileHorizontal_Click	Event	Tiles child forms horizontally in the MDI parent form
	mnuWinTileVertical_Click	Event	Tiles child forms vertically in the MDI parent form
Custom dialog box (frmFind)	btnCancel_Click	Event	Closes the search form
	btnFindNext_Click	Event	Searches and highlights text
	frmFindTemplate_Load	Event	Sets up references to the text box in the active Mid child form; Places previous search text in the search text box

Creating MDI Applications: A Recap

The MDI Notepad application involves many programming aspects. The following table summarizes the essentials to the creation of an MDI application.

Objective	What to Do	Remarks
To create an MDI	Set the form's IsMdiContainer Property to True.	
To make a form a child window of the MDI application	Set the form's MDIParent property To the Mdi form.	
To change the menu bar with the presence of a child form	Create multiple main menus in the MDI form and switch based on the child form count.	
To make a menu item show the titles of child forms	Set the WindowList property of the menu item to True.	
To create a new document (child window)	1. Declare a form variable. 2. Set the variable to a New child form.	For example: Dim MyForm As New frmTextDoc()
	3. Set the MdiParent property of the child form.	frmChild.MdiParent = Me
To open an existing document	1. Perform the two steps to create a new document.	For example, add the following code: Dim ExistingDoc As IO.StreamReader
	2. Open the existing file.	ExistingDoc = New IO.StreamReader(TheFile)
	3. Read the file content into the text box in the child form.	txtDoc.Text = ExistingDoc.ReadToEnd()

continues

Objective	What to Do	Remarks
To share variables and procedures among forms	Use Public variables and procedures in a standard module.	These elements alleviate the need to consider whether the form is loaded.
To reference a control in the active child form	1. Convert the active child form to the same form template.	For example: frmChild = Ctype(_mdiNotepad.ActiveMdiChild, _frmChildTemplate)
	2. Qualify the control with the form variable.	Console.WriteLine(frmChild.txtDocument) *Note:* In the MDI form, reference to the MDI form name can be omitted.
To cascade or tile child windows	Use the MDI form's LayoutMdi method.	For example: mdiNotePad.LayoutMdi(MdiLayout.Cascade)

Additional Remarks

As you start to review this notepad application, you may have realized that MDI is an interface style choice. If the user needs to refer to more than one document in an application that handles only a single document, such as the MS Notepad, they can load another copy of the application. If your application often involves multiple documents, however, it will be much easier for the user to work with an MDI interface. Your interface style choice should be based on this consideration.

It was noted in the preceding section that a standard module could be used to provide specific services to other forms, such as holding Public variables or procedures usable to various forms. In other cases, the procedures in the module can be made reusable if the code makes no specific reference to other modules. Apparently, the standard module in the example project is used for the former purpose, and therefore will not be reusable for other projects.

Admittedly, the project is highly simplified. The main purpose is to illustrate the key issues particularly pertaining to an MDI project. Hopefully, by working with the example, you have gained a good understanding of the use and design of MDI applications.

You can, of course, add several enhancements to the program. For example, you can do the following:

- Add the code to save a document.
- Add the find-and-replace capability to the custom dialog box.
- Include an Edit menu. Note, though, that the Edit context menu is automatically supported by VB for the text box.
- Show the saved document names (filenames) at the bottom of the File menu.
- Replace the text box with the rich text box, which supports varying fonts and other capabilities.

All of these enhancements are left to you to implement.

11.6 Designing a Large Project

As the size of a project grows, various problems and issues that do not seem obvious in a small project will start to surface. In some cases, efforts to patch the code can induce even more problems. Most of these problems relate to repetitive code, entangled code, and the hidden bugs that appear to be too many to ignore but too undetectable to catch. In developing a large project, it pays to put in a lot of effort upfront by carefully analyzing the requirements and designing the framework before any single line of code is started. The following are a few pointers worth careful consideration.

Modular Design

With the huge size of code, it is easy to get into a situation in which code in different procedures are entangled; that is, code in two or more procedures or modules may make reference to each other directly. The logic for such code structure becomes difficult to trace. Such code structure can cause great difficulty for maintenance. A minor change in the program requirements can call for a huge amount of maintenance effort.

For example, imagine a form named frmEmployee with a text box to enter the employee number. A button is provided to invoke a custom dialog box named frmSearchEmpNum, which allows the user to search for the employee number given a name. The dialog box is invoked in a typical manner:

```
Private Sub btnEmpSearch_Click(ByVal sender As System.Object,
    ByVal e As System.EventArgs) Handles btnEmpSearch.Click
        frmSearchEmpNum.ShowDialog()
End Sub
```

The Form Closing event procedure in frmSearchEmpNum, however, appears as follows:

```
Private Sub frmSearchEmpNum_Closing(ByVal sender As
    System.Object,
        ByVal e As System.ComponentModel.CancelEventArgs) Handles
         MyBase.Closing
        frmEmployee.txtEmpNum.Text = txtEmpNum.Text
End Sub
```

Notice that this event procedure places the employee number in the target text box before the custom dialog box closes. Such a design can cause several problems. If the target text box, for whatever reason, has to change its name or to be moved to another form, the code in the dialog box will have to be changed. Also, the dialog box is extremely specialized. It can provide service to only one control. If another text box in the same project needs the same service, either another dialog box with nearly the same code will have to be written or the code in the dialog box must be modified to identify the new target text box, making the code unnecessarily complex. Its maintainability and general applicability become an issue. (Note that in the preceding code, it is assume that the search form variable name and its template have the same name, frmSearchEmpNum. Also, the form name, frmEmployee is accessible from the search form.)

When developing code for large projects, be particularly careful in the design phase to ensure that code in each procedure is independent of the code in all other procedures. As implied in the previous discussion, to accomplish this, you should observe these rules:

* Avoid referencing objects in other forms or modules directly.
* Avoid declaring and sharing variables of a broader scope than necessary. In other words, declare and use variables with a scope as narrow as possible.

Procedures designed this way can then become the building block of a large project. Such a design is recognized as modular design.

Following this design approach, several alternatives to the preceding problem example can be considered:

* The dialog box places the result (employee number) in a Public variable either in the form module or in a standard module. The calling procedure can then obtain the result from the Public variable.
* The dialog box provides a Public procedure, such as EmployeeSearch, that takes the target text box in the calling form as the parameter. The result can then be placed in this control. The calling procedure calls EmployeeSearch in the custom dialog box instead of invoking the dialog box itself. Note that because the target control is passed as a parameter, any similar controls can be passed to the search procedure in the dialog box. Exercise 11-27 at the end of this chapter explores this design alternative.

In either of these design alternatives, any change to the name of the control that needs the service in the calling procedure will require no change in the code in the dialog box. In addition, any other text box requiring the same service can conveniently call the same dialog box.

Factoring to Minimize Code

Another problem in large projects is the potential of repeated code. Several forms can require the same computations and perform similar activities. Even in the same form, several procedures can require similar code to perform certain activities. Copying similar code to handle the repetitive needs can not only be boring and time-consuming, but also be error prone. In addition, the sheer number of lines of code can create problems for maintenance. Each time a revision of the repeated code is called for, the same correction will have to be done many times, increasing yet another possibility of introducing more errors.

One way to alleviate this problem is to analyze the program requirements carefully and code the required activities as Public general procedures in a standard module. Any event that needs to handle the activities can then simply call that procedure. An important advantage of this factoring approach is that if there is any error or required revision of the code, you need to look at only one place for correction. All procedures that use the function will automatically be corrected. The effort required for the revision is minimized, with much less chance to introduce additional errors.

Layered Standard Modules

The concept of modular design and code reusability can be carried out further by using multiple standard modules in a project. Some standard modules can be used to contain code and data that are particularly related to the current project, whereas others can be used to contain procedures that are useful to many projects. Procedures in each type of standard modules can be further classified by their commonality. For example, procedures that deal with files can be placed in one module. Modules of this nature can be added to any project that needs their capabilities.

Object-Oriented Programming

An additional approach to handling a large project is the use of the object-oriented programming technology. An object is a unit of code with data. It presents itself as a single unit (object or entity). A programmer using the object does not need to know anything about its inner working other than its interfaces: properties, methods, and events. A large project that involves a team can be divided into several subprojects (units). These units can then be coded As objects. The project can be assembled by putting the objects together, allowing all to interact with each other through their defined interfaces. Topics related to developing templates for objects are discussed in detail in Chapters 12 and 13.

Summary

- A typical large project can involve many forms and modules and its main form employs menus to invoke other forms.
- The Main Menu control allows the programmer to easily create a menu bar on a form. The text that is entered in a rectangle that the main menu displays becomes the text of the menu item, whose name can be set in the Properties window or through the Edit Name option of the menu's context menu along with other menu items.
- The Context Menu control allows the programmer to create a context menu that pops up when the user right-clicks on a control. The context menu can be set up in a way similar to the main menu. Each context menu can be associated with any number of controls, but a control can have only one context menu. To associate a control with a context menu, set the control's Context Menu property in its Properties window.
- The user can access a menu item by clicking on the item or the use of an access key or shortcut key. As explained in Chapter 10, "Special Topics in Data Entry," you can set up

an access key by placing an & before a letter in the item's text. The user can then access the menu item by pressing Alt+<letter>. You can set up a shortcut key for a menu item by selecting a key in its Shortcut property in the Properties window. The user can access the menu item by pressing the designated shortcut key.

- When a menu item is clicked, or accessed through an access or shortcut key, its Click event is triggered. The code placed in that event procedure will execute.

- When the menu structure becomes complex and involves several levels, a possible alternative is to use the tree view in place of the menu.

- The nodes in a tree view can be set up with the TreeNode Editor through the Nodes property in the Properties window. Nodes can also be added or removed using the Nodes.Add and Nodes.RemoveAt methods.

- Typically, the code to handle the user's selection of a tree view node is placed in the AfterSelect event. Inside the event, the current node's text is checked to take proper actions.

- In a multiple form application, you can choose a form or Sub Main as the startup object.

- To invoke a form, declare a variable and associate it with an instance of the form template using the New keyword; then use the form Show method to display the form.

- A form can also be invoked with the ShowDialog method. When invoked this way, the form stays on top of the application and is recognized as a modal form. Typically, a form invoked this way is used as a dialog box.

- A form can be made to disappear by its Close or Hide method. A closed form no longer exists in memory, cannot be shown again with the Show method, and must be created again; a hidden form stays in the memory and can be shown again with the Show method.

- Occasionally, you may need to place code in the form Activated event to handle the situation when the form appears; for example, after the form Show method is executed. Be aware that the event can also be triggered in various other situations, such as another active form gets closed. You should design your code to take care of these situations as well.

- Controls as well as Public and Friend variables in a form are accessible to other modules; however, the form must be still in memory—either appearing on the screen or being hidden with the Hide method. If you are not sure whether the form will be still in memory at time of access, assign the data to Public or Friend variables in a standard module. Other modules can then obtain the data by referencing the variables in the standard module.

- You can declare the same Public (or Friend) variable names in different standard modules. In that case, to reference the variables, qualify their names with the module name.

- The Sub Main procedure is usually placed in the standard module. It can be used to start a form, using the Application.Run method. When the form is declared as Public, other modules can reference this startup form.

- When the startup form closes, all other forms are also closed without triggering their respective Closing event. In general, this is the event that you place code to perform finishing touches for each form, such as saving unsaved data. When you have code in the Closing event in other forms, you should ensure that the Closing event is triggered when the startup form closes. You can use a Public collection object created in a standard module to keep track of the forms in memory, and place code in the startup form's Closing event to close these other forms.

- To recognize the events of a control that is created at runtime, declare the control variable with the WithEvents keyword. The declaration must be made at the module/class level.

- The number guessing game example is used to illustrate how a multiple form project can be developed.

- If an application can have many forms (windows) of the same nature appearing in a container form at one time, the application is a multiple document interface (MDI) application. The MDI application is technically different from the single document interface (SDI) application in that the former has a container form with one or more child forms, while the SDI does not have the parent-child relationship between forms.

- To create an MDI application, set the container form's IsMdiContainer property to True. Also by code, set the child form's MdiParent property to the container form.

- To reference the active MDI child form, use the syntax:

$$ParentForm.\texttt{ActiveMdiChild}$$

- To cascade or tile the child windows in the MDI container, use the container form's LayoutMdi method.

- If you set a form's AcceptButton property to a button, the button's Click event will be triggered when the user presses the Enter key. If you set a form's CancelButton property to a button, the button's Click event will be triggered when the user presses the Esc key.

- The MdiNotepad project is used to illustrate how to code an MDI project.

Explore and Discover

11-1. **Sequence of Mouse Click Events.** Four events can be associated with a mouse click: Click, MouseDown, MouseUp, and MouseMove; however, which event precedes which? Use the Console WriteLine method in each of these events for a form to find out; for example, place the following code in the Form Click event:

```
Console.WriteLine ("Form click event is raised.")
```

Code similarly for the other event procedures.

Run the project and then click the form. List the events in sequence of their occurrence.

11-2. **Who Gets the Mouse Click Events?** In exercise 11-1, add a text box on a form. Add the three mouse event procedures for the text box, and paraphrase the Console.WriteLine statement; for example, "Text box Click event is raised." Try the following actions and observe the messages in the immediate window:

1. Press and then release the mouse button in the form.
2. Press and then release the mouse button in the text box.
3. Press the mouse button in the form, and release it in the text box.
4. Press the mouse button in the text box, and release it in the form.

11-3. **Mouse Movement Events.** When the user moves the mouse on and around an object, several mouse events can be triggered: MouseMove, MouseEnter, MouseHover, and MouseLeave. In each of these events for the form, enter some code to identify the event; for example, enter the following code in the form MouseMove event:

```
Console.WriteLine("Form MouseMove")
```

Try the following actions by pressing the left and right buttons, and not pressing any button; then observe the messages in the immediate window:

1. Move the mouse on the form.
2. Move the mouse away from the form.
3. Move the mouse back onto the form, and gradually leave the form again.

11-4.   Are Menus Included? In a new form, set up a File menu with Open, Close, and Exit as its options by following the example earlier in this chapter. Draw a text box, a radio button, and check box on the form. Also, draw a button. Name it **btnShowControls,** and set its Text property to **Show Control Names**. Enter the following sub procedure, and call it from the button's Click event (*Hint:* Pass "Me" as the parameter, for example, ListControls(Me)).

```
Sub ListControls(ByVal TheControl As Control)
    Dim I As Integer
    For I = 0 To TheControl.Controls.Count - 1
        Console.WriteLine(TheControl.Controls(I).Name)
        If TheControl.Controls(I).Controls.Count > 0 Then
            ListControls(TheControl.Controls(I))
        End If
    Next I
End Sub
```

Run the project and then click the button. What do you see? Are the menus listed? Those controls that are not present on the form during runtime are not included in the Controls collection.

11-5.   Resizable and Nonresizable Forms. The form has a FormBorderStyle property that may interest you. Run a project with a new form. Can you resize the form by dragging an edge from one of its sides? End the program.

Set the form's FormBorderStyle property to FixedSingle, and run the project again. This time, can you resize the form?

The form's FormBorderStyle has several other settings. Some affect the title bar, while some affect the appearance of the outer edge of the form. Try each setting, and run the project to see the effect.

11-6.   Is the Minimized Form Idle or Active? Does a minimized form continue to work? To test, enter the following code in the form Resize event:

```
Dim ComeBackTime As Date
If Me.WindowState = FormWindowState.Minimized Then
    ComeBackTime = DateAdd(DateInterval.Second, 5, Now)
    Do Until Now > ComeBackTime
        Application.DoEvents()
    Loop
    Me.WindowState = FormWindowState.Normal
End If
```

Run the project. Click the Minimize button on the form's title bar. The form should come back in five seconds. A minimized form is not really idle, is it?

11-7.   Ending a Project. How does the Close method differ from the End statement in terminating a project? To test, draw two buttons on the form. Name them **btnClose** and **btnEnd**. Set their Text properties to **Close** and **End**, respectively. Enter the following code:

Code	Event Procedure
End	btnEnd_Click
Me.Close	btnClose_Click
MsgBox("Closing the form")	Form1_Closing

Run the project, and click the End button. Do you see any message? The program terminates abruptly.

Run the project again, and click the Close button. Do you see any message? Run the project again. This time, click the Close (X) button on the form's title bar instead of the Close button. Do you see any message?

You can place code in the form's Closing or Closed event to take care of unfinished business for the form before it is closed; however, the code will be triggered only if your code uses the form's Close method—not the End statement—to quit.

11-8. **What's the Difference: Different Ways to Declare the Form.** Add a new form to a new project. Name the second form **Form2Template**. Add a button in the startup form. Set its Text property to **Show,** and name it **btnShow**. In the startup form, enter the following code:

Code	Event Procedure
Dim Form2 As Form2Template	(General declaration area)
Form2 = New Form2Template()	
Form2.Show	btnShow_Click

In Form2Template, add a button. Set its Text property to **Disappear,** and name it **btnDisappear**. In the btnDisappear_Click event, enter the following code:

```
Me.Close
```

Run the project and then do the following:

1. Click the Show button in the startup form.
2. Click the Disappear button in the second form.
3. Click the Show button in the startup form again.

Does the second form appear without any problem? Now change the code in the startup form as follows:

Code	Event Procedure
Dim Form2 As New Form2Template()	(General declaration area)
Form2.Show	btnShow_Click

Run the project, and repeat the three preceding three activities. This time, do you encounter any problem? After a form is closed, you cannot use just the Show method to make it reappear. It must be re-created (reinitialized) with the New keyword first.

11-9. **How Many Forms Can You Create?** Add a new form to your new project, and name the second form **Form2Template**. In the startup form, add a button; name it **btnShow**, and set its Text property to **Show**. In the same form, enter the following code:

Code	Event Procedure
Dim Form2 As New Form2Template()	(General declaration area)
Form2.Show	btnShow_Click

Run the project. Click the Show button several times without closing the second form. How many of the second form do you see? You should see only one. The Show method does not create a new form object.

Now change the code in the startup form as follows:

Code	Event Procedure
Dim Form2 As Form2Template	(General declaration area)
Form2 = New Form2Template()	
Form2.Show	btnShow_Click

Run the project, and click the Show button on the startup form several times. How many forms do you see? You should see as many as the number of times you click. The New keyword creates (initializes) a new form.

Now change the code in the startup form as follows:

Code	Event Procedure
(None)	(General declaration area)
Dim Form2 As Form2Template	
Form2 = New Form2Template()	
Form2.Show	btnShow_Click

Run the project, and click the Show button on the startup form several times. How many forms do you see? You should see as many as the number of times you click. The New keyword creates (initializes) a new form.

So, what's the difference between this way and the preceding way of declaration? In the last way of declaration, the Form2 variable is not recognizable by any other procedure, while in the preceding one, Form2 is recognizable by other procedures. Note, however, it is associated only with the most recently created form. Set up another procedure in the startup form to verify.

11-10.   The Activated Event. The Activated event can be triggered unexpectedly. Add a new form to a new project, and name the second form **Form2Template**. In the startup form, add a button, name it **btnShow**, and set its Text property to **Show**. Enter the following code:

Code	Event Procedure
Dim Form2 As New Form2Template()	(General declaration area)
Form2.Show	btnShow_Click
Console.WriteLine("Startup form activated")	Form1_Activated

In the second form, add the following code in the form's Activated event:

```
Console.WriteLine("Form2 activated")
```

Run the project, and click the Show button on the startup form. Look into the immediate window. You should see activated messages from both forms. Now close the second form by clicking its Close button in the control box. Do you see another activated message from the startup form? Be aware of this situation to avoid unexpected execution of the code in that event.

11-11.   What's the Difference: The Startup Form for MDI Applications. Work with a new project. Set the form's IsMdiContainer property to True. Add a new form, and name it **frmChild**. Add a button to the parent form. Name it **btnShow** and then set its text to Show. Add the following code in its Click event:

```
Dim MyChild As New frmChild()
MyChild.MdiParent = Me
MyChild.Show()
```

In the child form, try to add the following code in its form Click event:

```
Form1.btnShow.Text = "Don't Show"
```

Are you successful? What's the error message? The parent form (startup form) template is not recognizable to any other form. Now change the code to the following:

```
Dim frmMdiParent As New Form1()
frmMdiParent.btnShow.Text = "Don't Show"
```

Is the code accepted? Run the project, and click the Show button in the parent form. Do you see the child form? Now click the child form. Do you see any result? The Dim statement in the form Click event is not referencing the same parent form. It is a different object. Now you know why the standard module is used to start up the parent form.

11-12. **Are the Child Forms Really Closed Gracefully?** You know that in an SDI application, when the startup form is closed, all the other forms are closed abruptly; however, the text claims that the child forms will close gracefully with each form's Closing event triggered when the MDI (parent) form closes. Design a project to verify.

11-13. **Start Position for the Form.** The form has a StartPosition property that allows five different settings. Run the project, and observe the form position after selecting a setting. Try all five settings. This property provides a neat way to set the form start position without any single line of code.

11-14. **Timing of Destructing a Form.** An object is supposed to be destroyed and not accessible when it is out of scope or when it is dissociated with its object variable (no longer accessible), but what actually happens to the form? The following experiment should shed some lights: Add another form to a new project. In the second form, declare two class level variables as follows:

```
Public Shared Count As Integer
Public ReadOnly ID As Integer
```

Expand the region, "Windows Form Designer generated code." Modify Sub New and Sub Dispose as follows:

```
Public Sub New()
    MyBase.New()

    'This call is required by the Windows Form Designer.
    InitializeComponent()

    'Add any initialization after the InitializeComponent() call
    Count += 1 'This line is inserted
    ID = Count 'This line is inserted
End Sub

Protected Overloads Overrides Sub Dispose(ByVal disposing As
  Boolean)
    If disposing Then
        If Not (components Is Nothing) Then
            components.Dispose()
        End If
    End If
    Count -= 1 'This line is inserted
    MyBase.Dispose(disposing)
End Sub
```

Note that two lines are inserted in Sub New and one line is inserted in Sub Dispose. The Sub New method is automatically called when the form is created with the New keyword. The Dispose method is called when the form object is being destroyed. The Shared variable, Count, tracks how many copies of the form are in memory.

Now go back to Form1, and enter the following code:

```
Private Sub Form1_Click(ByVal sender As System.Object, ByVal e As
    System.EventArgs) Handles MyBase.Click
    Dim MYForm As Form2
    Dim I As Integer
    For I = 1 To 1000
        MYForm = New Form2()
        MYForm.Text = MYForm.ID
        'MYForm.Show()
    Next I
    Console.WriteLine("Count=" & Form2.Count)
    Console.WriteLine("ID=" & MYForm.ID)
End Sub
```

Run the project, and click the form. What numbers do you see in the immediate window? If they are both 1,000, click the form one more time. (The same numbers for both Count and ID verify that MYForm refers to the most recent copy of the form.) You should eventually see two numbers smaller than 1,000. If the form object is immediately destroyed after it is dissociated with the variable (replaced by another object), there should be only one copy after executing the For loop. The results are obtained because the garbage collection function is not immediately performed until a need for memory arises.

Now remove the comment mark for the MyForm.Show statement. Run the project and then click the form. You should see 1,000 for both. Click one more time; you may see 2,000, or encounter runtime error. Click the form until you encounter an error. The error pertains to running out of memory, but you should never see the numbers decrease as the previous case. Why? There is a handle associated with each visible object onscreen. Each form that appears always has a reference, and will not be destroyed even if its associated variable is out of scope.

11-15.   **Timing of Destructing a Form**. (continued from exercise 11-14) Refer to the preceding exercise. Modify the Form1 Click procedure as follows:

```
Private Sub Form1_Click(ByVal sender As System.Object, ByVal e As
    System.EventArgs) Handles MyBase.Click
    Dim MYForm As Form2
    Dim I As Integer
    For I = 1 To 1000
        MYForm = New Form2()
        MYForm.Text = MYForm.ID
        MYForm.Show()
        Form.Close
    Next I
    Console.WriteLine("Count=" & Form2.Count)
    Console.WriteLine("ID=" & MYForm.ID)
End Sub
```

Note that the MyForm.Close statement is inserted in the For loop.

Run the project again, and click the form. What numbers do you see in the immediate window? Click a few more times and inspect the results. You should obtain the same results. Compare these results with those in exercise 11-14. A closed form is destructed as soon as it goes out of scope. Do you see the proof?

Exercises

11-16. **Creating Menus for a General Ledger Application.** In a new project, create a menu system that has the following:

On the menu bar, there are two items: File and Maintenance with both items' first letter underlined.

In the File menu, there are four options: New, Open, Close, and Exit, with the N, O, C, and x underlined in each respective item. There should be a separator between Exit and Close.

In the Maintenance menu, there are three options: Account Classification, Account Entry/Edit, and Statement Format. The letters underlined for the respective items are C, A, and S.

Add the code so that the program will end when the user clicks the Exit option at runtime.

11-17. **Creating a Menu for a Clinic.** In a new project, create a menu system that has the following:

On the menu bar, there are three items: Code Maintenance, Service, and Account/Patient. The first letter of each item is underlined.

In the Code Maintenance menu, there are three items: Service Code, Diagnosis Code, and Billing Adjustment Code. The first letter of each item should be underlined.

In the service menu, there are two items: Service and Reports (first letter of each is underlined). There is a separator between the two items. The reports item has three options (third-level menu items): Daily Service by Patient Report (S in Service is underlined; shortcut key is Ctrl+S), Daily Service by Service Code Report (C in code is underlined), and Daily Patient Payment Report (P in payment is underlined; shortcut key is Ctrl+P).

In the Account/Patient menu, there are two items: Account Entry/Edit and Patient Entry/Edit. The first letter of each item is underlined.

11-18. **Creating a tree view for a General Ledger Application**. (refer to exercise 11-16) Use a tree view instead of the menu to satisfy the requirements. Ignore the underline, shortcut, and access key requirements, but add code to ensure that when the Exit node is clicked, the form is closed.

11-19. **Creating a Treeview for a Clinic**. (refer to exercise 11-17) Use a tree view instead of the menu to satisfy the requirements. Ignore the underline, shortcut, and access key requirements, but add code to invoke another form when the Service Code option is clicked.

11-20. **Creating a Pop-Up Menu for a Clinic.** (continued from 11-17) Add a context menu to the clinic project. Name the menu mnuOther, which should have three options: Doctor, Hospital, and Lab. The menu should pop up when the form is a right-clicked.

11-21. **An Application with Two Forms**. Design a project that does the following:

As soon as the project starts, a login form appears to solicit a password from the user. The password is "master key." The text that the user enters into the password text box should be masked with "*." The password should be case sensitive.

If the password entered by the user is not correct, an error message to that effect should be displayed. Also, if the user fails three times, the program will terminate.

If the password entered is correct, this password form is closed. Another form (the form designed for exercise 11-16) is displayed until the user decides to quit.

11-22.   Unique Key for Each Form in the Collection Object. In the text, when a form is added to the Collection object, the form's Text property is used as the key; however, if multiple copies of the same form are created, the key will not be unique and will cause a runtime exception. Modify the project so that the key will be unique and easy to identify when the form needs to be removed from the Collection object. (*Hint:* Use a Shared variable to count the same form, and another Private variable to keep its identity.)

11-23.   To Save Only When There Is a Change. Refer to the MDI example in section 11.4. In the Closing event of the child form, the program prompts the user whether to save the document indiscriminately. Design a scheme so that the program will prompt the user only when some changes have been made to the document. (Hint: Use a Boolean variable to track changes in the TextChanged event.)

11-24.   An Application with a Sub Main Procedure. Modify exercise 11-17 by adding the following:

1. Add Sub Main in a standard module that will become the startup object. The Sub Main will display a splash form for three seconds and then the menu form, which will serve as the main form from then on.
2. The splash form will display a logo with the title "Clinic Receivable Management System, Version 1." (*Hint:* Use a picture that will cover the entire form as its background. Select a font of your choice to make the title succinct and neat. Set the form's ControlBox property to False so that it cannot be resized or closed by the user. If you want the text to appear in the form instead of the title bar, read Appendix B, "Graphics, Animation, and Drag and Drop," for additional hints.)
3. Add a File menu as the first menu in the menu bar. This menu should have New, Open, Close, and Exit as its menu options. There should be a separator between Exit and Close.
4. The program should terminate when the user clicks the Exit option.

11-25.   Saving a Document for an MDI Application. (refer to exercise 11-23) The SaveDoc Sub was not presented. Add the Sub procedure to the project.

11-26.   The Find and Replace Dialog Box. (refer to exercise 11-25) Suppose the Find menu is revised to include Find and Find & Replace as its menu options. The Find (Search) dialog box has been presented in the example. Add the Find and Replace capability to the project.

11-27.   A Generalized Find Dialog Box: Design for Code Reusability. The Find dialog box in the MDI example makes specific reference to the form and its text box. Such a design makes the dialog box difficult to use by other forms or projects. One way to avoid referring to the calling form is not to call the dialog box directly. The mnuFind Click event procedure in the MDI form will instead call a Sub (call it FindText) in the dialog box form, and pass the text box (the object, not just the Text property) to be searched as a parameter. Its header should look similar to the following:

```
Public Sub FindText(TextBoxFromCaller As TextBox)
```

This Sub then sets this text box to yet another class-level text box variable (call it WorkingTextBox) so that other procedures in this form can refer to it. In addition, the FindText Sub should invoke the dialog box as a modal form. That is:

```
WorkingTextBox = TextBoxFromCaller
Me.ShowDialog()
```

where WorkingTextBox is declared at the form level as follows:

```
Dim WorkingTextBox As TextBox
```

In this way, WorkingTextBox is actually referring to the text box in the form that calls the FindText Sub. Any searching or highlighting performed on the variable, WorkingTextBox is actually performed on the text box in the calling form. The btnFindNext event procedure can access this variable because it is declared at the class level. This scheme has the advantage that neither the FindText Sub nor the btnFindNext event procedure in the dialog box makes any direct reference to the MDI child form or the text box therein.

Notice that the FindText Sub does not really perform any Find Text, but sets the text box to the working text box variable and invokes the form's ShowDialog method; however, this Sub is what another developer sees to provide the search text service. Because the dialog box form is named frmSearch, and the text box to search on (in the calling form) is named txtDocument, this Sub can be invoked with the following statement:

```
frmSearch.FindText(txtDocument)
```

Modify the code for the text search functionality in the MDI project by implementing this design. (Note: an exercise in Chapter 12 provides yet another possible solution.)

Projects

11-28.   A Form with a Custom Dialog Box (Sales Application). (refer to exercise 9-19 in Chapter 9, "Database and ADO.NET," for the product table of the inventory database) Create another table, Sales, with four columns: OrderID, Date, ProductID, and Quantity Sold; then design a project for the sales order entry application. The form should have all the four fields (use a masked edit box for Date and text boxes for all other fields) and three buttons (Save, Search, and Quit).

When the Save button is clicked, data will be saved. The Search button is placed by the ProductID. When it is clicked, a custom dialog box will appear to help the user find the ProductID given a product name. When the Quit button is clicked, the program quits.

The dialog box has a text box for the user to enter a portion of the product name. When the user clicks the Search button by the text box, all products matching the name will appear in a grid (use the data grid), which has two columns: Product Name and Product ID. When the user clicks a row in the grid, the corresponding data will show in the two labels above the grid. When the user clicks the OK button, this dialog box disappears.

The data-entry form should incorporate all data validation routines necessary to ensure data validity before the record is saved into the Sales table.

11-29.   An Application with a Menu Form and Two Additional Forms. (continued from exercise 11-28) Modify exercise 11-28 in the following manner:

1. The project will start with a menu bar, which appears as follows:

<u>F</u>ile	<u>M</u>aintenance	<u>T</u>ransaction
<u>O</u>pen	<u>P</u>roduct	<u>S</u>ales
E<u>x</u>it	<u>C</u>ustomer	<u>P</u>urchase

2. The Open option of the File menu will invoke an open dialog box for the user to specify the location of the Inventory database. The Exit option will end the application.

3. The Product option of the Maintenance menu will invoke the form you created for exercise 9-19.

4. The Sales option of the Transaction menu will invoke the form you created for exercise 11-28.

5. When the Customer or Purchase option is clicked, display the message "Sorry! But the application is still under development."

Object-Based Programming

Forms and controls are recognized as objects, so you have been working with objects since the first day you worked with VB. You can see these objects while you are designing your project; however, there are objects such as the stream reader and the dataset of ADO.NET that are not visible on your form. All these objects have been defined and provided by others (Microsoft), not developed by yourself.

This chapter takes a different angle. You will learn how to develop your own templates of objects that you and other programmers can use. Before you can develop these objects, you will need to learn object-specific terminology. Section 12.1 discusses some of these terms. The remaining sections of this chapter deal with features that you can implement for the objects you develop.

After completing this chapter, you should be able to:

- Explain the relationship and differences between a class and an object.
- Develop code to create interfaces (properties, methods, and events) for a class.
- Implement additional features for a class, including enumerated constants, setting initial property values, raising events, and raising errors for improper uses of the object.
- Create and use an object from the class you have developed.
- Treat the form as a class.

12.1   Classes and Objects: Basic Concepts

You have seen and worked with objects such as controls, the stream reader, and ADO.NET. An object consists of code and data that work together as a unit. As a programmer who uses objects, you can think of objects as black boxes because you do not know how they work internally. You do not see any code of these objects. As you are aware, however, objects do have defined behaviors. They provide properties and methods that you can use to perform desired activities. They also recognize events to which you can write code in response. These defined features and behaviors are the interfaces of the object, and are exposed to its outside world (externally). All other code and data of the object are insulated from other programs (kept internally). This arrangement is recognized as *encapsulation*.

Object and Class Defined

Objects are derived—or more precisely, instantiated—from classes. A *class* is a code template or blueprint that defines the characteristics of an object; therefore, an object is a special instance of a class. To differentiate between a class and an object, consider the TextBox icon in the Toolbox, and a text box in your form. You know the general features that you can derive from the text box while it is in the Toolbox. The appearances and behaviors of the text boxes you draw on a form can be quite different from each other. Each text box on the form is a special instance of the text box in the Toolbox. The TextBox icon in the Toolbox is a template and, thus, a class. On the other hand, a text box in the form is a special instance of the text box class and, thus, is an object.

In daily language, we tend not to differentiate an object from a class. For example, an instance of the text box class is usually referred to as a text box, or just the text box, which in turn can really mean the text box class itself. Such references are harmless because a clear differentiation between the two is not really necessary in their context. In this chapter, however, you do need to understand the difference between the two. In Section 12.2, you will learn how to build a class—that is, a template. You will then create special instances of that class; that is, objects that your program can use.

Instance and Static Members

As you already know, objects have methods and properties that are defined in the objects' code template, class. Methods and properties are collectively recognized as *members* of the class. Depending on how it is declared in the class, a member may or may not be instantiated. Members that can be instantiated are recognized as *instance members*. Members that cannot be instantiated (can have only one copy for the class) are recognized as *static members*. Typically, members are declared as instance members. Static members are used for special purposes, as you will see later in this chapter.

Advantages of Object-Oriented Programming

When you start to build your own classes and use your own objects, your thinking process and the resulting code can be quite different from the programs you write in the "traditional" way. In essence, you will be doing object-oriented programming. Instead of attacking the programming problem directly, you will be thinking in terms of building a class to solve a generic class of problems and creating an object from the class to handle the problem at hand. While you are developing the class, you are one step away from a particular programming problem.

Why build classes? Why use objects? The following are the advantages of this programming approach:

- *Encapsulation:* As already explained, each object keeps its own data, free from the interference of any part of the code in a project. The performance and accuracy of an object is independent of the other code in a project.

- *Code Reusability and Maintainability:* A class/object has well-defined interfaces (properties, methods, and events) and boundaries (encapsulation). You can easily incorporate a new object/class into your project. These interfaces are all you need to know about the class/object to use the class properly. In addition, code update and maintenance can be much more convenient. For example, if there is a change in the class/object, the new version can easily replace the old one. When the class/object is provided through a Dynamic Link Library (DLL), replacing the old DLL with the new DLL is all it takes to update all the projects using that class. A project that is compiled using objects provided by a DLL does not embed (statically link) the code of these objects, but rather just makes references to them. These objects are linked to the project dynamically at run-time. There is no need to tear down or recompile the project. Code reusability is further enhanced when a class is *inheritable*. An inheritable class allows another class to extends it methods and properties. This feature is recognized as *inheritance*. The first class serves as the base class, and the second (new) class is the derived class. As a programmer, you can add functionality in the derived class without the need to modify the code in the base class; therefore, inheritance greatly enhances code reusability. Inheritance is discussed in detail in Chapter 13, "Object-Oriented Programming."

- *Uniform Data Validation Rules:* An interesting application of objects in business is their representation as a business entity. For example, an object can be used to represent a student, an employee, or a product. This appears to be a very different use compared with a text box as an object. All the data associated with such a business object can then be coded as the properties of the entity. You can code all the data validation rules for each property in the object's property procedures as explained in Section 12.2. A company can require that all the programs dealing with the business entity (object) use that object instead of using their own definition. Imposing such a requirement on all programs will result in uniform data validation rules. The advantages should be obvious: no unexpected exception will occur, and any change of validation rules can be revised in only one location—where the class is defined. This point should become clear after you complete Section 12.2.

- *Easier Project Management:* A big project can be more easily divided into smaller subprojects defined in terms of objects/classes that can be assigned to project team members. Each member can more easily focus on the member's own assignment because the interactions of the member's products are defined by the interfaces of the objects. These subprojects can then be assembled and tested by focusing on the behaviors of the interfaces.

12.2   Building and Using a Class

So, how do you build a class from which you can create objects? You build a class by writing code in a *class module*. You can think of a class module as a form module without its visual element; that is, a class module behaves like the code window of the form.

Differences Between the Class Module and the Standard Module

The class module is also similar to the standard module in that they both can contain only code, with no visual element; however, they are different in several respects:

- Each standard module can have only one copy in a project, and it can contain unrelated data and code (variables and procedures). On the other hand, each class module can have multiple instances (objects) in the same project, but it should not contain unrelated code or data.

- A standard module exists for as long as the project runs. An object (instance of a class) exists when it is created but is destroyed when it is out of scope. For example, if an object is created with an object variable in a procedure, the object is destroyed after the procedure ends. In addition, an object can be destroyed by being set to Nothing, such as ObjVar = Nothing. Note that the object may continue to reside in memory until the *garbage collector* (discussed in Section 12.2) is invoked and reclaims the resources that the object used. There is no way to destroy a standard module in a project other than ending the project.

- Public Sub and Function procedures in standard modules are recognized as Subs and Functions accordingly. To invoke a procedure in a standard module, your code makes a reference to the procedure name; however, Public Sub and Function procedures in a class module are methods of the object. They can be accessible only when the object exists. To invoke a method in a class module, your code must qualify the name of the method with the object name, not the class name; that is, the code must have the following syntax:

  ```
  Object.Method
  ```

- Public variables in a standard module are accessible to all other modules in the duration of the project. Public variables of a class are properties of the object; thus they are accessible only when the object exists, and must be referenced with the object name as the qualifier. That is, you refer to the Public variables of a class module by the following syntax:

  ```
  Object.Variable
  ```

Note again that the qualifier of the variable is the object name, not the class name. Recall that you code the Text property of a text box named txtEmployee as follows:

```
txtEmployee.Text
```

not

```
TextBox.Text
```

- Because public variables and procedures (subs and functions) are properties and methods of the object, there can be as many copies of these properties and methods as the number of instances (objects) of the class. These copies are independent of each other. In contrast, there is only one copy of the variables and procedures for each standard module in the project.

These differences are summarized in the following table.

Difference in	Class Module	Standard Module
Number of copies in a project	Multiple copies of the same module can be loaded.	Only one copy is loaded.
Data and code relationship	All data and code in one module should be related to the same class.	Unrelated code and data can exist in the same module.
Life duration	An object exists when it is created from the class module, and disappears when it is destroyed.	A standard module exists throughout the life of the project.
Copies of Public procedures	As many as the number of the objects created from the same module.	Only one copy exists.
Reference to the Public procedures	*Object.Method* (A Public procedure is a method of an object and can be accessible only when the object exists.)	*ProcedureName* or *ModuleName.ProcedureName.*
Copies of Public variables	As many as the number of the objects created from the same module.	Only one copy per project.
Reference to the Public variables	*Object.Variable* (Public variables are properties of the object and can be accessible only when the object exists.)	*VariableName* or *ModuleName.VariableName.*

Recall that properties and methods of a class are collectively recognized as members of the class. Note that the above discussion does not apply to *static members* of the class. Static members are declared with the *Shared* keyword. A class has only one copy of each static member. All instances of the class (objects) share the same static members of that class. The lifetime of the shared (static) members does not depend on any instance of the class. In addition, static members can be referenced either by the class name or by object name as follows:

```
ClassName.Member
ObjectName.Member
```

Adding a Class Module to a Project

To build a class, you need to add a class module to your project. Adding a class module is similar to adding a form and can be done by following these steps:

1. Click the Project menu.
2. Click the Add Class option to open the Add New Item dialog box.
3. Enter a name for the class in the Name box.
4. Click the Open button. A code window with the following code template should appear in place of the form.

```
Public Class ClassName
End Class
```

You can then place code in the code window (class module) to build a class. You can include as many class modules as you need in a project. Although you can place multiple classes in a class module by enclosing code within pairs of "Class. . . End Class" statements, this practice is not recommended. You may have difficulty in the future with locating the classes that you previously developed.

Scope of Class Modules. In general, a class is declared as Public. As such, it is accessible to all other modules in the project as well other projects. You can also declare a class as Friend. In such a case, the class is accessible only to the current project.

Creating the Fixed Asset Class

To illustrate how a class can be created and used, consider the creation of a FixedAsset class step by step. Suppose you would like to create this class with the following interfaces:

- Three properties:
  - Cost
  - Estimated life (in years)
  - The depreciation (accounting) method

- One method: net book value. This method will return the net book value of the fixed asset using the aforementioned three properties and a parameter to be discussed next.

How do you proceed? In general, the major steps are as follows:

1. Add a new class module to a new project, and assign a proper name. This was explained in the preceding subsection.
2. Add property procedures to create properties.
3. Add Public Sub and/or Function procedures for methods.

The following discussion assumes that you have added a class module to a new project and named it FixedAsset. All code should be placed inside the class definition:

```
Public Class FixedAsset
End Class
```

Creating a Property

To create a property, start your code in the class module with the following syntax:

```
Public [ReadOnly|WriteOnly] Property PropertyName() As Type
```

For example, you can declare an Account property as follows:

```
Public Property Account() As String
```

Typically, a property is expected to return a single value. If it is expected to return an array, a pair of parentheses should follow the type declaration of the property definition (similar to the header of a function). For example, if the Accounts property is expected to return a string array, it should be declared as follows:

```
'  The following declaration specifies that
'  the Accounts property will return an array
Public ReadOnly Property Accounts As String()
```

When you press the Enter key at the end of the statement, the IDE automatically provides you with the following code template:

```
Public Property PropertyName() As Type
    Get
    End Get
    Set(ByVal Value As Type)
    End Set
End Property
```

The Get procedure is used to return the value of the property; the Set procedure allows the client code (the code that uses an instance of this class) to set the value (setting) for the property.

Notice that the Property name can be declared with the Public, Friend, Protected (discussed in Chapter 13), and Private access. The default is Public. A Public property can be accessible to other modules. Notice also that you can place code only in either the Get or the Set procedure within the property definition. Inside the Set procedure, you should assign the parameter (named Value) to a variable that is private to the class module. You use a Private (instead of Public) variable so that the data passed to the class/object is insulated from other modules. In this way, data can be encapsulated.

In this example, you want the fixed asset class to have a Cost property; therefore, in the class module, you will create the following code template first:

```
Public Property Cost() As Double
    Get
    End Get
    Set(ByVal Value As Double)
    End Set
End Property
```

To keep a private copy of the Cost property, you will need to declare a class level Private variable to be associated with the property. For example, you can make the following declaration:

```
Private mCost As Double
```

The Set procedure can be coded as follows:

```
Set(ByVal Value As Double)
    mCost = Value
End Set
```

Using the Class and the Property. To see the effect of this property procedure, you need to make changes to the project's form. Double-click Form1 in the Solution Explorer window, draw a button, name it **btnCompute,** and set its Text property to **Compute.** In the button's Click event procedure, code the following:

```
Private Sub btnCompute_Click(ByVal sender As System.Object, ByVal
    e As System.EventArgs) Handles btnCompute.Click
    Dim Land As New FixedAsset()
    Land.Cost = 100000
End Sub
```

The Dim statement declares a variable Land of the FixedAsset type. It also creates a new instance of FixedAsset, and assigns it to Land. The creation of the Cost property in the FixedAsset class module now allows you to set the Cost property of Land to 100,000.

Compare the preceding code with what you learned in Chapter 9, "Database and ADO.NET," when working with ADO.NET objects. You should notice that there is no difference between the way you declare and use an object from a class you create for yourself and that from a class provided by others (as in the case of ADO.NET).

Returning the Property Value. The Set procedure allows the code in other modules to set the property value of the object. What do you code to make the object return the value of the same property? For example, in your form, you would like to inspect the value of the Cost property by coding the following:

```
MsgBox("Cost of the land is " & Land.Cost)
```

What code/procedure do you need to add in the class module to enable this? (*Note:* Go back to the class module. All code from this point on should be placed in the class module.) It is the Property Get procedure, as mentioned previously, in the Cost property definition. To enable the Cost property to return a value, you can code the following:

```
Get
    Cost = mCost 'Return the property setting
End Get
```

Note that the Cost property name is placed on the left side of the assignment statement so that the property will return a value. This is similar to the way you write code for a function to return a value. You can also use the Return statement to return the value. In that case, you will code:

```
Get
    Return(mCost)  'Return the property setting
End Get
```

Also note that mCost is the Private variable that accepts the value of the same property in the Set procedure discussed previously. Variables that are used to associate their values with Public properties such as mCost with Cost are recognized as the *private copies* of the properties. They are sometimes referenced as member variables and are typically named with a prefix of m or mvar.

Read and Write Capabilities. In general, it is said that the Set procedure enables the code to write (set) the value for the property, whereas the Get procedure enables the code to read (return) the property. As shown previously, when you declare a property without either the *ReadOnly* or *WriteOnly* specification, it is both read- and write-enabled. The IDE editor provides both the Get and Set procedure templates. You can declare a property to be ReadOnly or WriteOnly. In that case, the editor will provide only either the Get or the Set procedure depending on your specification. The read-only specification can be useful for properties such as Count or Balance that should be maintained (computed) in the object internally. The following code shows an example ReadOnly property definition for Balance:

```
Private mBalance As Double
Public ReadOnly Property Balance() As Double
    Get
        Return (mBalance)
    End Get
End Property
```

The Complete Property Procedures. Now you understand the property definition and its relationship with the Set and Get procedures in the class module and the properties of the class as previously illustrated. You can proceed in the same manner to code all other property procedures for the other properties (life and depreciation method) as initially planned. The complete code for the property procedures of the FixedAsset class appears as follows:

```
Private mCost As Double
Private mLife As Double
Private mDepreMethod As Integer
Public Property Cost() As Double
    Get
        Cost = mCost
    End Get
    Set(ByVal Value As Double)
        mCost = Value
    End Set
End Property
Public Property Life() As Double
    Get
        Life = mLife
    End Get
    Set(ByVal Value As Double)
        mLife = Value
    End Set
End Property
Public Property DepreMethod() As Integer
    Get
        DepreMethod = mDepreMethod
    End Get
    Set(ByVal Value As Integer)
        mDepreMethod = Value
    End Set
End Property
```

Creating a Method

How do you create a method for a class? The code for a method of an object is no different from a typical general Sub or Function procedure. In fact, you use exactly the same keywords: Sub and Function. To illustrate, you will create the NetBookValue method for the FixedAsset class to compute, and return the net book value for the asset. In general, the net book value is computed by the following formula:

$$\text{Net Book Value} = \text{Cost} - \text{Accumulated Depreciation}$$

The amount of accumulated depreciation depends on the number of years the asset is in use and the depreciation method. For simplicity, assume the company uses only two accounting depreciation methods: no depreciation (0), and straight-line depreciation (1). The net book value of an asset can be computed as follows:

- If DepreMethod is 0, no depreciation needs to be taken for the asset, such as land. The asset's net book value should be the same as its cost.
- If the DepreMethod is 1, the straight-line depreciation is used. The annual depreciation can be computed by the following formula:

$$\text{Annual Depreciation} = (\text{Cost} - \text{Salvage Value}) / \text{Life in Years}$$

For simplicity again, assume a zero for the salvage value. The annual depreciation can be computed as follows:

$$\text{Annual Depreciation} = \text{Cost} / \text{Life in Years}$$

The accumulated depreciation will be computed as follows:

$$\text{Accumulated Depreciation} = \text{Years in use} \times \text{annual depreciation}$$

Note that the maximum amount of accumulated depreciation is the cost of the asset. If the number of years the asset in use is greater than the asset's life, the net book value should be zero because the asset has been fully depreciated; otherwise, the net book value should be equal to the cost minus the annual depreciation times the number of years in use. The years in use should be passed as a parameter to the NetBookValue procedure (method) so that it can perform the computation.

The code for the NetBookValue method should be placed in the class module and should appear as follows:

```
Public Function NetBookValue(ByVal Years As Integer) As Double
    If mDepreMethod = 0 Then
        ' This depreciation method does not depreciate the asset.
        NetBookValue = mCost
    Else
        ' Straight line depreciation method
        If Years >= mLife Then
            'Asset has been fully depreciated;
            'book value should be zero.
            NetBookValue = 0
        Else
            ' Compute net book value by subtracting accumulated
            ' depreciation from the cost
            NetBookValue = mCost - Years * (mCost / mLife)
        End If
    End If
End Function
```

Note that the parameter, Years (representing years in use) has to be passed to the method (function) for the method to compute the net book value. Also, carefully examine the variables used in the formula to compute the net book value. Both the variables mCost and mLife are variables private to the FixedAsset class. Where are the sources of their values? They obtain their values when your code sets the values for the Cost and Life properties through their respective Set procedures. The flow of data can be depicted as in Figure 12.1.

Different Types of Methods. As you can see, when invoked, your NetBookValue method returns a value, the net book value; therefore, you code it as a function. Not all methods need to return a value. If you need a method that only brings about a result, such as displaying data or moving an image, you can code it as a Sub.

Differences Between Methods and General Procedures. So, how are the methods in class modules different from those general procedures in standard modules? In logic and in syntax, there really is no difference; however, as noted, the way the data are handled can and should be different. When designing your code, you always want to encapsulate the data as much as possible; that is, you will take care to eliminate contamination (unintentional interference) in the data you use in a procedure or a method. When dealing with the class/object, you accomplish this by encapsulating the properties. When working with procedures in the standard module, you will need to pass all required data elements as parameters. The number of parameters passed to a general procedure will tend to be more than that for a method, all other things being equal.

Another difference is the way that a method and the procedure are invoked. To invoke a method, you use the following syntax:

Object.Method(Parameter list)

whereas you usually invoke a procedure with the following syntax:

[ModuleName.]ProcedureName(Parameter List)

Figure 12.1

How a property setting is passed and used

```
'***********Code in the Form**************

Private Sub btnCompute_Click(ByVal sender As System.Object, ByVal e
    As System.EventArgs) _
    Handles btnCompute.Click
        Dim Land As New FixedAsset() 'Declare and create Land as the
            FixedAsset type
        Land.Cost = 100000
End Sub
```

This diagram illustrates how a property setting is passed from a module and used in an object. The arrows show the direction of data flows.

```
'******Land Object Created from The Class Module******

Private mCost As Double 'local copy
    Public Property Cost() As Double
        Get
            Cost = mCost
        End Get
        Set(ByVal Value As Double)
            mCost = Value
        End Set
End Property
Public Function NetBookValue(ByVal Years As Integer) As Double
    If mDepreMethod = 0 Then
        ' This depreciation method does not depreciate the asset.
        NetBookValue = mCost
    Else
        'Other statements
    End If
End Function
```

Note that to invoke a procedure, you refer to its name directly, or qualify it with the module name, whereas you qualify the method with the object name, not the class name. Each object (instance) of the same class has its own data, so you need not be concerned about data within a method being accidentally altered by another object. On the other hand, a procedure in a standard module deals with only one set of data; therefore, you will need to be more careful about the possibility that some of its data can be a leftover from previous invocation or accidentally altered by other code.

These differences are summarized in the following table.

Difference in	Procedures in a Standard Module	Methods in a Class Module
Number of parameters	More	Less
Invocation (reference)	*ProcName or Module.ProcName*	*Object.Method* (not *Class.Method*)
Potential data contamination	Higher	Lower
Number of copies in a project	One	As many as objects created

Note, however, the preceding comparison pertains to methods declared as Public. Because these methods exist with each object (instance of the class), they are recognized as *instance methods*. You can also declare methods as Public Shared. As discussed previously in this chapter, Shared methods are static and are referred to as *static* (or *shared*) *methods*. Shared methods have characteristics that resemble procedures in standard modules; that is, they have only one copy per class (not per object), and can be referenced by the class name, using the syntax:

```
ClassName.Method
```

Using the FixedAsset Class

Now that you have created a FixedAsset class, how do you use it in your project? As explained previously, you need to declare object variables of the FixedAsset class and then associate these variables with the instances of the class created using the New keyword.

From that point on, using the objects you have created will be exactly the same as using all the objects you have seen before.

For example, suppose you would like to create two fixed assets: Land and Factory. Each will be assigned different values of their properties. You will then use the NetBookValue method to determine their net book values after 10 years in use, and use MsgBox to display the results.

You can rewrite the btnCompute Click event procedure shown in the preceding subsection to satisfy these requirements. The code can appear as follows:

```
' Code in the form
Private Sub btnCompute_Click(ByVal sender As System.Object, ByVal
    e As System.EventArgs) Handles btnCompute.Click
    ' Declare Land and Factory as variables of the FixedAsset class
    Dim Land As FixedAsset
    Dim Factory As FixedAsset
    Land = New FixedAsset()    'Create a new Land object
    ' Set properties for Land
    Land.Cost = 100000
    Land.Life = 1000
    Land.DepreMethod = 0
    Factory = New FixedAsset()    'Create a new Factory object
    ' Set properties for Factory
    Factory.Cost = 300000
    Factory.Life = 20
    Factory.DepreMethod = 1
    ' Display cost and net book value for Land
    MsgBox("Land cost is " & Land.Cost _
        & ". Net book value is  " & Land.NETBookValue(10)) '10 years
    ' Display cost and net book value for Factory
    MsgBox("Factory cost is " & Factory.Cost _
        & ". Net book value is  " & Factory.NETBookValue(10))
End Sub
```

In the code, both Land and Factory are instantiated the FixedAsset class (type). Notice that you use the NetBookValue method for both Land and Factory objects after their respective properties have been set. This is done intentionally for you to be able to inspect the results. You should see each object retains its assigned cost, and each object has a correct net book value: 100,000 and 150,000, respectively. The data for each object are encapsulated and isolated from each other so that the property settings in one object will not affect the others. Imagine the net book value for each object is computed in a standard module. You will need to take special care to separate the data for the land from the factory, won't you?

Default Property Setting and the Constructor

In this fixed asset example, if you forget to set the property value for DepreMethod for a fixed asset object, its default value will be zero—(that is, no depreciation)—because all numeric variables will be initialized to zero when an instance of the class is initialized. Most fixed assets are depreciable, however, so the straight-line depreciation (accounting) method would be a better default. Is there a way to set the straight-line depreciation (accounting) method as the default for each fixed asset?

When an object is being created from the class, the Sub New procedure in the class is automatically executed. This *New procedure* cannot be called by any other procedure (and therefore is executed only once for each instance) and is recognized as the *constructor*. This is the procedure that can be used to set the initial states for the object so that it is ready to perform.

You can use the New procedure to set the default value for a property. In the example, you can use it to set the default value of the DepreMethod property to 1 as follows:

```
Sub New()
    mDepreMethod = 1
End Sub
```

After you add this code in the fixed asset class module, all fixed asset objects will have a default straight-line depreciation method.

To see the effect of the preceding code, go back to the form. Add a button, name it **btnShow,** and set its Text property to **Show**; then add the following code:

```
Private Sub btnShow_Click(ByVal sender As System.Object, ByVal e
    As System.EventArgs) Handles btnShow.Click
    Dim Furniture As New FixedAsset()
    MsgBox("DepreMethod for furniture is " & _
      Furniture.DepreMethod)
End Sub
```

Keep in mind that in this event procedure, you have not yet set any value for any property of the Furniture object. If, however, you run the project and then click the button, you will see that the MsgBox displays the following message:

```
DepreMethod for furniture is 1
```

Additional Uses of the Constructor. Similar to all other procedures, the New procedure can be overloaded; that is, you can write more than one New procedure with the same parameter list of different types or with a different parameter list (of the same types or different types). You can then use different New procedures to initialize an instance of the class. Typically, this feature is used to initialize property settings. In the fixed asset example, you can use it to allow the programmer to initialize the value for cost and life. The *additional* New procedure can appear as follows:

```
Sub New(ByVal pCost As Double, Optional ByVal pLife As Double = 0,
    Optional ByVal pDepreMethod As Integer = 1)
    mCost = pCost
    mLife = pLife
    mDepreMethod = pDepreMethod
End Sub
```

This procedure will set mCost (the private copy of the Cost property) to the value of the first parameter. The second parameter is written as optional. When it is present, the value will be assigned to mLife, the Private copy of the Life property. If not, 0 will be assigned. Similarly, the absence of the third parameter will cause 1 to be the default setting for the DepreMethod property.

Notice that this New procedure overloads the previous one that sets default value for mDepreMethod. Only one of these New subs is called when an instance of the class is instantiated. The optional third parameter is included in the list so that the default setting for the DepreMethod property will be the same regardless of how an object of the FixedAsset class is instantiated.

In the calling procedure, the following code will initialize the Cost property of Furniture to $3,000:

```
Dim Furniture As New FixedAsset(3000)
```

Notice the position of the parameter list. Although the New procedure in the class module specifies the parameter list, the list is placed in the pair of parentheses following the class name.

Building and Using a Class: A Recapitulation

The following table summarizes what you need to do to build a class, and to use an object created from it.

Objective	Action
Code and actions in the class module	
To create a class	Add a class module to the project, and provide the class name in the Class statement; for example, `Public Class FixedAsset`

To create a property	Code the property definition with the following syntax:
	`Public [ReadOnly¦WriteOnly] Property`
	`PropertyName() As Type`

To create a method	Write a Function that will return a value, or Sub that does not return a value.
To set default value for a property	Write code in the Sub New procedure.
To initialize property settings at the same time of object instantiation	Write additional New procedures, taking the initial settings as parameters.
Code in other modules (form, standard, or class modules)	

To use an object	Declare an object variable of the class created; for example,
	`Dim Land As FixedAsset`
	Set the object variable to the object using the New keyword; for example,
	`Land = New FixedAsset()`
	or simply
	`Dim Land As New FixedAsset()`

To reference a property or method of an object	Use the syntax:
	`Object.Property or Object.Method; e.g.,`
	`Land.Cost`

To initialize the settings of properties at the same time as object instantiation	Place the parameter list in the pair of parentheses after the class name where the instance is created; for example, `Dim Furniture As New FixedAsset(3000, 10)` Note that the overloading procedure must exist in the class to handle the initialization.

12.3   Adding Features to the Class

Perhaps you have noticed some desirable improvements in the preceding example. This section considers several of these improvements.

This textbook has advocated for the use of meaningful names for both constants and variables. The depreciation (accounting) methods were coded with numbers: 0 for no depreciation and 1 for the straight-line depreciation method. Is there a way to represent these numbers with meaningful names? Yes, you can with the Enum statement.

Enumerated Constants

The Enum statement has the following syntax:

```
[Public ¦ Private] Enum name
    membername1 [= constant]
    membername2 [= constant]
        . . .
End Enum
```

where *name* represents a generic name for the data you are enumerating, and *membername* is the name for the specific value you are designating.

For example, instead of using 0 and 1 to represent the depreciation (accounting) method in the previous example, you can place the following code *in the FixedAsset class module*:

```
Public Enum DepreType
    NoDepreciation = 0
    StraightLine = 1
End Enum
```

Note that the assignment of values to the enumerated names is optional. When you just list all names, the first one in the list will be assigned a value of zero. All subsequent names will be assigned a value of 1 greater than the preceding one. You can also assign any unique value to any name. Again, any subsequent names without being assigned a value will be assigned with one increment of its preceding one.

Revising the Property Procedures for the DepreMethod Property. Because you are going to use DepreType to enumerate the available settings with the depreciation (accounting) method property, the property definition for the DepreMethod and its Set procedure should be revised as follows:

```
Private mDepreMethod As DepreType
Public Property DepreMethod() As DepreType
    Get
        DepreMethod = mDepreMethod
    End Get
    Set(ByVal Value As DepreType)
        mDepreMethod = Value
    End Set
End Property
```

Compare the header for the property definition and that for the Set procedure with the ones you had previously. The property definition (first line) and the parameter Value passed to the Property Set procedure now are declared to be the DepreType, instead of the Integer type. The code informs the procedure to expect/accept only one of the two values or names declared in the Enum statement. Note that the declaration for the property (first line) must be consistent with that for the parameter in the Set procedure; otherwise, the compiler will inform you of an error.

Effect of Enumeration on Code. How does this change affect your code? You can use the Enum data in both the class module and the form module. For example, in the class module, the NetBookValue method (function) contains an If block that tests the value of the mDepreMethod. The block of code can be revised as follows:

```
If mDepreMethod = DepreType.NoDepreciation Then
   ' This method does not depreciate the asset.
   NetBookValue = mCost
Else
   ' Straight line depreciation
   If Years >= mLife Then
      NetBookValue = 0
   Else
      NetBookValue = mCost - Years * (mCost / mLife)
   End If
End if
```

This revision should make the code more readable. In addition, you can now use the names in the Enum declaration in the form to set the value for the DepreMethod in the button Click event procedure. For example, you can now code the following:

```
Land.DepreMethod = FixedAsset.DepreType.NoDepreciation
Factory.DepreMethod = FixedAsset.DepreType.StraightLine
```

Again, this change should make your code clearer and more readable. Notice that the enumeration is qualified with FixedAsset because the enumeration is defined in that module. While you are revising the code, you should see the IDE IntelliSense displaying available choices as shown in Figure 12.2.

Figure 12.2

The Effect of Using Enum Declaration

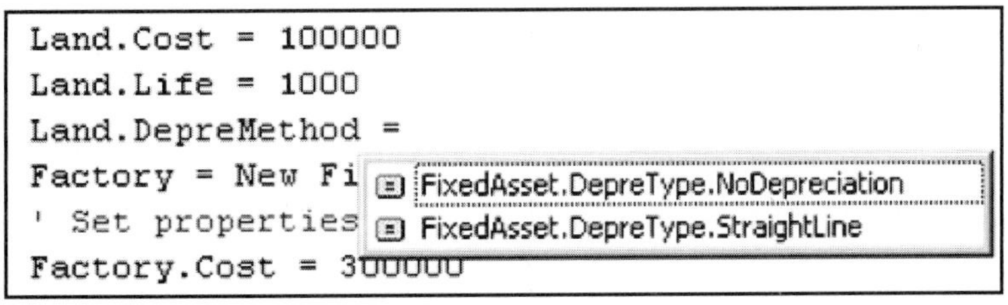

```
Land.Cost = 100000
Land.Life = 1000
Land.DepreMethod =
Factory = New Fi[  FixedAsset.DepreType.NoDepreciation  ]
' Set properties [  FixedAsset.DepreType.StraightLine  ]
Factory.Cost = 300000
```

With the Public Enum declaration in the class module
and revision in the property procedures, you should see
this box when you are revising your code in the form.

Throwing Exceptions

In the preceding example, what if you accidentally set the value of the DepreMethod property to 2 for a fixed asset object? This value is apparently out of the valid range of the DepreType we declared for the property. The invalid setting will be used for the property, but you will not be alerted to the error.

Displaying Error Message in a Property Procedure. One alternative, of course, is to provide an error-checking routine in the Set procedure for the property of interest, and to display an error message when the data is out of range. If you do so, when you test your program with an inappropriate property setting, you will encounter the message; however, the program continues to execute. You will have difficulty identifying the source of the error, and if another user uses the program, the error message will make no sense.

Throwing an Exception. A better alternative is to throw an exception in your class module, where you can specify the exception. An exception is a runtime error. It can be caused by wrong logic in code, wrong data such as bad property setting as in the example, or an action by the user such as failure to insert a disk in drive A. Throwing an exception emulates the exception you encounter in your code. For example, when your code attempts to read beyond the end of a file, the program will encounter the "System.IO.EndOfStreamException." If an error occurs when you throw an exception in a class module, the execution is halted at the point where your code attempts to set an invalid value. The error message will indicate the exception thrown in the class module. This can be helpful to other programmers who are using the class you have developed. How do you throw an exception? You use the *Throw statement*. The syntax appears as follows:

```
Throw New Exception(parameter list)
```

The exception can be a user-defined exception or a system defined exception. Most of the errors encountered are related to setting the property, and can be considered an argument error, as in this case. To help the programmer identify what went wrong, the exception thrown should be as specific as possible. In this example, the most appropriate exception to throw should be the ArgumentOutOfRangeException. Where can you find the list of exceptions that have been already defined? The most convenient place to locate them is the Debug menu. When you click the Debug menu and then select the Exceptions option, the Exceptions dialog box appears as shown in Figure 12.3. In most cases, you should be able to find the exception that is proper for the exception that you want to throw.

Incorporating Exception Throwing in a Property Procedure. If you apply this alternative to treating the error for the depreciation (accounting) method, you can revise the code for its Set procedure as follows:

```
Set(ByVal Value As DepreType)
    If Value>=0 AndlAlso Value <= DepreType.StraightLine Then
        mDepreMethod = Value
    Else
        Throw New ArgumentOutOfRangeException("DepreMethod",
            "Value should be in the range of 0 and 1")
    End If
End Set
```

Figure 12.3

The Exceptions dialog box

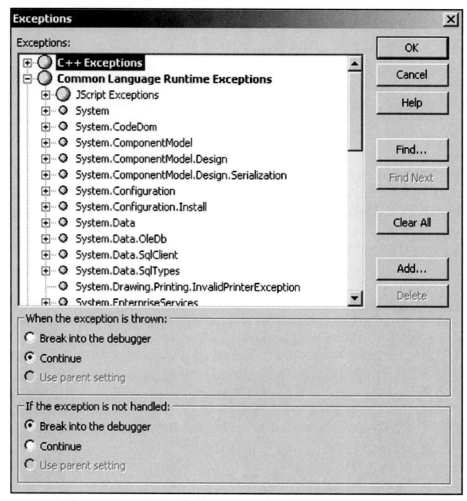

Click the Debug menu and select the Exceptions option. This dialog box will appear. Click the Expand (+) button by "Common Language Runtime Exceptions." And you should see a long list of exceptions from which you should be able to find one that fits your situation.

In this procedure, the If statement tests whether the Value parameter is within the valid range. If so, the property setting is assigned to the member variable mDepreMethod; otherwise, the "argument out of range" exception is thrown, with the message, "Value should be in the range of 0 and 1" displayed in the message box. You can explore the effect of this routine by using the following code in your btnCompute_Click event procedure (*Note:* To test the code, turn off Option Strict):

```
Land.DepreMethod = 2
```

When you test your program, execution will be halted on this line with an error message indicating System.ArgumentOutOfRangeException with "Additional information: Value should be in the range of 0 and 1."

Benefits of Throwing Exceptions. When you work for a company, most of the programming projects are fairly large. They are typically divided into smaller manageable subprojects, each assigned to different project team members. You will most likely be required to develop classes/objects to handle these subprojects. The classes/objects you have created will be used by your colleagues, while you will be using the classes/objects they have developed. You will appreciate it when your colleagues' classes and objects throw an exception to alert you to an error in your code. For the same reason, your colleagues will appreciate your classes that have similar implementations.

Additional Remarks. Admittedly, the fixed asset class you have created is simple, and can be enhanced in several ways. For example, you probably have noticed that various (accounting) depreciation methods exist. A complete fixed asset object should include all these methods for practical uses. Also, in reality, there are restrictive accounting rules governing the change of the depreciation method. You may want to incorporate an event such as **DepreMethodChanged** in the class when it detects an attempt to change the depreciation method. You can then place some code in that event to alert the user to the restriction when he or she attempts to change the depreciation method for an existing asset. In addition, you can also add methods for the class to compute the depreciation for the current year as well as the cumulative depreciation amount. These enhancements are left to you as exercise 12-18 at the end of the chapter. The implementation of events in a class is discussed in the next subsection.

Implementing Events in a Class

Recall that objects have three types of interfaces: properties, methods, and events. You have seen how properties and methods are created in a class, but how do you implement an event? In the class, you use the event declaration statement to declare an event, and the *RaiseEvent statement* to raise an event. The *event declaration statement* has the following syntax:

```
[Public] Event EventProcName(Parameter list)
```

where *EventProcName* is the name of the event procedure such as Click, and *Parameter list* is the list of parameters to pass to the procedure.

Notice that the event must be declared at the class level as Public. All events must be recognized by other modules in order to be used; therefore, an event declared as Private will not make any sense.

The following statement will declare an Insolvent event, with two parameters, both of the Double type:

```
Public Event Insolvent(Cash As Double, PaymentsDue As Double)
```

The *RaiseEvent statement* has the following syntax:

```
RaiseEvent EventProcName[(Parameter List)]
```

where *EventProcName* and *Parameter list* have the same meaning as in the event declaration. If there is no parameter, the pair of parentheses should be included.

The RaiseEvent statement will fire (raise) the event, and trigger the event procedure that is written to handle this event. The following code segment shows how the statement can be coded:

```
If Cash < PaymentsDue Then
    RaiseEvent Insolvent(Cash, PaymentsDue)
End If
```

After an event is properly declared and raised in the class module, it can be used in other modules similar to any typical event. The next subsection discusses additional details.

A Class with an Event: An Example

To illustrate how the two event statements are coded in a class, consider a simple example. Suppose you want to create a SortEngine class, in which you will provide a BubbleSort method that can be used to sort any array of the Integer type. Because you will be concerned about the amount of time that the method may take to sort the array, you would like to provide a means to inform the user of the progress in sorting. One way is to implement an event in the class. The event (call it PercentChanged) can be raised at each percentage of completion (1%, 2%, and so on), and will give the percentage as well as an estimated remaining time.

Bubble Sort Without an Event. You will begin with coding the sorting routine in a new project. Because the procedure is a method in a class module, you will need to do the following:

1. Add a class module to the new project, and name it **SortEngine**.
2. Enter the following code in the SortEngine class:

```
Public Sub BubbleSort(ByVal X() As Integer)
    Dim I As Integer
    Dim J As Integer
    Dim Temp As Integer
    For I = 0 To UBound(X) - 1
        For J = 0 To UBound(X) - I - 1
            If X(J) > X(J + 1) Then
                ' Out of order; swap
                Temp = X(J)
                X(J) = X(J + 1)
                X(J + 1) = Temp
            End If
        Next J
    Next I
End Sub
```

The bubble sort algorithm was explained in Chapter 8, "Arrays and Their Uses."

Declaring the Event. The first step to implement an event is to declare the event using the Event statement. As described previously in this subsection, the PercentChanged event will give two values: the percentage completed, and the remaining time. The Event statement should be declared in the class-level declaration area as follows:

```
Public Event PercentChanged(Percent As Integer, TimeLeft As
    Double)
```

As you can see, the declaration looks much like the header of a Sub procedure. The event must be declared as Public because you want it to be known to other modules in the projects. The Percent parameter is declared to be of the Integer type because you would like the number to be 1, 2, and 3 for 1%, 2%, and 3%, respectively. TimeLeft is declared to be a Double variable to show the estimated remaining time (in seconds). This statement should be placed in the general declaration area of the class module.

Raising the Event. The event should be raised each time the Percent variable increases by a percentile. The sorting time depends mainly on the number of comparisons to perform. As discussed in Chapter 8, for an array of N elements, the total number of comparisons for the bubble sort algorithm can be computed by the following formula:

$$\text{Comparisons} = (N - 1) + (N - 2) + \ldots + 2 + 1$$
$$= N * (N - 1) / 2$$

The number of comparisons that has been performed can be computed in the inner loop with a variable (call it Counter) as follows:

```
Counter += 1
```

The percentage can then be computed by the following formula:

```
Percent = CInt(100 * (Counter / Comparisons))
```

Assume the time at which the computation started (StartTime) has been obtained; then the remaining time can be estimated as follows:

```
TimeLeft = (Microsoft.VisualBasic.Timer - StartTime) /
    CDbl(Percent) * CDbl(100 - Percent)
```

The preceding line explicitly converts Percent and (100 - Percent) to the Double type using the CDbl function. Both TimeLeft and StartTime should be of the Double type to keep track of time in seconds. (Recall that the Timer function returns a Double value representing the number of seconds elapsed since midnight.) Percent should be declared as Integer, however, as implied in the preceding discussion. The use of CDbl function makes the data type of all elements in the expression compatible.

For efficiency, the event should not be raised until the value of Percent actually changes. To detect the change, another variable, OldPercent, can be used. When the procedure (method) is invoked, both Percent and OldPercent will initially be zero; therefore, the following If statement should detect the change:

```
If Percent > OldPercent Then
End If
```

Inside the If block, the RaiseEvent statement can be used to fire the event. In addition, OldPercent should be assigned with the value of Percent, ready to check for another change in Percent; therefore, you can code the following:

```
If Percent > OldPercent Then
    TimeLeft = (Microsoft.VisualBasic.Timer - StartTime) /
      CDbl(Percent) * CDbl(100  Percent)
    RaiseEvent PercentChanged(Percent, TimeLeft)
    ' Revise OldPercent, so that this block will execute
    ' only when Percent has changed again.
    OldPercent = Percent
End If
```

Notice that the two arguments enclosed in the pair of parentheses correspond to the event declaration statement. The variable names do not have to be exactly the same as in the event declaration. The relationship of the argument list between RaiseEvent and Event declaration is the same as that between Call and Sub.

The Complete Code for SortEngine. The complete code for the SortEngine class appears as follows:

```
Public Event PercentChanged(ByVal Percent As Integer, ByVal
  TimeLeft As Double)
Public Sub BubbleSort(ByVal X() As Integer)
    Dim I As Integer
    Dim J As Integer
    Dim Temp As Integer
    Dim N As Integer
    Dim Counter As Integer
    Dim Comparisons As Integer
    Dim Percent As Integer
    Dim OldPercent As Integer
    Dim StartTime As Double
    Dim TimeLeft As Double
    N = UBound(X) + 1 'Number of elements in array
    Comparisons = N * (N - 1) \ 2 'Number of comparisons
    StartTime = Microsoft.VisualBasic.Timer 'starting time to sort
    For I = 0 To UBound(X) - 1
        For J = 0 To UBound(X) - I - 1
            ' Compare and order
            If X(J) > X(J + 1) Then
                ' Out of order; swap
                Temp = X(J)
                X(J) = X(J + 1)
                X(J + 1) = Temp
            End If
            ' Code to handle event raising
            Counter += 1 'Count number of comparisons
            Percent = CInt(100 * (Counter / Comparisons))
            If Percent > OldPercent Then
                TimeLeft = (Microsoft.VisualBasic.Timer -
                    StartTime) / CDbl(Percent) * CDbl(100 - Percent)
                RaiseEvent PercentChanged(Percent, TimeLeft)
```

```
                            ' Revise OldPercent, so that this block will
                            ' execute only when Percent has changed again.
                            OldPercent = Percent
                      End If
                Next J
          Next I
    End Sub
```

Declaring and Using the Event. To use the event created in a class, the object must be declared at the module (form) level with the WithEvents keyword. For example, assume an object named Sorter is created from the preceding class to sort arrays in a form. The Sorter object should be declared at the form/class level as follows:

```
' This code is placed in the form
' that will use the SortEngine class
Dim WithEvents Sorter As New SortEngine()
```

Note that after the preceding line is placed in the code window of the form, you should be able to find the Sorter object in the code window's object box and the event in the procedure box as shown in Figure 12.4.

With this declaration, you can place code in the event in exactly the same manner as you can in all other events recognized by other objects.

Completing the Example. To continue and complete the example, go back to the form; then draw a text box, two buttons, two labels, and a progress bar.

The text box will be used to specify the upper bound for the array to sort. One button will be used to generate random numbers, and the other will be used to call the BubbleSort method. One label will be used to display the percentage; the other will be used to show the time remaining. The progress bar will be used to indicate the percentage of progress in sorting. The following table indicates how the properties of these controls should be set.

Control	Property	Setting	Remarks
Text box	Name	txtNumber	To specify the upper limit for the array to hold
	Text	(Cleared)	Numbers
Button	Name	btnGenerate	To generate the specified random numbers
	Text	Generate	
Button	Name	btnSort	To call the bubble sort routine in the SortEngine class module
	Text	Sort	
	Text	(cleared)	
Label	Name	lblPercent	To display percentage of completion
	Text	(Cleared)	
Label	Name	lblTimeLeft	To show remaining time to sort
Progress bar	Name	prgPercent	To indicate percentage of completion

Figure 12.5 shows a sample visual interface in action.

Figure 12.4

An object variable declared with events

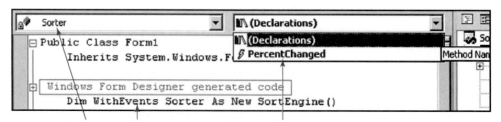

Once the Sorter object is declared **WithEvents**, you should be able to find both the object and its event(s) in the dropdown boxes on top of the code window.

Figure 12.5

Sample visual interface for the SortEngine project

When the user clicks the Generate button, the computer will generate an array of the Integer type with its upper bound equal to the number specified in the text box txtNumber. The code in the *btnGenerate_Click procedure* appears as follows:

```
Dim A() As Integer
Private Sub btnGenerate_Click(ByVal sender As System.Object, ByVal
    e As System.EventArgs) Handles btnGenerate.Click
    Dim N As Integer
    Dim I As Integer
    Dim Generator As New System.Random()
    If Len(Trim(txtNumber.Text)) = 0 Then
        MsgBox("Please enter a number")
        Exit Sub
    End If
    N = CInt(txtNumber.Text)
    ReDim A(N)
    For I = 0 To N
        'Generate a random number in the range of 0 and N - 1
        A(I) = Generator.Next(0, N)
    Next I
    prgPercent.Value = 0 'Clear the progress bar
    'Tell the user, it's done.
    MsgBox(N + 1 & " random numbers generated.")
End Sub
```

Note that for user feedback purposes, you also added two statements at the end of the procedure. One statement assigns a value of 0 to the Value property of the progress bar, and should clear the progress bar. The other statement displays a message box to inform the user of the number of random numbers generated.

When the user clicks the Sort button, your code will create a new Sorter object and then use its BubbleSort method to sort the array generated in the btnGenerate Click procedure. The ***btnSort_Click procedure*** can appear as follows:

```
Private Sub btnSort_Click(ByVal sender As System.Object, ByVal e
    As System.EventArgs) Handles btnSort.Click
    Sorter.BubbleSort(A)
End Sub
```

Because the object variable Sorter has been declared and created with New in the general declaration area, it should not be declared again. This procedure simply calls Sorter's BubbleSort method to sort array A.

How do you code the PercentChanged event? This event is triggered when the percentage of comparisons changes by a full percentile. You can use it to display the change in the labels and the progress bar. The code should appear as follows:

```
Private Sub Sorter_PercentChanged(ByVal Percent As Integer, ByVal
    TimeLeft As Double) Handles Sorter.PercentChanged
    Dim Remaining As DateTime
    lblPercent.Text = Percent & "%"
    prgPercent.Value = Percent
    Remaining = DateAdd(DateInterval.Second, TimeLeft, Today)
    lblTimeLeft.Text = "Time Left: " & Format(Remaining, "mm:ss")
    Application.DoEvents()
End Sub
```

Notice that you should obtain the event procedure template from the procedure box, not by writing your own. There is no difference between handling this event and handling any events generated by any VB objects. Notice that TimeLeft provided by the Sorter object is a Double value in seconds. You'd like to display the time in the HH:mm:ss format; therefore, that value is converted to a Date/Time value using the DateAdd function. The result is assigned to the Date/Time variable, Remaining, which is declared at the beginning of this procedure and displayed with the Format function. Percent is used to set the progress bar, and is also displayed in lblPercent. Notice also that the Application.DoEvents statement is needed for the operating system to update the appearance (Texts) of the labels.

Test this project by trying several different numbers for the upper bound of the array to get a feel. For a computer with a 1.4 gHz processor with an upper bound set to 40,000, you should see that it takes a few minutes to sort the array. Note that the bubble sort algorithm is used in this example to illustrate how the PercentChanged event can be implemented. Recall that this algorithm is the least efficient among all available sorting algorithms. You can think of its use here as a representation of a process that takes a long time.

Why Events? The sorting example illustrated thus far should give you a good appreciation of implementing events in classes. Without the PercentChanged event, a programmer using the SortEngine class will have no way to implement code to inform the user of the progress in sorting. One possible alternative is to rewrite the method (BubbleSort) so that it will take two labels and a progress bar as its parameters. It can then display the progress in these controls; however, such a design is inflexible. The programmer who uses the method will be forced to provide these controls. In addition, these controls must be of the classes of the label and the progress bar.

On the other hand, when the PercentChanged event is implemented in the class, the programmer who uses the class has complete flexibility in determining what to do with the object created from the class. The programmer can ignore the event or code the event in any manner the programmer sees fit. The combination of labels and the progress bar used in the preceding example is but one of the many possibilities.

Hooking Event Handlers

So far, you have been coding event handlers in the event procedures designated by the IDE designer. If you examine the procedure header again, you will find that each header ends with the following syntax:

```
Handles Object.Event
```

Does it have any significance? If you delete that portion from the header and test the event again, you will notice that the event procedure no longer gets invoked. This clause hooks the event handler (the event procedure you write) to the event trigger, the statement in the object that raises the event. Recall in the SortEngine class, you have a RaiseEvent statement. This is the statement that looks for an event procedure to execute (call). The *"Handles" clause* indicates which event(s) the event procedure handles.

You can actually use the same event procedure to handle more than one event as long as these events have the same parameter list. For example, suppose you have two text boxes named txtAmount1 and txtAmount2 that you want to respond the same way, such as check for numeric keys, when the user presses a key. You can actually write only one KeyPress event procedure but list the two events after Handles as follows:

```
Private Sub txtAmount_KeyPress(ByVal sender As System.Object,
   ByVal e As System.Windows.Forms.KeyPressEventArgs) Handles
   txtAmount1.KeyPress, txtAmount2.KeyPress
   Dim KeyAscii As Integer
   KeyAscii = AscW(e.KeyChar)
   Select Case KeyAscii
      Case Is < Keys.Space, Keys.D0 To Keys.D9
         'control key or numeric key; do nothing
      Case Else
```

```
                MsgBox("Numeric keys only, please.",
                   MsgBoxStyle.Information)
                e.Handled = True 'suppress the key
         End Select
     End Sub
```

Pay particular attention to the header. The sub name does not have to be associated with any particular control. It is the Handles clause that indicates what events that the procedure handles. Thus, the Handles clause allows you to hook events to their handlers at design time.

You can also hook an event with its handler at runtime by the use of the *AddHandler statement,* which has the following syntax:

```
    AddHandler Event, AddressOf Handler
```

For example, in the preceding example, if you would rather hook the events to the event handlers at runtime, you can remove the Handles clause and add the following two statements:

```
    AddHandler txtAmount1.KeyPress, AddressOf txtAmount_KeyPress
    AddHandler txtAmount2.KeyPress, AddressOf txtAmount_KeyPress
```

Of course, these two statements should be executed before the event procedures can be invoked. You can have more than one handler hooked to the same event. You can also remove the handler when it is no longer needed by the use of the RemoveHandler statement, which has the following syntax:

```
    RemoveHandler Event, AddressOf Handler
```

Hooking Event Handlers with Events of Controls Created during Runtime. The Add Handler statement is most useful when controls/objects are created during runtime. Consider the case of the data entry screen for cash flows that was discussed in Chapter 8. It was noted that the text boxes created during runtime could not deal with events, but you are now equipped to solve this problem. How? Suppose you have created a KeyPress event handler suitable to handle the Keypress event for all these text boxes (say, txtCashFlow_KeyPress). You can declare a text box variable "WithEvents" at the class level (required); then in the procedure to create the text boxes, you can add an AddHandler statement to hook each of the events to the same handler. The code fragment should appear as follows:

```
            'In the general declaration area
            Dim WithEvents txtCashFlow As TextBox
            'In the procedure that creates text boxes
            For I =0 To N
                txtCashFlow = New TextBox() 'Create a new text box
                AddHandler txtCashFlow.KeyPress, AddressOf
                  txtCashFlow_KeyPress
                'Other statements
            Next I
```

The additional details in making the project work are left to you as exercise 12-23.

You may wonder how the AddHandler statement is different from the Call statement. In many ways, they are similar; however, recall that events are triggered from objects to which your code is expected to respond. In other words, the call is made from the object to the handler (the Sub you write). The AddHandler statement informs the object of which sub to use, while the Call statement informs your own routine of which sub to use.

12.4   Nested Classes

A class can contain one or more other classes, which can in turn contain yet others forming a class of *nested classes.* Usually, the *inner classes* are exposed as properties of the *outer classes.* This arrangement is similar to what you have seen in ADO.NET. For example, the dataset contains the datatable, which contains data rows and data columns, each in turn having its own methods and properties.

Scope of Inner Class. Recall that a class at the module level must be either Public or Friend. Inner classes, however, can have a narrower scope. They can be declared as Private. A Private class can be referenced only within the class that contains it. Private classes are typically used to support the operations of their outer classes. They tend to contain code that pertains only to the internal operations, and therefore should be encapsulated (hidden from the outside world).

Uses of Nested Classes. Is there any practical business application of nested class? Imagine a depositor object that has properties such as the depositor ID, address, and other profile information. In addition, it can have two accounts: checking and savings. Each of these accounts has its properties such as account number, balance, interest rate, compensating balance, and so on, and methods such as deposit and withdraw. These accounts logically belong in the depositor class, and should be treated as such. Notice that although the accounts are properties of the depositor, they have methods, so these properties themselves must be objects to be able to have methods. You can solve this problem in the following manner: Let the depositor class contain the account class with the required properties and methods; then the checking account and savings account objects can be instantiated from the account class, and present themselves as the properties of the depositor class. The following subsection illustrates how the code can be developed.

Developing the Depositor Class

To illustrate how to code the nested classes, use the depositor problem described previously as an example. For simplicity, the depositor will have the depositor ID, checking account, and savings account properties. Because the checking account and savings account properties are instantiated from the account class, you will write the account class inside the depositor class, creating a nested class with the depositor as the outer class and the account as the inner class.

Call this new project **BankDepositor**. Before writing any code, add a class module to this new project, and name it **Depositor**. You will first create the property for the DepositorID. This should be fairly straightforward and is left to you to complete. You can now pay full attention to creating the Account class. This is a class inside the depositor class. So, the code structure should appear as follows:

```
Public Class Depositor
    ' Statements for the Depositor ID property
    '
    Public Class Account
    End Class
End Class
```

Notice that the Account class is Public because it needs to be accessible to the code external to the Depositor class as properties.

Exposing the Account class as Properties of the Depositor.
Recall that the depositor has two types of accounts: checking and savings, which are exposed as properties. Setting up these two properties is similar to that for other typical properties. You have to be aware that these two properties should be read-only, and be of the Account class. To create the CheckingAccount property, you can first set up an internal member (inside the depositor but outside the Account class) as follows:

```
Private mCheckingAccount As New Account()
```

Notice that the variable has been instantiated with the New keyword, so mCheckingAccount is an instance (object) of the Account class (type). The read-only CheckingAccount property is defined as follows:

```
Public ReadOnly Property CheckingAccount() As Account
    Get
        Return (mCheckingAccount)
    End Get
End Property
```

The code in effect returns an instance of the Account class as the CheckingAccount property. Because Account is a class, CheckingAccount is an object with all the properties and methods that Account has (will have). In a similar fashion, you can create the SavingsAccount property. The code is shown later in this subsection.

Properties and Methods of the Account Class. Coding the properties and methods for the Account class is no different from that for a typical class. The class has two properties: AccountNo and Balance. Balance should be read-only so that the amount is changed by deposit and withdraw only, not by an accidental setting. The class has two methods: Deposit and Withdraw. The former increases the account balance; the later decreases.

Complete Code for the Depositor Class. The code for the Depositor class should appear as follows:

```
Public Class Depositor
    Private mDepositorID As Integer
    Private mSavingsAccount As New Account()
    Private mCheckingAccount As New Account()
    Public Property DepositorID() As Integer
        Get
            Return (mDepositorID)
        End Get
        Set(ByVal Value As Integer)
            mDepositorID = Value
        End Set
    End Property
    Public ReadOnly Property CheckingAccount() As Account
        Get
            Return (mCheckingAccount)
        End Get
    End Property
    Public ReadOnly Property SavingsAccount() As Account
        Get
            Return (mSavingsAccount)
        End Get
    End Property
    Public Class Account
        Private mBalance As Double
        Private mAccountNo As Integer
        Public ReadOnly Property Balance() As Double
            Get
                Return (mBalance)
            End Get
        End Property
        Public Property AccountNo() As Integer
            Get
                Return (mAccountNo)
            End Get
            Set(ByVal Value As Integer)
                mAccountNo = Value
            End Set
        End Property
        Public Function Deposit(ByVal Amount As Double) As Double
            mBalance += Amount
            Return (mBalance)
        End Function
        Public Function Withdraw(ByVal Amount As Double) As Double
            mBalance -= Amount
            Return (mBalance)
        End Function
    End Class
End Class
```

Figure 12.6

Visual interface for
depositor activity

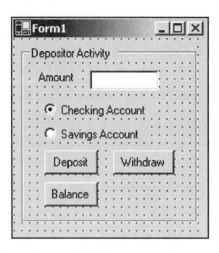

Using the Depositor Class

To illustrate how the Depositor class as developed can be used in code, go back to the form and create a visual interface as shown in Figure 12.6. The interface is used to keep track of the depositor's activities. For simplicity, assume the depositor is given. The user enters the amount, selects an account (checking or savings), and selects an action (deposit or withdraw). The account is updated accordingly. At anytime, the user can click the Balance button to find out the balance of the account of interest based on the radio button selected.

The following table shows the names of the controls used in code:

Control	Name	Remark
Text box	txtAmount	For the user to enter the amount
Radio button	rbtChecking	To indicate checking account (set its Checked property to True to make it the default)
Radio button	rbtSavings	To indicate savings account
Button	btnDeposit	To initiate deposit
Button	btnWithdraw	To initiate withdraw
Button	btnBalance	To show account balance

Because it is assumed that the depositor is given, the object is created with the New keyword at the form/class level where it is declared:

```
Dim TheDepositor As New Depositor()
```

Referencing the Accounts in the Depositor Class. Recall that you created two Account properties (CheckingAccount and SavingsAccount) for the Depositor class. How should they be referenced in the module that uses the Depositor object? They are referenced literally:

```
TheDepositor.CheckingAccount
TheDepositor.SavingsAccount
```

To call the Deposit method for the CheckingAccount property, you will code:

```
TheDepositor.CheckingAccount.Deposit(Amount)
```

Handling the Button Click Events. When the user clicks the Deposit button, the program should check which radio button is selected and deposit the amount to the proper account. The Withdraw and Balance button Click events can be handled similarly. The code should appear as follows:

```
Private Sub btnDeposit_Click(ByVal sender As System.Object, ByVal
    e As System.EventArgs) Handles btnDeposit.Click
    Dim Amount As Double
    Amount = Val(txtAmount.Text)
    If rbtChecking.Checked Then
        TheDepositor.CheckingAccount.Deposit(Amount)
    Else
        TheDepositor.SavingsAccount.Deposit(Amount)
    End If
End Sub
Private Sub btnWithdraw_Click(ByVal sender As System.Object, ByVal
    e As System.EventArgs) Handles btnWithdraw.Click
    Dim Amount As Double
    Amount = Val(txtAmount.Text)
    If rbtChecking.Checked Then
        TheDepositor.CheckingAccount.Withdraw(Amount)
    Else
        TheDepositor.SavingsAccount.Withdraw(Amount)
    End If
End Sub
Private Sub btnBalance_Click(ByVal sender As System.Object, ByVal
    e As System.EventArgs) Handles btnBalance.Click
    If rbtChecking.Checked Then
        MsgBox("Checking account balance is " &
            TheDepositor.CheckingAccount.Balance)
    Else
        MsgBox("Savings account balance is " &
            TheDepositor.SavingsAccount.Balance)
    End If
End Sub
```

Additional Remarks

The depositor class is used to illustrate how to code nested classes and create properties from the inner class. Of course, the class can be enhanced in several ways. Additional properties can be included at each level of classes. Events can also be added. For example, in the Withdraw method, you can create an NSF (insufficient fund) event, which is triggered when the amount to be drawn is greater than the account balance. The programmer using your Depositor class can then decide what to do with the situation, such as ignore or prompt for the user direction. These desirable refinements are left to you to complete.

Nested classes can make your code more complex. Use this kind of structure only when it is logical and necessary. Avoid creating very complex nested classes. They are harder to use. In general, a flat object model (class without nesting) is simpler and preferable.

12.5   The Visual Element in an Object

At the beginning of this chapter, it was stated that a class module is a form without the visual element. What if you need an object that requires the visual element? All you need is a form and then you can treat it like all other objects.

Treating the Form as an Object

A form is indeed a class. Take a look at the code window of a new form. Its first statement starts with Public Class followed by the form name. It differs from a plain class module in that it inherits from the Form class (second statement in a new form module) and therefore has the visual element that allows the programmer to further modify with the help of the IDE Designer.

The form has been treated the same as other class modules and code accordingly. Chapter 11, "Menus and Multiple-Form Applications," showed how multiple copies of the same form could be created in exactly the same manner as any class. For example, if you have created a form named frmEmployee, frmEmployee can be used in the following manner in another module:

```
Dim Smith As frmEmployee
Dim Johnson As frmEmployee
' Create an employee object and name it Smith
Smith = New frmEmployee()
' statements pertaining to Smith
' Create an employee object and name it Johnson
Johnson = New frmEmployee()
' statements pertaining to Johnson
```

Of course, if you intend to use the form as a class from which to create instances, you should code the form like a typical class. That is, you should design the form such that it has properties, methods, and events that other modules (form, class, or standard modules) can use. You should be careful in code design to avoid making specific references to members in other modules that you are coding in the same project. In addition, you should be aware that Public variables in the form are read-and-write properties, whereas Public procedures are methods; therefore, you should avoid using Public variables, but rather create Public properties in their place. Public variables allow the client code to set them at any values. In contrast, you can code data validation rules in the Set procedure in the property definition, ensuring the integrity of the value. Recall that the Set procedure of the DepreMethod property of the FixedAsset class was used to ensure that the setting is not out of range.

A Count Down Clock

To illustrate the use of a form as a visual object, consider a Count Down clock class. (Add a new form to a new project and then name this new form CountDownClock to create this class). Suppose you would like to have an object that you can set the initial length of time to count down and the interval that the timer ticks down. The programmer can also set the Disappear property, which when set to True (default) will make the object disappear when the countdown is complete. The countdown object also provides a Start method to start the countdown, and displays the remaining time on the visual interface that appears as shown in Figure 12.7.

The box used to display the remaining time (in seconds) is a label, and is named lblTimeLeft. The time left is tracked by a timer named tmrCountDown. These controls should not be accessible to any other module, and therefore their Modifiers property should be set to Private instead of the Friend default. The code for this CountDownClock class appears as follows:

```
Public Class CountDownClock
    Inherits System.Windows.Forms.Form
    Dim mTimeRemaining As Double
    Dim mInterval As Integer
    Dim mTickBy As Double = 0.1
    Dim mDisappear As Boolean = True
    WriteOnly Property TimeRemaining() As Double
        Set(ByVal Value As Double)
            mTimeRemaining = Value
        End Set
    End Property
    WriteOnly Property TickBy() As Double
        Set(ByVal Value As Double)
```

Figure 12.7

Visual appearance of the countdown object

```
                    If Value >= 0.001 Then
                        mTickBy = Value
                        mInterval = CInt(1000 * Value)
                        tmrCountDown.Interval = mInterval
                    End If
                End Set
            End Property
            WriteOnly Property Disappear() As Boolean
                Set(ByVal Value As Boolean)
                    mDisappear = Value
                End Set
            End Property
            Sub Start()
                Me.Show()
                tmrCountDown.Start()
            End Sub
            Private Sub tmrCountDown_Tick(ByVal sender As System.Object,
              ByVal e As System.EventArgs) Handles tmrCountDown.Tick
                mTimeRemaining -= mTickBy
                If mTimeRemaining > 0 Then
                    lblTimeLeft.Text = Format(mTimeRemaining, "####0.000")
                Else
                    mTimeRemaining = 0
                    tmrCountDown.Stop()
                    If mDisappear Then
                        Me.Close()
                    End If
                End If
            End Sub
        End Class
```

The class has three write-only properties: TimeRemaining, TickBy, and Disappear. The first
two properties are used to keep track of time in seconds. The Start method will display the form
and start the timer, using the timer's *Start method*, which enables the timer and will raise the Tick
event at a regular interval specified by the Interval property, which is set when the TickBy property is set. Recall that one unit of the Interval property is equal to one millisecond, while TickBy
is measured in seconds. Thus, one unit (second) of TickBy is equal to 1,000 units of Interval.
Both TickBy and Interval have a default of 1/10 of a second. Because the timer cannot handle
any interval value less than one millisecond, when an attempt is made to set the TickBy property
to a smaller value, the Set procedure will simply ignore the attempted setting.

In the timer Tick event, TimeRemaining is decreased by TickBy, the time length that has
elapsed since last Tick event. The remaining time will be displayed for as long as it is greater
than zero; then, it is reset to zero. The timer is disabled by its *Stop method*. If the Disappear property is set to True (default), the form (object) is also closed.

Using the Count Down Clock

Using the CountDownClock object is fairly straightforward. Create the object, and set the
RemainingTime and the TickBy properties; then, invoke the object's Start method. If you want
the visual display to continue to appear after the countdown becomes zero, you can also set its
Disappear property to False. The following code (in Form1) creates an object named
CountDownClock, sets its TimeRemaining to 15 seconds, sets its TickBy interval to one hun-
dredth of a second, and calls its Start method to start the countdown immediately.

```
Dim CountDownClock As New CountDownClock()
    With CountDownClock
        .TimeRemaining = 15 'Show 15 seconds when the count down
            starts
        .TickBy = .01 'Show change by every 1/100 of a second
        .Start()
End With
```

You can place the code in an event procedure to see how the countdown clock object works. Figure 12.7 shows the object in action.

One of the focal points of object-oriented programming is encapsulation. Data and code within the class should be completely isolated from other modules. The only parts that can be exposed to the outside world are the object's properties, methods, and events. In addition, the code should not make any direct reference to any members in another module that your class is designed to serve; otherwise, the code will become entangled. Hopefully, the examples in this chapter illustrate these points clearly.

Summary

- A class is a code template or blueprint that defines the characteristics of an object. An object is a special instance of a class.

- The advantages of object-oriented programming include encapsulation, code reusability and maintainability, uniform data validation rules, and easier project management.

- Classes are developed in class modules. A typical class module differs from a form module in that it does not have the visual elements. A class module differs from a standard module in that multiple copies (objects) can be instantiated from the class module, but there is only one copy of the standard module in the project.

- A class module can be added to the project in a way similar to adding a new form or a standard module.

- A class can be created by placing code within the Class. . . End Class block on the class module. Code in the class should be related to the purpose of the class and nothing else.

- Properties of a class can be created with Property procedures. The Get procedure returns the value (setting) of the property and the Set procedure allows the client code to set the value for the property. Data validation rules can be placed in the Set procedure to ensure the validity of the property setting.

- Public variables in a class are properties; however, use of public variables in place of property definitions is not advisable because it is not possible to implement data validation rules with public variable declarations.

- Public functions and subs in a class are exposed externally as methods of the class.

- There is no difference in instantiating and using the objects between classes developed in a project and classes provided by others, such as those in the .NET framework.

- The Sub New method is the constructor of the class, and is automatically executed when an instance of the class is instantiated. It is typically used to initialize properties and data used in the class.

- The FixedAsset class is used as an example to show how elements of a class can be coded.

- The Enum. . . End Enum block is used to enumerate constants for any particular group of data with meaningful names.

- When code outside of a class can cause an error in the class, one good way to handle the situation is to throw an exception. This allows the developer of the client code to identify and correct the error. The names of most exceptions are already available in the system. The list of exception names can be found in the Exceptions option of the Debug menu although user-defined exceptions can also be created.

- To create an event for a class, the event must be declared at the class level. It can then be raised in a procedure with the RaiseEvent statement.

- To use the event of a class in another module, the instance of the class must be declared with the WithEvents keyword. The event procedure can then be coded in exactly the same manner as all events recognized by those controls discussed in the textbook.

- The SortEngine example is used to illustrate how an event can be implemented in a class and used in another module (form).
- The Handles clause at the end of an event procedure header hooks the event procedure (handler) with the event. You can place more than one event in the Handles clause. If you do so, the event handler (procedure) will be invoked when any of these events is raised.
- Event handlers and events can be dynamically hooked and removed with the AddHandler and RemoveHandler statements. The Cashflow data entry project in Chapter 8 was revisited to illustrate the usefulness of the AddHandler statement to hook event handlers with events associated with controls created during runtime.
- A class can contain one or more other classes, which can in turn contain yet others, forming a class of nested classes. Usually, the inner classes are exposed as properties of the outer classes. To expose an inner class as a property, declare a property as the inner class type; then treat the property in a manner similar to any other types of properties.
- The example of the Depositor class and its inner Account class is used to illustrate how to code and expose an inner class as a property of its outer class.
- The form is a class, and can be used to create objects with visual elements. The CountDownClock class was used to illustrate how to create a class for this purpose.

Explore and Discover

12-1.   More Than One Class in a Class Module? Add a class module to a new form; then place the following code in the class module:

```
Public Class Class1
End Class
Public Class Class2
End Class
```

Next, place the following code in the form's Click event:

```
Dim MyObject1 As New Class1()
Dim MyObject2 As New Class2()
```

Run the project. Do you encounter any errors? You should not. You can have more than one class in a class module, and they will work just fine. The problem is how you will locate these classes in the future. Placing more than one class in a class module is not a good practice, although you are allowed to do so.

12-2.   Timing of Creation and Destruction of an Object. Add a class module to a new project, and place the following code in the class module in the preceding exercise as follows:

```
Public Class Class1
    Sub New()
        MyBase.new()
        MsgBox("I'm being initialized")
    End Sub
    Protected Overrides Sub Finalize()
        MsgBox("I'm being destroyed")
        MyBase.Finalize()
    End Sub
End Class
```

Place the following code in the form:

```
Dim MyObject1 As Class1
Private Sub Form1_Click(ByVal sender As System.Object, ByVal e As
   System.EventArgs) Handles MyBase.Click
   MyObject1 = New Class1()
End Sub
```

Notice the location of the object variable declaration.

Run the project. Do you see the "I'm being initialized" message? Now click the form. Do you
see the message? This indicates that the Sub New procedure is called automatically when the
object is being instantiated.

But do you see the "I'm being destroyed" message? Click the form's Close button. Do you see
the message? The Sub Finalize procedure is automatically called when an object is *actually*
destroyed. This also appears to suggest that objects are destroyed when their associated variables
are out of scope. But wait. Check out the experiment in the following exercise.

12-3.   **Timing of Creation and Destruction of an Object.** (continued from exercise 12-2)
Revise the code in the form in the preceding exercise as follows:

```
Private Sub Form1_Click(ByVal sender As System.Object, ByVal e As
   System.EventArgs) Handles MyBase.Click
   Dim MyObject1 As Class1
   MyObject1 = New Class1()
End Sub
```

Run the project and then click the form. Do you see the "I'm being initialized" message? But do
you see "I'm being destroyed" message? Objects are initialized with the New keyword, but they
are not necessarily automatically destroyed immediately after their associated names are out of
scope although you no longer are able to reference to them.

Click the form's Close button. Do you see the "I'm being destroyed" message? Objects may not
be destroyed until your project ends regardless of their scope.

12-4.   **Timing of Creation and Destruction of the Form Object.** Add a new form (Form2)
to a new project. Expand the code in Form2 in the #Region "Windows Form Designer generated
code" area; then add statements in the Sub New and Sub Dispose procedures as follows:

```
Public Sub New()
    MyBase.New()
    'This call is required by the Windows Form Designer.
    InitializeComponent()
    'Add any initialization after the InitializeComponent() call
    MsgBox("I'm being initialized") 'Add this line
End Sub
'Form overrides dispose to clean up the component list.
Protected Overloads Overrides Sub Dispose(ByVal disposing As
   Boolean)
    If disposing Then
        If Not (components Is Nothing) Then
            components.Dispose()
        End If
    End If
    MsgBox("I'm being destroyed") 'Add this line
    MyBase.Dispose(disposing)
End Sub
```

Place the following code in Form1:

```
Private Sub Form1_Click(ByVal sender As System.Object, ByVal e As
    System.EventArgs) Handles MyBase.Click
    Dim MyObject1 As Form2
    MyObject1 = New Form2()
End Sub
```

Run the project, and click the form. Is the "I'm being initialized" messages displayed? But is the "I'm being destroyed" message displayed? After it is instantiated, the form stays with the project until the user clicks its Close button, its Close method is called, or the project ends, regardless of the scope of the form variable.

12-5.   **Timing of Creation and Destruction of the Form Object.** (continued from exercise 12-4) Modify the code in Form1 as follows:

```
Private Sub Form1_Click(ByVal sender As System.Object, ByVal e As
    System.EventArgs) Handles MyBase.Click
    Dim MyObject1 As Form2
    MyObject1 = New Form2()
    MyObject1 = Nothing
End Sub
```

Run the project and then click the form. Are both the "I'm being initialized" and "I'm being destroyed" messages displayed? You should see only the "I'm initialized" message. The object is not immediately destroyed even when its associated variable is set to Nothing.

12-6.   **Timing of Creation and Destruction of the Form Object.** (continued from exercise 12-5) Modify the code in the preceding exercise as follows:

```
Private Sub Form1_Click(ByVal sender As System.Object, ByVal e As
    System.EventArgs) Handles MyBase.Click
    Dim MyObject1 As Form2
    MyObject1 = New Form2()
    MyObject1.Dispose()
End Sub
```

Run the project, and click the form. Are both "I'm being initialized" and "I'm being destroyed" messages displayed? You can explicitly call the object's Dispose method to destroy the object immediately, but you are not allowed to call the Finalize method to do the same. (See Chapter 13 for explanation of the two methods.)

12-7.   **You Can Raise Events in a Form, Too.** Add a new form (Form2) to a new project. Draw a button on this form (Form2), name the button **btnClick**, and set its Text property to **Click**. Place the following code in this form:

```
Public Event ActionOccurred()
Private Sub btnClick_Click(ByVal sender As System.Object, ByVal e
    As System.EventArgs) Handles btnClick.Click
    RaiseEvent ActionOccurred()
End Sub
```

Go back to Form1. Draw a button on the form, name the button **btnShow,** and set its Text property to **Show Form2**; then place the following code in this form:

```
Dim WithEvents ActionForm As Form2
Private Sub btnShow_Click(ByVal sender As System.Object, ByVal e
  As System.EventArgs) Handles btnShow.Click
    ActionForm = New Form2()
    ActionForm.Show()
End Sub
Private Sub ActionForm_ActionOccurred() Handles
  ActionForm.ActionOccurred
    MsgBox("Someone has clicked the Click button")
End Sub
```

Run the project, click the Show Form2 button, and click the Click button in Form2. Each time you do so, you should see the "Someone has clicked the Click button" message.

Can you see the use of this code arrangement? One form (Form1) can be used to monitor the activities in another form (Form2), which can inform the other of what happens by raising an event.

12-8. **Beware of the Difference.** (continued from exercise 12-7) Add the following code to Form1 in the preceding exercise:

```
Private Sub Form1_Click(ByVal sender As System.Object, ByVal e As
  System.EventArgs) Handles MyBase.Click
    Dim ActionForm As New Form2()
    ActionForm.Show()
End Sub
```

Run the project and click on Form1—the form itself, not the Show Form2 button. When Form2 appears, click its Click button. Do you see any message displayed? Why?

Click Form1's title bar to set focus on Form1; then click the Show Form2 button to display *another Form2*. Click the Click button on the newly displayed form. Do you see a message? Alternate the focus between the two Form2's and then click the Click button to confirm that one sends messages and the other does not.

How do you explain the difference? The ActionForm object created in the Button Click event procedure is associated with an object variable declared "WithEvents." It is capable of recognizing the event raised from the object. The ActionForm object created in the Form Click event procedure is not declared "WithEvents," and therefore cannot recognize the event.

12-9. **What Comes Next?** Enter the following code in a new form:

```
Enum TestType
    Test1
    Test2
    Test3
End Enum
Private Sub Form1_Click(ByVal sender As System.Object, ByVal e As
  System.EventArgs) Handles MyBase.Click
    Console.WriteLine(TestType.Test1 & TestType.Test2 &
      TestType.Test3)
End Sub
```

Run the project and then click the form. What numbers do you see in the immediate window?

Change Test1 in the Enum block as follows:

```
Test1 = 1
```

Run the project and then click the form again. This time what do you see?

Change the Enum block so that it will appear as follows:

```
Enum TestType
    Test1
    Test2 = 2
    Test3
End Enum
```

Run the project, and click the form again. What do you see this time? What is your conclusion concerning the items not being assigned with a value? (When nothing is assigned, the first member is zero. If a name is assigned with a value when the next one is not, the next one is one greater than the preceding value.)

12-10.   **The Handles Clause.** Draw a button on a new form. Name the button **btnTest,** and set its text to **Test**. Place the following in code window:

```
Private Sub btnTest_Click(ByVal sender As System.Object, ByVal e
    As System.EventArgs) Handles btnTest.Click
      MsgBox("Test")
End Sub
```

Run the project, and click the button to make sure that the "Test" message is displayed.

Add another button to the form. Name the button **btnTest1**, and set its text to Test1. Modify the Handles clause in the preceding procedure as follows:

```
Handles btnTest.Click, btnTest1.Click
```

Run the project, and click both buttons. Is the "Test" message displayed when each button is clicked?

Now remove the Handles clause so that the procedure header appears as follows:

```
Private Sub btnTest_Click(ByVal sender As System.Object, ByVal e
    As System.EventArgs)
```

Run the program again and then click both buttons. Is the "Test" message displayed when either of the buttons is clicked? Without the Handles clause, the event procedure (handler) is not invoked.

12-11.   The AddHandler Statement. (continued from exercise 12-10) Now add the following code in the Form Click event procedure to the preceding project.

```
AddHandler btnTest1.Click, AddressOf btnTest_Click
```

Run the project, and click both buttons. Is the "Test" message displayed when either of the buttons is clicked? Not yet. Now click the form and then click both buttons again. When is the "Test" message displayed? Notice that the event and the event handler are not hooked to each other until the AddHandler statement is executed. Notice also that in the AddHandler statement, btnTest1.Click is the event hooked to the event procedure. So, when you click the Test1 (not Test) button the message is displayed. The name of the event procedure itself does not determine which control's event is hooked. The AddHandler statement or the Handles clause does.

Now try to make the event procedure handle the click event of both buttons. (Either an AddHandler statement or the Handles clause should do.)

12-12.   How the Shared Property Works. Add a class module to a new project. Place the following code in the module:

```
Public Class Class1
    Public Shared Count As Integer
    Public ID As Integer
    Sub New()
        MyBase.new()
        Count += 1
        ID = +1
    End Sub
End Class
```

Place the following code in the form click event procedure:

```
Console.WriteLine(Class1.Count)
```

Do you see anything underlined? A Shared variable can be referenced with the class name. Now try to add the following statement:

```
Console.WriteLine(Class1.ID)
```

Is there an error? Public variables are properties and must be referenced with the object name. Remove this line from the code.

Add a button to the form. Name it **btnCreate** and then set its text to **Create Object**. Place the following code in the code window:

```
Private Sub btnCreate_Click(ByVal sender As System.Object, ByVal e
    As System.EventArgs) Handles btnCreate.Click
    Dim MyObject As New Class1()
    Console.WriteLine("Count = " & MyObject.Count)
    Console.WriteLine("ID = " & MyObject.ID)
End Sub
```

Run the project and then click the button several times. Inspect the results in the immediate window. You should see the value for Count increases each time you click the button, but the value for ID remains to be 1. Each instance of the class has its own ID property, but all instances share the same Count property because it is declared as Shared.

Also click the form. You should notice that it displays the same value as the value for Count in the Button Click event procedure. Class1.Count and MyObject.Count both refer to the same property. Actually, Shared methods work the same way, too. Design an experiment to verify for yourself.

Exercises

12-13.   An Employee Class. Create an employee class named Employee that has the following properties:

Field (Property)	Type
SSN	Long
Name	String
HourlyRate	Double

It has a GrossPay method that computes the gross pay of the employee. The method requires the number of hours worked (Double) as the parameter.

Draw a button in the form. Set its Text property to **Compute**. When the user clicks the button, your program will create an employee object named TheEmployee. Set its SSN, Name, and HourlyRate properties to 123456789, John Smith, and 70, respectively; then use its GrossPay method to compute the gross pay for working 50 hours in a week (overtime pay is 1.5 times of the regular rate). Use a message box to display the following message:

John Smith (employee number 123-45-6789) worked 50 hours, and is paid $x,xxx

(Replace x,xxx with proper amount.)

12-14.   **A Depositor Class.** Create a depositor class, and name it **Depositor**. The class should have the following properties:

Properties	Type
AccountNumber	Long
Name	String
Balance	Decimal (read-only)

It has two methods: Deposit and Withdraw. Both methods require one parameter (Amount) of the Decimal type. Deposit adds the value of the parameter to Balance, while Withdraw subtracts the value of the parameter from Balance. If the amount to be withdrawn is greater than the Balance, the object should raise an NSF event, which gives the Balance (before the withdrawal) and a Boolean variable, OK (with a default value, False). If OK is set to True in the calling module, the withdrawal is processed; otherwise, it is denied.

Test and use the class in a new project as follows:

1. Draw a text box, two radio buttons, and two buttons on the form. The text box will be used to enter the amount of deposit or withdrawal. The two radio buttons will be used to indicate whether the amount is a deposit or withdrawal. One button will have the text Process Transaction. When it is clicked, the amount in the text box will be processed either by the Deposit method or Withdraw method, depending on the radio button selected. The other button will have the text Quit. When this button is clicked, your program quits.
2. The object's Account Number and Name properties should be set to 1111 and Jane Doe, respectively. The initial balance is zero.
3. When the program runs, the user can enter an amount in the text box, select the proper radio button and then click the Process button. After the amount is processed, the balance is displayed in a message box, and the text box is cleared. When the object raises the NSF event, your program should display a message, ask the user whether to proceed with the transaction, and handle it accordingly.

12-15.   **A Student Class.** Create a Student class that has the following properties:

Property	Type	Description
Number	Long	Student ID number
Name	String	Student name
CourseCount	Long	Returns the number of courses enrolled; read-only

The number and name properties can be set only once in the duration of the object. Attempts to set these properties more than once should cause a "Property already set" exception.

The class has three methods:

The Enroll method takes Course ID as a parameter, and adds the Course ID to an array that tracks the courses enrolled. (*Hint:* Use ReDim Preserve to increase the size of the array to accommodate the new course.) An attempt to enroll a course already in the course list will cause an exception.

The Drop method removes a course from the Courses list. An attempt to remove a course not already in the list will cause an exception.

The Courses method returns a string array that contains the courses in which the student has enrolled.

Draw a text box and three buttons on the form. The text box with proper label will be used to enter the course ID. One button has the text Enroll. When it is clicked, the course ID in the text box will be added to the student's course list. Another button has the text Drop. When it is clicked, the course ID indicated in the text box will be removed from the course list. Finally, the third button has the text Show. When it is clicked, the courses in which the student has enrolled will be displayed in a message box.

The Number and Name properties will be set to 123456789 and John Doe, respectively, by code as soon as the project starts.

12-16. **A Student Class with Database Tables.** Modify exercise 12-15 so that when the Number property is set for the Student object, the student name and the courses enrolled are retrieved from the Students database, which contains two tables: Students and StudentCourse Tables.

The Students table has the following fields:

Field	Description
RecordNo	Record number; auto number; primary key
Number	Student ID number (SSN), Integer
Name	Student name, String

The StudentCourse table has the following fields:

Field	Description
Number	Student ID Number (SSN), Integer
Course	Course ID such as Acct5335-501

The form that uses the Student object has the following:

A text box (with a proper label) for the user to enter the student number

A label to display the student name (with a proper label)

A text box to enter/display a course ID

A list box to display the courses enrolled

A button to enroll a new course

A button to drop a course

A button to quit the application

When your program runs, as soon as the user leaves the Student Number field (except for going to the list box or the Quit button), the program sets the Number property of the Student object, which then will proceed to set all other pertinent properties or internal member variable(s) (Courses and CourseCount). (*Hint:* Add a routine in the class module to retrieve the student enrollment data; then use the retrieved data to set mCourseCount and the mCourses array).

A student must already exist before the student can enroll in or drop a course. The student name and courses enrolled should be displayed in the controls described previously. Note that the Enroll and Drop methods should be modified to take care of adding records to and deleting records from the StudentCourse table when called.

12-17.   Use of the Constructor. (refer to exercise 11-27 in Chapter 11) Modify the project so that the dialog box will appear and accept the calling form's text box as its parameter when the dialog box is instantiated. This modification should eliminate the need for the FindNext method described in exercise 11-27. (Hint: Use the Sub New constructor.)

12-18.   Revisiting the Fixed Asset Class. Modify the FixedAsset class in the text as follows:

Add an additional (accounting) depreciation method called the double declining balance method so that the DepreMethod will have three alternative settings (0, no depreciation; 1, straight line depreciation; and 2, double declining balance). This method is explained at the end of this exercise.

Add the Depreciation (class) method and the CumulativeDepreciation method. Both methods will take Years as their parameter, and return the current depreciation and the cumulative depreciation amount for the specified year(s), respectively.

Add the DepreMethodChanged event. This event will be raised when the user tries to change the depreciation method for an existing asset; that is, the user is allowed to set the DepreMethod once. Any subsequent attempt to change the depreciation (accounting) method will cause this event to be raised. This event should have three parameters: OriginalMethod, NewMethod, and Cancel. The first two show the pertinent depreciation methods. The last parameter allows the user to cancel the change.

Use the following formula to compute the depreciation of the double declining balance method for a given year:

$$Depreciation = (2 / N) * Current\ Net\ Book\ Value$$

Where N is the life of the asset in years and *Current Net Book Value* equals cost minus cumulative depreciation.

If the straight line method on the current net book value results in a higher depreciation amount, the straight line method should be used. That is,

If Current net book value / Remaining life > Current net book value * (2 / N), Depreciation = Current net book value / Remaining life.

Test the class module by designing a user interface in the form that allows the user to enter/specify the asset's cost, life, years in use, and the depreciation method. Use radio buttons for depreciation methods. Each time a radio button is clicked, the DepreMethod property is set. Clicking these buttons more than once should raise the DepreMethodChanged event. Your program should then warn the user of the change, and ask if the user means to change. A No answer should cancel the change. When the user clicks the Compute button, your program should show the current depreciation, cumulative depreciation, and book value in three text-boxes, respectively.

12-19.   An Apartment Class (Nested). Create an apartment class that has two properties: Bedroom and Kitchen. Each of these properties has the Size property expressed in squared feet, and the FurnitureList property returns a list of furniture and fixtures in the room. Each property also has an AddFurniture method that allows the user to add a furniture item to the furniture list. This method takes a string variable as its parameter, representing the furniture item. Because both the Bedroom and Kitchen properties have the same method and properties, you should write an inner class and then create the two properties from this class.

12-20.   The Search Engine. Create a search engine class that will allow the user to specify by code the database name, the table name, the field name on which to search, and the field name for which a value should be returned. The search engine should have a visual interface that allows the user to specify the search text (use a text box), to invoke the search method (use a button with a text Search), and to signal acceptance of the result (use another button with a text OK). There should also be a data grid. When the user clicks the Search button, the grid should show the two fields (field to search on and field to return value) of all records whose search on field values match the value of the search text. When the user clicks a cell in the data grid, the values of the two fields are displayed in two labels shown above the data grid. When the user clicks the OK button, the text of the label representing the field to search for (return) is returned in a read-only property named Result. See Figure 12.8 for a sample user interface in action. As soon as all the three database properties (the database name, search on field, and return field) are set, your class should verify that they exist and then throw an exception if one of them does not exist.

Test the engine in the following manner: In the main form, add a button. Name it **btnTest**. In its Click event, create a search engine object, set its DatabaseName property to a database familiar to you, such as grocertogo. Also set the TableName, SearchOnField, and ReturnField Properties available in the database, such as Products, ProductName, and ProductID.

Figure 12.8

Visual interface for the search engine

This search engine object allows the programmer to set the DatabaseName, TableName, SearchOnField, and ReturnField for a search in a database. After the user enters the search string and clicks the Search button, the data grid will show the two fields of all the rows whose search-on field values match the search text. When the user selects (clicks on) a row in the data grid, the field values of this row are displayed in the labels above the grid. The Text property of the right label is set as the Result when the user is done with the search.

Now place a text box for the return field such as ProductID, with a proper label, on the left side of the Test button. Add additional code in the button's Click event so that when the user clicks this button, the SearchEngine will be invoked, and when the user is done with the search by clicking the OK button in the search engine, the result will be displayed in the text box.

12-21.   A Simulation Engine. Refer to exercise 7-38 in Chapter 7, "Repetition." Modify the project so that the simulation process is done in an object. The visual interface in the form can then be used to accept input from the user and call the object.

12-22.   A Sort Class with an Event. Create a Sort class module with two of your favorite sorting algorithms. The SortAlgorithm property allows the user (or programmer) to specify the sorting algorithm to use. The programmer should be able to specify the sorting algorithm by a named constant, such as sortBubble or sortQuick. One of these algorithms should be set as the default. The class has an Exec method that will carry out the sorting. This method takes an array as its parameter, which will be sorted. In both sorting routines, implement an event called PercentChanged, which will be fired as the percentile of sort completion changes. The event should provide the following header template:

```
Private Sub Object_PercentChanged(Percent As Integer)
```

Draw two radio buttons, two buttons, a list box, and a label in a new form. The radio buttons will be used to specify the sorting algorithm to use. One button will have the text Generate. When it is clicked, 10,000 random numbers of the Long type will be generated. Another button will have the text Sort. When it is clicked, it will invoke the sort object's Exec method to perform the sorting. The result will be displayed in the list box. As the sorting is in progress, the label should display the (estimated) percentage of completion.

12-23.   Hooking Events to An Event Handler At Runtime. Refer to the Cashflow data entry example in section 8.4 and the subsection on hooking event handlers in section 12.3. Complete the project by adding an event handler that will check for numeric keys and hooking it to the KeyPress event of all text boxes created at runtime.

12-24.   A Data-Entry Server. Refer to exercise 10-20 in Chapter 10, "Special Topics in Data Entry." The exercise results in a project that includes various Sub procedures to check for valid keys, cumulative results starting from Exercise 10-15. Create a class module (call it EntryServer) that will include all these Subs at its Private procedures. The class module will provide a method, VerifyKey, which takes ActiveControl and KeyAscii as its parameters and returns a Boolean value to indicate whether there is a problem with the key. A True value will indicate that the key is wrong. The wrong key will be suppressed in the method. All controls should have their Tag properties set according to the specifications in those exercises in Chapter 10, "Special Topics in Data Entry."

Include a ClearScreen method in this class module. The method should take a form as its parameter. All the text boxes, masked edit boxes, check boxes, and radio buttons in the form should be cleared. All list boxes and combo boxes in the form should have their SelectedIndex properties set to -1. Also, clear all selections if a list box allows multi-selections because of its SelectionMode setting.

Test the class module using a form with a visual interface that includes all text boxes and masked edit boxes needed to test each type of key. In addition, add a check box, two radio buttons, a list box, and a combo box to test the ClearScreen method.

12-25.   A Progress Meter. Create a progress meter class that has two properties: Total and CurrentValue. Both are of the Integer type. The Total property represents the total expected iterations of a process, whereas CurrentValue gives the current iteration number. The class will display the percentage of completion in a progress bar and in a label. It will also display the estimated time remaining. This class should also have a Cancel button, which will raise the CancelByUser event when clicked. Test an instance of this class with exercise 12-22.

Projects

12-26.   A Tic-Tac-Toe Game Class. Develop a Tic-Tac-Toe game class that allows two players to use a visual interface (game board) to play the game against each other. The game board should be able to display a circle or a cross alternatively when the user clicks a square on the board. (*Hint:* Use labels for this purpose, and create them at runtime. You will need to declare these labels with the WithEvents keyword, and use the AddHandler statement to handle the Click event.) The class should be able to determine whether an attempted mark is legitimate, and should also be able to declare a winner when due. It should allow the user to specify the back color, font size, and board size (a number for both the width and height). Also, provide the Play method to start the game.

Test the class by creating a Tic-Tac-Toe object, and call its Play method from the main form.

12-27.   The Inventory Acquisition–Handling System. An inventory acquisition-handling system contains three classes: Vendor, Product, and Purchase.

The Vendor class has properties that correspond to data fields in the Vendors table of the Inventory database. These fields are as follows:

Field/Property	Type	Length
VendorID	Integer	5 digits
Name	String	32 characters
Address	String	32 characters
State	String	2 characters
Zip	Integer	5 or 9 digits
ContactName	String	24 characters
ContactPhone	Decimal	10 digits

The primary key of the table is VendorID.

The Vendor class has two methods: GetVendor and SaveVendor. Both methods take VendorID as the parameter. The GetVendor method will retrieve the vendor using the VendorID parameter to look for the record. If the record is found, the method will return a data row containing the record. In addition, it will set the properties of the object to the value of the fields. If the record is not found, it will return an empty row and clear the property setting.

The SaveVendor method will check whether VendorID exists in the Vendors table. If so, the corresponding record is updated; otherwise, a new record is added to the table.

The Product class has properties that correspond to data fields in the Products table of the Inventory database. These fields are as follows:

Field/Property	Type	Length
ProductID	String	five characters
ProductName	String	25 characters
Description	String	32 characters
VendorID	Long	five digits

The primary key of the Products table is ProductID.

The product class has two methods: GetProduct and SaveProduct. Both methods take ProductID as the parameter and work in exactly the same manner as the two methods for the Vendor class.

Finally, the Purchase class has properties that correspond to data fields in the Transactions table in the Inventory database. These data fields are as follows:

Field/Property	Type	Length
Date	Date/Time	MM/DD/YYYY
ProductID	String	five characters
Quantity	Integer	up to six digits
UnitCost	Decimal	six digits (including two decimal places)
VendorID	Integer	five digits

The Purchase class has a SavePurchase method that can be used to save a purchase transaction. None of these classes have a visual interface.

Required: Design a project as follows:

- Have a data-entry screen to enter, edit, and save vendors. This data entry form will use the Vendor object.
- Have a data-entry screen to enter, edit, and save products. This data entry form will use the Product object.
- Have a data-entry screen to enter and save the purchase transaction. This data entry form will use the Purchase class to handle the entry.
- Include and use the generalized Search Engine as described in exercise 12-20 to help identify/look up the VendorID and ProductID in the data-entry screens where the need is present.
- Implement all necessary data validation routines.

13. Object-Oriented Programming

This chapter continues the discussion of object-oriented programming, which includes three important features: encapsulation, inheritance, and polymorphism. Encapsulation was discussed in detail in Chapter 12, "Object-Based Programming." This chapter focuses on inheritance and polymorphism.

Inheritance allows a new class to extend the functionality of an existing class without having to change the source code of the existing class. Polymorphism allows different classes to provide functionality with some invariant methods or properties but different implementations. These features greatly enhance the flexibility of coding and using classes, as covered in this chapter.

After completing this chapter, you should be able to:

- Understand the basic concepts and terms in inheritance and polymorphism.
- Design and develop code for the base class.
- Develop code for classes, derived from a base class, that are developed from scratch or available in the .NET framework, including classes pertaining to event arguments.
- Create and design forms derived from existing forms and appreciate the implication of this feature.
- Develop code for base classes and derived classes to implement polymorphism.
- Develop code to implement interface-based polymorphism.

13.1   Inheritance

Inheritance allows the creation of a new class from an existing (base) class. The new class inherits all the properties, methods, and events from the *base class*. The new class is recognized as the *derived class*. In other languages, the base class is also called the *super class*, while the derived class is called *subclass*. You can add new code in the derived class to extend the functionality of the base class. To create a derived class, you use the *Inherits statement*. For example, suppose you have a base class called RealEstate from which you want to derive a new class called Residential. Your code for the Residential class will appear:

```
Public Class Residential
    Inherits RealEstate
    'Other statements
End Class
```

Inheritance Hierarchy

A class that does not explicitly inherit from any class actually inherits from the *System.Object class*. Because a class either inherits implicitly from the System.Object class or explicitly from another class, which in turn either inherits implicitly from System.Object or explicitly from yet another class, all classes can trace their heritage to the System.Object class; that is, all classes are derived from the System.Object base class.

A new class can inherit from a base class that is derived from yet another class, forming an *inheritance hierarchy*. There is no limit as to how tall this hierarchy can be; however, a tall inheritance hierarchy can cause maintenance problems. An update in a base class may affect countless derived classes, thus affecting many applications using these classes. (Imagine if the System.Object class is changed drastically, what could happen to all classes.) A practical suggestion is to limit the hierarchy to about five or six layers.

Why Inheritance?

The essence of object-oriented programming is inheritance. It provides a way to organize the code from the most general to the most specific. For example, you can design your hierarchy of classes for the real estate application beginning with a set of properties and methods for the "RealEstate" class to a more specific classification of residential property versus commercial property. Residential can be further classified into single-household dwelling, multiple-household dwelling, and so on. As the hierarchy goes down, more specific properties and methods can be added to each class. Through inheritance, all the functionality of the base class is provided to the derived class without any additional code, so inheritance enhances code reusability.

An Inheritance Example

Consider a simplified payroll application for a restaurant that has two classes of employees: salaried, and tip earners. All employees have common properties such as social security number, address, and date of employment. The formula to compute the payroll tax withholding is also the same for all employees. Basically, the withholding is based on the employee's gross earnings, which may be different from the gross pay. In the case of the salaried employee, the gross pay is the same per pay period, and is equal to the gross earnings. In the case of the tipped earner, however, the gross pay is computed by the hours worked times the wage rate. The gross earnings should include both the gross pay and tips, which are paid by the customer directly, not by the company. The net pay is the difference between gross pay (not gross earnings) and the withholding. The common and unique characteristics of each type of employee can be summarized as in the following table:

Common to all employees	Unique to the salaried employee	Unique to the tipped earner
SSN, name, address, date of employment	Gross pay = amount per period	Tips should be reported
Tax withholding = f(gross earnings)	Gross earnings = gross pay	Gross pay = hours worked × wage rate
Net pay = gross pay - withholding		Gross earnings = gross pay + tips

To code for the project you can create a class that contains the common characteristics of the all the employees and call the class **Employee**. The characteristics unique to each type of employee will be coded in separate classes. These classes can be called **SalariedPerson** and **TippedEarner**. Each should be derived from the Employee class so that it has the functionality of the Employee class.

The Employee Class. For simplicity, you will include only one property (SSN) in this class. Also, assume that the tax withholding is 15% of the gross earnings. Coding this class is no different from coding any class we have done so far. The code appears as follows:

```
Public Class Employee
    Private mSSN As Integer
    Public Property SSN() As Integer
        Get
            Return (mSSN)
        End Get
        Set(ByVal Value As Integer)
            mSSN = Value
        End Set
    End Property
    Function WithHolding(ByVal pGrossEarnings As Double) As Double
        'Assume 15% is the standard w/h
        Return (pGrossEarnings * 0.15)
    End Function
    Function NetPay(ByVal pGrossPay As Double, ByVal pWithHolding
      As Double) As Double
        Return (pGrossPay - pWithHolding)
    End Function
End Class
```

The Derived Classes. The Salaried class will be derived from the Employee class. The two methods used to compute the gross earnings and gross pay involve the straightforward assignment statements. The code should appear as follows and should be placed in a new class module within the same project.

```
Public Class SalariedPerson
    Inherits Employee
    Private mGrossPay As Double
    Private mGrossEarnings As Double

    Public ReadOnly Property GrossEarnings() As Double
        Get
            Return (mGrossEarnings)
        End Get
    End Property

    Public Function GrossPay(ByVal pSalary As Double) As Double
        mGrossPay = pSalary
        mGrossEarnings = mGrossPay
        Return (mGrossPay)
    End Function
End Class
```

Notice that there is an Inherits statement immediately following the Class definition. The statement in effect incorporates all the functionality of the Employee class in the SalariedPerson class. An object instantiated from this class automatically has the SSN property. In addition, it has the WithHolding and NetPay methods to compute the withholding and net pay for the salaried employee. Notice also that GrossEarnings is a read-only property, which should always be set equal to the gross pay for this class. If it is set up as both read and write, it can be accidentally set to a value different from the gross pay. Included also is a Private variable mGrossPay to retain the value of GrossPay in case it is needed for additional computations in this class.

The TippedEarner class has a Tips property. In addition, the gross pay is computed differently; however, it should still be derived from the Employee class so that it has the functionality of the Employee class. The code appears as follows:

```
Public Class TippedEarner
    Inherits Employee
    Dim mGrossEarnings As Double
    Dim mGrossPay As Double
    Dim mTips As Double

    Public ReadOnly Property GrossEarnings() As Double
        Get
            Return (mGrossEarnings)
        End Get
    End Property

    Public Property Tips() As Double
        Get
            Return (mTips)
        End Get
        Set(ByVal Value As Double)
            mTips = Value
            mGrossEarnings = mGrossPay + mTips
        End Set
    End Property

    Function GrossPay(ByVal HoursWorked As Double, ByVal WageRate
      As Double) As Double
        mGrossPay = HoursWorked * WageRate
        mGrossEarnings = mGrossPay + mTips
        Return (mGrossPay)
    End Function
End Class
```

Notice that GrossEarnings is a read-only property computed when the Tips property is set, or when the gross pay is computed. A Private copy of GrossPay is retained for other computations.

Using the Derived Classes. So, how can you use the derived classes? As mentioned, the derived classes have the functionality of their base class in addition to the additional features that are extended in the derived classes. The TippedEarner class now has the Tips and GrossEarnings properties as well as the GrossPay method on top of the Withholding and NetPay methods in the base Employee class. To test, place the following code in a button Click event procedure in a form:

```
Dim Tipped As New TippedEarner()
Dim I As Integer
Dim TheGrossPay As Double
Dim TheWithholding As Double
Dim TheNetPay As Double

Tipped.Tips = 1000
TheGrossPay = Tipped.GrossPay(160, 5)
TheWithholding = Tipped.Withholding(Tipped.GrossEarnings)
TheNetPay = Tipped.NETPay(TheGrossPay, TheWithholding)
    MsgBox("The net pay is " & TheNetPay)
```

When you click the button, you should see the message box display 530 as the net pay. The computation is correct because the withholding is based on the total earnings of 1800 (tips plus the gross pay), while net pay is the difference between gross pay (800) and the withholding (15% of 1800 = 270).

You might have noticed an inconvenience in using the object. You must explicitly call the WithHolding and NetPay methods to obtain the withholding and net pay amounts. Ideally, the object should automatically compute these two values after the tips are reported and gross pay is computed. This issue will be revisited later in this chapter when *Protected members* is discussed.

Inheriting from VS.NET Classes

The preceding discussion illustrates how to derive a new class from another class that is developed from scratch. You can create a new class from most of the VS.NET classes in developing your VB projects; that is, you can actually extend the functionality of any control. As an example, the Masked Edit control will be emulated by extending the text box.

The added functionality of the masked edit control comes from its mask property. You can add the Mask property and the needed code to make the property function properly in the derived class. For simplicity, the mask will recognize only the # symbol as the mask for the numeric key. Other characters in the mask will be treated as placeholder literals. When the mask is set at runtime, the placeholder literals will be displayed in the text box literally and cannot be changed by the user; however, all the positions with the # symbol will be displayed as blank spaces. Of course, these are the positions that the user can enter only numeric keys. When the user attempts to enter a non-numeric key, the routine will display the "numeric key only" message.

The initial code for the class module should appear as follows:

```
Public Class MaskEdit
    Inherits TextBox
    Private mMask As String
    Public Property Mask() As String
        Get
            Return (mMask)
        End Get
        Set(ByVal Value As String)

        End Set
    End Property
End Class
```

You have coded the read-side of the Mask property to return its private copy. Now consider the write-side. Recall that when the mask is set, all the literals in the mask should be displayed, while the # symbols are displayed as blank spaces. It is easier to handle this with another Private variable (call it mDisplayText). This variable will be initially assigned the same value as the mask. All the # symbols in it are replaced with blank spaces, and the result is then displayed in the Text property inherited from the text box class. It turns out that displaying the text is not exactly straightforward. You can write a sub procedure (called ShowDisplayText) to handle this. The Mask property's Set procedure appears as follows:

```
'Place this line immediately below mMask declaration
Private mDisplayText As String

Set(ByVal Value As String)
    mMask = Value
    'Replace all # with blank space
    mDisplayText = Replace(mMask, "#", " ")
    ShowDisplayText()
End Set
```

The ShowDisplayText sub procedure can also be used to display the text after the user enters a key. Consider the KeyPress event procedure first. This procedure is similar to the key validation procedure shown in Chapter 10, "Special Topics in Data Entry." The code appears as follows:

```
     Private Sub MaskEdit_KeyPress(ByVal sender As System.Object, ByVal
        e As System.Windows.Forms.KeyPressEventArgs)  Handles
        MyBase.KeyPress
        Dim KeyAscii As Integer
        Dim Pos As Integer
        'This is the position in which the key is entered
        Pos = SelectionStart + 1
        KeyAscii = AscW(e.KeyChar)
        If KeyAscii < Keys.Space Then
            'Control key; let the system handle it
            Exit Sub
        End If
        If Len(mMask) = 0 Then
            'no mask; take anything
        ElseIf Pos > Len(mMask) Then
            ' Beyond the mask area; no key accepted
            e.Handled = True
        Else
            Select Case Mid(mMask, Pos, 1)
                Case "#"
                    If KeyAscii>= Keys.D0 AndAlso KeyAscii <= Keys.D9
                        Then
                        ' Numeric key; accept and display
                            ShowDisplayText(Pos, KeyAscii)
                    Else
                        ' non-numeric key; display an error message
                        MsgBox("Numeric key only")
                    End If
                        ' the key has been handled;
                        'don't process any further
                        e.Handled = True
                Case Else
            End Select
        End If
     End Sub
```

Notice that you are coding in the MaskEdit class. The KeyPress event is inherited from the base class, the text box. To refer to an interface (method, property, or event) in the base class, qualify it with the *MyBase* keyword. The KeyPress event procedure header indicates that it handles the event in the MyBase.KeyPress text box class. Recall that when you code any event procedure for a form, the Handles clause always qualifies the event name with the MyBase keyword. On the other hand, the inherited properties and methods are generally referenced without any qualification; therefore, the text box's SelectionStart property is simply referenced as such in this event procedure.

The procedure first tests whether the key is a control key. If so, there is no need to handle it (exit the procedure and allow the system to handle the key). It then checks whether there is a mask. If there is no mask, nothing needs to be done; otherwise, if the current cursor position is beyond the mask, the key should be suppressed (no key should be entered). If a key is entered within the boundary of the mask, it is tested to see whether it is a numeric key. If so, it is displayed by the ShowDisplayText sub; otherwise, a "numeric key only" message is displayed. The key should not be further processed in either case, and therefore the Handled argument is set to True. In the first case, the key has already been displayed. In the other case, the key should be rejected.

Why does displaying a character in the text box take a special routine (ShowDisplayText)? The need stems from handling the cursor position after the key is displayed. Consider the simple mask ##-##-##. After the second digit is entered, the cursor should be moved to the fourth position, skipping the first "-" (which should never be overwritten). After a digit is displayed, the routine should look for the next # character to place to cursor. When there is no more # character, the cursor should be placed at the end of the text so that nothing else can be typed over. This need to place the cursor in the correct position also arises when the mask is initially set, although there is no particular digit to display but just the initial display text. The code for the ShowDisplayText sub appears as follows:

```
Private Sub ShowDisplayText(Optional ByVal Pos As Integer = 0,
    Optional ByVal KeyAscii As Integer = 0)
    Dim P As Integer
    If KeyAscii > 0 Then
        ' If there is a key, put it in its proper position
        Mid(mDisplayText, Pos, 1) = Chr(KeyAscii)
    End If
    ' Show the result in the text box
    Text = mDisplayText
    P = InStr(Pos + 1, mMask, "#") - 1
    If P >= 0 Then
        MyBase.Select(P, 0)
    Else
        MyBase.Select(Pos, 0)
    End If
End Sub
```

Notice that both of the parameters are optional. If the key code is passed, it is inserted to the specified position. The display text—mDisplayText, which holds what should appear in the text box—is assigned to the Text property so that it will appear in the text box; then the next "#" position is searched for. The text box's Select method is used to set the cursor position. Recall that the Select method takes up to two parameters. The first parameter specifies the position to place the cursor and the second specifies how many characters to highlight. A zero will indicate to highlight nothing. Notice the first position in the Select method is zero, while the first position for the InStr (and the Mid) function is 1; therefore, 1 is subtracted from what is returned from the InStr function.

Referencing the Class Itself and the Base Class. Notice also how the Select method is qualified. The method name conflicts with the reserved word for **Select Case**; therefore, it must be qualified by either *Me* or *MyBase*. Me refers to the current (derived) class, while MyBase refers to the base class. Because the method is inherited, either keyword will do. Again, notice that the Text property is used without being qualified because there is no name conflict.

Suppose you want to create another property with the same name Text in this derived class. Are you allowed? Yes. In this case, you will be shadowing the base property, so you must declare it with a special keyword, Shadows, as follows:

```
Shadows Property Text () As String
```

To refer to Text in the text box, you code MyBase.Text; to refer to the Text property in this derived class, you code Me.Text.

This emulated masked edit class is used to illustrate several points: how classes can be extended in VS.NET; how inherited events, properties, and methods are referenced in the derived class; and how to declare and reference properties and methods that shadow members in the base class. Notice, however, that this derived MaskEdit class has not been completely coded. It handles only one kind of mask character—#. Also, no code is provided to handle the arrow keys and the Backspace key. The desired refinements are left to you as exercise 13-19 at the end of this chapter.

Creating Event Arguments

In Chapter 12, it was shown in the SortEngine example how events can be declared and raised in a class. There, the event is created with two arguments: Percent and TimeLeft; however, all events provided by the system have a standardized format: The first argument is the sender object and the second is an event argument class. MS recommends that events be structured in this format, and that the event argument class be inherited from the System.EventArgs class. To conform to this format, you can modify the project as follows:

- Create an event class (call it SortEngineEventArgs) that inherits from System.EventArgs and will include Percent and TimeLeft as additional properties. This class should be Public, and can be separate from the SortEngine class (does not have to be an inner class of SortEngine).
- Change the event declaration.
- Change the arguments in the RaiseEvent statement.

The SortEngineEventArgs class can be coded as follows:

```
Public Class SortEngineEventArgs
    Inherits System.EventArgs
    Dim mPercent As Integer
    Dim mTimeLeft As Double

    Sub New(ByVal pPercent As Integer, ByVal pTimeLeft As Double)
        mPercent = pPercent
        mTimeLeft = pTimeLeft
    End Sub

    Public ReadOnly Property Percent() As Integer
        Get
            Return (mPercent)
        End Get
    End Property
    Public ReadOnly Property TimeLeft() As Double
        Get
            Return (mTimeLeft)
        End Get
    End Property
End Class
```

The two arguments Percent and TimeLeft are included in the class as read-only properties. Their values are initialized in the New constructor, which takes Percent and Timeleft as its two required parameters.

In the SortEngine class itself, the PercentChanged event can then be declared as follows:

```
Public Event PercentChanged(ByVal sender As System.Object, ByVal e
    As SortEngineEventArgs)
```

This declaration now conforms to the MS recommendation. In the sorting routine itself, everything remains the same except for the RaiseEvent statement, which should be changed as follows:

```
RaiseEvent PercentChanged(Me, New SortEngineEventArgs(Percent,
    TimeLeft))
```

Notice that the object that raises the event is the SortEngine class itself; therefore, Me is the first argument. The second parameter expects a SortEngineEventArgs object, so one instance of this class is created with the New keyword. Percent and TimeLeft are passed to the constructor, which expects these two parameters.

After these changes, in the module that uses the SortEngine class, you should see that the event procedure header appears as follows (assuming Sorter is declared WithEvents as SortEngine):

```
Private Sub Sorter_PercentChanged(ByVal sender As System.Object,
    ByVal e As SortEngineEvent.SortEngineEventArgs) Handles
    Sorter.PercentChanged
```

You can then reference Percent and TimeLeft by qualifying each with the e parameter as follows:

```
e.Percent
e.TimeLeft
```

Hiding Members from Classes Outside the Class Hierarchy

Consider the code in a base class. Suppose you would like for a method or property to be exposed to any class that inherits this base class, and yet the method or property should not be exposed to any other classes. Declaring such a member as Friend will not do because this member will still be visible to all other modules in the same project. Declaring it as Private, however, will make the member invisible to those derived classes. Solution? Declare the member as *Protected*. This access modifier does exactly what our situation needs: It makes the base member visible to its derived classes, but not visible to any classes that are not in the inheritance hierarchy.

To illustrate the use of this access modifier, consider the payroll project again. The base class exposes two methods: WithHolding and NetPay. They are to be called from other modules; however, as the remarks at the end of the example indicate, a better design would be that withholdings and net pay are computed automatically in the base class and the results made available to the other modules as read-only Public properties. These methods should not be declared as Public, but if these methods are called by the derived classes, all derived classes will end up with a lot of duplicate code with each other. A better design will be for the derived classes to pass the required payroll data to the base class and have the base class perform the computations in this central location. In this way, the base class also provides more services to the derived classes, and renders more uniformity to the modules using these payroll classes. With these considerations, you will redesign the code in the base class as follows:

- Withholding and NetPay will be exposed as properties (rather than as methods in the original design).
- There should be a procedure for the derived classes to use to set the payroll data. This procedure will be named SetPayData and declared as Protected because it will be used exclusively by the derived classes.
- The methods to compute Withholding and NetPay will be renamed as ComputeWithholding and ComputeNetPay. These methods should be only used to compute on the data made available by the SetPayData method, and will be declared as Private.
- Because gross pay is also passed to this class, the value can also be made as a read-only property in the base class so that each derived class will not have to set up a gross pay property. The modified base Employee class appears as follows:

```
Public Class Employee
    Private mGrossPay As Double
    Private mNetPay As Double
    Private mGrossEarnings As Double
    Private mTips As Double
    Private mWithholding As Double
    Private mSSN As Integer

    Protected Sub SetPayData(ByVal pGrossPay As Double,
      Optional ByVal pTips As Double = 0)
        mGrossPay = pGrossPay
        mTips = pTips
        mGrossEarnings = mGrossPay + mTips
        ComputeWithholding()
        ComputeNetPay()
    End Sub
    Private Sub ComputeWithholding()
        mWithholding = 0.15 * mGrossEarnings
    End Sub
    Private Sub ComputeNetPay()
        mNetPay = mGrossPay - mWithholding
    End Sub
    Public ReadOnly Property NetPay() As Double
        Get
            Return (mNetPay)
        End Get
    End Property
```

```
            Public ReadOnly Property Withholding() As Double
                Get
                    Return (mWithholding)
                End Get
            End Property

            Public ReadOnly Property GrossPay() As Double
                Get
                    Return (mGrossPay)
                End Get
            End Property

            Public ReadOnly Property GrossEarnings() As Double
                Get
                    Return (mGrossEarnings)
                End Get
            End Property
        End Class
```

The Protected SetPayData method allows the derived classes (only) to set gross pay and tip amounts and keeps a private copy of each. It then computes the gross earnings and calls the Private subs: ComputeWithholding and ComputeNetPay to perform additional computations. In these subs, a private copy of the withholding and net pay amount is also retained to serve as the return value for the public read-only properties, Withholding and NetPay, respectively.

The derived classes will simply take the basic pay data such as hours worked, wage rates, and tips, compute the gross pay, and pass the pay data to the SetPayData sub in the base class. The Tipped class still needs to provide the Public Tips property. The modified Salaried class appears as follows:

```
    Public Class SalariedPerson
        Inherits Employee
        Public Function ComputeGrossPay(ByVal pGrossPay As Double) As
          Double
            SetPayData(pGrossPay)
            Return (pGrossPay)
        End Function
    End Class
```

Notice that the previous gross pay method is now renamed as ComputeGrossPay to avoid the name conflict with the GrossPay property in the base class. Using the Shadowing feature will make the GrossPay property in the base class unavailable to other modules that use this derived class. As you can see, all it needs to do is to pass the gross pay data through the SetPayData method to the Employee class. All the computations and properties are handled in the base class. The modified TippedEarner class appears as follows:

```
    Public Class TippedEarner
        Inherits Employee
        Dim mGrossPay As Double
        Dim mTips As Double
        Public Function ComputeGrossPay(ByVal HoursWorked As Double,
          ByVal WageRate As Double) As Double
            mGrossPay = HoursWorked * WageRate
            SetPayData(mGrossPay, mTips)
            Return (mGrossPay)
        End Function

        Public Property Tips() As Double
            Get
                Return (mTips)
            End Get
            Set(ByVal Value As Double)
                mTips = Value
                SetPayData(mGrossPay, mTips)
            End Set
        End Property
    End Class
```

The ComputeGrossPay method computes gross pay using the hours worked and wage rate parameters. A private copy of the gross pay is retained. The Tips property is a read-write property. When it is set, and when the gross pay is computed, both the gross pay and the tips (private copy of both) are passed to the base class through the SetPayData method. This is necessary because the order in which either value is given first in the module using this class is undeterminable and should not be dictated.

These modified classes are much easier to use. All you have to do is to create an instance and provide the basic pay data. The resulting gross pay, gross earnings, withholdings, and net pay are automatically computed without any method calls. The following code shows how you may use these classes in a procedure in another module, such as a form:

```
Dim Salaried As New SalariedPerson()
Dim Tipped As New TippedEarner()
Salaried.ComputeGrossPay(1000) 'Set the salary
'And you can see the net pay and withholding
Console.WriteLine("Salaried gross pay is " & _
  Salaried.GrossEarnings & " and gross earning is " &  _
  Salaried.GrossEarnings)
Console.WriteLine("Salaried has a W/H of " &
  Salaried.Withholding & " and net pay of " & Salaried.NETPay)
'Report tips
Tipped.Tips = 500
'Provide hours worked and wage rate
Tipped.ComputeGrossPay(60, 4)
'And you can see the gross earnings, withholdings, and net pay
  Console.WriteLine("Tipped gross pay is " & Tipped.GrossPay &
  " and gross earnings of " & Tipped.GrossEarnings)
Console.WriteLine("Tipped has a W/H of " & Tipped.Withholding
  & " and net pay of " & Tipped.NETPay)
```

The MustInherit and NotInheritable Classes

The base class must be *inheritable* to allow inheritance. By default, classes are inheritable. If you have created a class that you believe should not be extended, you can mark it as *NotInheritable*. For example, the VS.NET Math class is marked NotInheritable. On the other hand, some classes cannot be used alone, and must be inherited to implement certain invariant methods. These classes should be marked as *MustInherit*. The syntax to specify whether a class is NotInheritable or MustInherit is as follows:

```
[Public¦Friend] [NotInheritable¦MustInherit] Class Name
```

A MustInherit class is also recognized as an *abstract class*. It typically requires the derived class to implement certain invariant methods. These methods are specified in the base class but their implementation details are left to the derived classes. In the base class, these methods are specified with the *MustOverride* keyword. Methods marked as such are recognized as *abstract methods*. Abstract classes and abstract methods are typically used for polymorphism, which is the topic of Section 13.3.

13.2   Inheriting a Form at Design Time

When coding applications for an organization, you may find that many forms appear similar to each other. It can be much more efficient if you can create a template and then copy and modify the template to create the needed new form. In VB.NET, you can do this in different ways. For example, you can develop by code a class that inherits a form you have designed. From there, you can add additional controls and code to the form programmatically. A possible drawback of this approach is the issue of designing the visual interface by code. Usually, this approach takes longer because you have to test the code repetitively to ensure that the visual elements appear on the form at the desired position with the proper size.

An easier and better alternative is to inherit the form template at design time, and work on the visual elements of the derived form directly at design time, too. You can do it this way in VB.NET. Here are the major steps:

1. Design a form template to be use as the base form.
2. Run or build the project.
3. Inherit the base form and obtain the derived form.
4. Add additional visual elements, and code to the derived form to make it a complete functional form.

You can then create and invoke the derived form in code similar to any other form.

A Data Entry Form Example

To illustrate the use of inherited form at design time, consider the data entry forms for sales and purchases. Both contain many of the same data fields (controls). To avoid duplicate efforts, you will create a data entry form template. Follow these steps:

1. Add a new (second) form to a new project, and name it **frmEntryTemplate**; then design this form so that it appears as shown in Figure 13.1.

The controls that can be involved in code are listed in the following table:

Control	Name	Use or comment
Text box	txtDate	For date of transaction
Text box	txtProductID	To enter product ID
Text box	txtQuantity	To enter quantity involved
Button	btnSave	For the user to invoke data saving operation
Button	btnQuit	To quit the program

Also place the following code in the code window:

```
Private Sub btnQuit_Click(ByVal sender As System.Object,
    ByVal e As System.EventArgs) Handles btnQuit.Click
      Me.Close()
End Sub
```

2. Press the F5 key to run and build the project. End the project. Alternatively, press Ctrl+Shift+B to build the project.

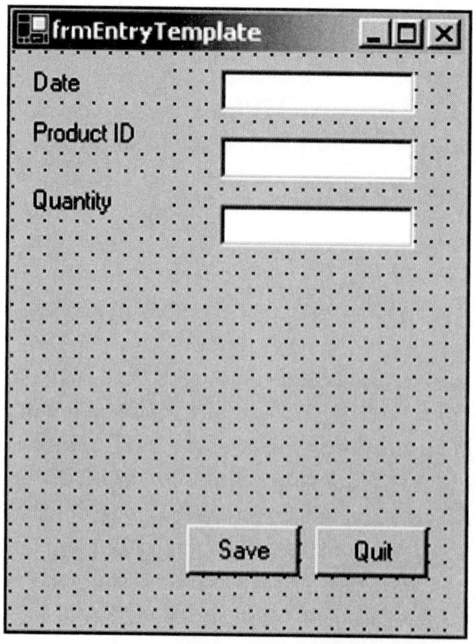

Figure 13.1

Visual interface for the data entry form template

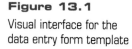

Figure 13.2

The Inheritance Picker
dialog box

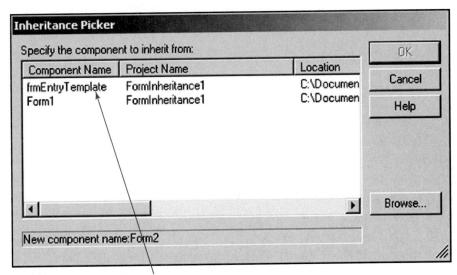

If you do not see this form name, cancel all operations and go
back to the IDE. Press the F5 key to build the project. End the
project and then follow Step 3 in the text to get here.

3. Create an inherited form from this base form.

   a. Click the Project menu and then select Add Inherited Form. The familiar Add New
       Item dialog box will appear.

   b. Enter frmSalesEntryTemplate as the form name, and click the Open button in the
       dialog box. The Inheritance Picker dialog box will appear, as shown in Figure 13.2.

   c. Double-click frmEntryTemplate in the dialog box to go back to the IDE. You will
       see frmSalesEntryTemplate form name in the Solution Explorer.

4. Design and edit the derived form. Double-click frmSalesEntryTemplate in the Solution
   Explorer so that the form appears. Add one label and one text box on the form so that it
   will appear as shown in Figure 13.3. Name the text box **txtCustomerID**.

Figure 13.3

The modified derived
form

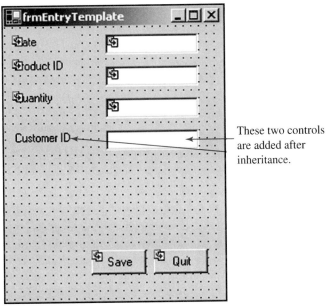

These two controls
are added after
inheritance.

Notice that all controls drawn in the base
form are marked as read-only, meaning
that their appearance cannot be changed.

Notice that all controls drawn on the base form are marked as read-only, meaning that their appearance or properties cannot be changed. If you find you need to change their tab order or any property, you will need to change them in the base form, not in the derived form. Notice also assuming that you have the tab indices for the three text boxes in the base form set to 0, 1, and 2, you should set the tab index for txtCustomerID to 2 in order for it to be the next data entry field when the program runs. Also, enter the following code in the code window of this derived form:

```
Private Sub btnSave_Click(ByVal sender As System.Object, ByVal e
    As System.EventArgs) Handles btnSave.Click
        Console.WriteLine(txtDate.Text)
        Console.WriteLine(txtCustomerID.Text)
        MsgBox("data saved")
End Sub
```

The code is designed to verify that the form works as expected; that is, controls in the base form and in this form are recognized properly. Note that you have to enter the procedure header manually; that is, the IDE does not provide the header template that you can normally get for the inherited controls. This completes the design of the derived sales data entry form. The design of the purchase entry form is left to you as exercise 13-24 at the end of this chapter.

To test this form, you can go back to the startup form, which is blank; in a real application, it should be the form containing the main menu. Add a button, and name it **btnShow**; then add the following code:

```
Private Sub btnShow_Click(ByVal sender As System.Object, ByVal e
    As System.EventArgs) Handles btnShow.Click
        Dim frmSalesEntry As New frmSalesEntryTemplate()
        frmSalesEntry.Text = "Sales Data Entry"
        frmSalesEntry.Show()
End Sub
```

Run the project, and click the Show button. The sales data entry form should appear. Verify the following:

- The title bar of the form shows "Sales Data Entry." This verifies that the derived form is properly recognized in the startup from.

- All the controls in the derived form appear. This verifies that the form invoked is indeed the derived form.

- Enter D in the date field and C in the customer field; then click the Save button in the sales entry form. The "Data saved" message should be displayed. In addition, you should also see D and C in the immediate window. This verifies that controls in the base form as well as the derived form are recognized properly.

- Click the Quit button in the sales entry form. The form should disappear. This verifies that the event and event handler in the base form are also recognized in the derived form (as all base and derived classes should behave). This also suggests that the base form can be used to implement all functionality common to its derived forms for efficient implementation.

13.3   Polymorphism

Polymorphism refers to the capability to define identically named methods or properties in multiple classes. Although these members have different implementations, the client code can use them at runtime interchangeably without having to deal with the differences in class or implementation. Polymorphism can be inheritance-based or interface-based. *Inheritance-based polymorphism* involves defining the methods or properties in the base class and requiring the derived class to implement these members. *Interface-based polymorphism* involves defining the methods or properties in an interface definition and allowing these members to be implemented in various classes.

Inheritance-Based Polymorphism

Consider inheritance-based polymorphism. As discussed previously, this type of polymorphism is defined through abstract classes that contain abstract methods or properties. To illustrate, consider the case of general ledger accounting. There are two types of accounts: real accounts and nominal accounts. Real accounts have substance and represent the company's assets, liabilities, or owners' equity. Nominal accounts are revenues or expenses that track the changes to owners' equity. At end of each accounting period, the two types of accounts *close* differently. Net changes in the nominal account are closed to an account called *income summary*. In addition, the amounts in the account (balance and changes) are cleared (set to zero). On the other hand, net changes in the real account are added to the beginning balance, which is carried forward to the next period as the beginning balance. While you can implement various details for all accounts the same way for both real and nominal accounts, you must have different implementations of the *Close* method depending on whether the account is real or nominal. In such a case, you can create a base Account class that provides common properties and methods for both types but defines the Close method in abstract. You can then create two Classes—RealAccount and NominalAccount—derived from the base class to implement the Close method.

The following provides additional implementation details about these classes:

- The Account class should have the following properties and methods:
  - Properties:
    - AccountNumber
    - AccountName
    - BeginningBalance—read only; the value is updated by the Close method explained later in this section
    - DebitTotal—representing all debit amounts posted to the account; a debit amount is represented with a positive value; read only, computed by the Post method explained later in this section
    - CreditTotal—representing all credit amounts posted to the account; a credit amount is represented with a negative value; read only, computed by the Post method explained later in this section
    - Balance—read only; representing the balance of the account; updated by the Post and Close methods explained later in this section
  - Methods:
    - Post—takes an amount as parameter to post to the account; a positive value is added to the private copy of DebitTotal while a negative value is added to the private copy of CreditTotal; this method also accumulates balance for the account internally
    - Close—takes the income summary account as its parameter and requires different implementations by this class' derived class
- The NominalAccount class should implement the Close method as follows:
  - Its balance is posted to the income summary account, using the Post method
  - All amount fields such as beginning balance, debit total, credit total, and balance are set to zero
- The RealAccount class should implement the Close method as follows:
  - Its beginning balance is set to the current balance, which has been updated by the Post method, to carry forward to the next accounting period
  - Its debit total and credit total are set to zero

Coding the Account Class. As mentioned earlier in this subsection, this base class should be an abstract class; therefore its header must be marked as MustInherit. The class definition appears as follows:

```
Public MustInherit Class Account
```

In addition, its abstract Close method must be defined with the MustOverride keyword and should appear as follows:

```
MustOverride Sub Close(ByVal IncomeSummary As Account)
```

Finally, those internal variables associated with amounts such as beginning balance, debit total, credit total, and balance must be accessible to the derived classes and therefore should be declared as Protected, instead of the typical Private access. The complete code for this class appears as follows:

```
Public MustInherit Class Account
    Private mAccountNumber As Integer
    Private mAccountName As String
    'The following variables are declared as Protected
    'so that this class' derived classes can access
    Protected mBeginningBalance As Double
    Protected mDebitTotal As Double
    Protected mCreditTotal As Double
    Protected mBalance As Double

    Public Property AccountNumber() As Integer
        Get
            Return (mAccountNumber)
        End Get
        Set(ByVal Value As Integer)
            mAccountNumber = Value
        End Set
    End Property

    Public Property AccountName() As String
        Get
            Return (mAccountName)
        End Get
        Set(ByVal Value As String)
            mAccountName = Value
        End Set
    End Property

    Public ReadOnly Property BeginningBalance() As Double
        Get
            Return (mBeginningBalance)
        End Get
    End Property

    Public ReadOnly Property DebitTotal() As Double
        Get
            Return (mDebitTotal)
        End Get
    End Property

    Public ReadOnly Property CreditTotal() As Double
        Get
            Return (mCreditTotal)
        End Get
    End Property

    Public ReadOnly Property Balance() As Double
        Get
            Return (mBalance)
        End Get
    End Property

    Public Function Post(ByVal Amount As Double) As Double
        If Amount >= 0 Then
```

```
            mDebitTotal += Amount
        Else
            mCreditTotal += Amount
        End If
        mBalance = mBeginningBalance + mDebitTotal + mCreditTotal
        Return (mBalance)
    End Function
    MustOverride Sub Close(ByVal IncomeSummary As Account)
End Class
```

The code for property definitions should be self-explanatory. Notice how the Post method is coded. If the parameter is a positive amount, it is added to DebitTotal; otherwise, it is added to CreditTotal. The method also computes (updates) the new balance, which is then returned to the caller. (Perhaps, you are wondering why not just combine the positive and negative amounts together. After all, the balance will be still the same. However, the accountant believes that separating the debit total from the credit total enhances the audit trail.)

Implementing the Close Method for the RealAccount class.

Recall that the Close method of this derived class takes its current balance (updated by the Post method) as its beginning balance and clears the amounts representing changes in the current period (debit total and credit total). The code appears as follows:

```
Public Class RealAccount
    Inherits Account
    Overrides Sub Close(ByVal IncomeSummary As Account)
        'Real account does not have to be closed to income summary
        'Just update the beginning balance
        mBeginningBalance = mBalance
        mDebitTotal = 0
        mCreditTotal = 0
    End Sub
End Class
```

Pay particular attention to the header for the Close method. The *Overrides keyword* must be specified because the method is defined as MustOverride in the base class. Notice that although the IncomeSummary account is passed to this method by definition, it is not used in the computation for the real account. Also notice how the Protected variables in the base class are referenced. They are referenced in exactly the same way as if they were declared in this class. Of course, they can also be qualified by the MyBase keyword.

Implementing the Close Method for the NominalAccount Class.

Recall that the Close method of this derived class requires the current balance be closed (posted) to the income summary account. In addition, all amount fields should also be cleared. The code appears as follows:

```
Public Class NominalAccount
    Inherits Account
    Overrides Sub Close(ByVal IncomeSummary As Account)
        'Nominal account is closed by adding its balance to
        'IncomeSummary and clearing all amounts
        'Post balance to income summary account
        IncomeSummary.Post(mBalance)
        'then set all pertinent amounts to zero
        mBeginningBalance = 0
        mDebitTotal = 0
        mCreditTotal = 0
        mBalance = 0
    End Sub
End Class
```

Using Polymorphism

As mentioned earlier in this section, polymorphism allows the client code to use the same methods or properties without regards to the differences in implementation between classes. In the preceding example, any object of the Account class (real or nominal) can be closed with the

Close method at runtime without encountering any problem, and the results will be correct. Before illustrating how polymorphism makes coding easier, it is necessary to introduce the CollectionBase class, which you need to use in the demonstration.

The CollectionBase Class. This class provides a way to create a collection of your own objects. Recall that in Chapter 8, "Arrays and Their Uses," you used the Collection object, which accepts any object into the collection as the generic object and may require a conversion back to the original type of object before specific members in the object can be referenced. The *CollectionBase class* allows you by inheritance to create a collection of a particular type, such as the Account class in the preceding sub-section. A class derived from the CollectionBase must implement the Add and Remove methods, usually through the class' *List property*, which provides the Add and RemoveAt method. To allow access (reference) to a particular item in the collection, you should also implement the Item property.

In this application, a collection of accounts will be used to demonstrate the usefulness of polymorphism. You will create an AccountCollection class that can accept and return objects of the Account type for this purpose. The following code shows how this class is created by inheritance of the CollectionBase:

```
Public Class AccountCollection
    Inherits CollectionBase
    Default Public ReadOnly Property Item(ByVal Index As Integer)
      As Account
        Get
            Return (List.Item(Index))
        End Get
    End Property

    Sub Add(ByVal TheAccount As Account)
        List.Add(TheAccount)
    End Sub

    Sub Remove(ByVal Index As Integer)
        list.RemoveAt(Index)
    End Sub
End Class
```

As mentioned, the Add and Remove methods are implemented with the base class' *List.Add* and *List.RemoveAt* methods; the read-only Item property is implemented using the *List.Item property*. Pay close attention to the header of the Item property definition. The *Default keyword* marks that this property is the default for this class/object. The property takes an Index parameter that indicates which element to return. A member can be marked as the default only when it requires a parameter. A default can be omitted from the reference as will demonstrated later. Notice also that the Item property is declared As Account; therefore, items to be added and retrieved from the collection must be of the Account type.

LOOK IT UP

For a walkthrough example of how to create a collection for a particular class, use the keyword Collection properties to search the search tab (not the index tab); then double-click the title "Walkthrough: Creating Your Own Collection Class" to read the page. It shows how the CollectionBase class can be used to create a collection class for the widget (defined in the example) class.

Testing the Classes. You are now ready to witness polymorphism in action in a form. For simplicity, assume that the general ledger system has four normal accounts: Cash, Payable, Sales, and Expense. The first two are real accounts, and the last two are nominal. In addition, you will have the IncomeSummary account (a real account) for closing purpose. You will create these accounts according to their types, assign their AccountName properties, and post some amounts to each account. You also create an Accounts object of the AccountCollection type to keep the first four accounts in this collection, which can be employed to demonstrate the use of the Close method. Assume you have a button named btnTest in the form. The code appears as follows:

```
Private Sub btnTest_Click(ByVal sender As System.Object, ByVal e
    As System.EventArgs) Handles btnTest.Click
    Dim Cash As New RealAccount()
    Dim Payable As New RealAccount()
    Dim Sales As New NominalAccount()
    Dim Expense As New NominalAccount()
    Dim IncomeSummary As New RealAccount()
    Dim Accounts As New AccountCollection()
    Dim I As Integer

    With Accounts
        .Add(Cash)
        .Add(Payable)
        .Add(Sales)
        .Add(Expense)
    End With

    Cash.AccountName = "Cash"
    Cash.Post(3000)
    Payable.AccountName = "A/P"
    Payable.Post(-1000)
    Sales.AccountName = "Sales revenue"
    Sales.Post(-9000)
    Expense.AccountName = "Various Expenses"
    Expense.Post(2000)
    IncomeSummary.AccountName = "Income Summary"

    ' Use the Close method regardless of the account type
    For I = 0 To Accounts.Count - 1
        Accounts(I).Close(IncomeSummary)
    Next I

    For I = 0 To Accounts.Count - 1
        Console.WriteLine(Accounts(I).AccountName & " " &
            Accounts(I).BeginningBalance)
    Next I
    Console.WriteLine(IncomeSummary.AccountName & " " &
      IncomeSummary.BeginningBalance)
    Console.WriteLine(IncomeSummary.AccountName & " " &
      IncomeSummary.DebitTotal)
    Console.WriteLine(IncomeSummary.AccountName & " " &
      IncomeSummary.CreditTotal)
    Console.WriteLine(IncomeSummary.AccountName & " " &
      IncomeSummary.Balance)
End Sub
```

In the code, the four accounts are added to the Accounts collection before each account's AccountName property is assigned and the amount is posted. The first For loop uses the Close method of each account in the Accounts collection to perform the closing. The second For loop writes out the resulting BeginningBalance of each account to verify the accuracy of the results. (You should see 3000, -1000, 0, and 0 because the first two accounts are real and the last two are nominal.) The last four statements display the effect of closing on the amounts in the IncomeSummary account. (You should see 0, 2000, -9000, -7000; indicating a 7000 credit balance.) Notice that the Accounts collection does not differentiate between real and nominal accounts, and uses the Close method indiscriminately. The results, however, are correct.

Have you noticed the effect of the Default keyword on this code? Without the default specification, you will have to reference each account in the Accounts collection as:

```
Accounts.Item(I)
```

With the default specification, however, you are able to reference to each account as:

```
Accounts(I)
```

Notice a difference between the Collection class and the classes derived from the CollectionBase class. The Collection class is One-based, where the CollectionBase class is zero-based (the first element has an index value of zero).

Again, Why Inheritance-Based Polymorphism? In the preceding example, if you do not use inheritance, you can still accomplish correct Close by the use of If blocks in the Account class: one block will handle the nominal account; the other will handle the real account. So, what is the advantage of using inheritance to deal with different type of closing? The answer lies in that many other programming problems are open-ended. At the time you are developing the base class, you may not be aware of all possible scenarios to incorporate in the If (or Select Case) blocks. As each new scenario is identified, you will have to go back and revise the class. On the other hand, using the inheritance-base polymorphism, there is no need to revise the base class. All you have to do is to develop another class derived from the base class to take care of the new scenario.

Interface-Based Polymorphism

In interface-based polymorphism, the interface defines the properties, methods, and/or events to be implemented similar to the definition of abstract members in a class. The interface, however, is not allowed to provide any implementation. (In contrast, recall that the base Account class in the previous example provides various implementations in addition to defining the abstract Close method.) The definitions in the interface represent a contract. Any class that implements the interface must implement every aspect of that interface exactly as defined. As a contract, after being published (the definition is made known and available to the software development team), the interface definition should never be changed. Any change to the definition will break the existing code that implements the particular interface.

Defining the Interface. The syntax to define the interface appears as follows:

```
[Public¦Friend¦Private¦Protected] Interface Name
     'Interface definition statements
End Interface
```

Inside the Interface block, you can define any methods (subs or functions), properties, and or events by giving their header definitions. The following represents a valid interface definition:

```
Public Interface ITest
     Sub sub1(ByVal Parm1 As Integer)
     Function Fun(ByVal Gamer As String) As String
     ReadOnly Property Item(ByVal Index As Integer) As Object
     Event SomethingOccurred(ByVal sender As System.Object, ByVal e
        As EventArgs)
End Interface
```

You can also use the Inherits statements to inherit another interface (not class). In that case, the Inherits statement must be the first statement in the block. An interface can inherit more than one base interface. Note that inside the block, the only allowed keywords are Overloads, Default, ReadOnly, and WriteOnly. No other modifier, such as Public, Private, Protected, Shared, Static, Overrides, MustOverride, or Overridable, is allowed. The interface itself, as defined in the first line, is Friend by default and can be explicitly declared Public, Friend, Private or Protected.

Placement of the Interface Definition. The interface can be defined in a class module or a standard module. When an interface has the Private or Protected modifier, it must be placed in a class; therefore, it must be in the class module in which the class belongs. When an interface has no modifier or has the Public or Friend access modifier, it can be placed inside or outside of the class or module definition. That is, any of the following placements is allowed:

- Inside a class definition:

```
Public Class ClassName
     [Public¦Friend¦Private¦Protected] Interface
      InterfaceName
          'Other statements
     End Interface
     'Other statements
End Class
```

- Outside any class definition in class module:

```
Public Class ClassName
     'Other statements
End Class
[Public¦Friend] Interface InterfaceName
     'Other statements
End Interface
```

- Inside a module definition:

```
Public Module ModuleName
     [Public¦Friend¦Private¦Protected] Interface
      InterfaceName
     'Other statements
     End Interface
     'Other statements
End Module
```

- Outside any module definition in standard module:

```
Public Module ModuleName
     'Other statements
End Module
[Public¦Friend] Interface InterfaceName
     'Other statements
End Interface
```

When the interface has either Public or Friend access, it is more appropriate to place the definition in a standard module because the interface cannot be instantiated and is meant to be implemented by a diverse group of classes. Placing the definition in a standard module makes it easily available to these classes, while placing it in a class module does not offer any obvious advantage.

Implementing an Interface. To implement an interface in a class, you use the *Implements keyword*. For example, to implement the ITest interface defined in the preceding example in a class named Class1, you will code:

```
Public Class Class1
     Implements ITest
     'Other statements
End Class
```

In addition, for each method, property, or event that you implement, you will also need to add an Implements clause at the end of the header to indicate which member you are implementing. For example, to implement Fun, the header of the method should appear:

```
Function Fun(ByVal Gamer As String) As String Implements ITest.Fun
```

Notice the Implements clause at the end of the header. The method to be implemented is expressed in the format *Interface.Method.*

Recall that everything defined in the interface must be implemented when you decide to implement an interface; therefore, in Class1, you will have to provide code to implement Sub1, Fun, Item, and SomethingOccurred after you code Implements ITest.

An IMove Example. To illustrate how an interface is actually implemented, consider a simple example. In the previous versions of VB, each control has a Move method; however, in VB.NET, this method is replaced with the SetBounds method because Move is now an event in the control. Suppose, however, you still want to define a Move method as a standard interface that you can choose to implement for any control of interest. How do you proceed?

You can first define an interface as follows (place the code in a standard module):

```
Public Interface IMove
    Sub Move(ByVal Left As Integer, _
      Optional ByVal Top As Integer = -1, _
      Optional ByVal Width As Integer = -1, _
      Optional ByVal Height As Integer = -1)
End Interface
```

Note the difference between the definition of Move and the SetBounds method. The SetBounds method requires all four parameters. On the other hand, the Move method requires only the first parameter although it takes up to four. The optional parameters will be replaced with their current values if omitted. Suppose you now want to implement the interface for the label and call the new label MyLabel. You can code the class as follows:

```
Public Class MyLabel
    Inherits Label
    Implements IMove
    Shadows Sub Move(ByVal Left As Integer, _
      Optional ByVal Top As Integer = -1, _
      Optional ByVal Width As Integer = -1, _
      Optional ByVal Height As Integer = -1) Implements IMove.Move
        If Top = -1 Then
            Top = Me.Top
        End If
        If Width = -1 Then
            Width = Me.Width
        End If
        If Height = -1 Then
            Height = Me.Height
        End If
        Me.SetBounds(Left, Top, Width, Height)
    End Sub
End Class
```

Within the class definition, the Inherits statement must be the first statement. The Implements statement must immediately follow the Inherits statement. Other property definitions or procedures can then follow. (Note that before you completely code the implementation of the interface definition, the Implements statement will be underlined as if there were an error in the statement.) Notice that you place the *Shadows keyword* at the beginning of the Sub Move header because Move is an event in the Label class. The Shadows keyword allows you to define the identifier in a different way. In the code, if you need to refer to the Move event in the base Label class, you will need to qualify it with the *MyBase keyword* as: MyBase.Move.

The remaining code should be self-explanatory. Any omitted parameter is replaced with the original value as defined in the parameter lists. After these parameter values are ascertained, the SetBounds method is called to move the label to the new position.

Testing the IMove Implementation. How does the new MyLabel control work? You can test it on a new form. You will declare and create a control of the MyLabel type, and make it appear on the form. To test the Move method, you will make it move horizontally to a random position when it is clicked. The test code appears as follows:

```
Dim WithEvents lblMover As New MyLabel()
Private Sub Form1_Load(ByVal sender As System.Object, ByVal e As
    System.EventArgs) Handles MyBase.Load
    With lblMover
        .AutoSize = True
        .Text = "Test Move"
        .BorderStyle = System.Windows.Forms.BorderStyle.Fixed3D
        .Location = New Point(Me.Width \ 2, Me.Height \ 2)
    End With
    Me.Controls.Add(lblMover)
End Sub

Private Sub lblMover_Click(ByVal sender As System.Object, ByVal e
    As System.EventArgs) Handles lblMover.Click
    Dim Rand As New Random()
    Dim L As Integer
    L = Rand.Next(0, Me.Width - lblMover.Width)
    lblMover.Move(L)
End Sub
```

The new label is declared WithEvents so that it can recognize the Click event. It is created and associated with the lblMover variable. The form Load procedure defines the appearance of the new label, placing the label with its Left and Top aligned at the center of the form. Note that the control must be added to the form's Controls collection using the collection's Add method for it to appear on the form.

The label's Click event procedure actually tests how the Move method works. The random number generator object, Random, is used to generate an integer number in the range of 0 and the difference between the form's width and the label's width. This value is passed to the new label's Move method, omitting the three optional parameters. When you run the project and then click the label, you should be able to verify that it moves to a random location at the same horizontal position. The formula to generate the random number ensures that the entire label appears on the form.

Why Interface-Based Polymorphism? Perhaps, you wonder why go through all the troubles of defining the interface and then implementing it in classes. After all, if you just code the classes with the properties and methods defined in an interface without explicitly implementing the interface, these classes will still behave the same way as if the interface had been implemented. So, why is there a need for the interface, and why the implements?

Keep in mind that classes can be developed by different individuals in an organization, and interfaces can be defined by other people. The published interface offers a way to standardize functionality of various methods and properties across classes regardless of the developers involved—even when the detailed implementations are different among the classes. Standardized interfaces make it easier to use the classes because developers, as users of the classes, will not be required to differentiate different implementations among various classes. Imagine the Move method is implemented in different controls by different developers, each with different order of the parameters such as height being the first parameter. The resulting confusion will most likely discourage most programmers from using the Move method of any control.

If there is already the inheritance-based polymorphism, however, is there truly a need for the interface-based polymorphism? Actually, each is suitable for a different situation. The inheritance-based polymorphism allows implementations in the base class, and is suitable for classes that are homogeneous and interrelated. The base class and the derived class should have an "is a" relationship— that is, the derived class "is a" base class such as a nominal account is a ledger account. The interface-based polymorphism is suitable for diverse classes that have no apparent relationships among themselves.

Multiple Inheritances

Can a class inherit from more than a base class? No. Such an inheritance is not allowed; however, a class is allowed to inherit from one base class and implements many interfaces. Also, an interface is allowed to inherit from multiple interfaces. One potential problem with the multiple-interface inheritance situation is the name conflict. Several interfaces may define elements that conflict with each other. The inheritance is still allowed in the situation. Some of the Explore and Discover exercises at the end of this chapter explore this issue.

13.4   Additional Topics

This section presents two sundry and yet important topics: garbage collection and user-defined exceptions. Understanding the garbage collection process enables you to manage system resources more efficiently; knowing how to create user-defined exceptions allows you to create exceptions that can be more meaningful to your program users.

Garbage Collection and the Finalizer

When an instance of a class is initialized, the Sub New method is automatically called. But what happens when the instance goes out of scope, or is set to Nothing? The system may not immediately reclaim the system resources used by the object, but waits until it determines that the resources have run low. The process of destroying those dead objects and reclaiming their associated resources is recognized as *garbage collection*. In this process, the object's Finalize method is called. Recall that all classes are based on the Object class. This class provides a Finalize method, so if your class does not provide a Finalize method, the method in the Object class will be called. If you want to perform any finishing touch when an instance of your class is being destroyed, be sure to use the following template:

```
Protected Overrides Sub Finalize()
    ' Place your finishing touch statements here
    MyBase.Finalize()
End Sub
```

The method should have the Protected access; that is, it should not be called from any client code. The method also overrides the same in the base class, and thus must call the base class' finalizer, using the MyBase qualifier, as shown in the code template. If the statement is not there, the Finalize method in the base class will not be executed. Resource leaks can result. Note also that calling the base class' Finalize method should be the last statement in the code because you want to finish all businesses in the current class before chaining execution of the finalizer up in the inheritance hierarchy. (Your code calls its base class' Finalize method, which in turns calls its base class' Finalize method and so forth.)

Because the Finalize method cannot be called by the client code, and the garbage collection process does not start immediately after an object is no longer accessible, you may find a need to provide a way for the client code to initiate destruction of the object explicitly. If your class is written and compiled as a component (discussed in Chapter 14, "Beyond the Core"), the *Dispose method* is typically the method for this purpose.

Creating User Defined Exceptions

Chapter 12, "Object Based Programming," showed how to throw an exception that is already defined. However, you may encounter conditions in which those defined exceptions may not describe exactly the types of the exceptions that you want your class to throw. You may find it more desirable to throw an exception that more precisely indicates the nature of the problem. For example, in the FixedAsset example, you may want the system to show DepreMethodException instead of ArgumentOutOfRangeException so that the programmer can more easily identify the coding error. In such a case, you can define your own exception. To do so, you need to be aware of the exception hierarchy.

The base class for all exceptions is *System.Exception* from which *SystemException* and *ApplicationException* are derived. The exceptions found in the Exceptions option of the Debug menu are all derived from SystemException. Microsoft recommends that the user-defined exception be derived from ApplicationException. This exception class has three overloaded constructors defined as follows:

```
Sub New()
Sub New(Message As String)
Sub New(Message As String, InnerException As System.Exception)
```

In the third overloaded constructor, the *InnerException* refers to an exception that is caught in a Catch block and is passed to the caller, allowing the code to determine the chain of exceptions.

With this understanding, you can create a DepreMethodException class as follows:

```
Public Class DepreMethodException
    Inherits ApplicationException
    Sub New()
        MyBase.New("Depreciation method setting not recognizable")
    End Sub
    Sub New(ByVal Message As String)
        MyBase.New(Message)
    End Sub
    Sub New(ByVal Message As String, ByVal InnerException As
      System.Exception)
        MyBase.New(Message, InnerException)
    End Sub
End Class
```

The default constructor (the one with no parameter) will give the message, "the depreciation method setting not recognizable," so that the user will realize that the DepreMethod property is given a bad setting. The exception throwing statement in Section 12.3 (in the Set procedure for the DepreMethod property, p. 527) can then be coded as:

```
Throw New DepreMethodException()
```

Of course, you can also incorporate additional information, using the second overloaded constructor. For example, you can also include the Value parameter as follows:

```
Throw New DepreMethodException(Value & " is not an allowed
    setting for DepreMethod")
```

Summary

- The three most significant features of object-oriented programming are encapsulation, inheritance, and polymorphism.
- Inheritance allows the creation of a new class from an existing (base) class. The new class inherits all the properties, methods, and events from the base class without having to deal with the source code of the base class. The derived class is the sub class and the base class is the super class.
- All classes are either directly or indirectly derived from the System.Object class.
- A new class can be derived not only from a class created in a project, but also from those existing in the .NET framework. All VB controls and the form are inheritable.
- The Employee, SalariedPerson, and TippedEarner classes were used to show how the latter two classes can be derived from the first class.
- The MaskEdit class was used to show how the TextBox class can be inherited to provide the functionality for a newly created Mask property.

- If a member (property or method) of a derived class has the same name as a member of the base class, the member in the derived class must be declared with the Shadows keyword. The member in the derived class is referenced as Me.MemberName or just the member name, while the member in the base class is referenced (in the derived class) as MyBase.MemberName.

- It is recommended that all events contain two parameters: sender and event arguments. The event arguments parameter should be derived from the System.EventArgs class. The SortEngineEventArgs class was used to show how to create a class for the purpose of passing event arguments.

- To allow a member of the base class to be accessed by only its derived classes, declare the member with the Protected access modifier. The modified Employee, SalariedPerson, and TippedEarner classes showed how the declaration of the Protected access for a member can facilitate implementation of desired features in these classes.

- A form with controls and code can be inherited at design time. The derived form can be further added with other controls and code at design time. The entry form and the sales entry form were used to illustrate the steps to accomplish the inheritance and additional modification at design time.

- Polymorphism refers to the capability to define identically named methods or properties in multiple classes. Although these members have different implementations, the client code can use them at runtime interchangeably without having to deal with the differences in class or implementation.

- There are two types of polymorphisms: inheritance-based and interface-based.

- Inheritance-based polymorphism involves defining the methods or properties in the base class and requiring the derived class to implement these members. The Account, RealAccount, and NominalAccount classes were used to illustrate inheritance-based polymorphism through the Close method.

- Interface-based polymorphism involves defining the methods or properties in an interface definition and allowing these members to be implemented in various classes. The IMove interface example was used to illustrate how to define and implement interfaces.

- Interface-based polymorphism ensures that classes implementing the interface provide standardized method (or property) calls, making these classes easier to use because of their uniformity.

- A class is not allowed to inherit from multiple base classes, but an interface is allowed to inherit from multiple interfaces.

- When an object is no longer accessible, the resources it used may not be immediately reclaimed by the system. Usually, the garbage collection process does not start until the system determines that the resources are running low. The garbage collector calls the Finalize method of each object before destroying and reclaiming resources used by the object.

- If you want to create your own exception, you should derive the new exception from the ApplicationException class.

Explore and Discover

13-1. Implicit Inheritance? The text claims that all objects are derived from the System.Object class. To see what this means, add a class module to a new project and then take the default file name **Class1**. You should see the following code in the class module:

```
Public Class Class1

End Class
```

Go back to the form. In the form Load event, type the following line:

```
Dim TheClass As New Class1()
TheClass.
```

When you key the period (.) after TheClass, do you see the IntelliSense display **GetType?** Complete the line (TheClass.GetType()). You have not coded any property or method in the class. If it did not inherit from any base class, the IntelliSense would have nothing to show. The GetType method is a method implemented in the System.Object class. Class1 must have implicitly inherited from that class.

13-2. **Static or Instance Method?** (continued from exercise 13-1) Add the following statement to the same event procedure:

```
Class1.GetType()
```

Does the compiler accept the statement? If so, the method is a Shared (static) method. If not, the method is an Instance method. What do you find? Remove the statement after your test.

13-3. **Access Modifier for the Class.** Use the class module in exercise 13-2. Change the access modifier Public to Friend, Protected, Private, and Shared (one at a time). Which ones does the compiler accept or reject? (Protected, Private and Shared are not allowed.)

13-4. **Access Modifier for the Inner Class.** Use the class module in exercise 13-3. Keep the following code in the module:

```
Public Class Class1
    Class Class2

    End Class
End Class
```

Change the access modifier for Class2 to Public, Friend, Protected, Private, and Shared (one at a time). Which ones does the compiler accept or reject? (Only Shared is not allowed.)

Change the access modifier for Class1 to Friend; then change the access modifier for Class2 to Public, Friend, Private, and Shared (one at a time). Which ones does the compiler accept or reject? (Only Shared is not allowed.) When Class2 is declared with the Public access modifier, is it really accessible to "all?" Not really because Class2's outer class is a Friend access. Class2 cannot be accessible when Class1 is not accessible.

13-5. **Name "Conflict" in Derived Class.** Add a class module to a new project and then take the default name. Code the class as follows:

```
Public Class Class1
    Function Name1() As Integer
        Return(1)
    End Sub
End Class
```

Add another class in the same module (but outside of Class1) as follows:

```
Class Class2
    Inherits Class1
    Property Name1() As Integer
        Get
            Return(0)
```

```
                End Get
                Set(ByVal Value As Integer)

                End Set
            End Property
        End Class
```

What does the compiler show? You can't declare in a derived class the same name of a member that is not Private in the base class. If you have to use the same property name in the derived class, qualify the property with the Shadows keyword as follows:

```
        Shadows Property Name1() As Integer
```

13-6. **Referencing a Shadowed Member.** (continued from exercise 13-5) Suppose you are coding for Class2 in the preceding exercise. How do you reference Name1 in Class1 and in Class2?

Add the following method to Class2.

```
        Sub Show()
            MsgBox(MyBase.Name1)
            MsgBox(Me.Name1)
        End Sub
```

The compiler accepts both, but what does each mean? Place the following code in the form's Click event:

```
            Dim TheClass As New Class2()
            TheClass.Show()
```

Run the project and then click the form. What do you see? If you see a 1, it comes from the base class (Class1). If you see a 0, it comes from the derived class (Class2).

13-7. **Name Conflict Again.** (continued from exercise 13-6) Change the code in Class2 as follows:

```
        Class Class2
            Inherits Class1
            Overloads Function Name1() As Integer
                Return (2)
            End Function
            Sub Show()
            MsgBox(MyBase.Name1())
                MsgBox(Name1())
            End Sub
        End Class
```

Notice the keyword to declare Name1. Do you see any error? You can also overload a member in the derived class. Run the project and then click the form. Do you see any difference?

13-8. **Can a Derived Form Be Inherited at Design Time?** Add a form (Form2) to a new project. Draw a label and a text box on the form. Run the project, and end it; then add a form inherited from Form2, and name it Form3. Add a list box and a combo box to this new form. Run the project and then end it again. Use the Add Inherited Form option of the Project menu, and verify that Form3 appears in the Inheritance Picker dialog box. Select Form3 from the dialog box, and verify that you can still perform any form design activity on this new inherited form.

13-9. **Interface Access Declaration.** Create a new project and add a new class module. In the class module inside the class definition, enter the following code:

```
Interface ITest
End Interface
```

Try to place the following access Modifiers before the Interface declaration: Public, Friend, Protected, Private, Shared. Which ones does the compiler accept or reject? (Shared is not allowed.)

Now move the interface definition out of the class definition, but still in the same module. Repeat the same experiment with the access modifiers. Which ones does the compiler accept or reject? (Only Friend and Public are accepted.)

13-10. **Interface Access Declaration.** (continued exercise from 13-9) Modify the code in the preceding exercise as follows:

```
Interface ITest
    Function Fun() As Integer
End Interface
```

Now try to place the following access Modifiers before the function definition: Public, Friend, Protected, Private, Shared. Which ones does the compiler accept or reject? (None are allowed.)

13-11. **Interface Access Implementation.** (continued from exercise 13-10) Add the following code to the class module in the preceding exercise:

```
Class Taker
    Implements ITest
    Function Fun() As Integer Implements ITest.Fun
    End Function
End Class
```

Now try to place the following access Modifiers before the function header in this class: Public, Friend, Protected, Private, Shared. Which ones does the compiler accept or reject? (Only Shared in not allowed.)

13-12. **Multiple Inheritances.** Can a class inherit from more than one class? Try the following code in a class module:

```
Class Class1
End Class
Class Class2
End Class
Class Class3
    Inherits Class1
    Inherits Class2
End Class
```

Does the compiler accept the second Inherits statement?

13-13. **Multiple Inheritances.** (continued from exercise 13-12) Can a class inherit from another class, and still implement more than one interface? Add the following code to the preceding module:

```
Interface ITest1
    Function Fun1() As Integer
End Interface
Interface ITest2
    Function Fun2() As Integer
End Interface
```

Modify the code for Class3 as follows:

```
Class Class3
    Inherits Class1
    Implements ITest1
    Implements ITest2
    Function Fun1() As Integer Implements ITest1.Fun1
    End Function
    Function Fun2() As Integer Implements ITest2.Fun2
    End Function
End Class
```

Do you see any compiler error after completing the code? You can implement as many interfaces in a class as you want.

13-14. **Multiple Inheritances.** (continued from exercise 13-13) Can an interface inherit from more than one interface? Add the following code to the preceding exercise.

```
Interface ITest3
    Inherits ITest1
    Inherits ITest2
End Interface
```

Do you see any error? An interface can inherit from many interfaces.

13-15. **Name Conflict in Interface Inheritance.** Add a class module to a new project, and retain the default name for the class module. Add the following code to the module:

```
Interface IConflict1
    Function Conf() As Integer
End Interface
Interface IConflict2
    ReadOnly Property Conf() As Integer
End Interface
Interface Iconflict
    Inherits IConflict1
    Inherits IConflict2
End Interface
```

Does the compiler accept the code? Notice that Conf is defined as a method in IConflict1 and as a read-only property in IConflict2. There is a name conflict, but the compiler still accepts.

How do you implement IConflict in a class? Try the following code in the same module:

```
Public Class Class1
    Implements Iconflict
    Function Conf1() As Integer Implements IConflict1.Conf
    End Function
    ReadOnly Property Conf2() As Integer Implements
      IConflict2.Conf
        Get
        End Get
    End Property
End Class
```

It works. Notice that you cannot have both the function and the property assigned the same name. Also notice how the Implements clause references the interface. It goes back to the base interface (IConflict1 or IConflict2). Try to change one of the interface names (to IConflict) in either of the Implements clause and see what happens.

Exercises

13-16. **Bank Accounts.** Create a base bank account that has a read-only Balance property and account number (read-write) property. It should also have a Deposit method that adds an amount (parameter of the Double type) to the balance, and a Withdraw method that subtracts an amount (parameter of the Double type) from the balance; then create two classes derived from this base class: SavingsAccount and CheckingAccount. The SavingsAccount should have the InterestRate (Double) property and the Update method, which assumes that the update is done monthly and adds 1/12 of the interest rate times the balance to the current balance. The CheckingAccount class has two properties: minimum compensation amount (Double), and monthly service fee (Double). The default minimum balance is $100,000. The class should have an Update method, which tests current balance against the minimum compensation amount. If the former is lower, the monthly service fee is subtracted from the current balance; otherwise, nothing is changed.

13-17. **Bank Accounts: Inheritance Polymorphism**. (continued from exercise 13-16) Revise the classes so that the Update method is an abstract method in the base bank account class, requiring the actual implementation in both the checking account and savings account class.

13-18. **The BankAccountCollection Class: Inheritance from the CollectionBase Class**. (continued from exercise 13-17) Create a BankAccountCollection class that inherits from the CollectionBase class. The derived class accepts only the bank account class into the collection (with the Add method), has a read-only Item property that takes a parameter of the Integer type, and returns the account as indexed by the parameter. The class should also implement a Remove method that removes an account in the position as specified by a parameter of the Integer type.

13-19. **Depositor and the Bank Account Classes (nested classes).** (continued from exercise 13-18) Create a Depositor class that has three properties: Depositor ID, Name, and Accounts. The Accounts property has an Item property and two methods, Add and Remove, as described in exercise 13-18. The BankAccount, CheckingAccount, SavingsAccount, and BankAccountCollection classes should all be inner classes of the Depositor.

13-20. **The MaskEdit class.** Refer to the MaskEdit class example in Section 13.1. Enhance the class so that it can handle the Backspace and Left arrow keys. In addition, it should also allow A and a as the mask character. The A mask requires that an uppercase letter be in that corresponding position; the a mask requires that either an upper- or lowercase letter be in that position.

13-21. **The Inventory Classes.** Create an inventory base class that has the ProductID and Description properties. It has two derived classes: SpecificItem and HomogeneousItem. The SpecificItem class has an ItemID, Cost, and SalesAmount properties. Its Valuation method tests whether the SalesAmount property is zero. If so, the method returns the Cost property value as its total cost; otherwise, it returns zero. The HomogeneousItem class has standard cost and quantity on hand (read-only) properties. Its Valuation method returns the product (extension) of quantity on hand times the standard cost as its total cost. It also has a Purchase method that adds a quantity (parameter) to the private copy of the quantity on hand property. It has a Sell method that subtracts a quantity (parameter) from the private copy of the quantity on hand property.

13-22. **The Inventory Classes: Inheritance Polymorphism.** (continued from exercise 13-21) Revise the classes so that the Valuation method is an abstract method in the base inventory class, requiring the actual implementation in both the SpecificItem class and the HomogeneousItem class.

13-23. **The InventoryCollection Class: Inheritance from the CollectionBase Class.** (continued from exercise 13-22) Create a InventoryCollection class that inherits from the CollectionBase class. This derived class accepts only the inventory class into the collection (with the Add method), and has a read-only Item property that takes a parameter of the Integer type and then returns the account as indexed by the parameter (make this the default property). The class should also implement a Remove method that removes an inventory in the position as specified by a parameter of the Integer type.

13-24. **A Student Class with an Inner Class.** (Refer to exercise 12-16 in Chapter 12.) Modify the project so that the CourseID is replaced with the Course object, which has the CourseID, ClassRoom, and Date/Time of course offering such as Monday and Wednesday 10:00-11:20 A.M. Also, the Courses should now be a property that has the Item property, and the Add and Remove methods similar to the Item property in the preceding exercise (13-23).

13-25. **Form Inheritance.** Refer to the form inheritance example in section 13.2. Modify the base form by inserting an Order Number field that appears before the date field. Name the label associated with this field **lblOrderNumber**. Complete the purchase entry form by adding one additional field (accompanied by proper labels) on the newly derived form: Vendor ID. At runtime, the Text property of lblOrderNumber will be changed to Purchase Order Number, and to Sales Order Number for the sales entry form. Add test code in the startup form to verify that the derived form works properly.

13-26. **Interface-Based Polymorphism.** (continued from exercise 13-25) Define an interface in a class module as follows:

```
Interface ISaver
    Sub SaveRecord()
    Sub ClearScreen()
End Interface
```

Implement the interface in both the sales and purchase entry forms. The SaveRecord method in the respective entry form will save the data on the form to a database table named tblSales or tblPurchase with the same corresponding fields. The ClearScreen method in each form will clear the data fields onscreen after the record is saved. Both tblSales and tblPurchase should be in the same Inventory database. Create one for this purpose.

13-27. **Implementing Event Arguments.** (Refer to exercise 12-18 in Chapter 12.) Implement the event with the two parameters as recommended by Microsoft. Call the second parameter **DepreMethodChangedArgs**.

13-28. **Implementing Event Arguments.** (Refer to exercise 12-22 in Chapter 12.) Add an event that will fire when the percentage of simulation is increased by one percentile. The event should have the two parameters as recommended by Microsoft. Name the second argument as **PercentChangedArgs**.

Projects

Note: Exercises 13-16 through 13-19 together can be considered as one project.

13-29.   **The Apartment Classes (Nested).** Develop an Apartment class that has two properties: ApartmentNumber and Address. This class is inherited by two classes: EfficientSuite and DeluxeSuite. The EfficientSuite class has two properties: Bedroom and Kitchen. Each of these properties has a Furnishing property. The Furnishing property has an Item property (default) and two methods, Add and Remove. The Item property is read-only, and takes a parameter of the Integer type. It returns a Furniture object at the position specified by the parameter. The Furniture object has four properties: AssetID, Description, DateAcquired, and Condition Index (a value ranging from 1 to 5; 1=Excellent, 5= to be junked). The DeluxeSuite class has two properties: Bedrooms and Kitchen. The DeluxeSuite's Bedrooms and Kitchen properties each have a Furnishing property that behaves the same way as the EfficientSuite's Furnishing property. The Bedrooms property has the Item property and two methods, Add and Remove, that behave in exactly the same way as those described for the EfficientSuite's Furnishing property. (*Hint:* Write the Furnishing and Bedrooms properties each respectively as a class inherited from the CollectionBase class.)

14 Beyond the Core

This chapter presents topics that are beyond the core of VB; however, these topics are important. A good understanding of the material covered in this chapter will enable you to extend VB's power beyond the level you can currently imagine.

The chapter begins with an introduction to the Windows registry, a database maintained by the Windows operating system to facilitate its own and other application program's operations. The discussion is limited to how the registry can be used to maintain data needed for the proper operation of your application.

Section 14.2 introduces you to creating components, which after created can be used by any other applications developed using the .NET framework. VB.NET provides you with templates that allow you to create components easily. You should be able to immediately appreciate how this capability enhances your ability to build applications rapidly and conveniently by assembling various components you create for yourself or others to use.

The remainder of the chapter presents ASP.NET framework, which allows rapid development of web applications (in particular in web forms) and creation of web services. Most of the applications that you will develop in the future will either directly or indirectly involve the web. The introduction to web forms paves the way for you to further explore into web programming. Web services provide functionality that can be accessed remotely. These services can be incorporated into your desktop or web applications. Section 14.4 illustrates how a web service can be created and used. Many articles, including some in the Harvard Business Review, have touted the potential of web services. After you learn the technique, it is up to you to put it to use in any innovative application you can imagine.

After completing this chapter, you should be able to:

- Save and retrieve data from the Windows registry.
- Comprehend the steps required to create components for use by other applications.
- Understand the concepts relevant to web applications using ASP.NET.
- Create web forms applications.
- Create and use web services.

14.1   Using the Windows Registry

You will most likely encounter a situation in which you would like your program to have some VB control properties set to certain values. However, you might be hesitant to hard-code the values because you want to allow your user to choose these values or because the computer in which your program will run may be different from the computer you use to develop the program, and the property values that are available in one computer may not be available in the other.

One possible solution to this problem is to create a special file that keeps track of these special settings, but this solution has several drawbacks. The code to handle the file can take many lines. Determining the proper file path can also be an issue. Finally, you will need to secure the file from the user's accidental alteration or destruction.

A better alternative is to use the Windows registry, which is a database that the operating system maintains to support the system's and applications' operations. This section illustrates how you can use the Windows registry in your program to handle some of its operational needs.

A Simple Text Browser Project

Consider the simple text viewer application whose visual interface is shown in Figure 14.1. The form has a button that allows a user to specify the text file that the user wants to read. After the filename is specified, your program proceeds to load the file content into the text box on the form. You also want to enable your user to view the text with any font and font size available in the system. The available fonts are listed in a combo box. When the user makes a selection from this box, the font in the text box changes accordingly. The challenge is this: You want your program to use this same font when it starts next time. This means your program must find some way to save this font before it quits and to retrieve the same font next time.

Selected settings of the controls used in the form are listed in the following table.

Figure 14.1
Visual interface for a text viewer

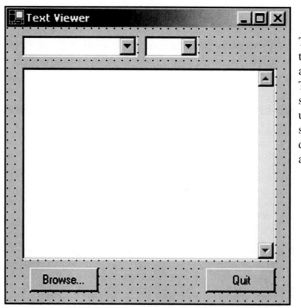

The program automatically populates the combo boxes with available fonts and selected font sizes at the start. The Browse button allows the user to specify a text file to view. When the user selects a font or changes the font size, the text box immediately displays the text with the new font and size.

Control	Property	Setting	Remarks
Text box	Name	txtTextBrowser	To display text read from a file
	MultiLine	True	
	Scrollbars	Vertical	
Combo box	Name	cboFontName	To display available fonts for selection
	DropdownStyle	Dropdown List	
Combo box	Name	cboFontSize	To set font size
	DropdownStyle	Dropdown	
Button	Name	BtnBrowse	To initiate browsing for a text file
	Text	Browse	
Button	Name	BtnQuit	To quit the application
	Text	Quit	
Open file dialog	Name	cdlOpenFile	

The code to populate the combo box with the available fonts appears as follows:

```
'Populate the combo box with available fonts
Dim TheFont As FontFamily
Dim FontName As String
For Each TheFont In System.Drawing.FontFamily.Families
    cboFontName.Items.Add(TheFont.Name)
Next TheFont
```

The Font Family Object. In the preceding code, the available fonts are obtained from the *Families collection* of the *FontFamily object*. The For Each loop enumerates all the available fonts, and adds the name of each font to the cboFontName combo box. At the start of the project, the routine should not only populate this combo box, but should also populate the combo box for font size. The form load event procedure appears as follows:

```
Private Sub Form1_Load(ByVal sender As Object, ByVal e As
    System.EventArgs) Handles MyBase.Load
    Dim I As Integer
    Dim FontSize As String
    Dim TheFont As FontFamily
    Dim FontName As String
    'Populate font size combo box with possible sizes; the user
      can also enter his/her own choice.
    For I = 6 To 20 Step 2
        cboFontSize.Items.Add(I)
    Next I
    'Populate the combo box with available fonts
    For Each TheFont In System.Drawing.FontFamily.Families
        cboFontName.Items.Add(TheFont.Name)
    Next TheFont
End Sub
```

Setting the Font. When the user selects a font or makes any changes in the font size, the text box should reflect this change by displaying the text with the updated font or size. The code to handle the change should appear as follows:

```
Private Sub cboFontName_SelectedIndexChanged(ByVal Sender As
    Object, ByVal e As System.EventArgs) Handles
    cboFontName.SelectedIndexChanged, cboFontSize.TextChanged
    ' Assign a Font object — Name and Size are required.
    If cboFontName.SelectedIndex >= 0 AndAlso
      Len(cboFontSize.Text) > 0 Then
        txtTextBrowser.Font = New
          System.Drawing.Font(cboFontName.Text,
          CSng(cboFontSize.Text))
    End If
End Sub
```

Notice that this event procedure handles two events: selected index changed in the font name combo box, and text changed in the font size combo box, as specified in the procedure's Handles clause. When the user selects an item in cboFontName, the control's SelectedIndexChanged event is triggered. (Note that the control's DropDownStyle property is set to DropDownList.) When the user enters or selects a font size in cboFontSize, the control's TextChanged event is triggered. In both cases, the code to handle the respective event is the same.

Remembering the Default Font

Suppose you want your program to remember the font and the size that the user has specified so that the program can use the same font and size next time as the default. How do you do this? One possibility is to create a file, and use it to keep the font name. This approach requires your program to handle several details, including the file path, and opening and closing the file. In addition, your program will need to ensure the file exists before it attempts to open the file. What initially appears to be a fairly simple problem seems to require some effort.

Accessing the Registry from VB. A better alternative to using the file is to use the Windows registry, which is a database maintained by the Windows operating system and available to all applications to keep track of information for their own uses. (Of course, the Windows operating system also uses the registry for various purposes; however, a discussion of these uses is beyond the scope of this book.) VB provides several procedures that you can use to easily access the registry. The following table lists three selected procedures.

Procedure	Type	Uses
GetSetting	Function	To retrieve data from the registry
SaveSetting	Statement	To save data in the registry
DeleteSetting	Statement	To delete data from the registry

In this example, you can use the registry to save the font name by using the SaveSetting statement, which has the following syntax:

```
SaveSetting(AppName, SectionName, Key, Setting)
```

where *AppName* = a string representing your application name

SectionName = a string representing the section name

Key = a string representing the key for your data (setting).

For example, to save the font given in the combo box into the registry, you can code the following:

```
SaveSetting ("TextBrowser", "TextFont", "FontName",
    cboFontName.Text)
```

If the font selected by the user is Courier, the preceding statement will save Courier in the location that represents an application named TextBrowser with the section name TextFont and key name FontName.

Where should the preceding statement be placed? Recall that the purpose of saving the font is to allow the same font to be used as the default for the next time. The most appropriate time to save it is before the program quits. You can place the code to save both the font and the size in the Closing event:

```
Private Sub Form1_Closing(ByVal sender As Object, ByVal e As
    System.ComponentModel.CancelEventArgs) Handles MyBase.Closing
    ' Save font and size for next time
    SaveSetting("TextBrowser", "TextFont", "FontName",
        cboFontName.Text)
    SaveSetting("TextBrowser", "TextFont", "FontSize",
        cboFontSize.Text)
End Sub
```

Retrieving the Setting. So, how can the setting be retrieved from the registry? You can use the GetSetting function, which has the following syntax:

```
Setting = GetSetting(AppName, SectionName, Key[,
  DefaultSetting])
```

where the *AppName, SectionName,* and *Key* parameters must match those specified when the setting was saved. You can also specify a value for the default setting, which will be the returned value if there is no previous setting in the registry. For this example problem, you can code the following:

```
' Retrieve Font name and size from registry
  FontName = GetSetting("TextBrowser", "TextFont", "FontName",
  txtTextBrowser.Font.Name)
FontSize = GetSetting("TextBrowser", "TextFont", "FontSize",
  CStr(txtTextBrowser.Font.Size))
```

Note that you use the text box's font name and size as the default settings in the preceding statements. This works well because when there is no previous setting, the safest thing to do is to use the same font as the current font of the text box. If you omit the default setting and nothing is found in the registry, the function will return a zero-length string.

Showing the Font in the Combo Box. After you retrieve the font from the registry, you also want the combo box to display the current setting. Recall that the combo box has its DropDownStyle property set to Dropdown List. Under this setting, its Text property cannot be assigned directly; however, you can set its SelectedIndex property to show its text. To set the proper value for the SelectedIndex property, the combo box's list must be searched for the item that matches the font retrieved from the registry. The easiest way will be to use the control's FindString method, which returns an Integer value representing the position in which the specified search string matches a portion of the item in that position. The statement appears as follows:

```
cboFontName.SelectedIndex = cboFontName.FindString(FontName)
cboFontSize.Text = FontSize
```

All the statements related to retrieving the font and size as well as setting the properties of the combo boxes should be coded in the Form Load event. The revised event procedure, including the proper declarations, appears as follows:

```
Private Sub Form1_Load(ByVal sender As Object, ByVal e As
  System.EventArgs) Handles MyBase.Load
    Dim I As Integer
    Dim FontSize As String
    Dim TheFont As FontFamily
    Dim FontName As String

    For I = 6 To 20 Step 2
        cboFontSize.Items.Add(I)
    Next I
    'Populate the combo box with available fonts
    For Each TheFont In System.Drawing.FontFamily.Families
        cboFontName.Items.Add(TheFont.Name)
    Next TheFont

    ' Retrieve Font name and size from registry
    FontName = GetSetting("TextBrowser", "TextFont", "FontName",
      txtTextBrowser.Font.Name)
    FontSize = GetSetting("TextBrowser", "TextFont", "FontSize",
      CStr(txtTextBrowser.Font.Size))
    cboFontName.SelectedIndex = cboFontName.FindString(FontName)
    cboFontSize.Text = FontSize
End Sub
```

Note again that setting the SelectedIndex Property of cboFontName will trigger the control's SelectedIndexChanged event, and setting of the Text property of cboFontSize will trigger its TextChanged event. Both events are handled by the cobFontName_SelectedIndexChanged event handler. This will work exactly the way you want: Whatever appears in the two combo boxes is the font and size used in the text box.

Deleting the Setting. If for any reason the setting should be removed from the registry, the DeleteSetting statement can be used. The statement has the following syntax:

DeleteSetting(*AppName, SectionName*[, *Key*])

To remove the font from the registry, you will code the following:

DeleteSetting("TextBrowser", "TextFont", "FontName")

Assume you have a button named btnDeleteSetting for the user to initiate the deletion. Your code will appear as follows:

```
Private Sub btnDeleteSetting_Click(ByVal sender As Object, ByVal e
    As System.EventArgs) Handles btnDeleteSetting.Click
    DeleteSetting ("TextBrowser", "TextFont", "FontName")
    DeleteSetting ("TextBrowser", "TextFont", "FontSize")
End Sub
```

As a side note, if you actually implement the preceding code to save the settings but want to permanently remove them from the registry, be sure that either the Delete Setting event procedure is placed in a different form, or the code in the Closing event is removed; otherwise, each time the form is invoked and then closed, the settings will be saved again.

Completing the Example. The example actually requires additional code. You should also provide the code for the user to specify the file to browse, open the file, and read the content into the text box. By now, you should be familiar enough with the code to handle this. The following code is provided without further explanation.

```
Private Sub btnBrowse_Click(ByVal Sender As Object, ByVal e As
    System.EventArgs) Handles btnBrowse.Click
    Dim FileName As String
    Dim TheTextFile As IO.StreamReader
    FileName = GetTheFileName()
    If Len(FileName) = 0 Then Exit Sub
    TheTextFile = New IO.StreamReader(FileName)
    txtTextBrowser.Text = TheTextFile.ReadToEnd
    TheTextFile.Close()
End Sub
Function GetTheFileName() As String
    With cdlOpenFile
        .Title = "Please specify text filename to open"
        .Filter = "Text File (*.txt)¦*.txt¦All Files (*.*)¦*.*"
        .ShowDialog()
        Return (.FileName)
    End With
End Function
```

Additional Remarks

As you can see from the preceding example, you can use the Windows registry to keep information that your program needs from one run to the next. Other examples of using the registry for this purpose include saving the user password (encrypted), keeping a file path as the default, and saving various settings of the visual interface, such as foreground and background colors, as the default.

Using the registry for such purposes has several advantages:

- It makes your program more flexible. Your program does not have to start with a setting that is hard-coded. The user can set the default and stay with it for as long as the user wants.

- Some specific systems may not have the hard-coded setting. This can cause problems. Avoiding hard-coding settings also enhances your program's applicability to different systems.

- Compared with using a file to save settings, it is much more convenient for the following reasons:

  - You don't have to worry about in which folder this file should be kept.

  - You don't have to check to ensure that the file exists before opening it.

  - The registry is less susceptible to user errors, such as mistakenly erasing the file or altering the file content.

Proper Use of the Registry. Because of the convenience, you may be tempted to use the registry to save anything that your program needs to read back in the future. Keep in mind, however, that the registry is used by the operating system to keep information for many other purposes. Overloading the registry will slow down the performance of the entire computer system.

You should use the registry only to maintain information that is pertinent to the operation of your program itself, not the type of data that the user needs to maintain for the user's application. For example, suppose your payroll program allows the user to set background colors for various controls. It would be appropriate to keep this type of information in the registry. On the other hand, the data that pertain to the payroll operations, such as employees' earnings records, should be kept in files or a database, rather than in the registry.

14.2   Creating Components

A *component* is a unit of code that can be reused as an object. Some components have visual elements, and are recognized as controls, such as the label and text box; others do not have visual elements, and are simply recognized as objects, such as the stream reader, database connection, and the dataset. VB.NET provides templates that make it easy to create components with or without visual elements. These templates also ensure compatibility across applications and languages supported by the .NET framework. This section presents two examples to illustrate how to create components without and with visual elements. Consider the case of creating a component without visual elements first.

Creating a Component with No Visual Element

The major steps in creating a component with no visual element are outlined as follows:

1. Create a new Class Library project.
2. Add the component template to the project.
3. Develop necessary code in the component template.
4. Build and debug the code.

You can then add a project to test the newly developed component to ensure that it is ready for use.

To illustrate, a project named **TinyDataLib** will be developed. In this project, you will create a component that allows the user to browse the schema of any specified Access database. This component has a DatabaseName property and two read-only properties: Tables and Columns. The Tables property returns a string array that contains all table names in a database and the

Columns property returns a string array that contains all the column names of a specified table in that same database. The Columns property requires an Integer parameter (Index) that specifies the position of the database table in the Tables array, so the Index specifies the table for which to return to column names. The user can specify the database name either at the time an instance of the component is being initialized or by setting its DatabaseName property.

Creating the TinyDataLib Project. Perform the following steps to create the project:

1. Click the File menu, select the New option, and click the Project option. The familiar New Project dialog box appears.

2. Click the Class Library icon in the Templates pane; then enter **TinyDataLib** in the Name box in place of the default name , as shown in Figure 14.2.

3. Click the OK button in the New Project dialog box.

4. Add a component class template to the project:

   a. Click the project menu and select the Add Component option to open the Add New Item dialog box. Ensure that the Component Class on the Templates pane is highlighted.

   b. Enter **DBSchemaBrowser** in the Name box in place of the default Component1.vb, as shown in Figure 14.3.

   c. Click the Open button in the Add New Item dialog box.

5. Delete the extra Class1 module.

   a. Right-click Class1.vb in the Solution Explorer.

   b. Click the Delete option in the context menu.

   c. Click the OK button in the message box.

6. Switch to the Code window for the component class. If you see two lines of message in the code window area, click "Click here to switch to code view."

Figure 14.2

Specifying the class library

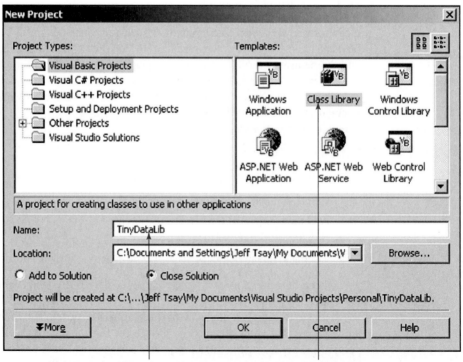

Make sure the Class Library is selected and enter "TinyDataLib" in the name box.

Figure 14.3

Specifying the component class

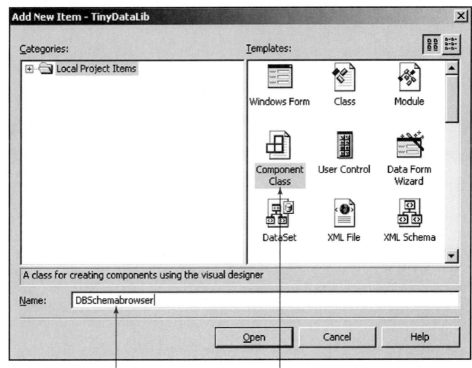

Make sure the Component Class icon is selected and enter DBSchemabrowser is entered in the name box.

Coding the Project. The basic code structure is taken from the example in Section 9.4 of Chapter 9, "Database and ADO.NET." Recall that the project involves a dataset that contains two data tables: one for the database tables, and the other for all the columns in the database. A relation between the two data tables is created so that the GetChildRows method can be used to extract all rows pertaining to a specified table. The code is modified in the following respects:

- The original code was developed for use in a form. The current code is written for a class, so all references to visual elements have been replaced with Private members in the class.
- Property procedures are added. The Private members for the Tables and Columns properties represent the output from the operations.
- The lstSchemaTables_SelectedIndexChanged event procedure is replaced with the GetColumns method, which is used to extract the pertinent column names for a specified table.

The modified code to browse the data base schema appears as follows:

```
Public Class DBSchemaBrowser
    Inherits System.ComponentModel.Component
    Private mDBName As String
    Private mTables() As String
    Private mColumns() As String

    ReadOnly Property Tables() As String()
        Get
            Return (mTables)
        End Get
    End Property
    ReadOnly Property Columns(ByVal Index As Integer) As String()
        Get
            'Return column names for Tables(Index)
            GetColumns(Index)
```

```
                        Return (mColumns)
                    End Get
                End Property

                Property DatabaseName() As String
                    Get
                        Return (mDBName)
                    End Get
                    Set(ByVal Value As String)
                        mDBName = Value
                        GetDBSchema()
                    End Set
                End Property
                Private relTable2Col As DataRelation
                Private dsSchema As New DataSet()
                Private cnnDatabase As New OleDb.OleDbConnection()
                Private tblSchemaTables As New DataTable()
                Private tblSchemaColumns As New DataTable()
                Private Sub GetDBSchema()
                    Dim Criteria(3) As Object
                    Dim I As Integer
                    Dim N As Integer
                    cnnDatabase.ConnectionString =
                      "Provider=Microsoft.Jet.OLEDB.4.0;Data Source=" &
                      mDBName
                    cnnDatabase.Open()
                    tblSchemaTables =
                      cnnDatabase.GetOleDbSchemaTable(OleDb.OleDbSchemaGuid.Ta
                      bles, Criteria)
                    tblSchemaColumns =
                      cnnDatabase.GetOleDbSchemaTable(OleDb.OleDbSchemaGuid.Co
                      lumns, Criteria)
                    cnnDatabase.Close()
                    'Recreate the dataset
                    dsSchema = Nothing 'Make the dataset nothing
                    dsSchema = New DataSet() 'Create a new dataset object
                    'Add the datatables to the dataset
                    dsSchema.Tables.Add(tblSchemaTables)
                    dsSchema.Tables.Add(tblSchemaColumns)
                    'Create the data relation
                    relTable2Col = dsSchema.Relations.Add("TableColumn",
                      tblSchemaTables.Columns("Table_Name"), _
                    tblSchemaColumns.Columns("Table_Name"))
                    'Place table names in mTables()
                    N = tblSchemaTables.Rows.Count - 1
                    ReDim mTables(N)
                    For I = 0 To N
                        mTables(I) =
                            CStr(tblSchemaTables.Rows(I)("Table_Name"))
                    Next I
                End Sub
                Private Sub GetColumns(ByVal Index As Integer)
                    Dim TheChildRows() As DataRow
                    Dim I As Integer
                    Dim N As Integer
                    TheChildRows =
                      tblSchemaTables.Rows(Index).GetChildRows(relTable2Col)
                    N = TheChildRows.Length - 1
                    ReDim mColumns(N)
                    For I = 0 To N
                        mColumns(I) =
                            CStr(TheChildRows(I).Item("Column_Name"))
                    Next I
                End Sub
            End Class
```

Pay particular attention to the Set procedure for the DatabaseName property. In addition to setting the value for the Private member of the property, it also calls the GetDBSchema procedure. This procedure sets up the connection with the database using the specified database name, reads the database tables and columns into two data tables, creates a dataset, adds the two data tables to the dataset, and sets up a relation between the two data tables. Note that the procedure also extracts the table names, and places them in the Private member of the Tables property.

Notice the pairs of parentheses following String in the property definitions of Tables and Columns. They are required because each property returns a string array. Notice also that the Columns property requires an Integer parameter that specifies the position of the table of interest. The Get property procedure in turn calls the (Private) GetColumns procedure to extract the pertinent column names for the specified table.

TIP

You may wonder why not just make GetColumns a Public method because there will be no need to implement the Columns property. If you look at the component from the user's viewpoint, however, you will notice that the component is much easier to use when both Tables and Columns are exposed as properties because of consistency.

Component Constructor. Recall that the user can also specify the database name when an instance of the class is initialized. You should also provide an overloading constructor as follows:

```
Sub New(ByVal DBName As String)
    mDBName = DBName
    GetDBSchema()
End Sub
```

As you can see, the constructor has exactly the same code as the Set procedure for the DatabaseName property.

Component Destructors. The Component class provides a Finalize method and a *Dispose method* for the system to reclaim resources (used by the component) when the component is no longer referenced. As you may recall, the Finalize method is called by the garbage collector (and is not callable by the client code) in the garbage collection process, which may not occur immediately after an instance of a class is no longer accessible. The Dispose method allows the client code to explicitly dispose of the resources. Any component that uses significant amount of system resources should implement the Dispose method.

If you inspect the components used in the DBSchemaBrowser class, you will find that the connection, dataset, data table, and data column provide the Dispose method. The connection is noted for using considerable amount of system resources, so its Dispose method should be called. The most appropriate time, however, is when the DBSchemaBrowser is to be disposed of. You should provide a Dispose method in this component.

Microsoft provides this guideline in writing the Dispose method: The method should release all of the resources that it owns. It should also release all resources owned by its base types by calling its parent's Dispose method. To ensure that resources are always cleaned up appropriately, the method should be safely callable multiple times without throwing an exception.

Microsoft also provides a template for the Dispose method for a derived class as follows:

```
Protected Overloads Overrides Sub Dispose(disposing As Boolean)
    If Not (Me.disposed) Then
        Try
            If disposing Then
                ' Release any managed resources here.
            End If
            ' Release unmanaged resources here.
            Me.disposed = True
        Finally
```

```
                            ' Call Dispose on your base class.
                            MyBase.Dispose(disposing)
                        End Try
                    End If
                End Sub
```

As you may recall, the Dispose method that the client code can call should be a Public method and has no parameter. The template here overloads that method and is of the Protected access. This method is not accessible externally, and is indeed *called* by the Public method (implemented in the Component class) to perform the disposition of the resources. Using this template, the code for the Dispose method for the DBSchemaBrowser appears as follows:

```
    Private Shadows Disposed As Boolean = False
    Protected Overloads Overrides Sub Dispose(ByVal disposing As
        Boolean)
        If Not (Me.Disposed) Then
            Try
                If disposing Then
                    ' Release any managed resources here.
                    cnnDatabase.Dispose()
                    cnnDatabase = Nothing
                    tblSchemaColumns.Dispose()
                    tblSchemaColumns = Nothing
                    tblSchemaTables.Dispose()
                    tblSchemaTables = Nothing
                    dsSchema.Dispose()
                    dsSchema = Nothing
                End If
                ' Release unmanaged resources here.
                Me.Disposed = True
            Finally
                ' Call Dispose on the base class.
                MyBase.Dispose(disposing)
            End Try
        End If
    End Sub
```

Because the Public Dispose method has already been implemented in the base Component class, there is no need to code another. When the client code calls for the Dispose method, the one in the Component class will be invoked.

Building the Project. To ensure that the project has no apparent errors, you should build the project by clicking the Build menu and then selecting the Build TinyDataLib option. This step also creates the DLL file from the project. After the build process encounters no error, the component is ready for further test.

Testing the DBSchemaBrowser Component

While the TinyDataLib project is still in the IDE, you can add another project to test how the DBSchemaBrowser component works. To do so, follow these steps:

1. Add a Windows Form test project.
   a. Click the File menu and then select the Add Project option (not the New or Open option). Select New project to open the Add New Project dialog box.
   b. Click the Windows Application icon in the Templates pane.
   c. Enter TestSchemaBrowser in the Name box; then click the OK button in the Add New Project dialog box.
2. Set this project as the startup project.
   a. Right-click the TestSchemaBrowser project in the Solution Explorer. The context menu appears.
   b. Select the Set as Startup Project option.

Figure 14.4

Adding reference to the test project

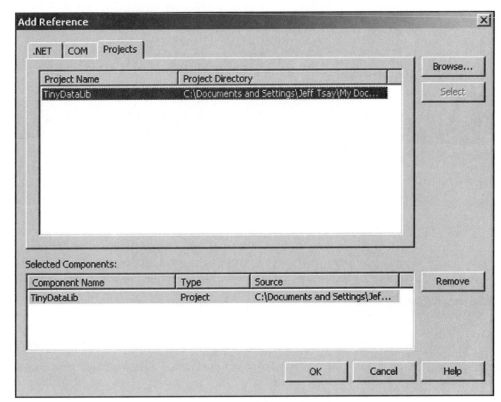

Make sure the Projects tab is selected. Double click TinyDataLib in the upper pane and it should appear in the lower (Selected Components) pane.

3. Add a reference to the TinyDataLib project.

   a. Right-click the TestSchemaBrowser project in the Solution Explorer to open the context menu.

   b. Select Add Reference to open the Add Reference dialog box.

   c. Click the Projects tab of the dialog box.

   d. Double-click the TinyDataLib project in the upper pane so that it is included in the lower pane, as shown in Figure 14.4.

   e. Click the OK button in the Add Reference dialog box.

4. Design the visual interface.

   a. Draw two list boxes on the form. Name them **lstTables** and **lstColumns**, respectively.

   b. Draw an OpenFileDialog on the form, and name it **cdlOpenFile**.

   c. Draw a button on the form, name it **btnBrowse,** and set its text to Browse.

5. Add the following code:

```
Dim SchemaBrowser As TinyDataLib.DBSchemaBrowser
Private Sub btnBrowse_Click(ByVal Sender As Object, ByVal e As
   System.EventArgs) Handles btnBrowse.Click
   With cdlOpenFile
       .Filter = "Access File (*.mdb)¦*.mdb"
       .ShowDialog()
       SchemaBrowser = New TinyDataLib.DBSchemaBrowser(.FileName)
   End With
   lstTables.DataSource = SchemaBrowser.Tables
End Sub
```

```
Private Sub lstTables_SelectedIndexChanged(ByVal Sender As Object,
   ByVal e As System.EventArgs) Handles
   lstTables.SelectedIndexChanged
     lstColumns.DataSource =
       SchemaBrowser.Columns(lstTables.SelectedIndex)
End Sub
```

Notice how the DBSchemaBrowser is referenced. It is qualified by the project name, TinyDataLib. The project name is the assembly name. The assembly can actually contain many components. To add more components to the project, click the project in the Solutions Explorer and then click the Project menu and select the Add Component option.

As you can tell from the code, the test project behaves as follows: When the user clicks the Browse button, the Open File dialog box prompts the user for the database name, which is passed to the component when an instance is initialized. The component's Tables property is used to return a string array, which is assigned to DataSource property of the lstTables list box so that the array is bound to the list box to display the table names. Also, when the user makes a selection in the list box that shows the table names, the selected index is passed to the component's Columns property for it to return the column names for the selected table. The returned array is bound to the lstColumns list box to display the column names. A sample result is shown in Figure 14.5.

Using the Component in Any Project

After the component is fully tested, you can use it in any new project. The steps are similar to those in step 3 of the preceding test project, and can be outlined as follows:

1. Right-click the project name in the Solution Explorer to open a context menu.

2. Select Add Reference to open the Add Reference dialog box.

3. Click the .NET tab of the dialog box.

4. Click the Browse button; then use the Select Component dialog box to browse the file directory to find the location of the assembly (TinyDataLib.dll). It should be in the Bin folder under the TinyDataLib folder.

5. Double-click TinyDataLib.dll; it should appear in the lower pane of the Add Reference dialog box.

6. Click the OK button in the dialog box.

You now have included the TinyDataLib in your project, and can create an instance of the DBSchemaBrowser in the following syntax:

```
Dim Name As TinyDataLib.DBSchemaBrowser
Name = New TinyDataLib.DBSchemaBrowser(DatabaseName)
```

Figure 14.5

Testing the
DBSchemaBrowser
component

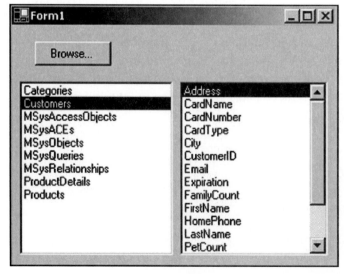

These two list boxes are bound to the Tables and Columns properties of the DBSchemaBrowser object. After the user clicks the Browse button and selects a database, the list box on the left displays all the table names in the database. When the user clicks an item in the left list box, all columns in that selected table name appear in the list box on the right.

Creating a Component with Visual Elements

Creating and testing a component with visual elements (a control) is not much different than creating a component with no visual elements. In most cases, you will extend the functionality of an existing control. Basically, you use a different template (Windows Control Library, instead of Class Library) to start and then develop your code from there.

To illustrate, create a control called KeyVerifierBox. This control will allow different types of keys in its box, depending on the setting of the KeyType property. If the property is set to Numeric, only numeric keys can be entered in the box. If the property is set to UpperCaseLetter, only uppercase letters can be entered. The default setting for this property is None, which will allow any kind of key in the box. Recall that in Chapter 10, "Special Topics in Data Entry," various key verification routines were written to ensure only valid keys are entered in the text box; therefore, you will create this new control by extending the text box. Here are the steps to create this new control:

1. Click the File menu, select the New option, and click the Project option in the sub menu to open the New Project dialog box.

2. Click the Windows Control Library icon in the Templates pane.

3. Enter KeyVerifierLib in the Name box and then click the OK button.

4. Rename the UserControl1.vb in the Solution Explorer to **KeyVerifierBox.vb**. To do this, right-click UserControl1.vb in the Solution Explorer, and select the Rename option; then change the name to **KeyVerifierBox.vb**.

5. Change the class name in the code window to **KeyVerifierBox**.

6. Change the Inherits statement in the class to:
   ```
   Inherits System.Windows.Forms.TextBox
   ```

7. Place the following code in the code window:

```
Public Class KeyVerifierBox
    Inherits System.Windows.Forms.TextBox
    ' Windows generated code is here
    Enum KeyTypeToVerify
        None = 0
        Numeric = 1
        UpperCaseLetter = 2
    End Enum
    Private mKeyType As KeyTypeToVerify
    Property KeyType() As KeyTypeToVerify
        Get
            Return (mKeyType)
        End Get
        Set(ByVal Value As KeyTypeToVerify)
            If Value < KeyTypeToVerify.None OrElse Value >
              KeyTypeToVerify.UpperCaseLetter Then
                Throw New System.ArgumentOutOfRangeException
                  ("KeyTypeToVerify")
                Exit Property
            End If
            mKeyType = Value
        End Set
    End Property
    Private Sub KeyVerifierBox_KeyPress(ByVal sender As Object,
      ByVal e As System.Windows.Forms.KeyPressEventArgs) Handles
      MyBase.KeyPress
        Dim KeyAscii As Integer
        KeyAscii = AscW(e.KeyChar)
        If KeyAscii < Keys.Space Then
            'Control keys; ignore
            Exit Sub
        End If
        Select Case mKeyType
            Case KeyTypeToVerify.None
            Case KeyTypeToVerify.Numeric
```

```
                        If IsNumericKey(KeyAscii) Then
                        Else
                            MsgBox("Numeric key only, please.")
                            e.Handled = True 'suppress the key
                        End If
                    Case KeyTypeToVerify.UpperCaseLetter
                        If IsUpperCase(KeyAscii) Then
                        Else
                            MsgBox("Upper case letter only, please.")
                            e.Handled = True 'suppress the key
                        End If
            End Select
        End Sub

        Private Function IsNumericKey(ByVal KeyAscii As Integer) As
          Boolean
            IsNumericKey = KeyAscii >= Keys.D0 AndAlso KeyAscii <=
              Keys.D9
        End Function

        Private Function IsUpperCase(ByVal KeyAscii As Integer) As
          Boolean
            IsUpperCase = KeyAscii >= Keys.A AndAlso KeyAscii <= Keys.Z
        End Function
    End Class
```

The routines to verify the keys entered are similar to those discussed in Chapter 10; however, notice the following points:

- The KeyType property decides what type of key to check. For clarity, the KeyTypeToVerify Enumeration is associated with the property. The enumeration lists three values: None (0), Numeric (1), and UpperCaseLetter (2). In Chapter 10, the user specifies the type of key to verify by setting a property character in the Tag property of the control. Also, the form's KeyPreview property must be set to True for those key verification routines to work properly. The introduction of the KeyType property eliminates the need to do any of these. All the user needs to do now is to select the proper setting for the KeyType property.

- The Set procedure of the KeyType property validates the value of the parameter. When the value is out of range, the exception is thrown.

- The KeyPress event handler is hooked to MyBase.KeyPress because the event is raised from the text box, from which the current class is derived.

After the code is in place, you can build the project to ensure that there is no error. The next step is to add a project to test the newly developed control.

Testing and Using the New Control

To test the new control involves the following major steps:

1. Add a new Windows form project to the solution, and name the project TestKeyVerifier.

2. Set this form project as the startup project.

3. Customize the Toolbox by adding the new control.

    a. Click the Tools menu and then select the Customize Toolbox option. The Customize Toolbox dialog appears.

    b. Click the .NET Framework Components tab in the dialog box, as shown in Figure 14.6.

    c. Click the Browse button in the dialog box. The Browse dialog box appears. Use the Open dialog box to find the location for KeyVerifierLib.dll. It should be in the Bin folder under the KeyVerifierLib folder (see Figure 14.6).

    d. Double-click KeyVerifierLib.dll. KeyverifierBox should appear in the .NET Framework Components list. If necessary, check the box on the left side of KeyVerifierBox in the dialog box and then click the OK button.

Figure 14.6

Adding the
KeyVerifierBox control to
the Toolbox

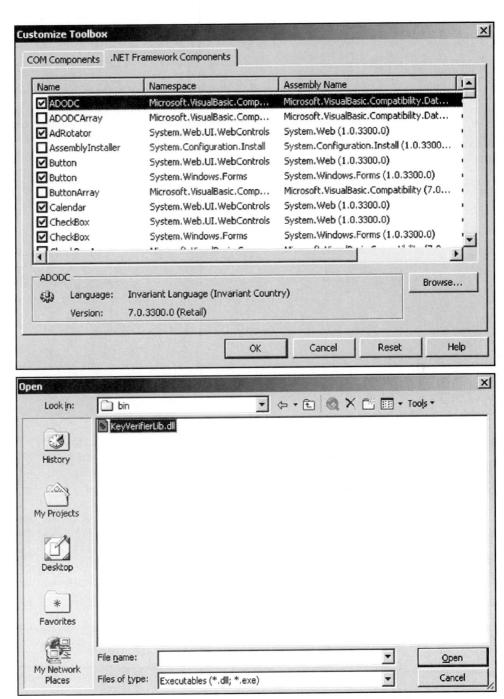

Make sure that .NET Framework Components tab is selected. Click the
Browse button and find the KeyVerifierLib.dll. Then click the Open
button. *Be sure to check KeyVerifierBox in the Customize Toolbox box
before clicking the OK button.*

The KeyVerifierBox control should appear at the bottom of the Windows Forms tab of the
Toolbox.

Draw two Key Verifier Boxes on the form. Set the KeyType property of one control to
Numeric, and another to UpperCaseLetter. Notice how these choices appear in the control's
Properties window; they are just like the enumerated settings of other controls! Run the project.
Try to enter different types of keys in each control, and see if these controls behave as expected.

Using the New Control in Any Project. After the control is included in the Toolbox, you can use it in any project just like any other control without involving any additional steps. If you really like what you have done, perhaps, you want to implement even more features in this control; for example, additional setting choices for the KeyType, such as Alphabetic to allow both upper- and lowercase letters, and Amount to allow commas and periods in proper position. You can even add a Mask property so that it will have features similar to the masked edit box. These enhancements are left to you as exercise 14-16 at the end of this chapter.

The User Control

Recall that when you created a new Windows Control Library project, the default class name was UserControl1 and the class inherits from UserControl. What is a user control? It is basically an empty control that allows you to design a new control visually. It is often used to combine several controls to provide some specific user interface functionality. For example, you may find that in your applications, you need to draw a visual interface for personal identification, which includes ID number, name, sex, and date of birth. Rather than drawing controls directly in all forms involved, you can create a user control (perhaps name it PersonalID control) that contains all these elements. You can also include all necessary code for data validation in the class. You can then have it built and included in the Toolbox. From then on, you can draw it on any form that involves personal identification. Exercises 14-17 and 14-18 at the end of this chapter provide you with an opportunity to explore the uses of this control.

14.3   Developing Web Forms Applications

This and the following section introduce you to ASP.NET. As mentioned at the beginning of this chapter, ASP.NET allows you to create web forms projects and web services. This section begins by explaining a few basic web concepts, and will continue with three examples to illustrate how to create web forms projects. The following section focuses on the steps required to create a web service.

Basic Concepts

Imagine that you have started a web browser, and entered a URL (uniform resource locator) that starts with HTTP://. Your browser then starts to display a page that includes various texts and images. What has happened at your computer and behind the scenes?

When you press the Enter key after typing in the URL, your computer sends a request to another computer asking for a document. The other computer sends back what your computer requested. Your web browser then interprets the document, and displays the result onscreen. In this context, your computer is the *client computer*; the other computer is the *web server*. The document that your computer receives most likely is written either in *HTML* (HyperText Markup Language) or *XML* (Extended Markup Language). Frequently, to provide additional functionality, the document (usually a form) may come with some additional scripts written in a scripting language such as *JavaScript* or *VBScript*. These scripts give your browser instructions to respond to your action, such as clicking a button after entering some data in some boxes, before the form is submitted to the server. Because these scripts work at the client computer, they are recognized as *client-side scripts*.

Scripts can also be developed to run at the server. This type of script is recognized as the *server-side script*. Some particular server software may be required to interpret these scripts. For example, the Microsoft Internet Information Server (IIS) can handle Active Server Pages (ASP), which can be written in either VBScript or JavaScript. Documents written as ASP have the ASP file extension, such as Course.ASP. When a document with the .ASP extension is requested from a server, the IIS interprets the scripts in the ASP page and generates a document (in XML or HTML, possibly plus some client-side scripts) that is actually sent to the client computer—that is, the generated document, instead of the original ASP, is sent to the client computer. Figure 14.7 depicts the interactions between a web browser at a client computer and the server computer. A developer writing a server-side script for the ASP that generates an HTML document must have an intimate knowledge of the HTML.

Figure 14.7

Between the web browser and the server computer

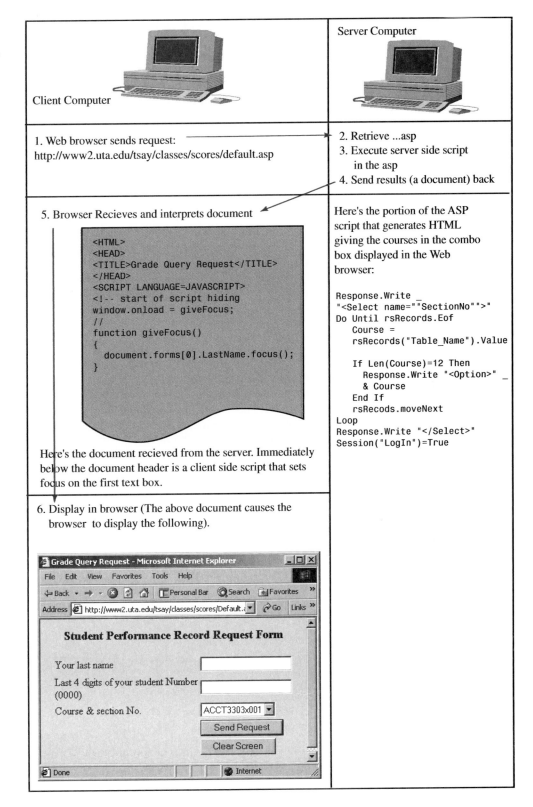

ASP.NET

As you can infer from the preceding discussion, under the ASP environment, it takes a clear understanding of the context in which computer—client or server—the script is to be run before a script can be developed properly and correctly. The .NET framework provides ASP.NET to make web programming easier and more intuitive. The ASP.NET page framework allows the developer to view the web application in an integrated fashion that makes separating the implementation details of client and server insignificant because the code to handle client events runs at the server. In addition, you do not need to have extensive knowledge of HTML or XML to develop a web-based application. You can indeed write the application in any language that the VS.NET supports, such as VB or C#. ASP.NET generates the HTML/XML code automatically from the code you develop in, say, VB.

ASP.NET allows the programmer to develop two types of web applications: *web forms* and *web services*. With web forms, the steps to develop a web application are similar to those for developing a Windows forms application. You can draw web controls on the web forms and design the visual interface at design time. You write code to support the page in your familiar language, VB. Because most types of events are handled at the server, you seldom have to concern yourself about differentiating between code for the client computer or the server computer, so web forms make developing the web application more intuitive.

Web services enable the server to provide functionality that can be used by other computers on the Internet. For example, suppose you have developed a special program capable of making accurate forecasts with a small collection of time series data and have made this functionality available on a server as a web service. Other computers at various remote sites can easily access or incorporate this forecasting capability offered at your server.

Requirements for ASP.NET Development

To develop and test ASP.NET applications, you need a server computer with the IIS and VS.NET (including its server components) installed. You must also have access permission to the server. If your own computer has all the required software installed, you can use it as your development computer. After you have developed the web application, you can deploy it by simply copying its compiled version onto the server. ASP.NET is based on the .NET framework. You have complete access to the .NET framework when you are developing an ASP.NET application; that is, ASP.NET is fully supported by the .NET framework.

Creating a Simple Web Forms Application

To illustrate how to develop a web forms application, you will learn to create a simple web Welcome page. In this Welcome page, when the program starts, the web browser will display a banner with the sign, "Welcome to ASP.NET" and a button with the text, "Change Color." When the user clicks the button, the fore- and background colors of the banner change. The major steps involved in developing this project are:

1. Create a new web forms project.
2. Design the visual interface.
3. Add the code behind (in VB).
4. Test the project.

Each of these steps is discussed in the following paragraphs.

Creating a New Web Forms Project. To create a new web forms project, follow the steps below:

1. Click the File menu. Select the New option and click Project in the submenu to open the New Project dialog box.
2. Click the ASP.NET Web Application icon in the Templates pane. Watch how the default name and location appear, as shown in Figure 14.8. The http://localhost default domain name (first part of the location name) indicates that the project is to be developed and tested on the same computer you are using (locally). If you are developing the project with a remote computer, enter the proper location, such as http://*Computer*.uta.edu/tsay.

Figure 14.8

Creating a new web form project

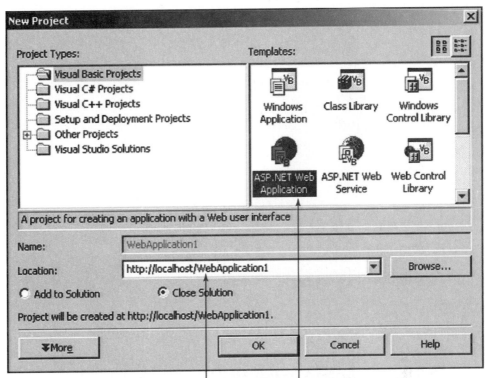

Make sure the ASP.NET Web Application is selected. You should see the default name and location boxes are specified differently. Enter the proper name in the Location box (change WebApplication1 to ASPBanner). The default "http://localhost" domain name indicates that the project is to be developed in the same computer you are using.

3. You may see Web Access Failed dialog box. If so, select the other access method—File Share or FrontPage Server Extensions—and click the OK button. The two *web access methods* are explained at the end of this example.

4. Change WebApplication1 in the Location box to **ASPBanner** and then click the OK button. You will see a blank web form in the area where a Windows form typically appears when you develop a desktop application.

5. Rename the file with the .aspx extension from WebForm1.aspx to **ASPBanner.aspx**:

    a.   Right-click WebForm1.aspx in the Solution Explorer.

    b.   Select the Rename option in the context menu.

    c.   Enter **ASPBanner.aspx** in place of WebForm1.aspx.

Take a moment to familiarize yourself with the new development environment. The Solution Explorer and Properties window appear as usual. Pay particular attention to the Toolbox area. The Web Forms tab as shown in Figure 14.9, now replaces the familiar Windows Forms tab. Notice that the controls available under this new environment are different from those in the Windows Forms tab. Even when the control names are the same, such as text box, their respective behavior and properties may not be exactly the same. You will see some of the differences later in this chapter. Note that these web form controls are handled by the server, not the client browser, and therefore are recognized as *web server controls*.

Designing the Visual Interface. The web form offers two modes in designing the visual interface: the *GridLayout mode* and the *FlowLayout mode*. With the GridLayout mode, you design the visual interface much like designing a Windows form. The controls and texts appear in the positions where you place them by drag and drop. With the FlowLayout mode, the

Figure 14.9

The Web Forms tab in
the Toolbox

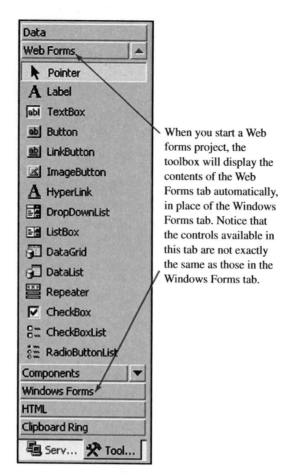

When you start a Web
forms project, the
toolbox will display the
contents of the Web
Forms tab automatically,
in place of the Windows
Forms tab. Notice that
the controls available in
this tab are not exactly
the same as those in the
Windows Forms tab.

controls and texts appear from left to right, top down, in the order you bring them to the web
form. You can switch between the two modes by setting the *pageLayout property* in the
Document object. This is the element similar to the Windows form that allows you to design the
visual interface at design time. You can choose the grid layout mode to design the visual interface because of familiarity, and follow these steps:

1. Draw a label at the center of the form; then set its Text property to **Welcome to
   ASP.NET!!!** and its ID property to **lblWelcome** using the familiar Properties window.

2. Draw a button on the form below the label. Using the ID property, name the button
   btnChangeColor, and set the button's Text property to **Change Color**.

3. Make the banner (label) more visually appealing. Set its back color to red and fore color
   to blue. Change its font to MonoType Corsiva (or choose one of your favorite) and the
   size to X-Large. The resulting visual interface should appear as shown in Figure 14.10.

Adding the Code Behind.   Recall that when the user clicks the Change Color button,
the banner color will change. To be more specific, suppose you want the back color to rotate
among blue, red, yellow, and green, and the fore color to be one color ahead; that is, when the
back color is blue, the fore color is red. You can declare an array, TheColors() at the module level
as follows:

```
Dim TheColors() As Color = {Color.Blue, Color.Red, Color.Yellow,
    Color.Green}
```

To support the computation for color rotation, you need a Shared variable such as I. The complete code to handle the button click event to perform color rotation appears as follows:

Figure 14.10

Visual interface for the Welcome banner

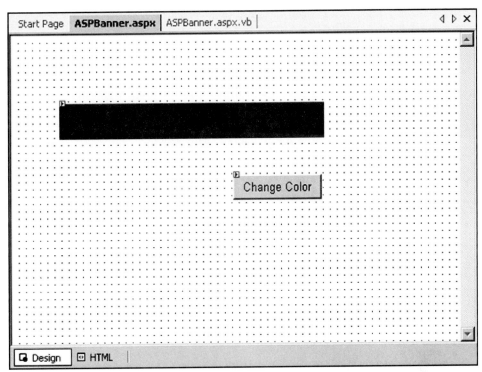

Here's the visual interface for the Welcome banner. Notice the tabs around the Web form. Currently we are on the design view. Click on a different tab and you will see a different content in this window. For example, click on the HTML tab, you should see to HTML associated with this design.

```
Dim TheColors() As Color = {Color.Blue, Color.Red, Color.Yellow,
    Color.Green}
Shared I As Integer
Private Sub btnChangeColor_Click(ByVal Sender As Object, ByVal e
    As System.EventArgs) Handles btnChangeColor.Click
    I += 1
    If I > 3 Then
        I = 0
    End If
    lblWelcome.BackColor = TheColors(I)
    If I = 3 Then
        lblWelcome.ForeColor = TheColors(0)
    Else
        lblWelcome.ForeColor = TheColors(I + 1)
    End If
End Sub
```

Notice that the I variable is declared as Shared instead of as Static inside the event procedure. This is necessary because when the user clicks on the button, the entire form is submitted to the server and is then posted back to the web browser; therefore, every variable in the module is reinitialized except for the Shared variable.

Testing the Project. You are now ready to test the project. Start the project; you should notice that the project takes a while to appear, and what appears is the web browser. Click the Change Color button in the browser several times, and observe that the colors in the browser change. Notice also that the web browser displays the progress at the bottom of the browser window after each click because the click causes the form to be submitted to the server and posted back. The Click event procedure is run at the server, not at the client computer.

To further test and verify that the project can be accessed as a web page, you can use your web browser, external to the VS.NET IDE. Suppose you develop this web forms project on your local computer. You can start your web browser and then enter the following address:

```
http://localhost/ASPBanner/ASPBanner.aspx
```

You should be able to verify that the page works in exactly the same way as when you were testing the project in the web forms development environment. Right-click in the browser window, and select the View Source option from the context menu. You should be able to see the following HTML text that is actually sent to the browser:

```
<!DOCTYPE HTML PUBLIC "-//W3C//DTD HTML 4.0 Transitional//EN">
<HTML>
  <HEAD>
    <title>WebForm1</title>
    <meta name="GENERATOR" content="Microsoft Visual Studio.NET
      7.0">
    <meta name="CODE_LANGUAGE" content="Visual Basic 7.0">
    <meta name="vs_defaultClientScript" content="JavaScript">
    <meta name="vs_targetSchema"
      content="http://schemas.microsoft.com/intellisense/ie5">
  </HEAD>
  <body MS_POSITIONING="GridLayout">
    <form name="Form1" method="post" action="ASPBanner.aspx"
      id="Form1">
<input type="hidden" name=
  "__VIEWSTATE"
    value="dDw2NjY0NzU4OTc7Oz5RmBt80cZOlbcK1TXJJTMJAwV+dg==" />
    <span id="lblWelcome" style="color:Blue;background-
    color:Red;font-family:Monotype Corsiva;
    font-size:X-Large;height:33px;width:300px;Z-INDEX: 101; LEFT:
      54px; POSITION: absolute;
    TOP: 75px">Welcome to ASP.NET!!!</span>
    <input type="submit" name="btnChangeColor" value="Change
      Color" id="btnChangeColor"
    style="height:27px;width:101px;Z-INDEX: 102; LEFT: 250px;
      POSITION: absolute;
    TOP: 154px" />
    </form>
  </body>
</HTML>
```

Notice that this is not the actual content of the ASPBanner.aspx, but rather the HTML code generated from that file. The .aspx file itself is generated by the VB code (code behind) that you wrote and is an aspx script. You can examine the contents of ASPBanner.aspx by clicking the HTML tab below the web form (see Figure 14.10). The following listing shows the code in that file. Compare the texts of the two files within the <body> </body> tags.

```
<%@ Page Language="vb" AutoEventWireup="false"
  Codebehind="ASPBanner.aspx.vb" Inherits="ASPBanner.WebForm1"%>
<!DOCTYPE HTML PUBLIC "-//W3C//DTD HTML 4.0 Transitional//EN">
<HTML>
  <HEAD>
    <title>WebForm1</title>
    <meta name="GENERATOR" content="Microsoft Visual Studio.NET
      7.0">
    <meta name="CODE_LANGUAGE" content="Visual Basic 7.0">
    <meta name="vs_defaultClientScript" content="JavaScript">
    <meta name="vs_targetSchema"
  content="http://schemas.microsoft.com/intellisense/ie5">
  </HEAD>
  <body MS_POSITIONING="GridLayout">
    <form id="Form1" method="post" runat="server">
    <asp:Label id="lblWelcome" style="Z-INDEX: 101; LEFT: 54px;
      POSITION: absolute;
```

```
      TOP: 75px" runat="server" Width="300px" Height="33px" Font-
        Names="Monotype Corsiva"
      Font-Size="X-Large" ForeColor="Blue" BackColor="Red">Welcome
        to ASP.NET!!!</asp:Label>
      <asp:Button id="btnChangeColor" style="Z-INDEX: 102; LEFT:
        250px; POSITION: absolute;
      TOP: 154px" runat="server" Width="101px" Height="27px"
        Text="Change Color"></asp:Button>
      </form>
    </body>
  </HTML>
```

To repeat, this file is generated by the VB code (code behind) you wrote. When a remote computer (client) requests this file from your computer (server) using the HTTP protocol, the IIS retrieves and executes the file, generating the HTML document as shown previously. The HTML document is what the client computer actually receives and displays in the web browser.

Web Access Methods. Recall at the beginning of this example, it was mentioned that you might encounter a Web Access Failed problem when you first tried to create a web forms project. There are two *web access methods*: *file share* and *FrontPage file extensions methods*. The default is the file share method. Under the file share access method, all files are managed using Windows-based file management commands. This option requires LAN (local area network) access to the server, so the sharing/access permissions for the files and folders involved in the project must be set properly to allow your access. Under the FrontPage file extensions method, all files are managed using the HTTP protocol. Projects to be developed over the Internet can use only this method.

After the project is set to use a particular web access method, it continues to use the same each time it is loaded into the IDE. To change the access method, follow these steps:

1. Right-click the project in the Solution Explorer to open the context menu.
2. Select Properties in the context menu to open the Property Pages dialog box.
3. Click the Common Properties folder in the left pane.
4. Click the Web Settings node in the same pane.
5. Select the desired web access method on the right pane.
6. Click the OK button in the dialog box.

LOOK IT UP

Use the web access methods keywords in the Index tab of the Help menu to find additional information on the two methods. The page provides guidelines to choosing the best method for your development environment.

Data Access with Web Forms

Most web applications involve access to databases. Quite often, the user visits a web site to obtain some information. For example, a student may visit the instructor's website to check out test scores that are stored in a scorebook (database). A more sophisticated application can involve making an appointment with the instructor. The application must not only be able to keep track of the available time slots and record the appointment, but also send email to the visitor to confirm the appointment, and to the instructor to inform the instructor of the appointment. An online bookstore application must be able to respond to the visitor's query of all available relevant titles, accept an order, calculate charges that may include shipping based on a complex table, and record the order. Regardless of the complexity of the application, one focal point is the use of databases to support the operations.

Data access with web forms is similar to that in a Windows form application, as discussed in Chapter 9. To illustrate, consider a simple grocery product query example. In this application, the user will enter a short string representing a portion of the products of interest, such as milk. When the user clicks a button, the web form will display all grocery products in the database that contain the short string. A sample result appears as in Figure 14.11.

Similar to developing the first web forms project, you will perform the following major steps to develop this application:

1. Create a new web forms project.
2. Design the visual interface.
3. Add the data access capability.
4. Add logic in the code behind (in VB).
5. Test the project.

The following discussion focuses on steps 2 through 4.

Designing the Visual Interface. After you have created the new web forms project (call it Grocery), do the following:

1. Draw a label, text box, button, and data grid on the form. Note that all these controls must be obtained from the Web Forms tab—not the Windows forms tab—in the Toolbox. Align these controls in the same positions as those in Figure 14.11.
2. Set the text box's ID property to **txtSearch**.
3. Set the button's ID property to **btnSearch**, and its Text property to **Search**.
4. Set the data grid's ID to **dtgProducts**. Also, set its EnableViewState to **False**. This setting is explained later in this section.

Adding the Data Access Capability. This step is exactly the same as discussed in Chapter 9. Here are the steps:

1. Draw a data adapter (oleDbDataAdapter) on the form. You will need to select the Data tab in the Toolbox to locate this control.

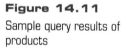

Figure 14.11

Sample query results of products

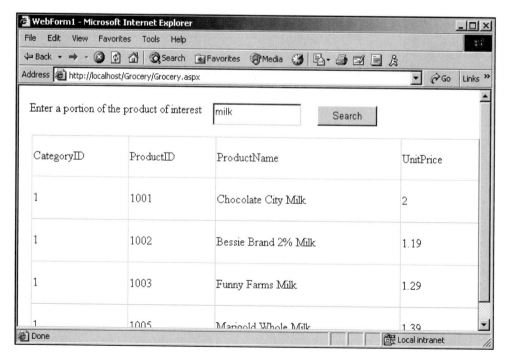

2. Set up the connection. If you can find the grocertogo.mdb in the Which data connection should the data adapter use? box, select it; otherwise, follow those steps outlined in Chapter 9 to set up the connection.

3. Choose the Use SQL Statements as the option for the query type; then set up the Select SQL statement as follows. Note that the Where clause uses the Like operator, not the = operator.

```
SELECT CategoryID, ProductID, ProductName, UnitPrice FROM Products
    WHERE  (ProductName Like ?)
```

4. Click the Finish button.

5. Rename the data adapter to **odaProducts**.

6. Generate the dataset.

   a. Click the Data menu and then select the Generate Dataset option.

   b. Select the New option in the Generate Dataset dialog box, and enter DsProducts in the New box.

   c. Click the OK button.

In the typical web application, the database location is predetermined and known, so it is more efficient to configure the data adapter and create the dataset at design time than to set up the connection and dataset at runtime.

Adding the Code Behind. When the user clicks the Search button, the web form is submitted to the server, and the event is handled at the server; then the page is returned to the browser (client) and reloaded. The data to be presented should be constructed at the time when the page is being loaded, not when the click event is triggered, so the code should be placed in the Page Load event procedure. The Page Load event will still be triggered and handled when the user clicks the Search button because the click will cause the form to be submitted to the server, and the page will be reloaded. The code should set up the parameter for ProductName, taking the value from the text box in which the user enters the query string. The code should then clear the dataset, refill the dataset, and bind it to the data grid. The procedure appears as follows:

```
Private Sub Page_Load(ByVal sender As System.Object, ByVal e As
    System.EventArgs) Handles MyBase.Load
    If Page.IsPostBack Then
        odaProducts.SelectCommand.Parameters(0).Value = "%" &
            Trim(txtSearch.Text) & "%"
        DsProducts1.Clear()
        odaProducts.Fill(DsProducts1)
        dtgProducts.DataSource = DsProducts1.Products
        dtgProducts.DataBind()
    End If
End Sub
```

The code first checks to see if the page load is a post back by testing the *IsPostBack property*; that is, it tests whether the page load is in response to a click. If the page is initially loaded in response to an HTTP request, the IsPostBack property will be False; but if it is reloaded after a click event, the property will be True. The data query routine will be executed only if it the page is loaded in response to a post back. The text that the user enters in the txtSearch text box is first trimmed to avoid the confusion with any extra spaces added either by the user or the browser and then concatenated with the wildcard % character on both ends. The result is then assigned to the only parameter in the Select SQL statement. The extra % specification allows the search to find all products containing the specified string regardless of its position in the product name.

> In referencing a parameter for a data command, it is more efficient to use a numeric index in the Parameters property such as Parameters(0); however, if there is more than one parameter in a query, using the field name such as Parameters("ProductName") will make the code easier to read.

Notice the last statement within the If block. The *DataBind method* of the data grid is called. This method resolves all data-binding expressions in the web form server control and must be called for the grid to display the data properly. Recall that no such statement was used in Chapter 9. This is one significant difference in data access between the web forms application and the Windows forms application.

In setting up the visual interface for this project, you indicate that the data grid's *EnableViewState property* should be set to False. In general, HTTP requests are stateless; that is, after a request for a document is performed, the server maintains no connection with the client and no longer remembers anything regarding the request. Each request is treated independent of the others. ASP.NET uses a special technique to maintain the view states across the HTTP requests. The EnableViewState property of the web server control specifies whether to keep track of the view states for the control. When set to True, this property allows the property values for the control to be preserved across the HTTP requests. In most cases, the property should be set to True (default) so that whatever was initially submitted to the form will remain the same on the page that is posted back; however, in the case of the data grid, new query results should appear. Preserving the original data serves no purpose, and will consume the computer resources unnecessarily.

If everything goes right, when you test the project, the web browser will initially appear with all controls except the data grid. After you enter **milk** in the text box and then click the Search button, you should see the results as shown in Figure 14.11.

Data Validation

In many web applications, the user is to enter data in a form. For example, in a startup form, the user may be required to enter the username and password before the user is allowed to use the application. The entered data typically should be validated. ASP.NET makes many of the data validation tasks automatic by providing a number of validation controls. The following table provides a selected list:

Control	Use
RequiredFieldValidator	Tests whether a specified field is filled with different data from what is specified in the InitialValue property, and verifies that the required information is supplied when the form is posted.
CompareValidator	Tests whether a specified field contains data that satisfies the test specified in the Operator property based on the value specified in the ValueToCompare property. The Operator property has seven possible settings: Equal (default), NotEqual, GreaterThan, GreaterThanEqual, LessThan, LessThanEqual, and DataTypeCheck.
RangeValidator	Tests whether a specified field contains data that is within a range, as specified in the MinimumValue and MaximumValue properties.
ValidationSummary	(See text)

Each of the first three controls performs a particular validation and is associated with a particular control (field) that is set in the validator's *ControlToValidate property*; therefore, if you want to perform three types of validations for a particular control, you will use three validation controls. Each validation control has an *IsValid property*, which is automatically set to True or False depending on the validation outcome when the form is submitted to the server (when the user clicks a button). For example, if a *CompareValidator*'s ControlToValidate property is set to a text box named txtPassword, its Operator property is set to Equal (default), and the text entered in the text box is not equal to the validator's ValueToCompare property, the validator's IsValid property will be False.

The *ValidationSummary control* summarizes the results of all validation controls in the web form. Depending on its *DisplayMode property*, the summary can be displayed as a list, a bulleted list, or a single paragraph. The error message displayed for each validation control is the *ErrorMessage property* of the control. You can show or hide the ValidationSummary control by setting the *ShowSummary property* to True or False. You can also show the summary in a message box by setting the *ShowMessageBox property* to True.

A Course Login Form

To illustrate how the validation controls can be used, consider a simple login form that requests the contents of a course. This login form requires the user to enter a predefined (static) username

Figure 14.12

The visual interface of a course login form

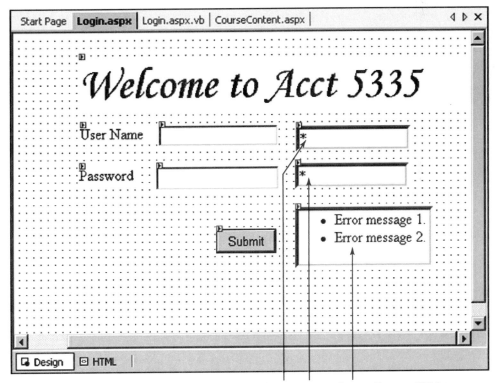

In addition to the typical data entry controls, two CompareValidator controls and a ValidationSummary control are also included to perform data validation for this web form. (These controls' BorderStyle properties have been set to Inset so that they are easier to see. You don't need to change their settings for your own project.)

and password. When the student enters both fields correctly and clicks the Submit button, the student will be presented with a page containing a list of hyperlinks pointing to specific course contents. If either field is incorrect, a pop-up message will display the pertinent error message. Figure 14.12 shows the visual interface at design time.

Notice that two CompareValidators and a ValidationSummary are also drawn on the form. The settings for the various properties of the controls used in the code are summarized in the following table:

Control	Property	Setting	Remark
Text box	ID	txtUserName	For the user to enter username.
Text box	ID	txtPassword	For the user to enter password.
	TextMode	Password	Entered key is displayed as a *.
Button	ID	btnSubmit	For the user to submit the form.
	Text	Submit	
CompareValidator	ID	comvUserName	To validate the username.
	Control to validate	txtUserName	To specify the control to validate.
	Error message	Must have a valid username	The validation summary will display this message when the username is incorrect.
	Text	*	If the username is entered incorrectly, a * will appear where this control is drawn.
	Value to compare	funplayer	The user must enter this string as the username.
CompareValidator	ID	comvPassword	To validate the password.
	Control to validate	txtPassword	To specify the control to validate.
	Error message	Must have a valid password	The validation summary will display this message when the username is incorrect.
	Text	*	If the username is entered incorrectly, a * will appear where this control is drawn.
	Value to compare	Horse99	The user must enter this string as the password.
ValidationSummary	DisplayMode	BulletList	Error messages are shown as a bullet list.
	Show Message Box	True	A pop-up message box will show the errors.
	Show Summary	False	To suppress the error message on the form.

These property settings for the controls will result in the following behavior of the form:

- The username field expects an entry of **funplayer**; and the password field expects **Horse99**.

- When an incorrect entry is made in the username or password field, a red (default color) * will be displayed next to the field. In addition, a pop-up message box will display "Must have a valid username" or "Must have a valid password."

The following code will cause the page named CourseContent.aspx to be sent to the web browser, replacing the login form if the username and password are entered correctly:

```
Private Sub btnSubmit_Click(ByVal Sender As Object, ByVal e As
    System.EventArgs) Handles btnSubmit.Click
        If comvUserName.IsValid AndAlso comvPassword.IsValid Then
            Response.Redirect("CourseContent.aspx")
        End If
End Sub
```

The code tests to determine whether both of the CompareValidator controls indicate the entries are valid. If so, the *Redirect method* of the *Response object* will redirect the request to a page named CourseContent.aspx, which given the specification should appear in the same folder. This page will be discussed later in this section.

The Response Object. The Response object is an ASP object that is used to send output to the client. Two of its methods are frequently used in the ASP script. Its *Write method* allows you to include text in a page. You can even use the method to write HTML code for the page. The Redirect method redirects the initial request to another page. In this example, when the user clicks the Submit button, the form is submitted to the server and the same page is requested. Recall that in the preceding examples after each button click, the same page is displayed in the web browser. The Redirect method allows a different page to be sent.

To see how the Response object works, try the following code in the course login example:

```
Private Sub Page_Load(ByVal Sender As Object, ByVal e As
    System.EventArgs) Handles MyBase.Load
        'Put user code to initialize the page here
        Response.Write("<Font color=red> <I><B>Oops! Something
            extra!</B></I></Font>")
End Sub
```

You should see "Oops! Something extra!" displayed in red, italicized, and bold-faced text. The HTML code is included in the page as a text string, and is interpreted by the web browser.

Adding Another Web Form to a Web Forms Project. The course login example calls for another web form to be included in the same project. Typically, all pages belonging to the same application are included in the same folder, assuming the number of pages is manageably small. The steps to add another web form to the project is similar to adding a Windows form to a typical Windows form application. You will click the Project menu, select the add Web Form option, enter the appropriate name for the new form in the familiar Add New Item dialog box, and click the Open button.

The course content page may appear as shown in Figure 14.13. Note that the page shows two hyperlinks, which are created with the *Hyperlink controll*. Its Text property allows you to display the link description. You should use its *NavigateUrl property* to provide the URL for the related page. For example, the NavigateUrl property of the first control can appear as follows:

```
HTTP://www2.uta.edu/tsay/courses/acct5335/libinstruction.pdf
```

14.4   Creating and Using Web Services

A web service is a component that can be called by other applications from a remote site. It performs a specific function, such as computing the effective interest rate for a bond, and returns values to the caller. Web services can be called across the web, and exchange data with other components using XML.

Figure 14.13

The redirected page

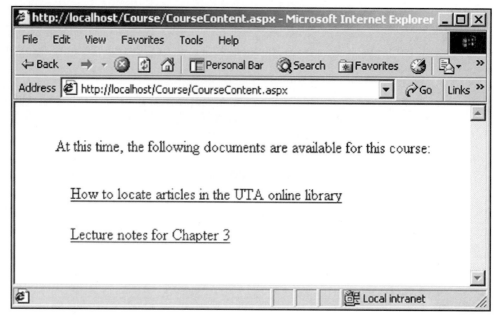

This page, redirected from the login page, shows two hyperlinks to other URLs. These hyperlinks are created with the Hyperlink control.

Web services have wide applicability both in terms of access and platforms. Recall that the components discussed in Section 14.2 can be used in various applications developed using any languages supported by the .NET framework; however, these components must be deployed on the computers that use the applications. In contrast, the web service components are located only in the computer providing the service. They do not require any additional deployment and are accessible to any computer—even with a different operating system—on the web. The service will work as long as the client and the server understand the messages they receive from each other. Technically, the client and server agree to a contract, described using WSDL (Web Services Description Language) and XSD (XML Schema Description), and then communicate by generating messages that honor the contract over a specified transfer protocol like HTTP.

Creating A Web Service

Creating a web service is similar to creating a class. The main differences are that the web service project requires the use of the VB.NET web service template, and that the class and the methods in the project must be marked with proper *attributes*. Attributes are keywords that allow you to specify additional information about entities, such as variables, classes, and methods. The extra information (meta-data) provided by attributes can be read by other applications to determine how the object should be used.

You specify the attribute for a program element, such as property, method, or class, by placing an attribute block before the element. An attribute block declaration consists of angle brackets < > enclosing a list of comma separated attribute declarations. A typical attribute declaration consists of the attribute name, a list of required positional parameters, and a list of optional named arguments. For example, the following line declares a *WebMethod attribute* for the Simulate function:

```
<WebMethod (Description:="This method simulates the blackjack
    game.")>
```

In creating a web service, you will need to provide attribute declarations for the WebService and for the web methods in the web service (class) as illustrated below.

As discussed previously, typically a web service represents some unique functionality that you can offer over the Internet. Recall that Chapter 7, "Repetition," showed a routine to compute the total output units under the learning curve model (Example 4). Assume this functionality is unique and therefore it is worth creating a web service for it. For the service to be complete, you also provide two additional methods to compute total hours and average hours for a given number of total output units. Here are the steps to create the service:

1. Create a new web service project.

    a. Click the File menu, select the New option, and click the Project option in the submenu to open the New Project dialog box.

    b. Click ASP.NET Web Service icon in the Templates pane. The dialog box should display a Name box and a Location box, with the Name box grayed out (similar to the dialog for setting up the web forms project).

    c. Change WebService1 in the Location box to **LearningCurve** so that the box will show http://localhost/LearningCurve as a result.

    d. Click the OK button in the dialog box. You should see a design template at the center of the IDE. Switch to code view.

2. Rename **Service1**.

    a. Right-click Service1.asmx in the Solution Explorer and then select the Rename option.

    b. Change the name to **LC.asmx**.

    c. Change Class Service1 in the code window to **Class LC**.

3. Update the contents of LC.asmx.

    a. Right-click LC.asmx in the Solution Explorer, and select the Open With option.

    b. Select Source Code (Text) Editor in the Open With dialog box, and click the Open button as shown in Figure 14.14). You should see the following text:

    ```
    <%WebService Language="vb" Codebdhind="LC.asmx.vb"
        Class="LearningCurve1.Service1" %>
    ```

    c. Replace Service1 with **LC** so that the text becomes:</P>

    ```
    <%WebService language="vb" Codebehind="LC.asmx.vb"
        Class="LearningCurve1.LC" %>
    ```

    d. Click the LC.asmx.vb* tab on the top of the Component Designer's design surface to go back to the code view, as shown in Figure 14.15.

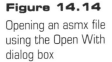

Figure 14.14

Opening an asmx file using the Open With dialog box

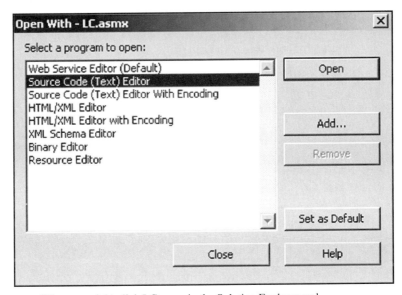

When you right click LC.asmx in the Solution Explorer and select the Open With option, you will see this dialog box. Select Source Code (Text) Editor and Click the Open button, you will see its contents.

Figure 14.15
Switching views

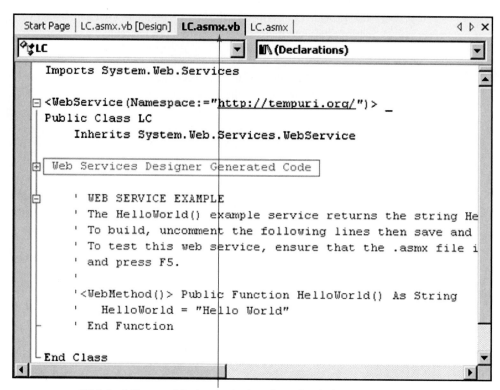

Click the LC.asmx.vb* tab to go back to the code window.

4. Develop code. The following code represents the service you provide. Modify the WebService attribute, and add the additional code. Do not delete the Web Services Designer Generated Code.

```
Imports System.Web.Services
<WebService(Namespace:="HTTP://AcctXpert.uta.edu/LearningCurve",  _
    Description:="This Web Service provides learning curve
        computation routines.")> _
Public Class LC
    Inherits System.Web.Services.WebService
<WebMethod(Description:= _
  "This method computes Average hours given hours required for the
     first units, rate of learning, and units of output.")> _
    Function AverageHours(ByVal FirstUnitHours As Double, ByVal
      RateOfLearning As Double, ByVal Units As Double) _
       As Double
       Dim B As Double
       B = Math.Log(RateOfLearning) / Math.Log(2)
       Return (FirstUnitHours * Units ^ B)
    End Function
    <WebMethod(Description:= _
  "This method computes Total hours given hours required for the
     first units, rate of learning, and units of output.")> _
    Function TotalHours(ByVal FirstUnitHours As Double, ByVal
      RateOfLearning As Double, ByVal Units As Double) _
        As Double
       Dim C As Double
       C = Math.Log(RateOfLearning) / Math.Log(2) + 1
       Return (FirstUnitHours * Units ^ C)
    End Function
    <WebMethod(Description:= _
  "This method computes total output units given hours required
     for the first units, rate of learning, " & _
```

```
    " and total hours available.")> _
    Function TotalOutputUnits(ByVal FirstUnitHours As Double,
       ByVal RateOfLearning As Double, _
       ByVal TotalHoursAvailable As Double) As Double
       Dim High As Double
       Dim Low As Double
       Dim X As Double
       Dim Y As Double
       Dim C As Double
       C = 1 + Math.Log(RateOfLearning) / Math.Log(2)
       X = 1
       Do
           X = X + X
           Y = FirstUnitHours * X ^ C 'Total hours required
       Loop Until Y >= TotalHoursAvailable
       ' Search for X using the half interval method
       Low = 0
       High = X
       Do
           X = (High + Low) / 2
           Y = FirstUnitHours * X ^ C
           If Y < TotalHoursAvailable Then
               ' Too low; adjust lower bound
               Low = X
           Else
               ' Too high; adjust upper bound
               High = X
           End If
       Loop Until (High - Low) / X < 0.000001
       Return (X)
    End Function
End Class
```

Press Ctrl+F5 to build and verify that there is no error in the code. If the build is successful, you will see a description of the web service in the browser window. Each method is listed and described using the Description parameter supplied in the associated WebMethod attribute.

Notice that the class is derived from System.Web.Services.WebService, enabling the base functionality required of the web service. Notice also the attribute declarations for the class and the three methods. The attribute name for the class is WebService. It also indicates where the service can be located. The attribute name for each of the methods is WebMethod; the Description parameter explains its use. These attribute declarations are necessary for other applications on the web to locate the service and use the methods.

Note also that the attributes are an integral part of the program element they describe, so the attributes within the attribute marker (<>) and the element they pertain to all constitute one statement. You must use the line continuation symbol (_) when the statement spans more than one line, as the preceding code shows. You will see the effects of these declarations in the next subsection.

Deploying the Web Service. After your web service is developed and fully debugged, you can deploy it by simply copying the project to the server if it is not the same as the development computer. To copy the project, follow these steps:

1. Click the Project menu and select the Copy Project option to open the Copy Project dialog box.
2. Select either FrontPage or File share from the Web access method options. If you are not successful with one method, try the other method. Also, you must be connected to the Internet to copy the files to the remote computer.
3. Enter the destination project folder name in the appropriate text box.
4. Select Only files needed to run this application in the Copy section of the dialog box, as shown in Figure 14.16; then click the OK button.

Figure 14.16

Deploying a web service with the Copy Project method

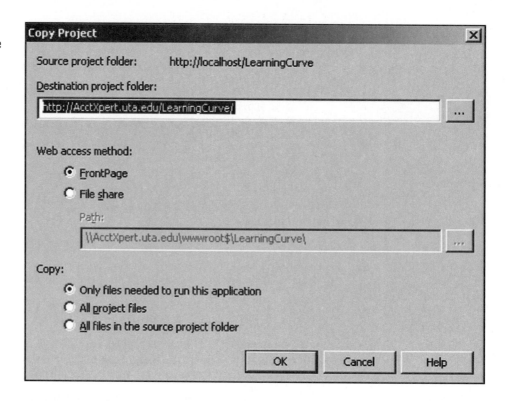

Accessing a Web Service

The preceding subsection explained how a web service is created and how it can be deployed, but how do you access and use a web service? The major steps include the following:

1. Create a new project; for example, **Web Forms**.
2. Add the web service to the web reference.
3. Design the visual interface on the web form.
4. Develop code to use the service, which can be treated as an object.

To illustrate, you will use the web service that you created in the preceding subsection as an example. Create a new web forms project and name it as **LCClient**. Follow the steps to create a web forms project as explained in the preceding subsection. The next major step is to add the web reference.

Adding a Web Reference.   To use the web service, your program needs to incorporate information such as the location and name of the web service. You provide this information by adding a web reference to the program. Here are the steps:

1. Right-click References in the Solution Explorer, and select the Add Web Reference option to open the Add Web Reference dialog box.
2. Enter the following string in the Address box.
   ```
   http://localhost/LearningCurve/LC.asmx?DISCO
   ```
   The dialog box will appear as shown in Figure 14.17. If your web service is located in a remote server, replace localhost with the proper server name.

   As a side note, if you click the View Documentation link in the Available references pane, the left pane of the dialog box will display the web service documentation as coded in the attributes for web service and web method descriptions, as shown in Figure 14.18.

Figure 14.17

The Add Web Reference
dialog box

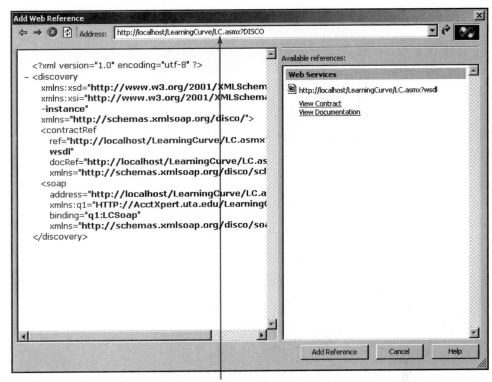

Enter the web service location in the Address box and you should see the address displayed
on the right pane along with the XML code on the left pane. A discovery document is
automatically generated for a web service when its URL is appended with "?DISCO."

Figure 14.18

Web service
documentation

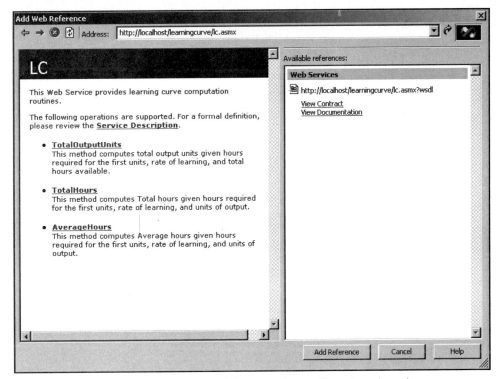

Click the View Documentation link on the right pane and you will see the web service
documentation displayed on the left pane. Notice that the description for each method is extracted
from the attribute description coded in the web service class.

Figure 14.19

The TotalOutputUnits
method for test

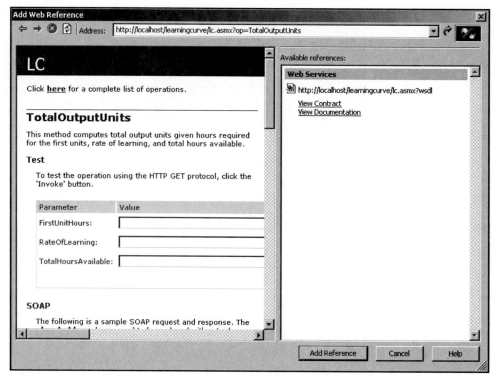

When you click the TotalOutputUnits link in the web service documentation (Figure 14.18),
you will see the required parameters for the method displayed on the left pane. If you enter
some test numbers in the boxes and click the Invoke button, another Internet Explorer window
will display the result.

You can even test any of these methods by clicking the link for the method. For example, if you click the TotalOutputUnits link, the dialog box will appear as shown in
Figure 14.19.

You can then enter some numbers, and click the Invoke button to obtain the result.

3. Click the Add Reference button in the dialog box.

Figure 14.20

Contents of web
references

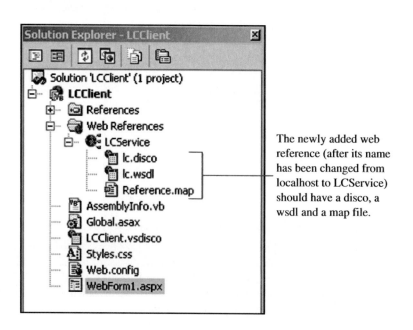

The newly added web
reference (after its name
has been changed from
localhost to LCService)
should have a disco, a
wsdl and a map file.

Figure 14.21

A sample result from the LC web service

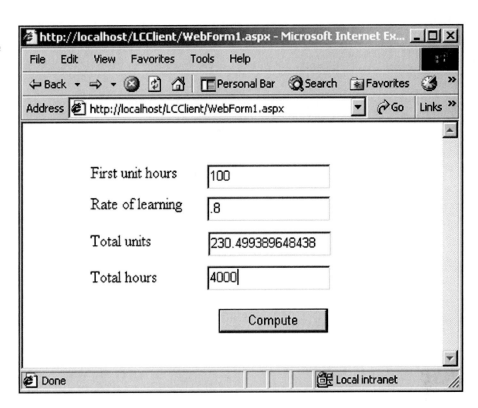

4. Rename the reference.

   a. Expand the Web References node in the Solution Explorer.

   b. Right-click localhost (or the server name in which your web service is located), and select the Rename option in the context menu.

   c. Change localhost (or the server name) to **LCService**. The web references should appear as shown in Figure 14.20. Notice the LC.wsdl file. This is an XML document written in Web Service Description Language (WSDL). The file defines how a web service behaves, and instructs the client how to interact with the service.

Design the Visual Interface. The next major step is to design the visual interface on the web form. Draw four labels, four text boxes, and a button. Align these controls, and set the Text properties for the labels and the button as shown in Figure 14.21.

Name the text boxes and the button as shown in the following table:

Control	ID
Text Box	txtFirstUnitHours
Text Box	txtRateOfLearning
Text Box	txtTotalUnits
Text Box	txtTotalHours
Button	btnCompute (also set its Text property to Compute)

Creating the Code to Test the Service. Using a web service is similar to using any class in the .NET framework. You declare a variable of the web service type and then create an instance of the service (technically recognized as a *proxy class*) with the New keyword in exactly the same manner as any class. And the reference is just like a typical namespace, so an instance of the LC class (web service) can be declared and created as follows:

```
Dim LCCalculator As New LCService.LC()
```

You can then use its methods just like those of any object. The following code tests two methods of the service: TotalHours and TotalOutputUnits.

```
Private Sub Page_Load(ByVal Sender As Object, ByVal e As
    System.EventArgs) Handles MyBase.Load
    'Put user code to initialize the page here
    Dim LCCalculator As New LCService.LC()
    If Page.IsPostBack Then
        Dim FirstUnitHours As Double
        Dim RateOfLearning As Double
        Dim TotalHours As Double
        Dim TotalUnits As Double
        FirstUnitHours = Val(txtFirstUnitHours.Text)
        RateOfLearning = Val(txtRateOfLearning.Text)
        TotalHours = Val(txtTotalHours.Text)
        TotalUnits = Val(txtTotalUnits.Text)
        If TotalHours = 0 Then
            txtTotalHours.Text =
                LCCalculator.TotalHours(FirstUnitHours,
                RateOfLearning, TotalUnits)
        Else
            txtTotalUnits.Text =
                LCCalculator.TotalOutputUnits(FirstUnitHours,
                RateOfLearning, TotalHours)
        End If
    End If
End Sub
```

The routine obtains the values entered by the user and tests whether an entry is made in the total hours field. If not, it calls the web service's TotalHours method and then displays the result in the text box for total hours. On the other hand, if there is an entry for total hours, the routine calls the web service's TotalOutputUnits method, and displays the result in the related text box. The sample result in Figure 14.21 is obtained when 4000 is entered in the total hours field. Notice that the routine is placed in the page load event because the results should be displayed when the page is to be sent back to the web browser, as explained previously.

Additional Remarks

A web service can serve various clients: web forms applications, other web services, and Windows form (desktop) applications. Although written as a class, it does not expose properties to web clients. Further, it does not keep track of values of Private variables the same way as a typical class. For example, consider the following code for the bank depositor web service (BankService):

```
<WebService(Namespace:="HTTP://AcctXpert.uta.edu/BankService", _
    Description:="This Web Service updates bank balance for a
        depositor.")> _
Public Class Depositor
    Inherits System.Web.Services.WebService
    Private mBalance As Double
    <WebMethod(Description:="This method returns the depositors
        balance.")> _
    Function Balance() As Double
        Return (mBalance)
    End Function
    <WebMethod(Description:= _
        "This method adds amount to balance.")> _
    Function Deposit(ByVal Amount As Double) As Double
        mBalance += Amount
        Return (mBalance)
    End Function
    <WebMethod(Description:="This method subtracts amount from
        balance.")> _
    Function Withdraw(ByVal Amount As Double) As Double
```

```
            mBalance -= Amount
            Return (mBalance)
        End Function
    End Class
```

Notice that the mBalance variable is meant to be used as a Private copy to keep track of the balance such as in a typical class. The Deposit method adds the amount specified in its parameter to the balance, and Withdraw subtracts the amount from the balance. If you use the following code to test the service, however, you will find the results displayed to be 2000, -500, and 0, respectively, suggesting that the balance (as tracked by the mBalance variable) has always been zero. (*Note:* First, create the web service named BankService, using the previous code; then create a Windows form project, add a web reference to BankService, and use a button named btnTest to perform the test.)

```
    Private Sub btnTest_Click(ByVal Sender As Object, ByVal e As
        System.EventArgs) Handles btnTest.Click
        Dim BC As New BankServiceLib.Depositor()
        MsgBox(BC.Deposit(2000))
        MsgBox(BC.Withdraw(500))
        MsgBox(BC.Balance())
    End Sub
```

The results are obtained because the service is accessed with the HTTP protocol, which is stateless; that is, the server does not keep track of the state of each request. To obtain the correct results, mBalance should be declared as Shared. Be aware of this difference between a web project and a typical Windows form project.

Summary

- The Windows registry is a database maintained by the Windows operating system to support the operations of the system and various applications. It allows each application to maintain information critical or useful to the application's functionality.

- VB functions (or statements) dealing with the registry include GetSetting, SaveSetting, and DeleteSetting.

- The registry offers a convenient location to keep data for your application, but be sure to use it properly. Save only the kind of data that is useful to the operations of your program, not the kind that the user maintains for the user's application. For example, you can save data regarding a payroll program's form location in the registry, but not the employees' earnings data.

- A component is a unit of compiled code that can be reused as an object. Some components have visual elements and are recognized as controls such as the label and text box, whereas some do not have visual elements and are simply recognized as objects such as the stream reader, database connection, and the dataset.

- A convenient way a create a component is to use the Add Component option in the Project menu. The option provides a code template for component development.

- The TinyDataLib project was used to illustrate how to create a component with no visual interface.

- The KeyVerifierLib project was used to illustrate how to create a component with visual interface.

- ASP.NET allows the programmer to develop two types of web applications: web forms and web services.

- With web forms, you can develop a web application similar to developing a Windows forms application. You can draw web controls on the web forms, and design the visual interface at design time. You write code to support the page in your familiar language, VB.

- The ASP Banner project was used to illustrate how to create a web forms project. The grocery product query project was used to illustrate how data access is performed in a web forms project. (Basically, the difference in data access between a web forms application and a desktop application is negligible.) The course login form project was used to illustrate how to perform data validation and redirect the request to another page.

- A web service is a component that can be called by other applications from a remote site. It performs a specific function; for example, determining the effective interest rate for a bond and returns values to the caller. Web services can be called across the web, and exchange data with other components using XML. Web services have wide applicability both in terms of access and platforms.

- The LearningCurve project was used to illustrate how to create and access a web service. A web service can serve various clients: desktop applications (and components), web forms applications, and even other web services.

- Coding a web service class is not exactly the same as coding a typical class. The web service does not expose properties, and does not keep track of variables the same way as the typical class. The BankingService project was used to illustrate the differences.

Explore And Discover

14-1. **The GetAllSettings Function**. After you have worked the registry example in this chapter, enter the following code in a new project:

```
Private Sub Form1_Click(ByVal sender As Object, ByVal e As
    System.EventArgs) Handles MyBase.Click
    Dim AllSettings(,) As String
    Dim I As Integer
    AllSettings = GetAllSettings("TextBrowser", "TextFont")
    For I = 0 To UBound(AllSettings, 1)
        Console.Write(AllSettings(I, 0))
        Console.WriteLine(" " & AllSettings(I, 1))
    Next I
End Sub
```

Run the project and then click the form. What do you see in the immediate window? The GetAllSettings function retrieves all settings for a particular section of an application. As you can see, the returned settings are placed in a two-dimensional array with the first column representing the names of the settings and the second, the values of the settings.

14-2. **Shell and SendKeys: A Way to Communicate with Other Applications.** You can use the Shell function to start another application and then use the Clipboard and SendKeys objects to communicate with another application. Draw a button on a new form. Name it **btnToNotePad** and set its Text property to **To Notepad**; then try the following code:

```
Private Sub btnToNotePad_Click(ByVal Sender As Object, ByVal e As
    System.EventArgs) Handles btnToNotePad.Click
    Dim D As Integer
    'Set up the Clipboard
    'Place text in the clipboard
    Clipboard.SetDataObject("This comes from my VB program.")
    D = Shell("Notepad", vbNormalFocus) 'Start notepad
    Application.DoEvents()
    AppActivate(D) 'Activate Notepad (set focus)
    Application.DoEvents()
    'Send Alt+E key & P key (Edit, paste)
    'This will paste the text in Clipboard in Notepad
    SendKeys.Send("%ep")
End Sub
```

Run the program and then click the button. What do you see?

The procedure first places a text string in the Clipboard object. It then starts the Notepad application, and sets the focus on it with the AppActivate statement. The SendKeys' Send method sends Alt+E (for the Edit menu) and P (for Paste) keys to the active window (Notepad), causing the text in the Clipboard to show in Notepad.

14-3.   What Is Exposed? It was stated in previous chapters that Public members are accessible to other projects (assemblies), but Friend members are accessible only within the project (assembly). Here is a way to verify:

1. Start a new Class Library project. Name it **ScopeExplorer**, and delete Class1.vb from the project.
2. Add two components to the project. Take their default names, such as **Component1** and **Component2**.
3. In Component1, enter the following code:

```
Public PublicVar As Integer
Friend FriendVar As Integer
Friend Sub FriendProc()
End Sub
Public Sub PublicProc()
End Sub
```

4. In Component2, enter the following code:

```
Public PublicVar As Integer
Friend FriendVar As Integer
Friend Sub FriendProc()
    Dim Comp1 As New Component1()
    Dim FV As Integer
    Dim PV As Integer
    Comp1.FriendProc()
    Comp1.PublicProc()
    FV = Comp1.FriendVar
    PV = Comp1.PublicVar
End Sub
Public Sub PublicProc()
    Dim Comp1 As New Component1()
    Dim FV As Integer
    Dim PV As Integer
    Comp1.FriendProc()
    Comp1.PublicProc()
    FV = Comp1.FriendVar
    PV = Comp1.PublicVar
End Sub
```

Did you run into any problem with the code? No. Both Public and Friend access modifiers make both the variables (and thus, properties) and methods accessible to classes in the same project.

5. Build the project.
6. Add a new Windows form project, name it **TestScope**, and set it as the startup project.
7. Add a reference in this Windows form project. Right-click Reference under the TestScope project in the Solution Explorer. Select the Add Reference option. Click the Projects tab in the Add Reference dialog box. Double-click ScopeExplorer in the top pane and then click the OK button in the dialog box.
8. Enter the following code in the form's code module:

```
Private Sub Form1_Load(ByVal Sender As Object, ByVal e As
    System.EventArgs) Handles MyBase.Load
        Dim TestComp As New ScopeExplorer.Component1()
```

```
Dim A As Integer
Dim B As Integer
A = TestComp.PublicVar
B = TestComp.Friendvar
TestComp.PublicProc()
TestComp.FriendProc()
End Sub
```

Where do you see errors? Only the component's Public variable and procedure (but not the Friend variable or procedure) are visible in this project.

14-4.   **Using MS Excel in VB**. Can you start MS Excel from VB? Yes. You can set up a reference to MS Excel. You can then treat it just like any object you have used. Here are the steps to set up the reference:

1. Click the Project menu and then select the Add Reference option. The Add Reference dialog box appears.
2. Click the Com tab.
3. Locate Microsoft Excel Object 9.0 Library (the version number may vary depending on the version of MS Office your computer has), click the item, and click the Select button.
4. Click the OK button. If you are prompted whether to generate a wrapper, click the Yes button.

    After you have the Excel reference in place, add a button to the form and name the button **btnExcel**; then enter the following code, which prompts the user to select an Excel file, and will start MS Excel and open the selected file.

```
Private Sub btnExcel_Click(ByVal Sender As Object, ByVal e
    As System.EventArgs) Handles btnExcel.Click
    Dim MyExcel As New Excel.Application()
    Dim FileName As String
    FileName = GetFileName("Excel File (*.xls)¦*.xls")
    With MyExcel
        .Workbooks.Open(FileName)
        .Visible = True
    End With
End Sub
Private Function GetFileName(ByVal TheFilter As String)
    Dim cdlOpenFile As New OpenFileDialog()
    With cdlOpenFile
        .Filter = TheFilter
        .ShowDialog()
        Return (.FileName)
    End With
End Function
```

Run the project, and click the button. Does Excel start with the file that you selected in the Open dialog box?

14-5.   **Using MS Word in VB.** (continued from exercise 14-4) Can you start MS Word from VB? Yes. You can set up a reference to MS Word. You can then treat it just like any object you have used. Here are the steps to set up the reference:

1. Click the Project menu, and select the Add Reference option. The Add Reference dialog box appears.
2. Click the Com tab.
3. Locate Microsoft Word Object 9.0 Library (the version number may vary depending on the version of MS Office your computer has), click the item, and click the Select button.
4. Click the OK button. If you are prompted whether to generate a wrapper, click the Yes button.

After you have the Word reference in place, add a button to the form and then name the button **btnWord**. Enter the following code, which prompts the user to select a Word file, and will then start MS Word and open the selected file.

```
Private Sub btnWord_Click(ByVal Sender As Object, ByVal e As
   System.EventArgs) Handles btnWord.Click
     Dim MyWord As New Word.Application()
     Dim FileName As String
     FileName = GetFileName("Word File (*.doc)¦*.doc")
     With MyWord
         .Documents.Open(FileName)
         .Visible = True
     End With
End Sub
```

(*Note:* Use the same GetFileName function as exercise 14-4.) Run the project, and click the button. Does the MS Word start with the file that you selected in the Open dialog box?

14-6.   **Differences between Web Forms Buttons and HTML Buttons.** Create a new ASP.NET web application project; then:

1. Draw two web forms controls on the form:
   a.   One button; name it **btnWeb,** and set its Text property to **Web**.
   b.   One text box; name it **txtWeb**.
2. Draw two HTML controls on the form. (Select the HTML tab in the Toolbox, and then find the proper controls.)
   a.   One Reset button; name it **btnReset**.
   b.   One text field; name it **txtHTML**.

Enter the following code:

```
Shared N As Integer
Private Sub Page_Load(ByVal Sender As Object, ByVal e As
   System.EventArgs) Handles MyBase.Load
     'Put user code to initialize the page here
     If IsPostBack Then
         N += 1
         txtWeb.Text = "Clicked " & N
     End If
End Sub
```

(Notice that btnReset and txtHTML are not visible in the code; that is, neither of them are recognized when you want to code them as controls.)

Run the project; then experiment the following in sequence:

1. Enter some text in each of the text fields. Click the Reset button. What happens to the texts? Both text fields are cleared.
2. Enter some text in each of the text fields. Click the Web button. What happen to the text fields? The txtWeb control should show Click 1, while the text in txtHTML disappears. Subsequent clicks on the Web button will cause the click count to increase.
3. Enter some text in each of the text fields. Click the Reset button. What happens to the texts? You should see the Web text box has its Click # restored, and the HTML text box has its text cleared.

   BtnWeb is a Server control, while btnReset works at the client (the browser). When you click a server control, the code in the server (in this case, Page load) is triggered. When you click the Reset button, it instructs the browser to clear the text fields without submitting the form back to the server. The value of the Web text box is embedded in HTML code sent from the server. The reset operation restores its value as demonstrated in experiment 3.

14-7. **Can You Include a Web Service in a Component?** (This exercise assumes that you have the LearningCurve web service as discussed in the text ready.) Start a new Class Library project. Add a new component to the project, and take the default names for both. In the Solution Explorer, right-click the References node and select the Add Web Reference node. Try to add the LearningCurve web service to the project. Are you successful? Yes. You can not only include a web service in a Windows form project, but also in a component.

Exercises

14-8. **Saving the Grocertogo.mdb File Path.** In many of your projects that involve using the grocertogo.mdb file, you have either hard-coded its file path or used the common dialog box to prompt for the file path. Add code to one of these projects so that when the project starts, it will do the following:

- Prompt for the file path (using the open file dialog box) if the program cannot find the setting from the registry.
- Save the file path in the registry when the program is quitting.
- Retrieve the file path when the program restarts. Your program should not prompt for the file path again, if the program can open the database without any problem.

14-9. **Saving the Form Location and WindowState.** Develop a project so that when the program restarts, it will appear at the previous location with the same previous WindowState; that is, if the form was previously maximized when it quit, it will be maximized when it runs again. (*Hint:* Save the form's Left, Top, and WindowState properties with three different keys in the Closing event, and retrieve these settings in the Form Load event.)

14-10. **A Login Form.** Design a login form that will be the first form in the project to greet the user when the user starts an application. The form should have two option buttons: Login and New User.

If the New User option button is clicked, the form displays three boxes: Username, Password, and Confirm. It also displays an OK button. The user is expected to enter the username in the Name box, and to enter the password twice: once in the Password box, and once in the Confirm box. The user then clicks the OK button. If the two passwords match, the username and the encrypted password should be saved in the registry. The password should be encrypted when the OK button is clicked. The password should be encrypted with a simple scheme of reversing the text, such as ABC is encrypted as CBA. (Hint: Use the StrReverse function.) If the passwords in the password and confirm boxes do not match, the form continues to prompt for the same.

If the user clicks the Login option button, the form should ask the user for the username and password. When the user finishes the entry, the user clicks a Login button. If the username exists, your program will compare the password with the one saved in the registry and proceed to the application if they match; otherwise, the login form will continue to prompt for the username and password.

14-11. **A Simulator Component.** (refer to exercise 8-33 in Chapter 8, "Arrays and Their Uses") This exercise requires an array representing the probability of obtaining the particular units of good output, such as Prob(100) is the probability for obtaining 100 units of good output, given spoilage rates for two sequential processes and the input units of raw materials. Create a SequentialProcess component that has three properties: spoilage rate for the first process, spoilage rate for the second process, and the input units of raw materials. It has a ComputeProb method that will use the values of the three properties to compute the probability for each level (number of units) of good output, and return it as an array of the Double type.

14-12.   The Depositor Component. (refer to exercise 13-18 in Chapter 13, "Object-Oriented Programming") Modify the project so that the depositor and its inner classes are accessible as a component. Name the assembly **DepositorLib**.

14-13.   The MaskEdit Component. (refer to exercise 13-19 in Chapter 13) Modify the project so that MaskEdit is accessible as a component. Name the assembly as **MaskEditLib**.

14-14.   The Inventory Component. (refer to exercise 13-22 in Chapter 13) Modify the project so that the inventory and its inner classes are accessible as a component. Name the assembly **InventoryLib**.

14-15.   The Tic-Tac-Toe Game Component. (refer to exercise 12-25 in Chapter 12, "Object-Based Programming") Modify the project so that the game board is a component and can be used by any project.

14-16.   Completing the KeyVerifierBox Component. (refer to the KeyVerifierBox example in Section 14.2) Add additional functionality to the component, including allowing commas and a period for a box specified with the KeyType, Amount. Modify the code so that when UpperCaseLetter is specified, all lowercase letters are automatically changed to the uppercase, instead of displaying an error message.

14-17.   The Address Control. Design an address control that contains a street address field, a city field, a state field, and Zip code field. Use text boxes with proper labels. The layout should look like a mailing label. (*Hint:* Use a user control to contain all these controls. Set these controls' Modifier properties to Public so that other projects can reference them.) Build and test the project; then add it to the Toolbox. Test it by adding a new Windows form project to the solution. Be sure to set this form project as the startup project.

14-18.   The Personal Identification Control (the User Control). Design a control that contains an ID number field, name field, (use text boxes with proper labels) and a date of birth field (use masked edit with proper label), plus two radio buttons to identify the person's sex. All these controls should be placed within a group box, whose Text property is ID. Also include data validation code in the class. (*Hint:* Use a user control to contain all these controls. Set these controls' Modifier properties to Public so that other projects can reference them.) Build and test the project; then add it to the Toolbox. Test it by adding a new Windows form project to the solution. Be sure to set this form project as the startup project.

14-19.   Answering Name Search Remotely. Create a web form that allows the user to enter a short string in a text box. When the user clicks the Search button, your form will display in a data grid all names (in the tblPhonebook table of the Phonebook database you created in Chapter 9) that match the search string.

14-20.   A Scoreboard Site. Create a web form that allows the user to enter the user's last name and the student number (a four digit number). When the user clicks the Submit button, your program will search the Scores table in your database, and display the student's scores of assignments and tests in a data grid. The data grid should show two columns: The left column gives the items (assignment or test), and right gives the corresponding scores.

14-21. A Login Web Form. Create a login web form that requires the user to enter the username, password, and password confirmation. These three fields should be validated as follows:

- The username field must contain data. (Use a RequiredFieldValidator.)
- The password field must contain data. (Use a RequiredFieldValidator.)
- The password confirmation field must have exactly the same data as the password field. (Use a CompareValidator and set its ControlToCompare property to the password field.)
- All entry errors are summarized with a ValidationSummary control.

The form should also have a button for the user to click and submit. If everything is valid, another form with two hyperlinks (one links to your university website, another to your favorite website) will replace the login form; otherwise, the login form continues to prompt for the username and password.

14-22. A Simulator Web Service. (refer to exercise 14-11) Instead of creating a component, create the simulator as a web service. Modify the code so that the three properties for the object are now three parameters of the ComputeProb method.

14-23. Creating A Component with A Web Service. (This exercise assumes that you have created the LearningCurve web service as discussed in this chapter.) Create a component project, and name it **LCLocalLib**. Add a component to the project, and name it **LCLocal**. In the component, develop a HoursForUnitX method that will return the number of hours expected to produce the Xth unit. The formula to compute this quantity is as follows:

Hours for the Xth Unit = Total hours for X units – Total hours for (X –1) units

Note that X represents the cumulative number of units counting from the first unit of production in the learning curve model. (*Hint:* Be sure to add a reference to the LearningCurve web service.)

14-24. Bond Model Web Service. (refer to project 7-39 in Chapter 7) Modify the requirements so that the project you create is a web service named BondModel that provides two web methods: BondPrice and MarketRate. The BondPrice method returns the bond price given the market rate, the coupon rate, and years to maturity (all of the Double type). The MarketRate method computes the effective market rate for the bond given the price, coupon rate, and years to maturity (all of the Double type). Both methods assume a face value of 100 for the bond. Test your project by adding a web forms project to the solution. Draw text boxes for the coupon rate, years to maturity, market rate, and bond price. The user will enter the first two fields and one of the last two. Your web forms project will use the web service to compute the solution for the field that the user leaves out.

14-25. A Bond Model Component. (refer to exercise 14-24) Instead of creating a web service for the bond model, create a component for it. Name the project **BondModelLib**. Modify the design by making the coupon rate and the years to maturity the properties of the bond model. The BondPrice method will take the market rate as its sole parameter, while the MarketRate method will take the bond price as it sole parameter.

Projects

14-26. A Component Login. Modify the project you created in exercise 14-10 so that it is suitable to be compiled as a component; then add a Windows form project to test the component. When the component performs properly, test the component version again, using a new Windows form project.

A Data Management Using Files

Chapter 9, "Database and ADO.NET," discussed the use of relational databases for data management. In business applications, the database approach to data management was introduced long after the file-oriented approach. Under the file-oriented approach, all data that need to be kept for use by the computer are stored in the secondary storage area as files. Chapter 6, "Input, Output, and Procedures," introduced the new StreamReader and StreamWriter to handle files. This appendix discusses the more traditional VB approaches to file handling. VB provides three different file types to handle data:

- Sequential files
- Binary files
- Random files

This appendix introduces these file types in the order as listed.

A.1 Working with Sequential Files

When you work with files for input and output, several key steps are involved:

1. Open the file. In this process, your program associates a file number with the physical file residing in the intermediate storage device, such as the hard drive or floppy disk.
2. Perform file operations such as reading/writing data from/onto the file. Most of the file activities of your program relate to this aspect.
3. Close the file. This process dissociates your program from the physical file and ensures that all I/O operations are completed by the system.

Opening a File

To open a file, you use the *FileOpen statement*. The syntax appears as follows:

```
FileOpen(FileNumber, FileName, Mode[, Access] [,Share]
    [,RecordLen])
```

where *FileNumber* = a number that you assign for the file to be referenced in your program
FileName = a string specifying the path and name of the file (e.g., **A:\MyFolder\Phones.txt**)
Mode = Input, Output, Append, Binary, or Random. The following table explains each of these modes:

Mode	Use
Input	Specifies that the file will be opened for the input mode. The file must exist before it is opened.
Output	Specifies that the file will be opened for the output mode. If the file specified does not exist, VB creates the file; if the file already exists, all its existing content will be lost.
Append	Specifies that the file will be opened for the append mode. If the file specified does not exist, VB creates the file; if the file already exists, all its existing contents are preserved; new data are added (appended) to the end of the file.
Binary	Specifies that the file will be opened for the binary mode to be explained later.
Random	Specifies that the file will be opened for the random mode to be explained later.

Access = Read, Write, or ReadWrite, or Default
Share = the operations restricted on the open file by other processes: Shared, Lock Read, Lock Write, and Lock Read Write (the default is Shared).
RecordLen = for sequential file access, this parameter specifies the number of bytes to be used as the buffer for the file; for random file access, this number specifies the record length (explained later).

The following statement will open an existing file named Phonebook.txt located in the Temp folder of Drive C for input.

```
FileOpen(1, "C:\Temp\Phonebook.txt", OpenMode.Input)
```

In this statement, the Access, Share, and RecordLen parameters are omitted, so the defaults are used. The default access for an input file is Read. The default share parameter is Share.

About the File Number. The use of a constant literal for the file number in the preceding code should raise concern for code clarity and a potential problem with file identification. Imagine that you need to open 10 files at the same time. It would be difficult to remember what file number is used for which file. A mistake in your code can cause unthinkable problems. In addition, it would be a challenge for someone, including yourself, to identify the files when reviewing the code in the future.

For this reason, it is a good practice to use a variable instead of a constant literal as the file number. You can declare a variable and assign a number to the variable. From then on, the variable can be used in placed of the constant literal. Suppose you want to open the file as soon as your program starts and use the file in several procedures. Using the variable PhoneFile for the file, your code can appear as follows:

```
Dim PhoneFile As Integer
Private Sub Form1_Load(ByVal sender As System.Object, ByVal e As
   System.EventArgs) Handles MyBase.Load
      PhoneFile = 1
      FileOpen(PhoneFile, "C:\Temp\Phonebook.txt", OpenMode.Input)
End Sub
```

After the file is opened in Input mode, you are ready to read data from the file sequentially.

Reading Data from a File

Data can be read from a sequential file in several ways. One commonly used statement is the Input statement, which has the following syntax:

```
Input(File Number, Variable)
```

where *File Number* = the file number associated with the input file as explained previously
Variable = a variable to hold the data read from the file

For example, suppose that you have opened the phone file shown in the preceding code example. The file contains your friends' names and phone numbers and appears as follows:

```
8172223838, John Dole
2145559999, Jane Smith
.
.
```

Assume your form has a button named btnRead. When you click the button, you want to read one line of data into the variables Phone and TheName and display the results. Your code should appear as follows:

```
Private Sub btnRead_Click(ByVal sender As System.Object, ByVal e
   As System.EventArgs) Handles btnRead.Click
      Dim Phone As Long
      Dim TheName As String
      Input(PhoneFile, Phone)
      Input(PhoneFile, TheName)
      MsgBox("Phone is " & Phone & ". Name is " & TheName & ".")
End Sub
```

The first time the procedure is executed, the variables Phone and TheName will hold the values of 8172223838 and "John Dole," respectively. The second time the procedure is executed, the variables will have the data on the second line.

As a technical side note, at the end of each line in a text file, there is an end of line marker that the computer uses to separate one line from the other. The marker consists of two character codes: Return (13; that is, Keys.Return) and Line Feed (10). VB provides the named constant vbCrLf for this marker. Recall that you used this constant in Chapter 3, "Visual Basic Controls and Events," to display texts on different lines. Although the marker is not visible to you, it is important to be aware of its existence. The awareness helps you understand how the sequential (text) file is handled internally by Visual Basic.

The Comma Delimiter for the Input Statement. In the preceding code, the Input statement looks for commas and the end of line markers (vbCrLf) to separate data fields and lines, respectively. Because the phone number and name are separated by a comma in each line, the Input statement will execute properly. What if each line appears as follows?

```
8172223838, Dole, John
```

The value 8172223838 will be correctly assigned to Phone, but TheName will contain only Dole instead of Dole, John. The comma between Dole and John will lead the Input statement to interpret that they are two separate data fields. What can be done to avoid or correct the problem? A typical way is to create a file with the names enclosed in a pair of double quotes:

```
8172223838, "Dole, John"
```

The string enclosed in quotes can then be read and interpreted by the Input statement as a single data field and assigned properly to the variable TheName.

What if you must read data from an existing file that was created without the double quotes? The workaround will take a bit more code. You will use the LineInput function to read in a line of data and perform your own string parsing.

The LineInput Function. Unlike the Input statement, the LineInput function reads and returns one line of data at a time from the file. This statement has the following syntax:

```
LineInput(File Number)
```

where *File Number* = the file number associated with the input file as explained previously.

The result obtained should be assigned to a variable. For example, the string variable PhoneName will contain an entire line of data as a result of executing the following statement:

```
PhoneName = LineInput(PhoneFile)
```

Note that the LineInput function does not filter out any characters in the input file, so if the file contains double quotes or commas, these characters will be preserved in the variable. If you need to remove any unneeded characters, you will need to provide the code for that purpose.

To continue the example, assume that the line read in is as follows:

```
8172223838, Dole, John
```

and you would like to put the number in Phone and the name in TheName. You can use the following code to obtain the result:

```
P = InStr(PhoneName, ",")
Phone = Microsoft.VisualBasic.Left(PhoneName, P - 1)
TheName = Mid(PhoneName, P + 2)
```

In the code, the InStr function is used to find the position of the first comma in PhoneName (the line read in). The substring on the left side of the comma is then assigned to Phone, and the right side is assigned to TheName.

The InputString Function. In addition to the Input statement and the LineInput function already described to read data from an input file, the *InputString function* can also be used for similar purposes. The Input function has the following syntax:

```
InputString(File Number, Chars)
```

Where *File Number* = same as explained previously for the Open statement

Chars = the number of characters to read in

To read the first phone number and name in the file in the previous example, you can code the following:

```
Phone = InputString(PhoneFile, 10)
TheName = InputString(PhoneFile, 12)
```

The InputString function does not skip any characters in a file, so the second statement in the code will also include both commas in the input stream; that is, the content of TheName will appear as follows:

```
, Dole, John
```

Notice the comma and the space before Dole, John. In addition, even the end of line marker, vbCrLf, will be included (and counted as two characters) when you use the InputString function.

The Relative Advantages of the Input Techniques. At this moment, you probably think that the InputString function is of limited use because it requires a lot of additional details, which you may not even be able to supply for the example we have at hand. In the previous example, all phone numbers and names respectively will have to be of equal length to use the InputString function.

Actually, there are relative advantages and disadvantages of each type of input technique:

- The *Input statement* provides a convenient way to read in data when the file has been created as comma delimited; however, not all the files are created in this format. Files that are to be exchanged between different software packages are usually exported (created by a software package for another software) in this format. You can then use the Input statement to import the data into your application. These files do not look very organized, and use much more storage space than files of other formats. Also, it requires more computer resources to parse the data in this format, so the Input statement is slow. You should avoid using it for high-volume repetitive data-processing applications.

- The *LineInput function* reads one line of data at a time. If you have files that contain data on a line-by-line basis, this statement can be used conveniently. As the previous example illustrates, it can also be used to parse data to overcome the problem that the Input statement can encounter with improperly delimited files; however, you will then need to provide the code to take care of the details, so the LineInput function is most often used as a technical supplement for the Input statement.

- The *InputString function* works the best when the data in a file are structured in a very precise format. It is the fastest technique among the three, so it is the technique most suitable for processing large-volume sequential files. (Note, however, "sequential files" are the precondition. Other file modes can be even faster, but the InputString function cannot be used in other file modes.) As you have already seen, when data in a file are not formatted precisely, it will be difficult to use this technique. Some of its uses are illustrated later in this appendix under the headings "LOF Function" and "Reading an Entire File."

The following table summarizes the advantages and disadvantages of the three sequential input techniques.

Input Technique	Feature	Advantages	Disadvantages
Input statement	Reads field by field	Simple, easy to use; good for import and export	Slow; files suitable for this operation require more storage and do not look neat.
LineInput function	Reads line by line	Faster than Input statement	Additional code is required to parse the string or each field must be of fixed length.
InputString function	Reads the number of characters as specified	Fastest among the three techniques	Length of each field must be known before the statement is executed.

The EOF Function. If you continue to execute the Input or the LineInput function, eventually the file will run out of data. When this happens, the end of file condition is raised. Further attempt to read the file will result in a runtime End Of File (EOF) error. To avoid encountering the EOF error, your code should check for the EOF condition before executing an Input/LineInput function. The EOF function returns the EOF condition of a file and can be used for this purpose. It has the following syntax:

```
EOF(File Number)
```

If the file specified has run out of data, the function returns a value of True; otherwise, it returns a value of False. In the previous example involving the Input statement, you can modify the code to take into account the EOF condition as follows:

```
Private Sub btnRead_Click(ByVal sender As System.Object, ByVal e
    As System.EventArgs) Handles btnRead.Click
    Dim Phone As Long
    Dim TheName As String
```

```
        If EOF(PhoneFile) Then
            MsgBox("Out of data")
            Exit Sub
        End If
        Input(PhoneFile, Phone)
        Input(PhoneFile, TheName)
        MsgBox("Phone is " & Phone & ". Name is " & TheName & ".")
    End Sub
```

The LOF Function. The EOF function works properly for the Input statement and LineInput function; however, it does not work for the InputString function. Why? This function reads in the number of characters as specified. It makes no attempt to identify the meaning of any characters it reads, which is why it takes the end of line marker vbCrLf as a part of the input.

To identify the EOF condition when using the InputString function, you should count the number of characters read in and compare the counter with the size of the file, which you can obtain using the LOF function. The *LOF function* has the same syntax as the EOF function, but it returns the size of the file. Suppose in the previous phone file that all phone numbers are saved as a 10-character string and names as a 20-character string. In addition, there is no carriage return character in the file; then, in the routine to read the data (say, the button btnInputString's Click event), you can code the following:

```
    Private Sub btnInputString_Click(ByVal sender As System.Object,
      ByVal e As System.EventArgs) Handles btnInputString.Click
        Dim Phone As Long
        Dim TheName As String
        Static CharsRead As Integer
        If CharsRead >= LOF(PhoneFile) Then
            MsgBox("All Phones and Names have been read.")
            Exit Sub
        End If
        Phone = InputString(PhoneFile, 10)
        TheName = InputString(PhoneFile, 20)
        MsgBox(Phone)
        MsgBox(TheName)
        'The above two lines read in a total of 30 characters.
        'Accumulate the number of chars read
        'to compare with the file length
        CharsRead = CharsRead + 30
    End Sub
```

Notice that the variable CharsRead is declared as a Static variable so that its value can be preserved between each event procedure call. It is used to keep track of the number of characters read and is compared with the file size at the beginning of the procedure. If it is greater than or equal to the file size, the entire file has been read. A message is displayed, and the procedure is terminated with the Exit Sub statement.

Reading an Entire File. The InputString function turns out to be a handy facility when you need to read the entire file in one operation. For example, suppose you would like to read the entire file into a text box named txtDoc from the file number TextFile, which has been opened properly. You can code the following:

```
    txtDoc.Text = InputString(TextFile, LOF(TextFile))
```

This is equivalent to the ReadToEnd method of the stream reader (as discussed in Chapter 6) and should be a handy way to display the file content in a text box. You can even allow the user to edit the text as in a word processing operation. Of course, to display the text properly, you should set the text box's MultiLine property to True and its Scrollbars property to Vertical or Both (vertical and horizontal).

The FreeFile Function. You have seen that you can designate a file number and use it to open the file. You have also been advised to use a variable for the file number instead of a constant literal in your code. When your program needs to handle many files simultaneously, it can be difficult for you to keep track of which number has been used to open a file. Because all you really need is to assign a legitimate number to the variable for each file, it would be nice if the system could handle this automatically for you. Is there a way? Yes, the *FreeFile function* provides exactly this service. It returns a number that you can safely use to open a file. Instead of designating a number for a file manually, you should always take advantage of this FreeFile function. For example, the following code from the previous example used to open the phone file:

```
PhoneFile = 1
FileOpen(PhoneFile, "C:\Temp\Phonebook.txt", OpenMode.Input)
```

should be changed to:

```
PhoneFile = FreeFile()
FileOpen(PhoneFile, "C:\Temp\Phonebook.txt", OpenMode.Input)
```

If you have only one file to open, the FreeFile function most likely will return a value of 1, the same number you would have designated. If you need to assign a number for another file in a separate part of your project, however, the use of the FreeFile function will relieve you from the tedious need to check which file number has been used and whether the associated file has been closed.

Always use the FreeFile function and the FileOpen statement as a pair in two consecutive statements. Inserting other code between the two lines can make the program harder to read. Further, an error can sneak in if the FreeFile function is used again with a new variable. For example, the following code will result in a "File already open" error.

```
FileOne = FreeFile()
FileTwo = FreeFile()
FileOpen(FileOne, "MyFileA.txt", OpenMode.Output)
FileOpen(FileTwo, "MyFileB.txt", OpenMode.Output)  X
```

Why? When the FreeFile function is used the second time, FileOne has not yet been opened; therefore, the system thinks the number used for FileOne is still available. The same number will be assigned to both FileOne and FileTwo, but the same number cannot be used to open two different files.

The correct code is:

```
FileOne = FreeFile()
FileOpen(FileOne, "MyFileA.txt", OpenMode.Output)
FileTwo = FreeFile()
FileOpen(FileTwo, "MyFileB.txt", OpenMode.Output)
```

The FileClose Statement. A file left open will be closed when the project ends. However, in many cases, you may need to close the file before the project ends; for example, when you need to open the same file with different mode, say, to switch from output mode to input mode. Indeed, it is a good practice to close the file when you are done with it. It eliminates the possibility that your program accidentally performs unexpected operations on the file. It releases the computer resources associated with that file and ensures that all file operations you have performed are actually carried out by the computer. The syntax to close a file is as follows:

```
FileClose([FileNumberList])
```

To close the phone file in the preceding example, you will write the following:

```
FileClose(PhoneFile)
```

Note that you can simply code:

```
FileClose()
```

In such a case, all open files will be closed.

Output with Sequential Files

To output data to a file, you need to open the file with either Output or Append mode. If you open a file with *Output mode*, any previous content of the file will be erased. In essence, you are creating a brand new file; however, in most cases, you would probably want to preserve the previous content of the file. In such cases, you should open the file with *Append mode*. The previous content will be preserved. The next output operation will be appended to the end of the current file content.

The following statements will open the Phone file discussed in the previous example. (Note that the file must first be closed if you have previously opened it for other purposes.)

```
Dim PhoneFile As Integer
PhoneFile = FreeFile()
FileOpen(PhoneFile, "C:\Temp\Phonebook.txt", OpenMode.Append)
```

You can then use either the Write (WriteLine) statement or Print (PrintLine) statement to add more phone numbers and names, depending on how you would like to create the data on the file.

The Write and WriteLine Statements.

The Write and WriteLine statements will create comma-delimited data, and enclose string data in pairs of double quotes. The WriteLine statement writes the variable list on a line and places the line end marker (vbCrLf) at the end, so the next output operation will start on the next line. On the other hand, the Write statement does not add the line end marker, so the next output operation will continue on the same line. Both statements have the same syntax as follows:

```
Write(File Number, Variable List)
WriteLine(File Number, Variable List)
```

where *File Number* = the file number associated with the output

Variable list = a list of variables to write onto the file

For example, you have a masked edit box named mskPhone, and a text box named txtFriend in a form. You would like to save the data entered by the user to the file just opened. If you use the following statement:

```
WriteLine(PhoneFile, mskPhone.ClipText, txtFriend.Text)
```

the line of output data in the file will appear as follows:

```
"2146668392", "Jones, Allen"
```

Note that the phone number is also enclosed in a pair of double quotes because the ClipText property is not considered numeric. To avoid the pair of quotes for the phone number, you should code the following:

```
WriteLine(PhoneFile, Val(mskPhone.ClipText), txtFriend.Text)
```

Recall that the Input statement explained previously expects this structure of data in the file. You can think of the Input and Write (and WriteLine) statements as complementary I/O statements.

The Print and PrintLine Statements.

The Print and PrintLine statements do not automatically provide any extra commas or quotes when outputting data. Similar to the Write statement, the Print statement does not add the line end marker (vbCrLf) at the end of the output line, but the PrintLine statement does. These statements have the following syntax:

```
Print(File Number, Variable List)
PrintLine(File Number, Variable List)
```

where *File Number* = the file number associated with the output file

Variable list = a list of variables to output data onto the file

If you output the data with the following statement:

```
PrintLine(PhoneFile, mskPhone.ClipText, txtFriend.Text)
```

the line of data in the file will appear as follows:

```
2146668392    Jones, Allen
```

Notice that the phone number and the name are separated with a proper tab position when the variables appear in the same PrintLine (Print) statement. If you want the data from each variable (property) to appear right next to the preceding variable, use the Print statement to output each variable separately. For example, the following statements will have a line of output as shown below:

```
'Next output will follow immediately
Print(PhoneFile, mskPhone.ClipText)
PrintLine(PhoneFile, txtFriend.Text)
```

2146668392Jones, Allen

Write Versus Print. The differences between the Write (WriteLine) statement and the Print (PrintLine) statement can be briefly stated as follows:

- The Write statement creates a *comma-delimited* file. The results can be used by other applications. The file can also conveniently be read by using the Input statement; however, the output operation is very slow, similar to its input counterpart, the Input statement. The resulting file does not look very neat and therefore is not suitable for reports. In addition, the file takes up more storage space, so you use the Write (WriteLine) statement only when the file is intended to be exported, or when the file size is very small and operational efficiency is not a concern.

- The Print (PrintLine) statement can generate files whose columns are neatly aligned, so you can use the Print (PrintLine) statement to generate files intended for reports. In addition, you can use it to generate files that take up less storage space than those generated by the Write (WriteLine) statement. If each field in a record is created as a fixed-length field, the resulting file can conveniently be read by the InputString function. I/O operations done in this way are more efficient than those using the Write (WriteLine) or Input statements; however, output from the Print (PrintLine) statement generally is not suitable for export.

This section has discussed many statements and functions related to file operations. The following table provides a summary.

Keyword	Statement or Function	Purpose	Code Example
FileOpen	Statement	To associate a file number with a physical file	`FileOpen(PhoneFile, MyFilePath, OpenMode.Input)`
FileClose	Statement	To close files	`FileClose(PhoneFile)`
Input	Statement	To read comma-delimited data from a file	`Input(PhoneFile, Phone)`
LineInput	Function	To read a line	`PhoneName=LineInput(PhoneFile)`
Write, WriteLine	Statement	To output comma-delimited data	`WriteLine(PhoneFile, ThePhone, TheName)`
Print, PrintLine	Statement	To output data with no extra quotes or comma	`PrintLine(PhoneFile, ThePhone, TheName)`
InputString	Function	To read data with a specified length	`Phone = InputString(PhoneFile, 10)`
EOF	Function	Returns a Boolean value indicating whether end of file has been reach	`If EOF(PhoneFile) Then Exit Sub`
LOF	Function	Returns the file size in bytes	`TheFileLength = LOF(PhoneFile)`
FreeFile	Function	Returns a value representing a file number that has not been used	`PhoneFile = FreeFile()`

This completes the discussion of input and output with the sequential file. Before exploring the binary and random files, it is desirable to introduce the *Structure*.

A.2 The Structure

The data types you learned in Chapter 4, "Data, Operations, and Built-In Functions," such as Boolean, Integer, Long, Single, and so on, are recognized as elementary data types. You can combine any of these data types together to form a new type, which is recognized as the *Structure*. When defined, it can be used as a data type to declare a variable, just like the keyword Integer can be used to declare an Integer variable.

Defining the Structure

To define a structure, you use the Structure block that appears as follows:

```
[Private¦Protected¦Friend¦Public] Structure Name
        Variable Declaration
            :
            :
    End Structure
```

where *Name* = a name for the Structure you are defining

Variable declaration = a declaration for a member in the Structure; e.g.,

```
Dim Phone As Long
```

Notice that the Structure must be declared at the class level, and that a Structure member cannot be declared as Protected. Notice also that string elements in a Structure can be of the fixed length (although VB.NET does not support the fixed length string as an elementary type). To declare a fixed-length member, you place a VBFixedString attribute in front of the variable declaration. For example, suppose you want to declare LastName as a fixed length string member (say, 12 characters long) of a structure. You code:

```
<VBFixedString(12)> Dim LastName As String
```

The following is an example of a Structure declaration:

```
Public Structure Sample
    <VBFixedString(20)> Dim Name As String
    Public Size As Integer
    Private Weight As Integer
End Structure
```

In this example, Name will have the Public access as a default for Dim.

Declaring and Using a Structure Variable

The Structure is not a variable but rather a type such as Integer or Long, but you can then declare a variable of the Structure and use it for any desirable purpose. Frequently, it is used to declare a variable that can be used as the record for input and output with the random file. The familiar Dim statement can be used for such purposes. For example, you may declare a TheSample variable of the preceding Structure as follows:

```
Dim TheSample As Sample
```

Note that you can declare as many variables of the same Structure as you want, just like you can declare as many Integer variables as you want.

How do you refer to an element in the record (structure)? You qualify the data element with the Structure variable. For example, the following expression refers to the Name in the TheSample record:

```
TheSample.Name
```

Structures are frequently used in handling data in the binary file and random file. The next section discusses how to work binary files.

A.3 Working with Binary Files

The binary file features extreme flexibility. You can read or write any part of the file at any point, provided you know what you are doing. Perhaps it is easier to understand how a binary file works by comparing it with a sequential file.

Differences between the Binary File and the Sequential File

The binary file differs from the sequential file in a number of ways. The following discussion considers these aspects in detail.

Input and Output Allowed. You can perform input from a sequential file only if it is opened with the Input mode and perform output only if it is opened in Output or Append mode; however, you can perform both input and output at the same time on a file opened with the binary mode.

Data Access. You can access data in a sequential file only sequentially; that is, you read or write one data element at a time. After you pass that element, you cannot go back until you close the file and reopen for another round. (*Note:* Technically, this is not exactly true with the case of the InputString function; however, it is still advisable to observe this general rule.) In contrast, you can have access to any position of a binary file in any order anytime, so you have complete freedom of movement around a binary file.

Data Conversion for Output. All output (numeric or string) to a sequential file is converted to strings before actual output is carried out. In contrast, no data conversion is performed on output to a binary file. So, a 9-digit number of the Integer type will be written onto a sequential file as a 9-digit character string (plus any delimiters) but on a binary file as a 4-byte field. (Recall that an Integer type variable requires 4 bytes of storage.) This difference in I/O operation can be tricky to a beginner and is further illustrated later in this appendix.

Data Conversion for Input. All numeric input from a sequential file is converted to the data type of the variable specified. In contrast, the data read from a binary file is taken at face value. The data obtained is assigned directly to the variable used in the FileGet statement (for binary input) without any data conversion.

Delimiters. In the sequential file output operation, delimiters are inserted automatically. Recall that if you use a Write or WriteLine statement to output a string, it adds a pair of double quotes to enclose the string, and a comma before it if it is not the first item in the output list. Each line in the sequential file (whether done by the WriteLine or PrintLine statement) is delimited by the character pair vbCrLf (Chr(13)Chr(10)); however, no delimiter characters are automatically inserted to any output in a binary file. If you create a file with the binary mode and reopen the file with the Input mode, you will most likely see only one long line of data.

These differences are summarized in the following table.

Difference in	Sequential File	Binary File
Mode and I/O	Either Input for input; or, Append or Output for output	Binary
Access	Sequential; either input or output	Direct; input and output at any byte position
Data conversion in output	Numeric data are converted to string before output	No conversion; each byte in memory is output as a byte in file
Data conversion in input	Strings read in for numeric variables will be converted to numbers	No conversion; each byte in file is read in as a byte into memory
Delimiters	Added automatically	No delimiter added

Opening a File with the Binary Mode

Suppose you want to open a file with a path C:\Payroll\Special.dat for the Binary mode, you can code the following:

```
Dim SpecialFile As Integer
SpecialFile = FreeFile()
FileOpen(SpecialFile, "C:\Payroll\Special.dat",
  OpenMode.Binary)
```

As you can see, the difference between opening a sequential file and a binary file is the enumeration value for the open mode. You use the Binary open mode to open a binary file.

Output and Input with a Binary File

When open, a binary file can be used to perform any input or output. To perform output, you use the FilePut statement, which has the following syntax:

```
FilePut(FileNumber, VariableName, [Position])
```

For example, to output a value 65 to the preceding file, you can code the following:

```
Dim SixtyFive As Integer
SixtyFive = 65
FilePut(SpecialFile, SixtyFive, 1)
```

The Position Value in the Binary File. The FilePut statement in the preceding code instructs the computer to output the variable SixtyFive to the binary file, SpecialFile, starting at position 1 (first position). The position is expressed in bytes. As explained, you can place the output in any position of the file. This holds even for the first output operation. So, if you change the position to 1,000,001 in the preceding statement, it will still work; however, you will leave the first 1,000,000 bytes unused. Unless you have something planned for that storage area, it is just not advisable to skip that many bytes in a file.

Retrieving Data from the Binary file. To retrieve the data from a binary file, you use the FileGet statement, which has the following syntax:

```
FileGet(FileNumber, VariableName, [Position])
```

For example, to read the data stored in the preceding example, you can code the following:

```
Dim RetrievedData As Integer
FileGet(SpecialFile, RetrievedData, 1)
```

If you encounter an error with the FileGet statement in conjunction with the use of a Structure, set Option Strict Off.

Notice that to retrieve the stored data correctly, the position and the data type of the variable must match that specified in the original Put statement. The binary file is very precise in this respect. Count on an unexpected result if you fail to observe this rule.

To ensure correct results, match the exact position and data type of the data you are retrieving with what is originally stored in a binary file.

Data Type and Binary I/O. Why is it so important to match the data type between input and output in a binary file? After all, you may recall that in working with the sequential file, any data can be read as a string without any errors in the results. This is certainly not the case for the binary file. Recall that data are saved in the binary file without any conversion, so the preceding FilePut statement will result in a 4-byte integer image being placed in the first four bytes of the file. After the data are left in the file, the computer no longer remembers the format of the data. It relies on your code to provide the correct format (data type) to retrieve the same data. A different data type will make the computer interpret the data differently and therefore incorrectly.

For example, consider the following code to retrieve the same data saved previously:

```
Structure TestStruc
    <VBFixedString(4)> Dim TestString As String
End Structure
Private Sub btnTest_Click(ByVal sender As System.Object, ByVal e
  As System.EventArgs) Handles btnTest.Click
    Dim MyStructure As TestStruc
    FileGet(SpecialFile, MyStructure, 1)
    MsgBox(MyStructure.TestString)
End Sub
```

The result will be quite different. The 4-byte Integer image will be retrieved from the file. No conversion is performed, so you should expect to see the character representation of the numeric value; that is, Chr(Value of first byte) & Chr(Value of second byte) & .... When you run the program and click the button, you should see the message box display an A.

TestString gives A because the first byte in the file has a code value of 65, the ASCII value for A. Incidentally, when the computer saves a numeric field, the lowest byte is saved first, as you might have inferred from these results.

You may wonder why you went through all the trouble of defining a fixed-length string to read the 4-byte field. Can't you just use the following code and obtain the same result?

```
Dim TestString As String
TestString = Space(4)
FileGet(SpecialFile, TestString, 1)      ?
```

No. The result is quite unexpected. When you attempt to read a data field into a variable string, the computer reads at the specified position to decide the length to read and reads in the data following that field into the string; that is, you will find after the FileGet statement, TestString will have a length of 65, containing whatever it reads from the file.

Omitting the Position Parameter? As implied in the preceding syntax, the position parameter in both FilePut and FileGet statements can be omitted. If left unspecified, the position that VB actually uses is the value that is determined by the Seek function, which returns a value representing a byte position in the file. In general, when you leave the position parameter unspecified, you leave the control at the mercy of the computer. Always specify the position parameter to ensure the accuracy of the results.

Handling String Data. Writing string data to the binary file is fairly simple and presents no problem. For example, the following statement will write the name "John Smith" to SpecialFile starting from byte position 3.

```
FilePut(SpecialFile, "John Smith", 3)
```

But how do you read it back? As just explained, using a string variable of variable length will not work. You must use a variable of fixed length string to handle it. And to declare a fixed length string variable, you must use the Structure. Note that the length of the string that is read from the file must be the same as the string previously output; therefore, it is advisable that a Structure be declared and used both to input and output strings.

Saving and Retrieving an Array

You can also save into and retrieve from a binary file an array of data. For example, the following code fragment will save 100 random numbers in a binary file called RandNumFile:

```
Dim RandNumFile As Integer
Dim I As Integer
Dim MyArray(99) As Integer
Dim Rand As New Random()
For I = 0 To 99
    MyArray(I) = Rand.Next(1, 1001)
Next I
RandNumFile = FreeFile()
FileOpen(RandNumFile, "RandNum.dat", OpenMode.Binary)
FilePut(RandNumFile, MyArray, 1)
FileClose(RandNumFile)
```

To retrieve the same data from the file into another array, you can code the following:

```
Dim RandNumFile As Integer
Dim YourArray(99) As Integer
RandNumFile = FreeFile()
FileOpen(RandNumFile, "RandNum.dat", OpenMode.Binary)
FileGet(RandNumFile, YourArray, 1)
FileClose(RandNumFile)
```

Note that you do not have to read the entire array at one time. After the data are saved, you can retrieve only the part that you need. For example, if you need to read only the last 50 elements of the number back, you can code the following:

```
Dim RandNumFile As Integer
Dim HisArray(49) As Integer
RandNumFile = FreeFile()
FileOpen(RandNumFile, "RandNum.dat", OpenMode.Binary)
FileGet(RandNumFile, HisArray, 201)
FileClose(RandNumFile)
```

Notice that HisArray has only 50 elements. Also, the byte position in the FileGet statement is 201 because each element of the Integer type is four bytes long. Finally, if HisArray is a scalar variable (not an array), the FileGet statement in the preceding code will read the fifty-first element from the file.

A.4 Working with Random Files

In many ways, the random file works similarly to the binary file. Indeed, after a file is created using the Random file mode, you can reopen the same file in the Binary mode and access the same data without any problem, provided that "you know what you are doing." The following are the similarities and differences between the binary file and the random file:

- Both file modes use the FileGet and FilePut statements for input and output; however, the third parameter (the number) in these statements has quite a different meaning. In the binary file, the number refers to the byte position, whereas in the random file, it refers to the record position. For example, consider the following statement:

```
FileGet(SpecialFile, TheName, 3)
```

  If SpecialFile is open with the Binary mode, 3 will refer to the third byte position of the file. If the file is open with the Random mode, 3 will refer to the third record. The actual byte position will depend on the specified record length. This also means that in the Binary mode, you can access data starting at any position in the file; however, in the Random mode, you can access data only at the beginning of a record position. You have much more flexibility in the Binary mode than in the Random mode.

- In the FileOpen statement, the sixth parameter (if specified) refers to the buffer size if the file mode is Binary; however, it refers to the record length if the file mode is Random. Omitting this parameter for the binary file will not cause any problem but can have serious unexpected consequences for the random file. In the Random file mode, the FileGet and FilePut statements rely on the specified record length to compute the byte position to store or retrieve a record. A wrong record length will result in accessing or writing over (and thus destroying) the wrong data.

- Because data in a random file can be accessed only at a record position (rather than at a byte position), it is only logical that the I/O operation involves an entire record instead of only a field (data element); therefore, the Structure is typically used.

- In Binary mode, the data type and length of data can vary from field to field. In Random mode, the maximum length of the record is defined in the FileOpen statement. Varying the record size in Random mode will result in waste of storage space.

These differences are summarized in the following table.

Differences in	Binary File	Random File
FileGet and FilePut statements	The third parameter refers to byte position.	The third parameter refers to record position.
Sixth parameter in FileOpen statement	Refers to buffer size.	Refers to the record size for address computation. Subsequent access to the file cannot specify any record size that exceeds this limit.
Access	By field.	By record.
Variability in data	Extremely flexible.	Limited.

An Example

To illustrate how the random file can be used, consider the familiar phonebook application. Suppose you would like to keep your friends' phone numbers, addresses, and email addresses in a random file. You have designed the visual interface as shown in Figure A.1.

The list box (named 1stNamePhone) will be used to display names and phone numbers. So that your user can easily find the name of interest, the list box's Sorted property is set to True; therefore, the list box will display names in alphabetical order when populated. When the user clicks a name, the record will be retrieved from the file and displayed on the form. When the user clicks the Save button, your program will determine whether it is a new record. If so, it will be added to the file; otherwise, the existing record will be updated.

Figure A.1

Visual interface for the phonebook application

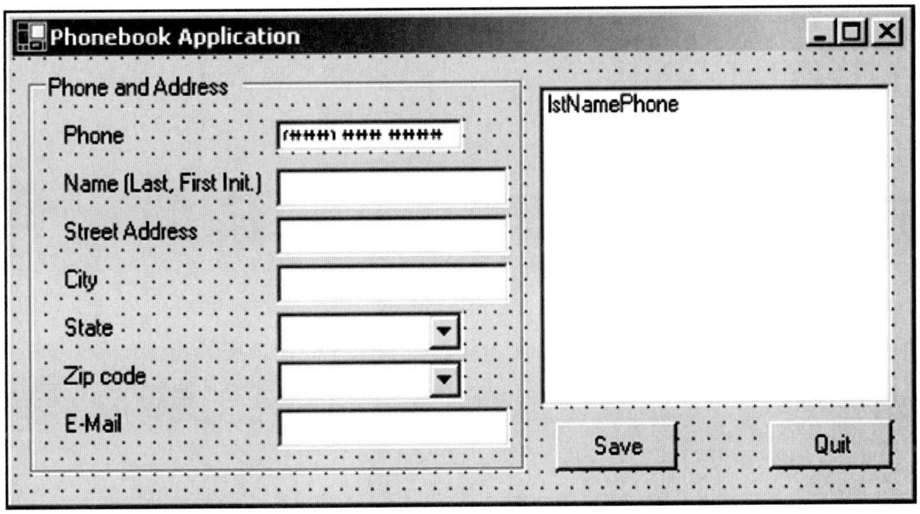

This project allows you to keep records in a random file. When the program starts, the list box will show phone numbers and names of existing records. Double-clicking an item in the list box will retrieve the corresponding record. The Save button will add the record if it is new; otherwise, it will update the record.

The following table shows the layout of each record and the name of the control for each field.

Field	Data Type	Field Length	Description	Control Name/Remark
Phone	String	10	Phone number	mskPhone; set Mask to "(###)-###-####"
Name	String	24	Last, First Init.	txtName; set MaxLength to 24
Address	String	32		txtAddress; set MaxLength to 32
City	String	28		txtCity; set MaxLength to 28
State Code	String	2		cboStateCode
Zip Code	Integer	4		cboZipCode
Email	String	48		txtEMail

Notice the length of the Zip Code field. Although externally you see the Zip code to be a five-digit number, its data type is Integer and will be saved as such, which takes four bytes of storage. Also, the Mask property of mskPhone should be set to "(###)-###-####" for proper entry in the field.

Recall from the previous discussion that each record in the file will have to be saved or retrieved in one FilePut or FileGet operation, so you will need to use the Structure. You can define a Structure as follows:

```
Structure PhoneRecStruc
    <VBFixedString(10)> Dim Phone As String
    <VBFixedString(24)> Dim Name As String
    <VBFixedString(32)> Dim Address As String
    <VBFixedString(28)> Dim City As String
    <VBFixedString(2)> Dim StateCode As String
    Dim ZipCode As Integer
    <VBFixedString(48)> Dim EMail As String
End Structure
```

Notice that all string elements are declared as fixed-length strings. As explained previously in this appendix, it is tricky to handle input with variable-length strings. You will be far better off using fixed-length strings in defining your records.

You can then use the Structure to declare a variable that can be used as the record for input and output with the random file. The familiar Dim statement can be used for such purposes:

```
Dim PhoneRecord As PhoneRecStruc
```

After you declare the record, you are ready to open a random file to perform I/O operations.

Opening a File for Random Mode

To open the preceding Phonebook file with the Random mode, you would code the following:

```
Dim PhoneFile As Integer
PhoneFile = FreeFile()
FileOpen(PhoneFile, "PhoneBook.dat", OpenMode.Random, , , 148)
```

The FileOpen statement specifies that each record in the file is 148 bytes long. As previously explained, under the Random mode, each record is expected to be of the same length. In general, however, it is not a good idea to hard-code the record length while your program is still under development. You may find a need to change the record structure and also its length. Each change will necessitate changing this number. An alternative is to use the Len function (explained in Chapter 4) to perform the length computation. The Open statement can be revised as follows:

```
FileOpen(PhoneFile, "PhoneBook.dat", OpenMode.Random, , ,
    Len(PhoneRecord))
```

> Be extremely careful in specifying the record length for a random file. A wrong length can create a huge chaos. The simplest way to specify the length of a record is to use the Len function as follows:
>
> ```
> TheLength = Len(YourRecord)
> ```

Performing Input and Output with a Random File

After the file is open and the record is defined, you can use the FileGet and FilePut statements to perform the I/O operation. For example, to read the first record from the Phonebook file, you can code the following:

```
FileGet(PhoneFile, PhoneRecord, 1)
```

Similarly, to save a phone record in the third record position, you can code as follows:

```
FilePut(PhoneFile, PhoneRecord, 3)
```

For this example, the record retrieved should be displayed in the visual interface, whereas the data source for the record to save comes from the visual interface. It is a good idea to write generalized Sub procedures to perform these operations. These procedures can then be called from wherever such activities need to be carried out. The ShowRecord procedure appears as follows:

```
Sub ShowRecord(ByVal RecNum As Integer)
    ' This Procedure displays a record in the visual interface
    FileGet(PhoneFile, PhoneRecord, RecNum)
    With PhoneRecord
        mskPhone.Text = Format(Val(.Phone), "(000)-000-0000")
        txtName.Text = .Name
        txtAddress.Text = .Address
        txtCity.Text = .City
        cboStateCode.Text = .StateCode
        cboZipCode.Text = .ZipCode
        txtEMail.Text = .EMail
    End With
End Sub
```

Notice that the phone number is formatted with the format string "(000)-000-0000." The masked edit box's Mask property has been set to "(###)-###-####." The data stored in the file, however, is a 10-digit string with no embedded parentheses or dashes, so it is converted to a number using the Val function first. The zeros in the format string ensure that a phone number shorter than 10 digits will be filled with leading zeros. The format string also adds the parentheses and the dashes so that the resulting string will fit the mask. The SaveRecord sub appears as follows:

```
Sub SaveRecord(ByVal RecNum As Integer)
    ' This procedure saves a record from the visual interface
    With PhoneRecord
        .Phone = mskPhone.ClipText
        .Name = txtName.Text
        .Address = txtAddress.Text
        .City = txtCity.Text
        .StateCode = cboStateCode.Text
        .ZipCode = CInt(cboZipCode.Text)
        .EMail = txtEMail.Text
    End With
    FilePut(PhoneFile, PhoneRecord, RecNum)
End Sub
```

Notice that the mskPhone's ClipText property (not the Text property) is moved to the Phone field in the record to save. Recall that the ClipText property extracts only those characters that are actually input by the user, not those literal constants added by the Mask property. The result-ing string should be a 10-digit number without parentheses or dashes.

In both procedures, the RecNum parameter gives the record position, which is used in the FileGet or FilePut statement to perform the necessary input or output operation.

TIP

If you have difficulties with the masked edit box's Text property, use its SelText property instead. Refer to the tip box dealing with clearing the Text property in Section 3.1 of Chapter 3 for specific information.

Completing the Example

With the two I/O procedures in place, you can now review the requirements of the project and complete the code. The program should do the following:

1. Open the file and populate the list box with names and phone numbers of the existing records in the file as soon as the program starts.

2. Display the record that the user selects from the list box by clicking the item.

3. Save the record in the visual interface when the user clicks the Save button. The pro-gram should determine whether the record exists by searching for the entered phone number (in the masked edit box) in the list box. If it is found, the data on the visual interface should be used to update the record in the file; otherwise, the record should be added as a new one.

General Declaration. The following code should be placed in the general declaration area:

```
Structure PhoneRecStruc
    <VBFixedString(10)> Dim Phone As String
    <VBFixedString(24)> Dim Name As String
    <VBFixedString(32)> Dim Address As String
    <VBFixedString(28)> Dim City As String
    <VBFixedString(2)> Dim StateCode As String
    Dim ZipCode As Integer
    <VBFixedString(48)> Dim EMail As String
End Structure
Dim PhoneRecord As PhoneRecStruc
Dim PhoneFile As Integer
```

As explained previously in this appendix, the Structure block is used to declare a data struc-ture. You use the block to declare a structure for the phone record. The Dim statement following the Structure block creates a variable, PhoneRecord, of the PhoneRecStruc type. This variable is used in the SaveRecord and ShowRecord Sub procedures. Also, the variable PhoneFile is declared as a class-level variable so that the file can be referenced in various procedures.

Populating the List Box. As soon as the program starts, it should open the Phonebook file and populate the list box with the existing data. The following procedure should accomplish this:

```
Private Sub Form1_Load(ByVal sender As System.Object, ByVal e As
    System.EventArgs) Handles MyBase.Load
    Dim R As Integer
    Dim Records As Integer
    PhoneFile = FreeFile()
    FileOpen(PhoneFile, "PhoneBook.dat", OpenMode.Random, , ,
      Len(PhoneRecord))
    Records = CInt(LOF(PhoneFile) / Len(PhoneRecord))
```

```
        'Populate the list box
        For R = 1 To Records
            FileGet(PhoneFile, PhoneRecord, R)
            lstPhoneName.Items.Add(Trim(PhoneRecord.Name) & vbTab & _
              Format(Val(PhoneRecord.Phone), "(000)-000-0000") & _
              vbTab & R)
        Next R
    End Sub
```

The procedure first opens the phone file with the random mode and a record length equal to that of PhoneRecord. It then proceeds to compute the number of records in the file in preparation for populating the list box. The number of records in the file is computed with the following formula:

```
    Records = CInt(LOF(PhoneFile) / Len(PhoneRecord))
```

Recall that the LOF function gives the number of bytes of the file and the Len function returns the length of the string (record). After the number of records is determined, the list box can be populated with a For loop, in which the records are read from the file and the names and the phone numbers are added to the list with the Items.Add method. Note that Name in the record has been declared as a fixed-string field of 24 characters. Its extra spaces are stripped with the Trim function before the content is placed in the list box. Note also that the record position, R, is also appended to the string. This number will be used to retrieve the record.

Retrieving Selected Record. When the user clicks an item in the list box, the program is expected to retrieve the data from the file and display the result in the visual interface. The record position is appended to the item as shown in the form load procedure. The code appears as follows:

```
    Private Sub lstPhoneName_SelectedIndexChanged(ByVal sender As
      System.Object, ByVal e As System.EventArgs) Handles
      lstPhoneName.SelectedIndexChanged
        Dim R As Integer
        Dim TheItem As String
        TheItem = lstPhoneName.SelectedItem
        'The record position is kept at the last part of
        'the item after the tab character
        R = CInt(Mid(TheItem, InStrRev(TheItem, vbTab) + 1))
        ShowRecord(R) 'Show record R, using the ShowRecord Sub
    End Sub
```

Saving a Record. When the user clicks the Save button, the program should check whether the current record (in the visual interface) exists in the file. Each record is identified by the phone number; that is, phone number is the record key. The phone number as shown in mskPhone is passed to the function FindPhone, which returns an Integer array with two elements. The first element indicates the record position in the file; the second, the position in the list box. If the phone number is not found in the list box, the function returns a value of -1 for both elements.

When the record does not exist, the program should do the following:

- Provide a record position for the new record. This value can be calculated by using the following formula:

```
    Records = CInt(LOF(PhoneFile) / Len(PhoneRecord) )+ 1
```

- Add the name and phone number to the list box. The record position of the new record should also be appended to the item for future retrieval.

All records, new or existing, can be saved with the same procedure, SaveRecord, which has been shown previously. The Save button's Click event procedure appears as follows:

```
Private Sub btnSave_Click(ByVal sender As System.Object, ByVal e
    As System.EventArgs) Handles btnSave.Click
    Dim R() As Integer
    'Note: Data validation should be performed here
    R = FindPhone(mskPhone.Text)
    If R(0) < 0 Then
        ' New record; add to the end of file
        R(0) = CInt(LOF(PhoneFile) / Len(PhoneRecord)) + 1
        ' Add phone & name to the list box
        lstPhoneName.Items.Add(txtName.Text & vbTab &
            mskPhone.Text & vbTab & R(0))
    Else
        ' Update the list box item
        lstPhoneName.Items(R(1)) = txtName.Text & vbTab &
            mskPhone.Text & vbTab & R(0)
    End If
    SaveRecord(R(0))
End Sub
```

The function to search for the phone number in the list box is given next:

```
Function FindPhone(ByVal Phone As String) As Integer()
    ' This function returns the record position
    ' for a given phone number.
    ' If the phone number is not found, -1 is returned.
    Dim I As Integer
    Dim TheItem As String
    With lstPhoneName
        'Assume Not found; return -1
        FindPhone = New Integer() {-1, -1}
        For I = 0 To .Items.Count - 1
            If InStr(CStr(.Items(I)), Phone) > 0 Then
                'Found; return the record position
                TheItem = CStr(.Items(I))
                Return (New Integer() {CInt(Mid(TheItem,
                InStrRev(TheItem, vbTab) + 1)), I})
            End If
        Next I
    End With
End Function
```

As you can see, in the function, the return values are first set to -1. If the ensuing search for the phone number is unsuccessful, these will be the values returned. In the For loop, the phone number being searched for is compared with the phone number in the list box (using the InStr function) one by one. When a match is found, the record position appended at the end of the item and the position of the item in the list box are returned.

Additional Remarks

You may have noticed that the visual interface includes two combo boxes: one for state code and another for Zip code. The DropDownStyle property of both boxes is set to its default, Dropdown, so that the user can enter the data like in a text box. In a real application, you can populate the combo boxes with known data so that the user can select from the list instead of actually keying the data. These data can come from a separate file, or they can be obtained from the existing phone records. Also, for real applications, data validation routines should be added and the screen should be cleared after the data are saved. These refinements are left to you as an exercise.

Because of its simplicity, the phonebook problem is used to illustrate the basic I/O operations not only here but also in Chapter 6 (basic I/O) and in Chapter 9, "Database and ADO.NET." You may want to compare these solutions to gain a good assessment of the relative advantages of different data management approaches in terms of design and code complexity. In terms of speed, using the random file should be the fastest and the sequential file should be the slowest.

Although the random file approach is the fastest, the current trend in data management is toward the use of the database approach. The latter approach has the advantages of developing new applications and handling complex queries much more easily and therefore more rapidly. All the complexities associated with data management are "absorbed" by the database management system (software), which offers SQL capability.

If you use the random file approach for complex applications, you will need to develop all the capabilities to handle queries and other data management requirements. This can be a tremendous undertaking. In addition, it may not be easy to modify the code to deal with a new application. The development efforts and lead time for each application are typically much longer than what is required for the database approach; therefore, unless the application's requirements are fairly simple, the database approach is usually the way to go.

A Technical Note

Notice that the preceding random file can also be opened with the Binary mode. For example, the following code fragment will open the same file in Binary mode:

```
PhoneFile = FreeFile()
FileOpen(PhoneFile, "PhoneBook.dat", OpenMode.Binary)
```

To read the Ith record, you will code the following:

```
FileGet(PhoneFile, PhoneRecord, (I - 1) * Len(PhoneRecord) + 1)
```

You can even just access an individual byte (or field) in the file; however, as you can see, the computation of the byte position can become cumbersome. So, in general, the binary file has the most flexibility but it can become pretty tricky for your program to keep track of the location of data.

A.5 Design Considerations

Despite of the relative advantages of the database approach to data management, there will always be cases where the file-oriented approach is more suitable, especially when the application problem setting is fairly simple. The file-oriented approach has the advantage of requiring far fewer systems resources. This section provides a summary of the situations in which each of the three file structures (sequential, binary, and random) is most suitable.

File Characteristics and Suitable Applications

The characteristics of the three file types are summarized in the following table.

Factor	Sequential	Binary	Random
Access	Data can be accessed in only one direction. A file must be opened for output and input separately.	Data can be accessed at the byte level. Any position in the file can be read or written.	Data can be accessed at the record level. Record size must be defined in the FileOpen statement.
Speed	Slow	Fast	Fast
Remarks	Data in the file can be inspected easily or changed by use of other word processing applications such as Notepad or Word.	Numeric (binary) data are kept as is. The file is extremely flexible in handling any possible data structures; however, the programmer has to devise a systematic way of keeping track of the location of the data. A minor error can cause chaos.	Numeric (binary) data are kept as is. Each record should have the same length. The file type is not as flexible as the binary file in handling varying data structures in the same file but is capable of handling records of the same type in huge numbers.

continues

Factor	Sequential	Binary	Random
Potentially suitable applications	Text files for word processing applications; data for one-time processing only (import/export files); small system configuration files.	System configuration files; small tables (tax rate table); numeric arrays (statistic data); files requiring speed and/or complex structures such as index files.	Files for fairly large volume data processing applications, such as master files and transaction files for various business applications, when the database approach is not used.

This appendix discusses the use of binary and random files. The differences among sequential, binary, and random files are explained. They mainly differ in the way data are handled and accessed. Numeric data are converted to strings before being saved onto a sequential file, and strings are converted to numeric data type when they are read from a sequential file if the variable involved is a numeric variable. On the other hand, data are saved or retrieved from the file without any conversion when the file mode is either Binary or Random. Data in a sequential file can be accessed only sequentially, whereas data in a binary file or random file can be accessed randomly. In Binary mode, the file can be accessed at any byte position, whereas in Random mode, the file can be accessed only by the record position. Understanding these differences can help you select the right file type given a set of requirements for a file in a particular application. The preceding table provides a summary in this respect.

Because a random file can be accessed only by the record position, it is only logical that each I/O operation involves a record (not just a field). Section A.2 shows how the Structure can be used to construct a record for such purposes. Structures can also be used to build very complex data structures. Their introduction in this appendix gives you a preview to such possibilities.

Summary

- Three types of files that you can use to handle data are sequential, binary, and random.
- The FileOpen statement is used to open a file; the FileClose statement, to close a specified file or all active files.
- A sequential file can be opened with input, output, or append mode (OpenMode.Output, and so on). With the output mode, existing data will be erased; with the Append mode, existing data are preserved and new data are appended to the existing data.
- It is recommended that a variable be used to represent the file number associated with each file. The FreeFile function can be used to obtain a file number that can safely be used to open a file.
- The Input statement reads a field in a sequential file; the LineInput function reads a line of data in a sequential file; and the InputString function reads from the sequential file a specified number of characters.
- The EOF function returns a Boolean value indicating whether the end of the has been reached for a specified file. A value of True indicates the end of the file has been reached.
- The LOF function returns a Long integer that gives the length of the the file in bytes.
- The Write and WriteLine statements write comma-delimited data in a sequential file. The WriteLine statement adds an end of line marker each time it completes an output operation, but the Write statement does not. These two statements can be considered the complements of the Input statement.
- The Print and PrintLine statements output data on a sequential file without adding any extra comma or double quotes. The PrintLine statement adds an end of line marker each time it completes an output operation, but the Print statement does not.
- Multiple elementary data elements can be grouped together to form a structure, using the Structure block. A variable can then be declared to be of the Structure type and used to handle input and output in one operation (usually in conjunction with a binary or random file).

- A binary file is opened with the FileOpen statement with the binary file mode (OpenMode.Binary). A binary file can perform input and output at any position of the file. The I/O operation is done without involving any implicit data conversion; for example, an Integer field is stored as a 4-byte field, not a string of digits.

- Input and output involving variable-length strings for the binary file (and the random file) can be tricky. It is recommended that the fixed-length string be used instead. The fixed-length string can be specified only within a Structure using the <VBFixedString> attribute.

- Saving and retrieving arrays of numeric data is easy and flexible with the binary file.

- A random file is opened with the FileOpen statement with the random mode (OpenMode.Random). A random file can perform input and output at any record position, but not any byte position. The record length must be specified in the FileOpen statement. An incorrect record length can result in serious problems, ranging from inaccurate results to destruction of the original data if output is performed. Typically, a record is constructed by the use of the Structure.

- The phonebook application is used to illustrate how a random file can be used to perform input and output.

- Each file organization (sequential, binary, and random) has its advantages and disadvantages. The last section provided a guideline for choosing the appropriate file organization for an application at hand.

Explore and Discover

A-1.   Append Versus Output Mode. Draw two buttons on a new form. Name the first one **btnAppend**, and set its Text property to **Append**. Name the second one **btnOutput** and set its Text property to **Output**. Enter the following code:

```
Private Sub btnAppend_Click(ByVal sender As System.Object, ByVal e
    As System.EventArgs) Handles btnAppend.Click
    Dim TestFile As Integer
    TestFile = FreeFile()
    FileOpen(TestFile, "C:\Temp\TestFile.txt", OpenMode.Append)
    Print(TestFile, "ABCD")
    FileClose(TestFile)
End Sub

Private Sub btnOutput_Click(ByVal sender As System.Object, ByVal e
    As System.EventArgs) Handles btnOutput.Click
    Dim TestFile As Integer
    TestFile = FreeFile()
    FileOpen(TestFile, "C:\Temp\TestFile.txt", OpenMode.Output)
    Print(TestFile, "ABCD")
    FileClose(TestFile)
End Sub
```

Note that the only difference between the two procedures is the mode for the file (Append versus Output). Note also that to test this project, you need to have a Temp folder in Drive C. Change the path to another folder if you do not want to create a Temp folder.

Run the project and click the Append button; then use Notepad to inspect the file. Each time you click the Append button, you should see one more instance of ABCD when you reopen the file from Notepad.

Click the Output button and then inspect the file again. What do you see? Click as many times as you want. You should always see only one line of ABCD in the file. The Output mode erases the previous contents of the file, whereas the Append mode appends data at the end of the existing file.

A-2. Mismatching Data Types Between Input and Output. Enter the following code:

```
Private Sub Form1_Click(ByVal sender As System.Object, ByVal e As
   System.EventArgs) Handles MyBase.Click
    Dim TestFile As Integer
    Dim TheData As Integer
    TestFile = FreeFile()
    FileOpen(TestFile, "C:\Temp\TestFile.dat", OpenMode.Output)
    PrintLine(TestFile, "ABCD")
    FileClose(TestFile)
    FileOpen(TestFile, "C:\Temp\TestFile.dat", OpenMode.Binary)
    Console.WriteLine(LOF(TestFile))
    FileGet(TestFile, TheData, 1)
    Console.WriteLine(TheData & " " & Hex$(TheData))
    Console.WriteLine((&H44434241))
End Sub
```

Run the program and then click the form. You should see the following three lines in the immediate output window:

```
      6
1145258561  44434241
1145258561
```

The printLine statement should print ABCD in the file. Why does the LOF function return 6, instead of 4? (*Hint:* The vbCrLf characters have been added at the end.)

Why does TheData have a value 1145258561? The FileGet statement reads a 4-byte image ABCD, which has that corresponding numeric value. When you use the Hex$ function to show the Hex decimal representation of TheData, it gives 44434241. This means internally, TheData contains &H44434241. This is confirmed by the output of the last Console.WriteLine statement. Note that &H41, &H42, &H43, and &H44 are the ASCII values for A, B, C, and D, respectively. Recall again that when numeric data are output, the lowest byte is written first. Conversely, when a numeric field is read, the first byte is read as the lowest byte in the value.

A-3. **Binary File and File Size.** Draw a button on a new form. Name it **btnTest** and set its Text property to **Test**. Enter the following code:

```
Private Sub btnTest_Click(ByVal sender As System.Object, ByVal e
   As System.EventArgs) Handles btnTest.Click
    Dim BinaryFile As Integer
    Dim A As Integer
    BinaryFile = FreeFile()
    FileOpen(BinaryFile, "C:\Temp\Binary.dat", OpenMode.Binary)
    FilePut(BinaryFile, A, 2001)
    MsgBox("File length = " & LOF(BinaryFile))
End Sub
```

Start the project and then click the button. What value do you see? You have just put an integer value 0 onto the file. Why does the LOF function return 2004?

A-4. **Variable-Length String and Length of the Structure.** Draw a button on a new form. Name it **btnShow** and set its Text property to **Show Length**. Enter the following code:

```
Private Structure MyDataStruc
    Dim TheString As String
    Dim TheInteger As Integer
End Structure

Dim MyData As MyDataStruc
```

```
Private Sub btnShow_Click(ByVal sender As System.Object, ByVal e
    As System.EventArgs) Handles btnShow.Click
    MsgBox(Len(MyData))
End Sub
```

Run the project and then click the button. What value do you see in the message box? The integer is four bytes long; however, you have not assigned any value to the string yet. Why is the length of the Structure variable 8? A variable-length string in VB is structured as a BSTR, which consists of a header and the string itself. The header contains information on the location and length of the string. What is included in the length count of the Structure is the length of the header, not the length of the string.

A-5. **Variable-Length Strings, Structure, and Input/Output.** (continued from exercise A-4) Add one more button to the preceding project. Name it **btnPut** and set its Text property to **Put**. Add the following code:

```
Dim UDTFile As Integer
Private Sub btnPut_Click(ByVal sender As System.Object, ByVal e As
    System.EventArgs) Handles btnPut.Click
    UDTFile = FreeFile()
    MsgBox("Length of MyData is " & Len(MyData))
    FileOpen(UDTFile, "C:\Temp\UDTFile.dat", OpenMode.Random, , ,
      Len(MyData))
    MyData.TheString = "ABC"
    MyData.TheInteger = 100
    FilePut(UDTFile, MyData, 1)
End Sub
```

Run the project and then click the button. What do you see? Why is there a bad record length error? Change the Len parameter in the FileOpen line above to the following:

```
Len(MyData) + 3
```

Run the project again. Does it work this time? Why? (See the following exercise.)

A-6. **Variable-Length Strings, Structure, and Input/Output.** (continued from exercise A-5) To be sure the data can be retrieved, add another button to your preceding project. Name it **btnGet** and set its Text property to **Get**. Add the following code:

```
Private Sub btnGet_Click(ByVal sender As System.Object, ByVal e As
    System.EventArgs) Handles btnGet.Click
    FileGet(UDTFile, MyData, 1)
    Console.WriteLine(MyData.TheString)
    Console.WriteLine(MyData.TheInteger)
End Sub
```

Run the project. Click the Put button and then the Get button. Is everything working properly? The reason 3 has to be added to the record length is that both the string and the string header are included in the output. The record length declared in the FileOpen statement must be at least the same as the record size used in the I/O operation. Keep in mind that the record lengths for all records in the file are assumed to be the same by the system; therefore, variable-length strings are not really suitable for random file I/O.

Exercises

A-7. A Mini Word Processor. Design a form suitable for simple word processing. It should have three buttons (Open, Save, and Quit) and a text box. The text box should be able to handle multiple lines of text. When the user clicks the Open button, your program should display an open file dialog for the user to specify a text file to open. The file content will then be displayed in the text box. When the user clicks the Save button, your program should display a save file dialog for the user to specify the file name to save the content of the text box. When the user clicks the Quit button, your program will quit. Whether the user clicks the Quit button or the Close (X) button, if the text box content has be changed, your program will ask the user whether to save the changes and act accordingly before it quits.

A-8. FICA Tax Brackets. A while back, the FICA taxes for each employee per year were as follows:

Medicare tax: 1.45% for all amount of payroll

Social Security tax: 6.2% for the first $72,600 of pay, 0% beyond $72,600

Design a file structure to save the data for future use to determine withholdings for employees during payroll calculation. There should be a user interface to display and update the saved data.

A-9. Income Tax Rate Brackets. A while back, two of the four Income Tax Rate schedules were as follow:

Schedule X (For Head of Household)

Taxable Income Between	Applicable Rate (on the Indicate Range)
0-24,650	15%
24,650-59,750	28%
59,750-124,650	31%
124,650-271,050	36%
271,050-. . .	39.6%

Schedule Z (For Single)

Taxable Income Between	Applicable Rate (on the Indicate Range)
0-33,050	15%
33,050-85,350	28%
85,350-138,200	31%
138,200-271,050	36%
271,050-. . .	39.6%

Develop a project to save and retrieve these tables. There should be a user interface to display and update the retrieved/saved data. (*Hint:* You can save these data as arrays in a binary file. Notice that although the tax income brackets are shown in two columns, a one-dimensional array should be able to take care of each schedule. The tax rates can be saved in another array. If you are concerned about the possibility that the number of brackets can change in the future, you can store that number as the first element in the file. Because you are working with multiple tables, you should find the Tab control useful in your interface design.)

A-10.   **General Ledger Account File.** Each of the general ledger accounts in a file is structured as follows:

Field Name	Data Type	Internal Length	External Length
Account Number	Integer	4	5
Account Name	String	24	24
Beginning Balance	Decimal	16	12
Y-T-D Debit Amount	Decimal	16	12
Y-T-D Credit Amount	Decimal	16	12

Develop a project with a visual interface to enter, edit, and save the account records. In real applications, the three amounts should be updated by transactions; however, for the purpose of this exercise, include them in your interface. (*Hint:* Use a visual interface design similar to the phonebook example in this appendix.)

A-11.   **Clinic Account Holder Basic Info File.** Each of the account holders of a clinic is structured as follows:

Field Name	Data Type	Internal Length	External Length
Account Number	Integer	4	5
Account Holder Name (Last, First Init.)	String	32	32
Date of Birth	Date/Time	8	10 (with "-")
S-S-N	Integer	4	11 (with "-")
Street Address	String	32	32
City	String	24	24
Sex	String	1	1
State	String	2	2
Zip Code	Integer	4	5 or 9
Home Phone	Long	8	14; for example, (817)-222-3333
Work Phone	Long	8	14 (see above)
Employer	String	32	32

Develop a project that will allow the user to enter and update account holder information. (*Hint:* You can still design a user interface similar to the phonebook application in this appendix. The actual number of accounts can be much more than that of a phonebook. This means for a real application, your routine for looking up an account can be much more complex using the file-oriented approach than using the database approach.)

A-12.   **Clinic Patient Basic ID Info File.** (continued from exercise A-11) The Clinic Patient Basic Info file has the following fields:

Field Name	Data Type	Internal Length	External Length
Account Number	Integer	4	5
Sequence Number	Integer	4	2
Patient Name (Last, First Init.)	String	24	24
Date of Birth	Date/Time	8	10
Sex	String	1	1

Develop a project that will allow the user to enter and update patient information records using the random file structure. Keep in mind that a patient record cannot exist without an account holder record. The sequence number 0 should be reserved for the account holder; 1 for spouse; and 2 and on for other dependents. Note also that not all records pertaining to a family will be entered consecutively. (*Hint:* Use two list boxes: one to hold account holders, and another to hold patients. The former can be used to verify the existence of an account. The latter can be used to determine whether to add or update a patient record. Of course, this approach assumes that the number of records for both files is relatively small. For large files, a more complex algorithm will have to be used. Identify the patient by combining the account number and sequence number.) (*Question:* If both the account holder and patient info data had been presented to you as one problem, would your design for the files be different? Notice that some fields in the account holder info record have to be repeated in the patient info file.)

A-13.   **Clinic Patient Visit File.** Each time a patient visits the clinic, a transaction record should be created. A simplified layout is given as follows:

Field Name	Data Type	Internal Length	External Length
Date	Date/Time	8	10
Account Number	Integer	4	5
Sequence Number	Integer	4	2
Diagnostic Code	String	8	3 to 8
Service Code	Decimal	16	5 to 8
Total Service Fee	Decimal	16	8
Insurance Company Code	String	12	12

Develop a project to allow the user to enter patient visit/service records. Keep in mind that the patient record must exist before any patient visit record can be entered. Again, identify the patient by combining the account number with the sequence number.

B. Graphics, Animation, Drag and Drop

This appendix discusses topics related to graphics. The first section discusses how to draw graphs in a control. After you have an understanding of graphic techniques, you will be able to consider topics in animation, which is discussed in Section B.2. Another interesting application of graphics is the drag-and-drop operation, which can provide the user a convenient way to specify operations that can otherwise be fairly complex to describe. This type of application can be exciting and dynamic. Drag and drop is discussed in Section B.3.

B.1 Drawing Graphs

VB.NET provides support for graphics with several namespaces: The ***System.Drawing*** namespace provides access to GDI+ (improved version of Graphic Device Interface) basic graphics functionality. More advanced functionality is provided in the System.Drawing.Drawing2D, System.Drawing.Imaging, and System.Drawing.Text namespaces.

The discussion here is limited to the functionality provided in the System.Drawing namespace. To draw a graph on a control, there must be a graphics object (representing the drawing surface) associated with the control. The graphics object provides various methods to perform drawing. The following table gives a selected list of these methods:

Method	Use
DrawEllipse	Draw an ellipse within a specified rectangle.
DrawLine	Draw a line between two specified points.
DrawPolygon	Draw a polygon with the specified points.
DrawRectangle	Draw a rectangle over two specified points.
DrawString	Write specified text with a specified font at a specified location.

Each method requires a pen that specifies the color and the pen size in pixels. Different methods require different additional parameters. For example, the DrawEllipse and the DrawRectangle methods require a rectangle structure as the second parameter, while the DrawLine method requires two points.

The drawing methods draw an outline for the specified shapes. To paint the interior of the shape with a color, you use the corresponding fill methods. For example, to fill an ellipse, you will use the ***FillEllipse method***. Before discussing these methods in detail, first take a look at a few concepts that are fundamental to graphics.

Basic Concepts

When you are drawing a graph, you will always need to decide the position to begin or end your drawing. The coordinate determines the numeric value of the position. The color you choose can affect the attractiveness of a graph significantly. This subsection introduces you to the basics of coordinates and colors.

Coordinates. VB.NET supports drawing on several controls, including the form, picture box, label, and the panel. The object on which you draw a graph has a coordinate system that is different than the familiar Cartesian coordinate system. In the latter system, the horizontal coordinate, x, increases from left to right, and the vertical coordinate, y, increases from bottom to top. With an object, the horizontal coordinate, x, also increases from left to right, with the leftmost margin being 0. The vertical coordinate, y, however, starts from top to bottom, with the topmost margin being 0. (The standard measurement unit is the pixel.) This system is depicted in Figure B.1.

You need to be aware of this difference so that you can draw on an object correctly.

Figure B.1

VB object's coordinate

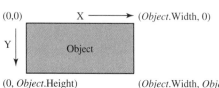

The coordinate of an object starts with left upper corner as (0,0) with its right lower corner being (Width, Height). Note that in the case of the form, the height goes up to Me.ClientSize.Height. The client region does not include the title bar.

Colors. In Visual Basic.NET, colors are of type System.Drawing.Color. The System.Drawing namespace provides a list of standard colors, so to specify the blue color, you code:

```
Color.Blue
```

At runtime, you can allow the user to visually choose a color using the ***color dialog***. For example, its ***ShowDialog method*** will display a dialog box with all available basic colors. If the user clicks its Define Custom Color button, the right pane will show a color pane from which he or she can select the desired color (Figure B.2).

The Graphic Object

To draw any graph on a control, there must be a Graphic object associated with the control. You can use the control's ***CreateGraphic method*** to create the Graphic object. The object is also available as an argument of the Control's ***Paint event***, which occurs when the control is drawn or redrawn. In the case of the form, the event occurs after the form is activated. You can also trigger this event by invoking the control's ***Invalidate method***. To illustrate, draw a horizontal line between Point (0, 100) and Point (100, 100) on the form. You can use the Graphics object's ***DrawLine method***, which has the following syntax:

```
Object.DrawLine(Pen, Point1, Point2)
```

Where Pen = a Pen object specifying the color and an optional parameter specifying the pen width

Point1, Point2 = Point object specifying the coordinate of the point; each can also be specified by two numbers representing the coordinate without the explicit Point type.

Figure B.2

The Color dialog box

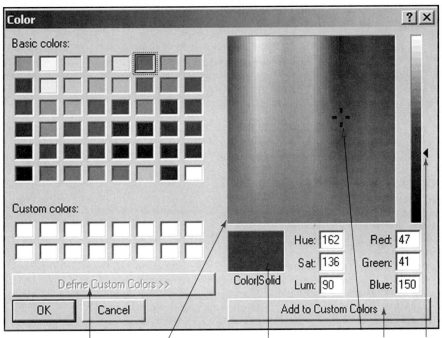

Click this button to make the color pane show. (It is disabled afterwards.)

Select the desired color to make it show in the selected color box. Then you can click the Add to custom Colors button to add to the Customer colors on the left pane.

The following code will draw a blue line with a pen size of three pixels between the specified points on the form:

```
Private Sub Form1_Paint(ByVal sender As Object, ByVal e As
    System.Windows.Forms.PaintEventArgs) Handles MyBase.Paint
        e.Graphics.DrawLine(New Pen(Color.Blue, 3), New Point(0, 100),
        New Point(100, 100))
End Sub
```

The Pen object specifies the blue color and a draw width of 3 (pixels). The first point specifies a coordinate of (0, 100). The first value gives the X value; the second, the Y value. Note that the statement can also be coded as:

```
e.Graphics.DrawLine(New Pen(Color.Blue, 3), 0, 100, 100, 100)
```

If you are a reviewer of the code, you may prefer the first format because it gives a clearer meaning of those numbers used in the statement.

Free-Hand Drawing. The DrawLine method can be used to provide the user the free-hand drawing capability with the mouse. For example, the MouseDown event is triggered when the user presses the mouse down. Its event arguments return the button (left, middle, or right) and the coordinate at which the button is pressed. You can use the event to provide the drawing capability as follows:

- When the right mouse button is pressed, the program will start the drawing process. Each time the right mouse button is pressed thereafter, a line is drawn between the current point and the previous point where the mouse was pressed.
- When a different mouse button is pressed, the drawing process discontinues.

Because you will write the code in the MouseDown event (which does not provide a graphic object as an event argument), you must create a graphic object that is associated with the form to be able to perform the drawing. You can create the object as soon as the project starts. The code appears as follows:

```
Dim TheGraph As Graphics
Private Sub Form1_Load(ByVal sender As Object, ByVal e As
    System.EventArgs) Handles MyBase.Load
        'Create a graphic object associated with the form
        TheGraph = Me.CreateGraphics()
End Sub
```

When performing the freehand drawing, the routine needs to decide whether to draw the line when the MouseDown event is triggered. It should draw a line only if the right mouse button is pressed. You will use a Boolean variable, IsDrawing, to track this state. The button pressed can be tested with the following If statement:

```
If e.Button = MouseButtons.Right Then
```

The event procedure appears as follows:

```
Private Sub Form1_MouseDown(ByVal sender As Object, ByVal e As
    System.Windows.Forms.MouseEventArgs) Handles MyBase.MouseDown
        Static IsDrawing As Boolean
        Static PreviousPoint As New Point()
        Dim CurrentPoint As New Point()
        Dim ThePen As New Pen(Color.Blue, 2)
        If e.Button = MouseButtons.Right Then
            CurrentPoint = New Point(e.X, e.Y)
            If IsDrawing Then
                'Draw a line only when the right mouse button
                'is pressed
                TheGraph.DrawLine(ThePen, PreviousPoint, CurrentPoint)
            Else
```

```
            'Set to start drawing
            IsDrawing = True
        End If
        'Keep the current point to draw the next line
        PreviousPoint = CurrentPoint
    Else
        IsDrawing = False
    End If
End Sub
```

As you can see from the code, the procedure first tests whether the button pressed is the right button. If it is, the position of the mouse is kept as CurrentPoint. It then decides whether to draw the line based on the value of IsDrawing, which is turned on by the first right button press and turned off when the button pressed in not the right button. Note that IsDrawing and PreviousPoint are declared to be Static because their values need to be preserved between the event procedure calls.

The DrawRectangle and DrawEllipse Methods

The DrawRectangle method draws a specified rectangle on the object. If the width and height are the same, the result is a square. The method has the following syntax:

Object.DrawRectangle(*Pen, Rectangle*)

The Rectangle is a structure (structure is explained in Appendix A, "Data Management Using Files") defined by a point specifying the location of its upper left corner, and a size specifying the width and height.

The DrawEllipse method draws an ellipse within a specified rectangle on the object. If the width and height are the same (and thus the shape is actually a square), the result is a circle. The method has the following syntax:

Object.DrawEllipse(*Pen, Rectangle*)

The following code example produces the graphs shown in Figure B.3.

```
Private Sub Form1_Paint(ByVal sender As Object, ByVal e As
    System.Windows.Forms.PaintEventArgs) Handles MyBase.Paint
    e.Graphics.DrawRectangle(New Pen(Color.Blue), New
        Rectangle(New Point(10, 10), New Size(100, 50)))
    e.Graphics.DrawEllipse(New Pen(Color.Blue), New Rectangle(New
        Point(10, 10), New Size(100, 50)))
    e.Graphics.DrawEllipse(New Pen(Color.Red), New Rectangle(New
        Point(150, 10), New Size(50, 50)))
End Sub
```

The first statement draws a rectangle of 100 x 50. The second statement draws an ellipse of the same size at the same point. As you can see, the ellipse is defined by the boundary of the rectangle. The third statement draws an ellipse defined by a rectangle of the same width and height of 50. The result is a circle.

Figure B.3

Drawing rectangle and ellipses

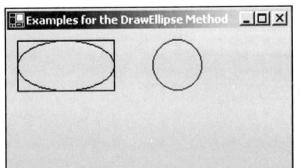

The DrawEllipse method draws an ellipse defined within a rectangle. When the width and height are the same, the result is a circle.

The Fill Methods and the Brushes

As mentioned at the beginning of this appendix, the draw methods draw the outlines of shapes, while the fill methods paint the shapes with colors. For example, the *FillEllipse method* fills an ellipse with a color. Instead of using a pen as in the case of the draw methods, the fill methods use a brush. The System.Drawing namespace provides several brush objects, which are listed in the following table:

Type of Brush	Explanation	Code Example (reference)
SolidBrush	Fills the specified area with the color specified for the brush	`New SolidBrush(Color.Red)`
Brushes	Provides the specified solid brush with named standard color	`Drawing.Brushes.AliceBlue`
SystemBrushes	Provides the specified brush with named system color (such as Control, Window)	`Drawing.SystemBrushes.ActiveCaption`
TextureBrush	Uses an image to fill the specified area	`New Drawing.TextureBrush(TheImage)`

The Brushes object provides brushes for all standard colors. The SolidBrush object allows any color of your choice. If you choose a standard color for the SolidBrush, the effect will be exactly the same as using one of the brushes provided by the Brushes object. The SystemBrushes object provides brushes of the system colors. These are the colors you can find in the System tab for the foreground or background color property in the Properties window.

The FillEllipse method has the following syntax:

```
Object.FillEllipse(Brush, Rectangle)
```

The following code produces the three circles as given in Figure B.4.

```
Dim TheColor As Color
Private Sub Form1_Load(ByVal sender As Object, ByVal e As
   System.EventArgs) Handles MyBase.Load
     cdlColor.ShowDialog()
     TheColor = cdlColor.Color
End Sub
Private Sub Form1_Paint(ByVal sender As Object, ByVal e As
   System.Windows.Forms.PaintEventArgs) Handles MyBase.Paint
     With e.Graphics
        .FillEllipse(Drawing.Brushes.Aqua, New Rectangle(New
          Point(10, 10), New Size(50, 50)))
        .FillEllipse(Drawing.SystemBrushes.ActiveCaptionText, New
          Rectangle(New Point(70, 10), New Size(50, 50)))
        .FillEllipse(New SolidBrush(TheColor), New Rectangle(New
          Point(130, 10), New Size(50, 50)))
     End With
End Sub
```

Figure B.4

Circles painted with colors specified by different types of brushes

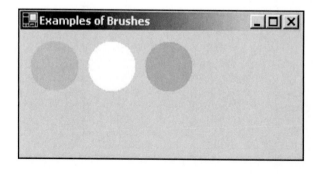

When the project starts, it prompts for a color from the user, using the color dialog. (To test the program, draw a ColorDialog control on the form and name it **cdlColor**.) This color is then used as the parameter of the SolidBrush in the third statement in the Form Paint event procedure. The first statement uses the Aqua brush of the Brushes object to paint the circle, while the second statement uses the ActiveCaptionText brush of the SystemBrushes object to paint the second circle.

The TextureBrush object uses a specified image to fill an area. The following code initially paints a circle with the AliceBlue color when the project starts, but when the user clicks a Find Image button and selects an image, the circle is filled with that image. Figure B.5 shows a sample result when the user chooses the Diamond.BMP file from the Common7\Graphics\Bitmaps\Assorted folder provided by Visual Studio.Net.

```
Dim TheImage As Image
Private Sub Form1_Paint(ByVal sender As Object, ByVal e As
    System.Windows.Forms.PaintEventArgs) Handles MyBase.Paint
    Dim TheBrush As Brush
    If TheImage Is Nothing Then
        TheBrush = Drawing.Brushes.AliceBlue
    Else
        TheBrush = New Drawing.TextureBrush(TheImage)
    End If
    e.Graphics.FillEllipse(TheBrush, New Rectangle(New Point(10,
        10), New Size(150, 150)))
End Sub
Private Sub btnFind_Click(ByVal Sender As Object, ByVal e As
    System.EventArgs) Handles btnFind.Click
    Dim TheImageFile As String
    cdlOpenFile.Title = "Open Image File"
    cdlOpenFile.ShowDialog()
    TheImageFile = cdlOpenFile.FileName
    TheImage = Image.FromFile(TheImageFile)
    'Force the form the repaint
    Me.Invalidate()
End Sub
```

Notice how the form is forced to repaint in the Find Image button's click event procedure. The form's *Invalidate method* is called. The method "invalidates" a region of the form, and therefore causes it to repaint that region. In this case, no region is specified, so the entire form is repainted when the form's Paint event is triggered.

Combined with colors, the different shapes produced by the FillEllipse method can produce an interesting presentation. For example, you can draw ellipses on the sides of a picture box with assorted colors. These ellipses can look like Christmas lights.

Figure B.5

Sample result of texture brush

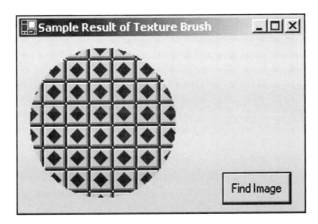

Figure B.6

Christmas lights

This project draws the Christmas lights around the sides of the picture box starting at the upper left corner. Lights are drawn clockwise as the arrows show. The Christmas tree is loaded to the Picture property at design time. You can download a similar picture from the Internet although you do not have to have the tree to work on this project.

An Example: Christmas Lights

This example develops a project that will draw Christmas lights on the sides of a picture box. When the picture is complete, it will look like Figure B.6.

To create the picture, follow these steps:

1. Draw a picture box on a new form, adjusting its size and location.
2. Name the picture box **picLights** and set its BackColor property to black.
3. Set the picture box's Image property to a Christmas tree picture. The Graphics folder that comes with VB.NET does not have one; however, you can download one from various websites on the Internet that feature clip art. You do not have to have a tree picture to do this project, although the result will look nicer if you do.
4. Draw a button on the form. Name it **btnShow** and set its Text property to **Show Lights**.
5. Develop the code to draw the lights.

To draw the lights, you need to answer the following questions:

1. How do I compute the size of the lights and the distance between them?
2. How do I compute the position of each light and draw it?
3. How do I alternate the colors for the lights?

Computing the Distance and Size of the Lights. As soon as the program starts, the distance and size of the lights can be computed. These parameters can then be used to determine the position of each light. To make your job easier, you will force the picture box to be square, using the longer of the width and height. You will draw 14 lights on each side.

Let *Distance* = the distance between the lights
BulbHeight = the height of each light
You can then compute the two variables as follows:

```
Distance  =  Width / 15
BulbHeight = 80% of Distance
BulbSize = (67 % of BulbHeight, BulbHeight)
```

Although you state that you will draw 14 lights on each side, each side will appear to have 15 lights because the first light of each side will start at a corner, which will overlap two sides. Consider a simple case of drawing two lights on each side. The graph will end up with three lights (two plus one extra) on each side as depicted in Figure B.7.

Figure B.7

Drawing two lights on each side

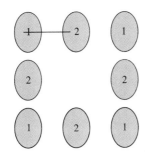

Draw two lights on each side. You will end up with three lights on each side because of the overlapping corner light.

Note also that the distance is measured from the upper left corner of the rectangle that defines each light; however, such a value will cause the lights to overlap each other. 80% of that maximum value appears to keep a proper distance between lights. This is how the preceding formula for the bulb height is derived. The bulb size will have a width of approximately two-thirds of the bulb height.

The following Form Load event procedure will carry out the needed computations.

```
Dim Distance As Integer
Dim BulbHeight As Integer
Dim TheGraph As Graphics
Dim TheBrush As SolidBrush
Dim BulbSize As Size
Private Sub Form1_Load(ByVal sender As Object, ByVal e As
   System.EventArgs) Handles MyBase.Load
    'Set the picture box squared
    With picLights
        If .Height > .Width Then
            .Width = .Height
        Else
            .Height = .Width
        End If
        'Compute distance between each light bulb
        Distance = CInt(.Width / 15)
    End With
    ' Radius is a bit shorter than half distance
    BulbHeight = CInt(0.8 * Distance)
    BulbSize = New Size(CInt(0.67 * BulbHeight), CInt(BulbHeight))
    TheGraph = picLights.CreateGraphics()
End Sub
```

Notice that both Distance and BulbSize will be used by other procedures; therefore, they are declared as the class-level variables.

In the procedure, the If block compares the picture box's height with its width and changes the shorter one to match the longer to make the picture box square. The Distance variable is then computed by dividing the picture box's Width property by 15. Notice also that a graph object associated with the picture box is created at the end of the procedure. It is important that this statement be executed only after the size of the picture box is fixed. If it is placed before a change in the picture box's size, the object may not perform the graphic method properly.

TIP

When creating a graphic object for a control, be sure that it is created after the location and size of the control is fixed. The graphic object is associated with a particular region at the time it is created. If there is a change, the object may not recognize the change and may not perform properly on the control's new region.

Computing the Position for Each Light. Recall that there are 56 lights. For computation, you will identify each light by its position counting clockwise from the upper left corner starting with number 0. With this scheme, the first 14 lights will be drawn on the top from left to right; the next 14, on the right side, top down; the next 14, at the bottom from right to left; and finally, the last 14 on the left side, bottom up. You can then compute the position of a light based on its number. (There are simpler ways to draw the lights. The reason to draw the lights this way is explained later.)

For example, consider the first light bulb (position 0). Its upper left corner should be placed at upper left corner (0, 0) of the picture box. The second light bulb (position 1) should be *a full distance from the first one*; and the third will be another full distance from the second light. This means the x coordinate will increase by a full distance for each next light, whereas the y coordinate remains the same.

Let X = the x coordinate of the light bulb

Y = the y coordinate of the light bulb

P = the position number of the light (0 = first position)

The positions of the *first 14 light bulbs* can then be computed as follows:

```
X =  P * Distance
Y = 0
```

The next 14 light bulbs will go on the right side and down vertically. The x coordinate for these light bulbs will remain the same, whereas y will increase by a full distance for each subsequent light. Their positions can be computed as follows:

```
X = 14 * Distance
Y = (P - 14) * Distance
```

Notice that in computing Y, 14 is subtracted from P so that light number 14 (the first light for this side) is on the corner (at the top); and light number 15 is one position below light number 14.

For the bottom side, the lights will go from the right to the left. As the position value increases, the X value decreases. This first light for this side (number 28) should be 14 times the distance from the left, same as all lights on the right side.

Let P = position of a light on this side

Then, the X value of the light position can be computed as follows:

```
X =  (42 - P) * Distance
Y = 14 * Distance
```

In a similar fashion, the formula for the light positions on the left side can be developed.

Drawing the Light Bulb. After the position is computed, it is fairly easy to draw the light bulb using the FillEllipse method. Let TheColor be the color to fill in the ellipse; then, the statement should appear as follows:

```
TheGraph.FillEllipse(New SolidBrush(TheColor), New
    Rectangle(New Point(X, Y), BulbSize))
```

Where the point (X, Y) and BulbSize are as computed as above.

The DrawBulb Procedure. Now, you are ready to write the procedure that computes the position and draws a light bulb. You will make it a sub procedure named DrawBulb. This procedure requires two parameters: P, the position number (0 through 55) of the light bulb; and TheColor, the color for the light bulb. The complete procedure appears as follows:

```
Private Sub DrawBulb(ByVal P As Integer, ByVal TheColor As Color)
    Dim X As Integer
    Dim Y As Integer
    'Step 1: Compute the position (x, y) of the light bulb
    Select Case P
        Case 0 To 13
            ' on the top
            X = P * Distance
            Y = 0  'Y is fixed for the top row
        Case 14 To 27
            ' on the right margin
            X = 14 * Distance 'X is fixed on the right
            Y = (P - 14) * Distance
```

```
            Case 28 To 41
                ' at the bottom
                X = (42 - P) * Distance
                Y = 14 * Distance 'Y is fixed
            Case 42 To 55
                'on the left
                X = 0 'X is fixed
                Y = (56 - P) * Distance
        End Select
        ' Step 2: Draw the light bulb
        TheGraph.FillEllipse(New SolidBrush(TheColor), New
          Rectangle(New Point(X, Y), BulbSize))
    End Sub
```

Calling the Procedure. The preceding procedure can be called to draw all 56 light bulbs. It should be called when the user clicks the Draw Lights button. You would like to alternate the light colors among green, red, white, and blue. For simplicity, you will use four lines of code, using a different color for each call. The complete procedure appears as follows:

```
    Private Sub btnShow_Click(ByVal Sender As Object, ByVal e As
      System.EventArgs) Handles btnShow.Click
        Dim I As Integer
        ' This loop draws 56 light bulbs starting with position 0
        ' The colors are: green, red, white, and blue
        For I = 0 To 52 Step 4
            DrawBulb(I, Color.Green)
            DrawBulb(I + 1, Color.Red)
            DrawBulb(I + 2, Color.White)
            DrawBulb(I + 3, Color.Blue)
        Next I
    End Sub
```

The procedure uses a For loop to call the DrawBulb Sub. Because each iteration calls DrawBulb four times using different color parameters, the loop counter is incremented by 4. Notice that the fourth call sets the bulb position to I + 3, so when I reaches 52, the last light bulb (number 55) will be drawn. The value of I should not increase beyond 52.

Why Compute the Bulb Positions That Way? The DrawBulb procedure appears to be a bit complex. You may have figured out a simpler way to compute the positions for the light bulbs given the program requirements, so you may wonder why such a complex procedure. There is a reason. The procedure can easily be modified to perform animation, which is discussed in the next section. You will revisit this project to illustrate how one type of animation can be implemented.

The DrawString Method and Fonts

The DrawString method draws a string (text) with a specified font and a specified brush starting at a specified location. The method has the following syntax:

```
    Object.DrawString(string, font, brush, x, y)
```

Where x, y = the coordinate for the starting point.

Creating a Font Object. The DrawString method requires a font object, which can be created with the following syntax:

```
    New Font(FontName, FontSize, FontStyle)
```

For example, the following statement defines a font named Times New Roman with a size of 24, italicized, and boldfaced:

```
    MyFont = New Font("Times New Roman", 24, FontStyle.Italic Or
      FontStyle.Bold)
```

The ***FontFamilies object*** provides a list of fonts available in the system. The following routine enumerates the available fonts and shows them in a combo box:

```
Dim TheFontFamily As FontFamily
For Each TheFontFamily In Drawing.FontFamily.Families
    cboFont.Items.Add(TheFontFamily.Name)
Next TheFontFamily
```

Measuring the String Length. Occasionally, you may have a need to compute the length of a string to properly draw it on an object. The ***MeasureString method*** returns a ***SizeF structure*** that gives the width and height of the string. The method has the following syntax:

```
Object.MeasureString(String, Font)
```

For example, the following expression using the MyFont object as defined previously will return a SizeF structure:

```
e.Graphics.MeasureString("Welcome to VB.NET", MyFont)
```

A "Welcome" Example. To put everything about drawing a string together, develop a project to draw "Welcome to VB.NET" at the center of the form. In this project, all the fonts available in the system will be displayed in a combo box named cboFont. When the user makes a font selection from the combo box, the text drawn on the form will immediately reflect the change. A sample result is shown in Figure B.8.

The following form load procedure should enumerate the available fonts and display them in the combo box:

```
Private Sub Form1_Load(ByVal sender As Object, ByVal e As
    System.EventArgs) Handles MyBase.Load
    Dim TheFontFamily As FontFamily
    For Each TheFontFamily In Drawing.FontFamily.Families
        cboFont.Items.Add(TheFontFamily.Name)
    Next TheFontFamily
    cboFont.SelectedIndex = cboFont.FindString(Me.Font.Name)
End Sub
```

Figure B.8

Drawing a string with a specified font at a computed position

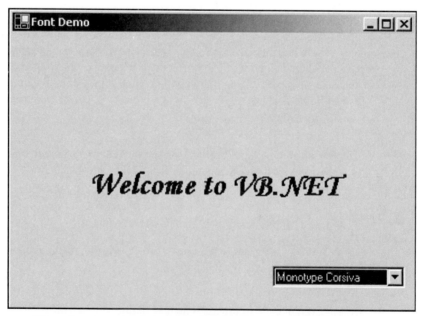

The welcome message is immediately redrawn *at the center* whenever the user makes a font selection from the combo box. The font names are obtained by enumerating through the font families available in the system.

The last statement in the procedure uses the FindString method to find the position of the form font in the combo box's item list and assigns the position to the combo box's SelectedIndex property. This statement makes the font used by the form appear as the selection for the combo box.

The following Form Paint event procedure draws the Welcome message at the center of the form:

```
Private Sub Form1_Paint(ByVal sender As Object, ByVal e As
   System.Windows.Forms.PaintEventArgs) Handles MyBase.Paint
   Dim MyText As String
   Dim TheBrush As Brush
   Dim MyFont As Font
   Dim MySizeF As SizeF
   MyText = "Welcome to VB.NET"
   TheBrush = Brushes.Blue
   MyFont = New Font(cboFont.Text, 24, FontStyle.Italic Or
     FontStyle.Bold)
   With e.Graphics
       MySizeF = .MeasureString(MyText, MyFont)
       .DrawString(MyText, MyFont, TheBrush, (Me.Width -
         MySizeF.Width) / 2, (Me.Height - MySizeF.Height) / 2)
   End With
End Sub
```

As explained previously, the SizeF structure has the Width and Height elements. These elements are used in conjunction with the form's width and height to compute the starting position for the Welcome message. Also note that the font name specified in the font is taken from the combo box's Text property. The font is then used by the DrawString method to draw the string.

TIP

Also notice a fine point: The form height includes the title bar, whereas the Y value (for the Top property) starts with a zero at the client region not including the title bar. The height available for drawing does not go as high as the form's height. The area available for drawing is represented by the ClientSize property and its height is referenced as Me.ClientSize.Height.

Because you would like the string to reflect the change as soon as the user makes a font selection, you should force the form to repaint whenever there is a change in the selected index. The following event procedure should take care of this requirement.

```
Private Sub cboFont_SelectedIndexChanged(ByVal Sender As Object,
   ByVal e As System.EventArgs) Handles
   cboFont.SelectedIndexChanged
     ' Force the form to repaint
     Me.Invalidate()
End Sub
```

B.2 Animation

Animations take different forms. For example, you can show different pictures at fixed time intervals in the same or different positions. While one picture is displayed, all other pictures of the same objects are made invisible. Usually, a timer is used to regulate the timing for displaying the pictures. This creates an illusion that the object is moving. You can also create animations by drawing instead of using existing pictures. For example, you can draw different colors on the same graph, again at a fixed time interval. This can create an impression that the object is blinking or the lights are moving. Also, you can create a rotating object (or an object with different motions) by drawing some part of the object at a different relative position while the object moves. In this section, you use three examples to illustrate how each of these effects can be achieved.

The Flying Butterfly

In this project, you show a butterfly flying at a random height and distance (width) from the lower left corner toward the upper right corner of the form. (This example assumes that your computer has Visual Studio Version 6. If it does not, replace the referenced image files with other files with similar images.) Follow these steps to set up the project:

1. Draw two picture boxes and a timer on a new form.

2. Name the picture boxes **picFly1** and **picFly2**; then set the Image properties to **Bfly1.bmp** and **Bfly2.bmp** for the two controls, respectively. (The images are located in Microsoft Visual Studio\MSDN98\98VS\1033\SAMPLES\VB98\Vcr.)

3. Name the timer control **tmrFly**. Set its Interval property to **300**. (You can change this setting depending on how fast you want the butterfly to flip and fly.)

4. Develop the code to perform the animation. The following discussion focuses on this aspect.

The initial form setup appears as in Figure B.9.

The Form Load Event Procedure. As soon the project starts, the program should perform several preparatory steps:

- Set the WindowState property to Maximized so that you can view the butterfly flying over the entire screen.

- Set the form's BackColor property to white so that it will correspond with that of the pictures.

- Move the pictures to the lower left corner so that they cannot be seen; that is, each picture is placed an entire width of itself to the left and entire height of itself below the form. Note that the Top property of the form starts with a value of zero below the title bar, but the form's Height property includes the title bar height. The area below the title bar is measured by the ClientSize property whose height is referenced as Me.ClientSize.Height. (See the sketch in Figure B.10.)

- Randomize the seed for the Rnd function because this function will be used.

The following procedure should accomplish these requirements.

```
Private Sub Form1_Load(ByVal Sender As Object, ByVal e As
    System.EventArgs) Handles MyBase.Load
    Me.WindowState = FormWindowState.Maximized  'maximize the form
    Me.BackColor = Color.White 'set background to white
    HideAtLowerLeft()
    Randomize() 'Randomize the seed
    tmrFly.Start()
End Sub
```

Figure B.9

Initial setup for the flying butterfly project

Note that the timer is started with its Start method, which sets the timer's Enabled property to True and thus starts the ticks. Notice that the routine to hide the images at the lower left corner of the form is written as a separate procedure named HideAtLowerLeft. Based on Figure B.10, the procedure appears as follows:

```
Private Sub HideAtLowerLeft()
    'Move picFly1 to lower left corner
    picFly1.Left = -picFly1.Width
    picFly1.Top = Me.ClientSize.Height
    'Move picFly2 to lower left corner
    picFly2.Left = -picFly2.Width
    picFly2.Top = Me.ClientSize.Height
End Sub
```

Toggling the Images. This animation involves only two pictures, so you can use a Static Boolean variable (IsFlyWingsOpen) to determine which picture should appear. The code structure can appear as follows:

```
Static IsFlyWingsOpen As Boolean
IsFlyWingsOpen = Not IsFlyWingsOpen 'Toggle wings open state
If IsFlyWingsOpen Then
    'Compute the Wings-open picture position
Else
    'Compute the wings-closed picture position
End If
picFly1.Visble = IsFlyWingsOpen
picFly2.Visible = Not IsFlyWingsOpen
```

The first Not statement will toggle the value of IsFlyWingsOpen. The Visible property of the first picture is set to the value of IsFlyWingsOpen, so if the variable is True, that picture will appear; otherwise, it will disappear. On the other hand, the second picture's Visible property is set to the opposite (Not) value of IsFlyWingsOpen, so when the variable is True, the second picture will not be visible; otherwise, it will be visible. The last two statements in the preceding code will make one picture appear and the other disappear depending on the value of IsFlyWingsOpen, which is toggled (with the Not statement) between procedure calls.

Computing the Picture Position. The current picture will move on average half its own width and a quarter of its own height from the position of the previous picture. That is, picFly1's position (x, y) can be computed as follows:

```
X = picFly2.Left + CInt(Rnd * picFly1.Width)
Y = picFly2.Top - CInt(Rnd * 0.5 * picFly1.Height)
```

Notice that the position of picFly1 is based on the previous position of picFly2 because the two images take turns to appear. Notice also that Rnd * picFly1.Width will result in a horizontal move on average by half of the first picture's width because Rnd generates a random number between 0 and 1, whose expected (average) value is 0.5. Multiplying this expected value by 0.5 should obtain an expected value of one-quarter, so the second formula should result in a vertical move up by one-quarter of the image's height. Similar formulas can be used to compute the new position for picFly2.

Figure B.10

Initial position of the two images

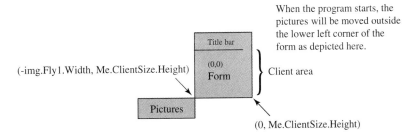

When the Butterfly Disappears from the Form. As soon as the butter-fly disappears from the form, you can start the two images from the lower right corner again. The butterfly disappears when the Left property of either image is greater than or equal to the form's width or when the image's Top property plus its Height is less than zero. For code simplicity you will test only the first image. The code structure will appear as follows:

```
If picFly1.Left >  Me.Width OrElse  picFly1.Top +
  picFly1.Height < 0 Then
     ' the butterfly has completely disappeared;
     ' start at the lower left corner again
     HideAtLowerLeft()
End If
```

The test for the control's position should be done before any computation of the control's new position; therefore, this block of code should appear at the top of the procedure.

The Complete Timer Tick Procedure. The placement and appearance of the butterfly should be regulated by the timer's interval, so the code to perform the anima-tion should be placed in the timer's Tick event. The complete timer Tick procedure appears as follows:

```
Private Sub tmrFly_Tick(ByVal Sender As Object, ByVal e As
  System.EventArgs) Handles tmrFly.Tick
     Static IsFlyWingsOpen As Boolean 'Declare a static variable
     If picFly1.Left > Me.Width OrElse picFly1.Top + picFly1.Height
     < 0 Then
          ' the butterfly has completely disappeared;
          ' start at the lower left corner again
          HideAtLowerLeft()
     End If
     IsFlyWingsOpen = Not IsFlyWingsOpen 'Toggle the state
     If IsFlyWingsOpen Then
          'Move the wings-open image
          picFly1.Left = picFly2.Left + CInt(Rnd() * picFly1.Width)
          picFly1.Top = picFly2.Top - CInt(Rnd() * 0.5 *
             picFly1.Height)
     Else
          ' Move the wings-closed image
          picFly2.Left = picFly1.Left + CInt(Rnd() * picFly2.Width)
          picFly2.Top = picFly1.Top - CInt(Rnd() * 0.5 *
             picFly2.Height)
     End If
     'Show wings-open picture if IsFlyWingsOpen is True
     picFly1.Visible = IsFlyWingsOpen
     'Make wings-closed image appear if IsFlyWingsOpen is False
     picFly2.Visible = Not IsFlyWingsOpen
End Sub
```

This project consists of two event procedures (the Form Load and the Timer Tick event pro-cedures) and the HideAtCorner sub procedure. Run the project, and you should see the butterfly fly from the lower left corner toward the upper right corner until it disappears. It will then reap-pear from the lower left corner again.

Rotating Light Colors

By rotating the colors for the light bulbs, you can create an impression that the lights are moving. The previous Christmas lights project can easily be modified to show this effect. Follow these steps:

1. Copy the entire ChristmasLight folder, and name the new folder **ChristmasLight2**.

2. Draw a timer control on the form. Name it **tmrLights**. Set its Interval property to 250.

3. Add code in the Timer event. The following discussion focuses on this aspect.

Actually, the code in the Timer Tick event should be similar to the one in the previous btnShow Click event. Consider the For loop in that procedure:

```
For I = 0 To 52 Step 4
    ' Statements to display green, red, white and blue lights
Next I
```

The loop begins with drawing a green light at position 0 and rotates among the four colors as it proceeds. After the loop is complete, 56 lights are drawn. Suppose the next time the procedure is called, the loop will begin with drawing a green light at position 1 and proceed from there to draw 56 lights. The fifty-sixth light will be drawn at position 56, one position beyond the last (55). Notice, however, position 0 has not yet been drawn, so if you subtract 56 from the position number when it exceeds 55, you make the drawing starting from position 0 again. The loop can then be made to draw a complete rotation from whichever position it begins to draw the lights. That is, if you let BegPos be the position the loop starts, you can modify the loop parameters as follows:

```
For I = BegPos To 52 + BegPos Step 4
    ' statements to draw the lights
Next I
```

You can increase the value of BegPos by 1 each time the procedure is called. There are four colors. There is no need to have this variable take on more than four values (from 0 to 3), so you can code the following:

```
BegPos = BegPos + 1
If BegPos > 3 Then
    BegPos = 0
End If
```

The complete Timer Tick event procedure can appear as follows:

```
Private Sub tmrLights_Tick(ByVal Sender As Object, ByVal e As
    System.EventArgs) Handles tmrLights.Tick
    Dim I As Integer
    Static BegPos As Integer
    'Draw 56 lights in rotation
    ' The colors are: green, red, white, and blue
    For I = BegPos To 52 + BegPos Step 4
        DrawBulb(I, Color.Green)
        DrawBulb(I + 1, Color.Red)
        DrawBulb(I + 2, Color.White)
        DrawBulb(I + 3, Color.Blue)
    Next I
    BegPos = BegPos + 1
    If BegPos > 3 Then
        BegPos = 0
    End If
End Sub
```

Notice that BegPos is declared as a Static variable so that its value can be preserved between the Timer Tick event procedure calls.

The event procedure does not really take care of the situation in which the light position exceeds 55. This can easily be handled in the DrawBulb procedure as follows:

```
Private Sub DrawBulb(ByVal P As Integer, ByVal TheColor As Color)
    Dim X As Integer
    Dim Y As Integer
    'Step 0: Adjust value for P
    If P > 55 Then
        P -= 56
    End If
    'Step 1: Compute the position of the light bulb
    ' Other statements (remain the same)
End Sub
```

You need to start the timer. One way, of course, is just to set its enabled property to True at design time. For the fun of it, you can place the code in the btnShow click event, replacing the code that you no longer need. You can make the button toggle between Show Lights and Stop. When the button's text shows Show Lights, a click will start the lights and the button will show the Stop text. Clicking on the button again will make the lights stop and the button show the Show Lights text. The code appears as follows:

```
Private Sub btnShow_Click(ByVal sender As Object, ByVal e As
    System.EventArgs) Handles btnShow.Click
        'Toggle between "Show Lights" and "Stop"
        If btnShow.Text = "Show Lights" Then
            tmrLights.Start()
            btnShow.Text = "Stop"
        Else
            tmrLights.Stop()
            btnShow.Text = "Show Lights"
        End If
End Sub
```

After you modify the project as shown, you are ready to see the effect. Run the program. Click the button, and you should be able to see lights rotating around the picture frame. Click it again, and you should see the lights stop.

The Rolling Wheel

This example project will emulate a rolling wheel on the form. The rolling wheel will appear from the right side and roll across the form. As soon as it disappears, it will appear from the right side again. To set up this project, bring a timer on a new form. Name the timer **tmrWheel** and set its interval to 100.

This project presents two issues. To "move" the wheel, you need not only to draw the wheel at the new position but also to erase the wheel at its previous location. Also, you need to show that the wheel not only moves forward but also rolls. To show the wheel is rolling, you can draw a line similar to the clock hand in the wheel and make it appear at different angles. A glimpse of the resulting form appears in Figure B.11.

As the wheel "turns," the hand will rotate. The distance that the wheel travels and the angle that the hand rotates should be consistent.

Let *WheelRadius* = the wheel radius
AngleTurned = the angle (in radians) that the hand rotates
The distance the wheel travels can then be computed as follows:

```
Distance = WheelRadius * AngleTurned
```

Here is a roundabout way of explaining how the preceding formula is derived:
The length of the whole circle is 2π WheelRadius.

The ratio of the distance traveled to the circle for an angle, AngleTurned (in radians), is AngledTurned / 2π; therefore:

Figure B.11

The rolling wheel

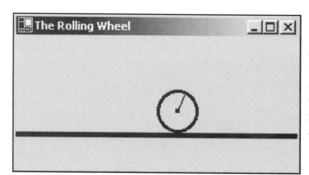

This project draws a wheel rolling across the form. As the wheel moves from right to left, its hand rotates, making the wheel appear to roll.

```
Distance = Circle × Ratio
         = (2 π WheelRadius) (AngleTurned / 2 π)
         = WheelRadius × AngleTurned
```

Assume that you will move the wheel 16 times to complete a full rotation (whole circle). The AngleTurned can be computed as follows:

```
AngleTurned = 2 π / 16; that is,
AngleTurned = π / 8
```

There should also be a "road" below the wheel. To show the road, you will draw a box at 60% of the form's height. You can use the *FillRectangle method* to draw the box. The method has the following syntax:

```
Object.FillRectangle(Brush, Rectangle)
```

where *Object* = the graphic object

Brush = the brush (e.g., SolidBrush) to use to fill the rectangle

Rectangle = a structure giving the location and size of the rectangle

For your purpose, you can draw the road as soon the form is ready, so you can place the code in the form Paint event as follows:

```
Private Sub Form1_Paint(ByVal sender As Object, ByVal e As
   System.Windows.Forms.PaintEventArgs) Handles MyBase.Paint
      e.Graphics.FillRectangle(Brushes.Black, _
         New Rectangle(New Point(0, CInt(0.6 * Me.Height)), _
         New Size(Me.Width, 5)))
End Sub
```

The code specifies a black brush. The rectangle will start at the coordinate (0, 60% of form height) with a width of the entire form and height of five pixels.

Setting the Initial Position of the Wheel. The wheel will go from right to left on the form. Initially, it will not be seen, so the center of its X coordinate should be the form's width plus it radius. The center of its Y coordinate should be immediately above the road. The wheel itself should not be drawn on the road to avoid drawing over it. Let WheelX and WheelY be the coordinates for the wheel's center. They can then be computed as follows:

```
' Compute the initial coordinate for wheel center
WheelX = Me.Width + WheelRadius 'On the form's right margin
'Place the bottom of the wheel two pixels above the road
WheelY = CInt(0.6 * Me.Height) - WheelRadius - 2
```

The formula for WheelY indicates that the lowest portion of the wheel will be drawn two pixels above the road. This should make the wheel barely touch the road surface since the wheel itself will be drawn with a pen size of three pixels.

The Form Load Procedure. All the preceding discussion pertains to the computations required as soon as the program starts. The code can be placed in the Form Load event as follows:

```
Dim TheGraph As Graphics
Dim Distance As Integer
Dim WheelRadius As Integer
Dim AngleTurned As Single 'angle turned in each period
Dim WheelX As Integer
Dim WheelY As Integer
Private Sub Form1_Load(ByVal sender As Object, ByVal e As
   System.EventArgs) Handles MyBase.Load
      ' Compute parameter values
      WheelRadius = CInt(Me.Height / 10)
      AngleTurned = Math.PI / 8
      Distance = CInt(WheelRadius * AngleTurned)
      ' Compute the initial coordinate for wheel center
```

```
        WheelX = Me.Width + WheelRadius 'On the form's right margin
        'Place the bottom of the wheel two pixels above the road
        WheelY = CInt(0.6 * Me.Height) - WheelRadius - 2
        TheGraph = Me.CreateGraphics()
        tmrWheel.Start()
    End Sub
```

Notice that all five variables have been declared as class-level variables because they will be used in other procedures. Notice also that a statement has been inserted to create the graph object and to start the timer. Finally, notice that the procedure uses the constant PI of the Math object that gives the value of π.

Drawing the Wheel. The wheel has three parts: the circle, the center point, and the hand. Given the wheel center at (Xc,Yc) with a Radius and a Color, the circle for the wheel can be drawn on the form with the following code:

```
'Draw the wheel
TheGraph.DrawEllipse(New Pen(TheColor, 3), _
    New Rectangle(New Point(Xc - Radius, Yc - Radius), _
    New Size(Radius + Radius, Radius + Radius)))
```

Recall that the rectangle to enclose the circle is defined with a point representing its upper left corner and a size of width by height. Both the width and height should be twice of the radius.

You would also like to draw a point at the center. This can be done with the following code:

```
' Draw the center point
TheGraph.FillEllipse(New SolidBrush(TheColor), _
    New Rectangle(New Point(Xc - 3, Yc - 3), New Size(5, 5)))
```

The center point is drawn with the FillEllipse method (instead of the DrawEllipse method) because you would like for it to show as a solid shape rather than a hollow circle.

The hand will connect the center point to the circle with a line. The hand's position on the circle depends on the angle. Given an angle, Theta (in radians), its coordinate can be computed with the following formula:

```
X = Xc + Cos(Theta) * Radius
Y = Yc - Sin(Theta) * Radius
```

Recall that by definition, at the point of origin (0, 0), Sin(Theta) = Y/Radius. (Refer to Figure B.12 for a visual hint.) At that point, Y = Sin(Theta) × Radius. Notice, however, that the Y value computed in this formula is based on the Cartesian coordinate. The Y coordinate of an object in VB goes the other way: the closer a position is to the top, the smaller the value is. The Y value should be subtracted from (rather than added to) Yc. This is how the formula to compute Y is derived.

Figure B.12

(x, y) with an angle Θ

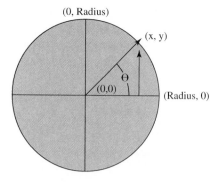

Given this chart in the Cartesian coordinate, the values of x and y can be computed as follows:
$Sin(\Theta) = y / radius$
Thus, $y = Sin(\Theta) \times radius$
$Cos(\Theta) = x / radius$
Thus, $x = Cos(\Theta) \times radius$

Similarly, at the point of origin, Cos(Theta) = X/Radius. Thus, X = Cos(Theta) × Radius. The X coordinate under the Cartesian system is consistent with that for the object in VB, so this value is added to Xc, the X coordinate of the wheel center. The hand then can be drawn with the DrawLine method as shown in following statement:

```
'Draw the hand from the center
TheGraph.DrawLine(New Pen(TheColor, 1), New Point(Xc, Yc), _
    New Point(CInt(Xc + Math.Cos(Theta) * Radius), CInt(Yc -
    Math.Sin(Theta) * Radius)))
```

The Sub procedure to draw a wheel (DrawWheel) appears as follows:

```
Sub DrawWheel(ByVal Xc As Integer, ByVal Yc As Integer, _
    ByVal Radius As Integer, ByVal Theta As Single, _
    ByVal TheColor As Color)
    'Draw the wheel
    TheGraph.DrawEllipse(New Pen(TheColor, 3), _
        New Rectangle(New Point(Xc - Radius, Yc - Radius), _
        New Size(Radius + Radius, Radius + Radius)))
    ' Draw the center
    TheGraph.FillEllipse(New SolidBrush(TheColor), _
        New Rectangle(New Point(Xc - 3, Yc - 3), New Size(5, 5)))
        'Draw the hand from the center
    TheGraph.DrawLine(New Pen(TheColor, 1), New Point(Xc, Yc), _
        New Point(CInt(Xc + Math.Cos(Theta) * Radius), CInt(Yc -
        Math.Sin(Theta) * Radius)))
End Sub
```

Rolling the Wheel. The DrawWheel Sub procedure can be used to roll the wheel across the form. This should be done in the Timer Tick event procedure. In each event call, the original wheel should be erased; then another wheel should be drawn at a new location.

To erase the wheel, you can draw it at the same location with the BackColor. This will restore every part of the wheel to the BackColor, making it disappear.

To draw another wheel at a new location, you will need to know the wheel's current coordinate. Recall that you have calculated the original coordinate for the wheel in the Form Load procedure. There, you also calculated the distance that the wheel would travel each time. The class-level variables for the coordinate are WheelX and WheelY, and the variable for the distance traveled is named Distance. WheelY should remain the same; however, WheelX should be decreased (because the wheel is going from right to left) by Distance for the distance the wheel travels; that is:

```
WheelX = WheelX - Distance
```

When the wheel completely disappears from the form, it will reappear from the right. If the wheel has disappeared from the left side, the WheelX value should be less than the negative value of the radius. You can code the following:

```
If WheelX < -WheelRadius Then
    ' wheel has disappeared; start from right again
    WheelX = Me.Width + WheelRadius
End If
```

The wheel rolls counter-clockwise. This means that as the wheel rolls, the angle Theta is increased by the angle turned, which is represented by the variable AngleTurned and was also computed in the form load procedure; therefore,

```
Theta = Theta + AngleTurned
```

You can start the value for Theta at zero and then check whether the value is greater than or equal to 2π. If so, the wheel has turned a complete round and Theta can be reset to 0. The code will appear as follows:

```
If Theta >= 2 * Math.Pi Then
    ' Set Theta to 0
    Theta = 0
End If
```

To put everything together, the complete Timer Tick event procedure should appear as follows:

```
Private Sub tmrWheel_Tick(ByVal Sender As Object, ByVal e As
    System.EventArgs) Handles tmrWheel.Tick
    Static Theta As Single
    ' Erase wheel drawn previously
    DrawWheel(WheelX, WheelY, WheelRadius, Theta, Me.BackColor)
    If WheelX < -WheelRadius Then
        ' wheel has disappeared; start from right again
        WheelX = Me.Width + WheelRadius
    End If
    'Change the angle (turn)
    Theta = Theta + AngleTurned
    If Theta >= 2 * Math.PI Then
        ' Set theta to 0 to start over
        Theta = 0
    End If
    ' Move the wheel by a fixed distance
    WheelX = WheelX - Distance
    DrawWheel(WheelX, WheelY, WheelRadius, Theta, Me.ForeColor)
End Sub
```

Notice that Theta is declared to be a Static variable in the procedure so that its value between event calls can be preserved. Notice also the DrawWheel Sub is called twice. The first time, the form's BackColor is used as the color parameter so that the previous wheel can be erased. The second time, the new wheel position, the new angle, and the ForeColor are passed to draw the wheel.

This rolling wheel project includes the Form Paint event procedure (to draw the road), Form Load event procedure (to initialize various variables), the DrawWheel Sub procedure, and the tmrWheel Tick event procedure. Try the project and get a feel for how the wheel turns. You can change the timer interval and the denominator for the AngleTurned formula to get a different speed for the wheel.

B.3 Drag and Drop

Drag and drop provides an interesting and easy way for the user to specify operations that can be too complex to express by some other means. A typical drag-and-drop operation involves dragging an icon to another icon at another location to initiate certain activities. For example, a file can be dragged into a trashcan to delete the file. Typically, in this type of operation, three icons are involved. In the case of dumping a file, one icon will represent the file (the *source*), another will represent an empty trashcan (the *target*; before the file is dragged), and the other will represent the trashcan containing the dumped file (after the file is dropped). Only one of the two trashcans will be visible at a given time.

Before a drag and drop operation can be performed, *the target control's **AllowDrop property** must be set to True* (False is the default). Each drag and drop involves three steps:

1. Set up what is to be dragged. This is done in the source control using the DoDragDrop method, typically in the control's MouseDown event, which occurs when the user presses the mouse on the source control.

2. When the drag enters the target control, examine the data type and decide what type of drag-drop effect will be allowed. This is done in the target control's ***DragEnter event***.

3. Accept the data or perform the desired operation in the target control's ***DragDrop event***, which occurs when the user drops the object on the target control by releasing the mouse.

TIP

When testing your drag and drop code, if nothing seems to be active, check the AllowDrop property of your target control first. Make sure your code sets the property to True or it is set to True if it is accessible in the Properties window.

The following two examples illustrate some of the basics of the drag and drop operation.

Keeping a Disk in the Holder: An Example

This project will allow the user to drag the disk and drop it in a disk holder. When the operation is complete, the disk will disappear as if it had been placed in the holder. The disk holder will change colors to indicate that it is holding the disk. (Note: This example assumes that your computer has Visual Studio Version 6. If it does not, replace the referenced image files with other files with similar images.)

Follow these steps to perform additional setup for the project:

1. Draw three picture boxes on the new form. Set all the controls' *SizeMode property* to StretchImage so that the icon will fill the box.

2. Name the first control **picDisk**. Set its Image property to **Disk03.ico**, which is located in the following folder:

   ```
   Microsoft Visual Studio\Common\Graphics\Icons\Computer
   ```

3. Name the second picture box **picDiskHolder1**. Name the third one **picDiskHolder2** and set its Visible property to **False**.

4. Set picDiskHolder1's Picture property to **Disks03.ico** and picDiskHolder2's Image property to **Disks04.ico**. (Note the names of both files. They start with "Disks," not just "Disk.")

5. Position the icons so that they will appear in the form as in Figure B.13.

You'd like for all three picture boxes to be of the same size. This is easier done with code than with visual adjustment. Also, when the project starts, the disk on the left can be dragged to the disk holder on the right, so picDiskHolder1 is the target control and its AllowDrop property should be set to True. The Form Load event procedure appears as follows:

```
Private Sub Form1_Load(ByVal Sender As Object, ByVal e As
   System.EventArgs) Handles MyBase.Load
      picDiskHolder1.AllowDrop = True
      'Make all picture boxes of the same size
      picDiskHolder1.Size = picDisk.Size
      picDiskHolder2.Size = picDisk.Size
End Sub
```

Figure B.13

Disk drag and drop

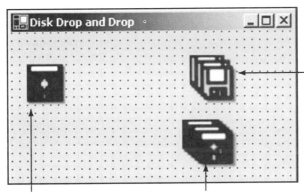

Place picDiskHolder1 here. When the program starts, this holder appears. But after the disk is dragged and dropped here, the other holder will appear here in its place.

Place picDisk here. Once this disk is dragged to the "empty holder" and dropped, it will disappear.

Place picDiskHolder2 here. When your program starts, this holder will not be visible.

As explained previously, when the drag operation starts, you need to indicate (with the DoDragDrop method) what types of drag-drop effects to have. The method has the following syntax:

Object.DoDragDrop(*Data, DragDropEffect*)

Where *Data* = the data to drag

DragDropEffect = Copy, Move, Link, None, or All.

The code should be placed in the MouseDown event and appears as follows:

```
Private Sub picDisk_MouseDown(ByVal sender As Object, ByVal e As
    System.Windows.Forms.MouseEventArgs) Handles picDisk.MouseDown
      picDisk.DoDragDrop(picDisk, DragDropEffects.Move)
End Sub
```

The code indicates that the data to be worked with is the control itself and the drag-drop effect is "move".

The next step is to indicate what kind of effect to allow in the target control's DragEnter event. It should allow the move effect. The event procedure appears as follows:

```
Private Sub picDiskHolder1_DragEnter(ByVal sender As Object, ByVal
    e As System.Windows.Forms.DragEventArgs) Handles
    picDiskHolder1.DragEnter
      e.Effect = DragDropEffects.Move
End Sub
```

Finally, when the DragDrop event occurs in picDiskHolder1, picDisk should disappear. In addition, picDiskHolder2 should take the place of picDiskHolder1; that is, picDiskHolder2 should appear at the location of picDiskHolder1, which should then disappear. This description yields the following code:

```
Private Sub picDiskHolder1_DragDrop(ByVal sender As Object, ByVal
    e As System.Windows.Forms.DragEventArgs) Handles
    picDiskHolder1.DragDrop
      picDisk.Visible = False
      picDiskHolder2.Location = picDiskHolder1.Location
      picDiskHolder2.Visible = True
      picDiskHolder1.Visible = False
End Sub
```

You can now test the program. When you drag and drop the disk on the disk holder, the disk should disappear. In addition, the disk holder changes color (disk holder 1 is replaced by disk holder 2).

The drag-and-drop operation is not limited to images. In addition, the operation can involve other kind of data. For example, the text in text boxes can be dragged and dropped into a list box. The next example shows how this can be done.

Dragging Texts Among Controls

This project illustrates how to perform drag-and-drop operation on the text. You can set up the visual interface with the following steps:

1. Draw two text boxes and a list box on a new form.

2. Name the two text boxes **txtSender1** and **txtSender2**.

3. Name the list box **lstRecipient** and set its AllowDrop property to **True**. (Note that some controls do not have this property accessible at design time.)

As discussed previously, the first step is to indicate in the source control's MouseDown event the data to be dragged and the type(s) of allowed effect(s). You'd like to drag the text to the list box, so the data to operate on is the Text property of the text box and the type of effect is "Copy." You need to do this for both text boxes. The two event procedures appear as follows:

```
Private Sub txtSender1_MouseDown(ByVal sender As Object, ByVal e
   As System.Windows.Forms.MouseEventArgs) Handles
   txtSender1.MouseDown
      txtSender1.DoDragDrop(txtSender1.Text, DragDropEffects.Copy)
End Sub
Private Sub txtsender2_MouseDown(ByVal sender As Object, ByVal e
   As System.Windows.Forms.MouseEventArgs) Handles
   txtSender2.MouseDown
      txtSender2.DoDragDrop(txtSender2.Text, DragDropEffects.Copy)
End Sub
```

The DoDragDrop method in effect sends the text to the ***ClipBoard***. In subsequent events, the event argument passes the data in the Clipboard as the Data object.

The second step is to allow the drop effect when the drag operation enters the target control. The drop effect should be allowed only if the data format is as expected. The code appears as follows:

```
Private Sub lstRecipient_DragEnter(ByVal sender As Object, ByVal e
   As System.Windows.Forms.DragEventArgs) Handles
   lstRecipient.DragEnter
      'Accept only text to drop
      If (e.Data.GetDataPresent(DataFormats.Text)) Then
         e.Effect = DragDropEffects.Copy
      Else
         e.Effect = DragDropEffects.None
      End If
End Sub
```

Notice how the If statement is coded. The event argument passes the data dragged (Data) and the data's GetDataPresent method tests whether the data dragged (in the Clipboard) is of the data format specified in the parameter, which is specified to be DataFormats.Text. (Other possible data formats include Bitmap, Html, UnicodeText, WaveAudio, and Tiff.) If the method returns a value of True, the copy effect of the drop operation will be allowed; otherwise, there will be no effect (none).

The third step is to handle the data when the Drag-Drop event occurs. The code appears as follows:

```
Private Sub lstRecipient_DragDrop(ByVal sender As Object, ByVal e
   As System.Windows.Forms.DragEventArgs) Handles
   lstRecipient.DragDrop
      lstRecipient.Items.Add(e.Data.GetData(DataFormats.Text))
End Sub
```

Notice what is added to the list box's Items list. The data (text) is not obtained directly from either of the text boxes. It is obtained from the event's Data argument, using the Data object's GetData method with a specified format of Text. Recall that the text was placed into the Clipboard in the first step of the drag-drop operation.

Summary

- Various draw methods draw the outline of a shape. For example, the DrawRectangle method draws a rectangle.

- Various fill methods paint the entire shape. For example, the FillRectangle method fills the rectangle with a color.

- To draw a graph on a control, such as label, panel, picture box, and form, there must be a graphic object associated with the control. The graphic object is one of the event arguments of the control's paint event. If you want draw something on the control when it first appears, you can perform the drawing in the paint event and use that graphic object. You can also use the control's CreateGraphics method to create graphic object.

- The freehand drawing example shows some of the basics about drawing using the DrawLine method.

- The DrawEllipse and FillEllipse methods draw ellipses and circles. The Christmas lights example illustrates the use of the FillEllipse method. It also suggests the potential computational complexity involved in drawing.

- Animation can be done using existing images or by drawing graphics. Typically, some code is placed in a Timer Tick event to move or rotate the images or draw shapes across the control surface to cause the animation effect.

- Three examples (flying butterfly, rotating Christmas lights, and rolling wheel) were used to illustrate how animation can be accomplished.

- Drag and drop operations are carried out in three steps. The first step involves coding in the source control's MouseDown event to place the data in the Clipboard based on the specified type of effect the drag is to have. The second step involves coding in the target control's DragEnter event to determine what type of drop effect is allowed. The third step involves coding in the target control's DragDrop event to take the data and put it in the proper place.

- Two examples (keeping a disk in the holder and dragging the text into a list box) were used to illustrate the basics of the drag and drop operation.

Explore and Discover

B-1.   **The Pens Class.** Enter the following code in a new form:

```
Private Sub Form1_Click(ByVal sender As Object, ByVal e As
   System.EventArgs) Handles MyBase.Click
      Dim ThePen As Pen
      ThePen = Pens.Beige
   End Sub
```

When you typed the period (.) after Pens, what did you notice? The IntelliSense provides you with a long list of standard colors, which are the same as those in the Brushes list. You can use a pen from the Pens list without using the Pen constructor.

B-2.   **The Graphics Clear Method.** Draw a button on the form. Name the button **btnClear** and enter the following code:

```
Private Sub btnClear_Click(ByVal Sender As Object, ByVal e As
   System.EventArgs) Handles btnClear.Click
      Dim TheGraph As Graphics
      TheGraph = Me.CreateGraphics
      TheGraph.Clear(Color.Red)
   End Sub
```

Run the project and then click the form. What do you see? The Clear method paints the entire region of a control with the specified color. To actually clear the surface of the control, use the control's BackColor property.

B-3.   **Additional Font Styles.** Draw a button on the form. Name it **btnWrite** and enter the following code:

```
Private Sub btnWrite_Click(ByVal Sender As Object, ByVal e As
   System.EventArgs) Handles btnWrite.Click
      Dim TheGraph As Graphics
      Dim TheFont As Font
      TheGraph = Me.CreateGraphics
      TheGraph.Clear(Me.BackColor)
      TheFont = New Font("Times New Roman", 16, FontStyle.Strikeout
        Or FontStyle.Underline)
```

```
        TheGraph.DrawString("Done!", TheFont, Drawing.Brushes.Black,
            10, 10)
    End Sub
```

Run the project and then click the button. What do you see on the form? Strikeout and Underline are the two additional font styles that you can use with a font.

B-4.   The Linear Gradient Brush. Draw a panel on a new form. Place the following line above the Class statement in the code window.

```
    Imports System.Drawing.Drawing2D
```

Enter the following code:

```
    Private Sub Panel1_Paint(ByVal sender As Object, ByVal e As
        System.Windows.Forms.PaintEventArgs) Handles Panel1.Paint
        Dim TheGraph As Graphics
        Dim LGBrush As LinearGradientBrush
        Dim Rect As Rectangle
        TheGraph = e.Graphics()

        Rect = New Rectangle(100, 10, 40, 80)
        LGBrush = New LinearGradientBrush(Rect, Color.Blue,
          Color.White, LinearGradientMode.Vertical)
        LGBrush.SetSigmaBellShape(0.5)
        TheGraph.FillEllipse(LGBrush, Rect)
    End Sub
```

Run the project. What do you see in the panel? The LinearGradient brush can be used to create various effects with different modes. For additional information, use LinearGradientBrush class as the keyword in the index tab of the help menu to find the relevant pages.

Exercises

B-5.   Draw Diagonal Cross. Draw a picture box on a new form. Write the code so that as soon as the program starts, the picture box will appear with a blue diagonal cross with a width of five pixels.

B-6.   Draw a Circle. Draw a picture box on the form. Write the code to draw a circle that touches all sides of the picture box. The circle should be drawn with a green pen of the pixels width and should appear as soon as the program starts. (*Hint:* Make sure the picture box's width and height have the same value.)

B-7.   Rotating Christmas Lights. Modify the first Christmas lights project in this appendix so that every fourth light will go out in rotation every quarter of a second. That is, the first quarter of a second, lights 0, 4, 8, and so on will go out; the second quarter of a second, lights 1, 5, 9, and so on will go out, whereas lights 0, 4, 8, and so on will come back on. (*Hint:* Fill the light bulb with the black color to make it "go out." Fill the light bulb with its original color to make it "come back on." Note that all lights to be restored are the same color.)

B-8.   Add Color to the Rolling Wheel. Modify the rolling wheel project in this appendix so that the wheel's color is white. Make sure the previous wheel is properly erased as the new one moves forward.

B-9.   **Emulating the Clock.** Draw a clock with a second hand. The hand will tick every second and complete a full rotation on the clock every minute.

B-10.   **Take the Sad Face to the Happy Home.** Draw two picture boxes and a group box on a new form. Name the two picture boxes **picSad** and **picHappy**. Set the Image properties of the two controls to **Sad.bmp** and **Happy.bmp**. These two files are located in the Assorted subfolder of the Bitmaps folder under the Graphics folder. Set the group box's Text property to **Happy Home** and name it **grpHappyHome**.

Provide the code so that at runtime the sad face will show but the happy face is not visible. When it is dragged into the Happy Home group box, it turns into the happy face.

B-11.   **Drag and Drop Between Two List Boxes.** Draw two list boxes onto a form. Populate both boxes with your friends' names. Provide the code so that at runtime you can drag any name from one control and drop it into another control.

B-12.   **Print Text on the Form.** Write a sub procedure that will take as its parameters a control, a string, and a pair of numbers (representing the location) and will print the string on the control at the specified location. The brush should have a black color. The font should be Times New Roman with a size of 16 (regular font style). Test the sub by writing "Hello" on the form.

B-13.   **Printing the Title.** Modify the sub in the preceding exercise (B-12) so that it will print the text at the center near the top of the "page." Note that the sub now needs only one number (y) (instead of a pair) in the parameter list. It should compute the value of x so that the title is printed at the center horizontally. Test the sub by writing **Annual Report** on a picture box.

B-14.   **Fancy Christmas Lights.** (refer to Exercise B-4) Now you know how to draw fancier light bulbs. Modify the first Christmas lights example so that the light bulbs look really fancy.

C Number Systems and Bit-Wise Operations

This appendix discusses two related topics: number systems and bit-wise operations. A discussion of the number systems should help build a foundation for a deeper understanding of numeric and bit-wise operations. Most of the VB.NET logical operators operate on a bit by bit basis. An understanding of how these operators work helps to eliminate unexpected errors resulting from code that performs operations that the programmer has not anticipated. It also helps the programmer takes advantages of these operators' special features.

C.1 Number Systems

Human beings use the decimal system for numbers. We count from 0 to 9 before adding another digit in presenting the number. Computers, on the other hand, operate on bits (binary digits) and bytes. A number is represented internally in the computer by setting various bits on or off. For example, the number zero is represented by setting off all bits used for that number; and one, the lowest bit, on. Because a bit has only two states (on and off), to go to the next number (2), the lowest bit is turned off, while the next lowest bit is turned on. Such a system is recognized as the binary number system. This coding system can be depicted as follows:

Binary system	Decimal system
0000	0
0001	1
0010	2
0011	3
0100	4
0101	5
0110	6
0111	7

Converting Between the Two Systems

If you examine the binary system closely, you may discover that each bit position represents a value of two raised to a certain power. For example, the lowest bit and the second lowest bit represent 2^0 and 2^1, respectively. This can be depicted as follows:

Binary number	1	1	1	1	1	1	1	1
Decimal value	2^7	2^6	2^5	2^4	2^3	2^2	2^1	2^0

From Binary to Decimal

To find the corresponding decimal value for any binary representation, multiply the bits by their corresponding positional value and sum the total. For example, a binary number, 10101, can have its decimal value computed as follows:

Binary value	1	0	1	0	1
multiply by	2^4	2^3	2^2	2^1	2^0
Results	16 + 0 + 4 + 0 + 1 = 21				

From Decimal to Binary

Conversely, to find the binary value for a decimal number, divide the number by two and find the remainder, which is the bit value for the lowest position; then divide the integer quotient by two again to obtain the bit value for the next higher position. Repeat this process to find the bit value for each successive position until the resulting quotient is zero. The following table shows how the binary representation for 13 can be obtained.

Step	4	3	2	1
Value To Be Divided by 2	1	3	6	13
Integer Quotient	0	1	3	6
Remainder (Binary Equivalent)	1	1	0	1

As the table shows, in the first step (last column), 13 is divided by 2, resulting in a quotient 6 and a remainder 1. In step 2, 6 (the previous quotient) is divided by 2, resulting in a quotient 3 and a remainder 0. This process continues until step 4, when the resulting quotient is 0. The remainder row shows the bit representation for 13, that is, 1101.

The Hex Decimal Representation

Although the binary number system corresponds to the internal coding exactly, it is inconvenient to show a long number with this system. To simplify the representation, the hex decimal system has been introduced. Under this system, each digit has 16 possible values (0 to 15), as opposed to 2 in the binary system and 10 in the decimal system. The numbers are represented as shown in the following table:

Decimal	Binary	Hex
0	0000	0
1	0001	1
2	0010	2
3	0011	3
4	0100	4
5	0101	5
6	0110	6
7	0111	7
8	1000	8
9	1001	9
10	1010	A
11	1011	B
12	1100	C
13	1101	D
14	1110	E
15	1111	F

As you can see from the table, the letters A, B, C, D, E, and F are used to represent 10, 11, 12, 13, 14, and 15, respectively, so that each of the 16 numbers in the hex decimal system is one digit. The next number after F will be 10 because we have exhausted all symbols to represent a number in one hex digit.

Notice that the letters used in this context have no direct association with the letters used in any text. They are simply symbols used to represent the numbers in the hex system. Notice also a hex decimal digit can be conveniently used to represent four bits in the binary system. For example, a hex number F0 will indicate that the lower four bits are zeros (off), while the upper four bits are 1s (on).

Converting Between Hex and Decimal Numbers

Converting numbers between the two systems is similar to converting between decimal and binary numbers. Each position, p, in the hex system represents a value of 16 raised to the power of p - 1, beginning from the lowest. To convert a hex decimal number to a decimal value, multiply each hex digit by its positional value and sum the total. For example, the hex number F3D can be converted to a decimal value as follows:

Hex number	F	3	D
Decimal equivalent	15	3	13
Multiply by	16^2	16^1	16^0
Result	3840 +	48 +	13 = 3901

To convert a decimal number to a hex representation, divide the number by 16 to find the integer quotient and the remainder, which gives the value at the lowest position. Divide the quotient by 16 again to obtain the remainder for the value at the next lowest position. Continue this process until the integer quotient is zero. For example, the following table illustrates how a decimal number, 3901, can be converted to a hex number:

Step	3	2	1
Number To Be Divided by 16	15	243	3901
Integer Quotient	0	15	243
Remainder	15	3	13
Result: Remainder in Hex	F	3	D

As you can see in step 1 (last column) from the table, the number 3901 is divided by 16, giving an integer quotient of 243 and a remainder of 13, which can be represented in the hex system as D. In a similar fashion, the previous quotient, 243, is divided by 16 to obtain the quotient and remainder for the second round. The process continues until the resulting quotient is zero in step 3. The remainder in hex representation F3D gives the solution.

Representing Hex Numbers in VB

VB allows a direct representation of hex numbers. You can code a hex number by preceding it with an &H. For example, to represent a hex number F, you code &HF. If the number is fairly large, attach an & at the end to indicate it is a Long integer. For example, code &HAB0CD0& instead of &HAB0CD0.

Why Discuss Number Systems?

Usually, VB shows results with decimal values. After all, the decimal system is what we are most familiar with. So, why discuss the other number systems? Here are some reasons:

- In some cases, it is much easier to think in terms of bits. In some applications, many "states" are represented by "Flags," which are collectively represented by an integer with its specific bits set on or off. An understanding of the binary number system will make it easier for us to see the relationship between "setting a bit on" and an integer value. Incidentally, a Boolean value is stored as a two-byte integer. The value False has all its bits off (&H0000), whereas True has all its bits on (&HFFFF). You can easily see that False has a numeric equivalent of 0. Also, when an integer's highest bit is on, it is a negative number. Its complement (a value that adds that number to make it zero) is the number's negative value. Because adding 1 to &HFFFF will clear all its bits, making it zero, you can see why True has a numeric value of -1. (See Explore and Discover exercise C-1 at the end of this Appendix.)

- Some operators operate bit-wise. For example, the logical operators such as And and Or operate by bit. When you understand the binary number system, you will be able to understand the results of the operations much more easily. The bit-wise logical operators are discussed in the next section.

- Some numbers are more conveniently represented by hex numbers. Each hex digit can represent a certain state more readily.

- Some constants are traditionally represented by hex numbers. For example, the parameter constants used in API (an acronym for Application Program Interface) calls are all in hex representation. Getting acquainted with the hex number system will alleviate your fear of the mystery associated with this representation.

C.2 Bit-Wise Operation of Logical Operators

Most VB logical operators actually operate on data on a bit-by-bit basis and can be used to perform operations not only on Boolean data but also on integer (Long, Integer and Short) data (see Figure C.1). In this context, a bit is considered True when it is on (with a value 1) and False when it is off (with a value 0). (Notice that the context is *a bit not a data field*.)

Figure C.1

Bitwise operation of logical operators

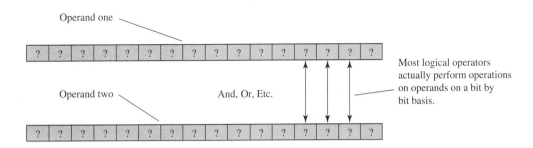

Operand one

And, Or, Etc.

Operand two

Most logical operators actually perform operations on operands on a bit by bit basis.

The Not, And, Or, Xor Operators

The following discussion focuses on four operators commonly used in the bit-wise operation: Not, And, Or, and Xor.

The Not Operator. Specifically, the *Not operator* will reverse the on or off state of each bit; that is, an on bit will become off, and an off bit will become on, as shown in Figure C.2.

Incidentally, recall that a Boolean variable takes two bytes of storage. False is coded with all the bits turned off, so in the hex decimal representation, it is &H0000, which, if assigned to a Short variable, should have a value of 0. Applying a Not operation on the value will result in all bits being turned on to become &HFFFF, representing True, equivalent to a value -1.

The And Operator. The *And operator* will produce a result of 1 (on) if both its operands' corresponding bits are 1 (on); otherwise, the result will be 0 (off), as shown in Figure C.3.

The Or Operator. The *Or operator* will produce a result of 1 if either of the corresponding bit operands is 1 (on); otherwise, the result will be 0 (off), as illustrated in Figure C.4.

The Xor Operator. The *Xor operator* will produce a result of 1 (on) if *one and only one* of the two bit operands is on; otherwise, the bit will be 0 (off), as shown in Figure C.5.

Various Uses of the Logical Operators

Now you know how the bit-wise operators work, but how are they used and for what? The following discussion highlights some of these operators' uses.

Setting a Flag. These operators can be used to set, test, or toggle Flags. A *Flag* is a bit of data representing the on/off state of something. A Flag is on when that particular bit is set to 1, and off when it is set to 0. Because a Short variable has 16 bits, it is often used to hold a group of

Figure C.2

The Not operation

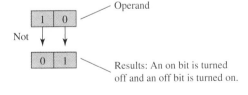

Operand

Not

Results: An on bit is turned off and an off bit is turned on.

Figure C.3

The And operation

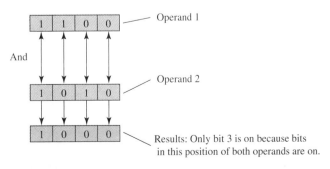

Operand 1

And

Operand 2

Results: Only bit 3 is on because bits in this position of both operands are on.

Figure C.4

The Or operation

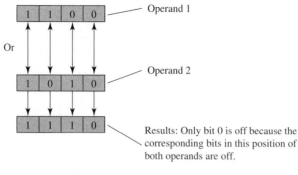

Operand 1

Or

Operand 2

Results: Only bit 0 is off because the corresponding bits in this position of both operands are off.

Figure C.5

The Xor operation

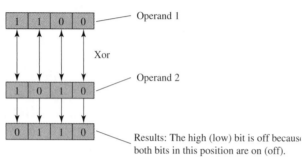

Operand 1

Xor

Operand 2

Results: The high (low) bit is off because both bits in this position are on (off).

Flags. As an illustration, suppose you have a Short variable, Flags that you want to use to represent several classifications of an account. You want to use the lowest bit to represent whether the account affects cash flow and the second lowest bit to represent whether the account is a control account. As you may recall from the preceding section (C.1), the lowest bit has a numeric value of 1 when it is on; and the second lowest bit has a numeric value of 2 when it is on. If you want to set the lowest bit on, you can code the following:

```
Flags = Flags Or 1
```

Recall that the Or operator will set the resulting bit to 1 when either of the operands (bits) is 1. In this case, the second operand has only its lowest bit set on (to 1). When the two operands are Ored, the result will be exactly the same as that for Flags, except that its lowest bit will be on regardless of its previous status. This result can then be assigned to Flags to reflect the Flags' new state. This operation is illustrated in Figure C.6.

By the same token, to set the second lowest bit on, you code the following:

```
Flags = Flags Or 2
```

Figure C.6

Setting a Flag with the Or operator

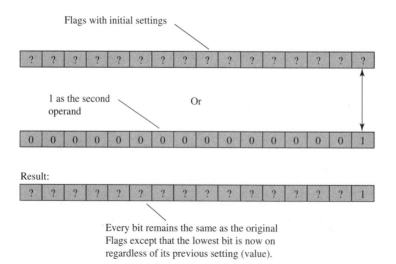

Flags with initial settings

1 as the second operand

Or

Result:

Every bit remains the same as the original Flags except that the lowest bit is now on regardless of its previous setting (value).

Testing a Flag. To test whether the lowest bit of Flags has been set on, you can use the And operator. For example, you can code the following:

```
Test = Flags And 1
```

Again, recall that the result of an And operation will be 1 (on) for a bit only if both corresponding operands are 1 (on). The result will be 1 only if Flags' lowest bit is also on, as illustrated in Figure C.7.

By the same token, you can test whether the second lowest bit is on by coding the following:

```
Test = Flags And 2
```

Testing for an Odd or Even Number. The previous illustration of testing whether the lowest bit of Flags is on has an additional interesting application. You may be aware that all odd integers have the lowest bit on, whereas even integers have it off. The same code can be used to test whether a number is odd or even. To experiment and verify, place a text box and a button on a new form. Name the text box **txtNumber** and the button **btnTest**. Also, set the Text property of the button to **Test**; then, type in the following code:

```
Private Sub btnTest_Click(ByVal Sender As Object, ByVal e As
   System.EventArgs) Handles btnTest.Click
      Dim Test As Integer
      Test = CInt(txtNumber.Text) And 1
      If Test = 0 Then
          'The lowest bit is off. This is an even number.
          MsgBox(txtNumber.Text & " is an even number.")
      Else
          'The lowest bit is on. This is an odd number.
          MsgBox(txtNumber.Text & " is an odd number.")
      End If
End Sub
```

After you run the project, enter a number and then click the Test button. The program should be able to tell you whether you have entered an odd or even number.

Toggling a Flag. The Xor operator also has a very interesting application. Often, it is used to toggle a Flag; that is, to turn a Flag from one state to the other. As explained earlier, this operator sets the result of a bit to 1 only when one of the two operands is 1 (on), so if you repetitively perform the Xor operation with a constant "on" bit to another operand, this latter operand will be off when it was originally on and on when it was originally off. That is, you can use the following code to change the setting of its lowest bit:

```
Flags = Flags Xor 1 'Toggle the lowest bit
```

Figure C.7

Testing a Flag with the And operator

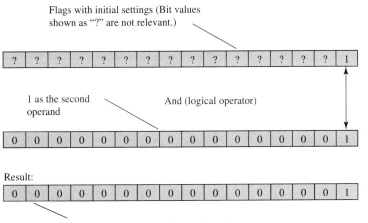

Flags with initial settings (Bit values shown as "?" are not relevant.)

| ? | ? | ? | ? | ? | ? | ? | ? | ? | ? | ? | ? | ? | ? | ? | 1 |

1 as the second operand   And (logical operator)

| 0 | 0 | 0 | 0 | 0 | 0 | 0 | 0 | 0 | 0 | 0 | 0 | 0 | 0 | 0 | 1 |

Result:

| 0 | 0 | 0 | 0 | 0 | 0 | 0 | 0 | 0 | 0 | 0 | 0 | 0 | 0 | 0 | 1 |

The result will be either 0 or 1 depending on the setting of the lowest bit in Flags; all other bits will be off (0) because of all the other zeros in the second operand.

In addition, if you execute the same line of code again, the setting of its lowest bit is restored to its original value. The Xor operation is illustrated in Figure C.8.

Again, by the same token, you can toggle the second lowest bit by coding the following:

```
Flags = Flags Xor 2 'Toggle the second lowest bit
```

Use of the Xor Operator for Encryption. The toggling capability of Xor makes it a popular operator to perform encryption operations. If some data is Xored with a "password" (or key), the data changes its original value; however, when the encrypted data is Xored again with the same password, the data is restored to its original value.

Here is a highly simplified example. Set up a new project as follows:

1. Place a text box and two labels on a new form.

2. Name the text box **txtOriginal**, the first label **lblEncrypted**, and the second **lblDecrypted**.

3. Clear the Text property of the text box, and set the properties of the two labels so that they look like blank text boxes (by setting BackColor to white and BorderStyle to fixed 3D).

Figure C.9 shows the visual interface in action.

Assume you want to use the letter X as the password for encryption. Enter the following code in your new project:

```
Private Sub txtOriginal_KeyPress(ByVal sender As Object, ByVal e
    As System.Windows.Forms.KeyPressEventArgs) Handles
    txtOriginal.KeyPress
    Dim Encrypted As Integer
    Dim Decrypted As Integer
    Dim KeyAscii As Integer
    ' Encrypt the key being entered with "X"
```

Figure C.8

Toggling a Flag with the Xor operator

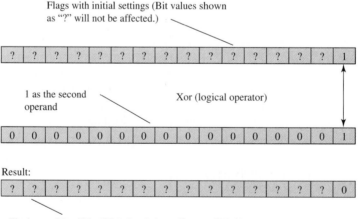

Flags with initial settings (Bit values shown as "?" will not be affected.)

1 as the second operand

Xor (logical operator)

Result:

The lowest bit will be either 0 or 1 depending on the setting of the lowest bit in Flags; repeating the same operation will thus reverse the current result. Other bits will not be affected. The second operand has all zeros in these bits. Any value Xored with a zero will still have the same value.

Figure C.9

Visual interface for the encryption example

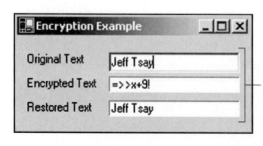

With the code below, whatever the user types into the textbox (txtOriginal), will be encrypted and shown in the second blank (lblEncrypted), which is then decrypted and displayed in the third blank (lblDecrypted).

```
        KeyAscii = AscW(e.KeyChar)
        Encrypted = KeyAscii Xor Keys.X
        ' Add the encrypted key to the encrypted label
        lblEncrypted.Text &= Chr(Encrypted)
        ' Restore the encryption by applying the same "password"
        Decrypted = Encrypted Xor Keys.X
        ' Add the restored key to the restored label
        lblDecrypted.Text &= Chr(Decrypted)
    End Sub
```

The encryption/decryption routine is placed in the text box's KeyPress event, which is triggered when the user enters a key into the text box. This procedure has an event argument, KeyChar that gives the key pressed. The code first obtains the key code (Asc) value of this key and then encrypts this value by Xoring it with the ASCII value of X (Keys.X). The encrypted character (along with all previously encrypted characters) is displayed in the label named lblEncrypted. The encrypted ASCII value is then transformed with another Xor operation using the same password (Keys.X). This operation should restore the key to what was originally entered. The decrypted key (along with all previously restored keys) is displayed in the label named lblDecrypted.

Run the project and enter some text into the text box. As you enter a key, you should be able to see the encrypted result in lblEncrypted. You should also be able to verify that the decrypted text in lblDecrypted is the same as the text you originally entered.

Note that this routine ignores the possibility that the user may press a control key such as the Enter key or the Backspace key. You should be able to fine tune the program before finishing this appendix. The refinement is left to you to complete.

The following table summarizes the use of logical operators in bit-wise operations.

Operator Example Result Remark	Operation	Example	Result	Remark
Not	Reverse the content	Not &HFFFF	&H0000	Not - 1 = 0; that is, Not True = False
And	1 only if both corresponding bits are 1	&H0F And &HF033	3	Can be used to test whether certain bits are on and to mask off certain bits
Or	1 if one of the corresponding bits is 1	&H0F Or &H03	&H0F	Can be used to turn on certain bits
Xor	1 only if one (but not both) of the corresponding its is one	&H0F Xor &H03	&H0C	Can be used to toggle certain bits and to encrypt data

Summary

- Human beings count from 0 to 9 before adding another digit in presenting the number. In contrast, computers operate on bits (binary digits) and bytes. The number system human beings use is recognized as the decimal system; the number system the computer operates is recognized as the binary system.
- To simplify the representation of a binary number, the hex decimal system has been introduced. Under this system, each digit has 16 possible values (0 to 15) and can be used to represent four bits.
- To find the corresponding decimal value for any binary or hex decimal representation, multiply the bits/hex digits by their corresponding positional value and sum the total.
- To find the binary/hex representation for a decimal number, divide the number by two/sixteen and find the remainder, which is the bit/hex value for the lowest position.

Then divide the integer quotient by two/sixteen again to obtain the bit/hex value for the next higher position. Repeat this process to find the bit/hex value for each successive position until the resulting quotient is zero.

- Most of the logical operators such as Not, And, Or, and Xor are bit-wise operators. They set the results of the operation on a bit-by-bit basis.

- The Not operator can be used to reverse the content or status of flags; the And operator can be used to test whether a particular bit is on or off as well as to test whether a number is odd or even; the Or operator can be used to turn on a bit; and the Xor operator can be used to toggle bits as well as to encrypt or decrypt data.

Explore and Discover

Note: To test any code in these Explore and Discover exercises, set Option Strict Off.

C-1. Some Hex Values of Interest. Enter the following code in the form's Click event procedure. Run the project, click any part of the form, and examine the results.

```
Console.WriteLine(&HFF)
Console.WriteLine(&HFF%)
Console.WriteLine(&HFFFFFFFF%)
Console.WriteLine(&HFFFFFFFF&)
```

What values do you get? The first two values should give you no surprises. But what about the last two values? Why are they different? The value &HFFFFFFFF% is of the Integer type. The four bytes holding the value have all the bits on. The highest bit of a number represents its sign. When it is on, it is a negative number. Its complement (whatever is required to add the value to zero) is the number's negative value. Adding 1 to &HFFFFFFFF% will clear all bits, making it zero; therefore, &HFFFFFFFF% is -1.

The value &HFFFFFFFF& is a Long integer (because an & type suffix is attached). Its lower four bytes are all on, but its higher four bytes are all zero; that is, its internal coding is actually &H00000000FFFFFFFF&. It is a positive number, and is 4294967295. (Perform the conversion as discussed in the text to verify.)

C-2. Numeric Value of True and False. Enter the following code in the form's Click event procedure. Run the project, click any part of the form, and examine the results. What numeric values do True and False have?

```
MsgBox("10 times True is " & 10 * True)
MsgBox("10 plus True is " & 10 + True)
MsgBox("10 times False is " & 10 * False)
MsgBox("10 plus False is " & 10 + False)
```

True is internally coded as a two-byte integer with all its bits on: &HFFFF, which is -1. False is internally coded as a two-byte integer with all its bits off: &H0000, so it is numerically zero.

C-3. Use of Logical Operators. Relational operators work on both numeric and string data. Can logical operators do the same? Try the following statements. (*Hint:* To test them, place these lines in the Form Click event procedure with a Dim A as Integer statement at the beginning; then insert a line of code to display the result between the lines below.)

```
A = "34" And "32"
A = "34" Or 32
A = "XY" Or "AB"
```

Why do the first two run, but not the last? (*Answer:* Logical operators work on numeric data only. Data type conversions are performed automatically by VB in the first two cases, making the code executable. It is impossible to convert the strings to numbers in the last case, so the operation fails.)

C-4.   The Value Property of the Radio Button. Place two radio buttons on a new form and then enter the following code:

```
Dim A As Integer
Private Sub RadioButton1_Click(ByVal sender As Object, ByVal e As
    System.EventArgs) Handles RadioButton1.Click
    A = RadioButton1.Checked
    MsgBox("A = " & A)
End Sub
Private Sub RadioButton2_Click(ByVal sender As Object, ByVal e As
    System.EventArgs) Handles RadioButton2.Click
    A = RadioButton1.Checked
    MsgBox("A = " & A)
End Sub
```

Run the project, and alternately click the two radio buttons. What value of A do you see each time? The numeric value for True is -1 (&HFFFF) and for False is 0 (&H0000).

C-5.   The Value Property of the Check Box. Place a check box on a new form. Enter the following code:

```
Dim A As Integer
Private Sub CheckBox1_Click(ByVal sender As Object, ByVal e As
    System.EventArgs) Handles CheckBox1.Click
    A = CheckBox1.Checked
    MsgBox("A = " & A)
End Sub
```

Run the project and then click the check box. What result do you see each time? When the box is checked? And when it is unchecked? Are they the same as the radio buttons?

C-6.   Assigning a Value to the Boolean Variable. Place a text box and a button on a new form. Name the text box **txtNumber** and the button **btnCheck**. Set the button's Text property to **Check**. Enter the following code:

```
Private Sub btnCheck_Click(ByVal Sender As Object, ByVal e As
    System.EventArgs) Handles btnCheck.Click
    Dim TheNumber As Single
    Dim BoolTest As Boolean
    TheNumber = Val(txtNumber.Text)
    BoolTest = TheNumber
    MsgBox("The resulting Boolean value is " & BoolTest)
    If BoolTest = TheNumber Then
        MsgBox("BoolTest and TheNumber are equal.")
    Else
        MsgBox("BoolTest and TheNumber are Not equal.")
    End If
End Sub
```

Run the program. Enter any number (try at least these numbers: 1000, -30, 0.005, and 0) and then click the button. What does the computer display? What conclusion can you draw from this experiment? What do you also learn? (*Answer:* Any nonzero value will be converted to True for a Boolean variable. Only a value of 0 is interpreted as False. Beware of the potential problem with comparing a Boolean variable with a variable of another data type after assigning the same value to both when you set Option Strict Off.)

C-7. **Playing with the Truth.** Enter the following code in the code window of a new project:

```
Private Sub Form1_Click(ByVal sender As Object, ByVal e As
    System.EventArgs) Handles MyBase.Click
        Dim B As Boolean
        Dim L As Integer
        Dim S As String
        B = 3 = 3
        L = 3 = 3
        S = 3 = 3
        MsgBox("B = " & B & ", L = " & L & ", S = " & S)
        MsgBox("Len(B) = " & Len(B) & ", Len(L) = " & Len(L) _
          & ", Len(S) = " & Len(S))
        S = L
        MsgBox("S = " & S & ", Len(S) = " & Len(S))
End Sub
```

Run the project and then click on the form. Does everything turn out to be as expected? Why does S have a length of 4 at one time and then 2 at another time? Should True have a length of two or four?

C-8. **Using the And Operator on the Same Value.** Draw a text box and a button on a new form. Name the text box **txtNumber** and clear its text. Name the button **btnAnd** and set its Text property to **And**. Place the following code in the code window:

```
Private Sub btnAnd_Click(ByVal Sender As Object, ByVal e As
    System.EventArgs) Handles btnAnd.Click
        Dim N As Integer
        Dim R As Integer
        R = Val(txtNumber.Text)
        N = R And R
        MsgBox("The result is " & N)
End Sub
```

Run the project. Enter an integer number and then click the And button. Repeat the same experiment with different numbers. What results do you see? (The corresponding bits of the two operands are the same. The result of the And operation should be the same as the operand.)

C-9. **Using the Or Operator on the Same Value.** (continued from exercise C-8) Add a button to the form in C-8. Name it **btnOr** and set its Text property to **Or**. Place the following code in the code window:

```
Private Sub btnOr_Click(ByVal Sender As Object, ByVal e As
    System.EventArgs) Handles btnOr.Click
        Dim N As Integer
        Dim R As Integer
        R = Val(txtNumber.Text)
        N = R Or R
        MsgBox("The result is " & N)
End Sub
```

Run the project. Enter an integer number and then click the Or button. Repeat the same experiment with different numbers. What results do you see? (The corresponding bits of the two operands are the same. The result of the Or operation should be the same as the operand.)

C-10. **Use of the Xor Operator on the Same Value.** (continued from exercise C-9) Add another button to the form in C-9. Name the button **btnXor** and set its Text property to **Xor**. Place the following code in the code window:

```
Private Sub btnXor_Click(ByVal Sender As Object, ByVal e As
    System.EventArgs) Handles btnXor.Click
      Dim N As Integer
      Dim R As Integer
      R = Val(txtNumber.Text)
      N = R Xor R
      MsgBox("The result is " & N)
End Sub
```

Run the project. Enter an integer number and then click the Xor button. Repeat the same experiment with different numbers. What result do you see? (The corresponding bits of the two operands are the same. The result of the Xor operation should give zero.) Can you generalize the results of performing the And, Or, and Xor operations on the same number?

Exercises

C-11.   Converting Numbers Between Systems.

   A. Convert the following numbers to binary values:
   - 41
   - 255
   - 4095

   B. Convert the following numbers to hex values:
   - 1000
   - 255
   - 32768 (*Hint:* Check the result in C below for verification.)

   C. What are the decimal values of the following hex numbers? (*Hint:* To verify your computation, write simple code to obtain the results; that is Console.WriteLine(&HFF) will print 255.)
   - &H1000
   - &HFFFE
   - &H10000
   - &H10000&

C-12.   **Testing Divisibility by 4.** In this appendix, you have learned how you can test whether an integer is an odd or even number. The same idea can also be used to test whether a number is divisible by 4 by using the And operator. A number is divisible by 4 when its lowest two bits are zero.

Place a text box and a button on a new form. Name the text box txtNumber and the button btnTest and then provide the code to test whether the number the user has entered into the text box is divisible by 4. (*Hint:* Use the And operator. A number with all bits off but the lowest two bits on has a value of 3.)

Use the MsgBox to display the result. Also, use the Mod operator to test the same (place the code in the Form Click event). Compare the results obtained from both approaches.

C-13.   **Encrypting a Number.** A company keeps its employees' salary data in a file in encrypted form. The data-entry screen for the salary data has a masked edit box for the employee number such as the Social Security number (SSN) and a text box for the salary amount. When the user clicks the Save button, the salary amount is encrypted and then saved. Both the SSN and the salary are internally treated as Integers. The Xor operation is performed on the salary using the SSN as the key. The result is displayed in a label. Your program then displays a message, "Salary saved." (*Note:* Just display the encrypted result and the message. Ignore the Save operation.)

C-14.   **Playing with the Flags.** You have three check boxes in a general ledger account entry form with the following captions:

- Is this a control account? (Question 1)
- Is this a contra account? (Question 2)
- Does this account affect cash flow? (Question 3)

You have decided to handle these questions internally with a Flags variable; that is, values in these check boxes will be collectively stored in only one Short variable named Flags. Bits 0, 1, and 2 will be used to keep track of questions 1, 2, and 3, respectively. When a check box is checked, its corresponding bit will be set on; when it is unchecked, its corresponding bit will be set off.

Provide the code to handle these Flags and display the results (the value of Flags) when a change occurs. (*Hint:* Place the code in the check boxes' Click event handlers. Use the And operator to turn a Flag off and the Or operator to turn a Flag on. Use a label [name it **lblResult**] to display the value of Flags at the end of each Click event. When all three Flags are on, Flags should have a value of 7.)

C-15.   **Rotating Background Colors.** Write a procedure that rotates the background color of a label, lblSign, in blue, red, green, yellow, and back to blue each time the user clicks a button named btnChange, captioned "Change." (*Hint:* Use a Static integer variable to keep track of the count. Use the And operator [although you could use Mod] to generate the number sequence 0, 1, 2, 3, 0, 1 . . . and so on, which can then be used in a Select Case block.)

C-16.   **Rotating Background Colors Automatically.** Modify the preceding project (C-15) so that the colors are rotated automatically every half of a second once your program starts.

C-17.   **Alternative Solution to the Exploration Problem.** Refer to the oil exploration investment decision example presented in Chapter 5, "Decision." The problem has an alternative solution. Write a line of code using relational and logical operators to come up with a correct value for the variable Invest. (*Question:* Which coding alternative executes more efficiently?)

Index

A

absolute termination criterion, 260
abstract classes/methods, 567
AcceptButton property, forms, 53
AcceptChanges method, datasets, 378–379
Access, MS Jet data engine, 357, 361–363.
  See also databases
access keys, 420–422, 449–451, 453, 463
accessing Web services, 626
Activated event, forms, 505
ActiveControl, Select statement, 429
ActiveX data objects (ADO), 361
Add method
  adding data tables to datasets, 398
  collection object, 326–327
  command parameter setup, ADO.NET, 383
Add New Item dialog box, adding forms, 468
Add Web Reference dialog box, 626
AddExtension property, file dialog boxes
  (Open/Save), 215
AddHandler statement, 535, 547
addition (+) operator, 131
AddRange method, collection object, 328–329
ADO (ActiveX data objects), 361
ADO.NET, 361–362
  code, 382
    binding datasets to controls, 384
    calling data commands directly,
      389–390
    coding data grids, 388
    command parameter setup, 383–384
    connection string setup, 383
    data adapter command object setup,
      383, 386–388
    DataReader object, 395–397
    declaring variables, 382, 386
    generating dataset schema, 384
    maintaining data in datasets, 388
    saving datasets locally, 390
  data adapter, 362–370
  data rows/columns, 362
  datasets, 362
  query parameters, 370–371
  updating databases, 374–382
  viewing single records, 372–374
AfterSelect event, TreeView control,
  467–468
algorithms for sorting data. See sorting data
alignment
  buttons, 52–53
  labels, 34, 4748, 54
  picture boxes, 87

Alphabetic icon (Properties window), 24
Alt key
  control access keys, 420–421
  representing with percentage symbol
    (%), 420
ampersand (&) character
  menu access keys, 421, 449, 463
  showing in text property, 421
  string concatenation, 32, 143–144
Anchor property
  buttons, 52
  labels, 104
And/AndAlso operators, 169
  And versus AndAlso, 195
angle brackets (< >)
  attribute marker, 625
  not equal relational operator (logical
    expressions), 166
apostrophe ('), code comments, 7, 31
Appearance property, Tab control, 422
application examples. See projects
Application object, 437
ApplicationException class, 581
applications. See also programs
  multiple document interface (MDI)
    applications. See MDI applications
  multiple-form applications. See
    multiple-form applications
  Web forms. See Web forms
    applications
arguments
  creating, 563–564
  positioning, 242
  relationship with parameters, 241
  Sub procedure argument position/type,
    220
arithmetic operations, 130–131, 135
arrays, 295
  appropriate usage, 337
  bubble sorts, 311–314, 351
  Clear method, 336
  collection object, 326–330
  copying data between arrays
    Copy method, 345
    CopyTo method, 336
  declarations
    one-dimensional arrays, 296
    position of named constants, 342
    static arrays, 342
    two-dimensional arrays, 330–331
    using variables, 342
  displaying contents in list boxes/combo
    boxes, 335
  Length property, 335

  one-dimensional, 296–300
  quick sorts, 319–324
  random sampling without replacement,
    307–310
  Rank property, 335
  ranks, 334, 346
  ReDim statement, 343
    preserving data, 335, 344
    syntax, 297–298
  reinitializing portions of array with
    Clear method, 336
  releasing (Erase statement), 335
  returning from functions, 345
  reversing order of elements, 336
  searching, 310, 324–326
    binary insertion sorts, 317,
      325–326, 351
    Binary Search method, 336
    sequential search with sorted data,
      324–325
  simplified selection, 300–301
  simulating/approximating
    probabilities, 305–307, 349,
      352–353
  sorting, 310–311
    bubble sorts, 311–314, 351
    comparison of performance of sorts,
      324
    efficiency, 314
    quick sorts, 319–324, 352
    shell sorts, 317–319, 351–352
    simple selection sorts, 314, 351
    Sort method, 336
    straight insertion sorts, 315–317
  static arrays, 342
  straight insertion sorts, 315–317
  table look up, 302–303
  tracking random occurrences,
    303–305
  two-dimensional arrays, 330–335,
    353–354
arrow keys (up/down), 420, 453
Asc function, 144–146
Asc keyword, sorting returned tables, 358
AscW function, 144–146
assignment statements, 42
  logical expressions, 168
  numeric data, 128–129
asterisk (*) character
  multiplication operator, 131
  specifying all fields in table, 358
attributes, 622
  attribute marker (<>), 625
  Web services, 622

Audio, Beep command, 53
Auto Hide, Toolbox, 22
AutoFlush property (StreamWriter object), 239–240
AutoSize property, labels, 37
autotabbing, masked edit boxes, 419

B

background color (BackColor property)
    buttons, 52
    forms, random, 55–57
    labels, 33, 36, 52–55
    Tab control, 422
BankDepositor project, 536–539
banners, *55, 56*
base classes, 558
BASIC language, 2
Beep command, 53
binary search algorithm, 325–326, 351
    insertion sorts, 317
Binary Search method, arrays, 336
binding
    data grids to datasets, 369
    datasets to controls, by code, 384
block-level declaration, 120
blocks, 31
    general applicability, 7
    If. See If blocks
    Select Case. See Select Case blocks
Boolean data type, 123–125
boolean variables, assigning values, 196
BorderStyle property
    labels, 52
    Tab control, 422
bound controls, displaying related table contents, 403–404
boundaries, arrays, 299–300
braces { }
    code syntax, 11
    sending symbols as their original keystrokes, 418, 420
brackets [ ], keywords in variable declarations, 117
breakpoints, Do . . . Loops, 256–258
browsing database schema, 390–395
    querying, 391–395
    using data relations, 398–400
bubble sorts, 311–314. See also sorting data
    adding a counter in inner loop, 351
    comparisons, 311–312
        swapping elements, 311
        performance of sorts, 324
    declaring arrays, 313
    displaying sort results, 314
    efficiency, 314
    generating random numbers, 313
    simple selection sorts, 314
    Sub procedure, 312
        calling sort procedure, 314
        computing sort time, 314
        testing sort procedure, 313
    versus insertion sorts, 317
building component projects, 602
built-in string functions, 144–148
    Asc, 144–146

button Click event, 90
buttons. See also objects
    Accept, 53
    access keys, 420–422, 449–451, 453
    adding to forms, 25–26
    alignment, 52, 53
    background color, 52
    Cancel button, 53
    clarity in labeling/messaging, 414
    Click event, 77, 101–102
    IDE toolbar, 20–21
    MsgBox buttons parameter, 206–208, 239
    Properties window, 24
    Quit, 49
    radio buttons, 74–76, 77, 78, 104, 110
    resizing, 26
    Solution Explorer, 23
    text
        font, 52
        Text property, 26
        TextAlign property, 104
    toggling, 199
    using both images and text, 105
    Web forms buttons versus HTML buttons, 635–636
ByRef keyword, 221–222, 243–244
Byte data type, 123–125
ByVal keyword, 221–222, 243–244

C

C or c (Currency) format, 136
calling
    Call keyword, 224–226
    procedures, standard modules, 475
    Sub procedures, 218–220
        argument position/type, 220
CancelButton property, forms, 53
cascading event procedures, 228
case, LCase/UCase functions, 145–147
Case statement. See Select Case blocks
Cashflow Entry Form, 327–330
    adding controls by code, 327–328
    creating specified number of text boxes, 328
    creating visual interface, 328–329
    invoking ShowBoxes sub, 329
    referencing text boxes in collection, 330
Categorized icon (Properties window), 24
CausesValidation property, 431
    checking for missing data, 431–432
    IsDate/IsNumeric functions, 433
    minimizing code, 433
    setting, 432–433
    troubleshooting, 435
    verifying input with users, 434
Char data type, 123–125
check box control, 76–78
    Checked property, 104
    CheckState property, 104
    Click event, 77, 91
    clicking repeatedly, 104
    enabling/disabling controls, 109
CheckDate function, 226
checked list box control, 81–82, 105

Checked property
    check boxes, 76–78, 104
    radio buttons, 74–76
CheckedChanged event, radio buttons, 78
CheckFileExists property, file dialog boxes (Open/Save), 215
CheckPathExists property, file dialog boxes (Open/Save), 215
CheckState property, check box control, 78, 104
child forms. See MDI applications
Chr function, 144–146
class modules, 118, 515
    adding to projects, 517
    scope, 517
    versus standard modules, 515–517
class-level declaration, 118–121
classes, 514–515. See also objects
    abstract classes, 567
    advantages of object-oriented programming, 514–515
    ApplicationException, 581
    building, 524–525
        adding class modules to projects, 517
        class modules versus standard modules, 515–517
        constructors, 523–524
        creating classes, 517
        creating methods, 520–522
        creating properties, 518–520
        setting default properties, 523–524
    collection classes, 574
    declaring events, 529
        benefits of events, 534
        event declaration syntax, 529
        example, 530
        using declared events, 532
    enumerated constants, 525–526
        effect on code, 526
        Enum statement, 525–526
        revising property procedures, 526
        throwing exceptions, 527–529
    hooking event handlers, 534–535, 547
    instantiation, 122
    members, 514, 517
    nested classes, 535–539
    raising events
        example, 530–531
        RaiseEvent statement syntax, 529
    using, 523–525
        properties, 518–519
    versus objects, 514
classification of data, 114
Clear method
    arrays, 336
    datasets, 371
Click event, 33, 90–91, 94
    buttons, 90
    check boxes, 77, 91
    DoubleClick event (list boxes), 91–92
    menu control, 463–464
    picture box, 87
    radio buttons, 77, 91
client computers, 608
client-side scripts, 608

Clipboard object, 632–633
Clipboard Ring tab (Toolbox), 21
Close method
    polymorphism, 571–573
    StreamReader object, 210, 212
    StreamWriter object, 213
        W–4 Form project, 281
code, 5. See also coding
    blocks, 31. See also blocks
    code behind, Web forms applications,
        612–613
    code modules, 474–478, 482–484, 480,
        488, 500
    comments, 7, 31
    effect of enumerated constants, 526
    line continuation, 32
    maintainability, 7
    minimizing code
        key verification, 427–428
        large projects, 500
        validating data at field level, 433
    modularity, 7
    object–oriented code structure, 3–4
    repetitive code, 427
    structure
        assignment statements, 42
        execution control, 42–43
    testing, 9
code window, 22
    adding code, 26–27
    class modules, 118
    general declaration area, 118
    Object box, 33
    placement of variable declaration
        statements, 118
    Procedure box, 33–34
    switching among code windows, 468
    toggling between form and code
        window, 22
    viewing available events, 33–34
coding, 31–32. See also ADO.NET. syntax
    adding code to code window, 26–27
        IntelliSense, 27
    blocks, 31
    comments, 31
    component projects, 599–601
        building projects, 602
        component constructors, 601
        component destructors, 601–602
        testing components, 602–604
        using components in projects, 604
    event procedures, 99–102
    If blocks
        code clarity/alternatives, 181–183
        comments, 179
        efficiency, 180–181
        indenting, 179
        syntax versus semantic, 180
    line continuation, 32
    mechanics, 6–7
    multiple statements on a line, 32
    standards for sound programs, 6–7
    TreeView control, 467–468
    With . . . End With structure, 150
collection classes, creating, 574
collection object, 326–330

collections, referencing objects by index
    using For . . . Next loops, 272
color
    buttons, 52
    forms, 55–57
    labels, 33, 36, 52–55
    rotating, 200
    foreground, labels, 54–55
    text boxes, 109
Color dialog box, 241
columns. See tables
combo box control, 83–86
    displaying array contents, 335
    FindString/FindStringExact methods,
        280
    methods, 84
    properties, 84–86
    SelectedIndex property, Form Load
        event, 90
    SelectedIndexChanged event, 92
    versus list box control, 85–86
comma (,) character
    Format function, 137
    handling in name text boxes, 427
    ranks (arrays), 334
    Select statement, separating field
        names, 358
commands
    creating menus. See menus
    data adapters, 383, 386–388, 402
        calling data commands directly,
            389–390
    File menu, 28, 29
    Help menu, 37, 38
    IDE menu bar, 20
    parameters, ADO.NET, 383–384
    Start menu, 50
    Tools menu, Customize Toolbox, 63
    View menu, 21, 23, 24
comments, 7, 31
    general procedures, 226–227
    If blocks, 179
common properties, 35–36
CompareValidator control, Web forms
    applications, 618
comparisons
    relational operators
        numeric, 166
        operand conversion issues, 167
        string, 167–168
compilers, 2
components, 597–608
    Dispose method, 580
    including Web services, 636
    user controls, 608
    with visual elements (controls),
        605–608
    without visual elements, 597–604
computations
    FICA withholding, 202, 247–248
    Net Sale project, 135
    performing computations using
        Do . . . Loops. See Do Loop
        structure
    restaurant guest checks, 202–203
concatenation, 143–144

conditional execution, 43
conditions, Do . . . Loop structure, 252, 283
configuring data adapter (ADO.NET),
    363–365
connection objects
    connection string setup, 383
    variable declaration, 382, 386
Const statement, 114
constants, 114
    array declaration, 342
    class level constants, 118
    declaring, 114–115, 121
        form (class)-level declaration,
            118–119
        Net Sale project, 134–135
        overlapping declarations in form
            and procedure, 120–121
        procedure-level declaration,
            118–119
        type suffixes, 115–116
    enumerated constants, 525–526
        effect on code, 526
        Enum statement, 525–526
        revising property procedures, 526
        throwing exceptions, 527–529
    lifetime, 118
        form (class)-level declaration,
            118–121
        procedure-level declaration,
            118–119
    local constants, 118–119
        overlapping declarations in form
            and procedure, 120–121
    named constants, 114
    naming conventions, 115–116, 123
    scope, 118
        form (class)-level declaration,
            118–121
        procedure-level declaration,
            118–119
    Select Case blocks, 187
    string constants, breaking into multiple
        lines, 32
    symbolic constants, 114
    system constants, 114
constructors, 523–524
    components, 601
containers, 69, 88
Contents tab (help file), 38
context (pop–up) menus, 463
context sensitive help, 38
ControlBox property, forms, 53
    keeping forms from unloading, 474
ControlChar.Cr, 418
ControlChars.Tab, 418
controls, 3, 30
    access keys, 420–422, 449–451, 453
    adding to forms, 327–328
    ADO.NET controls, 363
    binding datasets to controls by code,
        384
    checked list box control, 81–82
    clearing form controls, 292
    components, 605–608
    containers, 69
    Context Menu, 463

design principles, 87–88
displaying related table contents with
   bound controls, 403–404
enabling/disabling, 109, 110
focus, 62
formatting field contents with Leave
   event, 94
group box, 68–71, 74–76
hiding, 70–71
Hyperlink control, 621
Main Menu, 461. See also menus
masked edit box, 62–68
naming conventions, 88–89
progress bar, 446–448
properties, setting, 70
restoring field contents with Enter
   event, 93–94
tab control, 71–74, 422, 453
   creating tab pages on a form, 72
tab order, 89
user controls, 608
VB controls versus execution control, 33
conversions
   conversion functions, 139–140
   data, 197
      strict data type conversion (string
         data), 144
      strict implicit type conversion,
         127–128, 156
   data types, 131–132, 167, 196
   operand conversion issues (logical
      expressions), 167
Copy method, arrays, 345
CopyTo method, arrays, 336
Count property
   collection object, 326
   TreeView control, 467
Counter variable (For . . . Next loop), 261
   changing counter value, 285
   data types, 286–287
   value after Exit For, 286
counting
   frequency count (arrays), 303–304,
      305–307, 349, 352–353
   letters (arrays), 304–305
   list box items
Create Table statement (SQL), 361
criteria, Select Case blocks, 185–186,
   197–198
CType function (For Each . . . Next
   structure), 271
Currency (C or c) format, 136
cursor 415, 444–445
custom dialog boxes, 470–471
   building, 493–496
   invoking, 493
customizing
   debugger, 257
   IDE, 18–19
   Toolbox, 63–64

D

data
   classifications, 114
   converting, 197

erasing data fields, 236
passing data to Sub procedures
   by name, 221, 242
   by position, 220–221, 242
   ByVal versus ByRef, 221–222,
      243–244
protection against data loss, 415
   detecting unsaved data, 423–424
   handling unsaved data at Quit, 424
saving data fields, 236
sharing data between forms, 472–474
swapping between two variables,
   129–130
data access, Web forms, 615–618
Data Adapter Configuration Wizard, 363–365
data adapters
   ADO.NET, 362–370, 71, 375–376, 380
   command object setup, 383,
      386–388
   commands, 389–390, 402
   FillSchema method, 384
   Update method, 378–381
   variable declaration, 382, 386
data columns, 362
data conversion
   strict data type conversion (string
      data), 144
   strict implicit type conversion,
      127–128, 156
data definition language (DDL), 356
data entry. See also input
   checking for errors. See data
      validation
   error messages, 415
   inheriting forms at Design time
      example, 568–570
   interface design, 87–88
   unsaved data, 423–424
data grids, 369, 388
Data Link Properties dialog box, 363
data management, 355
data manipulation language (DML), 356
Data Reader, 395–397
data relations, 397–400, 403–404
data rows, 362
data sources, specifying in connection
   strings, 383
Data tab (Toolbox), 21
data tables, 362
   adding rows, 376–377
   adding to datasets, 398–399
   creating multiple data tables at Design
      time, 403
   deleting rows, 378, 381
   Select method, 376–377
data types
   checking, 429
   converting, 167, 196
   Counter variable (For . . . Next loop),
      286–287
   DataReader data typed accessor
      methods, 395–396
   numeric data, 123–127, 128–130,
      131–132, 156
   type suffixes, 115–116

data validation, 425–426, 454–457
   advantages of object-oriented
      programming, 515
   error handling, 438–442
   field level, 431–435
   If . . . Then . . . ElseIf . . . Then . . . Else
      . . . End block, 175–176
   KeyPress level, 426–431
   LostFocus event, 94
   masked edit box, 107–108
   screen level (Save Click event),
      435–438
   signaling errors from Validating
      procedures, 437–438
   Validated event, 94
   Validating event, 94
   Web forms applications, 618–619
database management system (DBMS),
   355–356
databases, 356
   ADO.NET. See ADO.NET
   fields, 356
   foreign keys, 356–357
   indexes, 356–357
   primary keys, 356–357
   query parameters, 370–371
   SQL (Structured Query Language),
      357–361
   tables, 356, 361
   updating, 374, 375–379, 388, 389
   viewing single records, 372–374
DataBind method, Web forms applications,
   618
datasets, 362
   AcceptChanges method, 378–379
   adding data tables, 398–399
   adding records, 388
   binding data grids, 369
   binding datasets to controls by code,
      384
   creating multiple data tables at Design
      time, 403
   deleting records, 388
   filling, 369–370
   generating, 368, 375–376, 380
   generating dataset schema (FillSchema
      method), 384
   Relations.Add method, 399
   saving datasets locally, 390
   typed/untyped datasets, 390
   updating, 377, 388
   updating records, 388
   variable declaration, 382, 386
DataSource property
   data grids, 369
   displaying array contents in list
      boxes/combo boxes, 335
   filling datasets, 369
Date data type, 124–126
date validation, 433, 455
Date/Time functions, 140–142, 157
   formatting Date data, 141–142
DateAdd function, 140, 157
DateSerial function, 140
DateValue function, 140

Day function, 140
DBMS (database management system), 355–356
DDL (data definition language), 356
debugger, customizing, 257
Decimal data type, 124–126
decision, 165
   If blocks. See If blocks
   logical expressions. See logical expressions
   Select Case blocks. See Select Case blocks
declaring
   arrays
     declaring dynamic arrays with initial values, 298
     one-dimensional arrays, 296
     position of named constants, 342
     static arrays, 342
     using variables for array declaration, 342
   collection object, 326
   constants, 114–115, 121
     benefits of events, 534
     event declaration syntax, 529
     example, 530
     form (class)-level declaration, 118–119
     Net Sale project, 134–135
     overlapping declarations in form and procedure, 120–121
     procedure-level declaration, 118–119
     Select Case blocks, 187
     type suffixes, 115–116
     using declared events, 532
   Function procedures, 224
   numeric data types, 126
   properties, 518
     read/write capabilities, 519
     returning property values, 519
     using classes/properties, 518–519
   static members, classes, 517
   StreamReader/StreamWriter object, 209–210
   two-dimensional variables, 330–331
   variables. See variable declaration
Default keyword, 574–575
default properties, 35–36
defining
   exceptions, 580–581
   interfaces (interface-based polymorphism). See also interface-based polymorphism
   interface definition placement, 576–577
   syntax, 576
   Move methods (interface-based polymorphism), 578
   testing Move implementation, 579
   tables/fields (table definitions), 356
   browsing table definitions. See browsing database schema
Delete method, data tables, 378, 381
Delete statement (SQL), 360–361

DeleteCommand property (ADO.NET data adapter), 371
DeleteSetting statement, 596
deploying Web services, 625
derived classes, 558–561
Desc keyword, sorting returned tables, 358
design
   controls, 87–88
   GUI design principles, 414–417
   interfaces, 479, 486–488
   large projects, 498–500
   menus, 460–461, 464
   unsaved data
     detecting, 423–424
     handling at Quit, 424
   user-friendly keyboards, 417–422
     access keys, 420–422, 449–453
     autotabbing, 419
     handling Enter key to move focus to next control, 417–418
     Tab control usage, 422, 453
     up/down arrow keys, 420, 453
   visual clues, 442–448
     mouse pointer, 415, 444–445
     progress bars, 446–448
     status messages, 445
Design time, 30
   group box behavior, 69–70
   inheriting forms, 567–570
destructors, components, 601–602
dialog boxes
   Add New Item, adding forms, 468
   Add Web Reference, 626
   Color, 241
   custom dialog boxes, 470–471
   Customize Toolbox, 63
   Data Link Properties, 363
   Exceptions, 527
   file dialog boxes (Open/Save), 214–216
   Font, 37
   Generate Dataset, 368
   Inheritance Picker, 569
   New Folder, 44
   New Project, 20
     setting project location, 44
   Notepad MDI example project
     building, 493–496
     invoking, 493
   Open Project, 28–29
   Project Location, 44
   Run, 50
   tab control, 71–74
   TabPage Collection Editor, 73
   Visual Studio.NET Combined Collection, 37. See also online help file
Dim statements, variable declaration, 115, 119
disabling controls, 109, 110
"Disk not ready" errors, 438–440
DisplayMember property, 393
Dispose method, 580
   component destructors, 601–602
division (/) operator, 131
DML (data manipulation language), 356
Do . . . Loop structure, 252

   breakpoints, 256–258
   computing value of infinite series, 255–258
   conditions, 252, 283
   displaying a sequence of numbers, 252–253
   endless loops, 255
   Exit Do statement, 256
   Exit While statement, 256
   loop without conditions, 255
   reading a name list and populating a list box, 253–255
   solving equations numerically, 258–261
   syntax, 252
   versus For structure, 272–273
Dock property
   buttons, 53
   picture box, 105
documenting general procedures, 226–227
DoEvents method (Application object), 437
dollar sign ($) character, Format function, 137
dot (.) character
   Format function (decimal place holder), 137
   handling in name text boxes, 427
   property syntax, 33
Double data type, 124–125, 156
double quotes (""), enclosing strings (SQL), 376
Double–Click event, 94
DoubleClick event (list boxes), 91–92
down/up arrow keys, 420, 453
drawing
   buttons, 25–26
   labels, 25
DropDownStyle property (combo box control), 84–86
dynamic arrays, ReDim statement, 297–298, 343
   assigning array values, 298
   declaring initial values, 298
   preserving data, 335, 344
   scope of ReDimed variables, 298

E

e (event argument), masked edit data validation, 430
E or e (Scientific) format, 136
elegant algorithms, 7
elements, arrays, 296
ellipses (. . .), usage in book, 11
Enabled property, 72
   forms/labels, 36
   group box control, 70–71
EnableViewState property, Web forms applications, 618
enabling controls
   depending on check boxes, 109
   depending on radio buttons, 110
encapsulation (objects), 514
encryption, 161
End Sub statement, 222–223, 236–237
   versus Exit Sub, 222–223

ending projects, 49, 472

endless loops, 255

Enter event, 93–95

Enter key, moving focus to next control, 417–418

entity integrity rule (primary keys), 357

enumeration

    Enum statement, 525–526

    enumerated constants, 525–526

    throwing exceptions, 527–529

        benefits, 528

        incorporating exception throwing in property procedures, 527–528

        pre-defined exceptions, 527

        Throw statement syntax, 527

equal (=) character

    assignment statements, 128

    IntelliSense, 27

    relational operator (logical expressions), 166

    selecting specific records, 358

Erase statement (arrays), 335

erasing data fields, Contacts project, 236

error messages, design principles, 415

errors, 9

    built-in string functions, 145

    common errors, 13

    handling, 438–442

    overflow errors, 124

    signaling errors from Validating procedures, 437–438

Esc key, 162

event argument (e), masked edit data validation, 430

event procedures, 33–34

    calling Validating procedures from Save Click event, 435–438

    template, 34

    versus general Sub procedures, 223

    viewing procedures in code window, 33–34

event-driven versus procedure-oriented languages, 4

events, 8, 33–34, 89, 529

    Activated, forms, 505

    AfterSelect, TreeView control, 467–468

    arguments, creating, 563–564

    CheckedChanged, radio buttons, 78

    Click, 33, 90–91, 94

        buttons, 90

        check boxes, 77, 91

        Environ-Pure project, 101–102

        menu control, 463–464

        picture box, 87

        radio buttons, 77, 91

    Closing

        allowing forms' Closing event to execute, 477–478, 482–484

        handling unsaved data, 424

    declaring, 529

        benefits of events, 534

        event declaration syntax, 529

        example, 530

        using declared events, 532

    Double–Click, 94

    DoubleClick (list boxes), 91–92

    Enter, 93–95

    event procedure syntax, 33

    Form Activated, 471–472

    Form Load, 90, 94

        label alignment, 47

    handling, 33

        AddHandler statement, 535, 547

        Handles clause, 534–535, 547

        hooking event handlers, 534–535

        MDI child forms, 489

        MDI parent forms, 489–493

        RemoveHandler statement, 535

    KeyDown, 420

    KeyPress, 93–94

        converting Enter key to Tab key, 418

        data validation, 426–427

    Leave, 94–95

    LostFocus, 94

    raising

        example, 530–531

        RaiseEvent statement syntax, 529

    SelectedIndexChanged, 94

        combo boxes, 92

        list boxes, 91–92

    TextChanged, text boxes, 67

    Tick event (timer), 48–49

    Validating, 94, 431

        calling Validating procedures from Save Click event, 435–438

        checking for missing data, 431–432

        IsDate/IsNumeric functions, 433

        minimizing code, 433

        signaling errors from Validating procedures, 437–438

        troubleshooting, 435

        verifying input with users, 434

    viewing available events in code window, 33–34

example applications. See projects

Excel, using in VB, 634

exceptions, 440. See also errors

    creating user defined exceptions, 580–581

    handling with Try . . . Catch . . . Finally . . . End Try, 440–441

    specifying exceptions, 441–442

    throwing, 527–529

Exceptions dialog box, 527

executable, 2

ExecuteNonQuery method, data commands, 389–390

ExecuteReader method, 395

execution control, 33, 42–43

Exit Do statement, 43, 256

Exit For statement, 43

Exit Function statement, 43

Exit Sub statement, 43, 222–223

Exit While statement, 256

expressions, 130–132

F

F or f (Fixed) format, 136

feedback, design principles, 415

fields

    databases, 356, 358–361, 390

    formatting field contents with Leave event, 94

    grouping (group box control), 68–71, 74–76

    validating data at field level, 431–435

File menu commands, 28–29

File menus, creating, 461–462. See also menus, creating

file share method, 615

FileName property, file dialog boxes (Open/Save), 215–216

files

    dialog boxes (Open/Save), 214–216

    extensions, AddExtension property, 215

    paths, CheckPathExists property, 215

    reading, 209

        closing StreamReader, 212

        combining declaration/creation of StreamReader object, 210

        creating StreamReader object, 210

        declaring StreamReader object, 209–210

        phone file (Contacts project), 235–236

        reading data from files, 210–211

        System.IO namespace, 209

        testing for end of file, 211–212

    writing, 209

        closing StreamWriter, 213, 281

        creating StreamReader object, 212–213

        declaring StreamWriter object, 209–210

        System.IO namespace, 209, 213–214

        writing text data, 213

Fill method

    filling datasets, 369–370

    OleDbDataAdapter, 376

FillSchema method, 384

Filter property, file dialog boxes (Open/Save), 215

Finalize method, 580

finding table items. See also searching

    finding arrays, 302

    populating arrays, 302–303

FindString/FindStringExact methods (list/combo boxes), 280

Fix function, 138

Fixed (F or f) format, 136

floating banners, 55

floating point, 125

Flush method (StreamWriter object), 240

focus, 62

    handling Enter key to move focus to next control, 417–418

    converting Enter key to Tab key, 418

    SendKeys object, 417–418

    LostFocus event, 94

    tab order (TabIndex property), 89

Focus method, Tab control, 422

folders

    creating solution folders, 24–25

    organizing project/solution folders, 30, 44–45

Font property
  buttons, 52
  forms/labels, 36–37
  Tab control, 422
For Each . . . Next structure, 270–273, 286
For . . . Next structure, 261–262
  changing parameters of For blocks, 284
  Counter variable, 261, 285–287
  *displaying a string on two lines,
    264–266*
  increments, 262
  listing every other item, 264
  listing numbers sequentially, 262–263
  listing selected items, 263–264
  nesting, 266–270
  *referencing objects in a collection by
    index, 272*
  syntax, 43, 261–262
  versus Do structure, 272–273
  versus For Each structure, 273
ForeColor property
  forms/labels, 36, 54–55
  Tab control, 422
foreign keys, 356–357
form (class)-level declaration, 118–119
  *overlapping declarations in form and
    procedure, 120–121*
form (IDE), 22
Form Activated event, 471–472
Form Closing event, MsgBox function, 208
Form Load event, 90, 94
  Contact project, 234–235
  label alignment, 47
Format function, 136–137
FormatNumber function, 137
FormBorderStyle property, keeping forms
  from unloading, 474
forms, 3. See also objects
  adding to projects, 468
  aligning labels, 47–49, 54
  background color, random, 55–57
  Beep command, 53
  buttons, 25–26, 74–76
  Cashflow Entry Form, 327–330
  closing
    *allowing forms' Closing event to
      execute, 477–478, 482–484*
    handling unsaved data, 424
    *title bar Close button (ControlBox
      property), 53*
  controls, 3
  *grouping fields (group box control),
    68–71, 74–76*
  icons, 52
  KeyPreview property, 420, 428–429
  Maximize/Minimize boxes, 53
  properties, 35–36
  random positioning, 56–57
  sharing data between forms, 472–474
  sizing
    dragging sizing handles, 25
    random size, 56–57
    WindowState property, 53
  startup forms, 469, 480–481
  startup objects, MDI applications, 505

  switching among forms, 468
  tab order, 89
  templates, 470
  treating as visual objects, 539–540
FORTRAN language, 2
fractional progression, 285–286
frequency count (arrays), 303–304
  *simulating/approximating
    probabilities, 305–307, 349,
    352–353*
Friend keyword
  *making variables available to other
    forms, 473*
  standard modules, 475
FrontPage file extensions method, 615
Function procedures, 216–217, 223–225
functions
  CheckDate, 226
  *CType (For Each . . . Next structure),
    271*
  DateAdd, 157
  Format, 136–137
  FormatNumber, 137
  GetTheFileName, 246
  IIf (immediate If), 181
  InputBox, 241
  IsDate/IsNumeric, data validation, 433
  LBound, 300
  MsgBox, 206–208
  returning arrays, 299, 345
  Rnd, 156–157
  Split, 333
  *TypeName (For Each . . . Next
    structure), 270*
  UBound, 299–300
  using functions, 142

G

G or g (General Number) format, 136
game boards (two-dimensional arrays),
  334–335, 353–354
garbage collection, 580
general applicability of code blocks, 7
general declaration area (code window), 118
General Number (G or g) format, 136
general procedures, 217, 225–230. See also
  Sub procedures; Function procedures
  cascading event procedures, 228
  CheckDate function, 226
  code reusability, 219–220
  documentation, 226–227
  Function procedures, 223–225
  Function versus Sub, 224–225
  headers, 228–229, 242–243
  naming, 226
  *optional parameters, 228–229,
    242–243*
  overloading procedures, 229, 243
  recursion, 227–228
  Sub procedures, 217–223, 242
  using, 230
  versus methods, 521–522
generating datasets, 368, 375–376, 384
Get procedure, returning property values,
  518–519

GetAllSettings function, Registry, 632
GetChildRows method, 399
GetOleDbSchemaTable method, 390–391,
  394
  *browsing database schema using data
    relations, 398–400*
  querying, 391–394
  syntax, 391–392
GetSchemaTable method, DataReader,
  396
GetSelected method, list box control,
  82–83, 86
GetSetting statement, 595
GetTheFileName function, 246
graphic user interface. See GUI
graphics (picture box), 86–87, 105
greater than (>) relational operator (logical
  expressions), 166
greater than or equal to (>=) relational
  operator (logical expressions), 166
group box control, 68–71, 74–76
GUI (graphic user interface), 2. See also
  user interfaces
GUI design. See also design
  design principles, 414–417
  unsaved data
    detecting, 423–424
    handling at Quit, 424
  visual clues, 442–448
    mouse pointer, 415, 444–445
    progress bars, 446–448
    status messages, 445
GW-BASIC language, 2

H

half interval method, 259
Handled property, KeyPress event, 93
Handles clause, 534–535, 547
handling
  *Enter key, to move focus to next
    control, 417–418*
  errors, 438–442
  events
    AddHandler statement, 535, 547
    Esc key, 162
    Handles clause, 534–535, 547
    hooking event handlers, 534–535
    MDI child forms, 489
    MDI parent forms, 489–493
    RemoveHandler statement, 535
    *radio buttons, Select Case block,
      189–190*
    special characters, 427
headers
  Function procedures, 224, 228–229
  procedure header syntax, 534–535
  quick sort procedures, 320
  Sub procedures, 228
    *specifying optional parameters,
      228–229*
help
  context sensitive help, 38
  Help menu, 37–39
  online help file, 13
  Start Page help options, 19

hiding
  controls, Visible property, 70–71
  forms, 471–472
  protecting members from classes
    outside inheritance hierarchies,
    565–567
  Toolbox, 21–22
highlighting data, 162–163. See also
  selecting
hooking event handlers, 534–535, 547
HorizontalScrollBar property, list boxes, 282
hot keys (access keys), 420–422, 449–451,
  453
HTML. See also Web forms; Web services
  syntax, 411
  Web forms buttons versus HTML
    buttons, 635–636
hyperlinks
  Help file, 38
  Hyperlink control, 621

I
I/O (input/output), 206
  file dialog boxes (Open/Save), 214–216
  MsgBox, 206, 244
    buttons parameter, 206–208
    default button, 239
    displaying simple messages, 207
    obtaining user response, 207–209
    syntax, 206
  reading files, 209–214
  writing files, 209–210, 212–214, 281
Icon property, forms, 52
icons. See buttons; progress indicators
IDE (Integrated Development
  Environment), 4–5, 17, 30
  code window, 22
  customizing IDE, 18–19
  exiting IDE, 24
  form, 22
  menu bar, 20
  program development, 30
  Properties window, 23–24
  Solution Explorer, 22–23
  starting IDE, 18
  starting new projects, 19–20, 24–25, 29
  toggling between form and code
    window, 22
  toolbar, 20–21
  Toolbox, 21–22
If blocks, 43, 171
  block level declaration, 193, 198
  code clarity/alternatives, 181–183
    IIf (immediate If) function, 181
    Select Case block, 183
  comments, 179
  converting into computational
    formulas, 182
  efficiency, 180–181
  If . . . Then . . . Else . . . End, 172–174
  If . . . Then . . . ElseIf . . . Then . . . Else
    . . . End, 174–176
  indenting, 179
  mixing with Select Case block, 191
  nesting, 176–178

  simple If block, 172
  syntax, 43, 178–179, 180
If statements. See also If blocks
  logical expressions, 166
  radio buttons, 76
  syntax, 166, 171
IIf (immediate If) function, 181
Image property, picture box, 87
ImageAlign property, picture box, 87
images
  buttons, 105
  picture box, 86–87, 105
immediate If (IIf) function, 181
implicit type conversion, 127–128, 156
increments, For . . . Next loops, 262
indenting, If blocks, 179
Index tab (help file), 37
indexes
  arrays, using variables as indexes, 297
  databases, 356–357
inheritance, 4, 515, 558
  creating derived classes, 558
  creating event arguments, 563–564
  hiding members from classes outside
    hierarchies, 565–567
  hierarchy, 558
  inheritance-based polymorphism,
    570–576
  inheriting forms at Design time,
    567–570
  inheriting from VS.NET classes,
    561–563
  Inherits statement, 558
  marking MustInherit and
    NotInheritable classes, 567
  multiple inheritances, 580, 585–586
  name conflicts in interface inheritance,
    586–587
Inheritance Picker dialog box, 569
inner classes, 535, 536. See also nested
  classes
inner joins (SQL), 359–360
input, 206
  controls
    design principles, 87–88
    grouping (group box control), 68–71
    naming conventions, 88–89
    tab order, 89
  file dialog boxes (Open/Save), 214–216
  formatting field contents with Leave
    event, 94
  input/process/output analysis, 132
  KeyPress event, 93
  MsgBox, 206, 244
    buttons parameter, 206–208
    default button, 239
    obtaining user response, 207–209
    syntax, 206
  reading files, 209–214
  restoring field contents with Enter
    event, 93–94
InputBox function, 241
Insert statement (SQL), 360–361
InsertComand property (ADO.NET data
  adapter), 371

insertion sorts, 315–317. See also sorting
  data
instance members, classes, 514
instance methods, 522
instantiation, 122
InStr function, 145–148
InStrRev function, 145–148
Int function, 138
Integer data type, 123–125
integer division (\) operator, 131
Integrated Development Environment. See
  IDE
IntelliSense, 27
interface-based polymorphism, 576–580,
  585–586
interfaces
  designing, 479, 486–488
  GUI design principles, 414–417
  Net Sale project, 132–134
  polymorphism. See interface–based
    polymorphism
  search engine class project, 552
  simple first program, 45–47
  SortEngine project, 532–533
  unsaved data
    detecting, 423–424
    handling at Quit, 424
  user-friendly keyboard design,
    417–422
    access keys, 420–422, 449–453
    autotabbing, 419
    handling Enter key to move focus to
      next control, 417–418
    Tab control usage, 422, 453
    up/down arrow keys, 420, 453
  visual clues, 442–448
    mouse pointer, 415, 444–445
    progress bars, 446–448
    status messages, 445
  W-4 Form project, 275–276
  Web forms, 611–612
  Web services, 629
interpreters, 2
intuitive approach, random sampling
  without replacement (arrays), 307–309,
  310
invoking Sub procedures, 218–220
IOException, 441
IsDate function, data validation, 433
IsNumeric function, data validation, 433
Item property, collection object, 326
Items property
  combo box control, 84–86
  list box control, 79–80, 83, 86
Items.Add method
  combo box control, 84
  list box control, 79, 81
Items.Count property
  combo box control, 84–85
  list box control, 81, 85
Items.RemoveAt method
  combo box control, 84
  list box control, 81

J–K

JavaScript, 608
Jet data engine, 357, 361–363
joins (SQL), 359–360
jumping (skipping) code, 43
keyboard design principles
reducing keystrokes, 414
user-friendliness, 417–422, 449–453
keyboards
Alt/Shift keys, representing with
symbols, 420
key code values, 449–451
key validation procedures, 420
sequence of keyboard events, 450–451
validating data when user presses a
key, 426–431
KeyChar property (KeyPress event), 93
KeyDown event, 420
KeyPress event, 93–94
converting Enter key to Tab key, 418
handling special characters, 427
text boxes, 426–427
KeyChar property, 93
KeyPreview property, 418, 420, 428–429
keys
foreign keys, 356–357
primary keys, 356–357
keywords. See also attributes
Asc, sorting returned tables, 358
ByRef, passing data to Sub procedures,
221–222, 243–244
ByVal, passing data to Sub procedures,
221–222, 243–244
Call, Sub procedures, 224–226
Default, 574–575
Desc, sorting returned tables, 358
Friend, 473, 475
Function, 224
Implements, implementing interfaces, 577
Me, derived class references
(inheritance), 563
MustOverride, 567
MyBase, base class references
(inheritance), 562–563
New
displaying forms, 469
StreamReader object, 210
StreamWriter object, 212
Overrides, 573
Private, standard modules, 475
Protected, inheritance, 565–567
Public
making variables available to other
forms, 473
standard modules, 475
Rem (Remark), 31
Shadows, 578
TypeOf (For Each . . . Next loops), 271
Until, 117, 253

L

1 (lowercase L) versus 1 (numeral 1), 28
labels. See also objects
Anchor property, 104
access keys, 421–422
adding to forms, 25, 327–328
aligning, 47
background color, 33, 36, 52–55
rotating, 200
border style, 52
disappearing from forms, 48–49
foreground color, 54–55
moving across forms, 34, 47–48, 54
names, changing, 39–42
properties, 35–36
sizing, 25, 37
text
alignment, 52
font, 37
UseMnemonic property, 421, 449
languages
BASIC versus Visual Basic, 3–4
evolution of Visual Basic, 2–3
language processors, 2
learning languages, 10
large project design, 498–500
LayoutMdi method, 493
LBound function, 300
Lcase function, 145–147
Leave event, 94–95
Left function, 145–147
Left property, labels, 47–48
Len function, 145, 148
Length property, arrays, 335
less than (<) relational operator (logical
expressions), 166
less than or equal to (<=) relational operator
(logical expressions), 166
lifetime, 118, 121
declaring constants, 121
form (class)-level declaration,
118–119, 120–121
procedure-level declaration,
118–120
Public/Private declaration, 121–122,
155–156
variables declared with Dim
statements, 119
variables declared with Static
statements, 119–120
line continuation, 32, 625
list box control, 78–83
checked list box, 81–82, 105
clearing selected items, 292
combining with text box controls. See
combo box control
counting items, 81, 83
DoubleClick event, 91–92
FindString/FindStringExact methods,
280
HorizontalScrollBar property, 282
identifying item position
(SelectedIndices property), 83
identifying selected items, 79, 82–83
indicating position of clicked item
(SelectedIndex property), 79
Items property, 83
removing items (Items.RemoveAt
method), 81
SelectedIndex property, Form Load
event, 90
SelectedIndexChanged event, 91–92
SelectedIndices property, 83
SelectedItems property, 83
setting number of possible selections
(SelectionMode property), 81
sorting items (Sorted property), 81
versatility of list box, 82
lists, collection object, 326–330
loading forms, Form Load event, 90
local variables/constants, 118–119
declaring variables
Dim statement, 119
Static statement, 119–120
overlapping declarations in form and
procedure, 120–121
Location property, forms/labels, 36
logic errors, 9
logical expressions, 166–171
assignment statements, 168
logical operators, 168–170, 195
operational precedence, 170–171
relational operators, 166–168
logical operators, 168–171, 195
Long data type, 123–125, 156
loops
counting letters (arrays), 304–305
Do structure versus For structure,
272–273
Do . . . Loop, 252–261, 283
efficiency, 273–275
For Each . . . Next, 270–272, 286
For structure versus For Each
structure, 273
For . . . Next, 43, 261–270, 272, 284,
285–287
frequency counts (arrays), 303–304
nesting, 266–270
random sampling without replacement
using arrays, 255, 256, 305–310,
349, 352–353, 440–442
LostFocus event, 94
Ltrim function, 145, 148

M

Main Menu control, 461, 463–464. See also
menus
marker approach, random sampling without
replacement, 309–310
masked edit box control, 62–65, 68, 104,
107–108, 291, 419, 429–430, 434
matching text (SQL), 358–359
Math object, 138–139
math operations, 130–131, 135
mathematical equations, solving using Do
Loops, 258–261
mathematical functions, 137–139
matrices, two-dimensional arrays, 334
Max Length property, text boxes, 419
MaximizeBox property, forms, 53
Maximum property, progress bar, 446
MDI (multiple document interface)
applications, 484–485. See also multiple-
form applications
creating, 485, 497–498
example Notepad project, 485–486
building Find dialog box, 493–496

handling events in child form, 489
handling events in parent form, 489–493
interface, 486–488
invoking Find dialog box, 493
procedure summary, 496–497
standard module code, 488
large project design, 498–500
startup forms, 505
versus SDI (single document interface) applications, 485
MdiList property, 488
Me keyword, derived class references (inheritance), 563
members of classes, 514, 517
menus, 460–464
access/shortcut keys, 463
Click event, 463–464
context (pop-up) menus, 463
creating, 460–464
IDE menu options. See commands
MDI applications, 486–488
menu bar, 20
Message property, error handling, 441
messages
error message design principles, 415
status messages, 445
methods, 34–35
abstract methods, 567
AcceptChanges, datasets, 378–379
Add
command parameter setup, ADO.NET, 383
collection object, 326–327
AddRange, collection object, 328–329
arrays, 336, 345
class members, 514, 517
Close
forms, 471
inheritance-based polymorphism example, 571–573
StreamReader object, 212
StreamWriter object, 210, 213, 281
creating, 520–522
DataBind, Web forms applications, 618
DataReader object
data typed accessor methods, 395–396
ExecuteReader, 395
GetSchemaTable, 396
Read, 395
Delete, data tables, 378, 381
Dispose, 580, 601–602
DoEvents (Application object), 437
ExecuteNonQuery, data commands, 389–390
ExecuteReader, 395
Fill, 369–370, 376
FillSchema, 384
Finalize, 580
FindString/FindStringExact, list/combo boxes, 280
Flush, StreamWriter object, 240
Focus, Tab control, 422

FrontPage file extensions, 615
GetChildRows, 399
GetOleDbSchemaTable, 390–391, 394
browsing database schema using data relations, 398–400
querying database schema, 391–394
querying table column names, 394–395
syntax, 391–392
GetSchemaTable, DataReader, 396
GetSelected, list box control, 86
Hide, forms, 471
instance methods, 522
Items.Add, 79–81, 84
Items.RemoveAt, 81, 84
LayoutMdi, 493
Math object, 138–139
Move, defining, 578
parameters, 34–35
Peek, StreamWriter object, 210
polymorphism. See polymorphism
Read
DataReader object, 395
StreamWriter object, 210
ReadLine, StreamWriter object, 210–212
ReadToEnd, StreamWriter object, 210, 212
ReadXML/ReadXMLSchema, saving datasets locally, 390
referencing object methods, 139
Relations.Add, 399
Remove, collection object, 326
Select, data tables, 376–377
Send, SendKeys object, 417–418
SetBounds, 34
shared/static methods, 522
Show, displaying forms, 470
ShowDialog, forms, 471
Start, Count Down Clock project, 541
Stop, Count Down Clock project, 541
syntax, 34–35
TreeView control, 467
Update, data adapters, 378, 380–381
Web access, 615
WriteLine, StreamWriter object, 213, 239
WriteXML/WriteXMLSchema, saving datasets locally, 390
Mid function, 145–147
MinimizeBox property, forms, 53
Minimum property, progress bar, 446
minus sign (–) character
Format function, 137
negation operator, 131
negative numbers, Select Case blocks, 187
subtraction operator, 131
Mod (modulus) operator, 131
modal/modeless style forms, 470–471
modularity, 7
modules, 474
class modules, 118, 515–517
standard, 474–478, 480, 482–484, 488, 500

modulus (Mod) operator, 131
Month function, 140
mouse, progress-indicating pointer, 415, 444–445
Move methods, defining, 578, 579
moving objects, SetBounds method, 34
MS Jet data engine, 357, 361–363
MsgBox function, 206, 244
buttons parameter, 206–208
default button, 239
displaying simple messages, 207
obtaining user response, 207–209
syntax, 206
Multiline property
tab control, 422
text box control, 103–104
multiple document interface (MDI) applications. See MDI applications
multiple-form applications. See also MDI applications
adding forms, 468
closing/hiding forms, 471–472
Close method, 471
closing versus hiding, 471
ending projects, 472
Form Activated event, 471–472
GuessingGame example project, 481–484
Hide method, 471
GuessingGame example project, 478
large project design, 498–500
modal/modeless forms, 470–471
project startup
changing startup form, 469
displaying other forms, 469–470
form templates/variables, 470
GuessingGame example project, 480–481
sharing data between forms, 472–474
declaring variables available to other forms, 473
keeping forms from unloading, 473–474
referencing properties of another form's controls, 472–473
standard modules. See multiple-form applications, standard modules
switching among forms/code windows, 468
multiple–form applications, standard modules, 474–478
adding to projects, 474
allowing forms' Closing event to execute, 477–478, 482–484
calling procedures, 475
declaring variables/procedures, 474–475
declaring in multiple modules, 476
duration, 475
GuessingGame example project, 480
making contents of startup form available, 476–477
Public/Friend/Private procedures, 475
using Sub Main as startup object, 476
multiplication (*) operator, 131

MustInherit classes, 567
MustOverride keyword, 567
My Profile, 19
MyBase keyword, base class references
(inheritance), 562–563

N

N or n (Standard) format, 136
named constants, 114
namespaces, 209, 213–214
naming
constants, 115–116, 123
controls, 88–89
general procedures, 226
menu items, 462
objects, 39–42
variables, 115–116, 123
NavigateUrl property (Hyperlink control),
621
negation (–) operator, 131, 187
nested classes, 535–539
nesting
If blocks, 176–178
loops, 266–270
Select Case block, 187–193
New Folder dialog box, 44
New keyword
displaying forms, 469
StreamReader object, 210
StreamWriter object, 212
New procedure, 523–524
New Project button (Start Page), 19–20
New Project dialog box, 20
setting project location, 44
new projects, starting, 19–20, 24–25, 29
nodes, tree view. See tree view
not equal (≠) relational operator (logical
expressions), 166
Not operator, 169
NotInheritable classes, 567
Now function, 140
numeric comparisons, relational operators,
166, 167
numeric data, 114
data types, 123–128
assignment statements, 128–130
data type conversions, 131–132
declaring, 126
floating point, 125
overflow errors, 124
precision, 123
range, 123
strict implicit type conversion,
127–128, 156
expressions, 130–131
operations, 130–131
rules of precedence, 131
use of parentheses, 131
sorting random numbers, 199
numeric functions, 137–142
numerically solving equations
using Do Loops, 258–261
using nested For . . . Next loops
(numerically by simulation),
268–270

O

O/o (letter O) versus 0 (numeral 0), 28
Object box, 23, 33
Object data type, 126–127
object program, 2
object-oriented code structure, 3–4
object-oriented programming. See also
objects; classes
advantages, 514–515
building classes, 524–525
class members, 514, 517
enumerated constants, 525–526,
527–529
objects versus classes, 514
using classes, 518–519, 523–525
objects, 122, 514–515. See also classes;
object-oriented programming
advantages of object-oriented
programming, 514–515
Clipboard, 632–633
collection, 326–330
connection string setup, 383
Cursor, 445
DataReader, 395–397
encapsulation, 514
events, 33–34
forms, treating as visual objects,
539–542
instantiation, 122
interfaces, 32
Math object, 138–139
methods, 34–35
creating, 520–522
parameters, 34–35
referencing object methods, 139
syntax, 34–35
types of methods, 521
versus general procedures,
521–522
names
changing object names, 39–42
naming conventions, 39
prefixes, 39
properties, 24, 32, 35–37
common properties, 35–36
constructors, 523–524
creating, 518–520
defaults, 35
read/write capabilities, 519
returning property values, 519
setting default properties,
523–524
using classes/properties, 518–519
Property pages, 24
Random, 138
Response, 621
SendKeys, 417–418, 632–633
up/down arrow keys, 420
timing of creation/destruction,
543–545
versus classes, 514
visual objects, 3. See also controls
ODBC (open database connectivity)
compliant servers, 361
OleDbDataAdapter. See data adapters

one-dimensional arrays, 296–300. See also
arrays
creating, 296–297, 342
determining boundaries, 299–300
displaying contents in list boxes/combo
boxes, 335
dynamic arrays, 297–299, 335
online help file, 13
Help menu, 37–39
Contents tab, 38
hyperlinks, 38
Index tab, 37
Visual Basic and Related in the
Filtered By option, 39
open database connectivity (ODBC)
compliant servers, 361
Open dialog box, 214–216
AddExtension property, 215
CheckFileExists property, 215
CheckPathExists property, 215
FileName property, 215
when user clicks Cancel
(OpenFileDialog), 216
Filter property, 215
Title property, 215
Open Project button (Start Page), 19
Open Project dialog box, 28–29
operations (numeric), 130–131
operators
logical, 168–171, 195
math, 130–131
relational, 166–168, 170–171
Option Explicit statement, checking for
variable declaration, 116–117
Option Strict, 127–128, 156
optional parameters, general procedures,
228–229, 242–243
Or/OrElse operators, 169
Or versus OrElse, 195
Order By clause, sorting returned tables,
358
organizing projects/solutions, 30, 44–45
outer classes, 535. See also nested classes
outer joins (SQL), 359–360
output, 206
file dialog boxes (Open/Save), 214–216
input/process/output analysis, 132
MsgBox, 206–209, 239, 244
writing files, 209–210, 212–214, 281
overflow errors, 124
overloading procedures, 229, 243
Overrides keyword, 573
OverwritePrompt property, SaveFileDialog,
216

P

parameters, 34–35
command parameter setup, ADO.NET,
383–384
events, 33
For . . . Next loops, 284
relationship with arguments, 241
SQL queries, 370–371
Sub procedures, 220–221, 228–229,
242–243

parent forms. See MDI (multiple document interface) applications
Parent property, TreeView control, 467
parent-child table relationships. See data relations
parentheses ( )
  arithmetic operations, 131
  event procedure syntax, 33
  method syntax, 34
  order of operations, logical expressions, 170
passing data to Sub procedures, 220–222, 242–244
PasswordChar property, text box control, 103
paths, 215, 234–235
Peek method, StreamReader object, 210
percent (%) character
  Alt key, 420
  Format function, 137
Percent format, 136
period (.) character
  Format function (decimal place holder), 137
  handling in name text boxes, 427
  property syntax, 33
picture box, 86–87, 105
pictures, buttons, 105
| (pipe) symbol
  code syntax, 11
  Filter property, Open/Save dialog boxes, 215
+ (plus sign) character
  addition operator, 131
  sending as its original keystrokes (versus the Shift key), 420
  Format function, 137
  Shift key, 420
  string concatenation, 143–144
  usage in book, 11
polymorphism, 570
  inheritance-based polymorphism, 571–576
  interface-based polymorphism, 576–580, 585–586
pop-up (context) menus, 463
populating
  arrays, 302–303
  list boxes, 79, 81, 277
pound sign (#) character
  date literals, 124
  Format function, 137
power (^) operator, 131
precedence, 131, 170–171
precision, numeric data types, 123
preferences, IDE, 18–19
prefixes, object names, 39
primary keys, 356–357
Private keyword, standard modules, 475
private properties, 518
private variables, 121–122, 155–156
probability
  calculating using nested For . . . Next loops, 268–270
  simulating/approximating probabilities with arrays, 305–307, 349, 352–353

Procedure box (code window), 33–34
procedure-level declaration, 118–121
procedure-oriented code structure (BASIC), 3
procedure-oriented versus event-driven languages, 4
procedures, 216–217. See also event procedures
  calling, standard modules, 475
  declaring, standard modules, 474–476
  event procedures, 217, 223
  Function procedures, 216–217, 223–225
  Function versus Sub, 217, 224–225
  general procedures, 217, 225–230
    cascading event procedures, 228
    CheckDate function, 226
    code reusability, 219–220
    documentation, 226–227
    event procedures versus general Sub procedures, 223
    Function versus Sub, 225
    headers, 228–229, 242–243
    naming, 226
    optional parameters, 228–229, 242–243
    overloading procedures, 229, 243
    recursion, 227–228
    using, 230
    versus methods, 521–522
  Get, returning property values, 518–519
  New, 523–524
    setting default properties, 523–524
  passing arrays to procedures, 299
  procedure header syntax, 534–535
  Set, setting property values, 518
  standard modules, 475
  Sub Main, using as startup object, 476
  Sub procedures, 216–217
    argument position/type, 220
    bubble sort routine, 312–314
    calling (invoking), 218–220
    insertion sort routine, 316–317
    passing data to Sub procedures, 220–222, 242
    quick sort routine, 323–324
    shell sort routine, 319
    terminating before reaching end, 222–223
    writing, 217–218
  templates, 34
  viewing procedures in code window, 33–34
processor, 4–5
program development, 5–10, 30
  benefits of hands-on practice, 11–13
  completing development cycle, 50–51
  criteria for sound application programs, 6–7
  steps, 8–10
program modularity, variable scope, 122–123
programs. See also projects
  adding programs to Start menu Programs submenu, 50–51
  closing programs without closing StreamWriter, 239

  running, 50
  testing, 9
Programs submenu (Start menu), adding programs, 50–51
progress indicators
  mouse pointer, 415, 444–445
  progress bar control, 446–448
  status messages, 445
Project icon (Solution Explorer), 23
Project Location dialog boxes, 44
projects, 23. See also programs
  adding class modules, 517
  closing, 27
  Design time, 30
  ending, 472
    GuessingGame project, 481–484
  large project design, 498–500
  multiple-form projects. See multiple-form applications
  opening saved projects, 28–29
  organizing project folders, 30, 44–45
  Run time, 30
  saving changes, 29
  starting new projects, 19–20, 24–25, 29
Prompt to Save Changes to Open Documents option, 29
PromptChar property, masked edit box, 104
properties, 24, 32, 35–37
  AcceptButton, forms, 53
  AddExtension, file dialog boxes, 215
  Anchor
    buttons, 52
    labels, 104
  Appearance, Tab control, 422
  AutoFlush, StreamWriter object, 239–240
  AutoSize, labels, 37
  AutoTab (autotabbing), masked edit box control, 419
  BackColor
    buttons, 52
    labels, 33, 36, 52
    Tab control, 422
  BorderStyle
    labels, 52
    Tab control, 422
  CancelButton, forms, 53
  CausesValidation, 431–435
  CheckFileExists, file dialog boxes, 215
  CheckPathExists, file dialog boxes, 215
  CheckState, check boxes, 78, 104
  class members, 514, 517
  ClipText (masked edit box control), 67–68
  common properties, 35–36
  Context Menu, 463
  ControlBox, forms, 53, 474
  Count, collection object, 326
  data adapter (ADO.NET) command properties, 371
  DataSource
    data grids, 369
    displaying array contents in list boxes/combo boxes, 335
  defaults, 35, 36
  DisplayMember, 393

Dock
   buttons, 53
   picture box, 105
DropDownStyle, combo box control,
   84–86
Enabled, 72, 70–71
EnableViewState, Web forms
   applications, 618
FileName, file dialog boxes, 215–216
Filter, file dialog boxes, 215
Font
   buttons, 52
   labels, 37
   Tab control, 422
ForeColor, Tab control, 422
FormBorderStyle, forms, 474
GetSelected, list box control, 82–83
Handled, KeyPress event, 93
help pages, 38
HorizontalScrollBar, list boxes, 282
Icon, forms, 52
Image, picture box, 87
ImageAlign, picture box, 87
incorporating exception throwing in
   property procedures, 527–528
Item, collection object, 326
Items
   combo box control, 84, 86
   list box control, 79–80, 83, 86
Items.Count
   combo box control, 84–85
   list box control, 81, 85
KeyChar, KeyPress event, 93
KeyPreview
   converting Enter key to Tab key, 418
   forms, 428–429
Left, labels, 47–48
Length, arrays, 335
marking defaults (Default keyword),
   574–575
Mask, masked edit box control, 62–65,
   68*
Max Length (autotabbing), text boxes,
   419*
MaximizeBox, forms, 53
Maximum, progress bar, 446
MdiList, 488
Message, error handling, 441
MinimizeBox, forms, 53
Minimum, progress bar, 446
Multiline
   Tab control, 422
   text box control, 103–104
OverwritePrompt, SaveFileDialog, 216
PasswordChar, text box control, 103
PromptChar, masked edit box, 104
Rank, arrays, 335
referencing properties of another
   form's controls, 472–473
revising property procedures, 526
ScrollBars, text box control, 103–104
SelectedIndex, 72
   combo box control, 84–85
   list box control, 79, 82, 85
   tab control, 72

SelectedIndices, list box control, 83
SelectedItem
   combo box control, 84–86
   list box control, 79, 82, 86
SelectedItems, list box control, 83,
   263–264
SelectedText, text box/masked edit
   controls, 66–68
SelectionLength, text box/masked edit
   controls, 66–68, 158–159
SelectionMode, list box control, 81, 86
SelectionStart, text box/masked edit
   controls, 66–68
setting, 70
   tab pages, 72–73
Shares, 548
SizeMode, picture box, 87
Sorted
   combo box control, 84–86
   list box control, 81, 86
TabIndex, 89
   setting control access keys, 421
Tag, key verification, 428–429
Text
   buttons, 26
   check boxes, 76–77
   combo boxes, 86
   masked edit boxes, 65–68, 434, 388
   radio buttons, 74
   text boxes, 60–62, 65–68
TextAlign
   buttons, 104
   labels, 52
   picture boxes, 87
Title, file dialog boxes, 215
Top, 54
TreeView control, 467
UseMnemonic, labels, 421, 449
using classes/properties, 518–519
Visible, 72l, 70–71
WindowState, forms, 53
Properties icon, 23, 24
Properties window, 23–24
Property pages, 24
Protected keyword, inheritance, 565–567
Public keyword, 473, 475
Public properties, 518
public variables, 121–122, 155–156

Q

qualifying namespaces, 214
queries
   database schema, 391–394
   parameters, 370–371
   SQL. See SQL (Structured Query
     Language)
   table column names, 394–395
question mark (?)
   command parameters, ADO.NET, 383
   SQL query parameters, 371
Quick BASIC language, 2
quick sorts, 319–324, 352. See also sorting
  data
quitting programs, 49
quotes (""), enclosing strings (SQL), 376

R

radio buttons, 74–76
   CheckedChanged event, 78
   Click event, 77, 91
   clicking repeatedly, 104
   enabling/disabling controls, 110
   group boxes, 74–76
   Select Case block, 189–190
raising events, 529–531
random colors, form backgrounds, 55–57
random numbers
   generating for bubble sorts, 313
   simulating/approximating probabilities
     with arrays, 305–307, 349, 352–353
   sorting, 199
Random object, 138
random occurrences, tracking with arrays
   counting letters, 304–305
   frequency count, 303–304
random positioning, forms, 56–57
random sampling without replacement
  using arrays, 307–310
   avoiding repetition, 307–308
   drawing random numbers, 307
   intuitive approach, 307–310
   marker approach, 309–310
random size, forms, 56–57
Randomize statement, 138
range
   numeric data types, 123
   specifying
     Case statement, 184
     database table ranges, 358
RangeValidator control, Web forms
  applications, 618
ranks (arrays), 334–346
Read method
   DataReader, 395
   StreamReader object, 210
reading text files, 209. See also input
   closing StreamReader, 212
   combining declaration/creation of
     StreamReader object, 210
   creating StreamReader object, 210
   declaring StreamReader object, 209–210
   phone file (Contacts project), 235–236
   reading data from files, 210–211
   System.IO namespace, 209, 213–214
   testing for end of file, 211–212
ReadLine method, StreamReader object,
  210–212
ReadOnly properties, declaring, 519
ReadToEnd method, StreamReader object,
  210, 212
ReadXML/ReadXMLSchema methods,
  saving datasets locally, 390
Recent Project command (File menu), 29
records. See tables; fields (databases)
recursion
   cascading event procedures, 228
   general procedures, 227–228
ReDim statement, resizing arrays, 343
   preserving data, 335, 344
   scope of ReDimed variables, 298
   syntax, 297–298

Refresh icon (Solution Explorer), 23
Registry, 592–597
    accessing the Registry from VB,
      594–596
    advantages, 596–597
    GetAllSettings function, 632
    proper usage, 597
    text viewer example application,
      592–596
relational operators, 166–168
    numeric comparisons, 166, 167
    operational precedence, 170–171
    string comparisons, 167–168
Relations.Add method, 399
relationships, tables, 397
    browsing database schema, 398–400
      displaying child rows, 399–400
    creating at Design time, 403
    displaying contents of related tables
      with bound controls, 403–404
relative termination criterion, 260
releasing arrays (Erase statement), 335
Rem (Remark) keyword, 31
remarks. See comments
Remove method, collection object, 326
RemoveAt method, TreeView control, 467
RemoveHandler statement, 535
reopening projects, 28–29
repetition, 43, 251
    Do structure versus For structure,
      272–273
    Do . . . Loop structure, 252–261, 283
    efficiency, 273–275
    For Each . . . Next structure, 270–272,
      286
    For structure versus For Each
      structure, 273
    For . . . Next structure, 261–262
      changing parameters of For blocks,
        284
      Counter variable, 261, 285–287
      displaying a string on two lines,
        264–266
      increments, 262
      listing every other item, 264
      listing matched items, 267–268
      listing numbers sequentially,
        262–263
      listing selected items, 263–264
      nesting, 266–267
      referencing objects in a collection by
        index, 272
      syntax, 261–262
    While . . . End While structure, 255,
      256
repetitive code, data validation, 427
Replace function, 145
replacing data, 162–163
RequiredFieldValidator control, Web forms
    applications, 618
resizing buttons/forms, 25–26. See also
    sizing
Response object, 621
restoring field contents with Enter event,
    93–94
Return statement, 222–224

returning arrays from functions, 345
reusing code, 514–515
Reverse method, arrays, 336
Right function, 145–147
Rnd function, 156–157, 138
rotating
    banners, 56
    label background colors, 200
rotation encryption, 161
rows, displaying child rows, 399–400
Rtrim function, 145, 148
Run dialog box, 50
Run time, 30
    group boxes, 70–71
    hooking event handlers with events of
      controls created during Run time,
      535
Run–time Error '71': "Disk not ready."
    errors, 438–440
running programs, 27, 50

S

Save dialog box, 214–216
SaveSetting statement, 594
saving
    calling Validating procedures from
      Save Click event, 435–438
    data fields, 236
    datasets, locally, 390
    project changes, 29
    unsaved data at Quit, 424
schema
    browsing table definitions, 390–395,
      398–400
    generating dataset schema (FillSchema
      method), 384
    XML, saving datasets locally, 390
Scientific (E or e) format, 136
scope, 118, 121, 157–159
    arrays, 296, 298
    block-level declaration, 120
    class modules, 517
    declaring constants, 121
    form (class)-level declaration,
      118–119, 120–121
    garbage collection, 580
    inner classes, 536
    object instantiate, 122
    procedure-level declaration,
      118–119
    program modularity, 122–123
    Public/Private declaration, 121–122,
      155–156
    static variables, 119–120
screen clearing, 280–281
screen level data validation (Save Click
    event), 435–438
scroll bars
    HorizontalScrollBar property, list
      boxes, 282
    ScrollBars property, text box control,
      103–104
SDI (single document interface)
    applications, 484, 485
search engine class project, 552–553
Search option, help, 38–39. See also help

searching, 310, 324–326
    arrays
      binary insertion sorts, 317
      binary search algorithm, 325–326,
        351
      Binary Search method, 336
      replacing data, 162–163
      sequential search with sorted data,
        324–325
      table items, using arrays, 302–303
Select Case blocks, 183–193
    block level declaration, 193, 198
    coding criteria, 185, 197–198
    If blocks, 183, 191
    nesting, 187–193
    Select Case structure versus arrays,
      301
    syntax, 183–187, 190–191
Select method, data tables, 376–377
Select statement
    ActiveControl, 429
    SQL, 357–360
SelectCommand property (ADO.NET data
    adapter), 371, 385
SelectedIndex property, 72
    combo box control, 84–85, 90
    list box control, 79, 82, 85, 90
    tab control, 72
SelectedIndexChanged event, 94
    combo boxes, 92
    list boxes, 91–92
SelectedIndices property, list box control,
    83
SelectedItem property
    combo box control, 84, 86
    list box control, 79, 82, 86
SelectedItems property (list box control),
    83, 263–264
SelectedNode property, TreeView control,
    467
SelectedText property, text box/masked edit
    controls, 66–68, 158–159
selecting
    list box items, 82–83
    text, 66–67
selection sorts, 314, 351
SelectionLength property
    text box/masked edit controls, 66–68
SelectionMode property, list box control,
    81, 86
SelectionStart property, text box/masked
    edit controls, 66–68
semantic errors, 9
semicolon (;), Select statement (SQL), 357
SendKeys object, 632–633
    handling Enter key to move focus to
      next control, 417
    Send method, 417–418
    up/down arrow keys, 420
separator lines, menus, 462
server-side scripts, 608
services, Web. See Web services
Set procedure, setting property values, 518
SetBounds method, 34
Shadows keyword, 578
shared methods, 522

Shared property, 548
Shell function, 632–633
shell sorts, 317–319, 324, 351–352. See
    also sorting data
Shift key, representing with plus sign (+),
    420
Short data type, 123–125
shortcut keys. See access keys
Show All Files icon (Solution Explorer), 23
Show method, displaying forms, 470
ShowDialog method, forms, 471
ShowSchema procedure, 399
ShowTwoLines project, 264–266
signaling errors from Validating
    procedures, 437–438
simple selection sorts, 314, 351
simulating/approximating probabilities with
    arrays, 305–307, 349, 352–353
Single data type, 124–125, 156
single document interface (SDI)
    applications, 484, 485
single quote ('), code comments, 7, 31
Size property, forms/labels, 36
SizeMode property, picture box, 87
sizing
    forms, 25, 53, 56–57
    labels, 25, 37
skipping (jumping) code, 43
Solution Explorer, 22–23
solutions, 23
    creating solution folders, 24–25
    organizing solution folders, 30, 44–45
solving equations numerically using Do
    Loops, 258–261
Sort method, arrays, 336
Sorted property
    combo box control, 84, 86
    list box control, 81, 86
sorting data, 310–311
    alphabetic order, 199
    bubble sorts, 311–314, 351
    comparison of performance of sorts, 324
    efficiency, 314
    list box items, 81
    quick sorts, 319–324, 352
    random numbers, 199
    returned tables (SQL), 358
    shell sorts, 317–319, 351–352
    simple selection sorts, 314, 351
    Sort method, 336
    straight insertion sorts, 315–317
sound, Beep command, 53
Space function, 145, 147
spaces, handling in name text boxes, 427
special characters, data validation, 427
speed, repetition structures, 272, 273
Split function, 333
SQL (Structured Query Language), 357–361
Standard (N or n) format, 136
standard modules, 474–478
    adding to projects, 474
    *allowing forms' Closing event to
        execute, 477–478, 482–484*
    calling procedures, 475
    *declaring variables/procedures,
        474–475, 476*

    duration, 475
    layering, 500
    *making contents of startup form
        available, 476–477*
    Public/Friend/Private procedures, 475
    using Sub Main as startup object, 476
    versus class modules, 515–517
standards, object naming, 39
Start menu
    *adding programs to Programs
        submenu, 50–51*
    Run command, 50
    *Settings, Taskbar & Start Menu
        command, 50*
Start method, 541
Start Page, customizing, 18–19
startup objects
    changing startup forms, 469
    *making contents of startup form
        available, 476–477*
    MDI applications, 505
    multiple-form applications, 480–481
    Sub Main procedure, 476
statements, 5, 42–43
static arrays, 342
static members, classes, 514, 517
static methods, 139, 522
static variables, 119–120
status messages, 445
Stop method, 541
Str function, 145–147
straight insertion sorts, 315–317. See also
    sorting data
    binary sorts, 317
    *comparison of performance of sorts,
        324*
    Insert Sub procedure, 316
    Insertion Sort Sub procedure, 316
    testing sort algorithm, 317
    versus bubble sorts, 317
StreamReader object, 209–212. See also
    input
    Close method, 212
    *combining declaration/creation of
        StreamReader object, 210*
    creating, 210, 240
    declaring, 209–210
    reading data from files, 210–211
    syntax, 209
    System.IO namespace, 213–214
    testing for end of file, 211–212
StreamWriter object, 209, 212–214. See
    also output
    AutoFlush property, 239–240
    *closing program without closing
        StreamWriter, 239*
    closing StreamWriter, 213, 281
    creating, 212–213, 240
    declaring object, 209–210
    Flush method, 240
    syntax, 209
    System.IO namespace, 213–214
    *writing text data (WriteLine method),
        213*
String Collection Editor, populating list
    boxes, 79–80

string comparisons, relational operators,
    167–168
string constants, breaking into multiple
    lines, 32
string data, 114, 142
    built-in string functions, 144–148
    *case (LCase/UCase functions),
        145–147*
    concatenation, 143–144
    declaring string variables, 143
    *displaying a string on two lines using
        For . . . Next loops, 264–266*
    *FindString/FindStringExact methods
        (list/combo boxes), 280*
    length (Len function), 148, 159
    strict data type conversion, 144
    variable–length strings, 143
StrReverse function, 145
Structured Query Language (SQL),
    357–361
Sub Main procedure, using as startup
    object, 476
Sub procedures, 216–217. See also general
    procedures
    calling (invoking), 218–220
    New, 523–524
    passing data to
        by name, 221, 242
        by position, 220–221, 242
        *ByVal versus ByRef, 221–222,
            243–244*
    sort routines
        bubble sorts, 312–314
        insertion sorts, 316–317
        quick sorts, 323–324
        shell sorts, 319
    *terminating before reaching end,
        222–223*
    versus event procedures, 223
    versus Function procedures, 224–225
        key difference, 217
    writing, 217–218
subclasses, 558. See also derived classes;
    inheritance
submenus, 464. See also menus
subschemata, 356
subtraction (–) operator, 131
suitability, repetition structures, 272–273
super classes, 558
swapping data between two variables,
    129–130
switching among forms/code windows, 468
symbolic constants, 114–116
syntax, 3–5, 11
    GetSelected method, 82
    Items.Add method (list box control), 79
    AddHandler statement, 535, 547
    arrays, 296, 297–298
    assignment statement, 129
    built–in string functions, 144–145
    Clear method (arrays), 336
    Close method, forms, 471
    code, 5
    collection object, 326–328
    Const statement, 114
    Create Table statement (SQL), 361

creating properties, 518
declaring string variables, 143
Delete statement (SQL), 361
DeleteSetting statement, 596
Dim statement, 115
Enum statement, 525–526
errors, 9
event declaration statement, 529
event procedures, 33
FillSchema method, 384
FindString/FindStringExact methods (list/combo boxes), 280
For . . . Next loop, 43
Format function, 136–137
Function procedures, 224, 228–229
GetChildRows method, 399
GetOleDbSchemaTable method, 391–392
GetSetting statement, 595
Hide method, forms, 471
HTML, 411
If blocks, 172–175, 178–179
  simple If block, 172
  syntax versus semantic, 180
If statements, 43, 166, 171
Insert statement (SQL), 360
InStr function, 147–148
interface definition (interface–based polymorphism), 576
LayoutMdi method, 493
loops, 252, 270, 261–262
MDI parent-child relationships, 485
methods, 34–35
MsgBox function, 206, 207
MustInherit classes, 567
NotInheritable classes, 567
numeric variable declaration, 126
Option Explicit statement, 116
procedure headers, 534–535
properties, 32–33
RaiseEvent statement, 529
referencing properties of another form's controls, 472–473
RemoveHandler statement, 535
SaveSetting statement, 594
Select Case block, 183–187, 190–191
Select statement (SQL), 357
Send method (SendKeys object), 417
Split function, 333
statements, 5
StreamReader object, 209–212
StreamWriter object, 209–210, 212–213
Sub procedures
  Call statement, 226
  calling (invoking) Sub procedures, 218–219
  headers, 228
  passing data to Sub procedures by name, 221
  passing data to Sub procedures by position, 220–221
  specifying optional parameters, 228–229
  writing Sub procedures, 217–218
symbolic constant declaration, 114

Throw statement, 527
two-dimensional variables, 330–331
Update statement (SQL), 360
With . . . End With structure, 150
system constants, 114
System.IO namespace, 209, 213–214. See also StreamReader object;

T

tab character, 149
tabbing
  autotabbing, 419
  converting Enter key to Tab key, 418
  Tab control, 71–74, 422, 453
  tab order, 89, 98-99
TabIndex property (labels/text boxes), setting access keys, 421
tables
  adding records, 360–361
  ADO.NET data tables, 362
  creating, 361
  definitions, 356
  deleting records, 360–361
  looking up items using arrays, 320–303
  matching text, 358–359
  querying table column names, 394–395
  relationships, 397
    browsing database schema, 398–400
    creating at Design time, 403
    displaying contents of related tables with bound controls, 403–404
  selecting specific records, 358
  sorting returned tables, 358
  specifying all fields in table, 358
  specifying ranges, 358
  two-dimensional arrays, 331–333
  updating, 374, 388
    adding rows to data tables, 376–377
    calling data adapter's Update method, 378, 389
    calling dataset's AcceptChanges method, 378–379
    configuring data adapters, 375–376
    deleting rows, 378
    determining whether data are new, 376–377
    generating datasets, 375–376
    modifying rows, 377
  updating immediately, 379–382
  updating records, 360–361
  viewing single records, 372–374
Tag property, key verification, 428–429
tags, HTML, 411
templates, 34, 470
terminating
  Do Loop criteria, 260
  programs, 49
  Sub procedures, 222–223, 236237
testing
  components, 602–604, 606–607
  programs, 9, 102, 282
  sort procedures, 313, 317
  Web forms projects, 613–615
  Web services, 629–630

text
  alignment, 52
  font, 52, 36–37
  matching (SQL), 358–359
  selecting, 66–67
text box control
  access keys, 421–422
  autotabbing (Max Length property), 419
  clearing, using For Each . . . Next loops, 271
  color, 109
  combining with list box controls. See combo box control
  data validation, 426–427
  focus, 62
  Multiline property, 103–104
  PasswordChar property, 103
  ScrollBars property, 103–104
  SelectedText property, 66–68, 66–68, 158–159
  SelectionLength property, 66–68
  SelectionStart property, 66–68
  Text property, 60–62, 65–68
  type over mode, 67
text files
  file dialog boxes (Open/Save), 214–216
  reading, 209
    closing StreamReader, 212
    combining declaration/creation of StreamReader object, 210
    creating StreamReader object, 210
    declaring StreamReader object, 209–210
    reading data from files, 210–211
    System.IO namespace, 209
    testing for end of file, 211–212
  writing, 209
    closing StreamWriter, 213, 281
    creating StreamReader object, 212–213
    declaring StreamWriter object, 209–210
    System.IO namespace, 209, 213–214
    writing text data, 213
Text property
  & symbol, 421
  access keys, 420–421, 449
  buttons, 26
  check boxes, 76–77
  combo box control, 86
  masked edit box, 388
  radio buttons, 74
  text box control, 60–62, 65–68
TextAlign property
  buttons, 104
  labels, 52
  picture box, 87
TextChanged event, 67
throwing exceptions, 527–529
  benefits, 528
  creating user defined exceptions, 580–581
  incorporating exception throwing in property procedures, 527–528

pre-defined exceptions, 527
Throw statement syntax, 527
Tick event (timer), 48–49
tick mark ('), code comments, 31
Time/Date functions, 140–142, 157
TimeOfDay function, 140
timer control, 47–49
Timer function, computing sort time
(bubble sorts), 314
Title parameter, MsgBox function, 206
Title property, file dialog boxes
(Open/Save), 215
Today function, 140
toggling buttons, 199
toolbar, 20–21
Toolbox, 21–22
customizing, 63–64
Data tab, ADO.NET controls, 363
displaying/hiding, 21–22
ToolTips, 21
Top property, 54
tree view, 464–468
Trim function, 145, 148
Try . . . Catch . . . Finally . . . End Try
structure, 440–442
two-dimensional arrays, 330–335. See also
arrays
type over mode, text boxes, 67
type suffixes, 115–116
type-declaration characters, 115. See also
type suffixes
typed datasets, 390
TypeName function (For Each . . . Next
structure), 270
TypeOf keyword (For Each . . . Next
loops), 271
types. See data types

U

UBound function, 299–300
Ucase function, 145–147
underscore (_)
event procedure syntax, 33
line continuation, 32, 625
Unicode, AscW/ChrW function, 146
unique indexes, 356–357
uniquely identified values (indexes), 357
unsaved data, handling at Quit, 424
Until keyword, Do . . . Loop structure, 253
untyped datasets, 390
Update method, data adapters, 378,
380–381
Update statement (SQL), 360–361
UpdateCommand property (ADO.NET data
adapter), 371
updating databases, 374
adding rows to data tables, 376–377
*calling data adapter's Update method,
378, 389*
*calling dataset's
AcceptChanges method, 378–379*
configuring data adapters, 375–376
deleting rows, 378
*determining whether data are new,
376–377*

generating datasets, 375–376
immediately, 379–382
maintaining data, 388
modifying rows, 377
records, 360–361
URLs, Hyperlink control, 621
UseMnemonic property, labels, 421, 449
user controls, 608
user input
controls
design principles, 87–88
grouping (group box control), 68–71
masked edit box, 62
naming conventions, 88–89
tab order, 89
*formatting field contents with Leave
event, 94*
KeyPress event, 93
*restoring field contents with Enter
event, 93–94*
user interfaces. See also input
graphics (picture box), 86–87
Image property, 87
SizeMode property, 87
Click event, 87
Dock property, 105
GUI design principles, 414–417
consistent appearance, 415
*flexibility in mobility and customiz-
ing the screen, 414–415*
*forgiveness for unintentional mis-
takes, 415–416*
immediate feedback, 415
pleasant appearance, 416–417
simple and clear layout, 414
unsaved data
detecting, 423–424
handling at Quit, 424
user-friendly keyboard design, 417–422
access keys, 420–422, 449–451, 453
autotabbing, 419
*handling Enter key to move focus to
next control, 417–418*
Tab control usage, 422, 453
up/down arrow keys, 420, 453
visual clues, 442–448
mouse pointer, 415, 444–445
progress bars, 446–448
status messages, 445
user-friendliness, 6
keyboard design, 417–422
access keys, 420–422, 449–451, 453
autotabbing, 419
*handling Enter key to move focus to
next control, 417–418*
Tab control usage, 422, 453
up/down arrow keys, 420, 453

V

Val function, 144–147
Validated event, 94
validating data, 425–426, 454–457
*advantages of object-oriented
programming, 515*
error handling, 438–442

field level, 431–435
*If . . . Then . . . ElseIf . . . Then . . . Else
. . . End block, 175–176*
KeyPress level, 426–431
LostFocus event, 94
masked edit box, 107–108
*screen level (Save Click event),
435–438*
*signaling errors from Validating
procedures, 437–438*
Web forms applications, 618–621
Validating event, 94, 431. See also
validating data
*calling Validating procedures from
Save Click event, 435–438*
checking for missing data, 431–432
IsDate/IsNumeric functions, 433
minimizing code, 433
*signaling errors from Validating
procedures, 437–438*
troubleshooting, 435
verifying input with users, 434
variable declaration, 115
*advantages of declaring all variables,
116*
*block–level declaration, 120, 193,
198*
*checking for variable declaration,
116–117*
Dim statement, 119
*form (class)-level declaration,
118–119, 120–121*
*making variables available to other
forms, 473*
Net Sale project, 134–135
numeric data types, 126
Object data type, 126–127
object instantiate, 122
*placement of variable declaration
statements in code window, 118*
procedure-level declaration, 118–119
Public/Private, 121–122, 155–156
rules for variable declaration, 117
standard modules, 474–475, 476
static declaration, 119–120
Static statement, 119–120
string variables, 143
type suffixes, 115–116
*working with ADO.NET by code,
382–386*
variable-length strings, 143
variables, 114
arrays, 297, 342
assignment statements, 128–129
*swapping data between two vari-
ables, 129–130*
*boolean variables, assigning values,
196*
class level variables, 118
Counter (For . . . Next loop), 261
changing counter value, 285
data types, 286–287
value after Exit For, 286
declaring. See variable declaration
form variables, 470

lifetime, *118–121*
  Dim statements, 119
  form (class)-level declaration,
    118–121
  procedure-level declaration,
    118–119
  static declaration, 119–120
  Static statements, 119–120
local variables, 118–119
  declaring with Dim statement, 119
  declaring with Static statement,
    119–120
  overlapping declarations in form
    and procedure, 120–121
naming conventions, 115–116, 123
scope, 118, 121
  block-level declaration, 120
  form (class)-level declaration,
    118–121
  procedure-level declaration,
    118–119
  program modularity, 122–123
  static variables, 119–120
scope of ReDimed variables, 298
static variables
  declaration, 119
  scope, 119–120
VB controls. See controls
VB. See Visual Basic
VB.NET editions/versions, 5. See also
  Visual Basic
VBScript, 608
vertical bars (|)
  code syntax, 11
  Filter property, Open/Save dialog
    boxes, 215
View Code icon (Solution Explorer), 23
View Designer icon (Solution Explorer), 23
View menu commands
  Properties Window, 24
  Solution Explorer, 23
  Toolbox, 21
viewing single records, 372–374
Virtual Vending Machine project, 164

Visible property, 72
  forms, 471
  group box control, 70–71
Visual Basic (VB), 2–5
  editions/versions, 2–5
  learning VB, 10
  processor, 4–5
  program development, 5–10
  syntax, 3–5
  versus BASIC, 3–4
visual clues, 442–448
  mouse pointer, 415, 444–445
  progress bars, 446–448
  status messages, 445
visual interfaces. See also user interfaces
  BankDepositor project, 538
  Contacts project, 231–232
  GuessingGame example multiple–form
    application, 479
  Notepad MDI project, 486–488
  search engine class project, 552
  simple first program, 45–47
  SortEngine project, 532–533
  Web forms, 275–276, 611–612
  Web services, 629
  Weight Lookup project, 331
visual objects, 3. See also controls
Visual Studio .NET (VS.NET), 5
Visual Studio.NET Combined Collection
  dialog box, 37. See also online help file

W–Z

Web forms applications, 608–610
  adding additional forms to projects,
    621
  creating, 610–615
  data access, 615–618
  data validation, 618–621
  Hyperlink control, 621
  requirements for ASP.NET
    development, 610
  testing projects, 613–615
  Web forms buttons versus HTML
    buttons, 635–636

Web references, adding to Web services,
  626–629
Web servers, 608
Web services, 621–631, 636
While . . . End While structure, 255–256
wildcard * character, specifying table
  fields, 358
Windows Forms tab (Toolbox), 21
Windows Registry, 592–597
  accessing the Registry from VB,
    594–596
  advantages, 596–597
  GetAllSettings function, 632
  proper usage, 597
  text viewer example application,
    592–596
WindowState property, forms, 53
With . . . End With structure, 150
word processor project, 248–249
Word, using in VB, 634–635
WriteLine method (StreamWriter object),
  213, 239
WriteOnly properties, declaring, 519
WriteXML method, saving datasets locally,
  390
writing. See also output
  Function procedures, 224–225
  Sub procedures, 217–218
  text files, 209
    closing StreamWriter, 213, 281
    creating StreamWriter object,
      212–213
    declaring StreamWriter object,
      209–210
    System.IO namespace, 209, 213–214
    writing text data (WriteLine
      method), 213
  XML, saving datasets locally, 390
Xor operator, 169–170
xsd files, 390, 402
Year function, 140